Justice Scalia
Decisions and Dissents

Edited by Robert Dittmer

Text Copyright © 2016 Robert Dittmer
All Rights Reserved

Note on the text: most italics and bold has been removed.

Table of Contents
Contents

Table of Contents 3

Acknowledgements 10

Decisions 11

Need warrant to move people's stuff in plain-view to record identifying information to check against database to see if it's stolen: Arizona v. Hicks (March 3, 1987) 11

A tax credit against the Ohio fuel sales tax for each gallon of ethanol, but only if the ethanol is produced in Ohio or in a State that grants similar tax advantages to ethanol produced in Ohio is unconstitutional: New Energy Company of Indiana v. Limbach (May 31, 1988) 15

Notes to New Energy Company of Indiana v. Limbach (May 31, 1988) 21

Somehow Michael's contention that procedural due process requires that he be afforded an opportunity to demonstrate his paternity in an evidentiary hearing fundamentally misconceives the nature of § 621: Michael H. v. Gerald D. (June 15, 1989) [Judgment and opinion] 21

Notes to Michael H. v. Gerald D. (June 15, 1989) 31

No exceptions for religious people: Employment Division, Department of Human Resources of Oregon v. Smith (April 17, 1990) 34

Notes to Employment Division, Department of Human Resources of Oregon v. Smith (April 17, 1990) 43

The Eleventh Amendment bars suits by Indian tribes against States without their consent: Blatchford v. Native Village of Noatak (June 24, 1991) 45

Notes to Blatchford v. Native Village of Noatak (June 24, 1991) 51

Life sentence for drug possession neither cruel nor unusual: Harmelin v. Michigan (June 27, 1991) [Judgment and opinion] 53

Notes to Harmelin v. Michigan (June 27, 1991) 71

Hate speech not automatically unprotected: R. A. V. v. City of St. Paul (June 22, 1992) 75

Notes to R.A.V. v. St. Paul (June 22, 1992) 83

Constitutional structures; separation of powers: Plaut v. Spendthrift Farm, Inc. (April 18, 1995) 86

Notes to Plaut v. Spendthrift Farm, Inc. (April 18, 1995) 101

State sovereignty: The Federal Government may not command the States' executive power in the absence of a particularized constitutional authorization: Printz v. United States (June 27, 1997) 103

Notes to Printz v. United States (June 27, 1997) 119

Non-party members can't vote in party primaries for the person to represent the party: California Democratic Party v. Jones (June 26, 2000) 125

Notes to California Democratic Party v. Jones (June 26, 2000) 134

No Thermal-Imaging (heat-sensing) without warrant: Kyllo v. United States (June 11, 2001) 136

Notes to Kyllo v. United States (June 11, 2001) 142

Can't prohibit candidates for judicial election in that State from announcing their views on disputed legal and political issues: Republican Party of Minnesota v. White (June 27, 2002) 144

Notes to Republican Party of Minnesota v. White (June 27, 2002) 154

The State admitted Sylvia's testimonial statement against petitioner, despite the fact that he had no opportunity to cross-examine her. That alone is sufficient to make out a violation of the Sixth Amendment: Crawford v. Washington (March 8, 2004) 157

Notes to Crawford v. Washington (March 8, 2004) 173

Political gerrymandering claims are nonjusticiable because there is no discernible and manageable standard for adjudicating them: Vieth v. Jubelirer (April 28, 2004) [Judgment and Opinion] 177

Notes to Vieth v. Jubelirer (April 28, 2004) 196

Second amendment protects an individual civilian right to keep and bear arms for traditionally lawful purposes like self-defense: District of Columbia v. Heller (June 26, 2008) 199

Notes to District of Columbia v. Heller, Majority Opinion (June 28, 2008) 231

Video Games are protected: Brown v. Entertainment Merchants Association (June 27, 2011) 237

Notes to Brown v. Entertainment Merchants Association (June 27, 2011) 245

GPS-tracking is a search that requires a warrant: United States v. Jones (January 23, 2012) 248

Notes to United States v. Jones (January 23, 2012) 254

Drug-sniffing dog on front porch requires warrant: Florida v. Jardines (March 26, 2013) 255

Notes to Florida v. Jardines (March 26, 2013) 260

The Government violates the Due Process Clause when it takes away someone's life, liberty, or property under a criminal law so vague that it fails to give ordinary people fair notice of the conduct it punishes, or so standardless that it invites arbitrary enforcement: Johnson v. United States (June 26, 2015) 261

Justice Scalia Concurrences and Dissents 270

"Secular purpose" requirement to be constitutional is impossible to prove, or disprove, and should end: Justice Scalia's dissent in Edwards v. Aguillard (June 19, 1987) 270

Notes to Justice Scalia's dissent in Edwards v. Aguillard (June 19, 1987) 287

Legislative history: Justice Scalia's concurrence in United States v. Taylor (June 24, 1988) 290

Separation of Powers: Justice Scalia's dissent in Morrison v. Olson (June 29, 1988) 291

Notes to Justice Scalia's dissent in Morrison v. Olson (June 29, 1988) 312

Cruel and Unusual Punishments: Justice Scalia's dissent in Thompson v. Oklahoma (June 29, 1988) 314

Notes to Justice Scalia's dissent in Thompson v. Oklahoma (June 29, 1988) 325

Congress cannot delegate its authority to make sentences for crimes: Justice Scalia's dissent in Mistretta v. United States (Jan. 18, 1989) 327

Notes to Justice Scalia's dissent in Mistretta v. United States (Jan. 18, 1989) ... 335

The benign purpose of compensating for social disadvantages, whether they have been acquired by reason of prior discrimination or otherwise, can no more be pursued by the illegitimate means of racial discrimination than can other assertedly benign purposes we have repeatedly rejected: Justice Scalia's concurrence in Richmond v. Croson (January 23, 1989) 336

Bodily search separate from arrest and without individualized suspicion of wrong-doing can only be done with respect to prison inmates, not customs service employees: Justice Scalia's dissent in Treasury Employees v. Von Raab (March 21, 1989) 341

Abortion: Justice Scalia's concurrence in Webster v. Reproductive Health Services (July 3, 1989) 346

The Court today endorses the principle that too much speech is an evil that the democratic majority can proscribe: Justice Scalia's dissent in Austin v. Michigan State Chamber of Commerce (March 27, 1990) 350

The new principle that the Court today announces will be enforced by a corps of judges who overwhelmingly owe their office to its violation. Something must be wrong here, and I suggest it is the Court: Justice Scalia's dissent in Rutan v. Republican Party of Illinois (June 21, 1990) 360

Notes to Justice Scalia's dissent in Rutan v. Republican Party of Illinois (June 21, 1990) 372

Confrontation Clause—doesn't exclude young children: Justice Scalia's dissent in Maryland v. Craig (June 27, 1990) 375

Miranda: Justice Scalia's dissent in Minnick v. Mississippi (December 3, 1990) 382

Although today's decision neither follows the law nor produces desirable concrete results, it certainly has great symbolic value: Justice Scalia's dissent in Edmonson v. Leesville Concrete Co. (June 3, 1991) 388

Legislative History: Justice Scalia's concurrence in United States v. R. L. C. (March 24, 1992) 390

Racial imbalances are not government-mandated segregation: Justice Scalia's concurrence in Freeman v. Pitts (March 31, 1992) 392

No traditions can violate the establishment clause: Justice Scalia's dissent in Lee v. Weisman (June 24, 1992) 396

Abortion: Justice Scalia's concurrence and dissent in Planned Parenthood of Southeastern Pa. v. Casey (June 29, 1992) 407

Notes to Justice Scalia's dissent in Planned Parenthood of Southeastern Pa. v. Casey (June 29, 1992) 419

In making life easier for ourselves we not appear to make it harder for the lower federal courts: Justice Scalia's concurrence in Herrera v. Collins (January 23, 1993) 422

Ordinary meaning: Justice Scalia's dissent in Smith v. United States (June 1, 1993) 423

Like some ghoul in a late-night horror movie: Justice Scalia's concurrence in Lamb's Chapel v. Center Moriches Union Free School District (June 7, 1993) ... 427

Overruling past decisions: Justice Scalia's concurrence in Harper v. Virginia Department of Taxation (June 18, 1993) 429

Quite obviously, not every restriction upon expression that did not exist in 1791 or in 1868 is ipso facto unconstitutional: Justice Scalia's dissent in McIntyre v. Ohio Elections Commission (April 19, 1995) 434

Government can never have a "compelling interest" in discriminating on the basis of race in order to "make up" for past racial discrimination: Justice Scalia's concurrence in Adarand Constructors, Inc. v. Pena (June 12, 1995) 443

Can't single out groups from disfavorable treatment: Justice Scalia's dissent in Romer v. Evans (May 20, 1996) 443

Notes to Justice Scalia's dissent in Romer v. Evans (May 20, 1996) 453

Single-Sex colleges constitutional: Justice Scalia's dissent in United States v. Virginia (June 26, 1996) 454

Notes to Justice Scalia's dissent in United States v. Virginia (June 26, 1996) 474

One would think it inconceivable that Elrod and Branti would be extended far beyond Rutan to the massive field of all government contracting : Justice Scalia's dissent in Board of Commissioners, Wabaunsee County, Kansas v. Umbehr (June 28, 1996) 477

Notes to Justice Scalia's dissent in Board of Commissioners, Wabaunsee County, Kansas v. Umbehr (June 28, 1996) 490

A sentencing enhancement based on a prior conviction should be subject to the Sixth Amendment requirement for a jury to determine the fact beyond a reasonable doubt: Justice Scalia's dissent in Almendarez-Torres v. United States (March 24, 1998) 493

Notes to Justice Scalia's dissent in Almendarez-Torres v. United States (March 24, 1998) 506

Standing and Line-Item Veto: Justice Scalia's concurrence and dissent in Clinton v. New York (June 25, 1998) 508

Miranda warning is not in the constitution: Justice Scalia's dissent in Dickerson v. United States (June 26, 2000) 518

Notes to Justice Scalia's dissent in Dickerson v. United States (June 26, 2000) 530

Justice Breyer proceeds on the erroneous and all-too-common assumption that the Constitution means what we think it ought to mean. It does not; it means what it says: Justice Scalia's concurrence in Apprendi v. New Jersey (June 26, 2000) 531

Speech, public forums: Justice Scalia's dissent in Hill v. Colorado (June 28, 2000) 532

Notes to Justice Scalia's dissent in Hill v. Colorado (June 28, 2000) 545

Americans with Disabilities Act (Golf): Justice Scalia's dissent in PGA Tour, Inc. v. Casey Martin (May 29, 2001) 547

Death Penalty: Justice Scalia's dissent in Atkins v. Virginia (June 20, 2002) 556

Notes to Justice Scalia's dissent in Atkins v. Virginia (June 20, 2002) 565

Using race in college admissions: Justice Scalia's concurrence and dissent in Grutter v. Bollinger (June 23, 2003) 566

Unenumerated Rights: Justice Scalia's dissent in Lawrence v. Texas (June 26, 2003) 568

Notes to Justice Scalia's dissent in Lawrence v. Texas (June 26, 2003) 579

Campaign finance limits: Justice Scalia's concurrence and dissent in McConnell v. Federal Election Commission (December 10, 2003) 580

Hamdi is entitled to a habeas decree requiring his release unless (1) criminal proceedings are promptly brought, or (2) Congress has suspended the writ of habeas corpus: Justice Scalia's dissent in Hamdi v. Rumsfeld (June 28, 2004) 590

Notes to Justice Scalia's dissent in Hamdi v. Rumsfeld (June 28, 2004) 604

Homegrown marijuana must be outlawed to prevent it going into other homes: Justice Scalia's concurrence in Gonzales v. Raich (June 6, 2005) 606

If a law states "as of that date" it includes anything pending as of that date: Justice Scalia's dissent in Hamdan v. Rumsfeld (June 29, 2006) 611

Notes to Justice Scalia's dissent in Hamdan v. Rumsfeld (June 29, 2006) 623

I would therefore reconsider the decision that sets us the unsavory task of separating issue-speech from election-speech with no clear criterion: Justice Scalia's concurrence and dissent in Federal Election Commission v. Wisconsin Right to Life (June 25, 2007) 626

Notes to Justice Scalia's concurrence and dissent in FEC v. Wisconsin Right to Life (June 25, 2007) 637

Association: Justice Scalia's dissent in Washington State Grange v. Washington State Republican Party (March 18, 2008) 639

Justice Scalia's statement in Kennedy v. Louisiana (October 1, 2008) 645

Facts necessary to lengthen sentence should have to be found by jury, not judge: Justice Scalia's dissent in Oregon v. Ice (January 14, 2009) 646

Corporate speech protected: Justice Scalia's concurrence in Citizens United v. Federal Elections Commission (January 21, 2010) 650

Notes to Justice Scalia's concurrence in Citizens United v. Federal Elections Commission (January 21, 2010) 653

Incorporation: Justice Scalia's concurrence in McDonald v. Chicago (June 28, 2010) 655

Notes to Justice Scalia's Concurrence in McDonald v. Chicago (June 28, 2010)662

California does not need to release 46,000 prisoners: Justice Scalia's dissent in Brown v. Plata (May 23, 2011) 665

Immigration law: Justice Scalia's concurrence and dissent in Arizona v. United States (June 25, 2012) 674

Notes to Justice Scalia's dissent in Arizona v. United States (June 25, 2012) 686

Mandatory Health Insurance: Justice Scalia's (or Justice Kennedy's?) dissent in National Federation of Independent Business v. Sebelius (June 28, 2012) 687

Notes to Justice Scalia (or Justice Kennedy's?) dissent in National Federation of Independent Business v. Sebelius (June 28, 2012) 722

Searches and Seizures of DNA: Justice Scalia's dissent in Maryland v. King (June 2, 2013) 724

Notes to Justice Scalia's dissent in Maryland v. King (June 2, 2013) 734

We have no power to decide this case, and the law is legal: Justice Scalia's dissent in United States v. Windsor (June 26, 2013) 735

Notes to Justice Scalia's dissent in United States v. Windsor (June 26, 2013) ... 748

Justice Scalia's dissent from denial of application for stay in Brown v. Plata [and Coleman] (August 2, 2013) 750

Equal Treatment and Non-discrimination: Justice Scalia's concurrence in Schuette v. BAMN (April 22, 2014) 751

Notes to Justice Scalia's dissent in Schuette v. BAMN (April 22, 2014) 759

Separation of Powers, Treaties: Justice Scalia's dissent in Bond v. United States (June 2, 2014) 761

Recess Appointments: Justice Scalia's concurrence in National Labor Relations Board v. Noel Canning (June 26, 2014) 771

Notes to Justice Scalia's concurrence in National Labor Relations Board v. Noel Canning (June 26, 2014) 796

Redistricting: Justice Scalia's dissent in Alabama Legislative Black Caucus v. Alabama (March 25, 2015) 800

Bait-and-Switch: Justice Scalia's concurrence and dissent in City and County of San Francisco v. Sheehan (May 18, 2015) 808

Exchanges established by the state: Justice Scalia's dissent in King v. Burwell (June 25, 2015) 810

Same-Sex Marriage: Justice Scalia's dissent in Obergefell v. Hodges (June 26, 2015) 822

Acknowledgements

Websites (in no particular order):

www.law.cornell.edu
supreme.justia.com
caselaw.findlaw.com
law.resource.org
openjurist.org
www.constitution.org
scholar.google.com
en.wikipedia.org

Decisions

Need warrant to move people's stuff in plain-view to record identifying information to check against database to see if it's stolen: Arizona v. Hicks (March 3, 1987)

JUSTICE SCALIA delivered the opinion of the Court.

In Coolidge v. New Hampshire, 403 U. S. 443 (1971), we said that, in certain circumstances, a warrantless seizure by police of an item that comes within plain view during their lawful search of a private area may be reasonable under the Fourth Amendment. See id. at 403 U. S. 465-471 (plurality opinion); id. at 465 U. S. 505-506 (Black, J., concurring and dissenting); id. at 465 U. S. 521-522 (WHITE, J., concurring and dissenting). We granted certiorari, 475 U.S. 1107 (1986), in the present case to decide whether this "plain view" doctrine may be invoked when the police have less than probable cause to believe that the item in question is evidence of a crime or is contraband.

I

On April 18, 1984, a bullet was fired through the floor of respondent's apartment, striking and injuring a man in the apartment below. Police officers arrived and entered respondent's apartment to search for the shooter, for other victims, and for weapons. They found and seized three weapons, including a sawed-off rifle, and in the course of their search also discovered a stocking-cap mask.

One of the policemen, Officer Nelson, noticed two sets of expensive stereo components, which seemed out of place in the squalid and otherwise ill-appointed four-room apartment. Suspecting that they were stolen, he read and recorded their serial numbers -- moving some of the components, including a Bang and Olufsen turntable, in order to do so -- which he then reported by phone to his headquarters. On being advised that the turntable had been taken in an armed robbery, he seized it immediately. It was later determined that some of the other serial numbers matched those on other stereo equipment taken in the same armed robbery, and a warrant was obtained and executed to seize that equipment as well. Respondent was subsequently indicted for the robbery.

The state trial court granted respondent's motion to suppress the evidence that had been seized. The Court of Appeals of Arizona affirmed. It was conceded that the initial entry and search, although warrantless, were justified by the exigent circumstance of the shooting. The Court of Appeals viewed the obtaining of the serial numbers, however, as an additional search, unrelated to that exigency. Relying upon a statement in Mincey v. Arizona, 437 U. S. 385 (1978), that a "warrantless search must be strictly circumscribed by the exigencies which justify its initiation,'" id. at 437 U. S. 393 (citation omitted), the Court of Appeals held that the police conduct violated the Fourth Amendment, requiring the evidence derived from that conduct to be excluded. 146 Ariz. 533, 534-535, 707 P.2d 331, 332-333 (1985). Both courts -- the trial court explicitly and the Court of Appeals by necessary implication -- rejected the State's contention that Officer Nelson's actions were justified under the "plain view" doctrine of Coolidge v. New Hampshire, supra. The Arizona Supreme Court denied review, and the State filed this petition.

II

As an initial matter, the State argues that Officer Nelson's actions constituted neither a "search" nor a "seizure" within the meaning of the Fourth Amendment. We agree that the mere recording of the serial numbers did not constitute a seizure. To be sure, that was the first step in a process by which respondent was eventually deprived of the stereo equipment. In and of itself, however, it did not "meaningfully interfere" with respondent's possessory interest in either the serial numbers or the equipment, and therefore did not amount to a seizure. See Maryland v. Macon, 472 U. S. 463, 472 U. S. 469 (1985).

Officer Nelson's moving of the equipment, however, did constitute a "search" separate and apart from the search for the shooter, victims, and weapons that was the lawful objective of his entry into the apartment. Merely inspecting those parts of the turntable that came into view during the latter search would not have constituted an independent search, because it would have produced no additional invasion of respondent's privacy interest. See Illinois v. Andreas, 463 U. S. 765, 463 U. S. 771 (1983). But taking action, unrelated to the objectives of the authorized intrusion, which exposed to view concealed portions of the apartment or its contents, did produce a new invasion of respondent's privacy unjustified by the exigent circumstance that validated the entry. This is why, contrary to JUSTICE POWELL's suggestion, post at 480 U. S. 333, the "distinction between looking' at a suspicious object in plain view and `moving' it even a few inches" is much more than trivial for purposes of the Fourth Amendment. It matters not that the search uncovered nothing of any great personal value to respondent -- serial numbers rather than (what might conceivably have been hidden behind or under the equipment) letters or photographs. A search is a search, even if it happens to disclose nothing but the bottom of a turntable.

III

The remaining question is whether the search was "reasonable" under the Fourth Amendment.

On this aspect of the case, we reject, at the outset, the apparent position of the Arizona Court of Appeals that, because the officers' action directed to the stereo equipment was unrelated to the justification for their entry into respondent's apartment, it was ipso facto unreasonable. That lack of relationship always exists with regard to action validated under the "plain view" doctrine; where action is taken for the purpose justifying the entry, invocation of the doctrine is superfluous. Mincey v. Arizona, supra, in saying that a warrantless search must be "strictly circumscribed by the exigencies which justify its initiation," 437 U.S. at 437 U. S. 393 (citation omitted), was addressing only the scope of the primary search itself, and was not overruling by implication the many cases acknowledging that the "plain view" doctrine can legitimate action beyond that scope.

We turn, then, to application of the doctrine to the facts of this case. "It is well established that, under certain circumstances, the police may seize evidence in plain view without a warrant," Coolidge v. New Hampshire, 403 U.S. at 403 U. S. 465 (plurality opinion) (emphasis added). Those circumstances include situations

"[w]here the initial intrusion that brings the police within plain view of such [evidence] is supported . . . by one of the recognized exceptions to the warrant requirement,"

ibid., such as the exigent circumstances intrusion here. It would be absurd to say that an object could lawfully be seized and taken from the premises, but could not be moved for closer examination. It is clear, therefore, that the search here was valid if the "plain view" doctrine would have sustained a seizure of the equipment.

There is no doubt it would have done so if Officer Nelson had probable cause to believe that the equipment was stolen. The State has conceded, however, that he had only a "reasonable suspicion," by which it means something less than probable cause. See Brief for Petitioner 18-19. * We have not ruled on the question whether probable cause is required in order to invoke the "plain view" doctrine. Dicta in Payton v. New York, 445 U. S. 573, 445 U. S. 587 (1980), suggested that the standard of probable cause must be met, but our later opinions in Texas v. Brown, 460 U. S. 730 (1983), explicitly regarded the issue as unresolved, see id. at 460 U. S. 742, n. 7 (plurality opinion); id. at 460 U. S. 746 (STEVENS, J., concurring in judgment).

We now hold that probable cause is required. To say otherwise would be to cut the "plain view" doctrine loose from its theoretical and practical moorings. The theory of that doctrine consists of extending to nonpublic places such as the home, where searches and seizures without a warrant are presumptively unreasonable, the police's longstanding authority to make warrantless seizures in public places of such objects as weapons and contraband. See Payton v. New York, supra, at 445 U. S. 586-587. And the practical justification for that extension is the desirability of sparing police, whose viewing of the object in the course of a lawful search is as legitimate as it would have been in a public place, the inconvenience and the risk -- to themselves or to preservation of the evidence -- of going to obtain a warrant. See Coolidge v. New Hampshire, supra, at 403 U. S. 468 (plurality opinion). Dispensing with the need for a warrant is worlds apart from permitting a lesser standard of cause for the seizure than a warrant would require, i.e., the standard of probable cause. No reason is apparent why an object should routinely be seizable on lesser grounds, during an unrelated search and seizure, than would have been needed to obtain a warrant for that same object if it had been known to be on the premises.

We do not say, of course, that a seizure can never be justified on less than probable cause. We have held that it can -- where, for example, the seizure is minimally intrusive and operational necessities render it the only practicable means of detecting certain types of crime. See, e.g., United States v. Cortez, 449 U. S. 411 (1981) (investigative detention of vehicle suspected to be transporting illegal aliens); United States v. Brignoni-Ponce, 422 U. S. 873 (1975) (same); United States v. Place, 462 U. S. 696, 462 U. S. 709, and n. 9 (1983) (dictum) (seizure of suspected drug dealer's luggage at airport to permit exposure to specially trained dog). No special operational necessities are relied on here, however -- but rather the mere fact that the items in question came lawfully within the officer's plain view. That alone cannot supplant the requirement of probable cause.

The same considerations preclude us from holding that, even though probable cause would have been necessary for a seizure, the search of objects in plain view that occurred here could be sustained on lesser grounds. A dwelling place search, no less than a dwelling place seizure, requires probable cause, and there is no reason in theory or practicality why application of the "plain view" doctrine would supplant that requirement. Although the interest protected by the Fourth Amendment injunction against unreasonable searches is quite different from that protected by its injunction against unreasonable seizures, see Texas v. Brown, supra, at 460 U. S. 747-748 (STEVENS, J., concurring in judgment), neither the one nor the other is of inferior worth or necessarily requires only lesser protection. We have not elsewhere drawn a categorical distinction between the two insofar as concerns the degree of justification needed to establish the reasonableness of police action, and we see no reason for a distinction in the particular circumstances before us here. Indeed, to treat searches more liberally would especially erode the plurality's warning in Coolidge that

"the 'plain view' doctrine may not be used to extend a general exploratory search from one object to another until something incriminating at last emerges."

403 U.S. at 403 U. S. 466. In short, whether legal authority to move the equipment could be found only as an inevitable concomitant of the authority to seize it, or also as a consequence of some independent power to search certain objects in plain view, probable cause to believe the equipment was stolen was required.

JUSTICE O'CONNOR's dissent suggests that we uphold the action here on the ground that it was a "cursory inspection," rather than a "full-blown search," and could therefore be justified by reasonable suspicion instead of probable cause. As already noted, a truly cursory inspection -- one that involves merely looking at what is already exposed to view, without disturbing it -- is not a "search" for Fourth Amendment purposes, and therefore does not even require reasonable suspicion. We are unwilling to send police and judges into a new thicket of Fourth Amendment law, to seek a creature of uncertain description that is neither a "plain view" inspection nor yet a "full-blown search." Nothing in the prior opinions of this Court supports such a distinction, not even the dictum from Justice Stewart's concurrence in Stanley v. Georgia, 394 U. S. 557, 394 U. S. 571 (1969), whose reference to a "mere inspection" describes, in our view, close observation of what lies in plain sight.

JUSTICE POWELL's dissent reasonably asks what it is we would have had Officer Nelson do in these circumstances. Post at 480 U. S. 332. The answer depends, of course, upon whether he had probable cause to conduct a search, a question that was not preserved in this case. If he had, then he should have done precisely what he did. If not, then he should have followed up his suspicions, if possible, by means other than a search -- just as he would have had to do if, while walking along the street, he had noticed the same suspicious stereo equipment sitting inside a house a few feet away from him, beneath an open window. It may well be that, in such circumstances, no effective means short of a search exist. But there is nothing new in the realization that the Constitution sometimes insulates the criminality of a few in order to protect the privacy of us all. Our disagreement with the dissenters pertains to where the proper balance should be struck; we choose to adhere to the textual and traditional standard of probable cause.

The State contends that, even if Officer Nelson's search violated the Fourth Amendment, the court below should have admitted the evidence thus obtained under the "good faith" exception to the exclusionary rule. That was not the question on which certiorari was granted, and we decline to consider it.

For the reasons stated, the judgment of the Court of Appeals of Arizona is
Affirmed.

* Contrary to the suggestion in JUSTICE O'CONNOR's dissent, post at 480 U. S. 339, this concession precludes our considering whether the probable cause standard was satisfied in this case.

A tax credit against the Ohio fuel sales tax for each gallon of ethanol, but only if the ethanol is produced in Ohio or in a State that grants similar tax advantages to ethanol produced in Ohio is unconstitutional: New Energy Company of Indiana v. Limbach (May 31, 1988)

Justice SCALIA delivered the opinion of the Court.

Appellant New Energy Company of Indiana has challenged the constitutionality of Ohio Rev.Code Ann. § 5735.145(B) (1986), a provision that awards a tax credit against the Ohio motor vehicle fuel sales tax for each gallon of ethanol sold (as a component of gasohol) by fuel dealers, but only if the ethanol is produced in Ohio or in a State that grants similar tax advantages to ethanol produced in Ohio. The question presented is whether § 5735.145(B) discriminates against interstate commerce in violation of the Commerce Clause, U.S. Const., Art. I, § 8, cl. 3.

* Ethanol, or ethyl alcohol, is usually made from corn. In the last decade it has come into widespread use as an automotive fuel, mixed with gasoline in a ratio of 1 to 9 to produce what is called gasohol. The interest in ethanol emerged in reaction to the petroleum market dislocations of the early 1970's. The product was originally promoted as a means of achieving energy independence while providing a market for surplus corn; more recently, emphasis has shifted to its environmental advantages as a replacement for lead in enhancing fuel octane. See United States Department of Agriculture, Ethanol:

Economic and Policy Tradeoffs 1 (1988). Ethanol was, however (and continues to be), more expensive than gasoline, and the emergence of ethanol production on a commercial scale dates from enactment of the first federal subsidy, in the form of an exemption from federal motor fuel excise taxes, in 1978. See Energy Tax Act of 1978, Pub.L. 95-618, § 221, 92 Stat. 3185, codified, as amended, at 26 U.S.C. 4041, 4081 (1982 ed. and Supp. IV). Since then, many States, particularly those in the grain-producing areas of the country, have enacted their own ethanol subsidies. See United States General Accounting Office, Importance and Impact of Federal Alcohol Fuel Tax Incentives 5 (1984). Ohio first passed such a measure in 1981, providing Ohio gasohol dealers a credit of so many cents per gallon of ethanol used in their product against the Ohio motor vehicle fuel sales tax payable on both ethanol and gasoline. This credit was originally available without regard to the source of the ethanol. See Act of June 10, 1981, § 1, 1981-1982 Ohio Leg. Acts 1693, 1731-1732. In 1984, however, Ohio enacted § 5735.145(B), which denies the credit to ethanol coming from States that do not grant a tax credit, exemption, or refund to ethanol from Ohio, or, if a State grants a smaller tax advantage than Ohio's, granting only an equivalent credit to ethanol from that State. 1

Appellant is an Indiana limited partnership that manufactures ethanol in South Bend, Indiana, for sale in several States, including Ohio. Indiana repealed its tax exemption for ethanol, effective July 1, 1985, see Act of Mar. 5, 1984, §§ 4, 5, 8, 1984 Ind. Acts 189, 194-195, at which time it also passed legislation providing a direct subsidy to Indiana ethanol producers (the sole one of which was appellant). See Ind.Code §§ 4-4-10.1-1 to 4-4-10.1-8 (Supp.1987). Thus, by reason of Ohio's reciprocity provision, appellant's ethanol sold in Ohio became ineligible for the Ohio tax credit. Appellant sought declaratory and injunctive relief in the Court of Common Pleas of Franklin County, Ohio, alleging that § 5735.145(B) violated the Commerce Clause by discriminating against out-of-state ethanol producers to the advantage of in-state industry. 2 The court denied relief, and the Ohio Court of Appeals affirmed. A divided Ohio Supreme Court initially reversed, finding that § 5735.145(B) discriminated without adequate justification against products of out-of-state origin, and shielded Ohio producers from out-of-state competition. The Ohio Supreme Court then granted appellees' motion for rehearing and reversed itself, a majority of the court finding that the provision was not protectionist or unreasonably burdensome. 32 Ohio St.3d 206, 513 N.E.2d 258 (1987). We noted probable jurisdiction. 484 U.S. 984, 108 S.Ct. 500, 98 L.Ed.2d 499 (1987).

II

It has long been accepted that the Commerce Clause not only grants Congress the authority to regulate commerce among the States, but also directly limits the power of the States to discriminate against interstate commerce. See, e.g., Hughes v. Oklahoma, 441 U.S. 322, 326, 99 S.Ct. 1727, 1731, 60 L.Ed.2d 250 (1979); H.P. Hood & Sons, Inc. v. Du Mond, 336 U.S. 525, 534-535, 69 S.Ct. 657, 663, 93 L.Ed. 865 (1949); Welton v. Missouri, 91 U.S. (1 Otto) 275, 23 L.Ed. 347 (1876). This "negative" aspect of the Commerce Clause prohibits economic protectionism—that is, regulatory measures designed to benefit in-state economic interests by burdening out-of-state competitors. See, e.g., Bacchus Imports, Ltd. v. Dias, 468 U.S. 263, 270-273, 104 S.Ct. 3049, 3054-3056, 82 L.Ed.2d 200 (1984); H.P. Hood & Sons, supra, 336 U.S., at 532-533, 69 S.Ct., at 662; Guy v. Baltimore, 100 U.S. (10 Otto) 434, 443, 25 L.Ed. 743 (1880). Thus, state statutes that clearly discriminate against interstate commerce are routinely struck down, see, e.g., Sporhase v. Nebraska ex rel. Douglas, 458 U.S. 941, 102 S.Ct. 3456, 73 L.Ed.2d 1254 (1982); Lewis v. BT Investment Managers, Inc., 447 U.S. 27, 100 S.Ct. 2009, 64 L.Ed.2d 702 (1980); Dean Milk Co. v. Madison, 340 U.S. 349, 71 S.Ct. 295, 95 L.Ed. 329 (1951), unless the discrimination is demonstrably justified by a valid factor unrelated to economic protectionism, see, e.g., Maine v. Taylor, 477 U.S. 131, 106 S.Ct. 2440, 91 L.Ed.2d 110 (1986).

The Ohio provision at issue here explicitly deprives certain products of generally available beneficial tax treatment because they are made in certain other States, and thus on its face appears to violate the cardinal requirement of nondiscrimination. Appellees argue, however, that the availability of the tax credit to some out-of-state manufacturers (those in States that give tax advantages to Ohio-produced ethanol) shows that the Ohio provision, far from discriminating against interstate commerce, is likely to promote it, by encouraging other States to enact similar tax advantages that will spur the interstate sale of ethanol. We rejected a similar contention in an earlier "reciprocity" case, Great Atlantic & Pacific Tea Co. v. Cottrell, 424 U.S. 366, 96 S.Ct. 923, 47 L.Ed.2d 55 (1976). The regulation at issue there permitted milk from out of State to be sold in Mississippi only if the State of origin accepted Mississippi milk on a reciprocal basis. Mississippi put forward, among other arguments, the assertion that "the reciprocity requirement is in effect a free-trade provision, advancing the identical national interest that is served by the Commerce Clause." Id., at 378, 96 S.Ct., at 932. In response, we said that "Mississippi may not use the threat of economic isolation as a weapon to force sister States to enter into even a desirable reciprocity agreement." Id., at 379, 96 S.Ct., at 932. More recently, we characterized a Nebraska reciprocity requirement for the export of ground water from the State as "facially discriminatory legislation" which merited " 'strictest scrutiny.' " Sporhase v. Nebraska ex rel. Douglas, supra, 458 U.S., at 958, 102 S.Ct., at 3465, quoting Hughes v. Oklahoma, supra, 441 U.S., at 337, 99 S.Ct., at 1736.

It is true that in Cottrell and Sporhase the effect of a State's refusal to accept the offered reciprocity was total elimination of all transport of the subject product into or out of the offering State; whereas in the present case the only effect of refusal is that the out-of-state product is placed at a substantial commercial disadvantage through discriminatory tax treatment. That makes no difference for purposes of Commerce Clause analysis. In the leading case of Baldwin v. G.A.F. Seelig, Inc., 294 U.S. 511, 55 S.Ct. 497, 79 L.Ed. 1032 (1935), the New York law excluding out-of-state milk did not impose an absolute ban, but rather allowed importation and sale so long as the initial purchase from the dairy farmer was made at or above the New York State-mandated price. In other words, just as the appellant here, in order to sell its product in Ohio, only has to cut its profits by reducing its sales price below the market price sufficiently to compensate the Ohio purchaser-retailer for the forgone tax credit, so also the milk wholesaler-distributor in Baldwin, in order to sell its product in New York, only had to cut its profits by increasing its purchase price above the market price sufficiently to meet the New York-prescribed minimum. We viewed the New York law as "an economic barrier against competition" that was "equivalent to a rampart of customs duties." Id., at 527, 55 S.Ct., at 502. Similarly, in Hunt v. Washington Apple Advertising Comm'n, 432 U.S. 333, 349-351, 97 S.Ct. 2434, 2444-2445, 53 L.Ed.2d 383 (1977), we found invalid under the Commerce Clause a North Carolina statute that did not exclude apples from other States, but merely imposed additional costs upon Washington sellers and deprived them of the commercial advantage of their distinctive grading system. The present law likewise imposes an economic disadvantage upon out-of-state sellers; and the promise to remove that if reciprocity is accepted no more justifies disparity of treatment than it would justify categorical exclusion. We have indicated that reciprocity requirements are not per se unlawful. See Cottrell, supra, 424 U.S., at 378, 96 S.Ct., at 931. But the case we cited for that proposition, Kane v. New Jersey, 242 U.S. 160, 167-168, 37 S.Ct. 30, 31-32, 61 L.Ed. 222 (1916), discussed a context in which, if a State offered the reciprocity did not accept it, the consequence was, to be sure, less favored treatment for its citizens, but nonetheless treatment that complied with the minimum requirements of the Commerce Clause. Here, quite to the contrary, the threat used to induce Indiana's acceptance is, in effect, taxing a product made by its manufacturers at a rate higher than the same product made by Ohio manufacturers, without (as we shall see) justification for the disparity.

Appellees argue that § 5735.145(B) should not be considered discrimination against interstate commerce because its practical scope is so limited. Apparently only one Ohio ethanol manufacturer exists (appellee South Point Ethanol) and only one out-of-state manufacturer (appellant) is clearly disadvantaged by the provision. Our cases, however, indicate that where discrimination is patent, as it is here, neither a widespread advantage to in-state interests nor a widespread disadvantage to out-of-state competitors need be shown. For example, in Bacchus Imports, Ltd. v. Dias, supra, we held unconstitutional under the Commerce Clause a special exemption from Hawaii's liquor tax for certain locally produced alcoholic beverages (okolehao and fruit wine), even though other locally produced alcoholic beverages were subject to the tax. Id., 468 U.S., at 265, 271, 104 S.Ct., at 3052, 3055. And in Lewis v. BT Investment Managers, Inc., supra, we held unconstitutional a Florida statute that excluded from certain business activities in Florida not all out-of-state entities, but only out-of-state bank holding companies, banks, or trust companies. In neither of these cases did we consider the size or number of the in-state businesses favored or the out-of-state businesses disfavored relevant to our determination. Varying the strength of the bar against economic protectionism according to the size and number of in-state and out-of-state firms affected would serve no purpose except the creation of new uncertainties in an already complex field.

Appellees contend that even if § 5735.145(B) is discriminatory, the discrimination is not covered by the Commerce Clause because of the so-called market-participant doctrine. That doctrine differentiates between a State's acting in its distinctive governmental capacity, and a State's acting in the more general capacity of a market participant; only the former is subject to the limitations of the negative Commerce Clause. See Hughes v. Alexandria Scrap Corp., 426 U.S. 794, 806-810, 96 S.Ct. 2488, 2496-2498, 49 L.Ed.2d 220 (1976). Thus, for example, when a State chooses to manufacture and sell cement, its business methods, including those that favor its residents, are of no greater constitutional concern than those of a private business. See Reeves, Inc. v. Stake, 447 U.S. 429, 438-439, 100 S.Ct. 2271, 2278, 65 L.Ed.2d 244 (1980).

The market-participant doctrine has no application here. The Ohio action ultimately at issue is neither its purchase nor its sale of ethanol, but its assessment and computation of taxes—a primeval governmental activity. To be sure, the tax credit scheme has the purpose and effect of subsidizing a particular industry, as do many dispositions of the tax laws. That does not transform it into a form of state participation in the free market. Our opinion in Alexandria Scrap, supra, a case on which appellees place great reliance, does not remotely establish such a proposition. There we examined, and upheld against Commerce Clause attack on the basis of the market-participant doctrine, a Maryland cash subsidy program that discriminated in favor of in-state auto-hulk processors. The purpose of the program was to achieve the removal of unsightly abandoned autos from the State, id., 426 U.S., at 796-797, 96 S.Ct., at 2491, and the Court characterized it as proprietary rather than regulatory activity, based on the analogy of the State to a private purchaser of the auto hulks, id., at 808-810, 96 S.Ct., at 2496-2498. We have subsequently observed that subsidy programs unlike that of Alexandria Scrap might not be characterized as proprietary. See Reeves, Inc., supra, 447 U.S., at 440, n. 14, 100 S.Ct., at 2279, n. 14. We think it clear that Ohio's assessment and computation of its fuel sales tax, regardless of whether it produces a subsidy, cannot plausibly be analogized to the activity of a private purchaser.

It has not escaped our notice that the appellant here, which is eligible to receive a cash subsidy under Indiana's program for in-state ethanol producers, is the potential beneficiary of a scheme no less discriminatory than the one that it attacks, and no less effective in conferring a commercial advantage over out-of-state competitors. To believe the Indiana scheme is valid, however, is not to believe that the Ohio scheme must be valid as well. The Commerce Clause does not prohibit all state action designed to give its residents an advantage in the marketplace, but only action of that description in connection with the State's regulation of interstate commerce. Direct subsidization of domestic industry does not ordinarily run afoul of that prohibition; discriminatory taxation of out-of-state manufacturers does. Of course, even if the Indiana subsidy were invalid, retaliatory violation of the Commerce Clause by Ohio would not be acceptable. See Cottrell, 424 U.S., at 379-380, 96 S.Ct., at 931-932.

III

Our cases leave open the possibility that a State may validate a statute that discriminates against interstate commerce by showing that it advances a legitimate local purpose that cannot be adequately served by reasonable nondiscriminatory alternatives. See, e.g., Maine v. Taylor, 477 U.S., at 138, 151, 106 S.Ct., at 2447, 2454; Sporhase v. Nebraska ex rel. Douglas, 458 U.S., at 958; Hughes v. Oklahoma, 441 U.S., at 336-337, 99 S.Ct., at 1736; Dean Milk Co. v. Madison, 340 U.S., at 354, 71 S.Ct., at 297. This is perhaps just another way of saying that what may appear to be a "discriminatory" provision in the constitutionally prohibited sense—that is, a protectionist enactment—may on closer analysis not be so. However it be put, the standards for such justification are high. Cf. Philadelphia v. New Jersey, 437 U.S. 617, 624, 98 S.Ct. 2531, 2535, 57 L.Ed.2d 475 (1978) ("Where simple economic protectionism is effected by state legislation, a virtually per se rule of invalidity has been erected"); Hughes v. Oklahoma, supra, 441 U.S., at 337, 99 S.Ct., at 1737 ("Facial discrimination by itself may be a fatal defect" and "at a minimum . . . invokes the strictest scrutiny").

Appellees advance two justifications for the clear discrimination in the present case: health and commerce. As to the first, they argue that the provision encourages use of ethanol (in replacement of lead as a gasoline octane-enhancer) to reduce harmful exhaust emissions, both in Ohio itself and in surrounding States whose polluted atmosphere may reach Ohio. Certainly the protection of health is a legitimate state goal, and we assume for purposes of this argument that use of ethanol generally furthers it. But § 5735.145(B) obviously does not, except perhaps by accident. As far as ethanol use in Ohio itself is concerned, there is no reason to suppose that ethanol produced in a State that does not offer tax advantages to ethanol produced in Ohio is less healthy, and thus should have its importation into Ohio suppressed by denial of the otherwise standard tax credit. And as far as ethanol use outside Ohio is concerned, surely that is just as effectively fostered by other States' subsidizing ethanol production or sale in some fashion other than giving a tax credit to Ohio-produced ethanol; but these helpful expedients do not qualify for the tax credit. It could not be clearer that health is not the purpose of the provision, but is merely an occasional and accidental effect of achieving what is its purpose, favorable tax treatment for Ohio -produced ethanol. 3 Essentially the same reasoning also responds to appellees' second (and related) justification for the discrimination, that the reciprocity requirement is designed to increase commerce in ethanol by encouraging other States to enact ethanol subsidies. What is encouraged is not ethanol subsidies in general, but only favorable treatment for Ohio-produced ethanol. In sum, appellees' health and commerce justifications amount to no more than implausible speculation, which does not suffice to validate this plain discrimination against products of out-of-state manufacture.

For the reasons stated, the judgment of the Ohio Supreme Court is
Reversed.

Notes to New Energy Company of Indiana v. Limbach (May 31, 1988)

1. Section 5735.145(B) provides:

"The qualified fuel otherwise eligible for the qualified fuel credit shall not contain ethanol produced outside Ohio unless the tax commissioner determines that the fuel claimed to be eligible for credit contains ethanol produced in a state that also grants an exemption, credit or refund from such state's motor vehicle fuel excise tax or sales tax for similar fuel containing ethanol produced in Ohio; provided however, that such credit shall not exceed the amount of the credit allowable for qualified fuel containing ethanol produced in Ohio."

This provision was passed in 1984 and took effect on January 1, 1985. After this litigation began, Ohio again amended its ethanol credit statute to reduce the amount of the credit and scheduled it for elimination in 1993. See Ohio Rev.Code Ann. § 5735.145 (Supp.1987).

2. Appellant also argued there, as it has here, that § 5735.145(B) was an excessive burden on commerce under the test set forth in Pike v. Bruce Church, Inc., 397 U.S. 137, 142, 90 S.Ct. 844, 847, 25 L.Ed.2d 174 (1970). To the extent that claim requires separate analysis we find it unnecessary to reach it, in light of our disposition of the discrimination claim. Appellant also alleged in the state courts violations of the Equal Protection Clause and the Privileges and Immunities Clause of the Fourteenth Amendment; those challenges are not at issue in this appeal.

3. We do not interpret the trial court's acceptance of appellees' proposed finding of fact of April 10, 1985, as a judicial finding that protecting health was in fact a purpose of the Ohio General Assembly, rather than merely one of several conceivable purposes for the enactment. In any event, a subjective purpose that has so little rational relationship to the provision in question is not merely implausible but, even if true, inadequate to validate patent discrimination against interstate commerce.

Somehow Michael's contention that procedural due process requires that he be afforded an opportunity to demonstrate his paternity in an evidentiary hearing fundamentally misconceives the nature of § 621: Michael H. v. Gerald D. (June 15, 1989) [Judgment and opinion]

JUSTICE SCALIA announced the judgment of the Court and delivered an opinion, in which THE CHIEF JUSTICE joins, and in all but footnote 6 of which JUSTICE O'CONNOR and JUSTICE KENNEDY join.

Under California law, a child born to a married woman living with her husband is presumed to be a child of the marriage. Cal. Evid. Code Ann. 621 (West Supp. 1989). The presumption of legitimacy may be rebutted only by the husband or wife, and then only in limited circumstances. Ibid. The instant appeal presents the claim that this presumption infringes upon the due process rights of a man who wishes to establish his paternity of a child born to the wife of another man, and the claim that it infringes upon the constitutional right of the child to maintain a relationship with her natural father.

I

The facts of this case are, we must hope, extraordinary. On May 9, 1976, in Las Vegas, Nevada, Carole D., an international model, and Gerald D., a top executive in a French oil company, were married. The couple established a home in Playa del Rey, California, in which they resided as husband and wife when one or the other was not out of the country on business. In the summer of 1978, Carole became involved in an adulterous affair with a neighbor, Michael H. In September 1980, she conceived a child, Victoria D., who was born on May 11, 1981. Gerald was listed as father on the birth certificate and has always held Victoria out to the world as his daughter. Soon after delivery of the child, however, Carole informed Michael that she believed he might be the father.

In the first three years of her life, Victoria remained always with Carole, but found herself within a variety of quasi-family units. In October 1981, Gerald moved to New York City to pursue his business interests, but Carole chose to remain in California. At the end of that month, Carole and Michael had blood tests of themselves and Victoria, which showed a 98.07% probability that Michael was Victoria's father. In January 1982, Carole visited Michael in St. Thomas, where his primary business interests were based. There Michael held Victoria out as his child. In March, however, Carole left Michael and returned to California, where she took up residence with yet another man, Scott K. Later that spring, and again in the summer, Carole and Victoria spent time with Gerald in New York City, as well as on vacation in Europe. In the fall, they returned to Scott in California.

In November 1982, rebuffed in his attempts to visit Victoria, Michael filed a filiation action in California Superior Court to establish his paternity and right to visitation. In March 1983, the court appointed an attorney and guardian ad litem to represent Victoria's interests. Victoria then filed a cross-complaint asserting that if she had more than one psychological or de facto father, she was entitled to maintain her filial relationship, with all of the attendant rights, duties, and obligations, with both. In May 1983, Carole filed a motion for summary judgment. During this period, from March through July 1983, Carole was again living with Gerald in New York. In August, however, she returned to California, became involved once again with Michael, and instructed her attorneys to remove the summary judgment motion from the calendar.

For the ensuing eight months, when Michael was not in St. Thomas he lived with Carole and Victoria in Carole's apartment in Los Angeles and held Victoria out as his daughter. In April 1984, Carole and Michael signed a stipulation that Michael was Victoria's natural father. Carole left Michael the next month, however, and instructed her attorneys not to file the stipulation. In June 1984, Carole reconciled with Gerald and joined him in New York, where they now live with Victoria and two other children since born into the marriage.

In May 1984, Michael and Victoria, through her guardian ad litem, sought visitation rights for Michael pendente lite. To assist in determining whether visitation would be in Victoria's best interests, the Superior Court appointed a psychologist to evaluate Victoria, Gerald, Michael, and Carole. The psychologist recommended that Carole retain sole custody, but that Michael be allowed continued contact with Victoria pursuant to a restricted visitation schedule. The court concurred and ordered that Michael be provided with limited visitation privileges pendente lite.

On October 19, 1984, Gerald, who had intervened in the action, moved for summary judgment on the ground that under Cal. Evid. Code 621 there were no triable issues of fact as to Victoria's paternity. This law provides that "the issue of a wife cohabiting with her husband, who is not impotent or sterile, is conclusively presumed to be a child of the marriage." Cal. Evid. Code Ann. 621(a) (West Supp. 1989). The presumption may be rebutted by blood tests, but only if a motion for such tests is made, within two years from the date of the child's birth, either by the husband or, if the natural father has filed an affidavit acknowledging paternity, by the wife. 621(c) and (d).

On January 28, 1985, having found that affidavits submitted by Carole and Gerald sufficed to demonstrate that the two were cohabiting at conception and birth and that Gerald was neither sterile nor impotent, the Superior Court granted Gerald's motion for summary judgment, rejecting Michael's and Victoria's challenges to the constitutionality of 621. The court also denied their motions for continued visitation pending the appeal under Cal. Civ. Code 4601, which provides that a court may, in its discretion, grant "reasonable visitation rights . . . to any . . . person having an interest in the welfare of the child." Cal. Civ. Code Ann. 4601 (West Supp. 1989). It found that allowing such visitation would "violat[e] the intention of the Legislature by impugning the integrity of the family unit." Supp. App. to Juris. Statement A-91.

On appeal, Michael asserted, inter alia, that the Superior Court's application of 621 had violated his procedural and substantive due process rights. Victoria also raised a due process challenge to the statute, seeking to preserve her de facto relationship with Michael as well as with Gerald. She contended, in addition, that as 621 allows the husband and, at least to a limited extent, the mother, but not the child, to rebut the presumption of legitimacy, it violates the child's right to equal protection. Finally, she asserted a right to continued visitation with Michael under 4601. After submission of briefs and a hearing, the California Court of Appeal affirmed the judgment of the Superior Court and upheld the constitutionality of the statute. 191 Cal. App. 3d 995, 236 Cal. Rptr. 810 (1987). It interpreted that judgment, moreover, as having denied permanent visitation rights under 4601, regarding that as the implication of the Superior Court's reliance upon 621 and upon an earlier California case, Vincent B. v. Joan R., 126 Cal. App. 3d 619, 179 Cal. Rptr. 9 (1981), appeal dism'd, 459 U.S. 807 (1982), which had held that once an assertion of biological paternity is "determined to be legally impossible" under

621, visitation against the wishes of the mother should be denied under 4601. 126 Cal. App. 3d, at 627-628, 179 Cal. Rptr., at 13.

The Court of Appeal denied Michael's and Victoria's petitions for rehearing, and, on July 30, 1987, the California Supreme Court denied discretionary review. On February 29, 1988, we noted probable jurisdiction of the present appeal. 485 U.S. 903 . Before us, Michael and Victoria both raise equal protection and due process challenges. We do not reach Michael's equal protection claim, however, as it was neither raised nor passed upon below. See Bankers Life & Casualty Co. v. Crenshaw, 486 U.S. 71 (1988).

II

The California statute that is the subject of this litigation is, in substance, more than a century old. California Code of Civ. Proc. 1962(5), enacted in 1872, provided that "[t]he issue of a wife cohabiting with her husband, who is not impotent, is indisputably presumed to be legitimate." In 1955, the legislature amended the statute by adding the preface: "Notwithstanding any other provision of law." 1955 Cal. Stats., ch. 948, p. 1835, 3. In 1965, when California's Evidence Code was adopted, the statute was codified as 621, with no substantive change except replacement of the word "indisputably" with "conclusively," 1965 Cal. Stats., ch. 299, 2, pp. 1297, 1308. When California adopted the Uniform Parentage Act, 1975 Cal. Stats., ch. 1244, 11, pp. 3196-3201, codified at Cal. Civ. Code Ann. 7000 et seq. (West 1983), it amended 621 by replacing the word "legitimate" with the phrase "a child of the marriage" and by adding nonsterility to nonimpotence and cohabitation as a predicate for the presumption. 1975 Cal. Stats., ch. 1244, 13, p. 3202. In 1980, the legislature again amended the statute to provide the husband an opportunity to introduce blood-test evidence in rebuttal of the presumption, 1980 Cal. Stats., ch. 1310, p. 4433; and in 1981 amended it to provide the mother such an opportunity, 1981 Cal. Stats., ch. 1180, p. 4761. In their present form, the substantive provisions of the statute are as follows:

" 621. Child of the marriage; notice of motion for blood tests

"(a) Except as provided in subdivision (b), the issue of a wife cohabiting with her husband, who is not impotent or sterile, is conclusively presumed to be a child of the marriage.

"(b) Notwithstanding the provisions of subdivision (a), if the court finds that the conclusions of all the experts, as disclosed by the evidence based upon blood tests performed pursuant to Chapter 2 (commencing with Section 890) of Division 7 are that the husband is not the father of the child, the question of paternity of the husband shall be resolved accordingly.

"(c) The notice of motion for blood tests under subdivision (b) may be raised by the husband not later than two years from the child's date of birth.

"(d) The notice of motion for blood tests under subdivision (b) may be raised by the mother of the child not later than two years from the child's date of birth if the child's biological father has filed an affidavit with the court acknowledging paternity of the child.

"(e) The provisions of subdivision (b) shall not apply to any case coming within the provisions of Section 7005 of the Civil Code [dealing with artificial insemination] or to any case in which the wife, with the consent of the husband, conceived by means of a surgical procedure."

III

We address first the claims of Michael. At the outset, it is necessary to clarify what he sought and what he was denied. California law, like nature itself, makes no provision for dual fatherhood. Michael was seeking to be declared the father of Victoria. The immediate benefit he evidently sought to obtain from that status was visitation rights. See Cal. Civ. Code Ann. 4601 (West 1983) (parent has statutory right to visitation "unless it is shown that such visitation would be detrimental to the best interests of the child"). But if Michael were successful in being declared the father, other rights would follow - most importantly, the right to be considered as the parent who should have custody, Cal. Civ. Code Ann. 4600 (West 1983), a status which "embrace[s] the sum of parental rights with respect to the rearing of a child, including the child's care; the right to the child's services and earnings; the right to direct the child's activities; the right to make decisions regarding the control, education, and health of the child; and the right, as well as the duty, to prepare the child for additional obligations, which includes the teaching of moral standards, religious beliefs, and elements of good citizenship." 4 California Family Law 60.021.[b] (C. Markey ed. 1987) (footnotes omitted). All parental rights, including visitation, were automatically denied by denying Michael status as the father. While Cal. Civ. Code Ann. 4601 places it within the discretionary power of a court to award visitation rights to a nonparent, the Superior Court here, affirmed by the Court of Appeal, held that California law denies visitation, against the wishes of the mother, to a putative father who has been prevented by 621 from establishing his paternity. See 191 Cal. App. 3d, at 1013, 236 Cal. Rptr., at 821, citing Vincent B. v. Joan R., 126 Cal. App. 3d, at 627-628 179 Cal. Rptr., at 13.

Michael raises two related challenges to the constitutionality of 621. First, he asserts that requirements of procedural due process prevent the State from terminating his liberty interest in his relationship with his child without affording him an opportunity to demonstrate his paternity in an evidentiary hearing. We believe this claim derives from a fundamental misconception of the nature of the California statute. While 621 is phrased in terms of a presumption, that rule of evidence is the implementation of a substantive rule of law. California declares it to be, except in limited circumstances, irrelevant for paternity purposes whether a child conceived during, and born into, an existing marriage was begotten by someone other than the husband and had a prior relationship with him. As the Court of Appeal phrased it:

"`The conclusive presumption is actually a substantive rule of law based upon a determination by the Legislature as a matter of overriding social policy, that given a certain relationship between the husband and wife, the husband is to be held responsible for the child, and that the integrity of the family unit should not be impugned.'" 191 Cal.

App. 3d, at 1005, 236 Cal. Rptr., at 816, quoting Vincent B. v. Joan R., supra, at 623, 179 Cal. Rptr., at 10.

Of course the conclusive presumption not only expresses the State's substantive policy but also furthers it, excluding inquiries into the child's paternity that would be destructive of family integrity and privacy. 1

This Court has struck down as illegitimate certain "irrebuttable presumptions." See, e. g., Stanley v. Illinois, 405 U.S. 645 (1972); Vlandis v. Kline, 412 U.S. 441 (1973); Cleveland Board of Education v. LaFleur, 414 U.S. 632 (1974). Those holdings did not, however, rest upon procedural due process. A conclusive presumption does, of course, foreclose the person against whom it is invoked from demonstrating, in a particularized proceeding, that applying the presumption to him will in fact not further the lawful governmental policy the presumption is designed to effectuate. But the same can be said of any legal rule that establishes general classifications, whether framed in terms of a presumption or not. In this respect there is no difference between a rule which says that the marital husband shall be irrebuttably presumed to be the father, and a rule which says that the adulterous natural father shall not be recognized as the legal father. Both rules deny someone in Michael's situation a hearing on whether, in the particular circumstances of his case, California's policies would best be served by giving him parental rights. Thus, as many commentators have observed, see, e. g., Bezanson, Some Thoughts on the Emerging Irrebuttable Presumption Doctrine, 7 Ind. L. Rev. 644 (1974); Nowak, Realigning the Standards of Review Under the Equal Protection Guarantee - Prohibited, Neutral, and Permissive Classifications, 62 Geo. L. J. 1071, 1102-1106 (1974); Note, Irrebuttable Presumptions: An Illusory Analysis, 27 Stan. L. Rev. 449 (1975); Note, The Irrebuttable Presumption Doctrine in the Supreme Court, 87 Harv. L. Rev. 1534 (1974), our "irrebuttable presumption" cases must ultimately be analyzed as calling into question not the adequacy of procedures but - like our cases involving classifications framed in other terms, see, e. g., Craig v. Boren, 429 U.S. 190 (1976); Carrington v. Rash, 380 U.S. 89 (1965) - the adequacy of the "fit" between the classification and the policy that the classification serves. See LaFleur, supra, at 652 (Powell, J., concurring in result); Vlandis, supra, at 456-459 (WHITE, J., concurring), 466-469 (REHNQUIST, J., dissenting); Weinberger v. Salfi, 422 U.S. 749 (1975). We therefore reject Michael's procedural due process challenge and proceed to his substantive claim.

Michael contends as a matter of substantive due process that, because he has established a parental relationship with Victoria, protection of Gerald's and Carole's marital union is an insufficient state interest to support termination of that relationship. This argument is, of course, predicated on the assertion that Michael has a constitutionally protected liberty interest in his relationship with Victoria.

It is an established part of our constitutional jurisprudence that the term "liberty" in the Due Process Clause extends beyond freedom from physical restraint. See, e. g., Pierce v. Society of Sisters, 268 U.S. 510 (1925); Meyer v. Nebraska, 262 U.S. 390 (1923). Without that core textual meaning as a limitation, defining the scope of the Due Process

Clause "has at times been a treacherous field for this Court," giving "reason for concern lest the only limits to . . . judicial intervention become the predilections of those who happen at the time to be Members of this Court." Moore v. East Cleveland, 431 U.S. 494, 502 (1977). The need for restraint has been cogently expressed by JUSTICE WHITE:

> "That the Court has ample precedent for the creation of new constitutional rights should not lead it to repeat the process at will. The Judiciary, including this Court, is the most vulnerable and comes nearest to illegitimacy when it deals with judge-made constitutional law having little or no cognizable roots in the language or even the design of the Constitution. Realizing that the present construction of the Due Process Clause represents a major judicial gloss on its terms, as well as on the anticipation of the Framers . . ., the Court should be extremely reluctant to breathe still further substantive content into the Due Process Clause so as to strike down legislation adopted by a State or city to promote its welfare. Whenever the Judiciary does so, it unavoidably pre-empts for itself another part of the governance of the country without express constitutional authority." Moore, supra, at 544 (dissenting opinion).

In an attempt to limit and guide interpretation of the Clause, we have insisted not merely that the interest denominated as a "liberty" be "fundamental" (a concept that, in isolation, is hard to objectify), but also that it be an interest traditionally protected by our society. 2 As we have put it, the Due Process Clause affords only those protections "so rooted in the traditions and conscience of our people as to be ranked as fundamental." Snyder v. Massachusetts, 291 U.S. 97, 105 (1934) (Cardozo, J.). Our cases reflect "continual insistence upon respect for the teachings of history [and] solid recognition of the basic values that underlie our society. . . ." Griswold v. Connecticut, 381 U.S. 479, 501 (1965) (Harlan, J., concurring in judgment).

This insistence that the asserted liberty interest be rooted in history and tradition is evident, as elsewhere, in our cases according constitutional protection to certain parental rights. Michael reads the landmark case of Stanley v. Illinois, 405 U.S. 645 (1972), and the subsequent cases of Quilloin v. Walcott, 434 U.S. 246 (1978), Caban v. Mohammed, 441 U.S. 380 (1979), and Lehr v. Robertson, 463 U.S. 248 (1983), as establishing that a liberty interest is created by biological fatherhood plus an established parental relationship - factors that exist in the present case as well. We think that distorts the rationale of those cases. As we view them, they rest not upon such isolated factors but upon the historic respect - indeed, sanctity would not be too strong a term - traditionally accorded to the relationships that develop within the unitary family. 3 See Stanley, supra, at 651; Quilloin, supra, at 254-255; Caban, supra, at 389; Lehr, supra, at 261. In Stanley, for example, we forbade the destruction of such a family when, upon the death of the mother, the State had sought to remove children from the custody of a father who had lived with and supported them and their mother for 18 years. As Justice Powell stated for the plurality in Moore v. East Cleveland, supra, at 503: "Our decisions establish that the Constitution protects the sanctity of the family precisely because the institution of the family is deeply rooted in this Nation's history and tradition."

Thus, the legal issue in the present case reduces to whether the relationship between persons in the situation of Michael and Victoria has been treated as a protected family unit under the historic practices of our society, or whether on any other basis it has been accorded special protection. We think it impossible to find that it has. In fact, quite to the contrary, our traditions have protected the marital family (Gerald, Carole, and the child they acknowledge to be theirs) against the sort of claim Michael asserts. 4

The presumption of legitimacy was a fundamental principle of the common law. H. Nicholas, Adulturine Bastardy 1 (1836). Traditionally, that presumption could be rebutted only by proof that a husband was incapable of procreation or had had no access to his wife during the relevant period. Id., at 9-10 (citing Bracton, De Legibus et Consuetudinibus Angliae, bk. i, ch. 9, p. 6; bk. ii, ch. 29, p. 63, ch. 32, p. 70 (1569)). As explained by Blackstone, nonaccess could only be proved "if the husband be out of the kingdom of England (or, as the law somewhat loosely phrases it, extra quatuor maria [beyond the four seas]) for above nine months. . . ." 1 Blackstone's Commentaries 456 (J. Chitty ed. 1826). And, under the common law both in England and here, "neither husband nor wife [could] be a witness to prove access or nonaccess." J. Schouler, Law of the Domestic Relations 225, p. 306 (3d ed. 1882); R. Graveson & F. Crane, A Century of Family Law: 1857-1957, p. 158 (1957). The primary policy rationale underlying the common law's severe restrictions on rebuttal of the presumption appears to have been an aversion to declaring children illegitimate, see Schouler, supra, 225, at 306-307; M. Grossberg, Governing the Hearth 201 (1985), thereby depriving them of rights of inheritance and succession, 2 J. Kent, Commentaries on American Law *175, and likely making them wards of the state. A secondary policy concern was the interest in promoting the "peace and tranquillity of States and families," Schouler, supra, 225, at 304, quoting Boullenois, Traite des Status, bk. 1, p. 62, a goal that is obviously impaired by facilitating suits against husband and wife asserting that their children are illegitimate. Even though, as bastardy laws became less harsh, "[j]udges in both [England and the United States] gradually widened the acceptable range of evidence that could be offered by spouses, and placed restraints on the `four seas rule' . . . [,] the law retained a strong bias against ruling the children of married women illegitimate." Grossberg, supra, at 202.

We have found nothing in the older sources, nor in the older cases, addressing specifically the power of the natural father to assert parental rights over a child born into a woman's existing marriage with another man. Since it is Michael's burden to establish that such a power (at least where the natural father has established a relationship with the child) is so deeply embedded within our traditions as to be a fundamental right, the lack of evidence alone might defeat his case. But the evidence shows that even in modern times - when, as we have noted, the rigid protection of the marital family has in other respects been relaxed - the ability of a person in Michael's position to claim paternity has not been generally acknowledged. For example, a 1957 annotation on the subject: "Who may dispute presumption of legitimacy of child conceived or born during wedlock," 53 A. L. R. 2d 572, shows three States (including California) with statutes limiting standing to the husband or wife and their descendants, one State (Louisiana) with a statute limiting it to the husband, two States (Florida and Texas) with judicial decisions limiting standing to the husband, and two States (Illinois and New York) with judicial decisions denying standing even to the mother. Not a single decision is set forth specifically according standing to the natural father, and "express indications of the nonexistence of any ... limitation" upon standing were found only "in a few jurisdictions." Id., at 579.

Moreover, even if it were clear that one in Michael's position generally possesses, and has generally always possessed, standing to challenge the marital child's legitimacy, that would still not establish Michael's case. As noted earlier, what is at issue here is not entitlement to a state pronouncement that Victoria was begotten by Michael. It is no conceivable denial of constitutional right for a State to decline to declare facts unless some legal consequence hinges upon the requested declaration. What Michael asserts here is a right to have himself declared the natural father and thereby to obtain parental prerogatives. 5 What he must establish, therefore, is not that our society has traditionally allowed a natural father in his circumstances to establish paternity, but that it has traditionally accorded such a father parental rights, or at least has not traditionally denied them. Even if the law in all States had always been that the entire world could challenge the marital presumption and obtain a declaration as to who was the natural father, that would not advance Michael's claim. Thus, it is ultimately irrelevant, even for purposes of determining current social attitudes towards the alleged substantive right Michael asserts, that the present law in a number of States appears to allow the natural father - including the natural father who has not established a relationship with the child - the theoretical power to rebut the marital presumption, see Note, Rebutting the Marital Presumption: A Developed Relationship Test, 88 Colum.L.Rev. 369, 373 (1988). What counts is whether the States in fact award substantive parental rights to the natural father of a child conceived within, and born into, an extant marital union that wishes to embrace the child. We are not aware of a single case, old or new, that has done so. This is not the stuff of which fundamental rights qualifying as liberty interests are made. 6

In Lehr v. Robertson, a case involving a natural father's attempt to block his child's adoption by the unwed mother's new husband, we observed that "[t]he significance of the biological connection is that it offers the natural father an opportunity that no other male possesses to develop a relationship with his offspring," 463 U.S., at 262, and we assumed that the Constitution might require some protection of that opportunity, id., at 262-265. Where, however, the child is born into an extant marital family, the natural father's unique opportunity conflicts with the similarly unique opportunity of the husband of the marriage; and it is not unconstitutional for the State to give categorical preference to the latter. In Lehr we quoted approvingly from Justice Stewart's dissent in Caban v. Mohammed, 441 U.S., at 397, to the effect that although "`[i]n some circumstances the actual relationship between father and child may suffice to create in the unwed father parental interests comparable to those of the married father,'" "`the absence of a legal tie with the mother may in such circumstances appropriately place a limit on whatever substantive constitutional claims might otherwise exist.'" 463 U.S., at 260, n. 16. In accord with our traditions, a limit is also imposed by the circumstance that the mother is, at the time of the child's conception and birth, married to, and cohabitating with, another man, both of whom wish to raise the child as the offspring of their union. 7 It is a question of legislative policy and not constitutional law whether California will allow the presumed parenthood of a couple desiring to retain a child conceived within and born into their marriage to be rebutted.

We do not accept JUSTICE BRENNAN's criticism that this result "squashes" the liberty that consists of "the freedom not to conform." Post, at 141. It seems to us that reflects the erroneous view that there is only one side to this controversy - that one disposition can expand a "liberty" of sorts without contracting an equivalent "liberty" on the other side. Such a happy choice is rarely available. Here, to provide protection to an adulterous natural father is to deny protection to a marital father, and vice versa. If Michael has a "freedom not to conform" (whatever that means), Gerald must equivalently have a "freedom to conform." One of them will pay a price for asserting that "freedom" - Michael by being unable to act as father of the child he has adulterously begotten, or Gerald by being unable to preserve the integrity of the traditional family unit he and Victoria have established. Our disposition does not choose between these two "freedoms," but leaves that to the people of California. JUSTICE BRENNAN's approach chooses one of them as the constitutional imperative, on no apparent basis except that the unconventional is to be preferred.

IV

We have never had occasion to decide whether a child has a liberty interest, symmetrical with that of her parent, in maintaining her filial relationship. We need not do so here because, even assuming that such a right exists, Victoria's claim must fail. Victoria's due process challenge is, if anything, weaker than Michael's. Her basic claim is not that California has erred in preventing her from establishing that Michael, not Gerald, should stand as her legal father. Rather, she claims a due process right to maintain filial relationships with both Michael and Gerald. This assertion merits little discussion, for, whatever the merits of the guardian ad litem's belief that such an arrangement can be of great psychological benefit to a child, the claim that a State must recognize multiple fatherhood has no support in the history or traditions of this country. Moreover, even if we were to construe Victoria's argument as forwarding the lesser proposition that, whatever her status vis-a-vis Gerald, she has a liberty interest in maintaining a filial relationship with her natural father, Michael, we find that, at best, her claim is the obverse of Michael's and fails for the same reasons.

Victoria claims in addition that her equal protection rights have been violated because, unlike her mother and presumed father, she had no opportunity to rebut the presumption of her legitimacy. We find this argument wholly without merit. We reject, at the outset, Victoria's suggestion that her equal protection challenge must be assessed under a standard of strict scrutiny because, in denying her the right to maintain a filial relationship with Michael, the State is discriminating against her on the basis of her illegitimacy. See Gomez v. Perez, 409 U.S. 535, 538 (1973). Illegitimacy is a legal construct, not a natural trait. Under California law, Victoria is not illegitimate, and she is treated in the same manner as all other legitimate children: she is entitled to maintain a filial relationship with her legal parents.

We apply, therefore, the ordinary "rational relationship" test to Victoria's equal protection challenge. The primary rationale underlying 621's limitation on those who may rebut the presumption of legitimacy is a concern that allowing persons other than the husband or wife to do so may undermine the integrity of the marital union. When the husband or wife contests the legitimacy of their child, the stability of the marriage has already been shaken. In contrast, allowing a claim of illegitimacy to be pressed by the child - or, more accurately, by a court-appointed guardian ad litem - may well disrupt an otherwise peaceful union. Since it pursues a legitimate end by rational means, California's decision to treat Victoria differently from her parents is not a denial of equal protection.

The judgment of the California Court of Appeal is

Affirmed.

Notes to Michael H. v. Gerald D. (June 15, 1989)

[1] In those circumstances in which California allows a natural father to rebut the presumption of legitimacy of a child born to a married woman, e. g., where the husband is impotent or sterile, or where the husband and wife have not been cohabiting, it is more likely that the husband already knows the child is not his, and thus less likely that the paternity hearing will disrupt an otherwise harmonious and apparently exclusive marital relationship.

[2] We do not understand what JUSTICE BRENNAN has in mind by an interest "that society traditionally has thought important . . . without protecting it." Post, at 140. The protection need not take the form of an explicit constitutional provision or statutory guarantee, but it must at least exclude (all that is necessary to decide the present case) a societal tradition of enacting laws denying the interest. Nor do we understand why our practice of limiting the Due Process Clause to traditionally protected interests turns the Clause "into a redundancy," post, at 141. Its purpose is to prevent future generations from lightly casting aside important traditional values - not to enable this Court to invent new ones.

[3] JUSTICE BRENNAN asserts that only a "pinched conception of `the family'" would exclude Michael, Carole, and Victoria from protection. Post, at 145. We disagree. The family unit accorded traditional respect in our society, which we have referred to as the "unitary family," is typified, of course, by the marital family, but also includes the household of unmarried parents and their children. Perhaps the concept can be expanded even beyond this, but it will bear no resemblance to traditionally respected relationships - and will thus cease to have any constitutional significance - if it is stretched so far as to

include the relationship established between a married woman, her lover, and their child, during a 3-month sojourn in St. Thomas, or during a subsequent 8-month period when, if he happened to be in Los Angeles, he stayed with her and the child.

[4] JUSTICE BRENNAN insists that in determining whether a liberty interest exists we must look at Michael's relationship with Victoria in isolation, without reference to the circumstance that Victoria's mother was married to someone else when the child was conceived, and that that woman and her husband wish to raise the child as their own. See post, at 145-146. We cannot imagine what compels this strange procedure of looking at the act which is assertedly the subject of a liberty interest in isolation from its effect upon other people - rather like inquiring whether there is a liberty interest in firing a gun where the case at hand happens to involve its discharge into another person's body. The logic of JUSTICE BRENNAN's position leads to the conclusion that if Michael had begotten Victoria by rape, that fact would in no way affect his possession of a liberty interest in his relationship with her.

[5] According to JUSTICE BRENNAN, Michael does not claim - and in order to prevail here need not claim - a substantive right to maintain a parental relationship with Victoria, but merely the right to "a hearing on the issue" of his paternity. Post, at 156, n. 12. "Michael's challenge . . . does not depend," we are told, "on his ability ultimately to obtain visitation rights." Post, at 147. To be sure it does not depend upon his ability ultimately to obtain those rights, but it surely depends upon his asserting a claim to those rights, which is precisely what JUSTICE BRENNAN denies. We cannot grasp the concept of a "right to a hearing" on the part of a person who claims no substantive entitlement that the hearing will assertedly vindicate.

[6] Justice Brennan criticized our methodology in using historical traditions specifically relating to the rights of an adulterous natural father, rather than inquiring more generally "whether parenthood is an interest that historically has received our attention and protection." Post, at 139, 105 L.Ed.2d, at 116. There seems to us no basis for the contention that this methodology is "nove[l]," post, at 140, 105 L.Ed.2d, at 117. For example, in Bowers v. Hardwick, 478 U.S. 186, 92 L.Ed.2d 140 (1986), we noted that at the time the Fourteenth Amendment was ratified all but 5 of the 37 States had criminal sodomy laws, that all 50 of the States had such laws prior to 1961, and that 24 States and the District of Columbia continued to have them; and we concluded from that record, regarding that very specific aspect of sexual conduct, that "to claim that a right to engage in such conduct is `deeply rooted in this Nation's history and tradition' or `implicit in the concept of ordered liberty' is, at best, facetious." Id., at 194. In Roe v. Wade, 410 U.S. 113, 35 L.Ed.2d 147 (1973), we spent about a fifth of our opinion negating the proposition that there was a longstanding tradition of laws proscribing abortion, Id., at 129-141.

We do not understand why, having rejected our focus upon the societal tradition regarding the natural father's rights vis-a-vis a child whose mother is married to another man, Justice Brennan would choose to focus instead upon "parenthood." Why should the relevant category not be even more general - perhaps "family relationships"; or "personal relationships"; or even "emotional attachments in general"? Though the dissent has no basis for the level of generality it would select, we do: We refer to the most specific level at which a relevant tradition protecting, or denying protection to, the asserted right can be identified. If, for example, there were no societal tradition, either way, regarding the rights of the natural father of a child adulterously conceived, we would have to consult, and ((if possible) reason from, the traditions regarding natural fathers in general. But there is such a more specific tradition, and it unqualifiedly denies protection to such a parent.

One would think that Justice Brennan would appreciate the value of consulting the most specific tradition available, since he acknowledges that "[e]ven if we can agree . . . that `family' and `parenthood' are part of the good life, it is absurd to assume that we can agree on the content of those terms and destructive to pretend that we do." Post, at 141, 105 L.Ed.2d, at 117. Because such general traditions provide such imprecise guidance, they permit judges to dictate rather than discern the society's views. The need, if arbitrary decisionmaking is to be avoided, to adopt the most specific tradition as the point of reference - or at least to announce, as Justice Brennan declines to do, some other criterion for selecting among the innumerable relevant traditions that could be consulted - is well enough exemplified by the fact that in the present case Justice Brennan's opinion and Justice O'Connor's opinion, post, p 132, 105 L.Ed.2d, at 111-112, which disapproves this footnote, both appeal to the tradition, but on the basis of the tradition they select reach opposite results. Although assuredly having the virtue (if it be that) of leaving judges free to decide as they think best when the unanticipated occurs, a rule of law that binds neither by text nor by any particular, identifiable tradition is no rule of law at all.

Finally, we may note that this analysis is not inconsistent with the result in cases such as Griswold v. Connecticut, 381 U.S. 479, 14 L.Ed.2d 510 (1965), or Eisenstadt v Baird, 405 U.S. 438, 31 L.Ed.2d 349 (1972). None of those cases acknowledged a longstanding and still extant societal tradition withholding the very right pronounced to be the subject of a liberty interest and then rejected it. Justice Brennan must do so here. In this case, the existence of such a tradition, continuing to the present day, refutes any possible contention that the alleged right is "so rooted in the traditions and conscience of our people as to be ranked as fundamental," Snyder v Massachusetts, 291 U.S. 97, 105 L.Ed. 674, 90 ALR 575 (1934), or "implicit in the concept of ordered liberty," Palko v. Connecticut, 302 U.S. 319, 325, 82 L.Ed. 288 (1937).

[7] JUSTICE BRENNAN chides us for thus limiting our holding to situations in which, as here, the husband and wife wish to raise her child jointly. The dissent believes that without this limitation we would be unable to "rely on the State's asserted interest in protecting the `unitary family' in denying that Michael and Victoria have been deprived of liberty." Post, at 147. As we have sought to make clear, however, and as the dissent elsewhere seems to understand, see post, at 139, 140-141, 145, 147, we rest our decision not upon our independent "balancing" of such interests, but upon the absence of any constitutionally protected right to legal parentage on the part of an adulterous natural

father in Michael's situation, as evidenced by long tradition. That tradition reflects a "balancing" that has already been made by society itself. We limit our pronouncement to the relevant facts of this case because it is at least possible that our traditions lead to a different conclusion with regard to adulterous fathering of a child whom the marital parents do not wish to raise as their own. It seems unfair for those who disagree with our holding to include among their criticisms that we have not extended the holding more broadly.

No exceptions for religious people: Employment Division, Department of Human Resources of Oregon v. Smith (April 17, 1990)

Justice SCALIA delivered the opinion of the Court.

This case requires us to decide whether the Free Exercise Clause of the First Amendment permits the State of Oregon to include religiously inspired peyote use within the reach of its general criminal prohibition on use of that drug, and thus permits the State to deny unemployment benefits to persons dismissed from their jobs because of such religiously inspired use.

I

Oregon law prohibits the knowing or intentional possession of a "controlled substance" unless the substance has been prescribed by a medical practitioner. Ore.Rev.Stat. § 475.992(4) (1987). The law defines "controlled substance" as a drug classified in Schedules I through V of the Federal Controlled Substances Act, 21 U.S.C. §§ 811-812 (1982 ed. and Supp. V), as modified by the State Board of Pharmacy. Ore.Rev.Stat. § 475.005(6) (1987). Persons who violate this provision by possessing a controlled substance listed on Schedule I are "guilty of a Class B felony." § 475.992(4)(a). As compiled by the State Board of Pharmacy under its statutory authority, see Ore.Rev.Stat. § 475.035 (1987), Schedule I contains the drug peyote, a hallucinogen derived from the plant Lophophorawilliamsii Lemaire. Ore.Admin. Rule 855-80-021(3)(s) (1988).

Respondents Alfred Smith and Galen Black were fired from their jobs with a private drug rehabilitation organization because they ingested peyote for sacramental purposes at a ceremony of the Native American Church, of which both are members. When respondents applied to petitioner Employment Division for unemployment compensation, they were determined to be ineligible for benefits because they had been discharged for work-related "misconduct". The Oregon Court of Appeals reversed that determination, holding that the denial of benefits violated respondents' free exercise rights under the First Amendment.

On appeal to the Oregon Supreme Court, petitioner argued that the denial of benefits was permissible because respondents' consumption of peyote was a crime under Oregon law. The Oregon Supreme Court reasoned, however, that the criminality of respondents' peyote use was irrelevant to resolution of their constitutional claim -- since the purpose of the "misconduct" provision under which respondents had been disqualified was not to enforce the State's criminal laws, but to preserve the financial integrity of the compensation fund, and since that purpose was inadequate to justify the burden that disqualification imposed on respondents' religious practice. Citing our decisions in Sherbert v. Verner, 374 U.S. 398 (1963), and Thomas v. Review Board, Indiana Employment Security Div., 450 U.S. 707 (1981), the court concluded that respondents were entitled to payment of unemployment benefits. Smith v. Employment Div., Dept. of Human Resources, 301 Or. 209, 217-219, 721 P.2d 445, 449-450 (1986). We granted certiorari. 480 U.S. 916 (1987).

Before this Court in 1987, petitioner continued to maintain that the illegality of respondents' peyote consumption was relevant to their constitutional claim. We agreed, concluding that

if a State has prohibited through its criminal laws certain kinds of religiously motivated conduct without violating the First Amendment, it certainly follows that it may impose the lesser burden of denying unemployment compensation benefits to persons who engage in that conduct.

Employment Div., Dept. of Human Resources of Oregon v. Smith, 485 U.S. 660, 670 (1988) (Smith I). We noted, however, that the Oregon Supreme Court had not decided whether respondents' sacramental use of peyote was in fact proscribed by Oregon's controlled substance law, and that this issue was a matter of dispute between the parties. Being "uncertain about the legality of the religious use of peyote in Oregon," we determined that it would not be "appropriate for us to decide whether the practice is protected by the Federal Constitution." Id. at 673. Accordingly, we vacated the judgment of the Oregon Supreme Court and remanded for further proceedings. Id. at 674.

On remand, the Oregon Supreme Court held that respondents' religiously inspired use of peyote fell within the prohibition of the Oregon statute, which "makes no exception for the sacramental use" of the drug. 307 Or. 68, 72-73, 763 P.2d 146, 148 (1988). It then considered whether that prohibition was valid under the Free Exercise Clause, and concluded that it was not. The court therefore reaffirmed its previous ruling that the State could not deny unemployment benefits to respondents for having engaged in that practice.

We again granted certiorari. 489 U.S. 1077 (1989).

II

Respondents' claim for relief rests on our decisions in Sherbert v. Verner, supra, Thomas v. Review Board, Indiana Employment Security Div., supra, and Hobbie v. Unemployment Appeals Comm'n of Florida, 480 U.S. 136 (1987), in which we held that a State could not condition the availability of unemployment insurance on an individual's willingness to forgo conduct required by his religion. As we observed in Smith I, however, the conduct at issue in those cases was not prohibited by law. We held that distinction to be critical, for if Oregon does prohibit the religious use of peyote, and if that prohibition is consistent with the Federal Constitution, there is no federal right to engage in that conduct in Oregon,

and

the State is free to withhold unemployment compensation from respondents for engaging in work-related misconduct, despite its religious motivation.

485 U.S. at 672. Now that the Oregon Supreme Court has confirmed that Oregon does prohibit the religious use of peyote, we proceed to consider whether that prohibition is permissible under the Free Exercise Clause.

A

The Free Exercise Clause of the First Amendment, which has been made applicable to the States by incorporation into the Fourteenth Amendment, see Cantwell v. Connecticut, 310 U.S. 296, 303 (1940), provides that "Congress shall make no law respecting an establishment of religion, or prohibiting the free exercise thereof. . . . " U.S. Const. Am. I (emphasis added). The free exercise of religion means, first and foremost, the right to believe and profess whatever religious doctrine one desires. Thus, the First Amendment obviously excludes all "governmental regulation of religious beliefs as such." Sherbert v. Verner, supra, 374 U.S. at 402. The government may not compel affirmation of religious belief, see Torcaso v. Watkins, 367 U.S. 488 (1961), punish the expression of religious doctrines it believes to be false, United States v. Ballard, 322 U.S. 78, 86-88 (1944), impose special disabilities on the basis of religious views or religious status, see McDaniel v. Paty, 435 U.S. 618 (1978); Fowler v. Rhode Island, 345 U.S. 67, 69 (1953); cf. Larson v. Valente, 456 U.S. 228, 245 (1982), or lend its power to one or the other side in controversies over religious authority or dogma, see Presbyterian Church v. Hull Church, 393 U.S. 440, 445-452 (1969); Kedroff v. St. Nicholas Cathedral, 344 U.S. 94, 95-119 (1952); Serbian Eastern Orthodox Diocese v. Milivojevich, 426 U.S. 696, 708-725 (1976).

But the "exercise of religion" often involves not only belief and profession but the performance of (or abstention from) physical acts: assembling with others for a worship service, participating in sacramental use of bread and wine, proselytizing, abstaining from certain foods or certain modes of transportation. It would be true, we think (though no case of ours has involved the point), that a state would be "prohibiting the free exercise [of religion]" if it sought to ban such acts or abstentions only when they are engaged in for religious reasons, or only because of the religious belief that they display. It would doubtless be unconstitutional, for example, to ban the casting of "statues that are to be used for worship purposes," or to prohibit bowing down before a golden calf.

Respondents in the present case, however, seek to carry the meaning of "prohibiting the free exercise [of religion]" one large step further. They contend that their religious motivation for using peyote places them beyond the reach of a criminal law that is not specifically directed at their religious practice, and that is concededly constitutional as applied to those who use the drug for other reasons. They assert, in other words, that "prohibiting the free exercise [of religion]" includes requiring any individual to observe a generally applicable law that requires (or forbids) the performance of an act that his religious belief forbids (or requires). As a textual matter, we do not think the words must be given that meaning. It is no more necessary to regard the collection of a general tax, for example, as "prohibiting the free exercise [of religion]" by those citizens who believe support of organized government to be sinful than it is to regard the same tax as "abridging the freedom . . . of the press" of those publishing companies that must pay the tax as a condition of staying in business. It is a permissible reading of the text, in the one case as in the other, to say that, if prohibiting the exercise of religion (or burdening the activity of printing) is not the object of the tax, but merely the incidental effect of a generally applicable and otherwise valid provision, the First Amendment has not been offended. Compare Citizen Publishing Co. v. United States, 394 U.S. 131, 139 (1969) (upholding application of antitrust laws to press), with Grosjean v. American Press Co., 297 U.S. 233, 250-251 (1936) (striking down license tax applied only to newspapers with weekly circulation above a specified level); see generally Minneapolis Star & Tribune Co. v. Minnesota Commissioner of Revenue, 460 U.S. 575, 581 (1983).

  Our decisions reveal that the latter reading is the correct one. We have never held that an individual's religious beliefs excuse him from compliance with an otherwise valid law prohibiting conduct that the State is free to regulate. On the contrary, the record of more than a century of our free exercise jurisprudence contradicts that proposition. As described succinctly by Justice Frankfurter in Minersville School Dist. Bd. of Educ. v. Gobitis, 310 U.S. 586, 594-595 (1940):

  Conscientious scruples have not, in the course of the long struggle for religious toleration, relieved the individual from obedience to a general law not aimed at the promotion or restriction of religious beliefs. The mere possession of religious convictions which contradict the relevant concerns of a political society does not relieve the citizen from the discharge of political responsibilities.

  (Footnote omitted.) We first had occasion to assert that principle in Reynolds v. United States, 98 U.S. 145 (1879), where we rejected the claim that criminal laws against polygamy could not be constitutionally applied to those whose religion commanded the practice. "Laws," we said,

  are made for the government of actions, and while they cannot interfere with mere religious belief and opinions, they may with practices. . . . Can a man excuse his practices to the contrary because of his religious belief? To permit this would be to make the professed doctrines of religious belief superior to the law of the land, and in effect to permit every citizen to become a law unto himself.

  Id. at 166-167.

  Subsequent decisions have consistently held that the right of free exercise does not relieve an individual of the obligation to comply with a

  valid and neutral law of general applicability on the ground that the law proscribes (or prescribes) conduct that his religion prescribes (or proscribes).

United States v. Lee, 455 U.S. 252, 263, n. 3 (1982) (STEVENS, J., concurring in judgment); see Minersville School Dist. Bd. of Educ. v. Gobitis, supra, 310 U.S. at 595 (collecting cases). In Prince v. Massachusetts, 321 U.S. 158 (1944), we held that a mother could be prosecuted under the child labor laws for using her children to dispense literature in the streets, her religious motivation notwithstanding. We found no constitutional infirmity in "excluding [these children] from doing there what no other children may do." Id. at 171. In Braunfeld v. Brown, 366 U.S. 599 (1961) (plurality opinion), we upheld Sunday closing laws against the claim that they burdened the religious practices of persons whose religions compelled them to refrain from work on other days. In Gillette v. United States, 401 U.S. 437, 461 (1971), we sustained the military selective service system against the claim that it violated free exercise by conscripting persons who opposed a particular war on religious grounds.

Our most recent decision involving a neutral, generally applicable regulatory law that compelled activity forbidden by an individual's religion was United States v. Lee, 455 U.S. at 258-261. There, an Amish employer, on behalf of himself and his employees, sought exemption from collection and payment of Social Security taxes on the ground that the Amish faith prohibited participation in governmental support programs. We rejected the claim that an exemption was constitutionally required. There would be no way, we observed, to distinguish the Amish believer's objection to Social Security taxes from the religious objections that others might have to the collection or use of other taxes.

If, for example, a religious adherent believes war is a sin, and if a certain percentage of the federal budget can be identified as devoted to war-related activities, such individuals would have a similarly valid claim to be exempt from paying that percentage of the income tax. The tax system could not function if denominations were allowed to challenge the tax system because tax payments were spent in a manner that violates their religious belief.

Id. at 260. Cf. Hernandez v. Commissioner, 490 U.S. 680 (1989) (rejecting free exercise challenge to payment of income taxes alleged to make religious activities more difficult).

The only decisions in which we have held that the First Amendment bars application of a neutral, generally applicable law to religiously motivated action have involved not the Free Exercise Clause alone, but the Free Exercise Clause in conjunction with other constitutional protections, such as freedom of speech and of the press, see Cantwell v. Connecticut, 310 U.S. at 304, 307 (invalidating a licensing system for religious and charitable solicitations under which the administrator had discretion to deny a license to any cause he deemed nonreligious); Murdock v. Pennsylvania, 319 U.S. 105 (1943) (invalidating a flat tax on solicitation as applied to the dissemination of religious ideas); Follett v. McCormick, 321 U.S. 573 (1944) (same), or the right of parents, acknowledged in Pierce v. Society of Sisters, 268 U.S. 510 (1925), to direct the education of their children, see Wisconsin v. Yoder, 406 U.S. 205 (1972) (invalidating compulsory school attendance laws as applied to Amish parents who refused on religious grounds to send their children to school). [n1] Some of our cases prohibiting compelled expression, decided exclusively upon free speech grounds, have also involved freedom of religion, cf. Wooley v. Maynard, 430 U.S. 705 (1977) (invalidating compelled display of a license plate slogan that offended individual religious beliefs); West Virginia Board of Education v. Barnette, 319 U.S. 624 (1943) (invalidating compulsory flag salute statute challenged by religious objectors). And it is easy to envision a case in which a challenge on freedom of association grounds would likewise be reinforced by Free Exercise Clause concerns. Cf. Roberts v. United States Jaycees, 468 U.S. 609, 622 (1983) ("An individual's freedom to speak, to worship, and to petition the government for the redress of grievances could not be vigorously protected from interference by the State [if] a correlative freedom to engage in group effort toward those ends were not also guaranteed.").

The present case does not present such a hybrid situation, but a free exercise claim unconnected with any communicative activity or parental right. Respondents urge us to hold, quite simply, that when otherwise prohibitable conduct is accompanied by religious convictions, not only the convictions but the conduct itself must be free from governmental regulation. We have never held that, and decline to do so now. There being no contention that Oregon's drug law represents an attempt to regulate religious beliefs, the communication of religious beliefs, or the raising of one's children in those beliefs, the rule to which we have adhered ever since Reynolds plainly controls.

Our cases do not at their farthest reach support the proposition that a stance of conscientious opposition relieves an objector from any colliding duty fixed by a democratic government.

Gillette v. United States, supra, 401 U.S. at 461.

B

Respondents argue that, even though exemption from generally applicable criminal laws need not automatically be extended to religiously motivated actors, at least the claim for a religious exemption must be evaluated under the balancing test set forth in Sherbert v. Verner, 374 U.S. 398 (1963). Under the Sherbert test, governmental actions that substantially burden a religious practice must be justified by a compelling governmental interest. See id. at 402-403; see also Hernandez v. Commissioner, supra, 490 U.S. at 699. Applying that test, we have, on three occasions, invalidated state unemployment compensation rules that conditioned the availability of benefits upon an applicant's willingness to work under conditions forbidden by his religion. See Sherbert v. Verner, supra; Thomas v. Review Board, Indiana Employment Div., 450 U.S. 707 (1981); Hobbie v. Unemployment Appeals Comm'n of Florida, 480 U.S. 136 (1987). We have never invalidated any governmental action on the basis of the Sherbert test except the denial of unemployment compensation. Although we have sometimes purported to apply the Sherbert test in contexts other than that, we have always found the test satisfied, see United States v. Lee, 455 U.S. 252 (1982); Gillette v. United States, 401 U.S. 437 (1971). In recent years we have abstained from applying the Sherbert test (outside the unemployment compensation field) at all. In Bowen v. Roy, 476 U.S. 693 (1986), we declined to apply Sherbert analysis to a federal statutory scheme that required benefit applicants and recipients to provide their Social Security numbers. The plaintiffs in that case asserted that it would violate their religious beliefs to obtain and provide a Social Security number for their daughter. We held the statute's application to the plaintiffs valid regardless of whether it was necessary to effectuate a compelling interest. See id. at 699-701. In Lyng v. Northwest Indian Cemetery Protective Assn., 485 U.S. 439 (1988), we declined to apply Sherbert analysis to the Government's logging and road construction activities on lands used for religious purposes by several Native American Tribes, even though it was undisputed that the activities "could have devastating effects on traditional Indian religious practices," 485 U.S. at 451. In Goldman v. Weinberger, 475 U.S. 503 (1986), we rejected application of the Sherbert test to military dress regulations that forbade the wearing of yarmulkes. In O'Lone v. Estate of Shabazz, 482 U.S. 342 (1987), we sustained, without mentioning the Sherbert test, a prison's refusal to excuse inmates from work requirements to attend worship services.

Even if we were inclined to breathe into Sherbert some life beyond the unemployment compensation field, we would not apply it to require exemptions from a generally applicable criminal law. The Sherbert test, it must be recalled, was developed in a context that lent itself to individualized governmental assessment of the reasons for the relevant conduct. As a plurality of the Court noted in Roy, a distinctive feature of unemployment compensation programs is that their eligibility criteria invite consideration of the particular circumstances behind an applicant's unemployment:

The statutory conditions [in Sherbert and Thomas] provided that a person was not eligible for unemployment compensation benefits if, "without good cause," he had quit work or refused available work. The "good cause" standard created a mechanism for individualized exemptions.

Bowen v. Roy, supra, 476 U.S. at 708 (opinion of Burger, C.J., joined by Powell and REHNQUIST, JJ.). See also Sherbert, supra, 374 U.S. at 401, n. 4 (reading state unemployment compensation law as allowing benefits for unemployment caused by at least some "personal reasons"). As the plurality pointed out in Roy, our decisions in the unemployment cases stand for the proposition that where the State has in place a system of individual exemptions, it may not refuse to extend that system to cases of "religious hardship" without compelling reason. Bowen v. Roy, supra, 476 U.S. at 708.

Whether or not the decisions are that limited, they at least have nothing to do with an across-the-board criminal prohibition on a particular form of conduct. Although, as noted earlier, we have sometimes used the Sherbert test to analyze free exercise challenges to such laws, see United States v. Lee, supra, 455 U.S. at 257-260; Gillette v. United States, supra, 401 U.S. at 462, we have never applied the test to invalidate one. We conclude today that the sounder approach, and the approach in accord with the vast majority of our precedents, is to hold the test inapplicable to such challenges. The government's ability to enforce generally applicable prohibitions of socially harmful conduct, like its ability to carry out other aspects of public policy, "cannot depend on measuring the effects of a governmental action on a religious objector's spiritual development." Lyng, supra, 485 U.S. at 451. To make an individual's obligation to obey such a law contingent upon the law's coincidence with his religious beliefs, except where the State's interest is "compelling" -- permitting him, by virtue of his beliefs, "to become a law unto himself," Reynolds v. United States, 98 U.S. at 167 -- contradicts both constitutional tradition and common sense. [n2]

The "compelling government interest" requirement seems benign, because it is familiar from other fields. But using it as the standard that must be met before the government may accord different treatment on the basis of race, see, e.g., Palmore v. Sidoti, 466 U.S. 429, 432 (1984), or before the government may regulate the content of speech, see, e.g., Sable Communications of California v. FCC, 492 U.S. 115 (1989), is not remotely comparable to using it for the purpose asserted here. What it produces in those other fields -- equality of treatment, and an unrestricted flow of contending speech -- are constitutional norms; what it would produce here -- a private right to ignore generally applicable laws -- is a constitutional anomaly. [n3]

Nor is it possible to limit the impact of respondents' proposal by requiring a "compelling state interest" only when the conduct prohibited is "central" to the individual's religion. Cf. Lyng v. Northwest Indian Cemetery Protective Assn., supra, 485 U.S. at 474-476 (BRENNAN, J., dissenting). It is no more appropriate for judges to determine the "centrality" of religious beliefs before applying a "compelling interest" test in the free exercise field than it would be for them to determine the "importance" of ideas before applying the "compelling interest" test in the free speech field. What principle of law or logic can be brought to bear to contradict a believer's assertion that a particular act is "central" to his personal faith? Judging the centrality of different religious practices is akin to the unacceptable "business of evaluating the relative merits of differing religious claims." United States v. Lee, 455 U.S. at 263 n. 2 (STEVENS, J., concurring). As we reaffirmed only last Term,

[i]t is not within the judicial ken to question the centrality of particular beliefs or practices to a faith, or the validity of particular litigants' interpretation of those creeds.

Hernandez v. Commissioner, 490 U.S. at 699. Repeatedly and in many different contexts, we have warned that courts must not presume to determine the place of a particular belief in a religion or the plausibility of a religious claim. See, e.g., Thomas v. Review Board, Indiana Employment Security Div., 450 U.S. at 716; Presbyterian Church v. Hull Church, 393 U.S. at 450; Jones v. Wolf, 443 U.S. 595, 602-606 (1979); United States v. Ballard, 322 U.S. 78, 85-87 (1944). [n4]

If the "compelling interest" test is to be applied at all, then, it must be applied across the board, to all actions thought to be religiously commanded. Moreover, if "compelling interest" really means what it says (and watering it down here would subvert its rigor in the other fields where it is applied), many laws will not meet the test. Any society adopting such a system would be courting anarchy, but that danger increases in direct proportion to the society's diversity of religious beliefs, and its determination to coerce or suppress none of them. Precisely because "we are a cosmopolitan nation made up of people of almost every conceivable religious preference," Braunfeld v. Brown, 366 U.S. at 606, and precisely because we value and protect that religious divergence, we cannot afford the luxury of deeming presumptively invalid, as applied to the religious objector, every regulation of conduct that does not protect an interest of the highest order. The rule respondents favor would open the prospect of constitutionally required religious exemptions from civic obligations of almost every conceivable kind -- ranging from compulsory military service, see, e.g., Gillette v. United States, 401 U.S. 437 (1971), to the payment of taxes, see, e.g., United States v. Lee, supra; to health and safety regulation such as manslaughter and child neglect laws, see, e.g., Funkhouser v. State, 763 P.2d 695 (Okla.Crim.App.1988), compulsory vaccination laws, see, e.g., Cude v. State, 237 Ark. 927, 377 S.W.2d 816 (1964), drug laws, see, e.g., Olsen v. Drug Enforcement Administration, 279 U.S.App.D.C. 1, 878 F.2d 1458 (1989), and traffic laws, see Cox v. New Hampshire, 312 U.S. 569 (1941); to social welfare legislation such as minimum wage laws, see Susan and Tony Alamo Foundation v. Secretary of Labor, 471 U.S. 290 (1985), child labor laws, see Prince v. Massachusetts, 321 U.S. 158 (1944), animal cruelty laws, see, e.g., Church of the Lukumi Babalu Aye Inc. v. City of Hialeah, 723 F.Supp. 1467 (S.D.Fla.1989), cf. State v. Massey, 229 N.C. 734, 51 S.E.2d 179, appeal dism'd, 336 U.S. 942 (1949), environmental protection laws, see United States v. Little, 638 F.Supp. 337 (Mont.1986), and laws providing for equality of opportunity for the races, see, e.g., Bob Jones University v. United States, 461 U.S. 574, 603-604 (1983). The First Amendment's protection of religious liberty does not require this. [n5]

    Values that are protected against government interference through enshrinement in the Bill of Rights are not thereby banished from the political process. Just as a society that believes in the negative protection accorded to the press by the First Amendment is likely to enact laws that affirmatively foster the dissemination of the printed word, so also a society that believes in the negative protection accorded to religious belief can be expected to be solicitous of that value in its legislation as well. It is therefore not surprising that a number of States have made an exception to their drug laws for sacramental peyote use. See, e.g., Ariz.Rev.Stat.Ann. § 13-3402(B)(1) (3) (1989); Colo.Rev.Stat. § 12-22-317(3) (1985); N.M.Stat.Ann. § 30-31-6(D) (Supp.1989). But to say that a nondiscriminatory religious practice exemption is permitted, or even that it is desirable, is not to say that it is constitutionally required, and that the appropriate occasions for its creation can be discerned by the courts. It may fairly be said that leaving accommodation to the political process will place at a relative disadvantage those religious practices that are not widely engaged in; but that unavoidable consequence of democratic government must be preferred to a system in which each conscience is a law unto itself or in which judges weigh the social importance of all laws against the centrality of all religious beliefs.

    * * * *

Because respondents' ingestion of peyote was prohibited under Oregon law, and because that prohibition is constitutional, Oregon may, consistent with the Free Exercise Clause, deny respondents unemployment compensation when their dismissal results from use of the drug. The decision of the Oregon Supreme Court is accordingly reversed.

It is so ordered.

Notes to Employment Division, Department of Human Resources of Oregon v. Smith (April 17, 1990)

1. Both lines of cases have specifically adverted to the non-free exercise principle involved. Cantwell, for example, observed that

[t]he fundamental law declares the interest of the United States that the free exercise of religion be not prohibited and that freedom to communicate information and opinion be not abridged.

310 U.S. at 307. Murdock said:

We do not mean to say that religious groups and the press are free from all financial burdens of government. . . . We have here something quite different, for example, from a tax on the income of one who engages in religious activities or a tax on property used or employed in connection with those activities. It is one thing to impose a tax on the income or property of a preacher. It is quite another thing to exact a tax from him for the privilege of delivering a sermon. . . . Those who can deprive religious groups of their colporteurs can take from them a part of the vital power of the press which has survived from the Reformation.

319 U.S. at 112.

Yoder said that

the Court's holding in Pierce stands as a charter of the rights of parents to direct the religious upbringing of their children. And, when the interests of parenthood are combined with a free exercise claim of the nature revealed by this record, more than merely a "reasonable relation to some purpose within the competency of the State" is required to sustain the validity of the State's requirement under the First Amendment.

406 U.S. at 233.

2. Justice O'CONNOR seeks to distinguish Lyng v. Northwest Indian Cemetery Protective Assn., supra, and Bowen v. Roy, supra, on the ground that those cases involved the government's conduct of "its own internal affairs," which is different because, as Justice Douglas said in Sherbert,

"the Free Exercise Clause is written in terms of what the government cannot do to the individual, not in terms of what the individual can exact from the government."

Post at 900 (O'CONNOR, J., concurring), quoting Sherbert, supra, at 412 (Douglas, J., concurring). But since Justice Douglas voted with the majority in Sherbert, that quote obviously envisioned that what "the government cannot do to the individual" includes not just the prohibition of an individual's freedom of action through criminal laws, but also the running of its programs (in Sherbert, state unemployment compensation) in such fashion as to harm the individual's religious interests. Moreover, it is hard to see any reason in principle or practicality why the government should have to tailor its health and safety laws to conform to the diversity of religious belief, but should not have to tailor its management of public lands, Lyng, supra, or its administration of welfare programs, Roy, supra.

3. Justice O'CONNOR suggests that "[t]here is nothing talismanic about neutral laws of general applicability," and that all laws burdening religious practices should be subject to compelling interest scrutiny because

the First Amendment unequivocally makes freedom of religion, like freedom from race discrimination and freedom of speech, a "constitutional norm," not an "anomaly."

Post at 901 (O'CONNOR, J., concurring). But this comparison with other fields supports, rather than undermines, the conclusion we draw today. Just as we subject to the most exacting scrutiny laws that make classifications based on race, see Palmore v. Sidoti, supra, or on the content of speech, see Sable Communications, supra, so too we strictly scrutinize governmental classifications based on religion, see McDaniel v. Paty, 435 U.S. 618 (1978); see also Torcaso v. Watkins, 367 U.S. 488 (1961). But we have held that race-neutral laws that have the effect of disproportionately disadvantaging a particular racial group do not thereby become subject to compelling interest analysis under the Equal Protection Clause, see Washington v. Davis, 426 U.S. 229 (1976) (police employment examination); and we have held that generally applicable laws unconcerned with regulating speech that have the effect of interfering with speech do not thereby become subject to compelling interest analysis under the First Amendment, see Citizen Publishing Co. v. United States, 394 U.S. 131, 139 (1969) (antitrust laws). Our conclusion that generally applicable, religion-neutral laws that have the effect of burdening a particular religious practice need not be justified by a compelling governmental interest is the only approach compatible with these precedents.

4. While arguing that we should apply the compelling interest test in this case, Justice O'CONNOR nonetheless agrees that

our determination of the constitutionality of Oregon's general criminal prohibition cannot, and should not, turn on the centrality of the particular religious practice at issue,

post at 906-907 (O'CONNOR, J., concurring). This means, presumably, that compelling interest scrutiny must be applied to generally applicable laws that regulate or prohibit any religiously motivated activity, no matter how unimportant to the claimant's religion. Earlier in her opinion, however, Justice O'CONNOR appears to contradict this, saying that the proper approach is

to determine whether the burden on the specific plaintiffs before us is constitutionally significant and whether the particular criminal interest asserted by the State before us is compelling.

Post at 899. "Constitutionally significant burden" would seem to be "centrality" under another name. In any case, dispensing with a "centrality" inquiry is utterly unworkable. It would require, for example, the same degree of "compelling state interest" to impede the practice of throwing rice at church weddings as to impede the practice of getting married in church. There is no way out of the difficulty that, if general laws are to be subjected to a "religious practice" exception, both the importance of the law at issue and the centrality of the practice at issue must reasonably be considered.

Nor is this difficulty avoided by Justice BLACKMUN's assertion that

although courts should refrain from delving into questions of whether, as a matter of religious doctrine, a particular practice is "central" to the religion, I do not think this means that the courts must turn a blind eye to the severe impact of a State's restrictions on the adherents of a minority religion.

Post at 919 (dissenting opinion). As Justice BLACKMUN's opinion proceeds to make clear, inquiry into "severe impact" is no different from inquiry into centrality. He has merely substituted for the question "How important is X to the religious adherent?" the question "How great will be the harm to the religious adherent if X is taken away?" There is no material difference.

5. Justice O'CONNOR contends that the "parade of horribles" in the text only

demonstrates . . . that courts have been quite capable of strik[ing] sensible balances between religious liberty and competing state interests.

Post at 902 (O'CONNOR, J., concurring). But the cases we cite have struck "sensible balances" only because they have all applied the general laws, despite the claims for religious exemption. In any event, Justice O'CONNOR mistakes the purpose of our parade: it is not to suggest that courts would necessarily permit harmful exemptions from these laws (though they might), but to suggest that courts would constantly be in the business of determining whether the "severe impact" of various laws on religious practice (to use Justice BLACKMUN's terminology) or the "constitutiona[l] significan[ce]" of the "burden on the particular plaintiffs" (to use Justice O'CONNOR's terminology) suffices to permit us to confer an exemption. It is a parade of horribles because it is horrible to contemplate that federal judges will regularly balance against the importance of general laws the significance of religious practice.

The Eleventh Amendment bars suits by Indian tribes against States without their consent: Blatchford v. Native Village of Noatak (June 24, 1991)

Justice Scalia delivered the opinion of the Court.
We are asked once again to mark the boundaries of state sovereign immunity from suit in federal court. The Court of Appeals for the Ninth Circuit found that immunity did not extend to suits by Indian tribes, and Alaska seeks review of that determination.

I

In 1980, Alaska enacted a revenue-sharing statute that provided annual payments of $25,000 to each "Native village government" located in a community without a state-chartered municipal corporation. Alaska Stat. Ann. 29.89.050 (1984). The State's attorney general believed the statute to be unconstitutional. In his view, Native village governments were "racially exclusive groups" or "racially exclusive organizations" whose status turned exclusively on the racial ancestry of their members; therefore, the attorney general believed, funding these groups would violate the equal protection clause of Alaska's Constitution. Acting on the attorney general's advice, the Commissioner of Alaska's Department of Community and Regional Affairs (petitioner here), enlarged the program to include all unincorporated communities, whether administered by Native governments or not. Shortly thereafter, the legislature increased funding under the program to match its increased scope. Funding, however, never reached the full $25,000 initially allocated to each unincorporated Native community.

The legislature repealed the revenue-sharing statute in 1985, see 1985 Alaska Sess. Laws, ch. 90, and replaced it with one that matched the program as expanded by the Commissioner. In the same year, respondents filed this suit, challenging the Commissioner's action on federal equal protection grounds, and seeking an order requiring the Commissioner to pay them the money that they would have received had the Commissioner not enlarged the program. The District Court initially granted an injunction to preserve sufficient funds for the 1986 fiscal year, but then dismissed the suit as violating the Eleventh Amendment. The Court of Appeals for the Ninth Circuit reversed, first on the ground that 28 U.S.C. 1362 constituted a congressional abrogation of Eleventh Amendment immunity, Native Village of Noatak v. Hoffman, 872 F. 2d 1384 (1989) (later withdrawn), and then, upon reconsideration, on the ground that Alaska had no immunity against suits by Indian tribes. 896 F. 2d 1157 (1989). We granted certiorari. 498 U. S. — (1990).

II

The Eleventh Amendment provides as follows:

"The Judicial power of the United States shall not be construed to extend to any suit in law or equity, commenced or prosecuted against one of the United States by Citizens of another State, or by Citizens or Subjects of any Foreign State."

Despite the narrowness of its terms, since Hans v. Louisiana, 134 U.S. 1 (1890), we have understood the Eleventh Amendment to stand not so much for what it says, but for the presupposition of our constitutional structure which it confirms: that the States entered the federal system with their sovereignty intact; that the judicial authority in Article III is limited by this sovereignty, Welch v. Texas Dept. of Highways and Public Transportation, 483 U.S. 468, 472 (1987) (opinion of Powell, J.); Employees v. Missouri Dept. of Public Health and Welfare, 411 U.S. 279, 290-294 (1973) (Marshall, J., concurring in result); and that a State will therefore not be subject to suit in federal court unless it has consented to suit, either expressly or in the "plan of the convention." See Port Authority Trans-Hudson Corp. v. Feeney, 494 U. S. —, — (1990); Welch, supra, at

474 (opinion of Powell, J); Atascadero State Hospital v. Scanlon, 473 U.S. 234, 238 (1985); Pennhurst State School and Hospital v. Halderman, 465 U.S. 89, 99 (1984).

Respondents do not ask us to revisit Hans; instead they argue that the traditional principles of immunity presumed by Hans do not apply to suits by sovereigns like Indian tribes. And even if they did, respondents contend, the States have consented to suits by tribes in the "plan of the convention." We consider these points in turn.

In arguing that sovereign immunity does not restrict suit by Indian tribes, respondents submit, first, that sovereign immunity only restricts suits by individuals against sovereigns, not by sovereigns against sovereigns, and as we have recognized, Oklahoma Tax Commission v. Citizen Band Potawatomi Indian Tribe of Okla., 498 U. S. —, — (1991), Indian tribes are sovereigns. Respondents' conception of the nature of sovereign immunity finds some support both in the apparent understanding of the Founders, and in dicta of our own opinions. [n.1] But whatever the reach or meaning of these early statements, the notion that traditional principles of sovereign immunity only restrict suits by individuals was rejected in Monaco v. Mississippi, 292 U.S. 313 (1934). It is with that opinion, and the conception of sovereignty that it embraces, that we must begin.

In Monaco, the Principality had come into possession of Mississippi state bonds, and had sued Mississippi in federal court to recover amounts due under those bonds. Mississippi defended on grounds of the Eleventh Amendment, among others. Had respondents' understanding of sovereign immunity been the Court's, the Eleventh Amendment would not have limited the otherwise clear grant of jurisdiction in Article III to hear controversies "between a State . . . and foreign States." But we held that it did.

"Manifestly, we cannot rest with a mere literal application of the words of 2 of Article III, or assume that the letter of the Eleventh Amendment exhausts the restrictions upon suits against non-consenting States. Behind the words of the constitutional provisions are postulates which limit and control. . . . There is . . . the postulate that States of the Union, still possessing attributes of sovereignty, shall be immune from suits, without their consent, save where there has been a `surrender of this immunity in the plan of the convention.' The Federalist, No. 81." Monaco, supra, at 322-323 (footnote omitted).

Our clear assumption in Monaco was that sovereign immunity extends against both individuals and sovereigns, so that there must be found inherent in the plan of the convention a surrender by the States of immunity as to either. Because we perceived in the plan "no ground upon which it can be said that any waiver or consent by a State of the Union has run in favor of a foreign State," id., at 330, we concluded that foreign states were still subject to the immunity of the States.

We pursue the same inquiry in the present case, and thus confront respondents' second contention: that the States waived their immunity against Indian tribes when they adopted the Constitution. Just as in Monaco with regard to foreign sovereigns, so also here with regard to Indian tribes, there is no compelling evidence that the Founders thought such a surrender inherent in the constitutional compact. [n.2] We have hitherto found a surrender of immunity against particular litigants in only two contexts: suits by sister States, South Dakota v. North Carolina, 192 U.S. 286, 318 (1904), and suits by the United States, United States v. Texas, 143 U.S. 621 (1892). We have not found a surrender by the United States to suit by the States, Kansas v. United States, 204 U.S. 331, 342 (1907); see Jackson, The Supreme Court, the Eleventh Amendment, and State Sovereign Immunity, 98 Yale L. J. 1, 79-80 (1988), nor, again, a surrender by the States to suit by foreign sovereigns, Monaco.

Respondents argue that Indian tribes are more like States than foreign sovereigns. That is true in some respects: they are, for example, domestic. The relevant difference between States and foreign sovereigns, however, is not domesticity, but the role of each in the convention within which the surrender of immunity was for the former, but not for the latter, implicit. What makes the States' surrender of immunity from suit by sister States plausible is the mutuality of that concession. There is no such mutuality with either foreign sovereigns or Indian tribes. We have repeatedly held that Indian tribes enjoy immunity against suits by States, Potawatomi Indian Tribe, supra, at —, as it would be absurd to suggest that the tribes surrendered immunity in a convention to which they were not even parties. But if the convention could not surrender the tribes' immunity for the benefit of the States, we do not believe that it surrendered the States' immunity for the benefit of the tribes.

III

Respondents argue that, if the Eleventh Amendment operates to bar suits by Indian tribes against States without their consent, 28 U.S.C. 1362 operates to void that bar. They press two very different arguments, which we consider in turn.

A

In United States v. Minnesota, 270 U.S. 181 (1926), we held that the United States had standing to sue on behalf of Indian tribes as guardians of the tribes' rights, and that, since "the immunity of the State is subject to the constitutional qualification that she may be sued in this Court by the United States," id., at 195, no Eleventh Amendment bar would limit the United States' access to federal courts for that purpose. Relying upon our decision in Moe v. Confederated Salish and Kootenai Tribes, 425 U.S. 463 (1976), respondents argue that we have read 1362 to embody a general delegation of the authority to sue on the tribes' behalf from the Federal Government back to tribes themselves. Hence, respondents suggest, because the United States would face no sovereign immunity limitation, in no case brought under 1362 can sovereign immunity be a bar.

Section 1362 provides as follows:

"The district courts shall have original jurisdiction of all civil actions, brought by any Indian tribe or band with a governing body duly recognized by the Secretary of the Interior, wherein the matter in controversy arises under the Constitution, laws, or treaties of the United States."

What is striking about this most unremarkable statute is its similarity to any number of other grants of jurisdiction to district courts to hear federal-question claims. Compare it, for example, with 1331(a) as it existed at the time 1362 was enacted:

"The district courts shall have original jurisdiction of all civil actions wherein the matter in controversy exceeds the sum or value of $10,000 exclusive of interest and costs, and arises under the Constitution, laws, or treaties of the United States." 28 U.S.C. 1331(a) (1964 ed.).

Considering the text of 1362 in the context of its enactment, one might well conclude that its sole purpose was to eliminate any jurisdictional minimum for "arising under" claims brought by Indian tribes. Tribes already had access to federal courts for "arising under" claims under 1331, where the amount in controversy was greater than $10,000; for all that appears from its text, 1362 merely extends that jurisdiction to claims below that minimum. Such a reading, moreover, finds support in the very title of the Act that adopted 1362: "To amend the Judicial Code to permit Indian tribes to maintain civil actions in Federal district courts without regard to the $10,000 limitation, and for other purposes." 80 Stat. 880.

Moe, however, found something more in the title's "other purposes" — an implication that "a tribe's access to federal court to litigate [federal question cases] would be at least in some respects as broad as that of the United States suing as the tribe's trustee," 425 U. S., at 473 (emphasis added). The "respect" at issue in Moe was access to federal court for the purpose of obtaining injunctive relief from state taxation. The Tax Injunction Act, 28 U.S.C. 1341 denied such access to persons other than the United States; we held that 1362 revoked that denial as to Indian tribes. Moe did not purport to be saying that 1362 equated tribal access with the United States' access generally, but only "at least in some respects," 425 U. S., at 473, or "in certain respects," id., at 474. Respondents now urge us, in effect, to eliminate this limitation utterly — for it is impossible to imagine any more extreme replication of the United States' ability to sue than replication even to the point of allowing unconsented suit against state sovereigns. This is a vast expansion upon Moe. Section 1341, which Moe held 1362 to eliminate in its application to tribal suits, was merely a limitation that Congress itself had created — commiting state tax-injunction suits to state courts as a matter of comity. Absent that statute, state taxes could constitutionally be enjoined. See Will v. Michigan Dept. of State Police, 491 U.S. 58, 71, n. 10 (1989). [n.3] The obstacle to suit in the present case, by contrast, is a creation not of Congress but of the Constitution. A willingness to eliminate the former in no way bespeaks a willingness to eliminate the latter, especially when limitation to "certain respects" has explicitly been announced.

Moreover, as we shall discuss in Part III-B, our cases require Congress' exercise of the power to abrogate state sovereign immunity, where it exists, to be exercised with unmistakeable clarity. To avoid that difficulty, respondents assert that 1362 represents not an abrogation of the States' sovereign immunity, but rather a delegation to tribes of the Federal Government's exemption from state sovereign immunity. We doubt, to begin with, that that sovereign exemption can be delegated — even if one limits the permissibility of delegation (as respondents propose) to persons on whose behalf the United States itself might sue. The consent, "inherent in the convention," to suit by the United States — at the instance and under the control of responsible federal officers — is not consent to suit by anyone whom the United States might select; and even consent to suit by the United States for a particular person's benefit is not consent to suit by that person himself.

But in any event, assuming that delegation of exemption from state sovereign immunity is theoretically possible, there is no reason to believe that Congress ever contemplated such a strange notion. Even if our decision in Moe could be regarded as in any way related to sovereign immunity, see n. 3, supra, it could nevertheless not be regarded as in any way related to congressional "delegation." The opinion does not mention that word, and contains not the slightest suggestion of such an analysis. To say that " 1362 . . . suggests that in certain respects tribes suing under this section were to be accorded treatment similar to that of the United States had it sued on their behalf," 425 U. S., at 474, does not remotely imply delegation — only equivalence of treatment. The delegation theory is entirely a creature of respondents' own invention.

B

Finally, respondents ask us to recognize 1362 as a congressional abrogation of Eleventh Amendment immunity. We have repeatedly said that this power to abrogate can only be exercised by a clear legislative statement. As we said in Dellmuth v. Muth, 491 U.S. 223 (1989),

"To temper Congress' acknowledged powers of abrogation with due concern for the Eleventh Amendment's role as an essential component of our constitutional structure, we have applied a simple but stringent test: `Congress may abrogate the States' constitutionally secured immunity from suit in federal court only by making its intention unmistakably clear in the language of the statute.' " Id., at 227-228.

We agree with petitioner that 1362 does not reflect an "unmistakably clear" intent to abrogate immunity, made plain "in the language of the statute." As we have already noted, the text is no more specific than 1331, the grant of general federal-question jurisdiction to district courts, and no one contends that 1331 suffices to abrogate immunity for all federal questions. [n.4]

Respondents' argument, however, is not that 1362 is a "clear statement" under the standard of Dellmuth, but rather that it was a sufficiently clear statement under the standard of Parden v. Terminal Railway of Alabama Docks Dept., 377 U.S. 184 (1964), the existing authority for "abrogation" at the time of 1362's enactment in 1966. In Parden, we found a sufficiently clear intent to avoid state immunity in a statute that subjected to liability "every" common carrier in interstate commerce, where the State, after the statute's enactment, chose to become a carrier in interstate commerce. Id., at 187-188. Similarly, respondents argue, a statute that grants jurisdiction to district courts to hear "all civil actions, brought by any Indian tribe" should constitute a sufficiently clear expression of intent to abrogate immunity. Dellmuth is not to the contrary, respondents maintain, since the statute there was enacted in the mid-1970's, long after the rule of Parden had been drawn into question. Dellmuth, supra, at 231.

We shall assume for the sake of argument (though we by no means accept) that Congress must be presumed to have had as relatively obscure a decision as Parden in mind as a backdrop to all its legislation. But even if Congress were aware of Parden's minimal clarity requirement, nothing in Parden could lead Congress to presume that that requirement applied to the abrogation of state immunity. Parden itself neither mentioned nor was premised upon abrogation. Its theory was that, by entering a field of economic activity that is federally regulated, the State impliedly "consent[s]" to be bound by that regulation and to be subject to suit in federal court on the same terms as other regulated parties, thus "waiv[ing]" its Eleventh Amendment immunity. 377 U. S., at 186. Not until 1976 (10 years after the passage of 1362) did we first acknowledge a congressional power to abrogate state immunity — under 5 of the Fourteenth Amendment. Fitzpatrick v. Bitzer, 427 U.S. 445 (1976). Thus, Parden would have given Congress no reason to believe it could abrogate state sovereign immunity, and gives us no reason to believe that Congress intended abrogation by a means so subtle as 1362. At the time 1362 was enacted, abrogation would have been regarded as such a novel (not to say questionable) course that a general "arising under" statute like 1362 would not conceivably have been thought to imply it. We conclude that neither under the current standard of Dellmuth nor under any standard in effect at the time of Parden was 1362 an abrogation of state sovereign immunity. [n.5]

IV

Finally, respondents argue that even if the Eleventh Amendment bars their claims for damages, they still seek injunctive relief, which the Eleventh Amendment would not bar. The Court of Appeals of course did not address this point, and we leave it for that court's initial consideration on remand.

The judgment of the Court of Appeals is reversed, and the cases remanded for further proceedings consistent with this opinion.

It is so ordered.

Notes to Blatchford v. Native Village of Noatak (June 24, 1991)

1 As Alexander Hamilton said, "It is inherent in the nature of sovereignty, not to be amendable to the suit of an individual without its consent." The Federalist No. 81, pp. 548-549 (J. Cooke ed. 1961) (emphasis added and deleted). James Madison expressed a similar understanding at the Virginia Convention ("It is not in the power of individuals to call any state into court"), 3 J. Elliot, The Debates in the Several State Conventions on the Adoption of the Federal Constitution 533 (2d ed. 1863) (emphasis added), as did Chief Justice Marshall ("[A]n individual cannot proceed to obtain judgment against a state, though he may be sued by a state.") Id., at 555-556 (emphasis added). In United States v.

Texas, 143 U.S. 621, 645 (1892), we adverted to respondents' distinction explicitly, describing Hans v. Louisiana, 134 U.S. 1, (1890), as having "proceeded upon the broad ground that `it is inherent in the nature of sovereignty not to be amenable to the suit of an individual without its consent,' " 143 U. S., at 645-646, and concluding that "the suability of one government by another government . . . does no violence to the inherent nature of sovereignty." Id., at 646.

2 The only evidence alluded to by respondents is a statement by President Washington to Chief Cornplanter of the Seneca Nation:

"Here, then, is the security for the remainder of your lands. No State, nor person, can purchase your lands, unless at some public treaty, held under the authority of the United States.

. . . . .

"If . . . you have any just cause of complaint against [a purchaser], and can make satisfactory proof thereof, the federal courts will be open to you for redress, as to all other persons." 4 American State Papers, Indian Affairs, Vol. 1, p. 142 (1832). But of course, denying Indian tribes the right to sue States in federal court does not disadvantage them in relation to "all other persons." Respondents are asking for access more favorable than that which others enjoy.

3 Such injunction suits can only be brought against state officers in their official capacity, and not against the State in its own name. Missouri v. Fiske, 290 U.S. 18, 27 (1933). Respondents argue that since the plaintiffs in Moe v. Confederated Salish and Kootenai Tribes, 425 U.S. 463 (1976), named the State of Montana as a defendant, as well as individual officers, the decision in that case held that 1362 eliminated not only the statutory bar of 1341 but sovereign immunity as well. We think not. Since Montana had not objected in this Court on sovereign immunity grounds, its immunity had been waived and was not at issue.

4 In asserting that 1362's grant of jurisdiction to "all civil actions" suffices to abrogate a state's defense of immunity, post, at 8, the minority has just repeated the mistake of the Court in Chisolm v. Georgia, 2 Dall. 419 (1793), see id., at 434-450 (Iredell, J., dissenting), the case that occasioned the Eleventh Amendment itself. The fact that Congress grants jurisdiction to hear a claim does not suffice to show Congress has abrogated all defenses to that claim. The issues are wholly distinct. A state may waive its Eleventh Amendment immunity, and if it does, 1362 certainly would grant a district court jurisdiction to hear the claim. The minority's view returns us, like Sisyphus, to the beginning of this 200-year struggle.

5 Because we find that 1362 does not enable tribes to overcome Alaska's sovereign immunity, we express no view on whether these respondents qualify as "tribes" within the meaning of that statute.

Life sentence for drug possession neither cruel nor unusual: Harmelin v. Michigan (June 27, 1991) [Judgment and opinion]

Justice Scalia announced the judgment of the Court and delivered the opinion of the Court with respect to Part V, and an opinion with respect to Parts I, II, III, and IV, in which The Chief Justice joins.

Petitioner was convicted of possessing 672 grams of cocaine and sentenced to a mandatory term of life in prison without possibility of parole. [n.1] The Michigan Court of Appeals initially reversed his conviction because evidence supporting it had been obtained in violation of the Michigan Constitution. 176 Mich. App. 524, 440 N. W. 2d 75 (1989). On petition for rehearing, the Court of Appeals vacated its prior decision and affirmed petitioner's sentence, rejecting his argument that the sentence was "cruel and unusual" within the meaning of the Eighth Amendment. Id., at 535, 440 N. W. 2d, at 80. The Michigan Supreme Court denied leave to appeal, 434 Mich. 863 (1990), and we granted certiorari. 495 U. S. — (1990).

Petitioner claims that his sentence is unconstitutionally "cruel and unusual" for two reasons. First, because it is "significantly disproportionate" to the crime he committed. Second, because the sentencing judge was statutorily required to impose it, without taking into account the particularized circumstances of the crime and of the criminal.

I

A The Eighth Amendment, which applies against the States by virtue of the Fourteenth Amendment, see Robinson v. California, 370 U.S. 660 (1962), provides: "Excessive bail shall not be required, nor excessive fines imposed, nor cruel and unusual punishments inflicted." In Rummel v. Estelle, 445 U.S. 263 (1980), we held that it did not constitute "cruel and unusual punishment" to impose a life sentence, under a recidivist statute, upon a defendant who had been convicted, successively, of fraudulent use of a credit card to obtain $80 worth of goods or services, passing a forged check in the amount of $28.36, and obtaining $120.75 by false pretenses. We said that "one could argue without fear of contradiction by any decision of this Court that for crimes concededly classified and classifiable as felonies, that is, as punishable by significant terms of imprisonment in a state penitentiary, the length of the sentence actually imposed is purely a matter of legislative prerogative." Id., at 274. We specifically rejected the proposition asserted by the dissent, id., at 295 (Powell, J.), that unconstitutional disproportionality could be established by weighing three factors: (1) gravity of the offense compared to severity of the penalty, (2) penalties imposed within the same jurisdiction for similar crimes, and (3) penalties imposed in other jurisdictions for the same offense. Id., at 281-282, and n. 27. A footnote in the opinion, however, said: "This is not to say that a proportionality principle would not come into play in the extreme example mentioned by the dissent, . . . if a legislature made overtime parking a felony punishable by life imprisonment." Id., at 274, n. 11.

Two years later, in Hutto v. Davis, 454 U.S. 370 (1982), we similarly rejected an Eighth Amendment challenge to a prison term of 40 years and fine of $20,000 for possession and distribution of approximately nine ounces of marijuana. We thought that result so clear in light of Rummel that our per curiam opinion said the Fourth Circuit, in sustaining the constitutional challenge, "could be viewed as having ignored, consciously or unconsciously, the hierarchy of the federal court system," which could not be tolerated "unless we wish anarchy to prevail," 454 U. S., at 374-375. And we again explicitly rejected application of the three factors discussed in the Rummel dissent. [n.2] See 454 U. S., at 373-374, and n. 2. However, whereas in Rummel we had said that successful proportionality challenges outside the context of capital punishment "have been exceedingly rare," 445 U. S., at 272 (discussing as the solitary example Weems v. United States, 217 U.S. 349 (1910), which we explained as involving punishment of a "unique nature," 445 U. S., at 274), in Davis we misdescribed Rummel as having said that " `successful challenges . . .' should be `exceedingly rare,' " 454 U. S., at 374 (emphasis added), and at that point inserted a reference to and description of the Rummel "overtime parking" footnote, 454 U. S., at 374, n. 3. The content of that footnote was imperceptibly (but, in the event, ominously) expanded: Rummel's "not [saying] that a proportionality principle would not come into play" in the fanciful parking example, 445 U. S., at 274, n. 11, became "not[ing] . . . that there could be situations in which the proportionality principle would come into play, such as" the fanciful parking example, Davis, supra, at 374, n. 3 (emphasis added). This combination of expanded text plus expanded footnote permitted the inference that gross disproportionality was an example of the "exceedingly rare" situations in which Eighth Amendment challenges "should be" successful. Indeed, one might say that it positively invited that inference, were that not incompatible with the sharp per curiam reversal of the Fourth Circuit's finding that 40 years for possession and distribution of nine ounces of marijuana was grossly disproportionate and therefore unconstitutional.

A year and a half after Davis we uttered what has been our last word on this subject to date. Solem v. Helm, 463 U.S. 277 (1983), set aside under the Eighth Amendment, because it was disproportionate, a sentence of life imprisonment without possibility of parole, imposed under a South Dakota recidivist statute for successive offenses that included three convictions of third-degree burglary, one of obtaining money by false pretenses, one of grand larceny, one of third-offense driving while intoxicated, and one of writing a "no account" check with intent to defraud. In the Solem account, Weems no longer involved punishment of a "unique nature," Rummel, supra, at 274, but was the "leading case," Solem, 463 U. S., at 287, exemplifying the "general principle of proportionality," id., at 288, which was "deeply rooted and frequently repeated in common-law jurisprudence," id., at 284, had been embodied in the English Bill of Rights "in language that was later adopted in the Eighth Amendment," id., at 285, and had been "recognized explicitly in this Court for almost a century," id., at 286. The most recent of those "recognitions" were the "overtime parking" footnotes in Rummel and Davis, 463 U.

S., at 288. As for the statement in Rummel that "one could argue without fear of contradiction by any decision of this Court that for crimes concededly classified and classifiable as felonies . . . the length of the sentence actually imposed is purely a matter of legislative prerogative," Rummel, supra, at 274: according to Solem, the really important words in that passage were " `one could argue,' " 463 U. S., at 288, n. 14 (emphasis added by Solem). "The Court [in Rummel] . . . merely recognized that the argument was possible. To the extent that the State . . . makes the argument here, we find it meritless." Id., at 289, n. 14. (Of course Rummel had not said merely "one could argue," but "one could argue without fear of contradiction by any decision of this Court.") Having decreed that a general principle of disproportionality exists, the Court used as the criterion for its application the three-factor test that had been explicitly rejected in both Rummel and Davis. 463 U. S., at 291-292. Those cases, the Court said, merely "indicated [that] no one factor will be dispositive in a given case," id., at 291, n. 17 — though Davis had expressly, approvingly, and quite correctly, described Rummel as having "disapproved each of [the] objective factors," 454 U. S., at 373 (emphasis added). See Rummel, 445 U. S., at 281-282, and n. 27.

It should be apparent from the above discussion that our 5to-4 decision eight years ago in Solem was scarcely the expression of clear and well accepted constitutional law. We have long recognized, of course, that the doctrine of stare decisis is less rigid in its application to constitutional precedents, see Payne v. Tennessee, ante, at —, (slip op., at 19); Smith v. Allwright, 321 U.S. 649, 665, and n. 10 (1944); Mitchell v. W. T. Grant Co., 416 U.S. 600, 627-628 (1974) (Powell, J., concurring); Burnet v. Coronado Oil & Gas Co., 285 U.S. 393, 406-408 (1932) (Brandeis, J., dissenting), and we think that to be especially true of a constitutional precedent that is both recent and in apparent tension with other decisions. Accordingly, we have addressed anew, and in greater detail, the question whether the Eighth Amendment contains a proportionality guarantee — with particular attention to the background of the Eighth Amendment (which Solem discussed in only two pages, see 463 U. S., at 284-286) and to the understanding of the Eighth Amendment before the end of the 19th century (which Solem discussed not at all). We conclude from this examination that Solem was simply wrong; the Eighth Amendment contains no proportionality guarantee.

B Solem based its conclusion principally upon the proposition that a right to be free from disproportionate punishments was embodied within the "cruel and unusuall Punishments" provision of the English Declaration of Rights of 1689, and was incorporated, with that language, in the Eighth Amendment. There is no doubt that the Declaration of Rights is the antecedent of our constitutional text. (This document was promulgated in February 1689 and was enacted into law as the Bill of Rights, 1 Wm. & Mary, Sess. 2, ch. 2, in December 1689. See Sources of Our Liberties 222-223 (R. Perry & J. Cooper eds. 1959); L. Schwoerer, Declaration of Rights, 1689 279, 295-298 (1981).) In 1791, five State Constitutions prohibited "cruel or unusual punishments," see Del. Declaration of Rights, 16 (1776); Md. Declaration of Rights, XXII (1776); Mass. Declaration of

Rights, Art. XXVI (1780); N. C. Declaration of Rights X (1776); N. H. Bill of Rights, XXXIII (1784), and two prohibited "cruel" punishments, Pa. Const., Art. IX, 13 (1790); S. C. Const., Art. IX, 4 (1790). The new Federal Bill of Rights, however, tracked Virginia's prohibition of "cruel and unusual punishments," see Va. Declaration of Rights 9 (1776), which most closely followed the English provision. In fact, the entire text of the Eighth Amendment is taken almost verbatim from the English Declaration of Rights, which provided "[t]hat excessive Baile ought not to be required nor excessive Fines imposed nor cruell and unusuall Punishments inflicted."

Perhaps the Americans of 1791 understood the Declaration's language precisely as the Englishmen of 1689 did — though as we shall discuss later, that seems unlikely. Or perhaps the colonists meant to incorporate the content of that antecedent by reference, whatever the content might have been. Solem suggested something like this, arguing that since Americans claimed "all the rights of English subjects," "their use of the language of the English Bill of Rights is convincing proof that they intended to provide at least the same protection," 463 U. S., at 286. Thus, not only is the original meaning of the 1689 Declaration of Rights relevant, but also the circumstances of its enactment, insofar as they display the particular "rights of English subjects" it was designed to vindicate.

As Solem observed, id., at 284-285, the principle of proportionality was familiar to English law at the time the Declaration of Rights was drafted. The Magna Carta provided that "[a] free man shall not be fined for a small offence, except in proportion to the measure of the offense; and for a great offence he shall be fined in proportion to the magnitude of the offence, saving his freehold . . . ." Art. 20 (translated in Sources of our Liberties, supra, at 15). When imprisonment supplemented fines as a method of punishment, courts apparently applied the proportionality principle while sentencing. Hodges v. Humkin, 2 Bulst. 139, 140, 80 Eng. Rep. 1015, 1016 (K. B. 1615) (Croke, J.) ("[I]mprisonment ought always to be according to the quality of the offence"). Despite this familiarity, the drafters of the Declaration of Rights did not explicitly prohibit "disproportionate" or "excessive" punishments. Instead, they prohibited punishments that were "cruell and unusuall." The Solem court simply assumed, with no analysis, that the one included the other. 463 U. S., at 285. As a textual matter, of course, it does not: a disproportionate punishment can perhaps always be considered "cruel," but it will not always be (as the text also requires) "unusual." The error of Solem's assumption is confirmed by the historical context and contemporaneous understanding of the English guarantee.

Most historians agree that the "cruell and unusuall Punishments" provision of the English Declaration of Rights was prompted by the abuses attributed to the infamous Lord Chief Justice Jeffreys of the King's Bench during the Stuart reign of James II. See, e. g., Schwoerer, supra, at 93; 4 W. Blackstone, Commentaries *372. They do not agree, however, on which abuses. See Ingraham v. Wright, 430 U.S. 651, 664-665 (1977); Furman v. Georgia, 408 U.S. 238, 317-319 (1972) (Marshall, J. concurring). Jeffreys is best known for presiding over the "Bloody Assizes" following the Duke of Monmouth's abortive rebellion in 1685; a special Commission led by Jeffreys tried, convicted, and executed hundreds of suspected insurgents. Some have attributed the Declaration of Rights provision to popular outrage against those proceedings. E. g., Sources of Our Liberties, supra, at 236, n. 103; Note, What Is Cruel and Unusual Punishment, 24 Harv. L. Rev. 54, 55, n. 2 (1910); see also 3 J. Story, Commentaries on the Constitution of the United States 1896 (1833). [n.3]

But the vicious punishments for treason decreed in the Bloody Assizes (drawing and quartering, burning of women felons, beheading, disembowling, etc.) were common in that period — indeed, they were specifically authorized by law and remained so for many years afterwards. See Granucci, "Nor Cruel and Unusual Punishments Inflicted:" The Original Meaning, 57 Calif. L. Rev. 839, 855-856 (1969); 4 Blackstone, supra, at *369-370. Thus, recently historians have argued, and the best historical evidence suggests, that it was not Jeffreys' management of the Bloody Assizes that led to the Declaration of Rights provision, but rather the arbitrary sentencing power he had exercised in administering justice from the King's Bench, particularly when punishing a notorious perjurer. See Granucci, supra, at 855-860; Schwoerer, supra, at 92-93. Accord, 1 J. Stephen, A History of the Criminal Law of England 490 (1883); 1 J. Chitty, Criminal Law 712 (5th Am. ed. 1847). Jeffreys was widely accused of "inventing" special penalties for the King's enemies, penalties that were not authorized by common-law precedent or statute. Letter to a Gentleman at Brussels, giving an account of the people's revolt (Windsor Dec. 2, 1688), cited in L. Schwoerer, The Declaration of Rights, 1689, p. 93 n. 207 (1981).

The preamble to the Declaration of Rights, a sort of indictment of James II that calls to mind the preface to our own Declaration of Independence, specifically referred to illegal sentences and King's Bench proceedings.

Whereas the late King James the Second, by the Assistance of diverse Evill Councellors Judges and Ministers imployed by him did endeavour to subvert and extirpate the Protestant Religion, and the Lawes and Liberties of this Kingdome.

"By Prosecutions in the Court of King's Bench for Matters and Causes cognizable onely in Parlyament and by diverse other Arbitrary and Illegall Courses.

"[E]xcessive Baile hath beene required of Persons committed in Criminall Cases to elude the Benefit of the Lawes made for the Liberty of the Subjects.

"And excessive Fines have been imposed.

"And illegall and cruell Punishments have been inflicted.

"All which are utterly and directly contrary to the knowne Lawes and Statutes and Freedome of this Realme." 1 Wm. & Mary, Sess. 2, ch. 2 (1689).

The only recorded contemporaneous interpretation of the "cruell and unusuall Punishments" clause confirms the focus upon Jeffreys' King's Bench activities, and upon the illegality rather than the disproportionality of his sentences. In 1685 Titus Oates, a Protestant cleric whose false accusations had caused the execution of 15 prominent Catholics for allegedly organizing a "Popish Plot" to overthrow King Charles II in 1679, was tried and convicted before the King's Bench for perjury. Oates' crime, "bearing false witness against another, with an express premeditated design to take away his life, so as the innocent person be condemned and executed" had, at one time, been treated as a species of murder, and punished with death. 4 Blackstone, supra, at *196. At sentencing, Jeffreys complained that death was no longer available as a penalty and lamented that "a proportionable punishment of that crime can scarce by our law, as it now stands, be inflicted upon him." Second Trial of Titus Oates, 10 How. St. Tr. 1227, 1314 (K. B. 1685). The law would not stand in the way, however. The judges met, and, according to Jeffreys, were in unanimous agreement that "crimes of this nature are left to be punished according to the discretion of this court, so far as that the judgment extend not to life or member." Ibid. Another Justice taunted Oates that "we have taken special care of you," see id., at 1316. The court then decreed that he should pay a fine of "1000 marks upon each Indictment," that he should be "stript of [his] Canonical Habits," that he should stand in the pillory annually at certain specified times and places, that on May 20 he should be whipped by "the common hangman" "from Aldgate to Newgate," that he should be similarly whipped on May 22 "from Newgate to Tyburn," and that he should be imprisoned for life. Ibid.

"The judges, as they believed, sentenced Oates to be scourged to death." 2 T. Macaulay, History of England 204 (1899) (hereinafter Macaulay). Accord, D. Ogg, England In The Reigns of James II and William III 154-155 (1984). Oates would not die, however. Four years later, and several months after the Declaration of Rights, he petitioned the House of Lords to set aside his sentence as illegal. 6 T. Macaulay 138-141. "Not a single peer ventured to affirm that the judgment was legal; but much was said about the odious character of the appellant" and the Lords affirmed the judgment. 6 id., at 140-141. A minority of the Lords dissented, however, and their statement sheds light on the meaning of the "cruell and unusuall Punishments" clause:

"1st, [T]he King's Bench, being a Temporal Court, made it a Part of the Judgment, That Titus Oates, being a Clerk, should, for his said Perjuries, be divested of his canonical and priestly Habit . . .; which is a Matter wholly out of their Power, belonging to the Ecclesiastical Courts only.

"2dly, [S]aid Judgments are barbarous, inhuman, and unchristian; and there is no Precedent to warrant the Punishments of whipping and committing to Prison for Life, for the Crime of Perjury; which yet were but Part of the Punishments inflicted upon him.

"4thly, [T]his will be an Encouragement and Allowance for giving the like cruel, barbarous and illegal Judgments hereafter, unless this Judgment be reversed.

"5thly, . . . [T]hat the said Judgments were contrary to Law and ancient Practice, and therefore erroneous, and ought to be reversed.

"6thly, Because it is contrary to the Declaration on the Twelfth of February last . . . that excessive Bail ought not to be required, nor excessive Fines imposed, nor cruel nor unusual Punishments aflicted." 1 Journals of the House of Lords 367 (May 31, 1689), quoted in Second Trial of Titus Oates, supra, at 1325.

Oates' cause then aroused support in the House of Commons, whose members proceeded to pass a bill to annul the sentence. A "free conference" was ultimately convened in which representatives of the House of Commons attempted to persuade the Lords to reverse their position. See 6 Macaulay 143-145. Though this attempt was not successful, the Commons' report of the conference confirms that the "cruell and unusuall Punishments" clause was directed at the Oates case (among others) in particular, and at illegality rather than disproportionality of punishment in general.

"[T]he Commons had hoped, That, after the Declaration [of Rights] presented to their Majesties upon their accepting the Crown (wherein their Lordships had joined with the Commons in complaining of the cruel and illegal Punishments of the last Reign; and in asserting it to be the ancient Right of the People of England that they should not be subjected to cruel and unusual Punishments; and that no Judgments to the Prejudice of the People in that kind ought in any wise to be drawn into Consequence, or Example); and after this Declaration had been so lately renewed in that Part of the Bill of Rights which the Lords have agreed to; they should not have seen Judgments of this Nature affirmed, and been put under a Necessity of sending up a Bill for reversing them; since those Declarations will not only be useless, but of pernicious Consequence to the People, if, so soon after, such Judgments as these stand affirmed, and be not taken as cruel and illegal within the Meaning of those Declarations.

"That the Commons had a particular Regard to these Judgments, amongst others, when that Declaration was first made; and must insist upon it, That they are erroneous, cruel, illegal, and of ill Example to future Ages . . . .

"That it seemed no less plain, That the Judgments were cruel, and of ill Example to future Ages.

"That it was surely of ill Example for a Temporal Court to give Judgment, `That a Clerk be divested of his Canonical Habits; and continue so divested during his Life.'

"That it was of ill example, and illegal, That a Judgment of perpetual Imprisonment should be given in a Case, where there is no express Law to warrant it.

"It was of ill Example, and unusual, That an Englishman should be exposed upon a Pillory, so many times a Year, during his Life.

"That it was illegal, cruel, and of dangerous Example, That a Freeman should be whipped in such a barbarous manner, as, in Probability, would determine in Death.

"That this was avowed, when these Judgments were given by the then Lord Chief Justice of the King's Bench; who declared; `That all the Judges had met; and unanimously agreed, That where the Subject was prosecuted at Common Law for a Misdemeanor, it was in the Discretion of the Court, to inflict what Punishment they pleased, not extending to Life, or Member.'

"That as soon as they had set up this Pretence to a discretionary Power, it was observable how they put it in Practice, not only in this, but in other Cases, and for other Offences, by inflicting such cruel and ignominious Punishments, as will be agreed to be far worse than Death itself to any Man who has a sense of Honour or Shame . . . ." 10 Journal of the House of Commons 247 (Aug. 2, 1689) (emphasis added).

In all these contemporaneous discussions, as in the prologue of the Declaration, a punishment is not considered objectionable because it is disproportionate, [n.4] but because it is "out of [the Judges'] Power," "contrary to Law and ancient practice," without "Precedents" or "express Law to warrant," "unusual," "illegal," or imposed by "Pretence to a discretionary Power." Accord, 2 Macaulay 204 (observing that Oates' punishment, while deserved, was unjustified by law). Moreover, the phrase "cruell and unusuall" is treated as interchangeable with "cruel and illegal." In other words, the "illegall and cruell Punishments" of the Declaration's prologue, see supra, at 9, are the same thing as the "cruell and unusuall Punishments" of its body. (Justice Marshall's concurrence in Furman v. Georgia, 408 U. S., at 318, observes that an earlier draft of the body prohibited "illegal" punishments, and that the change "appears to be inadvertent." See also 1 J. Chitty, Criminal Law 712 (5th Am. ed. 1847) (describing Declaration of Rights as prohibiting "cruel and illegal" punishments).) In the legal world of the time, and in the context of restricting punishment determined by the Crown (or the Crown's judges), "illegall" and "unusuall" were identical for practical purposes. Not all punishments were specified by statute; many were determined by the common law. Departures from the common law were lawful only if authorized by statute. See J. Stephen, A History of the Criminal Law of England 489-490 (1883); 1 J. Chitty, Criminal Law 710 (5th Am. ed. 1847). A requirement that punishment not be "unusuall" — that is, not contrary to "usage" (Lat. "usus") or "precedent" — was primarily a requirement that judges pronouncing sentence remain within the bounds of common-law tradition. 1 id., at 710-712; Ingraham v. Wright, 430 U. S., at 665 (English provision aimed at "judges acting beyond their lawful authority"); Granucci, 57 Calif. L. Rev., at 859; Cf. 4 W. Blackstone, Commentaries, *371-*373.

In sum, we think it most unlikely that the English Cruel and Unusual Punishments Clause was meant to forbid "disproportionate" punishments. There is even less likelihood that proportionality of punishment was one of the traditional "rights and privileges of Englishmen" apart from the Declaration of Rights, which happened to be included in the Eighth Amendment. Indeed, even those scholars who believe the principle to have been included within the Declaration of Rights do not contend that such a prohibition was reflected in English practice — nor could they. See Granucci, supra, at 847. [n.5] For, as we observed in Woodson v. North Carolina, 428 U.S. 280, 289 (1976), in 1791, England punished over 200 crimes with death. See also 1 Stephen, supra, at 458, 471-472 (until 1826, all felonies, except mayhem and petty larceny, were punishable by death). By 1830 the class of offenses punishable by death was narrowed to include "only" murder, attempts to murder by poisoning, stabbing, shooting etc.; administering poison to procure abortion, sodomy, rape, statutory rape, and certain classes of forgery. See 1 Stephen, supra, at 473-474. It is notable that, during his discussion of English capital punishment reform, Stephen does not once mention the Cruell and Unusuall Punishments Clause, though he was certainly aware of it. See 1 Stephen, supra, at 489-

490. Likewise, in his discussion of the suitability of punishments, Blackstone does not mention the Declaration. See 4 Blackstone, supra, at *9-*19.

C Unless one accepts the notion of a blind incorporation, however, the ultimate question is not what "cruell and unusuall punishments" meant in the Declaration of Rights, but what its meaning was to the Americans who adopted the Eighth Amendment. Even if one assumes that the Founders knew the precise meaning of that English antecedent, but see Granucci, supra, at 860-865, a direct transplant of the English meaning to the soil of American constitutionalism would in any case have been impossible. There were no common-law punishments in the federal system, see United States v. Hudson and Goodwin, 7 Cranch 32 (1812), so that the provision must have been meant as a check not upon judges but upon the Legislature. See, e. g., In re Kemmler, 136 U.S. 436, 446-447 (1890).

Wrenched out of its common-law context, and applied to the actions of a legislature, the word "unusual" could hardly mean "contrary to law." But it continued to mean (as it continues to mean today) "such as [does not] occu[r] in ordinary practice," Webster's 1828 edition, "[s]uch as is [not] in common use," Webster's 2d International. According to its terms, then, by forbidding "cruel and unusual punishments," see Stanford v. Kentucky, 492 U.S. 361, 378 (1989) (plurality opinion); In re Kemmler, supra, at 446-447, the Clause disables the Legislature from authorizing particular forms or "modes" of punishment — specifically, cruel methods of punishment that are not regularly or customarily employed. E. g., Louisiana ex rel. Francis v. Resweber, 329 U.S. 459, 464 (1947) (plurality opinion); In re Kemmler, supra, at 446-447. See also United States v. Collins, 25 F. Cas. (No. 14,836) 545 (CC R. I. 1854) (Curtis, J.).

The language bears the construction, however — and here we come to the point crucial to resolution of the present case — that "cruelty and unusualness" are to be determined not solely with reference to the punishment at issue ("Is life imprisonment a cruel and unusual punishment?") but with reference to the crime for which it is imposed as well ("Is life imprisonment cruel and unusual punishment for possession of unlawful drugs?"). The latter interpretation would make the provision a form of proportionality guarantee. [n.6] The arguments against it, however, seem to us conclusive.

First of all, to use the phrase "cruel and unusual punishment" to describe a requirement of proportionality would have been an exceedingly vague and oblique way of saying what Americans were well accustomed to saying more directly. The notion of "proportionality" was not a novelty (though then as now there was little agreement over what it entailed). In 1778, for example, the Virginia Legislature narrowly rejected a comprehensive "Bill for Proportioning Punishments" introduced by Thomas Jefferson. See 4 W. Blackstone, Commentaries 18 (H. Tucker ed. 1803) (discussing efforts at reform); 1 Writings of Thomas Jefferson 218-239 (A. Lipscomb 1903). Proportionality provisions had been included in several state constitutions. See, e. g., Pa. Const., 38 (1776) (punishments should be "in general more proportionate to the crimes"); S. C. Const., Art. XL (1778) (same); N. H. Bill of Rights, Art. I, XVIII (1784) ("all penalties ought to be proportioned to the nature of the offence"). There is little doubt that those who framed, proposed, and ratified the Bill of Rights were aware of such provisions, [n.7] yet chose not to replicate them. Both the New Hampshire Constitution, adopted 8 years before ratification of the Eighth Amendment, and the Ohio Constitution, adopted 12 years after, contain, in separate provisions, a prohibition of "cruel and unusual punishments" ("cruel or unusual," in New Hampshire's case) and a requirement that "all penalties ought to be proportioned to the nature of the offence." N. H. Bill of Rights, XVIII, XXXIII (1784). Ohio Const., Art. VIII, 13, 14 (1802). [n.8]

Secondly, it would seem quite peculiar to refer to cruelty and unusualness for the offense in question, in a provision having application only to a new government that had never before defined offenses, and that would be defining new and peculiarly national ones. Finally and most conclusively, as we proceed to discuss, the fact that what was "cruel and unusual" under the Eighth Amendment was to be determined without reference to the particular offense is confirmed by all available evidence of contemporary understanding. [n.9]

The Eighth Amendment received little attention during the proposal and adoption of the Federal Bill of Rights. However, what evidence exists from debates at the state ratifying conventions that prompted the Bill of Rights as well as the Floor debates in the First Congress which proposed it "confirm[s] the view that the cruel and unusual punishments clause was directed at prohibiting certain methods of punishment." Granucci, 57 Calif. L. Rev., at 842 (emphasis added). See Schwartz, Eighth Amendment Proportionality Analysis and the Compelling Case of William Rummell, 71 J. Crim. L. & Criminology 378, 378-382 (1980); Welling & Hipfner, Cruel and Unusual?: Capital Punishment in Canada, 26 U. Toronto L. J. 55, 61 (1976).

In the January 1788 Massachusetts Convention, for example, the objection was raised that Congress was

"nowhere restrained from inventing the most cruel and unheard-of punishments, and annexing them to crimes; and there is no constitutional check on [it], but that racks and gibbets may be amongst the most mild instruments of [its] discipline." 2 J. Elliot, Debates on the Federal Constitution 111 (2d ed. 1854) (emphasis added).

In the Virginia Convention, Patrick Henry decried the absence of a bill of rights, stating:

"What says our [Virginia] Bill of Rights? — `that excessive bail ought not be required, nor excessive fines imposed, nor cruel and unusual punishments inflicted.' . . .

"In this business of legislation, your members of Congress will loose the restriction of not imposing excessive fines, demanding excessive bail, and inflicting cruel and unusual punishments. These are prohibited by your declaration of rights. What has distinguished our ancestors? — That they would not admit of tortures, or cruel and barbarous punishment." 3 id., at 447.

The actions of the First Congress, which are of course persuasive evidence of what the Constitution means, Marsh v. Chambers, 463 U.S. 783, 788-790 (1983); Carroll

v. United States, 267 U.S. 132, 150-152 (1925); cf. McCulloch v. Maryland, 4 Wheat. 316, 401-402 (1819), belie any doctrine of proportionality. Shortly after this Congress proposed the Bill of Rights, it promulgated the Nation's first Penal Code. See 1 Stat. 112-119 (1790). As the then-extant New Hampshire Constitution's proportionality provision didactically observed, "[n]o wise legislature" — that is, no legislature attuned to the principle of proportionality — "will afix the same punishment to the crimes of theft, forgery and the like, which they do to those of murder and treason," N. H. Const., Art. I, XVIII (1784). Jefferson's Bill For Proportioning Crimes and Punishments punished murder and treason by death; counterfeiting of public securities by forfeiture of property plus six years at hard labor, and "run[ning] away with any sea-vessel or goods laden on board thereof" by treble damages to the victim and five years at hard labor. See 1 Writings of Thomas Jefferson 220-222, 229-231 (A. Lipscomb ed. 1903) (footnote omitted). Shortly after proposing the Bill of Rights, the First Congress ignored these teachings. It punished forgery of United States securities, "run[ning] away with [a] ship or vessel, or any goods or merchandise to the value of fifty dollars," treason, and murder on the high seas with the same penalty: death by hanging. 1 Stat. 114. The law books of the time are devoid of indication that anyone considered these newly enacted penalties unconstitutional by virtue of their disproportionality. Cf. United States v. Tully, 28 F. Cas. (No. 16, 545) 226 (CC Mass. 1812) (Story and Davis, JJ.) (Force or threat thereof not an element of "run[n]ing away with [a] ship or vessel").

The early commentary on the Clause contains no reference to disproportionate or excessive sentences, and again indicates that it was designed to outlaw particular modes of punishment. One commentator wrote:

"The prohibition of cruel and unusual punishments, marks the improved spirit of the age, which would not tolerate the use of the rack or the stake, or any of those horrid modes of torture, devised by human ingenuity for the gratification of fiendish passion." J. Bayard, A Brief Exposition of the Constitution of the United States 154 (2d ed. 1840).

Another commentator, after explaining (in somewhat convoluted fashion) that the "spirit" of the Excessive Bail and Excessive Fines Clauses forbade excessive imprisonments, went on to add:

"Under the [Eighth] amendment the infliction of cruel and unusual punishments, is also prohibited. The various barbarous and cruel punishments inflicted under the laws of some other countries, and which profess not to be behind the most enlightened nations on earth in civilization and refinement, furnish sufficient reasons for this express prohibition. Breaking on the wheel, flaying alive, rending assunder with horses, various species of horrible tortures inflicted in the inquisition, maiming, mutilating and scourging to death, are wholly alien to the spirit of our humane general constitution." B. Oliver, The Rights of An American Citizen 186 (1832).

Chancellor Kent, in a paragraph of his Commentaries arguing that capital punishment "ought to be confined to the few cases of the most atrocious character," does not suggest that the "cruel and unusual punishments" Clauses of State or Federal

Constitutions require such proportionality — even though the very paragraph in question begins with the statement that "cruel and unusual punishments are universally condemned." 2 J. Kent, Commentaries on American Law 10-11 (1827). And Justice Story had this to say:

"The provision [the Eighth Amendment] would seem wholly unecessary in a free government, since it is scarcely possible, that any department of such a government should authorize, or justify such atrocious conduct. It was, however, adopted as an admonition to all departments of the national government, to warn them against such violent proceedings, as had taken place in England in the arbitrary reigns of some of the Stuarts." 3 J. Story, Commentaries on the Constitution of the United States 1896 (1833).

Many other Americans apparently agreed that the clause only outlawed certain modes of punishment: during the 19th century several States ratified constitutions that prohibited "cruel and unusual," "cruel or unusual," or simply "cruel" punishments and required all punishments to be proportioned to the offense. Ohio Const., Art. VIII, 13, 14 (1802); Ind. Const., Art. I, 15-16 (1816); Me. Const., Art. I, 9 (1819); R. I. Const., Art. I, 8 (1842); W. Va. Const., Art. II, 2 (1861); Ga. Const., Art. I, 16, 21 (1868).

Perhaps the most persuasive evidence of what "cruel and unusual" meant, however, is found in early judicial constructions of the Eighth Amendment and its state counterparts. An early (perhaps the earliest) judicial construction of the Federal provision is illustrative. In Barker v. People, 20 Johns. *457 (N. Y. Sup. Ct. 1823), aff'd, 3 Cow. 686 (N. Y. 1824) the defendant, upon conviction of challenging another to a duel, had been disenfranchised. Chief Justice Spencer assumed that the Eighth Amendment applied to the States, and in finding that it had not been violated considered the proportionality of the punishment irrelevant. "The disenfranchisement of a citizen," he said, "is not an unusual punishment; it was the consequence of treason, and of infamous crimes, and it was altogether discretionary in the legislature to extend that punishment to other offences." Barker v. People, supra, at *459.

Throughout the 19th century, state courts interpreting state constitutional provisions with identical or more expansive wording (i. e., "cruel or unusual") concluded that these provisions did not proscribe disproportionality but only certain modes of punishment. For example, in Aldridge v. Commonwealth, 4 Va. 447 (1824), the General Court of Virginia had occasion to interpret the cruel and unusual punishments clause that was the direct ancestor of our federal provision, see supra, at 6. In rejecting the defendant's claim that a sentence of so many as 39 stripes violated the Virginia Constitution, the court said:

"As to the ninth section of the Bill of Rights, denouncing cruel and unusual punishments, we have no notion that it has any bearing on this case. That provision was never designed to control the Legislative right to determine ad libitum upon the adequacy of punishment, but is merely applicable to the modes of punishment. . . . [T]he best heads and hearts of the land of our ancestors, had long and loudly declaimed against the wanton cruelty of many of the punishments practised in other countries; and this section in the

Bill of Rights was framed effectually to exclude these, so that no future Legislature, in a moment perhaps of great and general excitement, should be tempted to disgrace our Code by the introduction of any of those odious modes of punishment." 4 Va., at 449-450 (emphasis in original).

    Accord Commonwealth v. Hitshings, 71 Mass. 482, 486 (1855); Garcia v. Territory, 1 N. M. 415, 417-419 (1869); Whitten v. Georgia, 47 Ga. 297, 301 (1872); Cummins v. People, 42 Mich. 142, 143-144, 3 N. W. 305 (1879); State v. Williams, 77 Mo. 310, 312-313 (1883); State v. White, 44 Kan. 514, 520-521, 25 P. 33, 34-35 (1890); People v. Morris, 80 Mich. 634, 638, 45 N. W. 591, 592 (1890); Hobbs v. State, 133 Ind. 404, 408-410, 32 N. E. 1019, 1020-1021 (1893); State v. Hogan, 63 Ohio St. 202, 218, 58 N. E. 572, 575 (1900); see also, In re Bayard, 32 N. Y. 546, 549-550 (1881). In the 19th century, judicial agreement that a "cruel and unusual" (or "cruel or unusual") provision did not constitute a proportionality requirement appears to have been universal. [n.10] One case, late in the century, suggested in dictum, not a fullfledged proportionality principle, but at least the power of the courts to intervene "in very extreme cases, where the punishment proposed is so severe and out of proportion to the offense as to shock public sentiment and violate the judgment of reasonable people." State v. Becker, 3 S. D. 29, 41, 51 N. W. 1018, 1022 (1892). That case, however, involved a constitutional provision proscribing all punishments that were merely "cruel," S. D. Const., Art. VI, 23 (1889). A few decisions early in the present century cited it (again in dictum) for the proposition that a sentence "so out of proportion to the offense . . . as to `shock public sentiment and violate the judgment of reasonable people' " would be "cruel and unusual." Jackson v. United States, 102 F. 473, 488 (CA9 1900); Territory v. Ketchum, 10 N. M. 718, 723, 65 P. 169, 171 (1901).

    III We think it enough that those who framed and approved the Federal Constitution chose, for whatever reason, not to include within it the guarantee against disproportionate sentences that some State Constitutions contained. It is worth noting, however, that there was good reason for that choice — a reason that reinforces the necessity of overruling Solem. While there are relatively clear historical guidelines and accepted practices that enable judges to determine which modes of punishment are "cruel and unusual," proportionality does not lend itself to such analysis. Neither Congress nor any state legislature has ever set out with the objective of crafting a penalty that is "disproportionate," yet as some of the examples mentioned above indicate, many enacted dispositions seem to be so — because they were made for other times or other places, with different social attitudes, different criminal epidemics, different public fears, and different prevailing theories of penology. This is not to say that there are no absolutes; one can imagine extreme examples that no rational person, in no time or place, could accept. But for the same reason these examples are easy to decide, they are certain never to occur. [n.11] The real function of a constitutional proportionality principle, if it exists, is to enable judges to evaluate a penalty that some assemblage of men and women has considered proportionate — and to say that it is not. For that real-world enterprise, the standards seem so inadequate that the proportionality principle becomes an invitation to imposition of subjective values.

This becomes clear, we think, from a consideration of the three factors that Solem found relevant to the proportionality determination: (1) the inherent gravity of the offense, (2) the sentences imposed for similarly grave offenses in the same jurisdiction, and (3) sentences imposed for the same crime in other jurisdictions. 463 U. S., at 290-291. As to the first factor: Of course some offenses, involving violent harm to human beings, will always and everywhere be regarded as serious, but that is only half the equation. The issue is what else should be regarded to be as serious as these offenses, or even to be more serious than some of them. On that point, judging by the statutes that Americans have enacted, there is enormous variation — even within a given age, not to mention across the many generations ruled by the Bill of Rights. The State of Massachusetts punishes sodomy more severely than assault and battery, compare Mass. Gen. Laws 272:34 (1988) ("not more than twenty years" in prison for sodomy) with 265:13A ("not more than two and one half years" in prison for assault and battery); whereas in several States, sodomy is not unlawful at all. In Louisiana, one who assaults another with a dangerous weapon faces the same maximum prison term as one who removes a shopping basket "from the parking area or grounds of any store . . . without authorization." La. Rev. Stat. Ann. 14:37; 14:68.1 (West 1986). A battery that results in "protracted and obvious disfigurement" merits imprisonment "for not more than five years," 14:34.1, one half the maximum penalty for theft of livestock or an oilfield seismograph, 14:67.1, 14:67.8. We may think that the First Congress punished with clear dis proportionality when it provided up to seven years in prison and up to $1,000 in fine for "cut[ting] off the ear or ears, . . . cut[ting] out or disabl[ing] the tongue, . . . put[ting] out an eye, . . . cut[ting] off . . . any limb or member of any person with intention . . . to maim or disfigure," but provided the death penalty for "run[ning] away with [a] ship or vessel, or any goods or merchandise to the value of fifty dollars." Act of Apr. 30, 1790, ch. 9, 8, 13, 1 Stat. 113-115. But then perhaps the citizens of 1791 would think that today's Congress punishes with clear disproportionality when it sanctions "assault by . . . wounding" with up to six months in prison, 18 U.S.C. 113(d), unauthorized reproduction of the "Smokey Bear" character or name with the same penalty, 18 U.S.C. 711 offering to barter a migratory bird with up to two years in prison, 16 U.S.C. 707(b), and purloining a "key suited to any lock adopted by the Post-Office Department" with a prison term of up to 10 years, 18 U.S.C. 1704. Perhaps both we and they would be right, but the point is that there are no textual or historical standards for saying so.

The difficulty of assessing gravity is demonstrated in the very context of the present case: Petitioner acknowledges that a mandatory life sentence might not be "grossly excessive" for possession of cocaine with intent to distribute, see Hutto v. Davis, 454 U.S. 370 (1982). But surely whether it is a "grave" offense merely to possess a significant quantity of drugs — thereby facilitating distribution, subjecting the holder to the temptation of distribution, and raising the possibility of theft by others who might distribute — depends entirely upon how odious and socially threatening one believes drug use to be. Would it be "grossly excessive" to provide life imprisonment for "mere possession" of a certain quantity of heavy weaponry? If not, then the only issue is whether the possible dissemination of drugs can be as "grave" as the possible dissemination of heavy weapons. Who are we to say no? The Members of the Michigan Legislature, and not we, know the situation on the streets of Detroit.

The second factor suggested in Solem fails for the same reason. One cannot compare the sentences imposed by the jurisdiction for "similarly grave" offenses if there is no objective standard of gravity. Judges will be comparing what they consider comparable. Or, to put the same point differently: when it happens that two offenses judicially determined to be "similarly grave" receive significantly dissimilar penalties, what follows is not that the harsher penalty is unconstitutional, but merely that the legislature does not share the judges' view that the offenses are similarly grave. Moreover, even if "similarly grave" crimes could be identified, the penalties for them would not necessarily be comparable, since there are many other justifications for a difference. For example, since deterrent effect depends not only upon the amount of the penalty but upon its certainty, crimes that are less grave but significantly more difficult to detect may warrant substantially higher penalties. Grave crimes of the sort that will not be deterred by penalty may warrant substantially lower penalties, as may grave crimes of the sort that are normally committed once-in-a-lifetime by otherwise law-abiding citizens who will not profit from rehabilitation. Whether these differences will occur, and to what extent, depends, of course, upon the weight the society accords to deterrence and rehabilitation, rather than retribution, as the objective of criminal punishment (which is an eminently legislative judgment). In fact, it becomes difficult even to speak intelligently of "proportionality," once deterrence and rehabilitation are given significant weight. Proportionality is inherently a retributive concept, and perfect proportionality is the talionic law. Cf. Bill For Proportioning Punishments, 1 Writings of Thomas Jefferson 218, 228-229 (A. Lipscomb 1903) ("[W]hoever . . . shall maim another, or shall disfigure him . . . shall be maimed or disfigured in like sort").

As for the third factor mentioned by Solem — the character of the sentences imposed by other States for the same crime — it must be acknowledged that that can be applied with clarity and ease. The only difficulty is that it has no conceivable relevance to the Eighth Amendment. That a State is entitled to treat with stern disapproval an act that other States punish with the mildest of sanctions follows a fortiori from the undoubted fact that a State may criminalize an act that other States do not criminalize at all. Indeed, a State may criminalize an act that other States choose to reward — punishing, for example, the killing of endangered wild animals for which other States are offering a bounty. What greater disproportion could there be than that? "Absent a constitutionally imposed uniformity inimical to traditional notions of federalism, some State will always bear the distinction of treating particular offenders more severely than any other State." Rummel, 445 U. S., at 282. Diversity not only in policy, but in the means of implementing policy, is the very raison d'être of our federal system. Though the different needs and concerns of other States may induce them to treat simple possession of 672 grams of cocaine as a relatively minor offense, see Wyo. Stat. 35-7-1031(c) (1988) (6 months); W. Va. Code 60A-4-401(c) (1989) (6 months), nothing in the Constitution requires Michigan to follow suit. The Eighth Amendment is not a ratchet, whereby a temporary consensus on leniency for a particular crime fixes a permanent constitutional maximum, disabling the States from giving effect to altered beliefs and responding to changed social conditions.

IV Our 20th-century jurisprudence has not remained entirely in accord with the proposition that there is no proportionality requirement in the Eighth Amendment, but neither has it departed to the extent that Solem suggests. In Weems v. United States, 217 U.S. 349 (1910), a government disbursing officer convicted of making false entries of small sums in his account book was sentenced by Philippine courts to 15 years of cadena temporal. That punishment, based upon the Spanish Penal Code, called for incarceration at " `hard and painful labor' " with chains fastened to the wrists and ankles at all times. Several "accessor[ies]" were superadded, including permanent disqualification from holding any position of public trust, subjection to "[government] surveillance" for life, and "civil interdiction," which consisted of deprivation of " `the rights of parental authority, guardianship of person or property, participation in the family council [, etc.]' " Weems, supra, at 364.

Justice McKenna, writing for himself and three others, held that the imposition of cadena temporal was "Cruel and Unusual Punishment." (Justice White, joined by Justice Holmes, dissented.) That holding, and some of the reasoning upon which it was based, was not at all out of accord with the traditional understanding of the provision we have described above. The punishment was both (1) severe and (2) unknown to Anglo-American tradition. As to the former, Justice McKenna wrote:

"No circumstance of degradation is omitted. It may be that even the cruelty of pain is not omitted. He must bear a chain night and day. He is condemned to painful as well as hard labor. What painful labor may mean we have no exact measure. It must be something more than hard labor. It may be hard labor pressed to the point of pain." Id., at 366-367.

As to the latter:

It has no fellow in American legislation. Let us remember that it has come to us from a government of a different form and genius from ours. It is cruel in its excess of imprisonment and that which accompanies and follows imprisonment. It is unusual in its character." Id., at 377.

Other portions of the opinion, however, suggest that mere disproportionality, by itself, might make a punishment cruel and unusual:

"Such penalties for such offenses amaze those who . . . believe that it is a precept of justice that punishment for crime should be graduated and proportioned to offense." Id., at 366-367.

"[T]he inhibition [of the Cruel and Unusual Punishments Clause] was directed, not only against punishments which inflict torture, `but against all punishments which by their excessive length or severity are greatly disproportioned to the offenses charged.' " Id., at 371, quoting O'Neil v. Vermont, 144 U.S. 323, 339-340 (1892) (Field, J., dissenting).

Since it contains language that will support either theory, our later opinions have used Weems, as the occasion required, to represent either the principle that "the Eighth Amendment bars not only those punishments that are `barbaric' but also those that are `excessive' in relation to the crime committed," Coker v. Georgia, 433 U.S. 584, 592 (1977), or the principle that only a "unique . . . punishmen[t]," a form of imprisonment different from the "more traditional forms . . . imposed under the Anglo-Saxon system," can violate the Eighth Amendment, Rummel, 445 U. S., at 274-275. If the proof of the pudding is in the eating, however, it is hard to view Weems as announcing a constitutional requirement of proportionality, given that it did not produce a decision implementing such a requirement, either here or in the lower federal courts, for six decades. In Graham v. West Virginia, 224 U.S. 616 (1912), for instance, we evaluated (and rejected) a claim that life imprisonment for a third offense of horse theft was "cruel and unusual." We made no mention of Weems, although the petitioner had relied upon that case. [n.12] See also Badders v. United States, 240 U.S. 391 (1916).

Opinions in the federal courts of appeals were equally devoid of evidence that this Court had announced a general proportionality principle. Some evaluated "cruel and unusual punishment" claims without reference to Weems. See, e. g., Bailey v. United States, 284 F. 126 (CA7 1922); Tincher v. United States, 11 F. 2d 18, 21 (CA4 1926). Others continued to echo (in dictum) variants of the dictum in State v. Becker, 3 S. D. 29, 51 N. W. 1018 (1892), to the effect that courts will not interfere with punishment unless it is "manifestly cruel and unusual," and cited Weems for the propostion that sentences imposed within the limits of a statute "ordinarily will not be regarded as cruel and unusual." See, e. g., Sansone v. Zerbst, 73 F. 2d 670, 672 (CA10 1934); Bailey v. United States, 74 F. 2d 451, 453 (CA10 1934). [n.13] Not until more than half a century after Weems did the Circuit Courts begin performing proportionality analysis. E. g., Hart v. Coiner, 483 F. 2d 136 (CA4 1973). Even then, some continued to state that "[a] sentence within the statutory limits is not cruel and unusual punishment." Page v. United States, 462 U.S. 932, 935 (CA3 1972). Accord, Rener v. Beto, 447 F. 2d 20, 23 (CA5 1971); Anthony v. United States, 331 F. 2d 687, 693 (CA9 1964).

The first holding of this Court unqualifiedly applying a requirement of proportionality to criminal penalties was issued 185 years after the Eighth Amendment was adopted. [n.14] In Coker v. Georgia, supra, the Court held that, because of the disproportionality, it was a violation of the Cruel and Unusual Punishments Clause to impose capital punishment for rape of an adult woman. Four years later, in Enmund v. Florida, 458 U.S. 782 (1982), we held that it violates the Eighth Amendment, because of disproportionality, to impose the death penalty upon a participant in a felony that results in murder, without any inquiry into the participant's intent to kill. Rummel, supra, treated this line of authority as an aspect of our death penalty jurisprudence, rather than a generalizable aspect of Eighth Amendment law. We think that is an accurate explanation, and we reassert it. Proportionality review is one of several respects in which we have held that "death is different," and have imposed protections that the Constitution nowhere else provides. See, e. g., Turner v. Murray, 476 U.S. 28, 36-37 (1986); Eddings v. Oklahoma, 455 U.S. 104 (1982); id., at 117 (O'Connor, J., concurring); Beck v. Alabama, 447 U.S. 625 (1980). We would leave it there, but will not extend it further.

V Petitioner claims that his sentence violates the Eighth Amendment for a reason in addition to its alleged disproportionality. He argues that it is "cruel and unusual" to impose a mandatory sentence of such severity, without any consideration of so-called mitigating factors such as, in his case, the fact that he had no prior felony convictions. He apparently contends that the Eighth Amendment requires Michigan to create a sentencing scheme whereby life in prison without possibility of parole is simply the most severe of a range of available penalties that the sentencer may impose after hearing evidence in mitigation and aggravation.

As our earlier discussion should make clear, this claim has no support in the text and history of the Eighth Amendment. Severe, mandatory penalties may be cruel, but they are not unusual in the constitutional sense, having been employed in various forms throughout our Nation's history. As noted earlier, mandatory death sentences abounded in our first Penal Code. They were also common in the several States — both at the time of the founding and throughout the 19th century. See Woodson v. North Carolina, 428 U. S., at 289-290. There can be no serious contention, then, that a sentence which is not otherwise cruel and unusual becomes so simply because it is "mandatory." See Chapman v. United States, 500 U. S. —, — — (1991) (slip op., at 12-13).

Petitioner's "required mitigation" claim, like his proportionality claim, does find support in our death-penalty jurisprudence. We have held that a capital sentence is cruel and unusual under the Eighth Amendment if it is imposed without an individualized determination that that punishment is "appropriate" — whether or not the sentence is "grossly disproportionate." See Woodson v. North Carolina, supra; Lockett v. Ohio, 438 U.S. 586 (1978); Eddings v. Oklahoma, supra; Hitchcock v. Dugger, 481 U.S. 393 (1987). Petitioner asks us to extend this so-called "individualized capitalsentencing doctrine," Sumner v. Shuman, 483 U.S. 66, 73 (1987), to an "individualized mandatory life in prison without parole sentencing doctrine." We refuse to do so.

Our cases creating and clarifying the "individualized capital sentencing doctrine" have repeatedly suggested that there is no comparable requirement outside the capital context, because of the qualitative difference between death and all other penalties. See Eddings v. Oklahoma, supra, at 110-112; id., at 117-118 (O'Connor, J. concurring); Lockett v. Ohio, supra, at 602-605; Woodson v. North Carolina, supra, at 303-305; Rummel v. Estelle, 445 U. S., at 272.

"The penalty of death differs from all other forms of criminal punishment, not in degree but in kind. It is unique in its total irrevocability. It is unique in its rejection of rehabilitation of the convict as a basic purpose of criminal justice. And it is unique, finally, in its ab solute renunciation of all that is embodied in our concept of humanity." Furman v. Georgia, 408 U. S., at 306 (Stewart, J., concurring).

It is true that petitioner's sentence is unique in that it is the second most severe known to the law; but life imprisonment with possibility of parole is also unique in that it is the third most severe. And if petitioner's sentence forecloses some "flexible techniques" for later reducing his sentence, see Lockett, supra, at 605 (Burger, C. J.) (plurality opinion), it does not foreclose all of them, since there remain the possibilities of retroactive legislative reduction and executive clemency. In some cases, moreover, there will be negligible difference between life without parole and other sentences of imprisonment — for example, a life sentence with eligibility for parole after 20 years, or even a lengthy term sentence without eligibility for parole, given to a 65-year-old man. But even where the difference is the greatest, it cannot be compared with death. We have drawn the line of required individualized sentencing at capital cases, and see no basis for extending it further.

The judgment of the Michigan Court of Appeals is

Affirmed.

Notes to Harmelin v. Michigan (June 27, 1991)

1 Mich. Comp. Laws Ann. 333.7403(2)(a)(i) (Supp. 1990-1991) pro- vides a mandatory sentence of life in prison for possession of 650 grams or more of "any mixture containing [a schedule 2] controlled substance"; 333.7214(a)(iv) defines cocaine as a schedule 2 controlled substance. Section 791.234(4) provides eligibility for parole after 10 years in prison, except for those convicted of either first-degree murder or "a major con- trolled substance offense"; 791.233b[1](b) defines "major controlled sub- stance offense" as, inter alia, a violation of 333.7403.

2 Specifically, we rejected, in some detail, the four-factor test promulgated by the Fourth Circuit in Hart v. Coiner, 483 F. 2d 136 (CA4 1973). This test included the three factors relied upon by the Rummel dissent. See Hart, supra, at 140-143.

3 Solem v. Helm, 463 U.S. 277 (1983), apparently adopted this interpretation, quoting, as it did, from one of these sources. See id., at 285 (quoting Sources of our Liberties 236).

4 Indeed, it is not clear that, by the standards of the age, Oates' sentence was disproportionate, given that his perjuries resulted in the deaths of 15 innocents. Granucci suggests that it was not. See Granucci, "Nor Cruel and Unusual Punishments Inflicted:" The Original Meaning, 57 Calif. L. Rev. 839, 859, and n. 97 (1969). And Macaulay observed that Oates' "sufferings, great as they might seem, had been trifling when compared with his crimes." 6 Macaulay, 137. See also, 2 id., at 203-204.

5 Contrary to Justice White's suggestion, post, at 3, n. 1, Granucci provides little (if any) direct evidence that the Declaration of Rights embodied a proportionality principle. He simply reasons that, because English law was concerned with proportionality, the Declaration of Rights must have embodied such a principle. Granucci, supra, at 844-847.

6 Justice White apparently agrees that the clause outlaws particular "modes" of punishment. He goes on to suggest, however, that because the Founders did not specifically exclude a proportionality component from words that "could reasonably be construed to include it," the Eighth Amendment must prohibit disproportionate punishments as well. Post, at 3. Surely this is an extraordinary method for determining what restrictions upon democratic self-government the Constitution contains. It seems to us that our task is not merely to identify various meanings that the text "could reasonably" bear, and then impose the one that from a policy standpoint pleases us best. Rather, we are to strive as best we can to select from among the various "reasonable" possibilities the most plausible meaning. We do not bear the burden of "proving an affirmative decision against the proportionality component," ibid.; rather, Justice White bears the burden of proving an affirmative decision in its favor. For if the Constitution does not affirmatively contain such a restriction, the matter of proportionality is left to state constitutions or to the democratic process.

7 Printed collections of State Constitutions were available to the Founders, see The Federalist No. 24, p. 159, n. (C. Rossiter ed. 1961) (A. Hamilton); see also id., No. 47, p. 304-307 (J. Madison) (comparing constitutions of all 13 States).

8 The New Hampshire proportionality provision, by far the most detailed of the genre, read: "All penalties ought to be proportioned to the nature of the offence. No wise legislature will affix the same punishment to the crimes of theft, forgery and the like, which they do to those of murder and treason; where the same undistinguishing severity is exerted against all offences; the people are led to forget the real distinction in the crimes themselves, and to commit the most flagrant with as little compunction as they do those of the lightest dye: For the same reason a multitude of san- guinary laws is both impolitic and unjust. The true design of all punish- ments being to reform, not to exterminate, mankind." N. H. Const., Art. I, 18 (1784).

The Ohio provision copied that of New Hampshire.

9 Justice White suggests that because the Framers prohibited "excessive fines" (which he asserts, and we will assume for the sake of argument, means "disproportionate fines"), they must have meant to prohibit "excessive" punishments as well. Post, at 1-2. This argument apparently did not impress state courts in the 19th century, and with good reason. The logic of the matter is quite the opposite. If "cruel and unusual punishments" included disproportionate punishments, the separate prohibition of disproportionate fines (which are certainly punishments) would have been entirely superfluous. When two parts of a provision (the Eighth Amend- ment) use different language to address the same

or similar subject matter, a difference in meaning is assumed. See Walton v. Arizona, 497 U. S. ---, --- (1990) (opinion concurring in part and concurring in judgment).

But, it might be argued, why would any rational person be careful to for- bid the disproportionality of fines but provide no protection against the disproportionality of more severe punishments? Does not the one suggest the existence of the other? Not at all. There is good reason to be concerned that fines, uniquely of all punishments, will be imposed in a measure out of accord with the penal goals of retribution and deterrence. Imprisonment, corporal punishment and even capital punishment cost a State money; fines are a source of revenue. As we have recognized in the con- text of other constitutional provisions, it makes sense to scrutinize govern- mental action more closely when the State stands to benefit. See United States Trust Co. of New York v. New Jersey, 431 U.S. 1, 25-26 (1977); Perry v. United States, 294 U. S. 330, 350-351 (1935). (We relied upon precisely the lack of this incentive for abuse in holding that "punitive dam- ages" were not "fines" within the meaning of the Eighth Amendment. Browning Ferris Industries of Vermont, Inc. v. Kelco Disposal, Inc., 492 U.S. 257, 271-276 (1989)). Thus, some early State Constitutions prohibited excessive fines without placing any restrictions on other modes of punishment. E. g., Conn. Declaration of Rights Art. I, 13 (1818) (prohibiting excessive fines only); Ga. Const., Art. LIX (1777) (same).

10 Neither State v. Driver, 78 N. C. 423 (1878), nor State ex rel. Garvey v. Whitaker, 48 La. 527, 19 So. 457 (1896) is to the contrary. They are examples of applying, not a proportionality principle, but rather the principle (curiously in accord with the original meaning of the phrase in the English Declaration of Rights, discussed above) that a punishment is "cruel and unusual" if it is illegal because not sanctioned by common law or statute. In Driver, the court had imposed a sentence of five years in county jail for the common-law offense of assault and battery, for which no statutory penalty had been established. The North Carolina Supreme Court held the sentence to violate the State's "cruel or unusual punishment" provision because a county jail is "a close prison, where life is soon in jeopardy," and no prisoner had ever "been imprisoned for five years in a County jail for any crime however aggravated." 78 N. C., at 425, 426-427. A subsequent North Carolina case makes it clear that when the legislature has prescribed a penalty of a traditional mode, the penalty's severity for the offense in question cannot violate the State's "cruel or unusual punishment" clause. State v. Blake, 157 N. C. 608, 611, 72 S. E. 1080, 1081-1082 (1911).

In Garvey, the defendants were sentenced to nearly six years in jail for trespassing on public property. The sentence prescribed by the relevant city ordinance was 30 days, but the defendants' one-hour forty-minute occupation had been made the subject of 72 separate counts, "each offence embracing only one and one-half minutes and one offence following after the other immediately and consecutively," 48 La., at 533, 19 So., at 459. The Louisiana Supreme Court found the sentence to have been cruel and unusual "considering the offence to have been a continuing one," ibid. We think it a fair reading of the case that the sentence was cruel and unusual because it was illegal.

11 Justice White argues that the Eighth Amendment must contain a proportionality principle because otherwise legislatures could "mak[e] overtime parking a felony punishable by life imprisonment." Post, at 10. We do not in principle oppose the "parade of horribles" form of argumentation, see Scalia, Assorted Canards of Contemporary Legal Analysis, 40 Case W. Res. L. Rev. 581, 590-593 (1989-1990); but its strength is in direct proportion to (1) the certitude that the provision in question was meant to exclude the very evil represented by the imagined parade, and (2) the probability that the parade will in fact materialize. Here, for the reasons we have discussed, there is no cause to believe that the provision was meant to exclude the evil of a disproportionate punishment. Justice White's argument has force only for those who believe that the Constitution prohibited everything that is intensely undesirable -- which is an obvious fallacy, see Art. I, 9 (implicitly permitting slavery); Monaghan, Our Perfect Constitution, 56 N. Y. U. L. Rev. 353 (1981). Nor is it likely that the horrible example imagined would ever in fact occur, unless, of course, overtime parking should one day become an arguably major threat to the common good, and the need to deter it arguably critical -- at which time the members of this Court would probably disagree as to whether the punishment really is "disproportionate," even as they disagree regarding the punishment for possession of cocaine today. As Justice Frankfurter reminded us, "[t]he process of Constitutional adjudication does not thrive on conjuring up horrible possibilities that never happen in the real world and devising doctrines sufficiently comprehensive in detail to cover the remotest contingency." New York v. United States, 326 U.S. 572, 583 (1946). It seems to us no more reasonable to hold that the Eighth Amendment for- bids "disproportionate punishment" because otherwise the State could impose life imprisonment for a parking offense, than it would be to hold that the Takings Clause forbids "disproportionate taxation" because otherwise the State could tax away all income above the subsistence level.

12 At the time we decided Graham, it was not clear that the Eighth Amendment was applicable to the States, but our opinion obviously assumed that it was. See Rummel v. Estelle, 445 U.S. 263, 277, n. 13 (1980).

13 State Supreme Courts reacted to Weems in various ways. The Virginia Supreme Court suggested that, since only four Justices had joined the majority opinion, the proportionality question "may be fairly said to be still an open question in so far as the authority of the Supreme Court is concerned." Hart v. Commonwealth, 131 Va. 726, 745, 109 S. E. 582, 588 (1921). Cf. North Georgia Fishing, Inc. v. Di-Chem, Inc., 419 U.S. 601, 616-619 (1975) (Blackmun, J., dissenting). The Supreme Court of Indiana apparently thought Weems to be in accord with the traditional view expressed in Hobbs v. State, 133 Ind. 404, 32 N. E. 1019 (1893). See Kistler v. State, 190 Ind. 149, 158 (1921). The North Carolina Supreme Court, after stating that Weems contained "an interesting historical re- view" went on to hold that, under North Carolina's "similar provision," punishment fixed by the legislature "cannot be excessive." State v. Blake, 157 N. C. 608, 611, 72 S. E. 1080, 1081-1082 (1911).

14 In Robinson v. California, 370 U.S. 660 (1962), the Court invalidated a 90-day prison sentence for the crime of being "addicted to the use of narcotics." The opinion does not cite Weems and rests upon the proposition that "[e]ven one day in prison would be a cruel and unusual punishment for the `crime' of having a common cold," 370 U. S., at 667. Despite the Court's statement to the contrary in Solem v. Helm, 463 U.S. 277, 287 (1983), there is no reason to believe that the decision was an application of the principle of proportionality. See Ingraham v. Wright, 430 U.S. 651, 667 (1977).

Hate speech not automatically unprotected: R. A. V. v. City of St. Paul (June 22, 1992)

Justice Scalia delivered the opinion of the Court.

In the predawn hours of June 21, 1990, petitioner and several other teenagers allegedly assembled a crudely made cross by taping together broken chair legs. They then allegedly burned the cross inside the fenced yard of a black family that lived across the street from the house where petitioner was staying. Although this conduct could have been punished under any of a number of laws, [n.1] one of the two provisions under which respondent city of St. Paul chose to charge petitioner (then a juvenile) was the St. Paul Bias Motivated Crime Ordinance, St. Paul, Minn. Legis. Code § 292.02 (1990), which provides:

"Whoever places on public or private property a symbol, object, appellation, characterization or graffiti, including, but not limited to, a burning cross or Nazi swastika, which one knows or has reasonable grounds to know arouses anger, alarm or resentment in others on the basis of race, color, creed, religion or gender commits disorderly conduct and shall be guilty of a misdemeanor."

Petitioner moved to dismiss this count on the ground that the St. Paul ordinance was substantially overbroad and impermissibly content based and therefore facially invalid under the First Amendment. [n.2] The trial court granted this motion, but the Minnesota Supreme Court reversed. That court rejected petitioner's overbreadth claim because, as construed in prior Minnesota cases, see, e. g., In re Welfare of S. L. J., 263 N. W. 2d 412 (Minn. 1978), the modifying phrase "arouses anger, alarm or resentment in others" limited the reach of the ordinance to conduct that amounts to "fighting words," i. e., "conduct that itself inflicts injury or tends to incite immediate violence . . .," In re Welfare of R. A. V., 464 N. W. 2d 507, 510 (Minn. 1991) (citing Chaplinsky v. New Hampshire, 315 U.S. 568, 572 (1942)), and therefore the ordinance reached only expression "that the first amendment does not protect." 464 N. W. 2d, at 511. The court also concluded that the ordinance was not impermissibly content based because, in its view, "the ordinance is a narrowly tailored means toward accomplishing the compelling governmental interest in protecting the community against bias motivated threats to public safety and order." Ibid. We granted certiorari, 501 U. S. ___ (1991).

In construing the St. Paul ordinance, we are bound by the construction given to it by the Minnesota court. Posadas de Puerto Rico Associates v. Tourism Co. of Puerto Rico, 478 U.S. 328, 339 (1986); New York v. Ferber, 458 U.S. 747,769, n. 24 (1982); Terminiello v. Chicago, 337 U.S. 1, 4 (1949). Accordingly, we accept the Minnesota Supreme Court's authoritative statement that the ordinance reaches only those expressions that constitute "fighting words" within the meaning of Chaplinsky. 464 N. W. 2d, at 510-511. Petitioner and his amici urge us to modify the scope of the Chaplinsky formulation, thereby invalidating the ordinance as "substantially overbroad," Broadrick v. Oklahoma, 413 U.S. 601, 610 (1973). We find it unnecessary to consider this issue. Assuming, arguendo, that all of the expression reached by the ordinance is proscribable under the "fighting words" doctrine, we nonetheless conclude that the ordinance is facially unconstitutional in that it prohibits otherwise permitted speech solely on the basis of the subjects the speech addresses. [n.3]

The First Amendment generally prevents government from proscribing speech, see, e. g., Cantwell v. Connecticut, 310 U.S. 296, 309-311 (1940), or even expressive conduct, see, e. g., Texas v. Johnson, 491 U.S. 397, 406 (1989), because of disapproval of the ideas expressed. Content based regulations are presumptively invalid. Simon & Schuster, Inc. v. Members of N. Y. State Crime Victims Bd., 502 U. S. ___, ___ (1991) (slip op., at 8-9); id., at ___ (Kennedy, J., concurring in judgment) (slip op., at 3-4); Consolidated Edison Co. of N. Y. v. Public Serv. Comm'n of N. Y., 447 U.S. 530, 536 (1980); Police Dept. of Chicago v. Mosley, 408 U.S. 92, 95 (1972). From 1791 to the present, however, our society, like other free but civilized societies, has permitted restrictions upon the content of speech in a few limited areas, which are "of such slight social value as a step to truth that any benefit that may be derived from them is clearly outweighed by the social interest in order and morality." Chaplinsky, supra, at 572. We have recognized that "the freedom of speech" referred to by the First Amendment does not include a freedom to disregard these traditional limitations. See, e. g., Roth v. United States, 354 U.S. 476 (1957) (obscenity); Beauharnais v. Illinois, 343 U.S. 250 (1952) (defamation); Chaplinsky v. New Hampshire, supra, ("fighting words"); see generally Simon & Schuster, supra, at ___ (Kennedy, J., concurring in judgment) (slip op., at 4). Our decisions since the 1960's have narrowed the scope of the traditional categorical exceptions for defamation, see New York Times Co. v.Sullivan, 376 U.S. 254 (1964); Gertz v. Robert Welch, Inc., 418 U.S. 323 (1974); see generally Milkovich v. Lorain Journal Co., 497 U.S. 1, 13-17 (1990), and for obscenity, see Miller v. California, 413 U.S. 15 (1973), but a limited categorical approach has remained an important part of our First Amendment jurisprudence.

We have sometimes said that these categories of expression are "not within the area of constitutionally protected speech," Roth, supra, at 483; Beauharnais, supra, at 266; Chaplinsky, supra, at 571-572, or that the "protection of the First Amendment does not extend" to them, Bose Corp. v. Consumers Union of United States, Inc., 466 U.S. 485, 504 (1984); Sable Communications of Cal., Inc. v. FCC, 492 U.S. 115, 124 (1989). Such statements must be taken in context, however, and are no more literally true than is the occasionally repeated shorthand characterizing obscenity "as not being speech at all," Sunstein, Pornography and the First Amendment, 1986 Duke L. J. 589, 615, n. 146. What they mean is that these areas of speech can, consistently with the First Amendment, be regulated because of their constitutionally proscribable content (obscenity, defamation, etc.)--not that they are categories of speech entirely invisible to the Constitution, so that they may be made the vehicles for content discrimination unrelated to their distinctively proscribable content. Thus, the government may proscribe libel; but it may not make the further content discrimination of proscribing only libel critical of the government. We recently acknowledged this distinction in Ferber, 458 U. S., at 763, where, in upholding New York's child pornography law, we expressly recognized that there was no "question here of censoring a particular literary theme . . . ." See also id., at 775 (O'Connor, J., concurring) ("As drafted, New York's statute does not attempt to suppress the communication of particular ideas").

Our cases surely do not establish the proposition that the First Amendment imposes no obstacle whatsoever toregulation of particular instances of such proscribable expression, so that the government "may regulate [them] freely," post, at 4 (White, J., concurring in judgment). That would mean that a city council could enact an ordinance prohibiting only those legally obscene works that contain criticism of the city government or, indeed, that do not include endorsement of the city government. Such a simplistic, all or nothing at all approach to First Amendment protection is at odds with common sense and with our jurisprudence as well. [n.4] It is not true that "fighting words" have at most a "*de minimis*" expressive content, ibid., or that their content is in all respects "worthless and undeserving of constitutional protection," post, at 6; sometimes they are quite expressive indeed. We have not said that they constitute "no part of the expression of ideas," but only that they constitute "no essential part of any exposition of ideas." Chaplinsky, 315 U. S., at 572 (emphasis added).

The proposition that a particular instance of speech can be proscribable on the basis of one feature (e. g., obscenity) but not on the basis of another (e. g., opposition to the city government) is commonplace, and has found application in many contexts. We have long held, for example, that nonverbal expressive activity can be banned because of the action it entails, but not because of the ideas it expresses--so that burning a flag in violation of an ordinance against outdoor fires could be punishable, whereas burning a flag in violation of an ordinance against dishonoring the flag is not. See Johnson, 491 U. S., at 406-407. See also Barnes v. Glen Theatre, Inc., 501 U. S. ___, ___ ___ (1991) (plurality) (slip op., at 4-6); id., at ___ ___ (Scalia, J., concurring in judgment) (slip op., at 5-6); id., at ___ ___ (Souter, J., concurring in judgment) (slip op., at 1-2); United States v. O'Brien, 391 U.S. 367, 376-377 (1968). Similarly, we have upheld reasonable "time, place, or manner" restrictions, but only if they are "justified without reference to the content of the regulated speech." Ward v. Rock Against Racism, 491 U.S. 781, 791 (1989) (internal quotation marks omitted); see also Clark v. Community for Creative Non

Violence, 468 U.S. 288, 298 (1984) (noting that the O'Brien test differs little from the standard applied to time, place, or manner restrictions). And just as the power to proscribe particular speech on the basis of a noncontent element (e. g., noise) does not entail the powerto proscribe the same speech on the basis of a content element; so also, the power to proscribe it on the basis of one content element (e. g., obscenity) does not entail the power to proscribe it on the basis of other content elements.

In other words, the exclusion of "fighting words" from the scope of the First Amendment simply means that, for purposes of that Amendment, the unprotected features of the words are, despite their verbal character, essentially a "nonspeech" element of communication. Fighting words are thus analogous to a noisy sound truck: Each is, as Justice Frankfurter recognized, a "mode of speech," Niemotko v. Maryland, 340 U.S. 268, 282 (1951) (Frankfurter, J., concurring in result); both can be used to convey an idea; but neither has, in and of itself, a claim upon the First Amendment. As with the sound truck, however, so also with fighting words: The government may not regulate use based on hostility--or favoritism--towards the underlying message expressed. Compare Frisby v. Schultz, 487 U.S. 474 (1988) (upholding, against facial challenge, a content neutral ban on targeted residential picketing) with Carey v. Brown, 447 U.S. 455 (1980) (invalidating a ban on residential picketing that exempted labor picketing). [n.5]

The concurrences describe us as setting forth a new First Amendment principle that prohibition of constitutionally proscribable speech cannot be "underinclusiv[e]," post, at 6 (White, J., concurring in judgment)--a First Amendment "absolutism" whereby "within a particular `proscribable' category of expression, . . . a government must either pro scribe all speech or no speech at all," post, at 4 (Stevens, J., concurring in judgment). That easy target is of the concurrences' own invention. In our view, the First Amendment imposes not an "underinclusiveness" limitation but a "content discrimination" limitation upon a State's prohibition of proscribable speech. There is no problem whatever, for example, with a State's prohibiting obscenity (and other forms of proscribable expression) only in certain media or markets, for although that prohibition would be "underinclusive," it would not discriminate on the basis of content. See, e. g., Sable Communications, 492 U. S., at 124-126 (upholding 47 U.S.C. § 223(b)(1) (1988), which prohibits obscene telephone communications).

Even the prohibition against content discrimination that we assert the First Amendment requires is not absolute. It applies differently in the context of proscribable speech than in the area of fully protected speech. The rationale of the general prohibition, after all, is that content discrimination "rais[es] the specter that the Government may effectively drive certain ideas or viewpoints from the marketplace," Simon & Schuster, 502 U. S., at ___ (slip op., at 9); Leathers v. Medlock, 499 U. S. ___, ___ (1991); FCC v. League of Women Voters of California, 468 U.S. 364, 383-384 (1984); Consolidated Edison Co., 447 U. S., at 536; Police Dept. of Chicago v. Mosley, 408 U. S., at 95-98. But content discrimination among various instances of a class of proscribable speech often does not pose this threat.

When the basis for the content discrimination consists entirely of the very reason the entire class of speech at issue is proscribable, no significant danger of idea or viewpoint discrimination exists. Such a reason, having been adjudged neutral enough to support exclusion of the entire class of speech from First Amendment protection, is also neutral enough to form the basis of distinction within the class. To illustrate: A State might choose to prohibit only that obscenity which is the most patently offensive in its prurience--i. e., that which involves the most lasciviousdisplays of sexual activity. But it may not prohibit, for example, only that obscenity which includes offensive political messages. See Kucharek v. Hanaway, 902 F. 2d 513, 517 (CA7 1990), cert. denied, 498 U. S. ___ (1991). And the Federal Government can criminalize only those threats of violence that are directed against the President, see 18 U.S.C. § 871--since the reasons why threats of violence are outside the First Amendment (protecting individuals from the fear of violence, from the disruption that fear engenders, and from the possibility that the threatened violence will occur) have special force when applied to the person of the President. See Watts v. United States, 394 U.S. 705, 707 (1969) (upholding the facial validity of § 871 because of the "overwhelmin[g] interest in protecting the safety of [the] Chief Executive and in allowing him to perform his duties without interference from threats of physical violence"). But the Federal Government may not criminalize only those threats against the President that mention his policy on aid to inner cities. And to take a final example (one mentioned by Justice Stevens, post, at 6-7), a State may choose to regulate price advertising in one industry but not in others, because the risk of fraud (one of the characteristics of commercial speech that justifies depriving it of full First Amendment protection, see Virginia Pharmacy Bd. v. Virginia Citizens Consumer Council, Inc., 425 U.S. 748, 771-772 (1976)) is in its view greater there. Cf. Morales v. Trans World Airlines, Inc., 504 U. S. ___ (1992) (state regulation of airline advertising); Ohralik v. Ohio State Bar Assn., 436 U.S. 447 (1978) (state regulation of lawyer advertising). But a State may not prohibit only that commercial advertising that depicts men in a demeaning fashion, see, e. g., L. A. Times, Aug. 8, 1989, section 4, p. 6, col. 1.

Another valid basis for according differential treatment to even a content defined subclass of proscribable speech is that the subclass happens to be associated with particular "secondary effects" of the speech, so that the regulation is%justified without reference to the content of the . . . speech," Renton v. Playtime Theatres, Inc., 475 U.S. 41, 48 (1986) (quoting, with emphasis, Virginia Pharmacy Bd., supra, at 771); see also Young v. American Mini Theatres, Inc., 427 U.S. 50, 71, n. 34 (1976) (plurality); id., at 80-82 (Powell, J., concurring); Barnes, 501 U. S., at ___ ___ (Souter, J., concurring in judgment) (slip op., at 3-7). A State could, for example, permit all obscene live performances except those involving minors. Moreover, since words can in some circumstances violate laws directed not against speech but against conduct (a law against treason, for example, is violated by telling the enemy the nation's defense secrets), a particular content based subcategory of a proscribable class of speech can be swept up incidentally within the reach of a statute directed at conduct rather than speech. See id., at ___ (plurality) (slip op., at 4); id., at ___ (Scalia, J., concurring in judgment) (slip op., at 5-6); id., at ___ (Souter, J., concurring in judgment) (slip op., at 1-2); FTC v. Superior Court Trial Lawyers Assn., 493 U.S. 411, 425-432 (1990); O'Brien, 391 U. S., at 376-377. Thus, for example, sexually derogatory "fighting words," among other words, may produce a violation of Title VII's general prohibition against sexual discrimination in employment practices, 42 U.S.C. § 2000e 2; 29 CFR § 1604.11 (1991). See also 18 U.S.C. § 242; 42 U.S.C. §§ 1981 1982. Where the government does not target conduct on the basis of its expressive content, acts are not shielded from regulation merely because they express a discriminatory idea or philosophy.

These bases for distinction refute the proposition that the selectivity of the restriction is "even arguably `conditioned upon the sovereign's agreement with what a speaker may intend to say.' " Metromedia, Inc. v. San Diego, 453 U.S. 490, 555 (1981) (Stevens, J., dissenting in part) (citation omitted). There may be other such bases as well. Indeed, to validate such selectivity (where totally proscribable speech is at issue) it may not even be necessary to identifyany particular "neutral" basis, so long as the nature of the content discrimination is such that there is no realistic possibility that official suppression of ideas is afoot. (We cannot think of any First Amendment interest that would stand in the way of a State's prohibiting only those obscene motion pictures with blue eyed actresses.) Save for that limitation, the regulation of "fighting words," like the regulation of noisy speech, may address some offensive instances and leave other, equally offensive, instances alone. See Posadas de Puerto Rico, 478 U. S., at 342-343. [n.6]

Applying these principles to the St. Paul ordinance, we conclude that, even as narrowly construed by the Minnesota Supreme Court, the ordinance is facially unconstitutional. Although the phrase in the ordinance, "arouses anger, alarm or resentment in others," has been limited by the Minnesota Supreme Court's construction to reach only those symbols or displays that amount to "fighting words," the remaining, unmodified terms make clear that the ordinanceapplies only to "fighting words" that insult, or provoke violence, "on the basis of race, color, creed, religion or gender." Displays containing abusive invective, no matter how vicious or severe, are permissible unless they are addressed to one of the specified disfavored topics. Those who wish to use "fighting words" in connection with other ideas--to express hostility, for example, on the basis of political affiliation, union membership, or homosexuality--are not covered. The First Amendment does not permit St. Paul to impose special prohibitions on those speakers who express views on disfavored subjects. See Simon & Schuster, 502 U. S., at ___ (slip op., at 8-9); Arkansas Writers' Project, Inc. v. Ragland, 481 U.S. 221, 229-230 (1987).

In its practical operation, moreover, the ordinance goes even beyond mere content discrimination, to actual viewpoint discrimination. Displays containing some words--odious racial epithets, for example--would be prohibited to proponents of all views. But "fighting words" that do not themselves invoke race, color, creed, religion, or gender--aspersions upon a person's mother, for example--would seemingly be usable ad libitum in the placards of those arguing in favor of racial, color, etc. tolerance and equality, but could not be used by that speaker's opponents. One could hold up a sign saying, for example, that all "anti Catholic bigots" are misbegotten; but not that all "papists" are, for that would insult and provoke violence "on the basis of religion." St. Paul has no such authority to license one side of a debate to fight freestyle, while requiring the other to follow Marquis of Queensbury Rules.

What we have here, it must be emphasized, is not a prohibition of fighting words that are directed at certain persons or groups (which would be facially valid if it met the requirements of the Equal Protection Clause); but rather, a prohibition of fighting words that contain (as the Minnesota Supreme Court repeatedly emphasized) messages of "bias motivated" hatred and in particular, as applied to this case, messages "based on virulent notions of racial supremacy." 464 N. W. 2d, at 508, 511. One must wholeheartedly agree with the Minnesota Supreme Court that "[i]t is the responsibility, even the obligation, of diverse communities to confront such notions in whatever form they appear," ibid., but the manner of that confrontation cannot consist of selective limitations upon speech. St. Paul's brief asserts that a general "fighting words" law would not meet the city's needs because only a content specific measure can communicate to minority groups that the "group hatred" aspect of such speech "is not condoned by the majority." Brief for Respondent 25. The point of the First Amendment is that majority preferences must be expressed in some fashion other than silencing speech on the basis of its content.

Despite the fact that the Minnesota Supreme Court and St. Paul acknowledge that the ordinance is directed at expression of group hatred, Justice Stevens suggests that this "fundamentally misreads" the ordinance. Post, at 18-19. It is directed, he claims, not to speech of a particular content, but to particular "injur[ies]" that are "qualitatively different" from other injuries. Post, at 9. This is word play. What makes the anger, fear, sense of dishonor, etc. produced by violation of this ordinance distinct from the anger, fear, sense of dishonor, etc. produced by other fighting words is nothing other than the fact that it is caused by a distinctive idea, conveyed by a distinctive message. The First Amendment cannot be evaded that easily. It is obvious that the symbols which will arouse "anger, alarm or resentment in others on the basis of race, color, creed, religion or gender" are those symbols that communicate a message of hostility based on one of these characteristics. St. Paul concedes in its brief that the ordinance applies only to "racial, religious, or gender specific symbols" such as "a burning cross, Nazi swastika or other instrumentality of like import." Brief for Respon dent 8. Indeed, St. Paul argued in the Juvenile Court that%[t]he burning of a cross does express a message and it is, in fact, the content of that message which the St. Paul Ordinance attempts to legislate." Memorandum from the Ramsey County Attorney to the Honorable Charles A. Flinn, Jr., dated July 13, 1990, in In re Welfare of R. A. V., No. 89-D%1231 (Ramsey Cty. Juvenile Ct.), p. 1, reprinted in App. to Brief for Petitioner C 1.

The content based discrimination reflected in the St. Paul ordinance comes within neither any of the specific exceptions to the First Amendment prohibition we discussed earlier, nor within a more general exception for content discrimination that does not threaten censorship of ideas. It assuredly does not fall within the exception for content discrimination based on the very reasons why the particular class of speech at issue (here, fighting words) is proscribable. As explained earlier, see supra, at 8, the reason why fighting words are categorically excluded from the protection of the First Amendment is not that their content communicates any particular idea, but that their content embodies a particularly intolerable (and socially unnecessary) mode of expressing whatever idea the speaker wishes to convey. St. Paul has not singled out an especially offensive mode of expression--it has not, for example, selected for prohibition only those fighting words that communicate ideas in a threatening (as opposed to a merely obnoxious) manner. Rather, it has proscribed fighting words of whatever manner that communicate messages of racial, gender, or religious intolerance. Selectivity of this sort creates the possibility that the city is seeking to handicap the expression of particular ideas. That possibility would alone be enough to render the ordinance presumptively invalid, but St. Paul's comments and concessions in this case elevate the possibility to a certainty.

St. Paul argues that the ordinance comes within another of the specific exceptions we mentioned, the one that allows content discrimination aimed only at the "secondary effects" of the speech, see Renton v. Playtime Theatres, Inc., 475 U.S. 41 (1986). According to St. Paul, the ordinance is intended, "not to impact on [sic] the right of free expression of the accused," but rather to "protect against the victimization of a person or persons who are particularly vulnerable because of their membership in a group that historically has been discriminated against." Brief for Respondent 28. Even assuming that an ordinance that completely proscribes, rather than merely regulates, a specified category of speech can ever be considered to be directed only to the secondary effects of such speech, it is clear that the St. Paul ordinance is not directed to secondary effects within the meaning of Renton. As we said in Boos v. Barry, 485 U.S. 312 (1988), "[l]isteners' reactions to speech are not the type of `secondary effects' we referred to in Renton." Id., at 321. "The emotive impact of speech on its audience is not a `secondary effect.' " Ibid. See also id., at 334 (opinion of Brennan, J.). [n.7]

It hardly needs discussion that the ordinance does not fall within some more general exception permitting all selectivity that for any reason is beyond the suspicion of official suppression of ideas. The statements of St. Paul in this very case afford ample basis for, if not full confirmation of, that suspicion.

Finally, St. Paul and its amici defend the conclusion of the Minnesota Supreme Court that, even if the ordinance regulates expression based on hostility towards its protected ideological content, this discrimination is nonetheless justified because it is narrowly tailored to serve compelling state interests. Specifically, they assert that the ordinance helps to ensure the basic human rights of members of groups that have historically been subjected to discrimination, including the right of such group members to live in peace where they wish. We do not doubt that these interests are compelling, and that the ordinance can be said to promote them. But the "danger of censorship" presented by a facially content based statute, Leathers v. Medlock, 499 U. S. ___, ___ (1991) (slip op., at 8), requires that that weapon be employed only where it is "necessary to serve the asserted [compelling] interest," Burson v. Freeman, 504 U. S. ___, ___ (1992) (plurality) (slip op., at 8) (emphasis added); Perry Education Assn. v. Perry Local Educators' Assn., 460 U.S. 37, 45 (1983). The existence of adequate content neutral alternatives thus "undercut[s] significantly" any defense of such a statute, Boos v. Barry, supra, at 329, casting considerable doubt on the government's protestations that "the asserted justification is in fact an accurate description of the purpose and effect of the law," Burson, supra, at ___ (Kennedy, J., concurring) (slip op., at 2). See Boos, supra, at 324-329; cf. Minneapolis Star & Tribune Co. v. Minnesota Comm'r of Revenue, 460 U.S. 575, 586-587 (1983). The dispositive question in this case, therefore, is whether content discrimination is reasonably necessary to achieve St. Paul's compelling interests; it plainly is not. An ordinance not limited to the favored topics, for example, would have precisely the same beneficial effect. In fact the only interest distinctively served by the content limitation is that of displaying the city council's special hostility towards the particular biases thus singled out. [n.8] That isprecisely what the First Amendment forbids. The politicians of St. Paul are entitled to express that hostility--but not through the means of imposing unique limitations upon speakers who (however benightedly) disagree.

* * *

Let there be no mistake about our belief that burning a cross in someone's front yard is reprehensible. But St. Paul has sufficient means at its disposal to prevent such behavior without adding the First Amendment to the fire.

The judgment of the Minnesota Supreme Court is reversed, and the case is remanded for proceedings not inconsistent with this opinion.

It is so ordered.

Notes to R.A.V. v. St. Paul (June 22, 1992)

1 The conduct might have violated Minnesota statutes carrying significant penalties. See, e. g., Minn. Stat. § 609.713(1) (1987) (providing for up to five years in prison for terroristic threats); § 609.563 (arson) (providing for up to five years and a $10,000 fine, depending on the value of the property intended to be damaged); § 606.595 (Supp. 1992) (criminal damage to property) (providing for up to one year and a $3,000 fine, depending upon the extent of the damage to the property).

2 Petitioner has also been charged, in Count I of the delinquency petition, with a violation of Minn. Stat. § 609.2231(4) (Supp. 1990) (racially motivated assaults). Petitioner did not challenge this count.

3 Contrary to Justice White's suggestion, post, at 1-2, petitioner's claim is "fairly included" within the questions presented in the petition for certiorari, see this Court's Rule 14.1(a). It was clear from the petition and from petitioner's other filings in this Court (and in the courts below) that his assertion that the St. Paul ordinance "violat[es] overbreadth . . . principles of the First Amendment," Pet. for Cert. i, was not just a technical "overbreadth" claim--i. e., a claim that the ordinance violated the rights of too many third parties--but included the contention that the ordinance was "overbroad" in the sense of restricting more speech than the Constitution permits, even in its application to him, because it is content based. An important component of petitioner's argument is, and has been all along, that narrowly construing the ordinance to cover only "fighting words" cannot cure this fundamental defect. Id., at 12, 14, 15-16. In his briefs in this Court, petitioner argued that a narrowing construction was ineffective because (1) its boundaries were vague, Brief for Petitioner 26, and because (2) denominating particular expression a "fighting word" because of the impact of its ideological content upon the audience is inconsistent with the First Amendment, Reply Brief for Petitioner 5; id., at 13 ("[The ordinance] is overbroad, viewpoint discriminatory and vague as `narrowly construed' ") (emphasis added). At oral argument, counsel for Petitioner reiterated this second point: "It is . . . one of my positions, that in [punishing only some fighting words and not others], even though it is a subcategory, technically, of unprotected conduct, [the ordinance] still is picking out an opinion, a disfavored message, and making that clear through the State." Tr. of Oral Arg. 8. In resting our judgment upon this contention, we have not departed from our criteria of what is "fairly included" within the petition. See Arkansas Electric Cooperative Corp. v. Arkansas Pub. Serv. Comm'n, 461 U.S. 375, 382, n. 6 (1983); Brown v. Socialist Workers '74 Campaign Comm., 459 U.S. 87, 94, n. 9 (1982); Eddings v. Oklahoma, 455 U.S. 104, 113, n. 9 (1982); see generally R. Stern, E. Gressman, & S. Shapiro, Supreme Court Practice 361 (6th ed. 1986).

4 Justice White concedes that a city council cannot prohibit only those legally obscene works that contain criticism of the city government, post, at 11, but asserts that to be the consequence, not of the First Amendment, but of the Equal Protection Clause. Such content based discrimination would not, he asserts, "be rationally related to a legitimate government interest," ibid. But of course the only reason that government interest is not a "legitimate" one is that it violates the First Amendment. This Court itself has occasionally fused the First Amendment into the Equal Protection Clause in this fashion, but at least with the acknowledgment (which Justice White cannot afford to make) that the First Amendment underlies its analysis. See Police Dept. of Chicago v. Mosley, 408 U.S. 92, 95 (1972) (ordinance prohibiting only nonlabor picketing violated the Equal Protection Clause because there was no "appropriate governmental interest" supporting the distinction inasmuch as "the First Amendment means that government has no power to restrict expression because of its message, its ideas, its subject matter, or its content"); Carey v. Brown, 447 U.S. 455 (1980). See generally Simon & Schuster, Inc.

v. Members of N. Y. State Crime Victims Bd., 502 U. S. ___, ___ (1991) (Kennedy, J., concurring in judgment) (slip op., at 2-3).

Justice Stevens seeks to avoid the point by dismissing the notion of obscene anti-government speech as "fantastical," post, at 3, apparently believing that any reference to politics prevents a finding of obscenity. Unfortunately for the purveyors of obscenity, that is obviously false. A shockingly hard core pornographic movie that contains a model sporting a political tattoo can be found, "taken as a whole [to] lac[k] serious literary, artistic, political, or scientific value," Miller v. California, 413 U.S. 15, 24 (1973) (emphasis added). Anyway, it is easy enough to come up with other illustrations of a content based restriction upon "unprotected speech" that is obviously invalid: the anti government libel illustration mentioned earlier, for one. See supra, at 5. And of course the concept of racist fighting words is, unfortunately, anything but a "highly speculative hypothetica[l]," post, at 4.

5 Although Justice White asserts that our analysis disregards "established principles of First Amendment law," post, at 19, he cites not a single case (and we are aware of none) that even involved, much less considered and resolved, the issue of content discrimination through regulation of "unprotected" speech--though we plainly recognized that as an issue in Ferber. It is of course contrary to all traditions of our jurisprudence to consider the law on this point conclusively resolved by broad language in cases where the issue was not presented or even envisioned.

6 Justice Stevens cites a string of opinions as supporting his assertion that "selective regulation of speech based on content" is not presumptively invalid. Post, at 6-7. Analysis reveals, however, that they do not support it. To begin with, three of them did not command a majority of the Court, Young v. American Mini Theatres, Inc., 427 U.S. 50, 63-73 (1976) (plurality); FCC v. Pacifica Foundation, 438 U.S. 726, 744-748 (1978) (plurality); Lehman v. City of Shaker Heights, 418 U.S. 298 (1974) (plurality), and two others did not even discuss the First Amendment, Morales v. Trans World Airlines, Inc., 504 U. S. ___ (1992); Jacob Siegel Co. v. FTC, 327 U.S. 608 (1946). In any event, all that their contents establish is what we readily concede: that presumptive invalidity does not mean invariable invalidity, leaving room for such exceptions as reasonable and viewpoint neutral content based discrimination in nonpublic forums, see Lehman, supra, at 301-304; see also Cornelius v. NAACP Legal Defense & Educational Fund, Inc., 473 U.S. 788, 806 (1985), or with respect to certain speech by government employees, see Broadrick v. Oklahoma, 413 U.S. 601 (1973); see also CSC v. Letter Carriers, 413 U.S. 548, 564-567 (1973).

7 St. Paul has not argued in this case that the ordinance merely regulates that subclass of fighting words which is most likely to provoke a violent response. But even if one assumes (as appears unlikely) that the categories selected may be so described, that would not justify selective regulation under a "secondary effects" theory. The only reason why such expressive conduct would be especially correlated with violence is that it conveys a particularly odious message; because the "chain of causation" thus necessarily

"run[s] through the persuasive effect of the expressive component" of the conduct, Barnes v. Glen Theatre, 501 U. S. ___, ___ (1991) (Souter, J., concurring in judgment) (slip op., at 6), it is clear that the St. Paul ordinance regulates on the basis of the "primary" effect of the speech--i. e., its persuasive (or repellant) force.

8 A plurality of the Court reached a different conclusion with regard to the Tennessee anti electioneering statute considered earlier this Termin Burson v. Freeman, 504 U. S. ___ (1992). In light of the "logical connection" between electioneering and the State's compelling interest in preventing voter intimidation and election fraud--an inherent connection borne out by a "long history" and a "wide spread and time tested consensus," id., at ___ ___ (slip op., at 14-19)--the plurality concluded that it was faced with one of those "rare case[s]" in which the use of a facially content based restriction was justified by interests unrelated to the suppression of ideas, id., at ___ (slip op., at 19); see also id., at ___ (Kennedy, J., concurring) (slip op., at 3). Justice White and Justice Stevens are therefore quite mistaken when they seek to convert the Burson plurality's passing comment that "[t]he First Amendment does not require States to regulate for problems that do not exist," id., at ___ (slip op., at 16), into endorsement of the revolutionary proposition that the suppression of particular ideas can be justified when only those ideas have been a source of trouble in the past. Post, at 10 (White, J.); post, at 19 (Stevens, J.).

Constitutional structures; separation of powers: Plaut v. Spendthrift Farm, Inc. (April 18, 1995)

Justice Scalia delivered the opinion of the Court.

In 1987, petitioners brought a civil action against respondents in the United States District Court for the Eastern District of Kentucky. The complaint alleged that in 1983 and 1984 respondents had committed fraud and deceit in the sale of stock in violation of §10(b) of the Securities Exchange Act of 1934 and Rule 10b-5 of the Securities and Exchange Commission. The case was mired in pretrial proceedings in the District Court until June 20, 1991, when we decided Lampf, Pleva, Lipkind, Prupis & Petigrow v. Gilbertson, 501 U.S. 350 (1991). Lampf held that "[l]itigation instituted pursuant to §10(b) and Rule 10b-5 . . . must be commenced within one year after the discovery of the facts constituting the violation and within three years after such violation." Id., at 364. We applied that holding to the plaintiff respondents in Lampf itself, found their suit untimely, and reinstated a summary judgment previously entered in favor of the defendant petitioners. Ibid. On the same day we decided James B. Beam Distilling Co. v. Georgia, 501 U.S. 529 (1991), in which a majority of the Court held, albeit in different opinions, that a new rule of federal law that is applied to the parties in the case announcing the rule must be applied as well to all cases pending on direct review. See Harper v. Virginia Dept. of Taxation, 509 U. S. ___, ___ (1993) (slip op., at 7-9). The joint effect of Lampf and Beam was to mandate application of the 1 year/3 year limitations period to petitioners' suit. The District Court, finding that petitioners' claims were untimely under the Lampf rule, dismissed their action with prejudice on August 13, 1991. Petitioners filed no appeal; the judgment accordingly became final 30 days later. See 28 U.S.C. § 2107(a) (1988 ed., Supp. V); Griffith v. Kentucky, 479 U.S. 314, 321, n. 6 (1987).

On December 19, 1991, the President signed the Federal Deposit Insurance Corporation Improvement Act of 1991, 105 Stat. 2236. Section 476 of the Act--a section that had nothing to do with FDIC improvements--became §27A of the Securities Exchange Act of 1934, and was later codified as 15 U.S.C. § 78aa-1 (1988 ed., Supp. V). It provides:

"(a) Effect on pending causes of action

"The limitation period for any private civil action implied under section 78j(b) of this title [§10(b) of the Securities Exchange Act of 1934] that was commenced on or before June 19, 1991, shall be the limitation period provided by the laws applicable in the jurisdiction, including principles of retroactivity, as such laws existed on June 19, 1991.

(b) Effect on dismissed causes of action

"Any private civil action implied under section 78j(b) of this title that was commenced on or before June 19, 1991--

(1) which was dismissed as time barred subsequent to June 19, 1991, and

(2) which would have been timely filed under the limitation period provided by the laws applicable in the jurisdiction, including principles of retroactivity, as such laws existed on June 19, 1991,

shall be reinstated on motion by the plaintiff not later than 60 days after December 19, 1991."

On February 11, 1992, petitioners returned to the District Court and filed a motion to reinstate the action previously dismissed with prejudice. The District Court found that the conditions set out in §§27A(b)(1) and (2) were met, so that petitioners' motion was required to be granted by the terms of the statute. It nonetheless denied the motion, agreeing with respondents that §27A(b) is unconstitutional. Memorandum Opinion and Order, Civ. Action No. 87-438 (ED Ky., Apr. 13, 1992). The United States Court of Appeals for the Sixth Circuit affirmed. 1 F. 3d 1487 (1993). We granted certiorari. 511 U. S. ____ (1994). [n.1]

Respondents bravely contend that §27A(b) does not require federal courts to reopen final judgments, arguing first that the reference to "the laws applicable in the jurisdiction . . . as such laws existed on June 19, 1991" (the day before Lampf was decided) may reasonably be construed to refer precisely to the limitations period provided in Lampf itself, in which case petitioners' action was time barred even under §27A. [n.2] It is true that "[a] judicial construction of a statute is an authoritative statement of what the statute meant before as well as after the decision of the case giving rise to that construction." Rivers v. Roadway Express, Inc., 511 U. S. ____, ____ (1994) (slip op., at

14); see also id., at ___, n. 12 (slip op., at 14, n. 12). But respondents' argument confuses the question of what the law in fact was on June 19, 1991, with the distinct question of what §27A means by its reference to what the law was. We think it entirely clear that it does not mean the law enunciated in Lampf, for two independent reasons. First, Lampf provides a uniform, national statute of limitations (instead of using the applicable state limitations period, as lower federal courts had previously done. See Lampf, supra, at 354, and n. 1). If the statute referred to that law, its reference to the "laws applicable in the jurisdiction" (emphasis added) would be quite inexplicable. Second, if the statute refers to the law enunciated in Lampf it is utterly without effect, a result to be avoided if possible. American Nat. Red Cross v. S. G., 505 U. S. ___, ___ (1992) (slip op., at 16-17); see 2A N. Singer, Sutherland on Statutory Construction §46.06 (4th ed. 1984). It would say, in subsection (a), that the limitation period is what the Supreme Court has held to be the limitation period; and in subsection(b), that suits dismissed as untimely under Lampf which were timely under Lampf (a null set) shall be reinstated. To avoid a constitutional question by holding that Congress enacted and the President approved a blank sheet of paper would indeed constitute "disingenuous evasion." George Moore Ice Cream Co. v. Rose, 289 U.S. 373, 379 (1933).

As an alternative reason why §27A(b) does not require the reopening of final judgments, respondents suggest that the subsection applies only to cases still pending in the federal courts when §27A was enacted. This has only half the defect of the first argument, for it makes only half of §27A purposeless--§27A(b). There is no need to "reinstate" actions that are still pending; §27A(a) (the new statute of limitations) could and would be applied by the courts of appeals. On respondents' reading, the only consequence of §27A(b) would be the negligible one of permitting the plaintiff in the pending appeal from a statute of limitations dismissal to return immediately to the district court, instead of waiting for the court of appeals' reversal. To enable §27A(b) to achieve such an insignificant consequence, one must disregard the language of the provision, which refers generally to suits "dismissed as time barred." It is perhaps arguable that this does not include suits that are not yet finally dismissed, i.e., suits still pending on appeal; but there is no basis for the contention that it includes only those. In short, there is no reasonable construction on which §27A(b) does not require federal courts to reopen final judgments in suits dismissed with prejudice by virtue of Lampf.

Respondents submit that §27A(b) violates both the separation of powers and the Due Process Clause of the Fifth Amendment. [n.3] Because the latter submission, if correct, might dictate a similar result in a challenge to state legislation under the Fourteenth Amendment, the former is the narrower ground for adjudication of the constitutional questions in the case, and we therefore consider it first. Ashwander v. TVA, 297 U.S. 288, 347 (1936) (Brandeis, J., concurring). We conclude that in §27A(b) Congress has exceeded its authority by requiring the federal courts to exercise "the judicial Power of the United States," U. S. Const., Art. III, §1, in a manner repugnant to the text, structure and traditions of Article III.

Our decisions to date have identified two types of legislation that require federal courts to exercise the judicial power in a manner that Article III forbids. The first appears in United States v. Klein, 13 Wall. 128 (1872), where we refused to give effect to a statute that was said "[t]o prescribe rules of decision to the Judicial Department of the government in cases pending before it." Id., at 146. Whatever the precise scope of Klein, however, later decisions have made clear that its prohibition does not take hold when Congress "amend[s] applicable law." Robertson v. Seattle Audubon Society, 503 U.S. 429, 441 (1992). Section 27A(b) indisputably does set out substantive legal standards for the Judiciary to apply, and in that sense changes the law (even if solely retroactively). The second type of unconstitutional restriction upon the exercise of judicial power identified by past cases is exemplified by Hayburn's Case, 2 Dall. 409 (1792), which stands for the principle that Congress cannot vest review of the decisions of Article III courts in officials of the Executive Branch. See, e.g., Chicago & Southern Air Lines, Inc. v. Waterman S. S. Corp., 333 U.S. 103 (1948). Yet under any application of §27A(b) only courts are involved; no officials of other departments sit in direct review of their decisions. Section 27A(b) therefore offends neither of these previously established prohibitions.

We think, however, that §27A(b) offends a postulate of Article III just as deeply rooted in our law as those we have mentioned. Article III establishes a "judicial department" with the "province and duty . . . to say what the law is" in particular cases and controversies. Marbury v. Madison, 1 Cranch 137, 177 (1803). The record of history shows that the Framers crafted this charter of the judicial department with an expressed understanding that it gives the Federal Judiciary the power, not merely to rule on cases, but to decide them, subject to review only by superior courts in the Article III hierarchy-- with an understanding, in short, that "a judgment conclusively resolves the case" because "a `judicial Power' is one to render dispositive judgments." Easterbrook, Presidential Review, 40 Case W. Res. L. Rev. 905, 926 (1990). By retroactively commanding the federal courts to reopen final judgments, Congress has violated this fundamental principle.

The Framers of our Constitution lived among the ruins of a system of intermingled legislative and judicial powers, which had been prevalent in the colonies long before the Revolution, and which after the Revolution had produced factional strife and partisan oppression. In the 17th and 18th centuries colonial assemblies and legislatures functioned as courts of equity of last resort, hearing original actions or providing appellate review of judicial judgments. G. Wood, The Creation of the American Republic 1776-1787, pp. 154-155 (1969). Often, however, they chose to correct the judicial process through special bills or other enacted legislation. It was common for such legislation not to prescribe a resolution of the dispute, but rather simply to set aside the judgment and order a new trial or appeal. M. Clarke, Parliamentary Privilege in the American Colonies 49-51 (1943). See, e.g., Judicial Action by the Provincial Legislature of Massachusetts, 15 Harv. L. Rev. 208 (1902) (collecting documents from 1708-1709); 5 Laws of New Hampshire, Including Public and Private Acts, Resolves, Votes, etc., 1784-

1792, p. ___ (Metcalf ed. 1916). Thus, as described in our discussion of Hayburn's Case, supra, at 6-7, such legislation bears not on the problem of interbranch review but on the problem of finality of judicial judgments.

The vigorous, indeed often radical, populism of the revolutionary legislatures and assemblies increased the frequency of legislative correction of judgments. Wood, supra, at 155-156, 407-408. See also INS v. Chadha, 462 U.S. 919, 961 (1983) (Powell, J., concurring). "The period 1780-1787 . . . was a period of `constitutional reaction' " to these developments, "which . . . leaped suddenly to its climax in the Philadelphia Convention." E. Corwin, The Doctrine of Judicial Review 37 (1914). Voices from many quarters, official as well as private, decried the increasing legislative interference with the private law judgments of the courts. In 1786 the Vermont Council of Censors issued an "Address of the Council of Censors to the Freemen of the State of Vermont," to fulfill the Council's duty, under the State Constitution of 1784, to report to the people " `whether the legislative and executive branches of government have assumed to themselves, or exercised, other or greater powers than they are entitled to by the Constitution.' " Vermont State Papers 1779-1786, pp. 531, 533 (Slade ed. 1823). A principal method of usurpation identified by the Censors was "[t]he instances . . . of judgments being vacated by legislative acts." Id., at 540. The Council delivered an opinion

"that the General Assembly, in all the instances where they have vacated judgments, recovered in due course of law, (except where the particular circumstances of the case evidently made it necessary to grant a new trial) have exercised a power not delegated, or intended to be delegated, to them, by the Constitution. . . . It supercedes the necessity of any other law than the pleasure of the Assembly, and of any other court than themselves: for it is an imposition on the suitor, to give him the trouble of obtaining, after several expensive trials, a final judgment agreeably to the known established laws of the land; if the Legislature, by a sovereign act, can interfere, reverse the judgment, and decree in such manner, as they, unfettered by rules, shall think proper." Ibid.

So too, the famous report of the Pennsylvania Council of Censors in 1784 detailed the abuses of legislative interference with the courts at the behest of private interests and factions. As the General Assembly had (they wrote) made a custom of "extending their deliberations to the cases of individuals," the people had "been taught to consider an application to the legislature, as a shorter and more certain mode of obtaining relief from hardships and losses, than the usual process of law." The Censors noted that because "favour and partiality have, from the nature of public bodies of men, predominated in the distribution of this relief . . . these dangerous procedures have been too often recurred to, since the revolution." Report of the Committee of the Council of Censors 6 (Bailey ed. 1784).

This sense of a sharp necessity to separate the legislative from the judicial power, prompted by the crescendo of legislative interference with private judgments of the courts, triumphed among the Framers of the new Federal Constitution. See Corwin, The Progress of Constitutional Theory Between the Declaration of Independence and the

Meeting of the Philadelphia Convention, 30 Am. Hist. Rev. 511, 514-517 (1925). The Convention made the critical decision to establish a judicial department independent of the Legislative Branch by providing that "the judicial Power of the United States shall be vested in one supreme Court, and in such inferior Courts as the Congress may from time to time ordain and establish." Before and during the debates on ratification, Madison, Jefferson, and Hamilton each wrote of the factional disorders and disarray that the system of legislative equity had produced in the years before the framing; and each thought that the separation of the legislative from the judicial power in the new Constitution would cure them. Madison's Federalist No. 48, the famous description of the process by which "[t]he legislative department is every where extending the sphere of its activity, and drawing all power into its impetuous vortex," referred to the report of the Pennsylvania Council of Censors to show that in that State "cases belonging to the judiciary department [had been] frequently drawn within legislative cognizance and determination." The Federalist No. 48, pp. 333, 337 (J. Cooke ed. 1961). Madison relied as well on Jefferson's Notes on the State of Virginia, which mentioned, as one example of the dangerous concentration of governmental powers into the hands of the legislature, that "the Legislature . . . in many instances decided rights which should have been left to judiciary controversy." Id., at 336 (emphasis deleted). [n.4]

If the need for separation of legislative from judicial power was plain, the principal effect to be accomplished by that separation was even plainer. As Hamilton wrote in his exegesis of Article III, §1, in Federalist No. 81:

"It is not true . . . that the parliament of Great Britain, or the legislatures of the particular states, can rectify the exceptionable decisions of their respective courts, in any other sense than might be done by a future legislature of the United States. The theory neither of the British, nor the state constitutions, authorises the revisal of a judicial sentence, by a legislative act. . . . A legislature without exceeding its province cannot reverse a determination once made, in a particular case; though it may prescribe a new rule for future cases." The Federalist No. 81, p. 545 (J. Cooke ed. 1961).

The essential balance created by this allocation of authority was a simple one. The Legislature would be possessed of power to "prescrib[e] the rules by which the duties and rights of every citizen are to be regulated," but the power of "[t]he interpretation of the laws" would be "the proper and peculiar province of the courts." The Federalist No. 78, p. 523, 525 (J. Cooke ed. 1961). See also Corwin, The Doctrine of Judicial Review, at 42. The Judiciary would be, "from the nature of its functions, . . . the [department] least dangerous to the political rights of the constitution," not because its acts were subject to legislative correction, but because the binding effect of its acts was limited to particular cases and controversies. Thus, "though individual oppression may now and then proceed from the courts of justice, the general liberty of the people can never be endangered from that quarter: . . . so long as the judiciary remains truly distinct from both the legislative and executive." The Federalist No. 78, pp. 522, 523 (J. Cooke ed. 1961).

Judicial decisions in the period immediately after ratification of the Constitution confirm the understanding that it forbade interference with the final judgments of courts. In Calder v. Bull, 3 Dall. 386 (1798), the Legislature of Connecticut had enacted a statute that set aside the final judgment of a state court in a civil case. Although the issue before this Court was the construction of the Ex Post-Facto Clause, Art. I, §10, Justice Iredell (a leading Federalist who had guided the Constitution to ratification in North Carolina) noted that

"the Legislature of [Connecticut] has been in the uniform, uninterrupted, habit of exercising a general superintending power over its courts of law, by granting new trials. It may, indeed, appear strange to some of us, that in any form, there should exist a power to grant, with respect to suits depending or adjudged, new rights of trial, new privileges of proceeding, not previously recognized and regulated by positive institutions .... The power ... is judicial in its nature; and whenever it is exercised, as in the present instance, it is an exercise of judicial, not of legislative, authority." Id., at 398.

The state courts of the era showed a similar understanding of the separation of powers, in decisions that drew little distinction between the federal and state constitutions. To choose one representative example from a multitude: in Bates v. Kimball, 2 Chipman 77 (Vt. 1824), a special Act of the Vermont Legislature authorized a party to appeal from the judgment of a court even though, under the general law, the time for appeal had expired. The court, noting that the unappealed judgment had become final, set itself the question "Have the Legislature power to vacate or annul an existing judgment between party and party?" Id., at 83. The answer was emphatic: "The necessity of a distinct and separate existence of the three great departments of government ... had been proclaimed and enforced by ... Blackstone, Jefferson and Madison," and had been "sanctioned by the people of the United States, by being adopted in terms more or less explicit, into all their written constitutions." Id., at 84. The power to annul a final judgment, the court held (citing Hayburn's Case, 2 Dall., at 410), was "an assumption of Judicial power," and therefore forbidden. Bates v. Kimball, supra, at 90. For other examples, see Merrill v. Sherburne, 1 N. H. 199 (1818) (legislature may not vacate a final judgment and grant a new trial); Lewis v. Webb, 3 Greenleaf 299 (Me. 1825) (same); T. Cooley, Constitutional Limitations 95-96 (1868) (collecting cases); J. Sutherland, Statutory Construction 18-19 (J. Lewis ed. 1904) (same).

By the middle of the 19th century, the constitutional equilibrium created by the separation of the legislative power to make general law from the judicial power to apply that law in particular cases was so well understood and accepted that it could survive even Dred Scott v. Sandford, 19 How. 393 (1857). In his First Inaugural Address, President Lincoln explained why the political branches could not, and need not, interfere with even that infamous judgment:

"I do not forget the position assumed by some, that constitutional questions are to be decided by the Supreme Court; nor do I deny that such decisions must be binding in any case, upon the parties to a suit, as to the object of that suit .... And while it is obviously possible that such decision may be erroneous in any given case, still the evil effect following it, being limited to that particular case, with the chance that it may be over ruled, and never become a precedent for other cases, can better be borne than could the evils of a different practice." 4 R. Basler, The Collected Works of Abraham Lincoln 268 (1953) (First Inaugural Address 1861).

And the great constitutional scholar Thomas Cooley addressed precisely the question before us in his 1868 treatise:

"If the legislature cannot thus indirectly control the action of the courts, by requiring of them a construction of the law according to its own views, it is very plain it cannot do so directly, by setting aside their judgments, compelling them to grant new trials, ordering the discharge of offenders, or directing what particular steps shall be taken in the progress of a judicial inquiry." T. Cooley, supra, at 94-95.

Section 27A(b) effects a clear violation of the separation of powers principle we have just discussed. It is, of course, retroactive legislation, that is, legislation that prescribes what the law was at an earlier time, when the act whose effect is controlled by the legislation occurred--in this case, the filing of the initial Rule 10b-5 action in the District Court. When retroactive legislation requires its own application in a case already finally adjudicated, it does no more and no less than "reverse a determination once made, in a particular case." The Federalist No. 81, p. 545 (J. Cooke ed. 1961). Our decisions stemming from Hayburn's Case--although their precise holdings are not strictly applicable here, see supra, at 6-7--have uniformly provided fair warning that such an act exceeds the powers of Congress. See, e.g., Chicago & Southern Air Lines, Inc., 333 U. S., at 113 ("[J]udgments within the powers vested in courts by the Judiciary Article of the Constitution may not lawfully be revised, overturned or refused faith and credit by another Department of Government"); United States v. O'Grady, 22 Wall. 641, 647-648 (1875) ("Judicial jurisdiction implies the power to hear and determine a cause, and . . . Congress cannot subject the judgments of the Supreme Court to the re examination and revision of any other tribunal"); Gordon v. United States, 117 U.S. 697, 700-704 (opinion of Taney, C. J.) (decided 1864, printed 1885) (judgments of Article III courts are "final and conclusive upon the rights of the parties"); Hayburn's Case, 2 Dall., at 411 (opinion of Wilson and Blair JJ., and Peters, D. J.) ("[R]evision and control" of Article III judgments is "radically inconsistent with the independence of that judicial power which is vested in the courts"); id., at 413 (opinion of Iredell, J., and Sitgreaves, D. J.) ("[N]o decision of any court of the United States can, under any circumstances, . . . be liable to a revision, or even suspension, by the [l]egislature itself, in whom no judicial power of any kind appears to be vested"). See also Pennsylvania v. Wheeling & Belmont Bridge Co., 18 How. 421, 431 (1856) ("[I]t is urged, that the act of congress cannot have the effect and operation to annul the judgment of the court already rendered, or the rights determined thereby . . . . This, as a general proposition, is certainly not to be denied, especially as it respects adjudication upon the private rights of parties. When they have passed into judgment the right becomes absolute, and it is the duty of the court to enforce it"). Today those clear statements must either be honored, or else proved false.

It is true, as petitioners contend, that Congress can always revise the judgments of Article III courts in one sense: When a new law makes clear that it is retroactive, an appellate court must apply that law in reviewing judgments still on appeal that were rendered before the law was enacted, and must alter the outcome accordingly. See United States v. Schooner Peggy, 1 Cranch 103 (1801); Landgraf v. USI Film Products, 511 U. S. ___, ___%___ (1994) (slip op., at 28-43). Since that is so, petitioners argue, federal courts must apply the "new" law created by §27A(b) in finally adjudicated cases as well; for the line that separates lower court judgments that are pending on appeal (or may still be appealed), from lower court judgments that are final, is determined by statute, see, e.g., 28 U.S.C. § 2107(a) (30 day time limit for appeal to federal court of appeals), and so cannot possibly be a constitutional line. But a distinction between judgments from which all appeals have been forgone or completed, and judgments that remain on appeal (or subject to being appealed), is implicit in what Article III creates: not a batch of unconnected courts, but a judicial department composed of "inferior Courts" and "one supreme Court." Within that hierarchy, the decision of an inferior court is not (unless the time for appeal has expired) the final word of the department as a whole. It is the obligation of the last court in the hierarchy that rules on the case to give effect to Congress's latest enactment, even when that has the effect of overturning the judgment of an inferior court, since each court, at every level, must "decide according to existing laws." Schooner Peggy, supra, at 109. Having achieved finality, however, a judicial decision becomes the last word of the judicial department with regard to a particular case or controversy, and Congress may not declare by retroactive legislation that the law applicable to that very case was something other than what the courts said it was. Finality of a legal judgment is determined by statute, just as entitlement to a government benefit is a statutory creation; but that no more deprives the former of its constitutional significance for separation of powers analysis than it deprives the latter of its significance for due process purposes. See, e.g., Cleveland Bd. of Ed. v. Loudermill, 470 U.S. 532 (1985); Meachum v. Fano, 427 U.S. 215 (1976).

To be sure, §27A(b) reopens (or directs the reopening of) final judgments in a whole class of cases rather than in a particular suit. We do not see how that makes any difference. The separation of powers violation here, if there is any, consists of depriving judicial judgments of the conclusive effect that they had when they were announced, not of acting in a manner--viz., with particular rather than general effect--that is unusual (though, we must note, not impossible) for a legislature. To be sure, a general statute such as this one may reduce the perception that legislative interference with judicial judgments was prompted by individual favoritism; but it is legislative interference with judicial judgments nonetheless. Not favoritism, nor even corruption, but power is the object of the separation of powers prohibition. The prohibition is violated when an individual final judgment is legislatively rescinded for even the very best of reasons, such as the legislature's genuine conviction (supported by all the law professors in the land) that the judgment was wrong; and it is violated 40 times over when 40 final judgments are legislatively dissolved.

It is irrelevant as well that the final judgments reopened by §27A(b) rested on the bar of a statute of limitations. The rules of finality, both statutory and judge made, treat a dismissal on statute of limitations grounds the same way they treat a dismissal for failure to state a claim, for failure to prove substantive liability, or for failure to prosecute: as a judgment on the merits. See, e.g., Fed. Rule Civ. Proc. 41(b); United States v. Oppenheimer, 242 U.S. 85, 87-88 (1916). Petitioners suggest, directly or by implication, two reasons why a merits judgment based on this particular ground may be uniquely subject to congressional nullification. First, there is the fact that the length and indeed even the very existence of a statute of limitations upon a federal cause of action is entirely subject to congressional control. But virtually all of the reasons why a final judgment on the merits is rendered on a federal claim are subject to congressional control. Congress can eliminate, for example, a particular element of a cause of action that plaintiffs have found it difficult to establish; or an evidentiary rule that has often excluded essential testimony; or a rule of offsetting wrong (such as contributory negligence) that has often prevented recovery. To distinguish statutes of limitations on the ground that they are mere creatures of Congress is to distinguish them not at all. The second supposedly distinguishing characteristic of a statute of limitations is that it can be extended, without violating the Due Process Clause, after the cause of the action arose and even after the statute itself has expired. See, e.g., Chase Securities Corp. v. Donaldson, 325 U.S. 304 (1945). But that also does not set statutes of limitations apart. To mention only one other broad category of judgment producing legal rule: rules of pleading and proof can similarly be altered after the cause of action arises, Landgraf v. USI Film Products, 511 U. S., at ___, and n. 29 (slip op., at 30-31, and n. 29), and even, if the statute clearly so requires, after they have been applied in a case but before final judgment has been entered. Petitioners' principle would therefore lead to the conclusion that final judgments rendered on the basis of a stringent (or, alternatively, liberal) rule of pleading or proof may be set aside for retrial under a new liberal (or, alternatively, stringent) rule of pleading or proof. This alone provides massive scope for undoing final judgments and would substantially subvert the doctrine of separation of powers.

The central theme of the dissent is a variant on these arguments. The dissent maintains that Lampf "announced" a new statute of limitations, post, at 1, in an act of "judicial . . . lawmaking," post, at 2, that "changed the law." Post, at 5. That statement, even if relevant, would be wrong. The point decided in Lampf had never before been addressed by this Court, and was therefore an open question, no matter what the lower courts had held at the time. But the more important point is that Lampf as such is irrelevant to this case. The dissent itself perceives that "[w]e would have the same issue to decide had Congress enacted the Lampf rule," and that the Lampf rule's genesis in judicial lawmaking rather than, shall we say, legislative lawmaking, "should not affect the separation of powers analysis." Post,, at 2. Just so. The issue here is not the validity or even the source of the legal rule that produced the Article III judgments, but rather the immunity from legislative abrogation of those judgments themselves. The separation of powers question before us has nothing to do with Lampf, and the dissent's attack on Lampf has nothing to do with the question before us.

Apart from the statute we review today, we know of no instance in which Congress has attempted to set aside the final judgment of an Article III court by retroactive legislation. That prolonged reticence would be amazing if such interference were not understood to be constitutionally proscribed. The closest analogue that the Government has been able to put forward is the statute at issue in United States v. Sioux Nation, 448 U.S. 371 (1980). That law required the Court of Claims, " `[n]otwithstanding any other provision of law . . . to review on the merits, without regard to the defense of res judicata or collateral estoppel,' " a Sioux claim for just compensation from the United States--even though the Court of Claims had previously heard and rejected that very claim. We considered and rejected separation of powers objections to the statute based upon Hayburn's Case and United States v. Klein. See 448 U. S., at 391-392. The basis for our rejection was a line of precedent (starting with Cherokee Nation v. United States, 270 U.S. 476 (1926)) that stood, we said, for the proposition that "Congress has the power to waive the res judicata effect of a prior judgment entered in the Government's favor on a claim against the United States." Sioux Nation, 448 U. S., at 397. And our holding was as narrow as the precedent on which we had relied: "In sum, . . . Congress' mere waiver of the res judicata effect of a prior judicial decision rejecting the validity of a legal claim against the United States does not violate the doctrine of separation of powers." Id., at 407. [n.5]

The Solicitor General suggests that even if Sioux Nation is read in accord with its holding, it nonetheless establishes that Congress may require Article III courts to reopen their final judgments, since "if res judicata were compelled by Article III to safeguard the structural independence of the courts, the doctrine would not be subject to waiver by any party litigant." Brief for United States 27 (citing Commodity Futures Trading Comm'n v. Schor, 478 U.S. 833, 850-851 (1986)). But the proposition that legal defenses based upon doctrines central to the courts' structural independence can never be waived simply does not accord with our cases. Certainly one such doctrine consists of the "judicial Power" to disregard an unconstitutional statute, see Marbury, 1 Cranch, at 177; yet none would suggest that a litigant may never waive the defense that a statute is unconstitutional. See, e.g., G. D. Searle & Co. v. Cohn, 455 U.S. 404, 414 (1982). What may follow from our holding that the judicial power unalterably includes the power to render final judgments, is not that waivers of res judicata are always impermissible, but rather that, as many federal Courts of Appeals have held, waivers of res judicata need not always be accepted-- that trial courts may in appropriate cases raise the res judicata bar on their own motion. See, e.g., Coleman v. Ramada Hotel Operating Co., 933 F. 2d 470, 475 (CA7 1991); In re Medomak Canning, 922 F. 2d 895, 904 (CA1 1990); Holloway Constr. Co. v. United States

Dept. of Labor, 891 F. 2d 1211, 1212 (CA6 1989). Waiver subject to the control of the courts themselves would obviously raise no issue of separation of powers, and would be precisely in accord with the language of the decision that the Solicitor General relies upon. We held in Schor that, although a litigant had consented to bring a state law counterclaim before an Article I tribunal, 478 U. S., at 849, we would nonetheless choose to consider his Article III challenge, because "where these Article III limitations are at issue, notions of consent and waiver cannot be dispositive." Id., at 851 (emphasis added). See also Freytag v. Commissioner, 501 U.S. 868, 878-879 (1991) (finding a "rare cas[e] in which we should exercise our discretion" to hear a waived claim based on the Appointments Clause, Art. II, §2, cl. 2). [n.6]

Petitioners also rely on a miscellany of decisions upholding legislation that altered rights fixed by the final judgments of non Article III courts, see, e.g., Sampeyreac v. United States, 7 Pet. 222, 238 (1833); Freeborn v. Smith, 2 Wall. 160 (1865), or administrative agencies, Paramino Lumber Co. v. Marshall, 309 U.S. 370 (1940), or that altered the prospective effect of injunctions entered by Article III courts, Wheeling & Belmont Bridge Co., 18 How., at 421. These cases distinguish themselves; nothing in our holding today calls them into question. Petitioners rely on general statements from some of these cases that legislative annulment of final judgments is not an exercise of judicial power. But even if it were our practice to decide cases by weight of prior dicta, we would find the many dicta that reject congressional power to revise the judgments of Article III courts to be the more instructive authority. See supra, at 14-15. [n.7]

Finally, petitioners liken §27A(b) to Federal Rule of Civil Procedure 60(b), which authorizes courts to relieve parties from a final judgment for grounds such as excusable neglect, newly discovered evidence, fraud, or "any other reason justifying relief . . . ." We see little resemblance. Rule 60(b), which authorizes discretionary judicial revision of judgments in the listed situations and in other "extraordinary circumstances," Liljeberg v. Health Services Acquisition Corp., 486 U.S. 847, 864 (1988), does not impose any legislative mandate to reopen upon the courts, but merely reflects and confirms the courts' own inherent and discretionary power, "firmly established in English practice long before the foundation of our Republic," to set aside a judgment whose enforcement would work inequity. Hazel Atlas Glass Co. v. Hartford Empire Co., 322 U.S. 238, 244 (1944). Thus, Rule 60(b), and the tradition that it embodies, would be relevant refutation of a claim that reopening a final judgment is always a denial of property without due process; but they are irrelevant to the claim that legislative instruction to reopen impinges upon the independent constitutional authority of the courts.

The dissent promises to provide "[a] few contemporary examples" of statutes retroactively requiring final judgments to be reopened, "to demonstrate that [such statutes] are ordinary products of the exercise of legislative power." Post, at 12. That promise is not kept. The relevant retroactivity, of course, consists not of the requirement that there be set aside a judgment that has been rendered prior to its being setting aside-- for example, a statute passed today which says that all default judgments rendered in the future may be reopened within 90 days after their entry. In that sense, all requirements to reopen are "retroactive," and the designation is superfluous. Nothing we say today precludes a law such as that. The finality that a court can pronounce is no more than what the law in existence at the time of judgment will permit it to pronounce. If the law then applicable says that the judgment may be reopened for certain reasons, that limitation is built into the judgment itself, and its finality is so conditioned. The present case, however, involves a judgment that Congress subjected to a reopening requirement which did not exist when the judgment was pronounced. The dissent provides not a single clear prior instance of such congressional action.

The dissent cites, first, Rule 60(b), which it describes as a "familiar remedial measure." Post, at 12. As we have just discussed, Rule 60(b) does not provide a new remedy at all, but is simply the recitation of pre-existing judicial power. The same is true of another of the dissent's examples, 28 U.S.C. § 2255 which provides federal prisoners a statutory motion to vacate a federal sentence. This procedure " `restates, clarifies and simplifies the procedure in the nature of the ancient writ of error coram nobis.' " United States v. Hayman, 342 U.S. 205, 218 (1952) (quoting the 1948 Reviser's Note to §2255). It is meaningless to speak of these statutes as applying "retroactively," since they simply codified judicial practice that pre-existed. Next, the dissent cites the provision of the Soldiers' and Sailors' Civil Relief Act of 1940, 54 Stat. 1178, 50 U. S. C. App. §520(4), which authorizes courts, upon application, to reopen judgments against members of the Armed Forces entered while they were on active duty. It could not be clearer, however, that this provision was not retroactive. It says: "If any judgment shall be rendered in any action or proceeding governed by this section against any person in military service during the period of such service . . . such judgment may . . . be opened . . . ." (Emphasis added).

The dissent also cites, post, at 14, a provision of the Handicapped Children's Protection Act of 1986, 82 Stat. 901, 20 U.S.C. § 1415(e)(4)(B) (1988 ed. and Supp. V), which provided for the award of attorney's fees under the Education for All Handicapped Children Act of 1975, 89 Stat. 773, 20 U.S.C. § 1411 et seq. (1988 ed. and Supp. V). This changed the law regarding attorney's fees under the Education for All Handicapped Children Act, after our decision in Smith v. Robinson, 468 U.S. 992 (1984), found such fees to be unavailable. The provision of the Statutes at Large adopting this amendment to the United States Code specified, in effect, that it would apply not only to proceedings brought after its enactment, but also to proceedings pending at the time of, or brought after, the decision in Smith. See 100 Stat. 798. The amendment says nothing about reopening final judgments, and the retroactivity provision may well mean nothing more than that it applies not merely to new suits commenced after the date of its enactment, but also to previously filed (but not yet terminated) suits of the specified sort. This interpretation would be consistent with the only case the dissent cites, which involved a court entered consent decree not yet fully executed. Counsel v. Dow, 849 F. 2d 731, 734, 738-739 (CA2 1988). Alternatively, the statute can perhaps be understood to create a new cause of action for attorney's fees attributable to already concluded litigation. That would create no separation of powers problem, and would be consistent with this Court's view that "[a]ttorney's fee determinations . . . are `collateral to the main cause of action' and `uniquely separable from the cause of action to be proved at trial.' " Landgraf v. USI Film Products, 511 U. S., at ___ (slip op., at 33) (quoting White v. NewHampshire Dept. of Employment Security, 455 U.S. 445, 451-452 (1982)). [n.8]

The dissent's perception that retroactive reopening provisions are to be found all about us is perhaps attributable to its inversion of the statutory presumption regarding retroactivity. Thus, it asserts that Rule 60(b) must be retroactive, since "[n]ot a single word in its text suggests that it does not apply to judgments entered prior to its effective date." Post, at 12-13. This reverses the traditional rule, confirmed only last Term, that statutes do not apply retroactively unless Congress expressly states that they do. See Landgraf, 511 U. S., at ___ (slip op., at 32-34). The dissent adds that "the traditional construction of remedial measures . . . support[s] construing [Rule 60(b)] to apply to past as well as future judgments." Post, at 13. But reliance on the vaguely remedial purpose of a statute to defeat the presumption against retroactivity was rejected in the companion cases of Landgraf, see 511 U. S., at ___ (slip op., at 40-42, n. 37) and Rivers v. Roadway Express, 511 U. S., at ___ (slip op., at 11-15). Compare Landgraf, 511 U. S. at ___ (slip op., at 2-4) (Blackmun, J., dissenting) ("This presumption [against retroactive legislation] need not be applied to remedial legislation . . . .") (citing Sampeyreac, 7 Pet., at 222).

The dissent sets forth a number of hypothetical horribles flowing from our assertedly "rigid holding"--for example, the inability to set aside a civil judgment that has become final during a period when a natural disaster prevented the timely filing of a certiorari petition. Post, at 18. That is horrible not because of our holding, but because the underlying statute itself enacts a "rigid" jurisdictional bar to entertaining untimely civil petitions. Congress could undoubtedly enact prospective legislation permitting, or indeed requiring, this Court to make equitable exceptions to an otherwise applicable rule of finality, just as district courts do pursuant to Rule 60(b). It is no indication whatever of the invalidity of the constitutional rule which we announce, that it produces unhappy consequences when a legislature lacks foresight, and acts belatedly to remedy a deficiency in the law. That is a routine result of constitutional rules. See, e.g., Collins v. Youngblood, 497 U.S. 37 (1990) (Ex Post-Facto Clause precludes post-offense statutory extension of a criminal sentence); United States Trust Co. of N. Y. v. New Jersey, 431 U.S. 1 (1977) (Contract Clause prevents retroactive alteration of contract with state bondholders); Louisville Joint Stock Land Bank v. Radford, 295 U.S. 555, 589-590, 601-602 (1935) (Takings Clause invalidates a bankruptcy law that abrogates a vested property interest). See also United States v. Security Industrial Bank, 459 U.S. 70, 78 (1982).

Finally, we may respond to the suggestion of the concurrence that this case should be decided more narrowly. The concurrence is willing to acknowledge only that "sometimes Congress lacks the power under Article I to reopen an otherwise closed court judgment," post, at 1. In the present context, what it considers critical is that §27A(b) is "exclusively retroactive" and "appli[es] to a limited number of individuals." Ibid. If Congress had only "provid[ed] some of the assurances against `singling out' that ordinary legislative activity normally provides--say, prospectivity and general applicability--we might have a different case." Post, at 3.

This seems to us wrong in both fact and law. In point of fact, §27A(b) does not "single out" any defendant for adverse treatment (or any plaintiff for favorable treatment). Rather, it identifies a class of actions (those filed pre-Lampf, timely under applicable state law, but dismissed as time barred post-Lampf) which embraces many plaintiffs and defendants, the precise number and identities of whom we even now do not know. The concurrence's contention that the number of covered defendants "is too small (compared with the number of similar, uncovered firms) to distinguish meaningfully the law before us from a similar law aimed at a single closed case," post, at 4 (emphasis added), renders the concept of "singling out" meaningless.

More importantly, however, the concurrence's point seems to us wrong in law. To be sure, the class of actions identified by §27A(b) could have been more expansive (e.g., all actions that were or could have been filed pre-Lampf) and the provision could have been written to have prospective as well as retroactive effect (e.g., "all post-Lampf dismissed actions, plus all future actions under Rule 10b-5, shall be timely if brought within 30 years of the injury"). But it escapes us how this could in any way cause the statute to be any less an infringement upon the judicial power. The nub of that infringement consists not of the Legislature's acting in a particularized and hence (according to the concurrence) nonlegislative fashion; [n.9] but rather of the Legislature's nullifying prior, authoritative judicial action. It makes no difference whatever to that separation of powers violation that it is in gross rather than particularized (e.g., "we hereby set aside all hitherto entered judicial orders"), or that it is not accompanied by an "almost" violation of the Bill of Attainder Clause, or an "almost" violation of any other constitutional provision.

Ultimately, the concurrence agrees with our judgment only "[b]ecause the law before us embodies risks of the very sort that our Constitution's `separation of powers' prohibition seeks to avoid." Post, at 7. But the doctrine of separation of powers is a structural safeguard rather than a remedy to be applied only when specific harm, or risk of specific harm, can be identified. In its major features (of which the conclusiveness of judicial judgments is assuredly one) it is a prophylactic device, establishing high walls and clear distinctions because low walls and vague distinctions will not be judicially defensible in the heat of interbranch conflict. It is interesting that the concurrence quotes twice, and cites without quotation a third time, the opinion of Justice Powell in INS v. Chadha, 462 U. S., at 959. But Justice Powell wrote only for himself in that case. He alone expressed dismay that "[t]he Court's decision . . . apparently will invalidate every use of the legislative veto," and opined that "[t]he breadth of this holding gives one pause." Ibid. It did not give pause to the six Justice majority, which put an end to the long simmering interbranch dispute that would otherwise have been indefinitely prolonged. We think legislated invalidation of judicial judgments deserves the same categorical treatment accorded by Chadha to congressional invalidation of executive action. The delphic alternative suggested by the concurrence (the setting aside of judgments is all right so long as Congress does not "impermissibly tr[y] to apply, as well as make, the law," post, at 1) simply prolongs doubt and multiplies confrontation. Separation of powers, a distinctively American political doctrine, profits from the advice authored by a distinctively American poet: Good fences make good neighbors.

* * *

We know of no previous instance in which Congress has enacted retroactive legislation requiring an Article III court to set aside a final judgment, and for good reason. The Constitution's separation of legislative and judicial powers denies it the authority to do so. Section 27A(b) is unconstitutional to the extent that it requires federal courts to reopen final judgments entered before its enactment. The judgment of the Court of Appeals is affirmed.

It is so ordered.

Notes to Plaut v. Spendthrift Farm, Inc. (April 18, 1995)

1 Last Term this Court affirmed, by an equally divided vote, a judgment of the United States Court of Appeals for the Fifth Circuit that held §27A(b) constitutional. Morgan Stanley & Co. v. Pacific Mut. Life Ins. Co., 511 U. S. ___ (1994) (per curiam). That ruling of course lacks precedential weight. Trans World Airlines, Inc. v. Hardison, 432 U.S. 63, 73, n. 8 (1977).

2 Since respondents' reading of the statute would avoid a constitutional question of undoubted gravity, we think it prudent to entertain the argument even though respondents did not make it in the Sixth Circuit. Of course the Sixth Circuit did decide (against respondents) the point to which the argument was directed. See 1 F. 3d 1487, 1490 (1993) ("The statute's language is plain and unambiguous. . . . [It] commands the Federal courts to reinstate cases which those courts have dismissed").

3 "No person shall be . . . deprived of life, liberty, or property, without due process of law." U. S. Const., Amdt. 5.

4 Read in the abstract these public pronouncements might be taken, as the Solicitor General does take them, see Brief for United States 28-30, to disapprove only the practice of having the legislature itself sit as a court of original or appellate jurisdiction. But against the backdrop of history, that reading is untenable. Many, perhaps a plurality, of the instances of legislative equity in the period before the framing simply involved duly enacted laws that nullified judgments so that new trials or judicial rulings on the merits could take place. See supra, at 7-8.

5 The dissent quotes a passage from the opinion saying that Congress " `only was providing a forum so that a new judicial review of the Black Hills claim could take place.' " Post, at 11 (quoting 448 U. S., at 407). That is quite consistent with the res judicata

holding. Any party who waives the defense of res judicata provides a forum for a new judicial review.

6 The statute at issue in United States v. Sioux Nation, 448 U.S. 371 (1980), seemingly prohibited courts from raising the res judicata defense sua sponte. See id., at 432-433 (Rehnquist, J., dissenting). The Court did not address that point; as far as appears it saw no reason to raise the defense on its own. Of course the unexplained silences of our decisions lack precedential weight. See, e.g., Brecht v. Abrahamson, 507 U. S. ___, ___ (1993) (slip op., at 9-11).

7 The dissent tries to turn the dicta of the territorial court cases, Sampeyreac and Freeborn, into holdings. It says of Sampeyreac that "the relevant judicial power that the [challenged] statute arguably supplanted was this Court's Article III appellate jurisdiction." Post, at 9. Even if it were true that the judicial power under discussion was that of this Court (which is doubtful), the point could still not possibly constitute a holding, since there was no "supplanted power" at issue in the case. One of the principal grounds of decision was that the finality of the territorial court's decree had not been retroactively abrogated. The decree had been entered under a previous statute which provided that a decree "shall be final and conclusive between the parties." Sampeyreac v. United States, 7 Pet. 222, 239 (1883) (emphasis in original). The asserted basis for reopening was fraud, in that Sampeyreac did not actually exist. We reasoned that "as Sampeyreac was a fictitious person, he was no party to the decree, and the act [under which the decree had allegedly become final] in strictness does not apply to the case." Ibid.

The dissent likewise says of Freeborn that "the `judicial power' to which the opinion referred was this Court's Article III appellate jurisdiction." Post, at 10. Once again, even if it was, the point remains dictum. No final judgment was at issue in Freeborn. The challenged statute reached only " `cases of appeal or writ of error heretofore prosecuted and now pending in the supreme court of the United States,' " see post, at 9, n. 8 (quoting 13 Stat. 441) (emphasis added). As we have explained, see supra, at 15-16, Congress may require (insofar as separation of powers limitations are concerned) that new statutes be applied in cases not yet final but still pending on appeal.

8 Even the dissent's scouring the 50 States for support has proved unproductive. It cites statutes from five States, post, at 14-15, nn. 13-14. Four of those statutes involve a virtually identical provision, which permits the state chartered entity that takes over an insolvent insurance company to apply to have any of the insurer's default judgments set aside. See Del. Code Ann., Tit. 18, §4418 (1989); Fla. Stat. §631.734 (1984); N. Y. Ins. Law §7717 (McKinney Supp. 1995); 40 Pa. Cons. Stat. §991.1716 (Supp. 1994). It is not at all clear, indeed it seems to us unlikely, that these statutes applied retroactively, to judgments that were final before enactment of the scheme that created the state chartered entity. The last statute involves a discretionary procedure for allowing appeal by pro se litigants, Va. Code Ann. §8.01-428(C) (Supp. 1994). It is obvious that the provision did not apply retroactively, to judgments rendered before the procedures were established.

9 The premise that there is something wrong with particularized legislative action is of course questionable. While legislatures usually act through laws of general applicability, that is by no means their only legitimate mode of action. Private bills in Congress are still common, and were even more so in the days before establishment of the Claims Court. Even laws that impose a duty or liability upon a single individual or firm are not on that account invalid--or else we would not have the extensive jurisprudence that we do concerning the Bill of Attainder Clause, including cases which say that it requires not merely "singling out" but also punishment, see, e.g., United States v. Lovett, 328 U.S. 303, 315-318 (1946), and a case which says that Congress may legislate "a legitimate class of one," Nixon v. Administrator of General Services, 433 U.S. 425, 472 (1977).

State sovereignty: The Federal Government may not command the States' executive power in the absence of a particularized constitutional authorization: Printz v. United States (June 27, 1997)

Justice Scalia delivered the opinion of the Court.

The question presented in these cases is whether certain interim provisions of the Brady Handgun Violence Prevention Act, Pub. L. 103-159, 107 Stat. 1536, commanding state and local law enforcement officers to conduct background checks on prospective handgun purchasers and to perform certain related tasks, violate the Constitution.

The Gun Control Act of 1968 (GCA), 18 U.S.C. § 921 et seq., establishes a detailed federal scheme governing the distribution of firearms. It prohibits firearms dealers from transferring handguns to any person under 21, not resident in the dealer's State, or prohibited by state or local law from purchasing or possessing firearms, §922(b). It also forbids possession of a firearm by, and transfer of a firearm to, convicted felons, fugitives from justice, unlawful users of controlled substances, persons adjudicated as mentally defective or committed to mental institutions, aliens unlawfully present in the United States, persons dishonorably discharged from the Armed Forces, persons who have renounced their citizenship, and persons who have been subjected to certain restraining orders or been convicted of a misdemeanor offense involving domestic violence. §§922(d) and (g).

In 1993, Congress amended the GCA by enacting the Brady Act. The Act requires the Attorney General to establish a national instant background check system by November 30, 1998, Pub. L. 103-159, as amended, Pub. L. 103-322, 103 Stat. 2074, note following 18 U.S.C. § 922 and immediately puts in place certain interim provisions until that system becomes operative. Under the interim provisions, a firearms dealer who proposes to transfer a handgun must first: (1) receive from the transferee a statement (the Brady Form), §922(s)(1)(A) (i)(I), containing the name, address and date of birth of the proposed transferee along with a sworn statement that the transferee is not among any of the classes of prohibited purchasers, §922(s)(3); (2) verify the identity of the transferee by examining an identification document, §922(s)(1)(A)(i)(II); and (3) provide the "chief law enforcement officer" (CLEO) of the transferee's residence with notice of the contents (and a copy) of the Brady Form, §§922(s)(1)(A)(i)(III) and (IV). With some exceptions, the dealer must then wait five business days before consummating the sale, unless the CLEO earlier notifies the dealer that he has no reason to believe the transfer would be illegal. §922(s)(1)(A)(ii).

The Brady Act creates two significant alternatives to the foregoing scheme. A dealer may sell a handgun immediately if the purchaser possesses a state handgun permit issued after a background check, §922(s)(1)(C), or if state law provides for an instant background check, §922(s)(1)(D). In States that have not rendered one of these alternatives applicable to all gun purchasers, CLEOs are required to perform certain duties. When a CLEO receives the required notice of a proposed transfer from the firearms dealer, the CLEO must "make a reasonable effort to ascertain within 5 business days whether receipt or possession would be in violation of the law, including research in whatever State and local record keeping systems are available and in a national system designated by the Attorney General." §922(s)(2). The Act does not require the CLEO to take any particular action if he determines that a pending transaction would be unlawful; he may notify the firearms dealer to that effect, but is not required to do so. If, however, the CLEO notifies a gun dealer that a prospective purchaser is ineligible to receive a handgun, he must, upon request, provide the would be purchaser with a written statement of the reasons for that determination. §922(s)(6)(C). Moreover, if the CLEO does not discover any basis for objecting to the sale, he must destroy any records in his possession relating to the transfer, including his copy of the Brady Form. §922(s)(6)(B)(i). Under a separate provision of the GCA, any person who "knowingly violates [the section of the GCA amended by the Brady Act] shall be fined under this title, imprisoned for no more than 1 year, or both." §924(a)(5).

Petitioners Jay Printz and Richard Mack, the CLEOs for Ravalli County, Montana, and Graham County, Arizona, respectively, filed separate actions challenging the constitutionality of the Brady Act's interim provisions. In each case, the District Court held that the provision requiring CLEOs to perform background checks was unconstitutional, but concluded that that provision was severable from the remainder of the Act, effectively leaving a voluntary background check system in place. 856 F. Supp. 1372 (Ariz. 1994); 854 F. Supp. 1503 (Mont. 1994). A divided panel of the Court of Appeals for the Ninth Circuit reversed, finding none of the Brady Act's interim provisions to be unconstitutional. 66 F. 3d 1025 (1995). We granted certiorari. 518 U. S. ___ (1996).

From the description set forth above, it is apparent that the Brady Act purports to direct state law enforcement officers to participate, albeit only temporarily, in the administration of a federally enacted regulatory scheme. Regulated firearms dealers are required to forward Brady Forms not to a federal officer or employee, but to the CLEOs, whose obligation to accept those forms is implicit in the duty imposed upon them to make "reasonable efforts" within five days to determine whether the sales reflected in the forms are lawful. While the CLEOs are subjected to no federal requirement that they prevent the sales determined to be unlawful (it is perhaps assumed that their state law duties will require prevention or apprehension), they are empowered to grant, in effect, waivers of the federally prescribed 5 day waiting period for handgun purchases by notifying the gun dealers that they have no reason to believe the transactions would be illegal.

The petitioners here object to being pressed into federal service, and contend that congressional action compelling state officers to execute federal laws is unconstitutional. Because there is no constitutional text speaking to this precise question, the answer to the CLEOs' challenge must be sought in historical understanding and practice, in the structure of the Constitution, and in the jurisprudence of this Court. We treat those three sources, in that order, in this and the next two sections of this opinion.

Petitioners contend that compelled enlistment of state executive officers for the administration of federal programs is, until very recent years at least, unprecedented. The Government contends, to the contrary, that-the earliest Congresses enacted statutes that required the participation of state officials in the implementation of federal laws," Brief for United States 28. The Government's contention demands our careful consideration, since early congressional enactments "provid[e] `contemporaneous and weighty evidence' of the Constitution's meaning," Bowsher v. Synar, 478 U.S. 714, 723-724 (1986) (quoting Marsh v. Chambers, 463 U.S. 783, 790 (1983)). Indeed, such "contemporaneous legislative exposition of the Constitution . . ., acquiesced in for a long term of years, fixes the construction to be given its provisions." Myers v. United States, 272 U.S. 52, 175 (1926) (citing numerous cases). Conversely if, as petitioners contend, earlier Congresses avoided use of this highly attractive power, we would have reason to believe that the power was thought not to exist.

The Government observes that statutes enacted by the first Congresses required state courts to record applications for citizenship, Act of Mar. 26, 1790, ch. 3, §1, 1 Stat. 103, to transmit abstracts of citizenship applications and other naturalization records to the Secretary of State, Act of June 18, 1798, ch. 54, §2, 1 Stat. 567, and to register aliens seeking naturalization and issue certificates of registry, Act of Apr. 14, 1802, ch. 28, §2, 2 Stat. 154-155. It may well be, however, that these requirements applied only in States that authorized their courts to conduct naturalization proceedings. See Act of Mar. 26, 1790, ch. 3, §1, 1 Stat. 103; Holmgren v. United States, 217 U.S. 509, 516-517 (1910) (explaining that the Act of March 26, 1790 "conferred authority upon state courts to admit aliens to citizenship" and refraining from addressing the question "whether the States can be required to enforce such naturalization laws against their consent"); United States v. Jones, 109 U.S. 513, 519-520 (1883) (stating that these obligations were imposed "with the consent of the States" and-could not be enforced against the consent of the States"). [n.1] Other statutes of that era apparently or at least arguably required state courts to perform functions unrelated to naturalization, such as resolving controversies between a captain and the crew of his ship concerning the seaworthiness of the vessel, Act of July

20, 1790, ch. 29, §3, 1 Stat. 132, hearing the claims of slave owners who had apprehended fugitive slaves and issuing certificates authorizing the slave's forced removal to the State from which he had fled, Act of Feb. 12, 1793, ch. 7, §3, 1 Stat. 302-305, taking proof of the claims of Canadian refugees who had assisted the United States during the Revolutionary War, Act of Apr. 7, 1798, ch. 26, §3, 1 Stat. 548, and ordering the deportation of alien enemies in times of war, Act of July 6, 1798, ch. 66, §2, 1 Stat. 577-578.

These early laws establish, at most, that the Constitution was originally understood to permit imposition of an obligation on state judges to enforce federal prescriptions, insofar as those prescriptions related to matters appropriate for the judicial power. That assumption was perhaps implicit in one of the provisions of the Constitution, and was explicit in another. In accord with the so called Madisonian Compromise, Article III, §1, established only a Supreme Court, and made the creation of lower federal courts optional with the Congress--even though it was obvious that the Supreme Court alone could not hear all federal cases throughout the United States. See C. Warren, The Making of the Constitution 325-327 (1928). And the Supremacy Clause, Art. VI, cl. 2, announced that "the Laws of the United States . . . shall be the supreme Law of the Land; and the Judges in every State shall be bound thereby." It is understandable why courts should have been viewed distinctively in this regard; unlike legislatures and executives, they applied the law of other sovereigns all the time. The principle underlying so called "transitory" causes of action was that laws which operated elsewhere created obligations in justice that courts of the forum state would enforce. See, e.g., McKenna v. Fisk, 1 How. 241, 247-249 (1843). The Constitution itself, in the Full Faith and Credit Clause, Art. IV, §1, generally required such enforcement with respect to obligations arising in other States. See Hughes v. Fetter, 341 U.S. 609 (1951).

For these reasons, we do not think the early statutes imposing obligations on state courts imply a power of Congress to impress the state executive into its service. Indeed, it can be argued that the numerousness of these statutes, contrasted with the utter lack of statutes imposing obligations on the States' executive (notwithstanding the attractiveness of that course to Congress), suggests an assumed absence of such power. [n.2] The only early federal law the Government has brought to our attention that imposed duties on state executive officers is the Extradition Act of 1793, which required the "executive authority" of a State to cause the arrest and delivery of a fugitive from justice upon the request of the executive authority of the State from which the fugitive had fled. See Act of Feb. 12, 1793, ch. 7, §1, 1 Stat. 302. That was in direct implementation, however, of the Extradition Clause of the Constitution itself, see Art. IV, §2. [n.3]

Not only do the enactments of the early Congresses, as far as we are aware, contain no evidence of an assumption that the Federal Government may command the States' executive power in the absence of a particularized constitutional authorization, they contain some indication of precisely the opposite assumption. On September 23, 1789--the day before its proposal of the Bill of Rights, see 1 Annals of Congress 912-913-- the First Congress enacted a law aimed at obtaining state assistance of the most rudimentary and necessary sort for the enforcement of the new Government's laws: the holding of federal prisoners in state jails at federal expense. Significantly, the law issued not a command to the States' executive, but a recommendation to their legislatures. Congress "recommended to the legislatures of the several States to pass laws, making it expressly the duty of the keepers of their gaols, to receive and safe keep therein all prisoners committed under the authority of the United States," and offered to pay 50 cents per month for each prisoner. Act of Sept. 23, 1789, 1 Stat. 96. Moreover, when Georgia refused to comply with the request, see L. White, The Federalists 402 (1948), Congress's only reaction was a law authorizing the marshal in any State that failed to comply with the Recommendation of September 23, 1789, to rent a temporary jail until provision for a permanent one could be made, see Resolution of Mar. 3, 1791, 1 Stat. 225.

In addition to early legislation, the Government also appeals to other sources we have usually regarded as indicative of the original understanding of the Constitution. It points to portions of The Federalist which reply to criticisms that Congress's power to tax will produce two sets of revenue officers--for example, "Brutus's" assertion in his letter to the New York Journal of December 13, 1787, that the Constitution "opens a door to the appointment of a swarm of revenue and excise officers to prey upon the honest and industrious part of the community, eat up their substance, and riot on the spoils of the country," reprinted in 1 Debate on the Constitution 502 (B. Bailyn ed. 1993). "Publius" responded that Congress will probably "make use of the State officers and State regulations, for collecting" federal taxes, The Federalist No. 36, p. 221 (C. Rossiter ed. 1961) (A. Hamilton) (hereinafter The Federalist), and predicted that "the eventual collection [of internal revenue] under the immediate authority of the Union, will generally be made by the officers, and according to the rules, appointed by the several States," id., No. 45, at 292 (J. Madison). The Government also invokes the Federalist's more general observations that the Constitution would "enable the [national] government to employ the ordinary magistracy of each [State] in the execution of its laws," id., No. 27, at 176 (A. Hamilton), and that it was "extremely probable that in other instances, particularly in the organization of the judicial power, the officers of the States will be clothed in the correspondent authority of the Union," id., No. 45, at 292 (J. Madison). But none of these statements necessarily implies--what is the critical point here--that Congress could impose these responsibilities without the consent of the States. They appear to rest on the natural assumption that the States would consent to allowing their officials to assist the Federal Government, see FERC v. Mississippi, 456 U.S. 742, 796, n. 35 (1982) (O'Connor, J., concurring in judgment in part and dissenting in part), an assumption proved correct by the extensive mutual assistance the States and Federal Government voluntarily provided one another in the early days of the Republic, see generally White, supra, at 401-404, including voluntary federal implementation of state law, see, e.g., Act of Apr. 2, 1790, ch. 5, §1, 1 Stat. 106 (directing federal tax collectors and customs officers to assist in enforcing state inspection laws).

Another passage of The Federalist reads as follows:

"It merits particular attention . . ., that the laws of the Confederacy as to the enumerated and legitimate objects of its jurisdiction will become the supreme law of the land; to the observance of which all officers, legislative, executive, and judicial in each State will be bound by the sanctity of an oath. Thus, the legislatures, courts, and magistrates, of the respective members will be incorporated into the operations of the national government as far as its just and constitutional authority extends; and will be rendered auxiliary to the enforcement of its laws." The Federalist No. 27, at 177 (A. Hamilton) (emphasis in original).

The Government does not rely upon this passage, but Justice Souter (with whose conclusions on this point the dissent is in agreement, see post, at 11) makes it the very foundation of his position; so we pause to examine it in some detail. Justice Souter finds "[t]he natural reading" of the phrases "will be incorporated into the operations of the national government" and "will be rendered auxiliary to the enforcement of its laws" to be that the National Government will have "authority . . ., when exercising an otherwise legitimate power (the commerce power, say), to require state `auxiliaries' to take appropriate action." Post, at 2. There are several obstacles to such an interpretation. First, the consequences in question ("incorporated into the operations of the national government" and "rendered auxiliary to the enforcement of its laws") are said in the quoted passage to flow automatically from the officers' oath to observe the "the laws of the Confederacy as to the enumerated and legitimate objects of its jurisdiction." [n.4] Thus, if the passage means that state officers must take an active role in the implementation of federal law, it means that they must do so without the necessity for a congressional directive that they implement it. But no one has ever thought, and no one asserts in the present litigation, that that is the law. The second problem with Justice Souter's reading is that it makes state legislatures subject to federal direction. (The passage in question, after all, does not include legislatures merely incidentally, as by referring to "all state officers"; it refers to legislatures specifically and first of all.) We have held, however, that state leglislatures are not subject to federal direction. New York v. United States, 505 U.S. 144 (1992). [n.5]

These problems are avoided, of course, if the calculatedly vague consequences the passage recites--"incorporated into the operations of the national government" and "rendered auxiliary to the enforcement of its laws"--are taken to refer to nothing more (or less) than the duty owed to the National Government, on the part of all state officials, to enact, enforce, and interpret state law in such fashion as not to obstruct the operation of federal law, and the attendant reality that all state actions constituting such obstruction, even legislative acts, are ipso facto invalid. [n.6] See Silkwood v. Kerr-McGee Corp., 464 U.S. 238, 248 (1984) (federal pre-emption of conflicting state law). This meaning accords well with the context of the passage, which seeks to explain why the new system of federal law directed to individual citizens, unlike the old one of federal law directed to the States, will "bid much fairer to avoid the necessity of using force" against the States, The Federalist No. 27, at 176 . It also reconciles the passage with Hamilton's statement in

Federalist No. 36, at 222, that the Federal Government would in some circumstances do well "to employ the state officers as much as possible, and to attach them to the Union by an accumulation of their emoluments"--which surely suggests inducing state officers to come aboard by paying them, rather than merely commandeering their official services. [n.7]

Justice Souter contends that his interpretation of Federalist No. 27 is "supported by No. 44," written by Madison, wherefore he claims that "Madison and Hamilton" together stand opposed to our view. Post, at 4. In fact, Federalist No. 44 quite clearly contradicts Justice Souter's reading. In that Number, Madison justifies the requirement that state officials take an oath to support the Federal Constitution on the ground that they "will have an essential agency in giving effect to the federal Constitution." If the dissent's reading of Federalist No. 27 were correct (and if Madison agreed with it), one would surely have expected that "essential agency" of state executive officers (if described further) to be described as their responsibility to execute the laws enacted under the Constitution. Instead, however, Federalist No. 44 continues with the following description:

"The election of the President and Senate will depend, in all cases, on the legislatures of the several States. And the election of the House of Representatives will equally depend on the same authority in the first instance; and will, probably, forever be conducted by the officers and according to the laws of the States." Id., at 287 (emphasis added).

It is most implausible that the person who labored for that example of state executive officers' assisting the Federal Government believed, but neglected to mention, that they had a responsibility to execute federal laws. [n.8] If it was indeed Hamilton's view that the Federal Government could direct the officers of the States, that view has no clear support in Madison's writings, or as far as we are aware, in text, history, or early commentary elsewhere. [n.9]

To complete the historical record, we must note that there is not only an absence of executive commandeering statutes in the early Congresses, but there is an absence of them in our later history as well, at least until very recent years. The Government points to the Act of August 3, 1882, ch. 376, §§2, 4, 22 Stat. 214, which enlisted state officials "to take charge of the local affairs of immigration in the ports within such State, and to provide for the support and relief of such immigrants therein landing as may fall into distress or need of public aid"; to inspect arriving immigrants and exclude any person found to be a "convict, lunatic, idiot," or indigent; and to send convicts back to their country of origin "without compensation." The statute did not, however, mandate those duties, but merely empowered the Secretary of the Treasury "to enter into contracts with such State . . . officers as may be designated for that purpose by the governor of any State." (Emphasis added.)

The Government cites the World War I selective draft law that authorized the President "to utilize the service of any or all departments and any or all officers or agents of the United States and of the several States, Territories, and the District of Columbia, and subdivisions thereof, in the execution of this Act," and made any person who refused to comply with the President's directions guilty of a misdemeanor. Act of May 18, 1917, ch. 15, §6, 40 Stat. 80-81 (emphasis added). However, it is far from clear that the authorization "to utilize the service" of state officers was an authorization to compel the service of state officers; and the misdemeanor provision surely applied only to refusal to comply with the President's authorized directions, which might not have included directions to officers of States whose governors had not volunteered their services. It is interesting that in implementing the Act President Wilson did not commandeer the services of state officers, but instead requested the assistance of the States' governors, see Proclamation of May 18, 1917, 40 Stat. 1665 ("call[ing] upon the Governor of each of the several States . . . and all officers and agents of the several States . . . to perform certain duties"); Registration Regulations Prescribed by the President Under the Act of Congress Approved May 18, 1917, Part I, §7 ("the governor [of each State] is requested to act under the regulations and rules prescribed by the President or under his direction") (emphasis added), obtained the consent of each of the governors, see Note, The President, the Senate, the Constitution, and the Executive Order of May 8, 1926, 21 Ill. L. Rev. 142, 144 (1926), and left it to the governors to issue orders to their subordinate state officers, see Selective Service Regulations Prescribed by the President Under the Act of May 18, 1917, §27 (1918); J. Clark, The Rise of a New Federalism 91 (1965). See generally Note, 21 Ill. L. Rev., at 144. It is impressive that even with respect to a wartime measure the President should have been so solicitous of state independence.

  The Government points to a number of federal statutes enacted within the past few decades that require the participation of state or local officials in implementing federal regulatory schemes. Some of these are connected to federal funding measures, and can perhaps be more accurately described as conditions upon the grant of federal funding than as mandates to the States; others, which require only the provision of information to the Federal Government, do not involve the precise issue before us here, which is the forced participation of the States' executive in the actual administration of a federal program. We of course do not address these or other currently operative enactments that are not before us; it will be time enough to do so if and when their validity is challenged in a proper case. For deciding the issue before us here, they are of little relevance. Even assuming they represent assertion of the very same congressional power challenged here, they are of such recent vintage that they are no more probative than the statute before us of a constitutional tradition that lends meaning to the text. Their persuasive force is far outweighed by almost two centuries of apparent congressional avoidance of the practice. Compare INS v. Chadha, 462 U.S. 919 (1983), in which the legislative veto, though enshrined in perhaps hundreds of federal statutes, most of which were enacted in the 1970's and the earliest of which was enacted in 1932, see id., at 967-975 (White, J., dissenting), was nonetheless held unconstitutional.

The constitutional practice we have examined above tends to negate the existence of the congressional power asserted here, but is not conclusive. We turn next to consideration of the structure of the Constitution, to see if we can discern among its "essential postulate[s]," Principality of Monaco v. Mississippi, 292 U.S. 313, 322 (1934), a principle that controls the present cases.

It is incontestible that the Constitution established a system of "dual sovereignty." Gregory v. Ashcroft, 501 U.S. 452, 457 (1991); Tafflin v. Levitt, 493 U.S. 455, 458 (1990). Although the States surrendered many of their powers to the new Federal Government, they retained "a residuary and inviolable sovereignty," The Federalist No. 39, at 245 (J. Madison). This is reflected throughout the Constitution's text, Lane County v. Oregon, 7 Wall. 71, 76 (1869); Texas v. White, 7 Wall. 700, 725 (1869), including (to mention only a few examples) the prohibition on any involuntary reduction or combination of a State's territory, Art. IV, §3; the Judicial Power Clause, Art. III, §2, and the Privileges and Immunities Clause, Art. IV, §2, which speak of the "Citizens" of the States; the amendment provision, Article V, which requires the votes of three fourths of the States to amend the Constitution; and the Guarantee Clause, Art. IV, §4, which "presupposes the continued existence of the states and . . . those means and instrumentalities which are the creation of their sovereign and reserved rights," Helvering v. Gerhardt, 304 U.S. 405, 414-415 (1938). Residual state sovereignty was also implicit, of course, in the Constitution's conferral upon Congress of not all governmental powers, but only discrete, enumerated ones, Art. I, §8, which implication was rendered express by the Tenth Amendment's assertion that "[t]he powers not delegated to the United States by the Constitution, nor prohibited by it to the States, are reserved to the States respectively, or to the people."

The Framers' experience under the Articles of Confederation had persuaded them that using the States as the instruments of federal governance was both ineffectual and provocative of federal state conflict. See The Federalist No. 15. Preservation of the States as independent political entities being the price of union, and "[t]he practicality of making laws, with coercive sanctions, for the States as political bodies" having been, in Madison's words, "exploded on all hands," 2 Records of the Federal Convention of 1787, p. 9 (M. Farrand ed. 1911), the Framers rejected the concept of a central government that would act upon and through the States, and instead designed a system in which the state and federal governments would exercise concurrent authority over the people--who were, in Hamilton's words, "the only proper objects of government," The Federalist No. 15, at 109. We have set forth the historical record in more detail elsewhere, see New York v. United States, 505 U. S., at 161-166, and need not repeat it here. It suffices to repeat the conclusion: "The Framers explicitly chose a Constitution that confers upon Congress the power to regulate individuals, not States." Id., at 166. [n.10] The great innovation of this design was that-our citizens would have two political capacities, one state and one federal, each protected from incursion by the other"--"a legal system unprecedented in form and design, establishing two orders of government, each with its own direct relationship, its own privity, its own set of mutual rights and obligations to the people who sustain it and are governed by it." U. S. Term Limits, Inc. v. Thornton, 514 U.S. 779, 838 (1995) (Kennedy, J., concurring). The Constitution thus contemplates that a State's government will represent and remain accountable to its own citizens. See New York, supra, at 168-169; United States v. Lopez, 514 U.S. 549, 576-577 (1995) (Kennedy, J., concurring). Cf. Edgar v. MITE Corp., 457 U.S. 624, 644 (1982) ("the State has no legitimate interest in protecting nonresident[s]"). As Madison expressed it: "[T]he local or municipal authorities form distinct and independent portions of the supremacy, no more subject, within their respective spheres, to the general authority than the general authority is subject to them, within its own sphere." The Federalist No. 39, at 245. [n.11]

This separation of the two spheres is one of the Constitution's structural protections of liberty. "Just as the separation and independence of the coordinate branches of the Federal Government serve to prevent the accumulation of excessive power in any one branch, a healthy balance of power between the States and the Federal Government will reduce the risk of tyranny and abuse from either front." Gregory, supra, at 458. To quote Madison once again:

"In the compound republic of America, the power surrendered by the people is first divided between two distinct governments, and then the portion allotted to each subdivided among distinct and separate departments. Hence a double security arises to the rights of the people. The different governments will control each other, at the same time that each will be controlled by itself." The Federalist No. 51, at 323.

See also The Federalist No. 28, at 180-181 (A. Hamilton). The power of the Federal Government would be augmented immeasurably if it were able to impress into its service--and at no cost to itself--the police officers of the 50 States.

We have thus far discussed the effect that federal control of state officers would have upon the first element of the "double security" alluded to by Madison: the division of power between State and Federal Governments. It would also have an effect upon the second element: the separation and equilibration of powers between the three branches of the Federal Government itself. The Constitution does not leave to speculation who is to administer the laws enacted by Congress; the President, it says, "shall take Care that the Laws be faithfully executed," Art. II, §3, personally and through officers whom he appoints (save for such inferior officers as Congress may authorize to be appointed by the "Courts of Law" or by "the Heads of Departments" who are themselves presidential appointees), Art. II, §2. The Brady Act effectively transfers this responsibility to thousands of CLEOs in the 50 States, who are left to implement the program without meaningful Presidential control (if indeed meaningful Presidential control is possible without the power to appoint and remove). The insistence of the Framers upon unity in the Federal Executive--to insure both vigor and accountability--is well known. See The Federalist No. 70 (A. Hamilton); 2 Documentary History of the Ratification of the Constitution 495 (M. Jensen ed. 1976) (statement of James Wilson); see also Calabresi & Prakash, The President's Power to Execute the Laws, 104 Yale L. J. 541 (1994). That unity would be shattered, and the power of the President would be subject to reduction, if Congress could act as effectively without the President as with him, by simply requiring state officers to execute its laws. [n.12]

The dissent of course resorts to the last, best hope of those who defend ultra vires congressional action, the Necessary and Proper Clause. It reasons, post, at 3-5, that the power to regulate the sale of handguns under the Commerce Clause, coupled with the power to "make all Laws which shall be necessary and proper for carrying into Execution the foregoing Powers," Art. I, §8, conclusively establishes the Brady Act's constitutional validity, because the Tenth Amendment imposes no limitations on the exercise of delegated powers but merely prohibits the exercise of powers "not delegated to the United States." What destroys the dissent's Necessary and Proper Clause argument, however, is not the Tenth Amendment but the Necessary and Proper Clause itself. [n.13] When a "La[w] . . . for carrying into Execution" the Commerce Clause violates the principle of state sovereignty reflected in the various constitutional provisions we mentioned earlier, supra, at 19-20, it is not a "La[w] . . . proper for carrying into Execution the Commerce Clause," and is thus, in the words of The Federalist, "merely [an] ac[t] of usurpation" which "deserve[s] to be treated as such." The Federalist No. 33, at 204 (A. Hamilton). See Lawson & Granger, The "Proper" Scope of Federal Power: A Jurisdictional Interpretation of the Sweeping Clause, 43 Duke L. J. 267, 297-326, 330-333 (1993). We in fact answered the dissent's Necessary and Proper Clause argument in New York: "[E]ven where Congress has the authority under the Constitution to pass laws requiring or prohibiting certain acts, it lacks the power directly to compel the States to require or prohibit those acts. . . . [T]he Commerce Clause, for example, authorizes Congress to regulate interstate commerce directly; it does not authorize Congress to regulate state governments' regulation of interstate commerce." 505 U. S., at 166.

The dissent perceives a simple answer in that portion of Article VI which requires that "all executive and judicial Officers, both of the United States and of the several States, shall be bound by Oath or Affirmation, to support this Constitution," arguing that by virtue of the Supremacy Clause this makes "not only the Constitution, but every law enacted by Congress as well," binding on state officers, including laws requiring state officer enforcement. Post, at 6. The Supremacy Clause, however, makes "Law of the Land" only "Laws of the United States which shall be made in Pursuance [of the Constitution]"; so the Supremacy Clause merely brings us back to the question discussed earlier, whether laws conscripting state officers violate state sovereignty and are thus not in accord with the Constitution.

Finally, and most conclusively in the present litigation, we turn to the prior jurisprudence of this Court. Federal commandeering of state governments is such a novel phenomenon that this Court's first experience with it did not occur until the 1970's, when the Environmental Protection Agency promulgated regulations requiring States to prescribe auto emissions testing, monitoring and retrofit programs, and to designate preferential bus and carpool lanes. The Courts of Appeals for the Fourth and Ninth

Circuits invalidated the regulations on statutory grounds in order to avoid what they perceived to be grave constitutional issues, see Maryland v. EPA, 530 F. 2d 215, 226 (CA4 1975); Brown v. EPA, 521 F. 2d 827, 838-842 (CA9 1975); and the District of Columbia Circuit invalidated the regulations on both constitutional and statutory grounds, see District of Columbia v. Train, 521 F. 2d 971, 994 (CADC 1975). After we granted certiorari to review the statutory and constitutional validity of the regulations, the Government declined even to defend them, and instead rescinded some and conceded the invalidity of those that remained, leading us to vacate the opinions below and remand for consideration of mootness. EPA v. Brown, 431 U.S. 99 (1977).

Although we had no occasion to pass upon the subject in Brown, later opinions of ours have made clear that the Federal Government may not compel the States to implement, by legislation or executive action, federal regulatory programs. In Hodel v. Virginia Surface Mining & Reclamation Assn., Inc., 452 U.S. 264 (1981), and FERC v. Mississippi, 456 U.S. 742 (1982), we sustained statutes against constitutional challenge only after assuring ourselves that they did not require the States to enforce federal law. In Hodel we cited the lower court cases in EPA v. Brown, supra, but concluded that the Surface Mining Control and Reclamation Act did not present the problem they raised because it merely made compliance with federal standards a precondition to continued state regulation in an otherwise pre-empted field, Hodel, supra, at 288. In FERC, we construed the most troubling provisions of the Public Utility Regulatory Policies Act of 1978, to contain only the "command" that state agencies "consider" federal standards, and again only as a precondition to continued state regulation of an otherwise pre-empted field. 456 U. S., at 764-765. We warned that "this Court never has sanctioned explicitly a federal command to the States to promulgate and enforce laws and regulations," id., at 761-762.

When we were at last confronted squarely with a federal statute that unambiguously required the States to enact or administer a federal regulatory program, our decision should have come as no surprise. At issue in New York v. United States, 505 U.S. 144 (1992), were the so called "take title" provisions of the Low Level Radioactive Waste Policy Amendments Act of 1985, which required States either to enact legislation providing for the disposal of radioactive waste generated within their borders, or to take title to, and possession of the waste--effectively requiring the States either to legislate pursuant to Congress's directions, or to implement an administrative solution. Id., at 175-176. We concluded that Congress could constitutionally require the States to do neither. Id., at 176. "The Federal Government," we held, "may not compel the States to enact or administer a federal regulatory program." Id., at 188.

The Government contends that New York is distinguishable on the following ground: unlike the "take title" provisions invalidated there, the background check provision of the Brady Act does not require state legislative or executive officials to make policy, but instead issues a final directive to state CLEOs. It is permissible, the Government asserts, for Congress to command state or local officials to assist in the implementation of federal law so long as "Congress itself devises a clear legislative solution that regulates private conduct" and requires state or local officers to provide only "limited, non policymaking help in enforcing that law." "[T]he constitutional line is crossed only when Congress compels the States to make law in their sovereign capacities." Brief for United States 16.

The Government's distinction between "making" law and merely "enforcing" it, between "policymaking" and mere "implementation," is an interesting one. It is perhaps not meant to be the same as, but it is surely reminiscent of, the line that separates proper congressional conferral of Executive power from unconstitutional delegation of legislative authority for federal separation of powers purposes. See A. L. A. Schechter Poultry Corp. v. United States, 295 U.S. 495, 530 (1935); Panama Refining Co. v. Ryan, 293 U.S. 388, 428-429 (1935). This Court has not been notably successful in describing the latter line; indeed, some think we have abandoned the effort to do so. See FPC v. New England Power Co., 415 U.S. 345, 352-353 (1974) (Marshall, J., concurring in result); Schoenbrod, The Delegation Doctrine: Could the Court Give it Substance? 83 Mich. L. Rev. 1223, 1233 (1985). We are doubtful that the new line the Government proposes would be any more distinct. Executive action that has utterly no policymaking component is rare, particularly at an executive level as high as a jurisdiction's chief law enforcement officer. Is it really true that there is no policymaking involved in deciding, for example, what "reasonable efforts" shall be expended to conduct a background check? It may well satisfy the Act for a CLEO to direct that (a) no background checks will be conducted that divert personnel time from pending felony investigations, and (b) no background check will be permitted to consume more than one half hour of an officer's time. But nothing in the Act requires a CLEO to be so parsimonious; diverting at least some felony investigation time, and permitting at least some background checks beyond one half hour would certainly not be unreasonable. Is this decision whether to devote maximum "reasonable efforts" or minimum "reasonable efforts" not preeminently a matter of policy? It is quite impossible, in short, to draw the Government's proposed line at "no policymaking," and we would have to fall back upon a line of "not too much policymaking." How much is too much is not likely to be answered precisely; and an imprecise barrier against federal intrusion upon state authority is not likely to be an effective one.

Even assuming, moreover, that the Brady Act leaves no "policymaking" discretion with the States, we fail to see how that improves rather than worsens the intrusion upon state sovereignty. Preservation of the States as independent and autonomous political entities is arguably less undermined by requiring them to make policy in certain fields than (as Judge Sneed aptly described it over two decades ago) by "reduc[ing] [them] to puppets of a ventriloquist Congress," Brown v. EPA, 521 F. 2d, at 839. It is an essential attribute of the States' retained sovereignty that they remain independent and autonomous within their proper sphere of authority. See Texas v. White, 7 Wall, at 725. It is no more compatible with this independence and autonomy that their officers be "dragooned" (as Judge Fernandez put it in his dissent below, 66 F. 3d, at 1035) into administering federal law, than it would be compatible with the independence and autonomy of the United States that its officers be impressed into service for the execution of state laws.

The Government purports to find support for its proffered distinction of New York in our decisions in Testa v. Katt, 330 U.S. 386 (1947), and FERC v. Mississippi, 456 U.S. 742 (1982). We find neither case relevant. Testa stands for the proposition that state courts cannot refuse to apply federal law--a conclusion mandated by the terms of the Supremacy Clause ("the Judges in every State shall be bound [by federal law]"). As we have suggested earlier, supra, at 6-7, that says nothing about whether state executive officers must administer federal law. Accord New York, 505 U. S., at 178-179. As for FERC, it stated (as we have described earlier) that "this Court never has sanctioned explicitly a federal command to the States to promulgate and enforce laws and regulations," 456 U. S., at 761-762, and upheld the statutory provisions at issue precisely because they did not commandeer state government, but merely imposed preconditions to continued state regulation of an otherwise pre-empted field, in accord with Hodel, 452 U. S., at 288, and required state administrative agencies to apply federal law while acting in a judicial capacity, in accord with Testa, See FERC, supra, at 759-771, and n. 24. [n.14]

The Government also maintains that requiring state officers to perform discrete, ministerial tasks specified by Congress does not violate the principle of New York because it does not diminish the accountability of state or federal officials. This argument fails even on its own terms. By forcing state governments to absorb the financial burden of implementing a federal regulatory program, Members of Congress can take credit for "solving" problems without having to ask their constituents to pay for the solutions with higher federal taxes. And even when the States are not forced to absorb the costs of implementing a federal program, they are still put in the position of taking the blame for its burdensomeness and for its defects. See Merritt, Three Faces of Federalism: Finding a Formula for the Future, 47 Vand. L. Rev. 1563, 1580, n. 65 (1994). Under the present law, for example, it will be the CLEO and not some federal official who stands between the gun purchaser and immediate possession of his gun. And it will likely be the CLEO, not some federal official, who will be blamed for any error (even one in the designated federal database) that causes a purchaser to be mistakenly rejected.

The dissent makes no attempt to defend the Government's basis for distinguishing New York, but instead advances what seems to us an even more implausible theory. The Brady Act, the dissent asserts, is different from the "take title" provisions invalidated in New York because the former is addressed to individuals-- namely CLEOs--while the latter were directed to the State itself. That is certainly a difference, but it cannot be a constitutionally significant one. While the Brady Act is directed to "individuals," it is directed to them in their official capacities as state officers; it controls their actions, not as private citizens, but as the agents of the State. The distinction between judicial writs and other government action directed against individuals in their personal capacity, on the one hand, and in their official capacity, on the other hand, is an ancient one, principally because it is dictated by common sense. We have observed that "a suit against a state official in his or her official capacity is not a suit against the official but rather is a suit against the official's office.... As such, it is no different from a suit against the State itself." Will v. Michigan Dept. of State Police, 491 U.S. 58, 71 (1989). And the same must be said of a directive to an official in his or her official capacity. To say that the Federal Government cannot control the State, but can control all of its officers, is to say nothing of significance. [n.15] Indeed, it merits the description "empty formalistic reasoning of the highest order," post, at 15. By resorting to this, the dissent not so much distinguishes New York as disembowels it. [n.16]

Finally, the Government puts forward a cluster of arguments that can be grouped under the heading: "The Brady Act serves very important purposes, is most efficiently administered by CLEOs during the interim period, and places a minimal and only temporary burden upon state officers." There is considerable disagreement over the extent of the burden, but we need not pause over that detail. Assuming all the mentioned factors were true, they might be relevant if we were evaluating whether the incidental application to the States of a federal law of general applicability excessively interfered with the functioning of state governments. See, e.g., Fry v. United States, 421 U.S. 542, 548 (1975); National League of Cities v. Usery, 426 U.S. 833, 853 (1976) (overruled by Garcia v. San Antonio Metropolitan Transit Authority, 469 U.S. 528 (1985)); South Carolina v. Baker, 485 U.S. 505, 529 (1988) (Rehnquist, C. J., concurring in judgment). But where, as here, it is the whole object of the law to direct the functioning of the state executive, and hence to compromise the structural framework of dual sovereignty, such a "balancing" analysis is inappropriate. [n.17] It is the very principle of separate state sovereignty that such a law offends, and no comparative assessment of the various interests can overcome that fundamental defect. Cf. Bowsher, 478 U. S., at 736 (declining to subject principle of separation of powers to a balancing test); Chadha, 462 U. S., at 944-946 (same); Plaut v. Spendthrift Farm, Inc., 514 U.S. 211, 239-240 (1995) (holding legislated invalidation of final judgments to be categorically unconstitutional). We expressly rejected such an approach in New York, and what we said bears repeating:

"Much of the Constitution is concerned with setting forth the form of our government, and the courts have traditionally invalidated measures deviating from that form. The result may appear `formalistic' in a given case to partisans of the measure at issue, because such measures are typically the product of the era's perceived necessity. But the Constitution protects us from our own best intentions: It divides power among sovereigns and among branches of government precisely so that we may resist the temptation to concentrate power in one location as an expedient solution to the crisis of the day." Id., at 187.

We adhere to that principle today, and conclude categorically, as we concluded categorically in New York: "The Federal Government may not compel the States to enact or administer a federal regulatory program." Id., at 188. The mandatory obligation imposed on CLEOs to perform background checks on prospective handgun purchasers plainly runs afoul of that rule.

What we have said makes it clear enough that the central obligation imposed upon CLEOs by the interim provisions of the Brady Act--the obligation to "make a reasonable effort to ascertain within 5 business days whether receipt or possession [of a handgun] would be in violation of the law, including research in whatever State and local record keeping systems are available and in a national system designated by the Attorney General," 18 U.S.C. § 922(s)(2)--is unconstitutional. Extinguished with it, of course, is the duty implicit in the background check requirement that the CLEO accept notice of the contents of, and a copy of, the completed Brady Form, which the firearms dealer is required to provide to him, §§922(s)(1)(A)(i)(III) and (IV).

Petitioners also challenge, however, two other provisions of the Act: (1) the requirement that any CLEO "to whom a [Brady Form] is transmitted" destroy the form and any record containing information derived from it, §922(s)(6)(B)(i), and (2) the requirement that any CLEO who "determines that an individual is ineligible to receive a handgun" provide the would be purchaser, upon request, a written statement of the reasons for that determination, §922(s)(6)(C). With the background check and implicit receipt of forms requirements invalidated, however, these provisions require no action whatsoever on the part of the CLEO. Quite obviously, the obligation to destroy all Brady Forms that he has received when he has received none, and the obligation to give reasons for a determination of ineligibility when he never makes a determination of ineligibility, are no obligations at all. These two provisions have conceivable application to a CLEO, in other words, only if he has chosen, voluntarily, to participate in administration of the federal scheme. The present petitioners are not in that position. [n.18] As to them, these last two challenged provisions are not unconstitutional, but simply inoperative.

There is involved in this Brady Act conundrum a severability question, which the parties have briefed and argued: whether firearms dealers in the jurisdictions at issue here, and in other jurisdictions, remain obliged to forward to the CLEO (even if he will not accept it) the requisite notice of the contents (and a copy) of the Brady Form, §§922(s)(1)(A)(i)(III) and (IV); and to wait five business days before consummating the sale, §922(s)(1)(A)(ii). These are important questions, but we have no business answering them in these cases. These provisions burden only firearms dealers and purchasers, and no plaintiff in either of those categories is before us here. We decline to speculate regarding the rights and obligations of parties not before the Court. Cf., e.g., New York, supra, at 186-187 (addressing severability where remaining provisions at issue affected the plaintiffs).

* * *

We held in New York that Congress cannot compel the States to enact or enforce a federal regulatory program. Today we hold that Congress cannot circumvent that prohibition by conscripting the State's officers directly. The Federal Government may neither issue directives requiring the States to address particular problems, nor command the States' officers, or those of their political subdivisions, to administer or enforce a federal regulatory program. It matters not whether policymaking is involved, and no case by case weighing of the burdens or benefits is necessary; such commands are fundamentally incompatible with our constitutional system of dual sovereignty. Accordingly, the judgment of the Court of Appeals for the Ninth Circuit is reversed.

It is so ordered.

Notes to Printz v. United States (June 27, 1997)

1 The dissent is wrong in suggesting, post, at 13, n. 9, that the Second Employers' Liability Cases, 223 U.S. 1 (1912), eliminate the possibility that the duties imposed on state courts and their clerks in connection with naturalization proceedings were contingent on the State's voluntary assumption of the task of adjudicating citizenship applications. The Second Employers' Liability Cases stand for the proposition that a state court must entertain a claim arising under federal law "when its ordinary jurisdiction as prescribed by local law is appropriate to the occasion and is invoked in conformity with those laws." Id., at 56-57. This does not necessarily conflict with Holmgren and Jones, as the States obviously regulate the "ordinary jurisdiction" of their courts. (Our references throughout this opinion to "the dissent" are to the dissenting opinion of Justice Stevens, joined by Justice Ginsburg

and Justice Breyer. The separate dissenting opinions of Justice Breyer and Justice Souter will be referred to as such.)

2 Bereft of even a single early, or indeed even pre-20th century, statute compelling state executive officers to administer federal laws, the dissent is driven to claim that early federal statutes compelled state judges to perform executive functions, which implies a power to compel state executive officers to do so as well. Assuming that this implication would follow (which is doubtful), the premise of the argument is in any case wrong. None of the early statutes directed to state judges or court clerks required the performance of functions more appropriately characterized as executive than judicial (bearing in mind that the line between the two for present purposes is not necessarily identical with the line established by the Constitution for federal separation of powers purposes, see Sweezy v. New Hampshire, 354 U.S. 234, 255 (1957)). Given that state courts were entrusted with the quintessentially adjudicative task of determining whether applicants for citizenship met the requisite qualifications, see Act of Mar. 26, 1790, ch. 3, §1, 1 Stat. 103, it is unreasonable to maintain that the ancillary functions of recording, registering, and certifying the citizenship applications were unalterably executive rather than judicial in nature.

The dissent's assertion that the Act of July 20, 1790, ch. 29, §3, 1 Stat. 132-133, which required state courts to resolve controversies between captain and crew regarding seaworthiness of a vessel, caused state courts to act "like contemporary regulatory agencies," post, at 14, is cleverly true--because contemporary regulatory agencies have been allowed to perform adjudicative ("quasi judicial") functions. See 5 U.S.C. § 554; Humphrey's Executor v. United States, 295 U.S. 602 (1935). It is foolish, however, to mistake the copy for the original, and to believe that 18th century courts were imitating agencies, rather than 20th century agencies imitating courts. The Act's requirement that the court appoint "three persons in the neighbourhood . . . most skilful in maritime affairs" to examine the ship and report on its condition certainly does not change the proceeding into one "supervised by a judge but otherwise more characteristic of executive activity," post, at 14; that requirement is not significantly different from the contemporary judicial practice of appointing expert witnesses, see e.g., Fed. Rule Evid. 706. The ultimate function of the judge under the Act was purely adjudicative; he was, after receiving the report, to "adjudge and determine . . . whether said ship or vessel is fit to proceed on the intended voyage . . . ." 1 Stat. 132.

3 Article IV, §2, cl. 2 provides:

"A Person charged in any State with Treason, Felony, or other Crime, who shall flee from Justice, and be found in another State, shall on Demand of the executive Authority of the State from which he fled, be delivered up, to be removed to the State having Jurisdiction of the Crime."

To the extent the legislation went beyond the substantive requirement of this provision and specified procedures to be followed in complying with the constitutional obligation, we have found that that was an exercise of the congressional power to "prescribe the Manner in which such Acts, Records and Proceedings, shall be proved, and the Effect thereof," Art. IV, §1. See California v. Superior Court of Cal., San Bernardino Cty., 482 U.S. 400, 407 (1987).

4 Both the dissent and Justice Souter dispute that the consequences are said to flow automatically. They are wrong. The passage says that (1) federal laws will be supreme, and (2) all state officers will be oath bound to observe those laws, and thus (3) state officers will be "incorporated" and "rendered auxiliary." The reason the progression is automatic is that there is not included between (2) and (3): "(2a) those laws will include laws compelling action by state officers." It is the mere existence of all federal laws that is said to make state officers "incorporated" and "auxiliary."

5 Justice Souter seeks to avoid incompatibility with New York (a decision which he joined and purports to adhere to), by saying, post, at 3-4, that the passage does not mean "any conceivable requirement maybe imposed on any state official," and that "the essence of legislative power . . . is a discretion not subject to command," so that legislatures, at least, cannot be commanded. But then why were legislatures mentioned in the passage? It seems to us assuredly not a "natural reading" that being "rendered auxiliary to the enforcement of [the national government's] laws" means impressibility into federal service for "courts and magistrates" but something quite different for "legislatures." Moreover, the novel principle of political science that Justice Souter invokes in order to bring forth disparity of outcome from parity of language--namely, that "[t]he essence of legislative power . . . is a discretion not subject to command"--seems to

us untrue. Perhaps legislatures are inherently uncommandable as to the outcome of their legislation, but they are commanded all the time as to what subjects they shall legislate upon--commanded, that is, by the people, in constitutional provisions that require, for example, the enactment of annual budgets or forbid the enactment of laws permitting gambling. We do not think that state legislatures would be betraying their very "essence" as legislatures (as opposed to their nature as sovereigns, a nature they share with the other two branches of government) if they obeyed a federal command to enact laws, for example, criminalizing the sale of marijuana.

6 If Justice Souter finds these obligations too insignificant, see post, at 3, n. 1, then perhaps he should subscribe to the interpretations of "essential agency" given by Madison, see infra, at 15 andn. 8, or by Story, see infra, n. 9. The point is that there is no necessity to give the phrase the problematic meaning which alone enables him to use it as a basis for deciding this case.

7 Justice Souter deduces from this passage in No. 36 that although the Federal Government may commandeer state officers, it must compensate them for their services. This is a mighty leap, which would create a constitutional jurisprudence (for determining when the compensation was adequate) that would make takings cases appear clear and simple.

8 Justice Souter's discussion of this passage omits to mention that it contains an example of state executives' "essential agency"--and indeed implies the opposite by observing that "other numbers of the Federalist give examples" of the "essential agency" of state executive officers. Post, at 4 (emphasis added). In seeking to explain the curiousness of Madison's not mentioning the state executives' obligation to administer federal law, Justice Souter says that in speaking of "an essential agency in giving effect to the Federal Constitution," Federalist No. 44, Madison "was not talking about executing congressional statutes; he was talking about putting the National Constitution into effect," post, at 4, n. 2. Quite so, which is our very point.

It is interesting to observe that Story's Commentaries on the Constitution, commenting upon the same issue of why state officials are required by oath to support the Constitution, uses the same "essential agency" language as Madison did in Federalist No. 44, and goes on to give more numerous examples of state executive agency than Madison did; all of them, however, involve not state administration of federal law, but merely the implementation of duties imposed on state officers by the Constitution itself: "The executive authority of the several states may be often called upon to exert Powers or allow Rights given by the Constitution, as in filling vacancies in the senate during the recess of the leislature; in issuing writs of election to fill vacancies in the house of representatives; in officering the militia, and giving effect to laws for calling them; and in the surrender of fugitives from justice." 2 Story, Commentaries on the Constitution of the United States 577 (1851).

9 Even if we agreed with Justice Souter's reading of the Federalist No. 27, it would still seem to us most peculiar to give the view expressed in that one piece, not

clearly confirmed by any other writer, the determinative weight he does. That would be crediting the most expansive view of federal authority ever expressed, and from the pen of the most expansive expositor of federal power. Hamilton was "from first to last the most nationalistic of all nationalists in his interpretation of the clauses of our federal Constitution." C. Rossiter, Alexander Hamilton and the Constitution 199 (1964). More specifically, it is widely recognized that "The Federalist reads with a split personality" on matters of federalism. See D. Braveman, W. Banks, & R. Smolla, Constitutional Law: Structure and Rights in Our Federal System 198-199 (3d ed. 1996). While overall The Federalist reflects a "large area of agreement between Hamilton and Madison," Rossiter, supra, at 58, that is not the case with respect to the subject at hand, see Braveman, supra, at 198-199. To choose Hamilton's view, as Justice Souter would, is to turn a blind eye to the fact that it was Madison's--not Hamilton's--that prevailed, not only at the Constitutional Convention and in popular sentiment, see Rossiter, supra, at 44-47, 194, 196; 1 Records of the Federal Convention (M. Farrand ed. 1911) 366, but in the subsequent struggle to fix the meaning of the Constitution by early congressional practice, see supra, at 5-10.

10 The dissent, reiterating Justice Stevens' dissent in New York, 505 U. S., at 210-213, maintains that the Constitution merely augmented the pre-existing power under the Articles to issue commands to the States with the additional power to make demands directly on individuals. See post, at 7-8. That argument, however, was squarely rejected by the Court in New York, supra, at 161-166, and with good reason. Many of Congress's powers under Art. I, § 8, were copied almost verbatim from the Articles of Confederation, indicating quite clearly that "[w]here the Constitution intends that our Congress enjoy a power once vested in the Continental Congress, it specifically grants it." Prakash, Field Office Federalism, 79 Va. L. Rev. 1957, 1972 (1993).

11 Justice Breyer's dissent would have us consider the benefits that other countries, and the European Union, believe they have derived from federal systems that are different from ours. We think such comparative analysis inappropriate to the task of interpreting a constitution, though it was of course quite relevant to the task of writing one. The Framers were familiar with many federal systems, from classical antiquity down to their own time; they are discussed in Nos. 18-20 of The Federalist. Some were (for the purpose here under discussion) quite similar to the modern "federal" systems that Justice Breyer favors. Madison's and Hamilton's opinion of such systems could not be clearer. Federalist No. 20, after an extended critique of the system of government established by the Union of Utrecht for the United Netherlands, concludes:

"I make no apology for having dwelt so long on the contemplation of these federal precedents. Experience is the oracle of truth; and where its responses are unequivocal, they ought to be conclusive and sacred. The important truth, which it unequivocally pronounces in the present case, is that a sovereignty over sovereigns, a government over governments, a legislation for communities, as contra distinguished from individuals, as it is a solecism in theory, so in practice it is subversive of the order and ends of civil polity . . . ." Id., at 138.

Antifederalists, on the other hand, pointed specifically to Switzerland--and its then 400 years of success as a "confederate republic"--as proof that the proposed Constitution and its federal structure was unnecessary. See Patrick Henry, Speeches given before the Virginia Ratifying Convention, 4 and 5 June, 1788, reprinted in The Essential Antifederalist 123, 135-136 (W. Allen & G. Lloyd ed. 1985). The fact is that our federalism is not Europe's. It is "the unique contribution of the Framers to political science and political theory." United States v. Lopez, 514 U.S. 549, 575 (1995) (Kennedy, J., concurring) (citing Friendly, Federalism: A Forward, 86 Yale L. J. 1019 (1977)).

12 There is not, as the dissent believes, post, at 23, "tension" between the proposition that impressing state police officers into federal service will massively augment federal power, and the proposition that it will also sap the power of the Federal Presidency. It is quite possible to have a more powerful Federal Government that is, by reason of the destruction of its Executive unity, a less efficient one. The dissent is correct, post, at 24, that control by the unitary Federal Executive is also sacrificed when States voluntarily administer federal programs, but the condition of voluntary state participation significantly reduces the ability of Congress to use this device as a means of reducing the power of the Presidency.

13 This argument also falsely presumes that the Tenth Amendment is the exclusive textual source of protection for principles of federalism. Our system of dual sovereignty is reflected in numerous constitutional provisions, see supra, at 19-20, and not only those, like the Tenth Amendment, that speak to the point explicitly. It is not at all unusual for our resolution of a significant constitutional question to rest upon reasonable implications. See, e.g., Myers v. United States, 272 U.S. 52(1926) (finding by implication from Art. II, §§1, 2, that the President has the exclusive power to remove executive officers); Plaut v. Spendthrift Farm, Inc., 514 U.S. 211 (1995) (finding that Article III implies a lack of congressional power to set aside final judgments).

14 The dissent points out that FERC cannot be construed as merely following the principle recognized in Testa that state courts must apply relevant federal law because "[a]lthough the commission was serving an adjudicative function, the commissioners were unquestionably not `judges' within the meaning of [the Supremacy Clause]." Post, at 33. That is true enough. But the answer to the question of which state officers must apply federal law (only " `judges' within the meaning of [the Supremacy Clause]") is different from the answer to the question of which state officers may be required by statute to apply federal law (officers who conduct adjudications similar to those traditionally performed by judges). It is within the power of the States, as it is within the power of the Federal Government, see Crowell v. Benson, 285 U.S. 22 (1932), to transfer some adjudicatory functions to administrative agencies, with opportunity for subsequent judicial review. But it is also within the power of Congress to prescribe, explicitly or by implication (as in the legislation at issue in FERC), that those adjudications must take

account of federal law. The existence of this latter power should not be unacceptable to a dissent that believes distinguishing among officers on the basis of their title rather than the function they perform is "empty formalistic reasoning of the highest order," post, at 15. We have no doubt that FERC would not have been decided the way it was if nonadjudicative responsibilities of the state agency were at issue.

15 Contrary to the dissent's suggestion, post, at 18-19, n. 16, and 29, the distinction in our Eleventh Amendment jurisprudence between States and municipalities is of no relevance here. We long ago made clear that the distinction is peculiar to the question of whether a governmental entity is entitled to Eleventh Amendment sovereign immunity, see Monell v. New York City Dept. of Social Servs., 436 U.S. 658, 690, n. 55 (1978); we have refused to apply it to the question of whether a governmental entity is protected by the Constitution's guarantees of federalism, including the Tenth Amendment, see National League of Cities v. Ursery, 426 U.S. 833, 855-856, n. 20 (1976) (overruled on other grounds by Garcia v. San Antonio Metropolitan Transit Authority, 469 U.S. 528 (1985)); see also Garcia, supra (resolving Tenth Amendment issues in suit brought by local transit authority).

16 The dissent's suggestion, post, at 28-29, n. 27, that New York v. United States, 505 U.S. 144 (1992), itself embraced the distinction between congressional control of States (impermissible) and congressional control of state officers (permissible) is based upon the most egregious wrenching of statements out of context. It would take too much to reconstruct the context here, but by examining the entire passage cited, id., at 178-179, the reader will readily perceive the distortion. The passage includes, for example, the following:

"Additional cases cited by the United States discuss the power of federal courts to order state officials to comply with federal law. . . . Again, however, the text of the Constitution plainly confers this authority on the federal courts . . . . The Constitution contains no analogous grant of authority to Congress." Id., at 179.

17 The dissent observes that "Congress could require private persons, such as hospital executives or school administrators, to provide arms merchants with relevant information about a prospective purchaser's fitness to own a weapon," and that "the burden on police officers [imposed by the Brady Act] would be permissible if a similar burden were also imposed on private parties with access to relevant data." Post, at 25. That is undoubtedly true, but it does not advance the dissent's case. The Brady Act does not merely require CLEOs to report information in their private possession. It requires them to provide information that belongs to the State and is available to them only in their official capacity; and to conduct investigation in their official capacity, by examining databases and records that only state officials have access to. In other words, the suggestion that extension of this statute to private citizens would eliminate the constitutional problem posits the impossible.

18 We note, in this regard, that both CLEOs before us here assert that they are prohibited from taking on these federal responsibilities under state law. That assertion is

clearly correct with regard to Montana law, which expressly enjoins any "county . . . or other local government unit" from "prohibit[ing] . . . or regulat[ing] the purchase, sale or other transfer (including delay in purchase, sale, or other transfer), ownership, [or] possession . . . of any . . . handgun," Mont. Code §45-8-351(1) (1995). It is arguably correct with regard to Arizona law as well, which states that "[a] political subdivision of this state shall not . . . prohibit the ownership, purchase, sale or transfer of firearms," Ariz. Rev. Stat. §13-3108(B) (1989). We need not resolve that question today; it is at least clear that Montana and Arizona do not require their CLEOs to implement the Brady Act, and CLEOs Printz and Mack have chosen not to do so.

Non-party members can't vote in party primaries for the person to represent the party: California Democratic Party v. Jones (June 26, 2000)

Justice Scalia delivered the opinion of the Court.

This case presents the question whether the State of California may, consistent with the First Amendment to the United States Constitution, use a so-called "blanket" primary to determine a political party's nominee for the general election.

I

Under California law, a candidate for public office has two routes to gain access to the general ballot for most state and federal elective offices. He may receive the nomination of a qualified political party by winning its primary, [n1] see Cal. Elec. Code Ann. §§15451, 13105(a) (West 1996); or he may file as an independent by obtaining (for a statewide race) the signatures of one percent of the State's electorate or (for other races) the signatures of three percent of the voting population of the area represented by the office in contest, see §8400.

Until 1996, to determine the nominees of qualified parties California held what is known as a "closed" partisan primary, in which only persons who are members of the political party-i.e., who have declared affiliation with that party when they register to vote, see Cal. Elec. Code Ann. §§2150, 2151 (West 1996 and Supp. 2000)-can vote on its nominee, see Cal. Elec. Code Ann. §2151 (West 1996). In 1996 the citizens of California adopted by initiative Proposition 198. Promoted largely as a measure that would "weaken" party "hard-liners" and ease the way for "moderate problem-solvers," App. 89-90 (reproducing ballot pamphlet distributed to voters), Proposition 198 changed California's partisan primary from a closed primary to a blanket primary. Under the new system, "[a]ll persons entitled to vote, including those not affiliated with any political party, shall have the right to vote ... for any candidate regardless of the candidate's political affiliation." Cal. Elec. Code Ann. §2001 (West Supp. 2000); see also §2151. Whereas under the closed primary each voter received a ballot limited to candidates of his own party, as a result of Proposition 198 each voter's primary ballot now lists every candidate regardless of party affiliation and allows the voter to choose freely among them.

It remains the case, however, that the candidate of each party who wins the greatest number of votes "is the nominee of that party at the ensuing general election." Cal. Elec. Code Ann. §15451 (West 1996). [n2]

Petitioners in this case are four political parties-the California Democratic Party, the California Republican Party, the Libertarian Party of California, and the Peace and Freedom Party-each of which has a rule prohibiting persons not members of the party from voting in the party's primary. [n3] Petitioners brought suit in the United States District Court for the Eastern District of California against respondent California Secretary of State, alleging, inter alia, that California's blanket primary violated their First Amendment rights of association, and seeking declaratory and injunctive relief. The group Californians for an Open Primary, also respondent, intervened as a party defendant. The District Court recognized that the new law would inject into each party's primary substantial numbers of voters unaffiliated with the party. 984 F. Supp. 1288, 1298-1299 (1997). It further recognized that this might result in selection of a nominee different from the one party members would select, or at the least cause the same nominee to commit himself to different positions. Id., at 1299. Nevertheless, the District Court held that the burden on petitioners' rights of association was not a severe one, and was justified by state interests ultimately reducing to this: "enhanc[ing] the democratic nature of the election process and the representativeness of elected officials." Id., at 1301. The Ninth Circuit, adopting the District Court's opinion as its own, affirmed. 169 F.3d 646 (1999). We granted certiorari. 528 U.S. 1133 (2000).

II

Respondents rest their defense of the blanket primary upon the proposition that primaries play an integral role in citizens' selection of public officials. As a consequence, they contend, primaries are public rather than private proceedings, and the States may and must play a role in ensuring that they serve the public interest. Proposition 198, respondents conclude, is simply a rather pedestrian example of a State's regulating its system of elections.

We have recognized, of course, that States have a major role to play in structuring and monitoring the election process, including primaries. See Burdick v. Takushi, 504 U.S. 428, 433 (1992); Tashjian v. Republican Party of Conn., 479 U.S. 208, 217 (1986). We have considered it "too plain for argument," for example, that a State may require parties to use the primary format for selecting their nominees, in order to assure that intraparty competition is resolved in a democratic fashion. American Party of Tex. v. White, 415 U.S. 767, 781 (1974); see also Tashjian, supra, at 237 (Scalia, J., dissenting). Similarly, in order to avoid burdening the general election ballot with frivolous candidacies, a State may require parties to demonstrate "a significant modicum of support" before allowing their candidates a place on that ballot. See Jenness v. Fortson, 403 U.S. 431, 442 (1971). Finally, in order to prevent "party raiding"-a process in which dedicated members of one party formally switch to another party to alter the outcome of that party's primary-a State may require party registration a reasonable period of time before a primary election. See Rosario v. Rockefeller, 410 U.S. 752 (1973). Cf. Kusper v. Pontikes, 414 U.S. 51 (1973) (23-month waiting period unreasonable).

What we have not held, however, is that the processes by which political parties select their nominees are, as respondents would have it, wholly public affairs that States may regulate freely. [n4] To the contrary, we have continually stressed that when States regulate parties' internal processes they must act within limits imposed by the Constitution. See, e.g., Eu v. San Francisco County Democratic Central Comm., 489 U.S. 214 (1989); Democratic Party of United States v. Wisconsin ex rel. La Follette, 450 U.S. 107 (1981). In this regard, respondents' reliance on Smith v. Allwright, 321 U.S. 649"] 321 U.S. 649 (1944), and Terry v. Adams, 345 U.S. 461 (1953), is misplaced. In Allwright, we invalidated the Texas Democratic Party's rule limiting participation in its primary to whites; in Terry, we invalidated the same rule promulgated by the Jaybird Democratic Association, a "self-governing voluntary club," 345 U.S., at 463. These cases held only that, when a State prescribes an election process that gives a special role to political parties, it "endorses, adopts and enforces the discrimination against Negroes," that the parties (or, in the case of the Jaybird Democratic Association, organizations that are "part and parcel" of the parties, see id., at 482 (Clark, J., concurring)) bring into the process-so that the parties' discriminatory action becomes state action under the Fifteenth Amendment. Allwright, supra, at 664; see also Terry, 345 U.S., at 484 (Clark, J., concurring); id., at 469 (opinion of Black, J.). They do not stand for the proposition that party affairs are public affairs, free of First Amendment protections-and our later holdings make that entirely clear. [n5] 321 U.S. 649 (1944), and Terry v. Adams, 345 U.S. 461 (1953), is misplaced. In Allwright, we invalidated the Texas Democratic Party's rule limiting participation in its primary to whites; in Terry, we invalidated the same rule promulgated by the Jaybird Democratic Association, a "self-governing voluntary club," 345 U.S., at 463. These cases held only that, when a State prescribes an election process that gives a special role to political parties, it "endorses, adopts and enforces the discrimination against Negroes," that the parties (or, in the case of the Jaybird Democratic Association, organizations that are "part and parcel" of the parties, see id., at 482 (Clark, J., concurring)) bring into the process-so that the parties' discriminatory action becomes state action under the Fifteenth Amendment. Allwright, supra, at 664; see also Terry, 345 U.S., at 484 (Clark, J., concurring); id., at 469 (opinion of Black, J.). They do not stand for the proposition that party affairs are public affairs, free of First Amendment protections-and our later holdings make that entirely clear. [n5] See, e.g., Tashjian, supra.

Representative democracy in any populous unit of governance is unimaginable without the ability of citizens to band together in promoting among the electorate candidates who espouse their political views. The formation of national political parties was almost concurrent with the formation of the Republic itself. See Cunningham, The Jeffersonian Republican Party, in 1 History of U.S. Political Parties 239, 241 (A. Schlesinger ed., 1973). Consistent with this tradition, the Court has recognized that the

First Amendment protects "the freedom to join together in furtherance of common political beliefs," Tashjian, supra, at 214-215, which "necessarily presupposes the freedom to identify the people who constitute the association, and to limit the association to those people only," La Follette, 450 U.S., at 122. That is to say, a corollary of the right to associate is the right not to associate. " 'Freedom of association would prove an empty guarantee if associations could not limit control over their decisions to those who share the interests and persuasions that underlie the association's being.' " Id., at 122, n. 22 (quoting L. Tribe, American Constitutional Law 791 (1978)). See also Roberts v. United States Jaycees, 468 U.S. 609, 623 (1984).

In no area is the political association's right to exclude more important than in the process of selecting its nominee. That process often determines the party's positions on the most significant public policy issues of the day, and even when those positions are predetermined it is the nominee who becomes the party's ambassador to the general electorate in winning it over to the party's views. See Timmons v. Twin Cities Area New Party, 520 U.S. 351, 372 (1997) (Stevens, J., dissenting) ("But a party's choice of a candidate is the most effective way in which that party can communicate to the voters what the party represents and, thereby, attract voter interest and support"). Some political parties-such as President Theodore Roosevelt's Bull Moose Party, the La Follette Progressives of 1924, the Henry Wallace Progressives of 1948, and the George Wallace American Independent Party of 1968-are virtually inseparable from their nominees (and tend not to outlast them). See generally E. Kruschke, Encyclopedia of Third Parties in the United States (1991).

Unsurprisingly, our cases vigorously affirm the special place the First Amendment reserves for, and the special protection it accords, the process by which a political party "select[s] a standard bearer who best represents the party's ideologies and preferences." Eu, supra, at 224 (internal quotation marks omitted). The moment of choosing the party's nominee, we have said, is "the crucial juncture at which the appeal to common principles may be translated into concerted action, and hence to political power in the community." Tashjian, 479 U.S., at 216; see also id., at 235-236 (Scalia, J., dissenting) ("The ability of the members of the Republican Party to select their own candidate ... unquestionably implicates an associational freedom"); Timmons, 520 U.S., at 359 ("[T]he New Party, and not someone else, has the right to select the New Party's standard bearer" (internal quotation marks omitted)); id., at 371 (Stevens, J., dissenting) ("The members of a recognized political party unquestionably have a constitutional right to select their nominees for public office").

In La Follette, the State of Wisconsin conducted an open presidential preference primary. [n6] Although the voters did not select the delegates to the Democratic Party's National Convention directly-they were chosen later at caucuses of party members-Wisconsin law required these delegates to vote in accord with the primary results. Thus allowing nonparty members to participate in the selection of the party's nominee conflicted with the Democratic Party's rules. We held that, whatever the strength of the state interests supporting the open primary itself, they could not justify this "substantial intrusion into the associational freedom of members of the National Party." [n7] 450 U.S., at 126.

California's blanket primary violates the principles set forth in these cases. Proposition 198 forces political parties to associate with-to have their nominees, and hence their positions, determined by-those who, at best, have refused to affiliate with the party, and, at worst, have expressly affiliated with a rival. In this respect, it is qualitatively different from a closed primary. Under that system, even when it is made quite easy for a voter to change his party affiliation the day of the primary, and thus, in some sense, to "cross over," at least he must formally become a member of the party; and once he does so, he is limited to voting for candidates of that party. [n8]

The evidence in this case demonstrates that under California's blanket primary system, the prospect of having a party's nominee determined by adherents of an opposing party is far from remote-indeed, it is a clear and present danger. For example, in one 1997 survey of California voters 37 percent of Republicans said that they planned to vote in the 1998 Democratic gubernatorial primary, and 20 percent of Democrats said they planned to vote in the 1998 Republican United States Senate primary. Tr. 668-669. Those figures are comparable to the results of studies in other States with blanket primaries. One expert testified, for example, that in Washington the number of voters crossing over from one party to another can rise to as high as 25 percent, id., at 511, and another that only 25 to 33 percent of all Washington voters limit themselves to candidates of one party throughout the ballot, App. 136. The impact of voting by nonparty members is much greater upon minor parties, such as the Libertarian Party and the Peace and Freedom Party. In the first primaries these parties conducted following California's implementation of Proposition 198, the total votes cast for party candidates in some races was more than double the total number of registered party members. California Secretary of State, Statement of Vote, Primary Election, June 2, 1998, http://primary98.ss.ca.gov/Final/

Official_Results.htm; California Secretary of State, Re-port of Registration, May 1998, http://www.ss.ca.gov/elections/elections_u.htm.

The record also supports the obvious proposition that these substantial numbers of voters who help select the nominees of parties they have chosen not to join often have policy views that diverge from those of the party faithful. The 1997 survey of California voters revealed significantly different policy preferences between party members and primary voters who "crossed over" from another party. Pl. Exh. 8 (Addendum to Mervin Field Report). One expert went so far as to describe it as "inevitable [under Proposition 198] that parties will be forced in some circumstances to give their official designation to a candidate who's not preferred by a majority or even plurality of party members." Tr. 421 (expert testimony of Bruce Cain).

In concluding that the burden Proposition 198 imposes on petitioners' rights of association is not severe, the Ninth Circuit cited testimony that the prospect of malicious crossover voting, or raiding, is slight, and that even though the numbers of "benevolent" crossover voters were significant, they would be determinative in only a small number of races. [n9] 169 F.3d, at 656-657. But a single election in which the party nominee is selected by nonparty members could be enough to destroy the party. In the 1860 presidential election, if opponents of the fledgling Republican Party had been able to cause its nomination of a pro-slavery candidate in place of Abraham Lincoln, the coalition of intraparty factions forming behind him likely would have disintegrated, endangering the party's survival and thwarting its effort to fill the vacuum left by the dissolution of the Whigs. See generally, 1 Political Parties & Elections in the United States: An Encyclopedia 398-408, 587 (L. Maisel ed. 1991). Ordinarily, however, being saddled with an unwanted, and possibly antithetical, nominee would not destroy the party but severely transform it. "[R]egulating the identity of the parties' leaders," we have said, "may ... color the parties' message and interfere with the parties' decisions as to the best means to promote that message." Eu, 489 U.S., at 231, n. 21.

In any event, the deleterious effects of Proposition 198 are not limited to altering the identity of the nominee. Even when the person favored by a majority of the party members prevails, he will have prevailed by taking somewhat different positions-and, should he be elected, will continue to take somewhat different positions in order to be renominated. As respondents' own expert concluded, "[t]he policy positions of Members of Congress elected from blanket primary states are ... more moderate, both in an absolute sense and relative to the other party, and so are more reflective of the preferences of the mass of voters at the center of the ideological spectrum." App. 109 (expert report of Elisabeth R. Gerber). It is unnecessary to cumulate evidence of this phenomenon, since, after all, the whole purpose of Proposition 198 was to favor nominees with "moderate" positions. Id., at 89. It encourages candidates-and officeholders who hope to be renominated-to curry favor with persons whose views are more "centrist" than those of the party base. In effect, Proposition 198 has simply moved the general election one step earlier in the process, at the expense of the parties' ability to perform the "basic function" of choosing their own leaders. Kusper, 414 U.S., at 58.

Nor can we accept the Court of Appeals' contention that the burden imposed by Proposition 198 is minor because petitioners are free to endorse and financially support the candidate of their choice in the primary. 169 F.3d, at 659. The ability of the party leadership to endorse a candidate is simply no substitute for the party members' ability to choose their own nominee. In Eu, we recognized that party-leadership endorsements are not always effective-for instance, in New York's 1982 gubernatorial primary, Edward Koch, the Democratic Party leadership's choice, lost out to Mario Cuomo. 489 U.S., at 228, n. 18. One study has concluded, moreover, that even when the leadership-endorsed candidate has won, the effect of the endorsement has been negligible. Ibid. (citing App. in Eu v. San Francisco County Democratic Central Comm., O. T. 1988, No. 87-1269, pp. 97-98). New York's was a closed primary; one would expect leadership endorsement to be even less effective in a blanket primary, where many of the voters are unconnected not only to the party leadership but even to the party itself. In any event, the ability of the party leadership to endorse a candidate does not assist the party rank and file, who may not themselves agree with the party leadership, but do not want the party's choice decided by outsiders.

We are similarly unconvinced by respondents' claim that the burden is not severe because Proposition 198 does not limit the parties from engaging fully in other traditional party behavior, such as ensuring orderly internal party governance, maintaining party discipline in the legislature, and conducting campaigns. The accuracy of this assertion is highly questionable, at least as to the first two activities. That party nominees will be equally observant of internal party procedures and equally respectful of party discipline when their nomination depends on the general electorate rather than on the party faithful seems to us improbable. Respondents themselves suggest as much when they assert that the blanket primary system " 'will lead to the election of more representative 'problem solvers' who are less beholden to party officials.' " Brief for Respondents 41 (emphasis added) (quoting 169 F.3d, at 661). In the end, however, the effect of Proposition 198 on these other activities is beside the point. We have consistently refused to overlook an unconstitutional restriction upon some First Amendment activity simply because it leaves other First Amendment activity unimpaired. See, e.g., Spence v. Washington, 418 U.S. 405, 411, n. 4 (1974) (per curiam); Kusper, 414 U.S., at 58. There is simply no substitute for a party's selecting its own candidates.

In sum, Proposition 198 forces petitioners to adulterate their candidate-selection process-the "basic function of a political party," ibid.-by opening it up to persons wholly unaffiliated with the party. Such forced association has the likely outcome-indeed, in this case the intended outcome-of changing the parties' message. We can think of no heavier burden on a political party's associational freedom. Proposition 198 is therefore unconstitutional unless it is narrowly tailored to serve a compelling state interest. See Timmons, 520 U.S., at 358 ("Regulations imposing severe burdens on [parties'] rights must be narrowly tailored and advance a compelling state interest"). It is to that question which we now turn.

III

Respondents proffer seven state interests they claim are compelling. Two of them-producing elected officials who better represent the electorate and expanding candidate debate beyond the scope of partisan concerns-are simply circumlocution for producing nominees and nominee positions other than those the parties would choose if left to their own devices. Indeed, respondents admit as much. For instance, in substantiating their interest in "representativeness," respondents point to the fact that "officials elected under blanket primaries stand closer to the median policy positions of their districts" than do those selected only by party members. Brief for Respondents 40. And in explaining their desire to increase debate, respondents claim that a blanket primary forces parties to reconsider long standing positions since it "compels [their] candidates to appeal to a larger segment of the electorate." Id., at 46. Both of these supposed interests, therefore, reduce to nothing more than a stark repudiation of freedom of political association: Parties should not be free to select their own nominees because those nominees, and the positions taken by those nominees, will not be congenial to the majority.

We have recognized the inadmissibility of this sort of "interest" before. In Hurley v. Irish-American Gay, Lesbian and Bisexual Group of Boston, Inc., 515 U.S. 557 (1995), the South Boston Allied War Veterans Council refused to allow an organization of openly gay, lesbian, and bisexual persons (GLIB) to participate in the council's annual St. Patrick's Day parade. GLIB sued the council under Massachusetts' public accommodation law, claiming that the council impermissibly denied them access on account of their sexual orientation. After noting that parades are expressive endeavors, we rejected GLIB's contention that Massachusetts' public accommodation law overrode the council's right to choose the content of its own message. Applying the law in such circumstances, we held, made apparent that its "object [was] simply to require speakers to modify the content of their expression to whatever extent beneficiaries of the law choose to alter it with messages of their own. ... [I]n the absence of some further, legitimate end, this object is merely to allow exactly what the general rule of speaker's autonomy forbids." Id., at 578.

Respondents' third asserted compelling interest is that the blanket primary is the only way to ensure that disenfranchised persons enjoy the right to an effective vote. By "disenfranchised," respondents do not mean those who cannot vote; they mean simply independents and members of the minority party in "safe" districts. These persons are disenfranchised, according to respondents, because under a closed primary they are unable to participate in what amounts to the determinative election-the majority party's primary; the only way to ensure they have an "effective" vote is to force the party to open its primary to them. This also appears to be nothing more than reformulation of an asserted state interest we have already rejected-recharacterizing nonparty members' keen desire to participate in selection of the party's nominee as "disenfranchisement" if that desire is not fulfilled. We have said, however, that a "nonmember's desire to participate in the party's affairs is overborne by the countervailing and legitimate right of the party to determine its own membership qualifications." Tashjian, 479 U.S., at 215-216, n. 6 (citing Rosario v. Rockefeller, 410 U.S. 752 (1973), and Nader v. Schaffer, 417 F. Supp. 837 (Conn.), summarily aff'd, 429 U.S. 989 (1976)). The voter's desire to participate does not become more weighty simply because the State supports it. Moreover, even if it were accurate to describe the plight of the non-party-member in a safe district as "disenfranchisement," Proposition 198 is not needed to solve the problem. The voter who feels himself disenfranchised should simply join the party. That may put him to a hard choice, but it is not a state-imposed restriction upon his freedom of association, whereas compelling party members to accept his selection of their nominee is a state-imposed restriction upon theirs.

Respondents' remaining four asserted state interests-promoting fairness, affording voters greater choice, increasing voter participation, and protecting privacy-are not, like the others, automatically out of the running; but neither are they, in the circumstances of this case, compelling. That determination is not to be made in the abstract, by asking whether fairness, privacy, etc., are highly significant values; but rather by asking whether the aspect of fairness, privacy, etc., addressed by the law at issue is highly significant. And for all four of these asserted interests, we find it not to be.

The aspect of fairness addressed by Proposition 198 is presumably the supposed inequity of not permitting nonparty members in "safe" districts to determine the party nominee. If that is unfair at all (rather than merely a consequence of the eminently democratic principle that-except where constitutional imperatives intervene-the majority rules), it seems to us less unfair than permitting nonparty members to hijack the party. As for affording voters greater choice, it is obvious that the net effect of this scheme-indeed, its avowed purpose-is to reduce the scope of choice, by assuring a range of candidates who are all more "centrist." This may well be described as broadening the range of choices favored by the majority-but that is hardly a compelling state interest, if indeed it is even a legitimate one. The interest in increasing voter participation is just a variation on the same theme (more choices favored by the majority will produce more voters), and suffers from the same defect. As for the protection of privacy: The specific privacy interest at issue is not the confidentiality of medical records or personal finances, but confidentiality of one's party affiliation. Even if (as seems unlikely) a scheme for administering a closed primary could not be devised in which the voter's declaration of party affiliation would not be public information, we do not think that the State's interest in assuring the privacy of this piece of information in all cases can conceivably be considered a "compelling" one. If such information were generally so sacrosanct, federal statutes would not require a declaration of party affiliation as a condition of appointment to certain offices. See, e.g., 47 U.S.C. § 154(b)(5) ("[M]aximum number of commissioners [of the Federal Communications Commission] who may be members of the same political party shall be a number equal to the least number of commissioners which constitutes a majority of the full membership of the Commission"); 47 U.S.C. § 396(c)(1) (1994 ed., Supp. III) (no more than five members of Board of Directors of Corporation for Public Broadcasting may be of same party); 42 U.S.C. § 2000e-4(a) (no more than three members of Equal Employment Opportunity Commission may be of same party).

Finally, we may observe that even if all these state interests were compelling ones, Proposition 198 is not a narrowly tailored means of furthering them. Respondents could protect them all by resorting to a nonpartisan blanket primary. Generally speaking, under such a system, the State determines what qualifications it requires for a candidate to have a place on the primary ballot-which may include nomination by established parties and voter-petition requirements for independent candidates. Each voter, regardless of party affiliation, may then vote for any candidate, and the top two vote getters (or however many the State prescribes) then move on to the general election. This system has all the characteristics of the partisan blanket primary, save the constitutionally crucial one: Primary voters are not choosing a party's nominee. Under a nonpartisan blanket primary, a State may ensure more choice, greater participation, increased "privacy," and a sense of "fairness"-all without severely burdening a political party's First Amendment right of association.

* * *

Respondents' legitimate state interests and petitioners' First Amendment rights are not inherently incompatible. To the extent they are in this case, the State of California has made them so by forcing political parties to associate with those who do not share their beliefs. And it has done this at the "crucial juncture" at which party members traditionally find their collective voice and select their spokesman. Tashjian, 479 U.S., at 216. The burden Proposition 198 places on petitioners' rights of political association is both severe and unnecessary. The judgment for the Court of Appeals for the Ninth Circuit is reversed.

It is so ordered.

Notes to California Democratic Party v. Jones (June 26, 2000)

1. A party is qualified if it meets one of three conditions: (1) in the last gubernatorial election, one of its statewide candidates polled at least two percent of the statewide vote; (2) the party's membership is at least one percent of the statewide vote at the last preceding gubernatorial election; or (3) voters numbering at least 10 percent of the statewide vote at the last gubernatorial election sign a petition stating that they intend to form a new party. See Cal. Elec. Code Ann. §5100 (West 1996 and Supp. 2000).

2. California's new blanket primary system does not apply directly to the apportionment of presidential delegates. See Cal. Elec. Code Ann. §§15151, 15375, 15500 (West Supp. 2000). Instead, the State tabulates the presidential primary in two ways: according to the number of votes each candidate received from the entire voter pool and according to the amount each received from members of his own party. The national parties may then use the latter figure to apportion delegates. Nor does it apply to the election of political party central or district committee members; only party members may vote in these elections. See Cal. Elec. Code Ann. §2151 (West 1996 and Supp. 2000).

3. Each of the four parties was qualified under California law when they filed this suit. Since that time, the Peace and Freedom Party has apparently lost its qualified status. See Brief for Petitioners 16 (citing Child of the '60s Slips, Los Angeles Times, Feb. 17, 1999, p. B-6).

4. On this point, the dissent shares respondents' view, at least where the selection process is a state-run election. The right not to associate, it says, "is simply inapplicable to participation in a state election." "[A]n election, unlike a convention or caucus, is a public affair." Post, at 6 (opinion of Stevens, J.). Of course it is, but when the election determines a party's nominee it is a party affair as well, and, as the cases to be discussed in text demonstrate, the constitutional rights of those composing the party cannot be disregarded.

5. The dissent is therefore wrong to conclude that Allwright and Terry demonstrate that "[t]he protections that the First Amendment affords to the internal processes of a political party do not encompass a right to exclude nonmembers from voting in a state-required, state-financed primary election." Post, at 6 (internal quotation marks and citation omitted). Those cases simply prevent exclusion that violates some independent constitutional proscription. The closest the dissent comes to identifying such a proscription in this case is its reference to "the First Amendment associational interests" of citizens to participate in the primary of a party to which they do not belong, and the "fundamental right" of citizens "to cast a meaningful vote for the candidate of their choice." Post, at 13. As to the latter: Selecting a candidate is quite different from voting for the candidate of one's choice. If the "fundamental right" to cast a meaningful vote were really at issue in this context, Proposition 198 would be not only constitutionally permissible but constitutionally required, which no one believes. As for the associational "interest" in selecting the candidate of a group to which one does not belong, that falls far short of a constitutional right, if indeed it can even fairly be characterized as an interest. It has been described in our cases as a "desire"-and rejected as a basis for disregarding the First Amendment right to exclude. See infra, at 16.

6. An open primary differs from a blanket primary in that, although as in the blanket primary any person, regardless of party affiliation, may vote for a party's nominee, his choice is limited to that party's nominees for all offices. He may not, for example, support a Republican nominee for Governor and a Democratic nominee for attorney general.

7. The dissent, in attempting to fashion its new rule-that the right not to associate does not exist with respect to primary elections, see post, at 6-rewrites Democratic Party of United States v. Wisconsin ex rel. La Follette, 450 U.S. 107 (1981), to stand merely for the proposition that a political party has a First Amendment right to "defin[e] the organization and composition of its governing units," post, at 3. In fact, however, the state-imposed burden at issue in La Follette was the " 'intrusion by those with adverse political principles' " upon the selection of the party's nominee (in that case its presidential nominee). 450 U.S., at 122 (quoting Ray v. Blair, 343 U.S. 154, 221-222 (1952) (per curiam)). See also 450 U.S., at 125 (comparing asserted state interests with burden created by the "imposition of voting requirements upon" delegates). Of course La Follette involved the burden a state regulation imposed on a national party, but that factor affected only the weight of the State's interest, and had no bearing upon the existence vel non of a party's First Amendment right to exclude. 450 U.S., at 121-122, 125-126. Although Justice Stevens now considers this interpretation of La Follette "specious", see post, at 4, n. 3, he once subscribed to it himself. His dissent from the order dismissing the appeals in Bellotti v. Connolly described La Follette thusly: "There this Court rejected Wisconsin's requirement that delegates to the party's Presidential nominating convention, selected in a primary open to nonparty voters, must cast their convention votes in accordance with the primary election results. In our view, the interests advanced

by the State ... did not justify its substantial intrusion into the associational freedom of members of the National Party... . Wisconsin required convention delegates to cast their votes for candidates who might have drawn their support from nonparty members. The results of the party's decisionmaking process might thereby have been distorted." 460 U.S. 1057, 1062-1063 (1983) (emphasis in original). Not only does the dissent's principle of no right to exclude conflict with our precedents, but it also leads to nonsensical results. In Tashjian v. Republican Party of Conn., 479 U.S. 208 (1986), we held that the First Amendment protects a party's right to invite independents to participate in the primary. Combining Tashjian with the dissent's rule affirms a party's constitutional right to allow outsiders to select its candidates, but denies a party's constitutional right to reserve candidate selection to its own members. The First Amendment would thus guarantee a party's right to lose its identity, but not to preserve it.

8. In this sense, the blanket primary also may be constitutionally distinct from the open primary, see n. 6, supra, in which the voter is limited to one party's ballot. See La Follette, supra, at 130, n. 2 (Powell, J., dissenting) ("[T]he act of voting in the Democratic primary fairly can be described as an act of affiliation with the Democratic Party... . The situation might be different in those States with 'blanket' primaries-i.e., those where voters are allowed to participate in the primaries of more than one party on a single occasion, selecting the primary they wish to vote in with respect to each individual elective office"). This case does not require us to determine the constitutionality of open primaries.

9. The Ninth Circuit defined a crossover voter as one "who votes for a candidate of a party in which the voter is not registered. Thus, the cross-over voter could be an independent voter or one who is registered to a competing political party." 169 F.3d 646, 656 (1999).

No Thermal-Imaging (heat-sensing) without warrant: Kyllo v. United States (June 11, 2001)

Justice Scalia delivered the opinion of the Court.
This case presents the question whether the use of a thermal-imaging device aimed at a private home from a public street to detect relative amounts of heat within the home constitutes a "search" within the meaning of the Fourth Amendment.

I

In 1991 Agent William Elliott of the United States Department of the Interior came to suspect that marijuana was being grown in the home belonging to petitioner Danny Kyllo, part of a triplex on Rhododendron Drive in Florence, Oregon. Indoor marijuana growth typically requires high-intensity lamps. In order to determine whether an amount of heat was emanating from petitioner's home consistent with the use of such lamps, at 3:20 a.m. on January 16, 1992, Agent Elliott and Dan Haas used an Agema

Thermovision 210 thermal imager to scan the triplex. Thermal imagers detect infrared radiation, which virtually all objects emit but which is not visible to the naked eye. The imager converts radiation into images based on relative warmth—black is cool, white is hot, shades of gray connote relative differences; in that respect, it operates somewhat like a video camera showing heat images. The scan of Kyllo's home took only a few minutes and was performed from the passenger seat of Agent Elliott's vehicle across the street from the front of the house and also from the street in back of the house. The scan showed that the roof over the garage and a side wall of petitioner's home were relatively hot compared to the rest of the home and substantially warmer than neighboring homes in the triplex. Agent Elliott concluded that petitioner was using halide lights to grow marijuana in his house, which indeed he was. Based on tips from informants, utility bills, and the thermal imaging, a Federal Magistrate Judge issued a warrant authorizing a search of petitioner's home, and the agents found an indoor growing operation involving more than 100 plants. Petitioner was indicted on one count of manufacturing marijuana, in violation of 21 U.S.C. § 841(a)(1). He unsuccessfully moved to suppress the evidence seized from his home and then entered a conditional guilty plea.

The Court of Appeals for the Ninth Circuit remanded the case for an evidentiary hearing regarding the intrusiveness of thermal imaging. On remand the District Court found that the Agema 210 "is a non-intrusive device which emits no rays or beams and shows a crude visual image of the heat being radiated from the outside of the house"; it "did not show any people or activity within the walls of the structure"; "[t]he device used cannot penetrate walls or windows to reveal conversations or human activities"; and "[n]o intimate details of the home were observed." Supp. App. to Pet. for Cert. 39—40. Based on these findings, the District Court upheld the validity of the warrant that relied in part upon the thermal imaging, and reaffirmed its denial of the motion to suppress. A divided Court of Appeals initially reversed, 140 F.3d 1249 (1998), but that opinion was withdrawn and the panel (after a change in composition) affirmed, 190 F.3d 1041 (1999), with Judge Noonan dissenting. The court held that petitioner had shown no subjective expectation of privacy because he had made no attempt to conceal the heat escaping from his home, id., at 1046, and even if he had, there was no objectively reasonable expectation of privacy because the imager "did not expose any intimate details of Kyllo's life," only "amorphous 'hot spots' on the roof and exterior wall," id., at 1047. We granted certiorari. 530 U.S. 1305 (2000).

II

The Fourth Amendment provides that "[t]he right of the people to be secure in their persons, houses, papers, and effects, against unreasonable searches and seizures, shall not be violated." "At the very core" of the Fourth Amendment "stands the right of a man to retreat into his own home and there be free from unreasonable governmental intrusion." Silverman v. United States, 365 U.S. 505, 511 (1961). With few exceptions, the question whether a warrantless search of a home is reasonable and hence constitutional must be answered no. See Illinois v. Rodriguez, 497 U.S. 177, 181 (1990); Payton v. New York, 445 U.S. 573, 586 (1980).

On the other hand, the antecedent question of whether or not a Fourth Amendment "search" has occurred is not so simple under our precedent. The permissibility of ordinary visual surveillance of a home used to be clear because, well into the 20th century, our Fourth Amendment jurisprudence was tied to common-law trespass. See, e.g., Goldman v. United States, 316 U.S. 129, 134–136 (1942); Olmstead v. United States, 277 U.S. 438,

464–466 (1928). Cf. Silverman v. United States, supra, at 510–512 (technical trespass not necessary for Fourth Amendment violation; it suffices if there is "actual intrusion into a constitutionally protected area"). Visual surveillance was unquestionably lawful because " 'the eye cannot by the laws of England be guilty of a trespass.' " Boyd v. United States, 116 U.S. 616, 628 (1886) (quoting Entick v. Carrington, 19 How. St. Tr. 1029, 95 Eng. Rep. 807 (K. B. 1765)). We have since decoupled violation of a person's Fourth Amendment rights from trespassory violation of his property, see Rakas v. Illinois, 439 U.S. 128, 143 (1978), but the lawfulness of warrantless visual surveillance of a home has still been preserved. As we observed in California v. Ciraolo, 476 U.S. 207, 213 (1986), "[t]he Fourth Amendment protection of the home has never been extended to require law enforcement officers to shield their eyes when passing by a home on public thoroughfares."

One might think that the new validating rationale would be that examining the portion of a house that is in plain public view, while it is a "search"[1] despite the absence of trespass, is not an "unreasonable" one under the Fourth Amendment. See Minnesota v. Carter, 525 U.S. 83, 104 (1998) (Breyer, J., concurring in judgment). But in fact we have held that visual observation is no "search" at all–perhaps in order to preserve somewhat more intact our doctrine that warrantless searches are presumptively unconstitutional. See Dow Chemical Co. v. United States, 476 U.S. 227, 234–235, 239 (1986). In assessing when a search is not a search, we have applied somewhat in reverse the principle first enunciated in Katz v. United States, 389 U.S. 347 (1967). Katz involved eavesdropping by means of an electronic listening device placed on the outside of a telephone booth–a location not within the catalog ("persons, houses, papers, and effects") that the Fourth Amendment protects against unreasonable searches. We held that the Fourth Amendment nonetheless protected Katz from the warrantless eavesdropping because he "justifiably relied" upon the privacy of the telephone booth. Id., at 353. As Justice Harlan's oft-quoted concurrence described it, a Fourth Amendment search occurs when the government violates a subjective expectation of privacy that society recognizes as reasonable. See id., at 361. We have subsequently applied this principle to hold that a Fourth Amendment search does not occur–even when the explicitly protected location of a house is concerned–unless "the individual manifested a subjective expectation of privacy in the object of the challenged search," and "society [is] willing to recognize that expectation as reasonable." Ciraolo, supra, at 211. We have applied this test in holding that it is not a search for the police to use a pen register at the phone company to determine what numbers were dialed in a private home, Smith v. Maryland, 442 U.S. 735, 743—744 (1979), and we have applied the test on two different occasions in holding that aerial surveillance of private homes and surrounding areas does not constitute a search, Ciraolo, supra; Florida v. Riley, 488 U.S. 445 (1989).

The present case involves officers on a public street engaged in more than naked-eye surveillance of a home. We have previously reserved judgment as to how much technological enhancement of ordinary perception from such a vantage point, if any, is too much. While we upheld enhanced aerial photography of an industrial complex in Dow Chemical, we noted that we found "it important that this is not an area immediately adjacent to a private home, where privacy expectations are most heightened," 476 U.S., at 237, n. 4 (emphasis in original).

III

It would be foolish to contend that the degree of privacy secured to citizens by the Fourth Amendment has been entirely unaffected by the advance of technology. For example, as the cases discussed above make clear, the technology enabling human flight has exposed to public view (and hence, we have said, to official observation) uncovered portions of the house and its curtilage that once were private. See Ciraolo, supra, at 215. The question we confront today is what limits there are upon this power of technology to shrink the realm of guaranteed privacy.

The Katz test—whether the individual has an expectation of privacy that society is prepared to recognize as reasonable—has often been criticized as circular, and hence subjective and unpredictable. See 1 W. LaFave, Search and Seizure §2.1(d), pp. 393—394 (3d ed. 1996); Posner, The Uncertain Protection of Privacy by the Supreme Court, 1979 S. Ct. Rev. 173, 188; Carter, supra, at 97 (Scalia, J., concurring). But see Rakas, supra, at 143—144, n. 12. While it may be difficult to refine Katz when the search of areas such as telephone booths, automobiles, or even the curtilage and uncovered portions of residences are at issue, in the case of the search of the interior of homes—the prototypical and hence most commonly litigated area of protected privacy—there is a ready criterion, with roots deep in the common law, of the minimal expectation of privacy that exists, and that is acknowledged to be reasonable. To withdraw protection of this minimum expectation would be to permit police technology to erode the privacy guaranteed by the Fourth Amendment. We think that obtaining by sense-enhancing technology any information regarding the interior of the home that could not otherwise have been obtained without physical "intrusion into a constitutionally protected area," Silverman, 365 U.S., at 512, constitutes a search—at least where (as here) the technology in question is not in general public use. This assures preservation of that degree of privacy against government that existed when the Fourth Amendment was adopted. On the basis of this criterion, the information obtained by the thermal imager in this case was the product of a search.[2]

The Government maintains, however, that the thermal imaging must be upheld because it detected "only heat radiating from the external surface of the house," Brief for United States 26. The dissent makes this its leading point, see post, at 1, contending that there is a fundamental difference between what it calls "off-the-wall" observations and "through-the-wall surveillance." But just as a thermal imager captures only heat emanating from a house, so also a powerful directional microphone picks up only sound emanating from a house—and a satellite capable of scanning from many miles away would pick up only visible light emanating from a house. We rejected such a mechanical interpretation of the Fourth Amendment in Katz, where the eavesdropping device picked up only sound waves that reached the exterior of the phone booth. Reversing that approach would leave the homeowner at the mercy of advancing technology—including imaging technology that could discern all human activity in the home. While the technology used in the present case was relatively crude, the rule we adopt must take account of more sophisticated systems that are already in use or in development.3 The dissent's reliance on the distinction between "off-the-wall" and "through-the-wall" observation is entirely incompatible with the dissent's belief, which we discuss below, that thermal-imaging observations of the intimate details of a home are impermissible. The most sophisticated thermal imaging devices continue to measure heat "off-the-wall" rather than "through-the-wall"; the dissent's disapproval of those more sophisticated thermal-imaging devices, see post, at 10, is an acknowledgement that there is no substance to this distinction. As for the dissent's extraordinary assertion that anything learned through "an inference" cannot be a search, see post, at 4–5, that would validate even the "through-the-wall" technologies that the dissent purports to disapprove. Surely the dissent does not believe that the through-the-wall radar or ultrasound technology produces an 8-by-10 Kodak glossy that needs no analysis (i.e., the making of inferences). And, of course, the novel proposition that inference insulates a search is blatantly contrary to United States v. Karo, 468 U.S. 705 (1984), where the police "inferred" from the activation of a beeper that a certain can of ether was in the home. The police activity was held to be a search, and the search was held unlawful.4

The Government also contends that the thermal imaging was constitutional because it did not "detect private activities occurring in private areas," Brief for United States 22. It points out that in Dow Chemical we observed that the enhanced aerial photography did not reveal any "intimate details." 476 U.S., at 238. Dow Chemical, however, involved enhanced aerial photography of an industrial complex, which does not share the Fourth Amendment sanctity of the home. The Fourth Amendment's protection of the home has never been tied to measurement of the quality or quantity of information obtained. In Silverman, for example, we made clear that any physical invasion of the structure of the home, "by even a fraction of an inch," was too much, 365 U.S., at 512, and there is certainly no exception to the warrant requirement for the officer who barely cracks open the front door and sees nothing but the nonintimate rug on the vestibule floor. In the home, our cases show, all details are intimate details, because the entire area is held safe from prying government eyes. Thus, in Karo, supra, the only thing detected was a can of ether in the home; and in Arizona v. Hicks, 480 U.S. 321 (1987), the only thing detected by a physical search that went beyond what officers lawfully present could observe in "plain view" was the registration number of a phonograph turntable. These were intimate details because they were details of the home, just as was the detail of how warm—or even how relatively warm—Kyllo was heating his residence.5

Limiting the prohibition of thermal imaging to "intimate details" would not only be wrong in principle; it would be impractical in application, failing to provide "a workable accommodation between the needs of law enforcement and the interests protected by the Fourth Amendment," Oliver v. United States, 466 U.S. 170, 181 (1984). To begin with, there is no necessary connection between the sophistication of the surveillance equipment and the "intimacy" of the details that it observes—which means that one cannot say (and the police cannot be assured) that use of the relatively crude equipment at issue here will always be lawful. The Agema Thermovision 210 might disclose, for example, at what hour each night the lady of the house takes her daily sauna and bath—a detail that many would consider "intimate"; and a much more sophisticated system might detect nothing more intimate than the fact that someone left a closet light on. We could not, in other words, develop a rule approving only that through-the-wall surveillance which identifies objects no smaller than 36 by 36 inches, but would have to develop a jurisprudence specifying which home activities are "intimate" and which are not. And even when (if ever) that jurisprudence were fully developed, no police officer would be able to know in advance whether his through-the-wall surveillance picks up "intimate" details—and thus would be unable to know in advance whether it is constitutional.

The dissent's proposed standard—whether the technology offers the "functional equivalent of actual presence in the area being searched," post, at 7—would seem quite similar to our own at first blush. The dissent concludes that Katz was such a case, but then inexplicably asserts that if the same listening device only revealed the volume of the conversation, the surveillance would be permissible, post, at 10. Yet if, without technology, the police could not discern volume without being actually present in the phone booth, Justice Stevens should conclude a search has occurred. Cf. Karo, supra, at 735 (Stevens, J., concurring in part and dissenting in part) ("I find little comfort in the Court's notion that no invasion of privacy occurs until a listener obtains some significant information by use of the device.... A bathtub is a less private area when the plumber is present even if his back is turned"). The same should hold for the interior heat of the home if only a person present in the home could discern the heat. Thus the driving force of the dissent, despite its recitation of the above standard, appears to be a distinction among different types of information—whether the "homeowner would even care if anybody noticed," post, at 10. The dissent offers no practical guidance for the application of this standard, and for reasons already discussed, we believe there can be none. The people in their houses, as well as the police, deserve more precision.6

We have said that the Fourth Amendment draws "a firm line at the entrance to the house," Payton, 445 U.S., at 590. That line, we think, must be not only firm but also bright—which requires clear specification of those methods of surveillance that require a warrant. While it is certainly possible to conclude from the videotape of the thermal imaging that occurred in this case that no "significant" compromise of the homeowner's privacy has occurred, we must take the long view, from the original meaning of the Fourth Amendment forward.

"The Fourth Amendment is to be construed in the light of what was deemed an unreasonable search and seizure when it was adopted, and in a manner which will conserve public interests as well as the interests and rights of individual citizens." Carroll v. United States, 267 U.S. 132, 149 (1925).

Where, as here, the Government uses a device that is not in general public use, to explore details of the home that would previously have been unknowable without physical intrusion, the surveillance is a "search" and is presumptively unreasonable without a warrant.

Since we hold the Thermovision imaging to have been an unlawful search, it will remain for the District Court to determine whether, without the evidence it provided, the search warrant issued in this case was supported by probable cause—and if not, whether there is any other basis for supporting admission of the evidence that the search pursuant to the warrant produced.

* * *

The judgment of the Court of Appeals is reversed; the case is remanded for further proceedings consistent with this opinion.

It is so ordered.

Notes to Kyllo v. United States (June 11, 2001)

1. When the Fourth Amendment was adopted, as now, to "search" meant "[t]o look over or through for the purpose of finding something; to explore; to examine by inspection; as, to search the house for a book; to search the wood for a thief." N. Webster, An American Dictionary of the English Language 66 (1828) (reprint 6th ed. 1989).

2. The dissent's repeated assertion that the thermal imaging did not obtain information regarding the interior of the home, post, at 3, 4 (opinion of Stevens, J.), is simply inaccurate. A thermal imager reveals the relative heat of various rooms in the home. The dissent may not find that information particularly private or important, see post, at 4, 5, 10, but there is no basis for saying it is not information regarding the interior of the home. The dissent's comparison of the thermal imaging to various circumstances in which outside observers might be able to perceive, without technology, the heat of the home—for example, by observing snowmelt on the roof, post, at 3—is quite irrelevant. The fact that equivalent information could sometimes be obtained by other means does not make lawful the use of means that violate the Fourth Amendment. The police might, for

example, learn how many people are in a particular house by setting up year-round surveillance; but that does not make breaking and entering to find out the same information lawful. In any event, on the night of January 16, 1992, no outside observer could have discerned the relative heat of Kyllo's home without thermal imaging.

3. The ability to "see" through walls and other opaque barriers is a clear, and scientifically feasible, goal of law enforcement research and development. The National Law Enforcement and Corrections Technology Center, a program within the United States Department of Justice, features on its Internet Website projects that include a "Radar-Based Through-the-Wall Surveillance System," "Handheld Ultrasound Through the Wall Surveillance," and a "Radar Flashlight" that "will enable law officers to detect individuals through interior building walls." www.nlectc.org/techproj/ (visited May 3, 2001). Some devices may emit low levels of radiation that travel "through-the-wall," but others, such as more sophisticated thermal imaging devices, are entirely passive, or "off-the-wall" as the dissent puts it.

4. The dissent asserts, post, at 5, n. 3, that we have misunderstood its point, which is not that inference insulates a search, but that inference alone is not a search. If we misunderstood the point, it was only in a good-faith effort to render the point germane to the case at hand. The issue in this case is not the police's allegedly unlawful inferencing, but their allegedly unlawful thermal-imaging measurement of the emanations from a house. We say such measurement is a search; the dissent says it is not, because an inference is not a search. We took that to mean that, since the technologically enhanced emanations had to be the basis of inferences before anything inside the house could be known, the use of the emanations could not be a search. But the dissent certainly knows better than we what it intends. And if it means only that an inference is not a search, we certainly agree. That has no bearing, however, upon whether hi-tech measurement of emanations from a house is a search.

5. The Government cites our statement in California v. Ciraolo, 476 U.S. 207 (1986), noting apparent agreement with the State of California that aerial surveillance of a house's curtilage could become " 'invasive' " if " 'modern technology' " revealed " 'those intimate associations, objects or activities otherwise imperceptible to police or fellow citizens.' " Id., at 215, n. 3 (quoting brief of the State of California). We think the Court's focus in this second-hand dictum was not upon intimacy but upon otherwise-imperceptibility, which is precisely the principle we vindicate today.

6. The dissent argues that we have injected potential uncertainty into the constitutional analysis by noting that whether or not the technology is in general public use may be a factor. See post, at 7—8. That quarrel, however, is not with us but with this Court's precedent. See Ciraolo, supra, at 215 ("In an age where private and commercial flight in the public airways is routine, it is unreasonable for respondent to expect that his marijuana plants were constitutionally protected from being observed with the naked eye from an altitude of 1,000 feet"). Given that we can quite confidently say that thermal imaging is not "routine," we decline in this case to reexamine that factor.

Can't prohibit candidates for judicial election in that State from announcing their views on disputed legal and political issues: Republican Party of Minnesota v. White (June 27, 2002)

Justice Scalia delivered the opinion of the Court.

The question presented in this case is whether the First Amendment permits the Minnesota Supreme Court to prohibit candidates for judicial election in that State from announcing their views on disputed legal and political issues.

I

Since Minnesota's admission to the Union in 1858, the State's Constitution has provided for the selection of all state judges by popular election. Minn. Const., Art. VI, §7. Since 1912, those elections have been nonpartisan. Act of June 19, ch. 2, 1912 Minn. Laws Special Sess., pp. 4-6. Since 1974, they have been subject to a legal restriction which states that a "candidate for a judicial office, including an incumbent judge," shall not "announce his or her views on disputed legal or political issues." Minn. Code of Judicial Conduct, Canon 5(A)(3)(d)(i) (2000). This prohibition, promulgated by the Minnesota Supreme Court and based on Canon 7(B) of the 1972 American Bar Association (ABA) Model Code of Judicial Conduct, is known as the "announce clause." Incumbent judges who violate it are subject to discipline, including removal, censure, civil penalties, and suspension without pay. Minn. Rules of Board on Judicial Standards 4(a)(6), 11(d) (2002). Lawyers who run for judicial office also must comply with the announce clause. Minn. Rule of Professional Conduct 8.2(b) (2002) ("A lawyer who is a candidate for judicial office shall comply with the applicable provisions of the Code of Judicial Conduct"). Those who violate it are subject to, inter alia, disbarment, suspension, and probation. Rule 8.4(a); Minn. Rules on Lawyers Professional Responsibility 8-14, 15(a) (2002).

In 1996, one of the petitioners, Gregory Wersal, ran for associate justice of the Minnesota Supreme Court. In the course of the campaign, he distributed literature criticizing several Minnesota Supreme Court decisions on issues such as crime, welfare, and abortion. A complaint against Wersal challenging, among other things, the propriety of this literature was filed with the Office of Lawyers Professional Responsibility, the agency which, under the direction of the Minnesota Lawyers Professional Responsibility Board, 1 investigates and prosecutes ethical violations of lawyer candidates for judicial office. The Lawyers Board dismissed the complaint; with regard to the charges that his campaign materials violated the announce clause, it expressed doubt whether the clause could constitutionally be enforced. Nonetheless, fearing that further ethical complaints would jeopardize his ability to practice law, Wersal withdrew from the election. In 1998, Wersal ran again for the same office. Early in that race, he sought an advisory opinion from the Lawyers Board with regard to whether it planned to enforce the announce clause. The Lawyers Board responded equivocally, stating that, although it had significant doubts about the constitutionality of the provision, it was unable to answer his question because he had not submitted a list of the announcements he wished to make.2

Shortly thereafter, Wersal filed this lawsuit in Federal District Court against respondents, 3 seeking, inter alia, a declaration that the announce clause violates the First Amendment and an injunction against its enforcement. Wersal alleged that he was forced to refrain from announcing his views on disputed issues during the 1998 campaign, to the point where he declined response to questions put to him by the press and public, out of concern that he might run afoul of the announce clause. Other plaintiffs in the suit, including the Minnesota Republican Party, alleged that, because the clause kept Wersal from announcing his views, they were unable to learn those views and support or oppose his candidacy accordingly. The parties filed cross-motions for summary judgment, and the District Court found in favor of respondents, holding that the announce clause did not violate the First Amendment. 63 F. Supp. 2d 967 (Minn. 1999). Over a dissent by Judge Beam, the United States Court of Appeals for the Eighth Circuit affirmed. 247 F. 3d 854 (2001). We granted certiorari. 534 U. S. 1054 (2001).

II

Before considering the constitutionality of the announce clause, we must be clear about its meaning. Its text says that a candidate for judicial office shall not "announce his or her views on disputed legal or political issues." Minn. Code of Judicial Conduct, Canon 5(A)(3)(d)(i) (2002).

We know that "announc[ing] . . . views" on an issue covers much more than promising to decide an issue a particular way. The prohibition extends to the candidate's mere statement of his current position, even if he does not bind himself to maintain that position after election. All the parties agree this is the case, because the Minnesota Code contains a so-called "pledges or promises" clause, which separately prohibits judicial candidates from making "pledges or promises of conduct in office other than the faithful and impartial performance of the duties of the office," ibid.--a prohibition that is not challenged here and on which we express no view.

There are, however, some limitations that the Minnesota Supreme Court has placed upon the scope of the announce clause that are not (to put it politely) immediately apparent from its text. The statements that formed the basis of the complaint against Wersal in 1996 included criticism of past decisions of the Minnesota Supreme Court. One piece of campaign literature stated that "[t]he Minnesota Supreme Court has issued decisions which are marked by their disregard for the Legislature and a lack of common sense." App. 37. It went on to criticize a decision excluding from evidence confessions by criminal defendants that were not tape-recorded, asking "[s]hould we conclude that because the Supreme Court does not trust police, it allows confessed criminals to go free?" Ibid. It criticized a decision striking down a state law restricting welfare benefits, asserting that "[i]t's the Legislature which should set our spending policies." Ibid. And it criticized a decision requiring public financing of abortions for poor women as "unprecedented" and a "pro-abortion stance." Id., at 38. Although one would think that all of these statements touched on disputed legal or political issues, they did not (or at least do not now) fall within the scope of the announce clause. The Judicial Board issued an opinion stating that judicial candidates may criticize past decisions, and the Lawyers Board refused to discipline Wersal for the foregoing statements because, in part, it thought they did not violate the announce clause. The Eighth Circuit relied on the Judicial Board's opinion in upholding the announce clause, 247 F. 3d, at 882, and the Minnesota Supreme Court recently embraced the Eighth Circuit's interpretation, In re Code of Judicial Conduct, 639 N. W. 2d 55 (2002).

There are yet further limitations upon the apparent plain meaning of the announce clause: In light of the constitutional concerns, the District Court construed the clause to reach only disputed issues that are likely to come before the candidate if he is elected judge. 63 F. Supp. 2d, at 986. The Eighth Circuit accepted this limiting interpretation by the District Court, and in addition construed the clause to allow general discussions of case law and judicial philosophy. 247 F. 3d, at 881-882. The Supreme Court of Minnesota adopted these interpretations as well when it ordered enforcement of the announce clause in accordance with the Eighth Circuit's opinion. In re Code of Judicial Conduct, supra.

It seems to us, however, that--like the text of the announce clause itself--these limitations upon the text of the announce clause are not all that they appear to be. First, respondents acknowledged at oral argument that statements critical of past judicial decisions are not permissible if the candidate also states that he is against stare decisis. Tr. of Oral Arg. 33-34.4 Thus, candidates must choose between stating their views critical of past decisions and stating their views in opposition to stare decisis. Or, to look at it more concretely, they may state their view that prior decisions were erroneous only if they do not assert that they, if elected, have any power to eliminate erroneous decisions. Second, limiting the scope of the clause to issues likely to come before a court is not much of a limitation at all. One would hardly expect the "disputed legal or political issues" raised in the course of a state judicial election to include such matters as whether the Federal Government should end the embargo of Cuba. Quite obviously, they will be those legal or political disputes that are the proper (or by past decisions have been made the improper) business of the state courts. And within that relevant category, "[t]here is almost no legal or political issue that is unlikely to come before a judge of an American court, state or federal, of general jurisdiction." Buckley v. Illinois Judicial Inquiry Bd., 997 F. 2d 224, 229 (CA7 1993). Third, construing the clause to allow "general" discussions of case law and judicial philosophy turns out to be of little help in an election campaign. At oral argument, respondents gave, as an example of this exception, that a candidate is free to assert that he is a " `strict constructionist.' " Tr. of Oral Arg. 29. But that, like most other philosophical generalities, has little meaningful content for the electorate unless it is exemplified by application to a particular issue of construction likely to come before a court--for example, whether a particular statute runs afoul of any provision of the Constitution. Respondents conceded that the announce clause would prohibit the candidate from exemplifying his philosophy in this fashion. Id., at 43. Without such application to real-life issues, all candidates can claim to be "strict constructionists" with equal (and unhelpful) plausibility.

In any event, it is clear that the announce clause prohibits a judicial candidate from stating his views on any specific nonfanciful legal question within the province of the court for which he is running, except in the context of discussing past decisions--and in the latter context as well, if he expresses the view that he is not bound by stare decisis.5

Respondents contend that this still leaves plenty of topics for discussion on the campaign trail. These include a candidate's "character," "education," "work habits," and "how [he] would handle administrative duties if elected." Brief for Respondents 35-36. Indeed, the Judicial Board has printed a list of preapproved questions which judicial candidates are allowed to answer. These include how the candidate feels about cameras in the courtroom, how he would go about reducing the caseload, how the costs of judicial administration can be reduced, and how he proposes to ensure that minorities and women are treated more fairly by the court system. Minnesota State Bar Association Judicial Elections Task Force Report & Recommendations, App. C (June 19, 1997), reprinted at App. 97-103. Whether this list of preapproved subjects, and other topics not prohibited by the announce clause, adequately fulfill the First Amendment's guarantee of freedom of speech is the question to which we now turn.

III

As the Court of Appeals recognized, the announce clause both prohibits speech on the basis of its content and burdens a category of speech that is "at the core of our First Amendment freedoms"--speech about the qualifications of candidates for public office. 247 F. 3d, at 861, 863. The Court of Appeals concluded that the proper test to be applied to determine the constitutionality of such a restriction is what our cases have called strict scrutiny, id., at 864; the parties do not dispute that this is correct. Under the strict-scrutiny test, respondents have the burden to prove that the announce clause is (1) narrowly tailored, to serve (2) a compelling state interest. E.g., Eu v. San Francisco County Democratic Central Comm., 489 U. S. 214, 222 (1989). In order for respondents to show that the announce clause is narrowly tailored, they must demonstrate that it does not "unnecessarily circumscrib[e] protected expression." Brown v. Hartlage, 456 U. S. 45, 54 (1982).

The Court of Appeals concluded that respondents had established two interests as sufficiently compelling to justify the announce clause: preserving the impartiality of the state judiciary and preserving the appearance of the impartiality of the state judiciary. 247 F. 3d, at 867. Respondents reassert these two interests before us, arguing that the first is compelling because it protects the due process rights of litigants, and that the second is compelling because it preserves public confidence in the judiciary.6 Respondents are rather vague, however, about what they mean by "impartiality." Indeed, although the term is used throughout the Eighth Circuit's opinion, the briefs, the Minnesota Code of Judicial Conduct, and the ABA Codes of Judicial Conduct, none of these sources bothers to define it. Clarity on this point is essential before we can decide whether impartiality is indeed a compelling state interest, and, if so, whether the announce clause is narrowly tailored to achieve it.

A

One meaning of "impartiality" in the judicial context--and of course its root meaning--is the lack of bias for or against either party to the proceeding. Impartiality in this sense assures equal application of the law. That is, it guarantees a party that the judge who hears his case will apply the law to him in the same way he applies it to any other party. This is the traditional sense in which the term is used. See Webster's New International Dictionary 1247 (2d ed. 1950) (defining "impartial" as "[n]ot partial; esp., not favoring one more than another; treating all alike; unbiased; equitable; fair; just"). It is also the sense in which it is used in the cases cited by respondents and amici for the proposition that an impartial judge is essential to due process. Tumey v. Ohio, 273 U. S. 510, 523, 531-534 (1927) (judge violated due process by sitting in a case in which it would be in his financial interest to find against one of the parties); Aetna Life Ins. Co. v. Lavoie, 475 U. S. 813, 822-825 (1986) (same); Ward v. Monroeville, 409 U. S. 57, 58-62 (1972) (same); Johnson v. Mississippi, 403 U. S. 212, 215-216 (1971) (per curiam) (judge violated due process by sitting in a case in which one of the parties was a previously successful litigant against him); Bracy v. Gramley, 520 U. S. 899, 905 (1997) (would violate due process if a judge was disposed to rule against defendants who did not bribe him in order to cover up the fact that he regularly ruled in favor of defendants who did bribe him); In re Murchison, 349 U. S. 133, 137-139 (1955) (judge violated due process by sitting in the criminal trial of defendant whom he had indicted).

We think it plain that the announce clause is not narrowly tailored to serve impartiality (or the appearance of impartiality) in this sense. Indeed, the clause is barely tailored to serve that interest at all, inasmuch as it does not restrict speech for or against particular parties, but rather speech for or against particular issues. To be sure, when a case arises that turns on a legal issue on which the judge (as a candidate) had taken a particular stand, the party taking the opposite stand is likely to lose. But not because of any bias against that party, or favoritism toward the other party. Any party taking that position is just as likely to lose. The judge is applying the law (as he sees it) evenhandedly.[7]

B

It is perhaps possible to use the term "impartiality" in the judicial context (though this is certainly not a common usage) to mean lack of preconception in favor of or against a particular legal view. This sort of impartiality would be concerned, not with guaranteeing litigants equal application of the law, but rather with guaranteeing them an equal chance to persuade the court on the legal points in their case. Impartiality in this sense may well be an interest served by the announce clause, but it is not a compelling state interest, as strict scrutiny requires. A judge's lack of predisposition regarding the relevant legal issues in a case has never been thought a necessary component of equal justice, and with good reason. For one thing, it is virtually impossible to find a judge who does not have preconceptions about the law. As then-Justice Rehnquist observed of our own Court: "Since most Justices come to this bench no earlier than their middle years, it would be unusual if they had not by that time formulated at least some tentative notions that would influence them in their interpretation of the sweeping clauses of the Constitution and their interaction with one another. It would be not merely unusual, but extraordinary, if they had not at least given opinions as to constitutional issues in their previous legal careers." Laird v. Tatum, 409 U. S. 824, 835 (1972) (memorandum opinion). Indeed, even if it were possible to select judges who did not have preconceived views on legal issues, it would hardly be desirable to do so. "Proof that a Justice's mind at the time he joined the Court was a complete tabula rasa in the area of constitutional adjudication would be evidence of lack of qualification, not lack of bias." Ibid. The Minnesota Constitution positively forbids the selection to courts of general jurisdiction of judges who are impartial in the sense of having no views on the law. Minn. Const., Art. VI, §5 ("Judges of the supreme court, the court of appeals and the district court shall be learned in the law"). And since avoiding judicial preconceptions on legal issues is neither possible nor desirable, pretending otherwise by attempting to preserve the "appearance" of that type of impartiality can hardly be a compelling state interest either.

C

A third possible meaning of "impartiality" (again not a common one) might be described as openmindedness. This quality in a judge demands, not that he have no preconceptions on legal issues, but that he be willing to consider views that oppose his preconceptions, and remain open to persuasion, when the issues arise in a pending case. This sort of impartiality seeks to guarantee each litigant, not an equal chance to win the legal points in the case, but at least some chance of doing so. It may well be that impartiality in this sense, and the appearance of it, are desirable in the judiciary, but we need not pursue that inquiry, since we do not believe the Minnesota Supreme Court adopted the announce clause for that purpose.

Respondents argue that the announce clause serves the interest in openmindedness, or at least in the appearance of openmindedness, because it relieves a judge from pressure to rule a certain way in order to maintain consistency with statements the judge has previously made. The problem is, however, that statements in election campaigns are such an infinitesimal portion of the public commitments to legal positions that judges (or judges-to-be) undertake, that this object of the prohibition is implausible. Before they arrive on the bench (whether by election or otherwise) judges have often committed themselves on legal issues that they must later rule upon. See, e.g., Laird, supra, at 831-833 (describing Justice Black's participation in several cases construing and deciding the constitutionality of the Fair Labor Standards Act, even though as a Senator he had been one of its principal authors; and Chief Justice Hughes's authorship of the opinion overruling Adkins v. Children's Hospital of D. C., 261 U. S. 525 (1923), a case he had criticized in a book written before his appointment to the Court).

More common still is a judge's confronting a legal issue on which he has expressed an opinion while on the bench. Most frequently, of course, that prior expression will have occurred in ruling on an earlier case. But judges often state their views on disputed legal issues outside the context of adjudication--in classes that they conduct, and in books and speeches. Like the ABA Codes of Judicial Conduct, the Minnesota Code not only permits but encourages this. See Minn. Code of Judicial Conduct, Canon 4(B) (2002) ("A judge may write, lecture, teach, speak and participate in other extra-judicial activities concerning the law ..."); Minn. Code of Judicial Conduct, Canon 4(B), Comment. (2002) ("To the extent that time permits, a judge is encouraged to do so ..."). That is quite incompatible with the notion that the need for openmindedness (or for the appearance of openmindedness) lies behind the prohibition at issue here.

The short of the matter is this: In Minnesota, a candidate for judicial office may not say "I think it is constitutional for the legislature to prohibit same-sex marriages." He may say the very same thing, however, up until the very day before he declares himself a candidate, and may say it repeatedly (until litigation is pending) after he is elected. As a means of pursuing the objective of open-mindedness that respondents now articulate, the announce clause is so woefully underinclusive as to render belief in that purpose a challenge to the credulous. See City of Ladue v. Gilleo, 512 U. S. 43, 52-53 (1994) (noting that underinclusiveness "diminish[es] the credibility of the government's rationale for restricting speech"); Florida Star v. B. J. F., 491 U. S. 524, 541-542 (1989) (Scalia, J., concurring in judgment) ("[A] law cannot be regarded as protecting an interest of the highest order, and thus as justifying a restriction upon truthful speech, when it leaves appreciable damage to that supposedly vital interest unprohibited" (internal quotation marks and citation omitted)).

Justice Stevens asserts that statements made in an election campaign pose a special threat to openmindedness because the candidate, when elected judge, will have a particular reluctance to contradict them. Post, at 5-6. That might be plausible, perhaps, with regard to campaign promises. A candidate who says "If elected, I will vote to uphold the legislature's power to prohibit same-sex marriages" will positively be breaking his word if he does not do so (although one would be na;ve not to recognize that campaign promises are--by long democratic tradition--the least binding form of human commitment). But, as noted earlier, the Minnesota Supreme Court has adopted a separate prohibition on campaign "pledges or promises," which is not challenged here. The proposition that judges feel significantly greater compulsion, or appear to feel significantly greater compulsion, to maintain consistency with nonpromissory statements made during a judicial campaign than with such statements made before or after the campaign is not self-evidently true. It seems to us quite likely, in fact, that in many cases the opposite is true. We doubt, for example, that a mere statement of position enunciated during the pendency of an election will be regarded by a judge as more binding--or as more likely to subject him to popular disfavor if reconsidered--than a carefully considered holding that the judge set forth in an earlier opinion denying some individual's claim to justice. In any event, it suffices to say that respondents have not carried the burden imposed by our strict-scrutiny test to establish this proposition (that campaign statements are uniquely destructive of openmindedness) on which the validity of the announce clause rests. See, e.g., Landmark Communications, Inc. v. Virginia, 435 U. S. 829, 841 (1978) (rejecting speech restriction subject to strict scrutiny where the State "offered little more than assertion and conjecture to support its claim that without criminal sanctions the objectives of the statutory scheme would be seriously undermined"); United States v. Playboy Entertainment Group, Inc., 529 U. S. 803, 816-825 (2000) (same).8

Moreover, the notion that the special context of electioneering justifies an abridgment of the right to speak out on disputed issues sets our First Amendment jurisprudence on its head. "[D]ebate on the qualifications of candidates" is "at the core of our electoral process and of the First Amendment freedoms," not at the edges. Eu, 370 U. S. 375, 395 (1962). "It is simply not the function of government to select which issues are worth discussing or debating in the course of a political campaign." Brown, 456 U. S., at 60 (internal quotation marks omitted). We have never allowed the government to prohibit candidates from communicating relevant information to voters during an election.

Justice Ginsburg would do so--and much of her dissent confirms rather than refutes our conclusion that the purpose behind the announce clause is not openmindedness in the judiciary, but the undermining of judicial elections. She contends that the announce clause must be constitutional because due process would be denied if an elected judge sat in a case involving an issue on which he had previously announced his view. Post, at 14-15, 18-19. She reaches this conclusion because, she says, such a judge would have a "direct, personal, substantial, and pecuniary interest" in ruling consistently with his previously announced view, in order to reduce the risk that he will be "voted off the bench and thereby lose [his] salary and emoluments," post, at 14-15 (internal quotation marks and alterations omitted). But elected judges--regardless of whether they have announced any views beforehand--always face the pressure of an electorate who might disagree with their rulings and therefore vote them off the bench. Surely the judge who frees Timothy McVeigh places his job much more at risk than the judge who (horror of horrors!) reconsiders his previously announced view on a disputed legal issue. So if, as Justice Ginsburg claims, it violates due process for a judge to sit in a case in which ruling one way rather than another increases his prospects for reelection, then--quite simply--the practice of electing judges is itself a violation of due process. It is not difficult to understand how one with these views would approve the election-nullifying effect of the announce clause.9 They are not, however, the views reflected in the Due Process Clause of the Fourteenth Amendment, which has coexisted with the election of judges ever since it was adopted, see infra, at 19-20.

Justice Ginsburg devotes the rest of her dissent to attacking arguments we do not make. For example, despite the number of pages she dedicates to disproving this proposition, post, at 1-6, we neither assert nor imply that the First Amendment requires campaigns for judicial office to sound the same as those for legislative office.10 What we do assert, and what Justice Ginsburg ignores, is that, even if the First Amendment allows greater regulation of judicial election campaigns than legislative election campaigns, the announce clause still fails strict scrutiny because it is woefully underinclusive, prohibiting announcements by judges (and would-be judges) only at certain times and in certain forms. We rely on the cases involving speech during elections, supra, at 16, only to make the obvious point that this underinclusiveness cannot be explained by resort to the notion that the First Amendment provides less protection during an election campaign than at other times.11

But in any case, Justice Ginsburg greatly exaggerates the difference between judicial and legislative elections. She asserts that "the rationale underlying unconstrained speech in elections for political office--that representative government depends on the public's ability to choose agents who will act at its behest--does not carry over to campaigns for the bench." Post, at 4. This complete separation of the judiciary from the enterprise of "representative government" might have some truth in those countries where judges neither make law themselves nor set aside the laws enacted by the legislature. It is not a true picture of the American system. Not only do state-court judges possess the power to "make" common law, but they have the immense power to shape the States' constitutions as well. See, e.g., Baker v. State, 170 Vt. 194, 744 A. 2d 864 (1999). Which is precisely why the election of state judges became popular.12

IV

To sustain the announce clause, the Eighth Circuit relied heavily on the fact that a pervasive practice of prohibiting judicial candidates from discussing disputed legal and political issues developed during the last half of the 20th century. 247 F. 3d, at 879-880. It is true that a "universal and long-established" tradition of prohibiting certain conduct creates "a strong presumption" that the prohibition is constitutional: "Principles of liberty fundamental enough to have been embodied within constitutional guarantees are not readily erased from the Nation's consciousness." McIntyre v. Ohio Elections Comm'n, 514 U. S. 334, 375-377 (1995) (Scalia, J., dissenting). The practice of prohibiting speech by judicial candidates on disputed issues, however, is neither long nor universal.

At the time of the founding, only Vermont (before it became a State) selected any of its judges by election. Starting with Georgia in 1812, States began to provide for judicial election, a development rapidly accelerated by Jacksonian democracy. By the time of the Civil War, the great majority of States elected their judges. E. Haynes, Selection and Tenure of Judges 99-135 (1944); Berkson, Judicial Selection in the United States: A Special Report, 64 Judicature 176 (1980). We know of no restrictions upon statements that could be made by judicial candidates (including judges) throughout the 19th and the first quarter of the 20th century. Indeed, judicial elections were generally partisan during this period, the movement toward nonpartisan judicial elections not even beginning until the 1870's. Id., at 176-177; M. Comisky & P. Patterson, The Judiciary--

Selection, Compensation, Ethics, and Discipline 4, 7 (1987). Thus, not only were judicial candidates (including judges) discussing disputed legal and political issues on the campaign trail, but they were touting party affiliations and angling for party nominations all the while.

      The first code regulating judicial conduct was adopted by the ABA in 1924. 48 ABA Reports 74 (1923) (report of Chief Justice Taft); P. McFadden, Electing Justice: The Law and Ethics of Judicial Campaigns 86 (1990). It contained a provision akin to the announce clause: "A candidate for judicial position ... should not announce in advance his conclusions of law on disputed issues to secure class support ... ." ABA Canon of Judicial Ethics 30 (1924). The States were slow to adopt the canons, however. "By the end of World War II, the canons ... were binding by the bar associations or supreme courts of only eleven states." J. MacKenzie, The Appearance of Justice 191 (1974). Even today, although a majority of States have adopted either the announce clause or its 1990 ABA successor, adoption is not unanimous. Of the 31 States that select some or all of their appellate and general-jurisdiction judges by election, see American Judicature Society, Judicial Selection in the States: Appellate and General Jurisdiction Courts (Apr. 2002), 4 have adopted no candidate-speech restriction comparable to the announce clause, 13 and 1 prohibits only the discussion of "pending litigation."14 This practice, relatively new to judicial elections and still not universally adopted, does not compare well with the traditions deemed worthy of our attention in prior cases. E.g., Burson v. Freeman, 504 U. S. 191, 205-206 (1992) (crediting tradition of prohibiting speech around polling places that began with the very adoption of the secret ballot in the late 19th century, and in which every State participated); id., at 214-216 (Scalia, J., concurring in judgment) (same); McIntyre, supra, at 375-377 (Scalia, J., dissenting) (crediting tradition of prohibiting anonymous election literature, which again began in 1890 and was universally adopted).

      * * *

      There is an obvious tension between the article of Minnesota's popularly approved Constitution which provides that judges shall be elected, and the Minnesota Supreme Court's announce clause which places most subjects of interest to the voters off limits. (The candidate-speech restrictions of all the other States that have them are also the product of judicial fiat.15) The disparity is perhaps unsurprising, since the ABA, which originated the announce clause, has long been an opponent of judicial elections. See ABA Model Code of Judicial Conduct Canon 5(C)(2), Comment (2000) ("[M]erit selection of judges is a preferable manner in which to select the judiciary"); An Independent Judiciary: Report of the ABA Commission on Separation of Powers and Judicial Independence 96 (1997) ("The American Bar Association strongly endorses the merit selection of judges, as opposed to their election ... . Five times between August 1972 and August 1984 the House of Delegates has approved recommendations stating the preference for merit selection and encouraging bar associations in jurisdictions where judges are elected ... to work for the adoption of merit selection and retention"). That opposition may be well taken (it certainly had the support of the Founders of the Federal Government), but the First Amendment does not permit it to achieve its goal by leaving the principle of elections in place while preventing candidates from discussing what the elections are about. "[T]he greater power to dispense with elections altogether does not include the lesser power to conduct elections under conditions of state-imposed voter ignorance. If the State chooses to tap the energy and the legitimizing power of the democratic process, it must accord the participants in that process ... the First Amendment rights that attach to their roles." Renne v. Geary, 501 U. S. 312, 349 (1991) (Marshall, J., dissenting); accord, Meyer v. Grant, 486 U. S. 414, 424-425 (1988) (rejecting argument that the greater power to end voter initiatives includes the lesser power to prohibit paid petition- circulators).

The Minnesota Supreme Court's canon of judicial conduct prohibiting candidates for judicial election from announcing their views on disputed legal and political issues violates the First Amendment. Accordingly, we reverse the grant of summary judgment to respondents and remand the case for proceedings consistent with this opinion.

It is so ordered.

Notes to Republican Party of Minnesota v. White (June 27, 2002)

1. The Eighth Circuit did not parse out the separate functions of these two entities in the case at hand, referring to the two of them collectively as the "Lawyers Board." We take the same approach.

2. Nor did Wersal have any success receiving answers from the Lawyers Board when he included "concrete examples," post, at 4, n. 2 (Stevens, J., dissenting), in his request for an advisory opinion on other subjects a month later: "As you are well aware, there is pending litigation over the constitutionality of certain portions of Canon 5. You are a plaintiff in this action and you have sued, among others, me as Director of the Office of Lawyers Professional Responsibility and Charles Lundberg as the Chair of the Board of Lawyers Professional Responsibility. Due to this pending litigation, I will not be answering your request for an advisory opinion at this time." App. 153.

3. Respondents are officers of the Lawyers Board and of the Minnesota Board on Judicial Standards (Judicial Board), which enforces the ethical rules applicable to judges.

4. Justice Ginsburg argues that we should ignore this concession at oral argument because it is inconsistent with the Eighth Circuit's interpretation of the announce clause. Post, at 8 (dissenting opinion). As she appears to acknowledge, however, the Eighth Circuit was merely silent on this particular question. Ibid. Silence is hardly inconsistent with what respondents conceded at oral argument.

5. In 1990, in response to concerns that its 1972 Model Canon–which was the basis for Minnesota's announce clause–violated the First Amendment, see L. Milord, The Development of the ABA Judicial Code 50 (1992), the ABA replaced that canon with a

provision that prohibits a judicial candidate from making "statements that commit or appear to commit the candidate with respect to cases, controversies or issues that are likely to come before the court." ABA Model Code of Judicial Conduct, Canon 5(A)(3)(d)(ii) (2000). At oral argument, respondents argued that the limiting constructions placed upon Minnesota's announce clause by the Eighth Circuit, and adopted by the Minnesota Supreme Court, render the scope of the clause no broader than the ABA's 1990 canon. Tr. of Oral Arg. 38. This argument is somewhat curious because, based on the same constitutional concerns that had motivated the ABA, the Minnesota Supreme Court was urged to replace the announce clause with the new ABA language, but, unlike other jurisdictions, declined. Final Report of the Advisory Committee to Review the ABA Model Code of Judicial Conduct and the Rules of the Minnesota Board on Judicial Standards 5—6 (June 29, 1994), reprinted at App. 367—368. The ABA, however, agrees with respondents' position, Brief for ABA as Amicus Curiae 5. We do not know whether the announce clause (as interpreted by state authorities) and the 1990 ABA canon are one and the same. No aspect of our constitutional analysis turns on this question.

6. Although the Eighth Circuit also referred to the compelling interest in an "independent" judiciary, 247 F.3d, at 864—868, both it and respondents appear to use that term, as applied to the issues involved in this case, as interchangeable with "impartial." See id., at 864 (describing a judge's independence as his "ability to apply the law neutrally"); Brief for Respondents 20, n. 4 ("[J]udicial impartiality is linked to judicial independence").

7. Justice Stevens asserts that the announce clause "serves the State's interest in maintaining both the appearance of this form of impartiality and its actuality." Post, at 5. We do not disagree. Some of the speech prohibited by the announce clause may well exhibit a bias against parties—including Justice Stevens' example of an election speech stressing the candidate's unbroken record of affirming convictions for rape, ibid. That is why we are careful to say that the announce clause is "barely tailored to serve that interest," supra, at 10 (emphasis added). The question under our strict scrutiny test, however, is not whether the announce clause serves this interest at all, but whether it is narrowly tailored to serve this interest. It is not.

8. We do not agree with Justice Stevens' broad assertion that "to the extent that [statements on legal issues] seek to enhance the popularity of the candidate by indicating how he would rule in specific cases if elected, they evidence a lack of fitness for office." Post, at 3 (emphasis added). Of course all statements on real-world legal issues "indicate" how the speaker would rule "in specific cases." And if making such statements (of honestly held views) with the hope of enhancing one's chances with the electorate displayed a lack of fitness for office, so would similarly motivated honest statements of judicial candidates made with the hope of enhancing their chances of confirmation by the Senate, or indeed of appointment by the President. Since such statements are made, we

think, in every confirmation hearing, Justice Stevens must contemplate a federal bench filled with the unfit.

9. Justice Ginsburg argues that the announce clause is not election nullifying because Wersal criticized past decisions of the Minnesota Supreme Court in his campaign literature and the Lawyers Board decided not to discipline him for doing so. Post, at 9—10. As we have explained, however, had Wersal additionally stated during his campaign that he did not feel bound to follow those erroneous decisions, he would not have been so lucky. Supra, at 5—7. This predicament hardly reflects "the robust communication of ideas and views from judicial candidate to voter." Post, at 10.

10. Justice Stevens devotes most of his dissent to this same argument that we do not make.

11. Nor do we assert that candidates for judicial office should be compelled to announce their views on disputed legal issues. Thus, Justice Ginsburg's repeated invocation of instances in which nominees to this Court declined to announce such views during Senate confirmation hearings is pointless. Post, at 5—6, n. 1, 17, n. 4. That the practice of voluntarily demurring does not establish the legitimacy of legal compulsion to demur is amply demonstrated by the unredacted text of the sentence she quotes in part, post, at 17, from Laird v. Tatum, 409 U.S. 824, 836, n. 5 (1972): "In terms of propriety, rather than disqualification, I would distinguish quite sharply between a public statement made prior to nomination for the bench, on the one hand, and a public statement made by a nominee to the bench." (Emphasis added.)

12. Although Justice Stevens at times appears to agree with Justice Ginsburg's premise that the judiciary is completely separated from the enterprise of representative government, post, at 3 ("[E]very good judge is fully aware of the distinction between the law and a personal point of view"), he eventually appears to concede that the separation does not hold true for many judges who sit on courts of last resort, post, at 3 ("If he is not a judge on the highest court in the State, he has an obligation to follow the precedent of that court, not his personal views or public opinion polls"); post, at 3, n. 2. Even if the policy making capacity of judges were limited to courts of last resort, that would only prove that the announce clause fails strict scrutiny. "[I]f announcing one's views in the context of a campaign for the State Supreme Court might be" protected speech, post, at 3, n. 2, then—even if announcing one's views in the context of a campaign for a lower court were not protected speech, ibid.—the announce clause would not be narrowly tailored, since it applies to high- and low-court candidates alike. In fact, however, the judges of inferior courts often "make law," since the precedent of the highest court does not cover every situation, and not every case is reviewed. Justice Stevens has repeatedly expressed the view that a settled course of lower court opinions binds the highest court. See, e.g., Reves v. Ernst & Young, 494 U.S. 56, 74 (1990) (concurring opinion); McNally v. United States, 483 U.S. 350, 376—377 (1987) (dissenting opinion).

13. Idaho Code Judicial Conduct, Canon 7 (2001); Mich. Code Judicial Conduct, Canon 7 (2002); N. C. Code Judicial Conduct, Canon 7 (2001); Ore. Code Judicial

Conduct, Rule 4—102 (2002). All of these States save Idaho have adopted the pledges or promises clause.

14. Ala. Canon of Judicial Ethics 7(B)(1)(c) (2002).

15. These restrictions are all contained in these states' codes of judicial conduct, App. to Brief for ABA as Amicus Curiae. "In every state, the highest court promulgates the Code of Judicial Conduct, either by express constitutional provision, statutory authorization, broad constitutional grant, or inherent power." In the Supreme Court of Texas: Per Curiam Opinion Concerning Amendments to Canons 5 and 6 of the Code of Judicial Conduct, 61 Tex. B. J. 64, 66 (1998) (collecting provisions).

The State admitted Sylvia's testimonial statement against petitioner, despite the fact that he had no opportunity to cross-examine her. That alone is sufficient to make out a violation of the Sixth Amendment: Crawford v. Washington (March 8, 2004)

Justice Scalia delivered the opinion of the Court.

Petitioner Michael Crawford stabbed a man who allegedly tried to rape his wife, Sylvia. At his trial, the State played for the jury Sylvia's tape-recorded statement to the police describing the stabbing, even though he had no opportunity for cross-examination. The Washington Supreme Court upheld petitioner's conviction after determining that Sylvia's statement was reliable. The question presented is whether this procedure complied with the Sixth Amendment's guarantee that, "[i]n all criminal prosecutions, the accused shall enjoy the right ... to be confronted with the witnesses against him."

I

On August 5, 1999, Kenneth Lee was stabbed at his apartment. Police arrested petitioner later that night. After giving petitioner and his wife Miranda warnings, detectives interrogated each of them twice. Petitioner eventually confessed that he and Sylvia had gone in search of Lee because he was upset over an earlier incident in which Lee had tried to rape her. The two had found Lee at his apartment, and a fight ensued in which Lee was stabbed in the torso and petitioner's hand was cut.

Petitioner gave the following account of the fight:

"Q. Okay. Did you ever see anything in [Lee's] hands?

"A. I think so, but I'm not positive.

"Q. Okay, when you think so, what do you mean by that?

"A. I coulda swore I seen him goin' for somethin' before, right before everything happened. He was like reachin', fiddlin' around down here and stuff ... and I just ... I don't know, I think, this is just a possibility, but I think, I think that he pulled somethin' out and I grabbed for it and that's how I got cut ... but I'm not positive. I, I, my mind goes blank when things like this happen. I mean, I just, I remember things wrong, I remember things that just doesn't, don't make sense to me later." App. 155 (punctuation added).

Sylvia generally corroborated petitioner's story about the events leading up to the fight, but her account of the fight itself was arguably different—particularly with respect to whether Lee had drawn a weapon before petitioner assaulted him:

"Q. Did Kenny do anything to fight back from this assault?

"A. (pausing) I know he reached into his pocket ... or somethin' ... I don't know what.

"Q. After he was stabbed?

"A. He saw Michael coming up. He lifted his hand ... his chest open, he might [have] went to go strike his hand out or something and then (inaudible).

"Q. Okay, you, you gotta speak up.

"A. Okay, he lifted his hand over his head maybe to strike Michael's hand down or something and then he put his hands in his ... put his right hand in his right pocket ... took a step back ... Michael proceeded to stab him ... then his hands were like ... how do you explain this ... open arms ... with his hands open and he fell down ... and we ran (describing subject holding hands open, palms toward assailant).

"Q. Okay, when he's standing there with his open hands, you're talking about Kenny, correct?

"A. Yeah, after, after the fact, yes.

"Q. Did you see anything in his hands at that point?

"A. (pausing) um um (no)." Id., at 137 (punctuation added).

The State charged petitioner with assault and attempted murder. At trial, he claimed self-defense. Sylvia did not testify because of the state marital privilege, which generally bars a spouse from testifying without the other spouse's consent. See Wash. Rev. Code §5.60.060(1) (1994). In Washington, this privilege does not extend to a spouse's out-of-court statements admissible under a hearsay exception, see State v. Burden, 120 Wash. 2d 371, 377, 841 P.2d 758, 761 (1992), so the State sought to introduce Sylvia's tape-recorded statements to the police as evidence that the stabbing was not in self-defense. Noting that Sylvia had admitted she led petitioner to Lee's apartment and thus had facilitated the assault, the State invoked the hearsay exception for statements against penal interest, Wash. Rule Evid. 804(b)(3) (2003).

Petitioner countered that, state law notwithstanding, admitting the evidence would violate his federal constitutional right to be "confronted with the witnesses against him." Amdt. 6. According to our description of that right in Ohio v. Roberts, 448 U.S. 56 (1980), it does not bar admission of an unavailable witness's statement against a criminal defendant if the statement bears "adequate 'indicia of reliability.' " Id., at 66. To meet that test, evidence must either fall within a "firmly rooted hearsay exception" or bear "particularized guarantees of trustworthiness." Ibid. The trial court here admitted the statement on the latter ground, offering several reasons why it was trustworthy: Sylvia was not shifting blame but rather corroborating her husband's story that he acted in self-defense or "justified reprisal"; she had direct knowledge as an eyewitness; she was describing recent events; and she was being questioned by a "neutral" law enforcement officer. App. 76—77. The prosecution played the tape for the jury and relied on it in closing, arguing that it was "damning evidence" that "completely refutes [petitioner's] claim of self-defense." Tr. 468 (Oct. 21, 1999). The jury convicted petitioner of assault.

The Washington Court of Appeals reversed. It applied a nine-factor test to determine whether Sylvia's statement bore particularized guarantees of trustworthiness, and noted several reasons why it did not: The statement contradicted one she had previously given; it was made in response to specific questions; and at one point she admitted she had shut her eyes during the stabbing. The court considered and rejected the State's argument that Sylvia's statement was reliable because it coincided with petitioner's to such a degree that the two "interlocked." The court determined that, although the two statements agreed about the events leading up to the stabbing, they differed on the issue crucial to petitioner's self-defense claim: "[Petitioner's] version asserts that Lee may have had something in his hand when he stabbed him; but Sylvia's version has Lee grabbing for something only after he has been stabbed." App. 32.

The Washington Supreme Court reinstated the conviction, unanimously concluding that, although Sylvia's statement did not fall under a firmly rooted hearsay exception, it bore guarantees of trustworthiness: " '[W]hen a codefendant's confession is virtually identical [to, i.e., interlocks with,] that of a defendant, it may be deemed reliable.' " 147 Wash. 2d 424, 437, 54 P.3d 656, 663 (2002) (quoting State v. Rice, 120 Wash. 2d 549, 570, 844 P.2d 416, 427 (1993)). The court explained:

"Although the Court of Appeals concluded that the statements were contradictory, upon closer inspection they appear to overlap... .

"[B]oth of the Crawfords' statements indicate that Lee was possibly grabbing for a weapon, but they are equally unsure when this event may have taken place. They are also equally unsure how Michael received the cut on his hand, leading the court to question when, if ever, Lee possessed a weapon. In this respect they overlap.

"[N]either Michael nor Sylvia clearly stated that Lee had a weapon in hand from which Michael was simply defending himself. And it is this omission by both that interlocks the statements and makes Sylvia's statement reliable." 147 Wash. 2d, at 438—439, 54 P.3d, at 664 (internal quotation marks omitted).1

We granted certiorari to determine whether the State's use of Sylvia's statement violated the Confrontation Clause. 539 U.S. 914 (2003).

II

The Sixth Amendment's Confrontation Clause provides that, "[i]n all criminal prosecutions, the accused shall enjoy the right ... to be confronted with the witnesses against him." We have held that this bedrock procedural guarantee applies to both federal and state prosecutions. Pointer v. Texas, 380 U.S. 400, 406 (1965). As noted above, Roberts says that an unavailable witness's out-of-court statement may be admitted so long as it has adequate indicia of reliability–i.e., falls within a "firmly rooted hearsay exception" or bears "particularized guarantees of trustworthiness." 448 U.S., at 66.

Petitioner argues that this test strays from the original meaning of the Confrontation Clause and urges us to reconsider it.

A

The Constitution's text does not alone resolve this case. One could plausibly read "witnesses against" a defendant to mean those who actually testify at trial, cf. Woodsides v. State, 3 Miss. 655, 664—665 (1837), those whose statements are offered at trial, see 3 J. Wigmore, Evidence §1397, p. 104 (2d ed. 1923) (hereinafter Wigmore), or something in-between, see infra, at 15—16. We must therefore turn to the historical background of the Clause to understand its meaning.

The right to confront one's accusers is a concept that dates back to Roman times. See Coy v. Iowa, 487 U.S. 1012, 1015 (1988); Herrmann & Speer, Facing the Accuser: Ancient and Medieval Precursors of the Confrontation Clause, 34 Va. J. Int'l L. 481 (1994). The founding generation's immediate source of the concept, however, was the common law. English common law has long differed from continental civil law in regard to the manner in which witnesses give testimony in criminal trials. The common-law tradition is one of live testimony in court subject to adversarial testing, while the civil law condones examination in private by judicial officers. See 3 W. Blackstone, Commentaries on the Laws of England 373—374 (1768).

Nonetheless, England at times adopted elements of the civil-law practice. Justices of the peace or other officials examined suspects and witnesses before trial. These examinations were sometimes read in court in lieu of live testimony, a practice that "occasioned frequent demands by the prisoner to have his 'accusers,' i.e. the witnesses against him, brought before him face to face." 1 J. Stephen, History of the Criminal Law of England 326 (1883). In some cases, these demands were refused. See 9 W. Holdsworth, History of English Law 216—217, 228 (3d ed. 1944); e.g., Raleigh's Case, 2 How. St. Tr. 1, 15—16, 24 (1603); Throckmorton's Case, 1 How. St. Tr. 869, 875—876 (1554); cf. Lilburn's Case, 3 How. St. Tr. 1315, 1318—1322, 1329 (Star Chamber 1637).

Pretrial examinations became routine under two statutes passed during the reign of Queen Mary in the 16th century, 1 & 2 Phil. & M., c. 13 (1554), and 2 & 3 id., c. 10 (1555). These Marian bail and committal statutes required justices of the peace to examine suspects and witnesses in felony cases and to certify the results to the court. It is doubtful that the original purpose of the examinations was to produce evidence admissible at trial. See J. Langbein, Prosecuting Crime in the Renaissance 21—34 (1974). Whatever the original purpose, however, they came to be used as evidence in some cases, see 2 M. Hale, Pleas of the Crown 284 (1736), resulting in an adoption of continental procedure. See 4 Holdsworth, supra, at 528—530.

The most notorious instances of civil-law examination occurred in the great political trials of the 16th and 17th centuries. One such was the 1603 trial of Sir Walter Raleigh for treason. Lord Cobham, Raleigh's alleged accomplice, had implicated him in an examination before the Privy Council and in a letter. At Raleigh's trial, these were read to the jury. Raleigh argued that Cobham had lied to save himself: "Cobham is absolutely in the King's mercy; to excuse me cannot avail him; by accusing me he may hope for favour." 1 D. Jardine, Criminal Trials 435 (1832). Suspecting that Cobham would recant, Raleigh demanded that the judges call him to appear, arguing that "[t]he Proof of the Common Law is by witness and jury: let Cobham be here, let him speak it. Call my accuser before my face ... ." 2 How. St. Tr., at 15—16. The judges refused, id., at 24, and, despite Raleigh's protestations that he was being tried "by the Spanish Inquisition," id., at 15, the jury convicted, and Raleigh was sentenced to death.

One of Raleigh's trial judges later lamented that " 'the justice of England has never been so degraded and injured as by the condemnation of Sir Walter Raleigh.' " 1 Jardine, supra, at 520. Through a series of statutory and judicial reforms, English law developed a right of confrontation that limited these abuses. For example, treason statutes required witnesses to confront the accused "face to face" at his arraignment. E.g., 13 Car. 2, c. 1, §5 (1661); see 1 Hale, supra, at 306. Courts, meanwhile, developed relatively strict rules of unavailability, admitting examinations only if the witness was demonstrably unable to testify in person. See Lord Morley's Case, 6 How. St. Tr. 769, 770—771 (H. L. 1666); 2 Hale, supra, at 284; 1 Stephen, supra, at 358. Several authorities also stated that a suspect's confession could be admitted only against himself, and not against others he implicated. See 2 W. Hawkins, Pleas of the Crown c. 46, §3, pp. 603—604 (T. Leach 6th ed. 1787); 1 Hale, supra, at 585, n. (k); 1 G. Gilbert, Evidence 216 (C. Lofft ed. 1791); cf. Tong's Case, Kel. J. 17, 18, 84 Eng. Rep. 1061, 1062 (1662) (treason). But see King v. Westbeer, 1 Leach 12, 168 Eng. Rep. 108, 109 (1739).

One recurring question was whether the admissibility of an unavailable witness's pretrial examination depended on whether the defendant had had an opportunity to cross-examine him. In 1696, the Court of King's Bench answered this question in the affirmative, in the widely reported misdemeanor libel case of King v. Paine, 5 Mod. 163, 87 Eng. Rep. 584. The court ruled that, even though a witness was dead, his examination was not admissible where "the defendant not being present when [it was] taken before the mayor ... had lost the benefit of a cross-examination." Id., at 165, 87 Eng. Rep., at 585. The question was also debated at length during the infamous proceedings against Sir John Fenwick on a bill of attainder. Fenwick's counsel objected to admitting the examination of a witness who had been spirited away, on the ground that Fenwick had had no opportunity to cross-examine. See Fenwick's Case, 13 How. St. Tr. 537, 591—592 (H. C. 1696) (Powys) ("[T]hat which they would offer is something that Mr. Goodman hath sworn when he was examined ...; sir J. F. not being present or privy, and no opportunity given to cross-examine the person; and I conceive that cannot be offered as evidence ..."); id., at 592 (Shower) ("[N]o deposition of a person can be read, though beyond sea, unless in cases where the party it is to be read against was privy to the examination, and might have cross-examined him ... . [O]ur constitution is, that the person shall see his accuser"). The examination was nonetheless admitted on a closely divided vote after several of those present opined that the common-law rules of procedure did not apply to parliamentary attainder proceedings—one speaker even admitting that the evidence would normally be inadmissible. See id., at 603—604 (Williamson); id., at 604—605 (Chancellor of the Exchequer); id., at 607; 3 Wigmore §1364, at 22—23, n. 54. Fenwick was condemned, but the proceedings "must have burned into the general consciousness the vital importance of the rule securing the right of cross-examination." Id., §1364, at 22; cf. Carmell v. Texas, 529 U.S. 513, 526—530 (2000).

Paine had settled the rule requiring a prior opportunity for cross-examination as a matter of common law, but some doubts remained over whether the Marian statutes prescribed an exception to it in felony cases. The statutes did not identify the circumstances under which examinations were admissible, see 1 & 2 Phil. & M., c. 13 (1554); 2 & 3 id., c. 10 (1555), and some inferred that no prior opportunity for cross-examination was required. See Westbeer, supra, at 12, 168 Eng. Rep., at 109; compare Fenwick's Case, 13 How. St. Tr., at 596 (Sloane), with id., at 602 (Musgrave). Many who expressed this view acknowledged that it meant the statutes were in derogation of the common law. See King v. Eriswell, 3 T. R. 707, 710, 100 Eng. Rep. 815, 817 (K. B. 1790) (Grose, J.) (dicta); id., at 722—723, 100 Eng. Rep., at 823—824 (Kenyon, C. J.) (same); compare 1 Gilbert, Evidence, at 215 (admissible only "by Force 'of the Statute' "), with id., at 65. Nevertheless, by 1791 (the year the Sixth Amendment was ratified), courts were applying the cross-examination rule even to examinations by justices of the peace in felony cases. See King v. Dingler, 2 Leach 561, 562—563, 168 Eng. Rep. 383, 383—384 (1791); King v. Woodcock, 1 Leach 500, 502—504, 168 Eng. Rep. 352, 353 (1789); cf. King v. Radbourne, 1 Leach 457, 459—461, 168 Eng. Rep. 330, 331—332 (1787); 3 Wigmore §1364, at 23. Early 19th-century treatises confirm that requirement. See 1 T. Starkie, Evidence 95 (1826); 2 id., at 484—492; T. Peake, Evidence 63—64 (3d ed. 1808). When Parliament amended the statutes in 1848 to make the requirement explicit, see 11 & 12 Vict., c. 42, §17, the change merely "introduced in terms" what was already afforded the defendant "by the equitable construction of the law." Queen v. Beeston, 29 Eng. L. & Eq. R. 527, 529 (Ct. Crim. App. 1854) (Jervis, C. J.).2

B

Controversial examination practices were also used in the Colonies. Early in the 18th century, for example, the Virginia Council protested against the Governor for having "privately issued several commissions to examine witnesses against particular men ex parte," complaining that "the person accused is not admitted to be confronted with, or defend himself against his defamers." A Memorial Concerning the Maladministrations of His Excellency Francis Nicholson, reprinted in 9 English Historical Documents 253, 257 (D. Douglas ed. 1955). A decade before the Revolution, England gave jurisdiction over Stamp Act offenses to the admiralty courts, which followed civil-law rather than common-law procedures and thus routinely took testimony by deposition or private judicial examination. See 5 Geo. 3, c. 12, §57 (1765); Pollitt, The Right of Confrontation: Its History and Modern Dress, 8 J. Pub. L. 381, 396—397 (1959). Colonial representatives protested that the Act subverted their rights "by extending the jurisdiction of the courts of admiralty beyond its ancient limits." Resolutions of the Stamp

Act Congress §8th (Oct. 19, 1765), reprinted in Sources of Our Liberties 270, 271 (R. Perry & J. Cooper eds. 1959). John Adams, defending a merchant in a high-profile admiralty case, argued: "Examinations of witnesses upon Interrogatories, are only by the Civil Law. Interrogatories are unknown at common Law, and Englishmen and common Lawyers have an aversion to them if not an Abhorrence of them." Draft of Argument in Sewall v. Hancock (1768—1769), in 2 Legal Papers of John Adams 194, 207 (K. Wroth & H. Zobel eds. 1965).

Many declarations of rights adopted around the time of the Revolution guaranteed a right of confrontation. See Virginia Declaration of Rights §8 (1776); Pennsylvania Declaration of Rights §IX (1776); Delaware Declaration of Rights §14 (1776); Maryland Declaration of Rights §XIX (1776); North Carolina Declaration of Rights §VII (1776); Vermont Declaration of Rights Ch. I, §X (1777); Massachusetts Declaration of Rights §XII (1780); New Hampshire Bill of Rights §XV (1783), all reprinted in 1 B. Schwartz, The Bill of Rights: A Documentary History 235, 265, 278, 282, 287, 323, 342, 377 (1971). The proposed Federal Constitution, however, did not. At the Massachusetts ratifying convention, Abraham Holmes objected to this omission precisely on the ground that it would lead to civil-law practices: "The mode of trial is altogether indetermined; ... whether [the defendant] is to be allowed to confront the witnesses, and have the advantage of cross-examination, we are not yet told.... [W]e shall find Congress possessed of powers enabling them to institute judicatories little less inauspicious than a certain tribunal in Spain, ... the Inquisition." 2 Debates on the Federal Constitution 110—111 (J. Elliot 2d ed. 1863). Similarly, a prominent Antifederalist writing under the pseudonym Federal Farmer criticized the use of "written evidence" while objecting to the omission of a vicinage right: "Nothing can be more essential than the cross examining [of] witnesses, and generally before the triers of the facts in question.... [W]ritten evidence ... [is] almost useless; it must be frequently taken ex parte, and but very seldom leads to the proper discovery of truth." R. Lee, Letter IV by the Federal Farmer (Oct. 15, 1787), reprinted in 1 Schwartz, supra, at 469, 473. The First Congress responded by including the Confrontation Clause in the proposal that became the Sixth Amendment.

Early state decisions shed light upon the original understanding of the common-law right. State v. Webb, 2 N. C. 103 (1794) (per curiam), decided a mere three years after the adoption of the Sixth Amendment, held that depositions could be read against an accused only if they were taken in his presence. Rejecting a broader reading of the English authorities, the court held: "[I]t is a rule of the common law, founded on natural justice, that no man shall be prejudiced by evidence which he had not the liberty to cross examine." Id., at 104.

Similarly, in State v. Campbell, 1 S. C. 124 (1844), South Carolina's highest law court excluded a deposition taken by a coroner in the absence of the accused. It held: "[I]f we are to decide the question by the established rules of the common law, there could not be a dissenting voice. For, notwithstanding the death of the witness, and whatever the respectability of the court taking the depositions, the solemnity of the occasion and the weight of the testimony, such depositions are ex parte, and, therefore, utterly incompetent." Id., at 125. The court said that one of the "indispensable conditions" implicitly guaranteed by the State Constitution was that "prosecutions be carried on to the conviction of the accused, by witnesses confronted by him, and subjected to his personal examination." Ibid.

Many other decisions are to the same effect. Some early cases went so far as to hold that prior testimony was inadmissible in criminal cases even if the accused had a previous opportunity to cross-examine. See Finn v. Commonwealth, 26 Va. 701, 708 (1827); State v. Atkins, 1 Tenn. 229 (1807) (per curiam). Most courts rejected that view, but only after reaffirming that admissibility depended on a prior opportunity for cross-examination. See United States v. Macomb, 26 F. Cas. 1132, 1133 (No. 15,702) (CC Ill. 1851); State v. Houser, 26 Mo. 431, 435—436 (1858); Kendrick v. State, 29 Tenn. 479, 485—488 (1850); Bostick v. State, 22 Tenn. 344, 345—346 (1842); Commonwealth v. Richards, 35 Mass. 434, 437 (1837); State v. Hill, 2 Hill 607, 608—610 (S. C. 1835); Johnston v. State, 10 Tenn. 58, 59 (1821). Nineteenth-century treatises confirm the rule. See 1 J. Bishop, Criminal Procedure §1093, p. 689 (2d ed. 1872); T. Cooley, Constitutional Limitations *318.

III

This history supports two inferences about the meaning of the Sixth Amendment.

A

First, the principal evil at which the Confrontation Clause was directed was the civil-law mode of criminal procedure, and particularly its use of ex parte examinations as evidence against the accused. It was these practices that the Crown deployed in notorious treason cases like Raleigh's; that the Marian statutes invited; that English law's assertion of a right to confrontation was meant to prohibit; and that the founding-era rhetoric decried. The Sixth Amendment must be interpreted with this focus in mind.

Accordingly, we once again reject the view that the Confrontation Clause applies of its own force only to in-court testimony, and that its application to out-of-court statements introduced at trial depends upon "the law of Evidence for the time being." 3 Wigmore §1397, at 101; accord, Dutton v. Evans, 400 U.S. 74, 94 (1970) (Harlan, J., concurring in result). Leaving the regulation of out-of-court statements to the law of evidence would render the Confrontation Clause powerless to prevent even the most flagrant inquisitorial practices. Raleigh was, after all, perfectly free to confront those who read Cobham's confession in court.

This focus also suggests that not all hearsay implicates the Sixth Amendment's core concerns. An off-hand, overheard remark might be unreliable evidence and thus a good candidate for exclusion under hearsay rules, but it bears little resemblance to the civil-law abuses the Confrontation Clause targeted. On the other hand, ex parte examinations might sometimes be admissible under modern hearsay rules, but the Framers certainly would not have condoned them.

The text of the Confrontation Clause reflects this focus. It applies to "witnesses" against the accused—in other words, those who "bear testimony." 1 N. Webster, An American Dictionary of the English Language (1828). "Testimony," in turn, is typically "[a] solemn declaration or affirmation made for the purpose of establishing or proving some fact." Ibid. An accuser who makes a formal statement to government officers bears testimony in a sense that a person who makes a casual remark to an acquaintance does not. The constitutional text, like the history underlying the common-law right of confrontation, thus reflects an especially acute concern with a specific type of out-of-court statement.

Various formulations of this core class of "testimonial" statements exist: "ex parte in-court testimony or its functional equivalent—that is, material such as affidavits, custodial examinations, prior testimony that the defendant was unable to cross-examine, or similar pretrial statements that declarants would reasonably expect to be used prosecutorially," Brief for Petitioner 23; "extrajudicial statements ... contained in formalized testimonial materials, such as affidavits, depositions, prior testimony, or confessions," White v. Illinois, 502 U.S. 346, 365 (1992) (Thomas, J., joined by Scalia, J., concurring in part and concurring in judgment); "statements that were made under circumstances which would lead an objective witness reasonably to believe that the statement would be available for use at a later trial," Brief for National Association of Criminal Defense Lawyers et al. as Amici Curiae 3. These formulations all share a common nucleus and then define the Clause's coverage at various levels of abstraction around it. Regardless of the precise articulation, some statements qualify under any definition—for example, ex parte testimony at a preliminary hearing.

Statements taken by police officers in the course of interrogations are also testimonial under even a narrow standard. Police interrogations bear a striking resemblance to examinations by justices of the peace in England. The statements are not sworn testimony, but the absence of oath was not dispositive. Cobham's examination was unsworn, see 1 Jardine, Criminal Trials, at 430, yet Raleigh's trial has long been thought a paradigmatic confrontation violation, see, e.g., Campbell, 1 S. C., at 130. Under the Marian statutes, witnesses were typically put on oath, but suspects were not. See 2 Hale, Pleas of the Crown, at 52. Yet Hawkins and others went out of their way to caution that such unsworn confessions were not admissible against anyone but the confessor. See supra, at 8.[3]

That interrogators are police officers rather than magistrates does not change the picture either. Justices of the peace conducting examinations under the Marian statutes were not magistrates as we understand that office today, but had an essentially investigative and prosecutorial function. See 1 Stephen, Criminal Law of England, at 221; Langbein, Prosecuting Crime in the Renaissance, at 34—45. England did not have a professional police force until the 19th century, see 1 Stephen, supra, at 194—200, so it is not surprising that other government officers performed the investigative functions now associated primarily with the police. The involvement of government officers in the production of testimonial evidence presents the same risk, whether the officers are police or justices of the peace.

In sum, even if the Sixth Amendment is not solely concerned with testimonial hearsay, that is its primary object, and interrogations by law enforcement officers fall squarely within that class.4

B

The historical record also supports a second proposition: that the Framers would not have allowed admission of testimonial statements of a witness who did not appear at trial unless he was unavailable to testify, and the defendant had had a prior opportunity for cross-examination. The text of the Sixth Amendment does not suggest any open-ended exceptions from the confrontation requirement to be developed by the courts. Rather, the "right ... to be confronted with the witnesses against him," Amdt. 6, is most naturally read as a reference to the right of confrontation at common law, admitting only those exceptions established at the time of the founding. See Mattox v. United States, 156 U.S. 237, 243 (1895); cf. Houser, 26 Mo., at 433–435. As the English authorities above reveal, the common law in 1791 conditioned admissibility of an absent witness's examination on unavailability and a prior opportunity to cross-examine. The Sixth Amendment therefore incorporates those limitations. The numerous early state decisions applying the same test confirm that these principles were received as part of the common law in this country.5

We do not read the historical sources to say that a prior opportunity to cross-examine was merely a sufficient, rather than a necessary, condition for admissibility of testimonial statements. They suggest that this requirement was dispositive, and not merely one of several ways to establish reliability. This is not to deny, as The Chief Justice notes, that "[t]here were always exceptions to the general rule of exclusion" of hearsay evidence. Post, at 5. Several had become well established by 1791. See 3 Wigmore §1397, at 101; Brief for United States as Amicus Curiae 13, n. 5. But there is scant evidence that exceptions were invoked to admit testimonial statements against the accused in a criminal case.6 Most of the hearsay exceptions covered statements that by their nature were not testimonial–for example, business records or statements in furtherance of a conspiracy. We do not infer from these that the Framers thought exceptions would apply even to prior testimony. Cf. Lilly v. Virginia, 527 U.S. 116, 134 (1999) (plurality opinion) ("[A]ccomplices' confessions that inculpate a criminal defendant are not within a firmly rooted exception to the hearsay rule").7

IV

Our case law has been largely consistent with these two principles. Our leading early decision, for example, involved a deceased witness's prior trial testimony. Mattox v. United States, 156 U.S. 237 (1895). In allowing the statement to be admitted, we relied on the fact that the defendant had had, at the first trial, an adequate opportunity to confront the witness: "The substance of the constitutional protection is preserved to the prisoner in the advantage he has once had of seeing the witness face to face, and of subjecting him to the ordeal of a cross-examination. This, the law says, he shall under no circumstances be deprived of ... ." Id., at 244.

Our later cases conform to Mattox's holding that prior trial or preliminary hearing testimony is admissible only if the defendant had an adequate opportunity to cross-examine. See Mancusi v. Stubbs, 408 U.S. 204, 213—216 (1972); California v. Green, 399 U.S. 149, 165—168 (1970); Pointer v. Texas, 380 U.S., at 406—408; cf. Kirby v. United States, 174 U.S. 47, 55—61 (1899). Even where the defendant had such an opportunity, we excluded the testimony where the government had not established unavailability of the witness. See Barber v. Page, 390 U.S. 719, 722—725 (1968); cf. Motes v. United States, 178 U.S. 458, 470—471 (1900). We similarly excluded accomplice confessions where the defendant had no opportunity to cross-examine. See Roberts v. Russell, 392 U.S. 293, 294—295 (1968) (per curiam); Bruton v. United States, 391 U.S. 123, 126—128 (1968); Douglas v. Alabama, 380 U.S. 415, 418—420 (1965). In contrast, we considered reliability factors beyond prior opportunity for cross-examination when the hearsay statement at issue was not testimonial. See Dutton v. Evans, 400 U.S., at 87—89 (plurality opinion).

Even our recent cases, in their outcomes, hew closely to the traditional line. Ohio v. Roberts, 448 U.S., at 67—70, admitted testimony from a preliminary hearing at which the defendant had examined the witness. Lilly v. Virginia, supra, excluded testimonial statements that the defendant had had no opportunity to test by cross-examination. And Bourjaily v. United States, 483 U.S. 171, 181—184 (1987), admitted statements made unwittingly to an FBI informant after applying a more general test that did not make prior cross-examination an indispensable requirement.8

Lee v. Illinois, 476 U.S. 530 (1986), on which the State relies, is not to the contrary. There, we rejected the State's attempt to admit an accomplice confession. The State had argued that the confession was admissible because it "interlocked" with the defendant's. We dealt with the argument by rejecting its premise, holding that "when the discrepancies between the statements are not insignificant, the codefendant's confession may not be admitted." Id., at 545. Respondent argues that "[t]he logical inference of this statement is that when the discrepancies between the statements are insignificant, then the codefendant's statement may be admitted." Brief for Respondent 6. But this is merely a possible inference, not an inevitable one, and we do not draw it here. If Lee had meant authoritatively to announce an exception–previously unknown to this Court's jurisprudence–for interlocking confessions, it would not have done so in such an oblique manner. Our only precedent on interlocking confessions had addressed the entirely different question whether a limiting instruction cured prejudice to codefendants from admitting a defendant's own confession against him in a joint trial. See Parker v. Randolph, 442 U.S. 62, 69—76 (1979) (plurality opinion), abrogated by Cruz v. New York, 481 U.S. 186 (1987).

Our cases have thus remained faithful to the Framers' understanding: Testimonial statements of witnesses absent from trial have been admitted only where the declarant is unavailable, and only where the defendant has had a prior opportunity to cross-examine.9

V

Although the results of our decisions have generally been faithful to the original meaning of the Confrontation Clause, the same cannot be said of our rationales. Roberts conditions the admissibility of all hearsay evidence on whether it falls under a "firmly rooted hearsay exception" or bears "particularized guarantees of trustworthiness." 448 U.S., at 66. This test departs from the historical principles identified above in two respects. First, it is too broad: It applies the same mode of analysis whether or not the hearsay consists of ex parte testimony. This often results in close constitutional scrutiny in cases that are far removed from the core concerns of the Clause. At the same time, however, the test is too narrow: It admits statements that do consist of ex parte testimony upon a mere finding of reliability. This malleable standard often fails to protect against paradigmatic confrontation violations.

Members of this Court and academics have suggested that we revise our doctrine to reflect more accurately the original understanding of the Clause. See, e.g., Lilly, 527 U.S., at 140–143 (Breyer, J., concurring); White, 502 U.S., at 366 (Thomas, J., joined by Scalia, J., concurring in part and concurring in judgment); A. Amar, The Constitution and Criminal Procedure 125–131 (1997); Friedman, Confrontation: The Search for Basic Principles, 86 Geo. L. J. 1011 (1998). They offer two proposals: First, that we apply the Confrontation Clause only to testimonial statements, leaving the remainder to regulation by hearsay law–thus eliminating the overbreadth referred to above. Second, that we impose an absolute bar to statements that are testimonial, absent a prior opportunity to cross-examine–thus eliminating the excessive narrowness referred to above.

In White, we considered the first proposal and rejected it. 502 U.S., at 352–353. Although our analysis in this case casts doubt on that holding, we need not definitively resolve whether it survives our decision today, because Sylvia Crawford's statement is testimonial under any definition. This case does, however, squarely implicate the second proposal.

A

Where testimonial statements are involved, we do not think the Framers meant to leave the Sixth Amendment's protection to the vagaries of the rules of evidence, much less to amorphous notions of "reliability." Certainly none of the authorities discussed above acknowledges any general reliability exception to the common-law rule. Admitting statements deemed reliable by a judge is fundamentally at odds with the right of confrontation. To be sure, the Clause's ultimate goal is to ensure reliability of evidence, but it is a procedural rather than a substantive guarantee. It commands, not that evidence be reliable, but that reliability be assessed in a particular manner: by testing in the crucible of cross-examination. The Clause thus reflects a judgment, not only about the desirability of reliable evidence (a point on which there could be little dissent), but about how reliability can best be determined. Cf. 3 Blackstone, Commentaries, at 373 ("This open examination of witnesses . . . is much more conducive to the clearing up of truth"); M. Hale, History and Analysis of the Common Law of England 258 (1713) (adversarial testing "beats and bolts out the Truth much better").

The Roberts test allows a jury to hear evidence, untested by the adversary process, based on a mere judicial determination of reliability. It thus replaces the constitutionally prescribed method of assessing reliability with a wholly foreign one. In this respect, it is very different from exceptions to the Confrontation Clause that make no claim to be a surrogate means of assessing reliability. For example, the rule of forfeiture by wrongdoing (which we accept) extinguishes confrontation claims on essentially equitable grounds; it does not purport to be an alternative means of determining reliability. See Reynolds v. United States, 98 U.S. 145, 158—159 (1879).

The Raleigh trial itself involved the very sorts of reliability determinations that Roberts authorizes. In the face of Raleigh's repeated demands for confrontation, the prosecution responded with many of the arguments a court applying Roberts might invoke today: that Cobham's statements were self-inculpatory, 2 How. St. Tr., at 19, that they were not made in the heat of passion, id., at 14, and that they were not "extracted from [him] upon any hopes or promise of Pardon," id., at 29. It is not plausible that the Framers' only objection to the trial was that Raleigh's judges did not properly weigh these factors before sentencing him to death. Rather, the problem was that the judges refused to allow Raleigh to confront Cobham in court, where he could cross-examine him and try to expose his accusation as a lie.

Dispensing with confrontation because testimony is obviously reliable is akin to dispensing with jury trial because a defendant is obviously guilty. This is not what the Sixth Amendment prescribes.

B

The legacy of Roberts in other courts vindicates the Framers' wisdom in rejecting a general reliability exception. The framework is so unpredictable that it fails to provide meaningful protection from even core confrontation violations.

Reliability is an amorphous, if not entirely subjective, concept. There are countless factors bearing on whether a statement is reliable; the nine-factor balancing test applied by the Court of Appeals below is representative. See, e.g., People v. Farrell, 34 P.3d 401, 406—407 (Colo. 2001) (eight-factor test). Whether a statement is deemed reliable depends heavily on which factors the judge considers and how much weight he accords each of them. Some courts wind up attaching the same significance to opposite facts. For example, the Colorado Supreme Court held a statement more reliable because its inculpation of the defendant was "detailed," id., at 407, while the Fourth Circuit found a statement more reliable because the portion implicating another was "fleeting," United States v. Photogrammetric Data Servs., Inc., 259 F.3d 229, 245 (2001). The Virginia Court of Appeals found a statement more reliable because the witness was in custody and charged with a crime (thus making the statement more obviously against her penal interest), see Nowlin v. Commonwealth, 40 Va. App. 327, 335–338, 579 S. E. 2d 367, 371–372 (2003), while the Wisconsin Court of Appeals found a statement more reliable because the witness was not in custody and not a suspect, see State v. Bintz, 2002 WI App. 204, ¶13, 257 Wis. 2d 177, 187, 650 N. W. 2d 913, 918. Finally, the Colorado Supreme Court in one case found a statement more reliable because it was given "immediately after" the events at issue, Farrell, supra, at 407, while that same court, in another case, found a statement more reliable because two years had elapsed, Stevens v. People, 29 P.3d 305, 316 (2001).

The unpardonable vice of the Roberts test, however, is not its unpredictability, but its demonstrated capacity to admit core testimonial statements that the Confrontation Clause plainly meant to exclude. Despite the plurality's speculation in Lilly, 527 U.S., at 137, that it was "highly unlikely" that accomplice confessions implicating the accused could survive Roberts, courts continue routinely to admit them. See Photogrammetric Data Servs., supra, at 245–246; Farrell, supra, at 406–408; Stevens, supra, at 314–318; Taylor v. Commonwealth, 63 S. W. 3d 151, 166–168 (Ky. 2001); State v. Hawkins, No. 2001–P–0060, 2002 WL 31895118, ¶¶34–37, *6 (Ohio App., Dec. 31, 2002); Bintz, supra, ¶¶7–14, 257 Wis. 2d, at 183–188, 650 N. W. 2d, at 916–918; People v. Lawrence, 55 P.3d 155, 160–161 (Colo. App. 2001); State v. Jones, 171 Ore. App. 375, 387–391, 15 P.3d 616, 623–625 (2000); State v. Marshall, 136 Ohio App. 3d 742, 747–748, 737 N. E. 2d 1005, 1009 (2000); People v. Schutte, 240 Mich. App. 713, 718–721, 613 N. W. 2d 370, 376–377 (2000); People v. Thomas, 313 Ill. App. 3d 998, 1005–1007, 730 N. E. 2d 618, 625–626 (2000); cf. Nowlin, supra, at 335–338, 579 S. E. 2d, at 371–372 (witness confessed to a related crime); People v. Campbell, 309 Ill. App. 3d 423, 431–432, 721 N. E. 2d 1225, 1230 (1999) (same). One recent study found that, after Lilly, appellate courts admitted accomplice statements to the authorities in 25 out of 70 cases—more than one-third of the time. Kirst, Appellate Court Answers to the Confrontation Questions in Lilly v. Virginia, 53 Syracuse L. Rev. 87, 105 (2003). Courts have invoked Roberts to admit other sorts of plainly testimonial statements despite the absence of any opportunity to cross-examine. See United States v. Aguilar, 295 F.3d 1018, 1021–1023 (CA9 2002) (plea allocution showing existence of a conspiracy); United States v. Centracchio, 265 F.3d 518, 527–530 (CA7 2001) (same); United States v. Dolah, 245 F.3d 98, 104–105 (CA2 2001) (same); United States v. Petrillo, 237 F.3d 119, 122–123 (CA2 2000) (same); United States v. Moskowitz, 215 F.3d 265, 268–269 (CA2 2000) (same); United States v. Gallego, 191 F.3d 156, 166–168 (CA2 1999) (same); United States v. Papajohn, 212 F.3d 1112, 1118–1120 (CA8 2000) (grand jury testimony); United States v. Thomas, 30 Fed. Appx. 277, 279 (CA4 2002) (same); Bintz, supra, ¶¶15–22, 257 Wis. 2d, at 188–191, 650 N. W. 2d, at 918–920 (prior trial testimony); State v. McNeill, 140 N. C. App. 450, 457–460, 537 S. E. 2d 518, 523–524 (2000) (same).

To add insult to injury, some of the courts that admit untested testimonial statements find reliability in the very factors that make the statements testimonial. As noted earlier, one court relied on the fact that the witness's statement was made to police while in custody on pending charges—the theory being that this made the statement more clearly against penal interest and thus more reliable. Nowlin, supra, at 335—338, 579 S. E. 2d, at 371—372. Other courts routinely rely on the fact that a prior statement is given under oath in judicial proceedings. E.g., Gallego, supra, at 168 (plea allocution); Papajohn, supra, at 1120 (grand jury testimony). That inculpating statements are given in a testimonial setting is not an antidote to the confrontation problem, but rather the trigger that makes the Clause's demands most urgent. It is not enough to point out that most of the usual safeguards of the adversary process attend the statement, when the single safeguard missing is the one the Confrontation Clause demands.

C

Roberts' failings were on full display in the proceedings below. Sylvia Crawford made her statement while in police custody, herself a potential suspect in the case. Indeed, she had been told that whether she would be released "depend[ed] on how the investigation continues." App. 81. In response to often leading questions from police detectives, she implicated her husband in Lee's stabbing and at least arguably undermined his self-defense claim. Despite all this, the trial court admitted her statement, listing several reasons why it was reliable. In its opinion reversing, the Court of Appeals listed several other reasons why the statement was not reliable. Finally, the State Supreme Court relied exclusively on the interlocking character of the statement and disregarded every other factor the lower courts had considered. The case is thus a self-contained demonstration of Roberts' unpredictable and inconsistent application.

Each of the courts also made assumptions that cross-examination might well have undermined. The trial court, for example, stated that Sylvia Crawford's statement was reliable because she was an eyewitness with direct knowledge of the events. But Sylvia at one point told the police that she had "shut [her] eyes and ... didn't really watch" part of the fight, and that she was "in shock." App. 134. The trial court also buttressed its reliability finding by claiming that Sylvia was "being questioned by law enforcement, and, thus, the [questioner] is ... neutral to her and not someone who would be inclined to advance her interests and shade her version of the truth unfavorably toward the defendant." Id., at 77. The Framers would be astounded to learn that ex parte testimony could be admitted against a criminal defendant because it was elicited by "neutral" government officers. But even if the court's assessment of the officer's motives was accurate, it says nothing about Sylvia's perception of her situation. Only cross-examination could reveal that.

The State Supreme Court gave dispositive weight to the interlocking nature of the two statements—that they were both ambiguous as to when and whether Lee had a weapon. The court's claim that the two statements were equally ambiguous is hard to accept. Petitioner's statement is ambiguous only in the sense that he had lingering doubts about his recollection: "A. I coulda swore I seen him goin' for somethin' before, right before everything happened... . [B]ut I'm not positive." Id., at 155. Sylvia's statement, on the other hand, is truly inscrutable, since the key timing detail was simply assumed in the leading question she was asked: "Q. Did Kenny do anything to fight back from this assault?" Id., at 137. Moreover, Sylvia specifically said Lee had nothing in his hands after he was stabbed, while petitioner was not asked about that.

The prosecutor obviously did not share the court's view that Sylvia's statement was ambiguous—he called it "damning evidence" that "completely refutes [petitioner's] claim of self-defense." Tr. 468 (Oct. 21, 1999). We have no way of knowing whether the jury agreed with the prosecutor or the court. Far from obviating the need for cross-examination, the "interlocking" ambiguity of the two statements made it all the more imperative that they be tested to tease out the truth.

We readily concede that we could resolve this case by simply reweighing the "reliability factors" under Roberts and finding that Sylvia Crawford's statement falls short. But we view this as one of those rare cases in which the result below is so improbable that it reveals a fundamental failure on our part to interpret the Constitution in a way that secures its intended constraint on judicial discretion. Moreover, to reverse the Washington Supreme Court's decision after conducting our own reliability analysis would perpetuate, not avoid, what the Sixth Amendment condemns. The Constitution prescribes a procedure for determining the reliability of testimony in criminal trials, and we, no less than the state courts, lack authority to replace it with one of our own devising.

We have no doubt that the courts below were acting in utmost good faith when they found reliability. The Framers, however, would not have been content to indulge this assumption. They knew that judges, like other government officers, could not always be trusted to safeguard the rights of the people; the likes of the dread Lord Jeffreys were not yet too distant a memory. They were loath to leave too much discretion in judicial hands. Cf. U.S. Const., Amdt. 6 (criminal jury trial); Amdt. 7 (civil jury trial); Ring v. Arizona, 536 U.S. 584, 611–612 (2002) (Scalia, J., concurring). By replacing categorical constitutional guarantees with open-ended balancing tests, we do violence to their design. Vague standards are manipulable, and, while that might be a small concern in run-of-the-mill assault prosecutions like this one, the Framers had an eye toward politically charged cases like Raleigh's—great state trials where the impartiality of even those at the highest levels of the judiciary might not be so clear. It is difficult to imagine Roberts' providing any meaningful protection in those circumstances.

* * *

Where nontestimonial hearsay is at issue, it is wholly consistent with the Framers' design to afford the States flexibility in their development of hearsay law—as does Roberts, and as would an approach that exempted such statements from Confrontation Clause scrutiny altogether. Where testimonial evidence is at issue, however, the Sixth Amendment demands what the common law required: unavailability and a prior opportunity for cross-examination. We leave for another day any effort to spell out a comprehensive definition of "testimonial."[10] Whatever else the term covers, it applies at a minimum to prior testimony at a preliminary hearing, before a grand jury, or at a former trial; and to police interrogations. These are the modern practices with closest kinship to the abuses at which the Confrontation Clause was directed.

In this case, the State admitted Sylvia's testimonial statement against petitioner, despite the fact that he had no opportunity to cross-examine her. That alone is sufficient to make out a violation of the Sixth Amendment. Roberts notwithstanding, we decline to mine the record in search of indicia of reliability. Where testimonial statements are at issue, the only indicium of reliability sufficient to satisfy constitutional demands is the one the Constitution actually prescribes: confrontation.

The judgment of the Washington Supreme Court is reversed, and the case is remanded for further proceedings not inconsistent with this opinion.

It is so ordered.

Notes to Crawford v. Washington (March 8, 2004)

1. The court rejected the State's argument that guarantees of trustworthiness were unnecessary since petitioner waived his confrontation rights by invoking the marital privilege. It reasoned that "forcing the defendant to choose between the marital privilege and confronting his spouse presents an untenable Hobson's choice." 147 Wash. 2d, at 432, 54 P.3d, at 660. The State has not challenged this holding here. The State also has not challenged the Court of Appeals' conclusion (not reached by the State Supreme Court) that the confrontation violation, if it occurred, was not harmless. We express no opinion on these matters.

2. There is some question whether the requirement of a prior opportunity for cross-examination applied as well to statements taken by a coroner, which were also authorized by the Marian statutes. See 3 Wigmore §1364, at 23 (requirement "never came to be conceded at all in England"); T. Peake, Evidence 64, n. (m) (3d ed. 1808) (not finding the point "expressly decided in any reported case"); State v. Houser, 26 Mo. 431, 436 (1858) ("there may be a few cases ... but the authority of such cases is questioned, even in [England], by their ablest writers on common law"); State v. Campbell, 1 S. C. 124, 130 (1844) (point "has not ... been plainly adjudged, even in the English cases"). Whatever the English rule, several early American authorities flatly rejected any special status for coroner statements. See Houser, supra, at 436; Campbell, supra, at 130; T. Cooley, Constitutional Limitations *318.

3. These sources—especially Raleigh's trial—refute The Chief Justice's assertion, post, at 3 (opinion concurring in judgment), that the right of confrontation was not particularly concerned with unsworn testimonial statements. But even if, as he claims, a general bar on unsworn hearsay made application of the Confrontation Clause to unsworn testimonial statements a moot point, that would merely change our focus from direct evidence of original meaning of the Sixth Amendment to reasonable inference. We find it implausible that a provision which concededly condemned trial by sworn ex parte affidavit thought trial by unsworn ex parte affidavit perfectly OK. (The claim that

unsworn testimony was self-regulating because jurors would disbelieve it, cf. post, at 2, n. 1, is belied by the very existence of a general bar on unsworn testimony.) Any attempt to determine the application of a constitutional provision to a phenomenon that did not exist at the time of its adoption (here, allegedly, admissible unsworn testimony) involves some degree of estimation—what The Chief Justice calls use of a "proxy," post, at 3—but that is hardly a reason not to make the estimation as accurate as possible. Even if, as The Chief Justice mistakenly asserts, there were no direct evidence of how the Sixth Amendment originally applied to unsworn testimony, there is no doubt what its application would have been.

4. We use the term "interrogation" in its colloquial, rather than any technical legal, sense. Cf. Rhode Island v. Innis, 446 U.S. 291, 300—301 (1980). Just as various definitions of "testimonial" exist, one can imagine various definitions of "interrogation," and we need not select among them in this case. Sylvia's recorded statement, knowingly given in response to structured police questioning, qualifies under any conceivable definition.

5. The Chief Justice claims that English law's treatment of testimonial statements was inconsistent at the time of the framing, post, at 4—5, but the examples he cites relate to examinations under the Marian statutes. As we have explained, to the extent Marian examinations were admissible, it was only because the statutes derogated from the common law. See supra, at 10. Moreover, by 1791 even the statutory-derogation view had been rejected with respect to justice-of-the-peace examinations—explicitly in King v. Woodcock, 1 Leach 500, 502—504, 168 Eng. Rep. 352, 353 (1789), and King v. Dingler, 2 Leach 561, 562—563, 168 Eng. Rep. 383, 383—384 (1791), and by implication in King v. Radbourne, 1 Leach 457, 459—461, 168 Eng. Rep. 330, 331—332 (1787). None of The Chief Justice's citations proves otherwise. King v. Westbeer, 1 Leach 12, 168 Eng. Rep. 108 (1739), was decided a half-century earlier and cannot be taken as an accurate statement of the law in 1791 given the directly contrary holdings of Woodcock and Dingler. Hale's treatise is older still, and far more ambiguous on this point, see 1 M. Hale, Pleas of the Crown 585—586 (1736); some who espoused the requirement of a prior opportunity for cross-examination thought it entirely consistent with Hale's views. See Fenwick's Case, 13 How. St. Tr. 537, 602 (H. C. 1696) (Musgrave). The only timely authority The Chief Justice cites is King v. Eriswell, 3 T. R. 707, 100 Eng. Rep. 815 (K. B. 1790), but even that decision provides no substantial support. Eriswell was not a criminal case at all, but a Crown suit against the inhabitants of a town to charge them with care of an insane pauper. Id., at 707—708, 100 Eng. Rep., at 815—816. It is relevant only because the judges discuss the Marian statutes in dicta. One of them, Buller, J., defended admission of the pauper's statement of residence on the basis of authorities that purportedly held ex parte Marian examinations admissible. Id., at 713—714, 100 Eng. Rep., at 819. As evidence writers were quick to point out, however, his authorities said no such thing. See Peake, Evidence, at 64, n. (m) ("Mr. J. Buller is reported to have said that it was so settled in 1 Lev. 180, and Kel. 55; certainly nothing of the kind appears in those

books"); 2 T. Starkie, Evidence 487—488, n. (c) (1826) ("Buller, J. ... refers to Radbourne's case ...; but in that case the deposition was taken in the hearing of the prisoner, and of course the question did not arise" (citation omitted)). Two other judges, Grose, J., and Kenyon, C. J., responded to Buller's argument by distinguishing Marian examinations as a statutory exception to the common-law rule, but the context and tenor of their remarks suggest they merely assumed the accuracy of Buller's premise without independent consideration, at least with respect to examinations by justices of the peace. See 3 T. R., at 710, 100 Eng. Rep., at 817 (Grose, J.); id., at 722—723, 100 Eng. Rep., at 823—824 (Kenyon, C. J.). In fact, the case reporter specifically notes in a footnote that their assumption was erroneous. See id., at 710, n. (c), 100 Eng. Rep., at 817, n. (c). Notably, Buller's position on pauper examinations was resoundingly rejected only a decade later in King v. Ferry Frystone, 2 East 54, 55, 102 Eng. Rep. 289 (K. B. 1801) ("The point ... has been since considered to be so clear against the admissibility of the evidence ... that it was abandoned by the counsel ... without argument"), further suggesting that his views on evidence were not mainstream at the time of the framing. In short, none of The Chief Justice's sources shows that the law in 1791 was unsettled even as to examinations by justices of the peace under the Marian statutes. More importantly, however, even if the statutory rule in 1791 were in doubt, the numerous early state-court decisions make abundantly clear that the Sixth Amendment incorporated the common-law right of confrontation and not any exceptions the Marian statutes supposedly carved out from it. See supra, at 13—14; see also supra, at 11, n. 2 (coroner statements). The common-law rule had been settled since Paine in 1696. See King v. Paine, 5 Mod. 163, 165, 87 Eng. Rep. 584, 585 (K. B.).

6. The one deviation we have found involves dying declarations. The existence of that exception as a general rule of criminal hearsay law cannot be disputed. See, e.g., Mattox v. United States, 156 U.S. 237, 243—244 (1895); King v. Reason, 16 How. St. Tr. 1, 24—38 (K. B. 1722); 1 D. Jardine, Criminal Trials 435 (1832); Cooley, Constitutional Limitations, at *318; 1 G. Gilbert, Evidence 211 (C. Lofft ed. 1791); see also F. Heller, The Sixth Amendment 105 (1951) (asserting that this was the only recognized criminal hearsay exception at common law). Although many dying declarations may not be testimonial, there is authority for admitting even those that clearly are. See Woodcock, supra, at 501—504, 168 Eng. Rep., at 353—354; Reason, supra, at 24—38; Peake, Evidence, at 64; cf. Radbourne, supra, at 460—462, 168 Eng. Rep., at 332—333. We need not decide in this case whether the Sixth Amendment incorporates an exception for testimonial dying declarations. If this exception must be accepted on historical grounds, it is sui generis.

7. We cannot agree with The Chief Justice that the fact "[t]hat a statement might be testimonial does nothing to undermine the wisdom of one of these [hearsay] exceptions." Post, at 6. Involvement of government officers in the production of testimony with an eye toward trial presents unique potential for prosecutorial abuse—a fact borne out time and again throughout a history with which the Framers were keenly

familiar. This consideration does not evaporate when testimony happens to fall within some broad, modern hearsay exception, even if that exception might be justifiable in other circumstances.

8. One case arguably in tension with the rule requiring a prior opportunity for cross-examination when the proffered statement is testimonial is White v. Illinois, 502 U.S. 346 (1992), which involved, inter alia, statements of a child victim to an investigating police officer admitted as spontaneous declarations. Id., at 349—351. It is questionable whether testimonial statements would ever have been admissible on that ground in 1791; to the extent the hearsay exception for spontaneous declarations existed at all, it required that the statements be made "immediat[ely] upon the hurt received, and before [the declarant] had time to devise or contrive any thing for her own advantage." Thompson v. Trevanion, Skin. 402, 90 Eng. Rep. 179 (K. B. 1694). In any case, the only question presented in White was whether the Confrontation Clause imposed an unavailability requirement on the types of hearsay at issue. See 502 U.S., at 348—349. The holding did not address the question whether certain of the statements, because they were testimonial, had to be excluded even if the witness was unavailable. We "[took] as a given ... that the testimony properly falls within the relevant hearsay exceptions." Id., at 351, n. 4.

9. The Chief Justice complains that our prior decisions have "never drawn a distinction" like the one we now draw, citing in particular Mattox v. United States, 156 U.S. 237 (1895), Kirby v. United States, 174 U.S. 47 (1899), and United States v. Burr, 25 F. Cas. 187 (No. 14, 694) (CC Va. 1807) (Marshall, C. J.). Post, at 4—6. But nothing in these cases contradicts our holding in any way. Mattox and Kirby allowed or excluded evidence depending on whether the defendant had had an opportunity for cross-examination. Mattox, supra, at 242—244; Kirby, supra, at 55—61. That the two cases did not extrapolate a more general class of evidence to which that criterion applied does not prevent us from doing so now. As to Burr, we disagree with The Chief Justice's reading of the case. Although Chief Justice Marshall made one passing reference to the Confrontation Clause, the case was fundamentally about the hearsay rules governing statements in furtherance of a conspiracy. The "principle so truly important" on which "inroad[s]" had been introduced was the "rule of evidence which rejects mere hearsay testimony." See 25 F. Cas., at 193. Nothing in the opinion concedes exceptions to the Confrontation Clause's exclusion of testimonial statements as we use the term. The Chief Justice fails to identify a single case (aside from one minor, arguable exception, see supra, at 22, n. 8), where we have admitted testimonial statements based on indicia of reliability other than a prior opportunity for cross-examination. If nothing else, the test we announce is an empirically accurate explanation of the results our cases have reached. Finally, we reiterate that, when the declarant appears for cross-examination at trial, the Confrontation Clause places no constraints at all on the use of his prior testimonial statements. See California v. Green, 399 U.S. 149, 162 (1970). It is therefore irrelevant that the reliability of some out-of-court statements " 'cannot be replicated, even if the

declarant testifies to the same matters in court.' " Post, at 6 (quoting United States v. Inadi, 475 U.S. 387, 395 (1986)). The Clause does not bar admission of a statement so long as the declarant is present at trial to defend or explain it. (The Clause also does not bar the use of testimonial statements for purposes other than establishing the truth of the matter asserted. See Tennessee v. Street, 471 U.S. 409, 414 (1985).)

10. We acknowledge The Chief Justice's objection, post, at 7—8, that our refusal to articulate a comprehensive definition in this case will cause interim uncertainty. But it can hardly be any worse than the status quo. See supra, at 27—30, and cases cited. The difference is that the Roberts test is inherently, and therefore permanently, unpredictable.

Political gerrymandering claims are nonjusticiable because there is no discernible and manageable standard for adjudicating them: Vieth v. Jubelirer (April 28, 2004) [Judgment and Opinion]

Justice Scalia announced the judgment of the Court and delivered an opinion, in which The Chief Justice, Justice O'Connor, and Justice Thomas join.

Plaintiffs-appellants Richard Vieth, Norma Jean Vieth, and Susan Furey challenge a map drawn by the Pennsylvania General Assembly establishing districts for the election of congressional Representatives, on the ground that the districting constitutes an unconstitutional political gerrymander.1 In Davis v. Bandemer, 478 U.S. 109 (1986), this Court held that political gerrymandering claims are justiciable, but could not agree upon a standard to adjudicate them. The present appeal presents the questions whether our decision in Bandemer was in error, and, if not, what the standard should be.

I

The facts, as alleged by the plaintiffs, are as follows. The population figures derived from the 2000 census showed that Pennsylvania was entitled to only 19 Representatives in Congress, a decrease in 2 from the Commonwealth's previous delegation. Pennsylvania's General Assembly took up the task of drawing a new districting map. At the time, the Republican party controlled a majority of both state Houses and held the Governor's office. Prominent national figures in the Republican Party pressured the General Assembly to adopt a partisan redistricting plan as a punitive measure against Democrats for having enacted pro-Democrat redistricting plans elsewhere. The Republican members of Pennsylvania's House and Senate worked together on such a plan. On January 3, 2002, the General Assembly passed its plan, which was signed into law by Governor Schweiker as Act 1.

Plaintiffs, registered Democrats who vote in Pennsylvania, brought suit in the United States District Court for the Middle District of Pennsylvania, seeking to enjoin implementation of Act 1 under Rev. Stat. §1979, 42 U.S.C. § 1983. Defendants-appellees were the Commonwealth of Pennsylvania and various executive and legislative officers responsible for enacting or implementing Act 1. The complaint alleged, among other things, that the legislation created malapportioned districts, in violation of the one-person, one-vote requirement of Article I, §2, of the United States Constitution, and that it constituted a political gerrymander, in violation of Article I and the Equal Protection Clause of the Fourteenth Amendment. With regard to the latter contention, the complaint alleged that the districts created by Act 1 were "meandering and irregular," and "ignor[ed] all traditional redistricting criteria, including the preservation of local government boundaries, solely for the sake of partisan advantage." Juris. Statement 136a, ¶22, 135a, ¶20.

A three-judge panel was convened pursuant to 28 U.S.C. § 2284. The defendants moved to dismiss. The District Court granted the motion with respect to the political gerrymandering claim, and (on Eleventh Amendment grounds) all claims against the Commonwealth; but it declined to dismiss the apportionment claim as to other defendants. See Vieth v. Pennsylvania, 188 F. Supp. 2d 532 (MD Pa. 2002) (Vieth I). On trial of the apportionment claim, the District Court ruled in favor of plaintiffs. See Vieth v. Pennsylvania, 195 F. Supp. 2d 672 (MD Pa. 2002) (Vieth II). It retained jurisdiction over the case pending the court's review and approval of a remedial redistricting plan. On April 18, 2002, Governor Schweiker signed into law Act No. 2002—34, Pa. Stat. Ann., Tit. 25, §3595.301 (Purdon Supp. 2003) (Act 34), a remedial plan that the Pennsylvania General Assembly had enacted to cure the apportionment problem of Act 1.

Plaintiffs moved to impose remedial districts, arguing that the District Court should not consider Act 34 to be a proper remedial scheme, both because it was malapportioned, and because it constituted an unconstitutional political gerrymander like its predecessor. The District Court denied this motion, concluding that the new districts were not malapportioned, and rejecting the political gerrymandering claim for the reasons previously assigned in Vieth I. Vieth v. Pennsylvania, 241 F. Supp. 2d 478, 484—485 (MD Pa. 2003) (Vieth III). The plaintiffs appealed the dismissal of their Act 34 political gerrymandering claim.[2] We noted probable jurisdiction. 539 U.S. 957 (2003).

II

Political gerrymanders are not new to the American scene. One scholar traces them back to the Colony of Pennsylvania at the beginning of the 18th century, where several counties conspired to minimize the political power of the city of Philadelphia by refusing to allow it to merge or expand into surrounding jurisdictions, and denying it additional representatives. See E. Griffith, The Rise and Development of the Gerrymander 26—28 (1974) (hereinafter Griffith). In 1732, two members of His Majesty's Council and the attorney general and deputy inspector and comptroller general of affairs of the Province of North Carolina reported that the Governor had proceeded to "divide old Precincts established by Law, & to enact new Ones in Places, whereby his Arts he has endeavored to prepossess People in a future election according to his desire, his Designs herein being ... either to endeavor by his means to get a Majority of his creatures in the Lower House" or to disrupt the assembly's proceedings. 3 Colonial Records of North

Carolina 380—381 (W. Saunders ed. 1886); see also Griffith 29. The political gerrymander remained alive and well (though not yet known by that name) at the time of the framing. There were allegations that Patrick Henry attempted (unsuccessfully) to gerrymander James Madison out of the First Congress. See 2 W. Rives, Life and Times of James Madison 655, n. 1 (reprint 1970); Letter from Thomas Jefferson to William Short, Feb. 9, 1789, reprinted in 5 Works of Thomas Jefferson 451 (P. Ford ed. 1904). And in 1812, of course, there occurred the notoriously outrageous political districting in Massachusetts that gave the gerrymander its name—an amalgam of the names of Massachusetts Governor Elbridge Gerry and the creature ("salamander") which the outline of an election district he was credited with forming was thought to resemble. See Webster's New International Dictionary 1052 (2d ed. 1945). "By 1840 the gerrymander was a recognized force in party politics and was generally attempted in all legislation enacted for the formation of election districts. It was generally conceded that each party would attempt to gain power which was not proportionate to its numerical strength." Griffith 123.

It is significant that the Framers provided a remedy for such practices in the Constitution. Article 1, §4, while leaving in state legislatures the initial power to draw districts for federal elections, permitted Congress to "make or alter" those districts if it wished.3 Many objected to the congressional oversight established by this provision. In the course of the debates in the Constitutional Convention, Charles Pinkney and John Rutledge moved to strike the relevant language. James Madison responded in defense of the provision that Congress must be given the power to check partisan manipulation of the election process by the States:

"Whenever the State Legislatures had a favorite measure to carry, they would take care so to mould their regulations as to favor the candidates they wished to succeed. Besides, the inequality of the Representation in the Legislatures of particular States, would produce a like inequality in their representation in the Natl. Legislature, as it was presumable that the Counties having the power in the former case would secure it to themselves in the latter. What danger could there be in giving a controuling power to the Natl. Legislature?" 2 Records of the Federal Convention of 1787, pp. 240—241 (M. Farrand ed. 1911).

Although the motion of Pinkney and Rutledge failed, opposition to the "make or alter" provision of Article I, §4—and the defense that it was needed to prevent political gerrymandering—continued to be voiced in the state ratifying debates. A delegate to the Massachusetts convention warned that state legislatures

"might make an unequal and partial division of the states into districts for the election of representatives, or they might even disqualify one third of the electors. Without these powers in Congress, the people can have no remedy; But the 4th section provides a remedy, a controlling power in a legislature, composed of senators and representatives of twelve states, without the influence of our commotions and factions, who will hear impartially, and preserve and restore to the people their equal and sacred rights of election." 2 Debates on the Federal Constitution 27 (J. Elliot 2d ed. 1876).

The power bestowed on Congress to regulate elections, and in particular to restrain the practice of political gerrymandering, has not lain dormant. In the Apportionment Act of 1842, 5 Stat. 491, Congress provided that Representatives must be elected from single-member districts "composed of contiguous territory." See Griffith 12 (noting that the law was "an attempt to forbid the practice of the gerrymander"). Congress again imposed these requirements in the Apportionment Act of 1862, 12 Stat. 572, and in 1872 further required that districts "contai[n] as nearly as practicable an equal number of inhabitants," 17 Stat. 28, §2. In the Apportionment Act of 1901, Congress imposed a compactness requirement. 31 Stat. 733. The requirements of contiguity, compactness, and equality of population were repeated in the 1911 apportionment legislation, 37 Stat. 13, but were not thereafter continued. Today, only the single-member-district-requirement remains. See 2 U.S.C. § 2c. Recent history, however, attests to Congress's awareness of the sort of districting practices appellants protest, and of its power under Article I, §4 to control them. Since 1980, no fewer than five bills have been introduced to regulate gerrymandering in congressional districting. See H. R. 5037, 101st Cong., 2d Sess. (1990); H. R. 1711, 101st Cong., 1st Sess. (1989); H. R. 3468, 98th Cong., 1st Sess. (1983); H. R. 5529, 97th Cong., 2d Sess. (1982); H. R. 2349, 97th Cong., 1st Sess. (1981).4

Eighteen years ago, we held that the Equal Protection Clause grants judges the power—and duty—to control political gerrymandering, see Davis v. Bandemer, 478 U.S. 109 (1986). It is to consideration of this precedent that we now turn.

III

As Chief Justice Marshall proclaimed two centuries ago, "[i]t is emphatically the province and duty of the judicial department to say what the law is." Marbury v. Madison, 1 Cranch 137, 177 (1803). Sometimes, however, the law is that the judicial department has no business entertaining the claim of unlawfulness—because the question is entrusted to one of the political branches or involves no judicially enforceable rights. See, e.g., Nixon v. United States, 506 U.S. 224 (1993) (challenge to procedures used in Senate impeachment proceedings); Pacific States Telephone & Telegraph Co. v. Oregon, 223 U.S. 118 (1912) (claims arising under the Guaranty Clause of Article IV, §4). Such questions are said to be "nonjusticiable," or "political questions."

In Baker v. Carr, 369 U.S. 186 (1962), we set forth six independent tests for the existence of a political question:

"[1] a textually demonstrable constitutional commitment of the issue to a coordinate political department; or [2] a lack of judicially discoverable and manageable standards for resolving it; or [3] the impossibility of deciding without an initial policy determination of a kind clearly for nonjudicial discretion; or [4] the impossibility of a court's undertaking independent resolution without expressing lack of the respect due coordinate branches of the government; or [5] an unusual need for unquestioning adherence to a political decision already made; or [6] the potentiality of embarrassment from multifarious pronouncements by various departments on one question." Id., at 217.

These tests are probably listed in descending order of both importance and certainty. The second is at issue here, and there is no doubt of its validity. "The judicial Power" created by Article III, §1, of the Constitution is not whatever judges choose to do, see Valley Forge Christian College v. Americans United for Separation of Church and State, Inc., 454 U.S. 464, 487 (1982); cf. Grupo Mexicano de Desarrollo, S. A. v. Alliance Bond Fund, Inc., 527 U.S. 308, 332—333 (1999), or even whatever Congress chooses to assign them, see Lujan v. Defenders of Wildlife, 504 U.S. 555, 576—577 (1992); Chicago & Southern Air Lines, Inc. v. Waterman S. S. Corp., 333 U.S. 103, 110—114 (1948). It is the power to act in the manner traditional for English and American courts. One of the most obvious limitations imposed by that requirement is that judicial action must be governed by standard, by rule. Laws promulgated by the Legislative Branch can be inconsistent, illogical, and ad hoc; law pronounced by the courts must be principled, rational, and based upon reasoned distinctions.

Over the dissent of three Justices, the Court held in Davis v. Bandemer that, since it was "not persuaded that there are no judicially discernible and manageable standards by which political gerrymander cases are to be decided," 478 U.S., at 123, such cases were justiciable. The clumsy shifting of the burden of proof for the premise (the Court was "not persuaded" that standards do not exist, rather than "persuaded" that they do) was necessitated by the uncomfortable fact that the six-Justice majority could not discern what the judicially discernable standards might be. There was no majority on that point. Four of the Justices finding justiciability believed that the standard was one thing, see id., at 127 (plurality opinion of White, J., joined by Brennan, Marshall, and Blackmun, JJ.); two believed it was something else, see id., at 161 (Powell, J., joined by Stevens, J., concurring in part and dissenting in part). The lower courts have lived with that assurance of a standard (or more precisely, lack of assurance that there is no standard), coupled with that inability to specify a standard, for the past 18 years. In that time, they have considered numerous political gerrymandering claims; this Court has never revisited the unanswered question of what standard governs.

Nor can it be said that the lower courts have, over 18 years, succeeded in shaping the standard that this Court was initially unable to enunciate. They have simply applied the standard set forth in Bandemer's four-Justice plurality opinion. This might be thought to prove that the four-Justice plurality standard has met the test of time—but for the fact that its application has almost invariably produced the same result (except for the incurring of attorney's fees) as would have obtained if the question were nonjusticiable: judicial intervention has been refused. As one commentary has put it, "[t]hroughout its subsequent history, Bandemer has served almost exclusively as an invitation to litigation without much prospect of redress." S. Issacharoff, P. Karlan, & R. Pildes, The Law of Democracy 886 (rev. 2d ed. 2002). The one case in which relief was provided (and merely preliminary relief, at that) did not involve the drawing of district lines5; in all of the cases we are aware of involving that most common form of political gerrymandering, relief was denied.6 Moreover, although the case in which relief was provided seemingly involved the ne plus ultra of partisan manipulation, see n. 5, supra, we would be at a loss to explain why the Bandemer line should have been drawn just there, and should not have embraced several districting plans that were upheld despite allegations of extreme partisan discrimination, bizarrely shaped districts, and disproportionate results. See, e.g., Session v. Perry, 298 F. Supp. 2d 451 (ED Tex. 2004) (per curiam); O'Lear v. Miller, 222 F. Supp. 2d 850 (ED Mich.), summarily aff'd, 537 U.S. 997 (2002); Badham v. Eu, 694 F. Supp. 664, 670 (ND Cal. 1988), summarily aff'd, 488 U.S. 1024 (1989). To think that this lower-court jurisprudence has brought forth "judicially discernible and manageable standards" would be fantasy.

Eighteen years of judicial effort with virtually nothing to show for it justify us in revisiting the question whether the standard promised by Bandemer exists. As the following discussion reveals, no judicially discernible and manageable standards for adjudicating political gerrymandering claims have emerged. Lacking them, we must conclude that political gerrymandering claims are nonjusticiable and that Bandemer was wrongly decided.

A

We begin our review of possible standards with that proposed by Justice White's plurality opinion in Bandemer because, as the narrowest ground for our decision in that case, it has been the standard employed by the lower courts. The plurality concluded that a political gerrymandering claim could succeed only where plaintiffs showed "both intentional discrimination against an identifiable political group and an actual discriminatory effect on that group." 478 U.S., at 127. As to the intent element, the plurality acknowledged that "[a]s long as redistricting is done by a legislature, it should not be very difficult to prove that the likely political consequences of the reapportionment were intended." Id., at 129. However, the effects prong was significantly harder to satisfy. Relief could not be based merely upon the fact that a group of persons banded together for political purposes had failed to achieve representation commensurate with its numbers, or that the apportionment scheme made its winning of elections more difficult. Id., at 132. Rather, it would have to be shown that, taking into account a variety of historic factors and projected election results, the group had been "denied its chance to effectively influence the political process" as a whole, which could be achieved even without electing a candidate. Id., at 132—133. It would not be enough to establish, for example, that Democrats had been "placed in a district with a supermajority of other Democratic voters" or that the district "departs from pre-existing political boundaries." Id., at 140—141. Rather, in a challenge to an individual district the inquiry would focus "on the opportunity of members of the group to participate in party deliberations in the slating and nomination of candidates, their opportunity to register and vote, and hence their chance to directly influence the election returns and to secure the attention of the winning candidate." Id., at 133. A statewide challenge, by contrast, would involve an analysis of "the voters' direct or indirect influence on the elections of the state legislature as a whole." Ibid. (emphasis added). With what has proved to be a gross understatement, the plurality acknowledged this was "of necessity a difficult inquiry." Id., at 143.

In her Bandemer concurrence, Justice O'Connor predicted that the plurality's standard "will over time either prove unmanageable and arbitrary or else evolve towards some loose form of proportionality." Id., at 155 (opinion concurring in judgment, joined by Burger, C. J., and Rehnquist, J.). A similar prediction of unmanageability was expressed in Justice Powell's opinion, making it the prognostication of a majority of the Court. See id., at 171 ("The ... most basic flaw in the plurality's opinion is its failure to enunciate any standard that affords guidance to legislatures and courts"). That prognostication has been amply fulfilled.

In the lower courts, the legacy of the plurality's test is one long record of puzzlement and consternation. See, e.g., Session, supra, at 474 ("Throughout this case we have borne witness to the powerful, conflicting forces nurtured by Bandemer's holding that the judiciary is to address 'excessive' partisan line-drawing, while leaving the issue virtually unenforceable"); Vieth I, 188 F. Supp. 2d, at 544 (noting that the "recondite standard enunciated in Bandemer offers little concrete guidance"); Martinez v. Bush, 234 F. Supp. 2d 1275, 1352 (SD Fla. 2002) (three-judge court) (Jordan, J., concurring) (the "lower courts continue to struggle in an attempt to interpret and apply the 'discriminatory effect' prong of the [Bandemer] standard"); O'Lear, supra, at 855 (describing Bandemer's standard for assessing discriminatory effect as "somewhat murky"). The test has been criticized for its indeterminacy by a host of academic commentators. See, e.g., L. Tribe, American Constitutional Law §13—9, p. 1083 (2d ed. 1988) ("Neither Justice White's nor Justice Powell's approach to the question of partisan apportionment gives any real guidance to lower courts forced to adjudicate this issue ..."); Still, Hunting of the Gerrymander, 38 UCLA L. Rev. 1019, 1020 (1991) (noting that the plurality opinion has "confounded legislators, practitioners, and academics alike"); Schuck, The Thickest Thicket: Partisan Gerrymandering and Judicial Regulation of Politics, 87 Colum. L. Rev. 1325, 1365 (1987) (noting that the Bandemer plurality's standard requires judgments that are "largely subjective and beg questions that lie at the heart of political competition in a democracy"); Issacharoff, Judging Politics: The Elusive Quest for Judicial Review of Political Fairness, 71 Texas L. Rev. 1643, 1671 (1993) ("Bandemer begot only confusion"); Grofman, An Expert Witness Perspective on Continuing and Emerging Voting Rights Controversies, 21 Stetson L. Rev. 783, 816 (1992) ("[A]s far as I am aware I am one of only two people who believe that Bandemer makes sense. Moreover, the other person, Daniel Lowenstein, has a diametrically opposed view as to what the plurality opinion means"). Because this standard was misguided when proposed, has not been improved in subsequent application, and is not even defended before us today by the appellants, we decline to affirm it as a constitutional requirement.

B

Appellants take a run at enunciating their own workable standard based on Article I, §2, and the Equal Protection Clause. We consider it at length not only because it reflects the litigant's view as to the best that can be derived from 18 years of experience, but also because it shares many features with other proposed standards, so that what is said of it may be said of them as well. Appellants' proposed standard retains the two-pronged framework of the Bandemer plurality—intent plus effect—but modifies the type of showing sufficient to satisfy each.

To satisfy appellants' intent standard, a plaintiff must "show that the mapmakers acted with a predominant intent to achieve partisan advantage," which can be shown "by direct evidence or by circumstantial evidence that other neutral and legitimate redistricting criteria were subordinated to the goal of achieving partisan advantage." Brief for Appellants 19 (emphasis added). As compared with the Bandemer plurality's test of mere intent to disadvantage the plaintiff's group, this proposal seemingly makes the standard more difficult to meet—but only at the expense of making the standard more indeterminate.

"Predominant intent" to disadvantage the plaintiff political group refers to the relative importance of that goal as compared with all the other goals that the map seeks to pursue—contiguity of districts, compactness of districts, observance of the lines of political subdivision, protection of incumbents of all parties, cohesion of natural racial and ethnic neighborhoods, compliance with requirements of the Voting Rights Act of 1965 regarding racial distribution, etc. Appellants contend that their intent test must be discernible and manageable because it has been borrowed from our racial gerrymandering cases. See Miller v. Johnson, 515 U.S. 900 (1995); Shaw v. Reno, 509 U.S. 630 (1993). To begin with, in a very important respect that is not so. In the racial gerrymandering context, the predominant intent test has been applied to the challenged district in which the plaintiffs voted. See Miller, supra; United States v. Hays, 515 U.S. 737 (1995). Here, however, appellants do not assert that an apportionment fails their intent test if any single district does so. Since "it would be quixotic to attempt to bar state legislatures from considering politics as they redraw district lines," Brief for Appellants 3, appellants propose a test that is satisfied only when "partisan advantage was the predominant motivation behind the entire statewide plan," id., at 32 (emphasis added). Vague as the "predominant motivation" test might be when used to evaluate single districts, it all but evaporates when applied statewide. Does it mean, for instance, that partisan intent must outweigh all other goals—contiguity, compactness, preservation of neighborhoods, etc.—statewide? And how is the statewide "outweighing" to be determined? If three-fifths of the map's districts forgo the pursuit of partisan ends in favor of strictly observing political-subdivision lines, and only two-fifths ignore those lines to disadvantage the plaintiffs, is the observance of political subdivisions the "predominant" goal between those two? We are sure appellants do not think so.

Even within the narrower compass of challenges to a single district, applying a "predominant intent" test to racial gerrymandering is easier and less disruptive. The

Constitution clearly contemplates districting by political entities, see Article I, §4, and unsurprisingly that turns out to be root-and-branch a matter of politics. See Miller, supra, at 914 ("[R]edistricting in most cases will implicate a political calculus in which various interests compete for recognition ..."); Shaw, supra, at 662 (White, J., dissenting) ("[D]istricting inevitably is the expression of interest group politics ..."); Gaffney v. Cummings, 412 U.S. 735, 753 (1973) ("The reality is that districting inevitably has and is intended to have substantial political consequences"). By contrast, the purpose of segregating voters on the basis of race is not a lawful one, and is much more rarely encountered. Determining whether the shape of a particular district is so substantially affected by the presence of a rare and constitutionally suspect motive as to invalidate it is quite different from determining whether it is so substantially affected by the excess of an ordinary and lawful motive as to invalidate it. Moreover, the fact that partisan districting is a lawful and common practice means that there is almost always room for an election-impeding lawsuit contending that partisan advantage was the predominant motivation; not so for claims of racial gerrymandering. Finally, courts might be justified in accepting a modest degree of unmanageability to enforce a constitutional command which (like the Fourteenth Amendment obligation to refrain from racial discrimination) is clear; whereas they are not justified in inferring a judicially enforceable constitutional obligation (the obligation not to apply too much partisanship in districting) which is both dubious and severely unmanageable. For these reasons, to the extent that our racial gerrymandering cases represent a model of discernible and manageable standards, they provide no comfort here.

The effects prong of appellants' proposal replaces the Bandemer plurality's vague test of "denied its chance to effectively influence the political process," 478 U.S., at 132—133, with criteria that are seemingly more specific. The requisite effect is established when "(1) the plaintiffs show that the districts systematically 'pack' and 'crack' the rival party's voters,[7] and (2) the court's examination of the 'totality of circumstances' confirms that the map can thwart the plaintiffs' ability to translate a majority of votes into a majority of seats." Brief for Appellants 20 (emphasis and footnote added). This test is loosely based on our cases applying §2 of the Voting Rights Act, 42 U.S.C. § 1973 to discrimination by race, see, e.g., Johnson v. De Grandy, 512 U.S. 997 (1994). But a person's politics is rarely as readily discernible—and never as permanently discernible—as a person's race. Political affiliation is not an immutable characteristic, but may shift from one election to the next; and even within a given election, not all voters follow the party line. We dare say (and hope) that the political party which puts forward an utterly incompetent candidate will lose even in its registration stronghold. These facts make it impossible to assess the effects of partisan gerrymandering, to fashion a standard for evaluating a violation, and finally to craft a remedy. See Bandemer, supra, at 156 (O'Connor, J., concurring in judgment).[8]

Assuming, however, that the effects of partisan gerrymandering can be determined, appellants' test would invalidate the districting only when it prevents a majority of the electorate from electing a majority of representatives. Before considering whether this particular standard is judicially manageable we question whether it is judicially discernible in the sense of being relevant to some constitutional violation. Deny it as appellants may (and do), this standard rests upon the principle that groups (or at least political-action groups) have a right to proportional representation. But the Constitution contains no such principle. It guarantees equal protection of the law to persons, not equal representation in government to equivalently sized groups. It nowhere says that farmers or urban dwellers, Christian fundamentalists or Jews, Republicans or Democrats, must be accorded political strength proportionate to their numbers.9

    Even if the standard were relevant, however, it is not judicially manageable. To begin with, how is a party's majority status to be established? Appellants propose using the results of statewide races as the benchmark of party support. But as their own complaint describes, in the 2000 Pennsylvania statewide elections some Republicans won and some Democrats won. See Juris. Statement 137a—138a (describing how Democrat candidates received more votes for President and auditor general, and Republicans received more votes for United States Senator, attorney general, and treasurer). Moreover, to think that majority status in statewide races establishes majority status for district contests, one would have to believe that the only factor determining voting behavior at all levels is political affiliation. That is assuredly not true. As one law review comment has put it:

    "There is no statewide vote in this country for the House of Representatives or the state legislature. Rather, there are separate elections between separate candidates in separate districts, and that is all there is. If the districts change, the candidates change, their strengths and weaknesses change, their campaigns change, their ability to raise money changes, the issues change—everything changes. Political parties do not compete for the highest statewide vote totals or the highest mean district vote percentages: They compete for specific seats." Lowenstein & Steinberg, The Quest for Legislative Districting in the Public Interest: Elusive or Illusory, 33 UCLA L. Rev. 1, 59—60 (1985).

    See also Schuck, Partisan Gerrymandering: A Political Problem Without Judicial Solution, in Political Gerrymandering and the Courts 240, 241 (B. Grofman ed. 1990).

    But if we could identify a majority party, we would find it impossible to assure that that party wins a majority of seats—unless we radically revise the States' traditional structure for elections. In any winner-take-all district system, there can be no guarantee, no matter how the district lines are drawn, that a majority of party votes statewide will produce a majority of seats for that party. The point is proved by the 2000 congressional elections in Pennsylvania, which, according to appellants' own pleadings, were conducted under a judicially drawn district map "free from partisan gerrymandering." Juris. Statement 137a. On this "neutral playing fiel[d]," the Democrats' statewide majority of the major-party vote (50.6%) translated into a minority of seats (10, versus 11 for the Republicans). Id., at 133a, 137a. Whether by reason of partisan districting or not, party constituents may always wind up "packed" in some districts and "cracked" throughout others. See R. Dixon, Democratic Representation 462 (1968) ("All Districting is 'Gerrymandering' "); Schuck, 87 Colum. L. Rev., at 1359. Consider, for example, a legislature that draws district lines with no objectives in mind except compactness and respect for the lines of political subdivisions. Under that system, political groups that tend to cluster (as is the case with Democratic voters in cities) would be systematically affected by what might be called a "natural" packing effect. See Bandemer, 478 U.S., at 159 (O'Connor, J., concurring in judgment).

Our one-person, one-vote cases, see Reynolds v. Sims, 377 U.S. 533 (1964); Wesberry v. Sanders, 376 U.S. 1 (1964), have no bearing upon this question, neither in principle nor in practicality. Not in principle, because to say that each individual must have an equal say in the selection of representatives, and hence that a majority of individuals must have a majority say, is not at all to say that each discernable group, whether farmers or urban dwellers or political parties, must have representation equivalent to its numbers. And not in practicality, because the easily administrable standard of population equality adopted by Wesberry and Reynolds enables judges to decide whether a violation has occurred (and to remedy it) essentially on the basis of three readily determined factors—where the plaintiff lives, how many voters are in his district, and how many voters are in other districts; whereas requiring judges to decide whether a districting system will produce a statewide majority for a majority party casts them forth upon a sea of imponderables, and asks them to make determinations that not even election experts can agree upon.

For these reasons, we find appellants' proposed standards neither discernible nor manageable.

C

For many of the same reasons, we also reject the standard suggested by Justice Powell in Bandemer. He agreed with the plurality that a plaintiff should show intent and effect, but believed that the ultimate inquiry ought to focus on whether district boundaries had been drawn solely for partisan ends to the exclusion of "all other neutral factors relevant to the fairness of redistricting." 478 U.S., at 161 (opinion concurring in part and dissenting in part); see also id., at 164–165. Under that inquiry, the courts should consider numerous factors, though "[n]o one factor should be dispositive." Id., at 173. The most important would be "the shapes of voting districts and adherence to established political subdivision boundaries." Ibid. "Other relevant considerations include the nature of the legislative procedures by which the apportionment law was adopted and legislative history reflecting contemporaneous legislative goals." Ibid. These factors, which "bear directly on the fairness of a redistricting plan," combined with "evidence concerning population disparities and statistics tending to show vote dilution," make out a claim of unconstitutional partisan gerrymandering. Ibid.

While Justice Powell rightly criticized the Bandemer plurality for failing to suggest a constitutionally based, judicially manageable standard, the standard proposed in his opinion also falls short of the mark. It is essentially a totality-of-the-circumstances analysis, where all conceivable factors, none of which is dispositive, are weighed with an eye to ascertaining whether the particular gerrymander has gone too far—or, in Justice Powell's terminology, whether it is not "fair." "Fairness" does not seem to us a judicially manageable standard. Fairness is compatible with noncontiguous districts, it is compatible with districts that straddle political subdivisions, and it is compatible with a party's not winning the number of seats that mirrors the proportion of its vote. Some criterion more solid and more demonstrably met than that seems to us necessary to enable the state legislatures to discern the limits of their districting discretion, to meaningfully constrain the discretion of the courts, and to win public acceptance for the courts' intrusion into a process that is the very foundation of democratic decisionmaking.

IV

We turn next to consideration of the standards proposed by today's dissenters. We preface it with the observation that the mere fact that these four dissenters come up with three different standards—all of them different from the two proposed in Bandemer and the one proposed here by appellants—goes a long way to establishing that there is no constitutionally discernible standard.

A

Justice Stevens concurs in the judgment that we should not address plaintiffs' statewide political gerrymandering challenges. Though he reaches that result via standing analysis, post, at 12, 13 (dissenting opinion), while we reach it through political-question analysis, our conclusions are the same: these statewide claims are nonjusticiable.

Justice Stevens would, however, require courts to consider political gerrymandering challenges at the individual-district level. Much of his dissent is addressed to the incompatibility of severe partisan gerrymanders with democratic principles. We do not disagree with that judgment, any more than we disagree with the judgment that it would be unconstitutional for the Senate to employ, in impeachment proceedings, procedures that are incompatible with its obligation to "try" impeachments. See Nixon v. United States, 506 U.S. 224 (1993). The issue we have discussed is not whether severe partisan gerrymanders violate the Constitution, but whether it is for the courts to say when a violation has occurred, and to design a remedy. On that point, Justice Stevens's dissent is less helpful, saying, essentially, that if we can do it in the racial gerrymandering context we can do it here.

We have examined, supra, at 15—18, the many reasons why that is not so. Only a few of them are challenged by Justice Stevens. He says that we "mistakenly assum[e] that race cannot provide a legitimate basis for making political judgments." Post, at 23. But we do not say that race-conscious decisionmaking is always unlawful. Race can be used, for example, as an indicator to achieve the purpose of neighborhood cohesiveness in districting. What we have said is impermissible is "the purpose of segregating voters on the basis of race," supra, at 16—that is to say, racial gerrymandering for race's sake, which would be the equivalent of political gerrymandering for politics' sake. Justice Stevens says we "er[r] in assuming that politics is 'an ordinary and lawful motive' " in districting, post, at 8—but all he brings forward to contest that is the argument that an excessive injection of politics is unlawful. So it is, and so does our opinion assume. That does not alter the reality that setting out to segregate voters by race is unlawful and hence rare, and setting out to segregate them by political affiliation is (so long as one doesn't go too far) lawful and hence ordinary.

Justice Stevens's confidence that what courts have done with racial gerrymandering can be done with political gerrymandering rests in part upon his belief that "the same standards should apply," post, at 20. But in fact the standards are quite different. A purpose to discriminate on the basis of race receives the strictest scrutiny under the Equal Protection Clause, while a similar purpose to discriminate on the basis of politics does not. "[N]othing in our case law compels the conclusion that racial and political gerrymanders are subject to precisely the same constitutional scrutiny. In fact, our country's long and persistent history of racial discrimination in voting—as well as our Fourteenth Amendment jurisprudence, which always has reserved the strictest scrutiny for discrimination on the basis of race—would seem to compel the opposite conclusion." Shaw, 509 U.S., at 650 (internal citation omitted). That quoted passage was in direct response to (and rejection of) the suggestion made by Justices White and Stevens in dissent that "a racial gerrymander of the sort alleged here is functionally equivalent to gerrymanders for nonracial purposes, such as political gerrymanders." Ibid. See also Bush v. Vera, 517 U.S. 952, 964 (1996) (plurality opinion) ("We have not subjected political gerrymandering to strict scrutiny").

Justice Stevens relies on First Amendment cases to suggest that politically discriminatory gerrymanders are subject to strict scrutiny under the Equal Protection Clause. See post, at 8–9. It is elementary that scrutiny levels are claim specific. An action that triggers a heightened level of scrutiny for one claim may receive a very different level of scrutiny for a different claim because the underlying rights, and consequently constitutional harms, are not comparable. To say that suppression of political speech (a claimed First Amendment violation) triggers strict scrutiny is not to say that failure to give political groups equal representation (a claimed equal protection violation) triggers strict scrutiny. Only an equal protection claim is before us in the present case—perhaps for the very good reason that a First Amendment claim, if it were sustained, would render unlawful all consideration of political affiliation in districting, just as it renders unlawful all consideration of political affiliation in hiring for non-policy-level government jobs. What cases such as Elrod v. Burns, 427 U.S. 347 (1976), require is not merely that Republicans be given a decent share of the jobs in a Democratic administration, but that political affiliation be disregarded.

Having failed to make the case for strict scrutiny of political gerrymandering, Justice Stevens falls back on the argument that scrutiny levels simply do not matter for purposes of justiciability. He asserts that a standard imposing a strong presumption of invalidity (strict scrutiny) is no more discernible and manageable than a standard requiring an evenhanded balancing of all considerations with no thumb on the scales (ordinary scrutiny). To state this is to refute it. As is well known, strict scrutiny readily, and almost always, results in invalidation. Moreover, the mere fact that there exist standards which this Court could apply—the proposition which much of Justice Stevens's opinion is devoted to establishing, see, e.g., post, at 5—11, 25—26—does not mean that those standard are discernible in the Constitution. This Court may not willy-nilly apply standards—even manageable standards—having no relation to constitutional harms. Justice Stevens points out, see post, at 11, n. 15, that Bandemer said differences between racial and political groups "may be relevant to the manner in which the case is adjudicated, but these differences do not justify a refusal to entertain such a case." 478 U.S., at 125. As 18 years have shown, Bandemer was wrong.

B

Justice Souter, like Justice Stevens, would restrict these plaintiffs, on the allegations before us, to district-specific political gerrymandering claims. Post, at 6, 12 (dissenting opinion). Unlike Justice Stevens, however, Justice Souter recognizes that there is no existing workable standard for adjudicating such claims. He proposes a "fresh start," post, at 4: a newly constructed standard loosely based in form on our Title VII cases, see McDonnell Douglas Corp. v. Green, 411 U.S. 792 (1973), and complete with a five-step prima facie test sewn together from parts of, among other things, our Voting Rights Act jurisprudence, law review articles, and apportionment cases. Even if these self-styled "clues" to unconstitutionality could be manageably applied, which we doubt, there is no reason to think they would detect the constitutional crime which Justice Souter is investigating—an "extremity of unfairness" in partisan competition. Post, at 2—3.

Under Justice Souter's proposed standard, in order to challenge a particular district, a plaintiff must show (1) that he is a member of a "cohesive political group"; (2) "that the district of his residence . . . paid little or no heed" to traditional districting principles; (3) that there were "specific correlations between the district's deviations from traditional districting principles and the distribution of the population of his group"; (4) that a hypothetical district exists which includes the plaintiff's residence, remedies the packing or cracking of the plaintiff's group, and deviates less from traditional districting principles; and (5) that "the defendants acted intentionally to manipulate the shape of the district in order to pack or crack his group." Post, at 5, 6, 7, 8, 9. When those showings have been made, the burden would shift to the defendants to justify the district "by reference to objectives other than naked partisan advantage." Post, at 10.

While this five-part test seems eminently scientific, upon analysis one finds that each of the last four steps requires a quantifying judgment that is unguided and ill suited to the development of judicial standards: How much disregard of traditional districting principles? How many correlations between deviations and distribution? How much remedying of packing or cracking by the hypothetical district? How many legislators must have had the intent to pack and crack—and how efficacious must that intent have been (must it have been, for example, a sine qua non cause of the districting, or a predominant cause)? At step two, for example, Justice Souter would require lower courts to assess whether mapmakers paid "little or no heed to . . . traditional districting principles." Post, at 6. What is a lower court to do when, as will often be the case, the district adheres to some traditional criteria but not others? Justice Souter's only response to this question is to evade it: "It is not necessary now to say exactly how a district court would balance a good showing on one of these indices against a poor showing on another, for that sort of detail is best worked out case by case." Post, at 7. But the devil lurks precisely in such detail. The central problem is determining when political gerrymandering has gone too far. It does not solve that problem to break down the original unanswerable question (How much political motivation and effect is too much?) into four more discrete but equally unanswerable questions.

Justice Souter's proposal is doomed to failure for a more basic reason: No test—yea, not even a five-part test—can possibly be successful unless one knows what he is testing for. In the present context, the test ought to identify deprivation of that minimal degree of representation or influence to which a political group is constitutionally entitled. As we have seen, the Bandemer test sought (unhelpfully, but at least gamely) to specify what that minimal degree was: "[a] chance to effectively influence the political process." 478 U.S., at 133. So did the appellants' proposed test: "[the] ability to translate a majority of votes into a majority of seats." Brief for Appellants 20. Justice Souter avoids the difficulties of those formulations by never telling us what his test is looking for, other than the utterly unhelpful "extremity of unfairness." He vaguely describes the harm he is concerned with as vote dilution, post, at 10, a term which usually implies some actual effect on the weight of a vote. But no element of his test looks to the effect of the gerrymander on the electoral success, the electoral opportunity, or even the political influence, of the plaintiff group. We do not know the precise constitutional deprivation his test is designed to identify and prevent.

Even if (though it is implausible) Justice Souter believes that the constitutional deprivation consists of merely "vote dilution," his test would not even identify that effect. Despite his claimed reliance on the McDonnell Douglas framework, Justice Souter would allow the plaintiff no opportunity to show that the mapmakers' compliance with traditional districting factors is pretextual.10 His reason for this is never stated, but it certainly cannot be that adherence to traditional districting factors negates any possibility of intentional vote dilution. As we have explained above, packing and cracking, whether intentional or no, are quite consistent with adherence to compactness and respect for political subdivision lines. See supra, at 20. An even better example is the traditional criterion of incumbency protection. Justice Souter has previously acknowledged it to be a traditional and constitutionally acceptable districting principle. See Vera, 517 U.S., at 1047–1048 (dissenting opinion). Since that is so, his test would not protect those who are packed, and often tightly so, to ensure the reelection of representatives of either party. Indeed, efforts to maximize partisan representation statewide might well begin with packing voters of the opposing party into the districts of existing incumbents of that party. By this means an incumbent is protected, a potential adversary to the districting mollified, and votes of the opposing party are diluted.

Like us, Justice Souter acknowledges and accepts that "some intent to gain political advantage is inescapable whenever political bodies devise a district plan, and some effect results from the intent." Post, at 2. Thus, again like us, he recognizes that "the issue is one of how much is too much." Ibid. And once those premises are conceded, the only line that can be drawn must be based, as Justice Souter again candidly admits, upon a substantive "notio[n] of fairness." Ibid. This is the same flabby goal that deprived Justice Powell's test of all determinacy. To be sure, Justice Souter frames it somewhat differently: courts must intervene, he says, when "partisan competition has reached an extremity of unfairness." Post, at 2—3 (emphasis added). We do not think the problem is solved by adding the modifier.

C

We agree with much of Justice Breyer's dissenting opinion, which convincingly demonstrates that "political considerations will likely play an important, and proper, role in the drawing of district boundaries." Post, at 4. This places Justice Breyer, like the other dissenters, in the difficult position of drawing the line between good politics and bad politics. Unlike them, he would tackle this problem at the statewide level.

The criterion Justice Breyer proposes is nothing more precise than "the unjustified use of political factors to entrench a minority in power." Post, at 6 (emphasis in original). While he invokes in passing the Equal Protection Clause, it should be clear to any reader that what constitutes unjustified entrenchment depends on his own theory of "effective government." Post, at 2. While one must agree with Justice Breyer's incredibly abstract starting point that our Constitution sought to create a "basically democratic" form of government, ibid., that is a long and impassable distance away from the conclusion that the judiciary may assess whether a group (somehow defined) has achieved a level of political power (somehow defined) commensurate with that to which they would be entitled absent unjustified political machinations (whatever that means).

Justice Breyer provides no real guidance for the journey. Despite his promise to do so, post, at 1, he never tells us what he is testing for, beyond the unhelpful "unjustified entrenchment." Post, at 6. Instead, he "set[s] forth several sets of circumstances that lay out the indicia of abuse," "along a continuum," post, at 12, proceeding (presumably) from the most clearly unconstitutional to the possibly unconstitutional. With regard to the first "scenario," he is willing to assert that the indicia "would be sufficient to support a claim." Post, at 12. This seems refreshingly categorical, until one realizes that the indicia consist not merely of the failure of the party receiving the majority of votes to acquire a majority of seats in two successive elections, but also of the fact that there is no "neutral" explanation for this phenomenon. Ibid. But of course there always is a neutral explanation—if only the time-honored criterion of incumbent protection. The indicia set forth in Justice Breyer's second scenario "could also add up to unconstitutional gerrymandering," post, at 12—13 (emphasis added); and for those in the third "a court may conclude that the map crosses the constitutional line," post, at 13 (emphasis added). We find none of this helpful. Each scenario suffers from at least one of the problems we have previously identified, most notably the difficulties of assessing partisan strength statewide and of ascertaining whether an entire statewide plan is motivated by political or neutral justifications, see supra, at 15—16, 19—20. And even at that, the last two scenarios do not even purport to provide an answer, presumably leaving it to each district court to determine whether, under those circumstances, "unjustified entrenchment" has occurred. In sum, we neither know precisely what Justice Breyer is testing for, nor precisely what fails the test.

But perhaps the most surprising omission from Justice Breyer's dissent, given his views on other matters, is the absence of any cost-benefit analysis. Justice Breyer acknowledges that "a majority normally can work its political will," post, at 8, and well describes the number of actors, from statewide executive officers, to redistricting commissions, to Congress, to the People in ballot initiatives and referenda, that stand ready to make that happen. See post, at 8—9. He gives no instance (and we know none) of permanent frustration of majority will. But where the majority has failed to assert itself for some indeterminate period (two successive elections, if we are to believe his first scenario), Justice Breyer simply assumes that "court action may prove necessary," post, at 10. Why so? In the real world, of course, court action that is available tends to be sought, not just where it is necessary, but where it is in the interest of the seeking party. And the vaguer the test for availability, the more frequently interest rather than necessity will produce litigation. Is the regular insertion of the judiciary into districting, with the delay and uncertainty that brings to the political process and the partisan enmity it brings upon the courts, worth the benefit to be achieved—an accelerated (by some unknown degree) effectuation of the majority will? We think not.

V

Justice Kennedy recognizes that we have "demonstrat[ed] the shortcomings of the other standards that have been considered to date," post, at 3 (opinion concurring in judgment). He acknowledges, moreover, that we "lack ... comprehensive and neutral principles for drawing electoral boundaries," post, at 1; and that there is an "absence of rules to limit and confine judicial intervention," ibid. From these premises, one might think that Justice Kennedy would reach the conclusion that political gerrymandering claims are nonjusticiable. Instead, however, he concludes that courts should continue to adjudicate such claims because a standard may one day be discovered.

The first thing to be said about Justice Kennedy's disposition is that it is not legally available. The District Court in this case considered the plaintiffs' claims justiciable but dismissed them because the standard for unconstitutionality had not been met. It is logically impossible to affirm that dismissal without either (1) finding that the unconstitutional-districting standard applied by the District Court, or some other standard that it should have applied, has not been met, or (2) finding (as we have) that the claim is nonjusticiable. Justice Kennedy seeks to affirm "[b]ecause, in the case before us, we have no standard." Post, at 8. But it is our job, not the plaintiffs', to explicate the standard that makes the facts alleged by the plaintiffs adequate or inadequate to state a claim. We cannot nonsuit them for our failure to do so.

Justice Kennedy asserts that to declare nonjusticiability would be incautious. Post, at 6. Our rush to such a holding after a mere 18 years of fruitless litigation "contrasts starkly" he says, "with the more patient approach" that this Court has taken in the past. Post, at 5. We think not. When it has come to determining what areas fall beyond our Article III authority to adjudicate, this Court's practice, from the earliest days of the Republic to the present, has been more reminiscent of Hannibal than of Hamlet. On July 18, 1793, Secretary of State Thomas Jefferson wrote the Justices at the direction of President Washington, asking whether they might answer "questions [that] depend for their solution on the construction of our treaties, on the laws of nature and nations, and on the laws of the land," but that arise "under circumstances which do not give a cognisance of them to the tribunals of the country." 3 Correspondence and Public Papers of John Jay 486—487 (H. Johnston ed. 1891) (emphasis in original). The letter specifically invited the Justices to give less than a categorical yes-or-no answer, offering to present the particular questions "from which [the Justices] will themselves strike out such as any circumstances might, in their opinion, forbid them to pronounce on." Id., at 487. On August 8, 1793, the Justices responded in a categorical and decidedly "impatient" manner, saying that the giving of advisory opinions—not just advisory opinions on particular questions but all advisory opinions, presumably even those concerning legislation affecting the Judiciary—was beyond their power. "[T]he lines of separation drawn by the Constitution between the three departments of the government" prevented it. Id., at 488. The Court rejected the more "cautious" course of not "deny[ing] all hopes of intervention," post, at 5, but leaving the door open to the possibility that at least some advisory opinions (on a theory we could not yet imagine) would not violate the separation of powers. In Gilligan v. Morgan, 413 U.S. 1, 7 (1973), a case filed after the Ohio National Guard's shooting of students at Kent State University, the plaintiffs sought "initial judicial review and continuing surveillance by a federal court over the training, weaponry, and orders of the Guard." The Court held the suit nonjusticiable; the matter was committed to the political branches because, inter alia, "it is difficult to conceive of an area of governmental activity in which the courts have less competence." Id., at 10. The Court did not adopt the more "cautious" course of letting the lower courts try their hand at regulating the military before we declared it impossible. Most recently, in Nixon v. United States, the Court, joined by Justice Kennedy, held that a claim that the Senate had employed certain impermissible procedures in trying an impeachment was a nonjusticiable political question. Our decision was not limited to the particular procedures under challenge, and did not reserve the possibility that sometime, somewhere, technology or the wisdom derived from experience might make a court challenge to Senate impeachment all right.

The only cases Justice Kennedy cites in defense of his never-say-never approach are Baker v. Carr and Bandemer. See post, at 5—6. Bandemer provides no cover. There, all of the Justices who concluded that political gerrymandering claims are justiciable proceeded to describe what they regarded as the discernible and manageable standard that rendered it so. The lower courts were set wandering in the wilderness for 18 years not because the Bandemer majority thought it a good idea, but because five Justices could not agree upon a single standard, and because the standard the plurality proposed turned out not to work.

As for Baker v. Carr: It is true enough that, having had no experience whatever in apportionment matters of any sort, the Court there refrained from spelling out the equal-protection standard. (It did so a mere two years later in Reynolds v. Sims.) But the judgment under review in Baker, unlike the one under review here, did not demand the determination of a standard. The lower court in Baker had held the apportionment claim of the plaintiffs nonjusticiable, and so it was logically possible to dispose of the appeal by simply disagreeing with the nonjusticiability determination. As we observed earlier, that is not possible here, where the lower court has held the claim justiciable but unsupported by the facts. We must either enunciate the standard that causes us to agree or disagree with that merits judgment, or else affirm that the claim is beyond our competence to adjudicate.

Justice Kennedy worries that "[a] determination by the Court to deny all hopes of intervention could erode confidence in the courts as much as would a premature decision to intervene." Post, at 5. But it is the function of the courts to provide relief, not hope. What we think would erode confidence is the Court's refusal to do its job—announcing that there may well be a valid claim here, but we are not yet prepared to figure it out. Moreover, that course does more than erode confidence; by placing the district courts back in the business of pretending to afford help when they in fact can give none, it deters the political process from affording genuine relief. As was noted by a lower court confronted with a political gerrymandering claim:

"When the Supreme Court resolves Vieth, it may choose to retreat from its decision that the question is justiciable, or it may offer more guidance on the nature of the required effect. . . . We have learned firsthand what will result if the Court chooses to do neither. Throughout this case we have borne witness to the powerful, conflicting forces nurtured by Bandemer's holding that the judiciary is to address 'excessive' partisan line-drawing, while leaving the issue virtually unenforceable. Inevitably, as the political party in power uses district lines to lock in its present advantage, the party out of power attempts to stretch the protective cover of the Voting Rights Act, urging dilution of critical standards that may, if accepted, aid their party in the short-run but work to the detriment of persons now protected by the Act in the long-run. Casting the appearance both that there is a wrong and that the judiciary stands ready with a remedy, Bandemer as applied steps on legislative incentives for self-correction." Session, 298 F. Supp. 2d, at 474.

But the conclusive refutation of Justice Kennedy's position is the point we first made: it is not an available disposition. We can affirm because political districting presents a nonjusticiable question; or we can affirm because we believe the correct standard which identifies unconstitutional political districting has not been met; we cannot affirm because we do not know what the correct standard is. Reduced to its essence, Justice Kennedy's opinion boils down to this: "As presently advised, I know of no discernible and manageable standard that can render this claim justiciable. I am unhappy about that, and hope that I will be able to change my opinion in the future." What are the lower courts to make of this pronouncement? We suggest that they must treat it as a reluctant fifth vote against justiciability at district and statewide levels—a vote that may change in some future case but that holds, for the time being, that this matter is nonjusticiable.

VI

We conclude that neither Article I, §2, nor the Equal Protection Clause, nor (what appellants only fleetingly invoke) Article I, §4, provides a judicially enforceable limit on the political considerations that the States and Congress may take into account when districting.

Considerations of stare decisis do not compel us to allow Bandemer to stand. That case involved an interpretation of the Constitution, and the claims of stare decisis are at their weakest in that field, where our mistakes cannot be corrected by Congress. See Payne v. Tennessee, 501 U.S. 808, 828 (1991). They are doubly weak in Bandemer because the majority's inability to enunciate the judicially discernible and manageable standard that it thought existed (or did not think did not exist) presaged the need for reconsideration in light of subsequent experience. And they are triply weak because it is hard to imagine how any action taken in reliance upon Bandemer could conceivably be frustrated—except the bringing of lawsuits, which is not the sort of primary conduct that is relevant.

While we do not lightly overturn one of our own holdings, "when governing decisions are unworkable or are badly reasoned, 'this Court has never felt constrained to follow precedent.' " Id., at 827 (quoting Smith v. Allwright, 321 U.S. 649, 665 (1944)). Eighteen years of essentially pointless litigation have persuaded us that Bandemer is incapable of principled application. We would therefore overrule that case, and decline to adjudicate these political gerrymandering claims.

The judgment of the District Court is affirmed.

It is so ordered.

Notes to Vieth v. Jubelirer (April 28, 2004)

1. The term "political gerrymander" has been defined as "[t]he practice of dividing a geographical area into electoral districts, often of highly irregular shape, to give

one political party an unfair advantage by diluting the opposition's voting strength." Black's Law Dictionary 696 (7th ed. 1999).

2. The plaintiffs apparently never amended their complaint to allege that Act 34 was a political gerrymander, yet the District Court's decision in Vieth III resolved that claim on the merits. Because subject-matter jurisdiction is not implicated and neither party has raised the point, we assume that the District Court deemed the plaintiffs' original complaint to have been constructively amended.

3. Article I, §4, provides as follows: "The Times, Places and Manner of holding Elections for Senators and Representatives, shall be prescribed in each State by the Legislature thereof; but the Congress may at any time by Law make or alter such Regulations, except as to the Places of chusing Senators."

4. The States, of course, have taken their own steps to prevent abusive districting practices. A number have adopted standards for redistricting, and measures designed to insulate the process from politics. See, e.g., Iowa Code §42.4(5) (2003); N. J. Const., Art. II, §2; Haw. Rev. Stat. §25—2 (1993); Idaho Code §72—1506 (1948—1999); Me. Rev. Stat. Ann., Tit. 21—A, §§1206, 1206—A (West Supp. 2003); Mont. Code Ann. §5—1—115 (2003); Wash. Rev. Code §44.05.090 (1994).

5. See Republican Party of North Carolina v. Martin, 980 F.2d 943 (CA4 1992) (upholding denial of Federal Rule of Civil Procedure 12(b)(6) judgment for the defendants); Republican Party of North Carolina v. North Carolina State Board of Elections, 27 F.3d 563 (CA4 1994) (unpublished opinion) (upholding, as modified, a preliminary injunction). Martin dealt with North Carolina's system of electing superior court judges statewide, a system that had resulted in the election of only a single Republican judge since 1900. 980 F.2d, at 948. Later developments in the case are described in n. 8, infra.

6. For cases in which courts rejected prayers for relief under Davis v. Bandemer, 478 U.S. 109 (1986), see, e.g., Duckworth v. State Administrative Bd. of Election Laws, 332 F.3d 769 (CA4 2003); Smith v. Boyle, 144 F.3d 1060 (CA7 1998); La Porte County Republican Central Comm. v. Bd. of Comm'rs of County of La Porte, 43 F.3d 1126 (CA7 1994); Session v. Perry, 298 F. Supp. 2d 451 (ED Tex. 2004) (per curiam); Martinez v. Bush, 234 F. Supp. 2d 1275 (SD Fla. 2002) (three-judge panel); O'Lear v. Miller, 222 F. Supp. 2d 850 (ED Mich.), summarily aff'd, 537 U.S. 997 (2002); Marylanders for Fair Representation, Inc. v. Schaefer, 849 F. Supp. 1022 (Md. 1994) (three-judge panel); Terrazas v. Slagle, 821 F. Supp. 1162 (WD Tex. 1993) (three-judge panel); Pope v. Blue, 809 F. Supp. 392 (WDNC) (three-judge panel), summarily aff'd, 506 U.S. 801 (1992); Illinois Legislative Redistricting Comm'n v. LaPaille, 782 F. Supp. 1272 (ND Ill. 1992); Fund for Accurate and Informed Representation, Inc. v. Weprin, 796 F. Supp. 662 (NDNY) (three-judge panel), summarily aff'd, 506 U.S. 1017 (1992); Holloway v. Hechler, 817 F. Supp. 617 (SD W. Va. 1992) (three-judge panel), summarily aff'd, 507 U.S. 956 (1993); Hastert v. State Bd. of Elections, 777 F. Supp. 634 (ND Ill. 1991) (three-judge panel); Anne Arundel County Republican Central Comm. v. State Administrative Bd. of

Election Laws, 781 F. Supp. 394 (Md. 1991) (three-judge panel), summarily aff'd, 504 U.S. 938 (1992); Republican Party of Virginia v. Wilder, 774 F. Supp. 400 (WD Va. 1991) (three-judge panel); Badham v. Eu, 694 F. Supp. 664, 670 (ND Cal. 1988), summarily aff'd, 488 U.S. 1024 (1989); In re 2003 Legislative Apportionment of House of Representatives, 2003 ME 81, 827 A. 2d 810; McClure v. Secretary of Commonwealth, 436 Mass. 614, 766 N. E. 2d 847 (2002); Legislative Redistricting Cases, 331 Md. 574, 629 A. 2d 646 (1993); Kenai Peninsula Borough v. State, 743 P.2d 1352 (Alaska 1987).

7. "Packing" refers to the practice of filling a district with a supermajority of a given group or party. "Cracking" involves the splitting of a group or party among several districts to deny that group or party a majority in any of those districts.

8. A delicious illustration of this is the one case we have found—alluded to above—that provided relief under Bandemer. See n. 5, supra. In Republican Party of North Carolina v. Hunt, No. 94–2410, 1996 WL 60439 (CA4, Feb. 12, 1996) (per curiam) (unpublished), judgt. order reported at 77 F.3d 470, the district court, after a trial with no less than 311 stipulations by the parties, 132 witness statements, approximately 300 exhibits, and 2 days of oral argument, concluded that North Carolina's system of electing superior court judges on a statewide basis "had resulted in Republican candidates experiencing a consistent and pervasive lack of success and exclusion from the electoral process as a whole and that these effects were likely to continue unabated into the future." 1996 WL 60439, at *1. In the elections for superior court judges conducted just five days after this pronouncement, "every Republican candidate standing for the office of superior court judge was victorious at the state level," ibid., a result which the Fourth Circuit thought (with good reason) "directly at odds with the recent prediction by the district court," id., at *2, causing it to remand the case for reconsideration.

9. The Constitution also does not share appellants' alarm at the asserted tendency of partisan gerrymandering to create more partisan representatives. Assuming that assertion to be true, the Constitution does not answer the question whether it is better for Democratic voters to have their State's congressional delegation include 10 wishy-washy Democrats (because Democratic voters are "effectively" distributed so as to constitute bare majorities in many districts), or 5 hardcore Democrats (because Democratic voters are tightly packed in a few districts). Choosing the former "dilutes" the vote of the radical Democrat; choosing the latter does the same to the moderate. Neither Article I, §2, nor the Equal Protection Clause takes sides in this dispute.

10. Justice Souter would allow a State, in proving its affirmative defense, to demonstrate that the reasons given for the district's shape "were more than a mere pretext for an old-fashioned gerrymander." Post, at 11. But the need to establish that affirmative defense does not arise until the plaintiff has established his prima facie case. And that prima facie case fails when, under step two, the district on its face complies with traditional districting criteria.

Second amendment protects an individual civilian right to keep and bear arms for traditionally lawful purposes like self-defense: District of Columbia v. Heller (June 26, 2008)

Justice Scalia delivered the opinion of the Court.

We consider whether a District of Columbia prohibition on the possession of usable handguns in the home violates the Second Amendment to the Constitution.

I

The District of Columbia generally prohibits the possession of handguns. It is a crime to carry an unregistered firearm, and the registration of handguns is prohibited. See D. C. Code §§7–2501.01(12), 7–2502.01(a), 7–2502.02(a)(4) (2001). Wholly apart from that prohibition, no person may carry a handgun without a license, but the chief of police may issue licenses for 1-year periods. See §§22–4504(a), 22–4506. District of Columbia law also requires residents to keep their lawfully owned firearms, such as registered long guns, "unloaded and dissembled or bound by a trigger lock or similar device" unless they are located in a place of business or are being used for lawful recreational activities. See §7–2507.02.1

Respondent Dick Heller is a D. C. special police officer authorized to carry a handgun while on duty at the Federal Judicial Center. He applied for a registration certificate for a handgun that he wished to keep at home, but the District refused. He thereafter filed a lawsuit in the Federal District Court for the District of Columbia seeking, on Second Amendment grounds, to enjoin the city from enforcing the bar on the registration of handguns, the licensing requirement insofar as it prohibits the carrying of a firearm in the home without a license, and the trigger-lock requirement insofar as it prohibits the use of "functional firearms within the home." App. 59a. The District Court dismissed respondent's complaint, see Parker v. District of Columbia, 311 F. Supp. 2d 103, 109 (2004). The Court of Appeals for the District of Columbia Circuit, construing his complaint as seeking the right to render a firearm operable and carry it about his home in that condition only when necessary for self-defense, 2 reversed, see Parker v. District of Columbia, 478 F. 3d 370, 401 (2007). It held that the Second Amendment protects an individual right to possess firearms and that the city's total ban on handguns, as well as its requirement that firearms in the home be kept nonfunctional even when necessary for self-defense, violated that right. See id., at 395, 399–401. The Court of Appeals directed the District Court to enter summary judgment for respondent.

We granted certiorari. 552 U. S. ____ (2007).

II

We turn first to the meaning of the Second Amendment .

A

The Second Amendment provides: "A well regulated Militia, being necessary to the security of a free State, the right of the people to keep and bear Arms, shall not be infringed." In interpreting this text, we are guided by the principle that "[t]he

Constitution was written to be understood by the voters; its words and phrases were used in their normal and ordinary as distinguished from technical meaning." United States v. Sprague, 282 U. S. 716, 731 (1931); see also Gibbons v. Ogden, 9 Wheat. 1, 188 (1824). Normal meaning may of course include an idiomatic meaning, but it excludes secret or technical meanings that would not have been known to ordinary citizens in the founding generation.

The two sides in this case have set out very different interpretations of the Amendment. Petitioners and today's dissenting Justices believe that it protects only the right to possess and carry a firearm in connection with militia service. See Brief for Petitioners 11–12; post, at 1 (Stevens, J., dissenting). Respondent argues that it protects an individual right to possess a firearm unconnected with service in a militia, and to use that arm for traditionally lawful purposes, such as self-defense within the home. See Brief for Respondent 2–4.

The Second Amendment is naturally divided into two parts: its prefatory clause and its operative clause. The former does not limit the latter grammatically, but rather announces a purpose. The Amendment could be rephrased, "Because a well regulated Militia is necessary to the security of a free State, the right of the people to keep and bear Arms shall not be infringed." See J. Tiffany, A Treatise on Government and Constitutional Law §585, p. 394 (1867); Brief for Professors of Linguistics and English as Amici Curiae 3 (hereinafter Linguists' Brief). Although this structure of the Second Amendment is unique in our Constitution, other legal documents of the founding era, particularly individual-rights provisions of state constitutions, commonly included a prefatory statement of purpose. See generally Volokh, The Commonplace Second Amendment, 73 N. Y. U. L. Rev. 793, 814–821 (1998).

Logic demands that there be a link between the stated purpose and the command. The Second Amendment would be nonsensical if it read, "A well regulated Militia, being necessary to the security of a free State, the right of the people to petition for redress of grievances shall not be infringed." That requirement of logical connection may cause a prefatory clause to resolve an ambiguity in the operative clause ("The separation of church and state being an important objective, the teachings of canons shall have no place in our jurisprudence." The preface makes clear that the operative clause refers not to canons of interpretation but to clergymen.) But apart from that clarifying function, a prefatory clause does not limit or expand the scope of the operative clause. See F. Dwarris, A General Treatise on Statutes 268–269 (P. Potter ed. 1871) (hereinafter Dwarris); T. Sedgwick, The Interpretation and Construction of Statutory and Constitutional Law 42–45 (2d ed. 1874).3 " 'It is nothing unusual in acts ... for the enacting part to go beyond the preamble; the remedy often extends beyond the particular act or mischief which first suggested the necessity of the law.' " J. Bishop, Commentaries on Written Laws and Their Interpretation §51, p. 49 (1882) (quoting Rex v. Marks, 3 East, 157, 165 (K. B. 1802)). Therefore, while we will begin our textual analysis with the operative clause, we will return to the prefatory clause to ensure that our reading of the operative clause is consistent with the announced purpose.4

1. Operative Clause.

a. "Right of the People." The first salient feature of the operative clause is that it codifies a "right of the people." The unamended Constitution and the Bill of Rights use the phrase "right of the people" two other times, in the First Amendment's Assembly-and-Petition Clause and in the Fourth Amendment's Search-and-Seizure Clause. The Ninth Amendment uses very similar terminology ("The enumeration in the Constitution, of certain rights, shall not be construed to deny or disparage others retained by the people"). All three of these instances unambiguously refer to individual rights, not "collective" rights, or rights that may be exercised only through participation in some corporate body.5

Three provisions of the Constitution refer to "the people" in a context other than "rights"—the famous preamble ("We the people"), §2 of Article I (providing that "the people" will choose members of the House), and the Tenth Amendment (providing that those powers not given the Federal Government remain with "the States" or "the people"). Those provisions arguably refer to "the people" acting collectively—but they deal with the exercise or reservation of powers, not rights. Nowhere else in the Constitution does a "right" attributed to "the people" refer to anything other than an individual right.6

What is more, in all six other provisions of the Constitution that mention "the people," the term unambiguously refers to all members of the political community, not an unspecified subset. As we said in United States v. Verdugo-Urquidez, 494 U. S. 259, 265 (1990) :

" '[T]he people' seems to have been a term of art employed in select parts of the Constitution.... [Its uses] sugges[t] that 'the people' protected by the Fourth Amendment, and by the First and Second Amendment s, and to whom rights and powers are reserved in the Ninth and Tenth Amendment s, refers to a class of persons who are part of a national community or who have otherwise developed sufficient connection with this country to be considered part of that community."

This contrasts markedly with the phrase "the militia" in the prefatory clause. As we will describe below, the "militia" in colonial America consisted of a subset of "the people"—those who were male, able bodied, and within a certain age range. Reading the Second Amendment as protecting only the right to "keep and bear Arms" in an organized militia therefore fits poorly with the operative clause's description of the holder of that right as "the people."

We start therefore with a strong presumption that the Second Amendment right is exercised individually and belongs to all Americans.

b. "Keep and bear Arms." We move now from the holder of the right—"the people"—to the substance of the right: "to keep and bear Arms."

Before addressing the verbs "keep" and "bear," we interpret their object: "Arms." The 18th-century meaning is no different from the meaning today. The 1773 edition of Samuel Johnson's dictionary defined "arms" as "weapons of offence, or armour of defence." 1 Dictionary of the English Language 107 (4th ed.) (hereinafter Johnson). Timothy Cunningham's important 1771 legal dictionary defined "arms" as "any thing that a man wears for his defence, or takes into his hands, or useth in wrath to cast at or strike another." 1 A New and Complete Law Dictionary (1771); see also N. Webster, American Dictionary of the English Language (1828) (reprinted 1989) (hereinafter Webster) (similar).

The term was applied, then as now, to weapons that were not specifically designed for military use and were not employed in a military capacity. For instance, Cunningham's legal dictionary gave as an example of usage: "Servants and labourers shall use bows and arrows on Sundays, &c. and not bear other arms." See also, e.g., An Act for the trial of Negroes, 1797 Del. Laws ch. XLIII, §6, p. 104, in 1 First Laws of the State of Delaware 102, 104 (J. Cushing ed. 1981 (pt. 1)); see generally State v. Duke, 42Tex. 455, 458 (1874) (citing decisions of state courts construing "arms"). Although one founding-era thesaurus limited "arms" (as opposed to "weapons") to "instruments of offence generally made use of in war," even that source stated that all firearms constituted "arms." 1 J. Trusler, The Distinction Between Words Esteemed Synonymous in the English Language37 (1794) (emphasis added).

Some have made the argument, bordering on the frivolous, that only those arms in existence in the 18th century are protected by the Second Amendment . We do not interpret constitutional rights that way. Just as the First Amendment protects modern forms of communications, e.g., Reno v. American Civil Liberties Union, 521 U. S. 844, 849 (1997), and the Fourth Amendment applies to modern forms of search, e.g., Kyllo v. United States, 533 U. S. 27, 35–36 (2001), the Second Amendment extends, prima facie,to all instruments that constitute bearable arms, even those that were not in existence at the time of the founding.

We turn to the phrases "keep arms" and "bear arms." Johnson defined "keep" as, most relevantly, "[t]o retain; not to lose," and "[t]o have in custody." Johnson 1095. Webster defined it as "[t]o hold; to retain in one's power or possession." No party has apprised us of an idiomatic meaning of "keep Arms." Thus, the most natural reading of "keep Arms" in the Second Amendment is to "have weapons."

The phrase "keep arms" was not prevalent in the written documents of the founding period that we have found, but there are a few examples, all of which favor viewing the right to "keep Arms" as an individual right unconnected with militia service. William Blackstone, for example, wrote that Catholics convicted of not attending service in the Church of England suffered certain penalties, one of which was that they were not permitted to "keep arms in their houses." 4 Commentaries on the Laws of England 55 (1769) (hereinafter Blackstone); see also 1 W. & M., c. 15, §4, in 3 Eng. Stat. at Large 422 (1689) ("[N]o Papist ... shall or may have or keep in his House ... any Arms ... "); 1 Hawkins, Treatise on the Pleas of the Crown 26 (1771) (similar). Petitioners point to militia laws of the founding period that required militia members to "keep" arms in connection with militia service, and they conclude from this that the phrase "keep Arms" has a militia-related connotation. See Brief for Petitioners 16–17 (citing laws of Delaware, New Jersey, and Virginia). This is rather like saying that, since there are many statutes that authorize aggrieved employees to "file complaints" with federal agencies, the phrase "file complaints" has an employment-related connotation. "Keep arms" was simply a common way of referring to possessing arms, for militiamen and everyone else.7

At the time of the founding, as now, to "bear" meant to "carry." See Johnson 161; Webster; T. Sheridan, A Complete Dictionary of the English Language (1796); 2 Oxford English Dictionary 20 (2d ed. 1989) (hereinafter Oxford). When used with "arms," however, the term has a meaning that refers to carrying for a particular purpose—confrontation. In Muscarello v. United States, 524 U. S. 125 (1998), in the course of analyzing the meaning of "carries a firearm" in a federal criminal statute, Justice Ginsburg wrote that "[s]urely a most familiar meaning is, as the Constitution's Second Amendment ... indicate[s]: 'wear, bear, or carry ... upon the person or in the clothing or in a pocket, for the purpose ... of being armed and ready for offensive or defensive action in a case of conflict with another person.'" Id., at 143 (dissenting opinion) (quoting Black's Law Dictionary 214 (6th ed. 1998)). We think that Justice Ginsburg accurately captured the natural meaning of "bear arms." Although the phrase implies that the carrying of the weapon is for the purpose of "offensive or defensive action," it in no way connotes participation in a structured military organization.

From our review of founding-era sources, we conclude that this natural meaning was also the meaning that "bear arms" had in the 18th century. In numerous instances, "bear arms" was unambiguously used to refer to the carrying of weapons outside of an organized militia. The most prominent examples are those most relevant to the Second Amendment : Nine state constitutional provisions written in the 18th century or the first two decades of the 19th, which enshrined a right of citizens to "bear arms in defense of themselves and the state" or "bear arms in defense of himself and the state." 8 It is clear from those formulations that "bear arms" did not refer only to carrying a weapon in an organized military unit. Justice James Wilson interpreted the Pennsylvania Constitution's arms-bearing right, for example, as a recognition of the natural right of defense "of one's person or house"—what he called the law of "self preservation." 2 Collected Works of James Wilson 1142, and n. x (K. Hall & M. Hall eds. 2007) (citing Pa. Const., Art. IX, §21 (1790)); see also T. Walker, Introduction to American Law 198 (1837) ("Thus the right of self-defence [is] guaranteed by the [Ohio] constitution"); see also id., at 157 (equating Second Amendment with that provision of the Ohio Constitution). That was also the interpretation of those state constitutional provisions adopted by pre-Civil War state courts.9 These provisions demonstrate—again, in the most analogous linguistic context—that "bear arms" was not limited to the carrying of arms in a militia.

The phrase "bear Arms" also had at the time of the founding an idiomatic meaning that was significantly different from its natural meaning: "to serve as a soldier, do military service, fight" or "to wage war." See Linguists' Brief 18; post, at 11 (Stevens, J., dissenting). But it unequivocally bore that idiomatic meaning only when followed by the preposition "against," which was in turn followed by the target of the hostilities. See 2 Oxford 21. (That is how, for example, our Declaration of Independence ¶28, used the phrase: "He has constrained our fellow Citizens taken Captive on the high Seas to bear Arms against their Country ... .") Every example given by petitioners' amici for the idiomatic meaning of "bear arms" from the founding period either includes the preposition "against" or is not clearly idiomatic. See Linguists' Brief 18–23. Without the preposition, "bear arms" normally meant (as it continues to mean today) what Justice Ginsburg's opinion in Muscarello said.

In any event, the meaning of "bear arms" that petitioners and Justice Stevens propose is not even the (sometimes) idiomatic meaning. Rather, they manufacture a hybrid definition, whereby "bear arms" connotes the actual carrying of arms (and therefore is not really an idiom) but only in the service of an organized militia. No dictionary has ever adopted that definition, and we have been apprised of no source that indicates that it carried that meaning at the time of the founding. But it is easy to see why petitioners and the dissent are driven to the hybrid definition. Giving "bear Arms" its idiomatic meaning would cause the protected right to consist of the right to be a soldier or to wage war—an absurdity that no commentator has ever endorsed. See L. Levy, Origins of the Bill of Rights 135 (1999). Worse still, the phrase "keep and bear Arms" would be incoherent. The word "Arms" would have two different meanings at once: "weapons" (as the object of "keep") and (as the object of "bear") one-half of an idiom. It would be rather like saying "He filled and kicked the bucket" to mean "He filled the bucket and died." Grotesque.

Petitioners justify their limitation of "bear arms" to the military context by pointing out the unremarkable fact that it was often used in that context—the same mistake they made with respect to "keep arms." It is especially unremarkable that the phrase was often used in a military context in the federal legal sources (such as records of congressional debate) that have been the focus of petitioners' inquiry. Those sources would have had little occasion to use it except in discussions about the standing army and the militia. And the phrases used primarily in those military discussions include not only "bear arms" but also "carry arms," "possess arms," and "have arms"—though no one thinks that those other phrases also had special military meanings. See Barnett, Was the Right to Keep and Bear Arms Conditioned on Service in an Organized Militia?, 83 Tex. L. Rev. 237, 261 (2004). The common references to those "fit to bear arms" in congressional discussions about the militia are matched by use of the same phrase in the few nonmilitary federal contexts where the concept would be relevant. See, e.g., 30 Journals of Continental Congress 349–351 (J. Fitzpatrick ed. 1934). Other legal sources frequently used "bear arms" in nonmilitary contexts.10 Cunningham's legal dictionary, cited above, gave as an example of its usage a sentence unrelated to military affairs ("Servants and labourers shall use bows and arrows on Sundays, &c. and not bear other arms"). And if one looks beyond legal sources, "bear arms" was frequently used in nonmilitary contexts.

See Cramer & Olson, What Did "Bear Arms" Mean in the Second Amendment ?, 6 Georgetown J. L. & Pub. Pol'y (forthcoming Sept. 2008), online at http://papers.ssrn.com/abstract=1086176 (as visited June 24, 2008, and available in Clerk of Court's case file) (identifying numerous nonmilitary uses of "bear arms" from the founding period).

Justice Stevens points to a study by amici supposedly showing that the phrase "bear arms" was most frequently used in the military context. See post, at 12–13, n. 9; Linguists' Brief 24. Of course, as we have said, the fact that the phrase was commonly used in a particular context does not show that it is limited to that context, and, in any event, we have given many sources where the phrase was used in nonmilitary contexts. Moreover, the study's collection appears to include (who knows how many times) the idiomatic phrase "bear arms against," which is irrelevant. The amici also dismiss examples such as " 'bear arms ... for the purpose of killing game' " because those uses are "expressly qualified." Linguists' Brief 24. (Justice Stevens uses the same excuse for dismissing the state constitutional provisions analogous to the Second Amendment that identify private-use purposes for which the individual right can be asserted. See post, at 12.) That analysis is faulty. A purposive qualifying phrase that contradicts the word or phrase it modifies is unknown this side of the looking glass (except, apparently, in some courses on Linguistics). If "bear arms" means, as we think, simply the carrying of arms, a modifier can limit the purpose of the carriage ("for the purpose of self-defense" or "to make war against the King"). But if "bear arms" means, as the petitioners and the dissent think, the carrying of arms only for military purposes, one simply cannot add "for the purpose of killing game." The right "to carry arms in the militia for the purpose of killing game" is worthy of the mad hatter. Thus, these purposive qualifying phrases positively establish that "to bear arms" is not limited to military use.11

Justice Stevens places great weight on James Madison's inclusion of a conscientious-objector clause in his original draft of the Second Amendment : "but no person religiously scrupulous of bearing arms, shall be compelled to render military service in person." Creating the Bill of Rights 12 (H. Veit, K. Bowling, & C. Bickford eds. 1991) (hereinafter Veit). He argues that this clause establishes that the drafters of the Second Amendment intended "bear Arms" to refer only to military service. See post, at 26. It is always perilous to derive the meaning of an adopted provision from another provision deleted in the drafting process.12 In any case, what Justice Stevens would conclude from the deleted provision does not follow. It was not meant to exempt from military service those who objected to going to war but had no scruples about personal gunfights. Quakers opposed the use of arms not just for militia service, but for any violent purpose whatsoever—so much so that Quaker frontiersmen were forbidden to use arms to defend their families, even though "[i]n such circumstances the temptation to seize a hunting rifle or knife in self-defense ... must sometimes have been almost overwhelming." P. Brock, Pacifism in the United States 359 (1968); see M. Hirst, The Quakers in Peace and War 336–339 (1923); 3 T. Clarkson, Portraiture of Quakerism 103–104 (3d ed.

1807). The Pennsylvania Militia Act of 1757 exempted from service those "scrupling the use of arms"—a phrase that no one contends had an idiomatic meaning. See 5 Stat. at Large of Pa. 613 (J. Mitchell & H. Flanders eds. 1898) (emphasis added). Thus, the most natural interpretation of Madison's deleted text is that those opposed to carrying weapons for potential violent confrontation would not be "compelled to render military service," in which such carrying would be required.13

Finally, Justice Stevens suggests that "keep and bear Arms" was some sort of term of art, presumably akin to "hue and cry" or "cease and desist." (This suggestion usefully evades the problem that there is no evidence whatsoever to support a military reading of "keep arms.") Justice Stevens believes that the unitary meaning of "keep and bear Arms" is established by the Second Amendment's calling it a "right" (singular) rather than "rights" (plural). See post, at 16. There is nothing to this. State constitutions of the founding period routinely grouped multiple (related) guarantees under a singular "right," and the First Amendment protects the "right [singular] of the people peaceably to assemble, and to petition the Government for a redress of grievances." See, e.g., Pa. Declaration of Rights §§IX, XII, XVI, in 5 Thorpe 3083–3084; Ohio Const., Arts. VIII, §§11, 19 (1802), in id., at 2910–2911.14 And even if "keep and bear Arms" were a unitary phrase, we find no evidence that it bore a military meaning. Although the phrase was not at all common (which would be unusual for a term of art), we have found instances of its use with a clearly nonmilitary connotation. In a 1780 debate in the House of Lords, for example, Lord Richmond described an order to disarm private citizens (not militia members) as "a violation of the constitutional right of Protestant subjects to keep and bear arms for their own defense." 49 The London Magazine or Gentleman's Monthly Intelligencer 467 (1780). In response, another member of Parliament referred to "the right of bearing arms for personal defence," making clear that no special military meaning for "keep and bear arms" was intended in the discussion. Id., at 467–468.15

c. Meaning of the Operative Clause. Putting all of these textual elements together, we find that they guarantee the individual right to possess and carry weapons in case of confrontation. This meaning is strongly confirmed by the historical background of the Second Amendment . We look to this because it has always been widely understood that the Second Amendment, like the First and Fourth Amendment s, codified a pre-existing right. The very text of the Second Amendment implicitly recognizes the pre-existence of the right and declares only that it "shall not be infringed." As we said in United States v. Cruikshank, 92 U. S. 542, 553 (1876), "[t]his is not a right granted by the Constitution. Neither is it in any manner dependent upon that instrument for its existence. The Second amendment declares that it shall not be infringed ... ."16

Between the Restoration and the Glorious Revolution, the Stuart Kings Charles II and James II succeeded in using select militias loyal to them to suppress political dissidents, in part by disarming their opponents. See J. Malcolm, To Keep and Bear Arms 31–53 (1994) (hereinafter Malcolm); L. Schwoerer, The Declaration of Rights, 1689, p. 76 (1981). Under the auspices of the 1671 Game Act, for example, the Catholic James II had ordered general disarmaments of regions home to his Protestant enemies. See Malcolm 103–106. These experiences caused Englishmen to be extremely wary of concentrated military forces run by the state and to be jealous of their arms. They accordingly obtained an assurance from William and Mary, in the Declaration of Right (which was codified as the English Bill of Rights), that Protestants would never be disarmed: "That the subjects which are Protestants may have arms for their defense suitable to their conditions and as allowed by law." 1 W. & M., c. 2, §7, in 3 Eng. Stat. at Large 441 (1689). This right has long been understood to be the predecessor to our Second Amendment . See E. Dumbauld, The Bill of Rights and What It Means Today 51 (1957); W. Rawle, A View of the Constitution of the United States of America 122 (1825) (hereinafter Rawle). It was clearly an individual right, having nothing whatever to do with service in a militia. To be sure, it was an individual right not available to the whole population, given that it was restricted to Protestants, and like all written English rights it was held only against the Crown, not Parliament. See Schwoerer, To Hold and Bear Arms: The English Perspective, in Bogus 207, 218; but see 3 J. Story, Commentaries on the Constitution of the United States §1858 (1833) (hereinafter Story) (contending that the "right to bear arms" is a "limitatio[n] upon the power of parliament" as well). But it was secured to them as individuals, according to "libertarian political principles," not as members of a fighting force. Schwoerer, Declaration of Rights, at 283; see also id., at 78; G. Jellinek, The Declaration of the Rights of Man and of Citizens 49, and n. 7 (1901) (reprinted 1979).

By the time of the founding, the right to have arms had become fundamental for English subjects. See Malcolm 122–134. Blackstone, whose works, we have said, "constituted the preeminent authority on English law for the founding generation," Alden v. Maine, 527 U. S. 706, 715 (1999), cited the arms provision of the Bill of Rights as one of the fundamental rights of Englishmen. See 1 Blackstone 136, 139–140 (1765). His description of it cannot possibly be thought to tie it to militia or military service. It was, he said, "the natural right of resistance and self-preservation," id., at 139, and "the right of having and using arms for self-preservation and defence," id., at 140; see also 3 id., at 2–4 (1768). Other contemporary authorities concurred. See G. Sharp, Tracts, Concerning the Ancient and Only True Legal Means of National Defence, by a Free Militia 17–18, 27 (3d ed. 1782); 2 J. de Lolme, The Rise and Progress of the English Constitution 886–887 (1784) (A. Stephens ed. 1838); W. Blizard, Desultory Reflections on Police 59–60 (1785). Thus, the right secured in 1689 as a result of the Stuarts' abuses was by the time of the founding understood to be an individual right protecting against both public and private violence.

And, of course, what the Stuarts had tried to do to their political enemies, George III had tried to do to the colonists. In the tumultuous decades of the 1760's and 1770's, the Crown began to disarm the inhabitants of the most rebellious areas. That provoked polemical reactions by Americans invoking their rights as Englishmen to keep arms. A New York article of April 1769 said that "[i]t is a natural right which the people have reserved to themselves, confirmed by the Bill of Rights, to keep arms for their own defence." A Journal of the Times: Mar. 17, New York Journal, Supp. 1, Apr. 13, 1769, in Boston Under Military Rule 79 (O. Dickerson ed. 1936); see also, e.g., Shippen, Boston Gazette, Jan. 30, 1769, in 1 The Writings of Samuel Adams 299 (H. Cushing ed. 1968). They understood the right to enable individuals to defend themselves. As the most important early American edition of Blackstone's Commentaries (by the law professor and former Antifederalist St. George Tucker) made clear in the notes to the description of the arms right, Americans understood the "right of self-preservation" as permitting a citizen to "repe[l] force by force" when "the intervention of society in his behalf, may be too late to prevent an injury." 1 Blackstone's Commentaries 145–146, n. 42 (1803) (hereinafter Tucker's Blackstone). See also W. Duer, Outlines of the Constitutional Jurisprudence of the United States 31–32 (1833).

There seems to us no doubt, on the basis of both text and history, that the Second Amendment conferred an individual right to keep and bear arms. Of course the right was not unlimited, just as the First Amendment's right of free speech was not, see, e.g., United States v. Williams, 553 U. S. ___ (2008). Thus, we do not read the Second Amendment to protect the right of citizens to carry arms for any sort of confrontation, just as we do not read the First Amendment to protect the right of citizens to speak for any purpose. Before turning to limitations upon the individual right, however, we must determine whether the prefatory clause of the Second Amendment comports with our interpretation of the operative clause.

2. Prefatory Clause.

The prefatory clause reads: "A well regulated Militia, being necessary to the security of a free State ... ."

a. "Well-Regulated Militia." In United States v. Miller, 307 U. S. 174, 179 (1939), we explained that "the Militia comprised all males physically capable of acting in concert for the common defense." That definition comports with founding-era sources. See, e.g., Webster ("The militia of a country are the able bodied men organized into companies, regiments and brigades ... and required by law to attend military exercises on certain days only, but at other times left to pursue their usual occupations"); The Federalist No. 46, pp. 329, 334 (B. Wright ed. 1961) (J. Madison) ("near half a million of citizens with arms in their hands"); Letter to Destutt de Tracy (Jan. 26, 1811), in The Portable Thomas Jefferson 520, 524 (M. Peterson ed. 1975) ("[T]he militia of the State, that is to say, of every man in it able to bear arms").

Petitioners take a seemingly narrower view of the militia, stating that "[m]ilitias are the state- and congressionally-regulated military forces described in the Militia Clauses (art. I, §8, cls. 15–16)." Brief for Petitioners 12. Although we agree with petitioners' interpretive assumption that "militia" means the same thing in Article I and the Second Amendment, we believe that petitioners identify the wrong thing, namely, the organized militia. Unlike armies and navies, which Congress is given the power to create ("to raise ... Armies"; "to provide ... a Navy," Art. I, §8, cls. 12–13), the militia is assumed by Article I already to be in existence. Congress is given the power to "provide for calling forth the militia," §8, cl. 15; and the power not to create, but to "organiz[e]" it—and not to organize "a" militia, which is what one would expect if the militia were to be a federal creation, but to organize "the" militia, connoting a body already in existence, ibid., cl. 16. This is fully consistent with the ordinary definition of the militia as all able-bodied men. From that pool, Congress has plenary power to organize the units that will make up an effective fighting force. That is what Congress did in the first militia Act, which specified that "each and every free able-bodied white male citizen of the respective states, resident therein, who is or shall be of the age of eighteen years, and under the age of forty-five years (except as is herein after excepted) shall severally and respectively be enrolled in the militia." Act of May 8, 1792, 1 Stat. 271. To be sure, Congress need not conscript every able-bodied man into the militia, because nothing in Article I suggests that in exercising its power to organize, discipline, and arm the militia, Congress must focus upon the entire body. Although the militia consists of all able-bodied men, the federally organized militia may consist of a subset of them.

Finally, the adjective "well-regulated" implies nothing more than the imposition of proper discipline and training. See Johnson 1619 ("Regulate": "To adjust by rule or method"); Rawle 121–122; cf. Va. Declaration of Rights §13 (1776), in 7 Thorpe 3812, 3814 (referring to "a well-regulated militia, composed of the body of the people, trained to arms").

b. "Security of a Free State." The phrase "security of a free state" meant "security of a free polity," not security of each of the several States as the dissent below argued, see 478 F. 3d, at 405, and n. 10. Joseph Story wrote in his treatise on the Constitution that "the word 'state' is used in various senses [and in] its most enlarged sense, it means the people composing a particular nation or community." 1 Story §208; see also 3 id., §1890 (in reference to the Second Amendment's prefatory clause: "The militia is the natural defence of a free country"). It is true that the term "State" elsewhere in the Constitution refers to individual States, but the phrase "security of a free state" and close variations seem to have been terms of art in 18th-century political discourse, meaning a " 'free country' " or free polity. See Volokh, "Necessary to the Security of a Free State," 83 Notre Dame L. Rev. 1, 5 (2007); see, e.g., 4 Blackstone 151 (1769); Brutus Essay III (Nov. 15, 1787), in The Essential Antifederalist 251, 253 (W. Allen & G. Lloyd eds., 2d ed. 2002). Moreover, the other instances of "state" in the Constitution are typically accompanied by modifiers making clear that the reference is to the several States—"each state," "several states," "any state," "that state," "particular states," "one state," "no state." And the presence of the term "foreign state" in Article I and Article III shows that the word "state" did not have a single meaning in the Constitution.

There are many reasons why the militia was thought to be "necessary to the security of a free state." See 3 Story §1890. First, of course, it is useful in repelling invasions and suppressing insurrections. Second, it renders large standing armies unnecessary—an argument that Alexander Hamilton made in favor of federal control over the militia. The Federalist No. 29, pp. 226, 227 (B. Wright ed. 1961) (A. Hamilton). Third, when the able-bodied men of a nation are trained in arms and organized, they are better able to resist tyranny.

3. Relationship between Prefatory Clause and Operative Clause

We reach the question, then: Does the preface fit with an operative clause that creates an individual right to keep and bear arms? It fits perfectly, once one knows the history that the founding generation knew and that we have described above. That history showed that the way tyrants had eliminated a militia consisting of all the able-bodied men was not by banning the militia but simply by taking away the people's arms, enabling a select militia or standing army to suppress political opponents. This is what had occurred in England that prompted codification of the right to have arms in the English Bill of Rights.

The debate with respect to the right to keep and bear arms, as with other guarantees in the Bill of Rights, was not over whether it was desirable (all agreed that it was) but over whether it needed to be codified in the Constitution. During the 1788 ratification debates, the fear that the federal government would disarm the people in order to impose rule through a standing army or select militia was pervasive in Antifederalist rhetoric. See, e.g., Letters from The Federal Farmer III (Oct. 10, 1787), in 2 The Complete Anti-Federalist 234, 242 (H. Storing ed. 1981). John Smilie, for example, worried not only that Congress's "command of the militia" could be used to create a "select militia," or to have "no militia at all," but also, as a separate concern, that "[w]hen a select militia is formed; the people in general may be disarmed." 2 Documentary History of the Ratification of the Constitution 508–509 (M. Jensen ed. 1976) (hereinafter Documentary Hist.). Federalists responded that because Congress was given no power to abridge the ancient right of individuals to keep and bear arms, such a force could never oppress the people. See, e.g., A Pennsylvanian III (Feb. 20, 1788), in The Origin of the Second Amendment 275, 276 (D. Young ed., 2d ed. 2001) (hereinafter Young); White, To the Citizens of Virginia, Feb. 22, 1788, in id., at 280, 281; A Citizen of America, (Oct. 10, 1787) in id., at 38, 40; Remarks on the Amendments to the federal Constitution, Nov. 7, 1788, in id., at 556. It was understood across the political spectrum that the right helped to secure the ideal of a citizen militia, which might be necessary to oppose an oppressive military force if the constitutional order broke down.

It is therefore entirely sensible that the Second Amendment's prefatory clause announces the purpose for which the right was codified: to prevent elimination of the militia. The prefatory clause does not suggest that preserving the militia was the only reason Americans valued the ancient right; most undoubtedly thought it even more important for self-defense and hunting. But the threat that the new Federal Government would destroy the citizens' militia by taking away their arms was the reason that right— unlike some other English rights—was codified in a written Constitution. Justice Breyer's assertion that individual self-defense is merely a "subsidiary interest" of the right to keep and bear arms, see post, at 36, is profoundly mistaken. He bases that assertion solely upon the prologue—but that can only show that self-defense had little to do with the right's codification; it was the central component of the right itself.

Besides ignoring the historical reality that the Second Amendment was not intended to lay down a "novel principl[e]" but rather codified a right "inherited from our English ancestors," Robertson v. Baldwin, 165 U. S. 275, 281 (1897), petitioners' interpretation does not even achieve the narrower purpose that prompted codification of the right. If, as they believe, the Second Amendment right is no more than the right to keep and use weapons as a member of an organized militia, see Brief for Petititioners 8—if, that is, the organized militia is the sole institutional beneficiary of the Second Amendment 's guarantee—it does not assure the existence of a "citizens' militia" as a safeguard against tyranny. For Congress retains plenary authority to organize the militia, which must include the authority to say who will belong to the organized force.17 That is why the first Militia Act's requirement that only whites enroll caused States to amend their militia laws to exclude free blacks. See Siegel, The Federal Government's Power to Enact Color-Conscious Laws, 92 Nw. U. L. Rev. 477, 521–525 (1998). Thus, if petitioners are correct, the Second Amendment protects citizens' right to use a gun in an organization from which Congress has plenary authority to exclude them. It guarantees a select militia of the sort the Stuart kings found useful, but not the people's militia that was the concern of the founding generation.

B

Our interpretation is confirmed by analogous arms-bearing rights in state constitutions that preceded and immediately followed adoption of the Second Amendment . Four States adopted analogues to the Federal Second Amendment in the period between independence and the ratification of the Bill of Rights. Two of them—Pennsylvania and Vermont—clearly adopted individual rights unconnected to militia service. Pennsylvania's Declaration of Rights of 1776 said: "That the people have a right to bear arms for the defence of themselves, and the state ... ." §XIII, in 5 Thorpe 3082, 3083 (emphasis added). In 1777, Vermont adopted the identical provision, except for inconsequential differences in punctuation and capitalization. See Vt. Const., ch. 1, §15, in 6 id., at 3741.

North Carolina also codified a right to bear arms in 1776: "That the people have a right to bear arms, for the defence of the State ... ." Declaration of Rights §XVII, in id., at 2787, 2788. This could plausibly be read to support only a right to bear arms in a militia—but that is a peculiar way to make the point in a constitution that elsewhere repeatedly mentions the militia explicitly. See §§14, 18, 35, in 5 id., 2789, 2791, 2793. Many colonial statutes required individual arms-bearing for public-safety reasons—such as the 1770 Georgia law that "for the security and defence of this province from internal dangers and insurrections" required those men who qualified for militia duty individually "to carry fire arms" "to places of public worship." 19 Colonial Records of the State of Georgia 137–139 (A. Candler ed. 1911 (pt. 2)) (emphasis added). That broad public-safety understanding was the connotation given to the North Carolina right by that State's Supreme Court in 1843. See State v. Huntly, 3 Ired. 418, 422–423.

The 1780 Massachusetts Constitution presented another variation on the theme: "The people have a right to keep and to bear arms for the common defence... ." Pt. First, Art. XVII, in 3 Thorpe 1888, 1892. Once again, if one gives narrow meaning to the phrase "common defence" this can be thought to limit the right to the bearing of arms in a state-organized military force. But once again the State's highest court thought otherwise. Writing for the court in an 1825 libel case, Chief Justice Parker wrote: "The liberty of the press was to be unrestrained, but he who used it was to be responsible in cases of its abuse; like the right to keep fire arms, which does not protect him who uses them for annoyance or destruction." Commonwealth v. Blanding, 20 Mass. 304, 313–314. The analogy makes no sense if firearms could not be used for any individual purpose at all. See also Kates, Handgun Prohibition and the Original Meaning of the Second Amendment, 82 Mich. L. Rev. 204, 244 (1983) (19th-century courts never read "common defence" to limit the use of weapons to militia service).

We therefore believe that the most likely reading of all four of these pre-Second Amendment state constitutional provisions is that they secured an individual right to bear arms for defensive purposes. Other States did not include rights to bear arms in their pre-1789 constitutions—although in Virginia a Second Amendment analogue was proposed (unsuccessfully) by Thomas Jefferson. (It read: "No freeman shall ever be debarred the use of arms [within his own lands or tenements]."18 1 The Papers of Thomas Jefferson 344 (J. Boyd ed. 1950)).

Between 1789 and 1820, nine States adopted Second Amendment analogues. Four of them—Kentucky, Ohio, Indiana, and Missouri—referred to the right of the people to "bear arms in defence of themselves and the State." See n. 8, supra. Another three States—Mississippi, Connecticut, and Alabama—used the even more individualistic phrasing that each citizen has the "right to bear arms in defence of himself and the State." See ibid. Finally, two States—Tennessee and Maine—used the "common defence" language of Massachusetts. See Tenn. Const., Art. XI, §26 (1796), in 6 Thorpe 3414, 3424; Me. Const., Art. I, §16 (1819), in 3 id., at 1646, 1648. That of the nine state constitutional protections for the right to bear arms enacted immediately after 1789 at least seven unequivocally protected an individual citizen's right to self-defense is strong evidence that that is how the founding generation conceived of the right. And with one possible exception that we discuss in Part II–D–2, 19th-century courts and commentators interpreted these state constitutional provisions to protect an individual right to use arms for self-defense. See n. 9, supra; Simpson v. State, 5Yer. 356, 360 (Tenn. 1833).

The historical narrative that petitioners must endorse would thus treat the Federal Second Amendment as an odd outlier, protecting a right unknown in state constitutions or at English common law, based on little more than an overreading of the prefatory clause.

C

Justice Stevens relies on the drafting history of the Second Amendment —the various proposals in the state conventions and the debates in Congress. It is dubious to rely on such history to interpret a text that was widely understood to codify a pre-existing right, rather than to fashion a new one. But even assuming that this legislative history is relevant, Justice Stevens flatly misreads the historical record.

It is true, as Justice Stevens says, that there was concern that the Federal Government would abolish the institution of the state militia. See post, at 20. That concern found expression, however, not in the various Second Amendment precursors proposed in the State conventions, but in separate structural provisions that would have given the States concurrent and seemingly nonpre-emptible authority to organize, discipline, and arm the militia when the Federal Government failed to do so. See Veit 17, 20 (Virginia proposal); 4 J. Eliot, The Debates in the Several State Conventions on the Adoption of the Federal Constitution 244, 245 (2d ed. 1836) (reprinted 1941) (North Carolina proposal); see also 2 Documentary Hist. 624 (Pennsylvania minority's proposal). The Second Amendment precursors, by contrast, referred to the individual English right already codified in two (and probably four) State constitutions. The Federalist-dominated first Congress chose to reject virtually all major structural revisions favored by the Antifederalists, including the proposed militia amendments. Rather, it adopted primarily the popular and uncontroversial (though, in the Federalists' view, unnecessary) individual-rights amendments. The Second Amendment right, protecting only individuals' liberty to keep and carry arms, did nothing to assuage Antifederalists' concerns about federal control of the militia. See, e.g., Centinel, Revived, No. XXIX, Philadelphia Independent Gazetteer, Sept. 9, 1789, in Young 711, 712.

Justice Stevens thinks it significant that the Virginia, New York, and North Carolina Second Amendment proposals were "embedded ... within a group of principles that are distinctly military in meaning," such as statements about the danger of standing armies. Post, at 22. But so was the highly influential minority proposal in Pennsylvania, yet that proposal, with its reference to hunting, plainly referred to an individual right. See 2 Documentary Hist. 624. Other than that erroneous point, Justice Stevens has brought forward absolutely no evidence that those proposals conferred only a right to carry arms in a militia. By contrast, New Hampshire's proposal, the Pennsylvania minority's proposal, and Samuel Adams' proposal in Massachusetts unequivocally referred to individual rights, as did two state constitutional provisions at the time. See Veit 16, 17 (New Hampshire proposal); 6 Documentary Hist. 1452, 1453 (J. Kaminski & G. Saladino eds. 2000) (Samuel Adams' proposal). Justice Stevens' view thus relies on the proposition, unsupported by any evidence, that different people of the founding period had vastly different conceptions of the right to keep and bear arms. That simply does not comport with our longstanding view that the Bill of Rights codified venerable, widely understood liberties.

D

We now address how the Second Amendment was interpreted from immediately after its ratification through the end of the 19th century. Before proceeding, however, we take issue with Justice Stevens' equating of these sources with postenactment legislative history, a comparison that betrays a fundamental misunderstanding of a court's interpretive task. See post, at 27, n. 28. "Legislative history," of course, refers to the pre-enactment statements of those who drafted or voted for a law; it is considered persuasive by some, not because they reflect the general understanding of the disputed terms, but because the legislators who heard or read those statements presumably voted with that understanding. Ibid. "Postenactment legislative history," ibid., a deprecatory contradiction in terms, refers to statements of those who drafted or voted for the law that are made after its enactment and hence could have had no effect on the congressional vote. It most certainly does not refer to the examination of a variety of legal and other sources to determine the public understanding of a legal text in the period after its enactment or ratification. That sort of inquiry is a critical tool of constitutional interpretation. As we will show, virtually all interpreters of the Second Amendment in the century after its enactment interpreted the amendment as we do.

    1. Post-ratification Commentary

    Three important founding-era legal scholars interpreted the Second Amendment in published writings. All three understood it to protect an individual right unconnected with militia service.

    St. George Tucker's version of Blackstone's Commentaries, as we explained above, conceived of the Blackstonian arms right as necessary for self-defense. He equated that right, absent the religious and class-based restrictions, with the Second Amendment. See 2 Tucker's Blackstone 143. In Note D, entitled, "View of the Constitution of the United States," Tucker elaborated on the Second Amendment : "This may be considered as the true palladium of liberty ... . The right to self-defence is the first law of nature: in most governments it has been the study of rulers to confine the right within the narrowest limits possible. Wherever standing armies are kept up, and the right of the people to keep and bear arms is, under any colour or pretext whatsoever, prohibited, liberty, if not already annihilated, is on the brink of destruction." 1 id., at App. 300 (ellipsis in original). He believed that the English game laws had abridged the right by prohibiting "keeping a gun or other engine for the destruction of game." Ibid; see also 2 id., at 143, and nn. 40 and 41. He later grouped the right with some of the individual rights included in the First Amendment and said that if "a law be passed by congress, prohibiting" any of those rights, it would "be the province of the judiciary to pronounce whether any such act were constitutional, or not; and if not, to acquit the accused ... ." 1 id., at App. 357. It is unlikely that Tucker was referring to a person's being "accused" of violating a law making it a crime to bear arms in a state militia.19

    In 1825, William Rawle, a prominent lawyer who had been a member of the Pennsylvania Assembly that ratified the Bill of Rights, published an influential treatise, which analyzed the Second Amendment as follows:

"The first [principle] is a declaration that a well regulated militia is necessary to the security of a free state; a proposition from which few will dissent... .

"The corollary, from the first position is, that the right of the people to keep and bear arms shall not be infringed.

"The prohibition is general. No clause in the constitution could by any rule of construction be conceived to give to congress a power to disarm the people. Such a flagitious attempt could only be made under some general pretence by a state legislature. But if in any blind pursuit of inordinate power, either should attempt it, this amendment may be appealed to as a restraint on both." Rawle 121–122.20

Like Tucker, Rawle regarded the English game laws as violating the right codified in the Second Amendment . See id., 122–123. Rawle clearly differentiated between the people's right to bear arms and their service in a militia: "In a people permitted and accustomed to bear arms, we have the rudiments of a militia, which properly consists of armed citizens, divided into military bands, and instructed at least in part, in the use of arms for the purposes of war." Id., at 140. Rawle further said that the Second Amendment right ought not "be abused to the disturbance of the public peace," such as by assembling with other armed individuals "for an unlawful purpose"—statements that make no sense if the right does not extend to any individual purpose.

Joseph Story published his famous Commentaries on the Constitution of the United States in 1833. Justice Stevens suggests that "[t]here is not so much as a whisper" in Story's explanation of the Second Amendment that favors the individual-rights view. Post, at 34. That is wrong. Story explained that the English Bill of Rights had also included a "right to bear arms," a right that, as we have discussed, had nothing to do with militia service. 3 Story §1858. He then equated the English right with the Second Amendment :

"§1891. A similar provision [to the Second Amendment] in favour of protestants (for to them it is confined) is to be found in the bill of rights of 1688, it being declared, 'that the subjects, which are protestants, may have arms for their defence suitable to their condition, and as allowed by law.' But under various pretences the effect of this provision has been greatly narrowed; and it is at present in England more nominal than real, as a defensive privilege." (Footnotes omitted.)

This comparison to the Declaration of Right would not make sense if the Second Amendment right was the right to use a gun in a militia, which was plainly not what the English right protected. As the Tennessee Supreme Court recognized 38 years after Story wrote his Commentaries, "[t]he passage from Story, shows clearly that this right was intended ... and was guaranteed to, and to be exercised and enjoyed by the citizen as such, and not by him as a soldier, or in defense solely of his political rights." Andrews v. State, 50 Tenn. 165, 183 (1871). Story's Commentaries also cite as support Tucker and Rawle, both of whom clearly viewed the right as unconnected to militia service. See 3 Story §1890, n. 2; §1891, n. 3. In addition, in a shorter 1840 work Story wrote: "One of the ordinary modes, by which tyrants accomplish their purposes without resistance, is, by disarming the people, and making it an offence to keep arms, and by substituting a regular army in the stead of a resort to the militia." A Familiar Exposition of the Constitution of the United States §450 (reprinted in 1986).

Antislavery advocates routinely invoked the right to bear arms for self-defense. Joel Tiffany, for example, citing Blackstone's description of the right, wrote that "the right to keep and bear arms, also implies the right to use them if necessary in self defence; without this right to use the guaranty would have hardly been worth the paper it consumed." A Treatise on the Unconstitutionality of American Slavery 117–118 (1849); see also L. Spooner, The Unconstitutionality of Slavery 116 (1845) (right enables "personal defence"). In his famous Senate speech about the 1856 "Bleeding Kansas" conflict, Charles Sumner proclaimed:

"The rifle has ever been the companion of the pioneer and, under God, his tutelary protector against the red man and the beast of the forest. Never was this efficient weapon more needed in just self-defence, than now in Kansas, and at least one article in our National Constitution must be blotted out, before the complete right to it can in any way be impeached. And yet such is the madness of the hour, that, in defiance of the solemn guarantee, embodied in the Amendments to the Constitution, that 'the right of the people to keep and bear arms shall not be infringed,' the people of Kansas have been arraigned for keeping and bearing them, and the Senator from South Carolina has had the face to say openly, on this floor, that they should be disarmed—of course, that the fanatics of Slavery, his allies and constituents, may meet no impediment." The Crime Against Kansas, May 19–20, 1856, in American Speeches: Political Oratory from the Revolution to the Civil War 553, 606–607 (2006).

We have found only one early 19th-century commentator who clearly conditioned the right to keep and bear arms upon service in the militia—and he recognized that the prevailing view was to the contrary. "The provision of the constitution, declaring the right of the people to keep and bear arms, &c. was probably intended to apply to the right of the people to bear arms for such [militia-related] purposes only, and not to prevent congress or the legislatures of the different states from enacting laws to prevent the citizens from always going armed. A different construction however has been given to it." B. Oliver, The Rights of an American Citizen 177 (1832).

2. Pre-Civil War Case Law

The 19th-century cases that interpreted the Second Amendment universally support an individual right unconnected to militia service. In Houston v. Moore, 5 Wheat. 1, 24 (1820), this Court held that States have concurrent power over the militia, at least where not pre-empted by Congress. Agreeing in dissent that States could "organize, discipline, and arm" the militia in the absence of conflicting federal regulation, Justice Story said that the Second Amendment "may not, perhaps, be thought to have any important bearing on this point. If it have, it confirms and illustrates, rather than impugns the reasoning already suggested." Id., at 51–53. Of course, if the Amendment simply "protect[ed] the right of the people of each of the several States to maintain a well-regulated militia," post, at 1 (Stevens, J., dissenting), it would have enormous and obvious bearing on the point. But the Court and Story derived the States' power over the militia from the nonexclusive nature of federal power, not from the Second Amendment, whose preamble merely "confirms and illustrates" the importance of the militia. Even clearer was Justice Baldwin. In the famous fugitive-slave case of Johnson v. Tompkins, 13 F. Cas. 840, 850, 852 (CC Pa. 1833), Baldwin, sitting as a circuit judge, cited both the Second Amendment and the Pennsylvania analogue for his conclusion that a citizen has "a right to carry arms in defence of his property or person, and to use them, if either were assailed with such force, numbers or violence as made it necessary for the protection or safety of either."

Many early 19th-century state cases indicated that the Second Amendment right to bear arms was an individual right unconnected to militia service, though subject to certain restrictions. A Virginia case in 1824 holding that the Constitution did not extend to free blacks explained that "numerous restrictions imposed on [blacks] in our Statute Book, many of which are inconsistent with the letter and spirit of the Constitution, both of this State and of the United States as respects the free whites, demonstrate, that, here, those instruments have not been considered to extend equally to both classes of our population. We will only instance the restriction upon the migration of free blacks into this State, and upon their right to bear arms." Aldridge v. Commonwealth, 2 Va. Cas. 447, 449 (Gen. Ct.). The claim was obviously not that blacks were prevented from carrying guns in the militia.21 See also Waters v. State, 1Gill 302, 309 (Md. 1843) (because free blacks were treated as a "dangerous population," "laws have been passed to prevent their migration into this State; to make it unlawful for them to bear arms; to guard even their religious assemblages with peculiar watchfulness"). An 1829 decision by the Supreme Court of Michigan said: "The constitution of the United States also grants to the citizen the right to keep and bear arms. But the grant of this privilege cannot be construed into the right in him who keeps a gun to destroy his neighbor. No rights are intended to be granted by the constitution for an unlawful or unjustifiable purpose." United States v. Sheldon, in 5 Transactions of the Supreme Court of the Territory of Michigan 337, 346 (W. Blume ed. 1940) (hereinafter Blume). It is not possible to read this as discussing anything other than an individual right unconnected to militia service. If it did have to do with militia service, the limitation upon it would not be any "unlawful or unjustifiable purpose," but any nonmilitary purpose whatsoever.

In Nunn v. State, 1Ga. 243, 251 (1846), the Georgia Supreme Court construed the Second Amendment as protecting the "natural right of self-defence" and therefore struck down a ban on carrying pistols openly. Its opinion perfectly captured the way in which the operative clause of the Second Amendment furthers the purpose announced in the prefatory clause, in continuity with the English right:

"The right of the whole people, old and young, men, women and boys, and not militia only, to keep and bear arms of every description, and not such merely as are used by the militia, shall not be infringed, curtailed, or broken in upon, in the smallest degree;

and all this for the important end to be attained: the rearing up and qualifying a well-regulated militia, so vitally necessary to the security of a free State. Our opinion is, that any law, State or Federal, is repugnant to the Constitution, and void, which contravenes this right, originally belonging to our forefathers, trampled under foot by Charles I. and his two wicked sons and successors, re-established by the revolution of 1688, conveyed to this land of liberty by the colonists, and finally incorporated conspicuously in our own Magna Charta!"

Likewise, in State v. Chandler, 5La. Ann. 489, 490 (1850), the Louisiana Supreme Court held that citizens had a right to carry arms openly: "This is the right guaranteed by the Constitution of the United States, and which is calculated to incite men to a manly and noble defence of themselves, if necessary, and of their country, without any tendency to secret advantages and unmanly assassinations."

Those who believe that the Second Amendment preserves only a militia-centered right place great reliance on the Tennessee Supreme Court's 1840 decision in Aymette v. State, 21 Tenn. 154. The case does not stand for that broad proposition; in fact, the case does not mention the word "militia" at all, except in its quoting of the Second Amendment . Aymette held that the state constitutional guarantee of the right to "bear" arms did not prohibit the banning of concealed weapons. The opinion first recognized that both the state right and the federal right were descendents of the 1689 English right, but (erroneously, and contrary to virtually all other authorities) read that right to refer only to "protect[ion of] the public liberty" and "keep[ing] in awe those in power," id., at 158. The court then adopted a sort of middle position, whereby citizens were permitted to carry arms openly, unconnected with any service in a formal militia, but were given the right to use them only for the military purpose of banding together to oppose tyranny. This odd reading of the right is, to be sure, not the one we adopt—but it is not petitioners' reading either. More importantly, seven years earlier the Tennessee Supreme Court had treated the state constitutional provision as conferring a right "of all the free citizens of the State to keep and bear arms for their defence," Simpson, 5 Yer., at 360; and 21 years later the court held that the "keep" portion of the state constitutional right included the right to personal self-defense: "[T]he right to keep arms involves, necessarily, the right to use such arms for all the ordinary purposes, and in all the ordinary modes usual in the country, and to which arms are adapted, limited by the duties of a good citizen in times of peace." Andrews, 50 Tenn., at 178; see also ibid. (equating state provision with Second Amendment).

3. Post-Civil War Legislation.

In the aftermath of the Civil War, there was an outpouring of discussion of the Second Amendment in Congress and in public discourse, as people debated whether and how to secure constitutional rights for newly free slaves. See generally S. Halbrook, Freedmen, the Fourteenth Amendment, and the Right to Bear Arms, 1866–1876 (1998) (hereinafter Halbrook); Brief for Institute for Justice as Amicus Curiae. Since those discussions took place 75 years after the ratification of the Second Amendment, they do not provide as much insight into its original meaning as earlier sources. Yet those born and educated in the early 19th century faced a widespread effort to limit arms ownership by a large number of citizens; their understanding of the origins and continuing significance of the Amendment is instructive.

Blacks were routinely disarmed by Southern States after the Civil War. Those who opposed these injustices frequently stated that they infringed blacks' constitutional right to keep and bear arms. Needless to say, the claim was not that blacks were being prohibited from carrying arms in an organized state militia. A Report of the Commission of the Freedmen's Bureau in 1866 stated plainly: "[T]he civil law [of Kentucky] prohibits the colored man from bearing arms. . . . Their arms are taken from them by the civil authorities... . Thus, the right of the people to keep and bear arms as provided in the Constitution is infringed." H. R. Exec. Doc. No. 70, 39th Cong., 1st Sess., 233, 236. A joint congressional Report decried:

"in some parts of [South Carolina], armed parties are, without proper authority, engaged in seizing all fire-arms found in the hands of the freemen. Such conduct is in clear and direct violation of their personal rights as guaranteed by the Constitution of the United States, which declares that 'the right of the people to keep and bear arms shall not be infringed.' The freedmen of South Carolina have shown by their peaceful and orderly conduct that they can safely be trusted with fire-arms, and they need them to kill game for subsistence, and to protect their crops from destruction by birds and animals." Joint Comm. on Reconstruction, H. R. Rep. No. 30, 39th Cong., 1st Sess., pt. 2, p. 229 (1866) (Proposed Circular of Brigadier General R. Saxton).

The view expressed in these statements was widely reported and was apparently widely held. For example, an editorial in The Loyal Georgian (Augusta) on February 3, 1866, assured blacks that "[a]ll men, without distinction of color, have the right to keep and bear arms to defend their homes, families or themselves." Halbrook 19.

Congress enacted the Freedmen's Bureau Act on July 16, 1866. Section 14 stated:

"[T]he right ... to have full and equal benefit of all laws and proceedings concerning personal liberty, personal security, and the acquisition, enjoyment, and disposition of estate, real and personal, including the constitutional right to bear arms, shall be secured to and enjoyed by all the citizens ... without respect to race or color, or previous condition of slavery... . " 14 Stat. 176–177.

The understanding that the Second Amendment gave freed blacks the right to keep and bear arms was reflected in congressional discussion of the bill, with even an opponent of it saying that the founding generation "were for every man bearing his arms about him and keeping them in his house, his castle, for his own defense." Cong. Globe, 39th Cong., 1st Sess., 362, 371 (1866) (Sen. Davis).

Similar discussion attended the passage of the Civil Rights Act of 1871 and the Fourteenth Amendment . For example, Representative Butler said of the Act: "Section eight is intended to enforce the well-known constitutional provision guaranteeing the right of the citizen to 'keep and bear arms,' and provides that whoever shall take away, by force or violence, or by threats and intimidation, the arms and weapons which any person may have for his defense, shall be deemed guilty of larceny of the same." H. R. Rep. No. 37, 41st Cong., 3d Sess., pp. 7–8 (1871). With respect to the proposed Amendment, Senator Pomeroy described as one of the three "indispensable" "safeguards of liberty ... under the Constitution" a man's "right to bear arms for the defense of himself and family and his homestead." Cong. Globe, 39th Cong., 1st Sess., 1182 (1866). Representative Nye thought the Fourteenth Amendment unnecessary because "[a]s citizens of the United States [blacks] have equal right to protection, and to keep and bear arms for self-defense." Id., at 1073 (1866).

It was plainly the understanding in the post-Civil War Congress that the Second Amendment protected an individual right to use arms for self-defense.

4. Post-Civil War Commentators.

Every late-19th-century legal scholar that we have read interpreted the Second Amendment to secure an individual right unconnected with militia service. The most famous was the judge and professor Thomas Cooley, who wrote a massively popular 1868 Treatise on Constitutional Limitations. Concerning the Second Amendment it said:

"Among the other defences to personal liberty should be mentioned the right of the people to keep and bear arms.... The alternative to a standing army is 'a well-regulated militia,' but this cannot exist unless the people are trained to bearing arms. How far it is in the power of the legislature to regulate this right, we shall not undertake to say, as happily there has been very little occasion to discuss that subject by the courts." Id., at 350.

That Cooley understood the right not as connected to militia service, but as securing the militia by ensuring a populace familiar with arms, is made even clearer in his 1880 work, General Principles of Constitutional Law. The Second Amendment, he said, "was adopted with some modification and enlargement from the English Bill of Rights of 1688, where it stood as a protest against arbitrary action of the overturned dynasty in disarming the people." Id., at 270. In a section entitled "The Right in General," he continued:

"It might be supposed from the phraseology of this provision that the right to keep and bear arms was only guaranteed to the militia; but this would be an interpretation not warranted by the intent. The militia, as has been elsewhere explained, consists of those persons who, under the law, are liable to the performance of military duty, and are officered and enrolled for service when called upon. But the law may make provision for the enrolment of all who are fit to perform military duty, or of a small number only, or it may wholly omit to make any provision at all; and if the right were limited to those enrolled, the purpose of this guaranty might be defeated altogether by the action or neglect to act of the government it was meant to hold in check. The meaning of the provision undoubtedly is, that the people, from whom the militia must be taken, shall have the right to keep and bear arms; and they need no permission or regulation of law for the purpose. But this enables government to have a well-regulated militia; for to bear arms implies something more than the mere keeping; it implies the learning to handle and use them in a way that makes those who keep them ready for their efficient use; in other words, it implies the right to meet for voluntary discipline in arms, observing in doing so the laws of public order." Id., at 271.

All other post-Civil War 19th-century sources we have found concurred with Cooley. One example from each decade will convey the general flavor:

"[The purpose of the Second Amendment is] to secure a well-armed militia.... But a militia would be useless unless the citizens were enabled to exercise themselves in the use of warlike weapons. To preserve this privilege, and to secure to the people the ability to oppose themselves in military force against the usurpations of government, as well as against enemies from without, that government is forbidden by any law or proceeding to invade or destroy the right to keep and bear arms.... The clause is analogous to the one securing the freedom of speech and of the press. Freedom, not license, is secured; the fair use, not the libellous abuse, is protected." J. Pomeroy, An Introduction to the Constitutional Law of the United States 152–153 (1868) (hereinafter Pomeroy).

"As the Constitution of the United States, and the constitutions of several of the states, in terms more or less comprehensive, declare the right of the people to keep and bear arms, it has been a subject of grave discussion, in some of the state courts, whether a statute prohibiting persons, when not on a journey, or as travellers, from wearing or carrying concealed weapons, be constitutional. There has been a great difference of opinion on the question." 2 J. Kent, Commentaries on American Law *340, n. 2 (O. Holmes ed., 12th ed. 1873) (hereinafter Kent).

"Some general knowledge of firearms is important to the public welfare; because it would be impossible, in case of war, to organize promptly an efficient force of volunteers unless the people had some familiarity with weapons of war. The Constitution secures the right of the people to keep and bear arms. No doubt, a citizen who keeps a gun or pistol under judicious precautions, practices in safe places the use of it, and in due time teaches his sons to do the same, exercises his individual right. No doubt, a person whose residence or duties involve peculiar peril may keep a pistol for prudent self-defence." B. Abbott, Judge and Jury: A Popular Explanation of the Leading Topics in the Law of the Land 333 (1880) (hereinafter Abbott).

"The right to bear arms has always been the distinctive privilege of freemen. Aside from any necessity of self-protection to the person, it represents among all nations power coupled with the exercise of a certain jurisdiction. ... [I]t was not necessary that the right to bear arms should be granted in the Constitution, for it had always existed." J. Ordronaux, Constitutional Legislation in the United States 241–242 (1891).

E

We now ask whether any of our precedents forecloses the conclusions we have reached about the meaning of the Second Amendment .

United States v. Cruikshank, 92 U. S. 542, in the course of vacating the convictions of members of a white mob for depriving blacks of their right to keep and bear arms, held that the Second Amendment does not by its own force apply to anyone other than the Federal Government. The opinion explained that the right "is not a right granted by the Constitution [or] in any manner dependent upon that instrument for its existence. The second amendment ... means no more than that it shall not be infringed by Congress." 92 U. S., at 553. States, we said, were free to restrict or protect the right under their police powers. The limited discussion of the Second Amendment in Cruikshank supports, if anything, the individual-rights interpretation. There was no claim in Cruikshank that the victims had been deprived of their right to carry arms in a militia; indeed, the Governor had disbanded the local militia unit the year before the mob's attack, see C. Lane, The Day Freedom Died 62 (2008). We described the right protected by the Second Amendment as " 'bearing arms for a lawful purpose' "22 and said that "the people [must] look for their protection against any violation by their fellow-citizens of the rights it recognizes" to the States' police power. 92 U. S., at 553. That discussion makes little sense if it is only a right to bear arms in a state militia.23

Presser v. Illinois, 116 U. S. 252 (1886), held that the right to keep and bear arms was not violated by a law that forbade "bodies of men to associate together as military organizations, or to drill or parade with arms in cities and towns unless authorized by law." Id., at 264–265. This does not refute the individual-rights interpretation of the Amendment; no one supporting that interpretation has contended that States may not ban such groups. Justice Stevens presses Presser into service to support his view that the right to bear arms is limited to service in the militia by joining Presser's brief discussion of the Second Amendment with a later portion of the opinion making the seemingly relevant (to the Second Amendment) point that the plaintiff was not a member of the state militia. Unfortunately for Justice Stevens' argument, that later portion deals with the Fourteenth Amendment; it was the Fourteenth Amendment to which the plaintiff's nonmembership in the militia was relevant. Thus, Justice Stevens' statement that Presser "suggested that... nothing in the Constitution protected the use of arms outside the context of a militia," post, at 40, is simply wrong. Presser said nothing about the Second Amendment 's meaning or scope, beyond the fact that it does not prevent the prohibition of private paramilitary organizations.

Justice Stevens places overwhelming reliance upon this Court's decision in United States v. Miller, 307 U. S. 174 (1939) . "[H]undreds of judges," we are told, "have relied on the view of the amendment we endorsed there," post, at 2, and "[e]ven if the textual and historical arguments on both side of the issue were evenly balanced, respect for the well-settled views of all of our predecessors on this Court, and for the rule of law itself ... would prevent most jurists from endorsing such a dramatic upheaval in the law," post, at 4. And what is, according to Justice Stevens, the holding of Miller that demands such obeisance? That the Second Amendment "protects the right to keep and bear arms for certain military purposes, but that it does not curtail the legislature's power to regulate the nonmilitary use and ownership of weapons." Post, at 2.

Nothing so clearly demonstrates the weakness of Justice Stevens' case. Miller did not hold that and cannot possibly be read to have held that. The judgment in the case upheld against a Second Amendment challenge two men's federal convictions for transporting an unregistered short-barreled shotgun in interstate commerce, in violation of the National Firearms Act, 48 Stat. 1236. It is entirely clear that the Court's basis for saying that the Second Amendment did not apply was not that the defendants were "bear[ing] arms" not "for ... military purposes" but for "nonmilitary use," post, at 2. Rather, it was that the type of weapon at issue was not eligible for Second Amendment protection: "In the absence of any evidence tending to show that the possession or use of a [short-barreled shotgun] at this time has some reasonable relationship to the preservation or efficiency of a well regulated militia, we cannot say that the Second Amendment guarantees the right to keep and bear such an instrument." 307 U. S., at 178 (emphasis added). "Certainly," the Court continued, "it is not within judicial notice that this weapon is any part of the ordinary military equipment or that its use could contribute to the common defense." Ibid. Beyond that, the opinion provided no explanation of the content of the right.

This holding is not only consistent with, but positively suggests, that the Second Amendment confers an individual right to keep and bear arms (though only arms that "have some reasonable relationship to the preservation or efficiency of a well regulated militia"). Had the Court believed that the Second Amendment protects only those serving in the militia, it would have been odd to examine the character of the weapon rather than simply note that the two crooks were not militiamen. Justice Stevens can say again and again that Miller did "not turn on the difference between muskets and sawed-off shotguns, it turned, rather, on the basic difference between the military and nonmilitary use and possession of guns," post, at 42–43, but the words of the opinion prove otherwise. The most Justice Stevens can plausibly claim for Miller is that it declined to decide the nature of the Second Amendment right, despite the Solicitor General's argument (made in the alternative) that the right was collective, see Brief for United States, O. T. 1938, No. 696, pp. 4–5. Miller stands only for the proposition that the Second Amendment right, whatever its nature, extends only to certain types of weapons.

It is particularly wrongheaded to read Miller for more than what it said, because the case did not even purport to be a thorough examination of the Second Amendment . Justice Stevens claims, post, at 42, that the opinionreached its conclusion "[a]fter reviewing many of the same sources that are discussed at greater length by the Court today." Not many, which was not entirely the Court's fault. The respondent made no appearance in the case, neither filing a brief nor appearing at oral argument; the Court heard from no one but the Government (reason enough, one would think, not to make that case the beginning and the end of this Court's consideration of the Second Amendment). See Frye, The Peculiar Story of United States v. Miller, 3 N. Y. U. J. L. &

Liberty 48, 65–68 (2008). The Government's brief spent two pages discussing English legal sources, concluding "that at least the carrying of weapons without lawful occasion or excuse was always a crime" and that (because of the class-based restrictions and the prohibition on terrorizing people with dangerous or unusual weapons) "the early English law did not guarantee an unrestricted right to bear arms." Brief for United States, O. T. 1938, No. 696, at 9–11. It then went on to rely primarily on the discussion of the English right to bear arms in Aymette v. State, 21 Tenn. 154, for the proposition that the only uses of arms protected by the Second Amendment are those that relate to the militia, not self-defense. See Brief for United States, O. T. 1938, No. 696, at 12–18. The final section of the brief recognized that "some courts have said that the right to bear arms includes the right of the individual to have them for the protection of his person and property," and launched an alternative argument that "weapons which are commonly used by criminals," such as sawed-off shotguns, are not protected. See id., at 18–21. The Government's Miller brief thus provided scant discussion of the history of the Second Amendment —and the Court was presented with no counterdiscussion. As for the text of the Court's opinion itself, that discusses none of the history of the Second Amendment . It assumes from the prologue that the Amendment was designed to preserve the militia, 307 U. S., at 178 (which we do not dispute), and then reviews some historical materials dealing with the nature of the militia, and in particular with the nature of the arms their members were expected to possess, id., at 178–182. Not a word (not a word) about the history of the Second Amendment . This is the mighty rock upon which the dissent rests its case.24

We may as well consider at this point (for we will have to consider eventually) what types of weapons Miller permits. Read in isolation, Miller's phrase "part of ordinary military equipment" could mean that only those weapons useful in warfare are protected. That would be a startling reading of the opinion, since it would mean that the National Firearms Act's restrictions on machineguns (not challenged in Miller) might be unconstitutional, machineguns being useful in warfare in 1939. We think that Miller's "ordinary military equipment" language must be read in tandem with what comes after: "[O]rdinarily when called for [militia] service [able-bodied] men were expected to appear bearing arms supplied by themselves and of the kind in common use at the time." 307 U. S., at 179. The traditional militia was formed from a pool of men bringing arms "in common use at the time" for lawful purposes like self-defense. "In the colonial and revolutionary war era, [small-arms] weapons used by militiamen and weapons used in defense of person and home were one and the same." State v. Kessler, 289 Ore. 359, 368, 614 P. 2d 94, 98 (1980) (citing G. Neumann, Swords and Blades of the American Revolution 6–15, 252–254 (1973)). Indeed, that is precisely the way in which the Second Amendment 's operative clause furthers the purpose announced in its preface. We therefore read Miller to say only that the Second Amendment does not protect those weapons not typically possessed by law-abiding citizens for lawful purposes, such as short-barreled shotguns. That accords with the historical understanding of the scope of the right, see Part III, infra.25

We conclude that nothing in our precedents forecloses our adoption of the original understanding of the Second Amendment . It should be unsurprising that such a significant matter has been for so long judicially unresolved. For most of our history, the Bill of Rights was not thought applicable to the States, and the Federal Government did not significantly regulate the possession of firearms by law-abiding citizens. Other provisions of the Bill of Rights have similarly remained unilluminated for lengthy periods. This Court first held a law to violate the First Amendment 's guarantee of freedom of speech in 1931, almost 150 years after the Amendment was ratified, see Near v. Minnesota ex rel. Olson, 283 U. S. 697 (1931), and it was not until after World War II that we held a law invalid under the Establishment Clause, see Illinois ex rel. McCollum v. Board of Ed. of School Dist. No. 71, Champaign Cty., 333 U. S. 203 (1948) . Even a question as basic as the scope of proscribable libel was not addressed by this Court until 1964, nearly two centuries after the founding. See New York Times Co. v. Sullivan, 376 U. S. 254 (1964) . It is demonstrably not true that, as Justice Stevens claims, post, at 41–42,"for most of our history, the invalidity of Second-Amendment-based objections to firearms regulations has been well settled and uncontroversial." For most of our history the question did not present itself.

III

Like most rights, the right secured by the Second Amendment is not unlimited. From Blackstone through the 19th-century cases, commentators and courts routinely explained that the right was not a right to keep and carry any weapon whatsoever in any manner whatsoever and for whatever purpose. See, e.g., Sheldon, in 5 Blume 346; Rawle 123; Pomeroy 152–153; Abbott333. For example, the majority of the 19th-century courts to consider the question held that prohibitions on carrying concealed weapons were lawful under the Second Amendment or state analogues. See, e.g., State v. Chandler, 5 La. Ann., at 489–490; Nunn v. State, 1 Ga., at 251; see generally 2 Kent *340, n. 2; The American Students' Blackstone 84, n. 11 (G. Chase ed. 1884). Although we do not undertake an exhaustive historical analysis today of the full scope of the Second Amendment, nothing in our opinion should be taken to cast doubt on longstanding prohibitions on the possession of firearms by felons and the mentally ill, or laws forbidding the carrying of firearms in sensitive places such as schools and government buildings, or laws imposing conditions and qualifications on the commercial sale of arms.26

We also recognize another important limitation on the right to keep and carry arms. Miller said, as we have explained, that the sorts of weapons protected were those "in common use at the time." 307 U. S., at 179. We think that limitation is fairly supported by the historical tradition of prohibiting the carrying of "dangerous and unusual weapons." See 4 Blackstone 148–149 (1769); 3 B. Wilson, Works of the Honourable James Wilson 79 (1804); J. Dunlap, The New-York Justice 8 (1815); C. Humphreys, A Compendium of the Common Law in Force in Kentucky 482 (1822); 1 W. Russell, A Treatise on Crimes and Indictable Misdemeanors 271–272 (1831); H. Stephen,

Summary of the Criminal Law 48 (1840); E. Lewis, An Abridgment of the Criminal Law of the United States 64 (1847); F. Wharton, A Treatise on the Criminal Law of the United States 726 (1852). See also State v. Langford, 10 N. C. 381, 383–384 (1824); O'Neill v. State, 16Ala. 65, 67 (1849); English v. State, 35Tex. 473, 476 (1871); State v. Lanier, 71 N. C. 288, 289 (1874).

It may be objected that if weapons that are most useful in military service—M-16 rifles and the like—may be banned, then the Second Amendment right is completely detached from the prefatory clause. But as we have said, the conception of the militia at the time of the Second Amendment 's ratification was the body of all citizens capable of military service, who would bring the sorts of lawful weapons that they possessed at home to militia duty. It may well be true today that a militia, to be as effective as militias in the 18th century, would require sophisticated arms that are highly unusual in society at large. Indeed, it may be true that no amount of small arms could be useful against modern-day bombers and tanks. But the fact that modern developments have limited the degree of fit between the prefatory clause and the protected right cannot change our interpretation of the right.

IV

We turn finally to the law at issue here. As we have said, the law totally bans handgun possession in the home. It also requires that any lawful firearm in the home be disassembled or bound by a trigger lock at all times, rendering it inoperable.

As the quotations earlier in this opinion demonstrate, the inherent right of self-defense has been central to the Second Amendment right. The handgun ban amounts to a prohibition of an entire class of "arms" that is overwhelmingly chosen by American society for that lawful purpose. The prohibition extends, moreover, to the home, where the need for defense of self, family, and property is most acute. Under any of the standards of scrutiny that we have applied to enumerated constitutional rights, 27 banning from the home "the most preferred firearm in the nation to 'keep' and use for protection of one's home and family," 478 F. 3d, at 400, would fail constitutional muster.

Few laws in the history of our Nation have come close to the severe restriction of the District's handgun ban. And some of those few have been struck down. In Nunn v. State, the Georgia Supreme Court struck down a prohibition on carrying pistols openly (even though it upheld a prohibition on carrying concealed weapons). See 1 Ga., at 251. In Andrews v. State, the Tennessee Supreme Court likewise held that a statute that forbade openly carrying a pistol "publicly or privately, without regard to time or place, or circumstances," 50 Tenn., at 187, violated the state constitutional provision (which the court equated with the Second Amendment). That was so even though the statute did not restrict the carrying of long guns. Ibid. See also State v. Reid, 1 Ala. 612, 616–617 (1840) ("A statute which, under the pretence of regulating, amounts to a destruction of the right, or which requires arms to be so borne as to render them wholly useless for the purpose of defence, would be clearly unconstitutional").

It is no answer to say, as petitioners do, that it is permissible to ban the possession of handguns so long as the possession of other firearms (i.e., long guns) is allowed. It is enough to note, as we have observed, that the American people have considered the handgun to be the quintessential self-defense weapon. There are many reasons that a citizen may prefer a handgun for home defense: It is easier to store in a location that is readily accessible in an emergency; it cannot easily be redirected or wrestled away by an attacker; it is easier to use for those without the upper-body strength to lift and aim a long gun; it can be pointed at a burglar with one hand while the other hand dials the police. Whatever the reason, handguns are the most popular weapon chosen by Americans for self-defense in the home, and a complete prohibition of their use is invalid.

We must also address the District's requirement (as applied to respondent's handgun) that firearms in the home be rendered and kept inoperable at all times. This makes it impossible for citizens to use them for the core lawful purpose of self-defense and is hence unconstitutional. The District argues that we should interpret this element of the statute to contain an exception for self-defense. See Brief for Petitioners 56–57. But we think that is precluded by the unequivocal text, and by the presence of certain other enumerated exceptions: "Except for law enforcement personnel ..., each registrant shall keep any firearm in his possession unloaded and disassembled or bound by a trigger lock or similar device unless such firearm is kept at his place of business, or while being used for lawful recreational purposes within the District of Columbia." D. C. Code §7–2507.02. The nonexistence of a self-defense exception is also suggested by the D. C. Court of Appeals' statement that the statute forbids residents to use firearms to stop intruders, see McIntosh v. Washington, 395 A. 2d 744, 755–756 (1978).28

Apart from his challenge to the handgun ban and the trigger-lock requirement respondent asked the District Court to enjoin petitioners from enforcing the separate licensing requirement "in such a manner as to forbid the carrying of a firearm within one's home or possessed land without a license." App. 59a. The Court of Appeals did not invalidate the licensing requirement, but held only that the District "may not prevent [a handgun] from being moved throughout one's house." 478 F. 3d, at 400. It then ordered the District Court to enter summary judgment "consistent with [respondent's] prayer for relief." Id., at 401. Before this Court petitioners have stated that "if the handgun ban is struck down and respondent registers a handgun, he could obtain a license, assuming he is not otherwise disqualified," by which they apparently mean if he is not a felon and is not insane. Brief for Petitioners 58. Respondent conceded at oral argument that he does not "have a problem with ... licensing" and that the District's law is permissible so long as it is "not enforced in an arbitrary and capricious manner." Tr. of Oral Arg. 74–75. We therefore assume that petitioners' issuance of a license will satisfy respondent's prayer for relief and do not address the licensing requirement.

Justice Breyer has devoted most of his separate dissent to the handgun ban. He says that, even assuming the Second Amendment is a personal guarantee of the right to bear arms, the District's prohibition is valid. He first tries to establish this by founding-era historical precedent, pointing to various restrictive laws in the colonial period. These demonstrate, in his view, that the District's law "imposes a burden upon gun owners that seems proportionately no greater than restrictions in existence at the time the Second Amendment was adopted." Post, at 2. Of the laws he cites, only one offers even marginal support for his assertion. A 1783 Massachusetts law forbade the residents of Boston to "take into" or "receive into" "any Dwelling House, Stable, Barn, Out-house, Ware-house, Store, Shop or other Building" loaded firearms, and permitted the seizure of any loaded firearms that "shall be found" there. Act of Mar. 1, 1783, ch. 13, 1783 Mass. Acts p. 218. That statute's text and its prologue, which makes clear that the purpose of the prohibition was to eliminate the danger to firefighters posed by the "depositing of loaded Arms" in buildings, give reason to doubt that colonial Boston authorities would have enforced that general prohibition against someone who temporarily loaded a firearm to confront an intruder (despite the law's application in that case). In any case, we would not stake our interpretation of the Second Amendment upon a single law, in effect in a single city, that contradicts the overwhelming weight of other evidence regarding the right to keep and bear arms for defense of the home. The other laws Justice Breyer cites are gunpowder-storage laws that he concedes did not clearly prohibit loaded weapons, but required only that excess gunpowder be kept in a special container or on the top floor of the home. Post, at 6–7. Nothing about those fire-safety laws undermines our analysis; they do not remotely burden the right of self-defense as much as an absolute ban on handguns. Nor, correspondingly, does our analysis suggest the invalidity of laws regulating the storage of firearms to prevent accidents.

Justice Breyer points to other founding-era laws that he says "restricted the firing of guns within the city limits to at least some degree" in Boston, Philadelphia and New York. Post, at 4 (citing Churchill, Gun Regulation, the Police Power, and the Right to Keep Arms in Early America, 25Law & Hist. Rev. 139, 162 (2007)). Those laws provide no support for the severe restriction in the present case. The New York law levied a fine of 20 shillings on anyone who fired a gun in certain places (including houses) on New Year's Eve and the first two days of January, and was aimed at preventing the "great Damages ... frequently done on [those days] by persons going House to House, with Guns and other Firearms and being often intoxicated with Liquor." 5 Colonial Laws of New York 244–246 (1894). It is inconceivable that this law would have been enforced against a person exercising his right to self-defense on New Year's Day against such drunken hooligans. The Pennsylvania law to which Justice Breyer refers levied a fine of 5 shillings on one who fired a gun or set off fireworks in Philadelphia without first obtaining a license from the governor. See Act of Aug. 26, 1721, §4, in 3 Stat.at Large 253–254. Given Justice Wilson's explanation that the right to self-defense with arms was protected by the Pennsylvania Constitution, it is unlikely that this law (which in any event amounted to at most a licensing regime) would have been enforced against a person who used firearms for self-defense. Justice Breyer cites a Rhode Island law that simply levied a 5-shilling fine on those who fired guns in streets and taverns, a law obviously inapplicable to this case. See An Act for preventing Mischief being done in the town of Newport, or in any other town in this Government, 1731, Rhode Island Session Laws. Finally, Justice Breyer points to a Massachusetts law similar to the Pennsylvania law, prohibiting "discharg[ing] any Gun or Pistol charged with Shot or Ball in the Town of Boston." Act of May 28, 1746, ch. X, Acts and Laws of Mass. Bay 208. It is again implausible that this would have been enforced against a citizen acting in self-defense, particularly given its preambulatory reference to "the indiscreet firing of Guns." Ibid. (preamble) (emphasis added).

A broader point about the laws that Justice Breyer cites: All of them punished the discharge (or loading) of guns with a small fine and forfeiture of the weapon (or in a few cases a very brief stay in the local jail), not with significant criminal penalties.29 They are akin to modern penalties for minor public-safety infractions like speeding or jaywalking. And although such public-safety laws may not contain exceptions for self-defense, it is inconceivable that the threat of a jaywalking ticket would deter someone from disregarding a "Do Not Walk" sign in order to flee an attacker, or that the Government would enforce those laws under such circumstances. Likewise, we do not think that a law imposing a 5-shilling fine and forfeiture of the gun would have prevented a person in the founding era from using a gun to protect himself or his family from violence, or that if he did so the law would be enforced against him. The District law, by contrast, far from imposing a minor fine, threatens citizens with a year in prison (five years for a second violation) for even obtaining a gun in the first place. See D. C. Code §7–2507.06.

Justice Breyer moves on to make a broad jurisprudential point: He criticizes us for declining to establish a level of scrutiny for evaluating Second Amendment restrictions. He proposes, explicitly at least, none of the traditionally expressed levels (strict scrutiny, intermediate scrutiny, rational basis), but rather a judge-empowering "interest-balancing inquiry" that "asks whether the statute burdens a protected interest in a way or to an extent that is out of proportion to the statute's salutary effects upon other important governmental interests." Post, at 10. After an exhaustive discussion of the arguments for and against gun control, Justice Breyer arrives at his interest-balanced answer: because handgun violence is a problem, because the law is limited to an urban area, and because there were somewhat similar restrictions in the founding period (a false proposition that we have already discussed), the interest-balancing inquiry results in the constitutionality of the handgun ban. QED.

We know of no other enumerated constitutional right whose core protection has been subjected to a freestanding "interest-balancing" approach. The very enumeration of the right takes out of the hands of government—even the Third Branch of Government—the power to decide on a case-by-case basis whether the right is really worth insisting upon. A constitutional guarantee subject to future judges' assessments of its usefulness is no constitutional guarantee at all. Constitutional rights are enshrined with the scope they were understood to have when the people adopted them, whether or not future legislatures or (yes) even future judges think that scope too broad. We would notapply an "interest-balancing" approach to the prohibition of a peaceful neo-Nazi march through Skokie. See National Socialist Party of America v. Skokie, 432 U. S. 43 (1977) (per curiam). The First Amendment contains the freedom-of-speech guarantee that the people ratified, which included exceptions for obscenity, libel, and disclosure of state secrets, but not for the expression of extremely unpopular and wrong-headed views. The Second Amendment is no different. Like the First, it is the very product of an interest-balancing by the people—which Justice Breyer would now conduct for them anew. And whatever else it leaves to future evaluation, it surely elevates above all other interests the right of law-abiding, responsible citizens to use arms in defense of hearth and home.

Justice Breyer chides us for leaving so many applications of the right to keep and bear arms in doubt, and for not providing extensive historical justification for those regulations of the right that we describe as permissible. See post, at 42–43. But since this case represents this Court's first in-depth examination of the Second Amendment, one should not expect it to clarify the entire field, any more than Reynolds v. United States, 98 U. S. 145 (1879), our first in-depth Free Exercise Clause case, left that area in a state of utter certainty. And there will be time enough to expound upon the historical justifications for the exceptions we have mentioned if and when those exceptions come before us.

In sum, we hold that the District's ban on handgun possession in the home violates the Second Amendment, as does its prohibition against rendering any lawful firearm in the home operable for the purpose of immediate self-defense. Assuming that Heller is not disqualified from the exercise of Second Amendment rights, the District must permit him to register his handgun and must issue him a license to carry it in the home.

* * *

We are aware of the problem of handgun violence in this country, and we take seriously the concerns raised by the many amici who believe that prohibition of handgun ownership is a solution. The Constitution leaves the District of Columbia a variety of tools for combating that problem, including some measures regulating handguns, see supra, at 54–55, and n. 26. But the enshrinement of constitutional rights necessarily takes certain policy choices off the table. These include the absolute prohibition of handguns held and used for self-defense in the home. Undoubtedly some think that the Second Amendment is outmoded in a society where our standing army is the pride of our Nation, where well-trained police forces provide personal security, and where gun violence is a serious problem. That is perhaps debatable, but what is not debatable is that it is not the role of this Court to pronounce the Second Amendment extinct.

We affirm the judgment of the Court of Appeals.

It is so ordered.

Notes to District of Columbia v. Heller, Majority Opinion (June 28, 2008)

1 There are minor exceptions to all of these prohibitions, none of which is relevant here.

2 That construction has not been challenged here.

3 As Sutherland explains, the key 18th-century English case on the effect of preambles, Copeman v. Gallant, 1 P. Wms. 314, 24Eng. Rep. 404 (1716), stated that "the preamble could not be used to restrict the effect of the words of the purview." J. Sutherland, Statutes and Statutory Construction, 47.04 (N. Singer ed. 5th ed. 1992). This rule was modified in England in an 1826 case to give more importance to the preamble, but in America "the settled principle of law is that the preamble cannot control the enacting part of the statute in cases where the enacting part is expressed in clear, unambiguous terms." Ibid. Justice Stevens says that we violate the general rule that every clause in a statute must have effect. Post, at 8. But where the text of a clause itself indicates that it does not have operative effect, such as "whereas" clauses in federal legislation or the Constitution's preamble, a court has no license to make it do what it was not designed to do. Or to put the point differently, operative provisions should be given effect as operative provisions, and prologues as prologues.

4 Justice Stevens criticizes us for discussing the prologue last. Post, at 8. But if a prologue can be used only to clarify an ambiguous operative provision, surely the first step must be to determine whether the operative provision is ambiguous. It might be argued, we suppose, that the prologue itself should be one of the factors that go into the determination of whether the operative provision is ambiguous—but that would cause the prologue to be used to produce ambiguity rather than just to resolve it. In any event, even if we considered the prologue along with the operative provision we would reach the same result we do today, since (as we explain) our interpretation of "the right of the people to keep and bear arms" furthers the purpose of an effective militia no less than (indeed, more than) the dissent's interpretation. See infra, at 26–27.

5 Justice Stevens is of course correct, post, at 10, that the right to assemble cannot be exercised alone, but it is still an individual right, and not one conditioned upon membership in some defined "assembly," as he contends the right to bear arms is conditioned upon membership in a defined militia. And Justice Stevens is dead wrong to think that the right to petition is "primarily collective in nature." Ibid. See McDonald v. Smith, 472 U. S. 479, 482–484 (1985) (describing historical origins of right to petition).

6 If we look to other founding-era documents, we find that some state constitutions used the term "the people" to refer to the people collectively, in contrast to "citizen," which was used to invoke individual rights. See Heyman, Natural Rights and the Second Amendment, in The Second Amendment in Law and History 179, 193–195 (C. Bogus ed. 2000) (hereinafter Bogus). But that usage was not remotely uniform. See, e.g., N. C. Declaration of Rights §XIV (1776), in 5 The Federal and State Constitutions, Colonial Charters, and Other Organic Laws 2787, 2788 (F. Thorpe ed. 1909) (hereinafter

Thorpe) (jury trial); Md. Declaration of Rights §XVIII (1776), in 3 id., at 1686, 1688 (vicinage requirement); Vt. Declaration of Rights ch. 1, §XI (1777), in 6 id., at 3737, 3741 (searches and seizures); Pa. Declaration of Rights §XII (1776), in 5 id., at 3081, 3083 (free speech). And, most importantly, it was clearly not the terminology used in the Federal Constitution, given the First, Fourth, and Ninth Amendment s.

    7 See, e.g., 3 A Compleat Collection of State-Tryals 185 (1719) ("Hath not every Subject power to keep Arms, as well as Servants in his House for defence of his Person?"); T. Wood, A New Institute of the Imperial or Civil Law 282 (1730) ("Those are guilty of publick Force, who keep Arms in their Houses, and make use of them otherwise than upon Journeys or Hunting, or for Sale ..."); A Collection of All the Acts of Assembly, Now in Force, in the Colony of Virginia 596 (1733) ("Free Negros, Mulattos, or Indians, and Owners of Slaves, seated at Frontier Plantations, may obtain Licence from a Justice of Peace, for keeping Arms, &c."); J. Ayliffe, A New Pandect of Roman Civil Law 195 (1734) ("Yet a Person might keep Arms in his House, or on his Estate, on the Account of Hunting, Navigation, Travelling, and on the Score of Selling them in the way of Trade or Commerce, or such Arms as accrued to him by way of Inheritance"); J. Trusler, A Concise View of the Common Law and Statute Law of England 270 (1781) ("if [papists] keep arms in their houses, such arms may be seized by a justice of the peace"); Some Considerations on the Game Laws 54 (1796) ("Who has been deprived by [the law] of keeping arms for his own defence? What law forbids the veriest pauper, if he can raise a sum sufficient for the purchase of it, from mounting his Gun on his Chimney Piece ... ?"); 3 B. Wilson, The Works of the Honourable James Wilson 84 (1804) (with reference to state constitutional right: "This is one of our many renewals of the Saxon regulations. 'They were bound,' says Mr. Selden, 'to keep arms for the preservation of the kingdom, and of their own person' "); W. Duer, Outlines of the Constitutional Jurisprudence of the United States 31–32 (1833) (with reference to colonists' English rights: "The right of every individual to keep arms for his defence, suitable to his condition and degree; which was the public allowance, under due restrictions of the natural right of resistance and self-preservation"); 3 R. Burn, Justice of the Peace and the Parish Officer 88 (1815) ("It is, however, laid down by Serjeant Hawkins, ... that if a lessee, after the end of the term, keep arms in his house to oppose the entry of the lessor, ..."); State v. Dempsey, 31 N. C. 384, 385 (1849) (citing 1840 state law making it a misdemeanor for a member of certain racial groups "to carry about his person or keep in his house any shot gun or other arms").

    8 See Pa. Declaration of Rights §XIII, in 5 Thorpe 3083 ("That the people have a right to bear arms for the defence of themselves and the state... "); Vt. Declaration of Rights §XV, in 6 id., at 3741 ("That the people have a right to bear arms for the defence of themselves and the State..."); Ky. Const., Art. XII, cl. 23 (1792), in 3 id., at 1264, 1275 ("That the right of the citizens to bear arms in defence of themselves and the State shall not be questioned"); Ohio Const., Art. VIII, §20 (1802), in 5 id., at 2901, 2911 ("That the people have a right to bear arms for the defence of themselves and the State ... "); Ind. Const., Art. I, §20 (1816), in 2 id., at 1057, 1059 ("That the people have a right to bear

arms for the defense of themselves and the State... "); Miss. Const., Art. I, §23 (1817), in 4 id., at 2032, 2034 ("Every citizen has a right to bear arms, in defence of himself and the State"); Conn. Const., Art. I, §17 (1818), in 1 id., at 536, 538 ("Every citizen has a right to bear arms in defence of himself and the state"); Ala. Const., Art. I, §23 (1819), in 1 id., at 96, 98 ("Every citizen has a right to bear arms in defence of himself and the State"); Mo. Const., Art. XIII, §3 (1820), in 4 id., at 2150, 2163 ("[T]hat their right to bear arms in defence of themselves and of the State cannot be questioned"). See generally Volokh, State Constitutional Rights to Keep and Bear Arms, 11 Tex. Rev. L. & Politics 191 (2006).

9 See Bliss v. Commonwealth, 2 Litt. 90, 91–92 (Ky. 1822); State v. Reid, 1 Ala. 612, 616–617 (1840); State v. Schoultz, 25Mo. 128, 155 (1857); see also Simpson v. State, 5Yer. 356, 360 (Tenn. 1833) (interpreting similar provision with "common defence" purpose); State v. Huntly, 25 N. C. 418, 422–423 (1843) (same); cf. Nunn v. State, 1 Ga. 243, 250–251 (1846) (construing Second Amendment); State v. Chandler, 5 La. Ann. 489, 489–490 (1850) (same).

10 See J. Brydall, Privilegia Magnatud apud Anglos 14 (1704) (Privilege XXXIII) ("In the 21st Year of King Edward the Third, a Proclamation Issued, that no Person should bear any Arms within London, and the Suburbs"); J. Bond, A Compleat Guide to Justices of the Peace 43 (1707) ("Sheriffs, and all other Officers in executing their Offices, and all other persons pursuing Hu[e] and Cry may lawfully bear arms"); 1 An Abridgment of the Public Statutes in Force and Use Relative to Scotland (1755) (entry for "Arms": "And if any person above described shall have in his custody, use, or bear arms, being thereof convicted before one justice of peace, or other judge competent, summarily, he shall for the first offense forfeit all such arms" (quoting 1 Geo. 1, c. 54, §1)); Statute Law of Scotland Abridged 132–133 (2d ed. 1769) ("Acts for disarming the highlands" but "exempting those who have particular licenses to bear arms"); E. de Vattel, The Law of Nations, or, Principles of the Law of Nature 144 (1792) ("Since custom has allowed persons of rank and gentlemen of the army to bear arms in time of peace, strict care should be taken that none but these should be allowed to wear swords"); E. Roche, Proceedings of a Court-Martial, Held at the Council-Chamber, in the City of Cork 3 (1798) (charge VI: "With having held traitorous conferences, and with having conspired, with the like intent, for the purpose of attacking and despoiling of the arms of several of the King's subjects, qualified by law to bear arms"); C. Humphreys, A Compendium of the Common Law in force in Kentucky 482 (1822) ("[I]n this country the constitution guaranties to all persons the right to bear arms; then it can only be a crime to exercise this right in such a manner, as to terrify people unnecessarily").

11 Justice Stevens contends, post, at 15, that since we assert that adding "against" to "bear arms" gives it a military meaning we must concede that adding a purposive qualifying phrase to "bear arms" can alter its meaning. But the difference is that we do not maintain that "against" alters the meaning of "bear arms" but merely that it clarifies which of various meanings (one of which is military) is intended. Justice Stevens, however, argues that "[t]he term 'bear arms' is a familiar idiom; when used unadorned by

any additional words, its meaning is 'to serve as a soldier, do military service, fight.' " Post, at 11. He therefore must establish that adding a contradictory purposive phrase can alter a word's meaning.

12 Justice Stevens finds support for his legislative history inference from the recorded views of one Antifederalist member of the House. Post, at 26 n. 25. "The claim that the best or most representative reading of the [language of the] amendments would conform to the understanding and concerns of [the Antifederalists] is ... highly problematic." Rakove, The Second Amendment : The Highest Stage of Originalism, Bogus 74, 81.

13 The same applies to the conscientious-objector amendments proposed by Virginia and North Carolina, which said: "That any person religiously scrupulous of bearing arms ought to be exempted upon payment of an equivalent to employ another to bear arms in his stead." See Veit 19; 4 J. Eliot, The Debates in the Several State Constitutions on the Adoption of the Federal Constitution 243, 244 (2d ed. 1836) (reprinted 1941). Certainly their second use of the phrase ("bear arms in his stead") refers, by reason of context, to compulsory bearing of arms for military duty. But their first use of the phrase ("any person religiously scrupulous of bearing arms") assuredly did not refer to people whose God allowed them to bear arms for defense of themselves but not for defense of their country.

14 Faced with this clear historical usage, Justice Stevens resorts to the bizarre argument that because the word "to" is not included before "bear" (whereas it is included before "petition" in the First Amendment), the unitary meaning of "to keep and bear" is established. Post, at 16, n. 13. We have never heard of the proposition that omitting repetition of the "to" causes two verbs with different meanings to become one. A promise "to support and to defend the Constitution of the United States" is not a whit different from a promise "to support and defend the Constitution of the United States."

15 Cf. 3 Geo., 34, §3, in 7 Eng. Stat. at Large 126 (1748) ("That the Prohibition contained ... in this Act, of having, keeping, bearing, or wearing any Arms or Warlike Weapons ... shall not extend ... to any Officers or their Assistants, employed in the Execution of Justice ...").

16 Contrary to Justice Stevens' wholly unsupported assertion, post, at 17, there was no pre-existing right in English law "to use weapons for certain military purposes" or to use arms in an organized militia.

17 Article I, §8, cl. 16 of the Constitution gives Congress the power "[t]o provide for organizing, arming, and disciplining, the Militia, and for governing such Part of them as may be employed in the Service of the United States, reserving to the States respectively, the Appointment of the Officers, and the Authority of training the Militia according to the discipline prescribed by Congress." It could not be clearer that Congress's "organizing" power, unlike its "governing" power, can be invoked even for that part of the militia not "employed in the Service of the United States." Justice Stevens provides no support whatever for his contrary view, see post, at 19 n. 20. Both the

Federalists and Anti-Federalists read the provision as it was written, to permit the creation of a "select" militia. See The Federalist No. 29, pp. 226, 227 (B. Wright ed. 1961); Centinel, Revived, No. XXIX, Philadelphia Independent Gazetteer, Sept. 9, 1789, in Young 711, 712.

18 Justice Stevens says that the drafters of the Virginia Declaration of Rights rejected this proposal and adopted "instead" a provision written by George Mason stressing the importance of the militia. See post, at 24, and n. 24. There is no evidence that the drafters regarded the Mason proposal as a substitute for the Jefferson proposal.

19 Justice Stevens quotes some of Tucker's unpublished notes, which he claims show that Tucker had ambiguous views about the Second Amendment. See post, at 31, and n. 32. But it is clear from the notes that Tucker located the power of States to arm their militias in the Tenth Amendment, and that he cited the Second Amendment for the proposition that such armament could not run afoul of any power of the federal government (since the amendment prohibits Congress from ordering disarmament). Nothing in the passage implies that the Second Amendment pertains only to the carrying of arms in the organized militia.

20 Rawle, writing before our decision in Barron ex rel. Tiernan v. Mayor of Baltimore, 7Pet. 243 (1833), believed that the Second Amendment could be applied against the States. Such a belief would of course be nonsensical on petitioners' view that it protected only a right to possess and carry arms when conscripted by the State itself into militia service.

21 Justice Stevens suggests that this is not obvious because free blacks in Virginia had been required to muster without arms. See post, at 28, n. 29 (citing Siegel, The Federal Government's Power to Enact Color-Conscious Laws, 92 Nw. U. L. Rev. 477, 497 (1998)). But that could not have been the type of law referred to in Aldridge, because that practice had stopped 30 years earlier when blacks were excluded entirely from the militia by the First Militia Act. See Siegel, supra, at 498, n. 120. Justice Stevens further suggests that laws barring blacks from militia service could have been said to violate the "right to bear arms." But under Justice Stevens' reading of the Second Amendment (we think), the protected right is the right to carry arms to the extent one is enrolled in the militia, not the right to be in the militia. Perhaps Justice Stevens really does adopt the full-blown idiomatic meaning of "bear arms," in which case every man and woman in this country has a right "to be a soldier" or even "to wage war." In any case, it is clear to us that Aldridge's allusion to the existing Virginia "restriction" upon the right of free blacks "to bear arms" could only have referred to "laws prohibiting blacks from keeping weapons," Siegel, supra, at 497–498.

22 Justice Stevens' accusation that this is "not accurate," post, at 39, is wrong. It is true it was the indictment that described the right as "bearing arms for a lawful purpose." But, in explicit reference to the right described in the indictment, the Court stated that "The second amendment declares that it [i.e., the right of bearing arms for a lawful purpose] shall not be infringed." 92 U. S., at 553.

23 With respect to Cruikshank's continuing validity on incorporation, a question not presented by this case, we note that Cruikshank also said that the First Amendment did not apply against the States and did not engage in the sort of Fourteenth Amendment inquiry required by our later cases. Our later decisions in Presser v. Illinois, 116 U. S. 252, 265 (1886) and Miller v. Texas, 153 U. S. 535, 538 (1894), reaffirmed that the Second Amendment applies only to the Federal Government.

24 As for the "hundreds of judges," post, at 2, who have relied on the view of the Second Amendment Justice Stevens claims we endorsed in Miller: If so, they overread Miller. And their erroneous reliance upon an uncontested and virtually unreasoned case cannot nullify the reliance of millions of Americans (as our historical analysis has shown) upon the true meaning of the right to keep and bear arms. In any event, it should not be thought that the cases decided by these judges would necessarily have come out differently under a proper interpretation of the right.

25 Miller was briefly mentioned in our decision in Lewis v. United States, 445 U. S. 55 (1980), an appeal from a conviction for being a felon in possession of a firearm. The challenge was based on the contention that the prior felony conviction had been unconstitutional. No Second Amendment claim was raised or briefed by any party. In the course of rejecting the asserted challenge, the Court commented gratuitously, in a footnote, that "[t]hese legislative restrictions on the use of firearms are neither based upon constitutionally suspect criteria, nor do they trench upon any constitutionally protected liberties. See United States v. Miller ... (the Second Amendment guarantees no right to keep and bear a firearm that does not have 'some reasonable relationship to the preservation or efficiency of a well regulated militia')." Id., at 65–66, n. 8. The footnote then cites several Court of Appeals cases to the same effect. It is inconceivable that we would rest our interpretation of the basic meaning of any guarantee of the Bill of Rights upon such a footnoted dictum in a case where the point was not at issue and was not argued.

26 We identify these presumptively lawful regulatory measures only as examples; our list does not purport to be exhaustive.

27 Justice Breyer correctly notes that this law, like almost all laws, would pass rational-basis scrutiny. Post, at 8. But rational-basis scrutiny is a mode of analysis we have used when evaluating laws under constitutional commands that are themselves prohibitions on irrational laws. See, e.g., Engquist v. Oregon Dept. of Agriculture, 553 U. S. ___, ___ (2008) (slip op., at 9–10). In those cases, "rational basis" is not just the standard of scrutiny, but the very substance of the constitutional guarantee. Obviously, the same test could not be used to evaluate the extent to which a legislature may regulate a specific, enumerated right, be it the freedom of speech, the guarantee against double jeopardy, the right to counsel, or the right to keep and bear arms. See United States v. Carolene Products Co., 304 U. S. 144, n. 4 (1938) ("There may be narrower scope for operation of the presumption of constitutionality [i.e., narrower than that provided by rational-basis review] when legislation appears on its face to be within a specific

prohibition of the Constitution, such as those of the first ten amendments..."). If all that was required to overcome the right to keep and bear arms was a rational basis, the Second Amendment would be redundant with the separate constitutional prohibitions on irrational laws, and would have no effect.

28 McIntosh upheld the law against a claim that it violated the Equal Protection Clause by arbitrarily distinguishing between residences and businesses. See 395 A. 2d, at 755. One of the rational bases listed for that distinction was the legislative finding "that for each intruder stopped by a firearm there are four gun-related accidents within the home." Ibid. That tradeoff would not bear mention if the statute did not prevent stopping intruders by firearms.

29 The Supreme Court of Pennsylvania described the amount of five shillings in a contract matter in 1792 as "nominal consideration." Morris's Lessee v. Smith, 4Dall. 119, 120 (Pa. 1792). Many of the laws cited punished violation with fine in a similar amount; the 1783 Massachusetts gunpowder-storage law carried a somewhat larger fine of 10 (200 shillings) and forfeiture of the weapon.

Video Games are protected: Brown v. Entertainment Merchants Association (June 27, 2011)

Justice Scalia delivered the opinion of the Court.

We consider whether a California law imposing restrictions on violent video games comports with the First Amendment.

I

California Assembly Bill 1179 (2005), Cal. Civ. Code Ann. §§1746–1746.5 (West 2009) (Act), prohibits the sale or rental of "violent video games" to minors, and requires their packaging to be labeled "18." The Act covers games "in which the range of options available to a player includes killing, maiming, dismembering, or sexually assaulting an image of a human being, if those acts are depicted" in a manner that "[a] reasonable person, considering the game as a whole, would find appeals to a deviant or morbid interest of minors," that is "patently offensive to prevailing standards in the community as to what is suitable for minors," and that "causes the game, as a whole, to lack serious literary, artistic, political, or scientific value for minors." §1746(d)(1)(A). Violation of the Act is punishable by a civil fine of up to $1,000. §1746.3.

Respondents, representing the video-game and software industries, brought a preenforcement challenge to the Act in the United States District Court for the Northern District of California. That court concluded that the Act violated the First Amendment and permanently enjoined its enforcement. Video Software Dealers Assn. v. Schwarzenegger, No. C–05–04188 RMW (2007), App. to Pet. for Cert. 39a. The Court of Appeals affirmed, Video Software Dealers Assn. v. Schwarzenegger, 556 F. 3d 950 (CA9 2009), and we granted certiorari, 559 U. S. ____ (2010).

II

California correctly acknowledges that video games qualify for First Amendment protection. The Free Speech Clause exists principally to protect discourse on public matters, but we have long recognized that it is difficult to distinguish politics from entertainment, and dangerous to try. "Everyone is familiar with instances of propaganda through fiction. What is one man's amusement, teaches another's doctrine." Winters v. New York, 333 U. S. 507, 510 (1948) . Like the protected books, plays, and movies that preceded them, video games communicate ideas—and even social messages—through many familiar literary devices (such as characters, dialogue, plot, and music) and through features distinctive to the medium (such as the player's interaction with the virtual world). That suffices to confer First Amendment protection. Under our Constitution, "esthetic and moral judgments about art and literature ... are for the individual to make, not for the Government to decree, even with the mandate or approval of a majority." United States v. Playboy Entertainment Group, Inc., 529 U. S. 803, 818 (2000) . And whatever the challenges of applying the Constitution to ever-advancing technology, "the basic principles of freedom of speech and the press, like the First Amendment's command, do not vary" when a new and different medium for communication appears. Joseph Burstyn, Inc. v. Wilson, 343 U. S. 495, 503 (1952) .

The most basic of those principles is this: "[A]s a general matter, ... government has no power to restrict expression because of its message, its ideas, its subject matter, or its content." Ashcroft v. American Civil Liberties Union, 535 U. S. 564, 573 (2002) (internal quotation marks omitted). There are of course exceptions. " 'From 1791 to the present,' ... the First Amendment has 'permitted restrictions upon the content of speech in a few limited areas,' and has never 'include[d] a freedom to disregard these traditional limitations.' " United States v. Stevens, 559 U. S. ___, ___ (2010) (slip op., at 5) (quoting R. A. V. v. St. Paul, 505 U. S. 377, 382–383 (1992)). These limited areas—such as obscenity, Roth v. United States, 354 U. S. 476, 483 (1957), incitement, Brandenburg v. Ohio, 395 U. S. 444, 447–449 (1969) (per curiam), and fighting words, Chaplinsky v. New Hampshire, 315 U. S. 568, 572 (1942)—represent "well-defined and narrowly limited classes of speech, the prevention and punishment of which have never been thought to raise any Constitutional problem," id., at 571–572.

Last Term, in Stevens, we held that new categories of unprotected speech may not be added to the list by a legislature that concludes certain speech is too harmful to be tolerated. Stevens concerned a federal statute purporting to criminalize the creation, sale, or possession of certain depictions of animal cruelty. See 18 U. S. C. §48 (amended 2010). The statute covered depictions "in which a living animal is intentionally maimed, mutilated, tortured, wounded, or killed" if that harm to the animal was illegal where the "the creation, sale, or possession t[ook] place," §48(c)(1). A saving clause largely borrowed from our obscenity jurisprudence, see Miller v. California, 413 U. S. 15, 24 (1973), exempted depictions with "serious religious, political, scientific, educational, journalistic, historical, or artistic value," §48(b). We held that statute to be an impermissible content-based restriction on speech. There was no American tradition of forbidding the depiction of animal cruelty—though States have long had laws against committing it.

The Government argued in Stevens that lack of a historical warrant did not matter; that it could create new categories of unprotected speech by applying a "simple balancing test" that weighs the value of a particular category of speech against its social costs and then punishes that category of speech if it fails the test. Stevens, 559 U. S., at ___ (slip op., at 7). We emphatically rejected that "startling and dangerous" proposition. Ibid. "Maybe there are some categories of speech that have been historically unprotected, but have not yet been specifically identified or discussed as such in our case law." Id., at ___ (slip op., at 9). But without persuasive evidence that a novel restriction on content is part of a long (if heretofore unrecognized) tradition of proscription, a legislature may not revise the "judgment [of] the American people," embodied in the First Amendment, "that the benefits of its restrictions on the Government outweigh the costs." Id., at ___ (slip op., at 7).

That holding controls this case. 1 As in Stevens, California has tried to make violent-speech regulation look like obscenity regulation by appending a saving clause required for the latter. That does not suffice. Our cases have been clear that the obscenity exception to the First Amendment does not cover whatever a legislature finds shocking, but only depictions of "sexual conduct," Miller, supra, at 24. See also Cohen v. California, 403 U. S. 15, 20 (1971); Roth, supra, at 487, and n. 20.

Stevens was not the first time we have encountered and rejected a State's attempt to shoehorn speech about violence into obscenity. In Winters, we considered a New York criminal statute "forbid[ding] the massing of stories of bloodshed and lust in such a way as to incite to crime against the person," 333 U. S., at 514. The New York Court of Appeals upheld the provision as a law against obscenity. "[T]here can be no more precise test of written indecency or obscenity," it said, "than the continuing and changeable experience of the community as to what types of books are likely to bring about the corruption of public morals or other analogous injury to the public order. " Id., at 514 (internal quotation marks omitted). That is of course the same expansive view of governmental power to abridge the freedom of speech based on interest-balancing that we rejected in Stevens. Our opinion in Winters, which concluded that the New York statute failed a heightened vagueness standard applicable to restrictions upon speech entitled to First Amendment protection, 333 U. S., at 517–519, made clear that violence is not part of the obscenity that the Constitution permits to be regulated. The speech reached by the statute contained "no indecency or obscenity in any sense heretofore known to the law." Id., at 519.

Because speech about violence is not obscene, it is of no consequence that California's statute mimics the New York statute regulating obscenity-for-minors that we upheld in Ginsberg v. New York, 390 U. S. 629 (1968) . That case approved a prohibition on the sale to minors of sexual material that would be obscene from the perspective of a child. 2 We held that the legislature could "adjus[t] the definition of obscenity 'to social realities by permitting the appeal of this type of material to be assessed in terms of the sexual interests ...' of ... minors. " Id., at 638 (quoting Mishkin v. New York, 383 U. S. 502, 509 (1966)). And because "obscenity is not protected expression," the New York statute could be sustained so long as the legislature's judgment that the proscribed materials were harmful to children "was not irrational." 390 U. S., at 641.

The California Act is something else entirely. It does not adjust the boundaries of an existing category of unprotected speech to ensure that a definition designed for adults is not uncritically applied to children. California does not argue that it is empowered to prohibit selling offensively violent works to adults —and it is wise not to, since that is but a hair's breadth from the argument rejected in Stevens. Instead, it wishes to create a wholly new category of content-based regulation that is permissible only for speech directed at children.

That is unprecedented and mistaken. "[M]inors are entitled to a significant measure of First Amendment protection, and only in relatively narrow and well-defined circumstances may government bar public dissemination of protected materials to them." Erznoznik v. Jacksonville, 422 U. S. 205, 212–213 (1975) (citation omitted). No doubt a State possesses legitimate power to protect children from harm, Ginsberg, supra, at 640–641; Prince v. Massachusetts, 321 U. S. 158, 165 (1944), but that does not include a free-floating power to restrict the ideas to which children may be exposed. "Speech that is neither obscene as to youths nor subject to some other legitimate proscription cannot be suppressed solely to protect the young from ideas or images that a legislative body thinks unsuitable for them." Erznoznik, supra, at 213–214. 3

California's argument would fare better if there were a longstanding tradition in this country of specially restricting children's access to depictions of violence, but there is none. Certainly the books we give children to read—or read to them when they are younger—contain no shortage of gore. Grimm's Fairy Tales, for example, are grim indeed. As her just deserts for trying to poison Snow White, the wicked queen is made to dance in red hot slippers "till she fell dead on the floor, a sad example of envy and jealousy." The Complete Brothers Grimm Fairy Tales 198 (2006 ed.). Cinderella's evil stepsisters have their eyes pecked out by doves. Id., at 95. And Hansel and Gretel (children!) kill their captor by baking her in an oven. Id., at 54.

High-school reading lists are full of similar fare. Homer's Odysseus blinds Polyphemus the Cyclops by grinding out his eye with a heated stake. The Odyssey of Homer, Book IX, p. 125 (S. Butcher & A. Lang transls. 1909) ("Even so did we seize the fiery-pointed brand and whirled it round in his eye, and the blood flowed about the heated bar. And the breath of the flame singed his eyelids and brows all about, as the ball of the eye burnt away, and the roots thereof crackled in the flame"). In the Inferno, Dante and Virgil watch corrupt politicians struggle to stay submerged beneath a lake of boiling pitch, lest they be skewered by devils above the surface. Canto XXI, pp. 187–189 (A. Mandelbaum transl. Bantam Classic ed. 1982). And Golding's Lord of the Flies recounts how a schoolboy called Piggy is savagely murdered by other children while marooned on an island. W. Golding, Lord of the Flies 208–209 (1997 ed.). 4

This is not to say that minors' consumption of violent entertainment has never encountered resistance. In the 1800's, dime novels depicting crime and "penny dreadfuls" (named for their price and content) were blamed in some quarters for juvenile delinquency. See Brief for Cato Institute as Amicus Curiae 6–7. When motion pictures came along, they became the villains instead. "The days when the police looked upon dime novels as the most dangerous of textbooks in the school for crime are drawing to a close... . They say that the moving picture machine ... tends even more than did the dime novel to turn the thoughts of the easily influenced to paths which sometimes lead to prison." Moving Pictures as Helps to Crime, N. Y. Times, Feb. 21, 1909, quoted in Brief for Cato Institute, at 8. For a time, our Court did permit broad censorship of movies because of their capacity to be "used for evil," see Mutual Film Corp. v. Industrial Comm'n of Ohio, 236 U. S. 230, 242 (1915), but we eventually reversed course, Joseph Burstyn, Inc., 343 U. S., at 502; see also Erznoznik, supra, at 212–214 (invalidating a drive-in movies restriction designed to protect children). Radio dramas were next, and then came comic books. Brief for Cato Institute, at 10–11. Many in the late 1940's and early 1950's blamed comic books for fostering a "preoccupation with violence and horror" among the young, leading to a rising juvenile crime rate. See Note, Regulation of Comic Books, 68 Harv. L. Rev. 489, 490 (1955). But efforts to convince Congress to restrict comic books failed. Brief for Comic Book Legal Defense Fund as Amicus Curiae 11–15. 5 And, of course, after comic books came television and music lyrics.

California claims that video games present special problems because they are "interactive," in that the player participates in the violent action on screen and determines its outcome. The latter feature is nothing new: Since at least the publication of The Adventures of You: Sugarcane Island in 1969, young readers of choose-your-own-adventure stories have been able to make decisions that determine the plot by following instructions about which page to turn to. Cf. Interactive Digital Software Assn. v. St. Louis County, 329 F. 3d 954, 957–958 (CA8 2003). As for the argument that video games enable participation in the violent action, that seems to us more a matter of degree than of kind. As Judge Posner has observed, all literature is interactive. "[T]he better it is, the more interactive. Literature when it is successful draws the reader into the story, makes him identify with the characters, invites him to judge them and quarrel with them, to experience their joys and sufferings as the reader's own." American Amusement Machine Assn. v. Kendrick, 244 F. 3d 572, 577 (CA7 2001) (striking down a similar restriction on violent video games).

Justice Alito has done considerable independent re-search to identify, see post, at 14–15, nn. 13–18, video games in which "the violence is astounding," post, at 14. "Victims are dismembered, decapitated, disemboweled, set on fire, and chopped into little pieces. . . . Blood gushes, splatters, and pools." Ibid. Justice Alito recounts all these disgusting video games in order to disgust us—but disgust is not a valid basis for restricting expression. And the same is true of Justice Alito's description, post, at 14–15, of those video games he has discovered that have a racial or ethnic motive for their violence—"'ethnic cleansing' [of] . . . African Americans, Latinos, or Jews." To what end does he relate this? Does it somehow increase the "aggressiveness" that California wishes to suppress? Who knows? But it does arouse the reader's ire, and the reader's desire to put an end to this horrible message. Thus, ironically, Justice Alito's argument highlights the precise danger posed by the California Act: that the ideas expressed by speech—whether it be violence, or gore, or racism—and not its objective effects, may be the real reason for governmental proscription.

III

Because the Act imposes a restriction on the content of protected speech, it is invalid unless California can demonstrate that it passes strict scrutiny—that is, unless it is justified by a compelling government interest and is narrowly drawn to serve that interest. R. A. V., 505 U. S., at 395. The State must specifically identify an "actual problem" in need of solving, Playboy, 529 U. S., at 822–823, and the curtailment of free speech must be actually necessary to the solution, see R. A. V., supra, at 395. That is a demanding standard. "It is rare that a regulation restricting speech because of its content will ever be permissible." Playboy, supra, at 818.

California cannot meet that standard. At the outset, it acknowledges that it cannot show a direct causal link between violent video games and harm to minors. Rather, relying upon our decision in Turner Broadcasting System, Inc. v. FCC, 512 U. S. 622 (1994), the State claims that it need not produce such proof because the legislature can make a predictive judgment that such a link exists, based on competing psychological studies. But reliance on Turner Broadcasting is misplaced. That decision applied intermediate scrutiny to a content-neutral regulation. Id., at 661–662. California's burden is much higher, and because it bears the risk of uncertainty, see Playboy, supra, at 816–817, ambiguous proof will not suffice.

The State's evidence is not compelling. California relies primarily on the research of Dr. Craig Anderson and a few other research psychologists whose studies purport to show a connection between exposure to violent video games and harmful effects on children. These studies have been rejected by every court to consider them, 6 and with good reason: They do not prove that violent video games cause minors to act aggressively (which would at least be a beginning). Instead, "[n]early all of the research is based on correlation, not evidence of causation, and most of the studies suffer from significant, admitted flaws in methodology." Video Software Dealers Assn. 556 F. 3d, at 964. They show at best some correlation between exposure to violent entertainment and minuscule real-world effects, such as children's feeling more aggressive or making louder noises in the few minutes after playing a violent game than after playing a nonviolent game. 7

Even taking for granted Dr. Anderson's conclusions that violent video games produce some effect on children's feelings of aggression, those effects are both small and indistinguishable from effects produced by other media. In his testimony in a similar lawsuit, Dr. Anderson admitted that the "effect sizes" of children's exposure to violent video games are "about the same" as that produced by their exposure to violence on television. App. 1263. And he admits that the same effects have been found when children watch cartoons starring Bugs Bunny or the Road Runner, id., at 1304, or when they play video games like Sonic the Hedgehog that are rated "E" (appropriate for all ages), id., at 1270, or even when they "vie[w] a picture of a gun," id., at 1315–1316. 8

Of course, California has (wisely) declined to restrict Saturday morning cartoons, the sale of games rated for young children, or the distribution of pictures of guns. The consequence is that its regulation is wildly underinclusive when judged against its asserted justification, which in our view is alone enough to defeat it. Underinclusiveness raises serious doubts about whether the government is in fact pursuing the interest it invokes, rather than disfavoring a particular speaker or viewpoint. See City of Ladue v. Gilleo, 512 U. S. 43, 51 (1994); Florida Star v. B. J. F., 491 U. S. 524, 540 (1989) . Here, California has singled out the purveyors of video games for disfavored treatment—at least when compared to booksellers, cartoonists, and movie producers—and has given no persuasive reason why.

The Act is also seriously underinclusive in another respect—and a respect that renders irrelevant the contentions of the concurrence and the dissents that video games are qualitatively different from other portrayals of violence. The California Legislature is perfectly willing to leave this dangerous, mind-altering material in the hands of children so long as one parent (or even an aunt or uncle) says it's OK. And there are not even any requirements as to how this parental or avuncular relationship is to be verified; apparently the child's or putative parent's, aunt's, or uncle's say-so suffices. That is not how one addresses a serious social problem.

California claims that the Act is justified in aid of parental authority: By requiring that the purchase of violent video games can be made only by adults, the Act ensures that parents can decide what games are appropriate. At the outset, we note our doubts that punishing third parties for conveying protected speech to children just in case their parents disapprove of that speech is a proper governmental means of aiding parental authority. Accepting that position would largely vitiate the rule that "only in relatively narrow and well-defined circumstances may government bar public dissemination of protected materials to [minors]." Erznoznik, 422 U. S., at 212–213.

But leaving that aside, California cannot show that the Act's restrictions meet a substantial need of parents who wish to restrict their children's access to violent video games but cannot do so. The video-game industry has in place a voluntary rating system designed to inform consumers about the content of games. The system, implemented by the Entertainment Software Rating Board (ESRB), assigns age-specific ratings to each video game submitted: EC (Early Childhood); E (Everyone); E10+ (Everyone 10 and older); T (Teens); M (17 and older); and AO (Adults Only—18 and older). App. 86. The Video Software Dealers Association encourages retailers to prominently display information about the ESRB system in their stores; to refrain from renting or selling adults-only games to minors; and to rent or sell "M" rated games to minors only with parental consent. Id., at 47. In 2009, the Federal Trade Commission (FTC) found that, as a result of this system, "the video game industry outpaces the movie and music industries" in "(1) restricting target-marketing of mature-rated products to children; (2) clearly and prominently disclosing rating information; and (3) re-stricting children's access to mature-rated products at retail." FTC, Report to Congress, Marketing Violent Entertainment to Children 30 (Dec. 2009), online at http:// www.ftc.gov / os/ 2009 / 12/ P994511violententertainment.pdf (as visited June 24, 2011, and available in Clerk of Court's case file) (FTC Report). This system does much to ensure that minors cannot purchase seriously violent games on their own, and that parents who care about the matter can readily evaluate the games their children bring home. Filling the remaining modest gap in concerned-parents' control can hardly be a compelling state interest. 9

And finally, the Act's purported aid to parental authority is vastly overinclusive. Not all of the children who are forbidden to purchase violent video games on their own have parents who care whether they purchase violent video games. While some of the legislation's effect may indeed be in support of what some parents of the restricted children actually want, its entire effect is only in support of what the State thinks parents ought to want. This is not the narrow tailoring to "assisting parents" that restriction of First Amendment rights requires.

* * *

California's effort to regulate violent video games is the latest episode in a long series of failed attempts to censor violent entertainment for minors. While we have pointed out above that some of the evidence brought forward to support the harmfulness of video games is unpersuasive, we do not mean to demean or disparage the concerns that underlie the attempt to regulate them—concerns that may and doubtless do prompt a good deal of parental oversight. We have no business passing judgment on the view of the California Legislature that violent video games (or, for that matter, any other forms of speech) corrupt the young or harm their moral development. Our task is only to say whether or not such works constitute a "well-defined and narrowly limited clas[s] of speech, the prevention and punishment of which have never been thought to raise any Constitutional problem," Chaplinsky, 315 U. S., at 571–572 (the answer plainly is no); and if not, whether the regulation of such works is justified by that high degree of necessity we have described as a compelling state interest (it is not). Even where the protection of children is the object, the constitutional limits on governmental action apply.

California's legislation straddles the fence between (1) addressing a serious social problem and (2) helping concerned parents control their children. Both ends are legitimate, but when they affect First Amendment rights they must be pursued by means that are neither seriously underinclusive nor seriously overinclusive. See Church of Lukumi Babalu Aye, Inc. v. Hialeah, 508 U. S. 520, 546 (1993) . As a means of protecting children from portrayals of violence, the legislation is seriously underinclusive, not only because it excludes portrayals other than video games, but also because it permits a parental or avuncular veto. And as a means of assisting concerned parents it is seriously overinclusive because it abridges the First Amendment rights of young people whose parents (and aunts and uncles) think violent video games are a harmless pastime. And the overbreadth in achieving one goal is not cured by the underbreadth in achieving the other. Legislation such as this, which is neither fish nor fowl, cannot survive strict scrutiny.

We affirm the judgment below.

It is so ordered.

Notes to Brown v. Entertainment Merchants Association (June 27, 2011)

1 Justice Alito distinguishes Stevens on several grounds that seem to us ill founded. He suggests, post, at 10 (opinion concurring in judgment), that Stevens did not apply strict scrutiny. If that is so (and we doubt it), it would make this an a fortiori case. He says, post, at 9, 10, that the California Act punishes the sale or rental rather than the "creation" or "possession" of violent depictions. That distinction appears nowhere in Stevens itself, and for good reason: It would make permissible the prohibition of printing or selling books—though not the writing of them. Whether government regulation applies to creating, distributing, or consuming speech makes no difference. And finally, Justice Alito points out, post, at 10, that Stevens "left open the possibility that a more narrowly drawn statute" would be constitutional. True, but entirely irrelevant. Stevens said, 559 U. S., at ___ (slip op., at 19), that the "crush-video" statute at issue there might pass muster if it were limited to videos of acts of animal cruelty that violated the law where the acts were performed. There is no contention that any of the virtual characters depicted in the imaginative videos at issue here are criminally liable.

2 The statute in Ginsberg restricted the sale of certain depictions of "nudity, sexual conduct, sexual excitement, or sado-masochistic abuse," that were " '[h]armful to minors.' " A depiction was harmful to minors if it: "(i) predominantly appeals to the prurient, shameful or morbid interests of minors, and "(ii) is patently offensive to prevailing standards in the adult community as a whole with respect to what is suitable material for minors, and "(iii) is utterly without redeeming social importance for minors." 390 U. S., at 646 (Appendix A to opinion of the Court) (quoting N. Y. Penal Law §484–h(1)(f)).

3 Justice Thomas ignores the holding of Erznoznik, and denies that persons under 18 have any constitutional right to speak or be spoken to without their parents' consent. He cites no case, state or federal, supporting this view, and to our knowledge there is none. Most of his dissent is devoted to the proposition that parents have traditionally had the power to control what their children hear and say. This is true enough. And it perhaps follows from this that the state has the power to enforce parental prohibitions—to require, for example, that the promoters of a rock concert exclude those

minors whose parents have advised the promoters that their children are forbidden to attend. But it does not follow that the state has the power to prevent children from hearing or saying anything without their parents' prior consent. The latter would mean, for example, that it could be made criminal to admit persons under 18 to a political rally without their parents' prior written consent—even a political rally in support of laws against corporal punishment of children, or laws in favor of greater rights for minors. And what is good for First Amendment rights of speech must be good for First Amendment rights of religion as well: It could be made criminal to admit a person under 18 to church, or to give a person under 18 a religious tract, without his parents' prior consent. Our point is not, as Justice Thomas believes, post, at 16, n. 2, merely that such laws are "undesirable." They are obviously an infringement upon the religious freedom of young people and those who wish to proselytize young people. Such laws do not enforce parental authority over children's speech and religion; they impose governmental authority, subject only to a parental veto. In the absence of any precedent for state control, uninvited by the parents, over a child's speech and religion (Justice Thomas cites none), and in the absence of any justification for such control that would satisfy strict scrutiny, those laws must be unconstitutional. This argument is not, as Justice Thomas asserts, "circular," ibid. It is the absence of any historical warrant or compelling justification for such restrictions, not our ipse dixit, that renders them invalid.

4 Justice Alito accuses us of pronouncing that playing violent video games "is not different in 'kind' " from reading violent literature. Post, at 2. Well of course it is different in kind, but not in a way that causes the provision and viewing of violent video games, unlike the provision and reading of books, not to be expressive activity and hence not to enjoy First Amendment protection. Reading Dante is unquestionably more cultured and intellectually edifying than playing Mortal Kombat. But these cultural and intellectual differences are not constitutional ones. Crudely violent video games, tawdry TV shows, and cheap novels and magazines are no less forms of speech than The Divine Comedy, and restrictions upon them must survive strict scrutiny—a question to which we devote our attention in Part III, infra. Even if we can see in them "nothing of any possible value to society . . ., they are as much entitled to the protection of free speech as the best of literature." Winters v. New York, 333 U. S. 507, 510 (1948).

5 The crusade against comic books was led by a psychiatrist, Frederic Wertham, who told the Senate Judiciary Committee that "as long as the crime comic books industry exists in its present forms there are no secure homes." Juvenile Delinquency (Comic Books): Hearings before the Subcommittee to Investigate Juvenile Delinquency, 83d Cong., 2d Sess., 84 (1954). Wertham's objections extended even to Superman comics, which he described as "particularly injurious to the ethical development of children." Id., at 86. Wertham's crusade did convince the New York Legislature to pass a ban on the sale of certain comic books to minors, but it was vetoed by Governor Thomas Dewey on the ground that it was unconstitutional given our opinion in Winters, supra. See People v. Bookcase, Inc., 14 N. Y. 2d 409, 412–413, 201 N. E. 2d 14, 15–16 (1964).

6 See Video Software Dealers Assn. v. Schwarzenegger, 556 F. 3d 950, 963–964 (CA9 2009); Interactive Digital Software Assn. v. St. Louis County, 329 F. 3d 954 (CA8 2003); American Amusement Machine Assn. v. Kendrick, 244 F. 3d 572, 578–579 (CA7 2001); Entertainment Software Assn. v. Foti, 451 F. Supp. 2d 823, 832–833 (MD La. 2006); Entertainment Software Assn. v. Hatch, 443 F. Supp. 2d 1065, 1070 (Minn. 2006), aff'd, 519 F. 3d 768 (CA8 2008); Entertainment Software Assn. v. Granholm, 426 F. Supp. 2d 646, 653 (ED Mich. 2006); Entertainment Software Assn. v. Blagojevich, 404 F. Supp. 2d 1051, 1063 (ND Ill. 2005), aff'd, 469 F. 3d 641 (CA7 2006).

7 One study, for example, found that children who had just finished playing violent video games were more likely to fill in the blank letter in "explo_e" with a "d" (so that it reads "explode") than with an "r" ("explore"). App. 496, 506 (internal quotation marks omitted). The prevention of this phenomenon, which might have been anticipated with common sense, is not a compelling state interest.

8 Justice Alito is mistaken in thinking that we fail to take account of "new and rapidly evolving technology," post, at 1. The studies in question pertain to that new and rapidly evolving technology, and fail to show, with the degree of certitude that strict scrutiny requires, that this subject-matter restriction on speech is justified. Nor is Justice Alito correct in attributing to us the view that "violent video games really present no serious problem." Post, at 2. Perhaps they do present a problem, and perhaps none of us would allow our own children to play them. But there are all sorts of "problems"—some of them surely more serious than this one—that cannot be addressed by governmental restriction of free expression: for example, the problem of encouraging anti-Semitism (National Socialist Party of America v. Skokie, 432 U. S. 43 (1977) (per curiam)), the problem of spreading a political philosophy hostile to the Constitution (Noto v. United States, 367 U. S. 290 (1961)), or the problem of encouraging disrespect for the Nation's flag (Texas v. Johnson, 491 U. S. 397 (1989)). Justice Breyer would hold that California has satisfied strict scrutiny based upon his own research into the issue of the harmfulness of violent video games. See post, at 20–35 (Appendixes to dissenting opinion) (listing competing academic articles discussing the harmfulness vel non of violent video games). The vast preponderance of this research is outside the record—and in any event we do not see how it could lead to Justice Breyer's conclusion, since he admits he cannot say whether the studies on his side are right or wrong. Post, at 15. Similarly, Justice Alito says he is not "sure" whether there are any constitutionally dispositive differences between video games and other media. Post, at 2. If that is so, then strict scrutiny plainly has not been satisfied.

9 Justice Breyer concludes that the remaining gap is compelling because, according to the FTC's report, some "20% of those under 17 are still able to buy M-rated games." Post, at 18 (citing FTC Report 28). But some gap in compliance is unavoidable. The sale of alcohol to minors, for example, has long been illegal, but a 2005 study suggests that about 18% of retailers still sell alcohol to those under the drinking age. Brief for State of Rhode Island et al. as Amici Curiae 18. Even if the sale of violent video games

to minors could be deterred further by increasing regulation, the government does not have a compelling interest in each marginal percentage point by which its goals are advanced.

GPS-tracking is a search that requires a warrant: United States v. Jones (January 23, 2012)

Justice Scalia delivered the opinion of the Court.

We decide whether the attachment of a Global-Positioning-System (GPS) tracking device to an individual's vehicle, and subsequent use of that device to monitor the vehicle's movements on public streets, constitutes a search or seizure within the meaning of the Fourth Amendment.

I

In 2004 respondent Antoine Jones, owner and operator of a nightclub in the District of Columbia, came under suspicion of trafficking in narcotics and was made the target of an investigation by a joint FBI and Metropolitan Police Department task force. Officers employed various investigative techniques, including visual surveillance of the nightclub, installation of a camera focused on the front door of the club, and a pen register and wiretap covering Jones's cellular phone.

Based in part on information gathered from these sources, in 2005 the Government applied to the United States District Court for the District of Columbia for a warrant authorizing the use of an electronic tracking device on the Jeep Grand Cherokee registered to Jones's wife. A warrant issued, authorizing installation of the de-vice in the District of Columbia and within 10 days.

On the 11th day, and not in the District of Columbia but in Maryland, 1 agents installed a GPS tracking device on the undercarriage of the Jeep while it was parked in a public parking lot. Over the next 28 days, the Government used the device to track the vehicle's movements, and once had to replace the device's battery when the vehicle was parked in a different public lot in Maryland. By means of signals from multiple satellites, the device established the vehicle's location within 50 to 100 feet, and communicated that location by cellular phone to a Government computer. It relayed more than 2,000 pages of data over the 4-week period.

The Government ultimately obtained a multiple-count indictment charging Jones and several alleged co-conspirators with, as relevant here, conspiracy to distribute and possess with intent to distribute five kilograms or more of cocaine and 50 grams or more of cocaine base, in violation of 21 U. S. C. §§841 and 846. Before trial, Jones filed a motion to suppress evidence obtained through the GPS device. The District Court granted the motion only in part, suppressing the data obtained while the vehicle was parked in the garage adjoining Jones's residence. 451 F. Supp. 2d 71, 88 (2006). It held the remaining data admissible, because " '[a] person traveling in an automobile on public thoroughfares has no reasonable expectation of privacy in his movements from one place to another.' " Ibid. (quoting United States v. Knotts, 460 U. S. 276, 281 (1983)). Jones's trial in October 2006 produced a hung jury on the conspiracy count.

In March 2007, a grand jury returned another indictment, charging Jones and others with the same conspiracy. The Government introduced at trial the same GPS-derived locational data admitted in the first trial, which connected Jones to the alleged conspirators' stash house that contained $850,000 in cash, 97 kilograms of cocaine, and 1 kilogram of cocaine base. The jury returned a guilty verdict, and the District Court sentenced Jones to life imprisonment.

The United States Court of Appeals for the District of Columbia Circuit reversed the conviction because of admission of the evidence obtained by warrantless use of the GPS device which, it said, violated the Fourth Amendment. United States v. Maynard, 615 F. 3d 544 (2010). The D. C. Circuit denied the Government's petition for rehearing en banc, with four judges dissenting. 625 F. 3d 766 (2010). We granted certiorari, 564 U. S. ___ (2011).

II

A

The Fourth Amendment provides in relevant part that "[t]he right of the people to be secure in their persons, houses, papers, and effects, against unreasonable searches and seizures, shall not be violated." It is beyond dispute that a vehicle is an "effect" as that term is used in the Amendment. United States v. Chadwick, 433 U. S. 1, 12 (1977) . We hold that the Government's installation of a GPS device on a target's vehicle, 2 and its use of that device to monitor the vehicle's movements, constitutes a "search."

It is important to be clear about what occurred in this case: The Government physically occupied private property for the purpose of obtaining information. We have no doubt that such a physical intrusion would have been considered a "search" within the meaning of the Fourth Amendment when it was adopted. Entick v. Carrington, 95 Eng. Rep. 807 (C. P. 1765), is a "case we have described as a 'monument of English freedom' 'undoubtedly familiar' to 'every American statesman' at the time the Constitution was adopted, and considered to be 'the true and ultimate expression of constitutional law' " with regard to search and seizure. Brower v. County of Inyo, 489 U. S. 593, 596 (1989) (quoting Boyd v. United States, 116 U. S. 616, 626 (1886)). In that case, Lord Camden expressed in plain terms the significance of property rights in search-and-seizure analysis:

"[O]ur law holds the property of every man so sacred, that no man can set his foot upon his neighbour's close without his leave; if he does he is a trespasser, though he does no damage at all; if he will tread upon his neighbour's ground, he must justify it by law." Entick, supra, at 817.

The text of the Fourth Amendment reflects its close connection to property, since otherwise it would have referred simply to "the right of the people to be secure against unreasonable searches and seizures"; the phrase "in their persons, houses, papers, and effects" would have been superfluous.

Consistent with this understanding, our Fourth Amendment jurisprudence was tied to common-law trespass, at least until the latter half of the 20th century. Kyllo v. United States, 533 U. S. 27, 31 (2001); Kerr, The Fourth Amendment and New Technologies: Constitutional Myths and the Case for Caution, 102 Mich. L. Rev. 801, 816 (2004). Thus, in Olmstead v. United States, 277 U. S. 438 (1928), we held that wiretaps attached to telephone wires on the public streets did not constitute a Fourth Amendment search because "[t]here was no entry of the houses or offices of the defendants," id., at 464.

Our later cases, of course, have deviated from that exclusively property-based approach. In Katz v. United States, 389 U. S. 347, 351 (1967), we said that "the Fourth Amendment protects people, not places," and found a violation in attachment of an eavesdropping device to a public telephone booth. Our later cases have applied the analysis of Justice Harlan's concurrence in that case, which said that a violation occurs when government officers violate a person's "reasonable expectation of privacy," id., at 360. See, e.g., Bond v. United States, 529 U. S. 334 (2000); California v. Ciraolo, 476 U. S. 207 (1986); Smith v. Maryland, 442 U. S. 735 (1979).

The Government contends that the Harlan standard shows that no search occurred here, since Jones had no "reasonable expectation of privacy" in the area of the Jeep accessed by Government agents (its underbody) and in the locations of the Jeep on the public roads, which were visible to all. But we need not address the Government's contentions, because Jones's Fourth Amendment rightsdo not rise or fall with the Katz formulation. At bottom, we must "assur[e] preservation of that degree of privacy against government that existed when the Fourth Amendment was adopted." Kyllo, supra, at 34. As explained, for most of our history the Fourth Amendment was understood to embody a particular concern for government trespass upon the areas ("persons, houses, papers, and effects") it enumerates. 3 Katz did not repudiate that understanding. Less than two years later the Court upheld defendants' contention that the Government could not introduce against them conversations between other people obtained by warrantless placement of electronic surveillance devices in their homes. The opinion rejected the dissent's contention that there was no Fourth Amendment violation "unless the conversational privacy of the homeowner himself is invaded." 4 Alderman v. United States, 394 U. S. 165, 176 (1969). "[W]e [do not] believe that Katz, by holding that the Fourth Amendment protects persons and their private conversations, was intendedto withdraw any of the protection which the Amendment extends to the home . . . ." Id., at 180.

More recently, in Soldal v. Cook County, 506 U. S. 56 (1992), the Court unanimously rejected the argument that although a "seizure" had occurred "in a 'technical' sense" when a trailer home was forcibly removed, id., at 62, no Fourth Amendment violation occurred because law enforcement had not "invade[d] the [individuals'] privacy," id., at 60. Katz, the Court explained, established that "property rights are not the sole measure of Fourth Amendment violations," but did not "snuf[f] out the previously recognized protection for property." 506 U. S., at 64. As Justice Brennan explained in his concurrence in Knotts, Katz did not erode the principle "that, when the Government does engage in physical intrusion of a constitutionally protected area in order to obtain information, that intrusion may constitute a violation of the Fourth Amendment." 460 U. S., at 286 (opinion concurring in judgment). We have embodied that preservation of past rights in our very definition of "reasonable expectation of privacy" which we have said to be an expectation "that has a source outside of the Fourth Amendment, either by reference to concepts of real or personal property law or to understandings that are recognized and permitted by society." Minnesota v. Carter, 525 U. S. 83, 88 (1998) (internal quotation marks omitted). Katz did not narrow the Fourth Amendment's scope. 5

The Government contends that several of our post-Katz cases foreclose the conclusion that what occurred here constituted a search. It relies principally on two cases in which we rejected Fourth Amendment challenges to "beepers," electronic tracking devices that represent another form of electronic monitoring. The first case, Knotts, upheld against Fourth Amendment challenge the use of a "beeper" that had been placed in a container of chloroform, allowing law enforcement to monitor the location of the container. 460 U. S., at 278. We said that there had been no infringement of Knotts' reasonable expectation of privacy since the information obtained—the location of the automobile carrying the container on public roads, and the location of the off-loaded container in open fields near Knotts' cabin—had been voluntarily conveyed to the public. 6 Id., at 281–282. But as we have discussed, the Katz reasonable-expectation-of-privacy test has been added to, not substituted for, the common-law trespassory test. The holding in Knotts addressed only the former, since the latter was not at issue. The beeper had been placed inthe container before it came into Knotts' possession, with the consent of the then-owner. 460 U. S., at 278. Knotts did not challenge that installation, and we specifically de-clined to consider its effect on the Fourth Amendment analysis. Id., at 279, n. Knotts would be relevant, perhaps, if the Government were making the argument that what would otherwise be an unconstitutional search isnot such where it produces only public information. The Government does not make that argument, and we know of no case that would support it.

The second "beeper" case, United States v. Karo, 468 U. S. 705 (1984), does not suggest a different conclusion. There we addressed the question left open by Knotts, whether the installation of a beeper in a container amounted to a search or seizure. 468 U. S., at 713. As in Knotts, at the time the beeper was installed the container belonged to a third party, and it did not come into possession of the defendant until later. 468 U. S., at 708. Thus, the specific question we considered was whether the installation "with the consent of the original owner constitute[d] a search or seizure . . . when the container is delivered to a buyer having no knowledge of the presence of the beeper." Id., at 707 (emphasis added). We held not. The Government, we said, came into physical contact with the container only before it belonged to the defendant Karo; and the transfer of the container with the unmonitored beeper inside did not convey any information and thus did not invade Karo's privacy. See id., at 712. That conclusion is perfectly consistent with the one we reach here. Karo accepted the container as it came to him, beeper and all, and was therefore not entitled to object to the beeper's presence, even though it was used to monitor the container's location. Cf. On Lee v. United States, 343 U. S. 747–752 (1952) (no search or seizure where an informant, who was wearing a concealed microphone, was invited into the defendant's business). Jones, who possessed the Jeep at the time the Government trespassorily inserted the information-gathering device, is on much different footing.

The Government also points to our exposition in New York v. Class, 475 U. S. 106 (1986), that "[t]he exterior ofa car . . . is thrust into the public eye, and thus to examine it does not constitute a 'search.' " Id., at 114. That statement is of marginal relevance here since, as the Government acknowledges, "the officers in this case did more than conduct a visual inspection of respondent's vehicle," Brief for United States 41 (emphasis added). By attaching the device to the Jeep, officers encroached on a protected area. In Class itself we suggested that this would make a difference, for we concluded that an officer's momentary reaching into the interior of a vehicle did constitute a search. 7 475 U. S., at 114–115.

Finally, the Government's position gains little support from our conclusion in Oliver v. United States, 466 U. S. 170 (1984), that officers' information-gathering intrusion on an "open field" did not constitute a Fourth Amendment search even though it was a trespass at common law, id., at 183. Quite simply, an open field, unlike the curtilage of a home, see United States v. Dunn, 480 U. S. 294, 300 (1987), is not one of those protected areas enumerated in the Fourth Amendment. Oliver, supra, at 176–177. See also Hester v. United States, 265 U. S. 57, 59 (1924) . The Government's physical intrusion on such an area—unlike its intrusion on the "effect" at issue here—is of no Fourth Amendment significance. 8

B

The concurrence begins by accusing us of applying "18th-century tort law." Post, at 1. That is a distortion. What we apply is an 18th-century guarantee against unreasonable searches, which we believe must provide at a minimum the degree of protection it afforded when it was adopted. The concurrence does not share that belief. It would apply exclusively Katz's reasonable-expectation-of-privacy test, even when that eliminates rights that previously existed.

The concurrence faults our approach for "present[ing] particularly vexing problems" in cases that do not involve physical contact, such as those that involve the transmission of electronic signals. Post, at 9. We entirely fail to understand that point. For unlike the concurrence, which would make Katz the exclusive test, we do not make trespass the exclusive test. Situations involving merely the transmission of electronic signals without trespass would remain subject to Katz analysis.

In fact, it is the concurrence's insistence on the exclusivity of the Katz test that needlessly leads us into "particularly vexing problems" in the present case. This Court has to date not deviated from the understanding that mere visual observation does not constitute a search. See Kyllo, 533 U. S., at 31–32. We accordingly held in Knotts that "[a] person traveling in an automobile on public thoroughfares has no reasonable expectation of privacy in his movements from one place to another." 460 U. S., at 281. Thus, even assuming that the concurrence is correct tosay that "[t]raditional surveillance" of Jones for a 4-week period "would have required a large team of agents, multiple vehicles, and perhaps aerial assistance," post, at 12, our cases suggest that such visual observation is constitutionally permissible. It may be that achieving the same result through electronic means, without an accompany-ing trespass, is an unconstitutional invasion of privacy, but the present case does not require us to answer that question.

And answering it affirmatively leads us needlessly into additional thorny problems. The concurrence posits that "relatively short-term monitoring of a person's movements on public streets" is okay, but that "the use of longer term GPS monitoring in investigations of most offenses" is no good. Post, at 13 (emphasis added). That introduces yet another novelty into our jurisprudence. There is no precedent for the proposition that whether a search has occurred depends on the nature of the crime being investigated. And even accepting that novelty, it remains unexplained why a 4-week investigation is "surely" too long and why a drug-trafficking conspiracy involving sub-stantial amounts of cash and narcotics is not an "extra-ordinary offens[e]" which may permit longer observation. See post, at 13–14. What of a 2-day monitoring of asuspected purveyor of stolen electronics? Or of a 6-month monitoring of a suspected terrorist? We may have to grapple with these "vexing problems" in some future case where a classic trespassory search is not involved and resort must be had to Katz analysis; but there is no reason for rushing forward to resolve them here.

III

The Government argues in the alternative that even if the attachment and use of the device was a search, it was reasonable—and thus lawful—under the Fourth Amendment because "officers had reasonable suspicion, and in-deed probable cause, to believe that [Jones] was a leader in a large-scale cocaine distribution conspiracy." Brief for United States 50–51. We have no occasion to consider this argument. The Government did not raise it below, and the D. C. Circuit therefore did not address it. See 625 F. 3d, at 767 (Ginsburg, Tatel, and Griffith, JJ., concurring in denial of rehearing en banc). We consider the argument forfeited. See Sprietsma v. Mercury Marine, 537 U. S. 51, n. 4 (2002).

* * *

The judgment of the Court of Appeals for the D. C. Circuit is affirmed.

It is so ordered.

Notes to United States v. Jones (January 23, 2012)

 1 In this litigation, the Government has conceded noncompliance with the warrant and has argued only that a warrant was not required. United States v. Maynard, 615 F. 3d 544, 566, n. (CADC 2010).

 2 As we have noted, the Jeep was registered to Jones's wife. The Government acknowledged, however, that Jones was "the exclusive driver." Id., at 555, n. (internal quotation marks omitted). If Jones was not the owner he had at least the property rights of a bailee. The Court of Appeals concluded that the vehicle's registration did not affect his ability to make a Fourth Amendment objection, ibid., and the Government has not challenged that determination here. We therefore do not consider the Fourth Amendment significance of Jones's status.

 3 Justice Alito's concurrence (hereinafter concurrence) doubts the wisdom of our approach because "it is almost impossible to think of late-18th-century situations that are analogous to what took place in this case." Post, at 3 (opinion concurring in judgment). But in fact it posits a situation that is not far afield—a constable's concealing himself in the target's coach in order to track its movements. Ibid. There is no doubt that the information gained by that trespassory activity would be the product of an unlawful search—whether that information consisted of the conversations occurring in the coach, or of the destinations to which the coach traveled. In any case, it is quite irrelevant whether there was an 18th-century analog. Whatever new methods of investigation may be devised, our task, at a minimum, is to decide whether the action in question would have constituted a "search" within the original meaning of the Fourth Amendment. Where, as here, the Government obtains information by physically intruding on a constitutionally protected area, such a search has undoubtedly occurred.

 4 Thus, the concurrence's attempt to recast Alderman as meaning that individuals have a "legitimate expectation of privacy in all conversations that [take] place under their roof," post, at 6–7, is foreclosed by the Court's opinion. The Court took as a given that the homeowner's "conversational privacy" had not been violated.

 5 The concurrence notes that post-Katz we have explained that " 'an actual trespass is neither necessary nor sufficient to establish a constitutional violation.' " Post, at 6 (quoting United States v. Karo, 468 U. S. 705, 713 (1984)). That is undoubtedly true, and undoubtedly irrelevant. Karo was considering whether a seizure occurred, and as the concurrence explains, a seizure of property occurs, not when there is a trespass, but "when there is some meaningful interference with an individual's possessory interests in that property." Post, at 2 (internal quotation marks omitted). Likewise with a search. Trespass alone does not qualify, but there must be conjoined with that what was present here: an attempt to find something or to obtain information. Related to this, and similarly irrelevant, is the concurrence's point that, if analyzed separately, neither the installation of the device nor its use would constitute a Fourth Amendment search. See ibid. Of course

not. A trespass on "houses" or "effects," or a Katz invasion of privacy, is not alone a search unless it is done to obtain information; and the obtaining of information is not alone a search unless it is achieved by such a trespass or invasion of privacy.

6 Knotts noted the "limited use which the government made of the signals from this particular beeper," 460 U. S., at 284; and reserved the question whether "different constitutional principles may be applicable" to "dragnet-type law enforcement practices" of the type that GPS tracking made possible here, ibid.

7 The Government also points to Cardwell v. Lewis, 417 U. S. 583 (1974), in which the Court rejected the claim that the inspection of an impounded vehicle's tire tread and the collection of paint scrapings from its exterior violated the Fourth Amendment. Whether the plural-ity said so because no search occurred or because the search was reasonable is unclear. Compare id., at 591 (opinion of Blackmun, J.) ("[W]e fail to comprehend what expectation of privacy was infringed"), with id., at 592 ("Under circumstances such as these, where probable cause exists, a warrantless examination of the exterior of a car is not unreasonable . . . ").

8 Thus, our theory is not that the Fourth Amendment is concerned with "any technical trespass that led to the gathering of evidence." Post, at 3 (Alito, J., concurring in judgment) (emphasis added). The Fourth Amendment protects against trespassory searches only with regard to those items ("persons, houses, papers, and effects") that it enumerates. The trespass that occurred in Oliver may properly be understood as a "search," but not one "in the constitutional sense." 466 U. S., at 170, 183.

Drug-sniffing dog on front porch requires warrant: Florida v. Jardines (March 26, 2013)

Justice Scalia delivered the opinion of the Court.

We consider whether using a drug-sniffing dog on a homeowner's porch to investigate the contents of the home is a "search" within the meaning of the Fourth Amendment.

I

In 2006, Detective William Pedraja of the Miami-Dade Police Department received an unverified tip that marijuana was being grown in the home of respondent Joelis Jardines. One month later, the Department and the Drug Enforcement Administration sent a joint surveillance team to Jardines' home. Detective Pedraja was part of that team. He watched the home for fifteen minutes and saw no vehicles in the driveway or activity around the home, and could not see inside because the blinds were drawn. Detective Pedraja then approached Jardines' home accompanied by Detective Douglas Bartelt, a trained canine handler who had just arrived at the scene with his drug-sniffing dog. The dog was trained to detect the scent of marijuana, cocaine, heroin, and several other drugs, indicating the presence of any of these substances through particular behavioral changes recognizable by his handler.

Detective Bartelt had the dog on a six-foot leash, owing in part to the dog's "wild" nature, App. to Pet. for Cert. A–35, and tendency to dart around erratically while searching. As the dog approached Jardines' front porch, he apparently sensed one of the odors he had been trained to detect, and began energetically exploring the area for the strongest point source of that odor. As Detective Bartelt explained, the dog "began tracking that airborne odor by . . . tracking back and forth," engaging in what is called "bracketing," "back and forth, back and forth." Id., at A– 33 to A–34. Detective Bartelt gave the dog "the full six feet of the leash plus whatever safe distance [he could] give him" to do this—he testified that he needed to give the dog "as much distance as I can." Id., at A–35. And Detective Pedraja stood back while this was occurring, so that he would not "get knocked over" when the dog was "spinning around trying to find" the source. Id., at A–38.

After sniffing the base of the front door, the dog sat, which is the trained behavior upon discovering the odor's strongest point. Detective Bartelt then pulled the dog away from the door and returned to his vehicle. He left the scene after informing Detective Pedraja that there had been a positive alert for narcotics.

On the basis of what he had learned at the home, Detective Pedraja applied for and received a warrant to search the residence. When the warrant was executed later that day, Jardines attempted to flee and was arrested; the search revealed marijuana plants, and he was charged with trafficking in cannabis.

At trial, Jardines moved to suppress the marijuana plants on the ground that the canine investigation was an unreasonable search. The trial court granted the motion, and the Florida Third District Court of Appeal reversed. On a petition for discretionary review, the Florida Supreme Court quashed the decision of the Third District Court of Appeal and approved the trial court's decision to suppress, holding (as relevant here) that the use of the trained narcotics dog to investigate Jardines' home was a Fourth Amendment search unsupported by probable cause, rendering invalid the warrant based upon information gathered in that search. 73 So. 3d 34 (2011).

We granted certiorari, limited to the question of whether the officers' behavior was a search within the meaning of the Fourth Amendment. 565 U. S. ___ (2012).

II

The Fourth Amendment provides in relevant part that the "right of the people to be secure in their persons, houses, papers, and effects, against unreasonable searches and seizures, shall not be violated." The Amendment establishes a simple baseline, one that for much of our history formed the exclusive basis for its protections: When "the Government obtains information by physically intruding" on persons, houses, papers, or effects, "a 'search' within the original meaning of the Fourth Amendment" has "undoubtedly occurred." United States v. Jones, 565 U. S.___, ___, n. 3 (2012) (slip op., at 6, n. 3). By reason of our decision in Katz v. United States, 389 U. S. 347 (1967), property rights "are not the sole measure of Fourth Amendment violations," Soldal v. Cook County, 506 U. S. 56, 64 (1992) —but though Katz may add to the baseline, it does not subtract anything from the Amendment's protections "when the Government does engage in [a] physical intrusion of a constitutionally protected area," United States v. Knotts, 460 U. S. 276, 286 (1983) (Brennan, J., concurring in the judgment).

That principle renders this case a straightforward one. The officers were gathering information in an area belonging to Jardines and immediately surrounding his house—in the curtilage of the house, which we have held enjoys protection as part of the home itself. And they gathered that information by physically entering and occupying the area to engage in conduct not explicitly or implicitly permitted by the homeowner.

A

The Fourth Amendment "indicates with some precision the places and things encompassed by its protections": persons, houses, papers, and effects. Oliver v. United States, 466 U. S. 170, 176 (1984). The Fourth Amendment does not, therefore, prevent all investigations conducted on private property; for example, an officer may (subject to Katz) gather information in what we have called "open fields"—even if those fields are privately owned—because such fields are not enumerated in the Amendment's text. Hester v. United States, 265 U. S. 57 (1924).

But when it comes to the Fourth Amendment, the home is first among equals. At the Amendment's "very core" stands "the right of a man to retreat into his own home and there be free from unreasonable governmental intrusion." Silverman v. United States, 365 U. S. 505, 511 (1961). This right would be of little practical value if the State's agents could stand in a home's porch or side garden and trawl for evidence with impunity; the right to retreat would be significantly diminished if the police could enter a man's property to observe his repose from just outside the front window.

We therefore regard the area "immediately surrounding and associated with the home"—what our cases call the curtilage—as "part of the home itself for Fourth Amendment purposes." Oliver, supra, at 180. That principle has ancient and durable roots. Just as the distinction between the home and the open fields is "as old as the common law," Hester, supra, at 59, so too is the identity of home and what Blackstone called the "curtilage or homestall," for the "house protects and privileges all its branches and appurtenants." 4 W. Blackstone, Commentaries on the Laws of England 223, 225 (1769). This area around the home is "intimately linked to the home, both physically and psychologically," and is where "privacy expectations are most heightened." California v. Ciraolo, 476 U. S. 207, 213 (1986).

While the boundaries of the curtilage are generally "clearly marked," the "conception defining the curtilage" is at any rate familiar enough that it is "easily understood from our daily experience." Oliver, 466 U. S., at 182, n. 12. Here there is no doubt that the officers entered it: The front porch is the classic exemplar of an area adjacent to the home and "to which the activity of home life extends." Ibid.

B

Since the officers' investigation took place in a constitutionally protected area, we turn to the question of whether it was accomplished through an unlicensed physical intrusion. 1 While law enforcement officers need not "shield their eyes" when passing by the home "on public thoroughfares," Ciraolo, 476 U. S., at 213, an officer's leave to gather information is sharply circumscribed when he steps off those thoroughfares and enters the Fourth Amendment's protected areas. In permitting, for example, visual observation of the home from "public navigable airspace," we were careful to note that it was done "in a physically nonintrusive manner." Ibid. Entick v. Carrington, 2 Wils. K. B. 275, 95 Eng. Rep. 807 (K. B. 1765), a case "undoubtedly familiar" to "every American statesman" at the time of the Founding, Boyd v. United States, 116 U. S. 616(1886), states the general rule clearly: "[O]ur law holds the property of every man so sacred, that no man can set his foot upon his neighbour's close without his leave." 2 Wils. K. B., at 291, 95 Eng. Rep., at 817. As it is undisputed that the detectives had all four of their feet and all four of their companion's firmly planted on the constitutionally protected extension of Jardines' home, the only question is whether he had given his leave (even implicitly) for them to do so. He had not.

"A license may be implied from the habits of the country," notwithstanding the "strict rule of the English common law as to entry upon a close." McKee v. Gratz, 260 U. S. 127, 136 (1922) (Holmes, J.). We have accordingly recognized that "the knocker on the front door is treated as an invitation or license to attempt an entry, justifying ingress to the home by solicitors, hawkers and peddlers of all kinds." Breard v. Alexandria, 341 U. S. 622, 626 (1951) . This implicit license typically permits the visitor to approach the home by the front path, knock promptly, wait briefly to be received, and then (absent invitation to linger longer) leave. Complying with the terms of that traditional invitation does not require fine-grained legal knowledge; it is generally managed without incident by the Nation's Girl Scouts and trick-or-treaters. 2 Thus, a police officer not armed with a warrant may approach a home and knock, precisely because that is "no more than any private citizen might do." Kentucky v. King, 563 U. S. ___, ___ (2011) (slip op., at 16).

But introducing a trained police dog to explore the area around the home in hopes of discovering incriminating evidence is something else. There is no customary invitation to do that. An invitation to engage in canine forensic investigation assuredly does not inhere in the very act of hanging a knocker. 3 To find a visitor knocking on the door is routine (even if sometimes unwelcome); to spot that same visitor exploring the front path with a metal detector, or marching his bloodhound into the garden before saying hello and asking permission, would inspire most of us to—well, call the police. The scope of a license—express or implied—is limited not only to a particular area but also to a specific purpose. Consent at a traffic stop to an officer's checking out an anonymous tip that there is a body in the trunk does not permit the officer to rummage through the trunk for narcotics. Here, the background social norms that invite a visitor to the front door do not invite him there to conduct a search. 4

The State points to our decisions holding that the subjective intent of the officer is irrelevant. See Ashcroft v. al-Kidd, 563 U. S. ___ (2011); Whren v. United States, 517 U. S. 806 (1996) . But those cases merely hold that a stop or search that is objectively reasonable is not vitiated by the fact that the officer's real reason for making the stop or search has nothing to do with the validating reason. Thus, the defendant will not be heard to complain that although he was speeding the officer's real reason for the stop was racial harassment. See id., at 810, 813. Here, however, the question before the court is precisely whether the officer's conduct was an objectively reasonable search. As we have described, that depends upon whether the officers had an implied license to enter the porch, which in turn depends upon the purpose for which they entered. Here, their behavior objectively reveals a purpose to conduct a search, which is not what anyone would think he had license to do.

III

The State argues that investigation by a forensic narcotics dog by definition cannot implicate any legitimate privacy interest. The State cites for authority our decisions in United States v. Place, 462 U. S. 696 (1983), United States v. Jacobsen, 466 U. S. 109 (1984), and Illinois v. Caballes, 543 U. S. 405 (2005), which held, respectively, that canine inspection of luggage in an airport, chemical testing of a substance that had fallen from a parcel in transit, and canine inspection of an automobile during a lawful traffic stop, do not violate the "reasonable expectation of privacy" described in Katz.

Just last Term, we considered an argument much like this. Jones held that tracking an automobile's where-abouts using a physically-mounted GPS receiver is a Fourth Amendment search. The Government argued that the Katz standard "show[ed] that no search occurred," as the defendant had "no 'reasonable expectation of privacy' " in his whereabouts on the public roads, Jones, 565 U. S., at ___ (slip op., at 5)—a proposition with at least as much support in our case law as the one the State marshals here. See, e.g., United States v. Knotts, 460 U. S. 276, 278 (1983) . But because the GPS receiver had been physically mounted on the defendant's automobile (thus intruding on his "effects"), we held that tracking the vehicle's movements was a search: a person's " Fourth Amendment rights do not rise or fall with the Katz formulation." Jones, supra, at ___ (slip op., at 5). The Katz reasonable-expectations test "has been added to, not substitutedfor," the traditional property-based understanding of the Fourth Amendment, and so is unnecessary to consider when the government gains evidence by physically intruding on constitutionally protected areas. Jones, supra, at ___ (slip op., at 8).

Thus, we need not decide whether the officers' investigation of Jardines' home violated his expectation of privacy under Katz. One virtue of the Fourth Amendment'sproperty-rights baseline is that it keeps easy cases easy. That the officers learned what they learned only by physically intruding on Jardines' property to gather evidence is enough to establish that a search occurred.

For a related reason we find irrelevant the State's argument (echoed by the dissent) that forensic dogs have been commonly used by police for centuries. This argument is apparently directed to our holding in Kyllo v. United States, 533 U. S. 27 (2001), that surveillance of the home is a search where "the Government uses a device that is not in general public use" to "explore details of the home that would previously have been unknowable without physical intrusion." Id., at 40 (emphasis added). But the implication of that statement (*inclusio unius est exclusio alterius*) is that when the government uses a physical intrusion to explore details of the home (including its curtilage), the antiquity of the tools that they bring along is irrelevant.

* * *

The government's use of trained police dogs to investigate the home and its immediate surroundings is a "search" within the meaning of the Fourth Amendment. The judgment of the Supreme Court of Florida is therefore affirmed.

It is so ordered.

Notes to Florida v. Jardines (March 26, 2013)

1 At oral argument, the State and its amicus the Solicitor General argued that Jardines conceded in the lower courts that the officers had a right to be where they were. This misstates the record. Jardines conceded nothing more than the unsurprising proposition that the officers could have lawfully approached his home to knock on the front door in hopes of speaking with him. Of course, that is not what they did.

2 With this much, the dissent seems to agree—it would inquire into " 'the appearance of things,' " post, at 5 (opinion of Alito, J.), what is "typica[l]" for a visitor, ibid., what might cause "alarm" to a "resident of the premises," ibid., what is "expected" of "ordinary visitors," ibid., and what would be expected from a " 'reasonably respectful citizen,' " post, at 7. These are good questions. But their answers are incompatible with the dissent's outcome, which is presumably why the dissent does not even try to argue that it would be customary, usual, reasonable, respectful, ordinary, typical, nonalarming, etc., for a stranger to explore the curtilage of the home with trained drug dogs.

3 The dissent insists that our argument must rest upon "the particular instrument that Detective Bartelt used to detect the odor of marijuana"—the dog. Post, at 8. It is not the dog that is the problem, but the behavior that here involved use of the dog. We think a typical person would find it " 'a cause for great alarm' " (the kind of reaction the dis-sent quite rightly relies upon to justify its no-night-visits rule, post,at 5) to find a stranger snooping about his front porch with or without a dog. The dissent would let the police do whatever they want by way of gathering evidence so long as they stay on the base-path, to use a baseball analogy—so long as they "stick to the path that is typically used to approach a front door, such as a paved walkway." Ibid. From that vantage point they can presumably peer into the house through binoculars with impunity. That is not the law, as even the State con-cedes. See Tr. of Oral Arg. 6.

4 The dissent argues, citing King, that "gathering evidence—even damning evidence—is a lawful activity that falls within the scope of the license to approach." Post,

at 7. That is a false generalization. What King establishes is that it is not a Fourth Amendment search to approach the home in order to speak with the occupant, because all are invited to do that. The mere "purpose of discovering information," post, at 8, in the course of engaging in that permitted conduct does not cause it to violate the Fourth Amendment. But no one is impliedly invited to enter the protected premises of the home in order to do nothing but conduct a search.

The Government violates the Due Process Clause when it takes away someone's life, liberty, or property under a criminal law so vague that it fails to give ordinary people fair notice of the conduct it punishes, or so standardless that it invites arbitrary enforcement: Johnson v. United States (June 26, 2015)

Justice Scalia delivered the opinion of the Court.

Under the Armed Career Criminal Act of 1984, a defendant convicted of being a felon in possession of a firearm faces more severe punishment if he has three or more previous convictions for a "violent felony," a term defined to include any felony that "involves conduct that presents a serious potential risk of physical injury to another." 18 U. S. C. §924(e)(2)(B). We must decide whether this part of the definition of a violent felony survives the Constitution's prohibition of vague criminal laws.

I

Federal law forbids certain people—such as convicted felons, persons committed to mental institutions, and drug users—to ship, possess, and receive firearms. §922(g). In general, the law punishes violation of this ban by up to 10 years' imprisonment. §924(a)(2). But if the violator has three or more earlier convictions for a "serious drug offense" or a "violent felony," the Armed Career Criminal Act increases his prison term to a minimum of 15 years and a maximum of life. §924(e)(1); Johnson v. United States, 559 U. S. 133, 136 (2010) . The Act defines "violent felony" as follows:

"any crime punishable by imprisonment for a term exceeding one year . . . that—
"(i) has as an element the use, attempted use, or threatened use of physical force against the person of another; or
"(ii) is burglary, arson, or extortion, involves use of explosives, or *otherwise involves conduct that presents a serious potential risk of physical injury to another.*" §924(e)(2)(B) (emphasis added).

The closing words of this definition, italicized above, have come to be known as the Act's residual clause. Since 2007, this Court has decided four cases attempting to discern its meaning. We have held that the residual clause (1) covers Florida's offense of attempted burglary, James v. United States, 550 U. S. 192 (2007); (2) does not cover New Mexico's offense of driving under the influence, Begay v. United States, 553 U. S. 137 (2008); (3) does not cover Illinois' offense of failure to report to a penal institution,

Chambers v. United States, 555 U. S. 122 (2009); and (4) does cover Indiana's offense of vehicular flight from a law-enforcement officer, Sykes v. United States, 564 U. S. 1 (2011). In both James and Sykes, the Court rejected suggestions by dissenting Justices that the residual clause violates the Constitution's prohibition of vague criminal laws. Compare James, 550 U. S., at 210, n. 6, with id., at 230 (Scalia, J., dissenting); compare Sykes, 564 U. S., at ___ (slip op., at 13–14), with id., at ___ (Scalia, J., dissenting) (slip op., at 6–8).

This case involves the application of the residual clause to another crime, Minnesota's offense of unlawful possession of a short-barreled shotgun. Petitioner Samuel Johnson is a felon with a long criminal record. In 2010, the Federal Bureau of Investigation began to monitor him because of his involvement in a white-supremacist organization that the Bureau suspected was planning to commit acts of terrorism. During the investigation, Johnson disclosed to undercover agents that he had manufactured explosives and that he planned to attack "the Mexican consulate" in Minnesota, "progressive bookstores," and " 'liberals.' " Revised Presentence Investigation in No. 0:12CR00104–001 (D. Minn.), p. 15, ¶16. Johnson showed the agents his AK–47 rifle, several semiautomatic firearms, and over 1,000 rounds of ammunition.

After his eventual arrest, Johnson pleaded guilty to being a felon in possession of a firearm in violation of §922(g). The Government requested an enhanced sentence under the Armed Career Criminal Act. It argued that three of Johnson's previous offenses— including unlawful possession of a short-barreled shotgun, see Minn. Stat. §609.67 (2006)—qualified as violent felonies. The District Court agreed and sentenced Johnson to a 15-year prison term under the Act. The Court of Appeals affirmed. 526 Fed. Appx. 708 (CA8 2013) (per curiam). We granted certiorari to decide whether Minnesota's offense of unlawful possession of a short-barreled shotgun ranks as a violent felony under the residual clause. 572 U. S. ___ (2014). We later asked the parties to present reargument addressing the compatibility of the residual clause with the Constitution's prohibition of vague criminal laws. 574 U. S. ___ (2015).

II

The Fifth Amendment provides that "[n]o person shall . . . be deprived of life, liberty, or property, without due process of law." Our cases establish that the Government violates this guarantee by taking away someone's life, liberty, or property under a criminal law so vague that it fails to give ordinary people fair notice of the conduct it punishes, or so standardless that it invites arbitrary enforcement. Kolender v. Lawson, 461 U. S. 352–358 (1983). The prohibition of vagueness in criminal statutes "is a well-recognized requirement, consonant alike with ordinary notions of fair play and the settled rules of law," and a statute that flouts it "violates the first essential of due process." Connally v. General Constr. Co., 269 U. S. 385, 391 (1926). These principles apply not only to statutes defining elements of crimes, but also to statutes fixing sentences. United States v. Batchelder, 442 U. S. 114, 123 (1979).

In Taylor v. United States, 495 U. S. 575, 600 (1990), this Court held that the Armed Career Criminal Act requires courts to use a framework known as the categorical approach when deciding whether an offense "is burglary, arson, or extortion, involves use of explosives, or otherwise involves conduct that presents a serious potential risk of physical injury to another." Under the categorical approach, a court assesses whether a crime qualifies as a violent felony "in terms of how the law defines the offense and not in terms of how an individual offender might have committed it on a particular occasion." Begay, supra, at 141.

Deciding whether the residual clause covers a crime thus requires a court to picture the kind of conduct that the crime involves in "the ordinary case," and to judge whether that abstraction presents a serious potential risk of physical injury. James, supra, at 208. The court's task goes beyond deciding whether creation of risk is an element of the crime. That is so because, unlike the part of the definition of a violent felony that asks whether the crime "has as an element the use . . . of physical force," the residual clause asks whether the crime "involves conduct" that presents too much risk of physical injury. What is more, the inclusion of burglary and extortion among the enumerated offenses preceding the residual clause confirms that the court's task also goes beyond evaluating the chances that the physical acts that make up the crime will injure someone. The act of making an extortionate demand or breaking and entering into someone's homedoes not, in and of itself, normally cause physical injury. Rather, risk of injury arises because the extortionist might engage in violence after making his demand or because the burglar might confront a resident in the home after breaking and entering.

We are convinced that the indeterminacy of the wide-ranging inquiry required by the residual clause both denies fair notice to defendants and invites arbitrary enforcement by judges. Increasing a defendant's sentence under the clause denies due process of law.

A

Two features of the residual clause conspire to make it unconstitutionally vague. In the first place, the residual clause leaves grave uncertainty about how to estimate the risk posed by a crime. It ties the judicial assessment of risk to a judicially imagined "ordinary case" of a crime, not to real-world facts or statutory elements. How does one go about deciding what kind of conduct the "ordinary case" of a crime involves? "A statistical analysis of the state reporter? A survey? Expert evidence? Google? Gut instinct?" United States v. Mayer, 560 F. 3d 948, 952 (CA9 2009) (Kozinski, C. J., dissenting from denial of rehearing en banc). To take an example, does the ordinary instance of witness tampering involve offering a witness a bribe? Or threatening a witness with violence? Critically, picturing the criminal's behavior is not enough; as we have already discussed, assessing "potential risk" seemingly requires the judge to imagine how the idealized ordinary case of the crime subsequently plays out. James illustrates how speculative (and how detached from statutory elements) this enterprise can become. Explaining why attempted burglary poses a serious potential risk of physical injury, the Court said: "An armed would-be burglar may be spotted by a police officer, a private security guard, or a participant in a neighborhood watch program. Or a homeowner . . . may give chase, and a violent encounter may ensue." 550 U. S., at 211. The dissent, by contrast, asserted that any confrontation that occurs during an attempted burglary "is likely to consist of nothing more than the occupant's yelling 'Who's there?' from his window, and the burglar's running away." Id., at 226 (opinion of Scalia, J.). The residual clause offers no reliable way to choose between these competing accounts of what "ordinary" attempted burglary involves.

At the same time, the residual clause leaves uncertainty about how much risk it takes for a crime to qualify as a violent felony. It is one thing to apply an imprecise "serious potential risk" standard to real-world facts; it is quite another to apply it to a judge-imagined abstraction. By asking whether the crime "otherwise involves conduct that presents a serious potential risk," moreover, the residual clause forces courts to interpret "serious potential risk" in light of the four enumerated crimes—burglary, arson, extortion, and crimes involving the use of explosives. These offenses are "far from clear in respect to the degree of risk each poses." Begay, 553 U. S., at 143. Does the ordinary burglar invade an occupied home by night or an unoccupied home by day? Does the typical extortionist threaten his victim in person with the use of force, or does he threaten his victim by mail with the revelation of embarrassing personal information? By combining indeterminacy about how to measure the risk posed by a crime with indeterminacy about how much risk it takes for the crime to qualify as a violent felony, the residual clause produces more unpredictability and arbitrariness than the Due Process Clause tolerates.

This Court has acknowledged that the failure of "persistent efforts . . . to establish a standard" can provide evidence of vagueness. United States v. L. Cohen Grocery Co., 255 U. S. 81, 91 (1921) . Here, this Court's repeated attempts and repeated failures to craft a principled and objective standard out of the residual clause confirm its hopeless indeterminacy. Three of the Court's previous four decisions about the clause concentrated on the level of risk posed by the crime in question, though in each case we found it necessary to resort to a different ad hoc test to guide our inquiry. In James, we asked whether "the risk posed by attempted burglary is comparable to that posed by its closest analog among the enumerated offenses," namely completed burglary; we concluded that it was. 550 U. S., at 203. That rule takes care of attempted burglary, but offers no help at all with respect to the vast majority of offenses, which have no apparent analog among the enumerated crimes. "Is, for example, driving under the influence of alcohol more analogous to burglary, arson, extortion, or a crime involving use of explosives?" Id., at 215 (Scalia, J., dissenting).

Chambers, our next case to focus on risk, relied principally on a statistical report prepared by the Sentencing Commission to conclude that an offender who fails to report to prison is not "significantly more likely than others to attack, or physically to resist, an apprehender, thereby producing a 'serious potential risk of physical injury.' " 555 U. S., at 128–129. So much for failure to report to prison, but what about the tens of thousands of federal and state crimes for which no comparable reports exist? And even those studies that are available might suffer from methodological flaws, be skewed toward rarer forms of the crime, or paint widely divergent pictures of the riskiness of the conduct that the crime involves. See Sykes, 564 U. S., at ___–___ (Scalia, J., dissenting) (slip op., at 4–6); id., at ___, n. 4 (Kagan, J., dissenting) (slip op., at 6, n. 4).

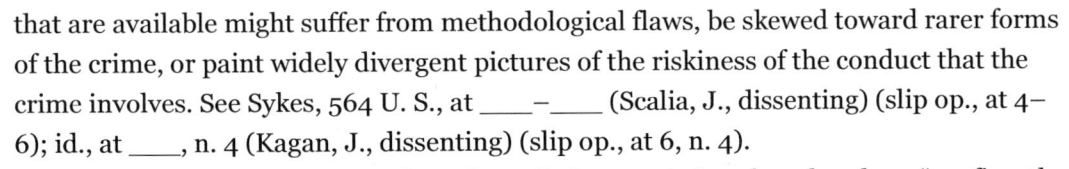

Our most recent case, Sykes, also relied on statistics, though only to "confirm the commonsense conclusion that Indiana's vehicular flight crime is a violent felony." Id., at ___ (majority opinion) (slip op., at 8). But common sense is a much less useful criterion than it sounds—as Sykes itself illustrates. The Indiana statute involved in that case covered everything from provoking a high-speed car chase to merely failing to stop immediately after seeing a police officer's signal. See id., at ___ (Kagan, J., dissenting) (slip op., at 3–4). How does common sense help a federal court discern where the "ordinary case" of vehicular flight in Indiana lies along this spectrum? Common sense has not even produced a consistent conception of the degree of risk posed by each of the four enumerated crimes; there is no reason to expect it to fare any better with respect to thousands of unenumerated crimes. All in all, James, Chambers, and Sykes failed to establish any generally applicable test that prevents the risk comparison required by the residual clause from devolving into guesswork and intuition.

The remaining case, Begay, which preceded Chambers and Sykes, took an entirely different approach. The Court held that in order to qualify as a violent felony under the residual clause, a crime must resemble the enumerated offenses "in kind as well as in degree of risk posed." 553 U. S., at 143. The Court deemed drunk driving insufficiently similar to the listed crimes, because it typically does not involve "purposeful, violent, and aggressive conduct." Id., at 144–145 (internal quotation marks omitted). Alas, Begay did not succeed in bringing clarity to the meaning of the residual clause. It did not (and could not) eliminate the need to imagine the kind of conduct typically involved in a crime. In addition, the enumerated crimes are not much more similar to one another in kind than in degree of risk posed, and the concept of "aggressive conduct" is far from clear. Sykes criticized the "purposeful, violent, and aggressive" test as an "addition to the statutory text," explained that "levels of risk" would normally be dispositive, and confined Begay to "strict liability, negligence, and recklessness crimes." 564 U. S., at ___–___ (slip op., at 10–11).

The present case, our fifth about the meaning of the residual clause, opens a new front of uncertainty. When deciding whether unlawful possession of a short-barreled shotgun is a violent felony, do we confine our attention to the risk that the shotgun will go off by accident while in someone's possession? Or do we also consider the possibility that the person possessing the shotgun will later use it to commit a crime? The inclusion of burglary and extortion among the enumerated offenses suggests that a crime may qualify under the residual clause even if the physical injury is remote from the criminal act. But how remote is too remote? Once again, the residual clause yields no answers.

This Court is not the only one that has had trouble making sense of the residual clause. The clause has "created numerous splits among the lower federal courts," where it has proved "nearly impossible to apply consistently." Chambers, 555 U. S., at 133 (Alito, J., concurring in judgment). The most telling feature of the lower courts' decisions is not division about whether the residual clause covers this or that crime (even clear laws produce close cases); it is, rather, pervasive disagreement about the nature of the inquiry one is supposed to conduct and the kinds of factors one is supposed to consider. Some judges have concluded that deciding whether conspiracy is a violent felony requires evaluating only the dangers posed by the "simple act of agreeing [to commit a crime]," United States v. Whitson, 597 F. 3d 1218, 1222 (CA11 2010) (per curiam); others have also considered the probability that the agreement will be carried out, United States v. White, 571 F. 3d 365, 370–371 (CA4 2009). Some judges have assumed that the battery of a police officer (defined to include the slightest touching) could "explode into violence and result in physical injury," United States v. Williams, 559 F. 3d 1143, 1149 (CA10 2009); others have felt that it "do[es] a great disservice to law enforcement officers" to assume that they would "explod[e] into violence" rather than "rely on their training and experience to determine the best method of responding," United States v. Carthorne, 726 F. 3d 503, 514 (CA4 2013). Some judges considering whether statutory rape qualifies as a violent felony have concentrated on cases involving a perpetrator much older than the victim, United States v. Daye, 571 F. 3d 225, 230–231 (CA2 2009); others have tried to account for the possibility that "the perpetrator and the victim [might be] close in age," United States v. McDonald, 592 F. 3d 808, 815 (CA7 2010). Disagreements like these go well beyond disputes over matters of degree.

It has been said that the life of the law is experience. Nine years' experience trying to derive meaning from the residual clause convinces us that we have embarked upon a failed enterprise. Each of the uncertainties in the residual clause may be tolerable in isolation, but "their sum makes a task for us which at best could be only guesswork." United States v. Evans, 333 U. S. 483, 495 (1948) . Invoking so shapeless a provision to condemn someone to prison for 15 years to life does not comport with the Constitution's guarantee of due process.

B

The Government and the dissent claim that there will be straightforward cases under the residual clause, because some crimes clearly pose a serious potential risk of physical injury to another. See post, at 14–15 (opinion of Alito, J.). True enough, though we think many of the cases the Government and the dissent deem easy turn out not to be so easy after all. Consider just one of the Government's examples, Connecticut's offense of "rioting at a correctional institution." See United States v. Johnson, 616 F. 3d 85 (CA2 2010). That certainly sounds like a violent felony—until one realizes that Connecticut defines this offense to include taking part in "any disorder, disturbance, strike, riot or other organized disobedience to the rules and regulations" of the prison. Conn. Gen. Stat. §53a–179b(a) (2012). Who is to say which the ordinary "disorder" most closely resembles—a full-fledged prison riot, a food-fight in the prison cafeteria, or a "passive and nonviolent [act] such as disregarding an order to move," Johnson, 616 F. 3d, at 95 (Parker, J., dissenting)?

In all events, although statements in some of our opinions could be read to suggest otherwise, our holdings squarely contradict the theory that a vague provision is constitutional merely because there is some conduct that clearly falls within the provision's grasp. For instance, we have deemed a law prohibiting grocers from charging an "unjust or unreasonable rate" void for vagueness—even though charging someone a thousand dollars for a pound of sugar would surely be unjust and unreasonable. L. Cohen Grocery Co., 255 U. S., at 89. We have similarly deemed void for vagueness a law prohibiting people on sidewalks from "conduct[ing] themselves in a manner annoying to persons passing by"—even though spitting in someone's face would surely be annoying. Coates v. Cincinnati, 402 U. S. 611 (1971) . These decisions refute any suggestion that the existence of some obviously risky crimes establishes the residual clause's constitutionality.

Resisting the force of these decisions, the dissent insists that "a statute is void for vagueness only if it is vague in all its applications." Post, at 1. It claims that the prohibition of unjust or unreasonable rates in L. Cohen Grocery was "vague in all applications," even though one can easily envision rates so high that they are unreasonable by any measure. Post, at 16. It seems to us that the dissent's supposed requirement of vagueness in all applications is not a requirement at all, but a tautology: If we hold a statute to be vague, it is vague in all its applications (and never mind the reality). If the existence of some clearly unreasonable rates would not save the law in L. Cohen Grocery, why should the existence of some clearly risky crimes save the residual clause?

The Government and the dissent next point out that dozens of federal and state criminal laws use terms like "substantial risk," "grave risk," and "unreasonable risk," suggesting that to hold the residual clause unconstitutional is to place these provisions in constitutional doubt. See post, at 7–8. Not at all. Almost none of the cited laws links a phrase such as "substantial risk" to a confusing list of examples. "The phrase 'shades of red,' standing alone, does not generate confusion or unpredictability; but the phrase 'fire-engine red, light pink, maroon, navy blue, or colors that otherwise involve shades of red' assuredly does so." James, 550 U. S., at 230, n. 7 (Scalia, J., dissenting). More importantly, almost all of the cited laws require gauging the riskiness of conduct in which an individual defendant engages on a particular occasion. As a general matter, we do not doubt the constitutionality of laws that call for the application of a qualitative standard such as "substantial risk" to real-world conduct; "the law is full of instances where a man's fate depends on his estimating rightly . . . some matter of degree," Nash v. United States, 229 U. S. 373, 377 (1913) . The residual clause, however, requires application of the "serious potential risk" standard to an idealized ordinary case of the crime. Because "the elements necessary to determine the imaginary ideal are uncertain both in nature and degree of effect," this abstract inquiry offers significantly less predictability than one "[t]hat deals with the actual, not with an imaginary condition other than the facts." International Harvester Co. of America v. Kentucky, 234 U. S. 216, 223 (1914) .

Finally, the dissent urges us to save the residual clause from vagueness by interpreting it to refer to the risk posed by the particular conduct in which the defendant engaged, not the risk posed by the ordinary case of the defendant's crime. See post, at 9–13. In other words, the dissent suggests that we jettison for the residual clause (though not for the enumerated crimes) the categorical approach adopted in Taylor, see 495 U. S., at 599–602, and reaffirmed in each of our four residual-clause cases, see James, 550 U. S., at 202; Begay, 553 U. S., at 141; Chambers, 555 U. S., at 125; Sykes, 564 U. S., ___ (slip op., at 5). We decline the dissent's invitation. In the first place, the Government has not asked us to abandon the categorical approach in residual-clause cases. In addition, Taylor had good reasons to adopt the categorical approach, reasons that apply no less to the residual clause than to the enumerated crimes. Taylor explained that the relevant part of the Armed Career Criminal Act "refers to 'a person who . . . has three previous convictions' for—not a person who has committed—three previous violent felonies or drug offenses." 495 U. S., at 600. This emphasis on convictions indicates that "Congress intended the sentencing court to look only to the fact that the defendant had been convicted of crimes falling within certain categories, and not to the facts underlying the prior convictions." Ibid. Taylor also pointed out the utter impracticability of requiring a sentencing court to reconstruct, long after the original conviction, the conduct underlying that conviction. For example, if the original conviction rested on a guilty plea, no record of the underlying facts may be available. "[T]he only plausible interpretation" of the law, therefore, requires use of the categorical approach. Id., at 602.

C

That brings us to stare decisis. This is the first case in which the Court has received briefing and heard argument from the parties about whether the residual clause is void for vagueness. In James, however, the Court stated in a footnote that it was "not persuaded by [the principal dissent's] suggestion . . . that the residual provision is unconstitutionally vague." 550 U. S., at 210, n. 6. In Sykes, the Court again rejected a dissenting opinion's claim of vagueness. 564 U. S., at ___–___ (slip op., at 13–14).

The doctrine of stare decisis allows us to revisit an earlier decision where experience with its application reveals that it is unworkable. Payne v. Tennessee, 501 U. S. 808, 827 (1991). Experience is all the more instructive when the decision in question rejected a claim of unconstitutional vagueness. Unlike other judicial mistakes that need correction, the error of having rejected a vagueness challenge manifests itself precisely in subsequent judicial decisions: the inability of later opinions to impart the predictability that the earlier opinion forecast. Here, the experience of the federal courts leaves no doubt about the unavoidable uncertainty and arbitrariness of adjudication under the residual clause. Even after Sykes tried to clarify the residual clause's meaning, the provision remains a "judicial morass that defies systemic solution," "a black hole of confusion and uncertainty" that frustrates any effort to impart "some sense of order and direction." United States v. Vann, 660 F. 3d 771, 787 (CA4 2011) (Agee, J., concurring).

This Court's cases make plain that even decisions rendered after full adversarial presentation may have to yield to the lessons of subsequent experience. See, e.g., United States v. Dixon, 509 U. S. 688, 711 (1993); Payne, 501 U. S., at 828–830 (1991). But James and Sykes opined about vagueness without full briefing or argument on that issue—a circumstance that leaves us "less constrained to follow precedent," Hohn v. United States, 524 U. S. 236, 251 (1998). The brief discussions of vagueness in James and Sykes homed in on the imprecision of the phrase "serious potential risk"; neither opinion evaluated the uncertainty introduced by the need to evaluate the riskiness of an abstract ordinary case of a crime. 550 U. S., at 210, n. 6; 564 U. S., at ___ (slip op., at 13–14). And departing from those decisions does not raise any concerns about upsetting private reliance interests.

Although it is a vital rule of judicial self-government, stare decisis does not matter for its own sake. It matters because it "promotes the evenhanded, predictable, and consistent development of legal principles." Payne, supra, at 827. Decisions under the residual clause have proved to be anything but evenhanded, predictable, or consistent. Standing by James and Sykes would undermine, rather than promote, the goals that stare decisis is meant to serve.

* * *

We hold that imposing an increased sentence under the residual clause of the Armed Career Criminal Act violates the Constitution's guarantee of due process. Our contrary holdings in James and Sykes are overruled. Today's decision does not call into question application of the Act to the four enumerated offenses, or the remainder of the Act's definition of a violent felony.

We reverse the judgment of the Court of Appeals for the Eighth Circuit and remand the case for further proceedings consistent with this opinion.

It is so ordered.

Justice Scalia Concurrences and Dissents

"Secular purpose" requirement to be constitutional is impossible to prove, or disprove, and should end: Justice Scalia's dissent in Edwards v. Aguillard (June 19, 1987)

JUSTICE SCALIA, with whom THE CHIEF JUSTICE joins, dissenting.

Even if I agreed with the questionable premise that legislation can be invalidated under the Establishment Clause on the basis of its motivation alone, without regard to its effects, I would still find no justification for today's decision. The Louisiana legislators who passed the "Balanced Treatment for Creation-Science and Evolution-Science Act" (Balanced Treatment Act), La.Rev.Stat.Ann. §§ 17:286.1-17:286.7 (West 1982), each of whom had sworn to support the Constitution, [n1] were well aware of the potential Establishment Clause problems, and considered that aspect of the legislation with great care. After seven hearings and several months of study, resulting in substantial revision of the original proposal, they approved the Act overwhelmingly, and specifically articulated the secular purpose they meant it to serve. Although the record contains abundant evidence of the sincerity of that purpose (the only issue pertinent to this case), the Court today holds, essentially on the basis of "its visceral knowledge regarding what must have motivated the legislators," 778 F.2d 225, 227 (CA5 1985) (Gee, J., dissenting) (emphasis added), that the members of the Louisiana Legislature knowingly violated their oaths and then lied about it. I dissent. Had requirements of the Balanced Treatment Act that are not apparent on its face been clarified by an interpretation of the Louisiana Supreme Court, or by the manner of its implementation, the Act might well be found unconstitutional; but the question of its constitutionality cannot rightly be disposed of on the gallop, by impugning the motives of its supporters.

I

This case arrives here in the following posture: the Louisiana Supreme Court has never been given an opportunity to interpret the Balanced Treatment Act, State officials have never attempted to implement it, and it has never been the subject of a full evidentiary hearing. We can only guess at its meaning. We know that it forbids instruction in either "creation science" or "evolution science" without instruction in the other, § 17:286.4A, but the parties are sharply divided over what creation science consists of. Appellants insist that it is a collection of educationally valuable scientific data that has been censored from classrooms by an embarrassed scientific establishment. Appellees insist it is not science at all, but thinly veiled religious doctrine. Both interpretations of the intended meaning of that phrase find considerable support in the legislative history.

At least at this stage in the litigation, it is plain to me that we must accept appellants' view of what the statute means. To begin with, the statute itself defines "creation science" as "the scientific evidences for creation and inferences from those scientific evidences." § 17:286.3(2) (emphasis added). If, however, that definition is not thought sufficiently helpful, the means by which the Louisiana Supreme Court will give the term more precise content is quite clear -- and again, at this stage in the litigation, favors the appellants' view. "Creation science" is unquestionably a "term of art," see Brief for 72 Nobel Laureates et al. as Amici Curiae 20, and thus, under Louisiana law, is "to be interpreted according to [its] received meaning and acceptation with the learned in the art, trade or profession to which [it] refer[s]." La.Civ.Code Ann., Art. 15 (West 1952). [n2] The only evidence in the record of the "received meaning and acceptation" of "creation science" is found in five affidavits filed by appellants. In those affidavits, two scientists, a philosopher, a theologian, and an educator, all of whom claim extensive knowledge of creation science, swear that it is essentially a collection of scientific data supporting the theory that the physical universe and life within it appeared suddenly, and have not changed substantially since appearing. See App. to Juris. Statement A-19 (Kenyon); id. at A-36 (Morrow); id. at A-41 (Miethe). These experts insist that creation science is a strictly scientific concept that can be presented without religious reference. See id. at A-19 - A-20, A-35 (Kenyon); id. at A-36 - A-38 (Morrow); id. at A-40, A-41, A-43 (Miethe); id. at A-47, A-48 (Most); id. at A-49 (Clinkert). At this point, then, we must assume that the Balanced Treatment Act does not require the presentation of religious doctrine.

Nothing in today's opinion is plainly to the contrary, but what the statute means and what it requires are of rather little concern to the Court. Like the Court of Appeals, 765 F.2d 1251, 1253, 1254 (CA5 1985), the Court finds it necessary to consider only the motives of the legislators who supported the Balanced Treatment Act, ante at 482 U.S. 586"]586, 593-594, 596. After examining the statute, its legislative history, and its historical and social context, the Court holds that the Louisiana Legislature acted without "a secular legislative purpose," and that the Act therefore fails the "purpose" prong of the three-part test set forth in 586, 593-594, 596. After examining the statute, its legislative history, and its historical and social context, the Court holds that the Louisiana Legislature acted without "a secular legislative purpose," and that the Act therefore fails the "purpose" prong of the three-part test set forth in Lemon v. Kurtzman, 403 U.S. 602, 612 (1971). As I explain below, infra at 636-640, I doubt whether that "purpose" requirement of Lemon is a proper interpretation of the Constitution; but even if it were, I could not agree with the Court's assessment that the requirement was not satisfied here.

This Court has said little about the first component of the Lemon test. Almost invariably, we have effortlessly discovered a secular purpose for measures challenged under the Establishment Clause, typically devoting no more than a sentence or two to the matter. See, e.g., Witters v. Washington Dept. of Services for Blind, 474 U.S. 481, 485-486 (1986); Grand Rapids School District v. Ball, 473 U.S. 373, 383 (1985); Mueller v. Allen, 463 U.S. 388, 394-395 (1983); Larkin v. Grendel's Den, Inc., 459 U.S. 116, 123-124 (1982); Widmar v. Vincent, 454 U.S. 263, 271 (1981); Committee for Public Education & Religious Liberty v. Regan, 444 U.S. 646, 654, 657 (1980); Wolman v. Walter, 433 U.S.

229, 236 (1977) (plurality opinion); Meek v. Pittenger, 421 U.S. 349, 363 (1975); Committee for Public Education & Religious Liberty v. Nyquist, 413 U.S. 756, 773 (1973); Levitt v. Committee for Public Education & Religious Liberty, 413 U.S. 472, 479-480, n. 7 (1973); Tilton v. Richardson, 403 U.S. 672, 678-679 (1971) (plurality opinion); Lemon v. Kurtzman, supra, at 613. In fact, only once before deciding Lemon, and twice since, have we invalidated a law for lack of a secular purpose. See Wallace v. Jaffree, 472 U.S. 38 (1985); Stone v. Graham, 449 U.S. 39 (1980) (per curiam); Epperson v. Arkansas, 393 U.S. 97 (1968).

Nevertheless, a few principles have emerged from our cases, principles which should, but to an unfortunately large extent do not, guide the Court's application of Lemon today. It is clear, first of all, that regardless of what "legislative purpose" may mean in other contexts, for the purpose of the Lemon test, it means the "actual" motives of those responsible for the challenged action. The Court recognizes this, see ante at 585, as it has in the past, see, e.g., Witters v. Washington Dept. of Services for Blind, supra, at 486; Wallace v. Jaffree, supra, at 56. Thus, if those legislators who supported the Balanced Treatment Act in fact acted with a "sincere" secular purpose, ante at 587, the Act survives the first component of the Lemon test, regardless of whether that purpose is likely to be achieved by the provisions they enacted.

Our cases have also confirmed that, when the Lemon Court referred to "a secular . . . purpose," 403 U.S. at 403 U.S. 612"]612, it meant "a secular purpose." The author of Lemon, writing for the Court, has said that invalidation under the purpose prong is appropriate when "there [is] no question that the statute or activity was motivated wholly by religious considerations." 612, it meant "a secular purpose." The author of Lemon, writing for the Court, has said that invalidation under the purpose prong is appropriate when "there [is] no question that the statute or activity was motivated wholly by religious considerations." Lynch v. Donnelly, 465 U.S. 668, 680 (1984) (Burger, C.J.) (emphasis added); see also id. at 681, n. 6; Wallace v. Jaffree, supra, at 56 ("[T]he First Amendment requires that a statute must be invalidated if it is entirely motivated by a purpose to advance religion") (emphasis added; footnote omitted). In all three cases in which we struck down laws under the Establishment Clause for lack of a secular purpose, we found that the legislature's sole motive was to promote religion. See Wallace v. Jaffree, supra, at 56, 57, 60; Stone v. Graham, supra, at 41, 43, n. 5; Epperson v. Arkansas, supra, at 103, 107-108; see also Lynch v. Donnelly, supra, at 680 (describing Stone and Epperson as cases in which we invalidated laws "motivated wholly by religious considerations"). Thus, the majority's invalidation of the Balanced Treatment Act is defensible only if the record indicates that the Louisiana Legislature had no secular purpose.

It is important to stress that the purpose forbidden by Lemon is the purpose to "advance religion." 403 U.S. at 613; accord, ante at 585 ("promote" religion); Witters v. Washington Dept. of Services for Blind, supra, at 486 ("endorse religion"); Wallace v. Jaffree, 472 U.S. at 56 ("advance religion"); ibid. ("endorse . . . religion"); Committee for Public Education & Religious Liberty v. Nyquist, supra, at 788 ("'advancing' . . . religion");

Levitt v. Committee for Public Education & Religious Liberty, supra, at 481 ("advancing religion"); Walz v. Tax Comm'n of New York City, 397 U.S. 664, 674 (1970) ("establishing, sponsoring, or supporting religion"); Board of Education v. Allen, 392 U.S. 236, 243 (1968) ("'advancement or inhibition of religion'") (quoting Abington School Dist. v. Schempp, 374 U.S. 203, 222 (1963)). Our cases in no way imply that the Establishment Clause forbids legislators merely to act upon their religious convictions. We surely would not strike down a law providing money to feed the hungry or shelter the homeless if it could be demonstrated that, but for the religious beliefs of the legislators, the funds would not have been approved. Also, political activism by the religiously motivated is part of our heritage. Notwithstanding the majority's implication to the contrary, ante at 589-591, we do not presume that the sole purpose of a law is to advance religion merely because it was supported strongly by organized religions or by adherents of particular faiths. See Walz v. Tax Comm'n of New York City, supra, at 670; cf. Harris v. McRae, 448 U.S. 297, 319-320 (1980). To do so would deprive religious men and women of their right to participate in the political process. Today's religious activism may give us the Balanced Treatment Act, but yesterday's resulted in the abolition of slavery, and tomorrow's may bring relief for famine victims.

Similarly, we will not presume that a law's purpose is to advance religion merely because it "'happens to coincide or harmonize with the tenets of some or all religions,'" Harris v. McRae, supra, at 319 (quoting McGowan v. Maryland, 366 U.S. 420, 442 (1961)), or because it benefits religion, even substantially. We have, for example, turned back Establishment Clause challenges to restrictions on abortion funding, Harris v. McRae, supra, and to Sunday closing laws, McGowan v. Maryland, supra, despite the fact that both "agre[e] with the dictates of [some] Judaeo-Christian religions," id. at 442.

In many instances, the Congress or state legislatures conclude that the general welfare of society, wholly apart from any religious considerations, demands such regulation.

Ibid. On many past occasions, we have had no difficulty finding a secular purpose for governmental action far more likely to advance religion than the Balanced Treatment Act. See, e.g., Mueller v. Allen, 463 U.S. at 394-395 (tax deduction for expenses of religious education); Wolman v. Walter, 433 U.S. at 236 (plurality opinion) (aid to religious schools); Meek v. Pittenger, 421 U.S. at 363 (same); Committee for Public Education & Religious Liberty v. Nyquist, 413 U.S. at 773 (same); Lemon v. Kurtzman, 403 U.S. at 613 (same); Walz v. Tax Comm'n of New York City, supra, at 672 (tax exemption for church property); Board of Education v. Allen, supra, at 243 (textbook loans to students in religious schools). Thus, the fact that creation science coincides with the beliefs of certain religions, a fact upon which the majority relies heavily, does not itself justify invalidation of the Act.

Finally, our cases indicate that even certain kinds of governmental actions undertaken with the specific intention of improving the position of religion do not "advance religion" as that term is used in Lemon. 403 U.S. at 613. Rather, we have said that, in at least two circumstances, government must act to advance religion, and that, in a third, it may do so.

First, since we have consistently described the Establishment Clause as forbidding not only state action motivated by the desire to advance religion, but also that intended to "disapprove," "inhibit," or evince "hostility" toward religion, see, e.g., ante at 585 ("'disapprove'") (quoting Lynch v. Donnelly, supra, at 690 (O'CONNOR, J., concurring)); Lynch v. Donnelly, supra, at 673 ("hostility"); Committee for Public Education & Religious Liberty v. Nyquist, supra, at 788 ("'inhibi[t]'"); and since we have said that governmental "neutrality" toward religion is the preeminent goal of the First Amendment, see, e.g., Grand Rapids School District v. Ball, 473 U.S. at 382; Roemer v. Maryland Public Works Bd., 426 U.S. 736, 747 (1976) (plurality opinion); Committee for Public Education & Religious Liberty v. Nyquist, supra, at 792-793; a State which discovers that its employees are inhibiting religion must take steps to prevent them from doing so, even though its purpose would clearly be to advance religion. Cf. Walz v. Tax Comm'n of New York City, supra, at 673. Thus, if the Louisiana Legislature sincerely believed that the State's science teachers were being hostile to religion, our cases indicate that it could act to eliminate that hostility without running afoul of Lemon's purpose test.

Second, we have held that intentional governmental advancement of religion is sometimes required by the Free Exercise Clause. For example, in Hobbie v. Unemployment Appeals Comm'n of Fla., 480 U.S. 136 (1987); Thomas v. Review Bd., Indiana Employment Security Div., 450 U.S. 707 (1981); Wisconsin v. Yoder, 406 U.S. 205 (1972); and Sherbert v. Verner, 374 U.S. 398 (1963), we held that, in some circumstances, States must accommodate the beliefs of religious citizens by exempting them from generally applicable regulations. We have not yet come close to reconciling Lemon and our Free Exercise cases, and typically we do not really try. See, e.g., Hobbie v. Unemployment Appeals Comm'n of Fla., supra, at 144-145; Thomas v. Review Bd., Indiana Employment Security Div., supra, at 719-720. It is clear, however, that members of the Louisiana Legislature were not impermissibly motivated for purposes of the Lemon test if they believed that approval of the Balanced Treatment Act was required by the Free Exercise Clause.

We have also held that, in some circumstances, government may act to accommodate religion, even if that action is not required by the First Amendment. See Hobbie v. Unemployment Appeals Comm'n of Fla., supra, at 144-145. It is well established that

[t]he limits of permissible state accommodation to religion are by no means coextensive with the noninterference mandated by the Free Exercise Clause.

Walz v. Tax Comm'n of New York City, supra, at 673; see also Gillette v. United States, 401 U.S. 437, 453 (1971). We have implied that voluntary governmental accommodation of religion is not only permissible, but desirable. See, e.g., ibid. Thus, few would contend that Title VII of the Civil Rights Act of 1964, which both forbids religious discrimination by private sector employers, 78 Stat. 255, 42 U.S.C. § 2000e-2(a)(1), and requires them reasonably to accommodate the religious practices of their employees, § 2000e(j), violates the Establishment Clause, even though its "purpose" is, of course, to advance religion, and even though it is almost certainly not required by the Free Exercise Clause. While we have warned that, at some point, accommodation may devolve into "an unlawful fostering of religion," Hobbie v. Unemployment Appeals Comm'n of Fla., supra, at 145, we have not suggested precisely (or even roughly) where that point might be. It is possible, then, that, even if the sole motive of those voting for the Balanced Treatment Act was to advance religion, and its passage was not actually required, or even believed to be required, by either the Free Exercise or Establishment Clauses, the Act would nonetheless survive scrutiny under Lemon's purpose test.

One final observation about the application of that test: although the Court's opinion gives no hint of it, in the past we have repeatedly affirmed "our reluctance to attribute unconstitutional motives to the States." Mueller v. Allen, supra, at 394; see also Lynch v. Donnelly, 465 U.S. at 699 (BRENNAN, J., dissenting). We "presume that legislatures act in a constitutional manner." Illinois v. Krull, 480 U.S. 340, 351 (1987); see also Clements v. Fashing, 457 U.S. 957, 963 (1982) (plurality opinion); Rostker v. Goldberg, 453 U.S. 57, 64 (1981); McDonald v. Board of Election Comm'rs of Chicago, 394 U.S. 802, 809 (1969). Whenever we are called upon to judge the constitutionality of an act of a state legislature,

we must have "due regard to the fact that this Court is not exercising a primary judgment, but is sitting in judgment upon those who also have taken the oath to observe the Constitution and who have the responsibility for carrying on government."

Rostker v. Goldberg, supra, at 64 (quoting Joint Anti-Fascist Refugee Committee v. McGrath, 341 U.S. 123, 164 (1951) (Frankfurter, J., concurring)). This is particularly true, we have said, where the legislature has specifically considered the question of a law's constitutionality. Ibid.

With the foregoing in mind, I now turn to the purposes underlying adoption of the Balanced Treatment Act.

II

A

We have relatively little information upon which to judge the motives of those who supported the Act. About the only direct evidence is the statute itself and transcripts of the seven committee hearings at which it was considered. Unfortunately, several of those hearings were sparsely attended, and the legislators who were present revealed little about their motives. We have no committee reports, no floor debates, no remarks inserted into the legislative history, no statement from the Governor, and no postenactment statements or testimony from the bill's sponsor or any other legislators. Cf. Wallace v. Jaffree, 472 U.S. at 43, 56-57. Nevertheless, there is ample evidence that the majority is wrong in holding that the Balanced Treatment Act is without secular purpose.

At the outset, it is important to note that the Balanced Treatment Act did not fly through the Louisiana Legislature on wings of fundamentalist religious fervor -- which would be unlikely, in any event, since only a small minority of the State's citizens belong to fundamentalist religious denominations. See B. Quinn, H. Anderson, M. Bradley, P. Goetting, & P. Shriver, Churches and Church Membership in the United States 16 (1982). The Act had its genesis (so to speak) in legislation introduced by Senator Bill Keith in June, 1980. After two hearings before the Senate Committee on Education, Senator Keith asked that his bill be referred to a study commission composed of members of both Houses of the Louisiana Legislature. He expressed hope that the joint committee would give the bill careful consideration and determine whether his arguments were "legitimate." 1 App. E-29 - E-30. The committee met twice during the interim, heard testimony (both for and against the bill) from several witnesses, and received staff reports. Senator Keith introduced his bill again when the legislature reconvened. The Senate Committee on Education held two more hearings, and approved the bill after substantially amending it (in part over Senator Keith's objection). After approval by the full Senate, the bill was referred to the House Committee on Education. That committee conducted a lengthy hearing, adopted further amendments, and sent the bill on to the full House, where it received favorable consideration. The Senate concurred in the House amendments, and, on July 20, 1981, the Governor signed the bill into law.

Senator Keith's statements before the various committees that considered the bill hardly reflect the confidence of a man preaching to the converted. He asked his colleagues to "keep an open mind," and not to be "biased" by misleading characterizations of creation science. Id. at E-33. He also urged them to "look at this subject on its merits, and not on some preconceived idea." Id. at E-34; see also 2 id. at E-491. Senator Keith's reception was not especially warm. Over his strenuous objection, the Senate Committee on Education voted 5-1 to amend his bill to deprive it of any force; as amended, the bill merely gave teachers permission to balance the teaching of creation science or evolution with the other. 1 id. at E-442 - E-461. The House Committee restored the "mandatory" language to the bill by a vote of only 6-5, 2 id. at E-626 - E-627, and both the full House (by vote of 52-35), id. at E-700 - E-706, and full Senate (23-15), id. at E-735 - E-738, had to repel further efforts to gut the bill.

The legislators understood that Senator Keith's bill involved a "unique" subject, 1 id. at E-106 (Rep. M. Thompson), and they were repeatedly made aware of its potential constitutional problems, see, e.g., id. at E-26 - E-28 (McGehee); id. at E-38 - E-39 (Sen. Keith); id. at E-241 - E-242 (Rossman); id. at E-257 (Probst); id. at E-261 (Beck); id. at E-282 (Sen. Keith). Although the Establishment Clause, including its secular purpose requirement, was of substantial concern to the legislators, they eventually voted overwhelmingly in favor of the Balanced Treatment Act: the House approved it 71-19 (with 15 members absent), 2 id. at E-716 - E-722; the Senate 26-12 (with all members present), id. at E-741 - E-744. The legislators specifically designated the protection of "academic freedom" as the purpose of the Act. La.Rev.Stat.Ann. § 17:286.2 (West 1982).

We cannot accurately assess whether this purpose is a "sham," ante at 587, until we first examine the evidence presented to the legislature far more carefully than the Court has done.

Before summarizing the testimony of Senator Keith and his supporters, I wish to make clear that I by no means intend to endorse its accuracy. But my views (and the views of this Court) about creation science and evolution are (or should be) beside the point. Our task is not to judge the debate about teaching the origins of life, but to ascertain what the members of the Louisiana Legislature believed. The vast majority of them voted to approve a bill which explicitly stated a secular purpose; what is crucial is not their wisdom in believing that purpose would be achieved by the bill, but their sincerity in believing it would be.

Most of the testimony in support of Senator Keith's bill came from the Senator himself, and from scientists and educators he presented, many of whom enjoyed academic credentials that may have been regarded as quite impressive by members of the Louisiana Legislature. To a substantial extent, their testimony was devoted to lengthy, and, to the layman, seemingly expert, scientific expositions on the origin of life. See, e.g., 1 App. E-11 - E-18 (Sunderland); id. at E-50 - E-60 (Boudreaux); id. at E-86 - E-89 (Ward); id. at E-130 - E-153 (Boudreaux paper); id. at E-321 - E-326 (Boudreaux); id. at E-423 - E-428 (Sen. Keith). These scientific lectures touched upon, inter alia, biology, paleontology, genetics, astronomy, astrophysics, probability analysis, and biochemistry. The witnesses repeatedly assured committee members that "hundreds and hundreds" of highly respected, internationally renowned scientists believed in creation science, and would support their testimony. See, e.g., id. at E-5 (Sunderland); id. at E-76 (Sen. Keith); id. at E-100 - E-101 (Reiboldt); id. at E-327 - E-328 (Boudreaux); 2 id. at E-503 - E-504 (Boudreaux).

Senator Keith and his witnesses testified essentially as set forth in the following numbered paragraphs:

(1) There are two and only two scientific explanations for the beginning of life [n3] -- evolution and creation science. 1 id. at E-6 (Sunderland); id. at E-34 (Sen. Keith); id. at E-280 (Sen. Keith); id. at E-417 - E-418 (Sen. Keith). Both are bona fide "sciences." Id. at E-6 - E-7 (Sunderland); id. at E-12 (Sunderland); id. at E-416 (Sen. Keith); id. at E-427 (Sen. Keith); 2 id. at E-491 - E-492 (Sen. Keith); id. at E-497 - E-498 (Sen. Keith). Both posit a theory of the origin of life, and subject that theory to empirical testing. Evolution posits that life arose out of inanimate chemical compounds and has gradually evolved over millions of years. Creation science posits that all life forms now on earth appeared suddenly and relatively recently, and have changed little. Since there are only two possible explanations of the origin of life, any evidence that tends to disprove the theory of evolution necessarily tends to prove the theory of creation science, and vice versa. For example, the abrupt appearance in the fossil record of complex life, and the extreme rarity of transitional life forms in that record, are evidence for creation science. 1 id. at E-7 (Sunderland); id. at E-12 - E-18 (Sunderland); id. at E-45 - E-60 (Boudreaux);

id. at E-67 (Harlow); id. at E-130 - E-153 (Boudreaux paper); id. at E-423 - E-428 (Sen. Keith).

(2) The body of scientific evidence supporting creation science is as strong as that supporting evolution. In fact, it may be stronger. Id. at E-214 (Young statement); id. at E-310 (Sen. Keith); id. at E-416 (Sen. Keith); 2 id. at E-492 (Sen. Keith). The evidence for evolution is far less compelling than we have been led to believe. Evolution is not a scientific "fact," since it cannot actually be observed in a laboratory. Rather, evolution is merely a scientific theory or "guess." 1 id. at E-20 - E-21 (Morris); id. at E-85 (Ward); id. at E-100 (Reiboldt); id. at E-328 - E-329 (Boudreaux); 2 id. at E-506 (Boudreaux). It is a very bad guess at that. The scientific problems with evolution are so serious that it could accurately be termed a "myth." 1 id. at E-85 (Ward); id. at E-92 - E-93 (Kalivoda); id. at E-95 - E-97 (Sen. Keith); id. at E-154 (Boudreaux paper); id. at E-329 (Boudreaux); id. at E-453 (Sen. Keith); 2 id. at E-505 - E-506 (Boudreaux); id. at E-516 (Young).

(3) Creation science is educationally valuable. Students exposed to it better understand the current state of scientific evidence about the origin of life. 1 id. at E-19 (Sunderland); id. at E-39 (Sen. Keith); id. at E-79 (Kalivoda); id. at E-308 (Sen. Keith); 2 id. at E-513 - E-514 (Morris). Those students even have a better understanding of evolution. 1 id. at E-19 (Sunderland). Creation science can and should be presented to children without any religious content. Id. at E-12 (Sunderland); id. at E-22 (Sanderford); id. at E-35 - E-36 (Sen. Keith); id. at E-101 (Reiboldt); id. at E-279 - E-280 (Sen. Keith); id. at E-282 (Sen. Keith).

(4) Although creation science is educationally valuable and strictly scientific, it is now being censored from or misrepresented in the public schools. Id. at E-19 (Sunderland); id. at E-21 (Morris); id. at E-34 (Sen. Keith); id. at E-37 (Sen. Keith); id. at E-42 (Sen. Keith); id. at E-92 (Kalivoda); id. at E-97 - E-98 (Reiboldt); id. at E-214 (Young statement); id. at E-218 (Young statement); id. at E-280 (Sen. Keith); id. at E-309 (Sen. Keith); 2 id. at E-513 (Morris). Evolution, in turn, is misrepresented as an absolute truth. 1 id. at E-63 (Harlow); id. at E-74 (Sen. Keith); id. at E-81 (Kalivoda); id. at E-214 (Young statement); 2 id. at E-507 (Harlow); id. at E-513 (Morris); id. at E-516 (Young). Teachers have been brainwashed by an entrenched scientific establishment composed almost exclusively of scientists to whom evolution is like a "religion." These scientists discriminate against creation scientists, so as to prevent evolution's weaknesses from being exposed. 1 id. at E-61 (Boudreaux); id. at E-63 - E-64 (Harlow); id. at E-78 - E-79 (Kalivoda); id. at E-80 (Kalivoda); id. at E-95 - E-97 (Sen. Keith); id. at E-129 (Boudreaux paper); id. at E-218 (Young statement); id. at E-357 (Sen. Keith); id. at E-430 (Boudreaux).

(5) The censorship of creation science has at least two harmful effects. First, it deprives students of knowledge of one of the two scientific explanations for the origin of life, and leads them to believe that evolution is proven fact; thus, their education suffers, and they are wrongly taught that science has proved their religious beliefs false. Second, it violates the Establishment Clause. The United States Supreme Court has held that secular

humanism is a religion. Id. at E-36 (Sen. Keith) (referring to Torcaso v. Watkins, 367 U.S. 488, 495, n. 11 (1961));1 App. E-418 (Sen. Keith); 2 id. at E-499 (Sen. Keith). Belief in evolution is a central tenet of that religion. 1 id. at E-282 (Sen. Keith); id. at E-312 - E-313 (Sen. Keith); id. at E-317 (Sen. Keith); id. at E-418 (Sen. Keith); 2 id. at E-499 (Sen. Keith). Thus, by censoring creation science and instructing students that evolution is fact, public school teachers are now advancing religion in violation of the Establishment Clause. 1 id. at E-2 - E-4 (Sen. Keith); id. at E-36 - E-37, E-39 (Sen. Keith); id. at E-154 - E-155 (Boudreaux paper); id. at E-281 - E-282 (Sen. Keith); id. at E-313 (Sen. Keith); id. at E-315 - E-316 (Sen. Keith); id. at E-317 (Sen. Keith); 2 id. at E-499 - E-500 (Sen. Keith).

Senator Keith repeatedly and vehemently denied that his purpose was to advance a particular religious doctrine. At the outset of the first hearing on the legislation, he testified:

We are not going to say today that you should have some kind of religious instructions in our schools. . . . We are not talking about religion today. . . . I am not proposing that we take the Bible in each science class and read the first chapter of Genesis.

1 id. at E-35. At a later hearing, Senator Keith stressed:

[T]o . . . teach religion and disguise it as creationism . . . is not my intent. My intent is to see to it that our textbooks are not censored.

Id. at E-280. He made many similar statements throughout the hearings. See, e.g., id. at E-41; id. at E-282; id. at E-310; id. at E-417; see also id. at E-44 (Boudreaux); id. at E-80 (Kalivoda).

We have no way of knowing, of course, how many legislators believed the testimony of Senator Keith and his witnesses. But in the absence of evidence to the contrary, [n4] we have to assume that many of them did. Given that assumption, the Court today plainly errs in holding that the Louisiana Legislature passed the Balanced Treatment Act for exclusively religious purposes.

B

Even with nothing more than this legislative history to go on, I think it would be extraordinary to invalidate the Balanced Treatment Act for lack of a valid secular purpose. Striking down a law approved by the democratically elected representatives of the people is no minor matter.

The cardinal principle of statutory construction is to save, and not to destroy. We have repeatedly held that, as between two possible interpretations of a statute, by one of which it would be unconstitutional and by the other valid, our plain duty is to adopt that which will save the act.

NLRB v. Jones & Laughlin Steel Corp., 301 U.S. 1, 30 (1937). So, too, it seems to me, with discerning statutory purpose. Even if the legislative history were silent or ambiguous about the existence of a secular purpose -- and here it is not -- the statute should survive Lemon's purpose test. But even more validation than mere legislative history is present here. The Louisiana Legislature explicitly set forth its secular purpose ("protecting academic freedom") in the very text of the Act. La.Rev.Stat. § 17:286.2 (West 1982). We have in the past repeatedly relied upon or deferred to such expressions, see, e.g., Committee for Public Education & Religious Liberty v. Regan, 444 U.S. at 654; Meek v. Pittenger, 421 U.S. at 363, 367-368; Committee for Public Education & Religious Liberty v. Nyquist, 413 U.S. at 773; Levitt v. Committee for Public Education & Religious Liberty, 413 U.S. at 479-480, n. 7; Tilton v. Richardson, 403 U.S. at 678-679 (plurality opinion); Lemon v. Kurtzman, 403 U.S. at 613; Board of Education v. Allen, 392 U.S. at 243.

The Court seeks to evade the force of this expression of purpose by stubbornly misinterpreting it, and then finding that the provisions of the Act do not advance that misinterpreted purpose, thereby showing it to be a sham. The Court first surmises that "academic freedom" means "enhancing the freedom of teachers to teach what they will," ante at 586 -- even though "academic freedom" in that sense has little scope in the structured elementary and secondary curriculums with which the Act is concerned. Alternatively, the Court suggests that it might mean "maximiz[ing] the comprehensiveness and effectiveness of science instruction," ante at 588 -- though that is an exceedingly strange interpretation of the words, and one that is refuted on the very face of the statute. See § 17:286.5. Had the Court devoted to this central question of the meaning of the legislatively expressed purpose a small fraction of the research into legislative history that produced its quotations of religiously motivated statements by individual legislators, it would have discerned quite readily what "academic freedom" meant: students' freedom from indoctrination. The legislature wanted to ensure that students would be free to decide for themselves how life began, based upon a fair and balanced presentation of the scientific evidence -- that is, to protect "the right of each [student] voluntarily to determine what to believe (and what not to believe) free of any coercive pressures from the State." Grand Rapids School District v. Ball, 473 U.S. at 385. The legislature did not care whether the topic of origins was taught; it simply wished to ensure that, when the topic was taught, students would receive "'all of the evidence.'" Ante at 586 (quoting Tr. of Oral Arg. 60).

As originally introduced, the "purpose" section of the Balanced Treatment Act read:

This Chapter is enacted for the purposes of protecting academic freedom . . . of students . . . and assisting students in their search for truth.

1 App. E-292 (emphasis added). Among the proposed findings of fact contained in the original version of the bill was the following:

Public school instruction in only evolution science . . . violates the principle of academic freedom because it denies students a choice between scientific models, and instead indoctrinates them in evolution science alone.

Id. at E-295 (emphasis added). [n5] Senator Keith unquestionably understood "academic freedom" to mean "freedom from indoctrination." See id. at E-36 (purpose of bill is "to protect academic freedom by providing student choice"); id. at E-283 (purpose of bill is to protect "academic freedom" by giving students a "choice," rather than subjecting them to "indoctrination on origins").

If one adopts the obviously intended meaning of the statutory term "academic freedom," there is no basis whatever for concluding that the purpose they express is a "sham." Ante at 587. To the contrary, the Act pursues that purpose plainly and consistently. It requires that, whenever the subject of origins is covered, evolution be "taught as a theory, rather than as proven scientific fact," and that scientific evidence inconsistent with the theory of evolution (viz., "creation science") be taught as well. La.Rev.Stat.Ann. § 17:286.4A (West 1982). Living up to its title of "Balanced Treatment for Creation-Science and Evolution-Science Act," § 17.286.1, it treats the teaching of creation the same way. It does not mandate instruction in creation science, § 17:286.5; forbids teachers to present creation science "as proven scientific fact," § 17:286.4A; and bans the teaching of creation science unless the theory is (to use the Court's terminology) "discredit[ed] '. . . at every turn'" with the teaching of evolution. Ante at 589 (quoting 765 F.2d at 1257). It surpasses understanding how the Court can see in this a purpose "to restructure the science curriculum to conform with a particular religious viewpoint," ante at 593, "to provide a persuasive advantage to a particular religious doctrine," ante at 592, "to promote the theory of creation science which embodies a particular religious tenet," ante at 593, and "to endorse a particular religious doctrine," ante at 594.

The Act's reference to "creation" is not convincing evidence of religious purpose. The Act defines creation science as "scientific evidenc[e]," § 17:286.3(2) (emphasis added), and Senator Keith and his witnesses repeatedly stressed that the subject can and should be presented without religious content. See supra, at 623. We have no basis on the record to conclude that creation science need be anything other than a collection of scientific data supporting the theory that life abruptly appeared on earth. See n. 4, supra. Creation science, its proponents insist, no more must explain whence life came than evolution must explain whence came the inanimate materials from which it says life evolved. But even if that were not so, to posit a past creator is not to posit the eternal and personal God who is the object of religious veneration. Indeed, it is not even to posit the "unmoved mover" hypothesized by Aristotle and other notably nonfundamentalist philosophers. Senator Keith suggested this when he referred to "a creator, however you define a creator." 1 App. E-280 (emphasis added).

The Court cites three provisions of the Act which, it argues, demonstrate a "discriminatory preference for the teaching of creation science" and no interest in "academic freedom." Ante at 482 U.S. 588"]588. First, the Act prohibits discrimination only against creation scientists and those who teach creation science. § 17:286.4C. Second, the Act requires local school boards to develop and provide to science teachers "a curriculum guide on presentation of creation-science." § 17:286.7A. Finally, the Act requires the Governor to designate seven creation scientists who shall, upon request, assist local school boards in developing the curriculum guides. § 17:286.7B. But none of these provisions casts doubt upon the sincerity of the legislators' articulated purpose of "academic freedom" -- unless, of course, one gives that term the obviously erroneous meanings preferred by the Court. The Louisiana legislators had been told repeatedly that creation scientists were scorned by most educators and scientists, who themselves had an almost religious faith in evolution. It is hardly surprising, then, that, in seeking to achieve a balanced, "nonindoctrinating" curriculum, the legislators protected from discrimination only those teachers whom they thought were suffering from discrimination. (Also, the legislators were undoubtedly aware of 588. First, the Act prohibits discrimination only against creation scientists and those who teach creation science. § 17:286.4C. Second, the Act requires local school boards to develop and provide to science teachers "a curriculum guide on presentation of creation-science." § 17:286.7A. Finally, the Act requires the Governor to designate seven creation scientists who shall, upon request, assist local school boards in developing the curriculum guides. § 17:286.7B. But none of these provisions casts doubt upon the sincerity of the legislators' articulated purpose of "academic freedom" -- unless, of course, one gives that term the obviously erroneous meanings preferred by the Court. The Louisiana legislators had been told repeatedly that creation scientists were scorned by most educators and scientists, who themselves had an almost religious faith in evolution. It is hardly surprising, then, that, in seeking to achieve a balanced, "nonindoctrinating" curriculum, the legislators protected from discrimination only those teachers whom they thought were suffering from discrimination. (Also, the legislators were undoubtedly aware of Epperson v. Arkansas, 393 U.S. 97 (1968), and thus could quite reasonably have concluded that discrimination against evolutionists was already prohibited.) The two provisions respecting the development of curriculum guides are also consistent with "academic freedom" as the Louisiana Legislature understood the term. Witnesses had informed the legislators that, because of the hostility of most scientists and educators to creation science, the topic had been censored from or badly misrepresented in elementary and secondary school texts. In light of the unavailability of works on creation science suitable for classroom use (a fact appellees concede, see Brief for Appellees 27, 40) and the existence of ample materials on evolution, it was entirely reasonable for the legislature to conclude that science teachers attempting to implement the Act would need a curriculum guide on creation science, but not on evolution, and that those charged with developing the guide would need an easily accessible group of creation scientists. Thus, the provisions of the Act of so much concern to the Court support the conclusion that the legislature acted to advance "academic freedom."

The legislative history gives ample evidence of the sincerity of the Balanced Treatment Act's articulated purpose. Witness after witness urged the legislators to support the Act so that students would not be "indoctrinated," but would instead be free to decide for themselves, based upon a fair presentation of the scientific evidence, about the origin of life. See, e.g., 1 App. E-18 (Sunderland) ("all that we are advocating" is presenting "scientific data" to students and "letting [them] make up their own mind[s]"); id. at E-19 - E-20 (Sunderland) (Students are now being "indoctrinated" in evolution through the use of "censored school books. . . . All that we are asking for is [the] open unbiased education in the classroom . . . your students deserve"); id. at E-21 (Morris) ("A student cannot [make an intelligent decision about the origin of life] unless he is well informed about both [evolution and creation science]"); id. at E-22 (Sanderford) ("We are asking very simply [that] . . . creationism [be presented] alongside . . . evolution, and let people make their own mind[s] up"); id. at E-23 (Young) (the bill would require teachers to live up to their "obligation to present all theories," and thereby enable "students to make judgments themselves"); id. at E-44 (Boudreaux) ("Our intention is truth, and, as a scientist, I am interested in truth"); id. at E-60 - E-61 (Boudreaux) ("[W]e [teachers] are guilty of a lot of rainwashing. . . . We have a duty to . . . [present the] truth" to students "at all levels from grade school on through the college level"); id. at E-79 (Kalivoda) ("This [hearing] is being held, I think, to determine whether children will benefit from freedom of information, or if they will be handicapped educationally by having little or no information about creation"); id. at E-80 (Kalivoda) ("I am not interested in teaching religion in schools. . . . I am interested in the truth, and [students'] having the opportunity to hear more than one side"); id. at E-98 (Reiboldt) ("The students have a right to know there is an alternate creationist point of view. They have a right to know the scientific evidences which suppor[t] that alternative"); id. at E-218 (Young statement) (passage of the bill will ensure that "communication of scientific ideas and discoveries may be unhindered"); 2 id. at E-514 (Morris) ("[A]re we going to allow [students] to look at evolution, to look at creationism, and to let one or the other stand or fall on its own merits, or will we, by failing to pass this bill, . . . deny students an opportunity to hear another viewpoint?"); id. at E-516 - E-517 (Young) ("We want to give the children here in this state an equal opportunity to see both sides of the theories"). Senator Keith expressed similar views. See, e.g., 1 id. at E-36; id. at E-41; id. at E-280; id. at E-283.

Legislators other than Senator Keith made only a few statements providing insight into their motives, but those statements cast no doubt upon the sincerity of the Act's articulated purpose. The legislators were concerned primarily about the manner in which the subject of origins was presented in Louisiana schools -- specifically, about whether scientifically valuable information was being censored, and students misled about evolution. Representatives Cain, Jenkins, and F. Thompson seemed impressed by the scientific evidence presented in support of creation science. See 2 id. at E-530 (Rep. F. Thompson); id. at E-533 (Rep. Cain); id. at E-613 (Rep. Jenkins). At the first study commission hearing, Senator Picard and Representative M. Thompson questioned Senator Keith about Louisiana teachers' treatment of evolution and creation science. See 1 id. at E-71 - E-74. At the close of the hearing, Representative M. Thompson told the audience:

We, as members of the committee, will also receive from the staff information of what is currently being taught in the Louisiana public schools. We really want to see [it]. I . . . have no idea in what manner [biology] is presented, and in what manner the creationist theories [are] excluded in the public school[s]. We want to look at what the status of the situation is.

Id. at E-104. Legislators made other comments suggesting a concern about censorship and misrepresentation of scientific information. See, e.g., id. at E-386 (Sen. McLeod); 2 id. at E-527 (Rep. Jenkins); id. at E-528 (Rep. M. Thompson); id. at E-534 (Rep. Fair).

It is undoubtedly true that what prompted the legislature to direct its attention to the misrepresentation of evolution in the schools (rather than the inaccurate presentation of other topics) was its awareness of the tension between evolution and the religious beliefs of many children. But even appellees concede that a valid secular purpose is not rendered impermissible simply because its pursuit is prompted by concern for religious sensitivities. Tr. of Oral Arg. 43, 56. If a history teacher falsely told her students that the bones of Jesus Christ had been discovered, or a physics teacher that the Shroud of Turin had been conclusively established to be inexplicable on the basis of natural causes, I cannot believe (despite the majority's implication to the contrary, see ante at 592-593) that legislators or school board members would be constitutionally prohibited from taking corrective action simply because that action was prompted by concern for the religious beliefs of the misinstructed students.

In sum, even if one concedes, for the sake of argument, that a majority of the Louisiana Legislature voted for the Balanced Treatment Act partly in order to foster (rather than merely eliminate discrimination against) Christian fundamentalist beliefs, our cases establish that that, alone, would not suffice to invalidate the Act, so long as there was a genuine secular purpose as well. We have, moreover, no adequate basis for disbelieving the secular purpose set forth in the Act itself, or for concluding that it is a sham enacted to conceal the legislators' violation of their oaths of office. I am astonished by the Court's unprecedented readiness to reach such a conclusion, which I can only attribute to an intellectual predisposition created by the facts and the legend of Scopes v. State, 154 Tenn. 105, 289 S.W. 363 (1927) -- an instinctive reaction that any governmentally imposed requirements bearing upon the teaching of evolution must be a manifestation of Christian fundamentalist repression. In this case, however, it seems to me the Court's position is the repressive one. The people of Louisiana, including those who are Christian fundamentalists, are quite entitled, as a secular matter, to have whatever scientific evidence there may be against evolution presented in their schools, just as Mr. Scopes was entitled to present whatever scientific evidence there was for it. Perhaps what the Louisiana Legislature has done is unconstitutional because there is no such evidence, and the scheme they have established will amount to no more than a presentation of the Book of Genesis. But we cannot say that on the evidence before us in this summary judgment context, which includes ample uncontradicted testimony that "creation science" is a body of scientific knowledge, rather than revealed belief. Infinitely less can we say (or should we say) that the scientific evidence for evolution is so conclusive that no one could be gullible enough to believe that there is any real scientific evidence to the contrary, so that the legislation's stated purpose must be a lie. Yet that illiberal judgment, that Scopes-in-reverse, is ultimately the basis on which the Court's facile rejection of the Louisiana Legislature's purpose must rest.

Since the existence of secular purpose is so entirely clear, and thus dispositive, I will not go on to discuss the fact that, even if the Louisiana Legislature's purpose were exclusively to advance religion, some of the well-established exceptions to the impermissibility of that purpose might be applicable -- the validating intent to eliminate a perceived discrimination against a particular religion, to facilitate its free exercise, or to accommodate it. See supra, at 617-618. I am not, in any case, enamored of those amorphous exceptions, since I think them no more than unpredictable correctives to what is (as the next Part of this opinion will discuss) a fundamentally unsound rule. It is surprising, however, that the Court does not address these exceptions, since the context of the legislature's action gives some reason to believe they may be applicable. [n6]

Because I believe that the Balanced Treatment Act had a secular purpose, which is all the first component of the Lemon test requires, I would reverse the judgment of the Court of Appeals and remand for further consideration.

III

I have to this point assumed the validity of the Lemon "purpose" test. In fact, however, I think the pessimistic evaluation that THE CHIEF JUSTICE made of the totality of Lemon is particularly applicable to the "purpose" prong: it is

a constitutional theory [that] has no basis in the history of the amendment it seeks to interpret, is difficult to apply, and yields unprincipled results. . . .

Wallace v. Jaffree, 472 U.S. at 112 (REHNQUIST, J., dissenting).

Our cases interpreting and applying the purpose test have made such a maze of the Establishment Clause that even the most conscientious governmental officials can only guess what motives will be held unconstitutional. We have said essentially the following: government may not act with the purpose of advancing religion, except when forced to do so by the Free Exercise Clause (which is now and then); or when eliminating existing governmental hostility to religion (which exists sometimes); or even when merely accommodating governmentally uninhibited religious practices, except that at some point (it is unclear where) intentional accommodation results in the fostering of religion, which is of course unconstitutional. See supra, at 614-618.

But the difficulty of knowing what vitiating purpose one is looking for is as nothing compared with the difficulty of knowing how or where to find it. For while it is possible to discern the objective "purpose" of a statute (i.e., the public good at which its provisions appear to be directed), or even the formal motivation for a statute where that is explicitly set forth (as it was, to no avail, here), discerning the subjective motivation of those enacting the statute is, to be honest, almost always an impossible task. The number of possible motivations, to begin with, is not binary, or indeed even finite. In the present case, for example, a particular legislator need not have voted for the Act either because he wanted to foster religion or because he wanted to improve education. He may have thought the bill would provide jobs for his district, or may have wanted to make amends with a faction of his party he had alienated on another vote, or he may have been a close friend of the bill's sponsor, or he may have been repaying a favor he owed the majority leader, or he may have hoped the Governor would appreciate his vote and make a fund-raising appearance for him, or he may have been pressured to vote for a bill he disliked by a wealthy contributor or by a flood of constituent mail, or he may have been seeking favorable publicity, or he may have been reluctant to hurt the feelings of a loyal staff member who worked on the bill, or he may have been settling an old score with a legislator who opposed the bill, or he may have been mad at his wife, who opposed the bill, or he may have been intoxicated and utterly unmotivated when the vote was called, or he may have accidentally voted "yes" instead of "no," or, of course, he may have had (and very likely did have) a combination of some of the above and many other motivations. To look for the sole purpose of even a single legislator is probably to look for something that does not exist.

Putting that problem aside, however, where ought we to look for the individual legislator's purpose? We cannot, of course, assume that every member present (if, as is unlikely, we know who or even how many they were) agreed with the motivation expressed in a particular legislator's preenactment floor or committee statement. Quite obviously, "[w]hat motivates one legislator to make a speech about a statute is not necessarily what motivates scores of others to enact it." United States v. O'Brien, 391 U.S. 367, 384 (1968). Can we assume, then, that they all agree with the motivation expressed in the staff-prepared committee reports they might have read -- even though we are unwilling to assume that they agreed with the motivation expressed in the very statute that they voted for? Should we consider postenactment floor statements? Or postenactment testimony from legislators, obtained expressly for the lawsuit? Should we consider media reports on the realities of the legislative bargaining? All of these sources, of course, are eminently manipulable. Legislative histories can be contrived and sanitized, favorable media coverage orchestrated, and postenactment recollections conveniently distorted. Perhaps most valuable of all would be more objective indications -- for example, evidence regarding the individual legislators' religious affiliations. And if that, why not evidence regarding the fervor or tepidity of their beliefs?

Having achieved, through these simple means, an assessment of what individual legislators intended, we must still confront the question (yet to be addressed in any of our cases) how many of them must have the invalidating intent. If a state senate approves a bill by vote of 26 to 25, and only one of the 26 intended solely to advance religion, is the law unconstitutional? What if 13 of the 26 had that intent? What if 3 of the 26 had the impermissible intent, but 3 of the 25 voting against the bill were motivated by religious hostility, or were simply attempting to "balance" the votes of their impermissibly motivated colleagues? Or is it possible that the intent of the bill's sponsor is alone enough to invalidate it -- on a theory, perhaps, that even though everyone else's intent was pure, what they produced was the fruit of a forbidden tree?

Because there are no good answers to these questions, this Court has recognized from Chief Justice Marshall, see Fletcher v. Peck, 6 Cranch 87, 130 (1810), to Chief Justice Warren, United States v. O'Brien, supra, at 383-384, that determining the subjective intent of legislators is a perilous enterprise. See also Palmer v. Thompson, 403 U.S. 217, 224-225 (1971); Epperson v. Arkansas, 393 U.S. at 113 (Black, J., concurring). It is perilous, I might note, not just for the judges who will very likely reach the wrong result, but also for the legislators who find that they must assess the validity of proposed legislation -- and risk the condemnation of having voted for an unconstitutional measure -- not on the basis of what the legislation contains, nor even on the basis of what they themselves intend, but on the basis of what others have in mind.

Given the many hazards involved in assessing the subjective intent of governmental decisionmakers, the first prong of Lemon is defensible, I think, only if the text of the Establishment Clause demands it. That is surely not the case. The Clause states that "Congress shall make no law respecting an establishment of religion." One could argue, I suppose, that any time Congress acts with the intent of advancing religion, it has enacted a "law respecting an establishment of religion"; but, far from being an unavoidable reading, it is quite an unnatural one. I doubt, for example, that the Clayton Act, 38 Stat. 730, as amended, 15 U.S.C. § 12 et seq., could reasonably be described as a "law respecting an establishment of religion" if bizarre new historical evidence revealed that it lacked a secular purpose, even though it has no discernible nonsecular effect. It is, in short, far from an inevitable reading of the Establishment Clause that it forbids all governmental action intended to advance religion; and, if not inevitable, any reading with such untoward consequences must be wrong.

In the past, we have attempted to justify our embarrassing Establishment Clause jurisprudence [n7] on the ground that it "sacrifices clarity and predictability for flexibility." Committee for Public Education & Religious Liberty v. Regan, 444 U.S. at 662. One commentator has aptly characterized this as "a euphemism . . . for . . . the absence of any principled rationale." Choper, supra, n. 7, at 681. I think it time that we sacrifice some "flexibility" for "clarity and predictability." Abandoning Lemon's purpose test -- a test which exacerbates the tension between the Free Exercise and Establishment Clauses, has no basis in the language or history of the Amendment, and, as today's decision shows, has wonderfully flexible consequences -- would be a good place to start.

Notes to Justice Scalia's dissent in Edwards v. Aguillard (June 19, 1987)

1. Article VI, cl. 3, of the Constitution provides that "the Members of the several State Legislatures . . . shall be bound by Oath or Affirmation, to support this Constitution."

2. Thus, the popular dictionary definitions cited by JUSTICE POWELL, ante at 598-599 (concurring opinion), and appellees, see Brief for Appellees 25, 26; Tr. of Oral Arg. 32, 34, are utterly irrelevant, as are the views of the school superintendents cited by

the majority, ante at 595, n. 18. Three-quarters of those surveyed had "[n]o" or "[l]imited" knowledge of "creation science theory," and not a single superintendent claimed "[e]xtensive" knowledge of the subject. 2 App. E-798.

3. Although creation scientists and evolutionists also disagree about the origin of the physical universe, both proponents and opponents of Senator Keith's bill focused on the question of the beginning of life.

4. Although appellees and amici dismiss the testimony of Senator Keith and his witnesses as pure fantasy, they did not bother to submit evidence of that to the District Court, making it difficult for us to agree with them. The State, by contrast, submitted the affidavits of two scientists, a philosopher, a theologian, and an educator, whose academic credentials are rather impressive. See App. to Juris. Statement A-17 - A-18 (Kenyon); id. at A-36 (Morrow); id. at A-39 - A-40 (Miethe); id. at A-46 - A-47 (Most); id. at A-49 (Clinkert). Like Senator Keith and his witnesses, the affiants swear that evolution and creation science are the only two scientific explanations for the origin of life, see id. at A-19 - A-20 (Kenyon); id. at A-38 (Morrow); id. at A-41 (Miethe); that creation science is strictly scientific, see id. at A-18 (Kenyon); id. at A-36 (Morrow); id. at A-40 - A-41 (Miethe); id. at A-49 (Clinkert); that creation science is simply a collection of scientific data that supports the hypothesis that life appeared on earth suddenly, and has changed little, see id. at A-19 (Kenyon); id. at A-36 (Morrow); id. at A-41 (Miethe); that hundreds of respected scientists believe in creation science, see id. at A-20 (Kenyon); that evidence for creation science is as strong as evidence for evolution, see id. at A-21 (Kenyon); id. at A-34 - A-35 (Kenyon); id. at A-37 - A-38 (Morrow); that creation science is educationally valuable, see id. at A-19 (Kenyon); id. at A-36 (Morrow); id. at A-38 - A-39 (Morrow); id. at A-49 (Clinkert); that creation science can be presented without religious content, see id. at A-19 (Kenyon); id. at A-35 (Kenyon); id. at A-36 (Morrow); id. at A-40 (Miethe); id. at A-43 - A-44 (Miethe); id. at A-47 (Most); id. at A-49 (Clinkert); and that creation science is now censored from classrooms, while evolution is misrepresented as proven fact, see id. at A-20 (Kenyon); id. at A-35 (Kenyon); id. at A-39 (Morrow); id. at A-50 (Clinkert). It is difficult to conclude on the basis of these affidavits -- the only substantive evidence in the record -- that the laymen serving in the Louisiana Legislature must have disbelieved Senator Keith or his witnesses.

5. The majority finds it "astonishing" that I would cite a portion of Senator Keith's original bill that was later deleted as evidence of the legislature's understanding of the phrase "academic freedom." Ante at 589, n. 8. What is astonishing is the majority's implication that the deletion of that section deprives it of value as a clear indication of what the phrase meant -- there and in the other, retained, sections of the bill. The Senate Committee on Education deleted most of the lengthy "purpose" section of the bill (with Senator Keith's consent) because it resembled legislative "findings of fact," which, committee members felt, should generally not be incorporated in legislation. The deletion had absolutely nothing to do with the manner in which the section described "academic freedom." See 1 App. E-314 - E-320; id. at E-440 - E-442.

6. As the majority recognizes, ante at 592, Senator Keith sincerely believed that "secular humanism is a bona fide religion," 1 App. E-36; see also id. at E-418; 2 id. at E-499, and that "evolution is the cornerstone of that religion," 1 id. at E-418; see also id. at E-282; id. at E-312 - E-313; id. at E-317; 2 id. at E-499. The Senator even told his colleagues that this Court had "held" that secular humanism was a religion. See 1 id. at E-36, id. at E-418; 2 id. at E-499. (In Torcaso v. Watkins, 367 U.S. 488, 495, n. 11 (1961), we did indeed refer to "Secular Humanism" as a "religio[n].") Senator Keith and his supporters raised the "religion" of secular humanism not, as the majority suggests, to explain the source of their "disdain for the theory of evolution," ante at 592, but to convince the legislature that the State of Louisiana was violating the Establishment Clause because its teachers were misrepresenting evolution as fact, and depriving students of the information necessary to question that theory. 1 App. E-2 - E-4 (Sen. Keith); id. at E-36 - E-37, E-39 (Sen. Keith); id. at E-154 - E-155 (Boudreaux paper); id. at E-281 - E-282 (Sen. Keith); id. at E-317 (Sen. Keith); 2 id. at E-499 - E-500 (Sen. Keith). The Senator repeatedly urged his colleagues to pass his bill to remedy this Establishment Clause violation by ensuring state neutrality in religious matters, see, e.g., 1 id. at E-36; id. at E-39; id. at E-313, surely a permissible purpose under Lemon. Senator Keith's argument may be questionable, but nothing in the statute or its legislative history gives us reason to doubt his sincerity or that of his supporters.

7. Professor Choper summarized our school aid cases thusly:

[A] provision for therapeutic and diagnostic health services to parochial school pupils by public employees is invalid if provided in the parochial school, but not if offered at a neutral site, even if in a mobile unit adjacent to the parochial school. Reimbursement to parochial schools for the expense of administering teacher-prepared tests required by state law is invalid, but the state may reimburse parochial schools for the expense of administering state-prepared tests. The state may lend school textbooks to parochial school pupils because, the Court has explained, the books can be checked in advance for religious content, and are "self-policing;" but the state may not lend other seemingly self-policing instructional items such as tape recorders and maps. The state may pay the cost of bus transportation to parochial schools, which the Court has ruled are "permeated" with religion; but the state is forbidden to pay for field trip transportation visits "to governmental, industrial, cultural, and scientific centers designed to enrich the secular studies of students."

Choper, The Religion Clauses of the First Amendment: Reconciling the Conflict, 41 U.Pitt.L.Rev. 673, 680-681 (1980) (footnotes omitted).

Since that was written, more decisions on the subject have been rendered, but they leave the theme of chaos securely unimpaired. See, e.g., Aguilar v. Felton, 473 U.S. 402 (1985); Grand Rapids School District v. Ball, 473 U.S. 373 (1985).

Legislative history: Justice Scalia's concurrence in United States v. Taylor (June 24, 1988)

Justice SCALIA, concurring in part.

I join the opinion of the Court except Part II-A, which is largely devoted to establishing, through the floor debate in the House, (1) that prejudice to the defendant is one of the factors that the phrase "among others" in § 3162(a)(2) refers to, and (2) that that factor is not necessarily determinative. Both these points seem to me so utterly clear from the text of the legislation that there is no justification for resort to the legislative history. Assume that there was nothing in the legislative history except statements that, unless the defendant had been harmed by the delay, dismissal with prejudice could not be granted. Would we permit that to govern, even though the text of the provision does not consider that factor dominant enough to be mentioned specifically, but just includes it within the phrase "among othe[r] [factors]," or perhaps within the phrase "facts and circumstances of the case which led to the dismissal"? Or assume the opposite, that there was nothing in the legislative history except statements that harm to the defendant could not be considered at all. Would we permit that to govern, even though impairment of the accused's defense is so obviously one of the "other factors" highly relevant to whether the Government should be permitted to reinstitute the prosecution?

I think the answer to both these questions is obviously no. The text is so unambiguous on these points that it must be assumed that what the Members of the House and the Senators thought they were voting for, and what the President thought he was approving when he signed the bill, was what the text plainly said, rather than what a few Representatives, or even a Committee Report, said it said. Where we are not prepared to be governed by what the legislative history says—to take, as it were, the bad with the good—we should not look to the legislative history at all. This text is eminently clear, and we should leave it at that.

It should not be thought that, simply because adverting to the legislative history produces the same result we would reach anyway, no harm is done. By perpetuating the view that legislative history can alter the meaning of even a clear statutory provision, we produce a legal culture in which the following statement could be made—taken from a portion of the floor debate alluded to in the Court's opinion:

"Mr. DENNIS. . . .
* * * * *

"I have an amendment here in my hand which could be offered, but if we can make up some legislative history which would do the same thing, I am willing to do it." 120 Cong.Rec. 41795 (1974).

We should not make the equivalency between making legislative history and making an amendment so plausible. It should not be possible, or at least should not be easy, to be sure of obtaining a particular result in this Court without making that result apparent on the face of the bill which both Houses consider and vote upon, which the President approves, and which, if it becomes law, the people must obey. I think we have an obligation to conduct our exegesis in a fashion which fosters that democratic process.

Separation of Powers: Justice Scalia's dissent in Morrison v. Olson (June 29, 1988)

JUSTICE SCALIA, dissenting.

It is the proud boast of our democracy that we have "a government of laws and not of men." Many Americans are familiar with that phrase; not many know its derivation. It comes from Part the First, Article XXX, of the Massachusetts Constitution of 1780, which reads in full as follows:

"In the government of this Commonwealth, the legislative department shall never exercise the executive and judicial powers, or either of them: The executive shall never exercise the legislative and judicial powers, or either of them: The judicial shall never exercise the legislative and executive powers, or either of them: to the end it may be a government of laws and not of men."

The Framers of the Federal Constitution similarly viewed the principle of separation of powers as the absolutely central guarantee of a just Government. In No. 47 of The Federalist, Madison wrote that "[n]o political truth is certainly of greater intrinsic value, or is stamped with the authority of more enlightened patrons of liberty." The Federalist No. 47, p. 301 (C. Rossiter ed. 1961) (hereinafter Federalist). Without a secure structure of separated powers, our Bill of Rights would be worthless, as are the bills of rights of many nations of the world that have adopted, or even improved upon, the mere words of ours.

The principle of separation of powers is expressed in our Constitution in the first section of each of the first three Articles. Article I, 1, provides that "[a]ll legislative Powers herein granted shall be vested in a Congress of the United States, which shall consist of a Senate and House of Representatives." Article III, 1, provides that "[t]he judicial Power of the United States, shall be vested in one supreme Court, and in such inferior Courts as the Congress may from time to time ordain and establish." And the provision at issue here, Art. II, 1, cl. 1, provides that "[t]he executive Power shall be vested in a President of the United States of America."

But just as the mere words of a Bill of Rights are not self-effectuating, the Framers recognized "[t]he insufficiency of a mere parchment delineation of the boundaries" to achieve the separation of powers. Federalist No. 73, p. 442 (A. Hamilton). "[T]he great security," wrote Madison, "against a gradual concentration of the several powers in the same department consists in giving to those who administer each department the necessary constitutional means and personal motives to resist encroachments of the others. The provision for defense must in this, as in all other cases, be made commensurate to the danger of attack." Federalist No. 51, pp. 321-322. Madison continued:

"But it is not possible to give to each department an equal power of self-defense. In republican government, the legislative authority necessarily predominates. The remedy for this inconveniency is to divide the legislature into different branches; and to render them, by different modes of election and different principles of action, as little connected with each other as the nature of their common functions and their common dependence on the society will admit. . . . As the weight of the legislative authority requires that it should be thus divided, the weakness of the executive may require, on the other hand, that it should be fortified." Id., at 322-323.

The major "fortification" provided, of course, was the veto power. But in addition to providing fortification, the Founders conspicuously and very consciously declined to sap the Executive's strength in the same way they had weakened the Legislature: by dividing the executive power. Proposals to have multiple executives, or a council of advisers with separate authority were rejected. See 1 M. Farrand, Records of the Federal Convention of 1787, pp. 66, 71-74, 88, 91-92 (rev. ed. 1966); 2 id., at 335-337, 533, 537, 542. Thus, while "[a]ll legislative Powers herein granted shall be vested in a Congress of the United States, which shall consist of a Senate and House of Representatives," U.S. Const., Art. I, 1 (emphasis added), "[t]he executive Power shall be vested in a President of the United States," Art. II, 1, cl. 1 (emphasis added).

That is what this suit is about. Power. The allocation of power among Congress, the President, and the courts in such fashion as to preserve the equilibrium the Constitution sought to establish - so that "a gradual concentration of the several powers in the same department," Federalist No. 51, p. 321 (J. Madison), can effectively be resisted. Frequently an issue of this sort will come before the Court clad, so to speak, in sheep's clothing: the potential of the asserted principle to effect important change in the equilibrium of power is not immediately evident, and must be discerned by a careful and perceptive analysis. But this wolf comes as a wolf.

I

The present case began when the Legislative and Executive Branches became "embroiled in a dispute concerning the scope of the congressional investigatory power," United States v. House of Representatives of United States, 556 F. Supp. 150, 152 (DC 1983), which - as is often the case with such interbranch conflicts - became quite acrimonious. In the course of oversight hearings into the administration of the Superfund by the Environmental Protection Agency (EPA), two Subcommittees of the House of Representatives requested and then subpoenaed numerous internal EPA documents. The President responded by personally directing the EPA Administrator not to turn over certain of the documents, see Memorandum of November 30, 1982, from President Reagan for the Administrator, Environmental Protection Agency, reprinted in H. R. Rep. No. 99-435, pp. 1166-1167 (1985), and by having the Attorney General notify the congressional Subcommittees of this assertion of executive privilege, see Letters of

November 30, 1982, from Attorney General William French Smith to Hon. John D. Dingell and Hon. Elliott H. Levitas, reprinted, id., at 1168-1177. In his decision to assert executive privilege, the President was counseled by appellee Olson, who was then Assistant Attorney General of the Department of Justice for the Office of Legal Counsel, a post that has traditionally had responsibility for providing legal advice to the President (subject to approval of the Attorney General). The House's response was to pass a resolution citing the EPA Administrator, who had possession of the documents, for contempt. Contempt of Congress is a criminal offense. See 2 U.S.C. 192. The United States Attorney, however, a member of the Executive Branch, initially took no steps to prosecute the contempt citation. Instead, the Executive Branch sought the immediate assistance of the Third Branch by filing a civil action asking the District Court to declare that the EPA Administrator had acted lawfully in withholding the documents under a claim of executive privilege. See ibid. The District Court declined (in my view correctly) to get involved in the controversy, and urged the other two branches to try "[c]ompromise and cooperation, rather than confrontation." 556 F. Supp., at 153. After further haggling, the two branches eventually reached an agreement giving the House Subcommittees limited access to the contested documents.

Congress did not, however, leave things there. Certain Members of the House remained angered by the confrontation, particularly by the role played by the Department of Justice. Specifically, the Judiciary Committee remained disturbed by the possibility that the Department had persuaded the President to assert executive privilege despite reservations by the EPA; that the Department had "deliberately and unnecessarily precipitated a constitutional confrontation with Congress"; that the Department had not properly reviewed and selected the documents as to which executive privilege was asserted; that the Department had directed the United States Attorney not to present the contempt certification involving the EPA Administrator to a grand jury for prosecution; that the Department had made the decision to sue the House of Representatives; and that the Department had not adequately advised and represented the President, the EPA, and the EPA Administrator. H. R. Rep. No. 99-435, p. 3 (1985) (describing unresolved "questions" that were the basis of the Judiciary Committee's investigation). Accordingly, staff counsel of the House Judiciary Committee were commissioned (apparently without the knowledge of many of the Committee's members, see id., at 731) to investigate the Justice Department's role in the controversy. That investigation lasted 2 1/2 years, and produced a 3,000-page report issued by the Committee over the vigorous dissent of all but one of its minority-party members. That report, which among other charges questioned the truthfulness of certain statements made by Assistant Attorney General Olson during testimony in front of the Committee during the early stages of its investigation, was sent to the Attorney General along with a formal request that he appoint an independent counsel to investigate Mr. Olson and others.

As a general matter, the Act before us here requires the Attorney General to apply for the appointment of an independent counsel within 90 days after receiving a request to do so, unless he determines within that period that "there are no reasonable grounds to believe that further investigation or prosecution is warranted." 28 U.S.C. 592(b)(1). As a practical matter, it would be surprising if the Attorney General had any choice (assuming this statute is constitutional) but to seek appointment of an independent counsel to pursue the charges against the principal object of the congressional request, Mr. Olson. Merely the political consequences (to him and the President) of seeming to break the law by refusing to do so would have been substantial. How could it not be, the public would ask, that a 3,000-page indictment drawn by our representatives over 2 1/2 years does not even establish "reasonable grounds to believe" that further investigation or prosecution is warranted with respect to at least the principal alleged culprit? But the Act establishes more than just practical compulsion. Although the Court's opinion asserts that the Attorney General had "no duty to comply with the [congressional] request," ante, at 694, that is not entirely accurate. He had a duty to comply unless he could conclude that there were "no reasonable grounds to believe," not that prosecution was warranted, but merely that "further investigation" was warranted, 28 U.S.C. 592(b)(1) (1982 ed., Supp. V) (emphasis added), after a 90-day investigation in which he was prohibited from using such routine investigative techniques as grand juries, plea bargaining, grants of immunity, or even subpoenas, see 592(a)(2). The Court also makes much of the fact that "the courts are specifically prevented from reviewing the Attorney General's decision not to seek appointment, 592(f)." Ante, at 695. Yes, 1 but Congress is not prevented from reviewing it. The context of this statute is acrid with the smell of threatened impeachment. Where, as here, a request for appointment of an independent counsel has come from the Judiciary Committee of either House of Congress, the Attorney General must, if he decides not to seek appointment, explain to that Committee why. See also 28 U.S.C. 595(c) (1982 ed., Supp. V) (independent counsel must report to the House of Representatives information "that may constitute grounds for an impeachment").

Thus, by the application of this statute in the present case, Congress has effectively compelled a criminal investigation of a high-level appointee of the President in connection with his actions arising out of a bitter power dispute between the President and the Legislative Branch. Mr. Olson may or may not be guilty of a crime; we do not know. But we do know that the investigation of him has been commenced, not necessarily because the President or his authorized subordinates believe it is in the interest of the United States, in the sense that it warrants the diversion of resources from other efforts, and is worth the cost in money and in possible damage to other governmental interests; and not even, leaving aside those normally considered factors, because the President or his authorized subordinates necessarily believe that an investigation is likely to unearth a violation worth prosecuting; but only because the Attorney General cannot affirm, as Congress demands, that there are no reasonable grounds to believe that further investigation is warranted. The decisions regarding the scope of that further investigation, its duration, and, finally, whether or not prosecution should ensue, are likewise beyond the control of the President and his subordinates.

II

If to describe this case is not to decide it, the concept of a government of separate and coordinate powers no longer has meaning. The Court devotes most of its attention to such relatively technical details as the Appointments Clause and the removal power, addressing briefly and only at the end of its opinion the separation of powers. As my prologue suggests, I think that has it backwards. Our opinions are full of the recognition that it is the principle of separation of powers, and the inseparable corollary that each department's "defense must . . . be made commensurate to the danger of attack," Federalist No. 51, p. 322 (J. Madison), which gives comprehensible content to the Appointments Clause, and determines the appropriate scope of the removal power. Thus, while I will subsequently discuss why our appointments and removal jurisprudence does not support today's holding, I begin with a consideration of the fountainhead of that jurisprudence, the separation and equilibration of powers.

First, however, I think it well to call to mind an important and unusual premise that underlies our deliberations, a premise not expressly contradicted by the Court's opinion, but in my view not faithfully observed. It is rare in a case dealing, as this one does, with the constitutionality of a statute passed by the Congress of the United States, not to find anywhere in the Court's opinion the usual, almost formulary caution that we owe great deference to Congress' view that what it has done is constitutional, see, e. g., Rostker v. Goldberg, 453 U.S. 57, 64 (1981); Fullilove v. Klutznick, 448 U.S. 448, 472 (1980) (opinion of Burger, C. J.); Columbia Broadcasting System, Inc. v. Democratic National Committee, 412 U.S. 94, 102 (1973); United States v. National Dairy Products Corp., 372 U.S. 29, 32 (1963), and that we will decline to apply the statute only if the presumption of constitutionality can be overcome, see Fullilove, supra, at 473; Columbia Broadcasting, supra, at 103. That caution is not recited by the Court in the present case because it does not apply. Where a private citizen challenges action of the Government on grounds unrelated to separation of powers, harmonious functioning of the system demands that we ordinarily give some deference, or a presumption of validity, to the actions of the political branches in what is agreed, between themselves at least, to be within their respective spheres. But where the issue pertains to separation of powers, and the political branches are (as here) in disagreement, neither can be presumed correct. The reason is stated concisely by Madison: "The several departments being perfectly coordinate by the terms of their common commission, neither of them, it is evident, can pretend to an exclusive or superior right of settling the boundaries between their respective powers . . . ." Federalist No. 49, p. 314. The playing field for the present case, in other words, is a level one. As one of the interested and coordinate parties to the underlying constitutional dispute, Congress, no more than the President, is entitled to the benefit of the doubt.

To repeat, Article II, 1, cl. 1, of the Constitution provides:

"The executive Power shall be vested in a President of the United States."

As I described at the outset of this opinion, this does not mean some of the executive power, but all of the executive power. It seems to me, therefore, that the decision of the Court of Appeals invalidating the present statute must be upheld on fundamental separation-of-powers principles if the following two questions are answered affirmatively: (1) Is the conduct of a criminal prosecution (and of an investigation to decide whether to prosecute) the exercise of purely executive power? (2) Does the statute deprive the President of the United States of exclusive control over the exercise of that power? Surprising to say, the Court appears to concede an affirmative answer to both questions, but seeks to avoid the inevitable conclusion that since the statute vests some purely executive power in a person who is not the President of the United States it is void.

The Court concedes that "[t]here is no real dispute that the functions performed by the independent counsel are `executive'," though it qualifies that concession by adding "in the sense that they are law enforcement functions that typically have been undertaken by officials within the Executive Branch." Ante, at 691. The qualifier adds nothing but atmosphere. In what other sense can one identify "the executive Power" that is supposed to be vested in the President (unless it includes everything the Executive Branch is given to do) except by reference to what has always and everywhere - if conducted by government at all - been conducted never by the legislature, never by the courts, and always by the executive. There is no possible doubt that the independent counsel's functions fit this description. She is vested with the "full power and independent authority to exercise all investigative and prosecutorial functions and powers of the Department of Justice [and] the Attorney General." 28 U.S.C. 594(a) (1982 ed., Supp. V) (emphasis added). Governmental investigation and prosecution of crimes is a quintessentially executive function. See Heckler v. Chaney, 470 U.S. 821, 832 (1985); Buckley v. Valeo, 424 U.S. 1, 138 (1976); United States v. Nixon, 418 U.S. 683, 693 (1974).

As for the second question, whether the statute before us deprives the President of exclusive control over that quintessentially executive activity: The Court does not, and could not possibly, assert that it does not. That is indeed the whole object of the statute. Instead, the Court points out that the President, through his Attorney General, has at least some control. That concession is alone enough to invalidate the statute, but I cannot refrain from pointing out that the Court greatly exaggerates the extent of that "some" Presidential control. "Most importan[t]" among these controls, the Court asserts, is the Attorney General's "power to remove the counsel for `good cause.'" Ante, at 696. This is somewhat like referring to shackles as an effective means of locomotion. As we recognized in Humphrey's Executor v. United States, 295 U.S. 602 (1935) - indeed, what Humphrey's Executor was all about - limiting removal power to "good cause" is an impediment to, not an effective grant of, Presidential control. We said that limitation was necessary with respect to members of the Federal Trade Commission, which we found to be "an agency of the legislative and judicial departments," and "wholly disconnected from the executive department," id., at 630, because "it is quite evident that one who holds his office only during the pleasure of another, cannot be depended upon to maintain an attitude of independence against the latter's will." Id., at 629. What we in Humphrey's Executor found to be a means of eliminating Presidential control, the Court today considers the "most importan[t]" means of assuring Presidential control. Congress, of course, operated under no such illusion when it enacted this statute, describing the "good cause" limitation as "protecting the independent counsel's ability to act independently of the President's direct control" since it permits removal only for "misconduct." H. R. Conf. Rep. 100-452, p. 37 (1987).

Moving on to the presumably "less important" controls that the President retains, the Court notes that no independent counsel may be appointed without a specific request from the Attorney General. As I have discussed above, the condition that renders such a request mandatory (inability to find "no reasonable grounds to believe" that further investigation is warranted) is so insubstantial that the Attorney General's discretion is severely confined. And once the referral is made, it is for the Special Division to determine the scope and duration of the investigation. See 28 U.S.C. 593(b) (1982 ed., Supp. V). And in any event, the limited power over referral is irrelevant to the question whether, once appointed, the independent counsel exercises executive power free from the President's control. Finally, the Court points out that the Act directs the independent counsel to abide by general Justice Department policy, except when not "possible." See 28 U.S.C. 594(f) (1982 ed., Supp. V). The exception alone shows this to be an empty promise. Even without that, however, one would be hard put to come up with many investigative or prosecutorial "policies" (other than those imposed by the Constitution or by Congress through law) that are absolute. Almost all investigative and prosecutorial decisions - including the ultimate decision whether, after a technical violation of the law has been found, prosecution is warranted - involve the balancing of innumerable legal and practical considerations. Indeed, even political considerations (in the nonpartisan sense) must be considered, as exemplified by the recent decision of an independent counsel to subpoena the former Ambassador of Canada, producing considerable tension in our relations with that country. See N. Y. Times, May 29, 1987, p. A12, col. 1. Another pre-eminently political decision is whether getting a conviction in a particular case is worth the disclosure of national security information that would be necessary. The Justice Department and our intelligence agencies are often in disagreement on this point, and the Justice Department does not always win. The present Act even goes so far as specifically to take the resolution of that dispute away from the President and give it to the independent counsel. 28 U.S.C. 594(a)(6) (1982 ed., Supp. V). In sum, the balancing of various legal, practical, and political considerations, none of which is absolute, is the very essence of prosecutorial discretion. To take this away is to remove the core of the prosecutorial function, and not merely "some" Presidential control.

As I have said, however, it is ultimately irrelevant how much the statute reduces Presidential control. The case is over when the Court acknowledges, as it must, that "[i]t is undeniable that the Act reduces the amount of control or supervision that the Attorney General and, through him, the President exercises over the investigation and prosecution of a certain class of alleged criminal activity." Ante, at 695. It effects a revolution in our constitutional jurisprudence for the Court, once it has determined that (1) purely executive functions are at issue here, and (2) those functions have been given to a person whose actions are not fully within the supervision and control of the President, nonetheless to proceed further to sit in judgment of whether "the President's need to control the exercise of [the independent counsel's] discretion is so central to the functioning of the Executive Branch" as to require complete control, ante, at 691 (emphasis added), whether the conferral of his powers upon someone else "sufficiently deprives the President of control over the independent counsel to interfere impermissibly with [his] constitutional obligation to ensure the faithful execution of the laws," ante, at 693 (emphasis added), and whether "the Act give[s] the Executive Branch sufficient control over the independent counsel to ensure that the President is able to perform his constitutionally assigned duties," ante, at 696 (emphasis added). It is not for us to determine, and we have never presumed to determine, how much of the purely executive powers of government must be within the full control of the President. The Constitution prescribes that they all are.

The utter incompatibility of the Court's approach with our constitutional traditions can be made more clear, perhaps, by applying it to the powers of the other two branches. Is it conceivable that if Congress passed a statute depriving itself of less than full and entire control over some insignificant area of legislation, we would inquire whether the matter was "so central to the functioning of the Legislative Branch" as really to require complete control, or whether the statute gives Congress "sufficient control over the surrogate legislator to ensure that Congress is able to perform its constitutionally assigned duties"? Of course we would have none of that. Once we determined that a purely legislative power was at issue we would require it to be exercised, wholly and entirely, by Congress. Or to bring the point closer to home, consider a statute giving to non-Article III judges just a tiny bit of purely judicial power in a relatively insignificant field, with substantial control, though not total control, in the courts - perhaps "clear error" review, which would be a fair judicial equivalent of the Attorney General's "for cause" removal power here. Is there any doubt that we would not pause to inquire whether the matter was "so central to the functioning of the Judicial Branch" as really to require complete control, or whether we retained "sufficient control over the matters to be decided that we are able to perform our constitutionally assigned duties"? We would say that our "constitutionally assigned duties" include complete control over all exercises of the judicial power - or, as the plurality opinion said in Northern Pipeline Construction Co. v. Marathon Pipe Line Co., 458 U.S. 50, 58 -59 (1982): "The inexorable command of [Article III] is clear and definite: The judicial power of the United States must be exercised by courts having the attributes prescribed in Art. III." We should say here that the President's constitutionally assigned duties include complete control over investigation and prosecution of violations of the law, and that the inexorable command of Article II is clear and definite: the executive power must be vested in the President of the United States.

Is it unthinkable that the President should have such exclusive power, even when alleged crimes by him or his close associates are at issue? No more so than that Congress should have the exclusive power of legislation, even when what is at issue is its own exemption from the burdens of certain laws. See Civil Rights Act of 1964, Title VII, 42 U.S.C. 2000e et seq. (prohibiting "employers," not defined to include the United States, from discriminating on the basis of race, color, religion, sex, or national origin). No more so than that this Court should have the exclusive power to pronounce the final decision on justiciable cases and controversies, even those pertaining to the constitutionality of a statute reducing the salaries of the Justices. See United States v. Will, 449 U.S. 200, 211 - 217 (1980). A system of separate and coordinate powers necessarily involves an acceptance of exclusive power that can theoretically be abused. As we reiterate this very day, "[i]t is a truism that constitutional protections have costs." Coy v. Iowa, post, at 1020. While the separation of powers may prevent us from righting every wrong, it does so in order to ensure that we do not lose liberty. The checks against any branch's abuse of its exclusive powers are twofold: First, retaliation by one of the other branch's use of its exclusive powers: Congress, for example, can impeach the executive who willfully fails to enforce the laws; the executive can decline to prosecute under unconstitutional statutes, cf. United States v. Lovett, 328 U.S. 303 (1946); and the courts can dismiss malicious prosecutions. Second, and ultimately, there is the political check that the people will replace those in the political branches (the branches more "dangerous to the political rights of the Constitution," Federalist No. 78, p. 465) who are guilty of abuse. Political pressures produced special prosecutors - for Teapot Dome and for Watergate, for example - long before this statute created the independent counsel. See Act of Feb. 8, 1924, ch. 16, 43 Stat. 5-6; 38 Fed. Reg. 30738 (1973).

The Court has, nonetheless, replaced the clear constitutional prescription that the executive power belongs to the President with a "balancing test." What are the standards to determine how the balance is to be struck, that is, how much removal of Presidential power is too much? Many countries of the world get along with an executive that is much weaker than ours - in fact, entirely dependent upon the continued support of the legislature. Once we depart from the text of the Constitution, just where short of that do we stop? The most amazing feature of the Court's opinion is that it does not even purport to give an answer. It simply announces, with no analysis, that the ability to control the decision whether to investigate and prosecute the President's closest advisers, and indeed the President himself, is not "so central to the functioning of the Executive Branch" as to be constitutionally required to be within the President's control. Apparently that is so because we say it is so. Having abandoned as the basis for our decisionmaking the text of Article II that "the executive Power" must be vested in the President, the Court does not even attempt to craft a substitute criterion - a "justiciable standard," see, e. g., Baker v. Carr, 369 U.S. 186, 210 (1962); Coleman v. Miller, 307 U.S. 433, 454 -455 (1939), however remote from the Constitution - that today governs, and in the future will govern, the decision of such questions. Evidently, the governing standard is to be what might be called the unfettered wisdom of a majority of this Court, revealed to an obedient people on a case-by-case basis. This is not only not the government of laws that the Constitution established; it is not a government of laws at all.

In my view, moreover, even as an ad hoc, standardless judgment the Court's conclusion must be wrong. Before this statute was passed, the President, in taking action disagreeable to the Congress, or an executive officer giving advice to the President or testifying before Congress concerning one of those many matters on which the two branches are from time to time at odds, could be assured that his acts and motives would be adjudged - insofar as the decision whether to conduct a criminal investigation and to prosecute is concerned - in the Executive Branch, that is, in a forum attuned to the interests and the policies of the Presidency. That was one of the natural advantages the Constitution gave to the Presidency, just as it gave members of Congress (and their staffs) the advantage of not being prosecutable for anything said or done in their legislative capacities. See U.S. Const., Art. I, 6, cl. 1; Gravel v. United States, 408 U.S. 606 (1972). It is the very object of this legislation to eliminate that assurance of a sympathetic forum. Unless it can honestly be said that there are "no reasonable grounds to believe" that further investigation is warranted, further investigation must ensure; and the conduct of the investigation, and determination of whether to prosecute, will be given to a person neither selected by nor subject to the control of the President - who will in turn assemble a staff by finding out, presumably, who is willing to put aside whatever else they are doing, for an indeterminate period of time, in order to investigate and prosecute the President or a particular named individual in his administration. The prospect is frightening (as I will discuss at some greater length at the conclusion of this opinion) even outside the context of a bitter, interbranch political dispute. Perhaps the boldness of the President himself will not be affected - though I am not even sure of that. (How much easier it is for Congress, instead of accepting the political damage attendant to the commencement of impeachment proceedings against the President on trivial grounds - or, for that matter, how easy it is for one of the President's political foes outside of Congress - simply to trigger a debilitating criminal investigation of the Chief Executive under this law.) But as for the President's high-level assistants, who typically have no political base of support, it is as utterly unrealistic to think that they will not be intimidated by this prospect, and that their advice to him and their advocacy of his interests before a hostile Congress will not be affected, as it would be to think that the Members of Congress and their staffs would be unaffected by replacing the Speech or Debate Clause with a similar provision. It deeply wounds the President, by substantially reducing the President's ability to protect himself and his staff. That is the whole object of the law, of course, and I cannot imagine why the Court believes it does not succeed.

Besides weakening the Presidency by reducing the zeal of his staff, it must also be obvious that the institution of the independent counsel enfeebles him more directly in his constant confrontations with Congress, by eroding his public support. Nothing is so politically effective as the ability to charge that one's opponent and his associates are not merely wrongheaded, naive, ineffective, but, in all probability, "crooks." And nothing so effectively gives an appearance of validity to such charges as a Justice Department investigation and, even better, prosecution. The present statute provides ample means for that sort of attack, assuring that massive and lengthy investigations will occur, not merely when the Justice Department in the application of its usual standards believes they are called for, but whenever it cannot be said that there are "no reasonable grounds to believe" they are called for. The statute's highly visible procedures assure, moreover, that unlike most investigations these will be widely known and prominently displayed. Thus, in the 10 years since the institution of the independent counsel was established by law, there have been nine highly publicized investigations, a source of constant political damage to two administrations. That they could not remotely be described as merely the application of "normal" investigatory and prosecutory standards is demonstrated by, in addition to the language of the statute ("no reasonable grounds to believe"), the following facts: Congress appropriates approximately $50 million annually for general legal activities, salaries, and expenses of the Criminal Division of the Department of Justice. See 1989 Budget Request of the Department of Justice, Hearings before a Subcommittee of the House Committee on Appropriations, 100th Cong., 2d Sess., pt. 6, pp. 284-285 (1988) (DOJ Budget Request). This money is used to support "[f]ederal appellate activity," "[o]rganized crime prosecution," "[p]ublic integrity" and "[f]raud" matters, "[n]arcotic & dangerous drug prosecution," "[i]nternal security," "[g]eneral litigation and legal advice," "special investigations," "[p]rosecution support," "[o]rganized crime drug enforcement," and "[m]anagement & administration." Id., at 284. By comparison, between May 1986 and August 1987, four independent counsel (not all of whom were operating for that entire period of time) spent almost $5 million (one-tenth of the amount annually appropriated to the entire Criminal Division), spending almost $1 million in the month of August 1987 alone. See Washington Post, Oct. 21, 1987, p. A21, col. 5. For fiscal year 1989, the Department of Justice has requested $52 million for the entire Criminal Division, DOJ Budget Request 285, and $7 million to support the activities of independent counsel, id., at 25.

In sum, this statute does deprive the President of substantial control over the prosecutory functions performed by the independent counsel, and it does substantially affect the balance of powers. That the Court could possibly conclude otherwise demonstrates both the wisdom of our former constitutional system, in which the degree of reduced control and political impairment were irrelevant, since all purely executive power had to be in the President; and the folly of the new system of standardless judicial allocation of powers we adopt today.

III

As I indicated earlier, the basic separation-of-powers principles I have discussed are what give life and content to our jurisprudence concerning the President's power to appoint and remove officers. The same result of unconstitutionality is therefore plainly indicated by our case law in these areas.

Article II, 2, cl. 2, of the Constitution provides as follows:

"[The President] shall nominate, and by and with the Advice and Consent of the the Senate, shall appoint Ambassadors, other public Ministers and Consuls, Judges of the supreme Court, and all other Officers of the United States, whose Appointments are not herein otherwise provided for, and which shall be established by Law: but the Congress may by Law vest the Appointment of such inferior Officers, as they think proper, in the President alone, in the Courts of Law, or in the Heads of Departments."

Because appellant (who all parties and the Court agree is an officer of the United States, ante, at 671, n. 12) was not appointed by the President with the advice and consent of the Senate, but rather by the Special Division of the United States Court of Appeals, her appointment is constitutional only if (1) she is an "inferior" officer within the meaning of the above Clause, and (2) Congress may vest her appointment in a court of law.

As to the first of these inquiries, the Court does not attempt to "decide exactly" what establishes the line between principal and "inferior" officers, but is confident that, whatever the line may be, appellant "clearly falls on the `inferior officer' side" of it. Ante, at 671. The Court gives three reasons: First, she "is subject to removal by a higher Executive Branch official," namely, the Attorney General. Ibid. Second, she is "empowered by the Act to perform only certain, limited duties." Ibid. Third, her office is "limited in jurisdiction" and "limited in tenure." Ante, at 672.

The first of these lends no support to the view that appellant is an inferior officer. Appellant is removable only for "good cause" or physical or mental incapacity. 28 U.S.C. 596(a) (1) (1982 ed., Supp. V). By contrast, most (if not all) principal officers in the Executive Branch may be removed by the President at will. I fail to see how the fact that appellant is more difficult to remove than most principal officers helps to establish that she is an inferior officer. And I do not see how it could possibly make any difference to her superior or inferior status that the President's limited power to remove her must be exercised through the Attorney General. If she were removable at will by the Attorney General, then she would be subordinate to him and thus properly designated as inferior; but the Court essentially admits that she is not subordinate. See ante, at 671. If it were common usage to refer to someone as "inferior" who is subject to removal for cause by another, then one would say that the President is "inferior" to Congress.

The second reason offered by the Court - that appellant performs only certain, limited duties - may be relevant to whether she is an inferior officer, but it mischaracterizes the extent of her powers. As the Court states: "Admittedly, the Act delegates to appellant [the] `full power and independent authority to exercise all investigative and prosecutorial functions and powers of the Department of Justice.'" Ibid., quoting 28 U.S.C. 594(a) (1982 ed., Supp. V) (emphasis added). 2 Moreover, in addition to this general grant of power she is given a broad range of specifically enumerated powers, including a power not even the Attorney General possesses: to "contes[t] in court

... any claim of privilege or attempt to withhold evidence on grounds of national security." 594(a)(6). 3 Once all of this is "admitted," it seems to me impossible to maintain that appellant's authority is so "limited" as to render her an inferior officer. The Court seeks to brush this away by asserting that the independent counsel's power does not include any authority to "formulate policy for the Government or the Executive Branch." Ante, at 671. But the same could be said for all officers of the Government, with the single exception of the President. All of them only formulate policy within their respective spheres of responsibility - as does the independent counsel, who must comply with the policies of the Department of Justice only to the extent possible. 594(f).

The final set of reasons given by the Court for why the independent counsel clearly is an inferior officer emphasizes the limited nature of her jurisdiction and tenure. Taking the latter first, I find nothing unusually limited about the independent counsel's tenure. To the contrary, unlike most high ranking Executive Branch officials, she continues to serve until she (or the Special Division) decides that her work is substantially completed. See 596(b)(1), (b)(2). This particular independent prosecutor has already served more than two years, which is at least as long as many Cabinet officials. As to the scope of her jurisdiction, there can be no doubt that is small (though far from unimportant). But within it she exercises more than the full power of the Attorney General. The Ambassador to Luxembourg is not anything less than a principal officer, simply because Luxembourg is small. And the federal judge who sits in a small district is not for that reason "inferior in rank and authority." If the mere fragmentation of executive responsibilities into small compartments suffices to render the heads of each of those compartments inferior officers, then Congress could deprive the President of the right to appoint his chief law enforcement officer by dividing up the Attorney General's responsibilities among a number of "lesser" functionaries.

More fundamentally, however, it is not clear from the Court's opinion why the factors it discusses - even if applied correctly to the facts of this case - are determinative of the question of inferior officer status. The apparent source of these factors is a statement in United States v. Germaine, 99 U.S. 508, 511 (1879) (discussing United States v. Hartwell, 6 Wall. 385, 393 (1868)), that "the term [officer] embraces the ideas of tenure, duration, emolument, and duties." See ante, at 672. Besides the fact that this was dictum, it was dictum in a case where the distinguishing characteristics of inferior officers versus superior officers were in no way relevant, but rather only the distinguishing characteristics of an "officer of the United States" (to which the criminal statute at issue applied) as opposed to a mere employee. Rather than erect a theory of who is an inferior officer on the foundation of such an irrelevancy, I think it preferable to look to the text of the Constitution and the division of power that it establishes. These demonstrate, I think, that the independent counsel is not an inferior officer because she is not subordinate to any officer in the Executive Branch (indeed, not even to the President). Dictionaries in use at the time of the Constitutional Convention gave the word "inferiour" two meanings which it still bears today: (1) "[l]ower in place, . . . station, . . . rank of life, . . . value or excellency," and (2) "[s]ubordinate." S. Johnson, Dictionary of the English Language (6th ed. 1785). In a document dealing with the structure (the constitution) of a government, one would naturally expect the word to bear the latter meaning - indeed, in such a context it would be unpardonably careless to use the word unless a relationship of subordination was intended. If what was meant was merely "lower in station or rank," one would use instead a term such as "lesser officers." At the only other point in the Constitution at which the word "inferior" appears, it plainly connotes a relationship of subordination. Article III vests the judicial power of the United States in "one supreme Court, and in such inferior Courts as the Congress may from time to time ordain and establish." U.S. Const., Art. III, 1 (emphasis added). In Federalist No. 81, Hamilton pauses to describe the "inferior" courts authorized by Article III as inferior in the sense that they are "subordinate" to the Supreme Court. See id., at 485, n., 490, n.

That "inferior" means "subordinate" is also consistent with what little we know about the evolution of the Appointments Clause. As originally reported to the Committee on Style, the Appointments Clause provided no "exception" from the standard manner of appointment (President with the advice and consent of the Senate) for inferior officers. 2 M. Farrand, Records of the Federal Convention of 1787, pp. 498-499, 599 (rev. ed. 1966). On September 15, 1787, the last day of the Convention before the proposed Constitution was signed, in the midst of a host of minor changes that were being considered, Gouverneur Morris moved to add the exceptions clause. Id., at 627. No great debate ensued; the only disagreement was over whether it was necessary at all. Id., at 627-628. Nobody thought that it was a fundamental change, excluding from the President's appointment power and the Senate's confirmation power a category of officers who might function on their own, outside the supervision of those appointed in the more cumbersome fashion. And it is significant that in the very brief discussion Madison mentions (as in apparent contrast to the "inferior officers" covered by the provision) "Superior Officers." Id., at 637. Of course one is not a "superior officer" without some supervisory responsibility, just as, I suggest, one is not an "inferior officer" within the meaning of the provision under discussion unless one is subject to supervision by a "superior officer." It is perfectly obvious, therefore, both from the relative brevity of the discussion this addition received, and from the content of that discussion, that it was intended merely to make clear (what Madison thought already was clear, see id., at 627) that those officers appointed by the President with Senate approval could on their own appoint their subordinates, who would, of course, by chain of command still be under the direct control of the President.

This interpretation is, moreover, consistent with our admittedly sketchy precedent in this area. For example, in United States v. Eaton, 169 U.S. 331 (1898), we held that the appointment by an Executive Branch official other than the President of a "vice-consul," charged with the duty of temporarily performing the function of the consul, did not violate the Appointments Clause. In doing so, we repeatedly referred to the "vice-consul" as a "subordinate" officer. Id., at 343. See also United States v. Germaine, supra, at 511 (comparing "inferior" commissioners and bureau officers to heads of department, describing the former as "mere . . . subordinates") (dicta); United States v. Hartwell, supra, at 394 (describing clerk appointed by Assistant Treasurer with approval of Secretary of the Treasury as a "subordinate office[r]") (dicta). More recently, in United States v. Nixon, 418 U.S. 683 (1974), we noted that the Attorney General's appointment of the Watergate Special Prosecutor was made pursuant to the Attorney General's "power to appoint subordinate officers to assist him in the discharge of his duties." Id., at 694 (emphasis added). The Court's citation of Nixon as support for its view that the independent counsel is an inferior officer is simply not supported by a reading of the case. We explicitly stated that the Special Prosecutor was a "subordinate office[r]," ibid., because, in the end, the President or the Attorney General could have removed him at any time, if by no other means than amending or revoking the regulation defining his authority. Id., at 696. Nor are any of the other cases cited by the Court in support of its view inconsistent with the natural reading that an inferior officer must at least be subordinate to another officer of the United States. In Ex parte Siebold, 100 U.S. 371 (1880), we upheld the appointment by a court of federal "Judges of Election," who were charged with various duties involving the overseeing of local congressional elections. Contrary to the Court's assertion, see ante, at 673, we did not specifically find that these officials were inferior officers for purposes of the Appointments Clause, probably because no one had contended that they were principal officers. Nor can the case be said to represent even an assumption on our part that they were inferior without being subordinate. The power of assisting in the judging of elections that they were exercising was assuredly not a purely executive power, and if we entertained any assumption it was probably that they, like the marshals who assisted them, see Siebold, 100 U.S., at 380, were subordinate to the courts, see id., at 397. Similarly, in GoBart Importing Co. v. United States, 282 U.S. 344 (1931), where we held that United States commissioners were inferior officers, we made plain that they were subordinate to the district courts which appointed them: "The commissioner acted not as a court, or as a judge of any court, but as a mere officer of the district court in proceedings of which that court had authority to take control at any time." Id., at 354.

To be sure, it is not a sufficient condition for "inferior" officer status that one be subordinate to a principal officer. Even an officer who is subordinate to a department head can be a principal officer. That is clear from the brief exchange following Gouverneur Morris' suggestion of the addition of the exceptions clause for inferior officers. Madison responded:

"It does not go far enough if it be necessary at all - Superior Officers below Heads of Departments ought in some cases to have the appointment of the lesser offices." 2 M. Farrand, Records of the Federal Convention, of 1787, p. 627 (rev. ed. 1966) (emphasis added).

But it is surely a necessary condition for inferior officer status that the officer be subordinate to another officer.

The independent counsel is not even subordinate to the President. The Court essentially admits as much, noting that "appellant may not be `subordinate' to the Attorney General (and the President) insofar as she possesses a degree of independent discretion to exercise the powers delegated to her under the Act." Ante, at 671. In fact, there is no doubt about it. As noted earlier, the Act specifically grants her the "full power and independent authority to exercise all investigative and prosecutorial functions of the Department of Justice," 28 U.S.C. 594(a) (1982 ed., Supp. V), and makes her removable only for "good cause," a limitation specifically intended to ensure that she be independent of, not subordinate to, the President and the Attorney General. See H. R. Conf. Rep. No. 100-452, p. 37 (1987).

Because appellant is not subordinate to another officer, she is not an "inferior" officer and her appointment other than by the President with the advice and consent of the Senate is unconstitutional.

IV

I will not discuss at any length why the restrictions upon the removal of the independent counsel also violate our established precedent dealing with that specific subject. For most of it, I simply refer the reader to the scholarly opinion of Judge Silberman for the Court of Appeals below. See In re Sealed Case, 267 U.S. App. D.C. 178, 838 F.2d 476 (1988). I cannot avoid commenting, however, about the essence of what the Court has done to our removal jurisprudence today.

There is, of course, no provision in the Constitution stating who may remove executive officers, except the provisions for removal by impeachment. Before the present decision it was established, however, (1) that the President's power to remove principal officers who exercise purely executive powers could not be restricted, see Myers v. United States, 272 U.S. 52, 127 (1926), and (2) that his power to remove inferior officers who exercise purely executive powers, and whose appointment Congress had removed from the usual procedure of Presidential appointment with Senate consent, could be restricted, at least where the appointment had been made by an officer of the Executive Branch, see ibid.; United States v. Perkins, 116 U.S. 483, 485 (1886). 4

The Court could have resolved the removal power issue in this case by simply relying upon its erroneous conclusion that the independent counsel was an inferior officer, and then extending our holding that the removal of inferior officers appointed by the Executive can be restricted, to a new holding that even the removal of inferior officers appointed by the courts can be restricted. That would in my view be a considerable and unjustified extension, giving the Executive full discretion in neither the selection nor the removal of a purely executive officer. The course the Court has chosen, however, is even worse.

Since our 1935 decision in Humphrey's Executor v. United States, 295 U.S. 602 - which was considered by many at the time the product of an activist, anti-New Deal Court bent on reducing the power of President Franklin Roosevelt - it has been established that the line of permissible restriction upon removal of principal officers lies at the point at which the powers exercised by those officers are no longer purely executive. Thus, removal restrictions have been generally regarded as lawful for so-called "independent regulatory agencies," such as the Federal Trade Commission, see ibid.; 15 U.S.C. 41, the Interstate Commerce Commission, see 49 U.S.C. 10301(c) (1982 ed., Supp. IV), and the Consumer Product Safety Commission, see 15 U.S.C. 2053(a), which engage substantially in what has been called the "quasi-legislative activity" of rulemaking, and for members of Article I courts, such as the Court of Military Appeals, see 10 U.S.C. 867(a)(2), who engage in the "quasi-judicial" function of adjudication. It has often been observed, correctly in my view, that the line between "purely executive" functions and "quasi-legislative" or "quasi-judicial" functions is not a clear one or even a rational one. See ante, at 689-691; Bowsher v. Synar, 478 U.S. 714, 761, n. 3 (1986) (WHITE, J., dissenting); FTC v. Ruberoid Co., 343 U.S. 470, 487 -488 (1952) (Jackson, J., dissenting). But at least it permitted the identification of certain officers, and certain agencies, whose functions were entirely within the control of the President. Congress had to be aware of that restriction in its legislation. Today, however, Humphrey's Executor is swept into the dustbin of repudiated constitutional principles. "[O]ur present considered view," the Court says, "is that the determination of whether the Constitution allows Congress to impose a `good cause'-type restriction on the President's power to remove an official cannot be made to turn on whether or not that official is classified as `purely executive.'" Ante, at 689. What Humphrey's Executor (and presumably Myers) really means, we are now told, is not that there are any "rigid categories of those officials who may or may not be removed at will by the President," but simply that Congress cannot "interefere with the President's exercise of the `executive power' and his constitutionally appointed duty to `take care that the laws be faithfully executed,'" ante, at 689-690.

One can hardly grieve for the shoddy treatment given today to Humphrey's Executor, which, after all, accorded the same indignity (with much less justification) to Chief Justice Taft's opinion 10 years earlier in Myers v. United States, 272 U.S. 52 (1926) - gutting, in six quick pages devoid of textual or historical precedent for the novel principle it set forth, a carefully researched and reasoned 70-page opinion. It is in fact comforting to witness the reality that he who lives by the ipse dixit dies by the ipse dixit. But one must grieve for the Constitution. Humphrey's Executor at least had the decency formally to observe the constitutional principle that the President had to be the repository of all executive power, see 295 U.S., at 627 -628, which, as Myers carefully explained, necessarily means that he must be able to discharge those who do not perform executive functions according to his liking. As we noted in Bowsher, once an officer is appointed "`it is only the authority that can remove him, and not the authority that appointed him, that he must fear and, in the performance of his functions, obey.'" 478 U.S., at 726, quoting Synar v. United States, 626 F. Supp. 1374, 1401 (DC 1986) (Scalia, Johnson, and Gasch, JJ.). By contrast, "our present considered view" is simply that any executive officer's removal can be restricted, so long as the President remains "able to accomplish his constitutional role." Ante, at 690. There are now no lines. If the removal of a prosecutor, the virtual embodiment of the power to "take care that the laws be faithfully executed," can be restricted, what officer's removal cannot? This is an open invitation for Congress to experiment. What about a special Assistant Secretary of State, with responsibility for one very narrow area of foreign policy, who would not only have to be confirmed by the Senate but could also be removed only pursuant to certain carefully designed restrictions? Could this possibly render the President "[un]able to accomplish his constitutional role"? Or a special Assistant Secretary of Defense for Procurement? The possibilities are endless, and the Court does not understand what the separation of powers, what "[a]mbition . . . counteract[ing] ambition." Federalist No. 51, p. 322 (Madison), is all about, if it does not expect Congress to try them. As far as I can discern from the Court's opinion, it is now open season upon the President's removal power for all executive officers, with not even the superficially principled restriction of Humphrey's Executor as cover. The Court essentially says to the President: "Trust us. We will make sure that you are able to accomplish your constitutional role." I think the Constitution gives the President - and the people - more protection than that.

V

The purpose of the separation and equilibration of powers in general, and of the unitary Executive in particular, was not merely to assure effective government but to preserve individual freedom. Those who hold or have held offices covered by the Ethics in Government Act are entitled to that protection as much as the rest of us, and I conclude my discussion by considering the effect of the Act upon the fairness of the process they receive.

Only someone who has worked in the field of law enforcement can fully appreciate the vast power and the immense discretion that are placed in the hands of a prosecutor with respect to the objects of his investigation. Justice Robert Jackson, when he was Attorney General under President Franklin Roosevelt, described it in a memorable speech to United States Attorneys, as follows:

> "There is a most important reason why the prosecutor should have, as nearly as possible, a detached and impartial view of all groups in his community. Law enforcement is not automatic. It isn't blind. One of the greatest difficulties of the position of prosecutor is that he must pick his cases, because no prosecutor can even investigate all of the cases in which he receives complaints. If the Department of Justice were to make even a pretense of reaching every probable violation of federal law, ten times its present staff will be inadequate. We know that no local police force can strictly enforce the traffic laws, or it would arrest half the driving population on any given morning. What every prosecutor is practically required to do is to select the cases for prosecution and to select those in which the offense is the most flagrant, the public harm the greatest, and the proof the most certain.

> "If the prosecutor is obliged to choose his case, it follows that he can choose his defendants. Therein is the most dangerous power of the prosecutor: that he will pick people that he thinks he should get, rather than cases that need to be prosecuted. With

the law books filled with a great assortment of crimes, a prosecutor stands a fair chance of finding at least a technical violation of some act on the part of almost anyone. In such a case, it is not a question of discovering the commission of a crime and then looking for the man who has committed it, it is a question of picking the man and then searching the law books, or putting investigators to work, to pin some offense on him. It is in this realm - in which the prosecutor picks some person whom he dislikes or desires to embarrass, or selects some group of unpopular persons and then looks for an offense, that the greatest danger of abuse of prosecuting power lies. It is here that law enforcement becomes personal, and the real crime becomes that of being unpopular with the predominant or governing group, being attached to the wrong political views, or being personally obnoxious to or in the way of the prosecutor himself." R. Jackson, The Federal Prosecutor, Address Delivered at the Second Annual Conference of United States Attorneys, April 1, 1940.

Under our system of government, the primary check against prosecutorial abuse is a political one. The prosecutors who exercise this awesome discretion are selected and can be removed by a President, whom the people have trusted enough to elect. Moreover, when crimes are not investigated and prosecuted fairly, nonselectively, with a reasonable sense of proportion, the President pays the cost in political damage to his administration. If federal prosecutors "pick people that [they] thin[k] [they] should get, rather than cases that need to be prosecuted," if they amass many more resources against a particular prominent individual, or against a particular class of political protesters, or against members of a particular political party, than the gravity of the alleged offenses or the record of successful prosecutions seems to warrant, the unfairness will come home to roost in the Oval Office. I leave it to the reader to recall the examples of this in recent years. That result, of course, was precisely what the Founders had in mind when they provided that all executive powers would be exercised by a single Chief Executive. As Hamilton put it, "[t]he ingredients which constitute safety in the republican sense are a due dependence on the people, and a due responsibility." Federalist No. 70, p. 424. The President is directly dependent on the people, and since there is only one President, he is responsible. The people know whom to blame, whereas "one of the weightiest objections to a plurality in the executive . . . is that it tends to conceal faults and destroy responsibility." Id., at 427.

That is the system of justice the rest of us are entitled to, but what of that select class consisting of present or former high-level Executive Branch officials? If an allegation is made against them of any violation of any federal criminal law (except Class B or C misdemeanors or infractions) the Attorney General must give it his attention. That in itself is not objectionable. But if, after a 90-day investigation without the benefit of normal investigatory tools, the Attorney General is unable to say that there are "no reasonable grounds to believe" that further investigation is warranted, a process is set in motion that is not in the full control of persons "dependent on the people," and whose flaws cannot be blamed on the President. An independent counsel is selected, and the scope of his or her authority prescribed, by a panel of judges. What if they are politically partisan, as judges have been known to be, and select a prosecutor antagonistic to the administration, or even to the particular individual who has been selected for this special treatment? There is no remedy for that, not even a political one. Judges, after all, have life tenure, and appointing a surefire enthusiastic prosecutor could hardly be considered an impeachable offense. So if there is anything wrong with the selection, there is effectively no one to blame. The independent counsel thus selected proceeds to assemble a staff. As I observed earlier, in the nature of things this has to be done by finding lawyers who are willing to lay aside their current careers for an indeterminate amount of time, to take on a job that has no prospect of permanence and little prospect for promotion. One thing is certain, however: it involves investigating and perhaps prosecuting a particular individual. Can one imagine a less equitable manner of fulfilling the executive responsibility to investigate and prosecute? What would be the reaction if, in an area not covered by this statute, the Justice Department posted a public notice inviting applicants to assist in an investigation and possible prosecution of a certain prominent person? Does this not invite what Justice Jackson described as "picking the man and then searching the law books, or putting investigators to work, to pin some offense on him"? To be sure, the investigation must relate to the area of criminal offense specified by the life-tenured judges. But that has often been (and nothing prevents it from being) very broad - and should the independent counsel or his or her staff come up with something beyond that scope, nothing prevents him or her from asking the judges to expand his or her authority or, if that does not work, referring it to the Attorney General, whereupon the whole process would recommence and, if there was "reasonable basis to believe" that further investigation was warranted, that new offense would be referred to the Special Division, which would in all likelihood assign it to the same independent counsel. It seems to me not conducive to fairness. But even if it were entirely evident that unfairness was in fact the result - the judges hostile to the administration, the independent counsel an old foe of the President, the staff refugees from the recently defeated administration - there would be no one accountable to the public to whom the blame could be assigned.

  I do not mean to suggest that anything of this sort (other than the inevitable self-selection of the prosecutory staff) occurred in the present case. I know and have the highest regard for the judges on the Special Division, and the independent counsel herself is a woman of accomplishment, impartiality, and integrity. But the fairness of a process must be adjudged on the basis of what it permits to happen, not what it produced in a particular case. It is true, of course, that a similar list of horribles could be attributed to an ordinary Justice Department prosecution - a vindictive prosecutor, an antagonistic staff, etc. But the difference is the difference that the Founders envisioned when they established a single Chief Executive accountable to the people: the blame can be assigned to someone who can be punished.

  The above described possibilities of irresponsible conduct must, as I say, be considered in judging the constitutional acceptability of this process. But they will rarely occur, and in the average case the threat to fairness is quite different. As described in the brief filed on behalf of three ex-Attorneys General from each of the last three administrations:

> "The problem is less spectacular but much more worrisome. It is that the institutional environment of the Independent Counsel - specifically, her isolation from the Executive Branch and the internal checks and balances it supplies - is designed to heighten, not to check, all of the occupational hazards of the dedicated prosecutor; the danger of too narrow a focus, of the loss of perspective, of preoccupation with the pursuit of one alleged suspect to the exclusion of other interests." Brief for Edward H. Levi, Griffin B. Bell, and William French Smith as Amici Curiae 11.

It is, in other words, an additional advantage of the unitary Executive that it can achieve a more uniform application of the law. Perhaps that is not always achieved, but the mechanism to achieve it is there. The mini-Executive that is the independent counsel, however, operating in an area where so little is law and so much is discretion, is intentionally cut off from the unifying influence of the Justice Department, and from the perspective that multiple responsibilities provide. What would normally be regarded as a technical violation (there are no rules defining such things), may in his or her small world assume the proportions of an indictable offense. What would normally be regarded as an investigation that has reached the level of pursuing such picayune matters that it should be concluded, may to him or her be an investigation that ought to go on for another year. How frightening it must be to have your own independent counsel and staff appointed, with nothing else to do but to investigate you until investigation is no longer worthwhile - with whether it is worthwhile not depending upon what such judgments usually hinge on, competing responsibilities. And to have that counsel and staff decide, with no basis for comparison, whether what you have done is bad enough, willful enough, and provable enough, to warrant an indictment. How admirable the constitutional system that provides the means to avoid such a distortion. And how unfortunate the judicial decision that has permitted it.

* * *

The notion that every violation of law should be prosecuted, including - indeed, especially - every violation by those in high places, is an attractive one, and it would be risky to argue in an election campaign that that is not an absolutely overriding value. Fiat justitia, ruat coelum. Let justice be done, though the heavens may fall. The reality is, however, that it is not an absolutely overriding value, and it was with the hope that we would be able to acknowledge and apply such realities that the Constitution spared us, by life tenure, the necessity of election campaigns. I cannot imagine that there are not many thoughtful men and women in Congress who realize that the benefits of this legislation are far outweighed by its harmful effect upon our system of government, and even upon the nature of justice received by those men and women who agree to serve in the Executive Branch. But it is difficult to vote not to enact, and even more difficult to vote to repeal, a statute called, appropriately enough, the Ethics in Government Act. If Congress is controlled by the party other than the one to which the President belongs, it has little incentive to repeal it; if it is controlled by the same party, it dare not. By its shortsighted action today, I fear the Court has permanently encumbered the Republic with an institution that will do it great harm.

Worse than what it has done, however, is the manner in which it has done it. A government of laws means a government of rules. Today's decision on the basic issue of fragmentation of executive power is ungoverned by rule, and hence ungoverned by law. It extends into the very heart of our most significant constitutional function the "totality of the circumstances" mode of analysis that this Court has in recent years become fond of. Taking all things into account, we conclude that the power taken away from the President here is not really too much. The next time executive power is assigned to someone other than the President we may conclude, taking all things into account, that it is too much. That opinion, like this one, will not be confined by any rule. We will describe, as we have today (though I hope more accurately) the effects of the provision in question, and will authoritatively announce: "The President's need to control the exercise of the [subject officer's] discretion is so central to the functioning of the Executive Branch as to require complete control." This is not analysis; it is ad hoc judgment. And it fails to explain why it is not true that - as the text of the Constitution seems to require, as the Founders seemed to expect, and as our past cases have uniformly assumed - all purely executive power must be under the control of the President.

The ad hoc approach to constitutional adjudication has real attraction, even apart from its work-saving potential. It is guaranteed to produce a result, in every case, that will make a majority of the Court happy with the law. The law is, by definition, precisely what the majority thinks, taking all things into account, it ought to be. I prefer to rely upon the judgment of the wise men who constructed our system, and of the people who approved it, and of two centuries of history that have shown it to be sound. Like it or not, that judgment says, quite plainly, that "[t]he executive Power shall be vested in a President of the United States."

Notes to Justice Scalia's dissent in Morrison v. Olson (June 29, 1988)

[1] I agree with the Court on this point, but not because of the section of the statute that it cites, 592(f). What that provides is that "[t]he Attorney General's determination . . . to apply to the division of the court for the appointment of an independent counsel shall not be reviewable in any court." Quite obviously, the determination to apply is not the same as the determination not to apply. In other contexts, we have sternly avoided "construing" a statute to mean what it plainly does not say, merely in order to avoid constitutional problems. See Commodity Futures Trading Comm'n v. Schor, 478 U.S. 833, 841 (1986). In my view, however, the Attorney General's decision not to refer would in any event be nonreviewable as the exercise of prosecutorial discretion. See Heckler v. Chaney, 470 U.S. 821 (1985).

[2] The Court omits the further provision that the independent counsel exercises within her sphere the "full power" of "the Attorney General, [with one minor exception relating to wiretap authorizations] and any other officer or employee of the Department of Justice[.]" 594(a). This is, of course, quite difficult to square with the Court's assertion that appellant is "`inferior' in rank and authority" to the Attorney General. Ante, at 671.

[3] The independent counsel's specifically enumerated powers include the following:

"(1) conducting proceedings before grand juries and other investigations;

"(2) participating in court proceedings and engaging in any litigation, including civil and criminal matters, that [the] independent counsel deems necessary;

"(3) appealing any decision of a court in any case or proceeding in which [the] independent counsel participates in an official capacity;

"(4) reviewing all documentary evidence available from any source;

"(5) determining whether to contest the assertion of any testimonial privilege;

"(6) receiving appropriate national security clearances and, if necessary contesting in court . . . any claim of privilege or attempt to withhold evidence on grounds of national security;

"(7) making applications to any Federal court for a grant of immunity to any witness . . . or for warrants, subpoenas, or other court orders, and for purposes of sections 6003, 6004, and 6005 of title 18, exercising the authority vested in a United States attorney or the Attorney General;

"(8) inspecting, obtaining, or using the original or a copy of any tax return . . .;

"(9) initiating and conducting prosecutions in any court of competent jurisdiction, framing and signing indictments, filing informations, and handling all aspects of any case filed in the name of the United States; and

"(10) consulting with the United States Attorney for the district in which the violation was alleged to have occurred." 594(a)(1)-(10).

In addition, the statute empowers the independent counsel to hire a staff of a size as large as she "deems necessary," 594(c), and to enlist and receive "where necessary to perform [her] duties" the assistance, personnel and resources of the Department of Justice, 594(d).

[4] The Court misunderstands my opinion to say that "every officer of the United States exercising any part of [the executive] power must serve at the pleasure of the President and be removable by him at will." Ante, at 690, n. 29. Of course, as my discussion here demonstrates, that has never been the law and I do not assert otherwise. What I do assert - and what the Constitution seems plainly to prescribe - is that the President must have control over all exercises of the executive power. See supra, at 705. That requires that he have plenary power to remove principal officers such as the independent counsel, but it does not require that he have plenary power to remove inferior officers. Since the latter are, as I have described, subordinate to, i. e., subject to the supervision of, principal officers who (being removable at will) have the President's

complete confidence, it is enough - at least if they have been appointed by the President or by a principal officer - that they be removable for cause, which would include, of course, the failure to accept supervision. Thus, Perkins is in no way inconsistent with my views.

Cruel and Unusual Punishments: Justice Scalia's dissent in Thompson v. Oklahoma (June 29, 1988)

JUSTICE SCALIA, with whom CHIEF JUSTICE REHNQUIST and JUSTICE WHITE join, dissenting.

If the issue before us today were whether an automatic death penalty for conviction of certain crimes could be extended to individuals younger than 16 when they commit the crimes, thereby preventing individualized consideration of their maturity and moral responsibility, I would accept the plurality's conclusion that such a practice is opposed by a national consensus, sufficiently uniform and of sufficiently long standing, to render it cruel and unusual punishment within the meaning of the Eighth Amendment. We have already decided as much, and more, in Lockett v. Ohio, 438 U.S. 586 (1978). I might even agree with the plurality's conclusion if the question were whether a person under 16 when he commits a crime can be deprived of the benefit of a rebuttable presumption that he is not mature and responsible enough to be punished as an adult. The question posed here, however, is radically different from both of these. It is whether there is a national consensus that no criminal so much as one day under 16, after individuated consideration of his circumstances, including the overcoming of a presumption that he should not be tried as an adult, can possibly be deemed mature and responsible enough to be punished with death for any crime. Because there seems to me no plausible basis for answering this last question in the affirmative, I respectfully dissent.

I

I begin by restating the facts, since I think that a fuller account of William Wayne Thompson's participation in the murder, and of his certification to stand trial as an adult, is helpful in understanding the case. The evidence at trial left no doubt that, on the night of January 22-23, 1983, Thompson brutally and with premeditation murdered his former brother-in-law, Charles Keene, the motive evidently being, at least in part, Keene's physical abuse of Thompson's sister. As Thompson left his mother's house that evening, in the company of three older friends, he explained to his girlfriend that "we're going to kill Charles." Several hours later, early in the morning of January 23, a neighbor, Malcolm "Possum" Brown, was awakened by the sound of a gunshot on his front porch. Someone pounded on his front door shouting: "Possum, open the door, let me in. They're going to kill me." Brown telephoned the police, and then opened the front door to see a man on his knees attempting to repel blows with his arms and hands. There were four other men on the porch. One was holding a gun and stood apart, while the other three were hitting and kicking the kneeling man, who never attempted to hit back. One of them was beating the victim with an object 12 to 18 inches in length. The police called back to see if the disturbance was still going on, and, while Brown spoke with them on the telephone, the men took the victim away in a car.

Several hours after they had left Thompson's mother's house, Thompson and his three companions returned. Thompson's girlfriend helped him take off his boots, and heard him say: "[W]e killed him. I shot him in the head and cut his throat, and threw him in the river." Subsequently, the former wife of one of Thompson's accomplices heard Thompson tell his mother that "he killed him. Charles was dead, and Vicki didn't have to worry about him anymore." During the days following the murder Thompson made other admissions. One witness testified that she asked Thompson the source of some hair adhering to a pair of boots he was carrying. He replied that was where he had kicked Charles Keene in the head. Thompson also told her that he had cut Charles' throat and chest and had shot him in the head. Another witness testified that, when she told Thompson that a friend had seen Keene dancing in a local bar, Thompson remarked that that would be hard to do with a bullet in his head. Ultimately, one of Thompson's codefendants admitted that, after Keene had been shot twice in the head, Thompson had cut Keene "so the fish could eat his body." Thompson and a codefendant had then thrown the body into the Washita River, with a chain and blocks attached so that it would not be found. On February 18, 1983, the body was recovered. The Chief Medical Examiner of Oklahoma concluded that the victim had been beaten, shot twice, and that his throat, chest, and abdomen had been cut.

On February 18, 1983, the State of Oklahoma filed an information and arrest warrant for Thompson, and on February 22, the State began proceedings to allow Thompson to be tried as an adult. Under Oklahoma law, anyone who commits a crime when he is under the age of 18 is defined to be a child, unless he is 16 or 17 and has committed murder or certain other specified crimes, in which case he is automatically certified to stand trial as an adult. Okla.Stat., Tit. 10, §§ 1101, 1104.2 (Supp.1987). In addition, under the statute the State invoked in the present case, juveniles may be certified to stand trial as adults if: (1) the State can establish the "prosecutive merit" of the case and (2) the court certifies, after considering six factors, that there are no reasonable prospects for rehabilitation of the child within the juvenile system. Okla.Stat., Tit. 10, § 1112(b) (1981).

At a hearing on March 29, 1983, the District Court found probable cause to believe that the defendant had committed first-degree murder, and thus concluded that the case had prosecutive merit. A second hearing was therefore held on April 21, 1983, to determine whether Thompson was amenable to the juvenile system, or whether he should be certified to stand trial as an adult. A clinical psychologist who had examined Thompson testified at the second hearing that, in her opinion, Thompson understood the difference between right and wrong, but had an antisocial personality that could not be modified by the juvenile justice system. The psychologist testified that Thompson believed that, because of his age, he was beyond any severe penalty of the law, and accordingly did not believe there would be any severe repercussions from his behavior. Numerous other witnesses testified about Thompson's prior abusive behavior. Mary Robinson, an employee of the Oklahoma juvenile justice system, testified about her contacts with Thompson during several of his previous arrests, which included arrests for assault and battery in August, 1980; assault and battery in October, 1981; attempted burglary in May, 1982; assault and battery with a knife in July, 1982; and assault with a deadly weapon in February, 1983. She testified that Thompson had been provided with all the counseling the State's Department of Human Services had available, and that none of the counseling or placements seemed to improve his behavior. She recommended that he be certified to stand trial as an adult. On the basis of the foregoing testimony, the District Court filed a written order certifying Thompson to stand trial as an adult. That was appealed and ultimately affirmed by the Oklahoma Court of Criminal Appeals.

Thompson was tried in the District Court of Grady County between December 4 and December 9, 1983. During the guilt phase of the trial, the prosecutor introduced three color photographs showing the condition of the victim's body when it was removed from the river. The jury found Thompson guilty of first-degree murder. At the sentencing phase of the trial, the jury agreed with the prosecution on the existence of one aggravating circumstance, that the murder was "especially heinous, atrocious, or cruel." As required by our decision in Eddings v. Oklahoma, 455 U.S. 104, 115-117 (1982), the defense was permitted to argue to the jury the youthfulness of the defendant as a mitigating factor. The jury recommended that the death penalty be imposed, and the trial judge, accordingly, sentenced Thompson to death. Thompson appealed, and his conviction and capital sentence were affirmed. Standing by its earlier decision in Eddings v. State, 616 P.2d 1159, 1166-1167 (1980), rev'd on other grounds, 455 U.S. 104 (1982), the Oklahoma Court of Criminal Appeals held that, "once a minor is certified to stand trial as an adult, he may also, without violating the Constitution, be punished as an adult." 724 P.2d 780, 784 (1986). It also held that admission of two of the three photographs was error in the guilt phase of the proceeding, because their prejudicial effect outweighed their probative value, but found that error harmless in light of the overwhelming evidence of Thompson's guilt. It held that their prejudicial effect did not outweigh their probative value in the sentencing phase, and that they were therefore properly admitted, since they demonstrated the brutality of the crime. Thompson petitioned for certiorari with respect to both sentencing issues, and we granted review. 479 U.S. 1084 (1987).

II

A

As the foregoing history of this case demonstrates, William Wayne Thompson is not a juvenile caught up in a legislative scheme that unthinkingly lumped him together with adults for purposes of determining that death was an appropriate penalty for him and for his crime. To the contrary, Oklahoma first gave careful consideration to whether, in light of his young age, he should be subjected to the normal criminal system at all. That question having been answered affirmatively, a jury then considered whether, despite his young age, his maturity and moral responsibility were sufficiently developed to justify the sentence of death. In upsetting this particularized judgment on the basis of a constitutional absolute, the plurality pronounces it to be a fundamental principle of our society that no one who is as little as one day short of his 16th birthday can have sufficient maturity and moral responsibility to be subjected to capital punishment for any crime. As a sociological and moral conclusion, that is implausible; and it is doubly implausible as an interpretation of the United States Constitution.

The text of the Eighth Amendment, made applicable to the States by the Fourteenth, prohibits the imposition of "cruel and unusual punishments." The plurality does not attempt to maintain that this was originally understood to prohibit capital punishment for crimes committed by persons under the age of 16; the evidence is unusually clear and unequivocal that it was not. The age at which juveniles could be subjected to capital punishment was explicitly addressed in Blackstone's Commentaries on the Laws of England, published in 1769 and widely accepted at the time the Eighth Amendment was adopted as an accurate description of the common law. According to Blackstone, not only was 15 above the age (viz., 7) at which capital punishment could theoretically be imposed; it was even above the age (14) up to which there was a rebuttable presumption of incapacity to commit a capital (or any other) felony. 4 W. Blackstone, Commentaries *23-*24. See also M. Hale, Pleas of the Crown *22 (describing the age of absolute incapacity as 12 and the age of presumptive incapacity as 14); Kean, The History of the Criminal Liability of Children, 53 L.Q.Rev. 364, 369-370 (1937); Streib, Death Penalty for Children: The American Experience with Capital Punishment for Crimes Committed While under Age Eighteen, 36 Okla.L.Rev. 613, 614-615 (1983) (hereinafter Streib, Death Penalty for Children). The historical practice in this country conformed with the common law understanding that 15-year-olds were not categorically immune from commission of capital crimes. One scholar has documented 22 executions, between 1642 and 1899, for crimes committed under the age of 16. See Streib, Death Penalty for Children 619.

Necessarily, therefore, the plurality seeks to rest its holding on the conclusion that Thompson's punishment as an adult is contrary to the "evolving standards of decency that mark the progress of a maturing society." Trop v. Dulles, 356 U.S. 86, 101 (1958) (plurality opinion) (Warren, C.J.). Ante at 821. Of course, the risk of assessing evolving standards is that it is all too easy to believe that evolution has culminated in one's own views. To avoid this danger, we have, when making such an assessment in prior cases, looked for objective signs of how today's society views a particular punishment. Furman v. Georgia, 408 U.S. 238, 277-279 (1972) (BRENNAN, J., concurring). See also Woodson v. North Carolina, 428 U.S. 280, 293 (1976) (plurality opinion) (Stewart, Powell, and STEVENS, JJ.); Coker v. Georgia, 433 U.S. 584, 593-597 (1977); Enmund v. Florida, 458 U.S. 782, 788-789 (1982). The most reliable objective signs consist of the legislation that the society has enacted. It will rarely, if ever, be the case that the Members of this Court will have a better sense of the evolution in views of the American people than do their elected representatives.

It is thus significant that, only four years ago, in the Comprehensive Crime Control Act of 1984, Pub.L. 98-473, 98 Stat. 2149, Congress expressly addressed the effect of youth upon the imposition of criminal punishment, and changed the law in precisely the opposite direction from that which the plurality's perceived evolution in social attitudes would suggest: it lowered from 16 to 15 the age at which a juvenile's case can, "in the interest of justice," be transferred from juvenile court to Federal District Court, enabling him to be tried and punished as an adult. 18 U.S.C. § 5032 (1982 ed., Supp. IV). This legislation was passed in light of Justice Department testimony that many juvenile delinquents were "cynical, street-wise, repeat offenders, indistinguishable, except for their age, from their adult criminal counterparts," Hearings on S. 829 before the Subcommittee on Criminal Law of the Senate Committee on the Judiciary, 98th Cong., 1st Sess., 551 (1983), and that, in 1979 alone, juveniles under the age of 15, i.e., almost a year younger than Thompson, had committed a total of 206 homicides nationwide, more than 1,000 forcible rapes, 10,000 robberies, and 10,000 aggravated assaults. Id. at 554. Since there are federal death penalty statutes [n1] which have not been determined to be unconstitutional, adoption of this new legislation could at least theoretically result in the imposition of the death penalty upon a 15-year-old. There is, to be sure, no reason to believe that the Members of Congress had the death penalty specifically in mind; but that does not alter the reality of what federal law now, on its face, permits. Moreover, if it is appropriate to go behind the face of the statutes to the subjective intentions of those who enacted them, it would be strange to find the consensus regarding criminal liability of juveniles to be moving in the direction the plurality perceives for capital punishment, while moving in precisely the opposite direction for all other penalties. [n2]

Turning to legislation at the state level, one observes the same trend of lowering, rather than raising, the age of juvenile criminal liability. [n3] As for the state status quo with respect to the death penalty in particular: the plurality chooses to "confine [its] attention" to the fact that all 18 of the States that establish a minimum age for capital punishment have chosen at least 16. Ante at 829. But it is beyond me why an accurate analysis would not include within the computation the larger number of States (19) that have determined that no minimum age for capital punishment is appropriate, leaving that to be governed by their general rules for the age at which juveniles can be criminally responsible. A survey of state laws shows, in other words, that a majority of the States for which the issue exists (the rest do not have capital punishment) are of the view that death is not different insofar as the age of juvenile criminal responsibility is concerned. And the latter age, while presumed to be 16 in all the States, see ante at 824, can, in virtually all the States, be less than 16 when individuated consideration of the particular case warrants it. Thus, what Oklahoma has done here is precisely what the majority of capital punishment States would do.

When the Federal Government, and almost 40% of the States, including a majority of the States that include capital punishment as a permissible sanction, allow for the imposition of the death penalty on any juvenile who has been tried as an adult, which category can include juveniles under 16 at the time of the offense, it is obviously impossible for the plurality to rely upon any evolved societal consensus discernible in legislation -- or at least discernible in the legislation of this society, which is assuredly all that is relevant. [n4] Thus, the plurality falls back upon what it promises will be an examination of "the behavior of juries." Ante at 831. It turns out not to be that, perhaps because of the inconvenient fact that no fewer than 5 murderers who committed their crimes under the age of 16 were sentenced to death, in five different States, between the years 1984 and 1986. V. Streib, Death Penalty for Juveniles 168-169 (1987). Instead, the plurality examines the statistics on capital executions, which are of course substantially lower than those for capital sentences because of various factors, most notably the exercise of executive clemency. See Streib, Death Penalty for Children 619. Those statistics show, unsurprisingly, that capital punishment for persons who committed crimes under the age of 16 is rare. We are not discussing whether the Constitution requires such procedures as will continue to cause it to be rare, but whether the Constitution prohibits it entirely. The plurality takes it to be persuasive evidence that social attitudes have changed to embrace such a prohibition -- changed so clearly and permanently as to be irrevocably enshrined in the Constitution -- that in this century all of the 18 to 20 executions of persons below 16 when they committed crimes occurred before 1948.

Even assuming that the execution, rather than the sentencing, statistics are the pertinent data, and further assuming that a 4-decade trend is adequate to justify calling a constitutional halt to what may well be a pendulum swing in social attitudes, the statistics are frail support for the existence of the relevant trend. There are many reasons that adequately account for the drop in executions other than the premise of general agreement that no 15-year-old murderer should ever be executed. Foremost among them, of course, was a reduction in public support for capital punishment in general. Of the 14 States (including the District of Columbia) that currently have no death penalty statute, 11 have acquired that status since 1950. V. Streib, Death Penalty for Juveniles 42, Table 3-1. That reduction in willingness to impose capital punishment (which may reasonably be presumed to have been felt even in those States that did not entirely abolish it), combined with the modern trend, constitutionalized in Lockett v. Ohio, 438 U.S. 586 (1978), towards individualized sentencing determinations, rather than automatic death sentences for certain crimes, reduced the total number of executions nationwide from an average of 1, 272 per decade in the first half of the century to 254 per decade since then. See V. Streib, Death Penalty for Juveniles 56, Table 4-1. A society less ready to impose the death penalty, and entirely unwilling to impose it without individualized consideration, will of course pronounce death for a crime committed by a person under 16 very rarely. There is absolutely no basis, however, for attributing that phenomenon to a modern consensus that such an execution should never occur -- any more than it would have been accurate to discern such a consensus in 1927, when, despite a level of total executions almost five times higher than that of the post-1950 period, there had been no execution for crime committed by juveniles under the age of 16 for almost 17 years. That that did not reflect a new societal absolute was demonstrated by the fact that, in approximately the next 17 years, there were 10 such executions. Id. at 191-208.

In sum, the statistics of executions demonstrate nothing except the fact that our society has always agreed that executions of 15-year-old criminals should be rare, and, in more modern times, has agreed that they (like all other executions) should be even rarer still. There is no rational basis for discerning in that a societal judgment that no one so much as a day under 16 can ever be mature and morally responsible enough to deserve that penalty; and there is no justification except our own predeliction for converting a statistical rarity of occurrence into an absolute constitutional ban. One must surely fear that, now that the Court has taken the first step of requiring individualized consideration in capital cases, today's decision begins a second stage of converting into constitutional rules the general results of that individuation. One could readily run the same statistical argument with respect to other classes of defendants. Between 1930 and 1955, for example, 30 women were executed in the United States. Only 3 were executed between then and 1986 -- and none in the 22-year period between 1962 and 1984. Proportionately, the drop is as impressive as that which the plurality points to in 15-year-old executions. (From 30 in 25 years to 3 in the next 31 years, versus from 18 in 50 years to potentially 1 -- the present defendant -- in the next 40 years.) Surely the conclusion is not that it is unconstitutional to impose capital punishment upon a woman. [n5]

If one believes that the data the plurality relies upon are effective to establish, with the requisite degree of certainty, a constitutional consensus in this society that no person can ever be executed for a crime committed under the age of 16, it is difficult to see why the same judgment should not extend to crimes committed under the age of 17, or of 18. The frequency of such executions shows an almost equivalent drop in recent years. Id. at 191-208; and, of the 18 States that have enacted age limits upon capital punishment, only 3 have selected the age of 16, only 4 the age of 17, and all the rest the age of 18, ante at 829, n. 29. It seems plain to me, in other words, that there is no clear line here, which suggests that the plurality is inappropriately acting in a legislative, rather than a judicial, capacity. Doubtless, at some age, a line does exist -- as it has always existed in the common law, see supra at 864 -- below which a juvenile can never be considered fully responsible for murder. The evidence that the views of our society, so steadfast and so uniform that they have become part of the agreed-upon laws that we live by, regard that absolute age to be 16 is nonexistent.

B

Having avoided any attempt to justify its holding on the basis of the original understanding of what was "cruel and unusual punishment," and having utterly failed in justifying its holding on the basis of "evolving standards of decency" evidenced by "the work product of state legislatures and sentencing juries," ante at 822, the plurality proceeds, in Part V of the opinion, to set forth its views regarding the desirability of ever imposing capital punishment for a murder committed by a 15-year-old. That discussion begins with the recitation of propositions upon which there is "broad agreement" within our society, namely, that "punishment should be directly related to the personal culpability of the criminal defendant," and that "adolescents as a class are less mature and responsible than adults." Ante at 834. It soon proceeds, however, to the conclusion that,

> [g]iven the lesser culpability of the juvenile offender, the teenager's capacity for growth, and society's fiduciary obligations to its children,

none of the rationales for the death penalty can apply to the execution of a 15-year-old criminal, so that it is "'nothing more than the purposeless and needless imposition of pain and suffering.'" Ante at 838, quoting Coker v. Georgia, 433 U.S. at 592. On this, as we have seen, there is assuredly not general agreement. Nonetheless, the plurality would make it one of the fundamental laws governing our society solely, because it has an "'abiding conviction'" that it is so, ante at 833, n. 40, quoting Coker v. Georgia, supra, at 598.

This is in accord with the proposition set out at the beginning of the plurality's discussion in Part V, that,

> "[a]lthough the judgments of legislatures, juries, and prosecutors weigh heavily in the balance, it is for us ultimately to judge whether the Eighth Amendment permits imposition of the death penalty."

Ante at 833, quoting Enmund v. Florida, 458 U.S. at 797. I reject that proposition in the sense intended here. It is assuredly "for us ultimately to judge" what the Eighth Amendment permits, but that means it is for us to judge whether certain punishments are forbidden because, despite what the current society thinks, they were forbidden under the original understanding of "cruel and unusual," compare Brown v. Board of Education, 347 U.S. 483 (1954); or because they come within current understanding of what is "cruel and unusual," because of the "evolving standards of decency" of our national society; but not because they are out of accord with the perceptions of decency, or of penology, or of mercy, entertained -- or strongly entertained, or even held as an "abiding conviction" -- by a majority of the small and unrepresentative segment of our society that sits on this Court. On its face, the phrase "cruel and unusual punishments" limits the evolving standards appropriate for our consideration to those entertained by the society, rather than those dictated by our personal consciences.

Because I think the views of this Court on the policy questions discussed in Part V of the plurality opinion to be irrelevant, I make no attempt to refute them. It suffices to say that there is another point of view, suggested in the following passage written by our esteemed former colleague Justice Powell, whose views the plurality several times invokes for support, ante at 823-825, 834:

Minors who become embroiled with the law range from the very young up to those on the brink of majority. Some of the older minors become fully "street-wise," hardened criminals, deserving no greater consideration than that properly accorded all persons suspected of crime.

Fare v. Michael C., 442 U.S. 707, 734, n. 4 (1979) (dissenting opinion). The view that it is possible for a 15-year-old to come within this category uncontestably prevailed when the Eighth and Fourteenth Amendments were adopted, and, judging from the actions of the society's democratically elected representatives, still persuades a substantial segment of the people whose "evolving standards of decency" we have been appointed to discern, rather than decree. It is not necessary, as the plurality's opinion suggests, that "we [be] persuaded," ante at 838, of the correctness of the people's views.

III

If I understand JUSTICE O'CONNOR's separate concurrence correctly, it agrees (1) that we have no constitutional authority to set aside this death penalty unless we can find it contrary to a firm national consensus that persons younger than 16 at the time of their crime cannot be executed, and (2) that we cannot make such a finding. It does not, however, reach the seemingly inevitable conclusion that (3) we therefore have no constitutional authority to set aside this death penalty. Rather, it proceeds (in Part II) to state that, since (a) we have treated the death penalty "differently from all other punishments," ante at 856, imposing special procedural and substantive protections not required in other contexts, and (b) although we cannot actually find any national consensus forbidding execution for crimes committed under 16, there may perhaps be such a consensus, therefore (c) the Oklahoma statutes plainly authorizing the present execution by treating 15-year-old felons (after individuated findings) as adults, and authorizing execution of adults, are not adequate, and what is needed is a statute explicitly stating that "15-year-olds can be guilty of capital crimes."

First, of course, I do not agree with (b) -- that there is any doubt about the nonexistence of a national consensus. The concurrence produces the doubt only by arbitrarily refusing to believe that what the laws of the Federal Government and 19 States clearly provide for represents a "considered judgment." Ante at 487 U.S. 852"]852. Second, I do not see how (c) follows from (b) -- how the problem of doubt about whether what the Oklahoma laws permit is contrary to a firm national consensus, and therefore unconstitutional, is solved by making absolutely sure that the citizens of Oklahoma really want to take this unconstitutional action. And finally, I do not see how the procedural and substantive protections referred to in (a) provide any precedent for what is done in (c). Those special protections for capital cases, such as the prohibition of unguided discretion, 852. Second, I do not see how (c) follows from (b) -- how the problem of doubt about whether what the Oklahoma laws permit is contrary to a firm national consensus, and therefore unconstitutional, is solved by making absolutely sure that the citizens of Oklahoma really want to take this unconstitutional action. And finally, I do not see how the procedural and substantive protections referred to in (a) provide any precedent for what is done in (c). Those special protections for capital cases, such as the prohibition of unguided discretion, Gregg v. Georgia, 428 U.S. 153, 176-196 (1976) (plurality opinion) (Stewart, Powell, and STEVENS, JJ.) and the prohibition of automatic death sentences for certain crimes, Woodson v. North Carolina, 428 U.S. at 289-301 (plurality opinion) (Stewart, Powell, and STEVENS, JJ.), were not drawn from a hat, but were thought to be (once again) what a national consensus required. I am unaware of any national consensus, and the concurrence does not suggest the existence of any, that the death penalty for felons under 16 can only be imposed by a single statute that explicitly addresses that subject. Thus, part (c) of the concurrence's argument, its conclusion, could be replaced with almost anything. There is no more basis for imposing the particular procedural protection it announces than there is for imposing a requirement that the death penalty for felons under 16 be adopted by a two-thirds vote of each house of the state legislature, or by referendum, or by bills printed in 10-point type. I am also left in some doubt whether this new requirement will be lifted (since its supposed rationale would disappear) when enough States have complied with it to render the nonexistence of a national consensus against such executions no longer doubtful; or only when enough States have done so to demonstrate that there is a national consensus in favor of such executions; or never.

It could not possibly be the concurrence's concern that this death sentence is a fluke -- a punishment not really contemplated by Oklahoma law, but produced as an accidental result of its interlocking statutes governing capital punishment and the age for treating juveniles as adults. The statutes, and their consequences, are quite clear. The present case, moreover, is of such prominence that it has received extensive coverage not only in the Oklahoma press, but nationally. It would not even have been necessary for the Oklahoma Legislature to act in order to remedy the miscarriage of its intent, if that is what this sentence was. The Governor of Oklahoma, who can certainly recognize a frustration of the will of the citizens of Oklahoma more readily than we, would certainly have used his pardon power if there was some mistake here. What the concurrence proposes is obviously designed to nullify, rather than effectuate, the will of the people of Oklahoma, even though the concurrence cannot find that will to be unconstitutional.

What the concurrence proposes is also designed, of course, to make it more difficult for all States to enact legislation resulting in capital punishment for murderers under 16 when they committed their crimes. It is difficult to pass a law saying explicitly "15-year-olds can be executed," just as it would be difficult to pass a law saying explicitly "blind people can be executed," or "white-haired grandmothers can be executed," or "mothers of two-year-olds can be executed." But I know of no authority whatever for our specifying the precise form that state legislation must take, as opposed to its constitutionally required content. We have in the past studiously avoided that sort of interference in the States' legislative processes, the heart of their sovereignty. Placing restraints upon the manner in which the States make their laws, in order to give 15-year-old criminals special protection against capital punishment, may well be a good idea, as perhaps is the abolition of capital punishment entirely. It is not, however, an idea it is ours to impose. Thus, while the concurrence purports to be adopting an approach more respectful of States' rights than the plurality, in principle it seems to me much more disdainful. It says to those jurisdictions that have laws like Oklahoma's: we cannot really say that what you are doing is contrary to national consensus, and therefore unconstitutional, but, since we are not entirely sure, you must in the future legislate in the manner that we say.

In my view, the concurrence also does not fulfill its promise of arriving at a more "narrow conclusion" than the plurality, and avoiding an "unnecessarily broad" constitutional holding. Ante at 858. To the contrary, I think it hoists on to the deck of our Eighth Amendment jurisprudence the loose cannon of a brand new principle. If the concurrence's view were adopted, henceforth a finding of national consensus would no longer be required to invalidate state action in the area of capital punishment. All that would be needed is uncertainty regarding the existence of a national consensus, whereupon various protective requirements could be imposed, even to the point of specifying the process of legislation. If 15-year-olds must be explicitly named in capital statutes, why not those of extremely low intelligence, or those over 75, or any number of other appealing groups as to which the existence of a national consensus regarding capital punishment may be in doubt for the same reason the concurrence finds it in doubt here, viz., because they are not specifically named in the capital statutes? Moreover, the motto that "death is different" would no longer mean that the firm view of our society demands that it be treated differently in certain identifiable respects, but rather that this Court can attach to it whatever limitations seem appropriate. I reject that approach, and would prefer to it even the misdescription of what constitutes a national consensus favored by the plurality. The concurrence's approach is a solomonic solution to the problem of how to prevent execution in the present case, while at the same time not holding that the execution of those under 16 when they commit murder is categorically unconstitutional. Solomon, however, was not subject to the constitutional constraints of the judicial department of a national government in a federal, democratic system.

IV

Since I find Thompson's age inadequate grounds for reversal of his sentence, I must reach the question whether the Constitution was violated by permitting the jury to consider in the sentencing stage the color photographs of Charles Keene's body. Thompson contends that this rendered his sentencing proceeding so unfair as to deny him due process of law.

The photographs in question, showing gunshot wounds in the head and chest, and knife slashes in the throat, chest and abdomen, were certainly probative of the aggravating circumstance that the crime was "especially heinous, atrocious, or cruel." The only issue, therefore, is whether they were unduly inflammatory. We have never before held that the excessively inflammatory character of concededly relevant evidence can form the basis for a constitutional attack, and I would decline to do so in this case. If there is a point at which inflammatoriness so plainly exceeds evidentiary worth as to violate the federal Constitution, it has not been reached here. The balancing of relevance and prejudice is generally a state evidentiary issue, which we do not sit to review. Lisenba v. California, 314 U.S. 219, 227-228 (1941).

For the foregoing reasons, I respectfully dissent from the judgment of the Court.

Notes to Justice Scalia's dissent in Thompson v. Oklahoma (June 29, 1988)

1. See 10 U.S.C. § 906a (peacetime espionage); 10 U.S.C. § 918 (murder while member of Armed Forces); 18 U.S.C. §§ 32 33, and 34 (1982 ed. and Supp. IV) (destruction of aircraft, motor vehicles, or related facilities resulting in death); 18 U.S.C. § 115(b)(3) (1982 ed., Supp. IV) (retaliatory murder of member of immediate family of law enforcement officials) (by cross-reference to 18 U.S.C. § 1111); 18 U.S.C. § 351 (1982 ed. and Supp. IV) (murder of Member of Congress, important Executive official, or Supreme Court Justice) (by cross-reference to 18 U.S.C. § 1111); 18 U.S.C. § 794 (espionage); 18 U.S.C. § 844(f) (1982 ed., Supp. IV) (destruction of government property resulting in death); 18 U.S.C. § 1111 (1982 ed. and Supp. IV) (first-degree murder within federal jurisdiction); 18 U.S.C. § 1716 (mailing of injurious articles with intent to kill resulting in death); 18 U.S.C. § 1751 (assassination or kidnaping resulting in death of President or Vice President) (by cross-reference to 18 U.S.C. § 1111); 18 U.S.C. § 1992 (willful wrecking of train resulting in death); 18 U.S.C. § 2113 (bank robbery-related murder or kidnaping); 18 U.S.C. § 2381 (treason); 49 U.S.C.App. §§ 1472 and 1473 (death resulting from aircraft hijacking).

2. The concurrence disputes the significance of Congress' lowering of the federal waiver age by pointing to a recently approved Senate bill that would set a minimum age of 18 before capital punishment could be imposed for certain narcotics-related offenses. This bill has not, however, been passed by the House of Representatives and signed into law by the President. Even if it eventually were, it would not result in the setting of a minimum age of 18 for any of the other federal death penalty statutes set forth in n. 1, supra. It would simply reflect a judgment by Congress that the death penalty is inappropriate for juvenile narcotics offenders. That would have minimal relevance to the question of consensus at issue here, which is not whether criminal offenders under 16 can be executed for all crimes, but whether they can be executed for any crimes. For the same reason, there is no significance to the concurrence's observation that the Federal Government has, by Treaty, agreed to a minimum death penalty age in certain very limited circumstances.

3. Compare S. Davis, Rights of Juveniles, App. B-l to B-26 (1987) with S. Davis, Rights of Juveniles 233-249 (1974). Idaho has twice lowered its waiver age, most recently from 15 to 14; Idaho Code § 16-1806 (Supp.1988); Illinois has added as excluded offenses: murder, criminal sexual assault, armed robbery with a firearm, and possession of a deadly weapon in a school committed by a child 15 or older; Ill.Ann.Stat., ch. 37, § 805-

4(6) (Supp.1988); Indiana has lowered its waiver age to 14 where aggravating circumstances are present, and it has made waiver mandatory where child is 10 or older and has been charged with murder; Ind.Code §§ 31-6-24(b) -- (e) (Supp.1987); Kentucky has established a waiver age of 14 for juveniles charged with capital offenses or Class A or B felonies; Ky.Rev.Stat. §§ 635.020(2)-(4), 640.010 (Supp.1986); Minnesota has made waiver mandatory for offenses committed by children 14 years or older who were previously certified for criminal prosecution and convicted of the offense or a lesser included offense; Minn.Stat. §§ 260.125, subd. 1, 3, and 3a (1986); and Montana has lowered its waiver age from 16 to 12 for children charged with sexual intercourse without consent, deliberate homicide, mitigated deliberate homicide, or attempted deliberate homicide or attempted mitigated deliberate homicide; Mont.Code Ann. § 41-5-206(1)(a) (1987); New Jersey lowered its waiver age from 16 to 14 for certain aggravated offenses; N.J.Stat.Ann. § 2A:4A-26 (West 1987); and New York recently amended its law to allow certain 13-, 14- and 15-year-olds to be tried and punished as adults; N.Y.Crim.Proc.Law § 190.71 (McKinney 1982).

 4. The plurality's reliance upon Amnesty International's account of what it pronounces to be civilized standards of decency in other countries, ante at 830-831, and n. 34, is totally inappropriate as a means of establishing the fundamental beliefs of this Nation. That 40% of our States do not rule out capital punishment for 15-year-old felons is determinative of the question before us here, even if that position contradicts the uniform view of the rest of the world. We must never forget that it is a Constitution for the United States of America that we are expounding. The practices of other nations, particularly other democracies, can be relevant to determining whether a practice uniform among our people is not merely an historical accident, but rather so "implicit in the concept of ordered liberty" that it occupies a place not merely in our mores but, text permitting, in our Constitution as well. See Palko v. Connecticut, 302 U.S. 319, 325 (1937) (Cardozo, J.). But where there is not first a settled consensus among our own people, the views of other nations, however enlightened the Justices of this Court may think them to be, cannot be imposed upon Americans through the Constitution. In the present case, therefore, the fact that a majority of foreign nations would not impose capital punishment upon persons under 16 at the time of the crime is of no more relevance than the fact that a majority of them would not impose capital punishment at all, or have standards of due process quite different from our own.

 5. I leave to a footnote my discussion of the plurality's reliance upon the fact that, in most or all States, juveniles under 16 cannot vote, sit on a jury, marry without parental consent, participate in organized gambling, patronize pool halls, pawn property, or purchase alcohol, pornographic materials, or cigarettes. Ante at 823, 824, and nn. 10-14. Our cases sensibly suggest that constitutional rules relating to the maturity of minors must be drawn with an eye to the decision for which the maturity is relevant. See Fare v. Michael C., 442 U.S. 707, 725-727 (1979) (totality of the circumstances test for juvenile waiver of Fifth Amendment rights permits evaluation of the juvenile's age, experience,

education, background, and intelligence, and into whether he has the capacity to understand the warnings given him); Bellotti v. Baird, 443 U.S. 622, 634-637, 642 (1979) (abortion decision differs in important ways from other decisions that may be made during minority). It is surely constitutional for a State to believe that the degree of maturity that is necessary fully to appreciate the pros and cons of smoking cigarettes, or even of marrying, may be somewhat greater than the degree necessary fully to appreciate the pros and cons of brutally killing a human being.

Congress cannot delegate its authority to make sentences for crimes: Justice Scalia's dissent in Mistretta v. United States (Jan. 18, 1989)

Justice SCALIA, dissenting.

While the products of the Sentencing Commission's labors have been given the modest name "Guidelines," see 28 U.S.C. 994(a)(1) (1982 ed., Supp. IV); United States Sentencing Commission Guidelines Manual (June 15, 1988), they have the force and effect of laws, prescribing the sentences criminal defendants are to receive. A judge who disregards them will be reversed, 18 U.S.C. 3742 (1982 ed., Supp. IV). I dissent from today's decision because I can find no place within our constitutional system for an agency created by Congress to exercise no governmental power other than the making of laws.

* There is no doubt that the Sentencing Commission has established significant, legally binding prescriptions governing application of governmental power against private individuals indeed, application of the ultimate governmental power, short of capital punishment. 1 Statutorily permissible sentences for particular crimes cover as broad a range as zero years to life, see, e.g., 18 U.S.C. 1201 (1982 ed. and Supp. IV) (kidnaping), and within those ranges the Commission was given broad discretion to prescribe the "correct" sentence, 28 U.S.C. 994(b)(2) (1982 ed., Supp. IV). Average prior sentences were to be a starting point for the Commission's inquiry, § 994(m), but it could and regularly did deviate from those averages as it thought appropriate. It chose, for example, to prescribe substantial increases over average prior sentences for white-collar crimes such as public corruption, antitrust violations, and tax evasion. Guidelines, at 2.31, 2.133, 2.140. For antitrust violations, before the Guidelines only 39% of those convicted served any imprisonment, and the average imprisonment was only 45 days, id., at 2.133, whereas the Guidelines prescribe base sentences (for defendants with no prior criminal conviction) ranging from 2-to-8 months to 10-to-16 months, depending upon the volume of commerce involved. See id., at 2.131, 5.2.

The Commission also determined when probation was permissible, imposing a strict system of controls because of its judgment that probation had been used for an "inappropriately high percentage of offenders guilty of certain economic crimes." Id., at 1.8. Moreover, the Commission had free rein in determining whether statutorily authorized fines should be imposed in addition to imprisonment, and if so, in what amounts. It ultimately decided that every nonindigent offender should pay a fine according to a schedule devised by the Commission. Id., at 5.18. Congress also gave the Commission discretion to determine whether 7 specified characteristics of offenses, and 11 specified characteristics of offenders, "have any relevance," and should be included among the factors varying the sentence. 28 U.S.C. 994(c), (d) (1982 ed., Supp. IV). Of the latter, it included only three among the factors required to be considered, and declared the remainder not ordinarily relevant. Guidelines, at 5.29-5.31.

It should be apparent from the above that the decisions made by the Commission are far from technical, but are heavily laden (or ought to be) with value judgments and policy assessments. This fact is sharply reflected in the Commission's product, as described by the dissenting Commissioner:

"Under the guidelines, the judge could give the same sentence for abusive sexual contact that puts the child in fear as for unlawfully entering or remaining in the United States. Similarly, the guidelines permit equivalent sentences for the following pairs of offenses: drug trafficking and a violation of the Wild Free-Roaming Horses and Burros Act; arson with a destructive device and failure to surrender a cancelled naturalization certificate; operation of a common carrier under the influence of drugs that causes injury and alteration of one motor vehicle identification number; illegal trafficking in explosives and trespass; interference with a flight attendant and unlawful conduct relating to contraband cigarettes; aggravated assault and smuggling $11,000 worth of fish." Dissenting View of Commissioner Paul H. Robinson on the Promulgation of the Sentencing Guidelines by the United States Sentencing Commission 6-7 (May 1, 1987) (citations omitted).

Petitioner's most fundamental and far-reaching challenge to the Commission is that Congress' commitment of such broad policy responsibility to any institution is an unconstitutional delegation of legislative power. It is difficult to imagine a principle more essential to democratic government than that upon which the doctrine of unconstitutional delegation is founded: Except in a few areas constitutionally committed to the Executive Branch, the basic policy decisions governing society are to be made by the Legislature. Our Members of Congress could not, even if they wished, vote all power to the President and adjourn sine die.

But while the doctrine of unconstitutional delegation is unquestionably a fundamental element of our constitutional system, it is not an element readily enforceable by the courts. Once it is conceded, as it must be, that no statute can be entirely precise, and that some judgments, even some judgments involving policy considerations, must be left to the officers executing the law and to the judges applying it, the debate over unconstitutional delegation becomes a debate not over a point of principle but over a question of degree. As Chief Justice Taft expressed the point for the Court in the landmark case of J.W. Hampton, Jr., & Co. v. United States, 276 U.S. 394, 406, 48 S.Ct. 348, 351, 72 L.Ed. 624 (1928), the limits of delegation "must be fixed according to common sense and the inherent necessities of the governmental co-ordination." Since Congress is no less endowed with common sense than we are, and better equipped to inform itself of the "necessities" of government; and since the factors bearing upon those necessities are both multifarious and (in the nonpartisan sense) highly political—including, for example, whether the Nation is at war, see Yakus v. United States, 321 U.S. 414, 64 S.Ct. 660, 88 L.Ed. 834 (1944), or whether for other reasons "emergency is instinct in the situation," Amalgamated Meat Cutters and Butcher Workmen of North America v. Connally, 337 F.Supp. 737, 752 (DC 1971) (three-judge court)—it is small wonder that we have almost never felt qualified to second-guess Congress regarding the permissible degree of policy judgment that can be left to those executing or applying the law. As the Court points out, we have invoked the doctrine of unconstitutional delegation to invalidate a law only twice in our history, over half a century ago. See Panama Refining Co. v. Ryan, 293 U.S. 388, 55 S.Ct. 241, 79 L.Ed. 446 (1935); A.L.A. Schechter Poultry Corp. v. United States, 295 U.S. 495, 55 S.Ct. 837, 79 L.Ed. 1570 (1935). What legislated standard, one must wonder, can possibly be too vague to survive judicial scrutiny, when we have repeatedly upheld, in various contexts, a "public interest" standard? See, e.g., National Broadcasting Co. v. United States, 319 U.S. 190, 216-217, 63 S.Ct. 997, 1009-1010, 87 L.Ed. 1344 (1943); New York Central Securities Corp. v. United States, 287 U.S. 12, 24-25, 53 S.Ct. 45, 48, 77 L.Ed. 138 (1932).

In short, I fully agree with the Court's rejection of petitioner's contention that the doctrine of unconstitutional delegation of legislative authority has been violated because of the lack of intelligible, congressionally prescribed standards to guide the Commission.

II

Precisely because the scope of delegation is largely uncontrollable by the courts, we must be particularly rigorous in preserving the Constitution's structural restrictions that deter excessive delegation. The major one, it seems to me, is that the power to make law cannot be exercised by anyone other than Congress, except in conjunction with the lawful exercise of executive or judicial power.

The whole theory of lawful congressional "delegation" is not that Congress is sometimes too busy or too divided and can therefore assign its responsibility of making law to someone else; but rather that a certain degree of discretion, and thus of lawmaking, inheres in most executive or judicial action, and it is up to Congress, by the relative specificity or generality of its statutory commands, to determine—up to a point—how small or how large that degree shall be. Thus, the courts could be given the power to say precisely what constitutes a "restraint of trade," see Standard Oil Co. of New Jersey v. United States, 221 U.S. 1, 31 S.Ct. 502, 55 L.Ed. 619 (1911), or to adopt rules of procedure, see Sibbach v. Wilson & Co., 312 U.S. 1, 22, 61 S.Ct. 422, 429, 85 L.Ed. 479 (1941), or to prescribe by rule the manner in which their officers shall execute their judgments, Wayman v. Southard,, 23 U.S. 1, 10 Wheat. 1, 45, 6 L.Ed. 253 (1825), because that "lawmaking" was ancillary to their exercise of judicial powers. And the Executive could be given the power to adopt policies and rules specifying in detail what radio and television licenses will be in the "public interest, convenience or necessity," because that was ancillary to the exercise of its executive powers in granting and policing licenses and making a "fair and equitable allocation" of the electromagnetic spectrum. See Federal Radio Comm'n v. Nelson Brothers Bond & Mortgage Co., 289 U.S. 266, 285, 53 S.Ct. 627, 636, 77 L.Ed. 1166 (1933). 2 Or to take examples closer to the case before us: Trial judges could be given the power to determine what factors justify a greater or lesser sentence within the statutorily prescribed limits because that was ancillary to their exercise of the judicial power of pronouncing sentence upon individual defendants. And the President, through the Parole Commission subject to his appointment and removal, could be given the power to issue Guidelines specifying when parole would be available, because that was ancillary to the President's exercise of the executive power to hold and release federal prisoners. See 18 U.S.C. 4203(a)(1) and (b); 28 CFR § 2.20 (1988).

As Justice Harlan wrote for the Court in Field v. Clark, 143 U.S. 649, 12 S.Ct. 495, 36 L.Ed. 294 (1892):

" 'The true distinction . . . is between the delegation of power to make the law, which necessarily involves a discretion as to what it shall be, and conferring authority or discretion as to its execution, to be exercised under and in pursuance of the law. The first cannot be done; to the latter no valid objection can be made.' " Id., at 693-694, 12 S.Ct., at 505 (emphasis added), quoting Cincinnati, W. & Z.R. Co. v. Commissioners of Clinton County, 1 Ohio St. 77, 88-89 (1852).

" 'Half the statutes on our books are in the alternative, depending on the discretion of some person or persons to whom is confided the duty of determining whether the proper occasion exists for executing them. But it cannot be said that the exercise of such discretion is the making of the law.' " Id., at 694, 12 S.Ct. at 505 (emphasis added), quoting Moers v. Reading, 21 Pa. 188, 202 (1853).

In United States v. Grimaud, 220 U.S. 506, 517, 31 S.Ct. 480, 483, 55 L.Ed. 563 (1911), which upheld a statutory grant of authority to the Secretary of Agriculture to make rules and regulations governing use of the public forests he was charged with managing, the Court said: "From the beginning of the Government various acts have been passed conferring upon executive officers power to make rules and regulations—not for the government of their departments, but for administering the laws which did govern. None of these statutes could confer legislative power." (Emphasis added.)

Or, finally, as Chief Justice Taft described it in Hampton & Co., 276 U.S., at 406, 48 S.Ct., at 351:

"The field of Congress involves all and many varieties of legislative action, and Congress has found it frequently necessary to use officers of the Executive Branch, within defined limits, to secure the exact effect intended by its acts of legislation, by vesting discretion in such officers to make public regulations interpreting a statute and directing the details of its execution, even to the extent of providing for penalizing a breach of such regulations." (Emphasis added.)

The focus of controversy, in the long line of our so-called excessive delegation cases, has been whether the degree of generality contained in the authorization for exercise of executive or judicial powers in a particular field is so unacceptably high as to amount to a delegation of legislative powers. I say "so-called excessive delegation" because although that convenient terminology is often used, what is really at issue is whether there has been any delegation of legislative power, which occurs (rarely) when Congress authorizes the exercise of executive or judicial power without adequate standards. Strictly speaking, there is no acceptable delegation of legislative power. As John Locke put it almost 300 years ago, "the power of the legislative being derived from the people by a positive voluntary grant and institution, can be no other, than what the positive grant conveyed, which being only to make laws, and not to make legislators, the leg- islative can have no power to transfer their authority of making laws, and place it in other hands." J. Locke, Second Treatise of Government 87 (R. Cox ed.1982) (emphasis added). Or as we have less epigrammatically said: "That Congress cannot delegate legislative power to the President is a principle universally recognized as vital to the integrity and maintenance of the system of government ordained by the Constitution." Field v. Clark, supra, 143 U.S. at 692, 12 S.Ct., at 504. In the present case, however, a pure delegation of legislative power is precisely what we have before us. It is irrelevant whether the standards are adequate, because they are not standards related to the exercise of executive or judicial powers; they are, plainly and simply, standards for further legislation.

The lawmaking function of the Sentencing Commission is completely divorced from any responsibility for execution of the law or adjudication of private rights under the law. It is divorced from responsibility for execution of the law not only because the Commission is not said to be "located in the Executive Branch" (as I shall discuss presently, I doubt whether Congress can "locate" an entity within one Branch or another for constitutional purposes by merely saying so); but, more importantly, because the Commission neither exercises any executive power on its own, nor is subject to the control of the President who does. The only functions it performs, apart from prescribing the law, 28 U.S.C. 994(a)(1), (3) (1982 ed., Supp. IV), conducting the investigations useful and necessary for prescribing the law, e.g., §§ 995(a)(13), (15), (16), (21), and clarifying the intended application of the law that it prescribes, e.g., §§ 994(a)(2), 995(a)(10), are data collection and intragovernmental advice giving and education, e.g., §§ 995(a)(8), (9), (12), (17), (18), (20). These latter activities—similar to functions performed by congressional agencies and even congressional staff—neither determine nor affect private rights, and do not constitute an exercise of governmental power. See Humphrey's Executor v. United States, 295 U.S. 602, 628, 55 S.Ct. 869, 874, 79 L.Ed. 1611 (1935). And the Commission's lawmaking is completely divorced from the exercise of judicial powers since, not being a court, it has no judicial powers itself, nor is it subject to the control of any other body with judicial powers. The power to make law at issue here, in other words, is not ancillary but quite naked. The situation is no different in principle from what would exist if Congress gave the same power of writing sentencing laws to a congressional agency such as the General Accounting Office, or to members of its staff.

The delegation of lawmaking authority to the Commission is, in short, unsupported by any legitimating theory to explain why it is not a delegation of legislative power. To disregard structural legitimacy is wrong in itself—but since structure has purpose, the disregard also has adverse practical consequences. In this case, as suggested earlier, the consequence is to facilitate and encourage judicially uncontrollable delegation. Until our decision last Term in Morrison v. Olson, 487 U.S. 654, 108 S.Ct. 2597, 101 L.Ed.2d 569 (1988), it could have been said that Congress could delegate lawmaking authority only at the expense of increasing the power of either the President or the courts. Most often, as a practical matter, it would be the President, since the judicial process is unable to conduct the investigations and make the political assessments essential for most policymaking. Thus, the need for delegation would have to be important enough to induce Congress to aggrandize its primary competitor for political power, and the recipient of the policymaking authority, while not Congress itself, would at least be politically accountable. But even after it has been accepted, pursuant to Morrison, that those exercising executive power need not be subject to the control of the President, Congress would still be more reluctant to augment the power of even an independent executive agency than to create an otherwise powerless repository for its delegation. Moreover, assembling the full-time senior personnel for an agency exercising executive powers is more difficult than borrowing other officials (or employing new officers on a short-term basis) to head an organization such as the Sentencing Commission.

By reason of today's decision, I anticipate that Congress will find delegation of its lawmaking powers much more attractive in the future. If rulemaking can be entirely unrelated to the exercise of judicial or executive powers, I foresee all manner of "expert" bodies, insulated from the political process, to which Congress will delegate various portions of its lawmaking responsibility. How tempting to create an expert Medical Commission (mostly M.D.'s, with perhaps a few Ph.D.'s in moral philosophy) to dispose of such thorny, "no-win" political issues as the withholding of life-support systems in federally funded hospitals, or the use of fetal tissue for research. This is an undemocratic precedent that we set—not because of the scope of the delegated power, but because its recipient is not one of the three Branches of Government. The only governmental power the Commission possesses is the power to make law; and it is not the Congress.

III

The strange character of the body that the Court today approves, and its incompatibility with our constitutional institutions, is apparent from that portion of the Court's opinion entitled "Location of the Commission." This accepts at the outset that the Commission is a "body within the Judicial Branch," ante, at 385, and rests some of its analysis upon that asserted reality. Separation-of-powers problems are dismissed, however, on the ground that "the Commission's powers are not united with the powers of the Judiciary in a way that has meaning for separation-of-powers analysis," since the Commission "is not a court, does not exercise judicial power, and is not controlled by or accountable to members of the Judicial Branch," ante, at 393. In light of the latter concession, I am at a loss to understand why the Commission is "within the Judicial Branch" in any sense that has relevance to today's discussion. I am sure that Congress can divide up the Government any way it wishes, and employ whatever terminology it desires, for non constitutional purposes—for example, perhaps the statutory designation that the Commission is "within the Judicial Branch" places it outside the coverage of certain laws which say they are inapplicable to that Branch, such as the Freedom of Information Act, see 5 U.S.C. 552(f) (1982 ed., Supp. IV). For such statutory purposes, Congress can define the term as it pleases. But since our subject here is the Constitution, to admit that that congressional designation "has no meaning for separation-of-powers analysis" is to admit that the Court must therefore decide for itself where the Commission is located for purposes of separation-of-powers analysis.

It would seem logical to decide the question of which Branch an agency belongs to on the basis of who controls its actions: If Congress, the Legislative Branch; if the President, the Executive Branch; if the courts (or perhaps the judges), the Judicial Branch. See, e.g., Bowsher v. Synar, 478 U.S. 714, 727-732, 106 S.Ct. 3181, 3188-3191, 92 L.Ed.2d 583 (1986). In Humphrey's Executor v. United States, 295 U.S. 602, 55 S.Ct. 869, 79 L.Ed. 1611 (1935), we approved the concept of an agency that was controlled by (and thus within) none of the Branches. We seem to have assumed, however, that that agency (the old Federal Trade Commission, before it acquired many of its current functions) exercised no governmental power whatever, but merely assisted Congress and the courts in the performance of their functions. See Id., at 628, 55 S.Ct., at 874. Where no governmental power is at issue, there is no strict constitutional impediment to a "branchless" agency, since it is only "all legislative Powers," Art. I, § 1, "the executive Power," Art. II, § 1, and "the judicial Power," Art. III, § 1, which the Constitution divides into three departments. (As an example of a "branchless" agency exercising no governmental powers, one can conceive of an Advisory Commission charged with reporting to all three Branches, whose members are removable only for cause and are thus subject to the control of none of the Branches.) Over the years, however, Humphrey's Executor has come in general contemplation to stand for something quite different—not an "independent agency" in the sense of an agency independent of all three Branches, but an "independent agency" in the sense of an agency within the Executive Branch (and thus authorized to exercise executive powers) independent of the control of the President.

We approved that concept last Term in Morrison. See 487 U.S., at 688-691, 108 S.Ct., at 2617-2619. I dissented in that case, essentially because I thought that concept illogical and destructive of the structure of the Constitution. I must admit, however, that today's next step—recognition of an independent agency in the Judicial Branch—makes Morrison seem, by comparison, rigorously logical. "The Commission," we are told, "is an independent agency in every relevant sense." Ante, at 393. There are several problems with this. First, once it is acknowledged that an "independent agency" may be within any of the three Branches, and not merely within the Executive, then there really is no basis for determining what Branch such an agency belongs to, and thus what governmental powers it may constitutionally be given, except (what the Court today uses) Congress' say-so. More importantly, however, the concept of an "independent agency" simply does not translate into the legislative or judicial spheres. Although the Constitution says that "the executive Power shall be vested in a President of the United States of America," Art. II, § 1, it was never thought that the President would have to exercise that power personally. He may generally authorize others to exercise executive powers, with full effect of law, in his place. See, e.g., Wolsey v. Chapman, 101 U.S. 755, 25 L.Ed. 915 (1880); Williams v. United States, 1 How. 290, 11 L.Ed. 135 (1843). It is already a leap from the proposition that a person who is not the President may exercise executive powers to the proposition we accepted in Morrison that a person who is neither the President nor subject to the President's control may exercise executive powers. But with respect to the exercise of judicial powers (the business of the Judicial Branch) the platform for such a leap does not even exist. For unlike executive power, judicial and legislative powers have never been thought delegable. A judge may not leave the decision to his law clerk, or to a master. See United States v. Raddatz, 447 U.S. 667, 683, 100 S.Ct. 2406, 2416, 65 L.Ed.2d 424 (1980); cf. Runkle v. United States, 122 U.S. 543, 7 S.Ct. 1141, 30 L.Ed. 1167 (1887). Senators and Members of the House may not send delegates to consider and vote upon bills in their place. See Rules of the House of Representatives, Rule VIII(3); Standing Rules of the United States Senate, Rule XII. Thus, however well established may be the "independent agencies" of the Executive Branch, here we have an anomaly beyond equal: an independent agency exercising governmental power on behalf of a Branch where all governmental power is supposed to be exercised personally by the judges of courts. 3

Today's decision may aptly be described as the Humphrey's Executor of the Judicial Branch, and I think we will live to regret it. Henceforth there may be agencies "within the Judicial Branch" (whatever that means), exercising governmental powers, that are neither courts nor controlled by courts, nor even controlled by judges. If an "independent agency" such as this can be given the power to fix sentences previously exercised by district courts, I must assume that a similar agency can be given the powers to adopt rules of procedure and rules of evidence previously exercised by this Court. The bases for distinction would be thin indeed.

* * *

Today's decision follows the regrettable tendency of our recent separation-of-powers jurisprudence, see Morrison, supra; Young v. United States ex rel. Vuitton et Fils S.A., 481 U.S. 787, 107 S.Ct. 2124, 95 L.Ed.2d 740 (1987), to treat the Constitution as though it were no more than a generalized prescription that the functions of the Branches should not be commingled too much—how much is too much to be determined, case-by-case, by this Court. The Constitution is not that. Rather, as its name suggests, it is a prescribed structure, a framework, for the conduct of government. In designing that structure, the Framers themselves considered how much commingling was, in the generality of things, acceptable, and set forth their conclusions in the document. That is the meaning of the statements concerning acceptable commingling made by Madison in defense of the proposed Constitution, and now routinely used as an excuse for disregarding it. When he said, as the Court correctly quotes, that separation of powers " 'does not mean that these three departments ought to have no partial agency in, or no controul over the acts of each other,' " ante, at 380—381, quoting The Federalist No. 47, pp. 325-326 (J. Cooke ed.1961), his point was that the commingling specifically provided for in the structure that he and his colleagues had designed—the Presidential veto over legislation, the Senate's confirmation of executive and judicial officers, the Senate's ratification of treaties, the Congress' power to impeach and remove executive and judicial officers—did not violate a proper understanding of separation of powers. He would be aghast, I think, to hear those words used as justification for ignoring that carefully designed structure so long as, in the changing view of the Supreme Court from time to time, "too much commingling" does not occur. Consideration of the degree of commingling that a particular disposition produces may be appropriate at the margins, where the outline of the framework itself is not clear; but it seems to me far from a marginal question whether our constitutional structure allows for a body which is not the Congress, and yet exercises no governmental powers except the making of rules that have the effect of laws.

    I think the Court errs, in other words, not so much because it mistakes the degree of commingling, but because it fails to recognize that this case is not about commingling, but about the creation of a new Branch altogether, a sort of junior-varsity Congress. It may well be that in some circumstances such a Branch would be desirable; perhaps the agency before us here will prove to be so. But there are many desirable dispositions that do not accord with the constitutional structure we live under. And in the long run the improvisation of a constitutional structure on the basis of currently perceived utility will be disastrous.

    I respectfully dissent from the Court's decision, and would reverse the judgment of the District Court.

Notes to Justice Scalia's dissent in Mistretta v. United States (Jan. 18, 1989)

    1. It is even arguable that the Commission has authority to establish guidelines and procedures for imposing the death penalty, thus reinstituting that sanction under federal statutes for which (by reason of our recent decisions) it has been thought unusable because of constitutionally inadequate procedures. The Justice Department believes such authority exists, and has encouraged the Commission to exercise it. See Gubiensio-Ortiz v. Kanahele, 857 F.2d 1245, 1256 (CA9 1988).

2. An executive agency can, of course, be created with no power other than the making of rules, as long as that agency is subject to the control of the President and the President has executive authority related to the rulemaking. In such circumstances, the rulemaking is ultimately ancillary to the President's executive powers.

3. There are of course agencies within the Judicial Branch (because they operate under the control of courts or judges) which are not themselves courts, see, e.g., 28 U.S.C. 601 et seq. (Administrative Office of the United States Courts), just as there are agencies within the Legislative Branch (because they operate under the control of Congress) which are not themselves Senators or Representatives, see, e.g., 31 U.S.C. 701 et seq. (General Accounting Office). But these agencies, unlike the Sentencing Commission, exercise no governmental powers, that is, they establish and determine neither private rights nor the prerogatives of the other Branches. They merely assist the courts and the Congress in their exercise of judicial and legislative powers.

The benign purpose of compensating for social disadvantages, whether they have been acquired by reason of prior discrimination or otherwise, can no more be pursued by the illegitimate means of racial discrimination than can other assertedly benign purposes we have repeatedly rejected: Justice Scalia's concurrence in Richmond v. Croson (January 23, 1989)

JUSTICE SCALIA, concurring in the judgment.

I agree with much of the Court's opinion, and, in particular, with JUSTICE O'CONNOR'S conclusion that strict scrutiny must be applied to all governmental classification by race, whether or not its asserted purpose is "remedial" or "benign." Ante, at 493, 495. I do not agree, however, with JUSTICE O'CONNOR'S dictum suggesting that, despite the Fourteenth Amendment, state and local governments may in some circumstances discriminate on the basis of race in order (in a broad sense) "to ameliorate the effects of past discrimination." Ante, at 476-477. The benign purpose of compensating for social disadvantages, whether they have been acquired by reason of prior discrimination or otherwise, can no more be pursued by the illegitimate means of racial discrimination than can other assertedly benign purposes we have repeatedly rejected. See, e. g., Wygant v. Jackson Board of Education, 476 U.S. 267, 274 -276 (1986) (plurality opinion) (discrimination in teacher assignments to provide "role models" for minority students); Palmore v. Sidoti, 466 U.S. 429, 433 (1984) (awarding custody of child to father, after divorced mother entered an interracial remarriage, in order to spare child social "pressures and stresses"); Lee v. Washington, 390 U.S. 333 (1968) (per curiam) (permanent racial segregation of all prison inmates, presumably to reduce possibility of racial conflict). The difficulty of overcoming the effects of past discrimination is as nothing compared with the difficulty of eradicating from our society the source of those effects, which is the tendency - fatal to a Nation such as ours - to classify and judge men and women on the basis of their country of origin or the color of their skin. A solution to the first problem that aggravates the second is no solution at all. I share the view expressed by Alexander Bickel that "[t]he lesson of the great decisions of the Supreme Court and the lesson of contemporary history have been the same for at least a generation: discrimination on the basis of race is illegal, immoral, unconstitutional, inherently wrong, and destructive of democratic society." A. Bickel, The Morality of Consent 133 (1975). At least where state or local action is at issue, only a social emergency rising to the level of imminent danger to life and limb - for example, a prison race riot, requiring temporary segregation of inmates, cf. Lee v. Washington, supra - can justify an exception to the principle embodied in the Fourteenth Amendment that "[o]ur Constitution is colorblind, and neither knows nor tolerates classes among citizens," Plessy v. Ferguson, 163 U.S. 537, 559 (1896) (Harlan, J., dissenting); accord, Ex parte Virginia, 100 U.S. 339, 345 (1880); 2 J. Story, Commentaries on the Constitution 1961, p. 677 (T. Cooley ed. 1873); T. Cooley, Constitutional Limitations 439 (2d ed. 1871).

We have in some contexts approved the use of racial classifications by the Federal Government to remedy the effects of past discrimination. I do not believe that we must or should extend those holdings to the States. In Fullilove v. Klutznick, 448 U.S. 448 (1980), we upheld legislative action by Congress similar in its asserted purpose to that at issue here. And we have permitted federal courts to prescribe quite severe, race-conscious remedies when confronted with egregious and persistent unlawful discrimination, see, e. g., United States v. Paradise, 480 U.S. 149 (1987); Sheet Metal Workers v. EEOC, 478 U.S. 421 (1986). As JUSTICE O'CONNOR acknowledges, however, ante, at 486-491, it is one thing to permit racially based conduct by the Federal Government - whose legislative powers concerning matters of race were explicitly enhanced by the Fourteenth Amendment, see U.S. Const., Amdt. 14, 5 - and quite another to permit it by the precise entities against whose conduct in matters of race that Amendment was specifically directed, see Amdt. 14, 1. As we said in Ex parte Virginia, supra, at 345, the Civil War Amendments were designed to "take away all possibility of oppression by law because of race or color" and "to be . . . limitations on the power of the States and enlargements of the power of Congress." Thus, without revisiting what we held in Fullilove (or trying to derive a rationale from the three separate opinions supporting the judgment, none of which commanded more than three votes, compare 448 U.S., at 453 -495 (opinion of Burger, C. J., joined by WHITE and Powell, JJ.), with id., at 495-517 (opinion of Powell, J.), and id., at 517-522 (opinion of MARSHALL, J., joined by BRENNAN and BLACKMUN, JJ.)), I do not believe our decision in that case controls the one before us here.

A sound distinction between federal and state (or local) action based on race rests not only upon the substance of the Civil War Amendments, but upon social reality and governmental theory. It is a simple fact that what Justice Stewart described in Fullilove as "the dispassionate objectivity [and] the flexibility that are needed to mold a race-conscious remedy around the single objective of eliminating the effects of past or present discrimination" - political qualities already to be doubted in a national legislature, Fullilove, supra, at 527 (Stewart, J., with whom REHNQUIST, J., joined, dissenting) - are substantially less likely to exist at the state or local level. The struggle for racial justice has historically been a struggle by the national society against oppression in the individual States. See, e. g., Ex parte Virginia, supra (denying writ of habeas corpus to a state judge in custody under federal indictment for excluding jurors on the basis of race); H. Hyman & W. Wiecek, Equal Justice Under Law, 1835-1875, pp. 312-334 (1982); Logan, Judicial Federalism in the Court of History, 66 Ore. L. Rev. 454, 494-515 (1988). And the struggle retains that character in modern times. See, e. g., Brown v. Board of Education, 349 U.S. 294 (1955) (Brown II); United States v. Montgomery Board of Education, 395 U.S. 225 (1969); Swann v. Charlotte-Mecklenburg Board of Education, 402 U.S. 1 (1971); Griffin v. Prince Edward County School Board, 377 U.S. 218 (1964); Cooper v. Aaron, 358 U.S. 1 (1958). Not all of that struggle has involved discrimination against blacks, see, e. g., Yick Wo v. Hopkins, 118 U.S. 356 (1886) (Chinese); Hernandez v. Texas, 347 U.S. 475 (1954) (Hispanics), and not all of it has been in the Old South, see, e. g., Columbus Board of Education v. Penick, 443 U.S. 449 (1979); Keyes v. School Dist. No. 1, Denver, Colorado, 413 U.S. 189 (1973). What the record shows, in other words, is that racial discrimination against any group finds a more ready expression at the state and local than at the federal level. To the children of the Founding Fathers, this should come as no surprise. An acute awareness of the heightened danger of oppression from political factions in small, rather than large, political units dates to the very beginning of our national history. See G. Wood, The Creation of the American Republic, 1776-1787, pp. 499-506 (1969). As James Madison observed in support of the proposed Constitution's enhancement of national powers:

"The smaller the society, the fewer probably will be the distinct parties and interests composing it; the fewer the distinct parties and interests, the more frequently will a majority be found of the same party; and the smaller the number of individuals composing a majority, and the smaller the compass within which they are placed, the more easily will they concert and execute their plan of oppression. Extend the sphere and you take in a greater variety of parties and interests; you make it less probable that a majority of the whole will have a common motive to invade the rights of other citizens; or if such a common motive exists, it will be more difficult for all who feel it to discover their own strength and to act in unison with each other." The Federalist No. 10, pp. 82-84 (C. Rossiter ed. 1961).

The prophesy of these words came to fruition in Richmond in the enactment of a set-aside clearly and directly beneficial to the dominant political group, which happens also to be the dominant racial group. The same thing has no doubt happened before in other cities (though the racial basis of the preference has rarely been made textually explicit) - and blacks have often been on the receiving end of the injustice. Where injustice is the game, however, turnabout is not fair play.

In my view there is only one circumstance in which the States may act by race to "undo the effects of past discrimination": where that is necessary to eliminate their own maintenance of a system of unlawful racial classification. If, for example, a state agency has a discriminatory pay scale compensating black employees in all positions at 20% less than their nonblack counterparts, it may assuredly promulgate an order raising the salaries of "all black employees" to eliminate the differential. Cf. Bazemore v. Friday, 478 U.S. 385, 395 -396 (1986). This distinction explains our school desegregation cases, in which we have made plain that States and localities sometimes have an obligation to adopt race-conscious remedies. While there is no doubt that those cases have taken into account the continuing "effects" of previously mandated racial school assignment, we have held those effects to justify a race-conscious remedy only because we have concluded, in that context, that they perpetuate a "dual school system." We have stressed each school district's constitutional "duty to dismantle its dual system," and have found that "[e]ach instance of a failure or refusal to fulfill this affirmative duty continues the violation of the Fourteenth Amendment." Columbus Board of Education v. Penick, supra, at 458-459 (emphasis added). Concluding in this context that race-neutral efforts at "dismantling the state-imposed dual system" were so ineffective that they might "indicate a lack of good faith," Green v. New Kent County School Board, 391 U.S. 430, 439 (1968); see also Raney v. Board of Education of Gould School Dist., 391 U.S. 443 (1968), we have permitted, as part of the local authorities' "affirmative duty to disestablish the dual school system[s]," such voluntary (that is, noncourt-ordered) measures as attendance zones drawn to achieve greater racial balance, and out-of-zone assignment by race for the same purpose. McDaniel v. Barresi, 402 U.S. 39, 40 -41 (1971). While thus permitting the use of race to declassify racially classified students, teachers, and educational resources, however, we have also made it clear that the remedial power extends no further than the scope of the continuing constitutional violation. See, e. g., Columbus Board of Education v. Penick, supra, at 465; Dayton Board of Education v. Brinkman, 433 U.S. 406, 420 (1977); Milliken v. Bradley, 418 U.S. 717, 744 (1974); Keyes v. School Dist. No. 1, Denver, Colorado, supra, at 213. And it is implicit in our cases that after the dual school system has been completely disestablished, the States may no longer assign students by race. Cf. Pasadena City Board of Education v. Spangler, 427 U.S. 424 (1976) (federal court may not require racial assignment in such circumstances).

Our analysis in Bazemore v. Friday, supra, reflected our unwillingness to conclude, outside the context of school assignment, that the continuing effects of prior discrimination can be equated with state maintenance of a discriminatory system. There we found both that the government's adoption of "wholly neutral admissions" policies for 4-H and Homemaker Clubs sufficed to remedy its prior constitutional violation of maintaining segregated admissions, and that there was no further obligation to use racial reassignments to eliminate continuing effects - that is, any remaining all-black and all-white clubs. 478 U.S., at 407 -408. "[H]owever sound Green [v. New Kent County School

Board, supra] may have been in the context of the public schools," we said, "it has no application to this wholly different milieu." Id., at 408. The same is so here.

A State can, of course, act "to undo the effects of past discrimination" in many permissible ways that do not involve classification by race. In the particular field of state contracting, for example, it may adopt a preference for small businesses, or even for new businesses - which would make it easier for those previously excluded by discrimination to enter the field. Such programs may well have racially disproportionate impact, but they are not based on race. And, of course, a State may "undo the effects of past discrimination" in the sense of giving the identified victim of state discrimination that which it wrongfully denied him - for example, giving to a previously rejected black applicant the job that, by reason of discrimination, had been awarded to a white applicant, even if this means terminating the latter's employment. In such a context, the white jobholder is not being selected for disadvantageous treatment because of his race, but because he was wrongfully awarded a job to which another is entitled. That is worlds apart from the system here, in which those to be disadvantaged are identified solely by race.

I agree with the Court's dictum that a fundamental distinction must be drawn between the effects of "societal" discrimination and the effects of "identified" discrimination, and that the situation would be different if Richmond's plan were "tailored" to identify those particular bidders who "suffered from the effects of past discrimination by the city or prime contractors." Ante, at 507-508. In my view, however, the reason that would make a difference is not, as the Court states, that it would justify race-conscious action - see, e. g., ante, at 504-506, 507-508 - but rather that it would enable race-neutral remediation. Nothing prevents Richmond from according a contracting preference to identified victims of discrimination. While most of the beneficiaries might be black, neither the beneficiaries nor those disadvantaged by the preference would be identified on the basis of their race. In other words, far from justifying racial classification, identification of actual victims of discrimination makes it less supportable than ever, because more obviously unneeded.

In this final book, Professor Bickel wrote:

"[A] racial quota derogates the human dignity and individuality of all to whom it is applied; it is invidious in principle as well as in practice. Moreover, it can easily be turned against those it purports to help. The history of the racial quota is a history of subjugation, not beneficence. Its evil lies not in its name, but in its effects: a quota is a divider of society, a creator of castes, and it is all the worse for its racial base, especially in a society desperately striving for an equality that will make race irrelevant." Bickel, The Morality of Consent, at 133.

Those statements are true and increasingly prophetic. Apart from their societal effects, however, which are "in the aggregate disastrous," id., at 134, it is important not to lose sight of the fact that even "benign" racial quotas have individual victims, whose very real injustice we ignore whenever we deny them enforcement of their right not to be disadvantaged on the basis of race. Johnson v. Transportation Agency, Santa Clara County, 480 U.S. 616, 677 (1987) (SCALIA, J., dissenting). As Justice Douglas observed: "A DeFunis who is white is entitled to no advantage by virtue of that fact; nor is he subject to any disability, no matter what his race or color. Whatever his race, he had a constitutional right to have his application considered on its individual merits in a racially neutral manner." DeFunis v. Odegaard, 416 U.S. 312, 337 (1974) (dissenting opinion). When we depart from this American principle we play with fire, and much more than an occasional DeFunis, Johnson, or Croson burns.

It is plainly true that in our society blacks have suffered discrimination immeasurably greater than any directed at other racial groups. But those who believe that racial preferences can help to "even the score" display, and reinforce, a manner of thinking by race that was the source of the injustice and that will, if it endures within our society, be the source of more injustice still. The relevant proposition is not that it was blacks, or Jews, or Irish who were discriminated against, but that it was individual men and women, "created equal," who were discriminated against. And the relevant resolve is that that should never happen again. Racial preferences appear to "even the score" (in some small degree) only if one embraces the proposition that our society is appropriately viewed as divided into races, making it right that an injustice rendered in the past to a black man should be compensated for by discriminating against a white. Nothing is worth that embrace. Since blacks have been disproportionately disadvantaged by racial discrimination, any race-neutral remedial program aimed at the disadvantaged as such will have a disproportionately beneficial impact on blacks. Only such a program, and not one that operates on the basis of race, is in accord with the letter and the spirit of our Constitution.

Since I believe that the appellee here had a constitutional right to have its bid succeed or fail under a decisionmaking process uninfected with racial bias, I concur in the judgment of the Court.

Bodily search separate from arrest and without individualized suspicion of wrong-doing can only be done with respect to prison inmates, not customs service employees: Justice Scalia's dissent in Treasury Employees v. Von Raab (March 21, 1989)

JUSTICE SCALIA, with whom JUSTICE STEVENS joins, dissenting.

The issue in this case is not whether Customs Service employees can constitutionally be denied promotion, or even dismissed, for a single instance of unlawful drug use, at home or at work. They assuredly can. The issue here is what steps can constitutionally be taken to detect such drug use. The Government asserts it can demand that employees perform "an excretory function traditionally shielded by great privacy," Skinner v. Railway Labor Executives' Assn., ante, at 626, while "a monitor of the same sex

... remains close at hand to listen for the normal sounds," ante, at 661, and that the excretion thus produced be turned over to the Government for chemical analysis. The Court agrees that this constitutes a search for purposes of the Fourth Amendment - and I think it obvious that it is a type of search particularly destructive of privacy and offensive to personal dignity.

Until today this Court had upheld a bodily search separate from arrest and without individualized suspicion of wrong-doing only with respect to prison inmates, relying upon the uniquely dangerous nature of that environment. See Bell v. Wolfish, 441 U.S. 520, 558 -560 (1979). Today, in Skinner, we allow a less intrusive bodily search of railroad employees involved in train accidents. I joined the Court's opinion there because the demonstrated frequency of drug and alcohol use by the targeted class of employees, and the demonstrated connection between such use and grave harm, rendered the search a reasonable means of protecting society. I decline to join the Court's opinion in the present case because neither frequency of use nor connection to harm is demonstrated or even likely. In my view the Customs Service rules are a kind of immolation of privacy and human dignity in symbolic opposition to drug use.

The Fourth Amendment protects the "right of the people to be secure in their persons, houses, papers, and effects, against unreasonable searches and seizures." While there are some absolutes in Fourth Amendment law, as soon as those have been left behind and the question comes down to whether a particular search has been "reasonable," the answer depends largely upon the social necessity that prompts the search. Thus, in upholding the administrative search of a student's purse in a school, we began with the observation (documented by an agency report to Congress) that "[m]aintaining order in the classroom has never been easy, but in recent years, school disorder has often taken particularly ugly forms: drug use and violent crime in the schools have become major social problems." New Jersey v. T. L. O., 469 U.S. 325, 339 (1985). When we approved fixed checkpoints near the Mexican border to stop and search cars for illegal aliens, we observed at the outset that "the Immigration and Naturalization Service now suggests there may be as many as 10 or 12 million aliens illegally in the country," and that "[i]nterdicting the flow of illegal entrants from Mexico poses formidable law enforcement problems." United States v. Martinez-Fuerte, 428 U.S. 543, 551 -552 (1976). And the substantive analysis of our opinion today in Skinner begins, "[t]he problem of alcohol use on American railroads is as old as the industry itself," and goes on to cite statistics concerning that problem and the accidents it causes, including a 1979 study finding that "23% of the operating personnel were `problem drinkers.'" Skinner, ante, at 606, and 607, n. 1.

The Court's opinion in the present case, however, will be searched in vain for real evidence of a real problem that will be solved by urine testing of Customs Service employees. Instead, there are assurances that "[t]he Customs Service is our Nation's first line of defense against one of the greatest problems affecting the health and welfare of our population," ante, at 668; that "[m]any of the Service's employees are often exposed to [drug smugglers] and to the controlled substances [they seek] to smuggle into the country," ante, at 669; that "Customs officers have been the targets of bribery by drug smugglers on numerous occasions, and several have been removed from the Service for accepting bribes and other integrity violations," ibid.; that "the Government has a compelling interest in ensuring that front-line interdiction personnel are physically fit, and have unimpeachable integrity and judgment," ante, at 670; that the "national interest in self-protection could be irreparably damaged if those charged with safeguarding it were, because of their own drug use, unsympathetic to their mission of interdicting narcotics," ibid.; and that "the public should not bear the risk that employees who may suffer from impaired perception and judgment will be promoted to positions where they may need to employ deadly force," ante, at 671. To paraphrase Churchill, all this contains much that is obviously true, and much that is relevant; unfortunately, what is obviously true is not relevant, and what is relevant is not obviously true. The only pertinent points, it seems to me, are supported by nothing but speculation, and not very plausible speculation at that. It is not apparent to me that a Customs Service employee who uses drugs is significantly more likely to be bribed by a drug smuggler, any more than a Customs Service employee who wears diamonds is significantly more likely to be bribed by a diamond smuggler - unless, perhaps, the addiction to drugs is so severe, and requires so much money to maintain, that it would be detectable even without benefit of a urine test. Nor is it apparent to me that Customs officers who use drugs will be appreciably less "sympathetic" to their drug-interdiction mission, any more than police officers who exceed the speed limit in their private cars are appreciably less sympathetic to their mission of enforcing the traffic laws. (The only difference is that the Customs officer's individual efforts, if they are irreplaceable, can theoretically affect the availability of his own drug supply - a prospect so remote as to be an absurd basis of motivation.) Nor, finally, is it apparent to me that urine tests will be even marginally more effective in preventing gun-carrying agents from risking "impaired perception and judgment" than is their current knowledge that, if impaired, they may be shot dead in unequal combat with unimpaired smugglers - unless, again, their addiction is so severe that no urine test is needed for detection.

What is absent in the Government's justifications - notably absent, revealingly absent, and as far as I am concerned dispositively absent - is the recitation of even a single instance in which any of the speculated horribles actually occurred: an instance, that is, in which the cause of bribetaking, or of poor aim, or of unsympathetic law enforcement, or of compromise of classified information, was drug use. Although the Court points out that several employees have in the past been removed from the Service for accepting bribes and other integrity violations, and that at least nine officers have died in the line of duty since 1974, ante, at 669, there is no indication whatever that these incidents were related to drug use by Service employees. Perhaps concrete evidence of the severity of a problem is unnecessary when it is so well known that courts can almost take judicial notice of it; but that is surely not the case here. The Commissioner of Customs himself has stated that he "believe[s] that Customs is largely drug-free," that "[t]he extent of illegal drug use by Customs employees was not the reason for establishing this program," and that he "hope[s] and expect[s] to receive reports of very few positive findings through drug screening." App. 10, 15. The test results have fulfilled those hopes and expectations. According to the Service's counsel, out of 3, 600 employees tested, no more than 5 tested positive for drugs. See ante, at 673.

The Court's response to this lack of evidence is that "[t]here is little reason to believe that American workplaces are immune from [the] pervasive social problem" of drug abuse. Ante, at 674. Perhaps such a generalization would suffice if the workplace at issue could produce such catastrophic social harm that no risk whatever is tolerable - the secured areas of a nuclear power plant, for example, see Rushton v. Nebraska Public Power District, 844 F.2d 562 (CA8 1988). But if such a generalization suffices to justify demeaning bodily searches, without particularized suspicion, to guard against the bribing or blackmailing of a law enforcement agent, or the careless use of a firearm, then the Fourth Amendment has become frail protection indeed. In Skinner, Bell, T. L. O., and Martinez-Fuerte, we took pains to establish the existence of special need for the search or seizure - a need based not upon the existence of a "pervasive social problem" combined with speculation as to the effect of that problem in the field at issue, but rather upon well-known or well-demonstrated evils in that field, with well-known or well-demonstrated consequences. In Skinner, for example, we pointed to a long history of alcohol abuse in the railroad industry, and noted that in an 8-year period 45 train accidents and incidents had occurred because of alcohol- and drug-impaired railroad employees, killing 34 people, injuring 66, and causing more than $28 million in property damage. Ante, at 608. In the present case, by contrast, not only is the Customs Service thought to be "largely drug-free," but the connection between whatever drug use may exist and serious social harm is entirely speculative. Except for the fact that the search of a person is much more intrusive than the stop of a car, the present case resembles Delaware v. Prouse, 440 U.S. 648 (1979), where we held that the Fourth Amendment prohibited random stops to check drivers' licenses and motor vehicle registrations. The contribution of this practice to highway safety, we concluded, was "marginal at best" since the number of licensed drivers that must be stopped in order to find one unlicensed one "will be large indeed." Id., at 660.

Today's decision would be wrong, but at least of more limited effect, if its approval of drug testing were confined to that category of employees assigned specifically to drug interdiction duties. Relatively few public employees fit that description. But in extending approval of drug testing to that category consisting of employees who carry firearms, the Court exposes vast numbers of public employees to this needless indignity. Logically, of course, if those who carry guns can be treated in this fashion, so can all others whose work, if performed under the influence of drugs, may endanger others - automobile drivers, operators of other potentially dangerous equipment, construction workers, school crossing guards. A similarly broad scope attaches to the Court's approval of drug testing for those with access to "sensitive information." 1 Since this category is not limited to Service employees with drug interdiction duties, nor to "sensitive information" specifically relating to drug traffic, today's holding apparently approves drug testing for all federal employees with security clearances - or, indeed, for all federal employees with valuable confidential information to impart. Since drug use is not a particular problem in the Customs Service, employees throughout the Government are no less likely to violate the public trust by taking bribes to feed their drug habit, or by yielding to blackmail. Moreover, there is no reason why this super-protection against harms arising from drug use must be limited to public employees; a law requiring similar testing of private citizens who use dangerous instruments such as guns or cars, or who have access to classified information, would also be constitutional.

There is only one apparent basis that sets the testing at issue here apart from all these other situations - but it is not a basis upon which the Court is willing to rely. I do not believe for a minute that the driving force behind these drug-testing rules was any of the feeble justifications put forward by counsel here and accepted by the Court. The only plausible explanation, in my view, is what the Commissioner himself offered in the concluding sentence of his memorandum to Customs Service employees announcing the program: "Implementation of the drug screening program would set an important example in our country's struggle with this most serious threat to our national health and security." App. 12. Or as respondent's brief to this Court asserted: "[I]f a law enforcement agency and its employees do not take the law seriously, neither will the public on which the agency's effectiveness depends." Brief for Respondent 36. What better way to show that the Government is serious about its "war on drugs" than to subject its employees on the front line of that war to this invasion of their privacy and affront to their dignity? To be sure, there is only a slight chance that it will prevent some serious public harm resulting from Service employee drug use, but it will show to the world that the Service is "clean," and - most important of all - will demonstrate the determination of the Government to eliminate this scourge of our society! I think it obvious that this justification is unacceptable; that the impairment of individual liberties cannot be the means of making a point; that symbolism, even symbolism for so worthy a cause as the abolition of unlawful drugs, cannot validate an otherwise unreasonable search.

There is irony in the Government's citation, in support of its position, of Justice Brandeis' statement in Olmstead v. United States, 277 U.S. 438, 485 (1928) that "[f]or good or for ill, [our Government] teaches the whole people by its example." Brief for Respondent 36. Brandeis was there dissenting from the Court's admission of evidence obtained through an unlawful Government wiretap. He was not praising the Government's example of vigor and enthusiasm in combatting crime, but condemning its example that "the end justifies the means," 277 U.S., at 485 . An even more apt quotation from that famous Brandeis dissent would have been the following:

"[I]t is . . . immaterial that the intrusion was in aid of law enforcement. Experience should teach us to be most on our guard to protect liberty when the

Government's purposes are beneficent. Men born to freedom are naturally alert to repel invasion of their liberty by evil-minded rulers. The greatest dangers to liberty lurk in insidious encroachment by men of zeal, well-meaning but without understanding." Id., at 479.

Those who lose because of the lack of understanding that be-got the present exercise in symbolism are not just the Customs Service employees, whose dignity is thus offended, but all of us - who suffer a coarsening of our national manners that ultimately give the Fourth Amendment its content, and who become subject to the administration of federal officials whose respect for our privacy can hardly be greater than the small respect they have been taught to have for their own.

Notes

[1] The Court apparently approves application of the urine tests to personnel receiving access to "sensitive information." Ante, at 677. Since, however, it is unsure whether "classified material" is "sensitive information," it remands with instructions that the Court of Appeals "examine the criteria used by the Service in determining what materials are classified and in deciding whom to test under this rubric." Ante, at 678. I am not sure what these instructions mean. Surely the person who classifies information always considers it "sensitive" in some sense - and the Court does not indicate what particular sort of sensitivity is crucial. Moreover, it seems to me most unlikely that "the criteria used by the Service in determining what materials are classified" are any different from those prescribed by the President in his Executive Order on the subject, see Exec. Order No. 12356, 3 CFR 166 (1982 Comp.) - and if there is a difference it is probably unlawful, see 5.4(b)(2), id., at 177. In any case, whatever idiosyncratic standards for classification the Customs Service might have would seem to be irrelevant, inasmuch as the rule at issue here is not limited to material classified by the Customs Service, but includes (and may well apply principally to) material classified elsewhere in the Government - for example, in the Federal Bureau of Investigation, the Drug Enforcement Administration, or the State Department - and conveyed to the Service. See App. 24-25.

Abortion: Justice Scalia's concurrence in Webster v. Reproductive Health Services (July 3, 1989)

JUSTICE SCALIA, concurring in part and concurring in the judgment.
I join Parts I, II-A, II-B, and II-C of the opinion of the Court. As to Part II-D, I share JUSTICE BLACKMUN's view, post at 556, that it effectively would overrule Roe v. Wade, 410 U.S. 113 (1973). I think that should be done, but would do it more explicitly. Since today we contrive to avoid doing it, and indeed to avoid almost any decision of national import, I need not set forth my reasons, some of which have been well recited in dissents of my colleagues in other cases. See, e.g., Thornburgh v. American College of

Obstetricians and Gynecologists, 476 U.S. 747, 786-797 (1986) (WHITE, J., dissenting); Akron v. Akron Center for Reproductive Health, Inc., 462 U.S. 416, 453-459 (1983) (O'CONNOR, J., dissenting); Roe v. Wade, supra, at 172-178 (REHNQUIST, J., dissenting); Doe v. Bolton, 410 U.S. 179, 221-223 (1973) (WHITE, J., dissenting).

The outcome of today's case will doubtless be heralded as a triumph of judicial statesmanship. It is not that, unless it is statesmanlike needlessly to prolong this Court's self-awarded sovereignty over a field where it has little proper business, since the answers to most of the cruel questions posed are political, and not juridical -- a sovereignty which therefore quite properly, but to the great damage of the Court, makes it the object of the sort of organized public pressure that political institutions in a democracy ought to receive.

JUSTICE O'CONNOR's assertion, ante at 526, that a "'fundamental rule of judicial restraint'" requires us to avoid reconsidering Roe, cannot be taken seriously. By finessing Roe we do not, as she suggests, ante at 526, adhere to the strict and venerable rule that we should avoid "'decid[ing] questions of a constitutional nature.'" We have not disposed of this case on some statutory or procedural ground, but have decided, and could not avoid deciding, whether the Missouri statute meets the requirements of the United States Constitution. The only choice available is whether, in deciding that constitutional question, we should use Roe v. Wade as the benchmark, or something else. What is involved, therefore, is not the rule of avoiding constitutional issues where possible, but the quite separate principle that we will not "'formulate a rule of constitutional law broader than is required by the precise facts to which it is to be applied.'" Ante at 526. The latter is a sound general principle, but one often departed from when good reason exists. Just this Term, for example, in an opinion authored by JUSTICE O'CONNOR, despite the fact that we had already held a racially based set-aside unconstitutional because unsupported by evidence of identified discrimination, which was all that was needed to decide the case, we went on to outline the criteria for properly tailoring race-based remedies in cases where such evidence is present. Richmond v. J. A. Croson Co., 488 U.S. 469, 506-508 (1989). Also this Term, in an opinion joined by JUSTICE O'CONNOR, we announced the constitutional rule that deprivation of the right to confer with counsel during trial violates the Sixth Amendment even if no prejudice can be shown, despite our finding that there had been no such deprivation on the facts before us -- which was all that was needed to decide that case. Perry v. Leeke, 488 U.S. 272, 278-280 (1989); see id. at 285 (KENNEDY, J., concurring in part). I have not identified with certainty the first instance of our deciding a case on broader constitutional grounds than absolutely necessary, but it is assuredly no later than Marbury v. Madison, 1 Cranch 137 (1803), where we held that mandamus could constitutionally issue against the Secretary of State, although that was unnecessary given our holding that the law authorizing issuance of the mandamus by this Court was unconstitutional.

The Court has often spoken more broadly than needed in precisely the fashion at issue here, announcing a new rule of constitutional law when it could have reached the identical result by applying the rule thereby displaced. To describe two recent opinions that JUSTICE O'CONNOR joined: In Daniels v. Williams, 474 U.S. 327 (1986), we overruled our prior holding that a "deprivation" of liberty or property could occur through negligent governmental acts, ignoring the availability of the alternative constitutional ground that, even if a deprivation had occurred, the State's postdeprivation remedies satisfied due process, see id. at 340-343 (STEVENS, J., concurring in judgment). In Illinois v. Gates, 462 U.S. 213 (1983), we replaced the preexisting "two-pronged" constitutional test for probable cause with a totality-of-the-circumstances approach, ignoring the concurrence's argument that the same outcome could have been reached under the old test, see id. at 267-272 (WHITE, J., concurring in judgment). It is rare, of course, that the Court goes out of its way to acknowledge that its judgment could have been reached under the old constitutional rule, making its adoption of the new one unnecessary to the decision, but even such explicit acknowledgment is not unheard of. See Commonwealth Edison Co. v. Montana, 453 U.S. 609 (1981); Perez v. Campbell, 402 U.S. 637 (1971). For a sampling of other cases where the availability of a narrower, well-established ground is simply ignored in the Court's opinion adopting a new constitutional rule, though pointed out in separate opinions of some Justices, see Michelin Tire Corp. v. Wages, 423 U.S. 276 (1976); Pointer v. Texas, 380 U.S. 400 (1965); and Mapp v. Ohio, 367 U.S. 643 (1961). It would be wrong, in any decision, to ignore the reality that our policy not to "formulate a rule of constitutional law broader than is required by the precise facts" has a frequently applied good-cause exception. But it seems particularly perverse to convert the policy into an absolute in the present case, in order to place beyond reach the inexpressibly "broader than was required by the precise facts" structure established by Roe v. Wade. The real question, then, is whether there are valid reasons to go beyond the most stingy possible holding today. It seems to me there are not only valid but compelling ones. Ordinarily, speaking no more broadly than is absolutely required avoids throwing settled law into confusion; doing so today preserves a chaos that is evident to anyone who can read and count. Alone sufficient to justify a broad holding is the fact that our retaining control, through Roe, of what I believe to be, and many of our citizens recognize to be, a political issue, continuously distorts the public perception of the role of this Court. We can now look forward to at least another Term with carts full of mail from the public, and streets full of demonstrators, urging us -- their unelected and life-tenured judges who have been awarded those extraordinary, undemocratic characteristics precisely in order that we might follow the law despite the popular will -- to follow the popular will. Indeed, I expect we can look forward to even more of that than before, given our indecisive decision today. And if these reasons for taking the unexceptional course of reaching a broader holding are not enough, then consider the nature of the constitutional question we avoid: in most cases, we do no harm by not speaking more broadly than the decision requires. Anyone affected by the conduct that the avoided holding would have prohibited will be able to challenge it himself and have his day in court to make the argument. Not so with respect to the harm that many States believed, pre-Roe, and many may continue to believe, is caused by largely unrestricted abortion. That will continue to occur if the States have the constitutional power to prohibit it, and would do so, but we skillfully avoid telling them so. Perhaps those abortions cannot constitutionally be proscribed. That is surely an arguable question, the question that reconsideration of Roe v. Wade entails. But what is not at all arguable, it seems to me, is that we should decide now, and not insist that we be run into a corner before we grudgingly yield up our judgment. The only sound reason for the latter course is to prevent a change in the law -- but to think that desirable begs the question to be decided.

It was an arguable question today whether § 188.029 of the Missouri law contravened this Court's understanding of Roe v. Wade, [*] and I would have examined Roe rather than examining the contravention. Given the Court's newly contracted abstemiousness, what will it take, one must wonder, to permit us to reach that fundamental question? The result of our vote today is that we will not reconsider that prior opinion, even if most of the Justices think it is wrong, unless we have before us a statute that in fact contradicts it -- and even then (under our newly discovered "no broader than necessary" requirement) only minor problematical aspects of Roe will be reconsidered, unless one expects state legislatures to adopt provisions whose compliance with Roe cannot even be argued with a straight face. It thus appears that the mansion of constitutionalized abortion law, constructed overnight in Roe v. Wade, must be disassembled doorjamb by doorjamb, and never entirely brought down, no matter how wrong it may be.

Of the four courses we might have chosen today -- to reaffirm Roe, to overrule it explicitly, to overrule it sub silentio, or to avoid the question -- the last is the least responsible. On the question of the constitutionality of § 188.029, I concur in the judgment of the Court and strongly dissent from the manner in which it has been reached.

* That question, compared with the question whether we should reconsider and reverse Roe, is hardly worth a footnote, but I think JUSTICE O'CONNOR answers that incorrectly as well. In Roe v. Wade, 410 U.S. 113, 165-166 (1973), we said that

the physician [has the right] to administer medical treatment according to his professional judgment up to the points where important state interests provide compelling justifications for intervention.

We have subsequently made clear that it is also a matter of medical judgment when viability (one of those points) is reached.

The time when viability is achieved may vary with each pregnancy, and the determination of whether a particular fetus is viable is, and must be, a matter for the judgment of the responsible attending physician.

Planned Parenthood of Central Mo. v. Danforth, 428 U.S. 52, 64 (1976). Section 188.029 conflicts with the purpose, and hence the fair import, of this principle, because it will sometimes require a physician to perform tests that he would not otherwise have performed to determine whether a fetus is viable. It is therefore a legislative imposition on the judgment of the physician, and one that increases the cost of an abortion.

JUSTICE O'CONNOR would nevertheless uphold the law because it "does not impose an undue burden on a woman's abortion decision." Ante at 492 U.S. 530"]530. This conclusion is supported by the observation that the required tests impose only a marginal cost on the abortion procedure, far less of an increase than the cost-doubling hospitalization requirement invalidated in 530. This conclusion is supported by the observation that the required tests impose only a marginal cost on the abortion procedure, far less of an increase than the cost-doubling hospitalization requirement invalidated in Akron v. Akron Center for Reproductive Health, Inc., 462 U.S. 416 (1983). See ante at 530-531. The fact that the challenged regulation is less costly than what we struck down in Akron tells us only that we cannot decide the present case on the basis of that earlier decision. It does not tell us whether the present requirement is an "undue burden," and I know of no basis for determining that this particular burden (or any other for that matter) is "due." One could with equal justification conclude that it is not. To avoid the question of Roe v. Wade's validity, with the attendant costs that this will have for the Court and for the principles of self-governance, on the basis of a standard that offers "no guide but the Court's own discretion," Baldwin v. Missouri, 281 U.S. 586, 595 (1930) (Holmes, J., dissenting), merely adds to the irrationality of what we do today.

Similarly irrational is the new concept that JUSTICE O'CONNOR introduces into the law in order to achieve her result, the notion of a State's "interest in potential life when viability is possible." Ante at 528. Since "viability" means the mere possibility (not the certainty) of survivability outside the womb, "possible viability" must mean the possibility of a possibility of survivability outside the womb. Perhaps our next opinion will expand the third trimester into the second even further, by approving state action designed to take account of "the chance of possible viability."

The Court today endorses the principle that too much speech is an evil that the democratic majority can proscribe: Justice Scalia's dissent in Austin v. Michigan State Chamber of Commerce (March 27, 1990)

JUSTICE SCALIA, dissenting.

"Attention all citizens. To assure the fairness of elections by preventing disproportionate expression of the views of any single powerful group, your Government has decided that the following associations of persons shall be prohibited from speaking or writing in support of any candidate: ____." In permitting Michigan to make private corporations the first object of this Orwellian announcement, the Court today endorses the principle that too much speech is an evil that the democratic majority can proscribe. I dissent because that principle is contrary to our case law and incompatible with the absolutely central truth of the First Amendment: that government cannot be trusted to assure, through censorship, the "fairness" of political debate.

I

A

The Court's opinion says that political speech of corporations can be regulated because "[s]tate law grants [them] special advantages," ante, at 658, and because this "unique state-conferred corporate structure . . . facilitates the amassing of large treasuries," ante, at 660. This analysis seeks to create one good argument by combining two bad ones. Those individuals who form that type of voluntary association known as a corporation are, to be sure, given special advantages - notably, the immunization of their personal fortunes from liability for the actions of the association - that the State is under no obligation to confer. But so are other associations and private individuals given all sorts of special advantages that the State need not confer, ranging from tax breaks to contract awards to public employment to outright cash subsidies. It is rudimentary that the State cannot exact as the price of those special advantages the forfeiture of First Amendment rights. See Pickering v. Board of Education of Township High School Dist. No. 205, Will County, 391 U.S. 563 (1968); Speiser v. Randall, 357 U.S. 513 (1958). The categorical suspension of the right of any person, or of any association of persons, to speak out on political matters must be justified by a compelling state need. See Buckley v. Valeo, 424 U.S. 1, 44-45 (1976) (per curiam). That is why the Court puts forward its second bad argument, the fact that corporations "amas[s] large treasuries." But that alone is also not sufficient justification for the suppression of political speech, unless one thinks it would be lawful to prohibit men and women whose net worth is above a certain figure from endorsing political candidates. Neither of these two flawed arguments is improved by combining them and saying, as the Court in effect does, that "since the State gives special advantages to these voluntary associations, and since they thereby amass vast wealth, they may be required to abandon their right of political speech."[*]

The Court's extensive reliance upon the fact that the objects of this speech restriction, corporations, receive "special advantages" is in stark contrast to our opinion issued just six years ago in FCC v. League of Women Voters of California, 468 U.S. 364 (1984). In that decision, striking down a congressionally imposed ban upon editorializing by noncommercial broadcasting stations that receive federal funds, the only respect in which we considered the receipt of that "special advantage" relevant was in determining whether the speech limitation could be justified under Congress' spending power, as a means of assuring that the subsidy was devoted only to the purposes Congress intended, which did not include political editorializing. We held it could not be justified on that basis, since "a noncommercial educational station that receives only 1% of its overall income from [federal] grants is barred absolutely from all editorializing. . . . The station has no way of limiting the use of its federal funds to all noneditorializing activities, and, more importantly, it is barred from using even wholly private funds to finance its editorial activity." Id., at 400. Of course the same is true here, even assuming that tax exemptions and other benefits accorded to incorporated associations constitute an exercise of the spending power. It is not just that portion of the corporation's assets attributable to the gratuitously conferred "special advantages" that is prohibited from being used for political endorsements, but all of the corporation's assets. I am at a loss to explain the vast difference between the treatment of the present case and League of Women Voters. Commercial corporations may not have a public persona as sympathetic as that of public broadcasters, but they are no less entitled to this Court's concern.

As for the second part of the Court's argumentation, the fact that corporations (or at least some of them) possess "massive wealth": Certain uses of "massive wealth" in the electoral process - whether or not the wealth is the result of "special advantages" conferred by the State - pose a substantial risk of corruption which constitutes a compelling need for the regulation of speech. Such a risk plainly exists when the wealth is given directly to the political candidate, to be used under his direction and control. We held in Buckley v. Valeo, supra, however, that independent expenditures to express the political views of individuals and associations do not raise a sufficient threat of corruption to justify prohibition. Id., at 45. Neither the Court's opinion nor either of the concurrences makes any effort to distinguish that case - except, perhaps, by misdescribing the case as involving "federal laws regulating individual donors," ante, at 659, or as involving "individual expenditures," ante, at 678 (STEVENS, J., concurring). Section 608(e)(1) of the Federal Election Campaign Act of 1971, 18 U.S.C. § 608(e)(1) (1970 ed., Supp. V), which we found unconstitutional in Buckley, was directed, like the Michigan law before us here, to expenditures made for the purpose of advocating the election or defeat of a particular candidate, see 424 U.S., at 42. It limited to $1,000 (a lesser restriction than the absolute prohibition at issue here) such expenditures not merely by "individuals," but by "persons," specifically defined to include corporations. See id., at 187 (setting forth § 591(g) of the statute). The plaintiffs in the case included corporations, see id., at 8, and we specifically discussed § 608(e)(1) as a restriction addressed not just to individuals but to "individuals and groups," id., at 39, 48, "persons and groups," id., at 45, "persons and organizations," ibid., "person[s] [and] association[s]," id., at 50. In support of our determination that the restriction was "wholly at odds with the guarantees of the First Amendment" we cited Miami Herald Publishing Co. v. Tornillo, 418 U.S. 241 (1974), which involved limitations upon a corporation. 424 U.S., at 50. Of course, if § 608(e)(1) had been unconstitutional only as applied to individuals and not as applied to corporations, we might nonetheless have invalidated it in toto for substantial overbreadth, see Broadrick v. Oklahoma, 413 U.S. 601, 611-613 (1973), but there is not a hint of that doctrine in our opinion. Our First Amendment law is much less certain than I had thought it to be if we are free to recharacterize each clear holding as a disguised "overbreadth" determination.

Buckley v. Valeo should not be overruled, because it is entirely correct. The contention that prohibiting overt advocacy for or against a political candidate satisfies a "compelling need" to avoid "corruption" is easily dismissed. As we said in Buckley, "[i]t would naively underestimate the ingenuity and resourcefulness of persons and groups desiring to buy influence to believe that they would have much difficulty devising expenditures that skirted the restriction on express advocacy of election or defeat but nevertheless benefited the candidate's campaign." 424 U.S., at 45. Independent advocacy, moreover, unlike contributions, "may well provide little assistance to the candidate's campaign and indeed may prove counterproductive," thus reducing the danger that it will be exchanged "as a quid pro quo for improper commitments from the candidate." Id., at 47. The latter point seems even more plainly true with respect to corporate advocates than it is with respect to individuals. I expect I could count on the fingers of one hand the candidates who would generally welcome, much less negotiate for, a formal endorsement by AT&T or General Motors. The advocacy of such entities that have "amassed great wealth" will be effective only to the extent that it brings to the people's attention ideas which - despite the invariably self-interested and probably uncongenial source - strike them as true.

The Court does not try to defend the proposition that independent advocacy poses a substantial risk of political "corruption," as English speakers understand that term. Rather, it asserts that that concept (which it defines as "`financial quid pro quo' corruption," ante, at 659) is really just a narrow subspecies of a hitherto unrecognized genus of political corruption. "Michigan's regulation," we are told, "aims at a different type of corruption in the political arena: the corrosive and distorting effects of immense aggregations of wealth that are accumulated with the help of the corporate form and that have little or no correlation to the public's support for the corporations's political ideas." Ante, at 659-660. Under this mode of analysis, virtually anything the Court deems politically undesirable can be turned into political corruption - by simply describing its effects as politically "corrosive," which is close enough to "corruptive" to qualify. It is sad to think that the First Amendment will ultimately be brought down not by brute force but by poetic metaphor.

The Court's opinion ultimately rests upon that proposition whose violation constitutes the "New Corruption": Expenditures must "reflect actual public support for the political ideas espoused." Ante, at 660. This illiberal free-speech principle of "one man, one minute" was proposed and soundly rejected in Buckley: "It is argued, however, that the ancillary governmental interest in equalizing the relative ability of individuals and groups to influence the outcome of elections serves to justify the limitation on express advocacy of the election or defeat of candidates imposed by § 608(e)(1)'s expenditure ceiling. But the concept that government may restrict the speech of some elements of our society in order to enhance the relative voice of others is wholly foreign to the First Amendment, which was designed `to secure "the widest possible dissemination of information from diverse and antagonistic sources,"' and `"to assure unfettered interchange of ideas for the bringing about of political and social changes desired by the people."'" 424 U.S., at 48-49 (citations omitted).

But it can be said that I have not accurately quoted today's decision. It does not endorse the proposition that government may ensure that expenditures "reflect actual public support for the political ideas espoused," but only the more limited proposition that government may ensure that expenditures "reflect actual public support for the political ideas espoused by corporations." Ante, at 660 (emphasis added). The limitation is of course entirely irrational. Why is it perfectly all right if advocacy by an individual billionaire is out of proportion with "actual public support" for his positions? There is no explanation, except the effort I described at the outset of this discussion to make one valid proposition out of two invalid ones: When the vessel labeled "corruption" begins to founder under weight too great to be logically sustained, the argumentation jumps to the good ship "special privilege"; and when that in turn begins to go down, it returns to "corruption." Thus hopping back and forth between the two, the argumentation may survive but makes no headway towards port, where its conclusion waits in vain.

B

JUSTICE BRENNAN's concurrence would have us believe that the prohibition adopted by Michigan and approved by the Court is a paternalistic measure to protect the corporate shareholders of America. It is designed, we are told, "to avert [the] danger" that "corporate funds drawn from the general treasury - which represents, after all, [the shareholder's] money," might be used on behalf of a political candidate he opposes. Ante, at 670 (BRENNAN, J., concurring). But such solicitude is a most implausible explanation for the Michigan statute, inasmuch as it permits corporations to take as many ideological and political positions as they please, so long as they are not "in assistance of, or in opposition to, the nomination or election of a candidate." Mich. Comp. Laws § 169.206(1) (1979). That is indeed the Court's sole basis for distinguishing First National Bank of Boston v. Bellotti, 435 U.S. 765 (1978), which invalidated restriction of a corporation's general political speech. The Michigan law appears to be designed, in other words, neither to protect shareholders, nor even (impermissibly) to "balance" general political debate, but to protect political candidates. Given the degree of political sophistication that ought to attend the exercise of our constitutional responsibilities, it is regrettable that this should come as a surprise.

But even if the object of the prohibition could plausibly be portrayed as the protection of shareholders (which the Court's opinion, at least, does not even assert), that would not suffice as a "compelling need" to support this blatant restriction upon core political speech. A person becomes a member of that form of association known as a for-profit corporation in order to pursue economic objectives, i. e., to make money. Some corporate charters may specify the line of commerce to which the company is limited, but even that can be amended by shareholder vote. Thus, in joining such an association, the shareholder knows that management may take any action that is ultimately in accord with what the majority (or a specified supermajority) of the shareholders wishes, so long as that action is designed to make a profit. That is the deal. The corporate actions to which the shareholder exposes himself, therefore, include many things that he may find politically or ideologically uncongenial: investment in South Africa, operation of an abortion clinic, publication of a pornographic magazine, or even publication of a newspaper that adopts absurd political views and makes catastrophic political endorsements. His only protections against such assaults upon his ideological commitments are (1) his ability to persuade a majority (or the requisite minority) of his fellow shareholders that the action should not be taken, and ultimately (2) his ability to sell his stock. (The latter course, by the way, does not ordinarily involve the severe psychic trauma or economic disaster that JUSTICE BRENNAN's opinion suggests.) It seems to me entirely fanciful, in other words, to suggest that the Michigan statute makes any significant contribution toward insulating the exclusively profit-motivated shareholder from the rude world of politics and ideology.

But even if that were not fanciful, it would be fanciful to think, as JUSTICE BRENNAN's opinion assumes, that there is any difference between for-profit and not-for-profit corporations insofar as the need for protection of the individual member's ideological psyche is concerned. Would it be any more upsetting to a shareholder of General Motors that it endorsed the election of Henry Wallace (to stay comfortably in the past) than it would be to a member of the American Civil Liberties Union that it endorsed the election of George Wallace? I should think much less so. Yet in the one case as in the other, the only protection against association-induced trauma is the will of the majority and, in the last analysis, withdrawal from membership.

C

In Part V of its opinion, the Court accurately sets forth our longstanding First Amendment law as follows: "Because the right to engage in political expression is fundamental to our constitutional system, statutory classifications impinging upon that right must be narrowly tailored to serve a compelling governmental interest." Ante, at 666.

The Court finds this requirement fully met for the following reason: "As we explained in the context of our discussions of whether the statute was overinclusive, supra, at 660-661, or underinclusive, supra, at 665 and this page, the State's decision to regulate only corporations is precisely tailored to serve the compelling state interest of eliminating from the political process the corrosive effect of political `war chests' amassed with the aid of the legal advantages given to corporations." Ibid.

That state interest (assuming it is compelling) does indeed explain why the State chose to silence "only corporations" rather than wealthy individuals as well. But it does not explain (what "narrow tailoring" pertains to) why the State chose to silence all corporations, rather than just those that possess great wealth. If narrow tailoring means anything, surely it must mean that action taken to counter the effect of amassed "war chests" must be targeted, if possible, at amassed "war chests." And surely such targeting is possible - either in the manner accomplished by the provision that we invalidated in Buckley, i. e., by limiting the prohibition to independent expenditures above a certain amount, or in some other manner, e. g., by limiting the expenditures of only those corporations with more than a certain amount of net worth or annual profit.

No more satisfactory explanation for the obvious lack of "narrow tailoring" is to be found in the Court's discussion of overinclusiveness, to which the above-quoted passage refers. That discussion asserts that we "rejected a similar argument" in FEC v. National Right to Work Comm., 459 U.S. 197 (1982) (NRWC), where we said that "`we accept Congress' judgment'" that "`the special characteristics of the corporate structure'" create a "`potential for . . . influence that demands regulation.'" Ante, at 661, quoting 459 U.S., at 209-210 (emphasis added by the Court). Today's opinion then continues: "Although some closely held corporations, just as some publicly held ones, may not have accumulated significant amounts of wealth, they receive from the State the special benefits conferred by the corporate structure and present the potential for distorting the political process. This potential for distortion justifies § 54(1)'s general applicability to all corporations." Ante, at 661.

The Court thus holds, for the first time since Justice Holmes left the bench, that a direct restriction upon speech is narrowly enough tailored if it extends to speech that has the mere potential for producing social harm. NRWC (which in any event involved not a direct restriction upon corporate speech but a restriction upon corporate solicitation of funds for candidates) is no authority for that startling proposition, since it did not purport to be applying the First Amendment narrow-tailoring requirement. The principle the Court abandons today - that the mere potential for harm does not justify a restriction upon speech - had its origin in the "clear and present danger" test devised by Justice Holmes in 1919, see Schenck v. United States, 249 U.S. 47, 49-51, and championed by him and Justice Brandeis over the next decade in a series of famous opinions opposing the affirmance of convictions for subversive speech, see Abrams v. United States, 250 U.S. 616, 624 (1919) (Holmes, J., dissenting); Gitlow v. New York, 268 U.S. 652, 672 (1925) (Holmes, J., dissenting); Whitney v. California, 274 U.S. 357, 374 (1927) (Brandeis, J., concurring). The Court finally adopted their view in 1937, see Herndon v. Lowry, 301 U.S. 242, 258; see also Bridges v. California, 314 U.S. 252, 263 (1941); Thornhill v. Alabama, 310 U.S. 88, 105 (1940); West Virginia Board of Education v. Barnette, 319 U.S. 624, 639 (1943); Terminiello v. Chicago, 337 U.S. 1, 4-5 (1949). Today's reversal of field will require adjustment of a fairly large number of significant First Amendment holdings. Presumably the State may now convict individuals for selling books found to have a potentially harmful influence on minors, Butler v. Michigan, 352 U.S. 380 (1957), ban indecent telephone communications that have the potential for reaching minors, Sable Communications of California v. FCC, 492 U.S. 115 (1989), restrain the press from publishing information that has the potential for jeopardizing a criminal defendant's right to a fair trial, Nebraska Press Assn. v. Stuart, 427 U.S. 539 (1976), or the potential for damaging the reputation of the subject of an investigation, Landmark Communications, Inc. v. Virginia, 435 U.S. 829 (1978), compel publication of the membership lists of organizations that have a potential for illegal activity, see NAACP v. Alabama ex rel.

Patterson, 357 U.S. 449, 464 (1958), and compel an applicant for bar membership to reveal her political beliefs and affiliations to eliminate the potential for subversive activity, Baird v. State Bar of Arizona, 401 U.S. 1 (1971).

It is perplexing, or perhaps revealing, to compare the Court's cavalier treatment of the narrow-tailoring requirement today with its elaborate discussion of that issue six years ago in League of Women Voters. See 468 U.S., at 392-395, 397-398. As my earlier discussion makes clear, it would make no difference if the law were narrowly tailored to serve its goal, since that goal is not compelling. But the fact that, even having made that first error, the Court must make yet a second in order to reach today's judgment suggests what an impregnable fortress our First Amendment jurisprudence has been. The Court's explicit acceptance of "potential danger" as adequate to establish narrow tailoring, even more than its recognition of an insubstantial interests as "compelling," greatly weakens those defenses.

D

Finally, a few words are in order concerning the Court's approval of the Michigan law's exception for "media corporations." This is all right, we are told, because of "the unique role that the press plays in `informing and educating the public, offering criticism, and providing a forum for discussion and debate.'" Ante, at 667 (citation omitted). But if one believes in the Court's rationale of "compelling state need" to prevent amassed corporate wealth from skewing the political debate, surely that "unique role" of the press does not give Michigan justification for excluding media corporations from coverage, but provides especially strong reason to include them. Amassed corporate wealth that regularly sits astride the ordinary channels of information is much more likely to produce the New Corruption (too much of one point of view) than amassed corporate wealth that is generally busy making money elsewhere. Such media corporations not only have vastly greater power to perpetrate the evil of overinforming, they also have vastly greater opportunity. General Motors, after all, will risk a stockholder suit if it makes a political endorsement that is not plausibly tied to its ability to make money for its shareholders. But media corporations make money by making political commentary, including endorsements. For them, unlike any other corporations, the whole world of politics and ideology is fair game. Yet the Court tells us that it is reasonable to exclude media corporations, rather than target them specially.

Members of the institutional press, despite the Court's approval of their illogical exemption from the Michigan law, will find little reason for comfort in today's decision. The theory of New Corruption it espouses is a dagger at their throats. The Court today holds merely that media corporations may be excluded from the Michigan law, not that they must be. We have consistently rejected the proposition that the institutional press has any constitutional privilege beyond that of other speakers. See Bellotti, 435 U.S., at 782, and cases cited. Thus, the Court's holding on this point must be put in the following unencouraging form: "Although the press' unique societal role may not entitle the press to greater protection under the Constitution, Bellotti, supra, at 782, and n. 18, it does provide a compelling reason for the State to exempt media corporations from the scope of political expenditure limitations." Ante, at 668. One must hope, I suppose, that Michigan will continue to provide this generous and voluntary exemption. II

I would not do justice to the significance of today's decision to discuss only its lapses from case precedent and logic. Infinitely more important than that is its departure from long-accepted premises of our political system regarding the benevolence that can be expected of government in managing the arena of public debate, and the danger that is to be anticipated from powerful private institutions that compete with government, and with one another, within that arena.

Perhaps the Michigan law before us here has an unqualifiedly noble objective - to "equalize" the political debate by preventing disproportionate expression of corporations' points of view. But governmental abridgment of liberty is always undertaken with the very best of announced objectives (dictators promise to bring order, not tyranny), and often with the very best of genuinely intended objectives (zealous policemen conduct unlawful searches in order to put dangerous felons behind bars). The premise of our Bill of Rights, however, is that there are some things - even some seemingly desirable things - that government cannot be trusted to do. The very first of these is establishing the restrictions upon speech that will assure "fair" political debate. The incumbent politician who says he welcomes full and fair debate is no more to be believed than the entrenched monopolist who says he welcomes full and fair competition. Perhaps the Michigan Legislature was genuinely trying to assure a "balanced" presentation of political views; on the other hand, perhaps it was trying to give unincorporated unions (a not insubstantial force in Michigan) political advantage over major employers. Or perhaps it was trying to assure a "balanced" presentation because it knows that with evenly balanced speech incumbent officeholders generally win. The fundamental approach of the First Amendment, I had always thought, was to assume the worst, and to rule the regulation of political speech "for fairness' sake" simply out of bounds.

I doubt that those who framed and adopted the First Amendment would agree that avoiding the New Corruption, that is, calibrating political speech to the degree of public opinion that supports it, is even a desirable objective, much less one that is important enough to qualify as a compelling state interest. Those Founders designed, of course, a system in which popular ideas would ultimately prevail; but also, through the First Amendment, a system in which true ideas could readily become popular. For the latter purpose, the calibration that the Court today endorses is precisely backwards: To the extent a valid proposition has scant public support, it should have wider rather than narrower public circulation. I am confident, in other words, that Jefferson and Madison would not have sat at these controls; but if they did, they would have turned them in the opposite direction.

Ah, but then there is the special element of corporate wealth: What would the Founders have thought of that? They would have endorsed, I think, what Tocqueville wrote in 1835: "When the members of an aristocratic community adopt a new opinion or conceive a new sentiment, they give it a station, as it were, beside themselves, upon the lofty platform where they stand; and opinions or sentiments so conspicuous to the eyes of the multitude are easily introduced into the minds or hearts of all around. In democratic countries the governing power alone is naturally in a condition to act in this manner; but it is easy to see that its action is always inadequate, and often dangerous. . . . No sooner does a government attempt to go beyond its political sphere and to enter upon this new track than it exercises, even unintentionally, an insupportable tyranny . . . . Worse still will be the case if the government really believes itself interested in preventing all circulation of ideas; it will then stand motionless and oppressed by the heaviness of voluntary torpor. Governments, therefore, should not be the only active powers; associations ought, in democratic nations, to stand in lieu of those powerful private individuals whom the equality of conditions has swept away." 2 A. de Tocqueville, Democracy in America 109 (P. Bradley ed. 1948).

While Tocqueville was discussing "circulation of ideas" in general, what he wrote is also true of candidate endorsements in particular. To eliminate voluntary associations - not only including powerful ones, but especially including powerful ones - from the public debate is either to augment the always dominant power of government or to impoverish the public debate. The case at hand is a good enough example. Why should the Michigan voters in the 93d House District be deprived of the information that private associations owning and operating a vast percentage of the industry of the State, and employing a large number of its citizens, believe that the election of a particular candidate is important to their prosperity? Contrary to the Court's suggestion, the same point cannot effectively be made through corporate PACs to which individuals may voluntarily contribute. It is important to the message that it represents the views of Michigan's leading corporations as corporations, occupying the "lofty platform" that they do within the economic life of the State - not just the views of some other voluntary associations to which some of the corporations' shareholders belong.

Despite all the talk about "corruption and the appearance of corruption" - evils that are not significantly implicated and that can be avoided in many other ways - it is entirely obvious that the object of the law we have approved today is not to prevent wrongdoing but to prevent speech. Since those private associations known as corporations have so much money, they will speak so much more, and their views will be given inordinate prominence in election campaigns. This is not an argument that our democratic traditions allow - neither with respect to individuals associated in corporations nor with respect to other categories of individuals whose speech may be "unduly" extensive (because they are rich) or "unduly" persuasive (because they are movie stars) or "unduly" respected (because they are clergymen). The premise of our system is that there is no such thing as too much speech - that the people are not foolish but intelligent, and will separate the wheat from the chaff. As conceded in Lincoln's aphorism about fooling "all of the people some of the time," that premise will not invariably accord with reality; but it will assuredly do so much more frequently than the premise the Court today embraces: that a healthy democratic system can survive the legislative power to prescribe how much political speech is too much, who may speak, and who may not. * * *

Because today's decision is inconsistent with unrepudiated legal judgments of our Court, but even more because it is incompatible with the unrepealable political wisdom of our First Amendment, I dissent.

[*] The Court's assertion that the Michigan law "does not impose an absolute ban on all forms of corporate political spending," ante, at 660, is true only in a respect that is irrelevant for purposes of First Amendment analysis. A corporation is absolutely prohibited from spending its own funds on this form of political speech, and would be guilty of misrepresentation if it asserted that a particular candidate was supported or opposed by the corporation. This is to say that the corporation as a corporation is prohibited from speaking. What the Michigan law permits the corporation to do is to serve as the founder and treasurer of a different association of individuals that can endorse or oppose political candidates. The equivalent, where an individual rather than an association is concerned, would be to prohibit John D. Rockefeller from making political endorsements, but to permit him to form an association to which others (though not he himself) can contribute for the purpose of making political endorsements. Just as political speech by that association is not speech by John D. Rockefeller, so also speech by a corporate PAC that the Michigan law allows is not speech by the corporation itself.

The new principle that the Court today announces will be enforced by a corps of judges who overwhelmingly owe their office to its violation. Something must be wrong here, and I suggest it is the Court: Justice Scalia's dissent in Rutan v. Republican Party of Illinois (June 21, 1990)

Justice Scalia, with whom The Chief Justice and Justice Kennedy join, and with whom Justice O'Connor joins as to Parts II and III, dissenting.

Today the Court establishes the constitutional principle that party membership is not a permissible factor in the dispensation of government jobs, except those jobs for the performance of which party affiliation is an "appropriate requirement." Ante, at 1. It is hard to say precisely (or even generally) what that exception means, but if there is any category of jobs for whose performance party affiliation is not an appropriate requirement, it is the job of being a judge, where partisanship is not only unneeded but positively undesirable. It is, however, rare that a federal administration of one party will appoint a judge from another party. And it has always been rare. See Marbury v. Madison, 1 Cranch 137 (1803). Thus, the new principle that the Court today announces will be enforced by a corps of judges (the Members of this Court included) who overwhelmingly owe their office to its violation. Something must be wrong here, and I suggest it is the Court.

The merit principle for government employment is probably the most favored in modern America, having been widely adopted by civil-service legislation at both the state and federal levels. But there is another point of view, described in characteristically Jacksonian fashion by an eminent practitioner of the patronage system, George Washington Plunkitt of Tammany Hall:

"I ain't up on sillygisms, but I can give you some arguments that nobody can answer.

"First, this great and glorious country was built up by political parties; second, parties can't hold together if their workers don't get offices when they win; third, if the parties go to pieces, the government they built up must go to pieces, too; fourth, then there'll be hell to pay." W. Riordon, Plunkitt of Tammany Hall 13 (1963).

It may well be that the Good Government Leagues of America were right, and that Plunkitt, James Michael Curley and their ilk were wrong; but that is not entirely certain. As the merit principle has been extended and its effects increasingly felt; as the Boss Tweeds, the Tammany Halls, the Pender gast Machines, the Byrd Machines and the Daley Machines have faded into history; we find that political leaders at all levels increasingly complain of the helplessness of elected government, unprotected by "party discipline," before the demands of small and cohesive interest-groups.

The choice between patronage and the merit principle — or, to be more realistic about it, the choice between the desirable mix of merit and patronage principles in widely varying federal, state, and local political contexts — is not so clear that I would be prepared, as an original matter, to chisel a single, inflexible prescription into the Constitution. Fourteen years ago, in Elrod v. Burns, 427 U.S. 347 (1976), the Court did that. Elrod was limited however, as was the later decision of Branti v. Finkel, 445 U.S. 507 (1980), to patronage firings, leaving it to state and federal legislatures to determine when and where political affiliation could be taken into account in hirings and promotions. Today the Court makes its constitutional civil-service reform absolute, extending to all decisions regarding government employment. Because the First Amendment has never been thought to require this disposition, which may well have disastrous consequences for our political system, I dissent.

I

The restrictions that the Constitution places upon the government in its capacity as lawmaker, i.e., as the regulator of private conduct, are not the same as the restrictions that it places upon the government in its capacity as employer. We have recognized this in many contexts, with respect to many different constitutional guarantees. Private citizens perhaps cannot be prevented from wearing long hair, but policemen can. Kelley v. Johnson, 425 U.S. 238, 247 (1976). Private citizens cannot have their property searched without probable cause, but in many circumstances government employees can. O'Connor v. Ortega, 480 U.S. 709, 723 (1987) (plurality opinion); id., at 732 (Scalia, J., concurring in judgment). Private citizens cannot be punished for refusing to provide the government information that may incriminate them, but government employees can be dismissed when the incriminating information that they refuse to provide relates to the performance of their job. Gardner v. Broderick, 392 U.S. 273, 277-278 (1968). With regard to freedom of speech in particular: Private citizens cannot be punished for speech of merely private concern, but government employees can be fired for that reason. Connick v. Myers, 461 U.S. 138, 147 (1983). Private citizens cannot be punished for partisan political activity, but federal and state employees can be dismissed and otherwise punished for that reason. Public Workers v. Mitchell, 330 U.S. 75, 101 (1947); CSC v. Letter Carriers, 413 U.S. 548, 556 (1973); Broadrick v. Oklahoma, 413 U.S. 601, 616-617 (1973).

Once it is acknowledged that the Constitution's prohibition against laws "abridging the freedom of speech" does not apply to laws enacted in the government's capacity as employer the same way it does to laws enacted in the government's capacity as regulator of private conduct, it may sometimes be difficult to assess what employment practices are permissible and what are not. That seems to me not a difficult question, however, in the present context. The provisions of the Bill of Rights were designed to restrain transient majorities from impairing long-recognized personal liberties. They did not create by implication novel individual rights overturning accepted political norms. Thus, when a practice not expressly prohibited by the text of the Bill of Rights bears the endorsement of a long tradition of open, widespread, and unchallenged use that dates back to the beginning of the Republic, we have no proper basis for striking it down. [n.1] Such a venerable and accepted tradition is not to be laid on the examining table and scrutinized for its conformity to some abstract principle of First-Amendment adjudication devised by this Court. To the contrary, such traditions are themselves the stuff out of which the Court's principles are to be formed. They are, in these uncertain areas, the very points of reference by which the legitimacy or illegitimacy of other practices are to be figured out. When it appears that the latest "rule," or "three-part test," or "balancing test" devised by the Court has placed us on a collision course with such a landmark practice, it is the former that must be recalculated by us, and not the latter that must be abandoned by our citizens. I know of no other way to formulate a constitutional jurisprudence that reflects, as it should, the principles adhered to, over time, by the American people, rather than those favored by the personal (and necessarily shifting) philosophical dispositions of a majority of this Court.

I will not describe at length the claim of patronage to landmark status as one of our accepted political traditions. Justice Powell discussed it in his dissenting opinions in Elrod and Branti. Elrod, 427 U.S., at 378-379 (Powell, J., dissenting); Branti, 445 U.S., at 522, n.1 (Powell, J., dissenting). Suffice it to say that patronage was, without any thought that it could be unconstitutional, a basis for government employment from the earliest days of the Republic until Elrod — and has continued unabated since Elrod, to the extent still permitted by that unfortunate decision. See, e.g., D. Price, Bringing Back the Parties 24, 32 (1984); Gardner, A Theory of the Spoils System, 54 Public Choice 171, 181 (1987); Toinet & Glenn, Clientelism and Corruption in the "Open" Society: The Case of the United

States, in Private Patronage and Public Power 193, 202 (C. Clapham ed. 1982). Given that unbroken tradition regarding the application of an ambiguous constitutional text, there was in my view no basis for holding that patronage-based dismissals violated the First Amendment — much less for holding, as the Court does today, that even patronage hiring does so. [n.2]

II

Even accepting the Court's own mode of analysis, however, and engaging in "balancing" a tradition that ought to be part of the scales, Elrod, Branti, and today's extension of them seem to me wrong.

A

The Court limits patronage on the ground that the individual's interest in uncoerced belief and expression outweighs the systemic interests invoked to justify the practice. Ante, at 68-72. The opinion indicates that the government may prevail only if it proves that the practice is "narrowly tailored to further vital government interests." Ante, at 74.

That strict-scrutiny standard finds no support in our cases. Although our decisions establish that government employees do not lose all constitutional rights, we have consistently applied a lower level of scrutiny when "the governmental function operating ... [is] not the power to regulate or license, as lawmaker, an entire trade or profession, or to control an entire branch of private business, but, rather, as proprietor, to manage [its] internal operatio[ns] ...." Cafeteria & Restaurant Workers v. McElroy, 367 U.S. 886, 896 (1961). When dealing with its own employees, the government may not act in a manner that is "patently arbitrary or discriminatory," id., at 898, but its regulations are valid if they bear a "rational connection" to the governmental end sought to be served, Kelley v. Johnson, 425 U.S., at 247.

In particular, restrictions on speech by public employees are not judged by the test applicable to similar restrictions on speech by nonemployees. We have said that "[a] governmental employer may subject its employees to such special restrictions on free expression as are reasonably necessary to promote effective government." Brown v. Glines, 444 U.S. 348, 356, n.13 (1980). In Public Workers v. Mitchell, 330 U.S., at 101, upholding provisions of the Hatch Act which prohibit political activities by federal employees, we said that "it is not necessary that the act regulated be anything more than an act reasonably deemed by Congress to interfere with the efficiency of the public service." We reaffirmed Mitchell in CSC v. Letter Carriers, 413 U.S., at 556, over a dissent by Justice Douglas arguing against application of a special standard to government employees, except insofar as their "job performance" is concerned, id., at 597. We did not say that the Hatch Act was narrowly tailored to meet the government's interest, but merely deferred to the judgment of Congress, which we were not "in any position to dispute." Id., at 567. Indeed, we recognized that the Act was not indispensably necessary to achieve those ends, since we repeatedly noted that "Congress at some time [may] come to a different view." Ibid., see also id., at 555, 564. In Broadrick v. Oklahoma, 413 U.S. 601

(1973), we upheld similar restrictions on state employees, though directed "at political expression which if engaged in by private persons would plainly be protected by the First and Fourteenth Amendments," Id., at 616.

To the same effect are cases that specifically concern adverse employment action taken against public employees because of their speech. In Pickering v. Board of Education of Township High School Dist., 391 U.S. 563, 568 (1968), we recognized:

"[T]he State has interests as an employer in regulating the speech of its employees that differ significantly from those it possesses in connection with regulation of the speech of the citizenry in general. The problem in any case is to arrive at a balance between the interests of the [employee], as a citizen, in commenting upon matters of public concern and the interests of the State, as an employer, in promoting the efficiency of the public services it performs through its employees."

Because the restriction on speech is more attenuated when the government conditions employment than when it imposes criminal penalties, and because "government offices could not function if every employment decision became a constitutional matter," Connick v. Myers, 461 U.S., at 143, we have held that government employment decisions taken on the basis of an employee's speech do not "abridg[e] the freedom of speech," U.S. Const., Amdt. 1, merely because they fail the narrow-tailoring and compelling-interest tests applicable to direct regulation of speech. We have not subjected such decisions to strict scrutiny, but have accorded "a wide degree of deference to the employer's judgment" that an employee's speech will interfere with close working relationships. 461 U.S., at 152.

When the government takes adverse action against an employee on the basis of his political affiliation (an interest whose constitutional protection is derived from the interest in speech), the same analysis applies. That is why both the Elrod plurality, 427 U.S., at 359, and the opinion concurring in the judgment, id., at 375, as well as Branti, 445 U.S., at 514-515, and the Court today, ante, at 89, rely on Perry v. Sindermann, 408 U.S. 593 (1972), a case that applied the test announced in Pickering, not the strict-scrutiny test applied to restrictions imposed on the public at large. Since the government may dismiss an employee for political speech "reasonably deemed by Congress to interfere with the efficiency of the public service," Public Workers v. Mitchell, supra, at 101, it follows a fortiori that the government may dismiss an employee for political affiliation if "reasonably necessary to promote effective government." Brown v. Glines, supra, at 356, n.13.

While it is clear from the above cases that the normal "strict scrutiny" that we accord to government regulation of speech is not applicable in this field, [n.3] the precise test that replaces it is not so clear; we have used various formulations. The one that appears in the case dealing with an employment practice closest in its effects to patronage is whether the practice could be "reasonably deemed" by the enacting legislature to further a legitimate goal. Public Workers v. Mitchell, supra, at 101. For purposes of my ensuing discussion, however, I will apply a less permissive standard that seems more in accord with our general "balancing" test: can the governmental advantages of this employment practice reasonably be deemed to outweigh its "coercive" effects?

B

Preliminarily, I may observe that the Court today not only declines, in this area replete with constitutional ambiguities, to give the clear and continuing tradition of our people the dispositive effect I think it deserves, but even declines to give it substantial weight in the balancing. That is contrary to what the Court has done in many other contexts. In evaluating so-called "substantive due process" claims we have examined our history and tradition with respect to the asserted right. See, e.g., Michael H. v. Gerald D., 491 U.S. (1989); Bowers v. Hardwick, 478 U.S. 186, 192-194 (1986). In evaluating claims that a particular procedure violates the Due Process Clause we have asked whether the procedure is traditional. See, e.g., Burnham v. Superior Court of California, Marin County, 495 U.S. (1990). And in applying the Fourth Amendment's reasonableness test we have looked to the history of judicial and public acceptance of the type of search in question. See, e.g., Camara v. Municipal Court of San Francisco, 387 U.S. 523, 537 (1967). See also Press-Enterprise Co. v. Superior Court of California, Riverside County, 478 U.S. 1, 8 (1986) (tradition of accessibility to judicial proceedings implies judgment of experience that individual's interest in access outweighs government's interest in closure); Richmond Newspapers, Inc. v. Virginia, 448 U.S. 555, 589 (1980) (Brennan, J., concurring in judgment) ("Such a tradition [of public access] commands respect in part because the Constitution carries the gloss of history"); Walz v. Tax Comm'n of New York, 397 U.S. 664, 678 (1970) ("unbroken practice of according the [property tax] exemption to churches" demonstrates that it does not violate Establishment Clause).

But even laying tradition entirely aside, it seems to me our balancing test is amply met. I assume, as the Court's opinion assumes, that the balancing is to be done on a generalized basis, and not case-by-case. The Court holds that the governmental benefits of patronage cannot reasonably be thought to outweigh its "coercive" effects (even the lesser "coercive" effects of patronage hiring as opposed to patronage firing) not merely in 1990 in the State of Illinois, but at any time in any of the numerous political subdivisions of this vast country. It seems to me that that categorical pronouncement reflects a naive vision of politics and an inadequate appreciation of the systemic effects of patronage in promoting political stability and facilitating the social and political integration of previously powerless groups.

The whole point of my dissent is that the desirability of patronage is a policy question to be decided by the people's representatives; I do not mean, therefore, to endorse that system. But in order to demonstrate that a legislature could reasonably determine that its benefits outweigh its "coercive" effects, I must describe those benefits as the proponents of patronage see them: As Justice Powell discussed at length in his Elrod dissent, patronage stabilizes political parties and prevents excessive political fragmentation — both of which are results in which States have a strong governmental interest. Party strength requires the efforts of the rank-and-file, especially in "the dull periods between elections," to perform such tasks as organizing precincts, registering new voters, and providing constituent services. Elrod, 427 U.S., at 385 (dissenting opinion). Even the most enthusiastic supporter of a party's program will shrink before such drudgery, and it is folly to think that ideological conviction alone will motivate sufficient numbers to keep the party going through the off-years. "For the most part, as every politician knows, the hope of some reward generates a major portion of the local political activity supporting parties." Ibid. Here is the judgment of one such politician, Jacob Arvey (best known as the promoter of Adlai Stevenson): Patronage is "'a necessary evil if you want a strong organization, because the patronage system permits of discipline, and without discipline, there's no party organization.'" Quoted in M. Tolchin & S. Tolchin, To the Victor 36 (1971). A major study of the patronage system describes the reality as follows:

"[A]lthough men have many motives for entering political life ... the vast underpinning of both major parties is made up of men who seek practical rewards. Tangible advantages constitute the unifying thread of most successful political practitioners" Id., at 22.

"With so little patronage cement, party discipline is relatively low; the rate of participation and amount of service the party can extract from [Montclair] county committeemen are minuscule compared with Cook County. The party considers itself lucky if 50 percent of its committeemen show up at meetings — even those labeled 'urgent' — while even lower percentages turn out at functions intended to produce crowds for visiting candidates." Id., at 123.

See also W. Grimshaw, The Political Economy of Machine Politics, 4 Corruption and Reform 15, 30 (1989); G. Pomper, Voters, Elections, and Parties 255 (1988); Wolfinger, Why Political Machines Have Not Withered Away and Other Revisionist Thoughts, 34 J. Politics 365, 384 (1972).

The Court simply refuses to acknowledge the link between patronage and party discipline, and between that and party success. It relies (as did the plurality in Elrod, 427 U.S., at 369, n.23) on a single study of a rural Pennsylvania county by Professor Sorauf, ante, at 13 — a work that has been described as "more persuasive about the ineffectuality of Democratic leaders in Centre County than about the generaliz ability of [its] findings." Wolfinger, supra, at 384, n.39. It is unpersuasive to claim, as the Court does, that party workers are obsolete because campaigns are now conducted through media and other money-intensive means. Ante, at 13. Those techniques have supplemented but not supplanted personal contacts. See Price, Bringing Back the Parties, at 25. Certainly they have not made personal contacts unnecessary in campaigns for the lower-level offices that are the foundations of party strength, nor have they replaced the myriad functions performed by party regulars not directly related to campaigning. And to the extent such techniques have replaced older methods of campaigning (partly in response to the limitations the Court has placed on patronage), the political system is not clearly better off. See Elrod, supra, at 384 (Powell, J., dissenting); Branti, 445 U.S., at 528 (Powell, J., dissenting). Increased reliance on money-intensive campaign techniques tends to entrench those in power much more effectively than patronage — but without the attendant benefit of strengthening the party system. A challenger can more easily obtain the support of party-workers (who can expect to be rewarded even if the candidate loses — if not this year, then the next) than the financial support of political action committees (which will generally support incumbents, who are likely to prevail).

It is self-evident that eliminating patronage will significantly undermine party discipline; and that as party discipline wanes, so will the strength of the two-party system. But, says the Court, "[p]olitical parties have already survived the substantial decline in patronage employment practices in this century." Ante, at 1213. This is almost verbatim what was said in Elrod, see 427 U.S., at 369. Fourteen years later it seems much less convincing. Indeed, now that we have witnessed, in 18 of the last 22 years, an Executive Branch of the Federal Government under the control of one party while the Congress is entirely or (for two years) partially within the control of the other party; now that we have undergone the most recent federal election, in which 98" of the incumbents, of whatever party, were returned to office; and now that we have seen elected officials changing their political affiliation with unprecedented readiness, Washington Post, Apr. 10, 1990, p.A1, the statement that "political parties have already survived" has a positively whistling-in-the-graveyard character to it. Parties have assuredly survived — but as what? As the forges upon which many of the essential compromises of American political life are hammered out? Or merely as convenient vehicles for the conducting of national presidential elections?

The patronage system does not, of course, merely foster political parties in general; it fosters the two-party system in particular. When getting a job, as opposed to effectuating a particular substantive policy, is an available incentive for party-workers, those attracted by that incentive are likely to work for the party that has the best chance of displacing the "ins," rather than for some splinter group that has a more attractive political philosophy but little hope of success. Not only is a two-party system more likely to emerge, but the differences between those parties are more likely to be moderated, as each has a relatively greater interest in appealing to a majority of the electorate and a relatively lesser interest in furthering philosophies or programs that are far from the mainstream. The stabilizing effects of such a system are obvious. See Toinet & Glenn, Clientelism and Corruption in the "Open" Society, at 208. In the context of electoral laws we have approved the States' pursuit of such stability, and their avoidance of the "splintered parties and unrestrained factionalism [that] may do significant damage to the fabric of government." Storer v. Brown, 415 U.S. 724, 736 (1974) (upholding law disqualifying persons from running as independents if affiliated with a party in the past year).

Equally apparent is the relatively destabilizing nature of a system in which candidates cannot rely upon patronage-based party loyalty for their campaign support, but must attract workers and raise funds by appealing to various interest-groups. See

Tolchin & Tolchin, To the Victor, at 127-130. There is little doubt that our decisions in Elrod and Branti, by contributing to the decline of party strength, have also contributed to the growth of interest-group politics in the last decade. See, e.g., Fitts, The Vice of Virtue, 136 U. Pa. L. Rev. 1567, 1603-1607 (1988). Our decision today will greatly accelerate the trend. It is not only campaigns that are affected, of course, but the subsequent behavior of politicians once they are in power. The replacement of a system firmly based in party discipline with one in which each office-holder comes to his own accommodation with competing interest groups produces "a dispersion of political influence that may inhibit a political party from enacting its programs into law." Branti, supra, at 531 (Powell, J., dissenting). [n.4]

Patronage, moreover, has been a powerful means of achieving the social and political integration of excluded groups. See, e.g., Elrod, supra, at 379 (Powell, J., dissenting); Cornwell, Bosses, Machines and Ethnic Politics, in Ethnic Group Politics 190, 195-197 (H. Bailey, Jr., & E. Katz eds. 1969). By supporting and ultimately dominating a particular party "machine," racial and ethnic minorities have — on the basis of their politics rather than their race or ethnicity — acquired the patronage awards the machine had power to confer. No one disputes the historical accuracy of this observation, and there is no reason to think that patronage can no longer serve that function. The abolition of patronage, however, prevents groups that have only recently obtained political power, especially blacks, from following this path to economic and social advancement.

"'Every ethnic group that has achieved political power in American cities has used the bureaucracy to provide jobs in return for political support. It's only when Blacks begin to play the same game that the rules get changed. Now the use of such jobs to build political bases becomes an "evil" activity, and the city insists on taking the control back "downtown."'" New York Amsterdam News, Apr. 1, 1978, p. A-4, quoted in Hamilton, The Patron-Recipient Relationship and Minority Politics in New York City, 94 Pol. Sci. Q. 211, 212 (1979).

While the patronage system has the benefits argued for above, it also has undoubted disadvantages. It facilitates financial corruption, such as salary kickbacks and partisan political activity on government-paid time. It reduces the efficiency of government, because it creates incentives to hire more and less-qualified workers and because highly qualified workers are reluctant to accept jobs that may only last until the next election. And, of course, it applies some greater or lesser inducement for individuals to join and work for the party in power.

To hear the Court tell it, this last is the greatest evil. That is not my view, and it has not historically been the view of the American people. Corruption and inefficiency, rather than abridgement of liberty, have been the major criticisms leading to enactment of the civil-service laws — for the very good reason that the patronage system does not have as harsh an effect upon conscience, expression, and association as the Court suggests. As described above, it is the nature of the pragmatic, patronage-based, two-party system to build alliances and to suppress rather than foster ideological tests for participation in the division of political "spoils." What the patronage system ordinarily demands of the party worker is loyalty to, and activity on behalf of, the organization itself rather than a set of political beliefs. He is generally free to urge within the organization the adoption of any political position; but if that position is rejected he must vote and work for the party nonetheless. The diversity of political expression (other than expression of party loyalty) is channeled, in other words, to a different stage — to the contests for party endorsement rather than the partisan elections. It is undeniable, of course, that the patronage system entails some constraint upon the expression of views, particularly at the partisan-election stage, and considerable constraint upon the employee's right to associate with the other party. It greatly exaggerates these, however, to describe them as a general "'coercion of belief,'" ante, at 9, quoting Branti, 445 U.S., at 516; see also ante, at 11-12; Elrod, 427 U.S., at 355 (plurality opinion). Indeed, it greatly exaggerates them to call them "coercion" at all, since we generally make a distinction between inducement and compulsion. The public official offered a bribe is not "coerced" to violate the law, and the private citizen offered a patronage job is not "coerced" to work for the party. In sum, I do not deny that the patronage system influences or redirects, perhaps to a substantial degree, individual political expression and political association. But like the many generations of Americans that have preceded us, I do not consider that a significant impairment of free speech or free association.

In emphasizing the advantages and minimizing the disadvantages (or at least minimizing one of the disadvantages) of the patronage system, I do not mean to suggest that that system is best. It may not always be; it may never be. To oppose our Elrod-Branti jurisprudence, one need not believe that the patronage system is necessarily desirable; nor even that it is always and everywhere arguably desirable; but merely that it is a political arrangement that may sometimes be a reasonable choice, and should therefore be left to the judgment of the people's elected representatives. The choice in question, I emphasize, is not just between patronage and a merit-based civil service, but rather among various combinations of the two that may suit different political units and different eras: permitting patronage hiring, for example, but prohibiting patronage dismissal; permitting patronage in most municipal agencies but prohibiting it in the police department; or permitting it in the mayor's office but prohibiting it everywhere else. I find it impossible to say that, always and everywhere, all of these choices fail our "balancing" test.

C

The last point explains why Elrod and Branti should be overruled, rather than merely not extended. Even in the field of constitutional adjudication, where the pull of stare decisis is at its weakest, see Glidden Co. v. Zdanok, 370 U.S. 530, 543 (1962) (opinion of Harlan, J.), one is reluctant to depart from precedent. But when that precedent is not only wrong, not only recent, not only contradicted by a long prior tradition, but also has proved unworkable in practice, then all reluctance ought to disappear. In my view that is the situation here. Though unwilling to leave it to the political process to draw the line between desirable and undesirable patronage, the Court has neither been prepared to rule that no such line exists (i.e., that all patronage is unconstitutional) nor able to design the line itself in a manner that judges, lawyers, and public employees can understand. Elrod allowed patronage dismissals of persons in "policymaking" or "confidential" positions. 427 U.S., at 367 (plurality opinion); id., at 375 (Stewart, J., concurring). Branti retreated from that formulation, asking instead "whether the hiring authority can demonstrate that party affiliation is an appropriate requirement for the effective performance of the public office involved." 445 U.S., at 518. What that means is anybody's guess. The Courts of Appeals have devised various tests for determining when "affiliation is an appropriate requirement." See generally Martin, A Decade of Branti Decisions: A Government Officials' Guide to Patronage Dismissals, 39 Am. U. L. Rev. 11, 23-42 (1989). These interpretations of Branti are not only significantly at variance with each other; they are still so general that for most positions it is impossible to know whether party affiliation is a permissible requirement until a court renders its decision.

A few examples will illustrate the shambles Branti has produced. A city cannot fire a deputy sheriff because of his political affiliation, [n.5] but then again perhaps it can, [n.6] especially if he is called the "police captain." [n.7] A county cannot fire on that basis its attorney for the department of social services, [n.8] nor its assistant attorney for family court, [n.9] but a city can fire its solicitor and his assistants, [n.10] or its assistant city attorney, [n.11] or its assistant state's attorney, [n.12] or its corporation counsel. [n.13] A city cannot discharge its deputy court clerk for his political affiliation, [n.14] but it can fire its legal assistant to the clerk on that basis. [n.15] Firing a juvenile court bailiff seems impermissible, [n.16] but it may be permissible if he is assigned permanently to a single judge. [n.17] A city cannot fire on partisan grounds its director of roads, [n.18] but it can fire the second in command of the water department. [n.19] A government cannot discharge for political reasons the senior vice president of its development bank, [n.20] but it can discharge the regional director of its rural housing administration. [n.21]

The examples could be multiplied, but this summary should make obvious that the "tests" devised to implement Branti have produced inconsistent and unpredictable results. That uncertainty undermines the purpose of both the nonpatronage rule and the exception. The rule achieves its objective of preventing the "coercion" of political affiliation, see supra, at, only if the employee is confident that he can engage in (or refrain from) political activities without risking dismissal. Since the current doctrine leaves many employees utterly in the dark about whether their jobs are protected, they are likely to play it safe. On the other side, the exception was designed to permit the government to implement its electoral mandate. Elrod, supra, at 367 (plurality opinion). But unless the government is fairly sure that dismissal is permitted, it will leave the politically uncongenial official in place, since an incorrect decision will expose it to lengthy litigation and a large damage award, perhaps even against the responsible officials personally.

This uncertainty and confusion are not the result of the fact that Elrod, and then Branti, chose the wrong "line." My point is that there is no right line — or at least no right line that can be nationally applied and that is known by judges. Once we reject as the criterion a long political tradition showing that party-based employment is entirely permissible, yet are unwilling (as any reasonable person must be) to replace it with the principle that party-based employment is entirely impermissible, we have left the realm of law and entered the domain of political science, seeking to ascertain when and where the undoubted benefits of political hiring and firing are worth its undoubted costs. The answer to that will vary from State to State, and indeed from city to city, even if one rejects out of hand (as the Branti line does) the benefits associated with party stability. Indeed, the answer will even vary from year to year. During one period, for example, it may be desirable for the manager of a municipally owned public utility to be a career specialist, insulated from the political system. During another, when the efficient operation of that utility or even its very existence has become a burning political issue, it may be desirable that he be hired and fired on a political basis. The appropriate "mix" of party-based employment is a political question if there ever was one, and we should give it back to the voters of the various political units to decide, through civil-service legislation crafted to suit the time and place, which mix is best.

III

Even were I not convinced that Elrod and Branti were wrongly decided, I would hold that they should not be extended beyond their facts, viz., actual discharge of employees for their political affiliation. Those cases invalidated patronage firing in order to prevent the "restraint it places on freedoms of belief and association." Elrod, 427 U.S., at 355 (plurality opinion); see also id., at 357 (patronage "compels or restrains" and "inhibits" belief and association). The loss of one's current livelihood is an appreciably greater constraint than such other disappointments as the failure to obtain a promotion or selection for an uncongenial transfer. Even if the "coercive" effect of the former has been held always to outweigh the benefits of party-based employment decisions, the "coercive" effect of the latter should not be. We have drawn a line between firing and other employment decisions in other contexts, see Wygant v. Jackson Bd. of Education, 476 U.S. 267, 282-283 (1986) (plurality opinion), and should do so here as well.

I would reject the alternative that the Seventh Circuit adopted in this case, which allows a cause of action if the employee can demonstrate that he was subjected to the "substantial equivalent of dismissal." 868 F. 2d 943, 950, 954 (CA7 1989). The trouble with that seemingly reasonable standard is that it is so imprecise that it will multiply yet again the harmful uncertainty and litigation that Branti has already created. If Elrod and Branti are not to be reconsidered in light of their demonstrably unsatisfactory consequences, I would go no further than to allow a cause of action when the employee has lost his position, that is, his formal title and salary. That narrow ground alone is enough to resolve the constitutional claims in the present case. Since none of the plaintiffs has alleged loss of his position because of affiliation, [n.22] I would affirm the

Seventh Circuit's judgment insofar as it affirmed the dismissal of petitioner Moore's claims, and would reverse the Seventh Circuit's judgment insofar as it reversed the dismissal of the claims of other petitioners and cross-respondents.

The Court's opinion, of course, not only declines to confine Elrod and Branti to dismissals in the narrow sense I have proposed, but, unlike the Seventh Circuit, even extends those opinions beyond "constructive" dismissals — indeed, even beyond adverse treatment of current employees — to all hiring decisions. In the long run there may be cause to rejoice in that extension. When the courts are flooded with litigation under that most unmanageable of standards (Branti) brought by that most persistent and tenacious of suitors (the disappointed office-seeker) we may be moved to reconsider our intrusion into this entire field.

In the meantime, I dissent.

Notes to Justice Scalia's dissent in Rutan v. Republican Party of Illinois (June 21, 1990)

1 The customary invocation of Brown v. Board of Education, 347 U.S. 483 (1954) as demonstrating the dangerous consequences of this principle, see ante, at 4 (Stevens, J., concurring), is unsupportable. I argue for the role of tradition in giving content only to ambiguous constitutional text; no tradition can supersede the Constitution. In my view the Fourteenth Amendment's requirement of "equal protection of the laws," combined with the Thirteenth Amendment's abolition of the institution of black slavery, leaves no room for doubt that laws treating people differently because of their race are invalid. Moreover, even if one does not regard the Fourteenth Amendment as crystal clear on this point, a tradition of unchallenged validity did not exist with respect to the practice in Brown. To the contrary, in the 19th century the principle of "separate-but-equal" had been vigorously opposed on constitutional grounds, litigated up to this Court, and upheld only over the dissent of one of our historically most respected Justices. See Plessy v. Ferguson, 163 U.S. 537, 555-556 (1896) (Harlan, J., dissenting).

2 Justice Stevens seeks to counteract this tradition by relying upon the supposed "unequivocal repudiation" of the right-privilege distinction. Ante, at 5. That will not do. If the right-privilege distinction was once used to explain the practice, and if that distinction is to be repudiated, then one must simply devise some other theory to explain it. The order of precedence is that a constitutional theory must be wrong if its application contradicts a clear constitutional tradition; not that a clear constitutional tradition must be wrong if it does not conform to the current constitutional theory. On Justice Stevens' view of the matter, this Court examines a historical practice, endows it with an intellectual foundation, and later, by simply undermining that foundation, relegates the constitutional tradition to the dustbin of history. That is not how constitutional adjudication works. Cf. Burnham v. Superior Court of California, Marin County, 495 U.S. (1990) (opinion of Scalia, J.). I am not sure, in any event, that the right-privilege

distinction has been as unequivocally rejected as Justice Stevens supposes. It has certainly been recognized that the fact that the government need not confer a certain benefit does not mean that it can attach any conditions whatever to the conferral of that benefit. But it remains true that certain conditions can be attached to benefits that cannot be imposed as prescriptions upon the public at large. If Justice Stevens chooses to call this something other than a right-privilege distinction, that is fine and good — but it is in any case what explains the nonpatronage restrictions upon federal employees that the Court continues to approve, and there is no reason why it cannot support patronage restrictions as well.

3 The Court calls our description of the appropriate standard of review "questionable," and suggests that these cases applied strict scrutiny ("even were Justice Scalia correct that less-than-strict scrutiny is appropriate"). Ante, at 7, n.4 (emphasis added). This suggestion is incorrect, does not aid the Court's argument, and if accepted would eviscerate the strict-scrutiny standard. It is incorrect because even a casual perusal of the cases reveals that the governmental actions were sustained, not because they were shown to be "narrowly tailored to further vital government interests," ante, at 1011, but because they were "reasonably" deemed necessary to promote effective government. It does not aid the Court's argument, moreover, because whatever standard those cases applied must be applied here, and if the asserted interests in patronage are as weighty as those proffered in the previous cases, then Elrod and Branti were wrongly decided. It eviscerates the standard, finally, because if the practices upheld in those cases survived strict scrutiny, then the so-called "strict scrutiny" test means nothing. Suppose a State made it unlawful for an employee of a privately owned nuclear power plant to criticize his employer. Can there be any doubt that we would reject out of hand the State's argument that the statute was justified by the compelling interest in maintaining the appearance that such employees are operating nuclear plants properly, so as to maintain public confidence in the plants' safety? But cf. CSC v. Letter Carriers, 413 U.S. 548, 565 (1973) (Hatch Act justified by need for government employees to "appear to the public to be avoiding [political partiality], if confidence in the system of representative Government is not to be eroded"). Suppose again that a State prohibited a private employee from speaking on the job about matters of private concern. Would we even hesitate before dismissing the State's claim that the compelling interest in fostering an efficient economy overrides the individual's interest in speaking on such matters? But cf. Connick v. Myers, 461 U.S. 138, 147 (1983) ("[W]hen a public employee speaks ... upon matters only of personal interest, absent the most unusual circumstances, a federal court is not the appropriate forum in which to review the wisdom of a personnel decision taken by a public agency allegedly in reaction to the employee's behavior"). If the Court thinks that strict scrutiny is appropriate in all these cases, then it should forthrightly admit that Public Workers v. Mitchell, 330 U.S. 75 (1947), Letter Carriers, Pickering v. Board of Education of Township High School Dist., 391 U.S. 563 (1968), Connick, and similar

cases were mistaken and should be overruled; if it rejects that course, then it should admit that those cases applied, as they said they did, a reasonableness test.

The Court's further contention that these cases are limited to the "interests that the government has in its capacity as an employer," ante, at 7, n. 4, as distinct from its interests "in the structure and functioning of society as a whole," ibid., is neither true nor relevant. Surely a principal reason for the statutes that we have upheld preventing political activity by government employees — and indeed the only substantial reason, with respect to those employees who are permitted to be hired and fired on a political basis — is to prevent the party in power from obtaining what is considered an unfair advantage in political campaigns. That is precisely the type of governmental interest at issue here. But even if the Court were correct, I see no reason in policy or principle why the government would be limited to furthering only its interests "as employer." In fact, we have seemingly approved the furtherance of broader governmental interests through employment restrictions. In Hampton v. Mow Sun Wong, 426 U.S. 88 (1976), we held unlawful a Civil Service Commission regulation prohibiting the hiring of aliens on the ground that the Commission lacked the requisite authority. We were willing, however, to "assume ... that if the Congress or the President had expressly imposed the citizenship requirement, it would be justified by the national interest in providing an incentive for aliens to become naturalized, or possibly even as providing the President with an expendable token for treaty negotiating purposes." Id., at 105. Three months after our opinion, the President adopted the restriction by Executive Order. Exec. Order No.11935, 3 CFR 146 (1976 Comp.). On remand, the lower courts denied the Mow Sun Wong plaintiffs relief, on the basis of this new Executive Order and relying upon the interest in providing an incentive for citizenship. Mow SunWong v. Hampton, 435 F. Supp. 37 (ND Cal. 1977), aff'd, 626 F. 2d 739 (CA9 1980). We denied certiorari, sub nom. Lum v. Campbell, 450 U.S. 959 (1981). In other cases, the lower federal courts have uniformly reached the same result. See, e.g., Jalil v. Campbell, 192 U.S. App. D.C. 4, 7, 590 F. 2d 1120, 1123, n.3 (1978); Vergara v. Hampton, 581 F. 2d 1281 (CA7 1978), cert. denied, 441 U.S. 905 (1979); Santin Ramos v. United States Civil Service Comm'n, 430 F. Supp. 422 (PR 1977) (three-judge court).

4 Justice Stevens discounts these systemic effects when he characterizes patronage as fostering partisan, rather than public, interests. Ante, at 9. But taking Justice Stevens at his word, one wonders why patronage can ever be an "appropriate requirement for the position involved," ante, at 1.

5 Jones v. Dodson, 727 F. 2d 1329, 1338 (CA4 1984).

6 McBee v. Jim Hogg County, Texas, 730 F. 2d 1009, 1014-1015 (CA5 1984) (en banc).

7 Joyner v. Lancaster, 553 F. Supp. 809, 818 (MDNC 1982), later proceeding, 815 F. 2d 20, 24 (CA4), cert. denied, 484 U.S. 830 (1987).

8 Layden v. Costello, 517 F. Supp. 860, 862 (NDNY 1981).

9 Tavano v. County of Niagara, New York, 621 F. Supp. 345, 349-350 (WDNY 1985), aff'd mem., 800 F. 2d 1128 (CA2 1986).

10 Ness v. Marshall, 660 F. 2d 517, 521-522 (CA3 1981); Montaquila v. St. Cyr, 433 A. 2d 206, 211 (R.I. 1981).

11 Finkelstein v. Barthelemy, 678 F. Supp. 1255, 1265 (ED La 1988).

12 Livas v. Petka, 711 F. 2d 798, 800-801 (CA7 1983).

13 Bavoso v. Harding, 507 F. Supp. 313, 316 (SDNY 1980).

14 Barnes v. Bosley, 745 F. 2d 501, 508 (CA8 1984), cert. denied, 471 U.S. 1017 (1985).

15 Bauer v. Bosley, 802 F. 2d 1058, 1063 (CA8 1986), cert. denied, 481 U.S. 1038 (1987).

16 Elrod v. Burns, 427 U.S. 347, 351 (1976).

17 Balogh v. Charron, 855 F. 2d 356 (CA6 1988).

18 Abraham v. Pekarski, 537 F. Supp. 858, 865 (ED Pa 1982), aff'd in part and dismissed in part, 728 F. 2d 167 (CA3), cert. denied, 467 U.S. 1242 (1984).

19 Tomczak v. Chicago, 765 F. 2d 633 (CA7), cert. denied, 474 U.S. 946 (1985).

20 De Choudens v. Government Development Bank of Puerto Rico, 801 F. 2d 5, 10 (CA1 1986) (en banc), cert. denied, 481 U.S. 1013 (1987).

21 Rosario Nevarez v. Torres Gaztambide, 820 F. 2d 525 (CA1 1987).

22 Standefer and O'Brien do not allege that their political affiliation was the reason they were laid off, but only that it was the reason they were not recalled. Complaint 9, 21-22, App. to Respondent's Brief in Opposition; 641 F. Supp. 249, 256, 257 (CDIll. 1986). Those claims are essentially identical to the claims of persons wishing to be hired; neither fall within the narrow rule of Elrod and Branti against patronage firing.

Confrontation Clause—doesn't exclude young children: Justice Scalia's dissent in Maryland v. Craig (June 27, 1990)

Justice Scalia, with whom Justice Brennan, Justice Marshall, and Justice Stevens join, dissenting.

Seldom has this Court failed so conspicuously to sustain a categorical guarantee of the Constitution against the tide of prevailing current opinion. The Sixth Amendment provides, with unmistakable clarity, that "[i]n all criminal prosecutions, the accused shall enjoy the right . . . to be confronted with the witnesses against him." The purpose of enshrining this protection in the Constitution was to assure that none of the many policy interests from time to time pursued by statutory law could overcome a defendant's right to face his or her accusers in court. The Court, however, says:

"We ... conclude today that a State's interest in the physical and psychological well-being of child abuse victims may be sufficiently important to outweigh, at least in some cases, a defendant's right to face his or her accusers in court. That a significant majority of States has enacted statutes to protect child witnesses from the trauma of giving testimony in child abuse cases attests to the widespread belief in the importance of such a public policy." Ante, at 13.

Because of this subordination of explicit constitutional text to currently favored public policy, the following scene can be played out in an American courtroom for the first time in two centuries: A father whose young daughter has been given over to the exclusive custody of his estranged wife, or a mother whose young son has been taken into custody by the State's child welfare department, is sentenced to prison for sexual abuse on the basis of testimony by a child the parent has not seen or spoken to for many months; and the guilty verdict is rendered without giving the parent so much as the opportunity to sit in the presence of the child, and to ask, personally or through counsel, "it is really not true, is it, that I — your father (or mother) whom you see before you — did these terrible things?" Perhaps that is a procedure today's society desires; perhaps (though I doubt it) it is even a fair procedure; but it is assuredly not a procedure permitted by the Constitution.

Because the text of the Sixth Amendment is clear, and because the Constitution is meant to protect against, rather than conform to, current "widespread belief," I respectfully dissent.

I

According to the Court, "we cannot say that [face-to-face] confrontation [with witnesses appearing at trial] is an in dispensable element of the Sixth Amendment's guarantee of the right to confront one's accusers." Ante, at 10. That is rather like saying "we cannot say that being tried before a jury is an indispensable element of the Sixth Amendment's guarantee of the right to jury trial." The Court makes the impossible plausible by recharacterizing the Confrontation Clause, so that confrontation (redesignated "face-to-face confrontation") becomes only one of many "elements of confrontation." Ante, at 7. The reasoning is as follows: The Confrontation Clause guarantees not only what it explicitly provides for — "face-to-face" confrontation — but also implied and collateral rights such as cross-examination, oath, and observation of demeanor (TRUE); the purpose of this entire cluster of rights is to ensure the reliability of evidence (TRUE); the Maryland procedure preserves the implied and collateral rights (TRUE), which adequately ensure the reliability of evidence (perhaps TRUE); therefore the Confrontation Clause is not violated by denying what it explicitly provides for — "face-to-face" confrontation (unquestionably FALSE). This reasoning abstracts from the right to its purposes, and then eliminates the right. It is wrong because the Confrontation Clause does not guarantee reliable evidence; it guarantees specific trial procedures that were thought to assure reliable evidence, undeniably among which was "face-to-face" confrontation. Whatever else it may mean in addition, the defendant's constitutional right "to be confronted with the witnesses against him" means, always and everywhere, at least what it explicitly says: the "`right to meet face to face all those who appear and give evidence at trial.'" Coy v. Iowa, 487 U.S. 1012, 1016 (1988), quoting California v. Green, 399 U.S. 149, 175 (1970) (Harlan, J. concurring).

The Court supports its antitextual conclusion by cobbling together scraps of dicta from various cases that have no bearing here. It will suffice to discuss one of them, since they are all of a kind: Quoting Ohio v. Roberts, 448 U.S. 56, 63 (1980), the Court says that "[i]n sum, our precedents establish that `the Confrontation Clause reflects a preference for face-to-face confrontation at trial,'" ante, at 10 (emphasis added by the Court). But Roberts, and all the other "precedents" the Court enlists to prove the implausible, dealt with the implications of the Confrontation Clause, and not its literal, unavoidable text. When Roberts said that the Clause merely "reflects a preference for face-to-face confrontation at trial," what it had in mind as the nonpreferred alternative was not (as the Court implies) the appearance of a witness at trial without confronting the defendant. That has been, until today, not merely "nonpreferred" but utterly unheardof. What Roberts had in mind was the receipt of other-than-first-hand testimony from witnesses at trial — that is, witnesses' recounting of hearsay statements by absent parties who, since they did not appear at trial, did not have to endure face-to-face confrontation. Rejecting that, I agree, was merely giving effect to an evident constitutional preference; there are, after all, many exceptions to the Confrontation Clause's hearsay rule. But that the defendant should be confronted by the witnesses who appear at trial is not a preference "reflected" by the Confrontation Clause; it is a constitutional right unqualifiedly guaranteed.

The Court claims that its interpretation of the Confrontation Clause "is consistent with our cases holding that other Sixth Amendment rights must also be interpreted in the context of the necessities of trial and the adversary process." Ante, at 1011. I disagree. It is true enough that the "necessities of trial and the adversary process" limit the manner in which Sixth Amendment rights may be exercised, and limit the scope of Sixth Amendment guarantees to the extent that scope is textually indeterminate. Thus (to describe the cases the Court cites): The right to confront is not the right to confront in a manner that disrupts the trial. Illinois v. Allen, 397 U.S. 337 (1970). The right "to have compulsory process for obtaining witnesses" is not the right to call witnesses in a manner that violates fair and orderly procedures. Taylor v. United States, 484 U.S. 400 (1988). The scope of the right "to have the assistance of counsel" does not include consultation with counsel at all times during the trial. Perry v. Leeke, 488 U.S. 272 (1989). The scope of the right to cross-examine does not include access to the State's investigative files. Pennsylvania v. Ritchie, 480 U.S. 39 (1987). But we are not talking here about denying expansive scope to a Sixth Amendment provision whose scope for the purpose at issue is textually unclear; "to confront" plainly means to encounter face-to-face, whatever else it may mean in addition. And we are not talking about the manner of arranging that face-to-face encounter, but about whether it shall occur at all. The "necessities of trial and the adversary process" are irrelevant here, since they cannot alter the constitutional text.

II

Much of the Court's opinion consists of applying to this case the mode of analysis we have used in the admission of hearsay evidence. The Sixth Amendment does not literally contain a prohibition upon such evidence, since it guarantees the defendant only the right to confront "the witnesses against him." As applied in the Sixth Amendment's context of a prosecution, the noun "witness" — in 1791 as today — could mean either (a) one "who knows or sees any thing; one personally present" or (b) "one who gives testimony" or who "testifies," i.e., "[i]n judicial proceedings, [one who] make[s] a solemn declaration under oath, for the purpose of establishing or making proof of some fact to a court." 2 N.Webster, An American Dictionary of the English Language (1828) (emphasis added). See also J.Buchanan, Linguae Britannicae Vera Pronunciatio (1757). The former meaning (one "who knows or sees") would cover hearsay evidence, but is excluded in the Sixth Amendment by the words following the noun: "witnesses against him." The phrase obviously refers to those who give testimony against the defendant at trial. We have nonetheless found implicit in the Confrontation Clause some limitation upon hearsay evidence, since otherwise the Government could subvert the confrontation right by putting on witnesses who know nothing except what an absent declarant said. And in determining the scope of that implicit limitation, we have focused upon whether the reliability of the hearsay statements (which are not expressly excluded by the Confrontation Clause) "is otherwise assured." Ante, at 11. The same test cannot be applied, however, to permit what is explicitly forbidden by the constitutional text; there is simply no room for interpretation with regard to "the irreducible literal meaning of the Clause." Coy, supra, at 1020-1021.

Some of the Court's analysis seems to suggest that the children's testimony here was itself hearsay of the sort permissible under our Confrontation Clause cases. See ante, at 12. That cannot be. Our Confrontation Clause conditions for the admission of hearsay have long included a "general requirement of unavailability" of the declarant. Idaho v. Wright, ante, p.8. "In the usual case ..., the prosecution must either produce or demonstrate the unavailability of, the declarant whose statement it wishes to use against the defendant." Ohio v. Roberts, 448 U.S., at 65. We have permitted a few exceptions to this general rule — e.g., for co-conspirators' statements, whose effect cannot be replicated by live testimony because they "derive [their] significance from the circumstances in which [they were] made," United States v. Inadi, 475 U.S. 387, 395 (1986). "Live" closed-circuit television testimony, however — if it can be called hearsay at all — is surely an example of hearsay as "a weaker substitute for live testimony," id., at 394, which can be employed only when the genuine article is unavailable. "When two versions of the same evidence are available, longstanding principles of the law of hearsay, applicable as well to Confrontation Clause analysis, favor the better evidence." Ibid. See also Roberts, supra (requiring unavailability as precondition for admission of prior testimony); Barber v. Page, 390 U.S. 719 (1968) (same).

The Court's test today requires unavailability only in the sense that the child is unable to testify in the presence of the defendant. [n.1] That cannot possibly be the relevant sense. If unconfronted testimony is admissible hearsay when the witness is unable to confront the defendant, then presumably there are other categories of admissible hearsay consisting of unsworn testimony when the witness is unable to risk perjury, uncross-examined testimony when the witness is unable to undergo hostile questioning, etc. California v. Green, 399 U.S. 149 (1970), is not precedent for such a silly system. That case held that the Confrontation Clause does not bar admission of prior testimony when the declarant is sworn as a witness but refuses to answer. But in Green, as in most cases of refusal, we could not know why the declarant refused to testify. Here, by contrast, we know that it is precisely because the child is unwilling to testify in the presence of the defendant. That unwillingness cannot be a valid excuse under the Confrontation Clause, whose very object is to place the witness under the sometimes hostile glare of the defendant. "That face-to-face presence may, unfortunately, upset the truthful rape victim or abused child; but by the same token it may confound and undo the false accuser, or reveal the child coached by a malevolent adult." Coy, 487 U.S., at 1020. To say that a defendant loses his right to confront a witness when that would cause the witness not to testify is rather like saying that the defendant loses his right to counsel when counsel would save him, or his right to subpoena witnesses when they would exculpate him, or his right not to give testimony against himself when that would prove him guilty.

III

The Court characterizes the State's interest which "outweigh[s]" the explicit text of the Constitution as an "interest in the physical and psychological well-being of child abuse victims," ante, at 13, an "interest in protecting" such victims "from the emotional trauma of testifying," ante, at 16. That is not so. A child who meets the Maryland statute's requirement of suffering such "serious emotional distress" from confrontation that he "cannot reasonably communicate" would seem entirely safe. Why would a prosecutor want to call a witness who cannot reasonably communicate? And if he did, it would be the State's own fault. Protection of the child's interest — as far as the Confrontation Clause is concerned [n.2] — is entirely within Maryland's control. The State's interest here is in fact no more and no less than what the State's interest always is when it seeks to get a class of evidence admitted in criminal proceedings: more convictions of guilty defendants. That is not an unworthy interest, but it should not be dressed up as a humanitarian one.

And the interest on the other side is also what it usually is when the State seeks to get a new class of evidence admitted: fewer convictions of innocent defendants — specifically, in the present context, innocent defendants accused of particularly heinous crimes. The "special" reasons that exist for suspending one of the usual guarantees of reliability in the case of children's testimony are perhaps matched by "special" reasons for being particularly insistent upon it in the case of children's testimony. Some studies show that children are substantially more vulnerable to suggestion than adults, and often unable to separate recollected fantasy (or suggestion) from reality. See Lindsay & Johnson, Reality Monitoring and Suggestibility: Children's Ability to Discriminate Among

Memories From Different Sources, in Children's Eyewitness Memory 92 (S.Ceci, M.Toglia, & D.Ross eds. 1987); Feher, The Alleged Molestation Victim, The Rules of Evidence, and the Constitution: Should Children Really Be Seen and Not Heard?, 14 Am. J. Crim. L. 227, 230-233 (1987); Christian sen, The Testimony of Child Witnesses: Fact, Fantasy, and the Influence of Pretrial Interviews, 62 Wash. L. Rev. 705, 708-711 (1987). The injustice their erroneous testimony can produce is evidenced by the tragic Scott County investigations of 1983-1984, which disrupted the lives of many (as far as we know) innocent people in the small town of Jordan, Minnesota. At one stage those investigations were pursuing allegations by at least eight children of multiple murders, but the prosecutions actually initiated charged only sexual abuse. Specifically, 24 adults were charged with molesting 37 children. In the course of the investigations, 25 children were placed in foster homes. Of the 24 indicted defendants, one pleaded guilty, two were acquitted at trial, and the charges against the remaining 21 were voluntarily dismissed. See Feher, supra, at 239-240. There is no doubt that some sexual abuse took place in Jordan; but there is no reason to believe it was as widespread as charged. A report by the Minnesota Attorney General's office, based on inquiries conducted by the Minnesota Bureau of Criminal Apprehension and the Federal Bureau of Investigation, concluded that there was an "absence of credible testimony and [a] lack of significant corroboration" to support reinstitution of sex-abuse charges, and "no credible evidence of murders." H. Humphrey, report on Scott County Investigation 8, 7 (1985). The report describes an investigation full of well-intentioned techniques employed by the prosecution team, police, child protection workers, and foster parents, that distorted and in some cases even coerced the children's recollection. Children were interrogated repeatedly, in some cases as many as 50 times, id., at 9; answers were suggested by telling the children what other witnesses had said, id., at 11; and children (even some who did not at first complain of abuse) were separated from their parents for months, id., at 9. The report describes the consequences as follows:

"As children continued to be interviewed the list of accused citizens grew. In a number of cases, it was only after weeks or months of questioning that children would `admit' their parents abused them.

"In some instances, over a period of time, the allegations of sexual abuse turned to stories of mutilations, and eventually homicide." Id., at 10-11.

The value of the confrontation right in guarding against a child's distorted or coerced recollections is dramatically evident with respect to one of the misguided investigative techniques the report cited: some children were told by their foster parents that reunion with their real parents would be hastened by "admission" of their parents' abuse. Id., at 9.Is it difficult to imagine how unconvincing such a testimonial admission might be to a jury that witnessed the child's delight at seeing his parents in the courtroom? Or how devastating it might be if, pursuant to a psychiatric evaluation that "trauma would impair the child's ability to communicate" in front of his parents, the child were permitted to tell his story to the jury on closed-circuit television?

In the last analysis, however, this debate is not an appropriate one. I have no need to defend the value of confrontation, because the Court has no authority to question it. It is not within our charge to speculate that, "where face-to-face confrontation causes significant emotional distress in a child witness," confrontation might "in fact disserve the Confrontation Clause's truth-seeking goal." Ante, at 17. If so, that is a defect in the Constitution — which should be amended by the procedures provided for such an eventuality, but cannot be corrected by judicial pronouncement that it is archaic, contrary to "widespread belief" and thus null and void. For good or bad, the Sixth Amendment requires confrontation, and we are not at liberty to ignore it. To quote the document one last time (for it plainly says all that need be said): "In all criminal prosecutions, the accused shall enjoy the right ... to be confronted with the witnesses against him" (emphasis added).

* * *

The Court today has applied "interest-balancing" analysis where the text of the Constitution simply does not permit it. We are not free to conduct a cost-benefit analysis of clear and explicit constitutional guarantees, and then to adjust their meaning to comport with our findings. The Court has convincingly proved that the Maryland procedure serves a valid interest, and gives the defendant virtually everything the Confrontation Clause guarantees (everything, that is, except confrontation). I am persuaded, therefore, that the Maryland procedure is virtually constitutional. Since it is not, however, actually constitutional I would affirm the judgment of the Maryland Court of Appeals reversing the judgment of conviction.

Notes

1 I presume that when the Court says "trauma would impair the child's ability to communicate," ante, at 18, it means that trauma would make it impossible for the child to communicate. That is the requirement of the Maryland law at issue here: "serious emotional distress such that the child cannot reasonably communicate." Md. Cts. & Jud. Proc. Code Ann. 9-102(a)(1)(ii) (1989). Any implication beyond that would in any event be dictum.

2 A different situation would be presented if the defendant sought to call the child. In that event, the State's refusal to compel the child to appear, or its insistence upon a procedure such as that set forth in the Maryland statute as a condition of its compelling him to do so, would call into questioning — itially, at least, and perhaps exclusively — the scope of the defendant's Sixth Amendment right "to have compulsory process for obtaining witnesses in his favor."

Miranda: Justice Scalia's dissent in Minnick v. Mississippi (December 3, 1990)

Justice Scalia, with whom The Chief Justice joins, dissenting.

The Court today establishes an irrebuttable presumption that a criminal suspect, after invoking his Miranda right to counsel, can never validly waive that right during any policeinitiated encounter, even after the suspect has been provided multiple Miranda warnings and has actually consulted his attorney. This holding builds on foundations already established in Edwards v. Arizona, 451 U.S. 477 (1981), but "the rule of Edwards is our rule, not a constitutional command; and it is our obligation to justify its expansion." Arizona v. Roberson, 486 U.S. 675, 688 (1988) (Kennedy, J., dissenting). Because I see no justification for applying the Edwards irrebuttable presumption when a criminal suspect has actually consulted with his attorney, I respectfully dissent.

I

Some recapitulation of pertinent facts is in order, given the Court's contention that "[t]he case before us well illustrates the pressures, and abuses, that may be concomitants of custody." Ante, at 7. It is undisputed that the FBI agents who first interviewed Minnick on Saturday, August 23, 1986, advised him of his Miranda rights before any questioning began. Although he refused to sign a waiver form, he agreed to talk to the agents, and described his escape from prison in Mississippi and the ensuing events. When he came to what happened at the trailer, however, Minnick hesitated. The FBI agents then reminded him that he did not have to answer questions without a lawyer present. Minnick indicated that he would finish his account on Monday, when he had a lawyer, and the FBI agents terminated the interview forthwith.

Minnick was then provided with an attorney, with whom he consulted several times over the weekend. As Minnick testified at a subsequent suppression hearing:

"I talked to [my attorney] two different times and — it might have been three different times. . . . He told me that first day that he was my lawyer and that he was appointed to me and not to talk to nobody and not tell nobody nothing and to not sign no waivers and not sign no extradition papers or sign anything and that he was going to get a court order to have any of the police — I advised him of the FBI talking to me and he advised me not to tell anybody anything that he was going to get a court order drawn up to restrict anybody talking to me outside of the San Diego Police Department." App. 46-47.

On Monday morning, Minnick was interviewed by Deputy Sheriff J. C. Denham, who had come to San Diego from Mississippi. Before the interview, Denham reminded Minnick of his Miranda rights. Minnick again refused to sign a waiver form, but he did talk with Denham, and did not ask for his attorney. As Minnick recalled at the hearing, he and Denham

"went through several different conversations about — first, about how everybody was back in the county jail and what everybody was doing, had he heard from Mama and had he went and talked to Mama and had he seen my brother, Tracy, and several different other questions pertaining to such things as that. And, we went off into how the escape went down at the county jail . . . ." App. 50.

Minnick then proceeded to describe his participation in the double murder at the trailer.

Minnick was later extradited and tried for murder in Mississippi. Before trial, he moved to suppress the statements he had given the FBI agents and Denham in the San Diego jail. The trial court granted the motion with respect to the statements made to the FBI agents, but ordered a hearing on the admissibility of the statements made to Denham. After receiving testimony from both Minnick and Denham, the court concluded that Minnick's confession had been "freely and voluntarily given from the evidence beyond a reasonable doubt," id., at 25, and allowed Denham to describe Minnick's confession to the jury.

The Court today reverses the trial court's conclusion. It holds that, because Minnick had asked for counsel during the interview with the FBI agents, he could not — as a matter of law — validly waive the right to have counsel present during the conversation initiated by Denham. That Minnick's original request to see an attorney had been honored, that Minnick had consulted with his attorney on several occasions, and that the attorney had specifically warned Minnick not to speak to the authorities, are irrelevant. That Minnick was familiar with the criminal justice system in general or Miranda warnings in particular (he had previously been convicted of robbery in Mississippi and assault with a deadly weapon in California) is also beside the point. The confession must be suppressed, not because it was "compelled," nor even because it was obtained from an individual who could realistically be assumed to be unaware of his rights, but simply because this Court sees fit to prescribe as a "systemic assuranc[e]," ante, at 9, that a person in custody who has once asked for counsel cannot thereafter be approached by the police unless counsel is present. Of course the Constitution's proscription of compelled testimony does not remotely authorize this incursion upon state practices; and even our recent precedents are not a valid excuse.

II

In Miranda v. Arizona, 384 U.S. 436 (1966), this Court declared that a criminal suspect has a right to have counsel present during custodial interrogation, as a prophylactic assurance that the "inherently compelling pressures," id. at 467, of such interrogation will not violate the Fifth Amendment. But Miranda did not hold that these "inherently compelling pressures" precluded a suspect from waiving his right to have counsel present. On the contrary, the opinion recognized that a State could establish that the suspect "knowingly and intelligently waived . . . his right to retained or appointed counsel." Id., at 475. For this purpose, the Court expressly adopted the "high standar[d] of proof for the waiver of constitutional rights," ibid., set forth in Johnson v. Zerbst, 304 U.S. 458 (1938).

The Zerbst waiver standard, and the means of applying it, are familiar: Waiver is "an intentional relinquishment or abandonment of a known right or privilege," id., at 464; and whether such a relinquishment or abandonment has occurred depends "in each case, upon the particular facts and circumstances surrounding that case, including the background, experience, and conduct of the accused," ibid. We have applied the Zerbst approach in many contexts where a State bears the burden of showing a waiver of constitutional criminal procedural rights. See, e. g., Faretta v. California, 422 U.S. 806, 835 (1975) (right to the assistance of counsel at trial); Brookhart v. Janis, 384 U.S. 1, 4 (1966) (right to confront adverse witnesses); Adams v. United States ex rel. McCann, 317 U.S. 269, 275-280 (1942) (right to trial by jury).

Notwithstanding our acknowledgment that Miranda rights are "not themselves rights protected by the Constitution but . . . instead measures to insure that the right against compulsory self-incrimination [is] protected," Michigan v. Tucker, 417 U.S. 433, 444 (1974), we have adhered to the principle that nothing less than the Zerbst standard for the waiver of constitutional rights applies to the waiver of Miranda rights. Until Edwards, however, we refrained from imposing on the States a higher standard for the waiver of Miranda rights. For example, in Michigan v. Mosley, 423 U.S. 96 (1975), we rejected a proposed irrebuttable presumption that a criminal suspect, after invoking the Miranda right to remain silent, could not validly waive the right during any subsequent questioning by the police. In North Carolina v. Butler, 441 U.S. 369 (1979) we rejected a proposed rule that waivers of Miranda rights must be deemed involuntary absent an explicit assertion of waiver by the suspect. And in Fare v. Michael C., 442 U.S. 707, 723-727 (1979) we declined to hold that waivers of Miranda rights by juveniles are per se involuntary.

Edwards, however, broke with this approach, holding that a defendant's waiver of his Miranda right to counsel, made in the course of a police-initiated encounter after he had requested counsel but before counsel had been provided, was per se involuntary. The case stands as a solitary exception to our waiver jurisprudence. It does, to be sure, have the desirable consequences described in today's opinion. In the narrow context in which it applies, it provides 100" assurance against confessions that are "the result of coercive pressures," ante, at 4; it " `prevent[s] police from badgering a defendant,' " ibid. (quoting Michigan v. Harvey, 494 U. S. —, — (1990)); it "conserves judicial resources which would otherwise be expended in making difficult determinations of voluntariness," ante, at 4; and it provides " ` "clear and unequivocal" guidelines to the law enforcement profession,' " ibid. (quoting Arizona v. Roberson, 486 U. S., at 682). But so would a rule that simply excludes all confessions by all persons in police custody. The value of any prophylactic rule (assuming the authority to adopt a prophylactic rule) must be assessed not only on the basis of what is gained, but also on the basis of what is lost. In all other contexts we have thought the above-described consequences of abandoning Zerbst outweighed by " `the need for police questioning as a tool for effective enforcement of criminal laws,' " Moran v. Burbine, 475 U.S. 412, 426 (1986). "Admissions of guilt," we have said, "are more than merely `desirable'; they are essential to society's compelling interest in finding, convicting, and punishing those who violate the law." Ibid. (citation omitted).

III

In this case, of course, we have not been called upon to reconsider Edwards, but simply to determine whether its irrebuttable presumption should continue after a suspect has actually consulted with his attorney. Whatever justifications might support Edwards are even less convincing in this context.

Most of the Court's discussion of Edwards — which stresses repeatedly, in various formulations, the case's emphasis upon "the `right to have counsel present during custodial interrogation,' " ante, at 5, quoting 451 U. S., at 482 (emphasis added by the Court) — is beside the point. The existence and the importance of the Miranda-created right "to have counsel present" are unquestioned here. What is questioned is why a State should not be given the opportunity to prove (under Zerbst) that the right was voluntarily waived by a suspect who, after having been read his Miranda rights twice and having consulted with counsel at least twice, chose to speak to a police officer (and to admit his involvement in two murders) without counsel present.

Edwards did not assert the principle that no waiver of the Miranda right "to have counsel present" is possible. It simply adopted the presumption that no waiver is voluntary in certain circumstances, and the issue before us today is how broadly those circumstances are to be defined. They should not, in my view, extend beyond the circumstances present in Edwards itself — where the suspect in custody asked to consult an attorney, and was interrogated before that attorney had ever been provided. In those circumstances, the Edwards rule rests upon an assumption similar to that of Miranda itself: that when a suspect in police custody is first questioned he is likely to be ignorant of his rights and to feel isolated in a hostile environment. This likelihood is thought to justify special protection against unknowing or coerced waiver of rights. After a suspect has seen his request for an attorney honored, however, and has actually spoken with that attorney, the probabilities change. The suspect then knows that he has an advocate on his side, and that the police will permit him to consult that advocate. He almost certainly also has a heightened awareness (above what the Miranda warning itself will provide) of his right to remain silent — since at the earliest opportunity "any lawyer worth his salt will tell the suspect in no uncertain terms to make no statement to the police under any circumstances." Watts v. Indiana, 338 U.S. 49, 59 (1949) (Opinion of Jackson, J.).

Under these circumstances, an irrebuttable presumption that any police-prompted confession is the result of ignorance of rights, or of coercion, has no genuine basis in fact. After the first consultation, therefore, the Edwards exclusionary rule should cease to apply. Does this mean, as the Court implies, that the police will thereafter have license to "badger" the suspect? Only if all one means by "badger" is asking, without such insistence or frequency as would constitute coercion, whether he would like to reconsider his decision not to confess. Nothing in the Constitution (the only basis for our intervention here) prohibits such inquiry, which may often produce the desirable result of a voluntary confession. If and when post-consultation police inquiry becomes so protracted or threatening as to constitute coercion, the Zerbst standard will afford the needed protection.

One should not underestimate the extent to which the Court's expansion of Edwards constricts law enforcement. Today's ruling, that the invocation of a right to counsel permanently prevents a police-initiated waiver, makes it largely impossible for the police to urge a prisoner who has initially declined to confess to change his mind — or indeed, even to ask whether he has changed his mind. Many persons in custody will invoke the Miranda right to counsel during the first interrogation, so that the permanent prohibition will attach at once. Those who do not do so will almost certainly request or obtain counsel at arraignment. We have held that a general request for counsel, after the Sixth Amendment right has attached, also triggers the Edwards prohibition of policesolicited confessions, see Michigan v. Jackson, 475 U.S. 625 (1986), and I presume that the perpetuality of prohibition announced in today's opinion applies in that context as well. "Perpetuality" is not too strong a term, since, although the Court rejects one logical moment at which the Edwards presumption might end, it suggests no alternative. In this case Minnick was reapproached by the police three days after he requested counsel, but the result would presumably be the same if it had been three months, or three years, or even three decades. This perpetual irrebuttable presumption will apply, I might add, not merely to interrogations involving the original crime but to those involving other subjects as well. See Arizona v. Roberson, 486 U.S. 675 (1988).

Besides repeating the uncontroverted proposition that the suspect has a "right to have counsel present," the Court stresses the clarity and simplicity that are achieved by today's holding. Clear and simple rules are desirable, but only in pursuance of authority that we possess. We are authorized by the Fifth Amendment to exclude confessions that are "compelled," which we have interpreted to include confessions that the police obtain from a suspect in custody without a knowing and voluntary waiver of his right to remain silent. Undoubtedly some bright-line rules can be adopted to implement that principle, marking out the situations in which knowledge or voluntariness cannot possibly be established — for example, a rule excluding confessions obtained after five hours of continuous interrogation. But a rule excluding all confessions that follow upon even the slightest police inquiry cannot conceivably be justified on this basis. It does not rest upon a reasonable prediction that all such confessions, or even most such confessions, will be unaccompanied by a knowing and voluntary waiver.

It can be argued that the same is true of the category of confessions excluded by the Edwards rule itself. I think that is so, but, as I have discussed above, the presumption of involuntariness is at least more plausible for that category. There is, in any event, a clear and rational line between that category and the present one, and I see nothing to be said for expanding upon a past mistake. Drawing a distinction between police-initiated inquiry before consultation with counsel and police-initiated inquiry after consultation with counsel is assuredly more reasonable than other distinctions Edwards has already led us into — such as the distinction between police-initiated inquiry after assertion of the Miranda right to remain silent, and police-initiated inquiry after assertion of the Miranda right to counsel, see Kamisar, The Edwards and Bradshaw Cases: The Court Giveth and the Court Taketh Away, in 5 The Supreme Court: Trends and Developments 157 (J. Choper, Y. Kamisar, & L. Tribe eds. 1984) ("[E]ither Mosley was wrongly decided or Edwards was"); or the distinction between what is needed to prove waiver of the Miranda right to have counsel present and what is needed to prove waiver of rights found in the Constitution.

The rest of the Court's arguments can be answered briefly. The suggestion that it will either be impossible or ethically impermissible to determine whether a "consultation" between the suspect and his attorney has occurred is alarmist. Since, as I have described above, the main purpose of the consultation requirement is to eliminate the suspect's feeling of isolation and to assure him the presence of legal assistance, any discussion between him and an attorney whom he asks to contact, or who is provided to him, in connection with his arrest, will suffice. The precise content of the discussion is irrelevant.

As for the "irony" that "the suspect whose counsel is prompt would lose the protection of Edwards, while the one whose counsel is dilatory would not," ante, at 9: There seems to me no irony in applying a special protection only when it is needed. The Edwards rule is premised on an (already tenuous) assumption about the suspect's psychological state, and when the event of consultation renders that assumption invalid the rule should no longer apply. One searching for ironies in the state of our law should consider, first, the irony created by Edwards itself: The suspect in custody who says categorically "I do not wish to discuss this matter" can be asked to change his mind; but if he should say, more tentatively, "I do not think I should discuss this matter without my attorney present" he can no longer be approached. To that there is added, by today's decision, the irony that it will be far harder for the state to establish a knowing and voluntary waiver of Fifth Amendment rights by a prisoner who has already consulted with counsel than by a newly arrested suspect.

Finally, the Court's concern that "Edwards' protection could pass in and out of existence multiple times," ante, at 8, does not apply to the resolution of the matter I have proposed. Edwards would cease to apply, permanently, once consultation with counsel has occurred.

* * *

Today's extension of the Edwards prohibition is the latest stage of prophylaxis built upon prophylaxis, producing a veritable fairyland castle of imagined constitutional restriction upon law enforcement. This newest tower, according to the Court, is needed to avoid "inconsisten[cy] with [the] purpose" of Edwards' prophylactic rule, ante, at 8, which was needed to protect Miranda's prophylactic right to have counsel present, which was needed to protect the right against compelled self-incrimination found (at last!) in the Constitution.

It seems obvious to me that, even in Edwards itself but surely in today's decision, we have gone far beyond any genuine concern about suspects who do not know their right to remain silent, or who have been coerced to abandon it. Both holdings are explicable, in my view, only as an effort to protect suspects against what is regarded as their own folly. The sharp-witted criminal would know better than to confess; why should the dull-witted suffer for his lack of mental endowment? Providing him an attorney at every stage where he might be induced or persuaded (though not coerced) to incriminate himself will even the odds. Apart from the fact that this protective enterprise is beyond our authority under the Fifth Amendment or any other provision of the Constitution, it is unwise. The procedural protections of the Constitution protect the guilty as well as the innocent, but it is not their objective to set the guilty free. That some clever criminals may employ those protections to their advantage is poor reason to allow criminals who have not done so to escape justice.

Thus, even if I were to concede that an honest confession is a foolish mistake, I would welcome rather than reject it; a rule that foolish mistakes do not count would leave most offenders not only unconvicted but undetected. More fundamentally, however, it is wrong, and subtly corrosive of our criminal justice system, to regard an honest confession as a "mistake." While every person is entitled to stand silent, it is more virtuous for the wrongdoer to admit his offense and accept the punishment he deserves. Not only for society, but for the wrongdoer himself, "admissio[n] of guilt . . ., if not coerced, [is] inherently desirable," United States v. Washington, 431 U.S. 181, 187 (1977), because it advances the goals of both "justice and rehabilitation." Michigan v. Tucker, 417 U. S., at 448, n. 23 (emphasis added). A confession is rightly regarded by the sentencing guidelines as warranting a reduction of sentence, because it "demonstrates a recognition and affirmative acceptance of personal responsibility for . . . criminal conduct," U. S. Sentencing Commission, Guidelines Manual 3E1.1 (1988), which is the beginning of reform. We should, then, rejoice at an honest confession, rather than pity the "poor fool" who has made it; and we should regret the attempted retraction of that good act, rather than seek to facilitate and encourage it. To design our laws on premises contrary to these is to abandon belief in either personal responsibility or the moral claim of just government to obedience. Cf. Caplan, Questioning Miranda, 38 Vand. L. Rev. 1417, 1471-1473 (1985). Today's decision is misguided, it seems to me, in so readily exchanging, for marginal, super-Zerbst protection against genuinely compelled testimony, investigators' ability to urge, or even ask, a person in custody to do what is right.

Although today's decision neither follows the law nor produces desirable concrete results, it certainly has great symbolic value: Justice Scalia's dissent in Edmonson v. Leesville Concrete Co. (June 3, 1991)

Justice Scalia, dissenting.

I join Justice O'Connor's dissent, which demonstrates that today's opinion is wrong in principle. I write to observe that it is also unfortunate in its consequences.

The concrete benefits of the Court's newly discovered constitutional rule are problematic. It will not necessarily be a net help rather than hindrance to minority litigants in obtaining racially diverse juries. In criminal cases, Batson v. Kentucky, 476 U.S. 79 (1986), already prevents the prosecution from using race-based strikes. The effect of today's decision (which logically must apply to criminal prosecutions) will be to prevent the defendant from doing so — so that the minority defendant can no longer seek to prevent an all-white jury, or to seat as many jurors of his own race as possible. To be sure, it is ordinarily more difficult to prove race-based strikes of white jurors, but defense counsel can generally be relied upon to do what we say the Constitution requires. So in criminal cases, today's decision represents a net loss to the minority litigant. In civil cases that is probably not true — but it does not represent an unqualified gain either. Both sides have peremptory challenges, and they are sometimes used to assure rather than to prevent a racially diverse jury.

The concrete costs of today's decision, on the other hand, are not at all doubtful; and they are enormous. We have now added to the duties of already-submerged state and federal trial courts the obligation to assure that race is not included among the other factors (sex, age, religion, political views, economic status) used by private parties in exercising their peremptory challenges. That responsibility would be burden enough if it were not to be discharged through the adversary process; but of course it is. When combined with our decision this Term in Powers v. Ohio, 499 U.S. Z (1991), which held that the party objecting to an allegedly race-based peremptory challenge need not be of the same race as the challenged juror, today's decision means that both sides, in all civil jury cases, no matter what their race (and indeed, even if they are artificial entities such as corporations), may lodge racial-challenge objections and, after those objections have been considered and denied, appeal the denials — with the consequence, if they are successful, of having the judgments against them overturned. Thus, yet another complexity is added to an increasingly Byzantine system of justice that devotes more and more of its energy to sideshows and less and less to the merits of the case. Judging by the number of Batson claims that have made their way even as far as this Court under the pre-Powers regime, it is a certainty that the amount of judges' and lawyers' time devoted to implementing today's newly discovered Law of the Land will be enormous. That time will be diverted from other matters, and the overall system of justice will certainly suffer. Alternatively, of course, the States and Congress may simply abolish peremptory challenges, which would cause justice to suffer in a different fashion. See Holland v. Illinois, 493 U.S. 474, 484 (1990).

Although today's decision neither follows the law nor produces desirable concrete results, it certainly has great symbolic value. To overhaul the doctrine of state action in this fashion — what a magnificent demonstration of this institution's uncompromising hostility to race-based judgments, even by private actors! The price of the demonstration is, alas, high, and much of it will be paid by the minority litigants who use our courts. I dissent.

Legislative History: Justice Scalia's concurrence in United States v. R. L. C. (March 24, 1992)

Justice Scalia, with whom Justice Kennedy and Justice Thomas join, concurring in part and concurring in the judgment.

In my view it is not consistent with the rule of lenity to construe a textually ambiguous penal statute against a criminal defendant on the basis of legislative history. Because Justice Souter's opinion assumes the contrary, I join only Parts I, II A, and III, and concur in the judgment.

The Court begins its analysis, quite properly, by examining the language of 18 U.S.C. § 5037(c)(1)(B) — which proves to be ambiguous. Reasonable doubt remains, the Court concludes, as to whether the provision refers (i) to the maximum punishment that could be imposed if the juvenile were being sentenced under the United States Sentencing Guidelines (15-21 months) or (ii) to the maximum punishment authorized by the statute defining the offense, see 18 U.S.C. § 1112(a) (36 months). Ante, at 5. With that conclusion I agree — and that conclusion should end the matter. The rule of lenity, in my view, prescribes the result when a criminal statute is ambiguous: the more lenient interpretation must prevail.

Yet the plurality continues. Armed with its warrant of textual ambiguity, the plurality conducts a search of § 5037's legislative history to determine whether that clarifies the statute. Happily for this defendant, the plurality's extratextual inquiry is benign: It uncovers evidence that the "better understood" reading of § 5037 is the more lenient one. Ante, at 12. But this methodology contemplates as well a different ending, one in which something said in a Committee Report causes the criminal law to be stricter than the text of the law displays. According to the plurality, "we resort to the [rule of lenity] only when `a reasonable doubt persists about a statute's intended scope even after resort to "the language and structure, legislative history, and motivating policies" of the statute.'" Ante, at 12 (quoting Moskal v. United States, 498 U.S. ___ (1990) (slip op., at 4)) (citation omitted). I doubt that Moskal accurately characterizes the law in this area, and I am certain that its treatment of "the venerable rule of lenity," ante, at 12, does not venerate the important values the old rule serves.

The Moskal formulation of the rule, in approving reliance on a statute's "motivating policies" (an obscure phrase), seems contrary to our statement in Hughey v. United States, 495 U.S. 411, 422 (1990), that "[e]ven [where] the statutory language . . . [is] ambiguous, longstanding principles of lenity . . . preclude our resolution of the ambiguity against [the criminal defendant] on the basis of general declarations of policy in the statute and legislative history." And insofar as Moskal requires consideration of legislative history at all, it compromises what we have described to be purposes of the lenity rule. "[A] fair warning," we have said, "should be given to the world in language that the common world will understand, of what the law intends to do if a certain line is passed. To make the warning fair, so far as possible the line should be clear." McBoyle v. United States, 283 U.S. 25, 27 (1931). "[T]he rule of lenity ensures that criminal statutes will provide fair warning concerning conduct rendered illegal." Liparota v. United States, 471 U.S. 419, 427 (1985). It may well be true that in most cases the proposition that the words of the United States Code or the Statutes at Large give adequate notice to the citizen is something of a fiction, see McBoyle, supra, at 27, albeit one required in any system of law; but necessaryfiction descends to needless farce when the public is charged even with knowledge of Committee Reports.

Moskal's mode of analysis also disserves the rule of lenity's other purpose: assuring that the society, through its representatives, has genuinely called for the punishment to be meted out. "[B]ecause of the seriousness of criminal penalties, and because criminal punishment usually represents the moral condemnation of the community, legislatures and not courts should define criminal activity." United States v. Bass, 404 U.S. 336, 348 (1971). See also Liparota, supra, at 427; United States v. Wiltberger, 5 Wheat. 76, 95 (1820). The rule reflects, as the plurality acknowledges, " ` "the instinctive distaste against men languishing in prison unless the lawmaker has clearly said they should." ' " Ante, at 12 (quoting Bass, supra, at 348, and H. Friendly, Benchmarks 209 (1967)). But legislative history can never provide assurance against that unacceptable result. After all, "[a] statute is a statute," ante, at 12, n. 5, and no matter how "authoritative" the history may be — even if it is that veritable Rosetta Stone of legislative archaeology, a crystal clear Committee Report — one can never be sure that the legislators who voted for the text of the bill were aware of it. The only thing that was authoritatively adopted for sure was the text of the enactment; the rest is necessarily speculation. Where it is doubtful whether the text includes the penalty, the penalty ought not be imposed. "[T]he moral condemnation of the community," Bass, supra, at 348, is no more reflected in the views of a majority of a single committee of congressmen (assuming, of course, they have genuinely considered what their staff has produced) than it is reflected in the views of a majority of an appellate court; we should feel no less concerned about "men languishing in prison" at the direction of the one than of the other.

We have in a number of cases other than Moskal done what the plurality has done here: inquired into legislative history and invoked it to support or at least permit themore lenient reading. But only once, to my knowledge, have we relied on legislative history to "clarify" a statute, explicitly found to be facially ambiguous, against the interest of a criminal defendant. In Dixson v. United States, 465 U.S. 482, 500-501, n. 19 (1984), the Court relied on legislative history to determine that defendants, officers of a corporation responsible for administering federal block grants, were "public officials" within the meaning of 18 U.S.C. § 201(a). The opinion does not trouble to discuss the "fair warning" or "condemnation of the community" implications of its decision, and both of the cases it cites in supposed support of its holding found the statute at hand not to be facially ambiguous. See United States v. Moore, 423 U.S. 122, 131 (1975) ("By its terms § 841 reaches `any person" and "does not exempt (as it could have) `all registrants' or `all persons registered under this Act' "); United States v. Brown, 333 U.S. 18, 22 (1948) ("The legislation reflects an unmistakable intention to provide punishment for escape or attempted escape to be superimposed upon the punishment meted out for previous offenses. This appears from the face of the statute itself"). I think Dixson weak (indeed, utterly unreasoned) foundation for a rule of construction that permits legislative history to satisfy the ancient requirement that criminal statutes speak "plainly and unmistakably," United States v. Gradwell, 243 U.S. 476, 485 (1917); see also Bass, supra, at 348.

In sum, I would not embrace, as the plurality does, the Moskal formulation of this canon of construction, lest lower courts take the dictum to heart. I would acknowledge the tension in our precedents, the absence of an examination of the consequences of the Moskal mode of analysis, and the consequent conclusion that Moskal may not be good law.

Racial imbalances are not government-mandated segregation: Justice Scalia's concurrence in Freeman v. Pitts (March 31, 1992)

JUSTICE SCALIA, concurring.

The District Court in the present case found that the imbalances in student assignment were attributable to private demographic shifts, rather than governmental action. Without disturbing this finding, and without finding that revision of student assignments was necessary to remedy some other unlawful government action, the Court of Appeals ordered DeKalb County to institute massive busing and other programs to achieve integration. The Court convincingly demonstrates that this cannot be reconciled with our cases, and I join its opinion.

Our decision will be of great assistance to the citizens of DeKalb County, who, for the first time since 1969, will be able to run their own public schools, at least so far as student assignments are concerned. It will have little effect, however, upon the many other school districts throughout the country that are still being supervised by federal judges, since it turns upon the extraordinarily rare circumstance of a finding that no portion of the current racial imbalance is a remnant of prior de jure discrimination. While it is perfectly appropriate for the Court to decide this case on that narrow basis, we must resolve -- if not today, then soon -- what is to be done in the vast majority of other districts where, though our cases continue to profess that judicial oversight of school operations is a temporary expedient, democratic processes remain suspended, with no prospect of restoration, 38 years after Brown v. Board of Education, 347 U.S. 483 (1954).

Almost a quarter-century ago, in Green v. School Bd., New Kent County, 391 U.S. 430, 437-438 (1968), this Court held that school systems which had been enforcing de jure segregation at the time of Brown I had not merely an obligation to assign students and resources on a race-neutral basis, but also an "affirmative duty" to "desegregate," that is, to achieve, insofar as practicable, racial balance in their schools. This holding has become such a part of our legal fabric that there is a tendency, reflected in the Court of Appeals opinion in this case, to speak as though the Constitution requires such racial balancing. Of course it does not: the Equal Protection Clause reaches only those racial imbalances shown to be intentionally caused by the State. As the Court reaffirms today, if "desegregation" (i.e., racial balancing) were properly to be ordered in the present case, it would be not because the extant racial imbalance in the DCSS public schools offends the Constitution, but rather because that imbalance is a "lingering effect" of the pre-1969 de jure segregation that offended the Constitution. For all our talk about "unitary status," "release from judicial supervision," and "affirmative duty to desegregate," the sole question in school desegregation cases (absent an allegation that current policies are intentionally discriminatory) is one of remedies for past violations.

Identifying and undoing the effects of some violations of the law is easy. Where, for example, a tax is found to have been unconstitutionally imposed, calculating the funds derived from that tax (which must be refunded), and distinguishing them from the funds derived from other taxes (which may be retained), is a simple matter. That is not so with respect to the effects of unconstitutionally operating a legally segregated school system; they are uncommonly difficult to identify and to separate from the effects of other causes. But one would not know that from our instructions to the lower courts on this subject, which tend to be at a level of generality that assumes facile reduction to specifics. "[Desegregation] decrees," we have said,

exceed appropriate limits if they are aimed at eliminating a condition that does not violate the Constitution or does not flow from such a violation,

Board of Education of Oklahoma City Public Schools v. Dowell, 498 U.S. 237, 247 (1991); Milliken v. Bradley, 433 U.S. 267, 282 (1977). We have never sought to describe how one identifies a condition as the effluent of a violation, or how a "vestige" or a "remnant" of past discrimination is to be recognized. Indeed, we have not even betrayed an awareness that these tasks are considerably more difficult than calculating the amount of taxes unconstitutionally paid. It is time for us to abandon our studied disregard of that obvious truth, and to adjust our jurisprudence to its reality.

Since parents and school boards typically want children to attend schools in their own neighborhood,

[t]he principal cause of racial and ethnic imbalance in . . . public schools across the country -- North and South -- is the imbalance in residential patterns.

Austin Independent School Dist. v. United States, 429 U.S. 990, 994 (1976) (Powell, J., concurring). That imbalance in residential patterns, in turn,

>doubtless result[s] from a melange of past happenings prompted by economic considerations, private discrimination, discriminatory school assignments, or a desire to reside near people of one's own race or ethnic background.

Columbus Bd. of Education v. Penick, 443 U.S. 449, 512 (1979) (REHNQUIST, J., dissenting); see also Pasadena City Bd. of Education v. Spangler, 427 U.S. 424, 435-437 (1976). Consequently, residential segregation "is a national, not a southern, phenomenon" which exists

>"regardless of the character of local laws and policies, and regardless of the extent of other forms of segregation or discrimination."

Keyes v. School Dist. No. 1, Denver, Colo., 413 U.S. 189, 223, and n. 9 (1973) (Powell, J., concurring in part and dissenting in part), quoting K. Taueber, Negroes in Cities 36 (1965).

Racially imbalanced schools are, hence, the product of a blend of public and private actions, and any assessment that they would not be segregated, or would not be as segregated, in the absence of a particular one of those factors is guesswork. It is similarly guesswork, of course, to say that they would be segregated, or would be as segregated, in the absence of one of those factors. Only in rare cases such as this one and Spangler, see 427 U.S. at 435-437, where the racial imbalance had been temporarily corrected after the abandonment of de jure segregation, can it be asserted with any degree of confidence that the past discrimination is no longer playing a proximate role. Thus, allocation of the burden of proof foreordains the result in almost all of the "vestige of past discrimination" cases. If, as is normally the case under our Equal Protection jurisprudence (and in the law generally), we require the plaintiffs to establish the asserted facts entitling them to relief -- that the racial imbalance they wish corrected is at least in part the vestige of an old de jure system -- the plaintiffs will almost always lose. Conversely, if we alter our normal approach and require the school authorities to establish the negative -- that the imbalance is not attributable to their past discrimination -- the plaintiffs will almost always win. See Penick, supra, 443 U.S. at 471 (Stewart, J., concurring in result).

Since neither of these alternatives is entirely palatable, an observer unfamiliar with the history surrounding this issue might suggest that we avoid the problem by requiring only that the school authorities establish a regime in which parents are free to disregard neighborhood school assignment, and to send their children (with transportation paid) to whichever school they choose. So long as there is free choice, he would say, there is no reason to require that the schools be made identical. The constitutional right is equal racial access to schools, not access to racially equal schools; whatever racial imbalances such a free choice system might produce would be the product of private forces. We apparently envisioned no more than this in our initial post-Brown cases. [n1] It is also the approach we actually adopted in Bazemore v. Friday, 478 U.S. 385, 407-409 (1986), which concerned remedies for prior de jure segregation of State university-operated clubs and services.

But we ultimately charted a different course with respect to public elementary and secondary schools. We concluded in Green that a "freedom of choice" plan was not necessarily sufficient, 391 U.S. at 439-440, and later applied this conclusion to all jurisdictions with a history of intentional segregation:

"Racially neutral" assignment plans proposed by school authorities to a district court may be inadequate; such plans may fail to counteract the continuing effects of past school segregation resulting from discriminatory location of school sites or distortion of school size in order to achieve or maintain an artificial racial separation. When school authorities present a district court with a "loaded game board," affirmative action in the form of remedial altering of attendance zones is proper to achieve truly nondiscriminatory assignments.

Swann v. Charlotte-Mecklenburg Bd. of Education, 402 U.S. 1, 28 (1971). Thus began judicial recognition of an "affirmative duty" to desegregate, id. at 15; Green, supra, at 437-438, achieved by allocating the burden of negating causality to the defendant. Our post-Green cases provide that, once state-enforced school segregation is shown to have existed in a jurisdiction in 1954, there arises a presumption, effectively irrebuttable (because the school district cannot prove the negative), that any current racial imbalance is the product of that violation, at least if the imbalance has continuously existed, see, e. g., Swann, supra, at 26; Keyes, 413 U.S. at 209-210.

In the context of elementary and secondary education, the presumption was extraordinary in law, but not unreasonable in fact.

Presumptions normally arise when proof of one fact renders the existence of another fact "so probable that it is sensible and timesaving to assume the truth of [the inferred] fact . . . until the adversary disproves it."

NLRB v. Curtin Matheson Scientific, Inc., 494 U.S. 775, 788-789 (1990), quoting E. Cleary, McCormick on Evidence §343, p. 969 (3d ed. 1984). The extent and recency of the prior discrimination, and the improbability that young children (or their parents) would use "freedom of choice" plans to disrupt existing patterns "warrant[ed] a presumption [that] schools that are substantially disproportionate in their racial composition" were remnants of the de jure system. Swann, supra, at 26.

But granting the merits of this approach at the time of Green, it is now 25 years later. "From the very first, federal supervision of local school systems was intended as a temporary measure to remedy past discrimination." Dowell, 498 U.S. at 247 (emphasis added). We envisioned it as temporary partly because "[n]o single tradition in public education is more deeply rooted than local control over the operation of schools," Milliken v. Bradley, 418 U.S. 717, 741 (1974) (Milliken I), and because no one's interest is furthered by subjecting the Nation's educational system to "judicial tutelage for the indefinite future," Dowell, supra, at 249; see also Dayton Bd. of Education v. Brinkman, 433 U.S. 406, 410 (1977); Spangler v. Pasadena City Bd. of Education, 611 F. 2d 1239, 1245, n. 5 (1979) (Kennedy, J., concurring). But we also envisioned it as temporary, I think, because the rational basis for the extraordinary presumption of causation simply must dissipate as the de jure system and the school boards who produced it recede further into the past. Since a multitude of private factors has shaped school systems in the years after abandonment of de jure segregation -- normal migration, population growth (as in this case), "white flight" from the inner cities, increases in the costs of new facilities -- the percentage of the current makeup of school systems attributable to the prior, government-enforced discrimination has diminished with each passing year, to the point where it cannot realistically be assumed to be a significant factor.

At some time, we must acknowledge that it has become absurd to assume, without any further proof, that violations of the Constitution dating from the days when Lyndon Johnson was President, or earlier, continue to have an appreciable effect upon current operation of schools. We are close to that time. While we must continue to prohibit, without qualification, all racial discrimination in the operation of public schools, and to afford remedies that eliminate not only the discrimination but its identified consequences, we should consider laying aside the extraordinary, and increasingly counterfactual, presumption of Green. We must soon revert to the ordinary principles of our law, of our democratic heritage, and of our educational tradition: that plaintiffs alleging equal protection violations must prove intent and causation, and not merely the existence of racial disparity, see Bazemore, supra, at 407-409 (WHITE, J., concurring); Washington v. Davis, 426 U.S. 229, 245 (1976); that public schooling, even in the South, should be controlled by locally elected authorities acting in conjunction with parents, see, e. g., Dowell, supra, at 248; Dayton, supra, at 410; Milliken I, supra, at 741-742; and that it is "desirable" to permit pupils to attend "schools nearest their homes," Swann, 402 U.S. at 28.

1. See, e.g., Cooper v. Aaron, 358 U.S. 1, 7 (1958) ("[O]bedience to the duty of desegregation would require the immediate general admission of Negro children . . . at particular schools"), Goss v. Board of Education of Knoxville, 373 U.S. 683, 687 (1963) (holding unconstitutional a minority-to-majority transfer policy which was unaccompanied by a policy allowing majority-to-minority transfers, but noting that, "if the transfer provisions were made available to all students, regardless of their race and regardless as well of the racial composition of the school to which he requested transfer, we would have an entirely different case. Pupils could then, at their option (or that of their parents), choose, entirely free of any imposed racial considerations, to remain in the school of their zone or transfer to another").

No traditions can violate the establishment clause: Justice Scalia's dissent in Lee v. Weisman (June 24, 1992)

JUSTICE SCALIA, with whom THE CHIEF JUSTICE, JUSTICE WHITE, and JUSTICE THOMAS join, dissenting.

Three Terms ago, I joined an opinion recognizing that the Establishment Clause must be construed in light of the

[g]overnment policies of accommodation, acknowledgment, and support for religion [that] are an accepted part of our political and cultural heritage.

That opinion affirmed that "the meaning of the Clause is to be determined by reference to historical practices and understandings." It said that

[a] test for implementing the protections of the Establishment Clause that, if applied with consistency, would invalidate longstanding traditions cannot be a proper reading of the Clause.

Allegheny County v. Greater Pittsburgh ACLU, 492 U.S. 573, 657, 670 (1989) (KENNEDY, J., concurring in judgment in part and dissenting in part).

These views, of course, prevent me from joining today's opinion, which is conspicuously bereft of any reference to history. In holding that the Establishment Clause prohibits invocations and benedictions at public school graduation ceremonies, the Court -- with nary a mention that it is doing so -- lays waste a tradition that is as old as public school graduation ceremonies themselves, and that is a component of an even more longstanding American tradition of nonsectarian prayer to God at public celebrations generally. As its instrument of destruction, the bulldozer of its social engineering, the Court invents a boundless, and boundlessly manipulable, test of psychological coercion, which promises to do for the Establishment Clause what the Durham rule did for the insanity defense. See Durham v. United States, 94 U.S.App.D.C. 228, 214 F.2d 862 (1954). Today's opinion shows more forcefully than volumes of argumentation why our Nation's protection, that fortress which is our Constitution, cannot possibly rest upon the changeable philosophical predilections of the Justices of this Court, but must have deep foundations in the historic practices of our people.

I

Justice Holmes' aphorism that "a page of history is worth a volume of logic," New York Trust Co. v. Eisner, 256 U.S. 345, 349 (1921), applies with particular force to our Establishment Clause jurisprudence. As we have recognized, our interpretation of the Establishment Clause should "compor[t] with what history reveals was the contemporaneous understanding of its guarantees." Lynch v. Donnelly, 465 U.S. 668, 673 (1984).

[T]he line we must draw between the permissible and the impermissible is one which accords with history and faithfully reflects the understanding of the Founding Fathers.

Abington School District v. Schempp, 374 U.S. 203, 294 (1963) (Brennan, J., concurring).

[H]istorical evidence sheds light not only on what the draftsmen intended the Establishment Clause to mean, but also on how they thought that Clause applied

to contemporaneous practices. Marsh v. Chambers, 463 U.S. 783, 790 (1983). Thus,

[t]he existence from the beginning of the Nation's life of a practice, [while] not conclusive of its constitutionality . . ., is a fact of considerable import in the interpretation of the Establishment Clause. Walz v. Tax Comm'n of New York City, 397 U.S. 664, 681 (1970) (Brennan, J., concurring).

The history and tradition of our Nation are replete with public ceremonies featuring prayers of thanksgiving and petition. Illustrations of this point have been amply provided in our prior opinions, see, e.g., Lynch, supra, 465 U.S. at 465 U.S. 674"]674-678; Marsh, supra, 463 U.S. at 786-788; see also Wallace v. Jaffree, 472 U.S. 38, 100-103 (1985) (REHNQUIST, J., dissenting); 674-678; Marsh, supra, 463 U.S. at 786-788; see also Wallace v. Jaffree, 472 U.S. 38, 100-103 (1985) (REHNQUIST, J., dissenting); Engel v. Vitale, 370 U.S. 421, 446-450, and n. 3 (1962) (Stewart, J., dissenting), but since the Court is so oblivious to our history as to suggest that the Constitution restricts "preservation and transmission of religious beliefs . . . to the private sphere," ante at 589, it appears necessary to provide another brief account.

From our Nation's origin, prayer has been a prominent part of governmental ceremonies and proclamations. The Declaration of Independence, the document marking our birth as a separate people, "appeal[ed] to the Supreme Judge of the world for the rectitude of our intentions" and avowed "a firm reliance on the protection of divine Providence." In his first inaugural address, after swearing his oath of office on a Bible, George Washington deliberately made a prayer a part of his first official act as President:

it would be peculiarly improper to omit in this first official act my fervent supplications to that Almighty Being who rules over the universe, who presides in the councils of nations, and whose providential aids can supply every human defect, that His benediction may consecrate to the liberties and happiness of the people of the United States a Government instituted by themselves for these essential purposes.

Inaugural Addresses of the Presidents of the United States 2 (1989). Such supplications have been a characteristic feature of inaugural addresses ever since. Thomas Jefferson, for example, prayed in his first inaugural address:

may that Infinite Power which rules the destinies of the universe lead our councils to what is best, and give them a favorable issue for your peace and prosperity.

Id. at 17. In his second inaugural address, Jefferson acknowledged his need for divine guidance and invited his audience to join his prayer:

I shall need, too, the favor of that Being in whose hands we are, who led our fathers, as Israel of old, from their native land and planted them in a country flowing with all the necessaries and comforts of life; who has covered our infancy with His providence and our riper years with His wisdom and power, and to whose goodness I ask you to join in supplications with me that He will so enlighten the minds of your servants, guide their councils, and prosper their measures that whatsoever they do shall result in your good, and shall secure to you the peace, friendship, and approbation of all nations.

Id. at 22-23. Similarly, James Madison, in his first inaugural address, placed his confidence in the guardianship and guidance of that Almighty Being whose power regulates the destiny of nations, whose blessings have been so conspicuously dispensed to this rising Republic, and to whom we are bound to address our devout gratitude for the past, as well as our fervent supplications and best hopes for the future.

Id. at 28. Most recently, President Bush, continuing the tradition established by President Washington, asked those attending his inauguration to bow their heads, and made a prayer his first official act as President. Id. at 346.

Our national celebration of Thanksgiving likewise dates back to President Washington. As we recounted in Lynch,

The day after the First Amendment was proposed, Congress urged President Washington to proclaim

a day of public thanksgiving and prayer, to be observed by acknowledging with grateful hearts the many and signal favours of Almighty God.

President Washington proclaimed November 26, 1789, a day of thanksgiving to

offe[r] our prayers and supplications to the Great Lord and Ruler of Nations, and beseech him to pardon our national and other transgressions. . . .

465 U.S. at 675, n. 2 (citations omitted). This tradition of Thanksgiving Proclamations -- with their religious theme of prayerful gratitude to God -- has been adhered to by almost every President. Id. at 675, and nn. 2 and 3; Wallace v. Jaffree, supra, 472 U.S. at 100-103 (REHNQUIST, J., dissenting).

The other two branches of the Federal Government also have a long-established practice of prayer at public events. As we detailed in Marsh, Congressional sessions have opened with a chaplain's prayer ever since the First Congress. 463 U.S. at 787-788. And this Court's own sessions have opened with the invocation "God save the United States and this Honorable Court" since the days of Chief Justice Marshall. 1 C. Warren, The Supreme Court in United States History 469 (1922).

In addition to this general tradition of prayer at public ceremonies, there exists a more specific tradition of invocations and benedictions at public school graduation exercises. By one account, the first public high school graduation ceremony took place in Connecticut in July. 1868 -- the very month, as it happens, that the Fourteenth Amendment (the vehicle by which the Establishment Clause has been applied against the States) was ratified -- when

15 seniors from the Norwich Free Academy marched in their best Sunday suits and dresses into a church hall and waited through majestic music and long prayers.

Brodinsky, Commencement Rites Obsolete? Not At All, A 10-Week Study Shows, 10 Updating School Board Policies, No. 4, p. 3 (Apr.1979). As the Court obliquely acknowledges in describing the "customary features" of high school graduations, ante at 583, and as respondents do not contest, the invocation and benediction have long been recognized to be "as traditional as any other parts of the [school] graduation program and are widely established." H. McKown, Commencement Activities 56 (1931); see also Brodinsky, supra, at 5.

II

The Court presumably would separate graduation invocations and benedictions from other instances of public "preservation and transmission of religious beliefs" on the ground that they involve "psychological coercion." I find it a sufficient embarrassment that our Establishment Clause jurisprudence regarding holiday displays, see Allegheny County v. Greater Pittsburgh ACLU, 492 U.S. 573 (1989), has come to "requir[e] scrutiny more commonly associated with interior decorators than with the judiciary." American Jewish Congress v. Chicago, 827 F.2d 120, 129 (Easterbrook, J., dissenting). But interior decorating is a rock-hard science compared to psychology practiced by amateurs. A few citations of "[r]esearch in psychology" that have no particular bearing upon the precise issue here, ante at 593, cannot disguise the fact that the Court has gone beyond the realm where judges know what they are doing. The Court's argument that state officials have "coerced" students to take part in the invocation and benediction at graduation ceremonies is, not to put too fine a point on it, incoherent.

The Court identifies two "dominant facts" that it says dictate its ruling that invocations and benedictions at public school graduation ceremonies violate the Establishment Clause. Ante at 586. Neither of them is, in any relevant sense, true.

A

The Court declares that students' "attendance and participation in the [invocation and benediction] are, in a fair and real sense, obligatory." Ibid. But what exactly is this "fair and real sense"? According to the Court, students at graduation who want "to avoid the fact or appearance of participation," ante at 588, in the invocation and benediction are psychologically obligated by "public pressure, as well as peer pressure, . . . to stand as a group or, at least, maintain respectful silence" during those prayers. Ante at 593. This assertion -- the very linchpin of the Court's opinion -- is almost as intriguing for what it does not say as for what it says. It does not say, for example, that students are psychologically coerced to bow their heads, place their hands in a Durer-like prayer position, pay attention to the prayers, utter "Amen," or in fact pray. (Perhaps further intensive psychological research remains to be done on these matters.) It claims only that students are psychologically coerced "to stand . . . or, at least, maintain respectful silence." Ibid. (emphasis added). Both halves of this disjunctive (both of which must amount to the fact or appearance of participation in prayer if the Court's analysis is to survive on its own terms) merit particular attention.

To begin with the latter: the Court's notion that a student who simply sits in "respectful silence" during the invocation and benediction (when all others are standing) has somehow joined -- or would somehow be perceived as having joined -- in the prayers is nothing short of ludicrous. We indeed live in a vulgar age. But surely "our social conventions," ibid., have not coarsened to the point that anyone who does not stand on his chair and shout obscenities can reasonably be deemed to have assented to everything said in his presence. Since the Court does not dispute that students exposed to prayer at graduation ceremonies retain (despite "subtle coercive pressures," ante at 588) the free will to sit, cf. ante at 593, there is absolutely no basis for the Court's decision. It is fanciful enough to say that "a reasonable dissenter," standing head erect in a class of bowed heads, "could believe that the group exercise signified her own participation or approval of it," ibid. It is beyond the absurd to say that she could entertain such a belief while pointedly declining to rise.

But let us assume the very worst, that the nonparticipating graduate is "subtly coerced" . . . to stand! Even that half of the disjunctive does not remotely establish a "participation" (or an "appearance of participation") in a religious exercise. The Court acknowledges that, "in our culture, standing . . . can signify adherence to a view or simple respect for the views of others." Ibid. (Much more often the latter than the former, I think, except perhaps in the proverbial town meeting, where one votes by standing.) But if it is a permissible inference that one who is standing is doing so simply out of respect for the prayers of others that are in progress, then how can it possibly be said that a "reasonable dissenter . . . could believe that the group exercise signified her own participation or approval"? Quite obviously, it cannot. I may add, moreover, that maintaining respect for the religious observances of others is a fundamental civic virtue that government (including the public schools) can and should cultivate -- so that, even if it were the case that the displaying of such respect might be mistaken for taking part in the prayer, I would deny that the dissenter's interest in avoiding even the false appearance of participation constitutionally trumps the government's interest in fostering respect for religion generally.

The opinion manifests that the Court itself has not given careful consideration to its test of psychological coercion. For if it had, how could it observe, with no hint of concern or disapproval, that students stood for the Pledge of Allegiance, which immediately preceded Rabbi Gutterman's invocation? Ante at 583. The government can, of course, no more coerce political orthodoxy than religious orthodoxy. West Virginia Board of Education v. Barnette, 319 U.S. 624, 642 (1943). Moreover, since the Pledge of Allegiance has been revised since Barnette to include the phrase "under God," recital of the Pledge would appear to raise the same Establishment Clause issue as the invocation and benediction. If students were psychologically coerced to remain standing during the invocation, they must also have been psychologically coerced, moments before, to stand for (and thereby, in the Court's view, take part in or appear to take part in) the Pledge. Must the Pledge therefore be barred from the public schools (both from graduation ceremonies and from the classroom)? In Barnette, we held that a public school student could not be compelled to recite the Pledge; we did not even hint that she could not be compelled to observe respectful silence -- indeed, even to stand in respectful silence -- when those who wished to recite it did so. Logically, that ought to be the next project for the Court's bulldozer.

I also find it odd that the Court concludes that high school graduates may not be subjected to this supposed psychological coercion, yet refrains from addressing whether "mature adults" may. Ante at 593. I had thought that the reason graduation from high school is regarded as so significant an event is that it is generally associated with transition from adolescence to young adulthood. Many graduating seniors, of course, are old enough to vote. Why, then, does the Court treat them as though they were first-graders? Will we soon have a jurisprudence that distinguishes between mature and immature adults?

B

The other "dominant fac[t]" identified by the Court is that "[s]tate officials direct the performance of a formal religious exercise" at school graduation ceremonies. Ante at 586. "Direct[ing] the performance of a formal religious exercise" has a sound of liturgy to it, summoning up images of the principal directing acolytes where to carry the cross, or showing the rabbi where to unroll the Torah. A Court professing to be engaged in a "delicate and fact-sensitive" line-drawing, ante at 597, would better describe what it means as "prescribing the content of an invocation and benediction." But even that would be false. All the record shows is that principals of the Providence public schools, acting within their delegated authority, have invited clergy to deliver invocations and benedictions at graduations; and that Principal Lee invited Rabbi Gutterman, provided him a two-page flyer, prepared by the National Conference of Christians and Jews, giving general advice on inclusive prayer for civic occasions, and advised him that his prayers at graduation should be nonsectarian. How these facts can fairly be transformed into the charges that Principal Lee "directed and controlled the content of [Rabbi Gutterman's] prayer," ante at 588, that school officials "monitor prayer," ante at 590, and attempted to "'compose official prayers,'" ante at 588, and that the "government involvement with religious activity in this case is pervasive," ante at 587, is difficult to fathom. The Court identifies nothing in the record remotely suggesting that school officials have ever drafted, edited, screened or censored graduation prayers, or that Rabbi Gutterman was a mouthpiece of the school officials.

These distortions of the record are, of course, not harmless error: without them, the Court's solemn assertion that the school officials could reasonably be perceived to be "enforc[ing] a religious orthodoxy," ante at 592, would ring as hollow, as it ought.

III

The deeper flaw in the Court's opinion does not lie in its wrong answer to the question whether there was state-induced "peer-pressure" coercion; it lies, rather, in the Court's making violation of the Establishment Clause hinge on such a precious question. The coercion that was a hallmark of historical establishments of religion was coercion of religious orthodoxy and of financial support by force of law and threat of penalty. Typically, attendance at the state church was required; only clergy of the official church could lawfully perform sacraments; and dissenters, if tolerated, faced an array of civil disabilities. L. Levy, The Establishment Clause 4 (1986). Thus, for example, in the colony of Virginia, where the Church of England had been established, ministers were required by law to conform to the doctrine and rites of the Church of England; and all persons were required to attend church and observe the Sabbath, were tithed for the public support of Anglican ministers, and were taxed for the costs of building and repairing churches. Id. at 3-4.

The Establishment Clause was adopted to prohibit such an establishment of religion at the federal level (and to protect state establishments of religion from federal interference). I will further acknowledge for the sake of argument that, as some scholars have argued, by 1790, the term "establishment" had acquired an additional meaning -- "financial support of religion generally, by public taxation" -- that reflected the development of "general or multiple" establishments, not limited to a single church. Id. at 8-9. But that would still be an establishment coerced by force of law. And I will further concede that our constitutional tradition, from the Declaration of Independence and the first inaugural address of Washington, quoted earlier, down to the present day, has, with a few aberrations, see Holy Trinity Church v. United States, 143 U.S. 457 (1892), ruled out of order government-sponsored endorsement of religion -- even when no legal coercion is present, and indeed even when no ersatz, "peer-pressure" psycho-coercion is present -- where the endorsement is sectarian, in the sense of specifying details upon which men and women who believe in a benevolent, omnipotent Creator and Ruler of the world, are known to differ (for example, the divinity of Christ). But there is simply no support for the proposition that the officially sponsored nondenominational invocation and benediction read by Rabbi Gutterman -- with no one legally coerced to recite them -- violated the Constitution of the United States. To the contrary, they are so characteristically American they could have come from the pen of George Washington or Abraham Lincoln himself.

Thus, while I have no quarrel with the Court's general proposition that the Establishment Clause "guarantees that government may not coerce anyone to support or participate in religion or its exercise," ante at 587, I see no warrant for expanding the concept of coercion beyond acts backed by threat of penalty -- a brand of coercion that, happily, is readily discernible to those of us who have made a career of reading the disciples of Blackstone, rather than of Freud. The Framers were indeed opposed to coercion of religious worship by the National Government; but, as their own sponsorship of nonsectarian prayer in public events demonstrates, they understood that "[s]peech is not coercive; the listener may do as he likes." American Jewish Congress v. Chicago, 827 F.2d at 132 (Easterbrook, J., dissenting).

This historical discussion places in revealing perspective the Court's extravagant claim that the State has, "for all practical purposes," ante at 589, and "in every practical sense," ante at 598, compelled students to participate in prayers at graduation. Beyond the fact, stipulated to by the parties, that attendance at graduation is voluntary, there is nothing in the record to indicate that failure of attending students to take part in the invocation or benediction was subject to any penalty or discipline. Contrast this with, for example, the facts of Barnette: schoolchildren were required by law to recite the Pledge of Allegiance; failure to do so resulted in expulsion, threatened the expelled child with the prospect of being sent to a reformatory for criminally inclined juveniles, and subjected his parents to prosecution (and incarceration) for causing delinquency. 319 U.S. at 629-630.

To characterize the "subtle coercive pressures," ante at 588, allegedly present here as the "practical" equivalent of the legal sanctions in Barnette is . . . well, let me just say it is not a "delicate and fact-sensitive" analysis.

The Court relies on our "school prayer" cases, Engel v. Vitale, 370 U.S. 421"] 370 U.S. 421 (1962), and 370 U.S. 421 (1962), and Abington School District v. Schempp, 374 U.S. 203"] 374 U.S. 203 (1963). Ante at 592. But whatever the merit of those cases, they do not support, much less compel, the Court's psychojourney. In the first place, Engel and Schempp do not constitute an exception to the rule, distilled from historical practice, that public ceremonies may include prayer, see supra at 633-636; rather, they simply do not fall within the scope of the rule (for the obvious reason that school instruction is not a public ceremony). Second, we have made clear our understanding that school prayer occurs within a framework in which legal coercion to attend school (i.e., coercion under threat of penalty) provides the ultimate backdrop. In Schempp, for example, we emphasized that the prayers were "prescribed as part of the curricular activities of students who are required by law to attend school." 374 U.S. at 223 (emphasis added). Engel's suggestion that the school prayer program at issue there -- which permitted students "to remain silent or be excused from the room," 370 U.S. at 430 -- involved "indirect coercive pressure," id. at 431, should be understood against this backdrop of legal coercion. The question whether the opt-out procedure in Engel sufficed to dispel the coercion resulting from the mandatory attendance requirement is quite different from the question whether forbidden coercion exists in an environment utterly devoid of legal compulsion. And finally, our school prayer cases turn in part on the fact that the classroom is inherently an instructional setting, and daily prayer there -- where parents are not present to counter "the students' emulation of teachers as role models and the children's susceptibility to peer pressure," 374 U.S. 203 (1963). Ante at 592. But whatever the merit of those cases, they do not support, much less compel, the Court's psychojourney. In the first place, Engel and Schempp do not constitute an exception to the rule, distilled from historical practice, that public ceremonies may include prayer, see supra at 633-636; rather, they simply do not fall within the scope of the rule (for the obvious reason that school instruction is not a public ceremony). Second, we have made clear our understanding that school prayer occurs within a framework in which legal coercion to attend school (i.e., coercion under threat of penalty) provides the ultimate backdrop. In Schempp, for example, we emphasized that the prayers were "prescribed as part of the curricular activities of students who are required by law to attend school." 374 U.S. at 223 (emphasis added). Engel's suggestion that the school prayer program at issue there -- which permitted students "to remain silent or be excused from the room," 370 U.S. at 430 -- involved "indirect coercive pressure," id. at 431, should be understood against this backdrop of legal coercion. The question whether the opt-out procedure in Engel sufficed to dispel the coercion resulting from the mandatory attendance requirement is quite different from the question whether forbidden coercion exists in an environment utterly devoid of legal compulsion. And finally, our school prayer cases turn in part on the fact that the classroom is inherently an instructional setting, and daily prayer there -- where parents are not present to counter "the students' emulation of teachers as role models and the children's susceptibility to peer pressure," Edwards v. Aguillard, 482 U.S. 578, 584 (1987) -- might be thought to raise special concerns regarding state interference with the liberty of parents to direct the religious upbringing of their children:

> Families entrust public schools with the education of their children, but condition their trust on the understanding that the classroom will not purposely be used to advance religious views that may conflict with the private beliefs of the student and his or her family.

Ibid; see Pierce v. Society of Sisters, 268 U.S. 510, 534-535 (1925). Voluntary prayer at graduation -- a one-time ceremony at which parents, friends and relatives are present -- can hardly be thought to raise the same concerns.

IV

Our religion-clause jurisprudence has become bedeviled (so to speak) by reliance on formulaic abstractions that are not derived from, but positively conflict with, our long-accepted constitutional traditions. Foremost among these has been the so-called Lemon test, see Lemon v. Kurtzman, 403 U.S. 602, 612-613 (1971), which has received well-earned criticism from many members of this Court. See, e.g., Allegheny County, 492 U.S. at 655-656 (opinion of KENNEDY, J.); Edwards v. Aguillard, supra, 482 U.S. at 636-640 (1987) (SCALIA, J., dissenting); Wallace v. Jaffree, 472 U.S. at 108-112 (REHNQUIST J., dissenting); Aguilar v. Felton, 473 U.S. 402, 426-430 (1985) (O'CONNOR, J., dissenting); Roemer v. Maryland Bd. of Public Works, 426 U.S. 736, 768-769 (1976) (WHITE, J., concurring in judgment). The Court today demonstrates the irrelevance of Lemon by essentially ignoring it, see ante at 587, and the interment of that case may be the one happy byproduct of the Court's otherwise lamentable decision. Unfortunately, however, the Court has replaced Lemon with its psycho-coercion test, which suffers the double disability of having no roots whatever in our people's historic practice and being as infinitely expandable as the reasons for psychotherapy itself.

Another happy aspect of the case is that it is only a jurisprudential disaster, and not a practical one. Given the odd basis for the Court's decision, invocations and benedictions will be able to be given at public school graduations next June, as they have for the past century and a half, so long as school authorities make clear that anyone who abstains from screaming in protest does not necessarily participate in the prayers. All that is seemingly needed is an announcement, or perhaps a written insertion at the beginning of the graduation Program, to the effect that, while all are asked to rise for the invocation and benediction, none is compelled to join in them, nor will be assumed, by rising, to have done so. That obvious fact recited, the graduates and their parents may proceed to thank God, as Americans have always done, for the blessings He has generously bestowed on them and on their country.

* * * *

The reader has been told much in this case about the personal interest of Mr. Weisman and his daughter, and very little about the personal interests on the other side. They are not inconsequential. Church and state would not be such a difficult subject if religion were, as the Court apparently thinks it to be, some purely personal avocation that can be indulged entirely in secret, like pornography, in the privacy of one's room. For most believers, it is not that, and has never been. Religious men and women of almost all denominations have felt it necessary to acknowledge and beseech the blessing of God as a people, and not just as individuals, because they believe in the "protection of divine Providence," as the Declaration of Independence put it, not just for individuals but for societies; because they believe God to be, as Washington's first Thanksgiving Proclamation put it, the "Great Lord and Ruler of Nations." One can believe in the effectiveness of such public worship, or one can deprecate and deride it. But the longstanding American tradition of prayer at official ceremonies displays with unmistakable clarity that the Establishment Clause does not forbid the government to accommodate it.

The narrow context of the present case involves a community's celebration of one of the milestones in its young citizens' lives, and it is a bold step for this Court to seek to banish from that occasion, and from thousands of similar celebrations throughout this land, the expression of gratitude to God that a majority of the community wishes to make. The issue before us today is not the abstract philosophical question whether the alternative of frustrating this desire of a religious majority is to be preferred over the alternative of imposing "psychological coercion," or a feeling of exclusion, upon nonbelievers. Rather, the question is whether a mandatory choice in favor of the former has been imposed by the United States Constitution. As the age-old practices of our people show, the answer to that question is not at all in doubt.

I must add one final observation: the founders of our Republic knew the fearsome potential of sectarian religious belief to generate civil dissension and civil strife. And they also knew that nothing, absolutely nothing, is so inclined to foster among religious believers of various faiths a toleration -- no, an affection -- for one another than voluntarily joining in prayer together, to the God whom they all worship and seek. Needless to say, no one should be compelled to do that, but it is a shame to deprive our public culture of the opportunity, and indeed the encouragement, for people to do it voluntarily. The Baptist or Catholic who heard and joined in the simple and inspiring prayers of Rabbi Gutterman on this official and patriotic occasion was inoculated from religious bigotry and prejudice in a manner that can not be replicated. To deprive our society of that important unifying mechanism in order to spare the nonbeliever what seems to me the minimal inconvenience of standing, or even sitting in respectful nonparticipation, is as senseless in policy as it is unsupported in law.

For the foregoing reasons, I dissent.

Abortion: Justice Scalia's concurrence and dissent in Planned Parenthood of Southeastern Pa. v. Casey (June 29, 1992)

Justice Scalia, with whom the Chief Justice, Justice White, and Justice Thomas join, concurring in the judgment in part and dissenting in part.

My views on this matter are unchanged from those I set forth in my separate opinions in Webster v. Reproductive Health Services, 492 U.S. 490, 532 (1989) (Scalia, J., concurring in part and concurring in judgment), and Ohio v. Akron Center for Reproductive Health, 497 U.S. 502, 520 (1990) (Akron II) (Scalia, J., concurring). The States may, if they wish, permit abortion on demand, but the Constitution does not require them to do so. The permissibility of abortion, and the limitations upon it, are to be resolved like most important questions in our democracy: by citizens trying to persuade one another and then voting. As the Court acknowledges, "where reasonable people disagree the government can adopt one position or the other." Ante, at 8. The Court is correct in adding the qualification that

this "assumes a state of affairs in which the choice does not intrude upon a protected liberty," ante, at 9--but the crucial part of that qualification is the penultimate word. A State's choice between two positions on which reasonable people can disagree is constitutional even when (as is often the case) it intrudes upon a "liberty" in the absolute sense. Laws against bigamy, for example--which entire societies of reasonable people disagree with--intrude upon men and women's liberty to marry and live with one another. But bigamy happens not to be a liberty specially "protected" by the Constitution.

That is, quite simply, the issue in this case: not whether the power of a woman to abort her unborn child is a "liberty" in the absolute sense; or even whether it is a liberty of great importance to many women. Of course it is both. The issue is whether it is a liberty protected by the Constitution of the United States. I am sure it is not. I reach that conclusion not because of anything so exalted as my views concerning the "concept of existence, of meaning, of the universe, and of the mystery of human life." Ibid. Rather, I reach it for the same reason I reach the conclusion that bigamy is not constitutionally protected--because of two simple facts: (1) the Constitution says absolutely nothing about it, and (2) the longstanding traditions of American society have permitted it to be legally proscribed. [n.1] Akron II, supra, at 520 (Scalia, J., concurring).

The Court destroys the proposition, evidently meant to represent my position, that "liberty" includes "only those practices, defined at the most specific level, that were protected against government interference by other rules of law when the Fourteenth Amendment was ratified," ante, at 5 (citing Michael H. v. Gerald D., 491 U.S. 110, 127, n. 6 (1989) (opinion of Scalia, J.). That is not, however, what Michael H. says; it merely observes that, in defining "liberty," we may not disregard a specific, "relevant tradition protecting, or denying protection to, the asserted right," 491 U. S., at 127, n. 6. But the Court does not wish to be fettered by any such limitations on its preferences. The Court's statement that it is "tempting" to acknowledge the authoritativeness of tradition in order to "cur[b] the discretion of federal judges," ante, at 5, is of course rhetoric rather than reality; no government official is "tempted" to place restraints upon his own freedom of action, which is why Lord Acton did not say "Power tends to purify." The Court's temptation is in the quite opposite and more natural direction--towards systematically eliminating checks upon its own power; and it succumbs.

Beyond that brief summary of the essence of my position, I will not swell the United States Reports with repetition of what I have said before; and applying the rational basis test, I would uphold the Pennsylvania statute in its entirety. I must, however, respond to a few of the more outrageous arguments in today's opinion, which it is beyondhuman nature to leave unanswered. I shall discuss each of them under a quotation from the Court's opinion to which they pertain.

" The inescapable fact is that adjudication of substantive due process claims may call upon the Court in interpreting the Constitution to exercise that same capacity which by tradition courts always have exercised: reasoned judgment. "

Ante, at 7.

Assuming that the question before us is to be resolved at such a level of philosophical abstraction, in such isolation from the traditions of American society, as by simply applying "reasoned judgment," I do not see how that could possibly have produced the answer the Court arrived at in Roe v. Wade, 410 U.S. 113 (1973). Today's opinion describes the methodology of Roe, quite accurately, as weighing against the woman's interest the State's " `important and legitimate interest in protecting the potentiality of human life.' " Ante, at 28-29 (quoting Roe, supra, at 162). But "reasoned judgment" does not begin by begging the question, as Roe and subsequent cases unquestionably did by assuming that what the State is protecting is the mere "potentiality of human life." See, e. g., Roe, supra, at 162; Planned Parenthood of Central Mo. v. Danforth, 428 U.S. 52, 61 (1976); Colautti v. Franklin, 439 U.S. 379, 386 (1979); Akron v. Akron Center for Reproductive Health, Inc., 462 U.S. 416, 428 (1983) (Akron I); Planned Parenthood Assn. of Kansas City, Mo., Inc. v. Ashcroft, 462 U.S. 476, 482 (1983). The whole argument of abortion opponents is that what the Court calls the fetus and what others call the unborn child is a human life. Thus, whatever answer Roe came up with after conducting its "balancing" is bound to be wrong, unless it is correct that the human fetus is in some critical sense merely potentially human. There is of course no way to determine that as a legal matter; it is in fact a value judgment. Some societies have considered newbornchildren not yet human, or the incompetent elderly no longer so.

The authors of the joint opinion, of course, do not squarely contend that Roe v. Wade was a correct application of "reasoned judgment"; merely that it must be followed, because of stare decisis. Ante, at 11, 18-19, 29. But in their exhaustive discussion of all the factors that go into the determination of when stare decisis should be observed and when disregarded, they never mention "how wrong was the decision on its face?" Surely, if "[t]he Court's power lies . . . in its legitimacy, a product of substance and perception," ante, at 23, the "substance" part of the equation demands that plain error be acknowledged and eliminated. Roe was plainly wrong--even on the Court's methodology of "reasoned judgment," and even more so (of course) if the proper criteria of text and tradition are applied.

The emptiness of the "reasoned judgment" that produced Roe is displayed in plain view by the fact that, after more than 19 years of effort by some of the brightest (and most determined) legal minds in the country, after more than 10 cases upholding abortion rights in this Court, and after dozens upon dozens of amicus briefs submitted in this and other cases, the best the Court can do to explain how it is that the word "liberty" must be thought to include the right to destroy human fetuses is to rattle off a collection of adjectives that simply decorate a value judgment and conceal a political choice. The right to abort, we are told, inheres in "liberty" because it is among "a person's most basic decisions," ante, at 7; it involves a "most intimate and personal choic[e]," ante, at 9; it is "central to personal dignity and autonomy," ibid.; it "originate[s] within the zone of conscience and belief," ibid.; it is "too intimate and personal" for state interference, ante, at 10; it reflects "intimate views" of a "deep, personal character," ante, at 11; it involves "intimate relationships," and notions of "personal autonomy and bodily integrity," ante, at 15; and it concerns a particularly " `important decisio[n],' " ante, at 16 (citationomitted). [n.2] But it is obvious to anyone applying "reasoned judgment" that the same adjectives can be applied to many forms of conduct that this Court (including one of the Justices in today's majority, see Bowers v. Hardwick, 478 U.S. 186 (1986)) has held are not entitled to constitutional protection--because, like abortion, they are forms of conduct that have long been criminalized in American society. Those adjectives might be applied, for example, to homosexual sodomy, polygamy, adult incest, and suicide, all of which are equally "intimate" and "deep[ly] personal" decisions involving "personal autonomy and bodily integrity," and all of which can constitutionally be proscribed because it is our unquestionable constitutional tradition that they are proscribable. It is not reasoned judgment that supports the Court's decision; only personal predilection. Justice Curtis's warning is as timely today as it was 135 years ago:

"[W]hen a strict interpretation of the Constitution, according to the fixed rules which govern the interpretation of laws, is abandoned, and the theoretical opinions of individuals are allowed to control its meaning, we have no longer a Constitution; we are under the government of individual men, who for the time being have power to declare what the Constitution is, according to their own views of what it ought tomean." Dred Scott v. Sandford, 19 How. 393, 621 (1857) (Curtis, J., dissenting).

" Liberty finds no refuge in a jurisprudence of doubt. "

Ante, at 1.

One might have feared to encounter this august and sonorous phrase in an opinion defending the real Roe v. Wade, rather than the revised version fabricated today by the authors of the joint opinion. The shortcomings of Roe did not include lack of clarity: Virtually all regulation of abortion before the third trimester was invalid. But to come across this phrase in the joint opinion--which calls upon federal district judges to apply an "undue burden" standard as doubtful in application as it is unprincipled in origin--is really more than one should have to bear.

The joint opinion frankly concedes that the amorphous concept of "undue burden" has been inconsistently applied by the Members of this Court in the few brief years since that "test" was first explicitly propounded by Justice O'Connor in her dissent in Akron I, supra. See Ante, at 34. [n.3] Because the three Justices now wish to "set forth astandard of general application," the joint opinion announces that "it is important to clarify what is meant by an undue burden," ibid. I certainly agree with that, but I do not agree that the joint opinion succeeds in the announced endeavor. To the contrary, its efforts at clarification make clear only that the standard is inherently manipulable and will prove hopelessly unworkable in practice.

The joint opinion explains that a state regulation imposes an "undue burden" if it "has the purpose or effect of placing a substantial obstacle in the path of a woman seeking an abortion of a nonviable fetus." Ibid.; see also ante, at 35-36. An obstacle is "substantial," we are told, if it is "calculated[,] [not] to inform the woman's free choice, [but to] hinder it." Ante, at 34. [n.4] This latter statement cannotpossibly mean what it says. Any regulation of abortion that is intended to advance what the joint opinion concedes is the State's "substantial" interest in protecting unborn life will be "calculated [to] hinder" a decision to have an abortion. It thus seems more accurate to say that the joint opinion would uphold abortion regulations only if they do not unduly hinder the woman's decision. That, of course, brings us right back to square one: Defining an "undue burden" as an "undue hindrance" (or a "substantial obstacle") hardly "clarifies" the test. Consciously or not, the joint opinion's verbal shell game will conceal raw judicial policy choices concerning what is "appropriate" abortion legislation.

The ultimately standardless nature of the "undue burden" inquiry is a reflection of the underlying fact that the concept has no principled or coherent legal basis. As The Chief Justice points out, Roe's strict scrutiny standard "at least had a recognized basis in constitutional law at thetime Roe was decided," ante, at 22, while "[t]he same cannot be said for the `undue burden' standard, which is created largely out of whole cloth by the authors of the joint opinion," ibid. The joint opinion is flatly wrong in asserting that "our jurisprudence relating to all liberties save perhaps abortion has recognized" the permissibility of laws that do not impose an "undue burden." Ante, at 31. It argues that the abortion right is similar to other rights in that a law "not designed to strike at the right itself, [but which] has the incidental effect of making it more difficult or more expensive to [exercise the right,]" is not invalid. Ante, at 31-32. I agree, indeed I have forcefully urged, that a law of general applicability which places only an incidental burden on a fundamental right does not infringe that right, see R. A. V. v. St. Paul, 505 U. S. ___, ___ (1992) (slip op., at 11); Employment Division, Dept. of Human Resources of Ore. v. Smith, 494 U.S. 872, 878-882 (1990), but that principle does not establish the quite different (and quite dangerous) proposition that a law which directly regulates a fundamental right will not be found to violate the Constitution unless it imposes an "undue burden." It is that, of course, which is at issue here: Pennsylvania has consciously and directly regulated conduct that our cases have held is constitutionally protected. The appropriate analogy, therefore, is that of a state law requiring purchasers of religious books to endure a 24-hour waiting period, or to pay a nominal additional tax of 1¢. The joint opinion cannot possibly be correct in suggesting that we would uphold such legislation on the ground that it does not impose a "substantial obstacle" to the exercise of First Amendment rights. The "undue burden" standard is not at all the generally applicable principle the joint opinion pretends it to be; rather, it is a unique concept created specially for this case, to preserve some judicial foothold in this ill gotten territory. In claiming otherwise, the three Justices show their willingness to place all constitutional rights at risk in an effort to preserve what they deem the-central holding in Roe," ante, at 31.

The rootless nature of the "undue burden" standard, a phrase plucked out of context from our earlier abortion decisions, see n. 3, supra, is further reflected in the fact that the joint opinion finds it necessary expressly to repudiate the more narrow formulations used in Justice O'Connor's earlier opinions. Ante, at 35. Those opinions stated that a statute imposes an "undue burden" if it imposes "absolute obstacles or severe limitations on the abortion decision," Akron I, 462 U. S., at 464 (O'Connor, J., dissenting) (emphasis added); see also Thornburgh v. American College of Obstetricians and Gynecologists, 476 U.S. 747, 828 (1986) (O'Connor, J., dissenting). Those strong adjectives are conspicuously missing from the joint opinion, whose authors have for some unexplained reason now determined that a burden is "undue" if it merely imposes a "substantial" obstacle to abortion decisions. See, e. g., ante, at 53, 59. Justice O'Connor has also abandoned (again without explanation) the view she expressed in Planned Parenthood Assn. of Kansas City, Mo., Inc. v. Ashcroft, 462 U.S. 476 (1983) (dissenting opinion), that a medical regulation which imposes an "undue burden" could nevertheless be upheld if it "reasonably relate[s] to the preservation and protection of maternal health," id., at 505 (citation and internal quotation marks omitted). In today's version, even health measures will be upheld only "if they do not constitute an undue burden," ante, at 35 (emphasis added). Gone too is Justice O'Connor's statement that "the State possesses compelling interests in the protection of potential human life . . . throughout pregnancy," Akron I, supra, at 461 (emphasis added); see also Ashcroft, supra, at 505 (O'Connor, J., concurring in judgment in part and dissenting in part); Thornburgh, supra, at 828 (O'Connor, J., dissenting); instead, the State's interest in unborn human life is stealthily downgraded to a merely "substantial" or "profound" interest, ante, at 34, 36. (That had to be done, of course, since designating the interest as "compelling" throughout pregnancy would have been, shall we say, a "substantial obstacle" to the joint opinion's determined effort to reaffirm what it views as the "central holding" of Roe. See Akron I, 462 U. S., at 420, n. 1.) And "viability" is no longer the "arbitrary" dividing line previously decried by Justice O'Connor in Akron I, id., at 461; the Court now announces that "the attainment of viability may continue to serve as the critical fact," ante, at 18. [n.5] It is difficult to maintain the illusion that we are interpreting a Constitution rather than inventing one, when we amend its provisions so breezily.

Because the portion of the joint opinion adopting and describing the undue burden test provides no more useful guidance than the empty phrases discussed above, one must turn to the 23 pages applying that standard to the present facts for further guidance. In evaluating Pennsylvania's abortion law, the joint opinion relies extensively on the factual findings of the District Court, and repeatedly qualifies its conclusions by noting that they are contingent upon the record developed in this case. Thus, the joint opinion would uphold the 24-hour waiting period contained in the Pennsylvania statute's informed consent provision, 18 Pa. Cons. Stat. § 3205 (1990), because "the record evidence shows that in the vast majority of cases, a 24-hour delay does not create any appreciable health risk," ante, at 43. The three Justices therefore conclude that "on the record before us, . . . we are not convinced that the 24-hour waiting period constitutes an undue burden." Ante, at 44-45. The requirement that a doctor provide the information pertinent to informed consent would also be upheld because "there is no evidence on this record that [this requirement] would amount in practical terms to a substantial obstacle to a woman seeking an abortion," ante, at 42. Similarly, the joint opinion would uphold the reporting requirements of the Act, §§ 3207, 3214, because "there is no . . . showing on the record before us" that these requirements constitute a "substantial obstacle" to abortion decisions. Ante, at 59. But at the same time the opinion pointedly observes that these reporting requirements may increase the costs of abortions and that "at some point [that fact] could become a substantial obstacle," ibid. Most significantly, the joint opinion's conclusion that the spousal notice requirement of the Act, see § 3209, imposes an "undue burden" is based in large measure on the District Court's "detailed findings of fact," which the joint opinion sets out at great length. Ante, at 45-49.

I do not, of course, have any objection to the notion that, in applying legal principles, one should rely only upon the facts that are contained in the record or that are properly subject to judicial notice. [n.6] But what is remarkable about the joint opinion's fact intensive analysis is that it does notresult in any measurable clarification of the "undue burden" standard. Rather, the approach of the joint opinion is, for the most part, simply to highlight certain facts in the record that apparently strike the three Justices as particularly significant in establishing (or refuting) the existence of an undue burden; after describing these facts, the opinion then simply announces that the provision either does or does not impose a "substantial obstacle" or an "undue burden." See, e. g., ante, at 38, 42, 44-45, 45, 52, 53, 59. We do not know whether the same conclusions could have been reached on a different record, or in what respects the record would have had to differ before an opposite conclusion would have been appropriate. The inherently standardless nature of this inquiry invites the district judge to give effect to his personal preferences about abortion. By finding and relying upon the right facts, he can invalidate, it would seem, almost any abortion restriction that strikes him as "undue"--subject, of course, to the possibility of being reversed by a Circuit Court or Supreme Court that is as unconstrained in reviewing his decision as he was in making it.

To the extent I can discern any meaningful content in the "undue burden" standard as applied in the joint opinion, it appears to be that a State may not regulate abortion in such a way as to reduce significantly its incidence. The joint opinion repeatedly emphasizes that an important factor in the "undue burden" analysis is whether the regulation "prevent[s] a significant number of women from obtaining an abortion," ante, at 52; whether a "significant number of women . . . are likely to be deterred from procuring an abortion," ibid.; and whether the regulation often "deters" women from seeking abortions, ante, at 55-56. We are not told, however, what forms of "deterrence" are impermissible or what degree of success in deterrence is too much to be tolerated. If, for example, a State required a woman to read a pamphlet describing, with illustrations, the facts of fetal development before she could obtain an abortion, the effect of such legislation mightbe to "deter" a "significant number of women" from procuring abortions, thereby seemingly allowing a district judge to invalidate it as an undue burden. Thus, despite flowery rhetoric about the State's "substantial" and "profound" interest in "potential human life," and criticism of Roe for undervaluing that interest, the joint opinion permits the State to pursue that interest only so long as it is not too successful. As Justice Blackmun recognizes (with evident hope), ante, at 5, the "undue burden" standard may ultimately require the invalidation of each provision upheld today if it can be shown, on a better record, that the State is too effectively "express[ing] a preference for childbirth over abortion," ante, at 41. Reason finds no refuge in this jurisprudence of confusion.

" While we appreciate the weight of the arguments . . . that Roe should be overruled, the reservations any of us may have in reaffirming the central holding of Roe are outweighed by the explication of individual liberty we have given combined with the force of stare decisis. "

Ante, at 11.

The Court's reliance upon stare decisis can best be described as contrived. It insists upon the necessity of adhering not to all of Roe, but only to what it calls the "central holding." It seems to me that stare decisis ought to be applied even to the doctrine of stare decisis, and I confess never to have heard of this new, keep what you want and throw away the rest version. I wonder whether, as applied to Marbury v. Madison, 1 Cranch 137 (1803), for example, the new version of stare decisis would be satisfied if we allowed courts to review the constitutionality of only those statutes that (like the one in Marbury) pertain to the jurisdiction of the courts.

I am certainly not in a good position to dispute that the Court has saved the "central holding" of Roe, since to dothat effectively I would have to know what the Court has saved, which in turn would require me to understand (as I do not) what the "undue burden" test means. I must confess, however, that I have always thought, and I think a lot of other people have always thought, that the arbitrary trimester framework, which the Court today discards, was quite as central to Roe as the arbitrary viability test, which the

Court today retains. It seems particularly ungrateful to carve the trimester framework out of the core of Roe, since its very rigidity (in sharp contrast to the utter indeterminability of the "undue burden" test) is probably the only reason the Court is able to say, in urging stare decisis, that Roe "has in no sense proven `unworkable,' " ante, at 13. I suppose the Court is entitled to call a "cen tral holding" whatever it wants to call a "central holding"-- which is, come to think of it, perhaps one of the difficulties with this modified version of stare decisis. I thought I might note, however, that the following portions of Roe have not been saved:

"Under Roe, requiring that a woman seeking an abortion be provided truthful information about abortion before giving informed written consent is unconstitutional, if the information is designed to influence her choice, Thornburgh, 476 U. S., at 759-765; Akron I, 462 U. S., at 442-445. Under the joint opinion's "undue burden" regime (as applied today, at least) such a requirement is constitutional, ante, at 38-42.

"Under Roe, requiring that information be provided by a doctor, rather than by nonphysician counselors, is unconstitutional, Akron I, supra, at 446-449. Under the "undue burden" regime (as applied today, at least) it is not, ante, at 42.

"Under Roe, requiring a 24-hour waiting period between the time the woman gives her informed consent and the time of the abortion is unconstitutional, Akron I, supra, at 449-451. Under the "undue burden" regime (as applied today, at least) it is not, ante, at 43-45.

"Under Roe, requiring detailed reports that include demographic data about each woman who seeks an abortion and various information about each abortion is unconstitutional, Thornburgh, supra, at 765-768. Under the "undue burden" regime (as applied today, at least) it generally is not, ante, at 58-59.

" Where, in the performance of its judicial duties, the Court decides a case in such a way as to resolve the sort of intensely divisive controversy reflected in Roe . . ., its decision has a dimension that the resolution of the normal case does not carry. It is the dimension present whenever the Court's interpretation of the Constitution calls the contending sides of a national controversy to end their national division by accepting a common mandate rooted in the Constitution. "

Ante, at 24.

The Court's description of the place of Roe in the social history of the United States is unrecognizable. Not only did Roe not, as the Court suggests, resolve the deeply divisive issue of abortion; it did more than anything else to nourish it, by elevating it to the national level where it is infinitely more difficult to resolve. National politics were not plagued by abortion protests, national abortion lobbying, or abortion marches on Congress, before Roe v. Wade was decided. Profound disagreement existed among our citizens over the issue--as it does over other issues, such as the death penalty--but that disagreement was being worked out at the state level. As with many other issues, the division of sentiment within each State was not as closely balanced as it was among the population of the Nation as a whole, meaning not only that more people would be satisfied with the results of state by state resolution, but also that those results would be more stable. Pre-Roe, moreover, political compromise was possible.

Roe's mandate for abortion on demand destroyed thecompromises of the past, rendered compromise impossible for the future, and required the entire issue to be resolved uniformly, at the national level. At the same time, Roe created a vast new class of abortion consumers and abortion proponents by eliminating the moral opprobrium that had attached to the act. ("If the Constitution guarantees abor tion, how can it be bad?"-- not an accurate line of thought, but a natural one.) Many favor all of those developments, and it is not for me to say that they are wrong. But to portray Roe as the statesmanlike "settlement" of a divisive issue, a jurisprudential Peace of Westphalia that is worth preserving, is nothing less than Orwellian. Roe fanned into life an issue that has inflamed our national politics in general, and has obscured with its smoke the selection of Justices to this Court in particular, ever since. And by keeping us in the abortion umpiring business, it is the perpetuation of that disruption, rather than of any pax Roeana, that the Court's new majority decrees.

" [T]o overrule under fire . . . would subvert the Court's legitimacy . . . .

" To all those who will be . . . tested by following, the Court implicitly undertakes to remain steadfast . . . . The promise of constancy, once given, binds its maker for as long as the power to stand by the decision survives and . . . the commitment [is not] obsolete. . . .

" [The American people's] belief in themselves as . . . a people [who aspire to live according to the rule of law] is not readily separable from their understanding of the Court invested with the authority to decide their constitutional cases and speak before all others for their constitutional ideals. If the Court's legitimacy should be undermined, then, so would the country be in its very ability to see itself through its constitutional ideals. "

Ante, at 25-26.

The Imperial Judiciary lives. It is instructive to compare this Nietzschean vision of us unelected, life tenured judges--leading a Volk who will be "tested by following," and whose very "belief in themselves" is mystically bound up in their "understanding" of a Court that "speak[s] before all others for their constitutional ideals"--with the somewhat more modest role envisioned for these lawyers by the Founders.

"The judiciary . . . has . . . no direction either of the strength or of the wealth of the society, and can take no active resolution whatever. It may truly be said to have neither Force nor Will but merely judgment . . . ." The Federalist No. 78, pp. 393-394 (G. Wills ed. 1982).

Or, again, to compare this ecstasy of a Supreme Court in which there is, especially on controversial matters, no shadow of change or hint of alteration ("There is a limit to the amount of error that can plausibly be imputed to prior courts," ante, at 24), with the more democratic views of a more humble man:

"[T]he candid citizen must confess that if the policy of the Government upon vital questions affecting the whole people is to be irrevocably fixed by decisions of the Supreme Court, . . . the people will have ceased to be their own rulers, having to that extent practically resigned their Government into the hands of that eminent tribunal." A. Lincoln, First Inaugural Address (Mar. 4, 1861), reprinted in Inaugural Addresses of the Presidents of the United States, S. Doc. No. 101-10, p. 139 (1989).

It is particularly difficult, in the circumstances of the present decision, to sit still for the Court's lengthy lecture upon the virtues of "constancy," ante, at 26, of "remain[ing] steadfast," id., at 25, of adhering to "principle," id., passim. Among the five Justices who purportedly adhere to Roe, atmost three agree upon the principle that constitutes adherence (the joint opinion's "undue burden" standard)--and that principle is inconsistent with Roe, see 410 U. S., at 154-156. [n.7] To make matters worse, two of the three, in order thus to remain steadfast, had to abandon previously stated positions. See n. 4 supra; see supra, at 11 12. It is beyond me how the Court expects these accommodations to be accepted "as grounded truly in principle, not as compromises with social and political pressures having, as such, no bearing on the principled choices that the Court is obliged to make." Ante, at 23. The only principle the Court "adheres" to, it seems to me, is the principle that the Court must be seen as standing by Roe. That is not a principle of law (which is what I thought the Court was talking about), but a principle of Realpolitik--and a wrong one at that.

I cannot agree with, indeed I am appalled by, the Court's suggestion that the decision whether to stand by an erroneous constitutional decision must be strongly influenced--against overruling, no less--by the substantial and continuing public opposition the decision has generated. The Court's judgment that any other course would "subvert the Court's legitimacy" must be another consequence of reading the error filled history book that described the deeply divided country brought together by Roe. In my history book, the Court was covered with dishonor and deprived of legitimacy by Dred Scott v. Sandford, 19 How. 393 (1857), an erroneous (and widely opposed) opinion that it did not abandon, rather than by West Coast Hotel Co. v.Parrish, 300 U.S. 379 (1937), which produced the famous "switch in time" from the Court's erroneous (and widely opposed) constitutional opposition to the social measures of the New Deal. (Both Dred Scott and one line of the cases resisting the New Deal rested upon the concept of "substantive due process" that the Court praises and employs today. Indeed, Dred Scott was "very possibly the first application of substantive due process in the Supreme Court, the original precedent for Lochner v. New York and Roe v. Wade." D. Currie, The Constitution in the Supreme Court 271 (1985) (footnotes omitted).)

But whether it would "subvert the Court's legitimacy" or not, the notion that we would decide a case differently from the way we otherwise would have in order to show that we can stand firm against public disapproval is frightening. It is a bad enough idea, even in the head of someone like me, who believes that the text of the Constitution, and our traditions, say what they say and there is no fiddling with them. But when it is in the mind of a Court that believes the Constitution has an evolving meaning, see ante, at 6; that the Ninth Amendment's reference to "othe[r]" rights is not a disclaimer, but a charter for action, ibid.; and that the function of this Court is to "speak before all others for [the people's] constitutional ideals" unrestrained by meaningful text or tradition--then the notion that the Court must adhere to a decision for as long as the decision faces "great opposition" and the Court is "under fire" acquires a character of almost czarist arrogance. We are offended by these marchers who descend upon us, every year on the anniversary of Roe, to protest our saying that the Constitution requires what our society has never thought the Constitution requires. These people who refuse to be "tested by following" must be taught a lesson. We have no Cossacks, but at least we can stubbornly refuse to abandon an erroneous opinion that we might otherwise change--to show how little they intimidate us.

Of course, as the Chief Justice points out, we have beensubjected to what the Court calls "political pressure" by both sides of this issue. Ante, at 21. Maybe today's decision not to overrule Roe will be seen as buckling to pressure from that direction. Instead of engaging in the hopeless task of predicting public perception--a job not for lawyers but for political campaign managers--the Justices should do what is legally right by asking two questions: (1) Was Roe correctly decided? (2) Has Roe succeeded in producing a settled body of law? If the answer to both questions is no, Roe should undoubtedly be overruled.

In truth, I am as distressed as the Court is--and expressed my distress several years ago, see Webster, 492 U. S., at 535--about the %political pressure" directed to the Court: the marches, the mail, the protests aimed at inducing us to change our opinions. How upsetting it is, that so many of our citizens (good people, not lawless ones, on both sides of this abortion issue, and on various sides of other issues as well) think that we Justices should properly take into account their views, as though we were engaged not in ascertaining an objective law but in determining some kind of social consensus. The Court would profit, I think, from giving less attention to the fact of this distressing phenomenon, and more attention to the cause of it. That cause permeates today's opinion: a new mode of constitutional adjudication that relies not upon text and traditional practice to determine the law, but upon what the Court calls "reasoned judgment," ante, at 7, which turns out to be nothing but philosophical predilection and moral intuition. All manner of "liberties," the Court tells us, inhere in the Constitution and are enforceable by this Court--not just those mentioned in the text or established in the traditions of our society. Ante, at 5-6. Why even the Ninth Amendment--which says only that "[t]he enumeration in the Constitution of certain rights shall not be construed to deny or disparage others retained by the people"--is, despite our contrary understanding for almost 200 years, a literally boundless source of additional, unnamed, unhinted at-rights," definable and enforceable by us, through "reasoned judgment." Ante, at 6-7.

What makes all this relevant to the bothersome application of "political pressure" against the Court are the twin facts that the American people love democracy and the

American people are not fools. As long as this Court thought (and the people thought) that we Justices were doing essentially lawyers' work up here--reading text and discerning our society's traditional understanding of that text--the public pretty much left us alone. Texts and traditions are facts to study, not convictions to demonstrate about. But if in reality our process of constitutional adjudication consists primarily of making value judgments; if we can ignore a long and clear tradition clarifying an ambiguous text, as we did, for example, five days ago in declaring unconstitutional invocations and benedictions at public high school graduation ceremonies, Lee v. Weisman, 505 U. S. ____ (1992); if, as I say, our pronouncement of constitutional law rests primarily on value judgments, then a free and intelligent people's attitude towards us can be expected to be (ought to be) quite different. The people know that their value judgments are quite as good as those taught in any law school--maybe better. If, indeed, the "liberties" protected by the Constitution are, as the Court says, undefined and unbounded, then the people should demonstrate, to protest that we do not implement their values instead of ours. Not only that, but confirmation hearings for new Justices should deteriorate into question and answer sessions in which Senators go through a list of their constituents' most favored and most disfavored alleged constitutional rights, and seek the nominee's commitment to support or oppose them. Value judgments, after all, should be voted on, not dictated; and if our Constitution has somehow accidently committed them to the Supreme Court, at least we can have a sort of plebiscite each time a new nominee to that body is put forward. Justice Blackmun

> not only regards this prospect with equanimity, he solicits it, ante, at 22-23.
> * * *

There is a poignant aspect to today's opinion. Its length, and what might be called its epic tone, suggest that its authors believe they are bringing to an end a troublesome era in the history of our Nation and of our Court. "It is the dimension" of authority, they say, to "cal[l] the contending sides of national controversy to end their national division by accepting a common mandate rooted in the Constitution." Ante, at 24.

There comes vividly to mind a portrait by Emanuel Leutze that hangs in the Harvard Law School: Roger Brooke Taney, painted in 1859, the 82d year of his life, the 24th of his Chief Justiceship, the second after his opinion in Dred Scott. He is all in black, sitting in a shadowed red armchair, left hand resting upon a pad of paper in his lap, right hand hanging limply, almost lifelessly, beside the inner arm of the chair. He sits facing the viewer, and staring straight out. There seems to be on his face, and in his deep set eyes, an expression of profound sadness and disillusionment. Perhaps he always looked that way, even when dwelling upon the happiest of thoughts. But those of us who know how the lustre of his great Chief Justiceship came to be eclipsed by Dred Scott cannot help believing that he had that case--its already apparent consequences for the Court, and its soon to be played out consequences for the Nation--burning on his mind. I expect that two years earlier he, too, had thought himself "call[ing] the contending sides of national controversy to end their national division by accepting a common mandate rooted in the Constitution."

It is no more realistic for us in this case, than it was for him in that, to think that an issue of the sort they both involved--an issue involving life and death, freedom and subjugation--can be "speedily and finally settled" by the Supreme Court, as President James Buchanan in hisinaugural address said the issue of slavery in the territories would be. See Inaugural Addresses of the Presidents of the United States, S. Doc. No. 101-10, p. 126 (1989). Quite to the contrary, by foreclosing all democratic outlet for the deep passions this issue arouses, by banishing the issue from the political forum that gives all participants, even the losers, the satisfaction of a fair hearing and an honest fight, by continuing the imposition of a rigid national rule instead of allowing for regional differences, the Court merely prolongs and intensifies the anguish.

We should get out of this area, where we have no right to be, and where we do neither ourselves nor the country any good by remaining.

Notes to Justice Scalia's dissent in Planned Parenthood of Southeastern Pa. v. Casey (June 29, 1992)

1 The Court's suggestion, ante, at 5, that adherence to tradition would require us to uphold laws against interracial marriage is entirely wrong. Any tradition in that case was contradicted by a text--an Equal Protec tion Clause that explicitly establishes racial equality as a constitutional value. See Loving v. Virginia, 388 U.S. 1, 9 (1967) ("In the case at bar, . . . we deal with statutes containing racial classifications, and the fact of equal application does not immunize the statute from the very heavy burden of justification which the Fourteenth Amendment has traditionally required of state statutes drawn according to race"); see also id., at 13 (Stewart, J., concurring in judgment). The enterprise launched in Roe, by contrast, sought to establish--in the teeth of a clear, contrarytradition--a value found nowhere in the constitutional text.

There is, of course, no comparable tradition barring recognition of a "liberty interest" in carrying one's child to term free from state efforts to kill it. For that reason, it does not follow that the Constitution does not protect childbirth simply because it does not protect abortion. The Court's contention, ante, at 17, that the only way to protect childbirth is to protect abortion shows the utter bankruptcy of constitutional analysis deprived of tradition as a validating factor. It drives one to say that the only way to protect the right to eat is to acknowledge the constitutional right to starve oneself to death.

2 Justice Blackmun's parade of adjectives is similarly empty: Abortion is among "the most intimate and personal choices," ante, at 2-3; it is a matter "central to personal dignity and autonomy," ibid.; and it involves "personal decisions that profoundly affect bodily integrity, identity, and destiny," ante, at 6. Justice Stevens is not much less conclusory: The decision to choose abortion is a matter of "the highest privacy and the

most personal nature," ante, at 5; it involves a "difficult choice having serious and personal consequences of major importance to [a woman's] future," ibid.; the authority to make this "traumatic and yet empowering decisio[n]" is "an element of basic human dignity," ibid.; and it is "nothing less than a matter of conscience," ibid.

3 The joint opinion is clearly wrong in asserting, ante, at 32, that "the Court's early abortion cases adhered to" the "undue burden" standard. The passing use of that phrase in Justice Blackmun's opinion for the Court in Bellotti v. Baird, 428 U.S. 132, 147 (1976) (Bellotti I), was not by way of setting forth the standard of unconstitutionality, as Justice O'Connor's later opinions did, but by way of expressing the conclusion of unconstitutionality. Justice Powell for a time appeared to employ a variant of "undue burden" analysis in several nonmajority opinions, see, e. g., Bellotti v. Baird, 443 U.S. 622, 647 (1979) (plurality opinion of Powell, J.) (Bellotti II); Carey v. Population Services International, 431 U.S. 678, 705 (1977) (Powell, J., concurring in part and concurring in judgment), but he too ultimately rejected that standard in his opinion for the Court in Akron v. Akron Center for Reproductive Health, 462 U.S. 416, 420, n. 1 (1983) (Akron I). The joint opinion's reliance on Maher v. Roe, 432 U.S. 464, 473 (1977), and Harris v. McRae, 448 U.S. 297, 314 (1980), is entirely misplaced, since those cases did not involve regulationof abortion but mere refusal to fund it. In any event, Justice O'Connor's earlier formulations have apparently now proved unsatisfactory to the three Justices, who--in the name of stare decisis no less--today find it necessary to devise an entirely new version of "undue burden" analysis, see ante, at 35.

4 The joint opinion further asserts that a law imposing an undue burden on abortion decisions is not a "permissible" means of serving "legitimate" state interests. Ante, at 34-35. This description of the undue burden standard in terms more commonly associated with the rational basis test will come as a surprise even to those who have followed closely our wanderings in this forsaken wilderness. See, e. g., Akron I, supra, at 463 (O'Connor, J., dissenting) ("The `undue burden' . . . represents the required threshold inquiry that must be conducted before this Court can require a State to justify its legislative actions under the exacting `compelling state interest' standard"); see also Hodgson v. Minnesota, 497 U.S. 417, ___ (1990) (O'Connor, J., concurring in part and concurring in judgment in part); Thornburgh v. American College of Obstetricians and Gynecologists, 476 U.S. 747, 828 (1986) (O'Connor, J., dissenting). This confusing equation of the two standards is apparently designed to explain how one of the Justices who joined the plurality opinion in Webster v. Reproductive Health Services, 492 U.S. 490 (1989), which adopted the rational basis test, could join an opinion expressly adopting the undue burden test. See id., at 520 (rejecting the view that abortion is a "fundamental right," instead inquiring whether a law regulating the woman's "liberty interest" inabortion is "reasonably designed" to further "legitimate" state ends). The same motive also apparently underlies the joint opinion's erroneous citation of the plurality opinion in Ohio v. Akron Center for Reproductive Health, 497 U.S. 502, ___ (1990) (Akron II) (opinion of Kennedy, J.), as applying the undue burden test. See ante, at 34

(using this citation to support the proposition that "two of us"--i. e., two of the authors of the joint opinion--have previously applied this test). In fact, Akron II does not mention the undue burden standard until the conclusion of the opinion, when it states that the statute at issue "does not impose an undue, or otherwise unconstitutional, burden." 497 U. S., at 519 (emphasis added). I fail to see how anyone can think that saying a statute does not impose an unconstitutional burden under any standard, including the undue burden test, amounts to adopting the undue burden test as the exclusive standard. The Court's citation of Hodgson as reflecting Justice Kennedy's and Justice O'Connor's "shared premises," ante, at 35-36, is similarly inexplicable, since the word "undue" was never even used in the former's opinion in that case. I joined Justice Kennedy's opinions in both Hodgson and Akron II; I should be grateful, I suppose, that the joint opinion does not claim that I, too, have adopted the undue burden test.

5 Of course Justice O'Connor was correct in her former view. The arbitrariness of the viability line is confirmed by the Court's inability to offer any justification for it beyond the conclusory assertion that it is only at that point that the unborn child's life "can in reason and all fairness" be thought to override the interests of the mother, ante, at 28. Precisely why is it that, at the magical second when machines currently in use (though not necessarily available to the particular woman) are able to keep an unborn child alive apart from its mother, the creature is suddenly able (under our Constitution) to be protected by law, whereas before that magical second it was not? That makes no more sense than according infants legal protection only after the point when they can feed themselves.

6 The joint opinion is not entirely faithful to this principle, however. In approving the District Court's factual findings with respect to the spousal notice provision, it relies extensively on nonrecord materials, and in reliance upon them adds a number of factual conclusions of its own. Ante, at 49-52. Because this additional factfinding pertains to matters that surely are "subject to reasonable dispute," Fed. Rule Evid. 201(b), the joint opinion must be operating on the premise that these are "legislative" rather than "adjudicative" facts, see Rule 201(a). But if a court can find an undue burden simply by selectively string citing the right social science articles, I do not see the point of emphasizing or requiring "detailed factual findings" in the District Court.

7 Justice Blackmun's effort to preserve as much of Roe as possible leads him to read the joint opinion as more "constan[t]" and "steadfast" than can be believed. He contends that the joint opinion's "undue burden" standard requires the application of strict scrutiny to "all non de minimis" abortion regulations, ante, at 5, but that could only be true if a "substantial obstacle," ante, at 34 (joint opinion), were the same thing as a non de minimis obstacle--which it plainly is not.

In making life easier for ourselves we not appear to make it harder for the lower federal courts: Justice Scalia's concurrence in Herrera v. Collins (January 23, 1993)

Justice Scalia, with whom Justice Thomas joins, concurring.

We granted certiorari on the question whether it violates due process or constitutes cruel and unusual punishment for a State to execute a person who, having been convicted of murder after a full and fair trial, later alleges that newly discovered evidence shows him to be "actually innocent." I would have preferred to decide that question, particularly since, as the Court's discussion shows, it is perfectly clear what the answer is: There is no basis in text, tradition, or even in contemporary practice (if that were enough), for finding in the Constitution a right to demand judicial consideration of newly discovered evidence of innocence brought forward after conviction. In saying that such a right exists, the dissenters apply nothing but their personal opinions to invalidate the rules of more than two thirds of the States, and a Federal Rule of Criminal Procedure for which this Court itself is responsible. If the system that has been in place for 200 years (and remains widely approved) "shocks" the dissenters' consciences, post, at 1, perhaps they should doubt the calibration of their consciences, or, better still, the usefulness of "conscience shocking" as a legal test.

I nonetheless join the entirety of the Court's opinion, including the final portion (pages 26-28)--because there is no legal error in deciding a case by assuming arguendo that an asserted constitutional right exists, and because I can understand, or at least am accustomed to, the reluctance of the present Court to admit publicly that Our Perfect Constitution [n.1] lets stand any injustice, much less the execution of an innocent man who has received, though to no avail, all the process that our society has traditionally deemed adequate. With any luck, we shall avoid ever having to face this embarrassing question again, since it is improbable that evidence of innocence as convincing as today's opinion requires would fail to produce an executive pardon.

My concern is that in making life easier for ourselves we not appear to make it harder for the lower federal courts, imposing upon them the burden of regularly analyzing newly discovered evidence of innocence claims in capital cases (in which event such federal claims, it can confidently be predicted, will become routine and even repetitive). A number of Courts of Appeals have hitherto held, largely in reliance on our unelaborated statement in Townsend v. Sain, 372 U.S. 293, 317 (1963), that newly discovered evidence relevant only to a state prisoner's guilt or innocence is not a basis for federal habeas corpus relief. See, e. g., Boyd v. Puckett, 905 F. 2d 895, 896-897 (CA5), cert. denied, 498 U.S. 988 (1990); Stockton v. Virginia, 852 F. 2d 740, 749 (CA4 1988), cert. denied, 489 U.S. 1071 (1989); Swindle v. Davis, 846 F. 2d 706, 707 (CA11 1988) (per curiam); Byrd v. Armontrout, 880 F. 2d 1, 8 (CA8 1989), cert. denied, 494 U.S. 1019 (1990); Burks v. Egeler, 512 F. 2d 221, 230 (CA6), cert. denied, 423 U.S. 937 (1975). I do not understand it to be theimport of today's decision that those holdings are to be replaced with a strange regime that assumes permanently, though only "arguendo," that a constitutional right exists, and expends substantial judicial resources on that assumption. The Court's extensive and scholarly discussion of the question presented in the present case does nothing but support our statement in Townsend, and strengthen the validity of the holdings based upon it.

Notes

1 My reference is to an article by Professor Monaghan, which discusses the unhappy truth that not every problem was meant to be solved by the United States Constitution, nor can be. See Monaghan, Our Perfect Constitution, 56 N. Y. U. L. Rev. 353 (1981).

Ordinary meaning: Justice Scalia's dissent in Smith v. United States (June 1, 1993)

Justice Scalia, with whom Justice Stevens and Justice Souter join, dissenting.

In the search for statutory meaning, we give nontechnical words and phrases their ordinary meaning. See Chapman v. United States, 500 U. S. ___, ___ (1991) (slip op., at 7); Perrin v. United States, 444 U.S. 37, 42 (1979); Minor v. Mechanics Bank of Alexandria, 1 Pet. 46, 64 (1828). To use an instrumentality ordinarily means to use it for its intended purpose. When someone asks "Do you use a cane?" he is not inquiring whether you have your grandfather's silver handled walking stick on display in the hall; he wants to know whether you walk with a cane. Similarly, to speak of "using a firearm" is to speak of using it for its distinctive purpose, i.e., as a weapon. To be sure, "one can use a firearm in a number of ways," ante, at 7, including as an article of exchange, just as one can "use" a cane as a hall decoration--but that is not the ordinary meaning of "using" the one or the other. [n.1] The Court does not appear to grasp the distinction between how a word can be used and how it ordinarily is used. It would, indeed, be "both reasonable and normal to say that petitioner `used' his MAC-10 in his drug trafficking offense by trading it for cocaine." Ibid. It would also be reasonable and normal to say that he "used" it to scratch his head. When one wishes to describe the action of employing the instrument of a firearm for such unusual purposes, "use" is assuredly a verb one could select. But that says nothing about whether the ordinary meaning of the phrase "uses a firearm" embraces such extraordinary employments. It is unquestionably not reasonable and normal, I think, to say simply "do not use firearms" when one means to prohibit selling or scratching with them.

The normal usage is reflected, for example, in the United States Sentencing Guidelines, which provide for enhanced sentences when firearms are "discharged," "brandished, displayed, or possessed," or "otherwise used." See, e. g., United States Sentencing Commission, Guidelines Manual § 2B3.1(b)(2) (Nov. 1992). As to the latter term, the Guidelines say: " `Otherwise used' with reference to a dangerous weapon (including a firearm) means that the conduct did not amount to the discharge of a firearm but was more than brandishing, displaying, or possessing a firearm or other dangerous weapon." USSG § 1B1.1, comment., n. 1(g) (definitions). "Otherwise used" in this provision obviously means "otherwise used as a weapon." [n.2]

Given our rule that ordinary meaning governs, and given the ordinary meaning of "uses a firearm," it seems to me inconsequential that "the words `as a weapon' appear nowhere in the statute," ante, at 5; they are reasonably implicit. Petitioner is not, I think, seeking to introduce an "additional requirement" into the text, ante, at 6, but is simply construing the text according to its normal import.

The Court seeks to avoid this conclusion by referring to the next subsection of the statute, § 924(d), which does not employ the phrase "uses a firearm," but provides for the confiscation of firearms that are "used in" referenced offenses which include the crimes of transferring, selling, or transporting firearms in interstate commerce. The Court concludes from this that whenever the term appears in this statute, "use" of a firearm must include nonweapon use. See ante, at 10-12. I do not agree. We are dealing here not with a technical word or an "artfully defined" legal term, compare Dewsnup v. Timm, 502 U. S. ___, ___ (1992) (Scalia, J., dissenting) (slip op., at 2-4), but with common words that are, as I have suggested, inordinately sensitive to context. Just as adding the direct object "a firearm" to the verb "use" narrows the meaning of that verb (it can no longer mean "partake of"), so also adding the modifier "in the offense of transferring, selling, or transporting firearms" to the phrase "use a firearm" expands the meaning of that phrase (it then includes, as it previously would not, nonweapon use). But neither the narrowing nor the expansion should logically be thought to apply to all appearances of the affected word or phrase. Just as every appearance of the word "use" in the statute need not be given the narrow meaning that word acquires in the phrase "use a firearm," so also every appearance of the phrase "use a firearm" need not be given the expansive connotation that phrase acquires in the broader context "use a firearm in crimes such as unlawful sale of firearms." When, for example, the statute provides that its prohibition on certain transactions in firearms "shall not apply to the loan or rental of a firearm to any person for temporary use for lawful sporting purposes," 18 U.S.C. §§ 922(a)(5)(B), (b)(3)(B), I have no doubt that the "use" referred to is only use as a sporting weapon, and not the use of pawning the firearm to pay for a ski trip. Likewise when, in § 924(c)(1), the phrase "uses . . . a firearm" is not employed in a context that necessarily envisions the unusual "use" of a firearm as a commodity, the normally understood meaning of the phrase should prevail.

Another consideration leads to the same conclusion: § 924(c)(1) provides increased penalties not only for one who "uses" a firearm during and in relation to any crime of violence or drug trafficking crime, but also for one who "carries" a firearm in those circumstances. The interpretation I would give the language produces an eminently reasonable dichotomy between "using a firearm" (as a weapon) and "carrying a firearm" (which in the context "uses or carries a firearm" means carrying it in such manner as to be ready for use as a weapon). The Court's interpretation, by contrast, produces a strange dichotomy between "using a firearm for any purpose whatever, including barter," and "carrying a firearm." [n.3]

Finally, although the present prosecution was brought under the portion of § 924(c)(1) pertaining to use of a firearm "during and in relation to any . . . drug trafficking crime," I think it significant that that portion is affiliated with the pre-existing provision pertaining to use of a firearm "during and in relation to any crime of violence," rather than with the firearm trafficking offenses defined in § 922 and referenced in § 924(d). The word "use" in the "crime of violence" context has the unmistakable import of use as a weapon, and that import carries over, in my view, to the subsequently added phrase "or drug trafficking crime." Surely the word "use" means the same thing as to both, and surely the 1986 addition of "drug trafficking crime" would have been a peculiar way to expand its meaning (beyond "use as a weapon") for crimes of violence.

Even if the reader does not consider the issue to be as clear as I do, he must at least acknowledge, I think, that it is eminently debatable--and that is enough, under the rule of lenity, to require finding for the petitioner here. "At the very least, it may be said that the issue is subject to some doubt. Under these circumstances, we adhere to the familiar rule that, `where there is ambiguity in a criminal statute, doubts are resolved in favor of the defendant.' " Adamo Wrecking Co. v. United States, 434 U.S. 275, 284-285 (1978), quoting United States v. Bass, 404 U. S.

336, 348 (1971). [n.4]

For the foregoing reasons, I respectfully dissent.

Notes

1 The Court asserts that the "significant flaw" in this argument is that "to say that the ordinary meaning of `uses a firearm' includes using a firearm as a weapon" is quite different from saying that the ordinary meaning "also excludes any other use." Ante, at 6 (emphases in original). The two are indeed different--but it is precisely the latter that I assert to be true: The ordinary meaning of "uses a firearm" does not include using it as an article of commerce. I think it perfectly obvious, for example, that the objective falsity requirement for a perjury conviction would not be satisfied if a witness answered "no" to a prosecutor's inquiry whether he had ever "used a firearm," even though he had once sold his grandfather's Enfield rifle to a collector.

2 The Court says that it is "not persuaded that [its] construction of the phrase `uses . . . a firearm' will produce anomalous applications." Ante, at 9. But as proof it points only to the fact that § 924(c)(1) fortuitously contains other language--the requirement that the use be "during and in relation to any crime of violence or drug trafficking crime"--that happens to prevent untoward results. Ibid. That language does not, in fact, prevent all untoward results: Though it excludes an enhanced penalty for the burglar who scratches his head with the barrel of a gun, it requires one for the burglar who happens to use a gun handle, rather than a rock, to break the window affording him

entrance--hardly a distinction that ought to make a sentencing difference if the gun has no other connection to the crime. But in any event, an excuse that turns upon the language of § 924(c)(1) is good only for that particular statute. The Court cannot avoid "anomalous applications" when it applies its anomalous meaning of "use a firearm" in other contexts--for example, the Guidelines provision just described in text.

In a vain attempt to show the contrary, it asserts that the phrase "otherwise used" in the Guidelines means used for any other purpose at all (the Court's preferred meaning of "use a firearm"), so long as it is more %culpable" than brandishing. See ante, at 8. But whence does it derive that convenient limitation? It appears nowhere in the text--as well it should not, since the whole purpose of the Guidelines is to take out of the hands of individual judges determinations as to what is "more culpable" and "less culpable." The definition of "otherwise used" in the Guidelines merely says that it means "more than" brandishing and less than firing. The Court is confident that "scratching one's head" with a firearm is not "more than" brandishing it. See ante, at 9. I certainly agree--but only because the "more" use referred to is more use as a weapon. Reading the Guidelines as they are written (rather than importing the Court's deusex machina of a culpability scale), and interpreting "use a firearm" in the strange fashion the Court does, produces, see ante, at 8, a full seven point upward sentence adjustment for firing a gun at a storekeeper during a robbery; a mere five point adjustment for pointing the gun at the storekeeper (which falls within the Guidelines' definition of "brandished," see USSG § 1B1.1, comment., n. 1(c)); but an intermediate six%point adjustment for using the gun to pry open the cash register or prop open the door. Quite obviously ridiculous. When the Guidelines speak of "otherwise us[ing]" a firearm, they mean, in accordance with normal usage, otherwise "using" it as a weapon--for example, placing the gun barrel in the mouth of the storekeeper to intimidate him.

3 The Court responds to this argument by abandoning all pretense of giving the phrase "uses a firearm" even a permissible meaning, much less its ordinary one. There is no problem, the Court says, because it is not contending that "uses a firearm" means "uses for any purpose," only that it means "uses as a weapon or for trade." See ante, at 12-13. Unfortunately, that is not one of the options that our mother tongue makes available. "Uses a firearm" can be given a broad meaning ("uses for any purpose") or its more ordinary narrow meaning ("uses as a weapon"); but it can not possibly mean "uses as a weapon or for trade."

4 The Court contends that giving the language its ordinary meaning would frustrate the purpose of the statute, since a gun "can be converted instantaneously from currency to cannon," ante, at 17. Stretching language in order to write a more effective statute than Congress devised is not an exercise we should indulge in. But in any case, the ready ability to use a gun that is at hand as a weapon is perhaps one of the reasons the statute sanctions not only using a firearm, but carrying one. Here, however, the Government chose not to indict under that provision. See ante, at 4.

Like some ghoul in a late-night horror movie: Justice Scalia's concurrence in Lamb's Chapel v. Center Moriches Union Free School District (June 7, 1993)

JUSTICE SCALIA, with whom JUSTICE THOMAS joins, concurring in the judgment.

I join the Court's conclusion that the District's refusal to allow use of school facilities for petitioners' film viewing, while generally opening the schools for community activities, violates petitioners' First Amendment free speech rights (as does N.Y.Educ.Law § 414 (McKinney 1988 and Supp.1993), to the extent it compelled the District's denial, see ante at ___). I also agree with the Court that allowing Lamb's Chapel to use school facilities poses "no realistic danger" of a violation of the Establishment Clause, ante at ___, but I cannot accept most of its reasoning in this regard. The Court explains that the showing of petitioners' film on school property after school hours would not cause the community to "think that the District was endorsing religion or any particular creed," and further notes that access to school property would not violate the three-part test articulated in Lemon v. Kurtzman, 403 U.S. 602 (1971). Ante at ___.

As to the Court's invocation of the Lemon test: like some ghoul in a late-night horror movie that repeatedly sits up in its grave and shuffles abroad after being repeatedly killed and buried, Lemon stalks our Establishment Clause jurisprudence once again, frightening the little children and school attorneys of Center Moriches Union Free School District. Its most recent burial, only last Term, was, to be sure, not fully six-feet under: our decision in Lee v. Weisman, 505 U.S. ___ (1992), conspicuously avoided using the supposed "test," but also declined the invitation to repudiate it. Over the years, however, no fewer than five of the currently sitting Justices have, in their own opinions, personally driven pencils through the creature's heart (the author of today's opinion repeatedly), and a sixth has joined an opinion doing so. See, e.g., Weisman, supra, 505 U.S. at ___ (SCALIA, J., joined by, inter alios, THOMAS, J., dissenting); Allegheny County v. American Civil Liberties Union, Greater Pittsburgh Chapter, 492 U.S. 573, 655-657 (1989) (KENNEDY, J., concurring in judgment in part and dissenting in part); Corporation of Presiding Bishop of Church of Jesus Christ of Latter-day Saints v. Amos, 483 U.S. 327, 346-349 (1987) (O'CONNOR, J., concurring); Wallace v. Jaffree, 472 U.S. 38, 107-113 (1985) (REHNQUIST, J., dissenting); id. at 90-91 (WHITE, J., dissenting); School Dist. of Grand Rapids v. Ball, 473 U.S. 373, 400 (1985) (WHITE, J., dissenting); Widmar v. Vincent, 454 U.S. 263, 282 (1981) (WHITE, J., dissenting); New York v. Cathedral Academy, 434 U.S. 125, 134-135 (1977) (WHITE, J., dissenting); Roemer v. Maryland Bd. of Public Works, 426 U.S. 736, 768 (1976) (WHITE, J., concurring in judgment); Committee for Public Education & Religious Liberty v. Nyquist, 413 U.S. 756, 820 (1973) (WHITE, J., dissenting).

The secret of the Lemon test's survival, I think, is that it is so easy to kill. It is there to scare us (and our audience) when we wish it to do so, but we can command it to return to the tomb at will. See, e.g., Lynch v. Donnelly, 465 U.S. 668, 679 (1984) (noting instances in which Court has not applied Lemon test). When we wish to strike down a practice it forbids, we invoke it, see, e.g., Aguilar v. Fenton, 473 U.S. 402 (1985) (striking down state remedial education program administered in part in parochial schools); when we wish to uphold a practice it forbids, we ignore it entirely, see Marsh v. Chambers, 463 U.S. 783 (1983) (upholding state legislative chaplains). Sometimes, we take a middle course, calling its three prongs "no more than helpful signposts," Hunt v. McNair, 413 U.S. 734, 741 (1973). Such a docile and useful monster is worth keeping around, at least in a somnolent state; one never knows when one might need him.

For my part, I agree with the long list of constitutional scholars who have criticized Lemon and bemoaned the strange Establishment Clause geometry of crooked lines and wavering shapes its intermittent use has produced. See, e.g., Choper, The Establishment Clause and Aid to Parochial Schools -- An Update, 75 Cal.L.Rev. 5 (1987); Marshall, "We Know It When We See It": The Supreme Court and Establishment, 59 S.Cal.L.Rev. 495 (1986); McConnell, Accommodation of Religion, 1985 S.Ct. Rev. 1; Kurland, The Religion Clauses and the Burger Court, 34 Cath.U.L.Rev. 1 (1984); R. Cord, Separation of Church and State (1982); Choper, The Religion Clauses of the First Amendment: Reconciling the Conflict, 41 U.Pitt.L.Rev. 673 (1980). I will decline to apply Lemon -- whether it validates or invalidates the government action in question -- and therefore cannot Join the opinion of the Court today. [*]

I cannot join for yet another reason: the Court's statement that the proposed use of the school's facilities is constitutional because (among other things) it would not signal endorsement of religion in general. Ante at ___. What a strange notion, that a Constitution which itself gives "religion in general" preferential treatment (I refer to the Free Exercise Clause) forbids endorsement of religion in general. The Attorney General of New York not only agrees with that strange notion, he has an explanation for it: "Religious advocacy," he writes, "serves the community only in the eyes of its adherents, and yields a benefit only to those who already believe." Brief for Respondent Attorney General 24. That was not the view of those who adopted our Constitution, who believed that the public virtues inculcated by religion are a public good. It suffices to point out that, during the summer of 1789, when it was in the process of drafting the First Amendment, Congress enacted the famous Northwest Territory Ordinance of 1789, Article III of which provides,

Religion, morality, and knowledge, being necessary to good government and the happiness of mankind, schools and the means of education shall forever be encouraged.

1 Stat. 52 (emphasis added). Unsurprisingly, then, indifference to "religion in general" is not what our cases, both old and recent, demand. See, e.g., Zorach v. Clauson, 343 U.S. 306, 313-314 (1952) ("When the state encourages religious instruction or cooperates with religious authorities by adjusting the schedule of public events to sectarian needs, it follows the best of our traditions"); Walz v. Tax Comm'n of New York City, 397 U.S. 664 (1970) (upholding property tax exemption for church property); Lynch,

465 U.S. at 673 (the Constitution "affirmatively mandates accommodation, not merely tolerance, of all religions.... Anything less would require the 'callous indifference' we have said was never intended" (citations omitted)); id. at 683 ("our precedents plainly contemplate that, on occasion, some advancement of religion will result from governmental action"); Marsh, supra; Presiding Bishop, supra, (exemption for religious organizations from certain provisions of Civil Rights Act).

* * * *

For the reasons given by the Court, I agree that the Free Speech Clause of the First Amendment forbids what respondents have done here. As for the asserted Establishment Clause justification, I would hold, simply and clearly, that giving Lamb's Chapel nondiscriminatory access to school facilities cannot violate that provision because it does not signify state or local embrace of a particular religious sect.

* The Court correctly notes, ante at ____, n. 7, that I joined the opinion in Corporation of Presiding Bishop of Church of Jesus Christ of Latterday Saints v. Amos, 483 U.S. 327 (1987), which considered the Lemon test. Lacking a majority at that time to abandon Lemon, we necessarily focused on that test, which had been the exclusive basis for the lower court's judgment. Here, of course, the lower court did not mention Lemon, and indeed did not even address any Establishment Clause argument on behalf of respondents. Thus, the Court is ultimately correct that Presiding Bishop provides a useful comparison: it was as impossible to avoid Lemon there as it is unnecessary to inject Lemon here.

Overruling past decisions: Justice Scalia's concurrence in Harper v. Virginia Department of Taxation (June 18, 1993)

Justice Scalia, concurring.

I joined the plurality opinion in Teague. Not only did I believe the rule it announced was correct, see Withrow v. Williams, 507 U. S. ___, ___ (1993) (Scalia, J., concurring in part and dissenting in part) (slip op., at 4), but I also believed that abandonment of our prior collateral review retroactivity rule was fully in accord with the doctrine of stare decisis, which as applied by our Court has never been inflexible. The Teague plurality opinion set forth good reasons for abandoning Linkletter--reasons justifying a similar abandonment of Chevron Oil Co. v. Huson, 404 U.S. 97 (1971). It noted, for example, that Linkletter "ha[d] not led to consistent results," Teague, supra, at 302; but neither has Chevron Oil. Proof that what it means is in the eye of the beholder is provided quite nicely by the separate opinions filed today: Of the four Justices who would still apply Chevron Oil, two find Davis v. Michigan Dept. of Treasury, 489 U.S. 803 (1989), retroactive, see, post, at 2 (Kennedy, J., concurring in part and concurring in judgment), two find it not retroactive, see post, at 11 (O'Connor, J., dissenting). Second, the Teague plurality opinion noted that Linkletter had been criticized by commentators,

Teague, supra, at 303; but the commentary cited in the opinion criticized not just Linkletter, but the Court's retroactivity jurisprudence in general, of which it considered Chevron Oil an integral part, see Beytagh, Ten Years of Non Retroactivity: A Critique and a Proposal, 61 Va. L. Rev. 1557, 1558, 1581-1582, 1606 (1975). Other commentary, of course, has also regarded the issue of retroactivity as a general problem of jurisprudence. See, e. g., Fallon & Meltzer, New Law, Non Retroactivity, and Constitutional Remedies, 104 Harv. L. Rev. 1731 (1991); Schaefer, Prospective Rulings: Two Perspectives, 1982 S. Ct. Rev. 1; Schaefer, The Control of "Sunbursts": Techniques of Prospective Overruling, 42 N. Y. U. L. Rev. 631 (1967); Mishkin, Forward: The High Court, The Great Writ, and the Due Process of Time and Law, 79 Harv. L. Rev. 56, 58-72 (1965).

Finally, the plurality opinion in Teague justified the departure from Linkletter by implicitly relying on the well settled proposition that stare decisis has less force where intervening decisions "have removed or weakened the conceptual underpinnings from the prior decision." Patterson v. McLean Credit Union, 491 U.S. 164, 173(1989). Justice O'Connor endorsed the reasoning expressed by Justice Harlan in his separate opinions in Mackey v. United States, 401 U.S. 667 (1971), andDesist v. United States, 394 U.S. 244 (1969), and noted that the Court had already adopted the first part of Justice Harlan's retroactivity views in Griffith v. Kentucky, 479 U.S. 314 (1987). See Teague, supra, at 303-305. Again, this argument equally--indeed, even more forcefully--supports reconsideration of Chevron Oil. Griffith returned this Court, in criminal cases, to the traditional view (which I shall discuss at greater length below) that prospective decisionmaking "violates basic norms of constitutional adjudication." Griffith, supra, at 322. One of the conceptual underpinnings of Chevron Oil was that retroactivity presents a similar problem in both civil and criminal contexts. See Chevron Oil, supra, at 106; see also Beytagh, supra, at 1606. Thus, after Griffith, Chevron Oil can be adhered to only by rejecting the reasoning of Chevron Oil--that is, only by asserting that the issue of retroactivity is different in the civil and criminal settings. That is a particularly difficult proof to make, inasmuch as Griffith rested on "basic norms of constitutional adjudication" and "the nature of judicial review." 479 U. S., at 322; see also Teague, supra, at 317 (White, J., concurring in part and concurring in judgment) (Griffith "appear[s] to have constitutional underpinnings"). [n.1]

What most provokes comment in the dissent, however, is not its insistence that today a rigid doctrine of stare decisis forbids tinkering with retroactivity, which four Terms ago did not; but rather the irony of its invoking stare decisis in defense of prospective decisionmaking at all. Prospective decisionmaking is the handmaid of judicial activism, and the born enemy of stare decisis. It was formulated in the heyday of legal realism and promoted as a "techniqu[e] of judicial lawmaking" in general, and more specifically as a means of making it easier to overrule prior precedent. B. Levy, Realist Jurisprudence and Prospective Overruling, 109 U. Pa. L. Rev. 1 (1960). Thus, the dissent is saying, in effect, that stare decisis demands the preservation of methods of destroying stare decisis recently invented in violation of stare decisis.

Contrary to the dissent's assertion that Chevron Oil articulated "our traditional retroactivity analysis," post, at 1, the jurisprudence it reflects "came into being," as Justice Harlan observed, less than 30 years ago with Linkletter v. Walker, 381 U.S. 618 (1965). Mackey, supra, at 676. It is so un ancient that one of the current members of this Court was sitting when it was invented. The true traditional view is that prospective decisionmaking is quite incompatible with the judicial power, and that courts have no authority to engage in the practice. See ante, at 6; James B. Beam Distilling Co. v. Georgia, 501 U. S. ___, ___ (1991) (slip op., at 4) (opinion of Souter, J.); American Trucking Assns., Inc. v. Smith, 496 U.S. 167, 201 (1990) (Scalia, J., concurring in judgment); Desist, supra, at 258-259 (Harlan, J., dissenting); Great Northern R. Co. v. Sunburst Oil & Refining Co., 287 U.S. 358, 365 (1932). Linkletter itself recognized that "[a]t common law there was no authority for the proposition that judicial decisions made law only for the future." 381 U. S., at 622-623. And before Linkletter, the academic proponents of prospective judicial decisionmaking acknowledged that their proposal contradicted traditional practice. See, e. g., Levy, supra, at 2, and n. 2; Carpenter, Court Decisions and the Common Law, 17 Colum. L. Rev. 593, 594 (1917). Indeed, the roots of the contrary tradition are so deep that Justice Holmes was prepared to hazard the guess that "[j]udicial decisions have had retrospective operation for near a thousand years." Kuhn v. Fairmont Coal Co., 215 U.S. 349, 372 (1910) (dissenting opinion).

Justice O'Connor asserts that " `[w]hen the Court changes its mind, the law changes with it.' " Post, at 4 (quoting Beam, supra, at ___ (O'Connor, J., dissenting) (slip op., at 1)). That concept is quite foreign to the American legal and constitutional tradition. It would have struck John Marshall as an extraordinary assertion of raw power. The conception of the judicial role that he possessed, and that was shared by succeeding generations of American judges until very recent times, took it to be "the province and duty of the judicial department to say what the law is," Marbury v. Madison, 1 Cranch 137, 177 (1803) (emphasis added)--not what the law shall be. That original and enduring American perception of the judicial role sprang not from the philosophy of Nietzsche but from the jurisprudence of Blackstone, which viewed retroactivity as an inherent characteristic of the judicial power, a power "not delegated to pronounce a new law, but to maintain and expound the old one." 1 W. Blackstone, Commentaries 69 (1765). Even when a "former determination is most evidently contrary to reason . . . [or] contrary to the divine law," a judge overruling that decision would "not pretend to make a new law, but to vindicate the old one from misrepresentation." Id., at 69-70. "For if it be found that the former decision is manifestly absurd or unjust, it is declared, not that such a sentence was bad law, but that it was not law." Id., at 70 (emphases in original). Fully retroactive decisionmaking was considered a principal distinction between the judicial and the legislative power: "[I]t is said that that which distinguishes a judicial from a legislative act is, that the one is a determination of what the existing law is in relation to some existing thing already done or happened, while the other is a predetermination of what the law shall be for the regulation of all future cases." T. Cooley, Constitutional Limitations 91

(1868). The critics of the traditional rule of full retroactivity were well aware that it was grounded in what one of them contemptuously called "another fiction known as the Separation of powers." Kocourek, Retrospective Decisions and Stare Decisis and a Proposal, 17 A. B. A. J. 180, 181 (1931).

Prospective decisionmaking was known to foe and friend alike as a practical tool of judicial activism, born out of disregard for stare decisis. In the eyes of its enemies, the doctrine "smack[ed] of the legislative process," Mishkin, 79 Harv. L. Rev., at 65, "encroach[ed] on the prerogatives of the legislative department of government," Von Moschzisker, Stare Decisis in Courts of Last Resort, 37 Harv. L. Rev. 409, 428 (1924), removed "one of the great inherent restraints upon this Court's depart[ing] from the field of interpretation to enter that of lawmaking," James v. United States, 366 U.S. 213, 225 (1961) (Black, J., concurring in part and dissenting in part), caused the Court's behavior to become "assimilated to that of a legislature," Kurland, Toward a Political Supreme Court, 37 U. Chi. L. Rev. 19, 34 (1969), and tended "to cut [the courts] loose from the force of precedent, allowing [them] to restructure artificially those expectations legitimately created by extant law and thereby mitigate the practical force of stare decisis." Mackey, 401 U. S., at 680 (Harlan, J., concurring in judgment). All this was not denied by the doctrine's friends, who also viewed it as a device to "augmen[t] the power of the courts to contribute to the growth of the law in keeping with the demands of society," Mallamud, Prospective Limitation and the Rights of the Accused, 56 Iowa L. Rev. 321, 359 (1970), as "a deliberate and conscious technique of judicial lawmaking," Levy, 109 U. Pa. L. Rev., at 6, as a means of "facilitating more effective and defensible judicial lawmaking," id., at 28.

Justice Harlan described this Court's embrace of the prospectivity principle as "the product of the Court's disquietude with the impacts of its fast moving pace of constitutional innovation," Mackey, supra, at 676. The Court itself, however, glowingly described the doctrine as the cause rather than the effect of innovation, extolling it as a "technique" providing the "impetus . . . for the implementation of long overdue reforms." Jenkins v. Delaware, 395 U.S. 213, 218 (1969). Whether cause or effect, there is no doubt that the era which gave birth to the prospectivity principle was marked by a newfound disregard for stare decisis. As one commentator calculated, "[b]y 1959, the number of instances in which the Court had reversals involving constitutional issues had grown to sixty; in the two decades which followed, the Court overruled constitutional cases on no less than forty seven occasions." Maltz, Some Thoughts on the Death of Stare Decisis in Constitutional Law, 1980 Wis. L. Rev. 467. It was an era when this Court cast overboard numerous settled decisions, and indeed even whole areas of law, with an unceremonious "heave ho." See, e. g., Mapp v. Ohio, 367 U.S. 643 (1961) (overruling Wolf v. Colorado, 338 U.S. 25 (1949)); Gideon v. Wainwright, 372 U.S. 335 (1963) (overruling Betts v. Brady, 316 U.S. 455 (1942)); Miranda v. Arizona, 384 U.S. 436, 479, n. 48 (1966) (overruling Crooker v. California, 357 U.S. 433 (1958), and Cicenia v. Lagay, 357 U.S. 504 (1958)); Katz v. United States, 389 U.S. 347 (1967) (overruling Olmstead v. United States,

277 U.S. 438 (1928), and Goldman v. United States, 316 U.S. 129 (1942)). To argue now that one of the jurisprudential tools of judicial activism from that period should be extended on grounds of stare decisis can only be described as paradoxical. [n.2]

In sum, I join the opinion of the Court because the doctrine of prospective decisionmaking is not in fact protected by our flexible rule of stare decisis; and because no friend of stare decisis would want it to be.

Notes

1 The dissent attempts to distinguish between retroactivity in civil and criminal settings on three grounds, none of which has ever been adopted by this Court. The dissent's first argument begins with the observation that "nonretroactivity in criminal cases historically has favored the government's reliance interests over the rights of criminal defendants." Post, at 9. But while it is true that prospectivity was usually employed in the past (during the brief period when it was used in criminal cases) to favor the government, there is no basis for the implicit suggestion that it would usually favor the government in the future. That phenomenon was a consequence, not of the nature of the doctrine, cf. James v. United States, 366 U.S. 213 (1961), but of the historical "accident" that during the period prospectivity was in fashion legal rules favoring the government were more frequently overturned. But more fundamentally, to base a rule of full retroactivity in the criminal law area upon what the dissent calls "the generalized policy of favoring individual rights over governmental prerogative," post, at 9, makes no more sense than to adopt, because of the same "generalized policy," a similarly gross rule that no decision favoring criminal defendants can ever be overruled. The law is more discerning than that. The dissent's next argument is based on the dubious empirical assumption that civil litigants, but not criminal defendants, will often receive some benefit from a prospective decision. That assumption does not hold even in this case: Prospective invalidation of Virginia's taxing scheme would afford petitioners the enormous future "benefit," post, at 10, of knowing that others in the State are being taxed more. But empirical problems aside, the dissent does not explain why, if a receipt of some benefit principle is important, we should use such an inaccurate proxy as the civil/criminal distinction, or how this newly discovered principle overcomes the "basic norms of constitutional adjudication" on which Griffith v. Kentucky, 479 U.S. 314, 322 (1987), rested. Finally, the dissent's "equal treatment" argument ably distinguishes between cases in which a prospectivity claim is properly raised, and those in which it is not. See post, at 10-11. But that does nothing to distinguish between civil and criminal cases; obviously, a party may procedurally default on a claim in either context.

2 Contrary to the suggestion in the dissent, I am not arguing that we should "cast overboard our entire retroactivity doctrine with . . . [an] unceremonious heave ho." Post, at 5 (emphasis added; internal quotation marks omitted). There is no need. We cast over the first half six Terms ago in Griffith, and deep sixed most of the rest two Terms ago in James B. Beam Distilling Co. v. Georgia, 501 U. S. ___ (1991)--in neither case

unceremoniously (in marked contrast to some of the overrulings cited in text). What little, if any, remains is teetering at the end of the plank and needs no more than a gentle nudge. But if the entire doctrine had been given a quick and unceremonious end, there could be no complaint on the grounds of stare decisis; as it was born, so should it die. I do not know the basis for the dissent's contention that I find the jurisprudence of the era that produced the doctrine of prospectivity "distasteful." Post, at 5. Much of it is quite appetizing. It is only the cavalier treatment of stare decisis and the invention of prospectivity that I have criticized here.

Quite obviously, not every restriction upon expression that did not exist in 1791 or in 1868 is ipso facto unconstitutional: Justice Scalia's dissent in McIntyre v. Ohio Elections Commission (April 19, 1995)

Justice Scalia, with whom The Chief Justice joins,

The question posed by the present case is not the easiest sort to answer for those who adhere to the Court's (and the society's) traditional view that the Constitution bears its original meaning and is unchanging. Under that view, "[o]n every question of construction, [we should] carry ourselves back to the time when the Constitution was adopted; recollect the spirit manifested in the debates; and instead of trying [to find] what meaning may be squeezed out of the text, or invented against it, conform to the probable one in which it was passed." T. Jefferson, Letter to William Johnson (June 12, 1823), in 15 Writings of Thomas Jefferson 439, 449 (A. Lipscomb ed. 1904). That technique is simple of application when government conduct that is claimed to violate the Bill of Rights or the Fourteenth Amendment is shown, upon investigation, to have been engaged in without objection at the very time the Bill of Rights or the Fourteenth Amendment was adopted. There is no doubt, for example, that laws against libel and obscenity do not violate "the freedom of speech" to which the First Amendment refers; they existed and were universally approved in 1791. Application of the principle of an unchanging Constitution is also simple enough at the other extreme, where the government conduct at issue was not engaged in at the time of adoption, and there is ample evidence that the reason it was not engaged in is that it was thought to violate the right embodied in the constitutional guarantee. Racks and thumbscrews, well known instruments for inflicting pain, were not in use because they were regarded as cruel punishments.

The present case lies between those two extremes. Anonymous electioneering was not prohibited by law in 1791 or in 1868. In fact, it was widely practiced at the earlier date, an understandable legacy of the revolutionary era in which political dissent could produce governmental reprisal. I need not dwell upon the evidence of that, since it is described at length in today's concurrence. See ante, at 3-13 (Thomas, J., concurring in judgment). The practice of anonymous electioneering may have been less general in 1868, when the

Fourteenth Amendment was adopted, but at least as late as 1837 it was respectable enough to be engaged in by Abraham Lincoln. See 1 A. Beveridge, Abraham Lincoln 1809-1858, pp. 215-216 (1928); 1 Uncollected Works of Abraham Lincoln 155-161 (R. Wilson ed. 1947).

But to prove that anonymous electioneering was used frequently is not to establish that it is a constitutional right. Quite obviously, not every restriction upon expression that did not exist in 1791 or in 1868 is ipso facto unconstitutional, or else modern election laws such as those involved in Burson v. Freeman, 504 U.S. 191 (1992), and Buckley v. Valeo, 424 U.S. 1 (1976), would be prohibited, as would (to mention only a few other categories) modern anti noise regulation of the sort involved in Kovacs v. Cooper, 336 U.S. 77 (1949), and Ward v. Rock Against Racism, 491 U.S. 781 (1989), and modern parade permitting regulation of the sort involved in Cox v. New Hampshire, 312 U.S. 569 (1941).

Evidence that anonymous electioneering was regarded as a constitutional right is sparse, and as far as I am aware evidence that it was generally regarded as such is nonexistent. The concurrence points to "freedom of the press" objections that were made against the refusal of some Federalist newspapers to publish unsigned essays opposing the proposed constitution (on the ground that they might be the work of foreign agents). See ante, at 7-9 (Thomas, J., concurring in judgment). But of course if every partisan cry of "freedom of the press" were accepted as valid, our Constitution would be unrecognizable; and if one were to generalize from these particular cries, the First Amendment would be not only a protection for newspapers but a restriction upon them. Leaving aside, however, the fact that no governmental action was involved, the Anti Federalists had a point, inasmuch as the editorial proscription of anonymity applied only to them, and thus had the vice of viewpoint discrimination. (Hence the comment by Philadelphiensis, quoted in the concurrence: " `Here we see pretty plainly through [the Federalists'] excellent regulation of the press, how things are to be carried on after the adoption of the new constitution.' " Ante, at 8 (quoting Philadelphiensis, Essay I, Independent Gazetteer, Nov. 7, 1787, in 3 Complete Anti Federalist 103 (H. Storing ed. 1981)).)

The concurrence recounts other pre-and post-Revolution examples of defense of anonymity in the name of "freedom of the press," but not a single one involves the context of restrictions imposed in connection with a free, democratic election, which is all that is at issue here. For many of them, moreover, such as the 1735 Zenger trial, ante, at 3-4, the 1779 "Leonidas" controversy in the Continental Congress, ante, at 4, and the 1779 action by the New Jersey Legislative Council against Isaac Collins, ante, at 5, the issue of anonymity was incidental to the (unquestionably free speech) issue of whether criticism of the government could be punished by the state.

Thus, the sum total of the historical evidence marshalled by the concurrence for the principle of constitutional entitlement to anonymous electioneering is partisan claims in the debate on ratification (which was almost like an election) that a viewpoint based restriction on anonymity by newspaper editors violates freedom of speech. This absence of historical testimony concerning the point before us is hardly remarkable. The issue of a governmental prohibition upon anonymous electioneering in particular (as opposed to a government prohibition upon anonymous publication in general) simply never arose. Indeed, there probably never arose even the abstract question of whether electoral openness and regularity was worth such a governmental restriction upon the normal right to anonymous speech. The idea of close government regulation of the electoral process is a more modern phenomenon, arriving in this country in the late 1800's. See Burson v. Freeman, supra, at 203-205.

What we have, then, is the most difficult case for determining the meaning of the Constitution. No accepted existence of governmental restrictions of the sort at issue here demonstrates their constitutionality, but neither can their nonexistence clearly be attributed to constitutional objections. In such a case, constitutional adjudication necessarily involves not just history but judgment: judgment as to whether the government action under challenge is consonant with the concept of the protected freedom (in this case, the freedom of speech and of the press) that existed when the constitutional protection was accorded. In the present case, absent other indication I would be inclined to agree with the concurrence that a society which used anonymous political debate so regularly would not regard as constitutional even moderate restrictions made to improve the election process. (I would, however, want further evidence of common practice in 1868, since I doubt that the Fourteenth Amendment time warped the post-Civil War States back to the Revolution.)

But there is other indication, of the most weighty sort: the widespread and longstanding traditions of our people. Principles of liberty fundamental enough to have been embodied within constitutional guarantees are not readily erased from the Nation's consciousness. A governmental practice that has become general throughout the United States, and particularly one that has the validation of long, accepted usage, bears a strong presumption of constitutionality. And that is what we have before us here. Section 3599.09(A) was enacted by the General Assembly of the State of Ohio almost 80 years ago. See Act of May 27, 1915, 1915 Ohio Leg. Acts 350. Even at the time of its adoption, there was nothing unique or extraordinary about it. The earliest statute of this sort was adopted by Massachusetts in 1890, little more than 20 years after the Fourteenth Amendment was ratified. No less than 24 States had similar laws by the end of World War I, [n.1] and today every State of the Union except California has one, [n.2] as does the District of Columbia, see D. C. Code Ann. §1-1420 (1992), and as does the Federal Government where advertising relating to candidates for federal office is concerned, see 2 U.S.C. § 441d(a). Such a universal [n.3] and long established American legislative practice must be given precedence, I think, over historical and academic speculation regarding a restriction that assuredly does not go to the heart of free speech.

It can be said that we ignored a tradition as old, and almost as widespread, in Texas v. Johnson, 491 U.S. 397 (1989), where we held unconstitutional a state law prohibiting desecration of the United States flag. See also United States v. Eichman, 496 U.S. 310 (1990). But those cases merely stand for the proposition that post-adoption tradition cannot alter the core meaning of a constitutional guarantee. As we said in Johnson, "[i]f there is a bedrock principle underlying the First Amendment, it is that the government may not prohibit the expression of an idea simply because society finds the idea itself offensive or disagreeable." 491 U. S., at 414. Prohibition of expression of contempt for the flag, whether by contemptuous words, see Street v. New York, 394 U.S. 576 (1969), or by burning the flag, came, we said, within that "bedrock principle." The law at issue here, by contrast, forbids the expression of no idea, but merely requires identification of the speaker when the idea is uttered in the electoral context. It is at the periphery of the First Amendment, like the law at issue in Burson, where we took guidance from tradition in upholding against constitutional attack restrictions upon electioneering in the vicinity of polling places, see 504 U. S., at 204-206 (plurality opinion); id., at 214-216 (Scalia, J., concurring in judgment).

The foregoing analysis suffices to decide this case for me. Where the meaning of a constitutional text (such as "the freedom of speech") is unclear, the widespread and long accepted practices of the American people are the best indication of what fundamental beliefs it was intended to enshrine. Even if I were to close my eyes to practice, however, and were to be guided exclusively by deductive analysis from our case law, I would reach the same result.

Three basic questions must be answered to decide this case. Two of them are readily answered by our precedents; the third is readily answered by common sense and by a decent regard for the practical judgment of those more familiar with elections than we are. The first question is whether protection of the election process justifies limitations upon speech that cannot constitutionally be imposed generally. (If not, Talley v. California, which invalidated a flat ban on all anonymous leafletting, controls the decision here.) Our cases plainly answer that question in the affirmative--indeed, they suggest that no justification for regulation is more compelling than protection of the electoral process. "Other rights, even the most basic, are illusory if the right to vote is undermined." Wesberry v. Sanders, 376 U.S. 1, 17 (1964). The State has a "compelling interest in preserving the integrity of its election process." Eu v. San Francisco Cty. Democratic Central Comm., 489 U.S. 214, 231 (1989). So significant have we found the interest in protecting the electoral process to be that we have approved the prohibition of political speech entirely in areas that would impede that process. Burson, supra, at 204-206 (plurality opinion).

The second question relevant to our decision is whether a "right to anonymity" is such a prominent value in our constitutional system that even protection of the electoral process cannot be purchased at its expense. The answer, again, is clear: no. Several of our cases have held that in peculiar circumstances the compelled disclosure of a person's identity would unconstitutionally deter the exercise of First Amendment associational rights. See, e.g., Brown v. Socialist Workers '74 Campaign Comm. (Ohio), 459 U.S. 87

(1982); Bates v. Little Rock, 361 U.S. 516 (1960); NAACP v. Alabama ex rel. Patterson, 357 U.S. 449 (1958). But those cases did not acknowledge any general right to anonymity, or even any right on the part of all citizens to ignore the particular laws under challenge. Rather, they recognized a right to an exemption from otherwise valid disclosure requirements on the part of someone who could show a "reasonable probability" that the compelled disclosure would result in "threats, harassment, or reprisals from either Government officials or private parties." This last quotation is from Buckley v. Valeo, 424 U.S. 1, 74 (1976) (per curiam), which prescribed the safety valve of a similar exemption in upholding the disclosure requirements of the Federal Election Campaign Act. That is the answer our case law provides to the Court's fear about the "tyranny of the majority," ante, at 23, and to its concern that " `[p]ersecuted groups and sects from time to time throughout history have been able to criticize oppressive practices and laws either anonymously or not at all,' " ante, at 8 (quoting Talley, 362 U. S., at 64). Anonymity can still be enjoyed by those who require it, without utterly destroying useful disclosure laws. The record in this case contains not even a hint that Mrs. McIntyre feared "threats, harassment, or reprisals"; indeed, she placed her name on some of her fliers and meant to place it on all of them. See App. 12, 36-40.

The existence of a generalized right of anonymity in speech was rejected by this Court in Lewis Publishing Co. v. Morgan, 229 U.S. 288 (1913), which held that newspapers desiring the privilege of second class postage could be required to provide to the Postmaster General, and to publish, a statement of the names and addresses of their editors, publishers, business managers and owners. We rejected the argument that the First Amendment forbade the requirement of such disclosure. Id., at 299. The provision that gave rise to that case still exists, see 39 U.S.C. § 3685 and is still enforced by the Postal Service. It is one of several federal laws seemingly invalidated by today's opinion.

The Court's unprecedented protection for anonymous speech does not even have the virtue of establishing a clear (albeit erroneous) rule of law. For after having announced that this statute, because it "burdens core political speech," requires "exacting scrutiny" and must be "narrowly tailored to serve an overriding state interest," ante, at 13 (ordinarily the kiss of death), the opinion goes on to proclaim soothingly (and unhelpfully) that "a State's enforcement interest might justify a more limited identification requirement." Ante, at 19. See also ante, at 2 (Ginsburg, J., concurring) ("We do not . . . hold that the State may not in other, larger circumstances, require the speaker to disclose its interest by disclosing its identity.") Perhaps, then, not all the State statutes I have alluded to are invalid, but just some of them; or indeed maybe all of them remain valid in "larger circumstances"! It may take decades to work out the shape of this newly expanded right to speak incognito, even in the elections field. And in other areas, of course, a whole new boutique of wonderful First Amendment litigation opens its doors. Must a parade permit, for example, be issued to a group that refuses to provide its identity, or that agrees to do so only under assurance that the identity will not be made public? Must a municipally owned theater that is leased for private productions book anonymously sponsored presentations? Must a government periodical that has a "letters to the editor" column disavow the policy that most newspapers have against the publication of anonymous letters? Must a public university that makes its facilities available for a speech by Louis Farrakhan or David Duke refuse to disclose the on campus or off campus group that has sponsored or paid for the speech? Must a municipal "public access" cable channel permit anonymous (and masked) performers? The silliness that follows upon a generalized right to anonymous speech has no end.

The third and last question relevant to our decision is whether the prohibition of anonymous campaigning is effective in protecting and enhancing democratic elections. In answering this question no, the Justices of the majority set their own views--on a practical matter that bears closely upon the real life experience of elected politicians and not upon that of unelected judges--up against the views of 49 (and perhaps all 50, see n. 4, supra) state legislatures and the federal Congress. We might also add to the list on the other side the legislatures of foreign democracies: Australia, Canada, and England, for example, all have prohibitions upon anonymous campaigning. See, e.g., Commonwealth Electoral Act 1918, §328 (Australia); Canada Elections Act, R.S.C., ch. E-2, §261 (1985); Representation of the People Act, 1983, §110 (England). How is it, one must wonder, that all of these elected legislators, from around the country and around the world, could not see what six Justices of this Court see so clearly that they are willing to require the entire Nation to act upon it: that requiring identification of the source of campaign literature does not improve the quality of the campaign?

The Court says that the State has not explained "why it can more easily enforce the direct bans on disseminating false documents against anonymous authors and distributors than against wrongdoers who might use false names and addresses in an attempt to avoid detection." Ante, at 19. I am not sure what this complicated comparison means. I am sure, however, that (1) a person who is required to put his name to a document is much less likely to lie than one who can lie anonymously, and (2) the distributor of a leaflet which is unlawful because it is anonymous runs much more risk of immediate detection and punishment than the distributor of a leaflet which is unlawful because it is false. Thus, people will be more likely to observe a signing requirement than a naked "no falsity" requirement; and, having observed that requirement, will then be significantly less likely to lie in what they have signed.

But the usefulness of a signing requirement lies not only in promoting observance of the law against campaign falsehoods (though that alone is enough to sustain it). It lies also in promoting a civil and dignified level of campaign debate--which the State has no power to command, but ample power to encourage by such undemanding measures as a signature requirement. Observers of the past few national elections have expressed concern about the increase of character assassination--"mudslinging" is the colloquial term--engaged in by political candidates and their supporters to the detriment of the democratic process. Not all of this, in fact not much of it, consists of actionable untruth; most is innuendo, or demeaning characterization, or mere disclosure of items of personal life that have no bearing upon suitability for office. Imagine how much all of this would increase if it could be done anonymously. The principal impediment against it is the reluctance of most individuals and organizations to be publicly associated with uncharitable and uncivil expression. Consider, moreover, the increased potential for "dirty tricks." It is not unheard of for campaign operatives to circulate material over the name of their opponents or their opponents' supporters (a violation of election laws) in order to attract or alienate certain interest groups. See, e.g., B. Felknor, Political Mischief: Smear, Sabotage, and Reform in U. S. Elections 111-112 (1992) (fake United Mine Workers' newspaper assembled by the National Republican Congressional Committee); New York v. Duryea, 76 Misc. 2d 948, 351 N. Y. S. 2d 978 (Sup. 1974) (letters purporting to be from the "Action Committee for the Liberal Party" sent by Republicans). How much easier--and sanction free!--it would be to circulate anonymous material (for example, a really tasteless, though not actionably false, attack upon one's own candidate) with the hope and expectation that it will be attributed to, and held against, the other side.

The Court contends that demanding the disclosure of the pamphleteer's identity is no different from requiring the disclosure of any other information that may reduce the persuasiveness of the pamphlet's message. See ante, at 14-15. It cites Miami Herald Publishing Co. v. Tornillo, 418 U.S. 241 (1974), which held it unconstitutional to require a newspaper that had published an editorial critical of a particular candidate to furnish space for that candidate to reply. But it is not usual for a speaker to put forward the best arguments against himself, and it is a great imposition upon free speech to make him do so. Whereas it is quite usual--it is expected--for a speaker to identify himself, and requiring that is (at least when there are no special circumstances present) virtually no imposition at all.

We have approved much more onerous disclosure requirements in the name of fair elections. In Buckley v. Valeo, 424 U.S. 1 (1976), we upheld provisions of the Federal Election Campaign Act that required private individuals to report to the Federal Election Commission independent expenditures made for communications advocating the election or defeat of a candidate for federal office. Id., at 80. Our primary rationale for upholding this provision was that it served an "informational interest" by "increas[ing] the fund of information concerning those who support the candidates," id., at 81. The provision before us here serves the same informational interest, as well as more important interests, which I have discussed above. The Court's attempt to distinguish Buckley, see ante, at 22-23, would be unconvincing, even if it were accurate in its statement that the disclosure requirement there at issue "reveals far less information" than requiring disclosure of the identity of the author of a specific campaign statement. That happens not to be accurate, since the provision there at issue required not merely "[d]isclosure of an expenditure and its use, without more," ante, at 22. It required, among other things:

"the identification of each person to whom expenditures have been made . . . within the calendar year in an aggregate amount or value in excess of $100, the amount, date, and purpose of each such expenditure and the name and address of, and office sought by, each candidate on whose behalf such expenditure was made." 2 U.S.C. § 434(b)(9) (1970 ed., Supp. IV) (emphasis added). See also 2 U.S.C. § 434(e) (1970 ed., Supp. IV). (Both reproduced in Appendix to Buckley, 424 U. S., at 158, 160).

Surely in many if not most cases, this information will readily permit identification of the particular message that the would be anonymous campaigner sponsored. Besides which the burden of complying with this provision, which includes the filing of quarterly reports, is infinitely more onerous than Ohio's simple requirement for signature of campaign literature. If Buckley remains the law, this is an easy case.

* * *

I do not know where the Court derives its perception that "anonymous pamphleteering is not a pernicious, fraudulent practice, but an honorable tradition of advocacy and of dissent." Ante, at 23. I can imagine no reason why an anonymous leaflet is any more honorable, as a general matter, than an anonymous phone call or an anonymous letter. It facilitates wrong by eliminating accountability, which is ordinarily the very purpose of the anonymity. There are of course exceptions, and where anonymity is needed to avoid "threats, harassment, or reprisals" the First Amendment will require an exemption from the Ohio law. Cf. NAACP v. Alabama ex rel. Patterson, 357 U.S. 449 (1958). But to strike down the Ohio law in its general application--and similar laws of 48 other States and the Federal Government--on the ground that all anonymous communication is in our society traditionally sacrosanct, seems to me a distortion of the past that will lead to a coarsening of the future.

I respectfully dissent.

Notes

1 See Act of June 19, 1915, No. 171, §9, 1915 Ala. Acts 250, 254-255; Act of Mar. 12, 1917, ch. 47, §1, 1917 Ariz. Sess. Laws 62, 62-63; Act of Apr. 2, 1913, No. 308, §6, 1913 Ark. Gen. Acts 1252, 1255; Act of Mar. 15, 1901, ch. 138, §1, 1901 Cal. Stats. 297; Act of June 6, 1913, ch. 6470, §9, 1913 Fla. Laws 268, 272-273; Act of June 26, 1917, §1, 1917 Ill. Laws 456, 456-457; Act of Mar. 14, 1911, ch. 137, §1, 1911 Kan. Sess. Laws 221; Act of July 11, 1912, No. 213, §14, 1912 La. Acts 447, 454; Act of June 3, 1890, ch. 381, 1890 Mass. Laws 342; Act of June 20, 1912, Ex. Sess. ch. 3, §7, 1912 Minn. Laws 23, 26; Act of Apr. 21, 1906, S. B. No. 191, 1906 Miss. Gen. Laws 295 (enacting Miss. Code §3728 (1906)); Act of Apr. 9, 1917, §1, 1917 Mo. Laws 272, 273; Act of Nov. 1912, §35, 1912 Mont. Laws 593, 608; Act of Mar. 31, 1913, ch. 282, §34, 1913 Nev. Stats. 476, 486-487; Act of Apr. 21, 1915, ch. 169, §7, 1915 N. H. Laws 234, 236; Act of Apr. 20, 1911, ch. 188, §9, 1911 N. J. Laws 329, 334; Act of Mar. 12, 1913, ch. 164, §1(k), 1913 N. C. Sess. Laws 259, 261; Act of May 27, 1915, 1915 Ohio Leg. Acts 350; Act of June 23, 1908, ch. 3, §35, 1909 Ore. Laws 15, 30; Act of June 26, 1895, No. 275, 1895 Pa. Laws 389; Act of Mar. 13, 1917, ch. 92, §23, 1917 Utah Laws 258, 267; Act of Mar. 12, 1909, ch. 82, §8, 1909 Wash. Laws 169, 177-178; Act of Feb. 20, 1915, ch. 27, §13, 1915 W. Va. Acts 246, 255; Act of July 11, 1911, ch. 650, §§94-14 to 94-16, 1911 Wis. Laws 883, 890.

2 See Ala. Code §17-22A%13 (Supp. 1994); Alaska Stat. Ann. §15.56.010 (1988); Ariz. Rev. Stat. Ann. §16-912 (Supp. 1994); Ark. Code Ann. §7-1-103 (1993); Colo. Rev. Stat. §1-13-108 (Supp. 1994); Conn. Gen. Stat. §9-333w (Supp. 1994); Del. Code Ann., Tit. 15, §§8021, 8023 (1993); Fla. Stat. §§106.143 and 106.1437 (1992); Ga.Code Ann. §21-2-415 (1993); Haw. Rev. Stat. §11-215 (1988); Idaho Code §67-6614A (Supp. 1994); Ill. Comp. Stat. §5/29-14 (1993); Ind. Code §3-14-1-4 (Supp. 1994); Iowa Code §56.14 (1991); Kan. Stat. Ann. §§25-2407 and 25-4156 (Supp. 1991); Ky. Rev. Stat. Ann. §121.190 (Baldwin Supp. 1994); La. Rev. Stat. Ann. §18:1463 (West Supp. 1994); Me. Rev. Stat. Ann., Tit. 21-A, §1014 (1993); Md. Ann. Code, Art. 33, §26-17 (1993); Mass. Gen. Laws §41 (1990); Mich. Comp. Laws Ann. §169.247 (West 1989); Minn. Stat. §211B.04 (1994); Miss. Code Ann. §23-15-899 (1990); Mo. Rev. Stat. §130.031 (Supp. 1994); Mont. Code Ann. §13-35-225 (1993); Neb. Rev. Stat. §49-1474.01 (1993); Nev. Rev. Stat. §294A.320 (Supp. 1993); N. H. Rev. Stat. Ann. §664:14 (Supp. 1992); N. J. Stat. Ann. §19:34-38.1 (1989); N. M. Stat. Ann. §§1-19-16 and 1-19-17 (1991); N. Y. Elec. Law §14-106 (McKinney 1978); N. C. Gen. Stat. §163-274 (Supp. 1994); N. D. Cent. Code §16.1-10-04.1 (1981); Ohio Rev. Code Ann. §3599.09(A) (1988); Okla. Stat., Tit. 21, §1840 (Supp. 1995); Ore. Rev. Stat. §260.522 (1991); 25 Pa. Cons. Stat. §3258 (1994); R. I. Gen. Laws §17-23-2 (1988); S. C. Code Ann. §8-13-1354 (Supp. 1993); S. D. Comp. Laws Ann. §12-25-4.1 (Supp. 1994); Tenn. Code Ann. §2-19-120 (Supp. 1994); Tex. Elec. Code Ann. §255.001 (Supp. 1995); Utah Code Ann. §20-14-24 (Supp. 1994); Vt. Stat. Ann., Tit. 17, §2022 (1982); Va. Code Ann. §24.2-1014 (1993); Wash. Rev. Code §42.17.510 (Supp. 1994); W. Va. Code §3-8-12 (1994); Wis. Stat. §11.30 (Supp. 1994); Wyo. Stat. §22-25-110 (1992).

Courts have declared some of these laws unconstitutional in recent years, relying upon our decision in Talley v. California, 362 U.S. 60 (1960). See, e.g., State v. Burgess, 543 So. 2d 1332 (La. 1989); State v. North Dakota Ed. Assn., 262 N. W. 2d 731 (N. D. 1978); People v. Duryea, 76 Misc. 2d 948, 351 N. Y. S. 2d 978 (Sup.), aff'd, 44 App. Div. 2d 663, 354 N. Y. S. 2d 129 (1974). Other decisions, including all pre-Talley decisions I am aware of, have upheld the laws. See, e.g., Commonwealth v. Evans, 156 Pa. Super. 321, 40 A. 2d 137 (1944); State v. Freeman, 143 Kan. 315, 55 P. 2d 362 (1936); State v. Babst, 104 Ohio St. 167, 135 N. E. 525 (1922).

3 It might be accurate to say that, insofar as the judicially unconstrained judgment of American legislatures is concerned, approval of the law before us here is universal. California, although it had enacted an election disclosure requirement as early as 1901, see Act of Mar. 15, 1901, ch. 138, §1, 1901 Cal. Stats. 297, abandoned its law (then similar to Ohio's) in 1983, see Act of Sept. 11, 1983, ch. 668, 1983 Cal. Stats. 2621, after a California Court of Appeal, relying primarily on our decision in Talley, had declared the provision unconstitutional, see Schuster v. Imperial County Municipal Court, 109 Cal. App. 3d 887, 167 Cal. Rptr. 447 (1980), cert. denied, 450 U.S. 1042 (1981).

Government can never have a "compelling interest" in discriminating on the basis of race in order to "make up" for past racial discrimination: Justice Scalia's concurrence in Adarand Constructors, Inc. v. Pena (June 12, 1995)

JUSTICE SCALIA, concurring in part and concurring in the judgment.

I join the opinion of the Court, except ___Part III-C, and except insofar as it may be inconsistent with the following: in my view, government can never have a "compelling interest" in discriminating on the basis of race in order to "make up" for past racial discrimination in the opposite direction. See Richmond v. J. A. Croson Co., 488 U.S. 469, 520 (1989) (SCALIA, J., concurring in judgment). Individuals who have been wronged by unlawful racial discrimination should be made whole, but, under our Constitution, there can be no such thing as either a creditor or a debtor race. That concept is alien to the Constitution's focus upon the individual, see Amdt. 14, § 1 ("[N]or shall any State . . . deny to any person" the equal protection of the laws) (emphasis added), and its rejection of dispositions based on race, see Amdt. 15, § 1 (prohibiting abridgment of the right to vote "on account of race") or based on blood, see Art. III, § 3 ("[N]o Attainder of Treason shall work Corruption of Blood"); Art. I, § 9 ("No Title of Nobility shall be granted by the United States"). To pursue the concept of racial entitlement -- even for the most admirable and benign of purposes -- is to reinforce and preserve for future mischief the way of thinking that produced race slavery, race privilege and race hatred. In the eyes of government, we are just one race here. It is American.

It is unlikely, if not impossible, that the challenged program would survive under this understanding of strict scrutiny, but I am content to leave that to be decided on remand.

Can't single out groups from disfavorable treatment: Justice Scalia's dissent in Romer v. Evans (May 20, 1996)

Justice Scalia, with whom The Chief Justice and Justice Thomas join, dissenting.

The Court has mistaken a Kulturkampf for a fit of spite. The constitutional amendment before us here is not the manifestation of a "`bare . . . desire to harm'" homosexuals, ante, at 13, but is rather a modest attempt by seemingly tolerant Coloradans to preserve traditional sexual mores against the efforts of a politically powerful minority to revise those mores through use of the laws. That objective, and the means chosen to achieve it, are not only unimpeachable under any constitutional doctrine hitherto pronounced (hence the opinion's heavy reliance upon principles of righteousness rather than judicial holdings); they have been specifically approved by the Congress of the United States and by this Court.

In holding that homosexuality cannot be singled out for disfavorable treatment, the Court contradicts a decision, unchallenged here, pronounced only 10 years ago, see

Bowers v. Hardwick, 478 U.S. 186 (1986), and places the prestige of this institution behind the proposition that opposition to homosexuality is as reprehensible as racial or religious bias. Whether it is or not is precisely the cultural debate that gave rise to the Colorado constitutional amendment (and to the preferential laws against which the amendment was directed). Since the Constitution of the United States says nothing about this subject, it is left to be resolved by normal democratic means, including the democratic adoption of provisions in state constitutions. This Court has no business imposing upon all Americans the resolution favored by the elite class from which the Members of this institution are selected, pronouncing that "animosity" toward homosexuality, ante, at 13, is evil. I vigorously dissent.

Let me first discuss Part II of the Court's opinion, its longest section, which is devoted to rejecting the State's arguments that Amendment 2 "puts gays and lesbians in the same position as all other persons," and "does no more than deny homosexuals special rights," ante, at 4. The Court concludes that this reading of Amendment 2's language is "implausible" under the "authoritative construction" given Amendment 2 by the Supreme Court of Colorado. Ibid.

In reaching this conclusion, the Court considers it unnecessary to decide the validity of the State's argument that Amendment 2 does not deprive homosexuals of the "protection [afforded by] general laws and policies that prohibit arbitrary discrimination in governmental and private settings." Ante, at 8. I agree that we need not resolve that dispute, because the Supreme Court of Colorado has resolved it for us. In Evans v. Romer, 882 P. 2d 1335 (1994), the Colorado court stated:

"[I]t is significant to note that Colorado law currently proscribes discrimination against persons who are not suspect classes, including discrimination based on age, §24-34-402(1)(a), 10A C. R. S. (1994 Supp.); marital or family status, §24-34-502(1)(a), 10A C. R. S. (1994 Supp.); veterans' status, §28-3-506, 11B C. R. S. (1989); and for any legal, off duty conduct such as smoking tobacco, §24-34-402.5, 10 AC. R. S. (1994 Supp.). Of course Amendment 2 is not intended to have any effect on this legislation, but seeks only to prevent the adoption of anti discrimination laws intended to protect gays, lesbians, and bisexuals." Id., at 1346, n. 9 (emphasis added).

The Court utterly fails to distinguish this portion of the Colorado court's opinion. Colorado Rev. Stat. §24-34-402.5 (Supp. 1995), which this passage authoritatively declares not to be affected by Amendment 2, was respondents' primary example of a generally applicable law whose protections would be unavailable to homosexuals under Amendment 2. See Brief for Respondents Evans et al. 11-12. The clear import of the Colorado court's conclusion that it is not affected is that "general laws and policies that prohibit arbitrary discrimination" would continue to prohibit discrimination on the basis of homosexual conduct as well. This analysis, which is fully in accord with (indeed, follows inescapably from) the text of the constitutional provision, lays to rest such horribles, raised in the course of oral argument, as the prospect that assaults upon homosexuals could not be prosecuted. The amendment prohibits special treatment of homosexuals, and nothing more. It would not affect, for example, a requirement of state law that pensions be paid to all retiring state employees with a certain length of service; homosexual employees, as well as others, would be entitled to that benefit. But it would prevent the State or any municipality from making death benefit payments to the "life partner" of a homosexual when it does not make such payments to the long time roommate of a nonhomosexual employee. Or again, it does not affect the requirement of the State's general insurance laws that customers be afforded coverage without discrimination unrelated to anticipated risk. Thus, homosexuals could not be denied coverage, or charged a greater premium, with respect to auto collision insurance; but neither the State nor any municipality could require that distinctive health insurance risks associated with homosexuality (if there are any) be ignored.

Despite all of its hand wringing about the potential effect of Amendment 2 on general antidiscrimination laws, the Court's opinion ultimately does not dispute all this, but assumes it to be true. See ante, at 9. The only denial of equal treatment it contends homosexuals have suffered is this: They may not obtain preferential treatment without amending the state constitution. That is to say, the principle underlying the Court's opinion is that one who is accorded equal treatment under the laws, but cannot as readily as others obtain preferential treatment under the laws, has been denied equal protection of the laws. If merely stating this alleged "equal protection" violation does not suffice to refute it, our constitutional jurisprudence has achieved terminal silliness.

The central thesis of the Court's reasoning is that any group is denied equal protection when, to obtain advantage (or, presumably, to avoid disadvantage), it must have recourse to a more general and hence more difficult level of political decisionmaking than others. The world has never heard of such a principle, which is why the Court's opinion is so long on emotive utterance and so short on relevant legal citation. And it seems to me most unlikely that any multilevel democracy can function under such a principle. For whenever a disadvantage is imposed, or conferral of a benefit is prohibited, at one of the higher levels of democratic decisionmaking (i.e., by the state legislature rather than local government, or by the people at large in the state constitution rather than the legislature), the affected group has (under this theory) been denied equal protection. To take the simplest of examples, consider a state law prohibiting the award of municipal contracts to relatives of mayors or city councilmen. Once such a law is passed, the group composed of such relatives must, in order to get the benefit of city contracts, persuade the state legislature--unlike all other citizens, who need only persuade the municipality. It is ridiculous to consider this a denial of equal protection, which is why the Court's theory is unheard of.

The Court might reply that the example I have given is not a denial of equal protection only because the same "rational basis" (avoidance of corruption) which renders constitutional the substantive discrimination against relatives (i.e., the fact that they alone cannot obtain city contracts) also automatically suffices to sustain what might be called the electoral procedural discrimination against them (i.e., the fact that they must go to the state level to get this changed). This is of course a perfectly reasonable response, and would explain why "electoral procedural discrimination" has not hitherto been heard of: a law that is valid in its substance is automatically valid in its level of enactment. But the Court cannot afford to make this argument, for as I shall discuss next, there is no doubt of a rational basis for the substance of the prohibition at issue here. The Court's entire novel theory rests upon the proposition that there is something special--something that cannot be justified by normal "rational basis" analysis--in making a disadvantaged group (or a nonpreferred group) resort to a higher decisionmaking level. That proposition finds no support in law or logic.

  I turn next to whether there was a legitimate rational basis for the substance of the constitutional amendment--for the prohibition of special protection for homosexuals. [n.1] It is unsurprising that the Court avoids discussion of this question, since the answer is so obviously yes. The case most relevant to the issue before us today is not even mentioned in the Court's opinion: In Bowers v. Hardwick, 478 U.S. 186 (1986), we held that the Constitution does not prohibit what virtually all States had done from the founding of the Republic until very recent years--making homosexual conduct a crime. That holding is unassailable, except by those who think that the Constitution changes to suit current fashions. But in any event it is a given in the present case: Respondents' briefs did not urge overruling Bowers, and at oral argument respondents' counsel expressly disavowed any intent to seek such overruling, Tr. of Oral Arg. 53. If it is constitutionally permissible for a State to make homosexual conduct criminal, surely it is constitutionally permissible for a State to enact other laws merely disfavoring homosexual conduct. (As the Court of Appeals for the District of Columbia Circuit has aptly put it: "If the Court [in Bowers] was unwilling to object to state laws that criminalize the behavior that defines the class, it is hardly open . . . to conclude that state sponsored discrimination against the class is invidious. After all, there can hardly be more palpable discrimination against a class than making the conduct that defines the class criminal." Padula v. Webster, 822 F. 2d 97, 103 (1987).) And a fortiori it is constitutionally permissible for a State to adopt a provision not even disfavoring homosexual conduct, but merely prohibiting all levels of state government from bestowing special protections upon homosexual conduct. Respondents (who, unlike the Court, cannot afford the luxury of ignoring inconvenient precedent) counter Bowers with the argument that a greater includes the lesser rationale cannot justify Amendment 2's application to individuals who do not engage in homosexual acts, but are merely of homosexual "orientation." Some courts of appeals have concluded that, with respect to laws of this sort at least, that is a distinction without a difference. See Equality Foundation of Greater Cincinnati, Inc. v. Cincinnati, 54 F. 3d 261, 267 (CA 6 1995) ("[F]or purposes of these proceedings, it is virtually impossible to distinguish or separate individuals of a particular orientation which predisposes them toward a particular sexual conduct from those who actually engage in that particular type of sexual conduct"); Steffan v. Perry, 41 F. 3d 677, 689-690 (CADC 1994). The Supreme Court of Colorado itself appears to be of this view. See 882 P.

2d, at 1349-1350 ("Amendment 2 targets this class of persons based on four characteristics: sexual orientation; conduct; practices; and relationships. Each characteristic provides a potentially different way of identifying that class of persons who are gay, lesbian, or bisexual. These four characteristics are not truly severable from one another because each provides nothing more than a different way of identifying the same class of persons") (emphasis added).

But assuming that, in Amendment 2, a person of homosexual "orientation" is someone who does not engage in homosexual conduct but merely has a tendency or desire to do so, Bowers still suffices to establish a rational basis for the provision. If it is rational to criminalize the conduct, surely it is rational to deny special favor and protection to those with a self avowed tendency or desire to engage in the conduct. Indeed, where criminal sanctions are not involved, homosexual-orientation" is an acceptable stand in for homosexual conduct. A State "does not violate the Equal Protection Clause merely because the classifications made by its laws are imperfect," Dandridge v. Williams, 397 U.S. 471, 485 (1970). Just as a policy barring the hiring of methadone users as transit employees does not violate equal protection simply because some methadone users pose no threat to passenger safety, see New York City Transit Authority v. Beazer, 440 U.S. 568 (1979), and just as a mandatory retirement age of 50 for police officers does not violate equal protection even though it prematurely ends the careers of many policemen over 50 who still have the capacity to do the job, see Massachusetts Bd. of Retirement v. Murgia, 427 U.S. 307 (1976) (per curiam), Amendment 2 is not constitutionally invalid simply because it could have been drawn more precisely so as to withdraw special antidiscrimination protections only from those of homosexual "orientation" who actually engage in homosexual conduct. As Justice Kennedy wrote, when he was on the Court of Appeals, in a case involving discharge of homosexuals from the Navy: "Nearly any statute which classifies people may be irrational as applied in particular cases. Discharge of the particular plaintiffs before us would be rational, under minimal scrutiny, not because their particular cases present the dangers which justify Navy policy, but instead because the general policy of discharging all homosexuals is rational." Beller v. Middendorf, 632 F. 2d 788, 808-809, n. 20 (CA9 1980) (citation omitted). See also Ben Shalom v. Marsh, 881 F. 2d 454, 464 (CA7 1989), cert. denied, 494 U.S. 1004 (1990).

Moreover, even if the provision regarding homosexual "orientation" were invalid, respondents' challenge to Amendment 2--which is a facial challenge--must fail. "A facial challenge to a legislative Act is, of course, the most difficult challenge to mount successfully, since the challenger must establish that no set of circumstances exists under which the Act would be valid." United States v. Salerno, 481 U.S. 739, 745 (1987). It would not be enough for respondents to establish (if they could) that Amendment 2 is unconstitutional as applied to those of homosexual "orientation"; since, under Bowers, Amendment 2 is unquestionably constitutional as applied to those who engage in homosexual conduct, the facial challenge cannot succeed. Some individuals of homosexual "orientation" who do not engage in homosexual acts might successfully bring an as applied challenge to Amendment 2, but so far as the record indicates, none of the respondents is such a person. See App. 4-5 (complaint describing each of the individual respondents as either "a gay man" or "a lesbian"). [n.2]

The foregoing suffices to establish what the Court's failure to cite any case remotely in point would lead one to suspect: No principle set forth in the Constitution, nor even any imagined by this Court in the past 200 years, prohibits what Colorado has done here. But the case for Colorado is much stronger than that. What it has done is not only unprohibited, but eminently reasonable, with close, congressionally approved precedent in earlier constitutional practice.

First, as to its eminent reasonableness. The Court's opinion contains grim, disapproving hints that Coloradans have been guilty of "animus" or "animosity" toward homosexuality, as though that has been established as Unamerican. Of course it is our moral heritage that one should not hate any human being or class of human beings. But I had thought that one could consider certain conduct reprehensible--murder, for example, or polygamy, or cruelty to animals--and could exhibit even "animus" toward such conduct. Surely that is the only sort of "animus" at issue here: moral disapproval of homosexual conduct, the same sort of moral disapproval that produced the centuries old criminal laws that we held constitutional in Bowers. The Colorado amendment does not, to speak entirely precisely, prohibit giving favored status to people who are homosexuals; they can be favored for many reasons--for example, because they are senior citizens or members of racial minorities. But it prohibits giving them favored status because of their homosexual conduct--that is, it prohibits favored status for homosexuality.

But though Coloradans are, as I say, entitled to be hostile toward homosexual conduct, the fact is that the degree of hostility reflected by Amendment 2 is the smallest conceivable. The Court's portrayal of Coloradans as a society fallen victim to pointless, hate filled "gay bashing" is so false as to be comical. Colorado not only is one of the 25 States that have repealed their antisodomy laws, but was among the first to do so. See 1971 Colo. Sess. Laws, ch. 121, §1. But the society that eliminates criminal punishment for homosexual acts does not necessarily abandon the view that homosexuality is morally wrong and socially harmful; often, abolition simply reflects the view that enforcement of such criminal laws involves unseemly intrusion into the intimate lives of citizens. Cf. Brief for Lambda Legal Defense and Education Fund, Inc., et al. as Amici Curiae in Bowers v. Hardwick, O. T. 1985, No. 85-140, p. 25, n. 21 (antisodomy statutes are "unenforceable by any but the most offensive snooping and wasteful allocation of law enforcement resources"); Kadish, The Crisis of Overcriminalization, 374 The Annals of the American Academy of Political and Social Science 157, 161 (1967) ("To obtain evidence [in sodomy cases], police are obliged to resort to behavior which tends to degrade and demean both themselves personally and law enforcement as an institution").

There is a problem, however, which arises when criminal sanction of homosexuality is eliminated but moral and social disapprobation of homosexuality is meant to be retained. The Court cannot be unaware of that problem; it is evident in many cities of the country, and occasionally bubbles to the surface of the news, in heated political disputes over such matters as the introduction into local schools of books teaching that homosexuality is an optional and fully acceptable "alternate life style." The problem (a problem, that is, for those who wish to retain social disapprobation of homosexuality) is that, because those who engage in homosexual conduct tend to reside in disproportionate numbers in certain communities, see Record, Exh. MMM, have high disposable income, see ibid.; App. 254 (affidavit of Prof. James Hunter), and of course care about homosexual rights issues much more ardently than the public at large, they possess political power much greater than their numbers, both locally and statewide. Quite understandably, they devote this political power to achieving not merely a grudging social toleration, but full social acceptance, of homosexuality. See, e.g., Jacobs, The Rhetorical Construction of Rights: The Case of the Gay Rights Movement, 1969-1991, 72 Neb. L. Rev. 723, 724 (1993) ("[T]he task of gay rights proponents is to move the center of public discourse along a continuum from the rhetoric of disapprobation, to rhetoric of tolerance, and finally to affirmation").

By the time Coloradans were asked to vote on Amendment 2, their exposure to homosexuals' quest for social endorsement was not limited to newspaper accounts of happenings in places such as New York, Los Angeles, San Francisco, and Key West. Three Colorado cities-- Aspen, Boulder, and Denver--had enacted ordinances that listed "sexual orientation" as an impermissible ground for discrimination, equating the moral disapproval of homosexual conduct with racial and religious bigotry. See Aspen Municipal Code §13-98 (1977); Boulder Rev. Municipal Code §§12-1-1 to 12-1-11 (1987); Denver Rev. Municipal Code, Art. IV §§28-91 to 28-116 (1991). The phenomenon had even appeared statewide: the Governor of Colorado had signed an executive order pronouncing that "in the State of Colorado we recognize the diversity in our pluralistic society and strive to bring an end to discrimination in any form," and directing state agency heads to "ensure non discrimination" in hiring and promotion based on, among other things, "sexual orientation." Executive Order No. D0035 (Dec. 10, 1990). I do not mean to be critical of these legislative successes; homosexuals are as entitled to use the legal system for reinforcement of their moral sentiments as are the rest of society. But they are subject to being countered by lawful, democratic countermeasures as well.

That is where Amendment 2 came in. It sought to counter both the geographic concentration and the disproportionate political power of homosexuals by (1) resolving the controversy at the statewide level, and (2) making the election a single issue contest for both sides. It put directly, to all the citizens of the State, the question: Should homosexuality be given special protection? They answered no. The Court today asserts that this most democratic of procedures is unconstitutional. Lacking any cases to establish that facially absurd proposition, it simply asserts that it must be unconstitutional, because it has never happened before.

"[Amendment 2] identifies persons by a single trait and then denies them protection across the board. The resulting disqualification of a class of persons from the right to seek specific protection from the law is unprecedented in our jurisprudence. The absence of precedent for Amendment 2 is itself instructive . . . .

"It is not within our constitutional tradition to enact laws of this sort. Central both to the idea of the rule of law and to our own Constitution's guarantee of equal protection is the principle that government and each of its parts remain open on impartial terms to all who seek its assistance." Ante, at 11-12.

As I have noted above, this is proved false every time a state law prohibiting or disfavoring certain conduct is passed, because such a law prevents the adversely affected group--whether drug addicts, or smokers, or gun owners, or motorcyclists--from changing the policy thus established in "each of [the] parts" of the State. What the Court says is even demonstrably false at the constitutional level. The Eighteenth Amendment to the Federal Constitution, for example, deprived those who drank alcohol not only of the power to alter the policy of prohibition locally or through state legislation, but even of the power to alter it through state constitutional amendment or federal legislation. The Establishment Clause of the First Amendment prevents theocrats from having their way by converting their fellow citizens at the local, state, or federal statutory level; as does the Republican Form of Government Clause prevent monarchists.

But there is a much closer analogy, one that involves precisely the effort by the majority of citizens to preserve its view of sexual morality statewide, against the efforts of a geographically concentrated and politically powerful minority to undermine it. The constitutions of the States of Arizona, Idaho, New Mexico, Oklahoma, and Utah to this day contain provisions stating that polygamy is "forever prohibited." See Ariz. Const., Art. XX, par. 2; Idaho Const., Art. I, §4; N. M. Const., Art. XXI, §1; Okla. Const., Art. I, §2; Utah Const., Art. III, §1. Polygamists, and those who have a polygamous "orientation," have been "singled out" by these provisions for much more severe treatment than merely denial of favored status; and that treatment can only be changed by achieving amendment of the state constitutions. The Court's disposition today suggests that these provisions are unconstitutional, and that polygamy must be permitted in these States on a state legislated, or perhaps even local option, basis--unless, of course, polygamists for some reason have fewer constitutional rights than homosexuals.

The United States Congress, by the way, required the inclusion of these anti polygamy provisions in the constitutions of Arizona, New Mexico, Oklahoma, and Utah, as a condition of their admission to statehood. See Arizona Enabling Act, 36 Stat. 569; New Mexico Enabling Act, 36 Stat. 558; Oklahoma Enabling Act, 34 Stat. 269; Utah Enabling Act, 28 Stat. 108. (For Arizona, New Mexico, and Utah, moreover, the Enabling Acts required that the anti polygamy provisions be "irrevocable without the consent of the United States and the people of said State"--so that not only were "each of [the] parts" of these States not "open on impartial terms" to polygamists, but even the States as a whole were not; polygamists would have to persuade the whole country to their way of thinking.) Idaho adopted the constitutional provision on its own, but the 51st Congress, which admitted Idaho into the Union, found its constitution to be "republican in form and . . . in conformity with the Constitution of the United States." Act of Admission of Idaho, 26 Stat. 215 (emphasis added). Thus, this "singling out" of the sexual practices of a single group for statewide, democratic vote--so utterly alien to our constitutional system, the Court would have us believe--has not only happened, but has received the explicit approval of the United States Congress.

I cannot say that this Court has explicitly approved any of these state constitutional provisions; but it has approved a territorial statutory provision that went even further, depriving polygamists of the ability even to achieve a constitutional amendment, by depriving them of the power to vote. In Davis v. Beason, 133 U.S. 333 (1890), Justice Field wrote for a unanimous Court:

"In our judgment, §501 of the Revised Statutes of Idaho Territory, which provides that `no person . . . who is a bigamist or polygamist or who teaches, advises, counsels, or encourages any person or persons to become bigamists or polygamists, or to commit any other crime defined by law, or to enter into what is known as plural or celestial marriage, or who is a member of any order, organization or association which teaches, advises, counsels, or encourages its members or devotees or any other persons to commit the crime of bigamy or polygamy, or any other crime defined by law . . . is permitted to vote at any election, or to hold any position or office of honor, trust, or profit within this Territory,' is not open to any constitutional or legal objection." Id., at 346-347 (emphasis added).

To the extent, if any, that this opinion permits the imposition of adverse consequences upon mere abstract advocacy of polygamy, it has of course been overruled by later cases. See Brandenburg v. Ohio, 395 U.S. 444 (1969) (per curiam). But the proposition that polygamy can be criminalized, and those engaging in that crime deprived of the vote, remains good law. See Richardson v. Ramirez, 418 U.S. 24, 53 (1974). Beason rejected the argument that "such discrimination is a denial of the equal protection of the laws." Brief for Appellant in Davis v. Beason, O. T. 1889, No. 1261, p. 41. Among the Justices joining in that rejection were the two whose views in other cases the Court today treats as equal protection lodestars--Justice Harlan, who was to proclaim in Plessy v. Ferguson, 163 U.S. 537, 559 (1896) (dissenting opinion), that the Constitution "neither knows nor tolerates classes among citizens," quoted ante, at 1, and Justice Bradley, who had earlier declared that "class legislation . . . [is] obnoxious to the prohibitions of the Fourteenth Amendment," Civil Rights Cases, 109 U.S. 3, 24 (1883), quoted ante, at 14. [n.3]

This Court cited Beason with approval as recently as 1993, in an opinion authored by the same Justice who writes for the Court today. That opinion said: "[A]dverse impact will not always lead to a finding of impermissible targeting. For example, a social harm may have been a legitimate concern of government for reasons quite apart from discrimination. . . . See, e.g., . . . Davis v. Beason, 133 U.S. 333 (1890)." Church of Lukumi

Babalu Aye, Inc. v. Hialeah, 508 U.S. 520, 535 (1993). It remains to be explained how §501 of the Idaho Revised Statutes was not an "impermissible targeting" of polygamists, but (the much more mild) Amendment 2 is an "impermissible targeting" of homosexuals. Has the Court concluded that the perceived social harm of polygamy is a "legitimate concern of government," and the perceived social harm of homosexuality is not?

I strongly suspect that the answer to the last question is yes, which leads me to the last point I wish to make: The Court today, announcing that Amendment 2 "defies . . . conventional [constitutional] inquiry," ante, at 10, and "confounds [the] normal process of judicial review," ante, at 11, employs a constitutional theory heretofore unknown to frustrate Colorado's reasonable effort to preserve traditional American moral values. The Court's stern disapproval of "animosity" towards homosexuality might be compared with what an earlier Court (including the revered Justices Harlan and Bradley) said in Murphy v. Ramsey, 114 U.S. 15 (1885), rejecting a constitutional challenge to a United States statute that denied the franchise in federal territories to those who engaged in polygamous cohabitation:

"[C]ertainly no legislation can be supposed more wholesome and necessary in the founding of a free, self governing commonwealth, fit to take rank as one of the co ordinate States of the Union, than that which seeks to establish it on the basis of the idea of the family, as consisting in and springing from the union for life of one man and one woman in the holy estate of matrimony; the sure foundation of all that is stable and noble in our civilization; the best guaranty of that reverent morality which is the source of all beneficent progress in social and political improvement." Id., at 45.

I would not myself indulge in such official praise for heterosexual monogamy, because I think it no business of the courts (as opposed to the political branches) to take sides in this culture war.

But the Court today has done so, not only by inventing a novel and extravagant constitutional doctrine to take the victory away from traditional forces, but even by verbally disparaging as bigotry adherence to traditional attitudes. To suggest, for example, that this constitutional amendment springs from nothing more than " `a bare . . . desire to harm a politically unpopular group,' " ante, at 13, quoting Department of Agriculture v. Moreno, 413 U.S. 528, 534 (1973), is nothing short of insulting. (It is also nothing short of preposterous to call "politically unpopular" a group which enjoys enormous influence in American media and politics, and which, as the trial court here noted, though composing no more than 4% of the population had the support of 46% of the voters on Amendment 2, see App. to Pet. for Cert. C-18.)

When the Court takes sides in the culture wars, it tends to be with the knights rather than the villains--and more specifically with the Templars, reflecting the views and values of the lawyer class from which the Court's Members are drawn. How that class feels about homosexuality will be evident to anyone who wishes to interview job applicants at virtually any of the Nation's law schools. The interviewer may refuse to offer a job because the applicant is a Republican; because he is an adulterer; because he went to the wrong prep school or belongs to the wrong country club; because he eats snails; because he is a womanizer; because she wears real animal fur; or even because he hates the Chicago Cubs. But if the interviewer should wish not to be an associate or partner of an applicant because he disapproves of the applicant's homosexuality, then he will have violated the pledge which the Association of American Law Schools requires all its member schools to exact from job interviewers: "assurance of the employer's willingness" to hire homosexuals. Bylaws of the Association of American Law Schools, Inc. §6-4(b); Executive Committee Regulations of the Association of American Law Schools §6.19, in 1995 Handbook, Association of American Law Schools. This law school view of what "prejudices" must be stamped out may be contrasted with the more plebeian attitudes that apparently still prevail in the United States Congress, which has been unresponsive to repeated attempts to extend to homosexuals the protections of federal civil rights laws, see, e.g., Employment Non Discrimination Act of 1994, S. 2238, 103d Cong., 2d Sess. (1994); Civil Rights Amendments of 1975, H. R. 5452, 94th Cong., 1st Sess. (1975), and which took the pains to exclude them specifically from the Americans With Disabilities Act of 1990, see 42 U.S.C. § 12211(a) (1988 ed., Supp. V).

* * *

Today's opinion has no foundation in American constitutional law, and barely pretends to. The people of Colorado have adopted an entirely reasonable provision which does not even disfavor homosexuals in any substantive sense, but merely denies them preferential treatment. Amendment 2 is designed to prevent piecemeal deterioration of the sexual morality favored by a majority of Coloradans, and is not only an appropriate means to that legitimate end, but a means that Americans have employed before. Striking it down is an act, not of judicial judgment, but of political will. I dissent.

Notes to Justice Scalia's dissent in Romer v. Evans (May 20, 1996)

1 The Court evidently agrees that "rational basis"--the normal test for compliance with the Equal Protection Clause--is the governing standard. The trial court rejected respondents' argument that homosexuals constitute a "suspect" or "quasi suspect" class, and respondents elected not to appeal that ruling to the Supreme Court of Colorado. See Evans v. Romer, 882 P. 2d 1335, 1341, n. 3 (1994). And the Court implicitly rejects the Supreme Court of Colorado's holding, see Evans v. Romer, 854 P. 2d 1270, 1282 (1993), that Amendment 2 infringes upon a "fundamental right" of "independently identifiable class[es]" to "participate equally in the political process." Ante, at 4.

2 The Supreme Court of Colorado stated: "We hold that the portions of Amendment 2 that would remain if only the provision concerning sexual orientation were stricken are not autonomous and thus, not severable," 882 P. 2d, at 1349. That statement was premised, however, on the proposition that "[the] four characteristics [described in the Amendment--sexual orientation, conduct, practices, and relationships] are not truly severable from one another because each provides nothing more than a different way of

identifying the same class of persons." Id., at 1349-1350 (emphasis added). As I have discussed above, if that premise is true--if the entire class affected by the Amendment takes part in homosexual conduct, practices and relationships--Bowers alone suffices to answer all constitutional objections. Separate consideration of persons of homosexual "orientation" is necessary only if one believes (as the Supreme Court of Colorado did not) that that is a distinct class.

    3 The Court labors mightily to get around Beason, see ante, at 12-13, but cannot escape the central fact that this Court found the statute at issue--which went much further than Amendment 2, denying polygamists not merely special treatment but the right to vote--"not open to any constitutional or legal objection," rejecting the appellant's argument (much like the argument of respondents today) that the statute impermissibly "single[d] him out," Brief for Appellant in Davis v. Beason, O. T. 1889, No. 1261, p. 41. The Court adopts my conclusions that (a) insofar as Beason permits the imposition of adverse consequences based upon mere advocacy, it has been overruled by subsequent cases, and (b) insofar as Beason holds that convicted felons may be denied the right to vote, it remains good law. To these conclusions, it adds something new: the claim that "[t]o the extent [Beason] held that the groups designated in the statute may be deprived of the right to vote because of their status, its ruling could not stand without surviving strict scrutiny, a most doubtful outcome." Ante, at 12-13. But if that is so, it is only because we have declared the right to vote to be a "fundamental political right," see, e.g., Dunn v. Blumstein, 405 U.S. 330, 336 (1972), deprivation of which triggers strict scrutiny. Amendment 2, of course, does not deny the fundamental right to vote, and the Court rejects the Colorado court's view that there exists a fundamental right to participate in the political process. Strict scrutiny is thus not in play here. See ante, at 10. Finally, the Court's suggestion that §501 of the Revised Statutes of Idaho, and Amendment 2, deny rights on account of "status" (rather than conduct) opens up a broader debate involving the significance of Bowers to this case, a debate which the Court is otherwise unwilling to join, see supra, at 6-9.

Single-Sex colleges constitutional: Justice Scalia's dissent in United States v. Virginia (June 26, 1996)

    Justice Scalia, dissenting.
    Much of the Court's opinion is devoted to deprecating the closed mindedness of our forebears with regard to women's education, and even with regard to the treatment of women in areas that have nothing to do with education. Closed minded they were--as every age is, including our own, with regard to matters it cannot guess, because it simply does not consider them debatable. The virtue of a democratic system with a First Amendment is that it readily enables the people, over time, to be persuaded that what they took for granted is not so, and to change their laws accordingly. That system is

destroyed if the smug assurances of each age are removed from the democratic process and written into the Constitution. So to counterbalance the Court's criticism of our ancestors, let me say a word in their praise: they left us free to change. The same cannot be said of this most illiberal Court, which has embarked on a course of inscribing one after another of the current preferences of the society (and in some cases only the counter majoritarian preferences of the society's law trained elite) into our Basic Law. Today it enshrines the notion that no substantial educational value is to be served by an all men's military academy--so that the decision by the people of Virginia to maintain such an institution denies equal protection to women who cannot attend that institution but can attend others. Since it is entirely clear that the Constitution of the United States--the old one--takes no sides in this educational debate, I dissent.

I shall devote most of my analysis to evaluating the Court's opinion on the basis of our current equal protection jurisprudence, which regards this Court as free to evaluate everything under the sun by applying one of three tests: "rational basis" scrutiny, intermediate scrutiny, or strict scrutiny. These tests are no more scientific than their names suggest, and a further element of randomness is added by the fact that it is largely up to us which test will be applied in each case. Strict scrutiny, we have said, is reserved for state "classifications based on race or national origin and classifications affecting fundamental rights," Clark v. Jeter, 486 U.S. 456, 461 (1988) (citation omitted). It is my position that the term "fundamental rights" should be limited to "interest[s] traditionally protected by our society," Michael H. v. Gerald D., 491 U.S. 110, 122 (1989) (plurality opinion of Scalia, J.); but the Court has not accepted that view, so that strict scrutiny will be applied to the deprivation of whatever sort of right we consider "fundamental." We have no established criterion for "intermediate scrutiny" either, but essentially apply it when it seems like a good idea to load the dice. So far it has been applied to content neutral restrictions that place an incidental burden on speech, to disabilities attendant to illegitimacy, and to discrimination on the basis of sex. See, e.g., Turner Broadcasting System, Inc. v. FCC, 512 U. S. ___, ___ (1994) (slip op., at 38); Mills v. Habluetzel, 456 U.S. 91, 98-99 (1982); Craig v. Boren, 429 U.S. 190, 197 (1976).

I have no problem with a system of abstract tests such as rational basis, intermediate, and strict scrutiny (though I think we can do better than applying strict scrutiny and intermediate scrutiny whenever we feel like it). Such formulas are essential to evaluating whether the new restrictions that a changing society constantly imposes upon private conduct comport with that "equal protection" our society has always accorded in the past. But in my view the function of this Court is to preserve our society's values regarding (among other things) equal protection, not to revise them; to prevent backsliding from the degree of restriction the Constitution imposed upon democratic government, not to prescribe, on our own authority, progressively higher degrees. For that reason it is my view that, whatever abstract tests we may choose to devise, they cannot supersede--and indeed ought to be crafted so as to reflect--those constant and unbroken national traditions that embody the people's understanding of ambiguous constitutional texts. More specifically, it is my view that "when a practice not expressly prohibited by the text of the Bill of Rights bears the endorsement of a long tradition of open, widespread, and unchallenged use that dates back to the beginning of the Republic, we have no proper basis for striking it down." Rutan v. Republican Party of Ill., 497 U.S. 62, 95 (1990) (Scalia, J., dissenting). The same applies, mutatis mutandis, to a practice asserted to be in violation of the post-Civil War Fourteenth Amendment. See, e.g., Burnham v. Superior Court of Cal., County of Marin, 495 U.S. 604 (1990) (plurality opinion of Scalia, J.) (Due Process Clause); J. E. B. v. Alabama ex rel. T. B., 511 U.S. 127, 156-163 (Scalia, J., dissenting) (Equal Protection Clause); Planned Parenthood of S. E. Pa. v. Casey, 505 U.S. 833, 979-984, 1000-1001 (1992) (Scalia, J., dissenting) (various alleged "penumbras").

    The all male constitution of VMI comes squarely within such a governing tradition. Founded by the Commonwealth of Virginia in 1839 and continuously maintained by it since, VMI has always admitted only men. And in that regard it has not been unusual. For almost all of VMI's more than a century and a half of existence, its single sex status reflected the uniform practice for government supported military colleges. Another famous Southern institution, The Citadel, has existed as a state funded school of South Carolina since 1842. And all the federal military colleges--West Point, the Naval Academy at Annapolis, and even the Air Force Academy, which was not established until 1954--admitted only males for most of their history. Their admission of women in 1976 (upon which the Court today relies, see ante, at 27-28, nn. 13, 15), came not by court decree, but because the people, through their elected representatives, decreed a change. See, e.g., Pub. L. 94-106, §803(a), 89 Stat. 537-538 (1975). In other words, the tradition of having government funded military schools for men is as well rooted in the traditions of this country as the tradition of sending only men into military combat. The people may decide to change the one tradition, like the other, through democratic processes; but the assertion that either tradition has been unconstitutional through the centuries is not law, but politics smuggled into law.

    And the same applies, more broadly, to single sex education in general, which, as I shall discuss, is threatened by today's decision with the cut off of all state and federal support. Government run nonmilitary educational institutions for the two sexes have until very recently also been part of our national tradition. "[It is] [c]oeducation, historically, [that] is a novel educational theory. From grade school through high school, college, and graduate and professional training, much of the Nation's population during much of our history has been educated in sexually segregated classrooms." Mississippi Univ. for Women v. Hogan, 458 U.S. 718, 736 (1982) (Powell, J., dissenting); see id., at 736-739. These traditions may of course be changed by the democratic decisions of the people, as they largely have been.

    Today, however, change is forced upon Virginia, and reversion to single sex education is prohibited nationwide, not by democratic processes but by order of this Court. Even while bemoaning the sorry, bygone days of "fixed notions" concerning women's education, see ante, at 18-19, and n. 10, 20-21, 25-27, the Court favors current notions so fixedly that it is willing to write them into the Constitution of the United States by application of custom built "tests." This is not the interpretation of a Constitution, but the creation of one.

To reject the Court's disposition today, however, it is not necessary to accept my view that the Court's made up tests cannot displace longstanding national traditions as the primary determinant of what the Constitution means. It is only necessary to apply honestly the test the Court has been applying to sex based classifications for the past two decades. It is well settled, as Justice O'Connor stated some time ago for a unanimous Court, that we evaluate a statutory classification based on sex under a standard that lies "[b]etween th[e] extremes of rational basis review and strict scrutiny." Clark v. Jeter, 486 U. S., at 461. We have denominated this standard "intermediate scrutiny" and under it have inquired whether the statutory classification is "substantially related to an important governmental objective." Ibid. See, e.g., Heckler v. Mathews, 465 U.S. 728, 744 (1984); Wengler v. Druggists Mutual Ins. Co., 446 U.S. 142, 150 (1980); Craig v. Boren, 429 U. S., at 197.

Before I proceed to apply this standard to VMI, I must comment upon the manner in which the Court avoids doing so. Notwithstanding our above described precedents and their " `firmly established principles,' " Heckler, supra, at 744 (quoting Hogan, supra, at 723), the United States urged us to hold in this case "that strict scrutiny is the correct constitutional standard for evaluating classifications that deny opportunities to individuals based on their sex." Brief for United States in No. 94-2107, p. 16. (This was in flat contradiction of the Government's position below, which was, in its own words, to "stat[e] unequivocally that the appropriate standard in this case is `intermediate scrutiny.' " 2 Record, Doc. No. 88, p. 3 (emphasis added).) The Court, while making no reference to the Government's argument, effectively accepts it.

Although the Court in two places recites the test as stated in Hogan, see ante, at 6, 15, which asks whether the State has demonstrated "that the classification serves important governmental objectives and that the discriminatory means employed are substantially related to the achievement of those objectives," 458 U. S., at 724 (internal quotation marks omitted), the Court never answers the question presented in anything resembling that form. When it engages in analysis, the Court instead prefers the phrase "exceedingly persuasive justification" from Hogan. The Court's nine invocations of that phrase, see ante, at 6, 11, 12, 13, 15, 16, 28, 29, 39, and even its fanciful description of that imponderable as "the core instruction" of the Court's decisions in J. E. B. v. Alabama ex rel. T. B., 511 U.S. 127 (1994), and Hogan, supra, see ante, at 13, would be unobjectionable if the Court acknowledged that whether a "justification" is "exceedingly persuasive" must be assessed by asking "[whether] the classification serves important governmental objectives and [whether] the discriminatory means employed are substantially related to the achievement of those objectives." Instead, however, the Court proceeds to interpret "exceedingly persuasive justification" in a fashion that contradicts the reasoning of Hogan and our other precedents.

That is essential to the Court's result, which can only be achieved by establishing that intermediate scrutiny is not survived if there are some women interested in attending VMI, capable of undertaking its activities, and able to meet its physical demands. Thus, the Court summarizes its holding as follows:

"In contrast to the generalizations about women on which Virginia rests, we note again these dispositive realities: VMI's implementing methodology is not inherently unsuitable to women; some women do well under the adversative model; some women, at least, would want to attend VMI if they had the opportunity; some women are capable of all of the individual activities required of VMI cadets and can meet the physical standards VMI now imposes on men." Ante, at 33 (internal quotation marks, citations, and punctuation omitted, emphasis added).

Similarly, the Court states that "[t]he State's justification for excluding all women from `citizen soldier' training for which some are qualified . . . cannot rank as `exceedingly persuasive'. . . ." Ante, at 28. [n.1]

Only the amorphous "exceedingly persuasive justification" phrase, and not the standard elaboration of intermediate scrutiny, can be made to yield this conclusion that VMI's single sex composition is unconstitutional because there exist several women (or, one would have to conclude under the Court's reasoning, a single woman) willing and able to undertake VMI's program. Intermediate scrutiny has never required a least restrictive means analysis, but only a "substantial relation" between the classification and the state interests that it serves. Thus, in Califano v. Webster, 430 U.S. 313 (1977) (per curiam), we upheld a congressional statute that provided higher Social Security benefits for women than for men. We reasoned that "women . . . as such have been unfairly hindered from earning as much as men," but we did not require proof that each woman so benefited had suffered discrimination or that each disadvantaged man had not; it was sufficient that even under the former congressional scheme "women on the average received lower retirement benefits than men." Id., at 318, and n. 5 (emphasis added). The reasoning in our other intermediate scrutiny cases has similarly required only a substantial relation between end and means, not a perfect fit. In Rostker v. Goldberg, 453 U.S. 57 (1981), we held that selective service registration could constitutionally exclude women, because even "assuming that a small number of women could be drafted for noncombat roles, Congress simply did not consider it worth the added burdens of including women in draft and registration plans." Id., at 81. In Metro Broadcasting, Inc. v. FCC, 497 U.S. 547, 579, 582-583 (1990), overruled on other grounds, Adarand Constructors, Inc. v. Pena, 515 U. S. ___, ___ ___ (1995) (slip op., at 25-26), we held that a classification need not be accurate "in every case" to survive intermediate scrutiny so long as, "in the aggregate," it advances the underlying objective. There is simply no support in our cases for the notion that a sex based classification is invalid unless it relates to characteristics that hold true in every instance.

Not content to execute a de facto abandonment of the intermediate scrutiny that has been our standard for sex based classifications for some two decades, the Court purports to reserve the question whether, even in principle, a higher standard (i.e., strict scrutiny) should apply. "The Court has," it says, "thus far reserved most stringent judicial scrutiny for classifications based on race or national origin . . .," ante, at 14, n. 6 (emphasis added); and it describes our earlier cases as having done no more than decline to "equat[e] gender classifications, for all purposes, to classifications based on race or national origin," ante, at 14 (emphasis added). The wonderful thing about these statements is that they are not actually false--just as it would not be actually false to say that "our cases have thus far reserved the `beyond a reasonable doubt' standard of proof for criminal cases," or that "we have not equated tort actions, for all purposes, to criminal prosecutions." But the statements are misleading, insofar as they suggest that we have not already categorically held strict scrutiny to be inapplicable to sex based classifications. See, e.g., Heckler v. Mathews, 465 U.S. 728 (1984) (upholding state action after applying only intermediate scrutiny); Michael M. v. Superior Court, Somoma Cty., 450 U.S. 464 (1981) (same) (plurality and both concurring opinions); Califano v. Webster, 430 U.S. 313 (1977) (same) (per curiam). And the statements are irresponsible, insofar as they are calculated to destabilize current law. Our task is to clarify the law--not to muddy the waters, and not to exact over compliance by intimidation. The States and the Federal Government are entitled to know before they act the standard to which they will be held, rather than be compelled to guess about the outcome of Supreme Court peek a boo.

The Court's intimations are particularly out of place because it is perfectly clear that, if the question of the applicable standard of review for sex based classifications were to be regarded as an appropriate subject for reconsideration, the stronger argument would be not for elevating the standard to strict scrutiny, but for reducing it to rational basis review. The latter certainly has a firmer foundation in our past jurisprudence: Whereas no majority of the Court has ever applied strict scrutiny in a case involving sex based classifications, we routinely applied rational basis review until the 1970's, see, e.g., Hoyt v. Florida, 368 U.S. 57 (1961); Goesaert v. Cleary, 335 U.S. 464 (1948). And of course normal, rational basis review of sex based classifications would be much more in accord with the genesis of heightened standards of judicial review, the famous footnote in United States v. Carolene Products Co., 304 U.S. 144 (1938), which said (intimatingly) that we did not have to inquire in the case at hand

"whether prejudice against discrete and insular minorities may be a special condition, which tends seriously to curtail the operation of those political processes ordinarily to be relied upon to protect minorities, and which may call for a correspondingly more searching judicial inquiry." Id., at 152-153, n. 4.

It is hard to consider women a "discrete and insular minorit[y]" unable to employ the "political processes ordinarily to be relied upon," when they constitute a majority of the electorate. And the suggestion that they are incapable of exerting that political power smacks of the same paternalism that the Court so roundly condemns. See, e.g., ante, at

18-20, 25-28 (and accompanying notes). Moreover, a long list of legislation proves the proposition false. See, e.g., Equal Pay Act of 1963, 29 U.S.C. § 206(d); Title VII of the Civil Rights Act of 1964, 42 U.S.C. § 2000e-2; Title IX of the Education Amendments of 1972, 20 U.S.C. § 1681; Women's Business Ownership Act of 1988, Pub. L. 100-533, 102 Stat. 2689; Violence Against Women Act of 1994, Pub. L. 103-322, Title IV, 108 Stat. 1902.

With this explanation of how the Court has succeeded in making its analysis seem orthodox--and indeed, if intimations are to be believed, even overly generous to VMI--I now proceed to describe how the analysis should have been conducted. The question to be answered, I repeat, is whether the exclusion of women from VMI is "substantially related to an important governmental objective."

It is beyond question that Virginia has an important state interest in providing effective college education for its citizens. That single sex instruction is an approach substantially related to that interest should be evident enough from the long and continuing history in this country of men's and women's colleges. But beyond that, as the Court of Appeals here stated: "That single gender education at the college level is beneficial to both sexes is a fact established in this case." 44 F. 3d 1229, 1238 (CA4 1995) (emphasis added).

The evidence establishing that fact was overwhelming--indeed, "virtually uncontradicted" in the words of the court that received the evidence, 766 F. Supp. 1407, 1415 (WD Va. 1991). As an initial matter, Virginia demonstrated at trial that "[a] substantial body of contemporary scholarship and research supports the proposition that, although males and females have significant areas of developmental overlap, they also have differing developmental needs that are deep seated." Id., at 1434. While no one questioned that for many students a coeducational environment was nonetheless not inappropriate, that could not obscure the demonstrated benefits of single sex colleges. For example, the District Court stated as follows:

"One empirical study in evidence, not questioned by any expert, demonstrates that single sex colleges provide better educational experiences than coeducational institutions. Students of both sexes become more academically involved, interact with faculty frequently, show larger increases in intellectual self esteem and are more satisfied with practically all aspects of college experience (the sole exception is social life) compared with their counterparts in coeducational institutions. Attendance at an all male college substantially increases the likelihood that a student will carry out career plans in law, business and college teaching, and also has a substantial positive effect on starting salaries in business. Women's colleges increase the chances that those who attend will obtain positions of leadership, complete the baccalaureate degree, and aspire to higher degrees." Id., at 1412.

See also id., at 1434-1435 (factual findings). "[I]n the light of this very substantial authority favoring single sex education," the District Court concluded that "the VMI Board's decision to maintain an all male institution is fully justified even without taking into consideration the other unique features of VMI's teaching and training." Id., at 1412.

This finding alone, which even this Court cannot dispute, see ante, at 17, should be sufficient to demonstrate the constitutionality of VMI's all male composition.

But besides its single sex constitution, VMI is different from other colleges in another way. It employs a "distinctive educational method," sometimes referred to as the "adversative, or doubting, model of education." 766 F. Supp., at 1413, 1421. "Physical rigor, mental stress, absolute equality of treatment, absence of privacy, minute regulation of behavior, and indoctrination in desirable values are the salient attributes of the VMI educational experience." Id., at 1421. No one contends that this method is appropriate for all individuals; education is not a "one size fits all" business. Just as a State may wish to support junior colleges, vocational institutes, or a law school that emphasizes case practice instead of classroom study, so too a State's decision to maintain within its system one school that provides the adversative method is "substantially related" to its goal of good education. Moreover, it was uncontested that "if the state were to establish a women's VMI type [i.e., adversative] program, the program would attract an insufficient number of participants to make the program work," 44 F. 3d, at 1241; and it was found by the District Court that if Virginia were to include women in VMI, the school "would eventually find it necessary to drop the adversative system altogether," 766 F. Supp., at 1413. Thus, Virginia's options were an adversative method that excludes women or no adversative method at all.

There can be no serious dispute that, as the District Court found, single sex education and a distinctive educational method "represent legitimate contributions to diversity in the Virginia higher education system." Id., at 1413. As a theoretical matter, Virginia's educational interest would have been best served (insofar as the two factors we have mentioned are concerned) by six different types of public colleges--an all men's, an all women's, and a coeducational college run in the "adversative method," and an all men's, an all women's, and a coeducational college run in the "traditional method." But as a practical matter, of course, Virginia's financial resources, like any State's, are not limitless, and the Commonwealth must select among the available options. Virginia thus has decided to fund, in addition to some 14 coeducational 4 year colleges, one college that is run as an all male school on the adversative model: the Virginia Military Institute.

Virginia did not make this determination regarding the make up of its public college system on the unrealistic assumption that no other colleges exist. Substantial evidence in the District Court demonstrated that the Commonwealth has long proceeded on the principle that " `[h]igher education resources should be viewed as a whole--public and private' "--because such an approach enhances diversity and because " `it is academic and economic waste to permit unwarranted duplication.' " Id., at 1420-1421 (quoting 1974 Report of the General Assembly Commission on Higher Education to the General Assembly of Virginia). It is thus significant that, whereas there are "four all female private [colleges] in Virginia," there is only "one private all male college," which "indicates that the private sector is providing for th[e] [former] form of education to a much greater extent that it provides for all male education." 766 F. Supp., at 1420-1421. In these circumstances, Virginia's election to fund one public all male institution and one on the adversarial model--and to concentrate its resources in a single entity that serves both these interests in diversity--is substantially related to the State's important educational interests.

The Court today has no adequate response to this clear demonstration of the conclusion produced by application of intermediate scrutiny. Rather, it relies on a series of contentions that are irrelevant or erroneous as a matter of law, foreclosed by the record in this case, or both.

1. I have already pointed out the Court's most fundamental error, which is its reasoning that VMI's all male composition is unconstitutional because "some women are capable of all of the individual activities required of VMI cadets," 766 F. Supp., at 1412, and would prefer military training on the adversarial model. See supra, at 6-9. This unacknowledged adoption of what amounts to (at least) strict scrutiny is without antecedent in our sex discrimination cases and by itself discredits the Court's decision.

2. The Court suggests that Virginia's claimed purpose in maintaining VMI as an all male institution--its asserted interest in promoting diversity of educational options--is not "genuin[e]," but is a pretext for discriminating against women. Ante, at 22; see ante, at 17-22. To support this charge, the Court would have to impute that base motive to VMI's Mission Study Committee, which conducted a 3 year study from 1983 to 1986 and recommended to VMI's Board of Visitors that the school remain all male. The Committee, a majority of whose members consisted of non VMI graduates, "read materials on education and on women in the military," "made site visits to single sex and newly coeducational institutions" including West Point and the Naval Academy, and "considered the reasons that other institutions had changed from single sex to coeducational status"; its work was praised as "thorough" in the accreditation review of VMI conducted by the Southern Association of Colleges and Schools. See 766 F. Supp., at 1413, 1428; see also id., at 1427-1430 (detailed findings of fact concerning the Mission Study Committee). The Court states that "[w]hatever internal purpose the Mission Study Committee served--and however well meaning the framers of the report--we can hardly extract from that effort any state policy evenhandedly to advance diverse educational options." Ante, at 22. But whether it is part of the evidence to prove that diversity was the Commonwealth's objective (its short report said nothing on that particular subject) is quite separate from whether it is part of the evidence to prove that anti feminism was not. The relevance of the Mission Study Committee is that its very creation, its sober 3 year study, and the analysis it produced, utterly refute the claim that VMI has elected to maintain its all male student body composition for some misogynistic reason.

The Court also supports its analysis of Virginia's "actual state purposes" in maintaining VMI's student body as all male by stating that there is no explicit statement in the record " `in which the Commonwealth has expressed itself' " concerning those purposes. Ante, at 18, 21 (quoting 976 F. 2d 890, 899 (CA4 1992)); see also ante, at 7. That is wrong on numerous grounds. First and foremost, in its implication that such an explicit statement of "actual purposes" is needed. The Court adopts, in effect, the argument of the United States that since the exclusion of women from VMI in 1839 was based on the "assumptions" of the time "that men alone were fit for military and leadership roles," and since "[b]efore this litigation was initiated, Virginia never sought to supply a valid, contemporary rationale for VMI's exclusionary policy," "[t]hat failure itself renders the VMI policy invalid." Brief for United States in No. 94-2107, at 10. This is an unheard of doctrine. Each state decision to adopt or maintain a governmental policy need not be accompanied--in anticipation of litigation and on pain of being found to lack a relevant state interest--by a lawyer's contemporaneous recitation of the State's purposes. The Constitution is not some giant Administrative Procedure Act, which imposes upon the States the obligation to set forth a "statement of basis and purpose" for their sovereign acts, see 5 U.S.C. § 553(c). The situation would be different if what the Court assumes to have been the 1839 policy had been enshrined and remained enshrined in legislation--a VMI charter, perhaps, pronouncing that the institution's purpose is to keep women in their place. But since the 1839 policy was no more explicitly recorded than the Court contends the present one is, the mere fact that today's Commonwealth continues to fund VMI "is enough to answer [the United States'] contention that the [classification] was the `accidental by product of a traditional way of thinking about females.' " Michael M., 450 U. S., at 471, n. 6 (plurality opinion) (quoting Califano v. Webster, 430 U.S. 313, 320 (1977)) (internal quotation marks omitted).

It is, moreover, not true that Virginia's contemporary reasons for maintaining VMI are not explicitly recorded. It is hard to imagine a more authoritative source on this subject than the 1990 Report of the Virginia Commission on the University of the 21st Century to the Governor and General Assembly (1990 Report). As the parties stipulated, that report "notes that the hallmarks of Virginia's educational policy are `diversity and autonomy.' " Stipulations of Fact, at 37, reprinted in Lodged Materials from the Record 64 (Lodged Materials). It said: "The formal system of higher education in Virginia includes a great array of institutions: state supported and independent, two year and senior, research and highly specialized, traditionally black and single sex." 1990 Report, quoted in relevant part at Lodged Materials 64-65 (emphasis added). [n.2] The Court's only response to this is repeated reliance on the Court of Appeals' assertion that " `the only explicit [statement] that we have found in the record in which the Commonwealth has expressed itself with respect to gender distinctions' " (namely, the statement in the 1990 Report that the Commonwealth's institutions must "deal with faculty, staff, and students without regard to sex") had nothing to do with the purpose of diversity. Ante, at 7, 21 (quoting 976 F. 2d, at 899). This proves, I suppose, that the Court of Appeals did not find a statement dealing with sex and diversity in the record; but the pertinent question (accepting the need for such a statement) is whether it was there. And the plain fact, which the Court does not deny, is that it was.

The Court contends that "[a] purpose genuinely to advance an array of educational options . . . is not served" by VMI. Ante, at 22. It relies on the fact that all of

Virginia's other public colleges have become coeducational. Ibid.; see also ante, at 3, n. 2. The apparent theory of this argument is that unless Virginia pursues a great deal of diversity, its pursuit of some diversity must be a sham. This fails to take account of the fact that Virginia's resources cannot support all possible permutations of schools, see supra, at 14-15, and of the fact that Virginia coordinates its public educational offerings with the offerings of in state private educational institutions that the Commonwealth provides money for its residents to attend and otherwise assists--which include four women's colleges. [n.3]

Finally, the Court unreasonably suggests that there is some pretext in Virginia's reliance upon decentralized decisionmaking to achieve diversity--its granting of substantial autonomy to each institution with regard to student body composition and other matters, see 766 F. Supp., at 1419. The Court adopts the suggestion of the Court of Appeals that it is not possible for "one institution with autonomy, but with no authority over any other state institution, [to] give effect to a state policy of diversity among institutions." Ante, at 22 (internal quotation marks omitted). If it were impossible for individual human beings (or groups of human beings) to act autonomously in effective pursuit of a common goal, the game of soccer would not exist. And where the goal is diversity in a free market for services, that tends to be achieved even by autonomous actors who act out of entirely selfish interests and make no effort to cooperate. Each Virginia institution, that is to say, has a natural incentive to make itself distinctive in order to attract a particular segment of student applicants. And of course none of the institutions is entirely autonomous; if and when the legislature decides that a particular school is not well serving the interest of diversity--if it decides, for example, that a men's school is not much needed--funding will cease. [n.4]

3. In addition to disparaging Virginia's claim that VMI's single sex status serves a state interest in diversity, the Court finds fault with Virginia's failure to offer education based on the adversative training method to women. It dismisses the District Court's " `findings' on `gender based developmental differences' " on the ground that "[t]hese `findings' restate the opinions of Virginia's expert witnesses, opinions about typically male or typically female `tendencies.' " Ante, at 23 (quoting 766 F. Supp., at 1434-1435). How remarkable to criticize the District Court on the ground that its findings rest on the evidence (i.e., the testimony of Virginia's witnesses)! That is what findings are supposed to do. It is indefensible to tell the Commonwealth that "[t]he burden of justification is demanding and it rests entirely on [you]," ante, at 15, and then to ignore the District Court's findings because they rest on the evidence put forward by the Commonwealth-- particularly when, as the District Court said, "[t]he evidence in the case . . . is virtually uncontradicted," 766 F. Supp., at 1415 (emphasis added).

Ultimately, in fact, the Court does not deny the evidence supporting these findings. See ante, at 24-29. It instead makes evident that the parties to this case could have saved themselves a great deal of time, trouble, and expense by omitting a trial. The Court simply dispenses with the evidence submitted at trial--it never says that a single finding of the District Court is clearly erroneous--in favor of the Justices' own view of the world, which the Court proceeds to support with (1) references to observations of someone who is not a witness, nor even an educational expert, nor even a judge who reviewed the record or participated in the judgment below, but rather a judge who merely dissented from the Court of Appeals' decision not to rehear this case en banc, see ante, at 24, (2) citations of nonevidentiary materials such as amicus curiae briefs filed in this Court, see ante, at 27, nn. 13, 14, and (3) various historical anecdotes designed to demonstrate that Virginia's support for VMI as currently constituted reminds the Justices of the "bad old days," see ante, at 25-28.

It is not too much to say that this approach to the case has rendered the trial a sham. But treating the evidence as irrelevant is absolutely necessary for the Court to reach its conclusion. Not a single witness contested, for example, Virginia's "substantial body of `exceedingly persuasive' evidence . . . that some students, both male and female, benefit from attending a single sex college" and "[that] [f]or those students, the opportunity to attend a single sex college is a valuable one, likely to lead to better academic and professional achievement." 766 F. Supp., at 1411-1412. Even the United States' expert witness "called himself a `believer in single sex education,' " although it was his "personal, philosophical preference," not one "born of educational benefit considerations," "that single sex education should be provided only by the private sector." Id., at 1412.

4. The Court contends that Virginia, and the District Court, erred, and "misperceived our precedent," by "train[ing] their argument on `means' rather than `end,' " ante, at 28. The Court focuses on "VMI's mission," which is to produce individuals "imbued with love of learning, confident in the functions and attitudes of leadership, possessing a high sense of public service, advocates of the American democracy and free enterprise system, and ready . . . to defend their country in time of national peril." 766 F. Supp., at 1425 (quoting Mission Study Committee of the VMI Board of Visitors, Report, May 16, 1986). "Surely," the Court says, "that goal is great enough to accommodate women." Ante, at 28.

This is law making by indirection. What the Court describes as "VMI's mission" is no less the mission of all Virginia colleges. Which of them would the Old Dominion continue to fund if they did not aim to create individuals "imbued with love of learning, etc." right down to being ready "to defend their country in time of national peril"? It can be summed up as "learning, leadership, and patriotism." To be sure, those general educational values are described in a particularly martial fashion in VMI's mission statement, in accordance with the military, adversative, and all male character of the institution. But imparting those values in that fashion--i.e., in a military, adversative, all male environment--is the distinctive mission of VMI. And as I have discussed (and both courts below found), that mission is not "great enough to accommodate women."

The Court's analysis at least has the benefit of producing foreseeable results. Applied generally, it means that whenever a State's ultimate objective is "great enough to accommodate women" (as it always will be), then the State will be held to have violated the Equal Protection Clause if it restricts to men even one means by which it pursues that objective--no matter how few women are interested in pursuing the objective by that means, no matter how much the single sex program will have to be changed if both sexes are admitted, and no matter how beneficial that program has theretofore been to its participants.

5. The Court argues that VMI would not have to change very much if it were to admit women. See, e.g., ante, at 22-25. The principal response to that argument is that it is irrelevant: If VMI's single sex status is substantially related to the government's important educational objectives, as I have demonstrated above and as the Court refuses to discuss, that concludes the inquiry. There should be no debate in the federal judiciary over "how much" VMI would be required to change if it admitted women and whether that would constitute "too much" change.

But if such a debate were relevant, the Court would certainly be on the losing side. The District Court found as follows: "[T]he evidence establishes that key elements of the adversative VMI educational system, with its focus on barracks life, would be fundamentally altered, and the distinctive ends of the system would be thwarted, if VMI were forced to admit females and to make changes necessary to accommodate their needs and interests." 766 F. Supp., at 1411. Changes that the District Court's detailed analysis found would be required include new allowances for personal privacy in the barracks, such as locked doors and coverings on windows, which would detract from VMI's approach of regulating minute details of student behavior, "contradict the principle that everyone is constantly subject to scrutiny by everyone else," and impair VMI's "total egalitarian approach" under which every student must be "treated alike"; changes in the physical training program, which would reduce "[t]he intensity and aggressiveness of the current program"; and various modifications in other respects of the adversative training program which permeates student life. See id., at 1412-1413, 1435-1443. As the Court of Appeals summarized it, "the record supports the district court's findings that at least these three aspects of VMI's program--physical training, the absence of privacy, and the adversative approach--would be materially affected by coeducation, leading to a substantial change in the egalitarian ethos that is a critical aspect of VMI's training." 976 F. 2d, at 896-897.

In the face of these findings by two courts below, amply supported by the evidence, and resulting in the conclusion that VMI would be fundamentally altered if it admitted women, this Court simply pronounces that "[t]he notion that admission of women would downgrade VMI's stature, destroy the adversative system and, with it, even the school, is a judgment hardly proved." Ante, at 25 (footnote omitted). The point about "downgrad[ing] VMI's stature" is a strawman; no one has made any such claim. The point about "destroy[ing] the adversative system" is simply false; the District Court not only stated that "[e]vidence supports this theory," but specifically concluded that while "[w]ithout a doubt" VMI could assimilate women, "it is equally without a doubt that

VMI's present methods of training and education would have to be changed" by a "move away from its adversative new cadet system." 766 F. Supp., at 1413, and n. 8, 1441. And the point about "destroy[ing] the school," depending upon what that ambiguous phrase is intended to mean, is either false or else sets a standard much higher than VMI had to meet. It sufficed to establish, as the District Court stated, that VMI would be "significantly different" upon the admission of women, 766 F. Supp., at 1412, and "would eventually find it necessary to drop the adversative system altogether," id., at 1413. [n.5]

6. Finally, the absence of a precise "all women's analogue" to VMI is irrelevant. In Mississippi Univ. for Women v. Hogan, 458 U.S. 718 (1982), we attached no constitutional significance to the absence of an all male nursing school. As Virginia notes, if a program restricted to one sex is necessarily unconstitutional unless there is a parallel program restricted to the other sex, "the opinion in Hogan could have ended with its first footnote, which observed that `Mississippi maintains no other single sex public university or college.' " Brief for Cross Petitioners in No. 94-2107, at 38 (quoting Mississippi Univ. for Women v. Hogan, supra, at 720, n. 1).

Although there is no precise female only analogue to VMI, Virginia has created during this litigation the Virginia Women's Institute for Leadership (VWIL), a state funded all women's program run by Mary Baldwin College. I have thus far said nothing about VWIL because it is, under our established test, irrelevant, so long as VMI's all male character is "substantially related" to an important state goal. But VWIL now exists, and the Court's treatment of it shows how far reaching today's decision is.

VWIL was carefully designed by professional educators who have long experience in educating young women. The program rejects the proposition that there is a "difference in the respective spheres and destinies of man and woman," Bradwell v. State, 16 Wall. 130, 141 (1872), and is designed to "provide an all female program that will achieve substantially similar outcomes [to VMI's] in an all female environment," 852 F. Supp. 471, 481 (WD Va. 1994). After holding a trial where voluminous evidence was submitted and making detailed findings of fact, the District Court concluded that "there is a legitimate pedagogical basis for the different means employed [by VMI and VWIL] to achieve the substantially similar ends." Ibid. The Court of Appeals undertook a detailed review of the record and affirmed. 44 F. 3d 1229 (CA4 1995). [n.6] But it is Mary Baldwin College, which runs VWIL, that has made the point most succinctly:

"It would have been possible to develop the VWIL program to more closely resemble VMI, with adversative techniques associated with the rat line and barracks like living quarters. Simply replicating an existing program would have required far less thought, research, and educational expertise. But such a facile approach would have produced a paper program with no real prospect of successful implementation." Brief for Mary Baldwin College as Amicus Curiae 5.

It is worth noting that none of the United States' own experts in the remedial phase of this case was willing to testify that VMI's adversative method was an appropriate methodology for educating women. This Court, however, does not care. Even though

VWIL was carefully designed by professional educators who have tremendous experience in the area, and survived the test of adversarial litigation, the Court simply declares, with no basis in the evidence, that these professionals acted on " `overbroad' generalizations," ante, at 24, 33.

A few words are appropriate in response to the concurrence, which finds VMI unconstitutional on a basis that is more moderate than the Court's but only at the expense of being even more implausible. The concurrence offers three reasons: First, that there is "scant evidence in the record," ante, at 5, that diversity of educational offering was the real reason for Virginia's maintaining VMI. "Scant" has the advantage of being an imprecise term. I have cited the clearest statements of diversity as a goal for higher education in the 1990 Report of the Virginia Commission on the University of the 21st Century to the Governor and General Assembly, the 1989 Virginia Plan for Higher Education, the Budget Initiatives prepared in 1989 by the State Council of Higher Education for Virginia, the 1974 Report of the General Assembly Commission on Higher Education, and the 1969 Report of the Virginia Commission on Constitutional Revision. See supra, at 14, 17-18, and n. 2, 19-20, n. 3. There is no evidence to the contrary, once one rejects (as the concurrence rightly does) the relevance of VMI's founding in days when attitudes towards the education of women were different. Is this conceivably not enough to foreclose rejecting as clearly erroneous the District Court's determination regarding "the Commonwealth's objective of educational diversity"? 766 F. Supp., at 1413. Especially since it is absurd on its face even to demand "evidence" to prove that the Commonwealth's reason for maintaining a men's military academy is that a men's military academy provides a distinctive type of educational experience (i.e., fosters diversity). What other purpose would the Commonwealth have? One may argue, as the Court does, that this type of diversity is designed only to indulge hostility towards women--but that is a separate point, explicitly rejected by the concurrence, and amply refuted by the evidence I have mentioned in discussing the Court's opinion. [n.7] What is now under discussion--the concurrence's making central to the disposition of this case the supposedly "scant" evidence that Virginia maintained VMI in order to offer a diverse educational experience--is rather like making crucial to the lawfulness of the United States Army record "evidence" that its purpose is to do battle. A legal culture that has forgotten the concept of res ipsa loquitur deserves the fate that it today decrees for VMI.

Second, the concurrence dismisses out of hand what it calls Virginia's "second justification for the single sex admissions policy: maintenance of the adversative method." Ante, at 7. The concurrence reasons that "this justification does not serve an important governmental objective" because, whatever the record may show about the pedagogical benefits of single sex education, "there is no similar evidence in the record that an adversative method is pedagogically beneficial or is any more likely to produce character traits than other methodologies." Ante, at 7-8. That is simply wrong. See, e.g., 766 F. Supp., at 1426 (factual findings concerning character traits produced by VMI's adversative methodology); id., at 1434 (factual findings concerning benefits for many college age men of an adversarial approach in general). In reality, the pedagogical benefits of VMI's adversative approach were not only proved, but were a given in this litigation. The reason the woman applicant who prompted this suit wanted to enter VMI was assuredly not that she wanted to go to an all male school; it would cease being all male as soon as she entered. She wanted the distinctive adversative education that VMI provided, and the battle was joined (in the main) over whether VMI had a basis for excluding women from that approach. The Court's opinion recognizes this, and devotes much of its opinion to demonstrating that " `some women . . . do well under [the] adversative model' " and that "[i]t is on behalf of these women that the United States has instituted this suit." Ante, at 33-34 (quoting 766 F. Supp., at 1434). Of course, in the last analysis it does not matter whether there are any benefits to the adversative method. The concurrence does not contest that there are benefits to single sex education, and that alone suffices to make Virginia's case, since admission of a woman will even more surely put an end to VMI's single sex education than it will to VMI's adversative methodology.

A third reason the concurrence offers in support of the judgment is that the Commonwealth and VMI were not quick enough to react to the "further developments" in this Court's evolving jurisprudence. Ante, at 4. Specifically, the concurrence believes it should have been clear after Hogan that "[t]he difficulty with [Virginia's] position is that the diversity benefited only one sex; there was single sex public education available for men at VMI, but no corresponding single sex public education available for women." Ante, at 6. If only, the concurrence asserts, Virginia had "made a genuine effort to devote comparable public resources to a facility for women, and followed through on such a plan, it might well have avoided an equal protection violation." Ante, at 7. That is to say, the concurrence believes that after our decision in Hogan (which held a program of the Mississippi University for Women to be unconstitutional--without any reliance on the fact that there was no corresponding Mississippi all men's program), the Commonwealth should have known that what this Court expected of it was . . . yes!, the creation of a state all women's program. Any lawyer who gave that advice to the Commonwealth ought to have been either disbarred or committed. (The proof of that pudding is today's 6-Justice majority opinion.) And any Virginia politician who proposed such a step when there were already 4 4-year women's colleges in Virginia (assisted by state support that may well exceed, in the aggregate, what VMI costs, see n. 3, supra) ought to have been recalled.

In any event, "diversity in the form of single sex, as well as coeducational, institutions of higher learning," is "available to women as well as to men" in Virginia. Ante, at 7. The concurrence is able to assert the contrary only by disregarding the four all women's private colleges in Virginia (generously assisted by public funds) and the Commonwealth's longstanding policy of coordinating public with private educational offerings, see supra, at 14-15, 17-18, and n. 2, 19, and n. 3. According to the concurrence, the reason Virginia's assistance to its four all women's private colleges does not count is that "[t]he private women's colleges are treated by the State exactly as all other private schools are treated." Ante, at 7. But if Virginia cannot get credit for assisting women's education if it only treats women's private schools as it does all other private schools, then why should it get blame for assisting men's education if it only treats VMI as it does all other public schools? This is a great puzzlement.

As is frequently true, the Court's decision today will have consequences that extend far beyond the parties to the case. What I take to be the Court's unease with these consequences, and its resulting unwillingness to acknowledge them, cannot alter the reality.

Under the constitutional principles announced and applied today, single sex public education is unconstitutional. By going through the motions of applying a balancing test--asking whether the State has adduced an "exceedingly persuasive justification" for its sex based classification--the Court creates the illusion that government officials in some future case will have a clear shot at justifying some sort of single sex public education. Indeed, the Court seeks to create even a greater illusion than that: It purports to have said nothing of relevance to other public schools at all. "We address specifically and only an educational opportunity recognized . . . as `unique' . . . ." Ante, at 16, n. 7.

The Supreme Court of the United States does not sit to announce "unique" dispositions. Its principal function is to establish precedent--that is, to set forth principles of law that every court in America must follow. As we said only this Term, we expect both ourselves and lower courts to adhere to the "rationale upon which the Court based the results of its earlier decisions." Seminole Tribe of Fla. v. Florida, 517 U. S. ____, ____ (1996) (slip op., at 21) (emphasis added). That is the principal reason we publish our opinions.

And the rationale of today's decision is sweeping: for sex based classifications, a redefinition of intermediate scrutiny that makes it indistinguishable from strict scrutiny. See supra, at 6-9. Indeed, the Court indicates that if any program restricted to one sex is "uniqu[e]," it must be opened to members of the opposite sex "who have the will and capacity" to participate in it. Ante, at 25. I suggest that the single sex program that will not be capable of being characterized as "unique" is not only unique but nonexistent. [n.8]

In any event, regardless of whether the Court's rationale leaves some small amount of room for lawyers to argue, it ensures that single sex public education is functionally dead. The costs of litigating the constitutionality of a single sex education program, and the risks of ultimately losing that litigation, are simply too high to be embraced by public officials. Any person with standing to challenge any sex based classification can haul the State into federal court and compel it to establish by evidence (presumably in the form of expert testimony) that there is an "exceedingly persuasive justification" for the classification. Should the courts happen to interpret that vacuous phrase as establishing a standard that is not utterly impossible of achievement, there is considerable risk that whether the standard has been met will not be determined on the basis of the record evidence--indeed, that will necessarily be the approach of any court that seeks to walk the path the Court has trod today. No state official in his right mind will buy such a high cost, high risk lawsuit by commencing a single sex program. The enemies of single sex education have won; by persuading only seven Justices (five would have been enough) that their view of the world is enshrined in the Constitution, they have effectively imposed that view on all 50 States.

This is especially regrettable because, as the District Court here determined, educational experts in recent years have increasingly come to "suppor[t] [the] view that substantial educational benefits flow from a single gender environment, be it male or female, that cannot be replicated in a coeducational setting." 766 F. Supp., at 1415 (emphasis added). "The evidence in th[is] case," for example, "is virtually uncontradicted" to that effect. Ibid. Until quite recently, some public officials have attempted to institute new single sex programs, at least as experiments. In 1991, for example, the Detroit Board of Education announced a program to establish three boys only schools for inner city youth; it was met with a lawsuit, a preliminary injunction was swiftly entered by a District Court that purported to rely on Hogan, see Garrett v. Board of Education of School Dist. of Detroit, 775 F. Supp. 1004, 1006 (ED Mich. 1991), and the Detroit Board of Education voted to abandon the litigation and thus abandon the plan, see Detroit Plan to Aid Blacks with All Boy Schools Abandoned, Los Angeles Times, Nov. 8, 1991, p. A4, col. 1. Today's opinion assures that no such experiment will be tried again.

There are few extant single sex public educational programs. The potential of today's decision for widespread disruption of existing institutions lies in its application to private single sex education. Government support is immensely important to private educational institutions. Mary Baldwin College--which designed and runs VWIL--notes that private institutions of higher education in the 1990-1991 school year derived approximately 19 percent of their budgets from federal, state, and local government funds, not including financial aid to students. See Brief for Mary Baldwin College as Amicus Curiae 22, n. 13 (citing U. S. Dept. of Education, National Center for Education Statistics, Digest of Education Statistics, p. 38 and Note (1993)). Charitable status under the tax laws is also highly significant for private educational institutions, and it is certainly not beyond the Court that rendered today's decision to hold that a donation to a single sex college should be deemed contrary to public policy and therefore not deductible if the college discriminates on the basis of sex. See Note, The Independent Sector and the Tax Laws: Defining Charity in an Ideal Democracy, 64 S. Cal. L. Rev. 461, 476 (1991). See also Bob Jones Univ. v. United States, 461 U.S. 574 (1983).

The Court adverts to private single sex education only briefly, and only to make the assertion (mentioned above) that "[w]e address specifically and only an educational opportunity recognized by the District Court and the Court of Appeals as `unique.' " Ante, at 16, n. 7. As I have already remarked, see supra, at 32-33, that assurance assures nothing, unless it is to be taken as a promise that in the future the Court will disclaim the reasoning it has used today to destroy VMI. The Government, in its briefs to this Court, at least purports to address the consequences of its attack on VMI for public support of private single sex education. It contends that private colleges which are the direct or indirect beneficiaries of government funding are not thereby necessarily converted into state actors to which the Equal Protection Clause is then applicable. See Brief for United States in No. 94-2107, at 35-37 (discussing Rendell Baker v. Kohn, 457 U.S. 830 (1982), and Blum v. Yaretsky, 457 U.S. 991 (1982)). That is true. It is also virtually meaningless.

The issue will be not whether government assistance turns private colleges into state actors, but whether the government itself would be violating the Constitution by providing state support to single sex colleges. For example, in Norwood v. Harrison, 413 U.S. 455 (1973), we saw no room to distinguish between state operation of racially segregated schools and state support of privately run segregated schools. "Racial discrimination in state operated schools is barred by the Constitution and `[i]t is also axiomatic that a state may not induce, encourage or promote private persons to accomplish what it is constitutionally forbidden to accomplish.' " Id., at 465 (quoting Lee v. Macon County Bd. of Ed., 267 F. Supp. 458, 475-476 (MD Ala. 1967)); see also Cooper v. Aaron, 358 U.S. 1, 19 (1958) ("State support of segregated schools through any arrangement, management, funds, or property cannot be squared with the [Fourteenth] Amendment's command that no State shall deny to any person within its jurisdiction the equal protection of the laws"); Grove City College v. Bell, 465 U.S. 555, 565 (1984) (case arising under Title IX of the Education Amendments of 1972 and stating that "[t]he economic effect of direct and indirect assistance often is indistinguishable"). When the Government was pressed at oral argument concerning the implications of these cases for private single sex education if government provided single sex education is unconstitutional, it stated that the implications will not be so disastrous, since States can provide funding to racially segregated private schools, "depend[ing] on the circumstances," Tr. of Oral Arg. 56. I cannot imagine what those "circumstances" might be, and it would be as foolish for private school administrators to think that that assurance from the Justice Department will outlive the day it was made, as it was for VMI to think that the Justice Department's "unequivoca[l]" support for an intermediate scrutiny standard in this case would survive the Government's loss in the courts below.

The only hope for state assisted single sex private schools is that the Court will not apply in the future the principles of law it has applied today. That is a substantial hope, I am happy and ashamed to say. After all, did not the Court today abandon the principles of law it has applied in our earlier sex classification cases? And does not the Court positively invite private colleges to rely upon our ad hocery by assuring them this case is "unique"? I would not advise the foundation of any new single sex college (especially an all male one) with the expectation of being allowed to receive any government support; but it is too soon to abandon in despair those single sex colleges already in existence. It will certainly be possible for this Court to write a future opinion that ignores the broad principles of law set forth today, and that characterizes as utterly dispositive the opinion's perceptions that VMI was a uniquely prestigious all male institution, conceived in chauvinism, etc., etc. I will not join that opinion.

* * *

Justice Brandeis said it is "one of the happy incidents of the federal system that a single courageous State may, if its citizens choose, serve as a laboratory; and try novel social and economic experiments without risk to the rest of the country." New State Ice Co. v. Liebmann, 285 U.S. 262, 311 (1932) (dissenting opinion). But it is one of the unhappy incidents of the federal system that a self righteous Supreme Court, acting on its Members' personal view of what would make a "more perfect Union," ante, at 41 (a criterion only slightly more restrictive than a "more perfect world"), can impose its own favored social and economic dispositions nationwide. As today's disposition, and others this single Term, show, this places it beyond the power of a "single courageous State," not only to introduce novel dispositions that the Court frowns upon, but to reintroduce, or indeed even adhere to, disfavored dispositions that are centuries old. See, e.g., BMW of North America, Inc. v. Gore, 517 U. S. ___ (1996); Romer v. Evans, 517 U. S. ___ (1996). The sphere of self government reserved to the people of the Republic is progressively narrowed.

In the course of this dissent, I have referred approvingly to the opinion of my former colleague, Justice Powell, in Mississippi Univ. for Women v. Hogan, 458 U.S. 718 (1982). Many of the points made in his dissent apply with equal force here--in particular, the criticism of judicial opinions that purport to be "narro[w]" but whose "logic" is "sweepin[g]." Id., at 745-746, n. 18. But there is one statement with which I cannot agree. Justice Powell observed that the Court's decision in Hogan, which struck down a single sex program offered by the Mississippi University for Women, had thereby "[l]eft without honor . . . an element of diversity that has characterized much of American education and enriched much of American life." Id., at 735. Today's decision does not leave VMI without honor; no court opinion can do that.

In an odd sort of way, it is precisely VMI's attachment to such old fashioned concepts as manly "honor" that has made it, and the system it represents, the target of those who today succeed in abolishing public single sex education. The record contains a booklet that all first year VMI students (the so called "rats") were required to keep in their possession at all times. Near the end there appears the following period piece, entitled "The Code of a Gentleman":

"Without a strict observance of the fundamental Code of Honor, no man, no matter how `polished,' can be considered a gentleman. The honor of a gentleman demands the inviolability of his word, and the incorruptibility of his principles. He is the descendant of the knight, the crusader; he is the defender of the defenseless and the champion of justice . . . or he is not a Gentleman.

A Gentleman . . .

Does not discuss his family affairs in public or with acquaintances.

Does not speak more than casually about his girl friend.

Does not go to a lady's house if he is affected by alcohol. He is temperate in the use of alcohol.

Does not lose his temper; nor exhibit anger, fear, hate, embarrassment, ardor or hilarity in public.

Does not hail a lady from a club window.

A gentleman never discusses the merits or demerits of a lady.

Does not mention names exactly as he avoids the mention of what things cost.

Does not borrow money from a friend, except in dire need. Money borrowed is a debt of honor, and must be repaid as promptly as possible. Debts incurred by a deceased parent, brother, sister or grown child are assumed by honorable men as a debt of honor.

Does not display his wealth, money or possessions.

Does not put his manners on and off, whether in the club or in a ballroom. He treats people with courtesy, no matter what their social position may be.

Does not slap strangers on the back nor so much as lay a finger on a lady.

Does not `lick the boots of those above' nor `kick the face of those below him on the social ladder.'

Does not take advantage of another's helplessness or ignorance and assumes that no gentleman will take advantage of him.

A Gentleman respects the reserves of others, but demands that others respect those which are his.

A Gentleman can become what he wills to be. . ."

I do not know whether the men of VMI lived by this Code; perhaps not. But it is powerfully impressive that a public institution of higher education still in existence sought to have them do so. I do not think any of us, women included, will be better off for its destruction.

Notes to Justice Scalia's dissent in United States v. Virginia (June 26, 1996)

1 Accord, ante, at 23 ("In sum . . ., neither the goal of producing citizen soldiers, VMI's raison d'être, nor VMI's implementing methodology is inherently unsuitable to women") (internal quotation marks omitted; emphasis added); ante, at 25 ("the question is whether the State can constitutionally deny to women who have the will and capacity, the training and attendant opportunities that VMI uniquely affords"); ante, at 31 (the "violation" is that "equal protection [has been] denied to women ready, willing, and able to benefit from educational opportunities of the kind VMI offers"); ante, at 33 ("As earlier stated, see supra, at 24, generalizations about `the way women are,' estimates of what is appropriate for most women, no longer justify denying opportunity to women whose talent and capacity place them outside the average description").

2 This statement is supported by other evidence in the record demonstrating, by reference to both public and private institutions, that Virginia actively seeks to foster its "rich heritage of pluralism and diversity in higher education, " 1969 Report of the Virginia Commission on Constitutional Revision, quoted in relevant part at Lodged Materials 53; that Virginia views " [o]ne special characteristic of the Virginia system [as being] its

diversity, " 1989 Virginia Plan for Higher Education, quoted in relevant part at Lodged Materials 64; and that in the Commonwealth's view "[h]igher education resources should be viewed as a whole--public and private" because "Virginia needs the diversity inherent in a dual system of higher education," 1974 Report of the General Assembly Commission on Higher Education to the General Assembly of Virginia, quoted in 766 F. Supp., at 1420. See also Budget Initiatives for 1990-1992 of the State Council of Higher Education for Virginia, p. 10 (June 21, 1989) (Budget Initiatives), quoted at infra, n. 3. It should be noted (for this point will be crucial to our later discussion) that these official reports quoted here, in text and footnote, regard the Commonwealth's educational system--public and private--as a unitary one.

3 The Commonwealth provides tuition assistance, scholarship grants, guaranteed loans, and work study funds for residents of Virginia who attend private colleges in the Commonwealth. See, e.g., Va. Code Ann. §§23-38.11 to 23-38.19 (1993 and Supp. 1995) (Tuition Assistance Grant Act); §§23-38.30 to 23-38.44:3 (Virginia Student Assistance Authorities); §§23-38.45 to 23-38.53 (1993) (College Scholarship Assistance Act); §§23-38.53:1 to 23-38.53:3 (Virginia Scholars Program); §§23-38.70, 23-38.71 (Virginia Work Study Program). These programs involve substantial expenditures: for example, Virginia appropriated $4, 413,750 (not counting federal funds it also earmarked) for the College Scholarship Assistance Program for both 1996 and 1997, and for the Tuition Assistance Grant Program appropriated $21, 568,000 for 1996 and $25,842,000 for 1997. See 1996 Va. Appropriations Act, ch. 912, pt. 1, §160.

In addition, as the parties stipulated in the District Court, the Commonwealth provides other financial support and assistance to private institutions--including single sex colleges--through low cost building loans, state funded services contracts, and other programs. See, e.g., Va. Code Ann. §§23-30.39 to 23.30.58 (Educational Facilities Authority Act). The State Council of Higher Education for Virginia, in a 1989 document not created for purposes of this litigation but introduced into evidence, has described these various programs as a "means by which the Commonwealth can provide funding to its independent institutions, thereby helping to maintain a diverse system of higher education." Budget Initiatives, p. 10.

4 The Court, unfamiliar with the Commonwealth's policy of diverse and independent institutions, and in any event careless of state and local traditions, must be forgiven by Virginians for quoting a reference to "the Charlottesville campus" of the University of Virginia. See ante, at 20. The University of Virginia, an institution even older than VMI, though not as old as another of the Commonwealth's universities, the College of William and Mary, occupies the portion of Charlottesville known, not as the "campus," but as "the grounds." More importantly, even if it were a "campus," there would be no need to specify "the Charlottesville campus," as one might refer to the Bloomington or Indianapolis campus of Indiana University. Unlike university systems with which the Court is perhaps more familiar, such as those in New York (e.g., the State University of New York at Binghamton or Buffalo), Illinois (University of Illinois at

Urbana Champaign or at Chicago), and California (University of California, Los Angeles or University of California, Berkeley), there is only one University of Virginia. It happens (because Thomas Jefferson lived near there) to be located at Charlottesville. To many Virginians it is known, simply, as "the University," which suffices to distinguish it from the Commonwealth's other institutions offering four year college instruction, which include Christopher Newport College, Clinch Valley College, the College of William and Mary, George Mason University, James Madison University, Longwood College, Mary Washington University, Norfolk State University, Old Dominion University, Radford University, Virginia Commonwealth University, Virginia Polytechnic Institute and State University, Virginia State University--and, of course, the Virginia Military Institute.

5 The Court's do it yourself approach to factfinding, which throughout is contrary to our well settled rule that we will not "undertake to review concurrent findings of fact by two courts below in the absence of a very obvious and exceptional showing of error," Graver Tank & Mfg. Co. v. Linde Air Products Co., 336 U.S. 271, 275 (1949) (and cases cited), is exemplified by its invocation of the experience of the federal military academies to prove that not much change would occur. See ante, at 25, n. 11; 27-28, and n. 15; 34, n. 19. In fact, the District Court noted that "the West Point experience" supported the theory that a coeducational VMI would have to "adopt a [different] system," for West Point found it necessary upon becoming coeducational to "move away" from its adversarial system. 766 F. Supp., at 1413, 1440. "Without a doubt . . . VMI's present methods of training and education would have to be changed as West Point's were." Id., at 1413, n. 8; accord, 976 F. 2d, at 896-897 (upholding District Court's findings that "the unique characteristics of VMI's program," including its "unique methodology," "would be destroyed by coeducation").

6 The Court is incorrect in suggesting that the Court of Appeals applied a "deferential" "brand of review inconsistent with the more exacting standard our precedent requires." Ante, at 38. That court "inquir[ed] (1) whether the state's objective is `legitimate and important,' and (2) whether `the requisite direct, substantial relationship between objective and means is present,' " 44 F. 3d, at 1235 (quoting Hogan, 458 U. S., at 1235). To be sure, such review is "deferential" to a degree that the Court's new standard is not, for it is intermediate scrutiny. (The Court cannot evade this point or prove the Court of Appeals too deferential by stating that that court "devised another test, a `substantive comparability' inquiry,' " ante, at 38 (quoting 44 F. 3d, at 1237), for as that court explained, its "substantive comparability" inquiry was an "additional step" that it engrafted on "th[e] traditional test" of intermediate scrutiny, 44 F. 3d, at 1237 (emphasis added).)

7 The concurrence states that it "read[s] the Court" not "as saying that the diversity rationale is a pretext" for discriminating against women, but as saying merely that the diversity rationale is not genuine. Ante, at 5, n. *. The Court itself makes no such disclaimer, which would be difficult to credit inasmuch as the foundation for its conclusion that the diversity rationale is not "genuin[e]," ante, at 22, is its antecedent

discussion of Virginia's "deliberate" actions over the past century and a half, based on "[f]amiliar arguments," that sought to enforce once "widely held views about women's proper place," ante, at 17-22.

8 In this regard, I note that the Court--which I concede is under no obligation to do so--provides no example of a program that would pass muster under its reasoning today: not even, for example, a football or wrestling program. On the Court's theory, any woman ready, willing, and physically able to participate in such a program would, as a constitutional matter, be entitled to do so.

One would think it inconceivable that Elrod and Branti would be extended far beyond Rutan to the massive field of all government contracting : Justice Scalia's dissent in Board of Commissioners, Wabaunsee County, Kansas v. Umbehr (June 28, 1996)

"This case is ultimately a reminder that the Federal Constitution does not prohibit everything that is intensely undesirable."
- Justice Thomas' concurrence in Bennis v. Michigan (March 4, 1996)

Justice Scalia, with whom Justice Thomas joins, dissenting.

Taken together, today's decisions in Board of Comm'rs, Waubansee Cty. v. Umbehr, ante, p. ___, and O'Hare Truck Service, Inc. v. Northlake, ante, p. ___, demonstrate why this Court's Constitution making process can be called "reasoned adjudication" only in the most formalistic sense.

Six years ago, by the barest of margins, the Court expanded Elrod v. Burns, 427 U.S. 347 (1976), and Branti v. Finkel, 445 U.S. 507 (1980), which had held that public employees cannot constitutionally be fired on the basis of their political affiliation, to establish the new rule that applicants for public employment cannot constitutionally be rejected on the basis of their political affiliation. Rutan v. Republican Party of Ill., 497 U.S. 62 (1990). The four dissenters argued that "the desirability of patronage is a policy question to be decided by the people's representatives" and "a political question if there ever was one." Id., at 104, 114 (Scalia, J., dissenting). They were "convinced" that Elrod and Branti had been "wrongly decided," 497 U. S., at 114; indeed, that those cases were "not only wrong, not only recent, not only contradicted by a long prior tradition, but also . . . unworkable in practice" and therefore "should be overruled," id., at 110-111. At the very least, the dissenters maintained, Elrod and Branti "should not be extended beyond their facts," 497 U. S., at 114.

Today, with the addition to the Court of another Justice who believes that we have no basis for proscribing as unconstitutional practices that do not violate any explicit text of the Constitution and that have been regarded as constitutional ever since the framing, see, e.g., Bennis v. Michigan, 516 U. S. ___, ___ (1996) (slip op., at 1-2)

(Thomas, J., concurring), one would think it inconceivable that Elrod and Branti would be extended far beyond Rutan to the massive field of all government contracting. Yet amazingly, that is what the Court does in these two opinions--and by lopsided votes, at that. It is profoundly disturbing that the varying political practices across this vast country, from coast to coast, can be transformed overnight by an institution whose conviction of what the Constitution means is so fickle.

The basic reason for my dissent today is the same as one of the reasons I gave (this one not joined by Justice O'Connor) in Rutan:

"[W]hen a practice not expressly prohibited by the text of the Bill of Rights bears the endorsement of a long tradition of open, widespread, and unchallenged use that dates back to the beginning of the Republic, we have no proper basis for striking it down. Such a venerable and accepted tradition is not to be laid on the examining table and scrutinized for its conformity to some abstract principle of First Amendment adjudication devised by this Court. To the contrary, such traditions are themselves the stuff out of which the Court's principles are to be formed. They are, in these uncertain areas, the very points of reference by which the legitimacy or illegitimacy of other practices is to be figured out. When it appears that the latest `rule,' or `three part test,' or `balancing test' devised by the Court has placed us on a collision course with such a landmark practice, it is the former that must be recalculated by us, and not the latter that must be abandoned by our citizens. I know of no other way to formulate a constitutional jurisprudence that reflects, as it should, the principles adhered to, over time, by the American people, rather than those favored by the personal (and necessarily shifting) philosophical dispositions of a majority of this Court." Rutan, supra, at 95-96 (Scalia, J., dissenting) (footnote omitted).

There can be no dispute that, like rewarding one's allies, the correlative act of refusing to reward one's opponents--and at bottom both of today's cases involve exactly that--is an American political tradition as old as the Republic. This is true not only with regard to employment matters, as Justice Powell discussed in his dissenting opinions in Elrod, supra, at 377-379, and Branti, supra, at 522, n. 1, but also in the area of government contracts, see, e.g., M. Tolchin & S. Tolchin, To the Victor: Political Patronage from the Clubhouse to the White House 14-15, 61, 233-241, 273-277 (1971); A. Heard, The Costs of Democracy 143-145 (1960); R. Caro, The Power Broker: Robert Moses and the Fall of New York 723-726, 738, 740-741, 775, 799, 927 (1975); M.Royko, Boss: Richard J. Daley of Chicago 69 (1971); Wolfinger, Why Political Machines Have Not Withered Away and Other Revisionist Thoughts, 34 J. Politics 365, 367-368, 372, 389 (1972); The Bond Game Remains the Same, Nat'l L. J., July 1, 1996, pp. A1, A20-A21. If that long and unbroken tradition of our people does not decide these cases, then what does? The constitutional text is assuredly as susceptible of one meaning as of the other; in that circumstance, what constitutes a "law abridging the freedom of speech" is either a matter of history or else it is a matter of opinion. Why are not libel laws such an "abridgment"? The only satisfactory answer is that they never were. What secret knowledge, one must wonder, is breathed into lawyers when they become Justices of this

Court, that enables them to discern that a practice which the text of the Constitution does not clearly proscribe, and which our people have regarded as constitutional for 200 years, is in fact unconstitutional?

The Court seeks to avoid the charge that it ignores the centuries old understandings and practices of our people by recounting, Umbehr, ante, at 13-14, shocking examples of raw political patronage in contracting, most of which would be unlawful under the most rudimentary bribery law. (It selects, of course, only the worst examples from the sources I have cited, omitting the more common practices that permit one author to say, with undeniable accuracy, that "honorable and prudent businessmen competing for government ventures make campaign contributions" out of "a desire to do what [is] thought necessary to remain eligible," and that "[m]any contractors routinely do so to both parties." Heard, supra, at 145.) These "examples of covert, widely condemned and sometimes illegal government action," it says, do not "legitimize the government discrimination." Umbehr, ante, at 14. But of course it is not the County's or City's burden (or mine) to "legitimize" all patronage practices; it is Umbehr's and O'Hare's (and the Court's) to show that all patronage practices are not only "illegitimate" in some vague moral or even precise legal sense, but that they are unconstitutional. It suffices to demonstrate the error of the Court's opinions that many contracting patronage practices have been open, widespread, and unchallenged since the beginning of the Republic; and that those that have been objected to have not been objected to on constitutional grounds. That the Court thinks it relevant that many patronage practices are "covert, widely condemned and sometimes illegal" merely displays its persistent tendency to equate those many things that are or should be proscribed as a matter of social policy with those few things that we have the power to proscribe under the Constitution. The relevant and inescapable point is this: No court ever held, and indeed no one ever thought, prior to our decisions in Elrod and Branti, that patronage contracting could violate the First Amendment. The Court's attempt to contest this point, or at least to becloud the issue, by appeal to obnoxious and universally condemned patronage practices simply displays the feebleness of its case.

In each case today, the Court observes that we "have long since rejected Justice Holmes' famous dictum, that a policeman 'may have a constitutional right to talk politics, but he has no constitutional right to be a policeman.'" Umbehr, ante, at 5 (quoting McAuliffe v. Mayor of New Bedford, 155 Mass. 216, 220, 29 N. E. 517 (1892)); see O'Hare, ante, at 3 (quoting same). But this activist Court also repeatedly rejects a more important aphorism of Justice Holmes, which expresses a fundamental philosophy that was once an inseparable part of our approach to constitutional law. In a case challenging the constitutionality of a federal estate tax on the ground that it was an unapportioned direct tax in violation of Article I, §9, Justice Holmes wrote:

"[The] matter . . . is disposed of . . ., not by an attempt to make some scientific distinction, which would be at least difficult, but on an interpretation of language by its traditional use--on the practical and historical ground that this kind of tax always has been regarded as the antithesis of a direct tax . . . . Upon this point a page of history is worth a volume of logic." New York Trust Co. v. Eisner, 256 U.S. 345, 349 (1921) (emphasis added).

The Court's decision to enter this field cannot be justified by the consideration (if it were ever a justification) that the democratic institutions of government have not been paying adequate attention to the problems it presents. The American people have evidently decided that political influence in government contracting, like many other things that are entirely constitutional, is not entirely desirable, and so they have set about passing laws to prohibit it in some but not all instances. As a consequence, government contracting is subject to the most extraordinary number of laws and regulations at the federal, state, and local levels.

The United States Code contains a categorical statutory prohibition on political contributions by those negotiating for or performing contracts with the Federal Government, 2 U.S.C. § 441c competitive bidding requirements for contracts with executive agencies, 41 U.S.C. §§ 252-253, public corruption and bribery statutes, e.g., 18 U.S.C. § 201 and countless other statutory requirements that restrict government officials' discretion in awarding contracts. "There are already over four thousand individual statutory provisions that affect the [Defense Department's] procurement process." Pyatt, Procurement Competition at Work: The Navy's Experience, 6 Yale J. Reg. 319, 319-320 (1989). Federal regulations are even more widespread. As one handbook in the area has explained, "[t]heir procedural and substantive requirements dictate, to an oftentimes astonishing specificity, how the entire contracting process will be conducted." ABA General Practice Section, Federal Procurement Regulations: Policy, Practice and Procedures 1 (1987). That is why it is no surprise in this area to find a 253-page book just setting forth "fundamentals," E. Massengale, Fundamentals of Federal Contract Law (1991), or a mere "deskbook" that runs 436 pages, ABA Section of Public Contract Law, Government Contract Law: The Deskbook for Procurement Professionals (1995). Such "summaries" are indispensable when, for example, the regulations that comprise the "Federal Acquisition Regulations System" total some 5,037 pages of fine print. See Title 48 CFR (1995).

Similar systems of detailed statutes and regulations exist throughout the States. In addition to the various statutes criminalizing bribes to government officials and other forms of public corruption, all 50 States have enacted legislation imposing competitive bidding requirements on various types of contracts with the government. [n.1] Government contracting is such a standard area for state regulation that a model procurement code has been developed, which is set forth in a 265-page book complete with proposed statutes, regulations, and explanations. See ABA Section of Urban, State and Local Government Law, Model Procurement Code for State and Local Governments (1981). As of 1989, 15 States had enacted legislation based on the model code. See ABA Section of Urban, State and Local Government Law, Annotations to the Model Procurement Code, at vii-viii (2d ed. 1992) (and statutes cited).

By 1992, more than 25 local jurisdictions had also adopted legislation based on the Model Procurement Code, see id., at ix, and thousands of other counties and municipalities have over time devised their own measures. New York City, for example, which "[e]ach year . . . enter[s] into approximately 40,000 contracts worth almost $6.5 billion," has regulated the public contracting process by a myriad of codes and regulations that seek to assure "scrupulous neutrality in choosing contractors and [consequently impose] multiple layers of investigation and accountability." Anechiarico & Jacobs, Purging Corruption from Public Contracting: The `Solutions' Are Now Part of the Problem, 40 N. Y. L. S. L. Rev. 143, 143-144 (1995) (hereinafter Anechiarico & Jacobs).

These examples of federal, state, and local statutes, codes, ordinances, and regulations could be multiplied to fill many volumes. They are the way in which government contracts have been regulated, and the way in which public policy problems that arise in the area have been addressed, since the founding of the Republic. See, e.g., Federal Procurement Regulations: Policy, Practice and Procedures, at 11-196 (describing the history of federal government procurement regulation). But these laws and regulations have brought to the field a degree of discrimination, discernment, and predictability that cannot be achieved by the blunt instrument of a constitutional prohibition.

Title 48 of the Code of Federal Regulations would not contain the 5,000+ pages it does if it did not make fine distinctions, permitting certain actions in some government acquisition areas and prohibiting them in others. Similarly, many of the competitive bidding statutes that I have cited contain exceptions for, or are simply written not to include, contracts under a particular dollar amount, [n.2] or those covering certain subject matters, [n.3] or those that are time sensitive. [n.4] A political unit's decision not to enact contracting regulations, or to suspend the regulations in certain circumstances, amounts to a decision to permit some degree of political favoritism. As I shall discuss shortly, O'Hare's and Umbehr's First Amendment permits no such selectivity--or at least none that can be known before litigation is over.

If inattention by the democratic organs of government is not a plausible reason for the Court's entry into the field, then what is? I believe the Court accepts (any sane person must accept) the premise that it is utterly impossible to erect, and enforce through litigation, a system in which no citizen is intentionally disadvantaged by the government because of his political beliefs. I say the Court accepts that, because the O'Hare opinion, in a rare brush with the real world, points out that "O'Hare was not part of a constituency that must take its chance of being favored or ignored in the larger political process--for example, by residing or doing business in a region the government rewards or spurns in the construction of public works." Ante, at 8. Of course. Government favors those who agree with its political views, and disfavors those who disagree, every day--in where it builds its public works, in the kinds of taxes it imposes and collects, in its regulatory prescriptions, in the design of its grant and benefit programs--in a million ways, including the letting of contracts for government business. What good reason has the

Court given for separating out this last way, and declaring it to be (as all the others for some reason are not) an "abridgment of the freedom of speech"?

As I have explained, I would separate the permissible from the impermissible on the basis of our Nation's traditions, which is what I believe sound constitutional adjudication requires. In Elrod and Branti, the Court rejected this criterion--but if what it said did not make good constitutional law, at least it made some sense: the loss of one's job is a powerful price to pay for one's politics. But the Court then found itself on the fabled slippery slope that Justice Holmes's aphorism about history and logic warned about: one logical proposition detached from history leads to another, until the Court produces a result that bears no resemblance to the America that we know. The next step was Rutan, which extended the prohibition of political motivation from firing to hiring. The third step is today's Umbehr, which extends it to the termination of a government contract. And the fourth step (as I shall discuss anon) is today's O'Hare, which extends it to the refusal to enter into contractual relationships.

If it is to be possible to dig in our cleats at some point on this slope--before we end up holding that the First Amendment requires the City of Chicago to have as few potholes in Republican wards (if any) as in Democratic ones--would not the most defensible point of termination for this indefensible exercise be public employment? A public employee is always an individual, and a public employee below the highest political level (which is exempt from Elrod) is virtually always an individual who is not rich; the termination or denial of a public job is the termination or denial of a livelihood. A public contractor, on the other hand, is usually a corporation; and the contract it loses is rarely its entire business, or even an indispensable part of its entire business. As Judge Posner put it:

"Although some business firms sell just to government, most government contractors also have private customers. If the contractor does not get the particular government contract on which he bids, because he is on the outs with the incumbent and the state does not have laws requiring the award of the contract to the low bidder (or the laws are not enforced), it is not the end of the world for him; there are other government entities to bid to, and private ones as well. It is not like losing your job." LaFalce v. Houston, 712 F. 2d 292, 294 (CA7 1983).

Another factor that suggests we should stop this new enterprise at government employment is the much greater volume of litigation that its extension to the field of contracting entails. The government contracting decisions worth litigating about are much more numerous than the number of personnel hirings and firings in that category; and the litigation resources of contractors are infinitely more substantial than those of fired employees or rejected applicants. Anyone who has had even brief exposure to the intricacies of federal contracting law knows that a lawsuit is often used as a device to stay or frustrate the award of a contract to a competitor. See, e.g., Delta Data Systems Corp. v. Webster, 744 F. 2d 197 (CADC 1984); Delta Data Systems Corp. v. Webster, 755 F. 2d 938 (CADC 1985). What the Court's decisions today mean is that all government entities, no matter how small, are at risk of §1983 lawsuits for violation of constitutional rights, unless they adopt (at great cost in money and efficiency) the detailed and cumbersome procedures that make a claim of political favoritism (and a §1983 lawsuit) easily defended against.

The Court's opinion in O'Hare shrugs off this concern with the response that "[w]e have no reason to believe that governments cannot bear a like burden [to that in the employment context] in defending against suits alleging the denial of First Amendment freedoms to public contractors." Ante, at 12. The burden is, as I have suggested, likely much greater than that in the employment context; and the relevant question (if one rejects history as the determinant) is not simply whether the governments "can bear" it, but whether the inconvenience of bearing it is outbalanced by the degree of abridgment of supposed First Amendment rights (of corporate shareholders, for the most part) that would occur if the burden were not imposed. [n.5] The Court in Umbehr dismisses the risk of litigation, not by analogy to the employment context, but by analogy to the many government contracting laws of the type I have discussed. "We are aware," it says, "of no evidence of excessive or abusive litigation under such provisions." Umbehr, ante, at 15. I am not sure the Court would be aware of such evidence if it existed, but if in fact litigation has been "nonexcessive" (a conveniently imprecise term) under these provisions, that is scant indication that it will be "nonexcessive" under the First Amendment. Uncertainty breeds litigation. Government contracting laws are clear and detailed, and whether they have been violated is typically easy to ascertain: the contract was put out for bid, or it was not. Umbehr's new First Amendment, by contrast, requires a sensitive "balancing" in each case; and the factual question of whether political affiliation or disfavored speech was the reason for the award or loss of the contract will usually be litigable. In short, experience under the government contracting laws has little predictive value.

The Court additionally asserts that the line cannot be drawn between employment and independent contracting, because " `the applicability of a provision of the Constitution has never depended on the vagaries of state or federal law.' " Umbehr, ante, at 11 (quoting Browning Ferris Industries of Vt., Inc. v. Kelco Disposal, Inc., 492 U.S. 257, 299 (1989) (O'Connor, J., concurring in part and dissenting in part)); see also Umbehr, ante, at 10-11 (citing other cases). That is not so. State law frequently plays a dispositive role in the issue of whether a constitutional provision is applicable. In fact, before we invented the First Amendment right not to be fired for political views, most litigation in this very field of government employment revolved around the Fourteenth Amendment's Due Process Clause, and asked whether the firing had deprived the plaintiff of a "property" interest without due process. And what is a property interest entitled to Fourteenth Amendment protection? " [P]roperty interests," we said, "are not created by the Constitution. Rather, they are created and their dimensions are defined by existing rules or understandings that stem from an independent source such as state law . . . . If it is the law of Texas that a teacher in the respondent's position has no contractual or other claim to job tenure, the respondent's [federal constitutional] claim would be defeated."

Perry v. Sindermann, 408 U.S. 593, 602, n. 7 (1972) (internal quotation marks and citation omitted). See also Mt. Healthy City Bd. of Ed. v. Doyle, 429 U.S. 274, 280-281 (1977) (whether a government entity possesses Eleventh Amendment immunity "depends, at least in part, upon the nature of the entity created by state law").

I have spoken thus far as though the only problem involved here were a practical one: as though, in the best of all possible worlds, if our judicial system and the resources of our governmental entities could only manage it, it would be desirable for an individual to suffer no disadvantage whatever at the hands of the government solely because of his political views--no denial of employment, no refusal of contracts, no discrimination in social programs, not even any potholes. But I do not believe that. The First Amendment guarantees that you and I can say and believe whatever we like (subject to a few tradition based exceptions, such as obscenity and "fighting words") without going to jail or being fined. What it ought to guarantee beyond that is not at all the simple question the Court assumes. The ability to discourage eccentric views through the mild means that have historically been employed, and that the Court has now set its face against, may well be important to social cohesion. To take an uncomfortable example from real life: An organization (I shall call it the White Aryan Supremacist Party, though that was not the organization involved in the actual incident I have in mind) is undoubtedly entitled, under the Constitution, to maintain and propagate racist and antisemitic views. But when the Department of Housing and Urban Development lets out contracts to private security forces to maintain law and order in units of public housing, must it really treat this bidder the same as all others? Or may it determine that the views of this organization are not political views that it wishes to "subsidize" with public funds, nor political views that it wishes to hold up as an exemplar of the law to the residents of public housing?

The state and local regulation I described earlier takes account of this reality. Even where competitive bidding requirements are applicable (which is far from always), they almost invariably require that a contract be awarded not to the lowest bidder but to the "lowest responsible bidder." [n.6] "The word `responsible' is as important as the word `lowest,' " H. Cohen, Public Construction Contracts and the Law 81 (1961), and has been interpreted in some States to permit elected officials to exercise political discretion. "Some New York courts," for example, "have upheld agency refusals to award a contract to a low bidder because the contractor, while technically and financially capable, was not morally responsible." Anechiarico & Jacobs 146-147. In the leading case of Picone v. New York, 176 Misc. 967, 29 N. Y. S. 2d 539 (Sup. Ct. N. Y. Cty. 1941), the court stated that in determining whether a lowest bidder for a particular contract was the "lowest responsible bidder," New York City officials had permissibly considered "whether [the bidder] possessed integrity and moral worth." Id., at 969, 29 N. Y. S. 2d, at 541. The New Jersey Supreme Court has similarly said "[i]t is settled that the legislative mandate that a bidder be `responsible' embraces moral integrity just as surely as it embraces a capacity to supply labor and materials." Trap Rock Industries, Inc. v. Kohl, 59 N. J. 471, 481, 284 A. 2d 161, 166 (1971). In the future, presumably, this will be permitted only if the disfavored moral views of the bidder have never been verbalized, for otherwise the First Amendment will produce entitlement to the contract, or at least guarantee a lawsuit.

In treading into this area, "we have left the realm of law and entered the domain of political science." Rutan, 497 U. S., at 113 (Scalia, J., dissenting). As Judge Posner rightly perceived, the issue that the Court today disposes of like some textbook exercise in logic "raises profound questions of political science that exceed judicial competence to answer." LaFalce v. Houston, 712 F. 2d, at 294.

If, however, the Court is newly to announce that it has discovered that the granting or withholding of a contract is a First Amendment issue, a coherent statement of the new law is the least that those who labor in the area are entitled to expect. They do not get it from today's decisions, which contradict each other on a number of fundamental points.

The decision in Umbehr appears to be an improvement on our Elrod-Branti-Rutan trilogy in one sense. Rutan, the most recent of these decisions, provided that the government could justify patronage employment practices only if it proved that such patronage was "narrowly tailored to further vital governmental interests." Rutan, supra, at 74. The four of us in dissent explained that "[t]hat strict scrutiny standard finds no support in our cases," and we argued that, if the new constitutional right was to be invented, the criterion for violation should be "the test announced in Pickering [v. Board of Ed. of Township High School Dist. 205, Will Cty., 391 U.S. 563 (1968)]." Rutan, supra, at 98, 100 (Scalia, J., dissenting). It thus appears a happy development that the Court in Umbehr explicitly rejects the suggestion, urged by Umbehr and by the United States as amicus curiae, that "on proof of viewpoint based retaliation for contractors' political speech, the government should be required to justify its actions as narrowly tailored to serve a compelling state interest," Umbehr, ante, at 7; accord, ante, at 9, and instead holds "that the Pickering balancing test, adjusted to weigh the government's interests as contractor rather than as employer, determines the extent of [independent contractors'] protection" under the First Amendment, ante, at 4. Pickering balancing, of course, requires a case by case assessment of the government's and the contractor's interests. "Pickering and its progeny . . . involve a post hoc analysis of one employee's speech and its impact on that employee's public responsibilities." United States v. Treasury Employees, 513 U. S. ___, ___ (1995) (slip op., at 11). See also id., at ___ (slip op., at 2) (O'Connor, J., concurring in judgment in part and dissenting in part) (Pickering requires "case by case application"); Rankin v. McPherson, 483 U.S. 378, 388-392 (1987); Connick v. Myers, 461 U.S. 138, 150-154 (1983); Pickering v. Board of Ed. of Township High School Dist. 205, Will Cty., 391 U.S. 563, 568-573 (1968). It is clear that this is what the Court's opinion in Umbehr anticipates: "a fact sensitive and deferential weighing of the government's legitimate interests," ante, at 8-9 (emphasis added), which accords "[d]eference . . . to the government's reasonable assessments of its interests as contractor," ante, at 9 (emphasis removed). "[S]uch a nuanced approach," Umbehr says, "which recognizes the variety of interests that may arise in independent contractor cases, is superior to a bright line rule." Ante, at 9-10.

What the Court sets down in Umbehr, however, it rips up in O'Hare. In Part III of that latter opinion, where the Court makes its application of the First Amendment to the facts of the case, there is to be found not a single reference to Pickering. See O'Hare, ante, at 7-13. Indeed, what is quite astonishing, the Court concludes that it "need not inquire" into any government interests that patronage contracting may serve--even generally, much less in the particular case at hand--"for Elrod and Branti establish that patronage does not justify the coercion of a person's political beliefs and associations." O'Hare, ante, at 5. Leaving aside that there is no coercion here, [n.7] the assertion obviously contradicts the need for "balancing" announced in the companion Umbehr decision. This rejection of "balancing" is evident elsewhere in O'Hare--as when the Court rejects as irrelevant the Seventh Circuit's observation in LaFalce v. Houston, 712 F. 2d 292 (1983), that some contractors elect to "curr[y] favor with diverse political parties," on the ground that the fact "[t]hat some citizens [thus] find a way to mitigate governmental overreaching, or refrain from complaining, does not excuse wrongs done to those who exercise their rights." O'Hare, ante, at 11. But whether the government action at issue here is a "wrong" is precisely the issue in this case, which we thought (per Umbehr) was to be determined by "balancing."

One would have thought these two opinions the products of the courts of last resort of two different legal systems, presenting fertile material for a comparative law course on freedom of speech . . . were it not for a single paragraph in O'Hare, a veritable deus ex machina of legal analysis, which reconciles the irreconcilable. The penultimate paragraph of that portion of the O'Hare opinion which sets forth the general principles of law governing the case, see ante, at 6-7, advises that henceforth "the freedom of speech" alluded to in the Bill of Rights will be divided into two categories: (1) the "right of free speech," where "we apply the balancing test from Pickering," and (since this "right of free speech" presumably does not exhaust the Free Speech Clause), (2) "political affiliation," where we apply the rigid rule of Elrod and Branti. The Court (or at least the O'Hare Court) says that "[t]here is an advantage in so confining the inquiry where political affiliation alone is concerned, for one's beliefs and allegiances ought not to be subject to probing or testing by the government." O'Hare, ante, at 6.

Frankly, the only "advantage" I can discern in this novel distinction is that it provides some explanation (no matter how difficult to grasp) of how these two opinions can issue from the same Court on the same day. It raises many questions. Does the "right of free speech" (category (1), that is) come into play if the contractor not only is a Republican, but says "I am a Republican"? (At that point, of course, the fatal need for "probing or testing" his allegiance disappears.) Or is the "right of free speech" at issue only if he goes still further, and says "I believe in the principles set forth in the Republican platform"? Or perhaps one must decide whether the Rubicon between the "right of free speech" and the more protected "political affiliation" has been crossed on the basis of the contracting authority's motivation, so that it does not matter whether the contractor says he is a Republican, or even says that he believes in the Republican platform, so long as the reason he is disfavored is simply that (whatever he says or believes) he is a Republican. But the analysis would change, perhaps, if the contracting authority really has nothing against Republicans as such, but can't stand people who believe what the Republican platform stands for. Except perhaps it would not change if the contractor never actually said he was a Republican--or perhaps only if he never actually said that he believed in the Republican platform. The many variations will provide endless diversion for the courts of appeals.

If one is so sanguine as to believe that facts involving the "right of free speech" and facts involving "political affiliation" can actually be segregated into separate categories, there arises, of course, the problem of what to do when both are involved. One would expect the more rigid test (Elrod nonbalancing) to prevail. That is certainly what happens elsewhere in the law. If one is categorically liable for a defamatory statement, but liable for a threatening statement only if it places the subject in immediate fear of physical harm, an utterance that which combines both ("Sir, I shall punch you in your lying mouth!") would be (at least as to the defamatory portion) categorically actionable. Not so, however, with our new First Amendment law. Where, we are told, "specific instances of the employee's speech or expression, which require balancing in the Pickering context, are intermixed with a political affiliation requirement," balancing rather than categorical liability will be the result. O'Hare, ante, at 6-7.

Were all this confusion not enough, the explanatory paragraph makes doubly sure it is not setting forth any comprehensible rule by adding, immediately after its description of how Elrod, rather than the Pickering balancing test, applies in "political affiliation" cases, the following: "It is true, on the other hand, . . . that the inquiry is whether the affiliation requirement is a reasonable one, so it is inevitable that some case by case adjudication will be required even where political affiliation is the test the government has imposed." O'Hare, ante, at 6. As I said in Rutan, "[w]hat that means is anybody's guess." 497 U. S., at 111 (Scalia, J., dissenting). Worse still, we learn that O'Hare itself, where the Court does not conduct balancing, may "perhaps [be] includ[ed]" among "those many cases . . . which require balancing" because it is one of the "intermixed" cases I discussed in the paragraph immediately above. O'Hare, ante, at 6. Why, then, one is inclined to ask, did not the Court conduct balancing?

The answer is contained in the next brief paragraph of the O'Hare opinion:

"The Court of Appeals, based on its understanding of the pleadings, considered this simply an affiliation case, and held, based on circuit precedent, there was no constitutional protection for one who was simply an outside contractor. We consider the case in those same terms, but we disagree with the Court of Appeals' conclusion." Ante, at 7.

This is a deus ex machina sent in to rescue the Court's deus ex machina, which was itself overwhelmed by the plot of this tragedy of inconsistency. Unfortunately, this adjutor adjutoris (to overextend, perhaps, my classical analogy) is also unequal to the task: The respondent in this case is entitled to defend the judgment in its favor on the basis of the facts as they were alleged, not as the Court of Appeals took them to be. When, as here, "the decision we review adjudicated a motion to dismiss, we accept all of the factual allegations in petitioners' complaint as true and ask whether, in these circumstances, dismissal of the complaint was appropriate." Berkovitz v. United States, 486 U.S. 531, 540 (1988) (emphasis added). It is at least highly arguable that the complaint alleged what the Court calls a violation of the "right of free speech" rather than merely the right of "political affiliation." The count at issue was entitled " FREEDOM OF SPEECH," see App. in No. 95-191, p. 15, and contended that petitioners had been retaliated against because of "the exercise of their constitutional right of freedom of speech," id., at 17. One of the two central factual allegations is the following: "John A. Gratzianna openly supported Paxson's opponent for the office of Mayor. Campaign posters for Paxson's opponent were displayed at plaintiff O'Hare's place of business." Id., at 16. It is particularly inexcusable to hide behind the Court of Appeals' treatment of this litigation as "simply an affiliation case," since when the Court of Appeals wrote its opinion the world had not yet learned that the Free Speech Clause is divided into the two categories of "right of free speech" and "political affiliation." As far as that court knew, it could have substituted "freedom of speech" for "freedom of political affiliation" whenever it used the term, with no effect on the outcome. It did not, in other words, remotely make a "finding" that the case involves only the right of political affiliation. Unavoidably, therefore, if what the O'Hare Court says in its first explanatory paragraph is to be believed--that is, what it says in the latter part of that paragraph, to the effect that "intermixed" cases are governed by Pickering--there is simply no basis for reversing the Court of Appeals without balancing, and directing that the case proceed, effectively depriving the City of its right to judgment on the pleadings.

 Unless, of course, Pickering balancing can never support the granting of a motion to dismiss. That is the proposition that today's O'Hare opinion, if it is not total confusion, must stand for. Nothing else explains how the Court can (1) assert that an "intermixed" case requires Pickering balancing, (2) acknowledge that the complaint here may set forth an "intermixed" case, and yet (3) reverse the dismissal without determining whether the complaint does set forth an "intermixed" case and, if so, proceeding to conduct at least a preliminary Pickering balancing. There is of course no reason in principle why this particular issue should be dismissal proof, and the consequence of making it so, given the burdens of pre-trial discovery (to say nothing of trial itself) will be to make litigation on this subject even more useful as a device for harassment and weapon of commercial competition. It must be acknowledged, however, that proceeding this way in the present case has one unquestionable advantage: it leaves it entirely to the district court to clean up, without any guidance or assistance from us, the mess that we have made--to figure out whether saying "Vote against Paxson," or "Paxson is a hack," or "Paxson's project for a 100,000-seat municipal stadium is wasteful," or whatever else Mr. Gratzianna's campaign posters might have said, removes this case from the Political Affiliation Clause of the Constitution and places it within the Right of Free Speech Clause.

One final observation about the sweep of today's holdings. The opinion in Umbehr, having swallowed the camel of First Amendment extension into contracting, in its penultimate paragraph demonstrates the Court's deep down judicial conservatism by ostentatiously straining out the following gnat: "Finally, we emphasize the limited nature of our decision today. Because Umbehr's suit concerns the termination of a pre-existing commercial relationship with the government, we need not address the possibility of suits by bidders or applicants for new government contracts who cannot rely on such a relationship." Umbehr, ante, at 17. The facts in Umbehr, of course, involved the termination of nothing so vague as a "commercial relationship with the government"; the Board of Commissioners had terminated Umbehr's contract. The fuzzier terminology is used, presumably, because O'Hare did not involve termination of a contract. As far as appears, O'Hare had not paid or promised anything to be placed on a list of tow truck operators who would be offered individual contracts as they came up. The company had no right to sue if the city failed to call it, nor the city any right to sue if the company turned down an offered tow. It had, in short, only what might be called (as an infinity of things might be called) "a pre-existing commercial relationship" with the city: it was one of the tow truck operators they regularly called. The quoted statement in Umbehr invites the bar to believe, therefore, that the Court which declined to draw the line of First Amendment liability short of firing from government employment (Elrod and Branti); short of nonhiring for government employment (Rutan); short of termination of a government contract (Umbehr); and short of denial of a government contract to someone who had a "pre existing commercial relationship with the government" (O'Hare); may take a firm stand against extending the Constitution into every little thing when it comes to denying a government contract to someone who had no "pre existing commercial relationship." Not likely; in fact, not even believable.

This Court has begun to make a habit of disclaiming the natural and foreseeable jurisprudential consequences of its pathbreaking (i.e., Constitution making) opinions. Each major step in the abridgment of the people's right to govern themselves is portrayed as extremely limited or indeed sui juris. In Romer v. Evans, 517 U. S. ___, ___ (1996) (slip op. at 11, 12), announced last month, the Court asserted that the Colorado constitutional amendment at issue was so distinctive that it "defies . . . conventional inquiry" and "confounds [the] normal process of judicial review." In United States v. Virginia, ante, at ___ n. 7 (1996), announced two days ago, the Court purported to address "specifically and only an educational opportunity recognized by the District Court and the Court of Appeals as `unique.' " And in the cases announced today, "we emphasize the limited nature of our decision." Umbehr, ante, at 17. The people should not be deceived. While the present Court sits, a major, undemocratic restructuring of our national institutions and mores is constantly in progress.

* * *

They say hard cases make bad law. The cases before the Court today set the blood boiling, with the arrogance that they seem to display on the part of elected officials. Shall the American System of Justice let insolent, petty tyrant politicians get away with this? What one tends to forget is that we have heard only the plaintiffs' tale. These suits were dismissed before trial, so the "facts" the Court recites in its opinions assume the truth of the allegations made (or the preliminary evidence presented) by the plaintiffs. We have no idea whether the allegations are true or false--but if they are true, they are certainly highly unusual. Elected officials do not thrive on arrogance.

For every extreme case of the sort alleged here, I expect there are thousands of contracts awarded on a "favoritism" basis that no one would get excited about. The Democratic mayor gives the city's municipal bond business to what is known to be a solid Democratic law firm--taking it away from the solid Republican law firm that had the business during the previous, Republican, administration. What else is new? Or he declines to give the construction contract for the new municipal stadium to the company that opposed the bond issue for its construction, and that in fact tried to get the stadium built across the river in the next State. What else would you expect? Or he awards the cable monopoly, not to the (entirely responsible) Johnny come lately, but to the local company that has always been a "good citizen"--which means it has supported with money, and the personal efforts of its management, civic initiatives that the vast majority of the electorate favor, though some oppose. Hooray! Favoritism such as this happens all the time in American political life, and no one has ever thought that it violated--of all things--the First Amendment to the Constitution of the United States.

The Court must be living in another world. Day by day, case by case, it is busy designing a Constitution for a country I do not recognize. Depending upon which of today's cases one chooses to consider authoritative, it has either (O'Hare) thrown out vast numbers of practices that are routine in American political life in order to get rid of a few bad apples; or (Umbehr) with the same purpose in mind subjected those routine practices to endless, uncertain, case by case, balance all the factors and who knows who will win litigation.

I dissent.

Notes to Justice Scalia's dissent in Board of Commissioners, Wabaunsee County, Kansas v. Umbehr (June 28, 1996)

1 See, e.g., Ala. Code §11-43C%70 (1989); id., §24-1-83 (1992); id., §41-16-20 (Supp. 1995); Alaska Stat. Ann. §36.30.100 (1992); Ariz. Rev. Stat. Ann. §41-2533 (1992); Ark. Code Ann. §§14-47-120, 14-47-138, 14-48-117, 14-48-129 (1987); Cal. Pub. Cont. Code Ann. §§10302, 10309, 10373, 10501, 10507.7, 20723, 20736, 20751, 20803, 20921, 21501, 21631 (West 1985 and Supp. 1996); Cal. Pub. Util. Code Ann. §131285 (West 1991); Cal. Rev. & Tax. Code Ann. §674 (West Supp. 1996); Colo. Rev. Stat. §24-103-202 (Supp. 1995); Conn. Gen. Stat. §4a-57 (Supp. 1996); Del. Code Ann., Tit. 9, §671 (1989); id., Tit.

29, §6903(a) (1991); Fla. Stat. §190.033 (Supp. 1996); id., §287.057 (1991 and Supp. 1996); Ga. Code Ann. §2-10-10 (1990); id., §§32-10-7, 32-10-68 (1991 and Supp. 1995); Haw. Rev. Stat. §103D-302 (Supp. 1995); Idaho Code §33-1510 (1995); id., §43-2508 (Supp. 1995); id., §50-1710 (1994); id., §67-5711C (1995); id., §67-5718 (1995 and 1996 Idaho Sess. Laws, ch. 198); Ill. Comp. Stat., ch. 50, §20/20 (1993); id., ch. 65, §5/8-10-3 (1993); id., ch. 70,§§205/25, 225/25, 265/25, 280/1-24, 280/2-24, 290/26, 310/5-24, 320/1-25, 320/2-25, 325/1-24, 325/2-24, 325/3-24, 325/5-24, 325/6-24, 325/7-24, 325/8-24, 340/25, 2305/11, 2405/11, 2805/14, 2905/5-4 (1993 and Supp. 1996); Ind. Code §§2-6-1.5-2, 10-7-2-28, 4-13.6-5-2, 8-16-3.5-5.5 (Supp. 1995); Iowa Code §18.6 (1995); Kan. Stat. Ann. §49-417(a) (Supp. 1990); id., §§75-3739 to 75-3741 (1989, Supp. 1990, and 1996 Kan. Sess. Laws); Ky. Rev. Stat. Ann. §162.070 (Baldwin 1990); La. Rev. Stat. Ann. §39:1594 (West 1989); Me. Rev. Stat. Ann., Tit. 5, §§1743, 1743-A (1989); Md. Ann. Code, Art. 25, §3(l) (Supp. 1995, and 1996 Md. Laws, ch. 66); id., Art. 25A, §5(F) (Supp. 1995); Md. Nat. Res. Code Ann. §§3-103(g)(3), 8-1005(c) (Supp. 1995); Mass. Gen. Laws, ch. 149, §§44A-44M (1989 and Supp. 1996); Mich. Comp. Laws Ann. §247.661c (West Supp. 1996); Minn. Stat. §16B.07 (1988 and Supp. 1996); Miss. Code Ann. §27-35-101 (1995); id., §§31-7-13, 37-151-17 (Supp. 1995); Mo. Rev. Stat. §§34.040.1, 34.042.1, 68.055.1 (Supp. 1996); Mont. Code Ann. §§7-3-1323, 7-5-2301, 7-5-2302, 7-5-4302, 7-14-2404 (1995); Neb. Rev. Stat. §§81-885.55, 84-1603 (1994); Nev. Rev. Stat. §332.065 (1984); N. H. Rev. Stat. Ann. §28:8 (1988); id., §186-C:22(VI) (Supp. 1995); id., §228:4 (1993); N. J. Stat. Ann. §28:1-7 (West 1981); N. M. Stat. Ann. §13-1-102 (1992); N. Y. Alt. County Govt. Law §401 (McKinney 1993); N. Y. Gen. Mun. Law §103 (McKinney 1986 and Supp. 1996); N. C. Gen. Stat. §133-10.1 (1995); id., §143-49 (1993); N. D. Cent. Code §54-44.4-05 (Supp. 1995); Ohio Rev. Code Ann. §§307.90, 511.12 (1994); id., §3381.11 (1995); Okla. Stat., Tit. 11, §24-114 (1994); id., Tit. 52, §318 (1991); id., Tit. 61, §101 (1989); Ore. Rev. Stat. §279.015 (1991); 53 Pa. Cons. Stat. §23308.1 (Supp. 1996); R. I. Gen. Laws §45-55-5 (Supp 1995); S. C. Code Ann. §11-35-1520 (Supp. 1995); S. D. Codified Laws §§5-18-2, 5-18-3 (1994); id., §5-18-9 (Supp. 1996); id., §9-42-5 (1995); id., §11-7-44 (1995); id., §13-49-16, 42-7A%5 (1991); Tenn. Code Ann. §§12-3-202, 12-3-203, 12-3-1007 (1992 and Supp. 1995); Tex. Educ. Code Ann. §51.907 (1987); Tex. Loc. Govt. Code Ann. §§252.021, 262.023, 262.027, 271.027, 375.221 (1988 and Supp. 1996); Utah Code Ann. §17A-2-1195 (1991); Vt. Stat. Ann., Tit. 29, §152(12) (1986); Va. Code Ann. §§11-41, 11-41.1 (1993); Wash. Rev. Code §§28A.160.140, 36.32.250 (Supp. 1996); W. Va. Code §§4-7-7, 5-6-7 (1994); Wis. Stat. §30.32 (1989 and Supp. 1995); id., §60.47 (1988 and Supp. 1995); Wyo. Stat. §35-2-429 (1994).

    2 See, e.g., 41 U.S.C. §§ 252a(b), 403(11) (certain federal contracting laws rendered inapplicable "to a contract or subcontract that is not greater than" $100,000); Cal. Pub. Cont. Code Ann. §10507.7 (West Supp. 1996) (lowest responsible bidder requirement for certain goods and materials only applicable to "contracts involving an [annual] expenditure of more than fifty thousand dollars"); Ill. Comp. Stat., ch. 50, §20/20 (1993) (lowest responsible bidder requirement for certain construction contracts

not applicable to contracts for more than $5,000); N. Y. Gen. Mun. Law §103.1 (McKinney Supp. 1996) (not covering public work contracts for $20,000 or less or purchase contracts for $10,000 or less); S. D. Codified Laws §5-18-3 (Supp. 1996) (requiring competitive bidding process for certain public improvement contracts "involv[ing] the expenditure of twenty five thousand dollars or more"); Texas Local Govt. Code Ann. §262.023(a) (Supp. 1996) (applying only to "a contract that will require an expenditure exceeding $15,000").

3 See, e. g., Idaho Code §33-1510 (1995); N. J. Stat. Ann. §28:1-7 (1981); Ohio Rev. Code Ann. §511.12 (Supp. 1995); Okla. Stat., Tit. 52, §318 (1991); Utah Code Ann. §17A-2-1195 (1991).

4 See, e.g., Del. Code Ann., Tit. 29, §6903(a)(2) (1991); Fla. Stat. §287.057(3)(a) (Supp. 1996); Minn. Stat. §16B.08(6) (1988); N. H. Rev. Stat. Ann. §228:4(I)(e) (1993); Tenn. Code Ann. §§12-3-202(3), 12-3-206 (1992).

5 O'Hare makes a brief attempt to minimize the seriousness of the litigation concern, pointing out that "[t]he amicus brief filed on behalf of respondents' position represents that in the six years since our opinion in [Rutan] . . . only 18 suits alleging First Amendment violations in employment decisions have been filed against Illinois state officials." Ante, at 11. In fact the brief said "at least eighteen cases," Brief for Illinois State Officials as Amici Curiae, at 3 (emphasis added), and that includes only suits against state officials, and not those against the officials of Illinois' 102 counties or its even more numerous municipalities. Those statistics pertain to employment suits, moreover--and as I have discussed, the contracting suits will be much more numerous.

O'Hare also says that "we have found no reported case in the Tenth Circuit involving a First Amendment patronage claim by an independent contractor in the six years since its Court of Appeals first recognized such claims, see Abercrombie v. Catoosa, 896 F. 2d 1228 (1990)." O'Hare, ante, at 11-12. With respect, Abercrombie (which discussed this issue in two short paragraphs) was such an obscure case that even the District Court in Umbehr, located in the Tenth Circuit, did not cite it, though it discussed cases in other jurisdictions. Umbehr v. McClure, 840 F. Supp. 837 (Kan. 1993). And when the Tenth Circuit reversed the District Court, it did not do so on the basis of Abercrombie--which, it noted, had "simply assumed that an independent contractor could assert a First Amendment retaliation claim" and had given "little reasoning" to the matter but merely so "suggested, without analysis." 44 F. 3d 876, 880 (1995) (emphasis added). Abercrombie was, in short, such a muffled clarion that even the courts did not hear it, much less the public at large.

6 See, e.g., Cal. Pub. Cont. Code Ann. §§10302, 10507.7, 20803 (West 1985 and Supp. 1996); Ill. Comp. Stat., ch. 50, §§20/20, 25/3; id., ch. 70, §§15/8, 15/9, 205/25, 220/1-24, 220/2-24 (1993); N. Y. Gen. Mun. Law §103.1 (McKinney Supp. 1996).

7 As the dissenters in Rutan v. Republican Party of Ill., 497 U.S. 62 (1990), agreed, "it greatly exaggerates [the constraints entailed by patronage] to call them `coercion' at all, since we generally make a distinction between inducement and

compulsion. The public official offered a bribe is not `coerced' to violate the law, and the private citizen offered a patronage job is not `coerced' to work for the party." Id., at 109-110 (Scalia, J., dissenting).

A sentencing enhancement based on a prior conviction should be subject to the Sixth Amendment requirement for a jury to determine the fact beyond a reasonable doubt: Justice Scalia's dissent in Almendarez-Torres v. United States (March 24, 1998)

Justice Scalia, with whom Justice Stevens, Justice Souter, and Justice Ginsburg join, dissenting.

Because Hugo Roman Almendarez-Torres illegally re-entered the United States after having been convicted of an aggravated felony, he was subject to a maximum possible sentence of 20 years imprisonment. See 8 U.S.C. § 1326(b)(2). Had he not been convicted of that felony, he would have been subject to a maximum of only two years. See 8 U.S.C. § 1326(a). The Court today holds that §1326(b)(2) does not set forth a separate offense, and that conviction of a prior felony is merely a sentencing enhancement for the offense set forth in §1326(a). This causes the Court to confront the difficult question whether the Constitution requires a fact which substantially increases the maximum permissible punishment for a crime to be treated as an element of that crime—to be charged in the indictment, and found beyond a reasonable doubt by a jury. Until the Court said so, it was far from obvious that the answer to this question was no; on the basis of our prior law, in fact, the answer was considerably doubtful.

In all our prior cases bearing upon the issue, however, we confronted a criminal statute or state-court criminal ruling that unambiguously relieved the prosecution of the burden of proving a critical fact to the jury beyond a reasonable doubt. In McMillan v. Pennsylvania, 477 U.S. 79 (1986), the statute provided that " 'visibl[e] possess[ion] [of] a firearm' " " 'shall not be an element of the crime[,]' " but shall be determined at sentencing by " '[t]he court . . . by a preponderance of the evidence,' " id., at 81, n. 1 (quoting 42 Pa. Cons. Stat. §9712 (1982)). In In re Winship, 397 U.S. 358 (1970), it provided that determinations of criminal action in juvenile cases " 'must be based on a preponderance of the evidence,' " id., at 360 (quoting N. Y. Family Court Act §744(b)). In Patterson v. New York, 432 U.S. 197 (1977), the statute provided that extreme emotional disturbance " 'is an affirmative defense,' " id., at 198, n. 2 (quoting N. Y. Penal Law §125.25 (McKinney 1975)). And in Mullaney v. Wilbur, 421 U.S. 684 (1975), Maine's highest court had held that in murder cases malice aforethought was presumed and had to be negated by the defendant, id., at 689 (citing State v. Lafferty, 309 A. 2d 647 (1973)).

In contrast to the provisions involved in these cases, 8 U.S.C. § 1326 does not, on its face, place the constitutional issue before us: it does not say that subsection (b)(2) is merely a sentencing enhancement. The text of the statute supports, if it does not indeed demand, the conclusion that subsection (b)(2) is a separate offense that includes the violation described in subsection (a) but adds the additional element of prior felony conviction. I therefore do not reach the difficult constitutional issue in this case because I adopt, as I think our cases require, that reasonable interpretation of §1326 which avoids the problem. Illegal re-entry simpliciter (§1326(a)) and illegal reentry after conviction of an aggravated felony (§1326(b)(2)) are separate criminal offenses. Prior conviction of an aggravated felony being an element of the latter offense, it must be charged in the indictment. Since it was not, petitioner's sentence must be set aside.

I

"[W]here a statute is susceptible of two constructions, by one of which grave and doubtful constitutional questions arise and by the other of which such questions are avoided, our duty is to adopt the latter." United States ex rel. Attorney General v. Delaware & Hudson Co., supra, at 408. This "cardinal principle," which "has for so long been applied by this Court that it is beyond debate," Edward J. DeBartolo Corp. v. Florida Gulf Coast Building & Constr. Trades Council, 485 U.S. 568, 575 (1988), requires merely a determination of serious constitutional doubt, and not a determination of unconstitutionality. That must be so, of course, for otherwise the rule would "mea[n] that our duty is to first decide that a statute is unconstitutional and then proceed to hold that such ruling was unnecessary because the statute is susceptible of a meaning, which causes it not to be repugnant to the Constitution." United States ex rel. Attorney General v. Delaware & Hudson Co., supra, at 408. The Court contends that neither of the two conditions for application of this rule is present here: that the constitutional question is not doubtful, and that the statute is not susceptible of a construction that will avoid it. I shall address the former point first.1

That it is genuinely doubtful whether the Constitution permits a judge (rather than a jury) to determine by a mere preponderance of the evidence (rather than beyond a reasonable doubt) a fact that increases the maximum penalty to which a criminal defendant is subject, is clear enough from our prior cases resolving questions on the margins of this one. In In re Winship, supra, we invalidated a New York statute under which the burden of proof in a juvenile delinquency proceeding was reduced to proof by a preponderance of the evidence. We held that "the Due Process Clause protects the accused against conviction except upon proof beyond reasonable doubt of every fact necessary to constitute the crime with which he is charged," 397 U.S., at 364, and that the same protection extends to "a juvenile . . . charged with an act which would constitute a crime if committed by an adult," id., at 359.

Five years later, in Mullaney v. Wilbur, supra, we unanimously extended Winship's protections to determinations that went not to a defendant's guilt or innocence, but simply to the length of his sentence. We invalidated Maine's homicide law, under which all intentional murders were presumed to be committed with malice aforethought (and, as such, were punishable by life imprisonment), unless the defendant could rebut this presumption with proof that he acted in the heat of passion (in which case the conviction would be reduced to manslaughter and the maximum sentence to 20 years). We acknowledged that "under Maine law these facts of intent [were] not general elements of the crime of felonious homicide[, but] [i]nstead, [bore] only on the appropriate punishment category." 421 U.S., at 699. Nonetheless, we rejected this distinction between guilt and punishment. "If Winship," we said, "were limited to those facts that constitute a crime as defined by state law, a State could undermine many of the interests that decision sought to protect without effecting any substantive change in its law. It would only be necessary to redefine the elements that constitute different crimes, characterizing them as factors that bear solely on the extent of punishment." Id., at 697—698.

In Patterson v. New York, we cut back on some of the broader implications of Mullaney. Although that case contained, we acknowledged, "some language . . . that ha[d] been understood as perhaps construing the Due Process Clause to require the prosecution to prove beyond a reasonable doubt any fact affecting 'the degree of criminal culpability,' " we denied that we "intend[ed] . . . such far-reaching effect." 432 U.S., at 214—215, n. 15. Accordingly, we upheld in Patterson New York's law casting upon the defendant the burden of proving as an "affirmative defense" to second-degree murder that he " 'acted under the influence of extreme emotional disturbance for which there was a reasonable explanation or excuse,' " id., at 198—199, n. 2, which defense would reduce his crime to manslaughter. We explained that "[p]roof of the nonexistence of all affirmative defenses has never been constitutionally required," and that the State need not "prove beyond a reasonable doubt every fact, the existence or nonexistence of which it is willing to recognize as an exculpatory or mitigating circumstance affecting the degree of culpability or the severity of the punishment." Id., at 207. We cautioned, however, that while our decision might "seem to permit state legislatures to reallocate burdens of proof by labeling as affirmative defenses at least some elements of the crimes now defined in their statutes[,] . . . [t]here are obviously constitutional limits beyond which the States may not go in this regard." Id., at 210.

Finally, and most recently, in McMillan v. Pennsylvania, 477 U.S., at 81, we upheld Pennsylvania's Mandatory Minimum Sentencing Act, which prescribed a mandatory minimum sentence of five years upon a judge's finding by a preponderance of the evidence that the defendant "visibly possessed a firearm" during the commission of certain enumerated offenses which all carried maximum sentences of more than five years. We observed that "we [had] never attempted to define precisely the constitutional limits noted in Patterson, i.e., the extent to which due process forbids the reallocation or reduction of burdens of proof in criminal cases," but explained that, whatever those limits, Pennsylvania's law did not transgress them, id., at 86, primarily because it "neither alter[ed] the maximum penalty for the crime committed nor create[d] a separate offense calling for a separate penalty; it operate[d] solely to limit the sentencing court's discretion in selecting a penalty within the range already available to it without the special finding of visible possession of a firearm," id., at 87—88.

The feebleness of the Court's contention that here there is no serious constitutional doubt is evidenced by the degree to which it must ignore or distort the analysis of McMillan. As just described, that opinion emphasized—and emphasized repeatedly—that an increase of the maximum penalty was not at issue. Beyond that, it specifically acknowledged that the outcome might have been different (i.e., the statute might have been unconstitutional) if the maximum sentence had been affected:

"Petitioners' claim that visible possession under the Pennsylvania statute is 'really' an element of the offenses for which they are being punished—that Pennsylvania has in effect defined a new set of upgraded felonies—would have at least more superficial appeal if a finding of visible possession exposed them to greater or additional punishment, cf. 18 U.S.C. § 2113(d) (providing separate and greater punishment for bank robberies accomplished through 'use of a dangerous weapon or device'), but it does not." Id., at 88.

The opinion distinguished one of our own precedents on this very ground, noting that the Colorado Sex Offenders Act invalidated in Specht v. Patterson, 386 U.S. 605 (1967), increased a sex offender's sentence from a 10—year maximum to an indefinite term up to and including life imprisonment. 477 U.S., at 88.

Despite all of that, the Court would have us believe that the present statute's alteration of the maximum permissible sentence—which it acknowledges is "the major difference between this case and McMillan," ante, at 20—militates in favor of, rather than against, this statute's constitutionality, because an increase of the minimum sentence (rather than the permissible maximum) is more disadvantageous to the defendant. Ibid. That is certainly an arguable position (it was argued, as the Court has the temerity to note, by the dissent in McMillan). But it is a position which McMillan not only rejected, but upon the converse of which McMillan rested its judgment.

In addition to inverting the consequence of this distinction (between statutes that prescribe a minimum sentence and those that increase the permissible maximum sentence) the Court seeks to minimize the importance of the distinction by characterizing it as merely one of five factors relied on in McMillan, and asserting that the other four factors here are the same. Ante, at 18-19. In fact, however, McMillan did not set forth any five-factor test; the Court selectively recruits "factors" from various parts of the discussion. Its first factor, for example, that " 'the [statute] plainly does not transgress the limits expressly set out in Patterson,' " ante, at 18, quoting from McMillan, 477 U. S, at 86–viz., that it does not "discar[d] the presumption of innocence" or "relieve the prosecution of its burden of proving guilt[,]" id., at 87—merely narrows the issue to the one before the Court, rather than giving any clue to the resolution of that issue. It is no more a factor in solving the constitutional problem before us than is the observation that §1326 is not an ex post facto law and does not effect an unreasonable search or seizure. The Court's second, fourth, and part of its fifth "factors" are in fact all subparts of the crucial third factor (the one that is absent here), since they are all culled from the general discussion in McMillan of how the Pennsylvania statute simply limited a sentencing judge's discretion. We said that, whereas in Mullaney the State had imposed " 'a differential in sentencing ranging from a nominal fine to a mandatory life sentence' " (the Court's "second" factor), Pennsylvania's law "neither alter[ed] the maximum penalty for the crime committed [the Court's "third" factor] nor create[d] a separate offense calling for a separate penalty [the Court's "fourth" factor]; it operate[d] solely to limit the sentencing court's discretion in selecting a penalty within the range already available to it without the special finding of visible possession of a firearm [the Court's "third" factor] . . . . The statute gives no impression of having been tailored to permit the visible possession finding to be a tail which wags the dog of the substantive offense [part of the Court's "fifth" factor]." 477 U.S., at 87—88.

The Court's recruitment of "factors" is, as I have said, selective. Omitted, for example, is McMillan's statement that "petitioners do not contend that the particular factor made relevant [by the statute] . . . has historically been treated 'in the Anglo-American legal tradition' as requiring proof beyond a reasonable doubt." Id., at 90, quoting Patterson, 432 U.S., at 226. Petitioner does make such an assertion in the present case—correctly, as I shall discuss. But even with its selective harvesting, the Court is incorrect in its assertion that "most" of the "factors" it recites, ante, at 19 (and in its implication that all except the third of them) exist in the present case as well. The second of them contrasted the consequence of the fact assumed in Mullaney (extension of the permissible sentence from as little as a nominal fine to as much as a mandatory life sentence) with the consequence of the fact at issue in McMillan (no extension of the permissible sentence at all, but merely a "limit[ation of] the sentencing court's discretion in selecting a penalty within the range already available," 477 U.S., at 88). The present case resembles Mullaney rather than McMillan in this regard, since the fact at issue increases the permissible sentence tenfold. And the only significant part of the fifth "factor"—that the statute in McMillan " 'dictated the precise weight to be given [the statutory] factor,' " ante, at 18, quoting McMillan, 477 U.S., at 89—90—is likewise a point of difference and not of similarity.

But this parsing of various factors is really beside the point. No one can read our pre-McMillan cases, and especially Mullaney (whose limits were adverted to in Patterson but never precisely described) without entertaining a serious doubt as to whether the statute as interpreted by the Court in the present case is constitutional. And no one can read McMillan, our latest opinion on the point, without perceiving that the determinative element in our validation of the Pennsylvania statute was the fact that it merely limited the sentencing judge's discretion within the range of penalty already available, rather than substantially increasing the available sentence. And even more than that: No one can read McMillan without learning that the Court was open to the argument that the Constitution requires a fact which does increase the available sentence to be treated as an element of the crime (such an argument, it said, would have "at least . . . superficial appeal," 477 U.S., at 88). If all that were not enough, there must be added the fact that many State Supreme Courts have concluded that a prior conviction which increases maximum punishment must be treated as an element of the offense under either their state constitutions, see, e.g., State v. McClay, 146 Me. 104, 112, 78 A. 2d 347, 352 (1951); Tuttle v. Commonwealth, 68 Mass. 505, 506 (1854) (prior conviction increasing maximum sentence must be set forth in indictment); State v. Furth, 5 Wash. 2d 1, 11—19, 104 P.2d 925, 930—933 (1940); State ex rel. Lockmiller v. Mayo, 88 Fla. 96, 98—99, 101 So. 228, 229 (1924); Roberson v. State, 362 P.2d 1115, 1118—1119 (Okla. Crim. App. 1961), or as a matter of common law, see, e.g., People ex rel. Cosgriff v. Craig, 195 N. Y. 190, 194—195, 88 N. E. 38, 39 (1909); People v. McDonald, 233 Mich. 98, 102, 105, 206 N. W. 516, 518, 519 (1925); State v. Smith, 129 Iowa 709, 710—715, 106 N. W. 187, 188—189 (1906) ("By the uniform current authority, the fact of prior convictions is to be taken as part of the offense instantly charged, at least to the extent of aggravating it and authorizing an increased punishment"); State v. Pennye, 102 Ariz. 207, 208—209, 427 P.2d 525, 526—527 (1967); State v. Waterhouse, 209 Ore. 424, 428—433, 307 P.2d 327, 329—331 (1957); Robbins v. State, 219 Ark. 376, 380—381, 242 S. W. 2d 640, 643 (1951); State v. Eichler, 248 Iowa 1267, 1270—1273, 83

N. W. 2d 576, 577—579 (1957).[2]

In the end, the Court cannot credibly argue that the question whether a fact which increases maximum permissible punishment must be found by a jury beyond a reasonable doubt is an easy one. That, perhaps, is why the Court stresses, and stresses repeatedly, the limited subject matter that §1326(b) addresses—recidivism. It even tries, with utter lack of logic, to limit its rejection of the fair reading of McMillan to recidivism cases. "For the reasons just given," it says, "and in light of the particular sentencing factor at issue in this case—recidivism—we should take McMillan's statement [regarding the "superficial appeal" the defendant's argument would have had if the factor at issue increased his maximum sentence] to mean no more than what it said, and therefore not to make a determinative difference here." Ante, at 21 (emphasis added). It is impossible to understand how McMillan could mean one thing in a later case where recidivism is at issue, and something else in a later case where some other sentencing factor is at issue. One might say, of course, that recidivism should be an exception to the general rule set forth in McMillan—but that more forthright characterization would display how doubtful the constitutional question is in light of our prior case law.

In any event, there is no rational basis for making recidivism an exception. The Court is of the view that recidivism need not be proved to a jury beyond a reasonable doubt (a view that, as I shall discuss, is precisely contrary to the common-law tradition) because it " 'goes to punishment only.' " It relies for this conclusion upon our opinion in Graham v. West Virginia, 224 U.S. 616 (1912). See ante, at 19, quoting Graham, supra, at 624; see also ante, at 23. The holding of Graham provides no support for the Court's position. It upheld against due process and double jeopardy objections a state recidivism law under which a defendant's prior convictions were charged and tried in a separate proceeding after he was convicted of the underlying offense. As the Court notes, ante, at 19, the prior convictions were not charged in the same indictment as the underlying offense; but they were charged in an "information" before the defendant was tried for the prior convictions, and, more importantly, the law explicitly preserved his right to a jury determination on the recidivism question. See Graham, supra, at 622–623; see also Oyler v. Boles, 368 U.S. 448, 453 (1962) (same). It is true, however, that if the basis for Graham's holding were accepted, one would have to conclude that recidivism need not be tried to the jury and found beyond a reasonable doubt. The essence of Graham's reasoning was that in the recidivism proceeding the defendant "was not held to answer for an offense," 224 U.S., at 624, since the recidivism charge " 'goes to the punishment only,' " ibid., quoting from McDonald v. Massachusetts, 180 U.S. 311, 312 (1901).

But that basis for dispensing with the protections of jury trial and findings beyond a reasonable doubt was explicitly rejected in Mullaney, which accorded these protections to facts that were "not general elements of the crime of felonious homicide ... [but bore] only on the appropriate punishment category," 421 U.S., at 699. Whatever else Mullaney stands for, it certainly stands for the proposition that what Graham used as the line of demarcation for double jeopardy and some due process purposes (the matter "goes only to the punishment") is not the line of demarcation for purposes of the right to jury trial and to proof beyond a reasonable doubt. So also does McMillan, which even while narrowing Mullaney made it very clear that the mere fact that a certain finding "goes only to the penalty" does not end the inquiry. The Court is certainly correct that the distinctive treatment of recidivism determinations for double jeopardy purposes takes some explaining; but it takes some explaining for the Court no less than for me. And the explanation assuredly is not (what the Court apparently suggests) that recidivism is never an element of the crime. It does much less violence to our jurisprudence, and to the traditional practice of requiring a jury finding of recidivism beyond a reasonable doubt, to explain Graham as a recidivism exception to the normal double jeopardy rule that conviction of a lesser included offense bars later trial for the greater crime. Our double jeopardy law, after all, is based upon traditional American and English practice, see United States v. Dixon, 509 U.S. 688, 704 (1993); United States v. Wilson, 420 U.S. 332, 339–344 (1975), and that practice has allowed recidivism to be charged and tried separately, see Spencer v. Texas, 385 U.S. 554, 566–567 (1967); Graham, supra, at 623, 625–626, 631; McDonald, supra, at 312–313. It has not allowed recidivism to be determined by a judge as more likely than not.

While I have given many arguments supporting the position that the Constitution requires the recidivism finding in this case to be made by a jury beyond a reasonable doubt, I do not endorse that position as necessarily correct. Indeed, that would defeat my whole purpose, which is to honor the practice of not deciding doubtful constitutional questions unnecessarily. What I have tried to establish–and all that I need to establish–is that on the basis of our jurisprudence to date, the answer to the constitutional question is not clear. It is the Court's burden, on the other hand, to establish that its constitutional answer shines forth clearly from our cases. That burden simply cannot be sustained. I think it beyond question that there was, until today's unnecessary resolution of the point, "serious doubt" whether the Constitution permits a defendant's sentencing exposure to be increased tenfold on the basis of a fact that is not charged, tried to a jury, and found beyond a reasonable doubt. If the Court wishes to abandon the doctrine of constitutional doubt, it should do so forthrightly, rather than by declaring certainty on a point that is clouded in doubt.

II

The Court contends that the doctrine of constitutional doubt is also inapplicable because §1326 is not fairly susceptible of the construction which avoids the constitutional problem—i.e., the construction whereby subsection (b)(2) sets forth a separate criminal offense. Ante, at 14. The Court begins its statutory analysis not by examining the text of §1326, but by demonstrating that the "subject matter [of the statute]—prior commission of a serious crime—is as typical a sentencing factor as one might imagine." Ante, at 5. That is eminently demonstrable, sounds powerfully good, but in fact proves nothing at all. It is certainly true that a judge (whether or not bound by the Federal Sentencing Guidelines) is likely to sentence nearer the maximum permitted for the offense if the defendant is a repeat offender. But the same can be said of many, perhaps most, factors that are used to define aggravated offenses. For example, judges will "typically" sentence nearer the maximum that a statute allows if the crime of conviction is committed with a firearm, or in the course of another felony; but that in no way suggests that armed robbery and felony murder are sentencing enhancements rather than separate crimes.

The relevant question for present purposes is not whether prior felony conviction is "typically" used as a sentencing factor, but rather whether, in statutes that provide higher maximum sentences for crimes committed by convicted felons, prior conviction is "typically" treated as a mere sentence enhancement or rather as an element of a separate offense. The answer to that question is the latter. That was the rule at common law, and was the near-uniform practice among the States at the time of the most recent study I am aware of. See Note, Recidivist Procedures, 40 N. Y. U. L. Rev. 332, 333—334 (1965); Note, The Pleading and Proof of Prior Convictions in Habitual Criminal Prosecutions, 33 N. Y. U. L. Rev. 210, 215—216 (1958). At common law, the fact of prior convictions had to be charged in the same indictment charging the underlying crime, and submitted to the jury for determination along with that crime. See, e.g., Spencer v. Texas, 385 U.S. 554, 566 (1967); Massey v. United States, 281 F. 293, 297 (CA8 1922); Singer v. United States, 278 F. 415, 420 (CA3 1922); People v. Sickles, 156 N. Y. 541, 545, 51 N. E. 288, 289 (1898). While several States later altered this procedure by providing a separate proceeding for the determination of prior convictions, at least as late as 1965 all but eight retained the defendant's right to a jury determination on this issue. See Note, Recidivist Procedures, 40

N. Y. U. L. Rev., supra, at 333—334, and 347. I am at a loss to explain the Court's assertion that it has "found no statute that clearly makes recidivism an offense element" added to another crime, ante, at 5—6. There are many such. 3

It is interesting that the Court drags the red herring of recidivism through both parts of its opinion–the "constitutional doubt" part and the "statutory interpretation" part alike. As just discussed, logic demonstrates that the nature of that charge (the fact that it is a "typical" sentencing factor) has nothing to do with what this statute means. And as discussed earlier, the text and reasoning of McMillan, and of the cases McMillan distinguishes, provide no basis for saying that recidivism is exempt from the Court's clear acknowledgment that taking away from the jury facts that increase the maximum sentence is constitutionally questionable. One wonders what state courts, and lower federal courts, are supposed to do with today's mysterious utterances. Are they to pursue logic, and conclude that all ambiguous statutes adding punishment for factors accompanying the principal offense are mere enhancements, or are they illogically to give this special treatment only to recidivism? Are they to deem the reasoning of McMillan superseded for all cases, or does it remain an open and doubtful question, for all cases except those involving recidivism, whether statutory maximums can be increased without the benefit of jury trial? Whatever else one may say about today's opinion, there is no doubt that it has brought to this area of the law more confusion than clarification.

Passing over the red herring, let me turn now to the statute at issue–§1326 as it stood when petitioner was convicted. The author of today's opinion for the Court once agreed that the "language and structure" of this enactment "are subject to two plausible readings," one of them being that recidivism constitutes a separate offense. United States v. Forbes, 16 F.3d 1294, 1298 (CA1 1994) (opinion of Coffin, J., joined by Breyer, C. J.).4 This would surely be enough to satisfy the requirement expressed by Justice Holmes, see United States v. Jin Fuey Moy, 241 U.S. 394, 401 (1916), and approved by the Court, ante, at 13, that the constitutional-doubt-avoiding construction be "fairly possible." Today, however, the Court relegates statutory language and structure to merely two of five "factors" that "help courts determine a statute's objectives and thereby illuminate its text," ante, at 4.

The statutory text reads, in relevant part, as follows:

"Reentry of deported alien; criminal penalties for reentry of certain deported aliens

"(a) Subject to subsection (b) of this section, any alien who [has been deported and thereafter reenters the United States] . . . shall be fined under title 18, or imprisoned not more than 2 years, or both.

"(b) Notwithstanding subsection (a) of this section, in the case of any alien described in such subsection–

"(1) whose deportation was subsequent to a conviction for commission of three or more misdemeanors involving drugs, crimes against the person, or both, or a felony (other than an aggravated felony), such alien shall be fined under title 18, imprisoned not more than 10 years, or both; or

"(2) whose deportation was subsequent to a conviction for commission of an aggravated felony, such alien shall be fined under such title, imprisoned not more than 20 years, or both." 8 U.S.C. § 1326(b).

One is struck at once by the parallel structure of subsections (a) and (b). Neither subsection says that the individual it describes "shall be guilty of a felony," and both subsections say that the individuals they describe "shall be fined under Title 18, or imprisoned not more than [2, 10, or 20] years." If this suffices to define a substantive offense in subsection (a) (as all agree it does), it is hard to see why it would not define a substantive offense in each paragraph of subsection (b) as well. Compare, for example, 21 U.S.C. § 841 which has a subsection (a) entitled "Unlawful acts," and a subsection (b) entitled "Penalties."

The opening phrase of subsection (b) certainly does not indicate that what follows merely supplements or enhances the penalty provision of subsection (a); what follows is to apply "notwithstanding" all of subsection (a), i.e., "in spite of" or "without prevention or obstruction from or by" subsection (a). See, e.g., Webster's New International Dictionary 1669 (2d ed. 1949). The next phrase ("in the case of any alien described in . . . subsection [(a)]") imports by reference the substantive acts attributed to the hypothetical alien (deportation and unauthorized reentry) in subsection (a). Significantly, this phrase does not apply subsection (b) to any alien "convicted under" subsection (a)–which is what one would expect if the provision was merely increasing the penalty for certain subsection (a) convictions. See, e.g., United States v. Davis, 801 F.2d 754, 755–756 (CA5 1986) (noting that "predicat[ing] punishment upon conviction" of another offense is one of the "common indicia of sentence-enhancement provisions"). Instead, subsection (b) applies to an alien "described in" subsection (a)–one who has been deported and has reentered illegally. And finally, subsection (a)'s provision that it applies "[s]ubject to subsection (b)" means that subsection (a) is inapplicable to an alien covered by subsection (b), just as subsection (b) applies "notwithstanding" that the alien would otherwise be covered by subsection (a).5

The Court relies on an earlier version of §1326 to support its interpretation of the statute in its current form. Ante, at 7–8. While I agree that such statutory history is a legitimate tool of construction, the statutory history of §1326 does not support, but rather undermines, the Court's interpretation. That earlier version contained a subsection (a) that, in addition to setting forth penalties (as did the subparts of subsection (b)), contained the phrase (which the subparts of subsection (b) did not) "shall be guilty of a felony, and upon conviction thereof, . . ." With such a formulation, of course, it would be easier to conclude that subsection (a) defines the crime and sets forth the basic penalty, and subsection (b) sets forth merely penalty enhancements. But if that was what the additional language in subsection (a) of the 1988 statute connoted, then what was the elimination of that additional language (in the 1990 version of the statute at issue here) meant to achieve? See §543(b)(3), 104 Stat. 5059. The more strongly the "shall be guilty of a felony" language suggests that subsection (b) of the 1988 statute contained only enhancements, the more strongly the otherwise inexplicable elimination of that language suggests that subsection (b) of the 1990 statute was meant to be parallel with subsection (a)—i.e., that both subsections were meant to set forth not merely penalties but also offenses. 6

After considering the subject matter and statutory language, the third factor the Court considers in arriving at its determination that this statute can only be read as a sentencing enhancement is the title of the 1988 amendment that added subsection (b)(2): "Criminal Penalties for Reentry of Certain Deported Aliens." See §7345, 102 Stat. 4471, cited ante, at 9. Of course, this title pertains to a subsection (b)(2) which, unlike the (b)(2) under which petitioner was convicted, was not parallel with the preceding subsection (a). But even disregarding that, the title of the amendment proves nothing at all. While "Criminal Penalties for Reentry" might normally be more suggestive of an enhancement than of a separate offense, there is good reason to believe it imports no such suggestion here. For the very next provision of the same enactment, which adjusts the substantive requirements for the crime of aiding and abetting the unlawful entry of an alien, is entitled "Criminal Penalties for Aiding or Assisting Certain Aliens to Enter the United States." See §7346, 102 Stat. 4471. Evidently, new substantive offenses that were penalized were simply entitled "Criminal Penalties" for the relevant offense. Moreover, the 1988 amendment kept the original title of §1326 ("Reentry of Deported Alien") intact, leaving it to apply to both subsection (a) and subsection (b). See §7345, supra; §276, 66 Stat. 229.

The Court's fourth factor leading it to conclude that this statute cannot reasonably be construed as establishing substantive offenses is legislative history. See ante, at 9. It is, again, the legislative history of the provision as it existed in 1988, before subsection (a) was stripped of the language "shall be guilty of a felony," thereby making subsections (a) and (b) parallel. Even so, it is of no help to the Court's case. The stray statements that the Court culls from the Congressional Record prove only that the new subsection (b) was thought to increase penalties for unlawful reentry. But there is no dispute that it does that! The critical question is whether it does it by adding penalties to the subsection (a) offense, or by creating additional, more severely punished, offenses. That technical point is not alluded to in any of the remarks the Court recites.

The Court's fifth and last argument in support of its interpretation of the statute is the contention that "the contrary interpretation . . . risks unfairness," ante, at 10, because it would require bringing the existence of the prior felony conviction to the attention of the jury. But it is also "unfair," of course, to deprive the defendant of a jury determination (and a beyond-a-reasonable-doubt burden of proof) on the critical question of the prior conviction. This Court's own assessment of which of those disadvantages is the greater can be of relevance here only insofar as we can presume that that perception would have been shared by the enacting Congress. We usually presume, however, not that an earlier Congress agreed with our current policy judgments, but rather that it agreed with the disposition provided by traditional practice or the common law. See United States v. Texas, 507 U.S. 529, 534 (1993); Astoria Fed. Sav. & Loan Assn. v. Solimino, 501 U.S. 104, 108 (1991); Norfolk Redevelopment and Housing Authority v. Chesapeake & Potomac Telephone Co. of Va., 464 U.S. 30, 35 (1983); Morissette v. United States, 342 U.S. 246, 263 (1952). As noted earlier, the Court's hostility to jury determination of prior convictions is quite simply at odds with the manner in which recidivism laws have historically been treated in this country.

Moreover, even if we were free to resolve this matter according to our current views of what is fair, the Court's judgment that avoiding jury "infection" is more important than affording a jury verdict (beyond a reasonable doubt) does not seem to me sound. The Court is not correct, to begin with, that the fact of prior conviction is "almost never contested," ante, at 10, particularly in unlawful-entry cases. That is clear from the very legislative history of the present statute. Senator Chiles explained that "identifying and prosecuting . . . illegal alien felons is a long and complex process" because "[i]t is not uncommon for an alien who has committed a certain felony to pay his bond and walk, only to be apprehended for a similar crime in the next county but with a new name and identification." 133 Cong. Rec. 8771. He went on to describe two specific aliens, one from whom police "seized 3 passports issued to him in 3 different names, 11 drivers licenses, immigration cards and numerous firearms and stolen property," and the other on whom immigration officials had "5 alien files . . . with 13 aliases, different birth dates and different social security cards." Id., at 8772. He said that "these aliens [were] not exceptions but rather common amongst the 100,000 illegal alien felons in the United States." Ibid. Representative Smith stated that aliens arrested for felonies "often are able to pay expensive bonds and disappear under a new identity often to reappear in court with a different name and a new offense. In some cases, they may return to their native lands and reenter the United States with new names and papers but committing the same crimes." Id., at 28840. And on the other side of the ledger, I doubt whether "infection" of the jury with knowledge of the prior crime is a serious problem. See, e.g., Spencer, supra, at 561 ("The defendants' interests [in keeping prejudicial prior convictions from the jury] are protected by limiting instructions and by the discretion residing with the trial judge to limit or forbid the admission of particularly prejudicial evidence even though admissible under an accepted rule of evidence") (citation omitted); Old Chief v. United States, 519 U.S. ___, ___ (slip op., at 18) (it is an abuse of discretion under Federal Rule of Evidence 403 to disallow defendant's stipulation to prior felony convictions where such convictions are an element of the offense); cf. Brief for National Association of Criminal Defense Lawyers as Amicus Curiae 30 ("In 1996, 98.2% of all Section 1326 defendants pleaded guilty"). If it is a problem, however, there are legislative and even judicial means for dealing with it, short of what today's decision does: taking the matter away from the jury in all cases. See 40 N. Y. U. L. Rev., at 333–334 (describing commonly used procedures under which defendant's right to a jury is invoked only "[i]f [he] denies the existence of prior convictions or stands mute"); Spencer, supra, at 567 (describing the English rule, under which the indictment alleges both the substantive offense and prior conviction, but the jury is not charged on the prior conviction until after it convicts the defendant of the substantive offense).

In sum, I find none of the four nontextual factors relied upon by the Court to support its interpretation ("typicality" of recidivism as a sentencing factor; titles; legislative history; and risk of unfairness) persuasive. What does seem to me significant, however, is a related statutory provision, introduced by a 1996 amendment, which explicitly refers to subsection (b)(2) as setting forth "offenses." See §334, 110 Stat. 3009–635 (instructing United States Sentencing Commission to amend sentencing guidelines "for offenses under . . . 1326(b)"). This later amendment can of course not cause subsection (b)(2) to have meant, at the time of petitioner's conviction, something different from what it then said. But Congress's expressed understanding that subsection (b) creates separate offenses is surely evidence that it is "fairly possible" to read the provision that way.7

I emphasize (to conclude this part of the discussion) that "fairly possible" is all that needs to be established. The doctrine of constitutional doubt does not require that the problem-avoiding construction be the preferable one–the one the Court would adopt in any event. Such a standard would deprive the doctrine of all function. "Adopt the interpretation that avoids the constitutional doubt if that is the right one" produces precisely the same result as "adopt the right interpretation." Rather, the doctrine of constitutional doubt comes into play when the statute is "susceptible of" the problem-avoiding interpretation, Delaware & Hudson Co., 213 U.S., at 408–when that interpretation is reasonable, though not necessarily the best. I think it quite impossible to maintain that this standard is not met by the interpretation of subsection (b) which regards it as creating separate offenses.

* * *

For the foregoing reasons, I think we must interpret the statute before us here as establishing a separate offense rather than a sentence enhancement. It can be argued that, once the constitutional doubts that require this course have been resolved, statutes no less ambiguous than the one before us here will be interpretable as sentence enhancements, so that not much will have been achieved. That begs the question, of course, as to how the constitutional doubt will be resolved. Moreover, where the doctrine of constitutional doubt does not apply, the same result may be dictated by the rule of lenity, which would preserve rather than destroy the criminal defendant's right to jury findings beyond a reasonable doubt. See, e.g., People ex rel. Cosgriff v. Craig, 195 N. Y., at 197, 88 N. E., at 40 ("It is unnecessary in this case to decide how great punishment the legislature may constitutionally authorize Courts of Special Sessions to impose on a conviction without a common-law jury. It is sufficient to say that in cases of doubtful construction or of conflicting statutory provisions, that interpretation should be given which best protects the rights of a person charged with an offense, to a trial according to the common law"). Whichever doctrine is applied for the purpose, it seems to me a sound principle that whenever Congress wishes a fact to increase the maximum sentence without altering the substantive offense, it must make that intention unambiguously clear. Accordingly, I would find that §1326(b)(2) establishes a separate offense, and would reverse the judgment below.

Notes to Justice Scalia's dissent in Almendarez-Torres v. United States (March 24, 1998)

1. The Court asserts that we have declined to apply the doctrine "in circumstances similar to those here–where a constitutional question, while lacking an obvious answer, does not lead a majority gravely to doubt that the statute is constitutional." Ante, at 14. The cases it cites, however, do not support this contention. In Rust v. Sullivan, 500 U.S. 173 (1991), the Court believed that "[t]here [was] no question but that the statutory prohibition . . . [was] constitutional," id., at 192 (emphasis added). And in United States v. Locke, 471 U.S. 84 (1985), the Court found the doctrine inapplicable not because of lack of constitutional doubt, but because the statutory language did not permit an interpretation that would "avoid a constitutional question," id., at 96. Similarly, in United States v. Monsanto, 491 U.S. 600 (1989), "the language of [the statute was] plain and unambiguous," id. at 606.

2. It would not be, as the Court claims, "anomalous" to require jury trial for a factor increasing the maximum sentence, "in light of existing case law that permits a judge, rather than a jury, to determine the existence of factors that can make a defendant eligible for the death penalty . . . ." Ante, at 23, citing Walton v. Arizona, 497 U.S. 639 (1990); Hildwin v. Florida, 490 U.S. 638 (1989) (per curiam); and Spaziano v. Florida, 468 U.S. 447 (1984). Neither the cases cited, nor any other case, permits a judge to determine the existence of a factor which makes a crime a capital offense. What the cited cases hold is that, once a jury has found the defendant guilty of all the elements of an offense which carries as its maximum penalty the sentence of death, it may be left to the judge to decide whether that maximum penalty, rather than a lesser one, ought to be imposed–even where that decision is constrained by a statutory requirement that certain "aggravating factors" must exist. The person who is charged with actions that expose him to to the death penalty has an absolute entitlement to jury trial on all the elements of the charge.

3. For federal statutes of this sort, see, e.g., 15 U.S.C. § 1264(a), 18 U.S.C. § 924(c), and 18 U.S.C. § 2114(a). In each of these provisions, recidivism is recited in a list of sentence-increasing aggravators that include, for example, intent to defraud or mislead (15 U.S.C. § 1264(a)), use of a firearm that is a machine gun, or a destructive device, or that is equipped with a silencer (18 U.S.C. § 924(c)), and wounding or threatening life with a dangerous weapon (§2114(a)). It would do violence to the text to treat recidivism as

a mere enhancement while treating the parallel provisions as aggravated offenses, which they obviously are.

4. The statutory text at issue in Forbes was in all relevant respects identical to the statute before us here, except that the years of imprisonment for the offenses were less; they were increased by a 1994 amendment, see §130001(b), 108 Stat. 2023.

5. The Court contends that treating subsection (b) as establishing substantive offenses renders the "notwithstanding" and "subject to" provisions redundant, because even without them our lesser included-offense jurisprudence would prevent a defendant from being convicted under both subsections (a) and (b). Ante, at 6. Redundancy, however, consists of the annoying practice of saying the same thing twice, not the sensible practice of saying once, with clarity and conciseness, what the law provides. The author of today's opinion once agreed that "[t]he fact that each subsection makes reference to the other is simply the logical way of indicating the relationship between the arguably two separate crimes." United States v. Forbes, 16 F.3d 1294, 1298 (CA1 1994). But if this be redundancy, it is redundancy that the Court's alternative reading does not cure—unless one believes that, without the "notwithstanding" and "subject to" language, our interpretive jurisprudence would permit the subsection (a) penalty to be added to the subsection (b) penalties.

6. Immediately after stressing the significance of the 1988 version of §1326(a), the Court dismisses the 1990 amendment that eliminated the 1988 language upon which it relies, as a "housekeeping measure" by which "Congress [did not] inten[d] to change, or to clarify, the fundamental relationship between" subsections (a) and (b). Ante, at 9. The Court offers no support for this confident characterization, unless it is the mistaken assumption that statutory changes or clarifications unconfirmed by legislative history are inoperative. "Suffice it to say that legislative history need not confirm the details of changes in the law effected by statutory language before we will interpret that language according to its natural meaning." Morales v. Trans World Airlines, Inc., 504 U.S. 374, 385, n. 2 (1992).

7. The Court is incorrect in its contention that the effective-date provision of the 1996 amendments reflects the opposite congressional understanding. See, ante, at 13. That provision states that the amendments "apply under [subsection (b)] . . . only to violations of [subsection (a)]," occurring on or after the date of enactment. §321(c), 110 Stat. 3009–628. There is no dispute, of course, that if subsection (b) creates separate offenses, one of the elements of the separate offenses is the lesser offense set forth in subsection (a). The quoted language is the clearest and simplest way of saying that that element of the subsection (b) offenses must have occurred after the date of enactment in order for the amendments to be applicable.

Standing and Line-Item Veto: Justice Scalia's concurrence and dissent in Clinton v. New York (June 25, 1998)

Justice Scalia, with whom Justice O'Connor joins, and with whom Justice Breyer joins as to Part III, concurring in part and dissenting in part.

Today the Court acknowledges the " 'overriding and time-honored concern about keeping the Judiciary's power within its proper constitutional sphere,' " ante, at 1—2, quoting Raines v. Byrd, 521 U.S. ___, ___ (1997) (slip op., at 8). It proceeds, however, to ignore the prescribed statutory limits of our jurisdiction by permitting the expedited-review provisions of the Line Item Veto Act to be invoked by persons who are not "individual[s]," 2 U.S.C. § 692 (1994 ed., Supp. II); and to ignore the constitutional limits of our jurisdiction by permitting one party to challenge the Government's denial to another party of favorable tax treatment from which the first party might, but just as likely might not, gain a concrete benefit. In my view, the Snake River appellees lack standing to challenge the President's cancellation of the "limited tax benefit," and the constitutionality of that action should not be addressed. I think the New York appellees have standing to challenge the President's cancellation of an "item of new direct spending"; I believe we have statutory authority (other than the expedited-review provision) to address that challenge; but unlike the Court I find the President's cancellation of spending items to be entirely in accord with the Constitution.

I

The Court's unrestrained zeal to reach the merits of this case is evident in its disregard of the statute's expedited-review provision, which extends that special procedure to "[a]ny Member of Congress or any individual adversely affected by [the Act]," §692. With the exception of Mike Cranney, a natural person, the appellees– corporations, cooperatives, and governmental entities–are not "individuals" under any accepted usage of that term. Worse still, the first provision of the United States Code confirms that insofar as this word is concerned, Congress speaks English like the rest of us: "In determining the meaning of any Act of Congress, unless the context indicates otherwise ... the wor[d] 'person' ... include[s] corporations, companies, associations, firms, partnerships, societies, and joint stock companies, as well as individuals." 1 U.S.C. § 1 (emphasis added). And doubly worse, one of the definitional provisions of this very Act expressly distinguishes "individuals" from "persons." A tax law does not create a "limited tax benefit," it says, so long as

"any difference in the treatment of persons is based solely on–

"(I) in the case of businesses and associations, the size or form of the business or association involved;

"(II) in the case of individuals, general demographic conditions, such as income, marital status, number of dependents, or tax return filing status ... ." 2 U.S.C. § 691e(9)(B)(iii) (1994 ed., Supp. II) (emphasis added).

The Court majestically sweeps the plain language of the statute aside, declaring that "[t]here is no plausible reason why Congress would have intended to provide for such special treatment of actions filed by natural persons and to have precluded entirely jurisdiction over comparable cases brought by corporate persons." Ante, at 10. Indeed, the Court says, it would be "absurd" for Congress to have done so. Ibid. But Congress treats individuals more favorably than corporations and other associations all the time. There is nothing whatever extraordinary—and surely nothing so bizarre as to permit this Court to declare a "scrivener's error"—in believing that individuals will suffer more seriously from delay in the receipt of "vetoed" benefits or tax savings than corporations will, and therefore according individuals (but not corporations) expedited review. It may be unlikely that this is what Congress actually had in mind; but it is what Congress said, it is not so absurd as to be an obvious mistake, and it is therefore the law.

The only individual who has sued, and thus the only appellee who qualifies for expedited review under §692, is Mike Cranney. Since §692 does not confer jurisdiction over the claims of the other appellees, we must dismiss them, unless we have jurisdiction under another statute. In their complaints, appellees sought declaratory relief not only under §692(a), but also under the Declaratory Judgment Act, 28 U.S.C. § 2201 invoking the District Court's jurisdiction under 28 U.S.C. § 1331. After the District Court ruled, the Government appealed directly to this Court, but it also filed a notice of appeal to the Court of Appeals for the District of Columbia. In light of the Government's representation that it desires "[t]o eliminate any possibility that the district court's decision might escape review," Reply Brief for Appellants 2, n. 1, I would deem its appeal to this Court a petition for writ of certiorari before judgment, see 28 U.S.C. § 2101(e), and grant it. Under this Court's Rule 11, "[a] petition for a writ of certiorari to review a case pending in a United States court of appeals, before judgment is entered in that court, will be granted only upon a showing that the case is of such imperative public importance as to justify deviation from normal appellate practice and to require immediate determination in this Court." In light of the public importance of the issues involved, and the little sense it would make for the Government to pursue its appeal against one appellee in this Court and against the others in the Court of Appeals, the entire case, in my view, qualifies for certiorari review before judgment.

II

Not only must we be satisfied that we have statutory jurisdiction to hear this case; we must be satisfied that we have jurisdiction under Article III. "To meet the standing requirements of Article III, '[a] plaintiff must allege personal injury fairly traceable to the defendant's allegedly unlawful conduct and likely to be redressed by the requested relief.'" Raines, 521 U.S., at ___ (slip op., at 6), quoting Allen v. Wright, 468 U.S. 737, 751 (1984).

In the first action before us, appellees Snake River Potato Growers, Inc. (Snake River) and Mike Cranney, Snake River's Director and Vice-Chairman, challenge the constitutionality of the President's cancellation of §968 of the Taxpayer Relief Act of 1997.

The Snake River appellees have standing, in the Court's view, because §968 gave them "the equivalent of a statutory 'bargaining chip,' " and "[b]y depriving them of their statutory bargaining chip, the cancellation inflicted a sufficient likelihood of economic injury to establish standing under our precedents." Ante, at 13, 14. It is unclear whether the Court means that deprivation of a "bargaining chip" itself suffices for standing, or that such deprivation suffices in the present case because it creates a likelihood of economic injury. The former is wrong as a matter of law, and the latter is wrong as a matter of fact, on the facts alleged.

For the proposition that "a denial of a benefit in the bargaining process" can suffice for standing the Court relies in a footnote, see ante, at 15, n. 22, on Northeastern Fla. Chapter, Associated Gen. Contractors of America v. Jacksonville, 508 U.S. 656 (1993). There, an association of contractors alleged that a city ordinance according racial preferences in the award of city contracts denied its members equal protection of the laws. Id., at 658—659. The association's members had regularly bid on and performed city contracts, and would have bid on designated set-aside contracts but for the ordinance. Id., at 659. We held that the association had standing even without proof that its members would have been awarded contracts absent the challenged discrimination. The reason, we explained, is that "[t]he 'injury in fact' in an equal protection case of this variety is the denial of equal treatment resulting from the imposition of the barrier, not the ultimate inability to obtain the benefit." Id., at 666, citing two earlier equal protection cases, Turner v. Fouche, 396 U.S. 346, 362 (1970), and Richmond v. J. A. Croson Co., 488 U.S. 469, 493 (1989). In other words, Northeastern Florida did not hold, as the Court suggests, that harm to one's bargaining position is an "injury in fact," but rather that, in an equal protection case, the denial of equal treatment is. Inasmuch as Snake River does not challenge the Line Item Veto Act on equal-protection grounds, Northeastern Florida is inapposite. And I know of no case outside the equal-protection field in which the mere detriment to one's "bargaining position," as opposed to a demonstrated loss of some bargain, has been held to confer standing. The proposition that standing is established by the mere reduction in one's chances of receiving a financial benefit is contradicted by Simon v. Eastern Ky. Welfare Rights Organization, 426 U.S. 26 (1976), which held that low-income persons who had been denied treatment at local hospitals lacked standing to challenge an Internal Revenue Service (IRS) ruling that reduced the amount of charitable care necessary for the hospitals to qualify for tax-exempt status. The situation in that case was strikingly similar to the one before us here: the denial of a tax benefit to a third party was alleged to reduce the chances of a financial benefit to the plaintiffs. And standing was denied.

But even if harm to one's bargaining position were a legally cognizable injury, Snake River has not alleged, as it must, facts sufficient to demonstrate that it personally has suffered that injury. See Warth v. Seldin, 422 U.S. 490, 502 (1975). In Eastern Ky. Welfare Rights, supra, the plaintiffs at least had applied for the financial benefit which had allegedly been rendered less likely of receipt; the present suit, by contrast, resembles a complaint asserting that the plaintiff's chances of winning the lottery were reduced, filed by a plaintiff who never bought a lottery ticket, or who tore it up before the winner was announced. Snake River has presented no evidence to show that it was engaged in bargaining, and that that bargaining was impaired by the President's cancellation of §968. The Court says that Snake River "was engaged in ongoing negotiations with the owner of a processing plant who had expressed an interest in structuring a tax-deferred sale when the President canceled §968," ante, at 13. There is, however, no evidence of "negotiations," only of two "discussions." According to the affidavit of Mike Cranney:

"On or about May 1997, I spoke with Howard Phillips, the principal owner of Idaho Potato Packers, concerning the possibility that, if the Cooperative Tax Act were passed, Snake River Potato Growers might purchase a Blackfoot, Idaho processing facility in a transaction that would allow the deferral of gain. Mr. Phillips expressed an interest in such a transaction if the Cooperative Tax Act were to pass. Mr. Phillips also acknowledged to me that Jim Chapman, our General Manager, had engaged him in a previous discussion concerning this matter." App. 112.

This affidavit would have set forth something of significance if it had said that Phillips had expressed an interest in the transaction "if and only if the Cooperative Tax Act were to pass." But of course it is most unlikely he said that; Idaho Potato Packers (IPP) could get just as much from the sale without the Act as with the Act, so long as the price was right. The affidavit would also have set forth something of significance if it had said that Phillips had expressed an interest in the sale "at a particular price if the Cooperative Tax Act were to pass." But it does not say that either. Nor does it even say that the President's action caused IPP to reconsider. Moreover, it was Snake River, not IPP, that terminated the discussions. According to Cranney, "[t]he President's cancellation of the Cooperative Tax Act caused me to terminate discussions with Phillips about the possibility of Snake River Potato Growers buying the Idaho Potato Packers facility," App. 114. So all we know from the record is that Snake River had two discussions with IPP concerning the sale of its processing facility on the tax deferred basis the Act would allow; that IPP was interested; and that Snake River ended the discussions after the President's action. We do not know that Snake River was prepared to offer a price—tax deferral or no—that would cross IPP's laugh threshold. We do not even know for certain that the tax deferral was a significant attraction to IPP; we know only that Cranney thought it was. On these facts—which never even bring things to the point of bargaining—it is pure conjecture to say that Snake River suffered an impaired bargaining position. As we have said many times, conjectural or hypothetical injuries do not suffice for Article III standing. See Lujan v. Defenders of Wildlife, 504 U.S. 555, 560 (1992).

Nor has Snake River demonstrated, as the Court finds, that "the cancellation inflicted a sufficient likelihood of economic injury to establish standing under our precedents." Ante, at 14. Presumably the economic injury the Court has in mind is Snake River's loss of a bargain purchase of a processing plant. But there is no evidence, and indeed not even an allegation, that before the President's action such a purchase was likely. The most that Snake River alleges is that the President's action rendered it "more difficult for plaintiffs to purchase qualified processors," App. 12. And even if that abstract "increased difficulty" sufficed for injury-in-fact (which it does not), the existence of even that is pure speculation. For all that appears, no owner of a processing plant would have been willing to sell to Snake River at any price that Snake River could afford—and the impossible cannot be made "more difficult." All we know is that a potential seller was "interested" in talking about the subject before the President's action, and that after the President's action Snake River itself decided to proceed no further. If this establishes a "likelihood" that Snake River would have made a bargain purchase but for the President's action, or even a "likelihood" that the President's action rendered "more difficult" a purchase that was realistically within Snake River's grasp, then we must adopt for our standing jurisprudence a new definition of likely: "plausible."

Twice before have we addressed whether plaintiffs had standing to challenge the Government's tax treatment of a third party, and twice before have we held that the speculative nature of a third party's response to changes in federal tax laws defeats standing. In Eastern Ky. Welfare Rights, 426 U.S. 26 (1976), we found it "purely speculative whether the denials of service ... fairly can be traced to [the IRS's] 'encouragement' or instead result from decisions made by the hospitals without regard to the tax implications." Id., at 42—43. We found it "equally speculative whether the desired exercise of the court's remedial powers in this suit would result in the availability to respondents of such services." Id., at 43. In Allen v. Wright, 468 U.S. 737 (1984), we held that parents of black children attending public schools lacked standing to challenge IRS policies concerning tax exemptions for private schools. The parents alleged, inter alia, that "federal tax exemptions to racially discriminatory private schools in their communities impair their ability to have their public schools desegregated." Id., at 752—753. We concluded that "the injury alleged is not fairly traceable to the Government conduct ... challenge[d] as unlawful," id., at 757, and that "it is entirely speculative ... whether withdrawal of a tax exemption from any particular school would lead the school to change its policies." Id., at 758. Likewise, here, it is purely speculative whether a tax-deferral would have prompted any sale, let alone one that reflected the tax benefit in the sale price.

The closest case the Court can appeal to as precedent for its finding of standing is Bryant v. Yellen, 447 U.S. 352 (1980). Even on its own terms, Bryant is distinguishable. As that case came to us, it involved a dispute between a class of some 800 landowners in the Imperial Valley, each of whom owned more than 160 acres, and a group of Imperial Valley residents who wished to purchase lands owned by that class. The point at issue was the application to those lands of a statutory provision that forbade delivery of water from a federal reclamation project to irrigable land held by a single owner in excess of 160 acres, and that limited the sale price of any lands so held in excess of 160 acres to a maximum amount, fixed the Secretary of the Interior, based on fair market value in 1929, before the Valley was irrigated by water from the Boulder Canyon Project. Id., at 366—

367. That price would of course be "far below [the lands'] current market values," id., at 367, n. 17. The Court concluded that the would-be purchasers "had a sufficient stake in the outcome of the controversy to afford them standing," id., at 368. It is true, as the Court today emphasizes, that the purchasers had not presented "detailed information about [their] financial resources," but the Court thought that unnecessary only because "purchasers of such land would stand to reap significant gains on resale." Id., at 367, n. 17. Financing, in other words, would be easy to come by. Here, by contrast, not only do we have no notion whether Snake River has the cash in hand to afford IPP's bottom-line price, but we also have no reason to believe that financing of the purchase will be readily available. Potato processing plants, unlike agricultural land in the Imperial Valley, do not have a readily available resale market. On the other side of the equation, it was also much clearer in Bryant that if the suit came out in the would-be purchasers' favor, many of the landowners would be willing to sell. The alternative would be withdrawing the land from agricultural production, whereas sale—even at bargain-basement prices for the land—would at least enable recoupment of the cost of improvements, such as drainage systems. Ibid. In the present case, by contrast, we have no reason to believe that IPP is not operating its processing plant at a profit, and will not continue to do so in the future; Snake River has proffered no evidence that IPP or any other processor would surely have sold if only the President had not cancelled the tax deferral. The only uncertainty in Bryant was whether any of the respondents would wind up as buyers of any of the excess land; that seemed probable enough, since "respondents are residents of the Imperial Valley who desire to purchase the excess land for purposes of farming." Ibid. We have no basis to say that it is "likely" that Snake River would have purchased a processing facility if §968 had not been cancelled.

More fundamentally, however, the reasoning of Bryant should not govern the present case because it represents a crabbed view of the standing doctrine that has been superseded. Bryant was decided at the tail-end of "an era in which it was thought that the only function of the constitutional requirement of standing was 'to assure that concrete adverseness which sharpens the presentation of issues,' " Spencer v. Kemna, 523 U.S. ___, ___ (1998) (slip op., at 9), quoting Baker v. Carr, 369 U.S. 186, 204 (1962). Thus, the Bryant Court ultimately afforded the respondents standing simply because they "had a sufficient stake in the outcome of the controversy," 447 U.S., at 368, not because they had demonstrated injury in fact, causation and redressability. "That parsimonious view of the function of Article III standing has since yielded to the acknowledgement that the constitutional requirement is a 'means of "defin[ing] the role assigned to the judiciary in a tripartite allocation of power," ' and 'a part of the basic charter ... provid[ing] for the interaction between [the federal] government and the governments of the several States,' " Spencer, supra, at ___ (slip op., at 10), quoting Valley Forge Christian College v. Americans United for Separation of Church and State, Inc., 454 U.S. 464, 474, 476 (1982). While Snake River in the present case may indeed have enough of a "stake" to assure adverseness, the matter it brings before us is inappropriate for our resolution because its allegations do not establish an injury in fact, attributable to the Presidential action it challenges, and remediable by this Court's invalidation of that Presidential action.

Because, in my view, Snake River has no standing to bring this suit, we have no jurisdiction to resolve its challenge to the President's authority to cancel a "limited tax benefit."

III

I agree with the Court that the New York appellees have standing to challenge the President's cancellation of §4722(c) of the Balanced Budget Act of 1997 as an "item of new direct spending." See ante, at 11–12. The tax liability they will incur under New York law is a concrete and particularized injury, fairly traceable to the President's action, and avoided if that action is undone. Unlike the Court, however, I do not believe that Executive cancellation of this item of direct spending violates the Presentment Clause.

The Presentment Clause requires, in relevant part, that "[e]very Bill which shall have passed the House of Representatives and the Senate, shall, before it becomes a Law, be presented to the President of the United States; If he approve he shall sign it, but if not he shall return it," U.S. Const., Art. I, §7, cl. 2. There is no question that enactment of the Balanced Budget Act complied with these requirements: the House and Senate passed the bill, and the President signed it into law. It was only after the requirements of the Presentment Clause had been satisfied that the President exercised his authority under the Line Item Veto Act to cancel the spending item. Thus, the Court's problem with the Act is not that it authorizes the President to veto parts of a bill and sign others into law, but rather that it authorizes him to "cancel"–prevent from "having legal force or effect"– certain parts of duly enacted statutes.

Article I, §7 of the Constitution obviously prevents the President from cancelling a law that Congress has not authorized him to cancel. Such action cannot possibly be considered part of his execution of the law, and if it is legislative action, as the Court observes, " 'repeal of statutes, no less than enactment, must conform with Art. I.' " Ante, at 19, quoting from INS v. Chadha, 462 U.S. 919, 954 (1983). But that is not this case. It was certainly arguable, as an original matter, that Art. I, §7 also prevents the President from cancelling a law which itself authorizes the President to cancel it. But as the Court acknowledges, that argument has long since been made and rejected. In 1809, Congress passed a law authorizing the President to cancel trade restrictions against Great Britain and France if either revoked edicts directed at the United States. Act of Mar. 1, 1809, §11, 2 Stat. 528. Joseph Story regarded the conferral of that authority as entirely unremarkable in The Orono, 18 F. Cas. 830 (No. 10, 585) (CCD Mass. 1812). The Tariff Act of 1890 authorized the President to "suspend, by proclamation to that effect" certain of its provisions if he determined that other countries were imposing "reciprocally unequal and unreasonable" duties. Act of Oct. 1, 1890, §3, 26 Stat. 612. This Court upheld the constitutionality of that Act in Field v. Clark, 143 U.S. 649 (1892), reciting the history since 1798 of statutes conferring upon the President the power to, inter alia, "discontinue the prohibitions and restraints hereby enacted and declared," id., at 684, "suspend the operation of the aforesaid act," id., at 685, and "declare the provisions of this act to be inoperative," id., at 688.

As much as the Court goes on about Art. I, §7, therefore, that provision does not demand the result the Court reaches. It no more categorically prohibits the Executive reduction of congressional dispositions in the course of implementing statutes that authorize such reduction, than it categorically prohibits the Executive augmentation of congressional dispositions in the course of implementing statutes that authorize such augmentation–generally known as substantive rulemaking. There are, to be sure, limits upon the former just as there are limits upon the latter–and I am prepared to acknowledge that the limits upon the former may be much more severe. Those limits are established, however, not by some categorical prohibition of Art. I, §7, which our cases conclusively disprove, but by what has come to be known as the doctrine of unconstitutional delegation of legislative authority: When authorized Executive reduction or augmentation is allowed to go too far, it usurps the nondelegable function of Congress and violates the separation of powers.

It is this doctrine, and not the Presentment Clause, that was discussed in the Field opinion, and it is this doctrine, and not the Presentment Clause, that is the issue presented by the statute before us here. That is why the Court is correct to distinguish prior authorizations of Executive cancellation, such as the one involved in Field, on the ground that they were contingent upon an Executive finding of fact, and on the ground that they related to the field of foreign affairs, an area where the President has a special "degree of discretion and freedom," ante, at 27 (citation omitted). These distinctions have nothing to do with whether the details of Art. I, §7 have been complied with, but everything to do with whether the authorizations went too far by transferring to the Executive a degree of political, law-making power that our traditions demand be retained by the Legislative Branch.

I turn, then, to the crux of the matter: whether Congress's authorizing the President to cancel an item of spending gives him a power that our history and traditions show must reside exclusively in the Legislative Branch. I may note, to begin with, that the Line Item Veto Act is not the first statute to authorize the President to "cancel" spending items. In Bowsher v. Synar, 478 U.S. 714 (1986), we addressed the constitutionality of the Balanced Budget and Emergency Deficit Control Act of 1985, 2 U.S.C. § 901 et seq. (1982 ed., Supp. III), which required the President, if the federal budget deficit exceeded a certain amount, to issue a "sequestration" order mandating spending reductions specified by the Comptroller General. §902. The effect of sequestration was that "amounts sequestered ... shall be permanently cancelled," §902(a)(4) (emphasis added). We held that the Act was unconstitutional, not because it impermissibly gave the Executive legislative power, but because it gave the Comptroller General, an officer of the Legislative Branch over whom Congress retained removal power, "the ultimate authority to determine the budget cuts to be made," 478 U.S., at 733, "functions ... plainly entailing execution of the law in constitutional terms." Id., at 732—733 (emphasis added). The President's discretion under the Line Item Veto Act is certainly broader than the Comptroller General's discretion was under the 1985 Act, but it is no broader than the discretion traditionally granted the President in his execution of spending laws.

Insofar as the degree of political, "law-making" power conferred upon the Executive is concerned, there is not a dime's worth of difference between Congress's authorizing the President to cancel a spending item, and Congress's authorizing money to be spent on a particular item at the President's discretion. And the latter has been done since the Founding of the Nation. From 1789—1791, the First Congress made lump-sum appropriations for the entire Government—"sum[s] not exceeding" specified amounts for broad purposes. Act of Sept. 29, 1789, ch. 23, §1, 1 Stat. 95; Act of Mar. 26, 1790, ch. 4, §1, 1 Stat. 104; Act of Feb. 11, 1791, ch. 6, 1 Stat. 190. From a very early date Congress also made permissive individual appropriations, leaving the decision whether to spend the money to the President's unfettered discretion. In 1803, it appropriated $50,000 for the President to build "not exceeding fifteen gun boats, to be armed, manned and fitted out, and employed for such purposes as in his opinion the public service may require," Act of Feb. 28, 1803, ch. 11, §3, 2 Stat. 206. President Jefferson reported that "[t]he sum of fifty thousand dollars appropriated by Congress for providing gun boats remains unexpended. The favorable and peaceable turn of affairs on the Mississippi rendered an immediate execution of that law unnecessary," 13 Annals of Cong. 14 (1803). Examples of appropriations committed to the discretion of the President abound in our history. During the Civil War, an Act appropriated over $76 million to be divided among various items "as the exigencies of the service may require," Act of Feb. 25, 1862, ch. 32, 12 Stat. 344—345. During the Great Depression, Congress appropriated $950 million "for such projects and/or purposes and under such rules and regulations as the President in his discretion may prescribe," Act of Feb. 15, 1934, ch. 13, 48 Stat. 351, and $4 billion for general classes of projects, the money to be spent "in the discretion and under the direction of the President," Emergency Relief Appropriation Act of 1935, 49 Stat. 115. The constitutionality of such appropriations has never seriously been questioned. Rather, "[t]hat Congress has wide discretion in the matter of prescribing details of expenditures for which it appropriates must, of course, be plain. Appropriations and other acts of Congress are replete with instances of general appropriations of large amounts, to be allotted and expended as directed by designated government agencies." Cincinnati Soap Co. v. United States, 301 U.S. 308, 321—322 (1937).

Certain Presidents have claimed Executive authority to withhold appropriated funds even absent an express conferral of discretion to do so. In 1876, for example, President Grant reported to Congress that he would not spend money appropriated for certain harbor and river improvements, see Act of Aug. 14, 1876, ch. 267, 19 Stat. 132, because "[u]nder no circumstances [would he] allow expenditures upon works not clearly national," and in his view, the appropriations were for "works of purely private or local interest, in no sense national," 4 Cong. Rec. 5628. President Franklin D. Roosevelt impounded funds appropriated for a flood control reservoir and levee in Oklahoma. See Act of Aug. 18, 1941, ch. 377, 55 Stat. 638, 645; Hearings on S. 373 before the Ad Hoc Subcommittee on Impoundment of Funds of the Committee on Government Operations and the Subcommittee on Separation of Powers of the Senate Committee on the Judiciary, 93d Cong., 1st Sess., 848—849 (1973). President Truman ordered the impoundment of hundreds of millions of dollars that had been appropriated for military aircraft. See Act of Oct. 29, 1949, ch. 787, 63 Stat. 987, 1013; Public Papers of the Presidents of the United States, Harry S. Truman, 1949, pp. 538—539 (W. Reid ed. 1964). President Nixon, the Mahatma Ghandi of all impounders, asserted at a press conference in 1973 that his "constitutional right" to impound appropriated funds was "absolutely clear." The President's News Conference of Jan. 31, 1973, 9 Weekly Comp. of Pres. Doc. 109—110 (1973). Our decision two years later in Train v. City of New York, 420 U.S. 35 (1975), proved him wrong, but it implicitly confirmed that Congress may confer discretion upon the executive to withhold appropriated funds, even funds appropriated for a specific purpose. The statute at issue in Train authorized spending "not to exceed" specified sums for certain projects, and directed that such "[s]ums authorized to be appropriated ... shall be allotted" by the Administrator of the Environmental Protection Agency, 33 U.S.C. § 1285 1287 (1970 ed., Supp. III). Upon enactment of this statute, the President directed the Administrator to allot no more than a certain part of the amount authorized. 420 U.S., at 40. This Court held, as a matter of statutory interpretation, that the statute did not grant the Executive discretion to withhold the funds, but required allotment of the full amount authorized. Id., at 44—47.

    The short of the matter is this: Had the Line Item Veto Act authorized the President to "decline to spend" any item of spending contained in the Balanced Budget Act of 1997, there is not the slightest doubt that authorization would have been constitutional. What the Line Item Veto Act does instead—authorizing the President to "cancel" an item of spending—is technically different. But the technical difference does not relate to the technicalities of the Presentment Clause, which have been fully complied with; and the doctrine of unconstitutional delegation, which is at issue here, is preeminently not a doctrine of technicalities. The title of the Line Item Veto Act, which was perhaps designed to simplify for public comprehension, or perhaps merely to comply with the terms of a campaign pledge, has succeeded in faking out the Supreme Court. The President's action it authorizes in fact is not a line-item veto and thus does not offend Art. I, §7; and insofar as the substance of that action is concerned, it is no different from what Congress has permitted the President to do since the formation of the Union.

    IV

    I would hold that the President's cancellation of §4722(c) of the Balanced Budget Act as an item of direct spending does not violate the Constitution. Because I find no party before us who has standing to challenge the President's cancellation of §968 of the Taxpayer Relief Act, I do not reach the question whether that violates the Constitution.

    For the foregoing reasons, I respectfully dissent.

Miranda warning is not in the constitution: Justice Scalia's dissent in Dickerson v. United States (June 26, 2000)

Justice Scalia, with whom Justice Thomas joins, dissenting.

Those to whom judicial decisions are an unconnected series of judgments that produce either favored or disfavored results will doubtless greet today's decision as a paragon of moderation, since it declines to overrule Miranda v. Arizona, 384 U.S. 436 (1966). Those who understand the judicial process will appreciate that today's decision is not a reaffirmation of Miranda, but a radical revision of the most significant element of Miranda (as of all cases): the rationale that gives it a permanent place in our jurisprudence.

Marbury v. Madison, 1 Cranch 137 (1803), held that an Act of Congress will not be enforced by the courts if what it prescribes violates the Constitution of the United States. That was the basis on which Miranda was decided. One will search today's opinion in vain, however, for a statement (surely simple enough to make) that what 18 U.S.C. § 3501 prescribes–the use at trial of a voluntary confession, even when a Miranda warning or its equivalent has failed to be given–violates the Constitution. The reason the statement does not appear is not only (and perhaps not so much) that it would be absurd, inasmuch as §3501 excludes from trial precisely what the Constitution excludes from trial, viz., compelled confessions; but also that Justices whose votes are needed to compose today's majority are on record as believing that a violation of Miranda is not a violation of the Constitution. See Davis v. United States, 512 U.S. 452, 457–458 (1994) (opinion of the Court, in which Kennedy, J., joined); Duckworth v. Eagan, 492 U.S. 195, 203 (1989) (opinion of the Court, in which Kennedy, J., joined); Oregon v. Elstad, 470 U.S. 298 (1985) (opinion of the Court by O'Connor, J.); New York v. Quarles, 467 U.S. 649 (1984) (opinion of the Court by Rehnquist, J.). And so, to justify today's agreed-upon result, the Court must adopt a significant new, if not entirely comprehensible, principle of constitutional law. As the Court chooses to describe that principle, statutes of Congress can be disregarded, not only when what they prescribe violates the Constitution, but when what they prescribe contradicts a decision of this Court that "announced a constitutional rule," ante, at 7. As I shall discuss in some detail, the only thing that can possibly mean in the context of this case is that this Court has the power, not merely to apply the Constitution but to expand it, imposing what it regards as useful "prophylactic" restrictions upon Congress and the States. That is an immense and frightening antidemocratic power, and it does not exist.

It takes only a small step to bring today's opinion out of the realm of power-judging and into the mainstream of legal reasoning: The Court need only go beyond its carefully couched iterations that "Miranda is a constitutional decision," ante, at 8, that "Miranda is constitutionally based," ante, at 10, that Miranda has "constitutional underpinnings," ante, at 10, n. 5, and come out and say quite clearly: "We reaffirm today that custodial interrogation that is not preceded by Miranda warnings or their equivalent violates the Constitution of the United States." It cannot say that, because a majority of the Court does not believe it. The Court therefore acts in plain violation of the Constitution when it denies effect to this Act of Congress.

I

Early in this Nation's history, this Court established the sound proposition that constitutional government in a system of separated powers requires judges to regard as inoperative any legislative act, even of Congress itself, that is "repugnant to the Constitution."

"So if a law be in opposition to the constitution; if both the law and the constitution apply to a particular case, so that the court must either decide that case conformably to the law, disregarding the constitution; or conformably to the constitution, disregarding the law; the court must determine which of these conflicting rules governs the case." Marbury, supra, at 178.

The power we recognized in Marbury will thus permit us, indeed require us, to "disregar[d]" §3501, a duly enacted statute governing the admissibility of evidence in the federal courts, only if it "be in opposition to the constitution"–here, assertedly, the dictates of the Fifth Amendment.

It was once possible to characterize the so-called Miranda rule as resting (however implausibly) upon the proposition that what the statute here before us permits– the admission at trial of un-Mirandized confessions–violates the Constitution. That is the fairest reading of the Miranda case itself. The Court began by announcing that the Fifth Amendment privilege against self-incrimination applied in the context of extrajudicial custodial interrogation, see 384 U.S., at 460—467–itself a doubtful proposition as a matter both of history and precedent, see id., at, at 510—511 (Harlan, J., dissenting) (characterizing the Court's conclusion that the Fifth Amendment privilege, rather than the Due Process

Clause, governed stationhouse confessions as a "trompe l'oeil"). Having extended the privilege into the confines of the station house, the Court liberally sprinkled throughout its sprawling 60-page opinion suggestions that, because of the compulsion inherent in custodial interrogation, the privilege was violated by any statement thus obtained that did not conform to the rules set forth in Miranda, or some functional equivalent. See id., at 458 ("Unless adequate protective devices are employed to dispel the compulsion inherent in custodial surroundings, no statement obtained from the defendant can truly be the product of his free choice") (emphases added); id., at 461 ("An individual swept from familiar surroundings into police custody, surrounded by antagonistic forces, and subjected to the techniques of persuasion described above cannot be otherwise than under compulsion to speak"); id., at 467 ("We have concluded that without proper safeguards the process of in-custody interrogation ... contains inherently compelling pressures which work to undermine the individual's will to resist and to compel him to speak where he would not otherwise do so freely"); id., 457, n. 26 (noting the "absurdity of denying that a confession obtained under these circumstances is compelled").

The dissenters, for their part, also understood Miranda's holding to be based on the "premise ... that pressure on the suspect must be eliminated though it be only the subtle influence of the atmosphere and surroundings." Id., at 512 (Harlan, J., dissenting). See also id., at 535 (White, J., dissenting) ("[I]t has never been suggested, until today, that such questioning was so coercive and accused persons so lacking in hardihood that the very first response to the very first question following the commencement of custody must be conclusively presumed to be the product of an overborne will"). And at least one case decided shortly after Miranda explicitly confirmed the view. See Orozco v. Texas, 394 U.S. 324, 326 (1969) ("[T]he use of these admissions obtained in the absence of the required warnings was a flat violation of the Self-Incrimination Clause of the Fifth Amendment as construed in Miranda").

So understood, Miranda was objectionable for innumerable reasons, not least the fact that cases spanning more than 70 years had rejected its core premise that, absent the warnings and an effective waiver of the right to remain silent and of the (thitherto unknown) right to have an attorney present, a statement obtained pursuant to custodial interrogation was necessarily the product of compulsion. See Crooker v. California, 357 U.S. 433 (1958) (confession not involuntary despite denial of access to counsel); Cicenia v. Lagay, 357 U.S. 504 (1958) (same); Powers v. United States, 223 U.S. 303 (1912) (lack of warnings and counsel did not render statement before United States Commisioner involuntary); Wilson v. United States, 162 U.S. 613 (1896) (same). Moreover, history and precedent aside, the decision in Miranda, if read as an explication of what the Constitution requires, is preposterous. There is, for example, simply no basis in reason for concluding that a response to the very first question asked, by a suspect who already knows all of the rights described in the Miranda warning, is anything other than a volitional act. See Miranda, supra, at 533—534 (White, J., dissenting). And even if one assumes that the elimination of compulsion absolutely requires informing even the most knowledgeable suspect of his right to remain silent, it cannot conceivably require the right to have counsel present. There is a world of difference, which the Court recognized under the traditional voluntariness test but ignored in Miranda, between compelling a suspect to incriminate himself and preventing him from foolishly doing so of his own accord. Only the latter (which is not required by the Constitution) could explain the Court's inclusion of a right to counsel and the requirement that it, too, be knowingly and intelligently waived. Counsel's presence is not required to tell the suspect that he need not speak; the interrogators can do that. The only good reason for having counsel there is that he can be counted on to advise the suspect that he should not speak. See Watts v. Indiana, 338 U.S. 49, 59 (1949) (Jackson, J., concurring in result in part and dissenting in part) ("[A]ny lawyer worth his salt will tell the suspect in no uncertain terms to make no statement to police under any circumstances").

Preventing foolish (rather than compelled) confessions is likewise the only conceivable basis for the rules (suggested in Miranda, see 384 U.S., at 444–445, 473–474), that courts must exclude any confession elicited by questioning conducted, without interruption, after the suspect has indicated a desire to stand on his right to remain silent, see Michigan v. Mosley, 423 U.S. 96, 105–106 (1975), or initiated by police after the suspect has expressed a desire to have counsel present, see Edwards v. Arizona, 451 U.S. 477, 484–485 (1981). Nonthreatening attempts to persuade the suspect to reconsider that initial decision are not, without more, enough to render a change of heart the product of anything other than the suspect's free will. Thus, what is most remarkable about the Miranda decision—and what made it unacceptable as a matter of straightforward constitutional interpretation in the Marbury tradition—is it's palpable hostility toward the act of confession per se, rather than toward what the Constitution abhors, compelled confession. See United States v. Washington, 431 U.S. 181, 187 (1977) ("[F]ar from being prohibited by the Constitution, admissions of guilt by wrongdoers, if not coerced, are inherently desirable"). The Constitution is not, unlike the Miranda majority, offended by a criminal's commendable qualm of conscience or fortunate fit of stupidity. Cf. Minnick v. Mississippi, 498 U.S. 146, 166–167 (1990) (Scalia, J., dissenting).

For these reasons, and others more than adequately developed in the Miranda dissents and in the subsequent works of the decision's many critics, any conclusion that a violation of the Miranda rules necessarily amounts to a violation of the privilege against compelled self-incrimination can claim no support in history, precedent, or common sense, and as a result would at least presumptively be worth reconsidering even at this late date. But that is unnecessary, since the Court has (thankfully) long since abandoned the notion that failure to comply with Miranda's rules is itself a violation of the Constitution.

II

As the Court today acknowledges, since Miranda we have explicitly, and repeatedly, interpreted that decision as having announced, not the circumstances in which custodial interrogation runs afoul of the Fifth or Fourteenth Amendment, but rather only "prophylactic" rules that go beyond the right against compelled self-incrimination. Of course the seeds of this "prophylactic" interpretation of Miranda were present in the decision itself. See Miranda, supra, at 439 (discussing the "necessity for procedures which assure that the [suspect] is accorded his privilege"); id., at 447 ("[u]nless a proper limitation upon custodial interrogation is achieved—such as these decisions will advance—there can be no assurance that practices of this nature will be eradicated"); id., at 457 ("[i]n these cases, we might not find the defendants' statements to have been involuntary in traditional terms"); ibid. (noting "concern for adequate safeguards to protect precious Fifth Amendment rights" and the "potentiality for compulsion" in Ernesto Miranda's interrogation). In subsequent cases, the seeds have sprouted and borne fruit: The Court has squarely concluded that it is possible—indeed not uncommon—for the police to violate Miranda without also violating the Constitution.

Michigan v. Tucker, 417 U.S. 433 (1974), an opinion for the Court written by then-Justice Rehnquist, rejected the true-to-Marbury, failure-to-warn-as-constitutional-violation interpretation of Miranda. It held that exclusion of the "fruits" of a Miranda violation—the statement of a witness whose identity the defendant had revealed while in custody—was not required. The opinion explained that the question whether the "police conduct complained of directly infringed upon respondent's right against compulsory self-incrimination" was a "separate question" from "whether it instead violated only the prophylactic rules developed to protect that right." Id., at 439. The "procedural safeguards" adopted in Miranda, the Court said, "were not themselves rights protected by the Constitution but were instead measures to insure that the right against compulsory self-incrimination was protected," and to "provide practical reinforcement for the right," id., at 444. Comparing the particular facts of the custodial interrogation with the "historical circumstances underlying the privilege," ibid., the Court concluded, unequivocally, that the defendant's statement could not be termed "involuntary as that term has been defined in the decisions of this Court," id., at 445, and thus that there had been no constitutional violation, notwithstanding the clear violation of the "procedural rules later established in Miranda," ibid. Lest there be any confusion on the point, the Court reiterated that the "police conduct at issue here did not abridge respondent's constitutional privilege against compulsory self-incrimination, but departed only from the prophylactic standards later laid down by this Court in Miranda to safeguard that privilege." Id., at 446. It is clear from our cases, of course, that if the statement in Tucker had been obtained in violation of the Fifth Amendment, the statement and its fruits would have been excluded. See Nix v. Williams, 467 U.S. 431, 442 (1984).

The next year, in Oregon v. Hass, 420 U.S. 714 (1975), the Court held that a defendant's statement taken in violation of Miranda that was nonetheless voluntary could be used at trial for impeachment purposes. This holding turned upon the recognition that violation of Miranda is not unconstitutional compulsion, since statements obtained in actual violation of the privilege against compelled self-incrimination, "as opposed to ... taken in violation of Miranda," quite simply "may not be put to any testimonial use whatever against [the defendant] in a criminal trial," including as impeachment evidence. New Jersey v. Portash, 440 U.S. 450, 459 (1979). See also Mincey v. Arizona, 437 U.S. 385, 397–398 (1978) (holding that while statements obtained in violation of Miranda may be used for impeachment if otherwise trustworthy, the Constitution prohibits "any criminal trial use against a defendant of his involuntary statement").

Nearly a decade later, in New York v. Quarles, 467 U.S. 649 (1984), the Court relied upon the fact that "[t]he prophylactic Miranda warnings ... are 'not themselves rights protected by the Constitution,'" id., at 654 (quoting Tucker, supra, at 444), to create a "public safety" exception. In that case, police apprehended, after a chase in a grocery store, a rape suspect known to be carrying a gun. After handcuffing and searching him (and finding no gun)—but before reading him his Miranda warnings—the police demanded to know where the gun was. The defendant nodded in the direction of some empty cartons and responded that "the gun is over there." The Court held that both the unwarned statement—"the gun is over there"—and the recovered weapon were admissible in the prosecution's case in chief under a "public safety exception" to the "prophylactic rules enunciated in Miranda." 467 U.S., at 653. It explicitly acknowledged that if the Miranda warnings were an imperative of the Fifth Amendment itself, such an exigency exception would be impossible, since the Fifth Amendment's bar on compelled self-incrimination is absolute, and its " 'strictures, unlike the Fourth's are not removed by showing reasonableness,' " 467 U.S., at 653, n. 3. (For the latter reason, the Court found it necessary to note that respondent did not "claim that [his] statements were actually compelled by police conduct which overcame his will to resist," id., at 654.)

The next year, the Court again declined to apply the "fruit of the poisonous tree" doctrine to a Miranda violation, this time allowing the admission of a suspect's properly warned statement even though it had been preceded (and, arguably, induced) by an earlier inculpatory statement taken in violation of Miranda. Oregon v. Elstad, 470 U.S. 298 (1985). As in Tucker, the Court distinguished the case from those holding that a confession obtained as a result of an unconstitutional search is inadmissible, on the ground that the violation of Miranda does not involve an "actual infringement of the suspect's constitutional rights," 470 U.S., at 308. Miranda, the Court explained, "sweeps more broadly than the Fifth Amendment itself," and "Miranda's preventive medicine provides a remedy even to the defendant who has suffered no identifiable constitutional harm." 470 U.S., at 307. "[E]rrors [that] are made by law enforcement officers in administering the prophylactic Miranda procedures … should not breed the same irremediable consequences as police infringement of the Fifth Amendment itself." Id., at 308–309.

In light of these cases, and our statements to the same effect in others, see, e.g., Davis v. United States, 512 U.S., at 457–458; Withrow v. Williams, 507 U.S. 680, 690–691 (1993); Eagan, 492 U.S., at 203, it is simply no longer possible for the Court to conclude, even if it wanted to, that a violation of Miranda's rules is a violation of the Constitution. But as I explained at the outset, that is what is required before the Court may disregard a law of Congress governing the admissibility of evidence in federal court. The Court today insists that the decision in Miranda is a "constitutional" one, ante, at 1, 8; that it has "constitutional underpinnings", ante, at 10, n. 5; a "constitutional basis" and a "constitutional origin", ante, at 9, n. 3; that it was "constitutionally based", ante, at 10; and that it announced a "constitutional rule," ante, at 7, 9, 11, 14. It is fine to play these word games; but what makes a decision "constitutional" in the only sense relevant here—in the sense that renders it impervious to supersession by congressional legislation such as §3501—is the determination that the Constitution requires the result that the decision announces and the statute ignores. By disregarding congressional action that concededly does not violate the Constitution, the Court flagrantly offends fundamental principles of separation of powers, and arrogates to itself prerogatives reserved to the representatives of the people.

The Court seeks to avoid this conclusion in two ways: First, by misdescribing these post-Miranda cases as mere dicta. The Court concedes only "that there is language in some of our opinions that supports the view" that Miranda's protections are not "constitutionally required." Ante, at 8. It is not a matter of language; it is a matter of holdings. The proposition that failure to comply with Miranda's rules does not establish a constitutional violation was central to the holdings of Tucker, Hass, Quarles, and Elstad.

The second way the Court seeks to avoid the impact of these cases is simply to disclaim responsibility for reasoned decisionmaking. It says:

"These decisions illustrate the principle—not that Miranda is not a constitutional rule—but that no constitutional rule is immutable. No court laying down a general rule can possibly foresee the various circumstances in which counsel will seek to apply it, and the sort of modifications represented by these cases are as much a normal part of constitutional law as the original decision." Ante, at 11.

The issue, however, is not whether court rules are "mutable"; they assuredly are. It is not whether, in the light of "various circumstances," they can be "modifi[ed]"; they assuredly can. The issue is whether, as mutated and modified, they must make sense. The requirement that they do so is the only thing that prevents this Court from being some sort of nine-headed Caesar, giving thumbs-up or thumbs-down to whatever outcome, case by case, suits or offends its collective fancy. And if confessions procured in violation of Miranda are confessions "compelled" in violation of the Constitution, the post-Miranda decisions I have discussed do not make sense. The only reasoned basis for their outcome was that a violation of Miranda is not a violation of the Constitution. If, for example, as the Court acknowledges was the holding of Elstad, "the traditional 'fruits' doctrine developed in Fourth Amendment cases" (that the fruits of evidence obtained unconstitutionally must be excluded from trial) does not apply to the fruits of Miranda violations, ante, at 11; and if the reason for the difference is not that Miranda violations are not constitutional violations (which is plainly and flatly what Elstad said); then the Court must come up with some other explanation for the difference. (That will take quite a bit of doing, by the way, since it is not clear on the face of the Fourth Amendment that evidence obtained in violation of that guarantee must be excluded from trial, whereas it is clear on the face of the Fifth Amendment that unconstitutionally compelled confessions cannot be used.) To say simply that "unreasonable searches under the Fourth Amendment are different from unwarned interrogation under the Fifth Amendment," ante, at 11—12, is true but supremely unhelpful.

Finally, the Court asserts that Miranda must be a "constitutional decision" announcing a "constitutional rule," and thus immune to congressional modification, because we have since its inception applied it to the States. If this argument is meant as an invocation of stare decisis, it fails because, though it is true that our cases applying Miranda against the States must be reconsidered if Miranda is not required by the

Constitution, it is likewise true that our cases (discussed above) based on the principle that Miranda is not required by the Constitution will have to be reconsidered if it is. So the stare decisis argument is a wash. If, on the other hand, the argument is meant as an appeal to logic rather than stare decisis, it is a classic example of begging the question: Congress's attempt to set aside Miranda, since it represents an assertion that violation of Miranda is not a violation of the Constitution, also represents an assertion that the Court has no power to impose Miranda on the States. To answer this assertion—not by showing why violation of Miranda is a violation of the Constitution—but by asserting that Miranda does apply against the States, is to assume precisely the point at issue. In my view, our continued application of the Miranda code to the States despite our consistent statements that running afoul of its dictates does not necessarily—or even usually—result in an actual constitutional violation, represents not the source of Miranda's salvation but rather evidence of its ultimate illegitimacy. See generally J. Grano, Confessions, Truth, and the Law 173—198 (1993); Grano, Prophylactic Rules in Criminal Procedure: A Question of Article III Legitimacy, 80 Nw. U. L. Rev. 100 (1985). As Justice Stevens has elsewhere explained, "[t]his Court's power to require state courts to exclude probative self-incriminatory statements rests entirely on the premise that the use of such evidence violates the Federal Constitution. ... If the Court does not accept that premise, it must regard the holding in the Miranda case itself, as well as all of the federal jurisprudence that has evolved from that decision, as nothing more than an illegitimate exercise of raw judicial power." Elstad, 470 U.S., at 370 (dissenting opinion). Quite so.

III

There was available to the Court a means of reconciling the established proposition that a violation of Miranda does not itself offend the Fifth Amendment with the Court's assertion of a right to ignore the present statute. That means of reconciliation was argued strenuously by both petitioner and the United States, who were evidently more concerned than the Court is with maintaining the coherence of our jurisprudence. It is not mentioned in the Court's opinion because, I assume, a majority of the Justices intent on reversing believes that incoherence is the lesser evil. They may be right.

Petitioner and the United States contend that there is nothing at all exceptional, much less unconstitutional, about the Court's adopting prophylactic rules to buttress constitutional rights, and enforcing them against Congress and the States. Indeed, the United States argues that "[p]rophylactic rules are now and have been for many years a feature of this Court's constitutional adjudication." Brief for United States 47. That statement is not wholly inaccurate, if by "many years" one means since the mid-1960's. However, in their zeal to validate what is in my view a lawless practice, the United States and petitioner greatly overstate the frequency with which we have engaged in it. For instance, petitioner cites several cases in which the Court quite simply exercised its traditional judicial power to define the scope of constitutional protections and, relatedly, the circumstances in which they are violated. See Loretto v. Teleprompter Manhattan CATV Corp., 458 U.S. 419, 436—437 (1982) (holding that a permanent physical occupation constitutes a per se taking); Maine v. Moulton, 474 U.S. 159, 176 (1985) (holding that the Sixth Amendment right to the assistance of counsel is actually "violated when the State obtains incriminating statements by knowingly circumventing the accused's right to have counsel present in a confrontation between the accused and a state agent").

Similarly unsupportive of the supposed practice is Bruton v. United States, 391 U.S. 123 (1968), where we concluded that the Confrontation Clause of the Sixth Amendment forbids the admission of a nontestifying co-defendant's facially incriminating confession in a joint trial, even where the jury has been given a limiting instruction. That decision was based, not upon the theory that this was desirable protection "beyond" what the Confrontation Clause technically required; but rather upon the self-evident proposition that the inability to cross-examine an available witness whose damaging out-of-court testimony is introduced violates the Confrontation Clause, combined with the conclusion that in these circumstances a mere jury instruction can never be relied upon to prevent the testimony from being damaging, see Richardson v. Marsh, 481 U.S. 200, 207–208 (1987).

The United States also relies on our cases involving the question whether a State's procedure for appointed counsel's withdrawal of representation on appeal satisfies the State's constitutional obligation to " 'affor[d] adequate and effective appellate review to indigent defendants.' " Smith v. Robbins, 528 U.S. ___, ___ (2000) (slip op., at 14) (quoting Griffin v. Illinois, 351 U.S. 12, 20 (1956). In Anders v. California, 386 U.S. 738 (1967), we concluded that California's procedure governing withdrawal fell short of the constitutional minimum, and we outlined a procedure that would meet that standard. But as we made clear earlier this Term in Smith, which upheld a procedure different from the one Anders suggested, the benchmark of constitutionality is the constitutional requirement of adequate representation, and not some excrescence upon that requirement decreed, for safety's sake, by this Court.

In a footnote, the United States directs our attention to certain overprotective First Amendment rules that we have adopted to ensure "breathing space" for expression. See Gertz v. Robert Welch, Inc., 418 U.S. 323, 340, 342 (1974) (recognizing that in New York Times Co. v. Sullivan, 376 U.S. 254 (1964), we "extended a measure of strategic protection to defamatory falsehood" of public officials); Freedman v. Maryland, 380 U.S. 51, 58 (1965) (setting forth "procedural safeguards designed to obviate the dangers of a censorship system" with respect to motion picture obscenity). In these cases, and others involving the First Amendment, the Court has acknowledged that in order to guarantee that protected speech is not "chilled" and thus forgone, it is in some instances necessary to incorporate in our substantive rules a "measure of strategic protection." But that is because the Court has viewed the importation of "chill" as itself a violation of the First Amendment—not because the Court thought it could go beyond what the First Amendment demanded in order to provide some prophylaxis.

Petitioner and the United States are right on target, however, in characterizing the Court's actions in a case decided within a few years of Miranda, North Carolina v. Pearce, 395 U.S. 711 (1969). There, the Court concluded that due process would be offended were a judge vindictively to resentence with added severity a defendant who had successfully appealed his original conviction. Rather than simply announce that vindictive sentencing violates the Due Process Clause, the Court went on to hold that "[i]n order to assure the absence of such a [vindictive] motivation, ... the reasons for [imposing the increased sentence] must affirmatively appear" and must "be based upon objective information concerning identifiable conduct on the part of the defendant occurring after the time of the original sentencing proceeding." Id., at 726. The Court later explicitly acknowledged Pearce's prophylactic character, see Michigan v. Payne, 412 U.S. 47, 53 (1973). It is true, therefore, that the case exhibits the same fundamental flaw as does Miranda when deprived (as it has been) of its original (implausible) pretension to announcement of what the Constitution itself required. That is, although the Due Process Clause may well prohibit punishment based on judicial vindictiveness, the Constitution by no means vests in the courts "any general power to prescribe particular devices 'in order to assure the absence of such a motivation,'" 395 U.S., at 741 (Black, J., dissenting). Justice Black surely had the right idea when he derided the Court's requirement as "pure legislation if there ever was legislation," ibid., although in truth Pearce's rule pales as a legislative achievement when compared to the detailed code promulgated in Miranda.1

The foregoing demonstrates that, petitioner's and the United States' suggestions to the contrary notwithstanding, what the Court did in Miranda (assuming, as later cases hold, that Miranda went beyond what the Constitution actually requires) is in fact extraordinary. That the Court has, on rare and recent occasion, repeated the mistake does not transform error into truth, but illustrates the potential for future mischief that the error entails. Where the Constitution has wished to lodge in one of the branches of the Federal Government some limited power to supplement its guarantees, it has said so. See Amdt. 14, §5 ("The Congress shall have power to enforce, by appropriate legislation, the provisions of this article"). The power with which the Court would endow itself under a "prophylactic" justification for Miranda goes far beyond what it has permitted Congress to do under authority of that text. Whereas we have insisted that congressional action under §5 of the Fourteenth Amendment must be "congruent" with, and "proportional" to, a constitutional violation, see City of Boerne v. Flores, 521 U.S. 507, 520 (1997), the Miranda nontextual power to embellish confers authority to prescribe preventive measures against not only constitutionally prohibited compelled confessions, but also (as discussed earlier) foolhardy ones.

I applaud, therefore, the refusal of the Justices in the majority to enunciate this boundless doctrine of judicial empowerment as a means of rendering today's decision rational. In nonetheless joining the Court's judgment, however, they overlook two truisms: that actions speak louder than silence, and that (in judge-made law at least) logic will out. Since there is in fact no other principle that can reconcile today's judgment with the post-Miranda cases that the Court refuses to abandon, what today's decision will stand for, whether the Justices can bring themselves to say it or not, is the power of the Supreme Court to write a prophylactic, extraconstitutional Constitution, binding on Congress and the States.

IV

Thus, while I agree with the Court that §3501 cannot be upheld without also concluding that Miranda represents an illegitimate exercise of our authority to review state-court judgments, I do not share the Court's hesitation in reaching that conclusion. For while the Court is also correct that the doctrine of stare decisis demands some "special justification" for a departure from longstanding precedent—even precedent of the constitutional variety—

that criterion is more than met here. To repeat Justice Stevens' cogent observation, it is "[o]bviou[s]" that "the Court's power to reverse Miranda's conviction rested entirely on the determination that a violation of the Federal Constitution had occurred." Elstad, 470 U.S., at 367, n. 9 (dissenting opinion) (emphasis added). Despite the Court's Orwellian assertion to the contrary, it is undeniable that later cases (discussed above) have "undermined [Miranda's] doctrinal underpinnings," ante, at 14, denying constitutional violation and thus stripping the holding of its only constitutionally legitimate support. Miranda's critics and supporters alike have long made this point. See Office of Legal Policy, U.S. Dept. of Justice, Report to Attorney General on Law of Pre-Trial Interrogation 97 (Feb. 12, 1986) ("The current Court has repudiated the premises on which Miranda was based, but has drawn back from recognizing the full implications of its decisions"); id., at 78 ("Michigan v. Tucker accordingly repudiated the doctrinal basis of the Miranda decision"); Sonenshein, Miranda and the Burger Court: Trends and Countertrends, 13 Loyola U. Chi. L. J. 405, 407—408 (1982) ("Although the Burger Court has not overruled Miranda, the Court has consistently undermined the rationales, assumptions, and values which gave Miranda life"); id., at 425—426 ("Seemingly, the Court [in Michigan v. Tucker] utterly destroyed both Miranda's rationale and its holding"); Stone, The Miranda Doctrine in the Burger Court, 1977 S. Ct. Rev. 99, 118 ("Mr. Justice Rehnquist's conclusion that there is a violation of the Self-Incrimination Clause only if a confession is involuntary ... is an outright rejection of the core premises of Miranda").

The Court cites Patterson v. McLean Credit Union, 491 U.S. 164, 173 (1989), as accurately reflecting our standard for overruling, see ante, at 14—which I am pleased to accept, even though Patterson was speaking of overruling statutory cases and the standard for constitutional decisions is somewhat more lenient. What is set forth there reads as though it was written precisely with the current status of Miranda in mind:

"In cases where statutory precedents have been overruled, the primary reason for the Court's shift in position has been the intervening development of the law, through either the growth of judicial doctrine or further action taken by Congress. Where such changes have removed or weakened the conceptual underpinnings from the prior decision, ... or where the later law has rendered the decision irreconcilable with competing legal doctrines or policies, ... the Court has not hesitated to overrule an earlier decision." 491 U.S., at 173.

Neither am I persuaded by the argument for retaining Miranda that touts its supposed workability as compared with the totality-of-the-circumstances test it purported to replace. Miranda's proponents cite ad nauseam the fact that the Court was called upon to make difficult and subtle distinctions in applying the "voluntariness" test in some 30-odd due process "coerced confessions" cases in the 30 years between Brown v. Mississippi, 297 U.S. 278 (1936), and Miranda. It is not immediately apparent, however, that the judicial burden has been eased by the "bright-line" rules adopted in Miranda. In fact, in the 34 years since Miranda was decided, this Court has been called upon to decide nearly 60 cases involving a host of Miranda issues, most of them predicted with remarkable prescience by Justice White in his Miranda dissent. 384 U.S., at 545.

Moreover, it is not clear why the Court thinks that the "totality-of-the-circumstances test ... is more difficult than Miranda for law enforcement officers to conform to, and for courts to apply in a consistent manner." Ante, at 14. Indeed, I find myself persuaded by Justice O'Connor's rejection of this same argument in her opinion in Williams, 507 U.S., at 711—712 (O'Connor, J., joined by Rehnquist, C. J., concurring in part and dissenting in part):

"Miranda, for all its alleged brightness, is not without its difficulties; and voluntariness is not without its strengths.... Miranda creates as many close questions as it resolves. The task of determining whether a defendant is in 'custody' has proved to be 'a slippery one.' And the supposedly 'bright' lines that separate interrogation from spontaneous declaration, the exercise of a right from waiver, and the adequate warning from the inadequate, likewise have turned out to be rather dim and ill defined. The totality-of-the-circumstances approach, on the other hand, permits each fact to be taken into account without resort to formal and dispositive labels. By dispensing with the difficulty of producing a yes-or-no answer to questions that are often better answered in shades and degrees, the voluntariness inquiry often can make judicial decisionmaking easier rather than more onerous." (Emphasis added; citations omitted.)

But even were I to agree that the old totality-of-the-circumstances test was more cumbersome, it is simply not true that Miranda has banished it from the law and replaced it with a new test. Under the current regime, which the Court today retains in its entirety, courts are frequently called upon to undertake both inquiries. That is because, as explained earlier, voluntariness remains the constitutional standard, and as such continues to govern the admissibility for impeachment purposes of statements taken in violation of Miranda, the admissibility of the "fruits" of such statements, and the admissibility of statements challenged as unconstitutionally obtained despite the interrogator's compliance with Miranda, see, e.g., Colorado v. Connelly, 479 U.S. 157 (1986).

Finally, I am not convinced by petitioner's argument that Miranda should be preserved because the decision occupies a special place in the "public's consciousness." Brief for Petitioner 44. As far as I am aware, the public is not under the illusion that we are infallible. I see little harm in admitting that we made a mistake in taking away from the people the ability to decide for themselves what protections (beyond those required by the Constitution) are reasonably affordable in the criminal investigatory process. And I see much to be gained by reaffirming for the people the wonderful reality that they govern themselves—which means that "[t]he powers not delegated to the United States by the Constitution" that the people adopted, "nor prohibited ... to the States" by that Constitution, "are reserved to the States respectively, or to the people," U.S. Const., Amdt. 10.2

* * *

Today's judgment converts Miranda from a milestone of judicial overreaching into the very Cheops' Pyramid (or perhaps the Sphinx would be a better analogue) of judicial arrogance. In imposing its Court-made code upon the States, the original opinion at least asserted that it was demanded by the Constitution. Today's decision does not pretend that it is—and yet still asserts the right to impose it against the will of the people's representatives in Congress. Far from believing that stare decisis compels this result, I believe we cannot allow to remain on the books even a celebrated decision—especially a celebrated decision—that has come to stand for the proposition that the Supreme Court has power to impose extraconstitutional constraints upon Congress and the States. This is not the system that was established by the Framers, or that would be established by any sane supporter of government by the people.

I dissent from today's decision, and, until §3501 is repealed, will continue to apply it in all cases where there has been a sustainable finding that the defendant's confession was voluntary.

Notes to Justice Scalia's dissent in Dickerson v. United States (June 26, 2000)

1. As for Michigan v. Jackson, 475 U.S. 625 (1986), upon which petitioner and the United States also rely, in that case we extended to the Sixth Amendment, postindictment, context the Miranda-based prophylactic rule of Edwards v. Arizona, 451 U.S. 477 (1981), that the police cannot initiate interrogation after counsel has been requested. I think it less a separate instance of claimed judicial power to impose constitutional prophylaxis than a direct, logic-driven consequence of Miranda itself.

2. The Court cites my dissenting opinion in Mitchell v. United States, 526 U.S. 314, 331—332 (1999), for the proposition that "the fact that a rule has found 'wide acceptance in the legal culture' is 'adequate reason not to overrule' it." Ante, at 13. But the legal culture is not the same as the "public's consciousness"; and unlike the rule at issue in Mitchell (prohibiting comment on a defendant's refusal to testify) Miranda has been

continually criticized by lawyers, law enforcement officials, and scholars since its pronouncement (not to mention by Congress, as §3501 shows). In Mitchell, moreover, the constitutional underpinnings of the earlier rule had not been demolished by subsequent cases.

Justice Breyer proceeds on the erroneous and all-too-common assumption that the Constitution means what we think it ought to mean. It does not; it means what it says: Justice Scalia's concurrence in Apprendi v. New Jersey (June 26, 2000)

Justice Scalia, concurring.

I feel the need to say a few words in response to Justice Breyer's dissent. It sketches an admirably fair and efficient scheme of criminal justice designed for a society that is prepared to leave criminal justice to the State. (Judges, it is sometimes necessary to remind ourselves, are part of the State—and an increasingly bureaucratic part of it, at that.) The founders of the American Republic were not prepared to leave it to the State, which is why the jury-trial guarantee was one of the least controversial provisions of the Bill of Rights. It has never been efficient; but it has always been free.

As for fairness, which Justice Breyer believes "[i]n modern times," post, at 1, the jury cannot provide: I think it not unfair to tell a prospective felon that if he commits his contemplated crime he is exposing himself to a jail sentence of 30 years—and that if, upon conviction, he gets anything less than that he may thank the mercy of a tenderhearted judge (just as he may thank the mercy of a tenderhearted parole commission if he is let out inordinately early, or the mercy of a tenderhearted governor if his sentence is commuted). Will there be disparities? Of course. But the criminal will never get more punishment than he bargained for when he did the crime, and his guilt of the crime (and hence the length of the sentence to which he is exposed) will be determined beyond a reasonable doubt by the unanimous vote of 12 of his fellow citizens.

In Justice Breyer's bureaucratic realm of perfect equity, by contrast, the facts that determine the length of sentence to which the defendant is exposed will be determined to exist (on a more-likely-than-not basis) by a single employee of the State. It is certainly arguable (Justice Breyer argues it) that this sacrifice of prior protections is worth it. But it is not arguable that, just because one thinks it is a better system, it must be, or is even more likely to be, the system envisioned by a Constitution that guarantees trial by jury. What ultimately demolishes the case for the dissenters is that they are unable to say what the right to trial by jury does guarantee if, as they assert, it does not guarantee—what it has been assumed to guarantee throughout our history—the right to have a jury determine those facts that determine the maximum sentence the law allows. They provide no coherent alternative.

Justice Breyer proceeds on the erroneous and all-too-common assumption that the Constitution means what we think it ought to mean. It does not; it means what it says. And the guarantee that "[i]n all criminal prosecutions, the accused shall enjoy the right to . . . trial, by an impartial jury" has no intelligible content unless it means that all the facts which must exist in order to subject the defendant to a legally prescribed punishment must be found by the jury.

Speech, public forums: Justice Scalia's dissent in Hill v. Colorado (June 28, 2000)

Justice Scalia, with whom Justice Thomas joins, dissenting.

The Court today concludes that a regulation requiring speakers on the public thoroughfares bordering medical facilities to speak from a distance of eight feet is "not a 'regulation of speech,' " but "a regulation of the places where some speech may occur," ante, at 14; and that a regulation directed to only certain categories of speech (protest, education, and counseling) is not "content-based." For these reasons, it says, the regulation is immune from the exacting scrutiny we apply to content-based suppression of speech in the public forum. The Court then determines that the regulation survives the less rigorous scrutiny afforded content-neutral time, place, and manner restrictions because it is narrowly tailored to serve a government interest—protection of citizens' "right to be let alone"—that has explicitly been disclaimed by the State, probably for the reason that, as a basis for suppressing peaceful private expression, it is patently incompatible with the guarantees of the First Amendment.

None of these remarkable conclusions should come as a surprise. What is before us, after all, is a speech regulation directed against the opponents of abortion, and it therefore enjoys the benefit of the "ad hoc nullification machine" that the Court has set in motion to push aside whatever doctrines of constitutional law stand in the way of that highly favored practice. Madsen v. Women's Health Center, Inc., 512 U.S. 753, 785 (1994) (Scalia, J., concurring in judgment in part and dissenting in part). Having deprived abortion opponents of the political right to persuade the electorate that abortion should be restricted by law, the Court today continues and expands its assault upon their individual right to persuade women contemplating abortion that what they are doing is wrong. Because, like the rest of our abortion jurisprudence, today's decision is in stark contradiction of the constitutional principles we apply in all other contexts, I dissent.

I

Colorado's statute makes it a criminal act knowingly to approach within 8 feet of another person on the public way or sidewalk area within 100 feet of the entrance door of a health care facility for the purpose of passing a leaflet to, displaying a sign to, or engaging in oral protest, education, or counseling with such person. Whatever may be said about the restrictions on the other types of expressive activity, the regulation as it applies to oral communications is obviously and undeniably content-based. A speaker wishing to approach another for the purpose of communicating any message except one of protest, education, or counseling may do so without first securing the other's consent. Whether a speaker must obtain permission before approaching within eight feet—and whether he will be sent to prison for failing to do so—depends entirely on what he intends to say when he gets there. I have no doubt that this regulation would be deemed content-based in an instant if the case before us involved antiwar protesters, or union members seeking to "educate" the public about the reasons for their strike. "[I]t is," we would say, "the content of the speech that determines whether it is within or without the statute's blunt prohibition," Carey v. Brown, 447 U.S. 455, 462 (1980). But the jurisprudence of this Court has a way of changing when abortion is involved.

The Court asserts that this statute is not content-based for purposes of our First Amendment analysis because it neither (1) discriminates among viewpoints nor (2) places restrictions on "any subject matter that may be discussed by a speaker." Ante, at 18. But we have never held that the universe of content-based regulations is limited to those two categories, and such a holding would be absurd. Imagine, for instance, special place-and-manner restrictions on all speech except that which "conveys a sense of contentment or happiness." This "happy speech" limitation would not be "viewpoint-based"—citizens would be able to express their joy in equal measure at either the rise or fall of the NASDAQ, at either the success or the failure of the Republican Party—and would not discriminate on the basis of subject matter, since gratification could be expressed about anything at all. Or consider a law restricting the writing or recitation of poetry—neither viewpoint-based nor limited to any particular subject matter. Surely this Court would consider such regulations to be "content-based" and deserving of the most exacting scrutiny1

"The vice of content-based legislation—what renders it deserving of the high standard of strict scrutiny—is not that it is always used for invidious, thought-control purposes, but that it lends itself to use for those purposes." Madsen, supra, at 794 (opinion of Scalia, J.) (emphasis omitted). A restriction that operates only on speech that communicates a message of protest, education, or counseling presents exactly this risk. When applied, as it is here, at the entrance to medical facilities, it is a means of impeding speech against abortion. The Court's confident assurance that the statute poses no special threat to First Amendment freedoms because it applies alike to "used car salesmen, animal rights activists, fundraisers, environmentalists, and missionaries," ante, at 18, is a wonderful replication (except for its lack of sarcasm) of Anatole France's observation that "[t]he law, in its majestic equality, forbids the rich as well as the poor to sleep under bridges ... ." see J. Bartlett, Familiar Quotations 550 (16th ed. 1992). This Colorado law is no more targeted at used car salesmen, animal rights activists, fund raisers, environmentalists, and missionaries than French vagrancy law was targeted at the rich. We know what the Colorado legislators, by their careful selection of content ("protest, education, and counseling"), were taking aim at, for they set it forth in the statute itself:

the "right to protest or counsel against certain medical procedures" on the sidewalks and streets surrounding health care facilities. Col. Rev. Stat. §18—9—122(1) (1999) (emphasis added).

The Court is unpersuasive in its attempt to equate the present restriction with content-neutral regulation of demonstrations and picketing—as one may immediately suspect from the opinion's wildly expansive definitions of demonstrations as " 'public display[s] of sentiment for or against a person or cause,' " and of picketing as an effort " 'to persuade or otherwise influence.' " Ante, at 16—17, quoting Webster's Third New International Dictionary 600, 1710 (1993). (On these terms, Nathan Hale was a demonstrator and Patrick Henry a picket.) When the government regulates "picketing," or "demonstrating," it restricts a particular manner of expression that is, as the author of today's opinion has several times explained, " 'a mixture of conduct and communication.' " Frisby v. Schultz, 487 U.S. 474, 497 (1988) (Stevens, J., dissenting), quoting NLRB v. Retail Store Employees, 447 U.S. 607, 618—619 (1980) (Stevens, J., concurring in part and concurring in result). The latter opinion quoted approvingly Justice Douglas's statement:

"Picketing by an organized group is more than free speech, since it involves patrol of a particular locality and since the very presence of a picket line may induce action of one kind or another, quite irrespective of the nature of the ideas which are being disseminated. Hence those aspects of picketing make it the subject of restrictive regulation." Bakery Drivers v. Wohl, 315 U.S. 769, 776—777 (1942) (concurring opinion).

As Justice Stevens went on to explain, "no doubt the principal reason why handbills containing the same message are so much less effective than labor picketing is that the former depend entirely on the persuasive force of the idea." Retail Store Employees, supra, at 619. Today, of course, Justice Stevens gives us an opinion restricting not only handbilling but even one-on-one conversation of a particular content. There comes a point—and the Court's opinion today passes it—at which the regulation of action intimately and unavoidably connected with traditional speech is a regulation of speech itself. The strictures of the First Amendment cannot be avoided by regulating the act of moving one's lips; and they cannot be avoided by regulating the act of extending one's arm to deliver a handbill, or peacefully approaching in order to speak. All of these acts can be regulated, to be sure; but not, on the basis of content, without satisfying the requirements of our strict-scrutiny First Amendment jurisprudence.

Even with regard to picketing, of course, we have applied strict scrutiny to content-based restrictions. See Carey, 447 U.S., at 461 (applying strict scrutiny to, and invalidating, an Illinois statute that made "permissibility of residential picketing ... dependent solely on the nature of the message being conveyed"). As discussed above, the prohibition here is content-based: those who wish to speak for purposes other than protest, counsel, or education may do so at close range without the listener's consent, while those who wish to speak for other purposes may not. This bears no resemblance to a blanket prohibition of picketing—unless, of course, one uses the fanciful definition of picketing ("an effort to persuade or otherwise influence") newly discovered by today's opinion. As for the Court's appeal to the fact that we often "examine the content of a communication" to determine whether it "constitutes a threat, blackmail, an agreement to fix prices, a copyright violation, a public offering of securities, or an offer to sell goods," ante, at 16, the distinction is almost too obvious to bear mention: Speech of a certain content is constitutionally proscribable. The Court has not yet taken the step of consigning "protest, education, and counseling" to that category.

Finally, the Court is not correct in its assertion that the restriction here is content-neutral because it is "justified without reference to the content of regulated speech," in the sense that "the State's interests in protecting access and privacy, and providing the police with clear guidelines, are unrelated to the content of the demonstrators' speech." Ante, at 14—15 (emphasis added). That is not an accurate statement of our law. The Court makes too much of the statement in Ward v. Rock Against Racism, 491 U.S. 781 (1989), that "[t]he principal inquiry in determining content neutrality … is whether the government has adopted a regulation of speech because of disagreement with the message it conveys." Id., at 791, quoted ante, at 14. That is indeed "the principal inquiry"–suppression of uncongenial ideas is the worst offense against the First Amendment–but it is not the only inquiry. Even a law that has as its purpose something unrelated to the suppression of particular content cannot irrationally single out that content for its prohibition. An ordinance directed at the suppression of noise (and therefore "justified without reference to the content of regulated speech") cannot be applied only to sound trucks delivering messages of "protest." Our very first use of the "justified by reference to content" language made clear that it is a prohibition in addition to, rather than in place of, the prohibition of facially content-based restrictions. "Selective exclusions from a public forum" we said, "may not be based on content alone, and may not be justified by reference to content alone." Police Dept. of Chicago v. Mosley, 408 U.S. 92, 96 (1972) (emphasis added).

But in any event, if one accepts the Court's description of the interest served by this regulation, it is clear that the regulation is both based on content and justified by reference to content. Constitutionally proscribable "secondary effects" of speech are directly addressed in subsection (2) of the statute, which makes it unlawful to obstruct, hinder, impede, or block access to a health care facility–a prohibition broad enough to include all physical threats and all physically threatening approaches. The purpose of subsection (3), however (according to the Court), is to protect "[t]he unwilling listener's interest in avoiding unwanted communication," ante, at 11. On this analysis, Colorado has restricted certain categories of speech–protest, counseling, and education–out of an apparent belief that only speech with this content is sufficiently likely to be annoying or upsetting as to require consent before it may be engaged in at close range. It is reasonable enough to conclude that even the most gentle and peaceful close approach by a so-called "sidewalk counselor"–who wishes to "educate" the woman entering an abortion clinic about the nature of the procedure, to "counsel" against it and in favor of other alternatives, and perhaps even (though less likely if the approach is to be successful) to "protest" her taking of a human life—will often, indeed usually, have what might be termed the "secondary effect" of annoying or deeply upsetting the woman who is planning the abortion. But that is not an effect which occurs "without reference to the content" of the speech. This singling out of presumptively "unwelcome" communications fits precisely the description of prohibited regulation set forth in Boos v. Barry, 485 U.S. 312, 321 (1988): It "targets the direct impact of a particular category of speech, not a secondary feature that happens to be associated with that type of speech." Ibid. (emphasis added).2

In sum, it blinks reality to regard this statute, in its application to oral communications, as anything other than a content-based restriction upon speech in the public forum. As such, it must survive that stringent mode of constitutional analysis our cases refer to as "strict scrutiny," which requires that the restriction be narrowly tailored to serve a compelling state interest. See United States v. Playboy Entertainment Group, Inc., 529 U.S. ___, ___ (2000) (slip op., at 8); Perry Ed. Assn. v. Perry Local Educators' Assn., 460 U.S. 37, 45 (1983). Since the Court does not even attempt to support the regulation under this standard, I shall discuss it only briefly. Suffice it to say that if protecting people from unwelcome communications (the governmental interest the Court posits) is a compelling state interest, the First Amendment is a dead letter. And if (as I shall discuss at greater length below) forbidding peaceful, nonthreatening, but uninvited speech from a distance closer than eight feet is a "narrowly tailored" means of preventing the obstruction of entrance to medical facilities (the governmental interest the State asserts) narrow tailoring must refer not to the standards of Versace, but to those of Omar the tentmaker. In the last analysis all of this does not matter, however, since as I proceed to discuss neither the restrictions upon oral communications nor those upon handbilling can withstand a proper application of even the less demanding scrutiny we apply to truly content-neutral regulations of speech in a traditional public forum.

II

As the Court explains, under our precedents even a content-neutral, time, place, and manner restriction must be narrowly tailored to advance a significant state interest, and must leave open ample alternative means of communication. Ward, 491 U.S., at 802. It cannot be sustained if it "burden[s] substantially more speech than is necessary to further the government's legitimate interests." Id., at 799.

This requires us to determine, first, what is the significant interest the State seeks to advance? Here there appears to be a bit of a disagreement between the State of Colorado (which should know) and the Court (which is eager to speculate). Colorado has identified in the text of the statute itself the interest it sought to advance: to ensure that the State's citizens may "obtain medical counseling and treatment in an unobstructed manner" by "preventing the willful obstruction of a person's access to medical counseling and treatment at a health care facility." Colo. Rev. Stat. §18—9—122(1) (1999). In its brief here, the State repeatedly confirms the interest squarely identified in the statute under review. See, e.g., Brief for Respondents 15 ("Each provision of the statute was chosen to precisely address crowding and physical intimidation: conduct shown to impede access, endanger safety and health, and strangle effective law enforcement"); id., at 14 ("[T]his provision narrowly addresses the conduct shown to interfere with access through crowding and physical threats"). The Court nevertheless concludes that the Colorado provision is narrowly tailored to serve . . . the State's interest in protecting its citizens' rights to be let alone from unwanted speech.

Indeed, the situation is even more bizarre than that. The interest that the Court makes the linchpin of its analysis was not only unasserted by the State; it is not only completely different from the interest that the statute specifically sets forth; it was explicitly disclaimed by the State in its brief before this Court, and characterized as a "straw interest" petitioners served up in the hope of discrediting the State's case. Id., at 25, n. 19. We may thus add to the lengthening list of "firsts" generated by this Court's relentlessly proabortion jurisprudence, the first case in which, in order to sustain a statute, the Court has relied upon a governmental interest not only unasserted by the State, but positively repudiated.

I shall discuss below the obvious invalidity of this statute assuming, first (in Part A), the fictitious state interest that the Court has invented, and then (in Part B), the interest actually recited in the statute and asserted by counsel for Colorado.

A

It is not without reason that Colorado claimed that, in attributing to this statute the false purpose of protecting citizens' right to be let alone, petitioners were seeking to discredit it. Just three Terms ago, in upholding an injunction against antiabortion activities, the Court refused to rely on any supposed " 'right of the people approaching and entering the facilities to be left alone.' " Schenck v. Pro-Choice Network of Western N. Y., 519 U.S. 357, 383 (1997). It expressed "doubt" that this "right ... accurately reflects our First Amendment jurisprudence." Ibid. Finding itself in something of a jam (the State here has passed a regulation that is obviously not narrowly tailored to advance any other interest) the Court today neatly re-packages the repudiated "right" as an "interest" the State may decide to protect, ante, at 11, n. 24, and then places it onto the scales opposite the right to free speech in a traditional public forum.

To support the legitimacy of its self-invented state interest, the Court relies upon a bon mot in a 1928 dissent (which we evidently overlooked in Schenck). It characterizes the "unwilling listener's interest in avoiding unwanted communication" as an "aspect of the broader 'right to be let alone' " Justice Brandeis coined in his dissent in Olmstead v. United States, 277 U.S. 438, 478. The amusing feature is that even this slim reed contradicts rather than supports the Court's position. The right to be let alone that Justice Brandeis identified was a right the Constitution "conferred, as against the government"; it was that right, not some generalized "common-law right" or "interest" to be free from hearing the unwanted opinions of one's fellow citizens, which he called the "most comprehensive" and "most valued by civilized men." Ibid. (emphasis added). To the extent that there can be gleaned from our cases a "right to be let alone" in the sense that Justice Brandeis intended, it is the right of the speaker in the public forum to be free from government interference of the sort Colorado has imposed here.

In any event, the Court's attempt to disguise the "right to be let alone" as a "governmental interest in protecting the right to be let alone" is unavailing for the simple reason that this is not an interest that may be legitimately weighed against the speakers' First Amendment rights (which the Court demotes to the status of First Amendment "interests," ante, at 9.) We have consistently held that "the Constitution does not permit the government to decide which types of otherwise protected speech are sufficiently offensive to require protection for the unwilling listener or viewer." Erznoznik v. Jacksonville, 422 U.S. 205, 210 (1975) (emphasis added). And as recently as in Schenck, the Court reiterated that "[a]s a general matter, we have indicated that in public debate our own citizens must tolerate insulting, and even outrageous, speech in order to provide adequate breathing space to the freedoms protected by the First Amendment." 519 U.S., at 383 (internal quotation marks omitted).

The Court nonetheless purports to derive from our cases a principle limiting the protection the Constitution affords the speaker's right to direct "offensive messages" at "unwilling" audiences in the public forum. Ante, at 10. There is no such principle. We have upheld limitations on a speaker's exercise of his right to speak on the public streets when that speech intrudes into the privacy of the home. Frisby, 487 U.S., at 483, upheld a content-neutral municipal ordinance prohibiting picketing outside a residence or dwelling. The ordinance, we concluded, was justified by, and narrowly tailored to advance, the government's interest in the "protection of residential privacy." Id., at 484. Our opinion rested upon the "unique nature of the home"; "the home," we said, "is different." Ibid. The reasoning of the case plainly assumed the nonexistence of the right– common law or otherwise–that the Court relies on today, the right to be free from unwanted speech when on the public streets and sidewalks. The home, we noted, was " 'the one retreat to which men and women can repair to escape from the tribulations of their daily pursuits.' " Ibid. (quoting Carey, 447 U.S., at 471). The limitation on a speaker's right to bombard the home with unwanted messages which we approved in Frisby–

and in Rowan v. Post Office Dept., 397 U.S. 728 (1970), upon which the Court also relies–was predicated on the fact that " 'we are often 'captives' outside the sanctuary of the home and subject to objectionable speech.' " Frisby, supra, at 484 (quoting Rowan, supra,, at 738) (emphasis added). As the universally understood state of First Amendment law is described in a leading treatise: "Outside the home, the burden is generally on the observer or listener to avert his eyes or plug his ears against the verbal assaults, lurid advertisements, tawdry books and magazines, and other 'offensive' intrusions which increasingly attend urban life." L. Tribe, American Constitutional Law §12—19, p. 948 (2d ed. 1988). The Court today elevates the abortion clinic to the status of the home.[3]

There is apparently no end to the distortion of our First Amendment law that the Court is willing to endure in order to sustain this restriction upon the free speech of abortion opponents. The labor movement, in particular, has good cause for alarm in the Court's extensive reliance upon American Steel Foundries v. Tri-City Central Trades Council, 257 U.S. 184 (1921), an opinion in which the Court held that the Clayton Act's prohibition of injunctions against lawful and peaceful labor picketing did not forbid the injunction in that particular case. The First Amendment was not at issue, and was not so much as mentioned in the opinion, so the case is scant authority for the point the Court wishes to make. The case is also irrelevant because it was "clear from the evidence that from the outset, violent methods were pursued from time to time in such a way as to characterize the attitude of the picketers as continuously threatening." Id., at 200. No such finding was made, or could be made, here. More importantly, however, as far as our future labor cases are concerned: If a "right to be free" from "persistence, importunity, following and dogging," id., at 204, short of actual intimidation was part of our infant First Amendment law in 1921, I am shocked to think that it is there today. The Court's assertion that "[n]one of our decisions has minimized the enduring importance of 'the right to be free' from persistent 'importunity, following and dogging' after an offer to communicate has been declined," ante, at 12, is belied by the fact that this passage from American Steel Foundries has never—not once—found its way into any of the many First Amendment cases this Court has decided since 1921. We will have cause to regret today's injection of this irrelevant anachronism into the mainstream of our First Amendment jurisprudence.

Of course even if one accepted the American Steel Foundries dictum as an accurate expression of First Amendment law, the statute here is plainly not narrowly tailored to protect the interest that dictum describes. Preserving the "right to be free" from "persistent importunity, following and dogging" does not remotely require imposing upon all speakers who wish to protest, educate, or counsel a duty to request permission to approach closer than eight feet. The only way the narrow-tailoring objection can be eliminated is to posit a state-created, First-Amendment-trumping "right to be let alone" as broad and undefined as Brandeis's Olmstead dictum, which may well (why not, if the Court wishes it?) embrace a right not to be spoken to without permission from a distance closer than eight feet. Nothing stands in the way of that solution to the narrow-tailoring problem—except, of course, its utter absurdity, which is no obstacle in abortion cases.

B

I turn now to the real state interest at issue here—the one set forth in the statute and asserted in Colorado's brief: the preservation of unimpeded access to health care facilities. We need look no further than subsection (2) of the statute to see what a provision would look like that is narrowly tailored to serve that interest. Under the terms of that subsection, any person who "knowingly obstructs, detains, hinders, impedes, or blocks another person's entry to or exit from a health care facility" is subject to criminal and civil liability. It is possible, I suppose, that subsection (2) of the Colorado statute will leave unrestricted some expressive activity that, if engaged in from within eight feet, may be sufficiently harassing as to have the effect of impeding access to health care facilities. In subsection (3), however, the State of Colorado has prohibited a vast amount of speech that cannot possibly be thought to correspond to that evil.

To begin with, the 8-foot buffer zone attaches to every person on the public way or sidewalk within 100 feet of the entrance of a medical facility, regardless of whether that person is seeking to enter or exit the facility. In fact, the State acknowledged at oral argument that the buffer zone would attach to any person within 100 feet of the entrance door of a skyscraper in which a single doctor occupied an office on the 18th floor. Tr. of Oral Arg. 41. And even with respect to those who are seeking to enter or exit the facilities, the statute does not protect them only from speech that is so intimidating or threatening as to impede access. Rather, it covers all unconsented-to approaches for the purpose of oral protest, education, or counseling (including those made for the purpose of the most peaceful appeals) and, perhaps even more significantly, every approach made for the purposes of leafletting or handbilling, which we have never considered, standing alone, obstructive or unduly intrusive. The sweep of this prohibition is breathtaking.

The Court makes no attempt to justify on the facts this blatant violation of the narrow-tailoring principle. Instead, it flirts with the creation of yet a new constitutional "first" designed for abortion cases: "[W]hen," it says, "a content-neutral regulation does not entirely foreclose any means of communication, it may satisfy the tailoring requirement even though it is not the least restrictive or least intrusive means of serving the statutory goal." Ante, at 21. The implication is that the availability of alternative means of communication permits the imposition of the speech restriction upon more individuals, or more types of communication, than narrow tailoring would otherwise demand. The Court assures us that "we have emphasized" this proposition "on more than one occasion," ibid. The only citation the Court provides, however, says no such thing. Ward v. Rock Against Racism, 491 U.S., at 798, quoted ante, at 21, n. 32, says only that narrow tailoring is not synonymous with "least restrictive alternative." It does not at all suggest—and to my knowledge no other case does either—that narrow tailoring can be relaxed when there are other speech alternatives.

The burdens this law imposes upon the right to speak are substantial, despite an attempt to minimize them that is not even embarrassed to make the suggestion that they might actually "assist ... the speakers' efforts to communicate their messages," ante, at 22. (Compare this with the Court's statement in a nonabortion case, joined by the author of today's opinion: "The First Amendment mandates that we presume that speakers, not the government, know best both what they want to say and how to say it." Riley v. National Federation of Blind of N. C., Inc., 487 U.S. 781, 790–791 (1988).) The Court displays a willful ignorance of the type and nature of communication affected by the statute's restrictions. It seriously asserts, for example, that the 8-foot zone allows a speaker to communicate at a "normal conversational distance," ante, at 22. I have certainly held conversations at a distance of eight feet seated in the quiet of my chambers, but I have never walked along the public sidewalk—and have not seen others do so—"conversing" at an 8-foot remove. The suggestion is absurd. So is the suggestion that the opponents of abortion can take comfort in the fact that the statute "places no limitation on the number of speakers or the noise level, including the use of amplification equipment," ante, at 21. That is good enough, I suppose, for "protesting"; but the Court must know that most of the "counseling" and "educating" likely to take place outside a health care facility cannot be done at a distance and at a high-decibel level. The availability of a powerful amplification system will be of little help to the woman who hopes to forge, in the last moments before another of her sex is to have an abortion, a bond of concern and intimacy that might enable her to persuade the woman to change her mind and heart. The counselor may wish to walk alongside and to say, sympathetically and as softly as the circumstances allow, something like: "My dear, I know what you are going through. I've been through it myself. You're not alone and you do not have to do this. There are other alternatives. Will you let me help you? May I show you a picture of what your child looks like at this stage of her human development?" The Court would have us believe that this can be done effectively—yea, perhaps even more effectively—by shouting through a bullhorn at a distance of eight feet.

The Court seems prepared, if only for a moment, see ante, at 22—23, to take seriously the magnitude of the burden the statute imposes on simple handbilling and leafletting. That concern is fleeting, however, since it is promptly assuaged by the realization that a leafletter may, without violating the statute, stand "near the path" of oncoming pedestrians and make his "proffe[r] ..., which the pedestrians can easily accept," ante, at 22—23. It does not take a veteran labor organizer to recognize—

although surely any would, see Brief for American Federation of Labor and Congress of Industrial Organization as Amicus Curiae 7—8—that leafletting will be rendered utterly ineffectual by a requirement that the leafletter obtain from each subject permission to approach, or else man a stationary post (one that does not obstruct access to the facility, lest he violate subsection (2) of statute) and wait for passersby voluntarily to approach an outstretched hand. That simply is not how it is done, and the Court knows it—or should. A leafletter, whether he is working on behalf of Operation Rescue, Local 109, or Bubba's Bar-B-Que, stakes out the best piece of real estate he can, and then walks a few steps toward individuals passing in his vicinity, extending his arm and making it as easy as possible for the passerby, whose natural inclination is generally not to seek out such distributions, to simply accept the offering. Few pedestrians are likely to give their "consent" to the approach of a handbiller (indeed, by the time he requested it they would likely have passed by), and even fewer are likely to walk over in order to pick up a leaflet. In the abortion context, therefore, ordinary handbilling, which we have in other contexts recognized to be a "classic for[m] of speech that lie[s] at the heart of the First Amendment," Schenck, 519 U.S., at 377, will in its most effective locations be rendered futile, the Court's implausible assertions to the contrary notwithstanding.

The Colorado provision differs in one fundamental respect from the "content-neutral" time, place, and manner restrictions the Court has previously upheld. Each of them rested upon a necessary connection between the regulated expression and the evil the challenged regulation sought to eliminate. So, for instance, in Ward v. Rock Against Racism, the Court approved the city's control over sound amplification because every occasion of amplified sound presented the evil of excessive noise and distortion disturbing the areas surrounding the public forum. The regulation we upheld in Ward, rather than "bann[ing] all concerts, or even all rock concerts, . . . instead focus[ed] on the source of the evils the city seeks to eliminate . . . and eliminates them without at the same time banning or significantly restricting a substantial quantity of speech that does not create the same evils." 491 U.S., at 799, n. 7. In Members of City Council of Los Angeles v. Taxpayers for Vincent, 466 U.S. 789, 808 (1984), the Court approved a prohibition on signs attached to utility poles which "did no more than eliminate the exact source of the evil it sought to remedy." In Heffron v. International Soc. for Krishna Consciousness, Inc., 452 U.S. 640, 652 (1981), the Court upheld a regulation prohibiting the sale or distribution on the state fairgrounds of any merchandise, including printed or written material, except from a fixed location, because that precisely served the State's interest in "avoiding congestion and maintaining the orderly movement of fair patrons on the fairgrounds."

In contrast to the laws approved in those cases, the law before us here enacts a broad prophylactic restriction which does not "respon[d] precisely to the substantive problem which legitimately concern[ed]" the State, Vincent, supra, at 810—namely (the only problem asserted by Colorado), the obstruction of access to health facilities. Such prophylactic restrictions in the First Amendment context—even when they are content-neutral—are not permissible. "Broad prophylactic rules in the area of free expression are suspect. . . . Precision of regulation must be the touchstone in an area so closely touching our most precious freedoms." NAACP v. Button, 371 U.S. 415, 438 (1963). In United States v. Grace, 461 U.S. 171 (1983), we declined to uphold a ban on certain expressive activity on the sidewalks surrounding the Supreme Court. The purpose of the restriction was the perfectly valid interest in security, just as the purpose of the restriction here is the perfectly valid interest in unobstructed access; and there, as here, the restriction furthered that interest—but it furthered it with insufficient precision and hence at excessive cost to the freedom of speech. There was, we said, "an insufficient nexus" between security and all the expressive activity that was banned, id., at 181—just as here there is an insufficient nexus between the assurance of access and forbidding unconsented communications within eight feet.4

Compare with these venerable and consistent descriptions of our First Amendment law the defenses that the Court makes to the contention that the present statute is overbroad. (To be sure, the Court is assuming its own invented state interest—protection of the "right to be let alone"—rather than the interest that the statute describes, but even so the statements are extraordinary.) "The fact," the Court says, "that the coverage of a statute is broader than the specific concern that led to its enactment is of no constitutional significance." Ante, at 26. That is true enough ordinarily, but it is not true with respect to restraints upon speech, which is what the doctrine of overbreadth is all about. (Of course it is also not true, thanks to one of the other proabortion "firsts" announced by the current Court, with respect to restrictions upon abortion, which—as our decision in Stenberg v. Carhart, post, p. ___, exemplifies—has been raised to First Amendment status, even as speech opposing abortion has been demoted from First Amendment status.) Again, the Court says that the overbreadth doctrine is not applicable because this law simply "does not 'ban' any signs, literature, or oral statements," but "merely regulates the places where communications may occur." Ante, at 27. I know of no precedent for the proposition that time, place, and manner restrictions are not subject to the doctrine of overbreadth. Our decision in Grace, supra, demonstrates the contrary: Restriction of speech on the sidewalks around the Supreme Court was invalidated because it went further than the needs of security justified. Surely New York City cannot require a parade permit and a security bond for any individual who carries a sign on the sidewalks of Fifth Avenue.

    The Court can derive no support for its approval of Colorado's overbroad prophylactic measure from our decision in Schenck. To be sure, there we rejected the argument that the court injunction on demonstrating within a fixed buffer zone around clinic entrances was unconstitutional because it banned even " 'peaceful nonobstructive demonstrations.' " 519 U.S., at 381. The Court upheld the injunction, however, only because the "District Court was entitled to conclude," "[b]ased on defendants' past conduct" and "the record in [that] case," that the specific defendants involved would, if permitted within the buffer zone, "continue to do what they had done before: aggressively follow and crowd individuals right up to the clinic door and then refuse to move, or purposefully mill around parking lot entrances in an effort to impede or block the progress of cars." Id., at 382. It is one thing to assume, as in Schenck, that a prophylactic injunction is necessary when the specific targets of that measure have demonstrated an inability or unwillingness to engage in protected speech activity without also engaging in conduct that the Constitution clearly does not protect. It is something else to assume that all those who wish to speak outside health care facilities across the State will similarly abuse their rights if permitted to exercise them. The First Amendment stands as a bar to exactly this type of prophylactic legislation. I cannot improve upon the Court's conclusion in Madsen that "it is difficult, indeed, to justify a prohibition on all uninvited approaches of persons seeking the services of the clinic, regardless of how peaceful the contact may be, without burdening more speech than necessary to prevent intimidation and to ensure access to the clinic. Absent evidence that the protestors' speech is independently proscribable (i.e., 'fighting words' or threats), or is so infused with violence as to be indistinguishable from a threat of physical harm, this provision cannot stand." 512 U.S., at 774 (citation omitted).

The foregoing discussion of overbreadth was written before the Court, in responding to Justice Kennedy, abandoned any pretense at compliance with that doctrine, and acknowledged—indeed, boasted—that the statute it approves "takes a prophylactic approach," ante, at 24, and adopts "[a] bright-line prophylactic rule," ante, at 25.5 I scarcely know how to respond to such an unabashed repudiation of our First Amendment doctrine. Prophylaxis is the antithesis of narrow tailoring, as the previously quoted passage from Button makes clear ("Broad prophylactic rules in the area of free expression are suspect. . . . Precision of regulation must be the touchstone in an area so closely touching our most precious freedoms." 371 U.S., at 438.) If the Court were going to make this concession, it could simply have dispensed with its earlier (unpersuasive) attempt to show that the statute was narrowly tailored. So one can add to the casualties of our whatever-it-takes proabortion jurisprudence the First Amendment doctrine of narrow tailoring and overbreadth. R. I. P.

* * *

Before it effectively threw in the towel on the narrow-tailoring point, the Court asserted the importance of taking into account " 'the place to which the regulations apply in determining whether these restrictions burden more speech than necessary.' " Ante, at 23 (quoting Madsen, supra, at 772). A proper regard for the "place" involved in this case should result in, if anything, a commitment by this Court to adhere to and rigorously enforce our speech-protective standards. The public forum involved here—the public spaces outside of health care facilities—has become, by necessity and by virtue of this Court's decisions, a forum of last resort for those who oppose abortion. The possibility of limiting abortion by legislative means—even abortion of a live-and-kicking child that is almost entirely out of the womb—has been rendered impossible by our decisions from Roe v. Wade, 410 U.S. 113 (1973), to Stenberg v. Carhart, post, p. ___. For those who share an abiding moral or religious conviction (or, for that matter, simply a biological appreciation) that abortion is the taking of a human life, there is no option but to persuade women, one by one, not to make that choice. And as a general matter, the most effective place, if not the only place, where that persuasion can occur, is outside the entrances to abortion facilities. By upholding these restrictions on speech in this place the Court ratifies the State's attempt to make even that task an impossible one.

Those whose concern is for the physical safety and security of clinic patients, workers, and doctors should take no comfort from today's decision. Individuals or groups intent on bullying or frightening women out of an abortion, or doctors out of performing that procedure, will not be deterred by Colorado's statute; bullhorns and screaming from eight feet away will serve their purposes well. But those who would accomplish their moral and religious objectives by peaceful and civil means, by trying to persuade individual women of the rightness of their cause, will be deterred; and that is not a good thing in a democracy. This Court once recognized, as the Framers surely did, that the freedom to speak and persuade is inseparable from, and antecedent to, the survival of self-government. The Court today rotates that essential safety valve on our democracy one-half turn to the right, and no one who seeks safe access to health care facilities in Colorado or elsewhere should feel that her security has by this decision been enhanced.

It is interesting to compare the present decision, which upholds an utterly bizarre proabortion "request to approach" provision of Colorado law, with Stenberg, post, p. ___, also announced today, which strikes down a live-birth abortion prohibition adopted by 30 States and twice passed by both Houses of Congress (though vetoed both times by the President). The present case disregards the State's own assertion of the purpose of its proabortion law, and posits instead a purpose that the Court believes will be more likely to render the law constitutional. Stenberg rejects the State's assertion of the very meaning of its antiabortion law, and declares instead a meaning that will render the law unconstitutional. The present case rejects overbreadth challenges to a proabortion law that regulates speech, on grounds that have no support in our prior jurisprudence and that instead amount to a total repudiation of the doctrine of overbreadth. Stenberg applies overbreadth analysis to an antiabortion law that has nothing to do with speech, even though until eight years ago overbreadth was unquestionably the exclusive preserve of the First Amendment. See Stenberg, post, at ___ (Thomas, J., dissenting); Janklow v. Planned Parenthood, Sioux Falls Clinic, 517 U.S. 1174, 1177–1181 (1996) (Scalia, J., dissenting from denial of cert.); Ada v. Guam Soc. of Obstetricians & Gynecologists, 506 U.S. 1011, 1013 (1992) (Scalia, J., dissenting from denial of cert.).

Does the deck seem stacked? You bet. As I have suggested throughout this opinion, today's decision is not an isolated distortion of our traditional constitutional principles, but is one of many aggressively proabortion novelties announced by the Court in recent years. See, e.g., Madsen v. Women's Health Center, Inc., 512 U.S. 753 (1994); Schenck v. Pro-Choice Network of Western N. Y., 519 U.S. 357 (1997); Thornburgh v. American College of Obstetricians and Gynecologists, 476 U.S. 747 (1986). Today's distortions, however, are particularly blatant. Restrictive views of the First Amendment that have been in dissent since the 1930's suddenly find themselves in the majority. "Uninhibited, robust, and wide open" debate is replaced by the power of the state to protect an unheard-of "right to be let alone" on the public streets. I dissent.

Notes to Justice Scalia's dissent in Hill v. Colorado (June 28, 2000)

1. The Court responds that statutes which restrict categories of speech—as opposed to subject matter or viewpoint—are constitutionally worrisome only if a "significant number of communications, raising the same problem that the statute was enacted to solve, . . . fall outside the statute's scope, while others fall inside." Ante, at 18–19. I am not sure that is correct, but let us assume, for the sake of argument, that it is. The Court then proceeds to assert that "[t]he statutory phrases, 'oral protest, education, or counseling,' distinguish speech activities likely to" present the problem of "harassment, . . . nuisance, . . . persistent importuning, . . . following, . . . dogging, and . . . implied threat

of physical touching," from "speech activities [such as my example of 'happy speech'] that are most unlikely to have those consequences," ibid. Well. That may work for "oral protest"; but it is beyond imagining why "education" and "counseling" are especially likely, rather than especially unlikely, to involve such conduct. (Socrates was something of a noodge, but even he did not go that far.) Unless, of course, "education" and "counseling" are code words for efforts to dissuade women from abortion—in which event the statute would not be viewpoint neutral, which the Court concedes makes it invalid.

2. The Court's contention that the statute is content-neutral because it is not a " 'regulation of speech' " but a "regulation of the places where some speech may occur," ante, at 14 (quoting Ward v. Rock Against Racism, 491 U.S. 781, 791 (1989)), is simply baffling. First, because the proposition that a restriction upon the places where speech may occur is not a restriction upon speech is both absurd and contradicted by innumerable cases. See, e.g., Madsen v. Women's Health Center, Inc., 512 U.S. 753 (1994); Burson v. Freeman, 504 U.S. 191 (1992); Frisby v. Schultz, 487 U.S. 474 (1988); Boos v. Barry, 485 U.S. 312 (1988); Heffron v. International Soc. for Krishna Consciousness, Inc., 452 U.S. 640 (1981); Carey v. Brown, 447 U.S. 455 (1980); Grayned v. City of Rockford, 408 U.S. 104 (1972); Police Dept. of Chicago v. Mosley, 408 U.S. 92 (1972). And second, because the fact that a restriction is framed as a "regulation of the places where some speech may occur" has nothing whatever to do with whether the restriction is content-neutral—which is why Boos held to be content-based the ban on displaying, within 500 feet of foreign embassies, banners designed to " 'bring into public odium any foreign government.' " 485 U.S., at 316.

3. I do not disagree with the Court that "our cases have repeatedly recognized the interests of unwilling listeners" in locations, such as public conveyances, where " 'the degree of captivity makes it impractical for the unwilling viewer or auditor to avoid exposure,' " ante, at 13 (quoting Erzoznick v. City of Jacksonville, 422 U.S. 205 (1975)). But we have never made the absurd suggestion that a pedestrian is a "captive" of the speaker who seeks to address him on the public sidewalks, where he may simply walk quickly by. Erzoznick itself, of course, invalidated a prohibition on the showing of films containing nudity on screens visible from the street, noting that "the burden normally falls upon the viewer to 'avoid further bombardment of [his] sensibilities simply by averting [his] eyes.' " Id., at 210—211 (quoting Cohen v. California, 403 U.S. 15, 21 (1971).

4. The Court's suggestion, ante, at 25, that the restrictions imposed by the Colorado ban are unobjectionable because they "interfer[e] far less with a speaker's ability to communicate," than did the regulations involved in Frisby and Heffron, and in cases requiring "silence" outside of a hospital (by which I presume the Court means Madsen v. Women's Health Center, Inc., 512 U.S. 753 (1994)), misses the point of narrow-tailoring analysis. We do not compare restrictions on speech to some Platonic ideal of speech restrictiveness, or to each other. Rather, our First Amendment doctrine requires us to consider whether the regulation in question burdens substantially more speech than necessary to achieve the particular interest the government has identified

and asserted. Ward, 491 U.S., at 799. In each of the instances the Court cites, we concluded that the challenged regulation contained the precision that our cases require and that Colorado's statute (which the Court itself calls "prophylactic," ante, at 24—25) manifestly lacks.

5. Of course the Court greatly understates the scope of the prophylaxis, saying that "the statute's prophylactic aspect is justified by the great difficulty of protecting, say, a pregnant woman from physical harassment with legal rules that focus exclusively on the individual impact of each instance of behavior," ante, at 24—25. But the statute prevents the "physically harassing" act of (shudder!) approaching within closer than eight feet not only when it is directed against pregnant women, but also (just to be safe) when it is directed against 300-pound, male, and unpregnant truck drivers—surely a distinction that is not "difficult to make accurately," ante, at 25.

Americans with Disabilities Act (Golf): Justice Scalia's dissent in PGA Tour, Inc. v. Casey Martin (May 29, 2001)

Justice Scalia, with whom Justice Thomas joins, dissenting.

In my view today's opinion exercises a benevolent compassion that the law does not place it within our power to impose. The judgment distorts the text of Title III, the structure of the ADA, and common sense. I respectfully dissent.

I

The Court holds that a professional sport is a place of public accommodation and that respondent is a "custome[r]" of "competition" when he practices his profession. Ante, at 17. It finds, ante, at 18, that this strange conclusion is compelled by the "literal text" of Title III of the Americans with Disabilities Act of 1990 (ADA), 42 U.S.C. § 12101 et seq., by the "expansive purpose" of the ADA, and by the fact that Title II of the Civil Rights Act of 1964, 42 U.S.C. § 2000a(a), has been applied to an amusement park and public golf courses. I disagree.

The ADA has three separate titles: Title I covers employment discrimination, Title II covers discrimination by government entities, and Title III covers discrimination by places of public accommodation. Title II is irrelevant to this case. Title I protects only "employees" of employers who have 15 or more employees, §§12112(a), 12111(5)(A). It does not protect independent contractors. See, e.g., Birchem v. Knights of Columbus, 116 F.3d 310, 312—313 (CA8 1997); cf. Nationwide Mut. Ins. Co. v. Darden, 503 U.S. 318, 322—323 (1992). Respondent claimed employment discrimination under Title I, but the District Court found him to be an independent contractor rather than an employee.

Respondent also claimed protection under §12182 of Title III. That section applies only to particular places and persons. The place must be a "place of public accommodation," and the person must be an "individual" seeking "enjoyment of the goods, services, facilities, privileges, advantages, or accommodations" of the covered place. §12182(a). Of course a court indiscriminately invoking the "sweeping" and "expansive" purposes of the ADA, ante, at 13, 18, could argue that when a place of public accommodation denied any "individual," on the basis of his disability, anything that might be called a "privileg[e]," the individual has a valid Title III claim. Cf. ante, at 14. On such an interpretation, the employees and independent contractors of every place of public accommodation come within Title III: The employee enjoys the "privilege" of employment, the contractor the "privilege" of the contract.

For many reasons, Title III will not bear such an interpretation. The provision of Title III at issue here (§12182, its principal provision) is a public-accommodation law, and it is the traditional understanding of public-accommodation laws that they provide rights for customers. "At common law, innkeepers, smiths, and others who made profession of a public employment, were prohibited from refusing, without good reason, to serve a customer." Hurley v. Irish-American Gay, Lesbian and Bisexual Group of Boston, Inc., 515 U.S. 557, 571 (1995) (internal quotation marks omitted). See also Heart of Atlanta Motel, Inc. v. United States, 379 U.S. 241 (1964). This understanding is clearly reflected in the text of Title III itself. Section 12181(7) lists 12 specific types of entities that qualify as "public accommodations," with a follow-on expansion that makes it clear what the "enjoyment of the goods, services, etc." of those entities consists of—and it plainly envisions that the person "enjoying" the "public accommodation" will be a customer. For example, Title III is said to cover an "auditorium" or "other place of public gathering," §12181(7)(D). Thus, "gathering" is the distinctive enjoyment derived from an auditorium; the persons "gathering" at an auditorium are presumably covered by Title III, but those contracting to clean the auditorium are not. Title III is said to cover a "zoo" or "other place of recreation," §12181(7)(I). The persons "recreat[ing]" at a "zoo" are presumably covered, but the animal handlers bringing in the latest panda are not. The one place where Title III specifically addresses discrimination by places of public accommodation through "contractual" arrangements, it makes clear that discrimination against the other party to the contract is not covered, but only discrimination against "clients or customers of the covered public accommodation that enters into the contractual, licensing or other arrangement." §12182(b)(1)(A)(iv). And finally, the regulations promulgated by the Department of Justice reinforce the conclusion that Title III's protections extend only to customers. "The purpose of the ADA's public accommodations requirements," they say, "is to ensure accessibility to the goods offered by a public accommodation." 28 CFR, Ch. 1, pt. 36, App. B, p. 650 (2000). Surely this has nothing to do with employees and independent contractors.

If there were any doubt left that §12182 covers only clients and customers of places of public accommodation, it is eliminated by the fact that a contrary interpretation would make a muddle of the ADA as a whole. The words of Title III must be read "in their context and with a view to their place in the overall statutory scheme." Davis v. Michigan Dept. of Treasury, 489 U.S. 803, 809 (1989). Congress expressly excluded employers of fewer than 15 employees from Title I. The mom-and-pop grocery store or laundromat need not worry about altering the nonpublic areas of its place of business to accommodate handicapped employees—or about the litigation that failure to do so will invite. Similarly, since independent contractors are not covered by Title I, the small business (or the large one, for that matter) need not worry about making special accommodations for the painters, electricians, and other independent workers whose services are contracted for from time to time. It is an entirely unreasonable interpretation of the statute to say that these exemptions so carefully crafted in Title I are entirely eliminated by Title III (for the many businesses that are places of public accommodation) because employees and independent contractors "enjoy" the employment and contracting that such places provide. The only distinctive feature of places of public accommodation is that they accommodate the public, and Congress could have no conceivable reason for according the employees and independent contractors of such businesses protections that employees and independent contractors of other businesses do not enjoy.

The United States apparently agrees that employee claims are not cognizable under Title III, see Brief for United States as Amicus Curiae 18—19, n. 17, but despite the implications of its own regulations, see 28 CFR, Ch. 1, pt. 36, App. B, p. 650 (2000), appears to believe (though it does not explicitly state) that claims of independent contractors are cognizable. In a discussion littered with entirely vague statements from the legislative history, cf. ante, at 12, the United States argues that Congress presumably wanted independent contractors with private entities covered under Title III because independent contractors with governmental entities are covered by Title II, see Brief for United States as Amicus Curiae 18, and n. 17—a line of reasoning that does not commend itself to the untutored intellect. But since the United States does not provide (and I cannot conceive of) any possible construction of the terms of Title III that will exclude employees while simultaneously covering independent contractors, its concession regarding employees effectively concedes independent contractors as well. Title III applies only to customers.

The Court, for its part, assumes that conclusion for the sake of argument, ante, at 17, but pronounces respondent to be a "customer" of the PGA TOUR or of the golf courses on which it is played. That seems to me quite incredible. The PGA TOUR is a professional sporting event, staged for the entertainment of a live and TV audience, the receipts from whom (the TV audience's admission price is paid by advertisers) pay the expenses of the tour, including the cash prizes for the winning golfers. The professional golfers on the tour are no more "enjoying" (the statutory term) the entertainment that the tour provides, or the facilities of the golf courses on which it is held, than professional baseball players "enjoy" the baseball games in which they play or the facilities of Yankee Stadium. To be sure, professional ballplayers participate in the games, and use the ballfields, but no one in his right mind would think that they are customers of the American League or of Yankee Stadium. They are themselves the entertainment that the customers pay to watch. And professional golfers are no different. It makes not a bit of difference, insofar as their "customer" status is concerned, that the remuneration for their performance (unlike most of the remuneration for ballplayers) is not fixed but contingent—viz., the purses for the winners in the various events, and the compensation from product endorsements that consistent winners are assured. The compensation of many independent contractors is contingent upon their success—real estate brokers, for example, or insurance salesmen.

As the Court points out, the ADA specifically identifies golf courses as one of the covered places of public accommodation. See §12181(7)(L) ("a gymnasium, health spa, bowling alley, golf course, or other place of exercise or recreation"); and the distinctive "goo[d], servic[e], facilit[y], privileg[e], advantag[e], or accommodatio[n]" identified by that provision as distinctive to that category of place of public accommodation is "exercise or recreation." Respondent did not seek to "exercise" or "recreate" at the PGA TOUR events; he sought to make money (which is why he is called a professional golfer). He was not a customer buying recreation or entertainment; he was a professional athlete selling it. That is the reason (among others) the Court's reliance upon Civil Rights Act cases like Daniel v. Paul, 395 U.S. 298 (1969), see ante, at 18-19, is misplaced. A professional golfer's practicing his profession is not comparable to John Q. Public's frequenting "a 232-acre amusement area with swimming, boating, sun bathing, picnicking, miniature golf, dancing facilities, and a snack bar." Daniel, supra, at 301.

The Court relies heavily upon the Q-School. It says that petitioner offers the golfing public the "privilege" of "competing in the Q-School and playing in the tours; indeed, the former is a privilege for which thousands of individuals from the general public pay, and the latter is one for which they vie." Ante, at 14—15. But the Q-School is no more a "privilege" offered for the general public's "enjoyment" than is the California Bar Exam.[1] It is a competition for entry into the PGA TOUR—an open tryout, no different in principle from open casting for a movie or stage production, or walk-on tryouts for other professional sports, such as baseball. See, e.g., Amateurs Join Pros for New Season of HBO's "Sopranos," Detroit News, Dec. 22, 2000, p. 2 (20,000 attend open casting for "The Sopranos"); Bill Zack, Atlanta Braves, Sporting News, Feb. 6, 1995 (1,300 would-be players attended an open tryout for the Atlanta Braves). It may well be that some amateur golfers enjoy trying to make the grade, just as some amateur actors may enjoy auditions, and amateur baseball players may enjoy open tryouts (I hesitate to say that amateur lawyers may enjoy taking the California Bar Exam). But the purpose of holding those tryouts is not to provide entertainment; it is to hire. At bottom, open tryouts for performances to be held at a place of public accommodation are no different from open bidding on contracts to cut the grass at a place of public accommodation, or open applications for any job at a place of public accommodation. Those bidding, those applying—and those trying out—are not converted into customers. By the Court's reasoning, a business exists not only to sell goods and services to the public, but to provide the "privilege" of employment to the public; wherefore it follows, like night the day, that everyone who seeks a job is a customer.[2]

II

Having erroneously held that Title III applies to the "customers" of professional golf who consist of its practitioners, the Court then erroneously answers—or to be accurate simply ignores—a second question. The ADA requires covered businesses to make such reasonable modifications of "policies, practices, or procedures" as are necessary to "afford" goods, services, and privileges to individuals with disabilities; but it explicitly does not require "modifications [that] would fundamentally alter the nature" of the goods, services, and privileges. §12182(b)(2)(A)(ii). In other words, disabled individuals must be given access to the same goods, services, and privileges that others enjoy. The regulations state that Title III "does not require a public accommodation to alter its inventory to include accessible or special goods with accessibility features that are designed for, or facilitate use by, individuals with disabilities." 28 CFR § 36.307 (2000); see also 28 CFR, ch. 1, pt. 36, App. B, p. 650 (2000). As one Court of Appeals has explained:

"The common sense of the statute is that the content of the goods or services offered by a place of public accommodation is not regulated. A camera store may not refuse to sell cameras to a disabled person, but it is not required to stock cameras specially designed for such persons. Had Congress purposed to impose so enormous a burden on the retail sector of the economy and so vast a supervisory responsibility on the federal courts, we think it would have made its intention clearer and would at least have imposed some standards. It is hardly a feasible judicial function to decide whether shoestores should sell single shoes to one-legged persons and if so at what price, or how many Braille books the Borders or Barnes and Noble bookstore chains should stock in each of their stores." Doe v. Mutual of Omaha Ins. Co., 179 F.3d 557, 560 (CA7 1999).

Since this is so, even if respondent here is a consumer of the "privilege" of the PGA TOUR competition, see ante, at 14, I see no basis for considering whether the rules of that competition must be altered. It is as irrelevant to the PGA TOUR's compliance with the statute whether walking is essential to the game of golf as it is to the shoe store's compliance whether "pairness" is essential to the nature of shoes. If a shoe store wishes to sell shoes only in pairs it may; and if a golf tour (or a golf course) wishes to provide only walk-around golf, it may. The PGA TOUR cannot deny respondent access to that game because of his disability, but it need not provide him a game different (whether in its essentials or in its details) from that offered to everyone else.

Since it has held (or assumed) professional golfers to be customers "enjoying" the "privilege" that consists of PGA TOUR golf; and since it inexplicably regards the rules of PGA TOUR golf as merely "policies, practices, or procedures" by which access to PGA TOUR golf is provided, the Court must then confront the question whether respondent's requested modification of the supposed policy, practice, or procedure of walking would "fundamentally alter the nature" of the PGA TOUR game, §12182(b)(2)(A)(ii). The Court attacks this "fundamental alteration" analysis by asking two questions: first, whether the "essence" or an "essential aspect" of the sport of golf has been altered; and second, whether the change, even if not essential to the game, would give the disabled player an advantage over others and thereby "fundamentally alter the character of the competition." Ante, at 20-21. It answers no to both.

Before considering the Court's answer to the first question, it is worth pointing out that the assumption which underlies that question is false. Nowhere is it writ that PGA TOUR golf must be classic "essential" golf. Why cannot the PGA TOUR, if it wishes, promote a new game, with distinctive rules (much as the American League promotes a game of baseball in which the pitcher's turn at the plate can be taken by a "designated hitter")? If members of the public do not like the new rules—if they feel that these rules do not truly test the individual's skill at "real golf" (or the team's skill at "real baseball") they can withdraw their patronage. But the rules are the rules. They are (as in all games) entirely arbitrary, and there is no basis on which anyone—not even the Supreme Court of the United States—can pronounce one or another of them to be "nonessential" if the rulemaker (here the PGA TOUR) deems it to be essential.

If one assumes, however, that the PGA TOUR has some legal obligation to play classic, Platonic golf—and if one assumes the correctness of all the other wrong turns the Court has made to get to this point—then we Justices must confront what is indeed an awesome responsibility. It has been rendered the solemn duty of the Supreme Court of the United States, laid upon it by Congress in pursuance of the Federal Government's power "[t]o regulate Commerce with foreign Nations, and among the several States," U.S. Const., Art. I, §8, cl. 3, to decide What Is Golf. I am sure that the Framers of the Constitution, aware of the 1457 edict of King James II of Scotland prohibiting golf because it interfered with the practice of archery, fully expected that sooner or later the paths of golf and government, the law and the links, would once again cross, and that the judges of this august Court would some day have to wrestle with that age-old jurisprudential question, for which their years of study in the law have so well prepared them: Is someone riding around a golf course from shot to shot really a golfer? The answer, we learn, is yes. The Court ultimately concludes, and it will henceforth be the Law of the Land, that walking is not a "fundamental" aspect of golf.

Either out of humility or out of self-respect (one or the other) the Court should decline to answer this incredibly difficult and incredibly silly question. To say that something is "essential" is ordinarily to say that it is necessary to the achievement of a certain object. But since it is the very nature of a game to have no object except amusement (that is what distinguishes games from productive activity), it is quite impossible to say that any of a game's arbitrary rules is "essential." Eighteen-hole golf courses, 10-foot-high basketball hoops, 90-foot baselines, 100-yard football fields—all are arbitrary and none is essential. The only support for any of them is tradition and (in more modern times) insistence by what has come to be regarded as the ruling body of the sport—both of which factors support the PGA TOUR's position in the present case. (Many, indeed, consider walking to be the central feature of the game of golf—hence Mark Twain's classic criticism of the sport: "a good walk spoiled.") I suppose there is some point at which the rules of a well-known game are changed to such a degree that no reasonable person would call it the same game. If the PGA TOUR competitors were required to dribble a large, inflated ball and put it through a round hoop, the game could no longer reasonably be called golf. But this criterion—destroying recognizability as the same generic game—is surely not the test of "essentialness" or "fundamentalness" that the Court applies, since it apparently thinks that merely changing the diameter of the cup might "fundamentally alter" the game of golf, ante, at 20.

Having concluded that dispensing with the walking rule would not violate federal-Platonic "golf" (and, implicitly, that it is federal-Platonic golf, and no other, that the PGA TOUR can insist upon) the Court moves on to the second part of its test: the competitive effects of waiving this nonessential rule. In this part of its analysis, the Court first finds that the effects of the change are "mitigated" by the fact that in the game of golf weather, a "lucky bounce," and "pure chance" provide different conditions for each competitor and individual ability may not "be the sole determinant of the outcome." Ante, at 25. I guess that is why those who follow professional golfing consider Jack Nicklaus the luckiest golfer of all time, only to be challenged of late by the phenomenal luck of Tiger Woods. The Court's empiricism is unpersuasive. "Pure chance" is randomly distributed among the players, but allowing respondent to use a cart gives him a "lucky" break every time he plays. Pure chance also only matters at the margin—a stroke here or there; the cart substantially improves this respondent's competitive prospects beyond a couple of strokes. But even granting that there are significant nonhuman variables affecting competition, that fact does not justify adding another variable that always favors one player.

In an apparent effort to make its opinion as narrow as possible, the Court relies upon the District Court's finding that even with a cart, respondent will be at least as fatigued as everyone else. Ante, at 28. This, the Court says, proves that competition will not be affected. Far from thinking that reliance on this finding cabins the effect of today's opinion, I think it will prove to be its most expansive and destructive feature. Because step one of the Court's two-part inquiry into whether a requested change in a sport will "fundamentally alter [its] nature," §12182(b)(2)(A)(ii), consists of an utterly unprincipled ontology of sports (pursuant to which the Court is not even sure whether golf's "essence" requires a 3-inch hole), there is every reason to think that in future cases involving requests for special treatment by would-be athletes the second step of the analysis will be determinative. In resolving that second step—determining whether waiver of the "nonessential" rule will have an impermissible "competitive effect"—by measuring the athletic capacity of the requesting individual, and asking whether the special dispensation would do no more than place him on a par (so to speak) with other competitors, the Court guarantees that future cases of this sort will have to be decided on the basis of individualized factual findings. Which means that future cases of this sort will be numerous, and a rich source of lucrative litigation. One can envision the parents of a Little League player with attention deficit disorder trying to convince a judge that their son's disability makes it at least 25% more difficult to hit a pitched ball. (If they are successful, the only thing that could prevent a court order giving the kid four strikes would be a judicial determination that, in baseball, three strikes are metaphysically necessary, which is quite absurd.)

The statute, of course, provides no basis for this individualized analysis that is the Court's last step on a long and misguided journey. The statute seeks to assure that a disabled person's disability will not deny him equal access to (among other things) competitive sporting events—not that his disability will not deny him an equal chance to win competitive sporting events. The latter is quite impossible, since the very nature of competitive sport is the measurement, by uniform rules, of unevenly distributed excellence. This unequal distribution is precisely what determines the winners and losers—and artificially to "even out" that distribution, by giving one or another player exemption from a rule that emphasizes his particular weakness, is to destroy the game. That is why the "handicaps" that are customary in social games of golf—which, by adding strokes to the scores of the good players and subtracting them from scores of the bad ones, "even out" the varying abilities—are not used in professional golf. In the Court's world, there is one set of rules that is "fair with respect to the able-bodied" but "individualized" rules, mandated by the ADA, for "talented but disabled athletes." Ante, at 29. The ADA mandates no such ridiculous thing. Agility, strength, speed, balance, quickness of mind, steadiness of nerves, intensity of concentration—these talents are not evenly distributed. No wild-eyed dreamer has ever suggested that the managing bodies of the competitive sports that test precisely these qualities should try to take account of the uneven distribution of God-given gifts when writing and enforcing the rules of competition. And I have no doubt Congress did not authorize misty-eyed judicial supervision of such a revolution.

* * *

My belief that today's judgment is clearly in error should not be mistaken for a belief that the PGA TOUR clearly ought not allow respondent to use a golf cart. That is a close question, on which even those who compete in the PGA TOUR are apparently divided; but it is a different question from the one before the Court. Just as it is a different question whether the Little League ought to give disabled youngsters a fourth strike, or some other waiver from the rules that makes up for their disabilities. In both cases, whether they ought to do so depends upon (1) how central to the game that they have organized (and over whose rules they are the master) they deem the waived provision to be, and (2) how competitive—how strict a test of raw athletic ability in all aspects of the competition—they want their game to be. But whether Congress has said they must do so depends upon the answers to the legal questions I have discussed above—not upon what this Court sententiously decrees to be "decent, tolerant,

[and] progressive," ante, at 13 (quoting Board of Trustees of Univ. of Ala. v. Garrett, 531 U.S. 356, 375 (2001) (Kennedy, J., concurring)).

And it should not be assumed that today's decent, tolerant, and progressive judgment will, in the long run, accrue to the benefit of sports competitors with disabilities. Now that it is clear courts will review the rules of sports for "fundamentalness," organizations that value their autonomy have every incentive to defend vigorously the necessity of every regulation. They may still be second-guessed in the end as to the Platonic requirements of the sport, but they will assuredly lose if they have at all wavered in their enforcement. The lesson the PGA TOUR and other sports organizations should take from this case is to make sure that the same written rules are set forth for all levels of play, and never voluntarily to grant any modifications. The second lesson is to end open tryouts. I doubt that, in the long run, even disabled athletes will be well served by these incentives that the Court has created.

Complaints about this case are not "properly directed to Congress," ante, at 27-28, n. 51. They are properly directed to this Court's Kafkaesque determination that professional sports organizations, and the fields they rent for their exhibitions, are "places of public accommodation" to the competing athletes, and the athletes themselves "customers" of the organization that pays them; its Alice in Wonderland determination that there are such things as judicially determinable "essential" and "nonessential" rules of a made-up game; and its Animal Farm determination that fairness and the ADA mean that everyone gets

to play by individualized rules which will assure that no one's lack of ability (or at least no one's lack of ability

so pronounced that it amounts to a disability) will be a handicap. The year was 2001, and "everybody was finally equal." K. Vonnegut, Harrison Bergeron, in Animal Farm and Related Readings 129 (1997).

Notes

1. The California Bar Exam is covered by the ADA, by the way, because a separate provision of Title III applies to "examinations . . . related to applications, licensing, certification, or credentialing for secondary or post-secondary education, professional, or trade purposes." 42 U.S.C. § 12189. If open tryouts were "privileges" under §12182, and participants in the tryouts "customers," §12189 would have been unnecessary.

2. The Court suggests that respondent is not an independent contractor because he "play[s] at [his] own pleasure," and is not subject to PGA TOUR control "over [his] manner of performance," ante, at 18 n. 33. But many independent contractors—composers of movie music, portrait artists, script writers, and even (some would say) plumbers—retain at least as much control over when and how they work as does respondent, who agrees to play in a minimum of 15 of the designated PGA TOUR events, and to play by the rules that the PGA TOUR specifies. Cf. Community for Creative Non-Violence v. Reid, 490 U.S. 730, 751-753 (1989) (discussing independent contractor status of a sculptor). Moreover, although, as the Court suggests in the same footnote, in rare cases a PGA TOUR winner will choose to forgo the prize money (in order, for example, to preserve amateur status necessary for continuing participation in college play) he is

contractually entitled to the prize money if he demands it, which is all that a contractual relationship requires.

Death Penalty: Justice Scalia's dissent in Atkins v. Virginia (June 20, 2002)

Justice Scalia, with whom the Chief Justice and Justice Thomas join, dissenting.

Today's decision is the pinnacle of our Eighth Amendment death-is-different jurisprudence. Not only does it, like all of that jurisprudence, find no support in the text or history of the Eighth Amendment; it does not even have support in current social attitudes regarding the conditions that render an otherwise just death penalty inappropriate. Seldom has an opinion of this Court rested so obviously upon nothing but the personal views of its members.

I

I begin with a brief restatement of facts that are abridged by the Court but important to understanding this case. After spending the day drinking alcohol and smoking marijuana, petitioner Daryl Renard Atkins and a partner in crime drove to a convenience store, intending to rob a customer. Their victim was Eric Nesbitt, an airman from Langley Air Force Base, whom they abducted, drove to a nearby automated teller machine, and forced to withdraw $200. They then drove him to a deserted area, ignoring his pleas to leave him unharmed. According to the co-conspirator, whose testimony the jury evidently credited, Atkins ordered Nesbitt out of the vehicle and, after he had taken only a few steps, shot him one, two, three, four, five, six, seven, eight times in the thorax, chest, abdomen, arms, and legs.

The jury convicted Atkins of capital murder. At resentencing (the Virginia Supreme Court affirmed his conviction but remanded for resentencing because the trial court had used an improper verdict form, 257 Va. 160, 179, 510 S. E. 2d 445, 457 (1999)), the jury heard extensive evidence of petitioner's alleged mental retardation. A psychologist testified that petitioner was mildly mentally retarded with an IQ of 59, that he was a "slow learne[r]," App. 444, who showed a "lack of success in pretty much every domain of his life," id., at 442, and that he had an "impaired" capacity to appreciate the criminality of his conduct and to conform his conduct to the law, id., at 453. Petitioner's family members offered additional evidence in support of his mental retardation claim (e.g., that petitioner is a "follower," id., at 421). The State contested the evidence of retardation and presented testimony of a psychologist who found "absolutely no evidence other than the IQ score ... indicating that [petitioner] was in the least bit mentally retarded" and concluded that petitioner was "of average intelligence, at least." Id., at 476.

The jury also heard testimony about petitioner's 16 prior felony convictions for robbery, attempted robbery, abduction, use of a firearm, and maiming. Id., at 491–522. The victims of these offenses provided graphic depictions of petitioner's violent tendencies: He hit one over the head with a beer bottle, id., at 406; he slapped a gun across another victim's face, clubbed her in the head with it, knocked her to the ground, and then helped her up, only to shoot her in the stomach, id., at 411–413. The jury sentenced petitioner to death. The Supreme Court of Virginia affirmed petitioner's sentence. 260 Va. 375, 534 S. E. 2d 312 (2000).

II

As the foregoing history demonstrates, petitioner's mental retardation was a central issue at sentencing. The jury concluded, however, that his alleged retardation was not a compelling reason to exempt him from the death penalty in light of the brutality of his crime and his long demonstrated propensity for violence. "In upsetting this particularized judgment on the basis of a constitutional absolute," the Court concludes that no one who is even slightly mentally retarded can have sufficient "moral responsibility to be subjected to capital punishment for any crime. As a sociological and moral conclusion that is implausible; and it is doubly implausible as an interpretation of the United States Constitution." Thompson v. Oklahoma, 487 U.S. 815, 863–864 (1988) (Scalia, J., dissenting).

Under our Eighth Amendment jurisprudence, a punishment is "cruel and unusual" if it falls within one of two categories: "those modes or acts of punishment that had been considered cruel and unusual at the time that the Bill of Rights was adopted," Ford v. Wainwright, 477 U.S. 399, 405 (1986), and modes of punishment that are inconsistent with modern "standards of decency," as evinced by objective indicia, the most important of which is "legislation enacted by the country's legislatures," Penry v. Lynaugh, 492 U.S. 302, 330–331 (1989).

The Court makes no pretense that execution of the mildly mentally retarded would have been considered "cruel and unusual" in 1791. Only the severely or profoundly mentally retarded, commonly known as "idiots," enjoyed any special status under the law at that time. They, like lunatics, suffered a "deficiency in will" rendering them unable to tell right from wrong. 4 W. Blackstone, Commentaries on the Laws of England 24 (1769) (hereinafter Blackstone); see also Penry, 492 U.S., at 331–332 ("[T]he term 'idiot' was generally used to describe persons who had a total lack of reason or understanding, or an inability to distinguish between good and evil"); id., at 333 (citing sources indicating that idiots generally had an IQ of 25 or below, which would place them within the "profound" or "severe" range of mental retardation under modern standards); 2 A. Fitz-Herbert, Natura Brevium 233B (9th ed. 1794) (originally published 1534) (An idiot is "such a person who cannot account or number twenty pence, nor can tell who was his father or mother, nor how old he is, etc., so as it may appear that he hath no understanding of reason what shall be for his profit, or what for his loss"). Due to their incompetence, idiots were "excuse[d] from the guilt, and of course from the punishment, of any criminal action committed under such deprivation of the senses." 4 Blackstone 25; see also Penry, supra, at 331. Instead, they were often committed to civil confinement or made wards of the State, thereby preventing them from "go[ing] loose, to the terror of the king's subjects." 4 Blackstone 25; see also S. Brakel, J. Parry, & B. Weiner, The Mentally

Disabled and the Law 12—14 (3d ed. 1985); 1 Blackstone 292—296; 1 M. Hale, Pleas of the Crown 33 (1st Am. ed. 1847). Mentally retarded offenders with less severe impairments–those who were not "idiots"–suffered criminal prosecution and punishment, including capital punishment. See, e.g., I. Ray, Medical Jurisprudence of Insanity 65, 87—92 (W. Overholser ed. 1962) (recounting the 1834 trial and execution in Concord, New Hampshire, of an apparent "imbecile"–imbecility being a less severe form of retardation which "differs from idiocy in the circumstance that while in [the idiot] there is an utter destitution of every thing like reason, [imbeciles] possess some intellectual capacity, though infinitely less than is possessed by the great mass of mankind"); A. Highmore, Law of Idiocy and Lunacy 200 (1807) ("The great difficulty in all these cases, is to determine where a person shall be said to be so far deprived of his sense and memory as not to have any of his actions imputed to him: or where notwithstanding some defects of this kind he still appears to have so much reason and understanding as will make him accountable for his actions …").

  The Court is left to argue, therefore, that execution of the mildly retarded is inconsistent with the "evolving standards of decency that mark the progress of a maturing society." Trop v. Dulles, 356 U.S. 86, 101 (1958) (plurality opinion) (Warren, C. J.). Before today, our opinions consistently emphasized that Eighth Amendment judgments regarding the existence of social "standards" "should be informed by objective factors to the maximum possible extent" and "should not be, or appear to be, merely the subjective views of individual Justices." Coker v. Georgia, 433 U.S. 584, 592 (1977) (plurality opinion); see also Stanford, supra, at 369; McCleskey v. Kemp, 481 U.S. 279, 300 (1987); Enmund v. Florida, 458 U.S. 782, 788 (1982). "First" among these objective factors are the "statutes passed by society's elected representatives," Stanford v. Kentucky, 492 U.S. 361, 370 (1989); because it "will rarely if ever be the case that the Members of this Court will have a better sense of the evolution in views of the American people than do their elected representatives," Thompson, supra, at 865 (Scalia, J., dissenting).

  The Court pays lipservice to these precedents as it miraculously extracts a "national consensus" forbidding execution of the mentally retarded, ante, at 12, from the fact that 18 States–less than half (47%) of the 38 States that permit capital punishment (for whom the issue exists)–have very recently enacted legislation barring execution of the mentally retarded. Even that 47% figure is a distorted one. If one is to say, as the Court does today, that all executions of the mentally retarded are so morally repugnant as to violate our national "standards of decency," surely the "consensus" it points to must be one that has set its righteous face against all such executions. Not 18 States, but only seven–18% of death penalty jurisdictions–have legislation of that scope. Eleven of those that the Court counts enacted statutes prohibiting execution of mentally retarded defendants convicted after, or convicted of crimes committed after, the effective date of the legislation;1 those already on death row, or consigned there before the statute's effective date, or even (in those States using the date of the crime as the criterion of retroactivity) tried in the future for murders committed many years ago, could be put to death. That is not a statement of absolute moral repugnance, but one of current preference between two tolerable approaches. Two of these States permit execution of the mentally retarded in other situations as well: Kansas apparently permits execution of all except the severely mentally retarded; 2 New York permits execution of the mentally retarded who commit murder in a correctional facility. N. Y. Crim. Proc. Law §400.27.12(d) (McKinney 2001); N. Y. Penal Law §125.27 (McKinney 202).

But let us accept, for the sake of argument, the Court's faulty count. That bare number of States alone—18—should be enough to convince any reasonable person that no "national consensus" exists. How is it possible that agreement among 47% of the death penalty jurisdictions amounts to "consensus"? Our prior cases have generally required a much higher degree of agreement before finding a punishment cruel and unusual on "evolving standards" grounds. In Coker, supra, at 595—596, we proscribed the death penalty for rape of an adult woman after finding that only one jurisdiction, Georgia, authorized such a punishment. In Enmund, supra, at 789, we invalidated the death penalty for mere participation in a robbery in which an accomplice took a life, a punishment not permitted in 28 of the death penalty States (78%). In Ford, 477 U.S., at 408, we supported the common-law prohibition of execution of the insane with the observation that "[t]his ancestral legacy has not outlived its time," since not a single State authorizes such punishment. In Solem v. Helm, 463 U.S. 277, 300 (1983), we invalidated a life sentence without parole under a recidivist statute by which the criminal "was treated more severely than he would have been in any other State." What the Court calls evidence of "consensus" in the present case (a fudged 47%) more closely resembles evidence that we found inadequate to establish consensus in earlier cases. Tison v. Arizona, 481 U.S. 137, 154, 158 (1987), upheld a state law authorizing capital punishment for major participation in a felony with reckless indifference to life where only 11 of the 37 death penalty States (30%) prohibited such punishment. Stanford, supra, at 372, upheld a state law permitting execution of defendants who committed a capital crime at age 16 where only 15 of the 36 death penalty States (42%) prohibited death for such offenders.

Moreover, a major factor that the Court entirely disregards is that the legislation of all 18 States it relies on is still in its infancy. The oldest of the statutes is only 14 years old; 3 five were enacted last year; 4 over half were enacted within the past eight years.5 Few, if any, of the States have had sufficient experience with these laws to know whether they are sensible in the long term. It is "myopic to base sweeping constitutional principles upon the narrow experience of [a few] years." Coker, 433 U.S., at 614 (Burger, C. J., dissenting); see also Thompson, 487 U.S., at 854—855 (O'Connor, J., concurring in judgment).

The Court attempts to bolster its embarrassingly feeble evidence of "consensus" with the following: "It is not so much the number of these States that is significant, but the consistency of the direction of change." Ante, at 10 (emphasis added). But in what other direction could we possibly see change? Given that 14 years ago all the death penalty statutes included the mentally retarded, any change (except precipitate undoing of what had just been done) was bound to be in the one direction the Court finds significant enough to overcome the lack of real consensus. That is to say, to be accurate the Court's "consistency-of-the-direction-of-change" point should be recast into the following unimpressive observation: "No State has yet undone its exemption of the mentally retarded, one for as long as 14 whole years." In any event, reliance upon "trends," even those of much longer duration than a mere 14 years, is a perilous basis for constitutional adjudication, as Justice O'Connor eloquently explained in Thompson:

"In 1846, Michigan became the first State to abolish the death penalty .... In succeeding decades, other American States continued the trend towards abolition .... Later, and particularly after World War II, there ensued a steady and dramatic decline in executions .... In the 1950's and 1960's, more States abolished or radically restricted capital punishment, and executions ceased completely for several years beginning in 1968... .

In 1972, when this Court heard arguments on the constitutionality of the death penalty, such statistics might have suggested that the practice had become a relic, implicitly rejected by a new societal consensus .... We now know that any inference of a societal consensus rejecting the death penalty would have been mistaken. But had this Court then declared the existence of such a consensus, and outlawed capital punishment, legislatures would very likely not have been able to revive it. The mistaken premise of the decision would have been frozen into constitutional law, making it difficult to refute and even more difficult to reject." 487 U.S., at 854–855.

Her words demonstrate, of course, not merely the peril of riding a trend, but also the peril of discerning a consensus where there is none.

The Court's thrashing about for evidence of "consensus" includes reliance upon the margins by which state legislatures have enacted bans on execution of the retarded. Ante, at 11. Presumably, in applying our Eighth Amendment "evolving-standards-of-decency" jurisprudence, we will henceforth weigh not only how many States have agreed, but how many States have agreed by how much. Of course if the percentage of legislators voting for the bill is significant, surely the number of people represented by the legislators voting for the bill is also significant: the fact that 49% of the legislators in a State with a population of 60 million voted against the bill should be more impressive than the fact that 90% of the legislators in a state with a population of 2 million voted for it. (By the way, the population of the death penalty States that exclude the mentally retarded is only 44% of the population of all death penalty States. U.S. Census Bureau, Statistical Abstract of the United States 21 (121st ed. 2001).) This is quite absurd. What we have looked for in the past to "evolve" the Eighth Amendment is a consensus of the same sort as the consensus that adopted the Eighth Amendment: a consensus of the sovereign States that form the Union, not a nose count of Americans for and against.

Even less compelling (if possible) is the Court's argument, ante, at 11, that evidence of "national consensus" is to be found in the infrequency with which retarded persons are executed in States that do not bar their execution. To begin with, what the

Court takes as true is in fact quite doubtful. It is not at all clear that execution of the mentally retarded is "uncommon," ibid., as even the sources cited by the Court suggest, see ante, at 11, n. 20 (citing D. Keyes, W. Edwards, & R. Perske, People with Mental Retardation are Dying Legally, 35 Mental Retardation (Feb. 1997) (updated by Death Penalty Information Center; available at http://www.advocacyone.org/ deathpenalty.html) (June 12, 2002) (showing that 12 States executed 35 allegedly mentally retarded offenders during the period 1984—2000)). See also Bonner & Rimer, Executing the Mentally Retarded Even as Laws Begin to Shift, N. Y. Times, Aug. 7, 2000 p. A1 (reporting that 10% of death row inmates are retarded). If, however, execution of the mentally retarded is "uncommon"; and if it is not a sufficient explanation of this that the retarded comprise a tiny fraction of society (1% to 3%), Brief for American Psychological Association et al. as Amici Curiae 7; then surely the explanation is that mental retardation is a constitutionally mandated mitigating factor at sentencing, Penry, 492 U.S., at 328. For that reason, even if there were uniform national sentiment in favor of executing the retarded in appropriate cases, one would still expect execution of the mentally retarded to be "uncommon." To adapt to the present case what the Court itself said in Stanford, 492 U.S., at 374: "[I]t is not only possible, but overwhelmingly probable, that the very considerations which induce [today's majority] to believe that death should never be imposed on [mentally retarded] offenders ... cause prosecutors and juries to believe that it should rarely be imposed."

But the Prize for the Court's Most Feeble Effort to fabricate "national consensus" must go to its appeal (deservedly relegated to a footnote) to the views of assorted professional and religious organizations, members of the so-called "world community," and respondents to opinion polls. Ante, at 11—12, n. 21. I agree with the Chief Jus-tice, ante, at 4—8 (dissenting opinion), that the views of professional and religious organizations and the results of opinion polls are irrelevant.6 Equally irrelevant are the practices of the "world community," whose notions of justice are (thankfully) not always those of our people. "We must never forget that it is a Constitution for the United States of America that we are expounding. ... [W]here there is not first a settled consensus among our own people, the views of other nations, however enlightened the Justices of this Court may think them to be, cannot be imposed upon Americans through the Constitution." Thompson, 487 U.S., at 868—869, n. 4 (Scalia, J., dissenting).

III

Beyond the empty talk of a "national consensus," the Court gives us a brief glimpse of what really underlies today's decision: pretension to a power confined neither by the moral sentiments originally enshrined in the Eighth Amendment (its original meaning) nor even by the current moral sentiments of the American people. " '[T]he Constitution,' " the Court says, "contemplates that in the end our own judgment will be brought to bear on the question of the acceptability of the death penalty under the Eighth Amendment.' " Ante, at 7 (quoting Coker, 433 U.S., at 597) (emphasis added). (The unexpressed reason for this unexpressed "contemplation" of the Constitution is presumably that really good lawyers have moral sentiments superior to those of the common herd, whether in 1791 or today.) The arrogance of this assumption of power takes one's breath away. And it explains, of course, why the Court can be so cavalier about the evidence of consensus. It is just a game, after all. "[I]n the end," it is the feelings and intuition of a majority of the Justices that count–"the perceptions of decency, or of penology, or of mercy, entertained ... by a majority of the small and unrepresentative segment of our society that sits on this Court." Thompson, supra, at 873 (Scalia, J., dissenting).

The genuinely operative portion of the opinion, then, is the Court's statement of the reasons why it agrees with the contrived consensus it has found, that the "diminished capacities" of the mentally retarded render the death penalty excessive. Ante, at 13–17. The Court's analysis rests on two fundamental assumptions: (1) that the Eighth Amendment prohibits excessive punishments, and (2) that sentencing juries or judges are unable to account properly for the "diminished capacities" of the retarded. The first assumption is wrong, as I explained at length in Harmelin v. Michigan, 501 U.S. 957, 966–990 (1991) (opinion of Scalia, J.). The Eighth Amendment is addressed to always-and-everywhere "cruel" punishments, such as the rack and the thumbscrew. But where the punishment is in itself permissible, "[t]he Eighth Amendment is not a ratchet, whereby a temporary consensus on leniency for a particular crime fixes a permanent constitutional maximum, disabling the States from giving effect to altered beliefs and responding to changed social conditions." Id., at 990. The second assumption–inability of judges or juries to take proper account of mental retardation–is not only unsubstantiated, but contradicts the immemorial belief, here and in England, that they play an indispensable role in such matters:

"[I]t is very difficult to define the indivisible line that divides perfect and partial insanity; but it must rest upon circumstances duly to be weighed and considered both by the judge and jury, lest on the one side there be a kind of inhumanity towards the defects of human nature, or on the other side too great an indulgence given to great crimes ... ." 1 Hale, Pleas of the Crown, at 30.

Proceeding from these faulty assumptions, the Court gives two reasons why the death penalty is an excessive punishment for all mentally retarded offenders. First, the "diminished capacities" of the mentally retarded raise a "serious question" whether their execution contributes to the "social purposes" of the death penalty, viz., retribution and deterrence. Ante, at 13–14. (The Court conveniently ignores a third "social purpose" of the death penalty–"incapacitation of dangerous criminals and the consequent prevention of crimes that they may otherwise commit in the future," Gregg v. Georgia, 428 U.S. 153, 183, n. 28 (1976) (joint opinion of Stewart, Powell, and Stevens, JJ.). But never mind; its discussion of even the other two does not bear analysis.) Retribution is not advanced, the argument goes, because the mentally retarded are no more culpable than the average murderer, whom we have already held lacks sufficient culpability to warrant the death penalty, see Godfrey v. Georgia, 446 U.S. 420, 433 (1980) (plurality opinion). Ante, at

14—15. Who says so? Is there an established correlation between mental acuity and the ability to conform one's conduct to the law in such a rudimentary matter as murder? Are the mentally retarded really more disposed (and hence more likely) to commit willfully cruel and serious crime than others? In my experience, the opposite is true: being childlike generally suggests innocence rather than brutality.

Assuming, however, that there is a direct connection between diminished intelligence and the inability to refrain from murder, what scientific analysis can possibly show that a mildly retarded individual who commits an exquisite torture-killing is "no more culpable" than the "average" murderer in a holdup-gone-wrong or a domestic dispute? Or a moderately retarded individual who commits a series of 20 exquisite torture-killings? Surely culpability, and deservedness of the most severe retribution, depends not merely (if at all) upon the mental capacity of the criminal (above the level where he is able to distinguish right from wrong) but also upon the depravity of the crime—which is precisely why this sort of question has traditionally been thought answerable not by a categorical rule of the sort the Court today imposes upon all trials, but rather by the sentencer's weighing of the circumstances (both degree of retardation and depravity of crime) in the particular case. The fact that juries continue to sentence mentally retarded offenders to death for extreme crimes shows that society's moral outrage sometimes demands execution of retarded offenders. By what principle of law, science, or logic can the Court pronounce that this is wrong? There is none. Once the Court admits (as it does) that mental retardation does not render the offender morally blameless, ante, at 13—14, there is no basis for saying that the death penalty is never appropriate retribution, no matter how heinous the crime. As long as a mentally retarded offender knows "the difference between right and wrong," ante, at 13, only the sentencer can assess whether his retardation reduces his culpability enough to exempt him from the death penalty for the particular murder in question.

As for the other social purpose of the death penalty that the Court discusses, deterrence: That is not advanced, the Court tells us, because the mentally retarded are "less likely" than their non-retarded counterparts to "process the information of the possibility of execution as a penalty and ... control their conduct based upon that information." Ante, at 15. Of course this leads to the same conclusion discussed earlier—that the mentally retarded (because they are less deterred) are more likely to kill—which neither I nor the society at large believes. In any event, even the Court does not say that all mentally retarded individuals cannot "process the information of the possibility of execution as a penalty and . . . control their conduct based upon that information"; it merely asserts that they are "less likely" to be able to do so. But surely the deterrent effect of a penalty is adequately vindicated if it successfully deters many, but not all, of the target class. Virginia's death penalty, for example, does not fail of its deterrent effect simply because some criminals are unaware that Virginia has the death penalty. In other words, the supposed fact that some retarded criminals cannot fully appreciate the death penalty has nothing to do with the deterrence rationale, but is simply an echo of the arguments denying a retribution rationale, discussed and rejected above. I am not sure that a murderer is somehow less blameworthy if (though he knew his act was wrong) he did not fully appreciate that he could die for it; but if so, we should treat a mentally retarded murderer the way we treat an offender who may be "less likely" to respond to the death penalty because he was abused as a child. We do not hold him immune from capital punishment, but require his background to be considered by the sentencer as a mitigating factor. Eddings v. Oklahoma, 455 U.S. 104, 113—117 (1982).

The Court throws one last factor into its grab bag of reasons why execution of the retarded is "excessive" in all cases: Mentally retarded offenders "face a special risk of wrongful execution" because they are less able "to make a persuasive showing of mitigation," "to give meaningful assistance to their counsel," and to be effective witnesses. Ante, at 16. "Special risk" is pretty flabby language (even flabbier than "less likely")–and I suppose a similar "special risk" could be said to exist for just plain stupid people, inarticulate people, even ugly people. If this unsupported claim has any substance to it (which I doubt) it might support a due process claim in all criminal prosecutions of the mentally retarded; but it is hard to see how it has anything to do with an Eighth Amendment claim that execution of the mentally retarded is cruel and unusual. We have never before held it to be cruel and unusual punishment to impose a sentence in violation of some other constitutional imperative.

* * *

Today's opinion adds one more to the long list of substantive and procedural requirements impeding imposition of the death penalty imposed under this Court's assumed power to invent a death-is-different jurisprudence. None of those requirements existed when the Eighth Amendment was adopted, and some of them were not even supported by current moral consensus. They include prohibition of the death penalty for "ordinary" murder, Godfrey, 446 U.S., at 433, for rape of an adult woman, Coker, 433 U.S., at 592, and for felony murder absent a showing that the defendant possessed a sufficiently culpable state of mind, Enmund, 458 U.S., at 801; prohibition of the death penalty for any person under the age of 16 at the time of the crime, Thompson, 487 U.S., at 838 (plurality opinion); prohibition of the death penalty as the mandatory punishment for any crime, Woodson v. North Carolina, 428 U.S. 280, 305 (1976) (plurality opinion), Sumner v. Shuman, 483 U.S. 66, 77—78 (1987); a requirement that the sentencer not be given unguided discretion, Furman v. Georgia, 408 U.S. 238 (1972) (per curiam), a requirement that the sentencer be empowered to take into account all mitigating circumstances, Lockett v. Ohio, 438 U.S. 586, 604 (1978) (plurality opinion), Eddings v. Oklahoma, supra, at 110; and a requirement that the accused receive a judicial evaluation of his claim of insanity before the sentence can be executed, Ford, 477 U.S., at 410—411 (plurality opinion). There is something to be said for popular abolition of the death penalty; there is nothing to be said for its incremental abolition by this Court.

This newest invention promises to be more effective than any of the others in turning the process of capital trial into a game. One need only read the definitions of mental retardation adopted by the American Association of Mental Retardation and the American Psychiatric Association (set forth in the Court's opinion, ante, at 2—3, n. 3) to realize that the symptoms of this condition can readily be feigned. And whereas the capital defendant who feigns insanity risks commitment to a mental institution until he can be cured (and then tried and executed), Jones v. United States, 463 U.S. 354, 370, and n. 20 (1983), the capital defendant who feigns mental retardation risks nothing at all. The mere pendency of the present case has brought us petitions by death row inmates claiming for the first time, after multiple habeas petitions, that they are retarded. See, e.g., Moore v. Texas, 535 U.S. __ (2002) (Scalia, J., dissenting from grant of applications for stay of execution).

Perhaps these practical difficulties will not be experienced by the minority of capital-punishment States that have very recently changed mental retardation from a mitigating factor (to be accepted or rejected by the sentencer) to an absolute immunity. Time will tell—and the brief time those States have had the new disposition in place (an average of 6.8 years) is surely not enough. But if the practical difficulties do not appear, and if the other States share the Court's perceived moral consensus that all mental retardation renders the death penalty inappropriate for all crimes, then that majority will presumably follow suit. But there is no justification for this Court's pushing them into the experiment—and turning the experiment into a permanent practice—on constitutional pretext. Nothing has changed the accuracy of Matthew Hale's endorsement of the common law's traditional method for taking account of guilt-reducing factors, written over three centuries ago:

"[Determination of a person's incapacity] is a matter of great difficulty, partly from the easiness of counterfeiting this disability ... and partly from the variety of the degrees of this infirmity, whereof some are sufficient, and some are insufficient to excuse persons in capital offenses. ...

"Yet the law of England hath afforded the best method of trial, that is possible, of this and all other matters of fact, namely, by a jury of twelve men all concurring in the same judgment, by the testimony of witnesses ..., and by the inspection and direction of the judge." 1 Hale, Pleas of the Crown, at 32—33.

Notes to Justice Scalia's dissent in Atkins v. Virginia (June 20, 2002)

1. See Ariz. Rev. Stat. Ann. §13—703.02(I) (Supp. 2001); Ark. Code Ann. §5—4—618(d)(1) (1997); Reams v. State, 322 Ark. 336, 340, 909 S. W. 2d 324, 326—327 (1995); Fla. Stat. §921.137(8) (Supp. 2002); Ga. Code Ann. §17—7—131(j) (1997); Ind. Code §35—36—9—6 (1998); Rondon v. State, 711 N. E. 2d 506, 512 (Ind. 1999); Kan. Stat. Ann. §§21—4623(d), 21—4631(c) (1995); Ky. Rev. Stat. Ann. §532.140(3) (1999); Md. Ann. Code, Art. 27, §412(g) (1996); Booth v. State, 327 Md. 142, 166—167, 608 A. 2d 162, 174 (1992); Mo. Rev. Stat. §565.030(7) (Supp. 2001); N. Y. Crim. Proc. Law §400.27.12(c)

(McKinney Supp. 2002); 1995 Sess. N. Y. Laws, ch. 1, §38; Tenn. Code Ann. §39—13—203(b) (1997); Van Tran v. State, 66 S. W. 2d 790, 798—799 (Tenn. 2001).

2. The Kansas statute defines "mentally retarded" as "having significantly subaverage general intellectual functioning ... to an extent which substantially impairs one's capacity to appreciate the criminality of one's conduct or to conform one's conduct to the requirements of law." Kan. Stat. Ann. §21—4623(e) (2001). This definition of retardation, petitioner concedes, is analogous to the Model Penal Code's definition of a "mental disease or defect" excusing responsibility for criminal conduct, see ALI, Model Penal Code §4.01 (1985), which would not include mild mental retardation. Reply Brief for petitioner 3, n. 4.

3. Ga. Code Ann. §17—7—131(j).

4. Ariz. Rev. Stat. Ann. §13—703.02; Conn. Gen. Stat. §53a—46a(h); Fla. Stat. Ann. §921.137; Mo. Rev. Stat. §§565.030(4)—(7); N. C. Gen. Stat. §15A—2005.

5. In addition to the statutes cited n. 3 supra, see S. D. Codified Laws §23A—27A—26.1 (enacted 2000); Neb. Rev. Stat. §§28—105.01(2)—(5) (1998); N. Y. Crim. Proc. Law §400.27(12) (1995); Ind. Code §35—36—9—6 (1994); Kan. Stat. Ann. §21—4623 (1994).

6. And in some cases positively counter-indicative. The Court cites, for example, the views of the United States Catholic Conference, whose members are the active Catholic Bishops of the United States. See ante, at 12, n. 21 (citing Brief for United States Catholic Conference et al. as Amici Curiae in McCarver v. North Carolina, O. T. 2001, No. 00—8727, p. 2). The attitudes of that body regarding crime and punishment are so far from being representative, even of the views of Catholics, that they are currently the object of intense national (and entirely ecumenical) criticism.

Using race in college admissions: Justice Scalia's concurrence and dissent in Grutter v. Bollinger (June 23, 2003)

Justice Scalia, with whom Justice Thomas joins, concurring in part and dissenting in part.

I join the opinion of The Chief Justice. As he demonstrates, the University of Michigan Law School's mystical "critical mass" justification for its discrimination by race challenges even the most gullible mind. The admissions statistics show it to be a sham to cover a scheme of racially proportionate admissions.

I also join Parts I through VII of Justice Thomas's opinion. I find particularly unanswerable his central point: that the allegedly "compelling state interest" at issue here is not the incremental "educational benefit" that emanates from the fabled "critical mass" of minority students, but rather Michigan's interest in maintaining a "prestige" law school whose normal admissions standards disproportionately exclude blacks and other minorities. If that is a compelling state interest, everything is.

I add the following: The "educational benefit" that the University of Michigan seeks to achieve by racial discrimination consists, according to the Court, of " 'cross-racial understanding,' " ante, at 18, and " 'better prepar[ation of] students for an increasingly diverse workforce and society,' " ibid., all of which is necessary not only for work, but also for good "citizenship," ante, at 19. This is not, of course, an "educational benefit" on which students will be graded on their Law School transcript (Works and Plays Well with Others: B+) or tested by the bar examiners (Q: Describe in 500 words or less your cross-racial understanding). For it is a lesson of life rather than law—essentially the same lesson taught to (or rather learned by, for it cannot be "taught" in the usual sense) people three feet shorter and twenty years younger than the full-grown adults at the University of Michigan Law School, in institutions ranging from Boy Scout troops to public-school kindergartens. If properly considered an "educational benefit" at all, it is surely not one that is either uniquely relevant to law school or uniquely "teachable" in a formal educational setting. And therefore: If it is appropriate for the University of Michigan Law School to use racial discrimination for the purpose of putting together a "critical mass" that will convey generic lessons in socialization and good citizenship, surely it is no less appropriate—indeed, particularly appropriate—for the civil service system of the State of Michigan to do so. There, also, those exposed to "critical masses" of certain races will presumably become better Americans, better Michiganders, better civil servants. And surely private employers cannot be criticized—indeed, should be praised—if they also "teach" good citizenship to their adult employees through a patriotic, all-American system of racial discrimination in hiring. The nonminority individuals who are deprived of a legal education, a civil service job, or any job at all by reason of their skin color will surely understand.

Unlike a clear constitutional holding that racial preferences in state educational institutions are impermissible, or even a clear anticonstitutional holding that racial preferences in state educational institutions are OK, today's Grutter-Gratz split double header seems perversely designed to prolong the controversy and the litigation. Some future lawsuits will presumably focus on whether the discriminatory scheme in question contains enough evaluation of the applicant "as an individual," ante, at 24, and sufficiently avoids "separate admissions tracks" ante, at 22, to fall under Grutter rather than Gratz. Some will focus on whether a university has gone beyond the bounds of a " 'good faith effort' " and has so zealously pursued its "critical mass" as to make it an unconstitutional de facto quota system, rather than merely " 'a permissible goal.' " Ante, at 23 (quoting Sheet Metal Workers v. EEOC, 478 U. S 421, 495 (1986) (O'Connor, J., concurring in part and dissenting in part)). Other lawsuits may focus on whether, in the particular setting at issue, any educational benefits flow from racial diversity. (That issue was not contested in Grutter; and while the opinion accords "a degree of deference to a university's academic decisions," ante, at 16, "deference does not imply abandonment or abdication of judicial review," Miller-El v. Cockrell, 537 U.S. 322, 340 (2003).) Still other suits may challenge the bona fides of the institution's expressed commitment to the educational benefits of diversity that immunize the discriminatory scheme in Grutter. (Tempting targets, one would suppose, will be those universities that talk the talk of multiculturalism and racial diversity in the courts but walk the walk of tribalism and racial segregation on their campuses—through minority-only student organizations, separate minority housing opportunities, separate minority student centers, even separate minority-only graduation ceremonies.) And still other suits may claim that the institution's racial preferences have gone below or above the mystical Grutter-approved "critical mass." Finally, litigation can be expected on behalf of minority groups intentionally short changed in the institution's composition of its generic minority "critical mass." I do not look forward to any of these cases. The Constitution proscribes government discrimination on the basis of race, and state-provided education is no exception.

Notes

*. Part VII of Justice Thomas's opinion describes those portions of the Court's opinion in which I concur. See post, at 27—31.

Unenumerated Rights: Justice Scalia's dissent in Lawrence v. Texas (June 26, 2003)

Justice Scalia, with whom The Chief Justice and Justice Thomas join, dissenting.

"Liberty finds no refuge in a jurisprudence of doubt." Planned Parenthood of Southeastern Pa. v. Casey, 505 U.S. 833, 844 (1992). That was the Court's sententious response, barely more than a decade ago, to those seeking to overrule Roe v. Wade, 410 U.S. 113 (1973). The Court's response today, to those who have engaged in a 17-year crusade to overrule Bowers v. Hardwick, 478 U.S. 186 (1986), is very different. The need for stability and certainty presents no barrier.

Most of the rest of today's opinion has no relevance to its actual holding—that the Texas statute "furthers no legitimate state interest which can justify" its application to petitioners under rational-basis review. Ante, at 18 (overruling Bowers to the extent it sustained Georgia's anti-sodomy statute under the rational-basis test). Though there is discussion of "fundamental proposition[s]," ante, at 4, and "fundamental decisions," ibid. nowhere does the Court's opinion declare that homosexual sodomy is a "fundamental right" under the Due Process Clause; nor does it subject the Texas law to the standard of review that would be appropriate (strict scrutiny) if homosexual sodomy were a "fundamental right." Thus, while overruling the outcome of Bowers, the Court leaves strangely untouched its central legal conclusion: "[R]espondent would have us announce ... a fundamental right to engage in homosexual sodomy. This we are quite unwilling to do." 478 U.S., at 191. Instead the Court simply describes petitioners' conduct as "an exercise of their liberty"—which it undoubtedly is—and proceeds to apply an unheard-of form of rational-basis review that will have far-reaching implications beyond this case. Ante, at 3.

I

I begin with the Court's surprising readiness to reconsider a decision rendered a mere 17 years ago in Bowers v. Hardwick. I do not myself believe in rigid adherence to stare decisis in constitutional cases; but I do believe that we should be consistent rather than manipulative in invoking the doctrine. Today's opinions in support of reversal do not bother to distinguish—or indeed, even bother to mention—the paean to stare decisis coauthored by three Members of today's majority in Planned Parenthood v. Casey. There, when stare decisis meant preservation of judicially invented abortion rights, the widespread criticism of Roe was strong reason to reaffirm it:

" Where, in the performance of its judicial duties, the Court decides a case in such a way as to resolve the sort of intensely divisive controversy reflected in Roe[,] ... its decision has a dimension that the resolution of the normal case does not carry.... [T]o overrule under fire in the absence of the most compelling reason ... would subvert the Court's legitimacy beyond any serious question." 505 U.S., at 866—867.

Today, however, the widespread opposition to Bowers, a decision resolving an issue as "intensely divisive" as the issue in Roe, is offered as a reason in favor of overruling it. See ante, at 15—16. Gone, too, is any "enquiry" (of the sort conducted in Casey) into whether the decision sought to be overruled has "proven 'unworkable,' " Casey, supra, at 855.

Today's approach to stare decisis invites us to overrule an erroneously decided precedent (including an "intensely divisive" decision) if: (1) its foundations have been "eroded" by subsequent decisions, ante, at 15; (2) it has been subject to "substantial and continuing" criticism, ibid.; and (3) it has not induced "individual or societal reliance" that counsels against overturning, ante, at 16. The problem is that Roe itself—which today's majority surely has no disposition to overrule—satisfies these conditions to at least the same degree as Bowers.

(1) A preliminary digressive observation with regard to the first factor: The Court's claim that Planned Parenthood v. Casey, supra, "casts some doubt" upon the holding in Bowers (or any other case, for that matter) does not withstand analysis. Ante, at 10. As far as its holding is concerned, Casey provided a less expansive right to abortion than did Roe, which was already on the books when Bowers was decided. And if the Court is referring not to the holding of Casey, but to the dictum of its famed sweet-mystery-of-life passage, ante, at 13 (" 'At the heart of liberty is the right to define one's own concept of existence, of meaning, of the universe, and of the mystery of human life' "): That "casts some doubt" upon either the totality of our jurisprudence or else (presumably the right answer) nothing at all. I have never heard of a law that attempted to restrict one's "right to define" certain concepts; and if the passage calls into question the government's power to regulate actions based on one's self-defined "concept of existence, etc.," it is the passage that ate the rule of law.

I do not quarrel with the Court's claim that Romer v. Evans, 517 U.S. 620 (1996), "eroded" the "foundations" of Bowers' rational-basis holding. See Romer, supra, at 640–643 (Scalia, J., dissenting).) But Roe and Casey have been equally "eroded" by Washington v. Glucksberg, 521 U.S. 702, 721 (1997), which held that only fundamental rights which are " 'deeply rooted in this Nation's history and tradition' " qualify for anything other than rational basis scrutiny under the doctrine of "substantive due process." Roe and Casey, of course, subjected the restriction of abortion to heightened scrutiny without even attempting to establish that the freedom to abort was rooted in this Nation's tradition.

(2) Bowers, the Court says, has been subject to "substantial and continuing [criticism], disapproving of its reasoning in all respects, not just as to its historical assumptions." Ante, at 15. Exactly what those nonhistorical criticisms are, and whether the Court even agrees with them, are left unsaid, although the Court does cite two books. See ibid. (citing C. Fried, Order and Law: Arguing the Reagan Revolution–A Firsthand Account 81–84 (1991); R. Posner, Sex and Reason 341–350 (1992)).1 Of course, Roe too (and by extension Casey) had been (and still is) subject to unrelenting criticism, including criticism from the two commentators cited by the Court today. See Fried, supra, at 75 ("Roe was a prime example of twisted judging"); Posner, supra, at 337 ("[The Court's] opinion in Roe ... fails to measure up to professional expectations regarding judicial opinions"); Posner, Judicial Opinion Writing, 62 U. Chi. L. Rev. 1421, 1434 (1995) (describing the opinion in Roe as an "embarrassing performanc[e]").

(3) That leaves, to distinguish the rock-solid, unamendable disposition of Roe from the readily overrulable Bowers, only the third factor. "[T]here has been," the Court says, "no individual or societal reliance on Bowers of the sort that could counsel against overturning its holding ... ." Ante, at 16. It seems to me that the "societal reliance" on the principles confirmed in Bowers and discarded today has been overwhelming. Countless judicial decisions and legislative enactments have relied on the ancient proposition that a governing majority's belief that certain sexual behavior is "immoral and unacceptable" constitutes a rational basis for regulation. See, e.g., Williams v. Pryor, 240 F.3d 944, 949 (CA11 2001) (citing Bowers in upholding Alabama's prohibition on the sale of sex toys on the ground that "[t]he crafting and safeguarding of public morality ... indisputably is a legitimate government interest under rational basis scrutiny"); Milner v. Apfel, 148 F.3d 812, 814 (CA7 1998) (citing Bowers for the proposition that "[l]egislatures are permitted to legislate with regard to morality ... rather than confined to preventing demonstrable harms"); Holmes v. California Army National Guard 124 F.3d 1126, 1136 (CA9 1997) (relying on Bowers in upholding the federal statute and regulations banning from military service those who engage in homosexual conduct); Owens v. State, 352 Md. 663, 683, 724 A. 2d 43, 53 (1999) (relying on Bowers in holding that "a person has no constitutional right to engage in sexual intercourse, at least outside of marriage"); Sherman v. Henry, 928 S. W. 2d 464, 469–473 (Tex. 1996) (relying on Bowers in rejecting a claimed constitutional right to commit adultery). We ourselves relied extensively on Bowers when

we concluded, in Barnes v. Glen Theatre, Inc., 501 U.S. 560, 569 (1991), that Indiana's public indecency statute furthered "a substantial government interest in protecting order and morality," ibid., (plurality opinion); see also id., at 575 (Scalia, J., concurring in judgment). State laws against bigamy, same-sex marriage, adult incest, prostitution, masturbation, adultery, fornication, bestiality, and obscenity are likewise sustainable only in light of Bowers' validation of laws based on moral choices. Every single one of these laws is called into question by today's decision; the Court makes no effort to cabin the scope of its decision to exclude them from its holding. See ante, at 11 (noting "an emerging awareness that liberty gives substantial protection to adult persons in deciding how to conduct their private lives in matters pertaining to sex" (emphasis added)). The impossibility of distinguishing homosexuality from other traditional "morals" offenses is precisely why Bowers rejected the rational-basis challenge. "The law," it said, "is constantly based on notions of morality, and if all laws representing essentially moral choices are to be invalidated under the Due Process Clause, the courts will be very busy indeed." 478 U.S., at 196.2

What a massive disruption of the current social order, therefore, the overruling of Bowers entails. Not so the overruling of Roe, which would simply have restored the regime that existed for centuries before 1973, in which the permissibility of and restrictions upon abortion were determined legislatively State-by-State. Casey, however, chose to base its stare decisis determination on a different "sort" of reliance. "[P]eople," it said, "have organized intimate relationships and made choices that define their views of themselves and their places in society, in reliance on the availability of abortion in the event that contraception should fail." 505 U.S., at 856. This falsely assumes that the consequence of overruling Roe would have been to make abortion unlawful. It would not; it would merely have permitted the States to do so. Many States would unquestionably have declined to prohibit abortion, and others would not have prohibited it within six months (after which the most significant reliance interests would have expired). Even for persons in States other than these, the choice would not have been between abortion and childbirth, but between abortion nearby and abortion in a neighboring State.

To tell the truth, it does not surprise me, and should surprise no one, that the Court has chosen today to revise the standards of stare decisis set forth in Casey. It has thereby exposed Casey's extraordinary deference to precedent for the result-oriented expedient that it is.

II

Having decided that it need not adhere to stare decisis, the Court still must establish that Bowers was wrongly decided and that the Texas statute, as applied to petitioners, is unconstitutional.

Texas Penal Code Ann. §21.06(a) (2003) undoubtedly imposes constraints on liberty. So do laws prohibiting prostitution, recreational use of heroin, and, for that matter, working more than 60 hours per week in a bakery. But there is no right to "liberty" under the Due Process Clause, though today's opinion repeatedly makes that claim. Ante, at 6 ("The liberty protected by the Constitution allows homosexual persons the right to make this choice"); ante, at 13 (" ' These matters ... are central to the liberty protected by the Fourteenth Amendment' "); ante, at 17 ("Their right to liberty under the Due Process Clause gives them the full right to engage in their conduct without intervention of the government"). The Fourteenth Amendment expressly allows States to deprive their citizens of "liberty," so long as "due process of law" is provided:

"No state shall ... deprive any person of life, liberty, or property, without due process of law." Amdt. 14 (emphasis added).

Our opinions applying the doctrine known as "substantive due process" hold that the Due Process Clause prohibits States from infringing fundamental liberty interests, unless the infringement is narrowly tailored to serve a compelling state interest. Washington v. Glucksberg, 521 U.S., at 721. We have held repeatedly, in cases the Court today does not overrule, that only fundamental rights qualify for this so-called "heightened scrutiny" protection–that is, rights which are " 'deeply rooted in this Nation's history and tradition,' " ibid. See Reno v. Flores, 507 U.S. 292, 303 (1993) (fundamental liberty interests must be "so rooted in the traditions and conscience of our people as to be ranked as fundamental" (internal quotation marks and citations omitted)); United States v. Salerno, 481 U.S. 739, 751 (1987) (same). See also Michael H. v. Gerald D., 491 U.S. 110, 122 (1989) ("[W]e have insisted not merely that the interest denominated as a 'liberty' be 'fundamental' ... but also that it be an interest traditionally protected by our society"); Moore v. East Cleveland, 431 U.S. 494, 503 (1977) (plurality opinion); Meyer v. Nebraska, 262 U.S. 390, 399 (1923) (Fourteenth Amendment protects "those privileges long recognized at common law as essential to the orderly pursuit of happiness by free men" (emphasis added)).3 All other liberty interests may be abridged or abrogated pursuant to a validly enacted state law if that law is rationally related to a legitimate state interest.

Bowers held, first, that criminal prohibitions of homosexual sodomy are not subject to heightened scrutiny because they do not implicate a "fundamental right" under the Due Process Clause, 478 U.S., at 191–194. Noting that "[p]roscriptions against that conduct have ancient roots," id., at 192, that "[s]odomy was a criminal offense at common law and was forbidden by the laws of the original 13 States when they ratified the Bill of Rights," ibid., and that many States had retained their bans on sodomy, id., at 193, Bowers concluded that a right to engage in homosexual sodomy was not " 'deeply rooted in this Nation's history and tradition,' " id., at 192.

The Court today does not overrule this holding. Not once does it describe homosexual sodomy as a "fundamental right" or a "fundamental liberty interest," nor does it subject the Texas statute to strict scrutiny. Instead, having failed to establish that the right to homosexual sodomy is " 'deeply rooted in this Nation's history and tradition,' " the Court concludes that the application of Texas's statute to petitioners' conduct fails the rational-basis test, and overrules Bowers' holding to the contrary, see id., at 196. "The Texas statute furthers no legitimate state interest which can justify its intrusion into the personal and private life of the individual." Ante, at 18.

I shall address that rational-basis holding presently. First, however, I address some aspersions that the Court casts upon Bowers' conclusion that homosexual sodomy is not a "fundamental right"–even though, as I have said, the Court does not have the boldness to reverse that conclusion.

III

The Court's description of "the state of the law" at the time of Bowers only confirms that Bowers was right. Ante, at 5. The Court points to Griswold v. Connecticut, 381 U.S. 479, 481—482 (1965). But that case expressly disclaimed any reliance on the doctrine of "substantive due process," and grounded the so-called "right to privacy" in penumbras of constitutional provisions other than the Due Process Clause. Eisenstadt v. Baird, 405 U.S. 438 (1972), likewise had nothing to do with "substantive due process"; it invalidated a Massachusetts law prohibiting the distribution of contraceptives to unmarried persons solely on the basis of the Equal Protection Clause. Of course Eisenstadt contains well known dictum relating to the "right to privacy," but this referred to the right recognized in Griswold–a right penumbral to the specific guarantees in the Bill of Rights, and not a "substantive due process" right.

Roe v. Wade recognized that the right to abort an unborn child was a "fundamental right" protected by the Due Process Clause. 410 U.S., at 155. The Roe Court, however, made no attempt to establish that this right was " 'deeply rooted in this Nation's history and tradition' "; instead, it based its conclusion that "the Fourteenth Amendment's concept of personal liberty ... is broad enough to encompass a woman's decision whether or not to terminate her pregnancy" on its own normative judgment that anti-abortion laws were undesirable. See id., at 153. We have since rejected Roe's holding that regulations of abortion must be narrowly tailored to serve a compelling state interest, see Planned Parenthood v. Casey, 505 U.S., at 876 (joint opinion of O'Connor, Kennedy, and Souter, JJ.); id., at 951—953 (Rehnquist, C. J., concurring in judgment in part and dissenting in part)–and thus, by logical implication, Roe's holding that the right to abort an unborn child is a "fundamental right." See 505 U.S., at 843—912 (joint opinion of O'Connor, Kennedy, and Souter, JJ.) (not once describing abortion as a "fundamental right" or a "fundamental liberty interest").

After discussing the history of antisodomy laws, ante, at 7—10, the Court proclaims that, "it should be noted that there is no longstanding history in this country of laws directed at homosexual conduct as a distinct matter," ante, at 7. This observation in no way casts into doubt the "definitive [historical] conclusion," id., on which Bowers relied: that our Nation has a longstanding history of laws prohibiting sodomy in general– regardless of whether it was performed by same-sex or opposite-sex couples:

"It is obvious to us that neither of these formulations would extend a fundamental right to homosexuals to engage in acts of consensual sodomy. Proscriptions against that conduct have ancient roots. Sodomy was a criminal offense at common law and was forbidden by the laws of the original 13 States when they ratified the Bill of Rights. In 1868, when the Fourteenth Amendment was ratified, all but 5 of the 37 States in the Union had criminal sodomy laws. In fact, until 1961, all 50 States outlawed sodomy, and today, 24 States and the District of Columbia continue to provide criminal penalties for sodomy performed in private and between consenting adults. Against this background, to claim that a right to engage in such conduct is 'deeply rooted in this Nation's history and tradition' or 'implicit in the concept of ordered liberty' is, at best, facetious." 478 U.S., at 192—194 (citations and footnotes omitted; emphasis added).

It is (as Bowers recognized) entirely irrelevant whether the laws in our long national tradition criminalizing homosexual sodomy were "directed at homosexual conduct as a distinct matter." Ante, at 7. Whether homosexual sodomy was prohibited by a law targeted at same-sex sexual relations or by a more general law prohibiting both homosexual and heterosexual sodomy, the only relevant point is that it was criminalized—which suffices to establish that homosexual sodomy is not a right "deeply rooted in our Nation's history and tradition." The Court today agrees that homosexual sodomy was criminalized and thus does not dispute the facts on which Bowers actually relied.

Next the Court makes the claim, again unsupported by any citations, that "[l]aws prohibiting sodomy do not seem to have been enforced against consenting adults acting in private." Ante, at 8. The key qualifier here is "acting in private"—since the Court admits that sodomy laws were enforced against consenting adults (although the Court contends that prosecutions were "infrequent," ante, at 9). I do not know what "acting in private" means; surely consensual sodomy, like heterosexual intercourse, is rarely performed on stage. If all the Court means by "acting in private" is "on private premises, with the doors closed and windows covered," it is entirely unsurprising that evidence of enforcement would be hard to come by. (Imagine the circumstances that would enable a search warrant to be obtained for a residence on the ground that there was probable cause to believe that consensual sodomy was then and there occurring.) Surely that lack of evidence would not sustain the proposition that consensual sodomy on private premises with the doors closed and windows covered was regarded as a "fundamental right," even though all other consensual sodomy was criminalized. There are 203 prosecutions for consensual, adult homosexual sodomy reported in the West Reporting system and official state reporters from the years 1880—1995. See W. Eskridge, Gaylaw: Challenging the Apartheid of the Closet 375 (1999) (hereinafter Gaylaw). There are also records of 20 sodomy prosecutions and 4 executions during the colonial period. J. Katz, Gay/Lesbian Almanac 29, 58, 663 (1983). Bowers' conclusion that homosexual sodomy is not a fundamental right "deeply rooted in this Nation's history and tradition" is utterly unassailable.

Realizing that fact, the Court instead says: "[W]e think that our laws and traditions in the past half century are of most relevance here. These references show an emerging awareness that liberty gives substantial protection to adult persons in deciding how to conduct their private lives in matters pertaining to sex." Ante, at 11 (emphasis added). Apart from the fact that such an "emerging awareness" does not establish a "fundamental right," the statement is factually false. States continue to prosecute all sorts of crimes by adults "in matters pertaining to sex": prostitution, adult incest, adultery, obscenity, and child pornography. Sodomy laws, too, have been enforced "in the past half century," in which there have been 134 reported cases involving prosecutions for consensual, adult, homosexual sodomy. Gaylaw 375. In relying, for evidence of an "emerging recognition," upon the American Law Institute's 1955 recommendation not to criminalize " 'consensual sexual relations conducted in private,' " ante, at 11, the Court ignores the fact that this recommendation was "a point of resistance in most of the states that considered adopting the Model Penal Code." Gaylaw 159.

In any event, an "emerging awareness" is by definition not "deeply rooted in this Nation's history and tradition[s]," as we have said "fundamental right" status requires. Constitutional entitlements do not spring into existence because some States choose to lessen or eliminate criminal sanctions on certain behavior. Much less do they spring into existence, as the Court seems to believe, because foreign nations decriminalize conduct. The Bowers majority opinion never relied on "values we share with a wider civilization," ante, at 16, but rather rejected the claimed right to sodomy on the ground that such a right was not " 'deeply rooted in this Nation's history and tradition,' " 478 U.S., at 193–194 (emphasis added). Bowers' rational-basis holding is likewise devoid of any reliance on the views of a "wider civilization," see id., at 196. The Court's discussion of these foreign views (ignoring, of course, the many countries that have retained criminal prohibitions on sodomy) is therefore meaningless dicta. Dangerous dicta, however, since "this Court ... should not impose foreign moods, fads, or fashions on Americans." Foster v. Florida, 537 U.S. 990, n. (2002) (Thomas, J., concurring in denial of certiorari).

IV

I turn now to the ground on which the Court squarely rests its holding: the contention that there is no rational basis for the law here under attack. This proposition is so out of accord with our jurisprudence–indeed, with the jurisprudence of any society we know–that it requires little discussion.

The Texas statute undeniably seeks to further the belief of its citizens that certain forms of sexual behavior are "immoral and unacceptable," Bowers, supra, at 196– the same interest furthered by criminal laws against fornication, bigamy, adultery, adult incest, bestiality, and obscenity. Bowers held that this was a legitimate state interest. The Court today reaches the opposite conclusion. The Texas statute, it says, "furthers no legitimate state interest which can justify its intrusion into the personal and private life of the individual," ante, at 18 (emphasis added). The Court embraces instead Justice Stevens' declaration in his Bowers dissent, that "the fact that the governing majority in a State has traditionally viewed a particular practice as immoral is not a sufficient reason for upholding a law prohibiting the practice," ante, at 17. This effectively decrees the end of all morals legislation. If, as the Court asserts, the promotion of majoritarian sexual morality is not even a legitimate state interest, none of the above-mentioned laws can survive rational-basis review.

V

Finally, I turn to petitioners' equal-protection challenge, which no Member of the Court save Justice O'Connor, ante, at 1 (opinion concurring in judgment), embraces: On its face §21.06(a) applies equally to all persons. Men and women, heterosexuals and homosexuals, are all subject to its prohibition of deviate sexual intercourse with someone of the same sex. To be sure, §21.06 does distinguish between the sexes insofar as concerns the partner with whom the sexual acts are performed: men can violate the law only with other men, and women only with other women. But this cannot itself be a denial of equal protection, since it is precisely the same distinction regarding partner that is drawn in state laws prohibiting marriage with someone of the same sex while permitting marriage with someone of the opposite sex.

The objection is made, however, that the antimiscegenation laws invalidated in Loving v. Virginia, 388 U.S. 1, 8 (1967), similarly were applicable to whites and blacks alike, and only distinguished between the races insofar as the partner was concerned. In Loving, however, we correctly applied heightened scrutiny, rather than the usual rational-basis review, because the Virginia statute was "designed to maintain White Supremacy." Id., at 6, 11. A racially discriminatory purpose is always sufficient to subject a law to strict scrutiny, even a facially neutral law that makes no mention of race. See Washington v. Davis, 426 U.S. 229, 241–242 (1976). No purpose to discriminate against men or women as a class can be gleaned from the Texas law, so rational-basis review applies. That review is readily satisfied here by the same rational basis that satisfied it in Bowers—society's belief that certain forms of sexual behavior are "immoral and unacceptable," 478 U.S., at 196. This is the same justification that supports many other laws regulating sexual behavior that make a distinction based upon the identity of the partner—

for example, laws against adultery, fornication, and adult incest, and laws refusing to recognize homosexual marriage.

Justice O'Connor argues that the discrimination in this law which must be justified is not its discrimination with regard to the sex of the partner but its discrimination with regard to the sexual proclivity of the principal actor.

"While it is true that the law applies only to conduct, the conduct targeted by this law is conduct that is closely correlated with being homosexual. Under such circumstances, Texas' sodomy law is targeted at more than conduct. It is instead directed toward gay persons as a class." Ante, at 5.

Of course the same could be said of any law. A law against public nudity targets "the conduct that is closely correlated with being a nudist," and hence "is targeted at more than conduct"; it is "directed toward nudists as a class." But be that as it may. Even if the Texas law does deny equal protection to "homosexuals as a class," that denial still does not need to be justified by anything more than a rational basis, which our cases show is satisfied by the enforcement of traditional notions of sexual morality.

Justice O'Connor simply decrees application of "a more searching form of rational basis review" to the Texas statute. Ante, at 2. The cases she cites do not recognize such a standard, and reach their conclusions only after finding, as required by conventional rational-basis analysis, that no conceivable legitimate state interest supports the classification at issue. See Romer v. Evans, 517 U.S., at 635; Cleburne v. Cleburne Living Center, Inc., 473 U.S. 432, 448—450 (1985); Department of Agriculture v. Moreno, 413 U.S. 528, 534—538 (1973). Nor does Justice O'Connor explain precisely what her "more searching form" of rational-basis review consists of. It must at least mean, however, that laws exhibiting " 'a … desire to harm a politically unpopular group,' " ante, at 2, are invalid even though there may be a conceivable rational basis to support them.

This reasoning leaves on pretty shaky grounds state laws limiting marriage to opposite-sex couples. Justice O'Connor seeks to preserve them by the conclusory statement that "preserving the traditional institution of marriage" is a legitimate state interest. Ante, at 7. But "preserving the traditional institution of marriage" is just a kinder way of describing the State's moral disapproval of same-sex couples. Texas's interest in §21.06 could be recast in similarly euphemistic terms: "preserving the traditional sexual mores of our society." In the jurisprudence Justice O'Connor has seemingly created, judges can validate laws by characterizing them as "preserving the traditions of society" (good); or invalidate them by characterizing them as "expressing moral disapproval" (bad).

* * *

Today's opinion is the product of a Court, which is the product of a law-profession culture, that has largely signed on to the so-called homosexual agenda, by which I mean the agenda promoted by some homosexual activists directed at eliminating the moral opprobrium that has traditionally attached to homosexual conduct. I noted in an earlier opinion the fact that the American Association of Law Schools (to which any reputable law school must seek to belong) excludes from membership any school that refuses to ban from its job-interview facilities a law firm (no matter how small) that does not wish to hire as a prospective partner a person who openly engages in homosexual conduct. See Romer, supra, at 653.

One of the most revealing statements in today's opinion is the Court's grim warning that the criminalization of homosexual conduct is "an invitation to subject homosexual persons to discrimination both in the public and in the private spheres." Ante, at 14. It is clear from this that the Court has taken sides in the culture war, departing from its role of assuring, as neutral observer, that the democratic rules of engagement are observed. Many Americans do not want persons who openly engage in homosexual conduct as partners in their business, as scoutmasters for their children, as teachers in their children's schools, or as boarders in their home. They view this as protecting themselves and their families from a lifestyle that they believe to be immoral and destructive. The Court views it as "discrimination" which it is the function of our judgments to deter. So imbued is the Court with the law profession's anti-anti-homosexual culture, that it is seemingly unaware that the attitudes of that culture are not obviously "mainstream"; that in most States what the Court calls "discrimination" against those who engage in homosexual acts is perfectly legal; that proposals to ban such "discrimination" under Title VII have repeatedly been rejected by Congress, see Employment Non-Discrimination Act of 1994, S. 2238, 103d Cong., 2d Sess. (1994); Civil Rights Amendments, H. R. 5452, 94th Cong., 1st Sess. (1975); that in some cases such "discrimination" is mandated by federal statute, see 10 U.S.C. § 654(b)(1) (mandating discharge from the armed forces of any service member who engages in or intends to engage in homosexual acts); and that in some cases such "discrimination" is a constitutional right, see Boy Scouts of America v. Dale, 530 U.S. 640 (2000).

Let me be clear that I have nothing against homosexuals, or any other group, promoting their agenda through normal democratic means. Social perceptions of sexual and other morality change over time, and every group has the right to persuade its fellow citizens that its view of such matters is the best. That homosexuals have achieved some success in that enterprise is attested to by the fact that Texas is one of the few remaining States that criminalize private, consensual homosexual acts. But persuading one's fellow citizens is one thing, and imposing one's views in absence of democratic majority will is something else. I would no more require a State to criminalize homosexual acts–or, for that matter, display any moral disapprobation of them–than I would forbid it to do so. What Texas has chosen to do is well within the range of traditional democratic action, and its hand should not be stayed through the invention of a brand-new "constitutional right" by a Court that is impatient of democratic change. It is indeed true that "later generations can see that laws once thought necessary and proper in fact serve only to oppress," ante, at 18; and when that happens, later generations can repeal those laws. But it is the premise of our system that those judgments are to be made by the people, and not imposed by a governing caste that knows best.

One of the benefits of leaving regulation of this matter to the people rather than to the courts is that the people, unlike judges, need not carry things to their logical conclusion. The people may feel that their disapproval of homosexual conduct is strong enough to disallow homosexual marriage, but not strong enough to criminalize private homosexual acts–and may legislate accordingly. The Court today pretends that it possesses a similar freedom of action, so that that we need not fear judicial imposition of homosexual marriage, as has recently occurred in Canada (in a decision that the Canadian Government has chosen not to appeal). See Halpern v. Toronto, 2003 WL 34950 (Ontario Ct. App.); Cohen, Dozens in Canada Follow Gay Couple's Lead, Washington Post, June 12, 2003, p. A25. At the end of its opinion–after having laid waste the foundations of our rational-basis jurisprudence–the Court says that the present case "does not involve whether the government must give formal recognition to any relationship that homosexual persons seek to enter." Ante, at 17. Do not believe it. More illuminating than this bald, unreasoned disclaimer is the progression of thought displayed by an earlier passage in the Court's opinion, which notes the constitutional protections afforded to "personal decisions relating to marriage, procreation, contraception, family relationships, child rearing, and education," and then declares that "[p]ersons in a homosexual relationship may seek autonomy for these purposes, just as heterosexual persons do." Ante, at 13 (emphasis added). Today's opinion dismantles the structure of constitutional law that has permitted a distinction to be made between heterosexual and homosexual unions, insofar as formal recognition in marriage is concerned. If moral disapprobation of homosexual conduct is "no legitimate state interest" for purposes of proscribing that conduct, ante, at 18; and if, as the Court coos (casting aside all pretense of neutrality), "[w]hen sexuality finds overt expression in intimate conduct with another person, the conduct can be but one element in a personal bond that is more enduring," ante, at 6; what justification could there possibly be for denying the benefits of marriage to homosexual couples exercising "[t]he liberty protected by the Constitution," ibid.? Surely not the encouragement of procreation, since the sterile and the elderly are allowed to marry. This case "does not involve" the issue of homosexual marriage only if one entertains the belief that principle and logic have nothing to do with the decisions of this Court. Many will hope that, as the Court comfortingly assures us, this is so.

The matters appropriate for this Court's resolution are only three: Texas's prohibition of sodomy neither infringes a "fundamental right" (which the Court does not dispute), nor is unsupported by a rational relation to what the Constitution considers a legitimate state interest, nor denies the equal protection of the laws. I dissent.

Notes to Justice Scalia's dissent in Lawrence v. Texas (June 26, 2003)

1. This last-cited critic of Bowers actually writes: "[Bowers] is correct nevertheless that the right to engage in homosexual acts is not deeply rooted in America's history and tradition." Posner, Sex and Reason, at 343.

2. While the Court does not overrule Bowers' holding that homosexual sodomy is not a "fundamental right," it is worth noting that the "societal reliance" upon that aspect of the decision has been substantial as well. See 10 U.S.C. § 654(b)(1) ("A member of the armed forces shall be separated from the armed forces ... if ... the member has engaged in ... a homosexual act or acts"); Marcum v. McWhorter, 308 F.3d 635, 640—642 (CA6 2002) (relying on Bowers in rejecting a claimed fundamental right to commit adultery); Mullins v. Oregon, 57 F.3d 789, 793—794 (CA9 1995) (relying on Bowers in rejecting a grandparent's claimed "fundamental liberty interes[t]" in the adoption of her grandchildren); Doe v. Wigginton, 21 F.3d 733, 739—740 (CA6 1994) (relying on Bowers in rejecting a prisoner's claimed "fundamental right" to on-demand HIV testing); Schowengerdt v. United States, 944 F.2d 483, 490 (CA9 1991) (relying on Bowers in upholding a bisexual's discharge from the armed services); Charles v. Baesler, 910 F.2d 1349, 1353 (CA6 1990) (relying on Bowers in rejecting fire department captain's claimed "fundamental" interest in a promotion); Henne v. Wright, 904 F.2d 1208, 1214—1215 (CA8 1990) (relying on Bowers in rejecting a claim that state law restricting surnames that could be given to children at birth implicates a "fundamental right"); Walls v. Petersburg, 895 F.2d 188, 193 (CA4 1990) (relying on Bowers in rejecting substantive-

due-process challenge to a police department questionnaire that asked prospective employees about homosexual activity); High Tech Gays v. Defense Industrial Security Clearance Office, 895 F.2d 563, 570—571 (CA9 1988) (relying on Bowers' holding that homosexual activity is not a fundamental right in rejecting—on the basis of the rational-basis standard—an equal-protection challenge to the Defense Department's policy of conducting expanded investigations into backgrounds of gay and lesbian applicants for secret and top-secret security clearance).

3. The Court is quite right that "history and tradition are the starting point but not in all cases the ending point of the substantive due process inquiry," ante, at 11. An asserted "fundamental liberty interest" must not only be "deeply rooted in this Nation's history and tradition," Washington v. Glucksberg, 521 U.S. 702, 721 (1997), but it must also be "implicit in the concept of ordered liberty," so that "neither liberty nor justice would exist if [it] were sacrificed," ibid. Moreover, liberty interests unsupported by history and tradition, though not deserving of "heightened scrutiny," are still protected from state laws that are not rationally related to any legitimate state interest. Id., at 722. As I proceed to discuss, it is this latter principle that the Court applies in the present case.

Campaign finance limits: Justice Scalia's concurrence and dissent in McConnell v. Federal Election Commission (December 10, 2003)

Justice Scalia, concurring with respect to BCRA Titles III and IV, dissenting with respect to BCRA Titles I and V, and concurring in the judgment in part and dissenting in part with respect to BCRA Title II.

With respect to Titles I, II, and V: I join in full the dissent of The Chief Justice; I join the opinion of Justice Kennedy, except to the extent it upholds new §323(e) of the Federal Election Campaign Act of 1971 (FECA) and §202 of the Bipartisan Campaign Reform Act of 2002 (BCRA) in part; and because I continue to believe that Buckley v. Valeo, 424 U.S. 1 (1976) (per curiam), was wrongly decided, I also join Parts I, II—A, and II—B of the opinion of Justice Thomas. With respect to Titles III and IV, I join The Chief Justice's opinion for the Court. Because these cases are of such extraordinary importance, I cannot avoid adding to the many writings a few words of my own.

This is a sad day for the freedom of speech. Who could have imagined that the same Court which, within the past four years, has sternly disapproved of restrictions upon such inconsequential forms of expression as virtual child pornography, Ashcroft v. Free Speech Coalition, 535 U.S. 234 (2002), tobacco advertising, Lorillard Tobacco Co. v. Reilly, 533 U.S. 525 (2001), dissemination of illegally intercepted communications, Bartnicki v. Vopper, 532 U.S. 514 (2001), and sexually explicit cable programming, United States v. Playboy Entertainment Group, Inc., 529 U.S. 803 (2000), would smile with favor upon a law that cuts to the heart of what the First Amendment is meant to protect: the right to criticize the government. For that is what the most offensive provisions of this legislation are all about. We are governed by Congress, and this legislation prohibits the criticism of Members of Congress by those entities most capable of giving such criticism loud voice: national political parties and corporations, both of the commercial and the not-for-profit sort. It forbids pre-election criticism of incumbents by corporations, even not-for-profit corporations, by use of their general funds; and forbids national-party use of "soft" money to fund "issue ads" that incumbents find so offensive.

To be sure, the legislation is evenhanded: It similarly prohibits criticism of the candidates who oppose Members of Congress in their reelection bids. But as everyone knows, this is an area in which evenhandedness is not fairness. If all electioneering were evenhandedly prohibited, incumbents would have an enormous advantage. Likewise, if incumbents and challengers are limited to the same quantity of electioneering, incumbents are favored. In other words, any restriction upon a type of campaign speech that is equally available to challengers and incumbents tends to favor incumbents.

Beyond that, however, the present legislation targets for prohibition certain categories of campaign speech that are particularly harmful to incumbents. Is it accidental, do you think, that incumbents raise about three times as much "hard money"–the sort of funding generally not restricted by this legislation–as do their challengers? See FEC, 1999—2000 Financial Activity of All Senate and House Campaigns (Jan. 1, 1999—Dec. 31, 2000) (last modified on May 15, 2001), http://www.fec.gov/press/ 051501congfinact/tables/allcong2000.xls (all Internet ma-terials as visited Dec. 4, 2003, and available in Clerk of Court's case file). Or that lobbyists (who seek the favor of incumbents) give 92 percent of their money in "hard" contributions? See U.S. Public Interest Research Group (PIRG), The Lobbyist's Last Laugh: How K Street Lob-byists Would Benefit from the McCain-Feingold Cam-paign Finance Bill 3 (July 5, 2001), http://www.pirg.org/ democracy/democracy.asp?id2=5068. Is it an oversight, do you suppose, that the so-called "millionaire provisions" raise the contribution limit for a candidate running against an individual who devotes to the campaign (as challengers often do) great personal wealth, but do not raise the limit for a candidate running against an individual who devotes to the campaign (as incumbents often do) a massive election "war chest"? See BCRA §§304, 316, and 319. And is it mere happenstance, do you estimate, that national-party funding, which is severely limited by the Act, is more likely to assist cash-strapped challengers than flush-with-hard-money incumbents? See A. Gierzynski & D. Breaux, The Financing Role of Parties, in Campaign Finance in State Legislative Elections 195—200 (J. Thompson & S. Moncrief eds. 1998). Was it unintended, by any chance, that incumbents are free personally to receive some soft money and even to solicit it for other organizations, while national parties are not? See new FECA §§323(a) and (e).

I wish to address three fallacious propositions that might be thought to justify some or all of the provisions of this legislation–only the last of which is explicitly embraced by the principal opinion for the Court, but all of which underlie, I think, its approach to these cases.

(a) Money is Not Speech

It was said by congressional proponents of this legislation, see 143 Cong. Rec. 20746 (1997) (remarks of Sen. Boxer), 145 Cong. Rec. S12612 (Oct. 14, 1999) (remarks of Sen. Cleland), 147 Cong. Rec. S2436 (Mar. 19, 2001) (remarks of Sen. Dodd), with support from the law reviews, see, e.g., Wright, Politics and the Constitution: Is Money Speech?, 85 Yale L. J. 1001 (1976), that since this legislation regulates nothing but the expenditure of money for speech, as opposed to speech itself, the burden it imposes is not subject to full First Amendment scrutiny; the government may regulate the raising and spending of campaign funds just as it regulates other forms of conduct, such as burning draft cards, see United States v. O'Brien, 391 U.S. 367 (1968), or camping out on the National Mall, see Clark v. Community for Creative Non&nbhyph;Violence, 468 U.S. 288 (1984). That proposition has been endorsed by one of the two authors of today's principal opinion: "The right to use one's own money to hire gladiators, [and] to fund 'speech by proxy,' ... [are] property rights ... not entitled to the same protection as the right to say what one pleases." Nixon v. Shrink Missouri Government PAC, 528 U.S. 377, 399 (2000) (Stevens, J., concurring). Until today, however, that view has been categorically rejected by our jurisprudence. As we said in Buckley, 424 U.S., at 16, "this Court has never suggested that the dependence of a communication on the expenditure of money operates itself to introduce a nonspeech element or to reduce the exacting scrutiny required by the First Amendment."

Our traditional view was correct, and today's cavalier attitude toward regulating the financing of speech (the "exacting scrutiny" test of Buckley, see ibid., is not uttered in any majority opinion, and is not observed in the ones from which I dissent) frustrates the fundamental purpose of the First Amendment. In any economy operated on even the most rudimentary principles of division of labor, effective public communication requires the speaker to make use of the services of others. An author may write a novel, but he will seldom publish and distribute it himself. A freelance reporter may write a story, but he will rarely edit, print, and deliver it to subscribers. To a government bent on suppressing speech, this mode of organization presents opportunities: Control any cog in the machine, and you can halt the whole apparatus. License printers, and it matters little whether authors are still free to write. Restrict the sale of books, and it matters little who prints them. Predictably, repressive regimes have exploited these principles by attacking all levels of the production and dissemination of ideas. See, e.g., Printing Act of 1662, 14 Car. II, c. 33, §§1, 4, 7 (punishing printers, importers, and booksellers); Printing Act of 1649, 2 Acts and Ordinances of the Interregnum 245, 246, 250 (punishing authors, printers, booksellers, importers, and buyers). In response to this threat, we have interpreted the First Amendment broadly. See, e.g., Bantam Books, Inc. v. Sullivan, 372 U.S. 58, 65, n. 6 (1963) ("The constitutional guarantee of freedom of the press embraces the circulation of books as well as their publication ...").

Division of labor requires a means of mediating exchange, and in a commercial society, that means is supplied by money. The publisher pays the author for the right to sell his book; it pays its staff who print and assemble the book; it demands payments from booksellers who bring the book to market. This, too, presents opportunities for repression: Instead of regulating the various parties to the enterprise individually, the government can suppress their ability to coordinate by regulating their use of money. What good is the right to print books without a right to buy works from authors? Or the right to publish newspapers without the right to pay deliverymen? The right to speak would be largely ineffective if it did not include the right to engage in financial transactions that are the incidents of its exercise.

This is not to say that any regulation of money is a regulation of speech. The government may apply general commercial regulations to those who use money for speech if it applies them evenhandedly to those who use money for other purposes. But where the government singles out money used to fund speech as its legislative object, it is acting against speech as such, no less than if it had targeted the paper on which a book was printed or the trucks that deliver it to the bookstore.

History and jurisprudence bear this out. The best early examples derive from the British efforts to tax the press after the lapse of licensing statutes by which the press was first regulated. The Stamp Act of 1712 imposed levies on all newspapers, including an additional tax for each advertisement. 10 Anne, c. 18, §113. It was a response to unfavorable war coverage, "obvious[ly] ... designed to check the publication of those newspapers and pamphlets which depended for their sale on their cheapness and sensationalism." F. Siebert, Freedom of the Press in England, 1476–1776, pp. 309–310 (1952). It succeeded in killing off approximately half the newspapers in England in its first year. Id., at 312. In 1765, Parliament applied a similar Act to the Colonies. 5 Geo. III, c. 12, §1. The colonial Act likewise placed exactions on sales and advertising revenue, the latter at 2s. per advertisement, which was "by any standard . . . excessive, since the publisher himself received only from 3 to 5s. and still less for repeated insertions." A. Schlesinger, Prelude to Independence: The Newspaper War on Britain, 1764–1776, p. 68 (1958). The founding generation saw these taxes as grievous incursions on the freedom of the press. See, e.g., 1 D. Ramsay, History of the American Revolution 61–62 (L. Cohen ed. 1990); J. Adams, A Dissertation on the Canon and Feudal Law (1765), reprinted in 3 Life and Works of John Adams 445, 464 (C. Adams ed. 1851). See generally Grosjean v. American Press Co., 297 U.S. 233, 245–249 (1936); Schlesinger, supra, at 67–84.

We have kept faith with the Founders' tradition by prohibiting the selective taxation of the press. Minneapolis Star & Tribune Co. v. Minnesota Comm'r of Revenue, 460 U.S. 575 (1983) (ink and paper tax); Grosjean, supra (advertisement tax). And we have done so whether the tax was the product of illicit motive or not. See Minneapolis Star & Tribune Co., supra, at 592. These press-taxation cases belie the claim that regulation of money used to fund speech is not regulation of speech itself. A tax on a newspaper's advertising revenue does not prohibit anyone from saying anything; it merely appropriates part of the revenue that a speaker would otherwise obtain. That is even a step short of totally prohibiting advertising revenue–

which would be analogous to the total prohibition of certain campaign-speech contributions in the present

cases. Yet it is unquestionably a violation of the First Amendment.

Many other cases exemplify the same principle that an attack upon the funding of speech is an attack upon speech itself. In Schaumburg v. Citizens for a Better Environment, 444 U.S. 620 (1980), we struck down an ordinance limiting the amount charities could pay their solicitors. In Simon & Schuster, Inc. v. Members of N. Y. State Crime Victims Bd., 502 U.S. 105 (1991), we held unconstitutional a state statute that appropriated the proceeds of criminals' biographies for payment to the victims. And in Rosenberger v. Rector and Visitors of Univ. of Va., 515 U.S. 819 (1995), we held unconstitutional a university's discrimination in the disbursement of funds to speakers on the basis of viewpoint. Most notable, perhaps, is our famous opinion in New York Times Co. v. Sullivan, 376 U.S. 254 (1964), holding that paid advertisements in a newspaper were entitled to full First Amendment protection:

"Any other conclusion would discourage newspapers from carrying 'editorial advertisements' of this type, and so might shut off an important outlet for the promulgation of information and ideas by persons who do not themselves have access to publishing facilities–who wish to exercise their freedom of speech even though they are not members of the press. The effect would be to shackle the First Amendment in its attempt to secure 'the widest possible dissemination of information from diverse and antagonistic sources.' " Id., at 266 (citations omitted).

This passage was relied on in Buckley for the point that restrictions on the expenditure of money for speech are equivalent to restrictions on speech itself. 424 U.S., at 16—17. That reliance was appropriate. If denying protection to paid-for speech would "shackle the First Amendment," so also does forbidding or limiting the right to pay for speech.

It should be obvious, then, that a law limiting the amount a person can spend to broadcast his political views is a direct restriction on speech. That is no different from a law limiting the amount a newspaper can pay its editorial staff or the amount a charity can pay its leafletters. It is equally clear that a limit on the amount a candidate can raise from any one individual for the purpose of speaking is also a direct limitation on speech. That is no different from a law limiting the amount a publisher can accept from any one shareholder or lender, or the amount a newspaper can charge any one advertiser or customer.

(b) Pooling Money is Not Speech

Another proposition which could explain at least some of the results of today's opinion is that the First Amendment right to spend money for speech does not include the right to combine with others in spending money for speech. Such a proposition fits uncomfortably with the concluding words of our Declaration of Independence: "And for the support of this Declaration, . . . we mutually pledge to each other our Lives, our Fortunes and our sacred Honor." (Emphasis added.) The freedom to associate with others for the dissemination of ideas—not just by singing or speaking in unison, but by pooling financial resources for expressive purposes—is part of the freedom of speech.

"Our form of government is built on the premise that every citizen shall have the right to engage in political expression and association. This right was enshrined in the First Amendment of the Bill of Rights. Exercise of these basic freedoms in America has traditionally been through the media of political associations. Any interference with the freedom of a party is simultaneously an interference with the freedom of its adherents." NAACP v. Button, 371 U.S. 415, 431 (1963) (internal quotation marks omitted).

"The First Amendment protects political association as well as political expression. The constitutional right of association explicated in NAACP v. Alabama, 357 U.S. 449, 460 (1958), stemmed from the Court's recognition that '[e]ffective advocacy of both public and private points of view, particularly controversial ones, is undeniably enhanced by group association.' Subsequent decisions have made clear that the First and Fourteenth Amendments guarantee ' "freedom to associate with others for the common advancement of political beliefs and ideas," ' . . . ." Buckley, supra, at 15.

We have said that "implicit in the right to engage in activities protected by the First Amendment" is "a corresponding right to associate with others in pursuit of a wide variety of political, social, economic, educational, religious, and cultural ends." Roberts v. United States Jaycees, 468 U.S. 609, 622 (1984). That "right to associate . . . in pursuit" includes the right to pool financial resources.

If it were otherwise, Congress would be empowered to enact legislation requiring newspapers to be sole proprietorships, banning their use of partnership or corporate form. That sort of restriction would be an obvious violation of the First Amendment, and it is incomprehensible why the conclusion should change when what is at issue is the pooling of funds for the most important (and most perennially threatened) category of speech: electoral speech. The principle that such financial association does not enjoy full First Amendment protection threatens the existence of all political parties.

(c) Speech by Corporations Can Be Abridged

The last proposition that might explain at least some of today's casual abridgment of free-speech rights is this: that the particular form of association known as a corporation does not enjoy full First Amendment protection. Of course the text of the First Amendment does not limit its application in this fashion, even though "[b]y the end of the eighteenth century the corporation was a familiar figure in American economic life." C. Cooke, Corporation, Trust and Company 92 (1951). Nor is there any basis in reason why First Amendment rights should not attach to corporate associations—and we have said so. In First Nat. Bank of Boston v. Bellotti, 435 U.S. 765 (1978), we held unconstitutional a state prohibition of corporate speech designed to influence the vote on referendum proposals. We said:

"[T]here is practically universal agreement that a major purpose of [the First] Amendment was to protect the free discussion of governmental affairs. If the speakers here were not corporations, no one would suggest that the State could silence their proposed speech. It is the type of speech indispensable to decisionmaking in a democracy, and this is no less true because the speech comes from a corporation rather than an individual. The inherent worth of the speech in terms of its capacity for informing the public does not depend upon the identity of its source, whether corporation, association, union, or individual." Id., at 776—777 (internal quotation marks, footnotes, and citations omitted).

In NAACP v. Button, supra, at 428—429, 431, we held that the NAACP could assert First Amendment rights "on its own behalf, . . . though a corporation," and that the activities of the corporation were "modes of expression and association protected by the First and Fourteenth Amendments." In Pacific Gas & Elec. Co. v. Public Util. Comm'n of Cal., 475 U.S. 1, 8 (1986), we held unconstitutional a state effort to compel corporate speech. "The identity of the speaker," we said, "is not decisive in determining whether speech is protected. Corporations and other associations, like individuals, contribute to the 'discussion, debate, and the dissemination of information and ideas' that the First Amendment seeks to foster." And in Buckley, 424 U.S. 1, we held unconstitutional FECA's limitation upon independent corporate expenditures.

The Court changed course in Austin v. Michigan Chamber of Commerce, 494 U.S. 652 (1990), upholding a state prohibition of an independent corporate expenditure in support of a candidate for state office. I dissented in that case, see id., at 679, and remain of the view that it was error. In the modern world, giving the government power to exclude corporations from the political debate enables it effectively to muffle the voices that best represent the most significant segments of the economy and the most passionately held social and political views. People who associate—who pool their financial resources—for purposes of economic enterprise overwhelmingly do so in the corporate form; and with increasing frequency, incorporation is chosen by those who associate to defend and promote particular ideas—such as the American Civil Liberties Union and the National Rifle Association, parties to these cases. Imagine, then, a government that wished to suppress nuclear power—or oil and gas exploration, or automobile manufacturing, or gun ownership, or civil liberties—and that had the power to prohibit corporate advertising against its proposals. To be sure, the individuals involved in, or benefited by, those industries, or interested in those causes, could (given enough time) form political action committees or other associations to make their case. But the organizational form in which those enterprises already exist, and in which they can most quickly and most effectively get their message across, is the corporate form. The First Amendment does not in my view permit the restriction of that political speech. And the same holds true for corporate electoral speech: A candidate should not be insulated from the most effective speech that the major participants in the economy and major incorporated interest groups can generate.

But what about the danger to the political system posed by "amassed wealth"? The most direct threat from that source comes in the form of undisclosed favors and payoffs to elected officials—which have already been criminalized, and will be rendered no more discoverable by the legislation at issue here. The use of corporate wealth (like individual wealth) to speak to the electorate is unlikely to "distort" elections—especially if disclosure requirements tell the people where the speech is coming from. The premise of the First Amendment is that the American people are neither sheep nor fools, and hence fully capable of considering both the substance of the speech presented to them and its proximate and ultimate source. If that premise is wrong, our democracy has a much greater problem to overcome than merely the influence of amassed wealth. Given the premises of democracy, there is no such thing as too much speech.

But, it is argued, quite apart from its effect upon the electorate, corporate speech in the form of contributions to the candidate's campaign, or even in the form of independent expenditures supporting the candidate, engenders an obligation which is later paid in the form of greater access to the officeholder, or indeed in the form of votes on particular bills. Any quid-pro-quo agreement for votes would of course violate criminal law, see 18 U.S.C. § 201 and actual payoff votes have not even been claimed by those favoring the restrictions on corporate speech. It cannot be denied, however, that corporate (like noncorporate) allies will have greater access to the officeholder, and that he will tend to favor the same causes as those who support him (which is usually why they supported him). That is the nature of politics—if not indeed human nature—and how this can properly be considered "corruption" (or "the appearance of corruption") with regard to corporate allies and not with regard to other allies is beyond me. If the Bill of Rights had intended an exception to the freedom of speech in order to combat this malign proclivity of the officeholder to agree with those who agree with him, and to speak more with his supporters than his opponents, it would surely have said so. It did not do so, I think, because the juice is not worth the squeeze. Evil corporate (and private affluent) influences are well enough checked (so long as adequate campaign-expenditure disclosure rules exist) by the politician's fear of being portrayed as "in the pocket" of so-called moneyed interests. The incremental benefit obtained by muzzling corporate speech is more than offset by loss of the information and persuasion that corporate speech can contain. That, at least, is the assumption of a constitutional guarantee which prescribes that Congress shall make no law abridging the freedom of speech.

But let us not be deceived. While the Government's briefs and arguments before this Court focused on the horrible "appearance of corruption," the most passionate floor statements during the debates on this legislation pertained to so-called attack ads, which the Constitution surely protects, but which Members of Congress analogized to "crack cocaine," 144 Cong. Rec. S868 (Feb. 24, 1998) (remarks of Sen. Daschle), "drive-by shooting[s]," id., at S879 (remarks of Sen. Durbin), and "air pollution," 143 Cong. Rec. 20505 (1997) (remarks of Sen. Dorgan). There is good reason to believe that the ending of negative campaign ads was the principal attraction of the legislation. A Senate sponsor said, "I hope that we will not allow our attention to be distracted from the real issues at hand—how to raise the tenor of the debate in our elections and give people real choices. No one benefits from negative ads. They don't aid our Nation's political dialog." Id., at 20521—20522 (remarks of Sen. McCain). He assured the body that "[y]ou cut off the soft money, you are going to see a lot less of that [attack ads]. Prohibit unions and corporations, and you will see a lot less of that. If you demand full disclosure for those who pay for those ads, you are going to see a lot less of that . . . ." 147 Cong. Rec. S3116 (Mar. 29, 2001) (remarks of Sen. McCain). See also, e.g., 148 Cong. Rec. S2117 (Mar. 20, 2002) (remarks of Sen. Cantwell) ("This bill is about slowing the ad war. . . . It is about slowing political advertising and making sure the flow of negative ads by outside interest groups does not continue to permeate the airwaves"); 143 Cong. Rec. 20746 (1997) (remarks of Sen. Boxer) ("These so-called issues ads are not regulated at all and mention candidates by name. They directly attack candidates without any accountability. It is brutal... . We have an opportunity in the McCain-Feingold bill to stop that . . ."); 145 Cong. Rec. S12606—S12607 (Oct. 14, 1999) (remarks of Sen. Wellstone) ("I think these issue advocacy ads are a nightmare. I think all of us should hate them... . [By passing the legislation], [w]e could get some of this poison politics off television").

Another theme prominent in the legislative debates was the notion that there is too much money spent on elections. The first principle of "reform" was that "there should be less money in politics." 147 Cong. Rec. S3236 (Apr. 2, 2001) (remarks of Sen. Murray). "The enormous amounts of special interest money that flood our political system have become a cancer in our democracy." 148 Cong. Rec. S2151 (Mar. 20, 2002) (remarks of Sen. Kennedy). "[L]arge sums of money drown out the voice of the average voter." 148 Cong. Rec. H373 (Feb. 13, 2002) (remarks of Rep. Langevin). The system of campaign finance is "drowning in money." Id., at H404 (remarks of Rep. Menendez). And most expansively:

"Despite the ever-increasing sums spent on campaigns, we have not seen an improvement in campaign discourse, issue discussion or voter education. More money does not mean more ideas, more substance or more depth. Instead, it means more of what voters complain about most. More 30-second spots, more negativity and an increasingly longer campaign period." 148 Cong. Rec. S2150 (Mar. 20, 2002) (remarks of Sen. Kerry).

Perhaps voters do detest these 30-second spots—though I suspect they detest even more hour-long campaign-debate interruptions of their favorite entertainment programming. Evidently, however, these ads do persuade voters, or else they would not be so routinely used by sophisticated politicians of all parties. The point, in any event, is that it is not the proper role of those who govern us to judge which campaign speech has "substance" and "depth" (do you think it might be that which is least damaging to incumbents?) and to abridge the rest.

And what exactly are these outrageous sums frittered away in determining who will govern us? A report prepared for Congress concluded that the total amount, in hard and soft money, spent on the 2000 federal elections was between $2.4 and $2.5 billion. J. Cantor, CRS Report for Congress, Campaign Finance in the 2000 Federal Elections: Overview and Estimates of the Flow of Money (2001). All campaign spending in the United States, including state elections, ballot initiatives, and judicial elections, has been estimated at $3.9 billion for 2000, Nelson, Spending in the 2000 Elections, in Financing the 2000 Election 24, Tbl. 2—1 (D. Magleby ed. 2002), which was a year that "shattered spending and contribution records," id., at 22. Even taking this last, larger figure as the benchmark, it means that Americans spent about half as much electing all their Nation's officials, state and federal, as they spent on movie tickets ($7.8 billion); about a fifth as much as they spent on cosmetics and perfume ($18.8 billion); and about a sixth as much as they spent on pork (the nongovernmental sort) ($22.8 billion). See U.S. Dept. of Commerce, Bureau of Economic Analysis, Tbl. 2.6U (Col. AS; Rows 356, 214, and 139), http:// www.bea.doc.gov/bea/dn/206u.csv. If our democracy is drowning from this much spending, it cannot swim.

* * *

Which brings me back to where I began: This litigation is about preventing criticism of the government. I cannot say for certain that many, or some, or even any, of the Members of Congress who voted for this legislation did so not to produce "fairer" campaigns, but to mute criticism of their records and facilitate reelection. Indeed, I will stipulate that all those who voted for the Act believed they were acting for the good of the country. There remains the problem of the Charlie Wilson Phenomenon, named after Charles Wilson, former president of General Motors, who is supposed to have said during the Senate hearing on his nomination as Secretary of Defense that "what's good for General Motors is good for the country."* Those in power, even giving them the benefit of the greatest good will, are inclined to believe that what is good for them is good for the country. Whether in prescient recognition of the Charlie Wilson Phenomenon, or out of fear of good old-fashioned, malicious, self-interested manipulation, "[t]he fundamental approach of the First Amendment . . . was to assume the worst, and to rule the regulation of political speech 'for fairness' sake' simply out of bounds." Austin, 494 U.S., at 693 (Scalia, J., dissenting). Having abandoned that approach to a limited extent in Buckley, we abandon it much further today.

We will unquestionably be called upon to abandon it further still in the future. The most frightening passage in the lengthy floor debates on this legislation is the following assurance given by one of the cosponsoring Senators to his colleagues:

"This is a modest step, it is a first step, it is an essential step, but it does not even begin to address, in some ways, the fundamental problems that exist with the hard money aspect of the system." 148 Cong. Rec. S2101 (Mar. 20, 2002) (statement of Sen. Feingold).

The system indeed. The first instinct of power is the retention of power, and, under a Constitution that requires periodic elections, that is best achieved by the suppression of election-time speech. We have witnessed merely the second scene of Act I of what promises to be a lengthy tragedy. In scene 3 the Court, having abandoned most of the First Amendment weaponry that Buckley left intact, will be even less equipped to resist the incumbents' writing of the rules of political debate. The federal election campaign laws, which are already (as today's opinions show) so voluminous, so detailed, so complex, that no ordinary citizen dare run for office, or even contribute a significant sum, without hiring an expert advisor in the field, can be expected to grow more voluminous, more detailed, and more complex in the years to come—and always, always, with the objective of reducing the excessive amount of speech.

Notes

*. * It is disillusioning to learn that the fabled quote is inaccurate. Wilson actually said: "[F]or years I thought what was good for our country was good for General Motors, and vice versa. The difference did not exist." Hearings before the Senate Committee on Armed Services, 83d Cong., 1st Sess., 26 (1953).

Hamdi is entitled to a habeas decree requiring his release unless (1) criminal proceedings are promptly brought, or (2) Congress has suspended the writ of habeas corpus: Justice Scalia's dissent in Hamdi v. Rumsfeld (June 28, 2004)

Justice Scalia, with whom Justice Stevens joins, dissenting.

Petitioner, a presumed American citizen, has been imprisoned without charge or hearing in the Norfolk and Charleston Naval Brigs for more than two years, on the allegation that he is an enemy combatant who bore arms against his country for the Taliban. His father claims to the contrary, that he is an inexperienced aid worker caught in the wrong place at the wrong time. This case brings into conflict the competing demands of national security and our citizens' constitutional right to personal liberty. Although I share the Court's evident unease as it seeks to reconcile the two, I do not agree with its resolution.

Where the Government accuses a citizen of waging war against it, our constitutional tradition has been to prosecute him in federal court for treason or some other crime. Where the exigencies of war prevent that, the Constitution's Suspension Clause, Art. I, §9, cl. 2, allows Congress to relax the usual protections temporarily. Absent suspension, however, the Executive's assertion of military exigency has not been thought sufficient to permit detention without charge. No one contends that the congressional Authorization for Use of Military Force, on which the Government relies to justify its actions here, is an implementation of the Suspension Clause. Accordingly, I would reverse the decision below.

I

The very core of liberty secured by our Anglo-Saxon system of separated powers has been freedom from indefinite imprisonment at the will of the Executive. Blackstone stated this principle clearly:

"Of great importance to the public is the preservation of this personal liberty: for if once it were left in the power of any, the highest, magistrate to imprison arbitrarily whomever he or his officers thought proper ... there would soon be an end of all other rights and immunities. ... To bereave a man of life, or by violence to confiscate his estate, without accusation or trial, would be so gross and notorious an act of despotism, as must at once convey the alarm of tyranny throughout the whole kingdom. But confinement of the person, by secretly hurrying him to gaol, where his sufferings are unknown or forgotten; is a less public, a less striking, and therefore a more dangerous engine of arbitrary government. ...

"To make imprisonment lawful, it must either be, by process from the courts of judicature, or by warrant from some legal officer, having authority to commit to prison; which warrant must be in writing, under the hand and seal of the magistrate, and express the causes of the commitment, in order to be examined into (if necessary) upon a habeas corpus. If there be no cause expressed, the gaoler is not bound to detain the prisoner. For the law judges in this respect, ... that it is unreasonable to send a prisoner, and not to signify withal the crimes alleged against him." 1 W. Blackstone, Commentaries on the Laws of England 132—133 (1765) (hereinafter Blackstone).

These words were well known to the Founders. Hamilton quoted from this very passage in The Federalist No. 84, p. 444 (G. Carey & J. McClellan eds. 2001). The two ideas central to Blackstone's understanding—due process as the right secured, and habeas corpus as the instrument by which due process could be insisted upon by a citizen illegally imprisoned—found expression in the Constitution's Due Process and Suspension Clauses. See Amdt. 5; Art. I, §9, cl. 2.

The gist of the Due Process Clause, as understood at the founding and since, was to force the Government to follow those common-law procedures traditionally deemed necessary before depriving a person of life, liberty, or property. When a citizen was deprived of liberty because of alleged criminal conduct, those procedures typically required committal by a magistrate followed by indictment and trial. See, e.g., 2 & 3 Phil. & M., c. 10 (1555); 3 J. Story, Commentaries on the Constitution of the United States §1783, p. 661 (1833) (hereinafter Story) (equating "due process of law" with "due presentment or indictment, and being brought in to answer thereto by due process of the common law"). The Due Process Clause "in effect affirms the right of trial according to the process and proceedings of the common law." Ibid. See also T. Cooley, General Principles of Constitutional Law 224 (1880) ("When life and liberty are in question, there must in every instance be judicial proceedings; and that requirement implies an accusation, a hearing before an impartial tribunal, with proper jurisdiction, and a conviction and judgment before the punishment can be inflicted" (internal quotation marks omitted)).

To be sure, certain types of permissible noncriminal detention—that is, those not dependent upon the contention that the citizen had committed a criminal act—did not require the protections of criminal procedure. However, these fell into a limited number of well-recognized exceptions—civil commitment of the mentally ill, for example, and temporary detention in quarantine of the infectious. See Opinion on the Writ of Habeas Corpus, 97 Eng. Rep. 29, 36—37 (H. L. 1758) (Wilmot, J.). It is unthinkable that the Executive could render otherwise criminal grounds for detention noncriminal merely by disclaiming an intent to prosecute, or by asserting that it was incapacitating dangerous offenders rather than punishing wrongdoing. Cf. Kansas v. Hendricks, 521 U.S. 346, 358 (1997) ("A finding of dangerousness, standing alone, is ordinarily not a sufficient ground upon which to justify indefinite involuntary commitment").

These due process rights have historically been vindicated by the writ of habeas corpus. In England before the founding, the writ developed into a tool for challenging executive confinement. It was not always effective. For example, in Darnel's Case, 3 How. St. Tr. 1 (K. B. 1627), King Charles I detained without charge several individuals for failing to assist England's war against France and Spain. The prisoners sought writs of habeas corpus, arguing that without specific charges, "imprisonment shall not continue on for a time, but for ever; and the subjects of this kingdom may be restrained of their liberties perpetually." Id., at 8. The Attorney General replied that the Crown's interest in protecting the realm justified imprisonment in "a matter of state ... not ripe nor timely" for the ordinary process of accusation and trial. Id., at 37. The court denied relief, producing widespread outrage, and Parliament responded with the Petition of Right, accepted by the King in 1628, which expressly prohibited imprisonment without formal charges, see 3 Car. 1, c. 1, §§5, 10.

The struggle between subject and Crown continued, and culminated in the Habeas Corpus Act of 1679, 31 Car. 2, c. 2, described by Blackstone as a "second magna charta, and stable bulwark of our liberties." 1 Blackstone 133. The Act governed all persons "committed or detained ... for any crime." §3. In cases other than felony or treason plainly expressed in the warrant of commitment, the Act required release upon appropriate sureties (unless the commitment was for a nonbailable offense). Ibid. Where the commitment was for felony or high treason, the Act did not require immediate release, but instead required the Crown to commence criminal proceedings within a specified time. §7. If the prisoner was not "indicted some Time in the next Term," the judge was "required ... to set at Liberty the Prisoner upon Bail" unless the King was unable to produce his witnesses. Ibid. Able or no, if the prisoner was not brought to trial by the next succeeding term, the Act provided that "he shall be discharged from his Imprisonment." Ibid. English courts sat four terms per year, see 3 Blackstone 275—277, so the practical effect of this provision was that imprisonment without indictment or trial for felony or high treason under §7 would not exceed approximately three to six months.

The writ of habeas corpus was preserved in the Constitution—the only common-law writ to be explicitly mentioned. See Art. I, §9, cl. 2. Hamilton lauded "the establishment of the writ of habeas corpus" in his Federalist defense as a means to protect against "the practice of arbitrary imprisonments ... in all ages, [one of] the favourite and most formidable instruments of tyranny." The Federalist No. 84, supra, at 444. Indeed, availability of the writ under the new Constitution (along with the requirement of trial by jury in criminal cases, see Art. III, §2, cl. 3) was his basis for arguing that additional, explicit procedural protections were unnecessary. See The Federalist No. 83, at 433.

II

The allegations here, of course, are no ordinary accusations of criminal activity. Yaser Esam Hamdi has been imprisoned because the Government believes he participated in the waging of war against the United States. The relevant question, then, is whether there is a different, special procedure for imprisonment of a citizen accused of wrongdoing by aiding the enemy in wartime.

A

Justice O'Connor, writing for a plurality of this Court, asserts that captured enemy combatants (other than those suspected of war crimes) have traditionally been detained until the cessation of hostilities and then released. Ante, at 10—11. That is probably an accurate description of wartime practice with respect to enemy aliens. The tradition with respect to American citizens, however, has been quite different. Citizens aiding the enemy have been treated as traitors subject to the criminal process.

As early as 1350, England's Statute of Treasons made it a crime to "levy War against our Lord the King in his Realm, or be adherent to the King's Enemies in his Realm, giving to them Aid and Comfort, in the Realm, or elsewhere." 25 Edw. 3, Stat. 5, c. 2. In his 1762 Discourse on High Treason, Sir Michael Foster explained:

"With regard to Natural-born Subjects there can be no Doubt. They owe Allegiance to the Crown at all Times and in all Places.

. . . . .

"The joining with Rebels in an Act of Rebellion, or with Enemies in Acts of Hostility, will make a Man a Traitor: in the one Case within the Clause of Levying War, in the other within that of Adhering to the King's enemies.

. . . . .

"States in Actual Hostility with Us, though no War be solemnly Declared, are Enemies within the meaning of the Act. And therefore in an Indictment on the Clause of Adhering to the King's Enemies, it is sufficient to Aver that the Prince or State Adhered to is an Enemy, without shewing any War Proclaimed... . And if the Subject of a Foreign Prince in Amity with Us, invadeth the Kingdom without Commission from his Sovereign, He is an Enemy. And a Subject of England adhering to Him is a Traitor within this Clause of the Act." A Report of Some Proceedings on the Commission ... for the Trial of the Rebels in the Year 1746 in the County of Surry, and of Other Crown Cases, Introduction, §1, p. 183; Ch. 2, §8, p. 216; §12, p. 219.

Subjects accused of levying war against the King were routinely prosecuted for treason. E.g., Harding's Case, 2 Ventris 315, 86 Eng. Rep. 461 (K. B. 1690); Trial of Parkyns, 13 How. St. Tr. 63 (K. B. 1696); Trial of Vaughan, 13 How. St. Tr. 485 (K. B. 1696); Trial of Downie, 24 How. St. Tr. 1 (1794). The Founders inherited the understanding that a citizen's levying war against the Government was to be punished criminally. The Constitution provides: "Treason against the United States, shall consist only in levying War against them, or in adhering to their Enemies, giving them Aid and Comfort"; and establishes a heightened proof requirement (two witnesses) in order to "convic[t]" of that offense. Art. III, §3, cl. 1.

In more recent times, too, citizens have been charged and tried in Article III courts for acts of war against the United States, even when their noncitizen co-conspirators were not. For example, two American citizens alleged to have participated during World War I in a spying conspiracy on behalf of Germany were tried in federal court. See United States v. Fricke, 259 F. 673 (SDNY 1919); United States v. Robinson, 259 F. 685 (SDNY 1919). A German member of the same conspiracy was subjected to military process. See United States ex rel. Wessels v. McDonald, 265 F. 754 (EDNY 1920). During World War II, the famous German saboteurs of Ex parte Quirin, 317 U.S. 1 (1942), received military process, but the citizens who associated with them (with the exception of one citizen-saboteur, discussed below) were punished under the criminal process. See Haupt v. United States, 330 U.S. 631 (1947); L. Fisher, Nazi Saboteurs on Trial 80—84 (2003); see also Cramer v. United States, 325 U.S. 1 (1945).

The modern treason statute is 18 U.S.C. § 2381; it basically tracks the language of the constitutional provision. Other provisions of Title 18 criminalize various acts of warmaking and adherence to the enemy. See, e.g., §32 (destruction of aircraft or aircraft facilities), §2332a (use of weapons of mass destruction), §2332b (acts of terrorism transcending national boundaries), §2339A (providing material support to terrorists), §2339B (providing material support to certain terrorist organizations), §2382 (misprision of treason), §2383 (rebellion or insurrection), §2384 (seditious conspiracy), §2390 (enlistment to serve in armed hostility against the United States). See also 31 CFR § 595.204 (2003) (prohibiting the "making or receiving of any contribution of funds, goods, or services" to terrorists); 50 U.S.C. § 1705(b) (criminalizing violations of 31 CFR § 595.204). The only citizen other than Hamdi known to be imprisoned in connection with military hostilities in Afghanistan against the United States was subjected to criminal process and convicted upon a guilty plea. See United States v. Lindh, 212 F. Supp. 2d 541 (ED Va. 2002) (denying motions for dismissal); Seelye, N. Y. Times, Oct. 5, 2002, p. A1, col. 5.

B

There are times when military exigency renders resort to the traditional criminal process impracticable. English law accommodated such exigencies by allowing legislative suspension of the writ of habeas corpus for brief periods. Blackstone explained:

"And yet sometimes, when the state is in real danger, even this [i.e., executive detention] may be a necessary measure. But the happiness of our constitution is, that it is not left to the executive power to determine when the danger of the state is so great, as to render this measure expedient. For the parliament only, or legislative power, whenever it sees proper, can authorize the crown, by suspending the habeas corpus act for a short and limited time, to imprison suspected persons without giving any reason for so doing.... In like manner this experiment ought only to be tried in case of extreme emergency; and in these the nation parts with it[s] liberty for a while, in order to preserve it for ever." 1 Blackstone 132.

Where the Executive has not pursued the usual course of charge, committal, and conviction, it has historically secured the Legislature's explicit approval of a suspension. In England, Parliament on numerous occasions passed temporary suspensions in times of threatened invasion or rebellion. E.g., 1 W. & M., c. 7 (1688) (threatened return of James II); 7 & 8 Will. 3, c. 11 (1696) (same); 17 Geo. 2, c. 6 (1744) (threatened French invasion); 19 Geo. 2, c. 1 (1746) (threatened rebellion in Scotland); 17 Geo. 3, c. 9 (1777) (the American Revolution). Not long after Massachusetts had adopted a clause in its constitution explicitly providing for habeas corpus, see Mass. Const. pt. 2, ch. 6, art. VII (1780), reprinted in 3 Federal and State Constitutions, Colonial Charters and Other Organic Laws 1888, 1910 (F. Thorpe ed. 1909), it suspended the writ in order to deal with Shay's Rebellion, see Act for Suspending the Privilege of the Writ of Habeas Corpus, ch. 10, 1786 Mass. Acts 510.

Our Federal Constitution contains a provision explicitly permitting suspension, but limiting the situations in which it may be invoked: "The privilege of the Writ of Habeas Corpus shall not be suspended, unless when in Cases of Rebellion or Invasion the public Safety may require it." Art. I, §9, cl. 2. Although this provision does not state that suspension must be effected by, or authorized by, a legislative act, it has been so understood, consistent with English practice and the Clause's placement in Article I. See Ex parte Bollman, 4 Cranch 75, 101 (1807); Ex parte Merryman, 17 F. Cas. 144, 151—152 (CD Md. 1861) (Taney, C. J., rejecting Lincoln's unauthorized suspension); 3 Story §1336, at 208—209.

The Suspension Clause was by design a safety valve, the Constitution's only "express provision for exercise of extraordinary authority because of a crisis," Youngstown Sheet & Tube Co. v. Sawyer, 343 U.S. 579, 650 (1952) (Jackson, J., concurring). Very early in the Nation's history, President Jefferson unsuccessfully sought a suspension of habeas corpus to deal with Aaron Burr's conspiracy to overthrow the Government. See 16 Annals of Congress 402—425 (1807). During the Civil War, Congress passed its first Act authorizing Executive suspension of the writ of habeas corpus, see Act of Mar. 3, 1863, 12 Stat. 755, to the relief of those many who thought President Lincoln's unauthorized proclamations of suspension (e.g., Proclamation No. 1, 13 Stat. 730 (1862)) unconstitutional. Later Presidential proclamations of suspension relied upon the congressional authorization, e.g., Proclamation No. 7, 13 Stat. 734 (1863). During Reconstruction, Congress passed the Ku Klux Klan Act, which included a provision authorizing suspension of the writ, invoked by President Grant in quelling a rebellion in nine South Carolina counties. See Act of Apr. 20, 1871, ch. 22, §4, 17 Stat. 14; A Proclamation [of Oct. 17, 1871], 7 Compilation of the Messages and Papers of the Presidents 136—138 (J. Richardson ed. 1899) (hereinafter Messages and Papers); id., at 138—139.

Two later Acts of Congress provided broad suspension authority to governors of U.S. possessions. The Philippine Civil Government Act of 1902 provided that the Governor of the Philippines could suspend the writ in case of rebellion, insurrection, or invasion. Act of July 1, 1902, ch. 1369, §5, 32 Stat. 691. In 1905 the writ was suspended for nine months by proclamation of the Governor. See Fisher v. Baker, 203 U.S. 174, 179–181 (1906). The Hawaiian Organic Act of 1900 likewise provided that the Governor of Hawaii could suspend the writ in case of rebellion or invasion (or threat thereof). Ch. 339, §67, 31 Stat. 153.

III

Of course the extensive historical evidence of criminal convictions and habeas suspensions does not necessarily refute the Government's position in this case. When the writ is suspended, the Government is entirely free from judicial oversight. It does not claim such total liberation here, but argues that it need only produce what it calls "some evidence" to satisfy a habeas court that a detained individual is an enemy combatant. See Brief for Respondents 34. Even if suspension of the writ on the one hand, and committal for criminal charges on the other hand, have been the only traditional means of dealing with citizens who levied war against their own country, it is theoretically possible that the Constitution does not require a choice between these alternatives.

I believe, however, that substantial evidence does refute that possibility. First, the text of the 1679 Habeas Corpus Act makes clear that indefinite imprisonment on reasonable suspicion is not an available option of treatment for those accused of aiding the enemy, absent a suspension of the writ. In the United States, this Act was read as "enforc[ing] the common law," Ex parte Watkins, 3 Pet. 193, 202 (1830), and shaped the early understanding of the scope of the writ. As noted above, see supra, at 5, §7 of the Act specifically addressed those committed for high treason, and provided a remedy if they were not indicted and tried by the second succeeding court term. That remedy was not a bobtailed judicial inquiry into whether there were reasonable grounds to believe the prisoner had taken up arms against the King. Rather, if the prisoner was not indicted and tried within the prescribed time, "he shall be discharged from his Imprisonment." 31 Car. 2, c. 2, §7. The Act does not contain any exception for wartime. That omission is conspicuous, since §7 explicitly addresses the offense of "High Treason," which often involved offenses of a military nature. See cases cited supra, at 7.

Writings from the founding generation also suggest that, without exception, the only constitutional alternatives are to charge the crime or suspend the writ. In 1788, Thomas Jefferson wrote to James Madison questioning the need for a Suspension Clause in cases of rebellion in the proposed Constitution. His letter illustrates the constraints under which the Founders understood themselves to operate:

"Why suspend the Hab. corp. in insurrections and rebellions? The parties who may be arrested may be charged instantly with a well defined crime. Of course the judge will remand them. If the publick safety requires that the government should have a man imprisoned on less probable testimony in those than in other emergencies; let him be taken and tried, retaken and retried, while the necessity continues, only giving him redress against the government for damages." 13 Papers of Thomas Jefferson 442 (July 31, 1788) (J. Boyd ed. 1956).

A similar view was reflected in the 1807 House debates over suspension during the armed uprising that came to be known as Burr's conspiracy:

"With regard to those persons who may be implicated in the conspiracy, if the writ of habeas corpus be not suspended, what will be the consequence? When apprehended, they will be brought before a court of justice, who will decide whether there is any evidence that will justify their commitment for farther prosecution. From the communication of the Executive, it appeared there was sufficient evidence to authorize their commitment. Several months would elapse before their final trial, which would give time to collect evidence, and if this shall be sufficient, they will not fail to receive the punishment merited by their crimes, and inflicted by the laws of their country." 16 Annals of Congress, at 405 (remarks of Rep. Burwell).

The absence of military authority to imprison citizens indefinitely in wartime—whether or not a probability of treason had been established by means less than jury trial—was confirmed by three cases decided during and immediately after the War of 1812. In the first, In re Stacy, 10 Johns. *328 (N. Y. 1813), a citizen was taken into military custody on suspicion that he was "carrying provisions and giving information to the enemy." Id., at *330 (emphasis deleted). Stacy petitioned for a writ of habeas corpus, and, after the defendant custodian attempted to avoid complying, Chief Justice Kent ordered attachment against him. Kent noted that the military was "without any color of authority in any military tribunal to try a citizen for that crime" and that it was "holding him in the closest confinement, and contemning the civil authority of the state." Id., at *333–*334.

Two other cases, later cited with approval by this Court in Ex parte Milligan, 4 Wall. 2, 128—129 (1866), upheld verdicts for false imprisonment against military officers. In Smith v. Shaw, 12 Johns. *257 (N. Y. 1815), the court affirmed an award of damages for detention of a citizen on suspicion that he was, among other things, "an enemy's spy in time of war." Id., at *265. The court held that "[n]one of the offences charged against Shaw were cognizable by a court-martial, except that which related to his being a spy; and if he was an American citizen, he could not be charged with such an offence. He might be amenable to the civil authority for treason; but could not be punished, under martial law, as a spy." Ibid. "If the defendant was justifiable in doing what he did, every citizen of the United States would, in time of war, be equally exposed to a like exercise of military power and authority." Id., at *266. Finally, in M'Connell v. Hampton, 12 Johns. *234 (N. Y. 1815), a jury awarded $9,000 for false imprisonment after a military officer confined a citizen on charges of treason; the judges on appeal did not question the verdict but found the damages excessive, in part because "it does not appear that [the defendant] … knew [the plaintiff] was a citizen." Id., at *238 (Spencer, J.). See generally Wuerth, The President's Power to Detain "Enemy Combatants": Modern Lessons from Mr. Madison's

Forgotten War, 98 Nw. U. L. Rev. (forthcoming 2004) (available in Clerk of Court's case file).

President Lincoln, when he purported to suspend habeas corpus without congressional authorization during the Civil War, apparently did not doubt that suspension was required if the prisoner was to be held without criminal trial. In his famous message to Congress on July 4, 1861, he argued only that he could suspend the writ, not that even without suspension, his imprisonment of citizens without criminal trial was permitted. See Special Session Message, 6 Messages and Papers 20—31.

Further evidence comes from this Court's decision in Ex parte Milligan, supra. There, the Court issued the writ to an American citizen who had been tried by military commission for offenses that included conspiring to overthrow the Government, seize munitions, and liberate prisoners of war. Id., at 6—7. The Court rejected in no uncertain terms the Government's assertion that military jurisdiction was proper "under the 'laws and usages of war,' " id., at 121:

"It can serve no useful purpose to inquire what those laws and usages are, whence they originated, where found, and on whom they operate; they can never be applied to citizens in states which have upheld the authority of the government, and where the courts are open and their process unobstructed." Ibid.[1]

Milligan is not exactly this case, of course, since the petitioner was threatened with death, not merely imprisonment. But the reasoning and conclusion of Milligan logically cover the present case. The Government justifies imprisonment of Hamdi on principles of the law of war and admits that, absent the war, it would have no such authority. But if the law of war cannot be applied to citizens where courts are open, then Hamdi's imprisonment without criminal trial is no less unlawful than Milligan's trial by military tribunal.

Milligan responded to the argument, repeated by the Government in this case, that it is dangerous to leave suspected traitors at large in time of war:

"If it was dangerous, in the distracted condition of affairs, to leave Milligan unrestrained of his liberty, because he 'conspired against the government, afforded aid and comfort to rebels, and incited the people to insurrection,' the law said arrest him, confine him closely, render him powerless to do further mischief; and then present his case to the grand jury of the district, with proofs of his guilt, and, if indicted, try him according to the course of the common law. If this had been done, the Constitution would have been vindicated, the law of 1863 enforced, and the securities for personal liberty preserved and defended." Id., at 122.

Thus, criminal process was viewed as the primary means—and the only means absent congressional action suspending the writ—not only to punish traitors, but to incapacitate them.

The proposition that the Executive lacks indefinite wartime detention authority over citizens is consistent with the Founders' general mistrust of military power permanently at the Executive's disposal. In the Founders' view, the "blessings of liberty" were threatened by "those military establishments which must gradually poison its very fountain." The Federalist No. 45, p. 238 (J. Madison). No fewer than 10 issues of the Federalist were devoted in whole or part to allaying fears of oppression from the proposed Constitution's authorization of standing armies in peacetime. Many safeguards in the Constitution reflect these concerns. Congress's authority "[t]o raise and support Armies" was hedged with the proviso that "no Appropriation of Money to that Use shall be for a longer Term than two Years." U.S. Const., Art. 1, §8, cl. 12. Except for the actual command of military forces, all authorization for their maintenance and all explicit authorization for their use is placed in the control of Congress under Article I, rather than the President under Article II. As Hamilton explained, the President's military authority would be "much inferior" to that of the British King:

"It would amount to nothing more than the supreme command and direction of the military and naval forces, as first general and admiral of the confederacy: while that of the British king extends to the declaring of war, and to the raising and regulating of fleets and armies; all which, by the constitution under consideration, would appertain to the legislature." The Federalist No. 69, p. 357.

A view of the Constitution that gives the Executive authority to use military force rather than the force of law against citizens on American soil flies in the face of the mistrust that engendered these provisions.

IV

The Government argues that our more recent jurisprudence ratifies its indefinite imprisonment of a citizen within the territorial jurisdiction of federal courts. It places primary reliance upon Ex parte Quirin, 317 U.S. 1 (1942), a World War II case upholding the trial by military commission of eight German saboteurs, one of whom, Hans Haupt, was a U.S. citizen. The case was not this Court's finest hour. The Court upheld the commission and denied relief in a brief per curiam issued the day after oral argument concluded, see id., at 18—19, unnumbered note; a week later the Government carried out the commission's death sentence upon six saboteurs, including Haupt. The Court eventually explained its reasoning in a written opinion issued several months later.

Only three paragraphs of the Court's lengthy opinion dealt with the particular circumstances of Haupt's case. See id., at 37—38, 45—46. The Government argued that Haupt, like the other petitioners, could be tried by military commission under the laws of war. In agreeing with that contention, Quirin purported to interpret the language of Milligan quoted above (the law of war "can never be applied to citizens in states which have upheld the authority of the government, and where the courts are open and their process unobstructed") in the following manner:

"Elsewhere in its opinion ... the Court was at pains to point out that Milligan, a citizen twenty years resident in Indiana, who had never been a resident of any of the states in rebellion, was not an enemy belligerent either entitled to the status of a prisoner of war or subject to the penalties imposed upon unlawful belligerents. We construe the Court's statement as to the inapplicability of the law of war to Milligan's case as having particular reference to the facts before it. From them the Court concluded that Milligan, not being a part of or associated with the armed forces of the enemy, was a nonbelligerent, not subject to the law of war ... ." 317 U.S., at 45.

In my view this seeks to revise Milligan rather than describe it. Milligan had involved (among other issues) two separate questions: (1) whether the military trial of Milligan was justified by the laws of war, and if not (2) whether the President's suspension of the writ, pursuant to congressional authorization, prevented the issuance of habeas corpus. The Court's categorical language about the law of war's inapplicability to citizens where the courts are open (with no exception mentioned for citizens who were prisoners of war) was contained in its discussion of the first point. See 4 Wall., at 121. The factors pertaining to whether Milligan could reasonably be considered a belligerent and prisoner of war, while mentioned earlier in the opinion, see id., at 118, were made relevant and brought to bear in the Court's later discussion, see id., at 131, of whether Milligan came within the statutory provision that effectively made an exception to Congress's authorized suspension of the writ for (as the Court described it) "all parties, not prisoners of war, resident in their respective jurisdictions, ... who were citizens of states in which the administration of the laws in the Federal tribunals was unimpaired," id., at 116. Milligan thus understood was in accord with the traditional law of habeas corpus I have described: Though treason often occurred in wartime, there was, absent provision for special treatment in a congressional suspension of the writ, no exception to the right to trial by jury for citizens who could be called "belligerents" or "prisoners of war."[2]

But even if Quirin gave a correct description of Milligan, or made an irrevocable revision of it, Quirin would still not justify denial of the writ here. In Quirin it was uncontested that the petitioners were members of enemy forces. They were "admitted enemy invaders," 317 U.S., at 47 (emphasis added), and it was "undisputed" that they had landed in the United States in service of German forces, id., at 20. The specific holding of the Court was only that, "upon the conceded facts," the petitioners were "plainly within [the] boundaries" of military jurisdiction, id., at 46 (emphasis added).[3] But where those jurisdictional facts are not conceded—where the petitioner insists that he is not a belligerent—Quirin left the pre-existing law in place: Absent suspension of the writ, a citizen held where the courts are open is entitled either to criminal trial or to a judicial decree requiring his release.[4]

V

It follows from what I have said that Hamdi is entitled to a habeas decree requiring his release unless (1) criminal proceedings are promptly brought, or (2) Congress has suspended the writ of habeas corpus. A suspension of the writ could, of course, lay down conditions for continued detention, similar to those that today's opinion prescribes under the Due Process Clause. Cf. Act of Mar. 3, 1863, 12 Stat. 755. But there is a world of difference between the people's representatives' determining the need for that suspension (and prescribing the conditions for it), and this Court's doing so.

The plurality finds justification for Hamdi's imprisonment in the Authorization for Use of Military Force, 115 Stat. 224, which provides:

"That the President is authorized to use all necessary and appropriate force against those nations, organizations, or persons he determines planned, authorized, committed, or aided the terrorist attacks that occurred on September 11, 2001, or harbored such organizations or persons, in order to prevent any future acts of international terrorism against the United States by such nations, organizations or persons." §2(a).

This is not remotely a congressional suspension of the writ, and no one claims that it is. Contrary to the plurality's view, I do not think this statute even authorizes detention of a citizen with the clarity necessary to satisfy the interpretive canon that statutes should be construed so as to avoid grave constitutional concerns, see Edward J. DeBartolo Corp. v. Florida Gulf Coast Building & Constr. Trades Council, 485 U.S. 568, 575 (1988); with the clarity necessary to comport with cases such as Ex parte Endo, 323 U.S. 283, 300 (1944), and Duncan v. Kahanamoku, 327 U.S. 304, 314–316, 324 (1946); or with the clarity necessary to overcome the statutory prescription that "[n]o citizen shall be imprisoned or otherwise detained by the United States except pursuant to an Act of Congress." 18 U.S.C. § 4001(a).5 But even if it did, I would not permit it to overcome Hamdi's entitlement to habeas corpus relief. The Suspension Clause of the Constitution, which carefully circumscribes the conditions under which the writ can be withheld, would be a sham if it could be evaded by congressional prescription of requirements other than the common-law requirement of committal for criminal prosecution that render the writ, though available, unavailing. If the Suspension Clause does not guarantee the citizen that he will either be tried or released, unless the conditions for suspending the writ exist and the grave action of suspending the writ has been taken; if it merely guarantees the citizen that he will not be detained unless Congress by ordinary legislation says he can be detained; it guarantees him very little indeed.

It should not be thought, however, that the plurality's evisceration of the Suspension Clause augments, principally, the power of Congress. As usual, the major effect of its constitutional improvisation is to increase the power of the Court. Having found a congressional authorization for detention of citizens where none clearly exists; and having discarded the categorical procedural protection of the Suspension Clause; the plurality then proceeds, under the guise of the Due Process Clause, to prescribe what procedural protections it thinks appropriate. It "weigh[s] the private interest ... against the Government's asserted interest," ante, at 22 (internal quotation marks omitted), and– just as though writing a new Constitution–comes up with an unheard-of system in which the citizen rather than the Government bears the burden of proof, testimony is by hearsay rather than live witnesses, and the presiding officer may well be a "neutral" military officer rather than judge and jury. See ante, at 26–27. It claims authority to engage in this sort of "judicious balancing" from Mathews v. Eldridge, 424 U.S. 319 (1976), a case involving ... the withdrawal of disability benefits! Whatever the merits of this technique when newly recognized property rights are at issue (and even there they are questionable), it has no place where the Constitution and the common law already supply an answer.

Having distorted the Suspension Clause, the plurality finishes up by transmogrifying the Great Writ—disposing of the present habeas petition by remanding for the District Court to "engag[e] in a factfinding process that is both prudent and incremental," ante, at 32. "In the absence of [the Executive's prior provision of procedures that satisfy due process], ... a court that receives a petition for a writ of habeas corpus from an alleged enemy combatant must itself ensure that the minimum requirements of due process are achieved." Ante, at 31—32. This judicial remediation of executive default is unheard of. The role of habeas corpus is to determine the legality of executive detention, not to supply the omitted process necessary to make it legal. See Preiser v. Rodriguez, 411 U.S. 475, 484 (1973) ("[T]he essence of habeas corpus is an attack by a person in custody upon the legality of that custody, and ... the traditional function of the writ is to secure release from illegal custody"); 1 Blackstone 132—133. It is not the habeas court's function to make illegal detention legal by supplying a process that the Government could have provided, but chose not to. If Hamdi is being imprisoned in violation of the Constitution (because without due process of law), then his habeas petition should be granted; the Executive may then hand him over to the criminal authorities, whose detention for the purpose of prosecution will be lawful, or else must release him.

There is a certain harmony of approach in the plurality's making up for Congress's failure to invoke the Suspension Clause and its making up for the Executive's failure to apply what it says are needed procedures—an approach that reflects what might be called a Mr. Fix-it Mentality. The plurality seems to view it as its mission to Make Everything Come Out Right, rather than merely to decree the consequences, as far as individual rights are concerned, of the other two branches' actions and omissions. Has the Legislature failed to suspend the writ in the current dire emergency? Well, we will remedy that failure by prescribing the reasonable conditions that a suspension should have included. And has the Executive failed to live up to those reasonable conditions? Well, we will ourselves make that failure good, so that this dangerous fellow (if he is dangerous) need not be set free. The problem with this approach is not only that it steps out of the courts' modest and limited role in a democratic society; but that by repeatedly doing what it thinks the political branches ought to do it encourages their lassitude and saps the vitality of government by the people.

VI

Several limitations give my views in this matter a relatively narrow compass. They apply only to citizens, accused of being enemy combatants, who are detained within the territorial jurisdiction of a federal court. This is not likely to be a numerous group; currently we know of only two, Hamdi and Jose Padilla. Where the citizen is captured outside and held outside the United States, the constitutional requirements may be different. Cf. Johnson v. Eisentrager, 339 U.S. 763, 769—771 (1950); Reid v. Covert, 354 U.S. 1, 74—75 (1957) (Harlan, J., concurring in result); Rasul v. Bush, ante, at 15—17 (Scalia, J., dissenting). Moreover, even within the United States, the accused citizen-enemy combatant may lawfully be detained once prosecution is in progress or in contemplation. See, e.g., County of Riverside v. McLaughlin, 500 U.S. 44 (1991) (brief detention pending judicial determination after warrantless arrest); United States v. Salerno, 481 U.S. 739 (1987) (pretrial detention under the Bail Reform Act). The Government has been notably successful in securing conviction, and hence long-term custody or execution, of those who have waged war against the state.

I frankly do not know whether these tools are sufficient to meet the Government's security needs, including the need to obtain intelligence through interrogation. It is far beyond my competence, or the Court's competence, to determine that. But it is not beyond Congress's. If the situation demands it, the Executive can ask Congress to authorize suspension of the writ—which can be made subject to whatever conditions Congress deems appropriate, including even the procedural novelties invented by the plurality today. To be sure, suspension is limited by the Constitution to cases of rebellion or invasion. But whether the attacks of September 11, 2001, constitute an "invasion," and whether those attacks still justify suspension several years later, are questions for Congress rather than this Court. See 3 Story §1336, at 208—209.6 If civil rights are to be curtailed during wartime, it must be done openly and democratically, as the Constitution requires, rather than by silent erosion through an opinion of this Court.

* * *

The Founders well understood the difficult tradeoff between safety and freedom. "Safety from external danger," Hamilton declared,

"is the most powerful director of national conduct. Even the ardent love of liberty will, after a time, give way to its dictates. The violent destruction of life and property incident to war; the continual effort and alarm attendant on a state of continual danger, will compel nations the most attached to liberty, to resort for repose and security to institutions which have a tendency to destroy their civil and political rights. To be more safe, they, at length, become willing to run the risk of being less free." The Federalist No. 8, p. 33.

The Founders warned us about the risk, and equipped us with a Constitution designed to deal with it.

Many think it not only inevitable but entirely proper that liberty give way to security in times of national crisis—that, at the extremes of military exigency, inter arma silent leges. Whatever the general merits of the view that war silences law or modulates its voice, that view has no place in the interpretation and application of a Constitution designed precisely to confront war and, in a manner that accords with democratic principles, to accommodate it. Because the Court has proceeded to meet the current emergency in a manner the Constitution does not envision, I respectfully dissent.

Notes to Justice Scalia's dissent in Hamdi v. Rumsfeld (June 28, 2004)

    1. As I shall discuss presently, see infra, at 17—19, the Court purported to limit this language in Ex parte Quirin, 317 U.S. 1, 45 (1942). Whatever Quirin's effect on Milligan's precedential value, however, it cannot undermine its value as an indicator of original meaning. Cf. Reid v. Covert, 354 U.S. 1, 30 (1957) (plurality opinion) (Milligan remains "one of the great landmarks in this Court's history").

    2. Without bothering to respond to this analysis, the plurality states that Milligan "turned in large part" upon the defendant's lack of prisoner-of-war status, and that the Milligan Court explicitly and repeatedly said so. See ante, at 14. Neither is true. To the extent, however, that prisoner-of-war status was relevant in Milligan, it was only because prisoners of war received different statutory treatment under the conditional suspension then in effect.

    3. The only two Court of Appeals cases from World War II cited by the Government in which citizens were detained without trial likewise involved petitioners who were conceded to have been members of enemy forces. See In re Territo, 156 F.2d 142, 143—145 (CA9 1946); Colepaugh v. Looney, 235 F.2d 429, 432 (CA10 1956). The plurality complains that Territo is the only case I have identified in which "a United States citizen [was] captured in a foreign combat zone," ante, at 16. Indeed it is; such cases must surely be rare. But given the constitutional tradition I have described, the burden is not upon me to find cases in which the writ was granted to citizens in this country who had been captured on foreign battlefields; it is upon those who would carve out an exception for such citizens (as the plurality's complaint suggests it would) to find a single case (other than one where enemy status was admitted) in which habeas was denied.

    4. The plurality's assertion that Quirin somehow "clarifies" Milligan, ante, at 15, is simply false. As I discuss supra, at 17—19, the Quirin Court propounded a mistaken understanding of Milligan; but nonetheless its holding was limited to "the case presented by the present record," and to "the conceded facts," and thus avoided conflict with the earlier case. See 317 U.S., at 45—46 (emphasis added). The plurality, ignoring this expressed limitation, thinks it "beside the point" whether belligerency is conceded or found "by some other process" (not necessarily a jury trial) "that verifies this fact with sufficient certainty." Ante, at 16. But the whole point of the procedural guarantees in the Bill of Rights is to limit the methods by which the Government can determine facts that the citizen disputes and on which the citizen's liberty depends. The plurality's claim that Quirin's one-paragraph discussion of Milligan provides a "[c]lear . . . disavowal" of two false imprisonment cases from the War of 1812, ante, at 15, thus defies logic; unlike the plaintiffs in those cases, Haupt was concededly a member of an enemy force. The Government also cites Moyer v. Peabody, 212 U.S. 78 (1909), a suit for damages against the Governor of Colorado, for violation of due process in detaining the alleged ringleader of a rebellion quelled by the state militia after the Governor's declaration of a state of insurrection and (he contended) suspension of the writ "as incident thereto." Ex parte

Moyer, 35 Colo. 154, 157, 91 P. 738, 740 (1905). But the holding of Moyer v. Peabody (even assuming it is transferable from state-militia detention after state suspension to federal standing-army detention without suspension) is simply that "[s]o long as such arrests [were] made in good faith and in the honest belief that they [were] needed in order to head the insurrection off," 212 U.S., at 85, an action in damages could not lie. This "good-faith" analysis is a forebear of our modern doctrine of qualified immunity. Cf. Scheuer v. Rhodes, 416 U.S. 232, 247—248 (1974) (understanding Moyer in this way). Moreover, the detention at issue in Moyer lasted about two and a half months, see 212 U.S., at 85, roughly the length of time permissible under the 1679 Habeas Corpus Act, see supra, at 4—5. In addition to Moyer v. Peabody, Justice Thomas relies upon Luther v. Borden, 7 How. 1 (1849), a case in which the state legislature had imposed martial law—a step even more drastic than suspension of the writ. See post, at 13—14 (dissenting opinion). But martial law has not been imposed here, and in any case is limited to "the theatre of active military operations, where war really prevails," and where therefore the courts are closed. Ex parte Milligan, 4 Wall. 2, 127 (1866); see also id., at 129—130 (distinguishing Luther).

5. The plurality rejects any need for "specific language of detention" on the ground that detention of alleged combatants is a "fundamental incident of waging war." Ante, at 12. Its authorities do not support that holding in the context of the present case. Some are irrelevant because they do not address the detention of American citizens. E.g., Naqvi, Doubtful Prisoner-of-War Status, 84 Int'l Rev. Red Cross 571, 572 (2002). The plurality's assertion that detentions of citizen and alien combatants are equally authorized has no basis in law or common sense. Citizens and noncitizens, even if equally dangerous, are not similarly situated. See, e.g., Milligan, supra; Johnson v. Eisentrager, 339 U.S. 763 (1950); Rev. Stat. 4067, 50 U.S.C. § 21 (Alien Enemy Act). That captivity may be consistent with the principles of international law does not prove that it also complies with the restrictions that the Constitution places on the American Government's treatment of its own citizens. Of the authorities cited by the plurality that do deal with detention of citizens, Quirin and Territo have already been discussed and rejected. See supra, at 19—20, and n. 3. The remaining authorities pertain to U.S. detention of citizens during the Civil War, and are irrelevant for two reasons: (1) the Lieber Code was issued following a congressional authorization of suspension of the writ, see Instructions for the Government of Armies of the United States in the Field, Gen. Order No. 100 (1863), reprinted in 2 Lieber, Miscellaneous Writings, p. 246; Act of Mar. 3, 1863, 12 Stat. 755, §§1, 2; and (2) citizens of the Confederacy, while citizens of the United States, were also regarded as citizens of a hostile power.

6. Justice Thomas worries that the constitutional conditions for suspension of the writ will not exist "during many ... emergencies during which ... detention authority might be necessary," post, at 16. It is difficult to imagine situations in which security is so seriously threatened as to justify indefinite imprisonment without trial, and yet the constitutional conditions of rebellion or invasion are not met.

Homegrown marijuana must be outlawed to prevent it going into other homes: Justice Scalia's concurrence in Gonzales v. Raich (June 6, 2005)

Justice Scalia, concurring in the judgment.

I agree with the Court's holding that the Controlled Substances Act (CSA) may validly be applied to respondents' cultivation, distribution, and possession of marijuana for personal, medicinal use. I write separately because my understanding of the doctrinal foundation on which that holding rests is, if not inconsistent with that of the Court, at least more nuanced.

Since Perez v. United States, 402 U.S. 146 (1971), our cases have mechanically recited that the Commerce Clause permits congressional regulation of three categories: (1) the channels of interstate commerce; (2) the instrumentalities of interstate commerce, and persons or things in interstate commerce; and (3) activities that "substantially affect" interstate commerce. Id., at 150; see United States v. Morrison, 529 U.S. 598, 608—609 (2000); United States v. Lopez, 514 U.S. 549, 558—559 (1995); Hodel v. Virginia Surface Mining & Reclamation Assn., Inc., 452 U.S. 264, 276—277 (1981). The first two categories are self-evident, since they are the ingredients of interstate commerce itself. See Gibbons v. Ogden, 9 Wheat. 1, 189—190 (1824). The third category, however, is different in kind, and its recitation without explanation is misleading and incomplete.

It is misleading because, unlike the channels, instrumentalities, and agents of interstate commerce, activities that substantially affect interstate commerce are not themselves part of interstate commerce, and thus the power to regulate them cannot come from the Commerce Clause alone. Rather, as this Court has acknowledged since at least United States v. Coombs, 12 Pet. 72 (1838), Congress's regulatory authority over intrastate activities that are not themselves part of interstate commerce (including activities that have a substantial effect on interstate commerce) derives from the Necessary and Proper Clause. Id., at 78; Katzenbach v. McClung, 379 U.S. 294, 301—302 (1964); United States v. Wrightwood Dairy Co., 315 U.S. 110, 119 (1942); Shreveport Rate Cases, 234 U.S. 342, 353 (1914); United States v. E. C. Knight Co., 156 U.S. 1, 39—40 (1895) (Harlan, J., dissenting).1 And the category of "activities that substantially affect interstate commerce," Lopez, supra, at 559, is incomplete because the authority to enact laws necessary and proper for the regulation of interstate commerce is not limited to laws governing intrastate activities that substantially affect interstate commerce. Where necessary to make a regulation of interstate commerce effective, Congress may regulate even those intrastate activities that do not themselves substantially affect interstate commerce.

I

Our cases show that the regulation of intrastate activities may be necessary to and proper for the regulation of interstate commerce in two general circumstances. Most directly, the commerce power permits Congress not only to devise rules for the governance of commerce between States but also to facilitate interstate commerce by eliminating potential obstructions, and to restrict it by eliminating potential stimulants. See NLRB v. Jones & Laughlin Steel Corp., 301 U.S. 1, 36—37 (1937). That is why the Court has repeatedly sustained congressional legislation on the ground that the regulated activities had a substantial effect on interstate commerce. See, e.g., Hodel, supra, at 281 (surface coal mining); Katzenbach, supra, at 300 (discrimination by restaurants); Heart of Atlanta Motel, Inc. v. United States, 379 U.S. 241, 258 (1964) (discrimination by hotels); Mandeville Island Farms v. American Crystal Sugar Co., 334 U.S. 219, 237 (1948) (intrastate price-fixing); Board of Trade of Chicago v. Olsen, 262 U.S. 1, 40 (1923) (activities of a local grain exchange); Stafford v. Wallace, 258 U.S. 495, 517, 524—525 (1922) (intrastate transactions at stockyard). Lopez and Morrison recognized the expansive scope of Congress's authority in this regard: "[T]he pattern is clear. Where economic activity substantially affects interstate commerce, legislation regulating that activity will be sustained." Lopez, supra, at 560; Morrison, supra, at 610 (same).

This principle is not without limitation. In Lopez and Morrison, the Court—conscious of the potential of the "substantially affects" test to " 'obliterate the distinction between what is national and what is local,' " Lopez, supra, at 566—567 (quoting A. L. A. Schechter Poultry Corp. v. United States, 295 U.S. 495, 554 (1935)); see also Morrison, supra, at 615—616—rejected the argument that Congress may regulate noneconomic activity based solely on the effect that it may have on interstate commerce through a remote chain of inferences. Lopez, supra, at 564—566; Morrison, supra, at 617—618. "[I]f we were to accept [such] arguments," the Court reasoned in Lopez, "we are hard pressed to posit any activity by an individual that Congress is without power to regulate." Lopez, supra, at 564; see also Morrison, supra, at 615—616. Thus, although Congress's authority to regulate intrastate activity that substantially affects interstate commerce is broad, it does not permit the Court to "pile inference upon inference," Lopez, supra, at 567, in order to establish that noneconomic activity has a substantial effect on interstate commerce.

As we implicitly acknowledged in Lopez, however, Congress's authority to enact laws necessary and proper for the regulation of interstate commerce is not limited to laws directed against economic activities that have a substantial effect on interstate commerce. Though the conduct in Lopez was not economic, the Court nevertheless recognized that it could be regulated as "an essential part of a larger regulation of economic activity, in which the regulatory scheme could be undercut unless the intrastate activity were regulated." 514 U.S., at 561. This statement referred to those cases permitting the regulation of intrastate activities "which in a substantial way interfere with or obstruct the exercise of the granted power." Wrightwood Dairy Co., 315 U.S., at 119; see also United States v. Darby, 312 U.S. 100, 118—119 (1941); Shreveport Rate Cases, 234 U.S., at 353. As the Court put it in Wrightwood Dairy, where Congress has the authority to enact a regulation of interstate commerce, "it possesses every power needed to make that regulation effective." 315 U.S., at 118—119.

Although this power "to make ... regulation effective" commonly overlaps with the authority to regulate economic activities that substantially affect interstate commerce,2 and may in some cases have been confused with that authority, the two are distinct. The regulation of an intrastate activity may be essential to a comprehensive regulation of interstate commerce even though the intrastate activity does not itself "substantially affect" interstate commerce. Moreover, as the passage from Lopez quoted above suggests, Congress may regulate even noneconomic local activity if that regulation is a necessary part of a more general regulation of interstate commerce. See Lopez, supra, at 561. The relevant question is simply whether the means chosen are "reasonably adapted" to the attainment of a legitimate end under the commerce power. See Darby, supra, at 121.

In Darby, for instance, the Court explained that "Congress, having ... adopted the policy of excluding from interstate commerce all goods produced for the commerce which do not conform to the specified labor standards," 312 U.S., at 121, could not only require employers engaged in the production of goods for interstate commerce to conform to wage and hour standards, id., at 119—121, but could also require those employers to keep employment records in order to demonstrate compliance with the regulatory scheme, id., at 125. While the Court sustained the former regulation on the alternative ground that the activity it regulated could have a "great effect" on interstate commerce, id., at 122—123, it affirmed the latter on the sole ground that "[t]he requirement for records even of the intrastate transaction is an appropriate means to a legitimate end," id., at 125.

As the Court said in the Shreveport Rate Cases, the Necessary and Proper Clause does not give "Congress ... the authority to regulate the internal commerce of a State, as such," but it does allow Congress "to take all measures necessary or appropriate to" the effective regulation of the interstate market, "although intrastate transactions ... may thereby be controlled." 234 U.S., at 353; see also Jones & Laughlin Steel Corp., 301 U.S., at 38 (the logic of the Shreveport Rate Cases is not limited to instrumentalities of commerce).

II

Today's principal dissent objects that, by permitting Congress to regulate activities necessary to effective interstate regulation, the Court reduces Lopez and Morrison to "little more than a drafting guide." Post, at 5 (opinion of O'Connor, J.). I think that criticism unjustified. Unlike the power to regulate activities that have a substantial effect on interstate commerce, the power to enact laws enabling effective regulation of interstate commerce can only be exercised in conjunction with congressional regulation of an interstate market, and it extends only to those measures necessary to make the interstate regulation effective. As Lopez itself states, and the Court affirms today, Congress may regulate noneconomic intrastate activities only where the failure to do so "could ... undercut" its regulation of interstate commerce. See Lopez, supra, at 561; ante, at 15, 21, 22. This is not a power that threatens to obliterate the line between "what is truly national and what is truly local." Lopez, supra, at 567—568.

Lopez and Morrison affirm that Congress may not regulate certain "purely local" activity within the States based solely on the attenuated effect that such activity may have in the interstate market. But those decisions do not declare noneconomic intrastate activities to be categorically beyond the reach of the Federal Government. Neither case involved the power of Congress to exert control over intrastate activities in connection with a more comprehensive scheme of regulation; Lopez expressly disclaimed that it was such a case, 514 U.S., at 561, and Morrison did not even discuss the possibility that it was. (The Court of Appeals in Morrison made clear that it was not. See Brzonkala v. Virginia Polytechnic Inst., 169 F.3d 820, 834—835 (CA4 1999) (en banc).) To dismiss this distinction as "superficial and formalistic," see post, at 6 (O'Connor, J., dissenting), is to misunderstand the nature of the Necessary and Proper Clause, which empowers Congress to enact laws in effectuation of its enumerated powers that are not within its authority to enact in isolation. See McCulloch v. Maryland, 4 Wheat. 316, 421—422 (1819).

And there are other restraints upon the Necessary and Proper Clause authority. As Chief Justice Marshall wrote in McCulloch v. Maryland, even when the end is constitutional and legitimate, the means must be "appropriate" and "plainly adapted" to that end. Id., at 421. Moreover, they may not be otherwise "prohibited" and must be "consistent with the letter and spirit of the constitution." Ibid. These phrases are not merely hortatory. For example, cases such as Printz v. United States, 521 U.S. 898 (1997), and New York v. United States, 505 U.S. 144 (1992), affirm that a law is not " 'proper for carrying into Execution the Commerce Clause' " "[w]hen [it] violates [a constitutional] principle of state sovereignty." Printz, supra, at 923—924; see also New York, supra, at 166.

III

The application of these principles to the case before us is straightforward. In the CSA, Congress has undertaken to extinguish the interstate market in Schedule I controlled substances, including marijuana. The Commerce Clause unquestionably permits this. The power to regulate interstate commerce "extends not only to those regulations which aid, foster and protect the commerce, but embraces those which prohibit it." Darby, 312 U.S., at 113. See also Hipolite Egg Co. v. United States, 220 U.S. 45, 58 (1911); Lottery Case, 188 U.S. 321, 354 (1903). To effectuate its objective, Congress has prohibited almost all intrastate activities related to Schedule I substances–both economic activities (manufacture, distribution, possession with the intent to distribute) and noneconomic activities (simple possession). See 21 U.S.C. § 841(a), 844(a). That simple possession is a noneconomic activity is immaterial to whether it can be prohibited as a necessary part of a larger regulation. Rather, Congress's authority to enact all of these prohibitions of intrastate controlled-substance activities depends only upon whether they are appropriate means of achieving the legitimate end of eradicating Schedule I substances from interstate commerce.

By this measure, I think the regulation must be sustained. Not only is it impossible to distinguish "controlled substances manufactured and distributed intrastate" from "controlled substances manufactured and distributed interstate," but it hardly makes sense to speak in such terms. Drugs like marijuana are fungible commodities. As the Court explains, marijuana that is grown at home and possessed for personal use is never more than an instant from the interstate market—and this is so whether or not the possession is for medicinal use or lawful use under the laws of a particular State.3 See ante, at 23—30. Congress need not accept on faith that state law will be effective in maintaining a strict division between a lawful market for "medical" marijuana and the more general marijuana market. See id., at 26—27, and n. 38. "To impose on [Congress] the necessity of resorting to means which it cannot control, which another government may furnish or withhold, would render its course precarious, the result of its measures uncertain, and create a dependence on other governments, which might disappoint its most important designs, and is incompatible with the language of the constitution." McCulloch, supra, at 424.

Finally, neither respondents nor the dissenters suggest any violation of state sovereignty of the sort that would render this regulation "inappropriate," id., at 421– except to argue that the CSA regulates an area typically left to state regulation. See post, at 6—7, 11 (opinion of O'Connor, J.); post, at 8—9 (opinion of Thomas, J.); Brief for Respondents 39—42. That is not enough to render federal regulation an inappropriate means. The Court has repeatedly recognized that, if authorized by the commerce power, Congress may regulate private endeavors "even when [that regulation] may pre-empt express state-law determinations contrary to the result which has commended itself to the collective wisdom of Congress." National League of Cities v. Usery, 426 U.S. 833, 840 (1976); see Cleveland v. United States, 329 U.S. 14, 19 (1946); McCulloch, supra, at 424. At bottom, respondents' state-sovereignty argument reduces to the contention that federal regulation of the activities permitted by California's Compassionate Use Act is not sufficiently necessary to be "necessary and proper" to Congress's regulation of the interstate market. For the reasons given above and in the Court's opinion, I cannot agree.

***

I thus agree with the Court that, however the class of regulated activities is subdivided, Congress could reasonably conclude that its objective of prohibiting marijuana from the interstate market "could be undercut" if those activities were excepted from its general scheme of regulation. See Lopez, 514 U.S., at 561. That is sufficient to authorize the application of the CSA to respondents.

Notes

1. See also Garcia v. San Antonio Metropolitan Transit Authority, 469 U.S. 528, 584—585 (1985) (O'Connor, J., dissenting) (explaining that it is through the Necessary

and Proper Clause that "an intrastate activity 'affecting' interstate commerce can be reached through the commerce power").

2. Wickard v. Filburn, 317 U.S. 111 (1942), presented such a case. Because the unregulated production of wheat for personal consumption diminished demand in the regulated wheat market, the Court said, it carried with it the potential to disrupt Congress's price regulation by driving down prices in the market. Id., at 127–129. This potential disruption of Congress's interstate regulation, and not only the effect that personal consumption of wheat had on interstate commerce, justified Congress's regulation of that conduct. Id., at 128–129.

3. The principal dissent claims that, if this is sufficient to sustain the regulation at issue in this case, then it should also have been sufficient to sustain the regulation at issue in United States v. Lopez, 514 U.S. 549 (1995). See post, at 11–12 (arguing that "we could have surmised in Lopez that guns in school zones are 'never more than an instant from the interstate market' in guns already subject to federal regulation, recast Lopez as a Necessary and Proper Clause case, and thereby upheld the Gun-Free School Zones Act"). This claim founders upon the shoals of Lopez itself, which made clear that the statute there at issue was "not an essential part of a larger regulation of economic activity." Lopez, supra, at 561 (emphasis added). On the dissent's view of things, that statement is inexplicable. Of course it is in addition difficult to imagine what intelligible scheme of regulation of the interstate market in guns could have as an appropriate means of effectuation the prohibition of guns within 1000 feet of schools (and nowhere else). The dissent points to a federal law, 18 U.S.C. § 922(b)(1), barring licensed dealers from selling guns to minors, see post, at 12, but the relationship between the regulatory scheme of which §922(b)(1) is a part (requiring all dealers in firearms that have traveled in interstate commerce to be licensed, see §922(a)) and the statute at issue in Lopez approaches the nonexistent—which is doubtless why the Government did not attempt to justify the statute on the basis of that relationship.

If a law states "as of that date" it includes anything pending as of that date: Justice Scalia's dissent in Hamdan v. Rumsfeld (June 29, 2006)

Justice Scalia, with whom Justice Thomas and Justice Alito join, dissenting.

On December 30, 2005, Congress enacted the Detainee Treatment Act (DTA). It unambiguously provides that, as of that date, "no court, justice, or judge" shall have jurisdiction to consider the habeas application of a Guantanamo Bay detainee. Notwithstanding this plain directive, the Court today concludes that, on what it calls the statute's most natural reading, every "court, justice, or judge" before whom such a habeas application was pending on December 30 has jurisdiction to hear, consider, and render judgment on it. This conclusion is patently erroneous. And even if it were not, the jurisdiction supposedly retained should, in an exercise of sound equitable discretion, not be exercised.

I

A

The DTA provides: "[N]o court, justice, or judge shall have jurisdiction to hear or consider an application for a writ of habeas corpus filed by or on behalf of an alien detained by the Department of Defense at Guantanamo Bay, Cuba." §1005(e)(1), 119 Stat. 2742 (internal division omitted). This provision "t[ook] effect on the date of the enactment of this Act," §1005(h)(1), id., at 2743, which was December 30, 2005. As of that date, then, no court had jurisdiction to "hear or consider" the merits of petitioner's habeas application. This repeal of jurisdiction is simply not ambiguous as between pending and future cases. It prohibits any exercise of jurisdiction, and it became effective as to all cases last December 30. It is also perfectly clear that the phrase "no court, justice, or judge" includes this Court and its Members, and that by exercising our appellate jurisdiction in this case we are "hear[ing] or consider[ing] ... an application for a writ of habeas corpus."

An ancient and unbroken line of authority attests that statutes ousting jurisdiction unambiguously apply to cases pending at their effective date. For example, in Bruner v. United States, 343 U. S. 112 (1952), we granted certiorari to consider whether the Tucker Act's provision denying district court jurisdiction over suits by "officers" of the United States barred a suit by an employee of the United States. After we granted certiorari, Congress amended the Tucker Act by adding suits by " 'employees' " to the provision barring jurisdiction over suits by officers. Id., at 114. This statute narrowing the jurisdiction of the district courts "became effective" while the case was pending before us, ibid., and made no explicit reference to pending cases. Because the statute "did not reserve jurisdiction over pending cases," id., at 115, we held that it clearly ousted jurisdiction over them. Summarizing centuries of practice, we said: "This rule—that, when a law conferring jurisdiction is repealed without any reservation as to pending cases, all cases fall with the law—has been adhered to consistently by this Court." Id., at 116–117. See also Landgraf v. USI Film Products, 511 U. S. 244, 274 (1994) (opinion for the Court by Stevens, J.) ("We have regularly applied intervening statutes conferring or ousting jurisdiction, whether or not jurisdiction lay when the underlying conduct occurred or when the suit was filed").

This venerable rule that statutes ousting jurisdiction terminate jurisdiction in pending cases is not, as today's opinion for the Court would have it, a judge-made "presumption against jurisdiction," ante, at 11, that we have invented to resolve an ambiguity in the statutes. It is simple recognition of the reality that the plain import of a statute repealing jurisdiction is to eliminate the power to consider and render judgment— in an already pending case no less than in a case yet to be filed.

"Without jurisdiction the court cannot proceed at all in any cause. Jurisdiction is power to declare the law, and when it ceases to exist, the only function remaining to the court is that of announcing the fact and dismissing the cause. And this is not less clear upon authority than upon principle." Ex parte McCardle, 7 Wall. 506, 514 (1869) (emphasis added).

To alter this plain meaning, our cases have required an explicit reservation of pending cases in the jurisdiction-repealing statute. For example, Bruner, as mentioned, looked to whether Congress made "any reservation as to pending cases." 343 U. S., at 116–117; see also id., at 115 ("Congress made no provision for cases pending at the effective date of the Act withdrawing jurisdiction and, for this reason, Courts of Appeals ordered pending cases terminated for want of jurisdiction"). Likewise, in Hallowell v. Commons, 239 U. S. 506 (1916), Justice Holmes relied on the fact that the jurisdiction-ousting provision "made no exception for pending litigation, but purported to be universal," id., at 508. And in Insurance Co. v. Ritchie, 5Wall. 541 (1867), we again relied on the fact that the jurisdictional repeal was made "without any saving of such causes as that before us," id., at 544. As in Bruner, Hallowell, and Ritchie, the DTA's directive that "no court, justice, or judge shall have jurisdiction," §1005(e)(1), 119 Stat. 2742, is made "without any reservation as to pending cases" and "purport[s] to be universal." What we stated in an earlier case remains true here: "[W]hen, if it had been the intention to confine the operation of [the jurisdictional repeal] ... to cases not pending, it would have been so easy to have said so, we must presume that Congress meant the language employed should have its usual and ordinary signification, and that the old law should be unconditionally repealed." Railroad Co. v. Grant, 98 U. S. 398, 403 (1879).

The Court claims that I "rea[d] too much into" the Bruner line of cases, ante, at 12, n. 7, and that "the Bruner rule" has never been "an inflexible trump," ante, at 19. But the Court sorely misdescribes Bruner—as if it were a kind of early-day Lindh v. Murphy, 521 U. S. 320 (1997), resolving statutory ambiguity by oblique negative inference. On the contrary, as described above, Bruner stated its holding as an unqualified "rule," which "has been adhered to consistently by this Court." 343 U. S., at 116–117. Though Bruner referred to an express savings clause elsewhere in the statute, id., at 115, n. 7, it disavowed any reliance on such oblique indicators to vary the plain meaning, quoting Ritchie at length: " 'It is quite possible that this effect of the [jurisdiction-stripping statute] was not contemplated by Congress.... . [B]ut when terms are unambiguous we may not speculate on probabilities of intention.' " 343 U. S., at 116 (quoting 5 Wall., at 544–545).

The Court also attempts to evade the Bruner line of cases by asserting that "the 'presumption' [of application to pending cases] that these cases have applied is more accurately viewed as the nonapplication of another presumption—viz., the presumption against retroactivity—in certain limited circumstances." Ante, at 11. I have already explained that what the Court calls a "presumption" is simply the acknowledgment of the unambiguous meaning of such provisions. But even taking it to be what the Court says, the effect upon the present case would be the same. Prospective applications of a statute are "effective" upon the statute's effective date; that is what an effective-date provision like §1005(h)(1) means.[1] " '[S]hall take effect upon enactment' is presumed to mean 'shall have prospective effect upon enactment,' and that presumption is too strong to be overcome by any negative inference [drawn from other provisions of the statute]." Landgraf, 511 U. S., at 288 (Scalia, J., concurring in judgments). The Court's "nonapplication of ... the presumption against retroactivity" to §1005(e)(1) is thus just another way of stating that the statute takes immediate effect in pending cases.

Though the Court resists the Bruner rule, it cannot cite a single case in the history of Anglo-American law (before today) in which a jurisdiction-stripping provision was denied immediate effect in pending cases, absent an explicit statutory reservation. By contrast, the cases granting such immediate effect are legion, and they repeatedly rely on the plain language of the jurisdictional repeal as an "inflexible trump," ante, at 19, by requiring an express reservation to save pending cases. See, e.g., Bruner, supra, at 115; Kline v. Burke Constr. Co., 260 U. S. 226, 234 (1922); Hallowell, 239 U. S., at 508; Gwin v. United States, 184 U. S. 669, 675 (1902); Gurnee v. Patrick County, 137 U. S. 141, 144 (1890); Sherman v. Grinnell, 123 U. S. 679, 680 (1887); Railroad Co. v. Grant, supra, at 403, Assessors v. Osbornes, 9Wall. 567, 575 (1870); Ex parte McCardle, 7 Wall., at 514; Ritchie, supra, at 544; Norris v. Crocker, 13How. 429, 440 (1852); Yeaton v. United States, 5 Cranch 281 (1809) (Marshall, C. J.), discussed in Gwin, supra, at 675; King v. Justices of the Peace of London, 3 Burr. 1456, 1457, 97 Eng. Rep. 924, 925 (K. B. 1764). Cf. National Exchange Bank of Baltimore v. Peters, 144 U. S. 570, 572 (1892) .

B

Disregarding the plain meaning of §1005(e)(1) and the requirement of explicit exception set forth in the foregoing cases, the Court instead favors "a negative inference ... from the exclusion of language from one statutory provision that is included in other provisions of the same statute," ante, at 13. Specifically, it appeals to the fact that §1005(e)(2) and (e)(3) are explicitly made applicable to pending cases (by §1005(h)(2)). A negative inference of the sort the Court relies upon might clarify the meaning of an ambiguous provision, but since the meaning of §1005(e)(1) is entirely clear, the omitted language in that context would have been redundant.

Even if §1005(e)(1) were at all ambiguous in its application to pending cases, the "negative inference" from §1005(h)(2) touted by the Court would have no force. The numerous cases in the Bruner line would at least create a powerful default "presumption against jurisdiction," ante, at 11. The negative inference urged by the Court would be a particularly awkward and indirect way of rebutting such a longstanding and consistent practice. This is especially true since the negative inference that might be drawn from §1005(h)(2)'s specification that certain provisions shall apply to pending cases is matched by a negative inference in the opposite direction that might be drawn from §1005(b)(2), which provides that certain provisions shall not apply to pending cases.

The Court's reliance on our opinion in Lindh v. Murphy, 521 U. S. 320 (1997), is utterly misplaced. Lindh involved two provisions of the Antiterrorism and Effective Death Penalty Act of 1996 (AEDPA): a set of amendments to chapter 153 of the federal habeas statute that redefined the scope of collateral review by federal habeas courts; and a provision creating a new chapter 154 in the habeas statute specially to govern federal collateral review of state capital cases. See 521 U. S., at 326–327. The latter provision explicitly rendered the new chapter 154 applicable to cases pending at the time of AEDPA's enactment; the former made no specific reference to pending cases. Id., at 327. In Lindh, we drew a negative inference from chapter 154's explicit reference to pending cases, to conclude that the chapter 153 amendments did not apply in pending cases. It was essential to our reasoning, however, that both provisions appeared to be identically difficult to classify under our retroactivity cases. First, we noted that, after Landgraf, there was reason for Congress to suppose that an explicit statement was required to render the amendments to chapter 154 applicable in pending cases, because the new chapter 154 "will have substantive as well as purely procedural effects." 521 U. S., at 327. The next step—and the critical step—in our reasoning was that Congress had identical reason to suppose that an explicit statement would be required to apply the chapter 153 amendments to pending cases, but did not provide it. Id., at 329. The negative inference of Lindh rested on the fact that "[n]othing ... but a different intent explain[ed] the different treatment." Ibid.

Here, by contrast, there is ample reason for the different treatment. The exclusive-review provisions of the DTA, unlike both §1005(e)(1) and the AEDPA amendments in Lindh, confer new jurisdiction (in the D. C. Circuit) where there was none before. For better or for worse, our recent cases have contrasted jurisdiction-creating provisions with jurisdiction-ousting provisions, retaining the venerable rule that the latter are not retroactive even when applied in pending cases, but strongly indicating that the former are typically retroactive. For example, we stated in Hughes Aircraft Co. v. United States ex rel. Schumer, 520 U. S. 939, 951 (1997), that a statute "that creates jurisdiction where none previously existed" is "as much subject to our presumption against retroactivity as any other." See also Republic of Austria v. Altmann, 541 U. S. 677, 695 (2004) (opinion for the Court by Stevens, J.); id., at 722 (Kennedy, J., dissenting). The Court gives our retroactivity jurisprudence a dazzling clarity in asserting that "subsections (e)(2) and (e)(3) 'confer' jurisdiction in a manner that cannot conceivably give rise to retroactivity questions under our precedents."[2] Ante, at 17–18. This statement rises to the level of sarcasm when one considers its author's description of the governing test of our retroactivity jurisprudence:

"The conclusion that a particular rule operates 'retroactively' comes at the end of a process of judgment concerning the nature and extent of the change in the law and the degree of connection between the operation of the new rule and a relevant past event. Any test of retroactivity will leave room for disagreement in hard cases, and is unlikely to classify the enormous variety of legal changes with perfect philosophical clarity. However, retroactivity is a matter on which judges tend to have 'sound ... instinct[s],' ... and familiar considerations of fair notice, reasonable reliance, and settled expectations offer sound guidance." Landgraf, 511 U. S., at 270 (opinion for the Court by Stevens, J.).

The only "familiar consideration," "reasonable reliance," and "settled expectation" I am aware of pertaining to the present case is the rule of Bruner—applicable to §1005(e)(1), but not to §1005(e)(2) and (3)—which the Court stubbornly disregards. It is utterly beyond question that §1005(e)(2)'s and (3)'s application to pending cases (without explicit specification) was not as clear as §1005(e)(1)'s. That is alone enough to explain the difference in treatment.

Another obvious reason for the specification was to stave off any Suspension Clause problems raised by the immediately effective ouster of jurisdiction brought about by subsection (e)(1). That is to say, specification of the immediate effectiveness of subsections (e)(2) and (e)(3) (which, unlike subsection (e)(1), would not fall within the Bruner rule and would not automatically be deemed applicable in pending cases) could reasonably have been thought essential to be sure of replacing the habeas jurisdiction that subsection (e)(1) eliminated in pending cases with an adequate substitute. See infra, at 16–18.

These considerations by no means prove that an explicit statement would be required to render subsections (e)(2) and (e)(3) applicable in pending cases. But they surely gave Congress ample reason to doubt that their application in pending cases would unfold as naturally as the Court glibly assumes. In any event, even if it were true that subsections (e)(2) and (e)(3) " 'confer' jurisdiction in a manner that cannot conceivably give rise to retroactivity questions," ante, at 17–18, this would merely establish that subsection (h)(2)'s reference to pending cases was wholly superfluous when applied to subsections (e)(2) and (e)(3), just as it would have been for subsection (e)(1). Lindh's negative inference makes sense only when Congress would have perceived "the wisdom of being explicit" with respect to the immediate application of both of two statutory provisions, 521 U. S., at 328, but chose to be explicit only for one of them—not when it would have perceived no need to be explicit for both, but enacted a redundancy only for one.

In short, it is simply untrue that Congress " 'should have been just as concerned about' " specifying the application of §1005(e)(1) to pending cases, ante, at 14 (quoting Lindh, 521 U. S., at 329). In fact, the negative-inference approach of Lindh is particularly inappropriate in this case, because the negative inference from §1005(h)(2) would tend to defeat the purpose of the very provisions that are explicitly rendered applicable in pending cases, §1005(e)(2) and (3). Those provisions purport to vest "exclusive" jurisdiction in the D. C. Circuit to consider the claims raised by petitioners here. See infra, at 16–18. By drawing a negative inference à la Lindh, the Court supplants this exclusive-review mechanism with a dual-review mechanism for petitioners who were expeditious enough to file applications challenging the CSRTs or military commissions before December 30, 2005. Whatever the force of Lindh's negative inference in other cases, it surely should not apply here to defeat the purpose of the very provision from which the negative inference is drawn.

C

Worst of all is the Court's reliance on the legislative history of the DTA to buttress its implausible reading of §1005(e)(1). We have repeatedly held that such reliance is impermissible where, as here, the statutory language is unambiguous. But the Court nevertheless relies both on floor statements from the Senate and (quite heavily) on the drafting history of the DTA. To begin with floor statements: The Court urges that some "statements made by Senators preceding passage of the Act lend further support to" the Court's interpretation, citing excerpts from the floor debate that support its view, ante, 15–16, n. 10. The Court immediately goes on to discount numerous floor statements by the DTA's sponsors that flatly contradict its view, because "those statements appear to have been inserted into the Congressional Record after the Senate debate." Ibid. Of course this observation, even if true, makes no difference unless one indulges the fantasy that Senate floor speeches are attended (like the Philippics of Demosthenes) by throngs of eager listeners, instead of being delivered (like Demosthenes' practice sessions on the beach) alone into a vast emptiness. Whether the floor statements are spoken where no Senator hears, or written where no Senator reads, they represent at most the views of a single Senator. In any event, the Court greatly exaggerates the one-sidedness of the portions of the floor debate that clearly occurred before the DTA's enactment. Some of the statements of Senator Graham, a sponsor of the bill, only make sense on the assumption that pending cases are covered.3 And at least one opponent of the DTA unmistakably expressed his understanding that it would terminate our jurisdiction in this very case.4 (Of course in its discussion of legislative history the Court wholly ignores the President's signing statement, which explicitly set forth his understanding that the DTA ousted jurisdiction over pending cases.5)

But selectivity is not the greatest vice in the Court's use of floor statements to resolve today's case. These statements were made when Members of Congress were fully aware that our continuing jurisdiction over this very case was at issue. The question was divisive, and floor statements made on both sides were undoubtedly opportunistic and crafted solely for use in the briefs in this very litigation. See, e.g., 151 Cong. Rec. S14257–S14258 (Dec. 21, 2005) (statement of Sen. Levin) (arguing against a reading that would "stri[p] the Federal courts of jurisdiction to consider pending cases, including the Hamdan case now pending in the Supreme Court," and urging that Lindh requires the same negative inference that the Court indulges today (emphasis added)). The Court's reliance on such statements cannot avoid the appearance of similar opportunism. In a virtually identical context, the author of today's opinion has written for the Court that "[t]he legislative history discloses some frankly partisan statements about the meaning of the final effective date language, but those statements cannot plausibly be read as reflecting any general agreement." Landgraf, 511 U. S., at 262 (opinion for the Court by Stevens, J.). Likewise, the handful of floor statements that the Court treats as authoritative do not "reflec[t] any general agreement." They reflect the now-common tactic—which the Court once again rewards—of pursuing through floor-speech ipse dixit what could not be achieved through the constitutionally prescribed method of putting language into a bill that a majority of both Houses vote for and the President signs.

With regard to the floor statements, at least the Court shows some semblance of seemly shame, tucking away its reference to them in a half-hearted footnote. Not so for its reliance on the DTA's drafting history, which is displayed prominently, see ante, at 14–15. I have explained elsewhere that such drafting history is no more legitimate or reliable an indicator of the objective meaning of a statute than any other form of legislative history. This case presents a textbook example of its unreliability. The Court, ante, at 14, trumpets the fact that a bill considered in the Senate included redundant language, not included in the DTA as passed, reconfirming that the abolition of habeas jurisdiction "shall apply to any application or other action that is pending on or after the date of the enactment of this Act." 151 Cong. Rec. S12655 (Nov. 10, 2005). But this earlier version of the bill also differed from the DTA in other material respects. Most notably, it provided for postdecision review by the D. C. Circuit only of the decisions of CSRTs, not military commissions, ibid.; and it limited that review to whether "the status determination ... was consistent with the procedures and standards specified by the Secretary of Defense," ibid., not whether "the use of such standards and procedures ... is consistent with the Constitution and laws of the United States," DTA §1005(e)(2)(C)(ii), 119 Stat. 2742. To say that what moved Senators to reject this earlier bill was the "action that is pending" provision surpasses the intuitive powers of even this Court's greatest Justices.6 And to think that the House and the President also had this rejection firmly in mind is absurd. As always—but especially in the context of strident, partisan legislative conflict of the sort that characterized enactment of this legislation—the language of the statute that was actually passed by both Houses of Congress and signed by the President is our only authoritative and only reliable guidepost.

D

A final but powerful indication of the fact that the Court has made a mess of this statute is the nature of the consequences that ensue. Though this case concerns a habeas application challenging a trial by military commission, DTA §1005(e)(1) strips the courts of jurisdiction to hear or consider any "application for a writ of habeas corpus filed by or on behalf of an alien detained by the Department of Defense at Guantanamo Bay, Cuba." The vast majority of pending petitions, no doubt, do not relate to military commissions at all, but to more commonly challenged aspects of "detention" such as the terms and conditions of confinement. See Rasul v. Bush, 542 U. S. 466, 498 (2004) (Scalia, J., dissenting). The Solicitor General represents that "[h]abeas petitions have been filed on behalf of a purported 600 [Guantanamo Bay] detainees," including one that "seek[s] relief on behalf of every Guantanamo detainee who has not already filed an action," Respondents' Motion to Dismiss for Lack of Jurisdiction 20, n. 10 (hereinafter Motion to Dismiss). The Court's interpretation transforms a provision abolishing jurisdiction over all Guantanamo-related habeas petitions into a provision that retains jurisdiction over cases sufficiently numerous to keep the courts busy for years to come.

II

Because I would hold that §1005(e)(1) unambiguously terminates the jurisdiction of all courts to "hear or consider" pending habeas applications, I must confront petitioner's arguments that the provision, so interpreted, violates the Suspension Clause. This claim is easily dispatched. We stated in Johnson v. Eisentrager, 339 U. S. 763, 768 (1950):

"We are cited to no instance where a court, in this or any other country where the writ is known, has issued it on behalf of an alien enemy who, at no relevant time and in no stage of his captivity, has been within its territorial jurisdiction. Nothing in the text of the Constitution extends such a right, nor does anything in our statutes."

Notwithstanding the ill-considered dicta in the Court's opinion in Rasul, 542 U. S., at 480–481, it is clear that Guantanamo Bay, Cuba, is outside the sovereign "territorial jurisdiction" of the United States. See id., at 500–505 (Scalia, J., dissenting). Petitioner, an enemy alien detained abroad, has no rights under the Suspension Clause.

But even if petitioner were fully protected by the Clause, the DTA would create no suspension problem. This Court has repeatedly acknowledged that "the substitution of a collateral remedy which is neither inadequate nor ineffective to test the legality of a person's detention does not constitute a suspension of the writ of habeas corpus." Swain v. Pressley, 430 U. S. 372, 381 (1977); see also INS v. St. Cyr, 533 U. S. 289, 314, n. 38 (2006) ("Congress could, without raising any constitutional questions, provide an adequate substitute through the courts of appeals").

Petitioner has made no showing that the postdecision exclusive review by the D. C. Circuit provided in §1005(e)(3) is inadequate to test the legality of his trial by military commission. His principal argument is that the exclusive-review provisions are inadequate because they foreclose review of the claims he raises here. Though petitioner's brief does not parse the statutory language, his argument evidently rests on an erroneously narrow reading of DTA §1005(e)(3)(D)(ii), 119 Stat. 2743. That provision grants the D. C. Circuit authority to review, "to the extent the Constitution and laws of the United States are applicable, whether the use of such standards and procedures to reach the final decision is consistent with the Constitution and laws of the United States." In the quoted text, the phrase "such standards and procedures" refers to "the standards and procedures specified in the military order referred to in subparagraph (A)," namely "Military Commission Order No. 1, dated August 31, 2005 (or any successor military order)." DTA §1005(e)(3)(D)(i), (e)(3)(A), ibid. This Military Commission Order (Order No. 1) is the Department of Defense's fundamental implementing order for the President's order authorizing trials by military commission. Order No. 1 establishes commissions, §2; delineates their jurisdiction, §3; provides for their officers, §4(A); provides for their prosecution and defense counsel, §4(B), (C); lays out all their procedures, both pretrial and trial, §5(A)–(P), §6(A)–(G); and provides for posttrial military review through the Secretary of Defense and the President, §6(H). In short, the "standards and procedures specified in" Order No. 1 include every aspect of the military commissions, including the fact of their existence and every respect in which they differ from courts-martial. Petitioner's claims that the President lacks legal authority to try him before a military commission constitute claims that "the use of such standards and procedures," as specified in Order No. 1, is "[in]consistent with the Constitution and laws of the United States," DTA §1005(e)(3)(D)(ii), 119 Stat. 2743. The D. C. Circuit thus retains jurisdiction to consider these claims on postdecision review, and the Government does not dispute that the DTA leaves unaffected our certiorari jurisdiction under 28 U. S. C. §1254(1) to review the D. C. Circuit's decisions. Motion to Dismiss 16, n. 8. Thus, the DTA merely defers our jurisdiction to consider petitioner's claims; it does not eliminate that jurisdiction. It constitutes neither an "inadequate" nor an "ineffective" substitute for petitioner's pending habeas application.7

Though it does not squarely address the issue, the Court hints ominously that "the Government's preferred reading" would "rais[e] grave questions about Congress' authority to impinge upon this Court's appellate jurisdiction, particularly in habeas cases." Ante, at 10–11 (citing Ex parte Yerger, 8Wall. 85 (1869); Felker v. Turpin, 518 U. S. 651 (1996); Durousseau v. United States, 6 Cranch 307 (1810); United States v. Klein, 13Wall. 128 (1872); and Ex parte McCardle, 7 Wall. 506). It is not clear how there could be any such lurking questions, in light of the aptly named "Exceptions Clause" of Article III, §2, which, in making our appellate jurisdiction subject to "such Exceptions, and under such Regulations as the Congress shall make," explicitly permits exactly what Congress has done here. But any doubt our prior cases might have created on this score is surely chimerical in this case. As just noted, the exclusive-review provisions provide a substitute for habeas review adequate to satisfy the Suspension Clause, which forbids the suspension of the writ of habeas corpus. A fortiori they provide a substitute adequate to satisfy any implied substantive limitations, whether real or imaginary, upon the Exceptions Clause, which authorizes such exceptions as §1005(e)(1).

III

Even if Congress had not clearly and constitutionally eliminated jurisdiction over this case, neither this Court nor the lower courts ought to exercise it. Traditionally, equitable principles govern both the exercise of habeas jurisdiction and the granting of the injunctive relief sought by petitioner. See Schlesinger v. Councilman, 420 U. S. 738, 754 (1975); Weinberger v. Romero-Barcelo, 456 U. S. 305, 311 (1982) . In light of Congress's provision of an alternate avenue for petitioner's claims in §1005(e)(3), those equitable principles counsel that we abstain from exercising jurisdiction in this case.

In requesting abstention, the Government relies principally on Councilman, in which we abstained from considering a serviceman's claim that his charge for marijuana possession was not sufficiently "service-connected" to trigger the subject-matter jurisdiction of the military courts-martial. See 420 U. S., at 740, 758. Admittedly, Councilman does not squarely control petitioner's case, but it provides the closest analogue in our jurisprudence. As the Court describes, ante, at 21, Councilman "identifie[d] two considerations of comity that together favor[ed] abstention pending completion of ongoing court-martial proceedings against service personnel." But the Court errs in finding these considerations inapplicable to this case. Both of them, and a third consideration not emphasized in Councilman, all cut in favor of abstention here.

First, the Court observes that Councilman rested in part on the fact that "military discipline and, therefore, the efficient operation of the Armed Forces are best served if the military justice system acts without regular interference from civilian courts," and concludes that "Hamdan is not a member of our Nation's Armed Forces, so concerns about military discipline do not apply." Ante, at 22. This is true enough. But for some reason, the Court fails to make any inquiry into whether military commission trials might involve other "military necessities" or "unique military exigencies," 420 U. S., at 757, comparable in gravity to those at stake in Councilman. To put this in context: The charge against the respondent in Councilman was the off-base possession and sale of marijuana while he was stationed in Fort Sill, Oklahoma, see id., at 739–740. The charge against the petitioner here is joining and actively abetting the murderous conspiracy that slaughtered thousands of innocent American civilians without warning on September 11, 2001. While Councilman held that the prosecution of the former charge involved "military necessities" counseling against our interference, the Court does not even ponder the same question for the latter charge.

The reason for the Court's "blinkered study" of this question, ante, at 19, is not hard to fathom. The principal opinion on the merits makes clear that it does not believe that the trials by military commission involve any "military necessity" at all: "The charge's shortcomings ... are indicative of a broader inability on the Executive's part here to satisfy the most basic precondition ... for establishment of military commissions: military necessity." Ante, at 48. This is quite at odds with the views on this subject expressed by our political branches. Because of "military necessity," a joint session of Congress authorized the President to "use all necessary and appropriate force," including military commissions, "against those nations, organizations, or persons [such as petitioner] he determines planned, authorized, committed, or aided the terrorist attacks that occurred on September 11, 2001." Authorization for Use of Military Force, §2(a), 115 Stat. 224, note following 50 U. S. C. §1541 (2000 ed., Supp. III). In keeping with this authority, the President has determined that "[t]o protect the United States and its citizens, and for the effective conduct of military operations and prevention of terrorist attacks, it is necessary for individuals subject to this order ... to be detained, and, when tried, to be tried for violations of the laws of war and other applicable laws by military tribunals." Military Order of Nov. 13, 2001, 3 CFR §918(e) (2002). It is not clear where the Court derives the authority—or the audacity—to contradict this determination. If "military necessities" relating to "duty" and "discipline" required abstention in Councilman, supra, at 757, military necessities relating to the disabling, deterrence, and punishment of the mass-murdering terrorists of September 11 require abstention all the more here.

The Court further seeks to distinguish Councilman on the ground that "the tribunal convened to try Hamdan is not part of the integrated system of military courts, complete with independent review panels, that Congress has established." Ante, at 22. To be sure, Councilman emphasized that "Congress created an integrated system of military courts and review procedures, a critical element of which is the Court of Military Appeals consisting of civilian judges completely removed from all military influence or persuasion, who would gain over time thorough familiarity with military problems." 420 U. S., at 758 (internal quotation marks and footnote omitted). The Court contrasts this "integrated system" insulated from military influence with the review scheme established by Order No. 1, which "provides that appeal of a review panel's decision may be had only to the Secretary of Defense himself, §6(H)(5), and then, finally, to the President, §6(H)(6)." Ante, at 23.

Even if we were to accept the Court's extraordinary assumption that the President "lack[s] the structural insulation from military influence that characterizes the Court of Appeals for the Armed Forces," ante, at 23,[8] the Court's description of the review scheme here is anachronistic. As of December 30, 2005, the "fina[l]" review of decisions by military commissions is now conducted by the D. C. Circuit pursuant to §1005(e)(3) of the DTA, and by this Court under 28 U. S. C. §1254(1). This provision for review by Article III courts creates, if anything, a review scheme more insulated from Executive control than that in Councilman.[9] At the time we decided Councilman, Congress had not "conferred on any Art[icle] III court jurisdiction directly to review court-martial determinations." 420 U. S., at 746. The final arbiter of direct appeals was the Court of Military Appeals (now the Court of Appeals for the Armed Forces), an Article I court whose members possessed neither life tenure, nor salary protection, nor the constitutional protection from removal provided to federal judges in Article III, §1. See 10 U. S. C. §867(a)(2) (1970 ed.).

Moreover, a third consideration counsels strongly in favor of abstention in this case. Councilman reasoned that the "considerations of comity, the necessity of respect for coordinate judicial systems" that motivated our decision in Younger v. Harris, 401 U. S. 37 (1971), were inapplicable to courts-martial, because "the particular demands of federalism are not implicated." 420 U. S., at 756, 757. Though military commissions likewise do not implicate "the particular demands of federalism," considerations of interbranch comity at the federal level weigh heavily against our exercise of equity jurisdiction in this case. Here, apparently for the first time in history, see Motion to Dismiss 6, a District Court enjoined ongoing military commission proceedings, which had been deemed "necessary" by the President "[t]o protect the United States and its citizens, and for the effective conduct of military operations and prevention of terrorist attacks." Military Order of Nov. 13, 3 CFR §918(e). Such an order brings the Judicial Branch into direct conflict with the Executive in an area where the Executive's competence is maximal and ours is virtually nonexistent. We should exercise our equitable discretion to avoid such conflict. Instead, the Court rushes headlong to meet it. Elsewhere, we have deferred exercising habeas jurisdiction until state courts have "the first opportunity to review" a petitioner's claim, merely to "reduc[e] friction between the state and federal court systems." O'Sullivan v. Boerckel, 526 U. S. 838, 844, 845 (1999) . The "friction" created today between this Court and the Executive Branch is many times more serious.

In the face of such concerns, the Court relies heavily on Ex parte Quirin, 317 U. S. 1 (1942) : "Far from abstaining pending the conclusion of military proceedings, which were ongoing, [in Quirin] we convened a special Term to hear the case and expedited our review." Ante, at 24. It is likely that the Government in Quirin, unlike here, preferred a hasty resolution of the case in this Court, so that it could swiftly execute the sentences imposed, see Hamdi v. Rumsfeld, 542 U. S. 507, 569 (2004) (Scalia, J., dissenting). But the Court's reliance on Quirin suffers from a more fundamental defect: Once again, it ignores the DTA, which creates an avenue for the consideration of petitioner's claims that did not exist at the time of Quirin. Collateral application for habeas review was the only vehicle available. And there was no compelling reason to postpone consideration of the Quirin application until the termination of military proceedings, because the only cognizable claims presented were general challenges to the authority of the commissions that would not be affected by the specific proceedings. See supra, at 8–9, n. 2. In the DTA, by contrast, Congress has expanded the scope of Article III review and has channeled it exclusively through a single, postverdict appeal to Article III courts. Because Congress has created a novel unitary scheme of Article III review of military commissions that was absent in 1942, Quirin is no longer governing precedent.

I would abstain from exercising our equity jurisdiction, as the Government requests.

* * *

For the foregoing reasons, I dissent.

Notes to Justice Scalia's dissent in Hamdan v. Rumsfeld (June 29, 2006)

1 The Court apparently believes that the effective-date provision means nothing at all. "That paragraph (1), along with paragraphs (2) and (3), is to 'take effect on the date of enactment,' DTA §1005(h)(1), 119 Stat. 2743, is not dispositive," says the Court, ante, at 14, n. 9. The Court's authority for this conclusion is its quote from INS v. St. Cyr, 533 U. S. 289, 317 (2001), to the effect that "a statement that a statute will become effective on a certain date does not even arguably suggest that it has any application to conduct that occurred at an earlier date." Ante, at 14, n. 9 (emphasis added, internal quotation marks omitted). But this quote merely restates the obvious: An effective-date provision does not render a statute applicable to "conduct that occurred at an earlier date," but of course it renders the statute applicable to conduct that occurs on the effective date and all future dates—such as the Court's exercise of jurisdiction here. The Court seems to suggest that, because the effective-date provision does not authorize retroactive application, it also fails to authorize prospective application (and is thus useless verbiage). This cannot be true.

2 A comparison with Lindh v. Murphy, 521 U. S. 320 (1997), shows this not to be true. Subsections (e)(2) and (e)(3) of §1005 resemble the provisions of AEDPA at issue in

Lindh (whose retroactivityas applied to pending cases the Lindh majority did not rule upon,see 521 U. S., at 326), in that they "g[o] beyond 'mere' procedure,"id., at 327. They impose novel and unprecedented disabilities onthe Executive Branch in its conduct of military affairs. Subsection (e)(2) imposes judicial review on the Combatant Status ReviewTribunals (CSRTs), whose implementing order did not subject themto review by Article III courts. See Memorandum from Deputy Secretary of Defense Paul Wolfowitz re: Order Establishing Com-batant Status Review Tribunals, at 3 §h (July 7, 2004), avail-able at http://www.defenselink.mil/news/Jul2004/d20040707review.pdf (all Internet materials as visited June 27, 2006, and availablein Clerk of Court's case file). Subsection (e)(3) authorizes the D. C. Circuit to review "the validity of any final decision rendered pursuant to Military Commission Order No. 1," §1005(e)(3)(A), 119 Stat. 2743. Historically, federal courts have never reviewed the validity of the final decision of any military commission; their jurisdiction has been restricted to considering the commission's "lawful authority to hear, decide and condemn," In re Yamashita, 327 U. S. 1, 8 (1946) (emphasis added). See also Johnson v. Eisentrager, 339 U. S. 763, 786–787 (1950) . Thus, contrary to the Court's suggestion, ante, at 17, subsections (e)(2) and (e)(3) confer new jurisdiction: They impose judicial oversight on a traditionally unreviewable exercise of military authority by the Commander in Chief. They arguably "spea[k] not just to the power of a particular court but to . . . substantive rights . . . as well," Hughes Aircraft Co. v. United States ex rel. Shumer, 520 U. S. 939, 951 (1997) —namely, the unreviewable powers of the President. Our recent cases had reiterated that the Executive is protected by the presumption against retroactivity in such comparatively trivial contexts as suits for tax refunds and increased pay, see Landgraf v. USI Film Products, 511 U. S. 244, 271, n. 25 (1994) .

3 "Because I have described how outrageous these claims are—about the exercise regime, the reading materials—most Americans would be highly offended to know that terrorists are suing us in our own courts about what they read." 151 Cong. Rec. S12756 (Nov. 14, 2005). "Instead of having unlimited habeas corpus opportunities under the Constitution, we give every enemy combatant, all 500, a chance to go to Federal court, the Circuit Court of Appeals for the District of Columbia... . It will be a one-time deal." Id., at S12754. "This Levin-Graham-Kyl amendment allows every detainee under our control to have their day in court. They are allowed to appeal their convictions." Id., at S12801 (Nov. 15, 2005); see also id., at S12799 (rejecting the notion that "an enemy combatant terrorist al-Qaida member should be able to have access to our Federal courts under habeas like an American citizen").

4 "An earlier part of the amendment provides that no court, justice, or judge shall have jurisdiction to consider the application for writ of habeas corpus... . Under the language of exclusive jurisdiction in the DC Circuit, the U. S. Supreme Court would not have jurisdiction to hear the Hamdan case ... ." Id., at S12796 (statement of Sen. Specter).

5 "[T]he executive branch shall construe section 1005 to preclude the Federal courts from exercising subject matter jurisdiction over any existing or future action,

including applications for writs of habeas corpus, described in section 1005." President's Statement on Signingof H. R. 2863, the "Department of Defense, Emergency Supplemental Appropriations to Address Hurricanes in the Gulf ofMexico, and Pandemic Influenza Act, 2006" (Dec. 30, 2005), availableat http://www.whitehouse.gov/news/releases/2005/12/print/200512308.html.

6 The Court asserts that "it cannot be said that the changes to subsection (h)(2) were inconsequential," ante, at 15, n. 10, but the Court's sole evidence is the self-serving floor statements that it selectively cites.

7 Petitioner also urges that he could be subject to indefinite delay if military officials and the President are deliberately dilatory in reviewing the decision of his commission. In reviewing the constitutionality of legislation, we generally presume that the Executive will implement its provisions in good faith. And it is unclear in any event that delay would inflict any injury on petitioner, who (after an adverse determination by his CSRT, see 344 F. Supp. 2d 152, 161 (DC 2004)) is already subject to indefinite detention under our decision in Hamdi v. Rumsfeld, 542 U. S. 507 (2004) . Moreover, the mere possibility of delay does not render an alternative remedy "inadequate [o]r ineffective to test the legality" of a military commission trial. Swain v. Pressley, 430 U. S. 372, 381 (1977) . In an analogous context, we discounted the notion that postponement of relief until postconviction review inflicted any cognizable injury on a serviceman charged before a military court-martial. Schlesinger v. Councilman, 420 U. S. 738, 754–755 (1975); see also Younger v. Harris, 401 U. S. 37, 46 (1971) .

8 The very purpose of Article II's creation of a civilian Commander in Chief in the President of the United States was to generate "structural insulation from military influence." See The Federalist No. 28 (A. Hamilton); id., No. 69 (same). We do not live under a military junta. It is a disservice to both those in the Armed Forces and the President to suggest that the President is subject to the undue control of the military.

9 In rejecting our analysis, the Court observes that appeals to the D. C. Circuit under subsection (e)(3) are discretionary, rather than as of right, when the military commission imposes a sentence less than 10 years' imprisonment, see ante, at 23, n. 19, 52–53; §1005(e)(3)(B), 119 Stat. 2743. The relevance of this observation to the abstention question is unfathomable. The fact that Article III review is discretionary does not mean that it lacks "structural insulation from military influence," ante, at 23, and its discretionary nature presents no obstacle to the courts' future review these cases. The Court might more cogently have relied on the discretionary nature of review to argue that the statute provides an inadequate substitute for habeas review under the Suspension Clause. See supra, at 16–18. But this argument would have no force, even if all appeals to the D. C. Circuit were discretionary. The exercise of habeas jurisdiction has traditionally been entirely a matter of the court's equitable discretion, see Withrow v. Williams, 507 U. S. 680, 715–718 (1993) (Scalia, J., concurring in part and dissenting in part), so the fact that habeas jurisdiction is replaced by discretionary appellate review does not render the substitution "inadequate." Swain, 430 U. S., at 381.

I would therefore reconsider the decision that sets us the unsavory task of separating issue-speech from election-speech with no clear criterion: Justice Scalia's concurrence and dissent in Federal Election Commission v. Wisconsin Right to Life (June 25, 2007)

Justice Scalia, with whom Justice Kennedy and Justice Thomas join, concurring in part and concurring in the judgment.

A Moroccan cartoonist once defended his criticism of the Moroccan monarch (lse majesté being a serious crime in Morocco) as follows: " 'I'm not a revolutionary, I'm just defending freedom of speech.... . I never said we had to change the king—no, no, no, no! But I said that some things the king is doing, I do not like. Is that a crime?' "1 Well, in the United States (making due allowance for the fact that we have elected representatives instead of a king) it is a crime, at least if the speaker is a union or a corporation (including not-for-profit public-interest corporations) and if the representative is identified by name within a certain period before a primary or congressional election in which he is running. That is the import of §203 of the Bipartisan Campaign Reform Act of 2002 (BCRA), the constitutionality of which we upheld three Terms ago in McConnell v. Federal Election Comm'n, 540 U. S. 93 (2003). As an element essential to that determination of constitutionality, our opinion left open the possibility that a corporation or union could establish that, in the particular circumstances of its case, the ban was unconstitutional because it was (to pursue the analogy) only the king's policies and not his tenure in office that was criticized. Today's cases present the question of what sort of showing is necessary for that purpose. For the reasons I set forth below, it is my view that no test for such a showing can both (1) comport with the requirement of clarity that unchilled freedom of political speech demands, and (2) be compatible with the facial validity of §203 (as pronounced in McConnell). I would therefore reconsider the decision that sets us the unsavory task of separating issue-speech from election-speech with no clear criterion.

I

Today's cases originated in the efforts of Wisconsin Right to Life, Inc. (WRTL), a Wisconsin nonprofit, nonstock ideological advocacy corporation, to lobby Wisconsin voters concerning the filibustering of the President's judicial nominees. The problem for WRTL was that, under §203 of BCRA, it would have been unlawful to air its television and radio ads within 30 days before the September 14, 2004, primary or within 60 days before the November 2, 2004, general election because the ads named Senator Feingold, who was then seeking reelection. Section 203(a) of BCRA amended §316(b)(2) of the Federal Election Campaign Act Amendments of 1974, which prohibited corporations and unions from "mak[ing] a contribution or expenditure in connection with any election to any political office, or in connection with any primary election … for any political office."

2 U. S. C. §441b(a). Prior to BCRA, that section covered only expenditures for communications that expressly advocated the election or defeat of a candidate (in campaign-finance speak, so-called "express advocacy"). McConnell, supra, at 204. As amended, however, that section was broadened to cover "electioneering communication[s]," §441b(b)(2) (2000 ed., Supp. IV), which include "any broadcast, cable, or satellite communication" that "refers to a clearly identified candidate for Federal office" and that is aired within 60 days before a general election, or 30 days before a primary election, in the jurisdiction in which the candidate is running. §434(f)(3) (2000 ed., Supp. IV).2 Under the new law, a corporation or union wishing to air advertisements covered by the definition of "electioneering communication" is prohibited by §203 from doing so unless it first creates a separate segregated fund run by a "political action committee," commonly known as a "PAC." §441b(b)(2)(C) (2000 ed., Supp. IV). Three Terms ago, in McConnell, supra, this Court upheld most of BCRA's provisions against constitutional challenge, including §203. The Court found that the "vast majority" of ads aired during the 30-day and 60-day periods before elections were "the functional equivalent of express advocacy," id., at 206, but suggested that "pure issue ads," id., at 207, or "genuine issue ads," id., at 206, would be protected.

The question in these cases is whether §203 can be applied to WRTL's ads consistently with the First Amendment. Last Term, this Court unanimously held, in Wisconsin Right to Life, Inc. v. Federal Election Comm'n, 546 U. S. 410, 411–412 (2006) (per curiam) (WRTL I), that as-applied challenges to §203 are available. The District Court in these cases subsequently held that §203 is unconstitutional as applied to the three ads at issue. The Court today affirms the judgment of the District Court. While I agree with that result, I disagree with the principal opinion's reasons.

II

A proper explanation of my views in these cases requires some discussion of the case law leading up to McConnell. I begin with the seminal case of Buckley v. Valeo, 424 U. S. 1 (1976) (per curiam), wherein this Court considered the constitutionality of various political contribution and expenditure limitations contained in the Federal Election Campaign Act of 1971 (FECA), 86 Stat. 3, as amended, 88 Stat. 1263. Buckley set forth a now-familiar framework for evaluating the constitutionality of campaign-finance regulations. The Court began with the recognition that contributing money to, and spending money on behalf of, political candidates implicates core First Amendment protections, and that restrictions on such contributions and expenditures "operate in an area of the most fundamental First Amendment activities." 424 U. S., at 14. The Court also recognized, however, that the Government has a compelling interest in "prevention of corruption and the appearance of corruption." Id., at 25. The "corruption" to which the Court repeatedly referred was of the "quid pro quo" variety, whereby an individual or entity makes a contribution or expenditure in exchange for some action by an official. Id., at 26, 27, 45, 47.

The Court then held that FECA's contribution limitations passed constitutional muster because they represented a "marginal restriction upon the contributor's ability to engage in free communication," id., at 20–21, and were thus subject to a lower level of scrutiny, id., at 25. The Court invalidated, however, FECA's limitation on independent expenditures (i.e., expenditures made to express one's own positions and not in coordination with a campaign). Id., at 39–51. In the Court's view, expenditure limitations restrict speech that is " 'at the core of our electoral process and of the First Amendment freedoms,' " id., at 39, and require the highest scrutiny, id., at 44–45.

The independent-expenditure restriction at issue in Buckley limited the amount of money that could be spent " 'relative to a clearly identified candidate.' " Id., at 41 (quoting 18 U. S. C. §608(e)(1) (1970 ed., Supp. IV) (repealed 1976)). Before striking down the expenditure limitation, the Court narrowly construed §608(e)(1), in light of vagueness concerns, to cover only express advocacy—that is, advertising that "in express terms advocate[s] the election or defeat of a clearly identified candidate for federal office" by use of such words of advocacy "as 'vote for,' 'elect,' 'support,' 'cast your ballot for,' 'Smith for Congress,' 'vote against,' 'defeat,' 'reject.' " 424 U. S., at 44, and n. 52. This narrowing construction excluded so-called "issue advocacy"—for example, an ad that refers to a clearly identified candidate's position on an issue, but does not expressly advocate his election or defeat. Even as narrowly construed to cover only express advocacy, however, §608(e)(1) was held to be unconstitutional because the narrowed prohibition was too narrow to be effective and (quite apart from that shortcoming) independent expenditures did not pose a serious enough threat of corruption. Id., at 45–46. Notably, the Court also found the Government's interest in "equalizing the relative ability of individuals and groups to influence the outcome of elections" insufficient to support limitations on independent expenditures. Id., at 48.

Buckley might well have been the last word on limitations on independent expenditures. Some argued, however, that independent expenditures by corporations should be treated differently. That argument should have been foreclosed by Buckley for several reasons: (1) the particular provision at issue in Buckley, §608(e)(1) of FECA, was directed to expenditures not just by "individuals," but by "persons," with " 'persons' " specifically defined to include " 'corporation[s],' " id., at 23, 39, n. 45; (2) the plaintiffs in Buckley included corporations, id., at 8; and (3) Buckley, id., at 50–51, cited a case that involved limitations on corporations in support of its striking down the restriction at issue, Miami Herald Publishing Co. v. Tornillo, 418 U. S. 241 (1974) . Moreover, pre-Buckley cases had accorded corporations full First Amendment protection. See, e.g., NAACP v. Button, 371 U. S. 415, 428–429, 431 (1963) (holding that the corporation's activities were "modes of expression and association protected by the First and Fourteenth Amendment s"); Grosjean v. American Press Co., 297 U. S. 233, 244 (1936) (holding that corporations are guaranteed the "freedom of speech and of the press ... safeguarded by the due process of law clause of the Fourteenth Amendment "). See also Pacific Gas & Elec. Co. v. Public Util. Comm'n of Cal., 475 U. S. 1, 8 (1986) (plurality opinion) ("The identity of the speaker is not decisive in determining whether speech is protected"; "[c]orporations and other associations, like individuals, contribute to the 'discussion, debate, and the dissemination of information and ideas' that the First Amendment seeks to foster").

Indeed, one would have thought the coup de grâce to the argument that corporations can be treated differently for these purposes was dealt by First Nat. Bank of Boston v. Bellotti, 435 U. S. 765 (1978), decided just two years after Buckley. In that case, the Court struck down a Massachusetts statute that prohibited corporations from spending money in connection with a referendum unless the referendum materially affected the corporation's property, business, or assets. As the Court explained: The principle that such advocacy is "at the heart of the First Amendment's protection" and is "indispensable to decisionmaking in a democracy" is "no less true because the speech comes from a corporation rather than an individual." 435 U. S., at 776–777. And the Court rejected the arguments that corporate participation "would exert an undue influence on the outcome of a referendum vote"; that corporations would "drown out other points of view" and "destroy the confidence of the people in the democratic process," id., at 789; and that the prohibition was needed to protect corporate shareholders "by preventing the use of corporate resources in furtherance of views with which some shareholders may disagree," id., at 792–793.3

The Court strayed far from these principles, however, in one post-Buckley case: Austin v. Michigan Chamber of Commerce, 494 U. S. 652 (1990) . This was the only pre-McConnell case in which this Court had ever permitted the Government to restrict political speech based on the corporate identity of the speaker. Austin upheld state restrictions on corporate independent expenditures in support of, or in opposition to, any candidate in elections for state office. 494 U. S., at 654–655. The statute had been modeled after the federal statute that BCRA §203 amended, which had been construed to reach only express advocacy, id., at 655, n. 1. And the ad at issue in Austin used the magical and forbidden words of express advocacy: "Elect Richard Bandstra." Id., at 714 (App. to opinion of Kennedy, J., dissenting). How did the Court manage to reach this result without overruling Bellotti? It purported to recognize a different class of corruption: "the corrosive and distorting effects of immense aggregations of wealth that are accumulated with the help of the corporate form and that have little or no correlation to the public's support for the corporation's political ideas." Austin, supra, at 660.

Among the many problems with this "new" theory of corruption was that it actually constituted "the same 'corrosive and distorting effects of immense aggregations of wealth,' found insufficient to sustain a similar prohibition just a decade earlier," in Bellotti. McConnell, 540 U. S., at 325 (opinion of Kennedy, J.) (quoting Austin, supra, at 660; citation omitted). Indeed, Buckley itself had cautioned that "[t]he First Amendment 's protection against governmental abridgment of free expression cannot properly be made to depend on a person's financial ability to engage in public discussion." 424 U. S., at 49. However, two Members of Austin's 6-to-3 majority appear to have thought it significant that Austin involved express advocacy whereas Bellotti involved issue advocacy. 494 U. S., at 675–676 (Brennan, J., concurring); id., at 678 (Stevens, J., concurring).4

Austin was a significant departure from ancient First Amendment principles. In my view, it was wrongly decided. The flawed rationale upon which it is based is examined at length elsewhere, including in a dissenting opinion in Austin that a Member of the 5-to-4 McConnell majority had joined, see Austin, 494 U. S., at 695–713 (opinion of Kennedy, J., joined by O'Connor, J.). See also id., at 679–695 (Scalia, J., dissenting); McConnell, 540 U. S., at 257–259 (opinion of Scalia, J.); id., at 325–330 (opinion of Kennedy, J.); id., at 273–275 (opinion of Thomas, J.). But at least Austin was limited to express advocacy, and nonexpress advocacy was presumed to remain protected under Buckley and Bellotti, even when engaged in by corporations.

Three Terms ago the Court extended Austin's flawed rationale to cover an even broader class of speech. In McConnell, the Court rejected a facial overbreadth challenge to BCRA §203's restrictions on corporate and union advertising, which were not limited to express advocacy but covered vast amounts of nonexpress advocacy (embraced within the term "electioneering communications"). 540 U. S., at 203–209. The Court held that, at least in light of the availability of the PAC option, the compelling governmental interest that supported restrictions on corporate expenditures for express advocacy also justified the extension of those restrictions to "electioneering communications," the "vast majority" of which were intended to influence elections. Id., at 206. Of course, the compelling interest to which the Court referred was " 'the corrosive and distorting effects of immense aggregations of [corporate] wealth,' " id., at 205 (quoting Austin, supra, at 660). "The justifications for the regulation of express advocacy," the Court explained, "apply equally" to ads run during the BCRA blackout period "to the extent ... [those ads] are the functional equivalent of express advocacy." 540 U. S., at 206 (emphasis added). The Court found that the "vast majority" of ads aired during the 30- and 60-day periods before elections fit that description. Finally, the Court concluded that, "[e]ven ... assum[ing] that BCRA will inhibit some constitutionally protected corporate and union speech" (i.e., "pure issue ads," id., at 207, or "genuine issue ads," id., at 206, and n. 88), its application to such ads was insubstantial, and thus the statute was not overbroad, id., at 207. But McConnell did not foreclose as-applied challenges to §203, WRTL I, 546 U. S., at 411–412, which brings me back to the present cases.

III

The question is whether WRTL meets the standard for prevailing in an as-applied challenge to BCRA §203. Answering that question obviously requires the Court to articulate the standard. The most obvious one, and the one suggested by the Federal Election Commission (FEC) and intervenors, is the standard set forth in McConnell itself: whether the advertisement is the "functional equivalent of express advocacy." McConnell, supra, at 206. See also Brief for Appellant FEC 18 (arguing that WRTL's "advertisements are the functional equivalent of the sort of express advocacy that this Court has long recognized may be constitutionally regulated"); Reply Brief for Appellant Sen. John McCain et al. in No. 06–970, p. 14 ("[C]ourts should apply the standard articulated in McConnell; Congress may constitutionally restrict corporate funding of ads that are the 'functional equivalent of express advocacy' for or against a candidate"). Intervenors flesh out the standard somewhat further: "[C]ourts should ask whether the ad's audience would reasonably understand the ad, in the context of the campaign, to promote or attack the candidate." Id., at 15. The District Court instead articulated a five-factor test that looks to whether the ad under review "(1) describes a legislative issue that is either currently the subject of legislative scrutiny or likely to be the subject of such scrutiny in the near future; (2) refers to the prior voting record or current position of the named candidate on the issue described; (3) exhorts the listener to do anything other than contact the candidate about the described issue; (4) promotes, attacks, supports, or opposes the named candidate; and (5) refers to the upcoming election, candidacy, and/or political party of the candidate." 466 F. Supp. 2d 195, 207 (DC 2006). The backup definition of "electioneering communications" contained in BCRA itself, see n. 2, supra, offers another possibility. It covers any communication that "promotes or supports a candidate for that office ... (regardless of whether the communication expressly advocates a vote for or against a candidate) and which also is suggestive of no plausible meaning other than an exhortation to vote for or against a specific candidate." And the principal opinion in this case offers a variation of its own (one bearing a strong likeness to BCRA's backup definition): whether "the ad is susceptible of no reasonable interpretation other than as an appeal to vote for or against a specific candidate." Ante, at 16.

There is a fundamental and inescapable problem with all of these various tests. Each of them (and every other test that is tied to the public perception, or a court's perception, of the import, the intent, or the effect of the ad) is impermissibly vague and thus ineffective to vindicate the fundamental First Amendment rights of the large segment of society to which §203 applies. Consider the application of these tests to WRTL's ads: There is not the slightest doubt that these ads had an issue-advocacy component. They explicitly urged lobbying on the pending legislative issue of appellate-judge filibusters. The question before us is whether something about them caused them to be the "functional equivalent" of express advocacy, and thus constitutionally subject to BCRA's criminal penalty. Does any of the tests suggested above answer this question with the degree of clarity necessary to avoid the chilling of fundamental political discourse? I think not.

The "functional equivalent" test does nothing more than restate the question (and make clear that the electoral advocacy need not be express). The test which asks how the ad's audience "would reasonably understand the ad" provides ample room for debate and uncertainty. The District Court's five-factor test does not (and could not possibly) specify how much weight is to be given to each factor—and includes the inherently vague factor of whether the ad "promotes, attacks, supports, or opposes the named candidate." (Does attacking the king's position attack the king?) The tests which look to whether the ad is "susceptible of no plausible meaning" or "susceptible of no reasonable interpretation" other than an exhortation to vote for or against a specific candidate seem tighter. They ultimately depend, however, upon a judicial judgment (or is it—worse still—a jury judgment?) concerning "reasonable" or "plausible" import that is far from certain, that rests upon consideration of innumerable surrounding circumstances which the speaker may not even be aware of, and that lends itself to distortion by reason of the decisionmaker's subjective evaluation of the importance or unimportance of the challenged speech. In this critical area of political discourse, the speaker cannot be compelled to risk felony prosecution with no more assurance of impunity than his prediction that what he says will be found susceptible of some "reasonable interpretation other than as an appeal to vote for or against a specific candidate." Under these circumstances, "[m]any persons, rather than undertake the considerable burden (and sometimes risk) of vindicating their rights through case-by-case litigation, will choose simply to abstain from protected speech—harming not only themselves but society as a whole, which is deprived of an uninhibited marketplace of ideas." Virginia v. Hicks, 539 U. S. 113, 119 (2003) (citation omitted).

It will not do to say that this burden must be accepted—that WRTL's antifilibustering, constitutionally protected speech can be constrained—in the necessary pursuit of electoral "corruption." We have rejected the "can't-make-an-omelet-without-breaking-eggs" approach to the First Amendment, even for the infinitely less important (and less protected) speech category of virtual child pornography. In Ashcroft v. Free Speech Coalition, 535 U. S. 234 (2002), the Government argued:

"the possibility of producing images by using computer imaging makes it very difficult for it to prosecute those who produce pornography by using real children. Experts ... may have difficulty in saying whether the pictures were made by using real children or by using computer imaging. The necessary solution ... is to prohibit both kinds of images." Id., at 254–255.

The Court rejected the principle that protected speech may be banned because it is difficult to distinguish from unprotected speech. Ibid. "[T]hat protected speech may be banned as a means to ban unprotected speech," it said, "turns the First Amendment upside down." Id., at 255. The same principle must be applied here. Indeed, it must be applied a fortiori, since laws targeting political speech are the principal object of the First-Amendment guarantee. The fact that the line between electoral advocacy and issue advocacy dissolves in practice is an indictment of the statute, not a justification of it.

Buckley itself compels the conclusion that these tests fall short of the clarity that the First Amendment demands. Recall that Buckley narrowed the ambiguous phrase "any expenditure ... relative to a clearly identified candidate" to mean any expenditure "advocating the election or defeat of a candidate." 424 U. S., at 42 (internal quotation marks omitted). But that construction alone did not eliminate the vagueness problem because "the distinction between discussion of issues and candidates and advocacy of election or defeat of candidates may often dissolve in practical application." Ibid. Any effort to distinguish between the two based on intent of the speaker or effect of the speech on the listener would " 'pu[t] the speaker ... wholly at the mercy of the varied understanding of his hearers,' " would " 'offe[r] no security for free discussion,' " and would " 'compe[l] the speaker to hedge and trim.' " Id., at 43 (quoting Thomas v. Collins, 323 U. S. 516, 535 (1945)). In order to avoid these "constitutional deficiencies," the Court was compelled to narrow the statutory language even further to cover only advertising that used the magic words of express advocacy. 424 U. S., at 43–44.

If a permissible test short of the magic-words test existed, Buckley would surely have adopted it. Especially since a consequence of the express-advocacy interpretationwas the invalidation ofthe entire limitation on independent expenditures, in part because the statute (as thus narrowed) could not be an effective limitation on expenditures for electoral advocacy. (It would be "naiv[e]," Buckley said, to pretend that persons and groups would have difficulty "devising expenditures that skirted the restriction on express advocacy of election or defeat but nevertheless benefited the candidate's campaign." Id., at 45.) Why did Buckley employ such a "highly strained" reading of the statute, McConnell, 540 U. S., at 280 (opinion of Thomas, J.), when broader readings, more faithful to the text, were available that might not have resulted in such underinclusiveness? In particular, after going to the trouble of narrowing the statute to cover "advocacy of [the] election or defeat of a candidat[e]," why not do what the principal opinion in these cases does, which is essentially to preface that phrase with the phrase "susceptible of no reasonable interpretation other than as"? Ante, at 16. There is only one plausible explanation: The Court eschewed narrowing constructions that would have been more faithful to the text and more effective at capturing campaign speech because those tests were all too vague. We cannot now adopt a standard held to be facially vague on the theory that it is somehow clear enough for constitutional as-applied challenges. If Buckley foreclosed such vagueness in a statutory test, it also must foreclose such vagueness in an as-applied test.

Though the principal opinion purports to recognize the "imperative for clarity" in this area of First Amendment law, its attempt to distinguish its test from the test found to be vague in Buckley falls far short. It claims to be "not so sure" that Buckley rejected its test because Buckley's holding did not concern "what the constitutional standard was in the abstract, divorced from specific statutory language." Ante, at 21, n. 7. Forget about abstractions: Thespecific statutory language at issue in Buckley was interpreted to mean " 'advocating the election or defeat of a candidate,' " and that is materially identical to the operative language in the principal opinion's test. The principal opinion's protestation that Buckley's vagueness holding "d[id] not dictate a constitutional test," ante, at 21, n. 7, is utterly compromised by the fact that the principal opinion itself relies on the very same vagueness holding to reject an intent-and-effect test in this case. See ante, at 13–14 (citing Buckley, supra, at 43–44). It is the same vagueness holding, and the principal opinion cannot invoke it on page 13 of its opinion and disclaim it on page 22. Finally, the principal opinion quotes McConnell for the proposition that "[t]he Buckley Court's 'express advocacy restriction was an endpoint of statutory interpretation, not a first principle of constitutional law.' " Ante, at 21, n. 7 (quoting McConnell, 540 U. S., at 190). I am not sure why this cryptic statement is at all relevant, since we are discussing here the principle of constitutional law that underlay Buckley's express-advocacy restriction. In any case, the statement is assuredly not a repudiation of Buckley's vagueness holding, since overbreadth and not vagueness was the issue in McConnell.<footcall num="5">

What, then, is to be done? We could adopt WRTL's proposed test, under which §203 may not be applied to any ad (1) that "focuses on a current legislative branch matter, takes a position on the matter, and urges the public to ask a legislator to take a particular position or action with respect to the matter," and (2) that "does not mention any election, candidacy, political party, or challenger, or the official's character, qualifications, or fitness for office," (3) whether or not it "say[s] that the public official is wrong or right on the issue," so long as it does not expressly say he is "wrong for [the] office." Brief for Appellee 56–57 (footnote omitted).6 Or we could of course adopt the Buckley test of express advocacy. The problem is that, although these tests are clear, they are incompatible with McConnell'sholding that §203 is facially constitutional, which was premised on the finding that a vast majority of ads proscribed by §203 are "sham issue ads," 540 U. S., at 185, that fall outside the First Amendment 's protection. Indeed, any clear rule that would protect all genuine issue ads would cover such a substantial number of ads prohibited by §203 that §203 would be rendered substantially overbroad. The Government claims that even the amorphous test adopted by the District Court "call[s] into question a substantial percentage of the statute's applications," Tr. of Oral Arg. 4,7 and that any test providing relief to WRTL is incompatible with McConnell's facial holding because WRTL's ads are in the "heartland" of what Congress meant to prohibit, Brief for Appellant FEC 18, 28, 36, n. 9. If that is so, then McConnell cannot be sustained.

Like the Buckley Court and the parties to these cases, I recognize the practical reality that corporations can evade the express-advocacy standard. I share the instinct that "[w]hat separates issue advocacy and political advocacy is a line in the sand drawn on a windy day." See McConnell, supra, at 126, n. 16 (internal quotation marks omitted); Brief for Appellant FEC 30; Brief for Appellant Sen. John McCain et al. in No. 06–970, p. 35. But the way to indulge that instinct consistently with the First Amendment is either to eliminate restrictions on independent expenditures altogether or to confine them to one side of the traditional line—the express-advocacy line, set in concrete on a calm day by Buckley, several decades ago. Section 203's line is bright, but it bans vast amounts of political advocacy indistinguishable from hitherto protected speech.

The foregoing analysis shows that McConnell was mistaken in its belief that as-applied challenges could eliminate the unconstitutional applications of §203. They can do so only if a test is adopted which contradicts the holding of McConnell—that §203 is facially valid because the vast majority of pre-election issue ads can constitutionally be proscribed. In light of the weakness in Austin's rationale, and in light of the longstanding acceptance of the clarity of Buckley's express-advocacy line, it was adventurous for

McConnell to extend Austin beyond corporate speech constituting express advocacy. Today's cases make it apparent that the adventure is a flop, and that McConnell's holding concerning §203 was wrong.8

IV

Which brings me to the question of stare decisis. "Stare decisis is not an inexorable command" or " 'a mechanical formula of adherence to the latest decision.' " Payne v. Tennessee, 501 U. S. 808, 828 (1991) (quoting Helvering v. Hallock, 309 U. S. 106, 119 (1940)). It is instead " 'a principle of policy,' " Payne, supra, at 828, and this Court has a "considered practice" not to apply that principle of policy "as rigidly in constitutional as in nonconstitutional cases." Glidden Co. v. Zdanok, 370 U. S. 530, 543 (1962) . This Court has not hesitated to overrule decisions offensive to the First Amendment (a "fixed star in our constitutional constellation," if there is one, West Virginia Bd. of Ed. v. Barnette, 319 U. S. 624, 642 (1943))—and to do so promptly where fundamental error was apparent. Just three years after our erroneous decision in Minersville School Dist. v. Gobitis, 310 U. S. 586 (1940), the Court corrected the error in Barnette. Overruling a constitutional case decided just a few years earlier is far from unprecedented.9

Of particular relevance to the stare decisis question in these cases is the impracticability of the regime created by McConnell. Stare decisis considerations carry little weight when an erroneous "governing decisio[n]" has created an "unworkable" legal regime. Payne, supra, at 827. As described above, the McConnell regime is unworkable because of the inability of any acceptable as-applied test to validate the facial constitutionality of §203—that is, its inability to sustain proscription of the vast majority of issue ads. We could render the regime workable only by effectively overruling McConnell without saying so—adopting a clear as-applied rule protective of speech in the "heartland" of what Congress prohibited. The promise of an administrable as-applied rule that is both effective in the vindication of First Amendment rights and consistent with McConnell's holding is illusory.

It is not as though McConnell produced a settled body of law. Indeed, it is far more accurate to say that McConnell unsettled a body of law. Not until 1947, with the enactment of the Taft-Hartley amendments to the Federal Corrupt Practices Act, 1925, did Congress even purport to regulate campaign-related expenditures of corporations and unions. See United States v. CIO, 335 U. S. 106, 107, 113–115 (1948) . In the three decades following, this Court expressly declined to pronounce upon the constitutionality of such restrictions on independent expenditures. See Pipefitters v. United States, 407 U. S. 385, 400 (1972); United States v. Automobile Workers, 352 U. S. 567, 591–592 (1957); CIO, supra, at 110, 124. When the Court finally did turn to that question, it struck them down. See Buckley, 424 U. S. 1 . Our subsequent pre-McConnell decisions, with the lone exception of Austin, disapproved limits on independent expenditures. The modest medicine of restoring First Amendment protection to nonexpress advocacy—speech that was protected until three Terms ago—does not unsettle an established body of law.

Neither do any of the other considerations relevant to stare decisis suggest adherence to McConnell. These cases do not involve property or contract rights, where reliance interests are involved. Payne, supra, at 828. And McConnell's §203 holding has assuredly not become "embedded" in our "national culture." Dickerson v. United States, 530 U. S. 428, 443–444 (2000) (declining to overrule Miranda v. Arizona, 384 U. S. 436 (1966), in part because it had become embedded in our national culture). If §203 has had any cultural impact, it has been to undermine the traditional and important role of grassroots advocacy in American politics by burdening the "budget-strapped nonprofit entities upon which many of our citizens rely for political commentary and advocacy." McConnell, 540 U. S., at 340 (opinion of Kennedy, J.).

Perhaps overruling this one part of McConnell with respect to one part of BCRA would not "ai[d] the legislative effort to combat real or apparent corruption." Id., at 194. But the First Amendment was not designed to facilitate legislation, even wise legislation. Indeed, the assessment of former House Minority Leader Richard Gephardt, a proponent of campaign-finance reform, may well be correct. He said that " '[w]hat we have is two important values in direct conflict: freedom of speech and our desire for healthy campaigns in a healthy democracy,' " and " '[y]ou can't have both.' " Gibbs, The Wake-Up Call, Time, Feb. 3, 1997, pp. 22, 25. (He was referring, presumably, to incumbents' notions of healthy campaigns.) If he was wrong, however, and the two values can coexist, it is pretty clear which side of the equation this institution is primarily responsible for. It is perhaps our most important constitutional task to assure freedom of political speech. And when a statute creates a regime as unworkable and unconstitutional as today's effort at as-applied review proves §203 to be, it is our responsibility to decline enforcement.

* * *

There is wondrous irony to be found in both the genesis and the consequences of BCRA. In the fact that the institutions it was designed to muzzle—unions and nearly all manner of corporations—for all the "corrosive and distorting effects" of their "immense aggregations of wealth," were utterly impotent to prevent the passage of this legislation that forbids them to criticize candidates (including incumbents). In the fact that the effect of BCRA has been to concentrate more political power in the hands of the country's wealthiest individuals and their so-called 527 organizations, unregulated by §203. (In the 2004 election cycle, a mere 24 individuals contributed an astounding total of $142 million to 527s. S. Weissman & R. Hassan, BCRA and the 527 Groups, in The Election After Reform 79, 92—96 (M. Malbin ed. 2006).) And in the fact that while these wealthy individuals dominate political discourse, it is this small, grass-roots organization of Wisconsin Right to Life that is muzzled.

I would overrule that part of the Court's decision in McConnell upholding §203(a) of BCRA. Accordingly, I join Parts I and II of today's principal opinion and otherwise concur only in the judgment.

Notes to Justice Scalia's concurrence and dissent in FEC v. Wisconsin Right to Life (June 25, 2007)

1 Whitlock, Satirist Continues to Prove Himself a Royal Pain, Washington Post, Apr. 26, 2005, pp. C1, C8.

2 BCRA also includes a backup definition of "electioneering communication" that will take effect in the event the primary definition is "held to be constitutionally insufficient ... to support the regulation provided herein." 2 U. S. C. §434(f)(3)(A)(ii) (2000 ed., Supp. IV). This defines "electioneering communication" as "any broadcast, cable, or satellite communication which promotes or supports a candidate for [a federal] office, or attacks or opposes a candidate for that office (regardless of whether the communication expressly advocates a vote for or against a candidate) and which also is suggestive of no plausible meaning other than an exhortation to vote for or against a specific candidate." Ibid.

3 In Federal Election Comm'n v. Massachusetts Citizens for Life, Inc., 479 U. S. 238, 248 (1986) (MCFL), we addressed the pre-BCRA version of 2 U. S. C. §441b, which was interpreted to ban corporate treasury expenditures for express advocacy in connection with federal elections. We held that, "[r]egardless of whether th[e] concern [for unfair advantage to organizations that amass great wealth] is adequate to support application of §441b to commercial enterprises, a question not before us, that justification" did not support application of the statute to the nonprofit organization that brought the challenge in MCFL. 479 U. S., at 263 (emphasis added).

4 The dissent asserts that Austin was faithful to Bellotti's principles, to prove which it quotes a footnote in Bellotti leaving open the possibility that independent expenditures by corporations might someday be demonstrated to beget quid-pro-quo corruption. Post, at 12, n. 6 (opinion of Souter, J.) (quoting Bellotti, 435 U. S., at 788, n. 26). That someday has never come. No one seriously believes that independent expenditures could possibly give rise to quid-pro-quo corruption without being subject to regulation as coordinated expenditures.

5 Justice Alito's concurrence at least hints that the principal opinion's test may impermissibly chill speech, and offers to reconsider McConnell's holding "[i]f it turns out that the implementation of the as-applied standard set out in the [principal opinion] impermissibly chills political speech." Post, at 1 (emphasis added). The wait-and-see approach makes no sense and finds no support in our cases. How will we know that would-be speakers have been chilled and have not spoken? If a tree does not fall in the forest, can we hear the sound it would have made had it fallen? Our normal practice is to assess ex ante the risk that a standard will have an impermissible chilling effect on First Amendment protected speech. Justice Alito seemed to recognize that as recently as, well, today. In another opinion released this morning, he finds that a proposed test for censoring student speech "can easily be manipulated in dangerous ways," wherefore he "would reject it before such abuse occurs." Morse v. Frederick, ante, at 2 (concurring

opinion) (emphasis added). I would accord the core First Amendment speech at issue here at least the same respect he accords speech in the classroom.

6 The principal opinion claims that its test is no more vague than WRTL's test. See ante, at 21, n. 7. I disagree. WRTL's test requires yes or no answers to a series of precise and focused questions: Does the ad take a position on a legislative matter? Does it mention the election? Does it expressly say the candidate is wrong for the office? A group of children—indeed, even a group of college students—could answer these questions with great consistency. The principal opinion's test, by contrast, hinges on assessment of the reasonableness of a determination that something does not constitute advocacy of the election or defeat of a candidate.

7 The same must be said, I think, of the test proposed by the principal opinion. While its coverage is not entirely clear, it would apparently protect even McConnell's paradigmatic example of the functional equivalent of express advocacy—the so-called "Jane Doe ad," which "condemned Jane Doe's record on a particular issue before exhorting viewers to 'call Jane Doe and tell her what you think,'" 540 U. S., at 126–127. Indeed, it at least arguably protects the most "striking" example of a so-called sham issue ad in the McConnell record, the notorious "Yellowtail ad," which accused Bill Yellowtail of striking his wife and then urged listeners to call him and "[t]ell him to support family values." Id., at 193–194, n. 78 (internal quotation marks omitted). The claim that §203 on its face does not reach a substantial amount of speech protected under the principal opinion's test—and that the test is therefore compatible with McConnell—seems to me indefensible. Indeed, the principal opinion's attempt at distinguishing McConnell is unpersuasive enough, and the change in the law it works is substantial enough, that seven Justices of this Court, having widely divergent views concerning the constitutionality of the restrictions at issue, agree that the opinion effectively overrules McConnell without saying so. See post, at 24–25 (Souter, J., dissenting). This faux judicial restraint is judicial obfuscation.

8 Justice Kennedy's opinion in McConnell explained why the possibility of corporations' funding speech out of a PAC does not save the statute from constitutional infirmity. See 540 U. S., at 330–333. McConnell's rejection of those arguments rested, of course, upon the assumption that for non-PAC genuine issue ads as-applied challenges would be available. See id., at 207; WRTL I, 546 U. S. 410, 411–412 (2006) (per curiam). The discussion today shows that to be mistaken. The dissent asserts, post, at 31, that there is no reason "why substituting the phrase 'Contact your Senators' for the phrase 'Contact Senators Feingold and Kohl' would have denied WRTL a constitutionally sufficient ... alternative." Surely that is not so. The purpose of the ad was to put political pressure upon Senator Feingold to change his position on the filibuster—not only through the constituents who accepted the invitation to contact him, but also through the very existence of an ad bringing to the public's attention that he, Senator Feingold, stood athwart the allowance of a vote on judicial nominees. (Unlike the principal opinion, I think that the fair import of the ad in context.)

9 See, e.g., Seminole Tribe of Fla. v. Florida, 517 U. S. 44 (1996) (overruling Pennsylvania v. Union Gas Co., 491 U. S. 1 (1989)); Adarand Constructors, Inc. v. Peña, 515 U. S. 200 (1995) (overruling in part Metro Broadcasting, Inc. v. FCC, 497 U. S. 547 (1990)); United States v. Dixon, 509 U. S. 688 (1993) (overruling Grady v. Corbin, 495 U. S. 508 (1990)); Payne v. Tennessee, 501 U. S. 808 (1991) (overruling South Carolina v. Gathers, 490 U. S. 805 (1989), and Booth v. Maryland, 482 U. S. 496 (1987)); Daniels v. Williams, 474 U. S. 327 (1986) (overruling in part Parratt v. Taylor, 451 U. S. 527 (1981)); Garcia v. San Antonio Metropolitan Transit Authority, 469 U. S. 528 (1985) (overruling National League of Cities v. Usery, 426 U. S. 833 (1976)); United States v. Scott, 437 U. S. 82 (1978) (overruling United States v. Jenkins, 420 U. S. 358 (1975)); National League of Cities, supra, (overruling Maryland v. Wirtz, 392 U. S. 183 (1968)); Edelman v. Jordan, 415 U. S. 651 (1974) (overruling in part Shapiro v. Thompson, 394 U. S. 618 (1969); State Dept. of Health and Rehabilitative Servs. of Fla. v. Zarate, 407 U. S. 918 (1972); and Sterrett v. Mothers' & Children's Rights Organization, 409 U. S. 809 (1972)); Miller v. California, 413 U. S. 15 (1973) (overruling Book Named "John Cleland's Memoirs of a Woman of Pleasure" v. Attorney General of Mass., 383 U. S. 413 (1966)); Perez v. Campbell, 402 U. S. 637 (1971) (overruling Kesler v. Department of Public Safety of Utah, 369 U. S. 153 (1962)).

Association: Justice Scalia's dissent in Washington State Grange v. Washington State Republican Party (March 18, 2008)

Justice Scalia, with whom Justice Kennedy joins, dissenting.

The electorate's perception of a political party's beliefs is colored by its perception of those who support the party; and a party's defining act is the selection of a candidate and advocacy of that candidate's election by conferring upon him the party's endorsement. When the state-printed ballot for the general election causes a party to be associated with candidates who may not fully (if at all) represent its views, it undermines both these vital aspects of political association. The views of the self-identified party supporter color perception of the party's message, and that self-identification on the ballot, with no space for party repudiation or party identification of its own candidate, impairs the party's advocacy of its standard bearer. Because Washington has not demonstrated that this severe burden upon parties' associational rights is narrowly tailored to serve a compelling interest—indeed, because it seems to me Washington's only plausible interest is precisely to reduce the effectiveness of political parties—I would find the law unconstitutional.

I

I begin with the principles on which the Court and I agree. States may not use election regulations to undercut political parties' freedoms of speech or association. See U. S. Term Limits, Inc. v. Thornton, 514 U. S. 779, 833–834 (1995) . Thus, when a State regulates political parties as a part of its election process, we consider "the 'character and magnitude' " of the burden imposed on the party's associational rights and "the extent to which the State's concerns make the burden necessary." Timmons v. Twin Cities Area New Party, 520 U. S. 351, 358 (1997) . Regulations imposing severe burdens must be narrowly tailored to advance a compelling state interest. Ibid.

Among the First Amendment rights that political parties possess is the right to associate with the persons whom they choose and to refrain from associating with persons whom they reject. Democratic Party of United States v. Wisconsin ex rel. La Follette, 450 U. S. 107, 122 (1981) . Also included is the freedom to choose and promote the " 'standard bearer who best represents the party's ideologies and preferences.' " Eu v. San Francisco County Democratic Central Comm., 489 U. S. 214, 224 (1989) .

When an expressive organization is compelled to associate with a person whose views the group does not accept, the organization's message is undermined; the organization is understood to embrace, or at the very least tolerate, the views of the persons linked with them. We therefore held, for example, that a State severely burdened the right of expressive association when it required the Boy Scouts to accept an openly gay scoutmaster. The scoutmaster's presence "would, at the very least, force the organization to send a message, both to the youth members and the world, that the Boy Scouts accepts homosexual conduct as a legitimate form of behavior." Boy Scouts of America v. Dale, 530 U. S. 640, 653 (2000) .

A political party's expressive mission is not simply, or even primarily, to persuade voters of the party's views. Parties seek principally to promote the election of candidates who will implement those views. See, e.g., Tashjian v. Republican Party of Conn., 479 U. S. 208, 216 (1986); Storer v. Brown, 415 U. S. 724, 745 (1974);M. Hershey & P. Beck, Party Politics in America13(10th ed. 2003). That is achieved in large part by marking candidates with the party's seal of approval. Parties devote substantial resources to making their names trusted symbols of certain approaches to governance. See, e.g., App. 239 (Declaration of Democratic Committee Chair Paul J. Berendt); J. Aldrich, Why Parties? 48–49 (1995). They then encourage voters to cast their votes for the candidates that carry the party name. Parties' efforts to support candidates by marking them with the party trademark, so to speak, have been successful enough to make the party name, in the words of one commentator, "the most important resource that the party possesses." Cain, Party Autonomy and Two-Party Electoral Competition, 149 U. Pa. L. Rev. 793, 804 (2001). And all evidence suggests party labels are indeed a central consideration for most voters. See, e.g., id., at 804, n. 34; Rahn, The Role of Partisan Stereotypes in Information Processing About Political Candidates, 37Am. J. Pol. Sci. 472 (1993); Klein & Baum, Ballot Information and Voting Decisions in Judicial Elections, 54 Pol. Research Q. 709 (2001).

II

A

The State of Washington need not like, and need not favor, political parties. It is entirely free to decline running primaries for the selection of party nominees and to hold nonpartisan general elections in which party labels have no place on the ballot. See California Democratic Party v. Jones, 530 U. S. 567, 585–586 (2000) . Parties would then be left to their own devices in both selecting and publicizing their candidates. But Washington has done more than merely decline to make its electoral machinery available for party building. Recognizing that parties draw support for their candidates by giving them the party imprimatur, Washington seeks to reduce the effectiveness of that endorsement by allowing any candidate to use the ballot for drawing upon the goodwill that a party has developed, while preventing the party from using the ballot to reject the claimed association or to identify the genuine candidate of its choice. This does not merely place the ballot off limits for party building; it makes the ballot an instrument by which party building is impeded, permitting unrebutted associations that the party itself does not approve.

These cases cannot be decided without taking account of the special role that a state-printed ballot plays in elections. The ballot comes into play "at the most crucial stage in the electoral process—the instant before the vote is cast." Anderson v. Martin, 375 U. S. 399, 402 (1964) . It is the only document that all voters are guaranteed tosee, and it is "the last thing the voter sees before he makes his choice," Cook v. Gralike, 531 U. S. 510, 532 (2001) (Rehnquist, C. J., concurring in judgment). Thus, we have held that a State cannot elevate a particular issue to prominence by making it the only issue for which the ballot sets forth the candidates' positions. Id., at 525–526 (opinion of the Court). And we held unconstitutional California's election system, which listed as the party's candidate on the general election ballot the candidate selected in a state-run "blanket primary" in which all citizens could determine who would be the party's nominee. Jones, 530 U. S., at 586. It was not enough to sustain the law that the party remained free to select its preferred candidate through another process, and could denounce or campaign against the candidate carrying the party's name on the general election ballot. Forced association with the party on the general election ballot was fatal. Id., at 575–577.

The Court makes much of the fact that the party names shown on the Washington ballot may be billed as mere statements of candidate "preference." See ante, at 11–14. To be sure, the party is not itself forced to display favor for someone it does not wish to associate with, as the Boy Scouts were arguably forced to do by employing the homosexual scoutmaster in Dale, and as the political parties were arguably forced to do by lending their ballot-endorsement as party nominee in Jones. But thrusting an unwelcome, self-proclaimed association upon the party on the election ballot itself is amply destructive of the party's associational rights. An individual's endorsement of a party shapes the voter's view of what the party stands for, no less than the party's endorsement of an individual shapes the voter's view of what the individual stands for. That is why party nominees are often asked (and regularly agree) to repudiate the support of persons regarded as racial extremists. On Washington's ballot, such repudiation is impossible. And because the ballot is the only document voters are guaranteed to see, and the last thing they see before casting their vote, there is "no means of replying" that "would be equally effective with the voter." Cook, supra, at 532 (Rehnquist, C. J., concurring in judgment).

Not only is the party's message distorted, but its goodwill is hijacked. There can be no dispute that candidate acquisition of party labels on Washington's ballot—even if billed as self-identification—is a means of garnering the support of those who trust and agree with the party. The "I prefer the D's" and "I prefer the R's" will not be on the ballot for esthetic reasons; they are designed to link candidates to unwilling parties (or at least parties who are unable to express their revulsion) and to encourage voters to cast their ballots based in part on the trust they place in the party's name and the party's philosophy. These harms will be present no matter how Washington's law is implemented. There is therefore "no set of circumstances" under which Washington's law would not severely burden political parties, see United States v. Salerno, 481 U. S. 739, 745 (1987), and no good reason to wait until Washington has undermined its political parties to declare that it is forbidden to do so.

B

The Chief Justice would wait to see if the law is implemented in a manner that no more harms political parties than allowing a person to state that he " 'like[s] Campbell's soup' " would harm the Campbell Soup Company. See ante, at 3 (concurring opinion). It is hard to know how to respond. First and most fundamentally, there is simply no comparison between statements of "preference" for an expressive association and statements of "preference" for soup. The robust First Amendment freedom to associate belongs only to groups "engage[d] in 'expressive association,' " Dale, 530 U. S., at 648. The Campbell Soup Company does not exist to promote a message, and "there is only minimal constitutional protection of the freedom of commercial association," Roberts v. United States Jaycees, 468 U. S. 609, 634 (1984) (O'Connor, J., concurring in part and concurring in judgment).

Second, I assuredly do not share The Chief Justice's view that the First Amendment will be satisfied so long as the ballot "is designed in such a manner that no reasonable voter would believe that the candidates listed there are nominees or members of, or otherwise associated with, the parties the candidates claimed to 'prefer.' " Ante, at 3. To begin with, it seems to me quite impossible for the ballot to satisfy a reasonable voter that the candidate is not "associated with" the party for which he has expressed a preference. He has associated himself with the party by his very expression of a preference—and that indeed is the whole purpose of allowing the preference to be expressed. If all The Chief Justice means by "associated with" is that the candidate "does not speak on the party's behalf or with the party's approval," ibid., none of my analysis in this opinion relies upon that misperception, nor upon the misperception that the candidate is a member or the nominee of the party. Avoiding those misperceptions is far from enough. Is it enough to say on the ballot that a notorious and despised racist who says that the party is his choice does not speak with the party's approval? Surely not. His unrebutted association of that party with his views distorts the image of the party nonetheless. And the fact that the candidate who expresses a "preference" for one or another party is shown not to be the nominee of that party does not deprive him of the boost from the party's reputation which the party wishes to confer only on its nominee. The Chief Justice claims that "the content of the ballots in the pertinent respect is yet to be determined," ibid. I disagree. We know all we need to know about the form of ballot. When pressed, Washington's Attorney General assured us at oral argument that the ballot will not say whether the party for whom the candidate expresses a preference claims or disavows him. (Of course it will not, for that would enable the party expression that it is the very object of this legislation to impair.)

And finally, while The Chief Justice earlier expresses his awareness that the special character of the ballot is what makes these cases different, ante, at 2, his Campbell's Soup example seems to forget that. If we must speak in terms of soup, Washington's law is like a law that encourages Oscar the Grouch (Sesame Street's famed bad-taste resident of a garbage can) to state a "preference" for Campbell's at every point of sale, while barring the soup company from disavowing his endorsement, or indeed using its name at all, in those same crucial locations. Reserving the most critical communications forum for statements of "preference" by a potentially distasteful speaker alters public perceptions of the entity that is "preferred"; and when this privileged connection undermines not a company's ability to identify and promote soup but an expressive association's ability to identify and promote its message and its standard bearer, the State treads on the constitutionally protected freedom of association.

The majority opinion and The Chief Justice's concurrence also endorse a wait-and-see approach on the grounds that it is not yet evident how the law will affect voter perception of the political parties. But contrary to the Court's suggestion, it is not incumbent on the political parties to adduce "evidence," ante, at 15, that forced association affects their ability to advocate for their candidates and their causes. We have never put expressive groups to this perhaps-impossible task. Rather, we accept their own assessments of the matter. The very cases on which The Chief Justice relies for a wait-and-see approach, ante, at 1–2, establish as much. In Dale, for example, we did not require the Boy Scouts to prove that forced acceptance of the openly homosexual scoutmaster would distort their message. See 530 U. S., at 653 (citing La Follette, 450 U. S., at 123–124). Nor in Hurley v. Irish-American Gay, Lesbian and Bisexual Group of Boston, Inc., 515 U. S. 557 (1995),did we require the organizers of the St. Patrick's Day Parade to demonstrate that including a gay contingent in the parade would distort their message. See id., at 577. Nor in Jones, 530 U. S. 567, did we require the political parties to demonstrate either that voters would incorrectly perceive the "nominee" labels on the ballot to be the products of party elections or that the labels would change voter perceptions of the party. It does not take a study to establish that when statements of party connection are the sole information listed next to candidate names on the ballot, those statements will affect voters' perceptions of what the candidate stands for, what the party stands for, and whom they should elect.

III

Since I conclude that Washington's law imposes a severe burden on political parties' associational rights, I would uphold the law only if it were "narrowly tailored" to advance "a compelling state interest." Timmons, 520 U. S., at 358. Neither the Court's opinion nor the State's submission claims that Washington's law passes such scrutiny. The State argues only that it "has a rational basis" for "providing voters with a modicum of relevant information about the candidates," Brief for Petitioners in No. 06–730, pp. 48–49. This is the only interest the Court's opinion identifies as well. Ante, at 15.

But "rational basis" is the least demanding of our tests; it is the same test that allows individuals to be taxed at different rates because they are in different businesses. See Allied Stores of Ohio, Inc. v. Bowers, 358 U. S. 522, 526–527 (1959) . It falls far, far short of establishing the compelling state interest that the First Amendment requires. And to tell the truth, here even the existence of a rational basis is questionable. Allowing candidates to identify themselves with particular parties on the ballot displays the State's view that adherence to party philosophy is "an important—perhaps paramount— consideration in the citizen's choice." Anderson, 375 U. S., at 402. If that is so, however, it seems to me irrational not to allow the party to disclaim that self-association, or to identify its own endorsed candidate.

It is no mystery what is going on here. There is no state interest behind this law except the Washington Legislature's dislike for bright-colors partisanship, and its desire to blunt the ability of political parties with noncentrist views to endorse and advocate their own candidates. That was the purpose of the Washington system that this enactment was adopted to replace—a system indistinguishable from the one we invalidated in Jones, which required parties to allow nonmembers to join in the selection of the candidates shown as their nominees on the election ballot. (The system was held unconstitutional in Democratic Party of Washington State v. Reed, 343 F. 3d 1198 (CA9 2003).) And it is the obvious purpose of Washington legislation enacted after this law, which requires political parties to repeat a candidate's self-declared party "preference" in electioneering communications concerning the candidate—even if the purpose of the communication is to criticize the candidate and to disavow any con-nection between him and the party. Wash. Rev. Code §42.17.510(1) (2006); see also Wash. Admin. Code §390–18–020 (2007).

Even if I were to assume, however, that Washington has a legitimate interest in telling voters on the ballot (above all other things) that a candidate says he favors a particular political party; and even if I were further to assume (per impossibile) that that interest was a compelling one; Washington would still have to "narrowly tailor" its law to protect that interest with minimal intrusion upon the parties' associational rights. There has been no attempt to do that here. Washington could, for example, have permitted parties to disclaim on the general-election ballot the asserted association or to designate on the ballot their true nominees. The course the State has chosen makes sense only as an effort to use its monopoly power over the ballot to undermine the expressive activities of the political parties.

* * *

The right to associate for the election of candidates is fundamental to the operation of our political system, and state action impairing that association bears a heavy burden of justification. Washington's electoral system permits individuals to appropriate the parties' trademarks, so to speak, at the most crucial stage of election, thereby distorting the parties' messages and impairing their endorsement of candidates. The State's justification for this (to convey a "modicum of relevant information") is not only weak but undeserving of credence. We have here a system which, like the one it replaced, does not merely refuse to assist, but positively impairs, the legitimate role of political parties. I dissent from the Court's conclusion that the Constitution permits this sabotage.

Justice Scalia's statement in Kennedy v. Louisiana (October 1, 2008)

Statement of Justice Scalia, with whom The Chief Justice joins, respecting the denial of rehearing.

Respondent has moved for rehearing of this case because there has come to light a federal statute enacted in 2006 permitting the death sentence under the Uniform Code of Military Justice for rape of a minor. See Pub L. 109–163, §552(b)(1), 119 Stat. 3263. This provision was not cited by either party, nor by any of the numerous amici in the case; it was first brought to the Court's attention after the opinion had issued, in a letter signed by 85 Members of Congress. Respondent asserts that rehearing is justified because this statute calls into question the majority opinion's conclusion that there is a national consensus against capital punishment for rape of a child.

I am voting against the petition for rehearing because the views of the American people on the death penalty for child rape were, to tell the truth, irrelevant to the majority's decision in this case. The majority opinion, after an unpersuasive attempt to show that a consensus against the penalty existed, in the end came down to this: "[T]he Constitution contemplates that in the end our own judgment will be brought to bear on the question of the acceptability of the death penalty under the Eighth Amendment ." Ante, at ___ (slip op., at 24). Of course the Constitution contemplates no such thing; the proposed Eighth Amendment would have been laughed to scorn if it had read "no criminal penalty shall be imposed which the Supreme Court deems unacceptable." But that is what the majority opinion said, and there is no reason to believe that absence of a national consensus would provoke second thoughts.

While the new evidence of American opinion is ultimately irrelevant to the majority's decision, let there be no doubt that it utterly destroys the majority's claim to be discerning a national consensus and not just giving effect to the majority's own preference. As noted in the letter from Members of Congress, the bill providing the death penalty for child rape passed the Senate 95–0; it passed the House 374–41, with the votes of a majority of each State's delegation; and was signed by the President. Justice Kennedy's statement posits two reasons why this act by Congress proves nothing about the national consensus regarding permissible penalties for child rape. First, it claims the statute merely "reclassif[ied]" the offense of child rape. Ante, at 2. But the law did more than that; it specifically established (as it would have to do)the penalty for the new offense of child rape—and that penalty was death: "For an offense under subsection (a) (rape) or subsection (b) (rape of a child), death or such other punishment as a court-martial may direct." §552(b)(1), 119 Stat. 3263 (emphasis added). By separate executive order, the President later expressly reauthorized the death penalty as a punishment for child rape. Exec. Order No. 13447, 72Fed. Reg. 56214 (2007). Based on these acts, there is infinitely more reason to think that Congress and the President made a judgment regarding the appropriateness of the death penalty for child rape than there is to think that the many non-enacting state legislatures upon which the majority relies did so—especially since it was widely believed that Coker took the capital-punishment option off the table. See Coker v. Georgia, 433 U. S. 584 (1977).

Second, Justice Kennedy speculates that the Eighth Amendment may permit subjecting a member of the military to a means of punishmentthat would be cruel and unusual if inflicted upon a civilian for the same crime. That is perhaps so where the fact of the malefactor's membership in the Armed Forces makes the offense more grievous. One can imagine, for example, a social judgment that treason by a military officer who has sworn to defend his country deserves the death penalty even though treason by a civilian does not. (That is not the social judgment our society has made, see 18 U. S. C. §2381, but one can imagine it.) It is difficult to imagine, however, how rape of a child could sometimes be deserving of death for a soldier but never for a civilian.

Facts necessary to lengthen sentence should have to be found by jury, not judge: Justice Scalia's dissent in Oregon v. Ice (January 14, 2009)

Justice Scalia, with whom The Chief Justice, Justice Souter, and Justice Thomas join, dissenting.

The rule of Apprendi v. New Jersey, 530 U. S. 466 (2000), is clear: Any fact—other than that of a prior conviction—that increases the maximum punishment to which a defendant may be sentenced must be admitted by the defendant or proved beyond a reasonable doubt to a jury. Oregon's sentencing scheme allows judges rather than juries to find the facts necessary to commit defendants to longer prison sentences, and thus directly contradicts what we held eight years ago and have reaffirmed several times since. The Court's justification of Oregon's scheme is a virtual copy of the dissents in those cases.

The judge in this case could not have imposed a sentence of consecutive prison terms without making the factual finding that the defendant caused "separate harms" to the victim by the acts that produced two convictions. See 343 Ore. 248, 268, 170 P. 3d 1049, 1060 (2007) (Kistler, J., dissenting). There can thus be no doubt that the judge's factual finding was "essential to" the punishment he imposed. United States v. Booker, 543 U. S. 220, 232 (2005). That "should be the end of the matter." Blakely v. Washington, 542 U. S. 296, 313 (2004).

Instead, the Court attempts to distinguish Oregon's sentencing scheme by reasoning that the rule of Apprendi applies only to the length of a sentence for an individual crime and not to the total sentence for a defendant. I cannot understand why we would make such a strange exception to the treasured right of trial by jury. Neither the reasoning of the Apprendi line of cases, nor any distinctive history of the factfinding necessary to imposition of consecutive sentences, nor (of course) logic supports such an odd rule.

We have taken pains to reject artificial limitations upon the facts subject to the jury-trial guarantee. We long ago made clear that the guarantee turns upon the penal consequences attached to the fact, and not to its formal definition as an element of the crime. Mullaney v. Wilbur, 421 U. S. 684, 698 (1975). More recently, we rejected the contention that the "aggravating circumstances" that qualify a defendant for the death penalty did not have to be found by the jury. "If," we said, "a State makes an increase in a defendant's authorized punishment contingent on the finding of a fact, that fact—no matter how the State labels it—must be found by a jury beyond a reasonable doubt." Ring v. Arizona, 536 U. S. 584, 602 (2002). A bare three years ago, in rejecting the contention that the facts determining application of the Federal Sentencing Guidelines did not have to be found by the jury, we again set forth the pragmatic, practical, nonformalistic rule in terms that cannot be mistaken: The jury must "find the existence of ' "any particular fact" ' that the law makes essential to [a defendant's] punishment." Booker, supra, at 232 (quoting Blakely, supra, at 301).

This rule leaves no room for a formalistic distinction between facts bearing on the number of years of imprisonment that a defendant will serve for one count (subject to the rule of Apprendi) and facts bearing on how many years will be served in total (now not subject to Apprendi). There is no doubt that consecutive sentences are a "greater punishment" than concurrent sentences, Apprendi, supra, at 494. We have hitherto taken note of the reality that "a concurrent sentence is traditionally imposed as a lesssevere sanction than a consecutive sentence." Ralston v. Robinson, 454 U. S. 201, 216, n. 9 (1981) (emphasis deleted). The decision to impose consecutive sentences alters the single consequence most important to convicted noncapital defendants: their date of release from prison. For many defendants, the difference between consecutive and concurrent sentences is more important than a jury verdict of innocence on any single count: Two consecutive 10-year sentences are in most circumstances a more severe punishment than any number of concurrent 10-year sentences.

    To support its distinction-without-a-difference, the Court puts forward the same (the very same) arguments regarding the history of sentencing that were rejected by Apprendi. Here, it is entirely irrelevant that common-law judges had discretion to impose either consecutive or concurrent sentences, ante, at 7; just as there it was entirely irrelevant that common-law judges had discretion to impose greater or lesser sentences (within the prescribed statutory maximum) for individual convictions. There is no Sixth Amendment problem with a system that exposes defendants to a known range of sentences after a guilty verdict: "In a system that says the judge may punish burglary with 10 to 40 years, every burglar knows he is risking 40 years in jail." Blakely, supra, at 309. The same analysis applies to a system where both consecutive and concurrent sentences are authorized after only a jury verdict of guilt; the burglar-rapist knows he is risking consecutive sentences. Our concern here is precisely the same as our concern in Apprendi: What happens when a State breaks from the common-law practice of discretionary sentences and permits the imposition of an elevated sentence only upon the showing of extraordinary facts? In such a system, the defendant "is entitled to" the lighter sentence "and by reason of the Sixth Amendment [,] the facts bearing upon that entitlement must be found by a jury." Blakely, 542 U. S., at 309.

    The Court protests that in this case there is no "encroachment" on or "erosion" of the jury's role because traditionally it was for the judge to determine whether there would be concurrent terms. Ante, at 8–9. Alas, this argument too was made and rejected in Apprendi. The jury's role was not diminished, the Apprendi dissent contended, because it was traditionally up to judges, not juries, to determine what the sentence would be. 530 U. S., at 556, 559 (opinion of Breyer, J.). The Court's opinion acknowledged that in the 19th century it was the practice to leave sentencing up to the judges, within limits fixed by law. But, it said, that practice had no bearing upon whether the jury must find the fact where a law conditions the higher sentence upon the fact. The jury's role is diminished when the length of a sentence is made to depend upon a fact removed from its determination. Id., at 482–483. The same is true here.

    The Court then observes that the results of the Oregon system could readily be achieved, instead, by a system in which consecutive sentences are the default rulebut judges are permitted to impose concurrent sentences when they find certain facts. Ante, at 9–10. Undoubtedly the Sixth Amendment permits a system in which judges are authorized (or even required) to impose consecutive sentences unless the defendant proves additional facts to the Court's satisfaction. See ibid. But the permissibility of that alternative means of achieving the same end obviously does not distinguish Apprendi,because the same argument (the very same argument) was raised and squarely rejected in that case:

"If the defendant can escape the statutory maximum by showing, for example, that he is a war veteran, then a judge that finds the fact of veteran status is neither exposing the defendant to a deprivation of liberty greater than that authorized by the verdict according to statute, nor is the judge imposing upon the defendant a greater stigma than that accompanying the jury verdict alone. Core concerns animating the jury and burden-of-proof requirements are thus absent from such a scheme." 530 U. S., at 491, n. 16.

Ultimately, the Court abandons its effort to provide analytic support for its decision, and turns to what it thinks to be the " 'salutary objectives' " of Oregon's scheme. Ante, at 9. "Limiting judicial discretion," we are told, promotes sentences proportionate to the gravity of the offense, and reduces disparities in sentence length. Ibid. The same argument (the very same argument) was made and rejected in Booker, see 543 U. S., at 244,and Blakely, see 542 U. S., at 313. The protection of the Sixth Amendment does not turn on this Court's opinion of whether an alternative scheme is good policy, or whether the legislature had a compassionate heart in adopting it. The right to trial by jury and proof beyond a reasonable doubt is a given, and all legislative policymaking—good and bad, heartless and compassionate—must work within the confines of that reality. Of course the Court probably exaggerates the benign effect of Oregon's scheme, as is suggested by the defense bar's vigorous objection, evidenced by the participation of the National Association of Criminal Defense Lawyers as amicus in favor of respondent. Even that exaggeration is a replay of the rejected dissentin one of our prior cases. There the Court responded: "It is hard to believe that the National Association of Criminal Defense Lawyers was somehow duped into arguing for the wrong side." Blakely, supra, at 312.

Finally, the Court summons up the parade of horribles assembled by the amicus brief of 17 States supporting Oregon. It notes that "[t]rial judges often find facts" in connection with "a variety of sentencing determinations other than the length of incarceration," and worries that even their ability to set the length of supervised release, impose community service, or order entry into a drug rehabilitation program, may be called into question. Ante, at 10. But if these courses reduce rather than augment the punishment that the jury verdict imposes, there is no problem. The last horrible the Court invokes is the prospect of bifurcated or even trifurcated trials in order to have the jury find the facts essential to consecutive sentencing without prejudicing the defendant's merits case. Ibid. That is another déjà vu and déjà rejeté; we have watched it parade past before, in several of our Apprendi-related opinions, and have not saluted. See Blakely, supra, at 336–337 (Breyer, J., dissenting); Apprendi, supra, at 557 (same).

* * *

The Court's peroration says that "[t]he jury-trial right is best honored through a 'principled rationale' that applies the rule of the Apprendi cases 'within the central sphere of their concern.' " Ante, at 11 (quoting Cunningham v. California, 549 U. S. 270, 295 (2007) (Kennedy, J., dissenting)). Undoubtedly so. But we have hitherto considered "the central sphere of their concern" to be facts necessary to the increase of the defendant's sentence beyond what the jury verdict alone justifies. "If the jury's verdict alone does not authorize the sentence, if, instead, the judge must find an additional fact to impose the longer term, the Sixth Amendment requirement is not satisfied." Id., at 290 (opinion of the Court). If the doubling or tripling of a defendant's jail time through fact-dependent consecutive sentencing does not meet this description, nothing does. And as for a "principled rationale": The Court's reliance upon a distinction without a difference, and its repeated exhumation of arguments dead and buried by prior cases, seems to me the epitome of the opposite. Today's opinion muddies the waters, and gives cause to doubt whether the Court is willing to stand by Apprendi's interpretation of the Sixth Amendment's jury-trial guarantee.

Corporate speech protected: Justice Scalia's concurrence in Citizens United v. Federal Elections Commission (January 21, 2010)

Justice Scalia, with whom Justice Alito joins, and with whom Justice Thomas joins in part, concurring.

I join the opinion of the Court. 1

I write separately to address Justice Stevens' discussion of " Original Understandings," post, at 34 (opinion concurring in part and dissenting in part) (hereinafter referred to as the dissent). This section of the dissent purports to show that today's decision is not supported by the original understanding of the First Amendment. The dissent attempts this demonstration, however, in splendid isolation from the text of the First Amendment. It never shows why "the freedom of speech" that was the right of Englishmen did not include the freedom to speak in association with other individuals, including association in the corporate form. To be sure, in 1791 (as now) corporations could pursue only the objectives set forth in their charters; but the dissent provides no evidence that their speech in the pursuit of those objectives could be censored.

Instead of taking this straightforward approach to determining the Amendment's meaning, the dissent embarks on a detailed exploration of the Framers' views about the "role of corporations in society." Post, at 35. The Framers didn't like corporations, the dissent concludes, and therefore it follows (as night the day) that corporations had no rights of free speech. Of course the Framers' personal affection or disaffection for corporations is relevant only insofar as it can be thought to be reflected in the understood meaning of the text they enacted—not, as the dissent suggests, as a freestanding substitute for that text. But the dissent's distortion of proper analysis is even worse than that. Though faced with a constitutional text that makes no distinction between types of speakers, the dissent feels no necessity to provide even an isolated statement from the founding era to the effect that corporations are not covered, but places the burden on petitioners to bring forward statements showing that they are ("there is not a scintilla of evidence to support the notion that anyone believed [the First Amendment] would preclude regulatory distinctions based on the corporate form," post, at 34–35).

Despite the corporation-hating quotations the dissent has dredged up, it is far from clear that by the end of the 18th century corporations were despised. If so, how came there to be so many of them? The dissent's statement that there were few business corporations during the eighteenth century—"only a few hundred during all of the 18th century"—is misleading. Post, at 35, n. 53. There were approximately 335 charters issued to business corporations in the United States by the end of the 18th century. 2 See 2 J. Davis, Essays in the Earlier History of American Corporations 24 (1917) (reprint 2006) (hereinafter Davis). This was a "considerable extension of corporate enterprise in the field of business," Davis 8, and represented "unprecedented growth," id., at 309. Moreover, what seems like a small number by today's standards surely does not indicate the relative importance of corporations when the Nation was considerably smaller. As I have previously noted, "[b]y the end of the eighteenth century the corporation was a familiar figure in American economic life." McConnell v. Federal Election Comm'n, 540 U. S. 93, 256 (2003) (Scalia, J., concurring in part, concurring in judgment in part, and dissenting in part) (quoting C. Cooke, Corporation Trust and Company 92 (1951) (hereinafter Cooke)).

Even if we thought it proper to apply the dissent's approach of excluding from First Amendment coverage what the Founders disliked, and even if we agreed that the Founders disliked founding-era corporations; modern corporations might not qualify for exclusion. Most of the Founders' resentment towards corporations was directed at the state-granted monopoly privileges that individually chartered corporations enjoyed. 3 Modern corporations do not have such privileges, and would probably have been favored by most of our enterprising Founders—excluding, perhaps, Thomas Jefferson and others favoring perpetuation of an agrarian society. Moreover, if the Founders' specific intent with respect to corporations is what matters, why does the dissent ignore the Founders' views about other legal entities that have more in common with modern business corporations than the founding-era corporations? At the time of the founding, religious, educational, and literary corporations were incorporated under general incorporation statutes, much as business corporations are today. 4 See Davis 16–17; R. Seavoy, Origins of the American Business Corporation, 1784–1855, p. 5 (1982); Cooke 94. There were also small unincorporated business associations, which some have argued were the " 'true progenitors' " of today's business corporations. Friedman 200 (quoting S. Livermore, Early American Land Companies: Their Influence on Corporate Development 216 (1939)); see also Davis 33. Were all of these silently excluded from the protections of the First Amendment?

The lack of a textual exception for speech by corporations cannot be explained on the ground that such organizations did not exist or did not speak. To the contrary, colleges, towns and cities, religious institutions, and guilds had long been organized as corporations at common law and under the King's charter, see 1 W. Blackstone, Commentaries on the Laws of England 455–473 (1765); 1 S. Kyd, A Treatise on the Law of Corporations 1–32, 63 (1793) (reprinted 2006), and as I have discussed, the practice of incorporation only expanded in the United States. Both corporations and voluntary associations actively petitioned the Government and expressed their views in newspapers and pamphlets. For example: An antislavery Quaker corporation petitioned the First Congress, distributed pamphlets, and communicated through the press in 1790. W. diGiacomantonio, "For the Gratification of a Volunteering Society": Antislavery and Pressure Group Politics in the First Federal Congress, 15 J. Early Republic 169 (1995). The New York Sons of Liberty sent a circular to colonies farther south in 1766. P. Maier, From Resistance to Revolution 79–80 (1972). And the Society for the Relief and Instruction of Poor Germans circulated a biweekly paper from 1755 to 1757. Adams, The Colonial German-language Press and the American Revolution, in The Press & the American Revolution 151, 161–162 (B. Bailyn & J. Hench eds. 1980). The dissent offers no evidence—none whatever—that the First Amendment 's unqualified text was originally understood to exclude such associational speech from its protection. 5

  Historical evidence relating to the textually similar clause "the freedom of . . . the press" also provides no support for the proposition that the First Amendment excludes conduct of artificial legal entities from the scope of its protection. The freedom of "the press" was widely understood to protect the publishing activities of individual editors and printers. See McIntyre v. Ohio Elections Comm'n, 514 U. S. 334, 360 (1995) (Thomas, J ., concurring in judgment); see also McConnell, 540 U. S., at 252–253 (opinion of Scalia, J .). But these individuals often acted through newspapers, which (much like corporations) had their own names, outlived the individuals who had founded them, could be bought and sold, were sometimes owned by more than one person, and were operated for profit. See generally F. Mott, American Journalism: A History of Newspapers in the United States Through 250 Years 3–164 (1941); J. Smith, Freedom's Fetters (1956). Their activities were not stripped of First Amendment protection simply because they were carried out under the banner of an artificial legal entity. And the notion which follows from the dissent's view, that modern newspapers, since they are incorporated, have free-speech rights only at the sufferance of Congress, boggles the mind. 6

  In passing, the dissent also claims that the Court's conception of corruption is unhistorical. The Framers "would have been appalled," it says, by the evidence of corruption in the congressional findings supporting the Bipartisan Campaign Reform Act of 2002. Post, at 61. For this proposition, the dissent cites a law review article arguing that "corruption" was originally understood to include "moral decay" and even actions taken by citizens in pursuit of private rather than public ends. Teachout, The Anti-Corruption Principle, 94 Cornell L. Rev. 341, 373, 378 (2009). It is hard to see how this has anything to do with what sort of corruption can be combated by restrictions on political speech. Moreover, if speech can be prohibited because, in the view of the

Government, it leads to "moral decay" or does not serve "public ends," then there is no limit to the Government's censorship power.

The dissent says that when the Framers "constitutionalized the right to free speech in the First Amendment, it was the free speech of individual Americans that they had in mind." Post, at 37. That is no doubt true. All the provisions of the Bill of Rights set forth the rights of individual men and women—not, for example, of trees or polar bears. But the individual person's right to speak includes the right to speak in association with other individual persons . Surely the dissent does not believe that speech by the Republican Party or the Democratic Party can be censored because it is not the speech of "an individual American." It is the speech of many individual Americans, who have associated in a common cause, giving the leadership of the party the right to speak on their behalf. The association of individuals in a business corporation is no different—or at least it cannot be denied the right to speak on the simplistic ground that it is not "an individual American." 7

But to return to, and summarize, my principal point, which is the conformity of today's opinion with the original meaning of the First Amendment . The Amendment is written in terms of "speech," not speakers. Its text offers no foothold for excluding any category of speaker, from single individuals to partnerships of individuals, to unincorporated associations of individuals, to incorporated associations of individuals—and the dissent offers no evidence about the original meaning of the text to support any such exclusion. We are therefore simply left with the question whether the speech at issue in this case is "speech" covered by the First Amendment . No one says otherwise. A documentary film critical of a potential Presidential candidate is core political speech, and its nature as such does not change simply because it was funded by a corporation. Nor does the character of that funding produce any reduction whatever in the "inherent worth of the speech" and "its capacity for informing the public," First Nat. Bank of Boston v. Bellotti, 435 U. S. 765, 777 (1978) . Indeed, to exclude or impede corporate speech is to muzzle the principal agents of the modern free economy. We should celebrate rather than condemn the addition of this speech to the public debate.

Notes to Justice Scalia's concurrence in Citizens United v. Federal Elections Commission (January 21, 2010)

1 Justice Thomas does not join Part IV of the Court's opinion.

2 The dissent protests that 1791 rather than 1800 should be the relevant date, and that "[m]ore than half of the century's total business charters were issued between 1796 and 1800." Post, at 35, n. 53. I used 1800 only because the dissent did. But in any case, it is surely fanciful to think that a consensus of hostility towards corporations was transformed into general favor at some magical moment between 1791 and 1796.

3 "[P]eople in 1800 identified corporations with franchised monopolies." L. Friedman, A History of American Law 194 (2d ed. 1985) (hereinafter Friedman). "The

chief cause for the changed popular attitude towards business corporations that marked the opening of the nineteenth century was the elimination of their inherent monopolistic character. This was accomplished primarily by an extension of the principle of free incorporation under general laws." 1 W. Fletcher, Cyclopedia of the Law of Corporations §2, p. 8 (rev. ed. 2006).

4 At times (though not always) the dissent seems to exclude such non-"business corporations" from its denial of free speech rights. See post, at 37. Finding in a seemingly categorical text a distinction between the rights of business corporations and the rights of non-business corporations is even more imaginative than finding a distinction between the rights of all corporations and the rights of other associations.

5 The best the dissent can come up with is that "[p]ostratification practice" supports its reading of the First Amendment . Post, at 40, n. 56. For this proposition, the dissent cites Justice White's statement (in dissent) that "[t]he common law was generally interpreted as prohibiting corporate political participation," First Nat. Bank of Boston v. Bellotti, 435 U. S. 765, 819 (1978) . The sole authority Justice White cited for this proposition, id., at 819, n. 14, was a law-review note that made no such claim. To the contrary, it stated that the cases dealing with the propriety of corporate political expenditures were "few." Note, Corporate Political Affairs Programs, 70 Yale L. J. 821, 852 (1961). More specifically, the note cites only two holdings to that effect, one by a Federal District Court, and one by the Supreme Court of Montana. Id., at 852, n. 197. Of course even if the common law was "generally interpreted" to prohibit corporate political expenditures as ultra vires, that would have nothing to do with whether political expenditures that were authorized by a corporation's charter could constitutionally be suppressed. As additional "[p]ostratification practice," the dissent notes that the Court "did not recognize any First Amendment protections for corporations until the middle part of the 20th century." Post, at 40, n. 56. But it did that in Grosjean v. American Press Co., 297 U. S. 233 (1936), a case involving freedom of the press—which the dissent acknowledges did cover corporations from the outset. The relative recency of that first case is unsurprising. All of our First Amendment jurisprudence was slow to develop. We did not consider application of the First Amendment to speech restrictions other than prior restraints until 1919, see Schenck v. United States, 249 U. S. 47 (1919); we did not invalidate a state law on First Amendment grounds until 1931, see Stromberg v. California, 283 U. S. 359 (1931), and a federal law until 1965, see Lamont v. Postmaster General, 381 U. S. 301 (1965) .

6 The dissent seeks to avoid this conclusion (and to turn a liability into an asset) by interpreting the Freedom of the Press Clause to refer to the institutional press (thus demonstrating, according to the dissent, that the Founders "did draw distinctions— explicit distinctions—between types of 'speakers,' or speech outlets or forms "). Post, at 40 and n. 57. It is passing strange to interpret the phrase "the freedom of speech, or of the press" to mean, not everyone's right to speak or publish, but rather everyone's right to speak or the institutional press's right to publish. No one thought that is what it meant.

Patriot Noah Webster's 1828 dictionary contains, under the word "press," the following entry: "Liberty of the press, in civil policy, is the free right of publishing books, pamphlets, or papers without previous restraint; or the unrestrained right which every citizen enjoys of publishing his thoughts and opinions, subject only to punishment for publishing what is pernicious to morals or to the peace of the state." 2 American Dictionary of the English Language (1828) (reprinted 1970). As the Court's opinion describes, ante, at 36, our jurisprudence agrees with Noah Webster and contradicts the dissent. "The liberty of the press is not confined to newspapers and periodicals. It necessarily embraces pamphlets and leaflets. . . . The press in its historical connotation comprehends every sort of publication which affords a vehicle of information and opinion." Lovell v. City of Griffin, 303 U. S. 444, 452 (1938).

7 The dissent says that " 'speech' " refers to oral communications of human beings, and since corporations are not human beings they cannot speak. Post, at 37, n. 55. This is sophistry. The authorized spokesman of a corporation is a human being, who speaks on behalf of the human beings who have formed that association—just as the spokesman of an unincorporated association speaks on behalf of its members. The power to publish thoughts, no less than the power to speak thoughts, belongs only to human beings, but the dissent sees no problem with a corporation's enjoying the freedom of the press. The same footnote asserts that "it has been 'claimed that the notion of institutional speech . . . did not exist in post-revolutionary America.' " This is quoted from a law-review article by a Bigelow Fellow at the University of Chicago (Fagundes, State Actors as First Amendment Speakers, 100 Nw. U. L. Rev. 1637, 1654 (2006)), which offers as the sole support for its statement a treatise dealing with government speech, M. Yudof, When Government Speaks 42–50 (1983). The cited pages of that treatise provide no support whatever for the statement—unless, as seems overwhelmingly likely, the "institutional speech" referred to was speech by the subject of the law-review article, governmental institutions. The other authority cited in the footnote, a law-review article by a professor at Washington and Lee Law School, Bezanson, Institutional Speech, 80 Iowa L. Rev. 735, 775 (1995), in fact contradicts the dissent, in that it would accord free-speech protection to associations.

Incorporation: Justice Scalia's concurrence in McDonald v. Chicago (June 28, 2010)

Justice Scalia, concurring.

I join the Court's opinion. Despite my misgivings about Substantive Due Process as an original matter, I have acquiesced in the Court's incorporation of certain guarantees in the Bill of Rights "because it is both long established and narrowly limited." Albright v. Oliver, 510 U. S. 266, 275 (1994) (Scalia, J., concurring). This case does not require me to reconsider that view, since straightforward application of settled doctrine suffices to decide it.

  I write separately only to respond to some aspects of Justice Stevens' dissent. Not that aspect which disagrees with the majority's application of our precedents to this case, which is fully covered by the Court's opinion. But much of what Justice Stevens writes is a broad condemnation of the theory of interpretation which underlies the Court's opinion, a theory that makes the traditions of our people paramount. He proposes a different theory, which he claims is more "cautiou[s]" and respectful of proper limits on the judicial role. Post, at 57. It is that claim I wish to address.

I

A

  After stressing the substantive dimension of what he has renamed the "liberty clause," post, at 4–7, 1 Justice Stevens proceeds to urge readoption of the theory of incorporation articulated in Palko v. Connecticut, 302 U. S. 319, 325 (1937), see post, at 14–20. But in fact he does not favor application of that theory at all. For whether Palko requires only that "a fair and enlightened system of justice would be impossible without" the right sought to be incorporated, 302 U. S., at 325, or requires in addition that the right be rooted in the "traditions and conscience of our people," ibid. (internal quotation marks omitted), many of the rights Justice Stevens thinks are incorporated could not pass muster under either test: abortion, post, at 7 (citing Planned Parenthood of Southeastern Pa. v. Casey, 505 U. S. 833, 847 (1992)); homosexual sodomy, post, at 16 (citing Lawrence v. Texas, 539 U. S. 558, 572 (2003)); the right to have excluded from criminal trials evidence obtained in violation of the Fourth Amendment, post, at 18 (citing Mapp v. Ohio, 367 U. S. 643, 650, 655–657 (1961)); and the right to teach one's children foreign languages, post, at 7 (citing Meyer v. Nebraska, 262 U. S. 390, 399–403 (1923)), among others.

  That Justice Stevens is not applying any version of Palko is clear from comparing, on the one hand, the rights he believes are covered, with, on the other hand, his conclusion that the right to keep and bear arms is not covered. Rights that pass his test include not just those "relating to marriage, procreation, contraception, family relationships, and child rearing and education," but also rights against "[g]overnment action that shocks the conscience, pointlessly infringes settled expectations, trespasses into sensitive private realms or life choices without adequate justification, [or] perpetrates gross injustice." Post, at 23 (internal quotation marks omitted). Not all such rights are in, however, since only " some fundamental aspects of personhood, dignity, and the like" are protected, post, at 24 (emphasis added). Exactly what is covered is not clear. But whatever else is in, he knows that the right to keep and bear arms is out, despite its being as "deeply rooted in this Nation's history and tradition," Washington v. Glucksberg, 521 U. S. 702, 721 (1997) (internal quotation marks omitted), as a right can be, see District of Columbia v. Heller, 554 U. S. ___, ___–___, ___–___, ___–___ (2008) (slip op., at 20–21, 26–30, 41–44). I can find no other explanation for such certitude except that Justice Stevens, despite his forswearing of "personal and private notions," post, at 21 (internal quotation marks omitted), deeply believes it should be out.

The subjective nature of Justice Stevens ' standard is also apparent from his claim that it is the courts' prerogative—indeed their duty —to update the Due Process Clause so that it encompasses new freedoms the Framers were too narrow-minded to imagine, post, at 19–20, and n. 21. Courts, he proclaims, must "do justice to [the Clause's] urgent call and its open texture" by exercising the "interpretive discretion the latter embodies." Post, at 21. (Why the people are not up to the task of deciding what new rights to protect, even though it is they who are authorized to make changes, see U. S. Const., Art. V, is never explained. 2) And it would be "judicial abdication" for a judge to "tur[n] his back" on his task of determining what the Fourteenth Amendment covers by "outsourc[ing]" the job to "historical sentiment," post, at 20—that is, by being guided by what the American people throughout our history have thought. It is only we judges, exercising our "own reasoned judgment," post, at 15, who can be entrusted with deciding the Due Process Clause's scope—which rights serve the Amendment's "central values," post, at 23—which basically means picking the rights we want to protect and discarding those we do not.

B

<tab>Justice Stevens resists this description, insisting that his approach provides plenty of "guideposts" and "constraints" to keep courts from "injecting excessive subjectivity" into the process. 3 Post, at 21. Plenty indeed—and that alone is a problem. The ability of omnidirectional guideposts to constrain is inversely proportional to their number. But even individually, each lodestar or limitation he lists either is incapable of restraining judicial whimsy or cannot be squared with the precedents he seeks to preserve.

He begins with a brief nod to history, post, at 21, but as he has just made clear, he thinks historical inquiry unavailing, post, at 19–20. Moreover, trusting the meaning of the Due Process Clause to what has historically been protected is circular, see post, at 19, since that would mean no new rights could get in.

<tab>Justice Stevens moves on to the "most basic" constraint on subjectivity his theory offers: that he would "esche[w] attempts to provide any all-purpose, top-down, totalizing theory of 'liberty.' " Post, at 22. The notion that the absence of a coherent theory of the Due Process Clause will somehow curtail judicial caprice is at war with reason. Indeterminacy means opportunity for courts to impose whatever rule they like; it is the problem, not the solution. The idea that interpretive pluralism would reduce courts' ability to impose their will on the ignorant masses is not merely naïve, but absurd. If there are no right answers, there are no wrong answers either.

<tab>Justice Stevens also argues that requiring courts to show "respect for the democratic process" should serve as a constraint. Post, at 23. That is true, but Justice Stevens would have them show respect in an extraordinary manner. In his view, if a right "is already being given careful consideration in, and subjected to ongoing calibration by,

the States, judicial enforcement may not be appropriate." Ibid. In other words, a right, such as the right to keep and bear arms, that has long been recognized but on which the States are considering restrictions, apparently deserves less protection, while a privilege the political branches (instruments of the democratic process) have withheld entirely and continue to withhold, deserves more . That topsy-turvy approach conveniently accomplishes the objective of ensuring that the rights this Court held protected in Casey, Lawrence, and other such cases fit the theory—but at the cost of insulting rather than respecting the democratic process.

 The next constraint Justice Stevens suggests is harder to evaluate. He describes as "an important tool for guiding judicial discretion" "sensitivity to the interaction between the intrinsic aspects of liberty and the practical realities of contemporary society." Post, at 24. I cannot say whether that sensitivity will really guide judges because I have no idea what it is. Is it some sixth sense instilled in judges when they ascend to the bench? Or does it mean judges are more constrained when they agonize about the cosmic conflict between liberty and its potentially harmful consequences? Attempting to give the concept more precision, Justice Stevens explains that "sensitivity is an aspect of a deeper principle: the need to approach our work with humility and caution." Ibid. Both traits are undeniably admirable, though what relation they bear to sensitivity is a mystery. But it makes no difference, for the first case Justice Stevens cites in support, see ibid., Casey, 505 U. S., at 849, dispels any illusion that he has a meaningful form of judicial modesty in mind.

 <tab>Justice Stevens offers no examples to illustrate the next constraint: stare decisis, post, at 25. But his view of it is surely not very confining, since he holds out as a "canonical" exemplar of the proper approach, see post, at 16, 54, Lawrence, which overruled a case decided a mere 17 years earlier, Bowers v. Hardwick, 478 U. S. 186 (1986), see 539 U. S., at 578 (it "was not correct when it was decided, and it is not correct today"). Moreover, Justice Stevens would apply that constraint unevenly: He apparently approves those Warren Court cases that adopted jot-for-jot incorporation of procedural protections for criminal defendants, post, at 11, but would abandon those Warren Court rulings that undercut his approach to substantive rights, on the basis that we have "cut back" on cases from that era before, post, at 12.

 <tab>Justice Stevens also relies on the requirement of a "careful description of the asserted fundamental liberty interest" to limit judicial discretion. Post, at 25 (internal quotation marks omitted). I certainly agree with that requirement, see Reno v. Flores, 507 U. S. 292, 302 (1993), though some cases Justice Stevens approves have not applied it seriously, see, e.g., Lawrence, supra, at 562 ("The instant case involves liberty of the person both in its spatial and in its more transcendent dimensions"). But if the "careful description" requirement is used in the manner we have hitherto employed, then the enterprise of determining the Due Process Clause's "conceptual core," post, at 23, is a waste of time. In the cases he cites we sought a careful, specific description of the right at issue in order to determine whether that right, thus narrowly defined, was fundamental .

See, e.g., Glucksberg, 521 U. S., at 722–728; Reno, supra, at 302–306; Collins v. Harker Heights, 503 U. S. 115, 125–129 (1992); Cruzan v. Director, Mo. Dept. of Health, 497 U. S. 261, 269–279 (1990); see also Vacco v. Quill, 521 U. S. 793, 801–808 (1997) . The threshold step of defining the asserted right with precision is entirely unnecessary, however, if (as Justice Stevens maintains) the "conceptual core" of the "liberty clause," post, at 23, includes a number of capacious, hazily defined categories. There is no need to define the right with much precision in order to conclude that it pertains to the plaintiff's "ability independently to define [his] identity," his "right to make certain unusually important decisions that will affect his own, or his family's, destiny," or some aspect of his "[s]elf-determination, bodily integrity, freedom of conscience, intimate relationships, political equality, dignity [or] respect." Ibid. (internal quotation marks omitted). Justice Stevens must therefore have in mind some other use for the careful-description requirement—perhaps just as a means of ensuring that courts "procee[d] slowly and incrementally," post, at 25. But that could be achieved just as well by having them draft their opinions in longhand. 4

II

If Justice Stevens' account of the constraints of his approach did not demonstrate that they do not exist, his application of that approach to the case before us leaves no doubt. He offers several reasons for concluding that the Second Amendment right to keep and bear arms is not fundamental enough to be applied against the States. 5 None is persuasive, but more pertinent to my purpose, each is either intrinsically indeterminate, would preclude incorporation of rights we have already held incorporated, or both. His approach therefore does nothing to stop a judge from arriving at any conclusion he sets out to reach.

 Justice Stevens begins with the odd assertion that "firearms have a fundamentally ambivalent relationship to liberty," since sometimes they are used to cause (or sometimes accidentally produce) injury to others. Post, at 35. The source of the rule that only nonambivalent liberties deserve Due Process protection is never explained—proof that judges applying Justice Stevens' approach can add new elements to the test as they see fit. The criterion, moreover, is inherently manipulable. Surely Justice Stevens does not mean that the Clause covers only rights that have zero harmful effect on anyone . Otherwise even the First Amendment is out. Maybe what he means is that the right to keep and bear arms imposes too great a risk to others' physical well-being. But as the plurality explains, ante, at 35–36, other rights we have already held incorporated pose similarly substantial risks to public safety. In all events, Justice Stevens supplies neither a standard for how severe the impairment on others' liberty must be for a right to be disqualified, nor (of course) any method of measuring the severity.

 Justice Stevens next suggests that the Second Amendment right is not fundamental because it is "different in kind" from other rights we have recognized. Post, at 37. In one respect, of course, the right to keep and bear arms is different from some other rights we have held the Clause protects and he would recognize: It is deeply grounded in our nation's history and tradition. But Justice Stevens has a different distinction in mind: Even though he does "not doubt for a moment that many Americans . . . see [firearms] as critical to their way of life as well as to their security," he pronounces that owning a handgun is not "critical to leading a life of autonomy, dignity, or political equality." 6 Post, at 37–38. Who says? Deciding what is essential to an enlightened, liberty-filled life is an inherently political, moral judgment—the antithesis of an objective approach that reaches conclusions by applying neutral rules to verifiable evidence. 7

No determination of what rights the Constitution of the United States covers would be complete, of course, without a survey of what other countries do. Post, at 40–41. When it comes to guns, Justice Stevens explains, our Nation is already an outlier among "advanced democracies"; not even our "oldest allies" protect as robust a right as we do, and we should not widen the gap. Ibid. Never mind that he explains neither which countries qualify as "advanced democracies" nor why others are irrelevant. For there is an even clearer indication that this criterion lets judges pick which rights States must respect and those they can ignore: As the plurality shows, ante, at 34–35, and nn. 28–29, this follow-the-foreign-crowd requirement would foreclose rights that we have held (and Justice Stevens accepts) are incorporated, but that other "advanced" nations do not recognize—from the exclusionary rule to the Establishment Clause. A judge applying Justice Stevens' approach must either throw all of those rights overboard or, as cases Justice Stevens approves have done in considering unenumerated rights, simply ignore foreign law when it undermines the desired conclusion, see, e.g., Casey, 505 U. S. 833 (making no mention of foreign law).

<tab>Justice Stevens also argues that since the right to keep and bear arms was codified for the purpose of "prevent[ing] elimination of the militia," it should be viewed as " 'a federalism provision' " logically incapable of incorporation. Post, at 41–42 (quoting Elk Grove Unified School Dist. v. Newdow, 542 U. S. 1, 45 (2004) (Thomas, J., concurring in judgment); some internal quotation marks omitted). This criterion, too, evidently applies only when judges want it to. The opinion Justice Stevens quotes for the "federalism provision" principle, Justice Thomas' s concurrence in <font i="1">Newdow, argued that incorporation of the Establishment Clause "makes little sense" because that Clause was originally understood as a limit on congressional interference with state establishments of religion. Id., at 49–51. Justice Stevens, of course, has no problem with applying the Establishment Clause to the States. See, e.g., id., at 8, n. 4 (opinion for the Court by Stevens, J.) (acknowledging that the Establishment Clause "appl[ies] to the States by incorporation into the Fourteenth Amendment "). While he insists that Clause is not a "federalism provision," post, at 42, n. 40, he does not explain why it is not, but the right to keep and bear arms is (even though only the latter refers to a "right of the people"). The "federalism" argument prevents the incorporation of only certain rights.

Justice Stevens next argues that even if the right to keep and bear arms is "deeply rooted in some important senses," the roots of States' efforts to regulate guns run just as deep. Post, at 44 (internal quotation marks omitted). But this too is true of other rights we have held incorporated. No fundamental right—not even the First Amendment—is absolute. The traditional restrictions go to show the scope of the right, not its lack of fundamental character. At least that is what they show (Justice Stevens would agree) for other rights. Once again, principles are applied selectively.

Justice Stevens' final reason for rejecting incorporation of the Second Amendment reveals, more clearly than any of the others, the game that is afoot. Assuming that there is a "plausible constitutional basis" for holding that the right to keep and bear arms is incorporated, he asserts that we ought not to do so for prudential reasons . Post, at 47. Even if we had the authority to withhold rights that are within the Constitution's command (and we assuredly do not), two of the reasons Justice Stevens gives for abstention show just how much power he would hand to judges. The States' "right to experiment" with solutions to the problem of gun violence, he says, is at its apex here because "the best solution is far from clear." Post, at 47–48 (internal quotation marks omitted). That is true of most serious social problems—whether, for example, "the best solution" for rampant crime is to admit confessions unless they are affirmatively shown to have been coerced, but see Miranda v. Arizona, 384 U. S. 436, 444–445 (1966), or to permit jurors to impose the death penalty without a requirement that they be free to consider "any relevant mitigating factor," see Eddings v. Oklahoma, 455 U. S. 104, 112 (1982), which in turn leads to the conclusion that defense counsel has provided inadequate defense if he has not conducted a "reasonable investigation" into potentially mitigating factors, see, e.g., Wiggins v. Smith, 539 U. S. 510, 534 (2003), inquiry into which question tends to destroy any prospect of prompt justice, see, e.g., Wong v. Belmontes, 558 U. S. ____ (2009) (per curiam) (reversing grant of habeas relief for sentencing on a crime committed in 1981). The obviousness of the optimal answer is in the eye of the beholder. The implication of Justice Stevens ' call for abstention is that if We The Court conclude that They The People's answers to a problem are silly, we are free to "interven[e]," post, at 47, but if we too are uncertain of the right answer, or merely think the States may be on to something, we can loosen the leash.

A second reason Justice Stevens says we should abstain is that the States have shown they are "capable" of protecting the right at issue, and if anything have protected it too much. Post, at 49. That reflects an assumption that judges can distinguish between a proper democratic decision to leave things alone (which we should honor), and a case of democratic market failure (which we should step in to correct). I would not—and no judge should—presume to have that sort of omniscience, which seems to me far more "arrogant," post, at 41, than confining courts' focus to our own national heritage.

III

Justice Stevens ' response to this concurrence, post, at 51–56, makes the usual rejoinder of "living Constitution" advocates to the criticism that it empowers judges to eliminate or expand what the people have prescribed: The traditional, historically focused method, he says, reposes discretion in judges as well. 8 Historical analysis can be difficult; it sometimes requires resolving threshold questions, and making nuanced judgments about which evidence to consult and how to interpret it.

I will stipulate to that. 9 But the question to be decided is not whether the historically focused method is a perfect means of restraining aristocratic judicial Constitution-writing; but whether it is the best means available in an imperfect world. Or indeed, even more narrowly than that: whether it is demonstrably much better than what Justice Stevens proposes. I think it beyond all serious dispute that it is much less subjective, and intrudes much less upon the democratic process. It is less subjective because it depends upon a body of evidence susceptible of reasoned analysis rather than a variety of vague ethico-political First Principles whose combined conclusion can be found to point in any direction the judges favor. In the most controversial matters brought before this Court—for example, the constitutionality of prohibiting abortion, assisted suicide, or homosexual sodomy, or the constitutionality of the death penalty— any historical methodology, under any plausible standard of proof, would lead to the same conclusion. 10 Moreover, the methodological differences that divide historians, and the varying interpretive assumptions they bring to their work, post, at 52–54, are nothing compared to the differences among the American people (though perhaps not among graduates of prestigious law schools) with regard to the moral judgments Justice Stevens would have courts pronounce. And whether or not special expertise is needed to answer historical questions, judges most certainly have no "comparative ... advantage," post, at 24 (internal quotation marks omitted), in resolving moral disputes. What is more, his approach would not eliminate, but multiply, the hard questions courts must confront, since he would not replace history with moral philosophy, but would have courts consider both .

And the Court's approach intrudes less upon the democratic process because the rights it acknowledges are those established by a constitutional history formed by democratic decisions; and the rights it fails to acknowledge are left to be democratically adopted or rejected by the people, with the assurance that their decision is not subject to judicial revision. Justice Stevens ' approach, on the other hand, deprives the people of that power, since whatever the Constitution and laws may say, the list of protected rights will be whatever courts wish it to be. After all, he notes, the people have been wrong before, post, at 55, and courts may conclude they are wrong in the future. Justice Stevens abhors a system in which "majorities or powerful interest groups always get their way," post, at 56, but replaces it with a system in which unelected and life-tenured judges always get their way. That such usurpation is effected unabashedly, see post, at 53—with "the judge's cards ... laid on the table," ibid. —makes it even worse. In a vibrant democracy, usurpation should have to be accomplished in the dark. It is Justice Stevens' approach, not the Court's, that puts democracy in peril.

Notes to Justice Scalia's Concurrence in McDonald v. Chicago (June 28, 2010)

1 I do not entirely understand Justice Stevens' renaming of the Due Process Clause. What we call it, of course, does not change what the Clause says, but shorthand should not obscure what it says. Accepting for argument's sake the shift in emphasis—from avoiding certain deprivations without that "process" which is "due," to avoiding the deprivations themselves—the Clause applies not just to deprivations of "liberty," but also to deprivations of "life" and even "property."

2 Justice Stevens insists that he would not make courts the sole interpreters of the "liberty clause"; he graciously invites "[a]ll Americans" to ponder what the Clause means to them today. Post, at 20, n. 22. The problem is that in his approach the people's ponderings do not matter, since whatever the people decide, courts have the last word.

3 Justice Breyer is not worried by that prospect. His interpretive approach applied to incorporation of the Second Amendment includes consideration of such factors as "the extent to which incorporation will further other, perhaps more basic, constitutional aims; and the extent to which incorporation will advance or hinder the Constitution's structural aims"; whether recognizing a particular right will "further the Constitution's effort to ensure that the government treats each individual with equal respect" or will "help maintain the democratic form of government"; whether it is "inconsistent ... with the Constitution's efforts to create governmental institutions well suited to the carrying out of its constitutional promises"; whether it fits with "the Framers' basic reason for believing the Court ought to have the power of judicial review"; courts' comparative advantage in answering empirical questions that may be involved in applying the right; and whether there is a "strong offsetting justification" for removing a decision from the democratic process. Post, at 7, 11–17 (dissenting opinion).

4 After defending the careful-description criterion, Justice Stevens quickly retreats and cautions courts not to apply it too stringently. Post, at 26. Describing a right too specifically risks robbing it of its "universal valence and a moral force it might otherwise have," ibid., and "loads the dice against its recognition," post, at 26, n. 25 (internal quotation marks omitted). That must be avoided, since it endangers rights Justice Stevens does like. See ibid. (discussing Lawrence v. Texas, 539 U. S. 558 (2003)). To make sure those rights get in, we must leave leeway in our description, so that a right that has not itself been recognized as fundamental can ride the coattails of one that has been.

5 Justice Stevens claims that I mischaracterize his argument by referring to the Second Amendment right to keep and bear arms, instead of "the interest in keeping a firearm of one's choosing in the home," the right he says petitioners assert. Post, at 38, n. 36. But it is precisely the " Second Amendment right to keep and bear arms" that petitioners argue is incorporated by the Due Process Clause. See, e.g., Pet. for Cert. i. Under Justice Stevens' own approach, that should end the matter. See post, at 26 ("[W]e must pay close attention to the precise liberty interest the litigants have asked us to vindicate"). In any event, the demise of watered-down incorporation, see ante, at 17–19,

means that we no longer subdivide Bill of Rights guarantees into their theoretical components, only some of which apply to the States. The First Amendment freedom of speech is incorporated—not the freedom to speak on Fridays, or to speak about philosophy.

6 Justice Stevens goes a step farther still, suggesting that the right to keep and bear arms is not protected by the "liberty clause" because it is not really a liberty at all, but a "property right." Post, at 38. Never mind that the right to bear arms sounds mighty like a liberty; and never mind that the "liberty clause" is really a Due Process Clause which explicitly protects "property," see United States v. Carlton, 512 U. S. 26, 41–42 (1994) (Scalia, J., concurring in judgment). Justice Stevens' theory cannot explain why the Takings Clause, which unquestionably protects property, has been incorporated, see Chicago, B. & Q. R. Co. v. Chicago, 166 U. S. 226, 241 (1897), in a decision he appears to accept, post, at 14, n. 14.

7 As Justice Stevens notes, see post, at 51–52, I accept as a matter of stare decisis the requirement that to be fundamental for purposes of the Due Process Clause, a right must be "implicit in the concept of ordered liberty," Lawrence, supra, at 593, n. 3 (Scalia, J., dissenting) (internal quotation marks omitted). But that inquiry provides infinitely less scope for judicial invention when conducted under the Court's approach, since the field of candidates is immensely narrowed by the prior requirement that a right be rooted in this country's traditions. Justice Stevens, on the other hand, is free to scan the universe for rights that he thinks "implicit in the concept, etc." The point Justice Stevens makes here is merely one example of his demand that an historical approach to the Constitution prove itself, not merely much better than his in restraining judicial invention, but utterly perfect in doing so. See Part III, infra.

8 Justice Stevens also asserts that his approach is "more faithful to this Nation's constitutional history" and to "the values and commitments of the American people, as they stand today," post, at 54. But what he asserts to be the proof of this is that his approach aligns (no surprise) with those cases he approves (and dubs "canonical," ibid.). Cases he disfavors are discarded as "hardly bind[ing]" "excesses," post, at 12, or less "enduring," post, at 17, n. 16. Not proven. Moreover, whatever relevance Justice Stevens ascribes to current "values and commitments of the American people" (and that is unclear, see post, at 48–49, n. 47), it is hard to see how it shows fidelity to them that he disapproves a different subset of old cases than the Court does.

9 That is not to say that every historical question on which there is room for debate is indeterminate, or that every question on which historians disagree is equally balanced. Cf. post, at 52–53. For example, the historical analysis of the principal dissent in Heller is as valid as the Court's only in a two-dimensional world that conflates length and depth.

10 By the way, Justice Stevens greatly magnifies the difficulty of an historical approach by suggesting that it was my burden in Lawrence to show the "ancient roots of proscriptions against sodomy," post, at 53 (internal quotation marks omitted). Au

contraire, it was his burden (in the opinion he joined) to show the ancient roots of the right of sodomy.

California does not need to release 46,000 prisoners: Justice Scalia's dissent in Brown v. Plata (May 23, 2011)

Justice Scalia, with whom Justice Thomas joins, dissenting.

Today the Court affirms what is perhaps the most radical injunction issued by a court in our Nation's history: an order requiring California to release the staggering number of 46,000 convicted criminals.

There comes before us, now and then, a case whose proper outcome is so clearly indicated by tradition and common sense, that its decision ought to shape the law, rather than vice versa. One would think that, before allowing the decree of a federal district court to release 46,000 convicted felons, this Court would bend every effort to read the law in such a way as to avoid that outrageous result. Today, quite to the contrary, the Court disregards stringently drawn provisions of the governing statute, and traditional constitutional limitations upon the power of a federal judge, in order to uphold the absurd.

The proceedings that led to this result were a judicial travesty. I dissent because the institutional reform the District Court has undertaken violates the terms of the governing statute, ignores bedrock limitations on the power of Article III judges, and takes federal courts wildly beyond their institutional capacity.

I

A

The Prison Litigation Reform Act (PLRA) states that "[p]rospective relief in any civil action with respect to prison conditions shall extend no further than necessary to correct the violation of the Federal right of a particular plaintiff or plaintiffs"; that such relief must be "narrowly drawn, [and] exten[d] no further than necessary to correct the violation of the Federal right"; and that it must be "the least intrusive means necessary to correct the violation of the Federal right." 18 U. S. C. §3626(a)(1)(A). In deciding whether these multiple limitations have been complied with, it is necessary to identify with precision what is the "violation of the Federal right of a particular plaintiff or plaintiffs" that has been alleged. What has been alleged here, and what the injunction issued by the Court is tailored (narrowly or not) to remedy is the running of a prison system with inadequate medical facilities. That may result in the denial of needed medical treatment to "a particular [prisoner] or [prisoners]," thereby violating (ac-cording to our cases) his or their Eighth Amendment rights. But the mere existence of the inadequate system does not subject to cruel and unusual punishment the entire prison population in need of medical care, including those who receive it.

The Court acknowledges that the plaintiffs "do not base their case on deficiencies in care provided on any one occasion"; rather, "[p]laintiffs rely on systemwide deficiencies in the provision of medical and mental health care that, taken as a whole, subject sick and mentally ill prisoners in California to 'substantial risk of serious harm' and cause the delivery of care in the prisons to fall below the evolving standards of decency that mark the progress of a maturing society." Ante, at 7, n. 3. But our judge-empowering "evolving standards of decency" jurisprudence (with which, by the way, I heartily disagree, see, e.g., Roper v. Simmons, 543 U. S. 551, 615–616 (2005) (Scalia, J., dissenting)) does not prescribe (or at least has not until today prescribed) rules for the "decent" running of schools, prisons, and other government institutions. It forbids "indecent" treatment of individuals—in the context of this case, the denial of medical care to those who need it . And the persons who have a constitutional claim for denial of medical care are those who are denied medical care—not all who face a "substantial risk" (whatever that is) of being denied medical care.

The Coleman litigation involves "the class of seriously mentally ill persons in California prisons," ante, at 8, and the Plata litigation involves "the class of state prisoners with serious medical conditions," ante, at 9. The plaintiffs do not appear to claim—and it would absurd to suggest—that every single one of those prisoners has personally experienced "torture or a lingering death," ante, at 13 (internal quotation marks omitted), as a consequence of that bad medical system. Indeed, it is inconceivable that anything more than a small proportion of prisoners in the plaintiff classes have personally received sufficiently atrocious treatment that their Eighth Amendment right was violated—which, as the Court recognizes, is why the plaintiffs do not premise their claim on "deficiencies in care provided on any one occasion." Ante, at 7, n. 3. Rather, the plaintiffs' claim is that they are all part of a medical system so defective that some number of prisoners will inevitably be injured by incompetent medical care, and that this number is sufficiently high so as to render the system, as a whole, unconstitutional.

But what procedural principle justifies certifying a class of plaintiffs so they may assert a claim of systemic unconstitutionality? I can think of two possibilities, both of which are untenable. The first is that although some or most plaintiffs in the class do not individually have viable Eighth Amendment claims, the class as a whole has collectively suffered an Eighth Amendment violation. That theory is contrary to the bedrock rule that the sole purpose of classwide adjudication is to aggregate claims that are individually viable. "A class action, no less than traditional joinder (of which it is a species), merely enables a federal court to adjudicate claims of multiple parties at once, instead of in separate suits. And like traditional joinder, it leaves the parties' legal rights and duties intact and the rules of decision unchanged." Shady Grove Orthopedic Associates, P. A. v. Allstate Ins. Co., 559 U. S. ___, ___ (2010) (plurality opinion) (slip op., at 14).

The second possibility is that every member of the plaintiff class has suffered an Eighth Amendment violation merely by virtue of being a patient in a poorly-run prison system, and the purpose of the class is merely to aggregate all those individually viable claims. This theory has the virtue of being consistent with procedural principles, but at the cost of a gross substantive departure from our case law. Under this theory, each and every prisoner who happens to be a patient in a system that has systemic weaknesses—such as "hir[ing] any doctor who had a license, a pulse and a pair of shoes," ante, at 10 (internal quotation marks omitted)—has suffered cruel or unusual punishment, even if that person cannot make an individualized showing of mistreatment. Such a theory of the Eighth Amendment is preposterous. And we have said as much in the past: "If ... a healthy inmate who had suffered no deprivation of needed medical treatment were able to claim violation of his constitutional right to medical care ... simply on the ground that the prison medical facilities were inadequate, the essential distinction between judge and executive would have disappeared: it would have become the function of the courts to assure adequate medical care in prisons." Lewis v. Casey, 518 U. S. 343, 350 (1996).

Whether procedurally wrong or substantively wrong, the notion that the plaintiff class can allege an Eighth Amendment violation based on "systemwide deficiencies" is assuredly wrong. It follows that the remedy decreed here is also contrary to law, since the theory of systemic unconstitutionality is central to the plaintiffs' case. The PLRA requires plaintiffs to establish that the systemwide injunction entered by the District Court was "narrowly drawn" and "extends no further than necessary" to correct "the violation of the Federal right of a particular plaintiff or plaintiffs." If (as is the case) the only viable constitutional claims consist of individual instances of mistreatment, then a remedy reforming the system as a whole goes far beyond what the statute allows.

It is also worth noting the peculiarity that the vast majority of inmates most generously rewarded by the re-lease order—the 46,000 whose incarceration will be ended—do not form part of any aggrieved class even under the Court's expansive notion of constitutional violation. Most of them will not be prisoners with medical conditions or severe mental illness; and many will undoubtedly be fine physical specimens who have developed intimidating muscles pumping iron in the prison gym.

B

Even if I accepted the implausible premise that the plaintiffs have established a systemwide violation of the Eighth Amendment, I would dissent from the Court's endorsement of a decrowding order. That order is an example of what has become known as a "structural injunction." As I have previously explained, structural injunctions are radically different from the injunctions traditionally issued by courts of equity, and presumably part of "the judicial Power" conferred on federal courts by Article III:

"The mandatory injunctions issued upon termination of litigation usually required 'a single simple act.' H. McClintock, Principles of Equity §15, pp. 32–33 (2d ed. 1948). Indeed, there was a 'historical prejudice of the court of chancery against rendering decrees which called for more than a single affirmative act.' Id., §61, at 160. And where specific performance of contracts was sought, it was the categorical rule that no decree would issue that required ongoing supervision. . . . Compliance with these 'single act' mandates could, in addition to being simple, be quick; and once it was achieved the contemnor's relationship with the court came to an end, at least insofar as the subject of the order was concerned. Once the document was turned over or the land conveyed, the litigant's obligation to the court, and the court's coercive power over the litigant, ceased... . The court did not engage in any ongoing supervision of the litigant's conduct, nor did its order continue to regulate its behavior." Mine Workers v. Bagwell, 512 U. S. 821, 841–842 (1994) (Scalia, J., concurring).

Structural injunctions depart from that historical practice, turning judges into long-term administrators of complex social institutions such as schools, prisons, and police departments. Indeed, they require judges to play a role essentially indistinguishable from the role ordinarily played by executive officials. Today's decision not only affirms the structural injunction but vastly expands its use, by holding that an entire system is unconstitutional because it may produce constitutional violations.

The drawbacks of structural injunctions have been described at great length elsewhere. See, e.g., Lewis, supra, at 385–393 (1996) (Thomas, J., concurring); Missouri v. Jenkins, 515 U. S. 70, 124–133 (1995) (Thomas, J., concurring); Horowitz, Decreeing Organizational Change: Judicial Supervision of Public Institutions, 1983 Duke L. J. 1265. This case illustrates one of their most pernicious aspects: that they force judges to engage in a form of factfinding-as-policymaking that is outside the traditional judicial role. The factfinding judges traditionally engage in involves the determination of past or present facts based (except for a limited set of materials of which courts may take "judicial notice") exclusively upon a closed trial record. That is one reason why a district judge's factual findings are entitled to plain-error review: because having viewed the trial first hand he is in a better position to evaluate the evidence than a judge reviewing a cold record. In a very limited category of cases, judges have also traditionally been called upon to make some predictive judgments: which custody will best serve the interests of the child, for example, or whether a particular one-shot injunction will remedy the plaintiff's grievance. When a judge manages a structural injunction, however, he will inevitably be required to make very broad empirical predictions necessarily based in large part upon policy views—the sort of predictions regularly made by legislators and executive officials, but inappropriate for the Third Branch.

This feature of structural injunctions is superbly illustrated by the District Court's proceeding concerning the decrowding order's effect on public safety. The PLRA requires that, before granting "[p]rospective relief in [a] civil action with respect to prison conditions," a court must "give substantial weight to any adverse impact on public safety or the operation of a criminal justice system caused by the relief." 18 U. S. C. §3626(a)(1)(A). Here, the District Court discharged that requirement by making the "factual finding" that "the state has available methods by which it could readily reduce the prison population to 137.5% design capacity or less without an adverse impact on public safety or the operation of the criminal justice system." Juris. Statement App., O. T. 2009, No. 09-416, p. 253a. It found the evidence "clear" that prison overcrowding would "perpetuate a criminogenic prison system that itself threatens public safety," id., at 186a, and volunteered its opinion that "[t]he population could be reduced even further with the reform of California's antiquated sentencing policies and other related changes to the laws." Id., at 253a. It "reject[ed] the testimony that inmates released early from prison would commit additional new crimes," id., at 200a, finding that "shortening the length of stay through earned credits would give inmates incentives to participate in programming designed to lower recidivism," id., at 204a, and that "slowing the flow of technical parole violators to prison, thereby substantially reducing the churning of parolees, would by itself improve both the prison and parole systems, and public safety." Id., at 209a. It found that "the diversion of offenders to community correctional programs has significant beneficial effects on public safety," id., at 214a, and that "additional rehabilitative programming would result in a significant population reduction while improving public safety," id., at 216a.

The District Court cast these predictions (and the Court today accepts them) as "factual findings," made in reliance on the procession of expert witnesses that testified at trial. Because these "findings" have support in the record, it is difficult to reverse them under a plain-error standard of review. Ante, at 38. And given that the District Court devoted nearly 10 days of trial and 70 pages of its opinion to this issue, it is difficult to dispute that the District Court has discharged its statutory obligation to give "substantial weight to any adverse impact on public safety."

But the idea that the three District Judges in this case relied solely on the credibility of the testifying expert witnesses is fanciful. Of course they were relying largely on their own beliefs about penology and recidivism. And of course different district judges, of different policy views, would have "found" that rehabilitation would not work and that releasing prisoners would increase the crime rate. I am not saying that the District Judges rendered their factual findings in bad faith. I am saying that it is impossible for judges to make "factual findings" without inserting their own policy judgments, when the factual findings are policy judgments. What occurred here is no more judicial factfinding in the ordinary sense than would be the factual findings that deficit spending will not lower the unemployment rate, or that the continued occupation of Iraq will decrease the risk of terrorism. Yet, because they have been branded "factual findings" entitled to deferential review, the policy preferences of three District Judges now govern the operation of California's penal system.

It is important to recognize that the dressing-up of pol-icy judgments as factual findings is not an error peculiar to this case. It is an unavoidable concomitant of institutional-reform litigation. When a district court issues an injunction, it must make a factual assessment of the anticipated consequences of the injunction. And when the injunction undertakes to restructure a social institution, assessing the factual consequences of the injunction is necessarily the sort of predictive judgment that our system of government allocates to other government officials.

But structural injunctions do not simply invite judges to indulge policy preferences. They invite judges to indulge incompetent policy preferences. Three years of law school and familiarity with pertinent Supreme Court precedents give no insight whatsoever into the management of social institutions. Thus, in the proceeding below the District Court determined that constitutionally adequate medical services could be provided if the prison population was 137.5% of design capacity. This was an empirical finding it was utterly unqualified to make. Admittedly, the court did not generate that number entirely on its own; it heard the numbers 130% and 145% bandied about by various witnesses and decided to split the difference. But the ability of judges to spit back or even average-out numbers spoon-fed to them by expert witnesses does not render them competent decisionmakers in areas in which they are otherwise unqualified.

The District Court also relied heavily on the views of the Receiver and Special Master, and those reports play a starring role in the Court's opinion today. The Court notes that "the Receiver and the Special Master filed reports stating that overcrowding posed a significant barrier to their efforts" and deems those reports "persuasive evidence that, absent a reduction in overcrowding, any remedy might prove unattainable and would at the very least require vast expenditures of resources by the State." Ante, at 31–32. The use of these reports is even less consonant with the traditional judicial role than the District Court's reliance on the expert testimony at trial. The latter, even when, as here, it is largely the expression of policy judgments, is at least subject to cross-examination. Relying on the un-cross-examined findings of an investigator, sent into the field to prepare a factual report and give suggestions on how to improve the prison system, bears no resemblance to ordinary judicial decisionmaking. It is true that the PLRA contemplates the appointment of Special Masters (although not Receivers), but Special Masters are authorized only to "conduct hearings and prepare proposed findings of fact" and "assist in the development of remedial plans," 18 U. S. C. §3626(f)(6). This does not authorize them to make factual findings (unconnected to hearings) that are given seemingly wholesale deference. Neither the Receiver nor the Special Master was selected by California to run its prisons, and the fact that they may be experts in the field of prison reform does not justify the judicial imposition of their perspectives on the state.

C

My general concerns associated with judges' running social institutions are magnified when they run prison systems, and doubly magnified when they force prison officials to release convicted criminals. As we have previously recognized:

"[C]ourts are ill equipped to deal with the increasingly urgent problems of prison administration and re- form... . [T]he problems of prisons in America are complex and intractable, and, more to the point, they are not readily susceptible of resolution by decree... . Running a prison is an inordinately difficult undertaking that requires expertise, planning, and the com-mitment of resources, all of which are peculiarly within the province of the legislative and executive branches of government. Prison is, moreover, a task that has been committed to the responsibility of those branches, and separation of powers concerns counsel a policy of judicial restraint. Where a state penal system is involved, federal courts have ... additional reason to accord deference to the appropriate prison authorities." Turner v. Safley, 482 U. S. 78, 84–85 (1987) (internal quotation marks omitted).

These principles apply doubly to a prisoner-release order. As the author of today's opinion explained earlier this Term, granting a writ of habeas corpus " 'disturbs the State's significant interest in repose for concluded litigation, denies society the right to punish some admitted offenders, and intrudes on state sovereignty to a degree matched by few exercises of federal judicial authority.' " Harrington v. Richter, 562 U. S. ___, ___ (2011) (slip op., at 13) (quoting Harris v. Reed, 489 U. S. 255, 282 (1989) (Kennedy, J., dissenting)). Recognizing that habeas relief must be granted sparingly, we have reversed the Ninth Circuit's erroneous grant of habeas relief to individual California prisoners four times this Term alone. Cullen v. Pinholster, 563 U. S. ___ (2011); Felkner v. Jackson, 562 U. S. ___ (2011) (per curiam); Swarthout v. Cooke, 562 U. S. ___ (2011) (per curiam); Harrington, supra . And yet here, the Court affirms an order granting the functional equivalent of 46,000 writs of habeas corpus, based on its paean to courts' "substantial flexibility when making these judgments." Ante, at 41. It seems that the Court's respect for state sovereignty has vanished in the case where it most matters.

II

The Court's opinion includes a bizarre coda noting that "[t]he State may wish to move for modification of the three-judge court's order to extend the deadline for the required reduction to five years." Ante, at 46–47. The District Court, it says, "may grant such a request provided that the State satisfies necessary and appropriate preconditions designed to ensure the measures are taken to implement the plan without undue delay"; and it gives vague suggestions of what these preconditions "may include," such as "interim benchmarks." Ante, at 47. It also invites the District Court to "consider whether it is appropriate to order the State to begin without delay to develop a system to identify prisoners who are unlikely to reoffend," and informs the State that it "should devise systems to select those prisoners least likely to jeopardize public safety." Ibid. (What a good idea!)

The legal effect of this passage is unclear—I suspect intentionally so. If it is nothing but a polite remainder to the State and to the District Court that the injunction is subject to modification, then it is entirely unnecessary. As both the State and the District Court are undoubtedly aware, a party is always entitled to move to modify an equitable decree, and the PLRA contains an express provision authorizing District Courts to modify or terminate prison injunctions. See 18 U. S. C. §3626(b).

I suspect, however, that this passage is a warning shot across the bow, telling the District Court that it had better modify the injunction if the State requests what we invite it to request. Such a warning, if successful, would achieve the benefit of a marginal reduction in the inevitable murders, robberies, and rapes to be committed by the released inmates. But it would achieve that at the expense of intellectual bankruptcy, as the Court's "warning" is entirely alien to ordinary principles of appellate review of injunctions. When a party moves for modification of an injunction, the district court is entitled to rule on that motion first, subject to review for abuse of discretion if it declines to modify the order. Horne v. Flores, 557 U. S. ____, ____, ____ (2009) (slip op., at 10, 20). Moreover, when a district court enters a new decree with new benchmarks, the selection of those benchmarks is also reviewed under a deferential, abuse-of-discretion standard of review—a point the Court appears to recognize. Ante, at 45. Appellate courts are not supposed to "affirm" injunctions while preemptively noting that the State "may" request, and the District Court "may" grant, a request to extend the State's deadline to release prisoners by three years based on some suggestions on what appropriate preconditions for such a modification "may" include.

Of course what is really happening here is that the Court, overcome by common sense, disapproves of the results reached by the District Court, but cannot remedy them (it thinks) by applying ordinary standards of appellate review. It has therefore selected a solution unknown in our legal system: A deliberately ambiguous set of suggestions on how to modify the injunction, just deferential enough so that it can say with a straight face that it is "affirming," just stern enough to put the District Court on notice that it will likely get reversed if it does not follow them. In doing this, the Court has aggrandized itself, grasping authority that appellate courts are not supposed to have, and using it to enact a compromise solution with no legal basis other than the Court's say-so. That we are driven to engage in these extralegal activities should be a sign that the entire project of permitting district courts to run prison systems is misbegotten.

But perhaps I am being too unkind. The Court, or at least a majority of the Court's majority, must be aware that the judges of the District Court are likely to call its bluff, since they know full well it cannot possibly be an abuse of discretion to refuse to accept the State's proposed modifications in an injunction that has just been approved (affirmed) in its present form. An injunction, after all, does not have to be perfect; only good enough for government work, which the Court today says this is. So perhaps the coda is nothing more than a ceremonial washing of the hands—making it clear for all to see, that if the terrible things sure to happen as a consequence of this outrageous order do happen, they will be none of this Court's responsibility. After all, did we not want, and indeed even suggest, something better?

III

In view of the incoherence of the Eighth Amendment claim at the core of this case, the nonjudicial features of institutional reform litigation that this case exemplifies, and the unique concerns associated with mass prisoner releases, I do not believe this Court can affirm this injunction. I will state my approach briefly: In my view, a court may not order a prisoner's release unless it determines that the prisoner is suffering from a violation of his constitutional rights, and that his release, and no other relief, will remedy that violation. Thus, if the court determines that a particular prisoner is being denied constitutionally required medical treatment, and the release of that prisoner (and no other remedy) would enable him to obtain medical treatment, then the court can order his release; but a court may not order the release of prisoners who have suffered no violations of their constitutional rights, merely to make it less likely that that will happen to them in the future.

This view follows from the PLRA's text that I discussed at the outset, 18 U. S. C. §3626(a)(1)(A). "[N]arrowly drawn" means that the relief applies only to the "particular [prisoner] or [prisoners]" whose constitutional rights are violated; "extends no further than necessary" means that prisoners whose rights are not violated will not obtain relief; and "least intrusive means necessary to correct the violation of the Federal right" means that no other relief is available. * *

I acknowledge that this reading of the PLRA would severely limit the circumstances under which a court could issue structural injunctions to remedy allegedly unconstitutional prison conditions, although it would not eliminate them entirely. If, for instance, a class representing all prisoners in a particular institution alleged that the temperature in their cells was so cold as to violate the Eighth Amendment, or that they were deprived of all exercise time, a court could enter a prisonwide injunction ordering that the temperature be raised or exercise time be provided. Still, my approach may invite the objection that the PLRA appears to contemplate structural injunctions in general and mass prisoner-release orders in particular. The statute requires courts to "give substantial weight to any adverse impact on public safety or the operation of a criminal justice system caused by the relief" and authorizes them to appoint Special Masters, §3626 (a)(1)(A), (f), provisions that seem to presuppose the possibility of a structural remedy. It also sets forth criteria under which courts may issue orders that have "the purpose or effect of reducing or limiting the prisoner population," §3626(g)(4).

I do not believe that objection carries the day. In addition to imposing numerous limitations on the ability of district courts to order injunctive relief with respect to prison conditions, the PLRA states that "[n]othing in this section shall be construed to ... repeal or detract from otherwise applicable limitations on the remedial powers of the courts." §3626(a)(1)(C). The PLRA is therefore best understood as an attempt to constrain the discretion of courts issuing structural injunctions—not as a mandate for their use. For the reasons I have outlined, structural injunctions, especially prisoner-release orders, raise grave separation-of-powers concerns and veer significantly from the historical role and institutional capability of courts. It is appropriate to construe the PLRA so as to constrain courts from entering injunctive relief that would exceed that role and capability.

* * *

The District Court's order that California release 46,000 prisoners extends "further than necessary to correct the violation of the Federal right of a particular plaintiff or plaintiffs" who have been denied needed medical care. 18 U. S. C. §3626(a)(1)(A). It is accordingly forbidden by the PLRA—besides defying all sound conception of the proper role of judges.

Notes

* * Any doubt on this last score, at least as far as prisoner-release orders are concerned, is eliminated by §3626(a)(3)(E) of the statute, which provides that to enter a prisoner-release order the court must find "by clear and convincing evidence that— (i) crowding is the primary cause of the violation of a Federal right; and (ii) no other relief will remedy the violation of the Federal right."

Immigration law: Justice Scalia's concurrence and dissent in Arizona v. United States (June 25, 2012)

Justice Scalia, concurring in part and dissenting in part.

The United States is an indivisible "Union of sovereign States." Hinderlider v. La Plata River & Cherry Creek Ditch Co., 304 U. S. 92, 104 (1938). Today's opinion, approving virtually all of the Ninth Circuit's injunction against enforcement of the four challenged provisions of Arizona's law, deprives States of what most would con-sider the defining characteristic of sovereignty: the power to exclude from the sovereign's territory people who have no right to be there. Neither the Constitution itself nor even any law passed by Congress supports this result. I dissent.

I

As a sovereign, Arizona has the inherent power to exclude persons from its territory, subject only to those limitations expressed in the Constitution or constitution-ally imposed by Congress. That power to exclude has long been recognized as inherent in sovereignty. Emer de Vattel's seminal 1758 treatise on the Law of Nations stated:

"The sovereign may forbid the entrance of his territory either to foreigners in general, or in particular cases, or to certain persons, or for certain particular purposes, according as he may think it advantageous to the state. There is nothing in all this, that does not flow from the rights of domain and sovereignty: every one is obliged to pay respect to the prohibition; and whoever dares violate it, incurs the penalty decreed to render it effectual." The Law of Nations, bk. II,ch. VII, §94, p. 309 (B. Kapossy & R. Whatmore eds. 2008).

See also I R. Phillimore, Commentaries upon International Law, pt. III, ch. X, p. 233 (1854) ("It is a received maxim of International Law that, the Government of a State may prohibit the entrance of strangers into the country"). 1

There is no doubt that "before the adoption of the constitution of the United States" each State had the author-ity to "prevent [itself] from being burdened by an influx of persons." Mayor of New York v. Miln, 11 Pet. 102, 132–133 (1837). And the Constitution did not strip the States of that authority. To the contrary, two of the Constitution's provisions were designed to enable the States to prevent "the intrusion of obnoxious aliens through other States." Letter from James Madison to Edmund Randolph (Aug. 27, 1782), in 1 The Writings of James Madison 226 (1900); accord, The Federalist No. 42, pp. 269–271 (C. Rossiter ed. 1961) (J. Madison). The Articles of

Confederation had provided that "the free inhabitants of each of these States, paupers, vagabonds and fugitives from justice excepted, shall be entitled to all privileges and immunities of free citizens in the several States." Articles of Confederation, Art. IV. This meant that an unwelcome alien could obtain all the rights of a citizen of one State simply by first becoming an inhabitant of another. To remedy this, the Constitution's Privileges and Immunities Clause provided that "[t]he Citizens of each State shall be entitled to all Privileges and Immunities of Citizens in the several States." Art. IV, §2, cl. 1 (emphasis added). Butif one State had particularly lax citizenship standards, it might still serve as a gateway for the entry of "obnoxious aliens" into other States. This problem was solved "by authorizing the general government to establish a uniform rule of naturalization throughout the United States." The Federalist No. 42, supra, at 271; see Art. I, §8, cl. 4. In other words, the naturalization power was given to Congress not to abrogate States' power to exclude those they did not want, but to vindicate it.

Two other provisions of the Constitution are an acknowledgment of the States' sovereign interest in protecting their borders. Article I provides that "[n]o State shall, without the Consent of the Congress, lay any Imposts or Duties on Imports or Exports, except what may be absolutely necessary for executing it's inspection Laws." Art. I, §10, cl. 2 (emphasis added). This assumed what everyone assumed: that the States could exclude from their territory dangerous or unwholesome goods. A later portion of the same section provides that "[n]o State shall, without the Consent of Congress, . . . engage in War, unless actually invaded, or in such imminent Danger as will not admit of delay." Art. I, §10, cl. 3 (emphasis added). This limits the States' sovereignty (in a way not relevant here) but leaves intact their inherent power to protect their territory.

Notwithstanding "[t]he myth of an era of unrestricted immigration" in the first 100 years of the Republic, the States enacted numerous laws restricting the immigration of certain classes of aliens, including convicted criminals, indigents, persons with contagious diseases, and (in Southern States) freed blacks. Neuman, The Lost Century of American Immigration (1776–1875), 93 Colum. L. Rev. 1833, 1835, 1841–1880 (1993). State laws not only pro-vided for the removal of unwanted immigrants but also imposed penalties on unlawfully present aliens and those who aided their immigration. 2 Id., at 1883.

In fact, the controversy surrounding the Alien and Sedition Acts involved a debate over whether, under the Constitution, the States had exclusive authority to enact such immigration laws. Criticism of the Sedition Act has become a prominent feature of our First Amendment jurisprudence, see, e.g., New York Times Co. v. Sullivan, 376 U. S. 254–276 (1964), but one of the Alien Acts 3 also aroused controversy at the time:

"Be it enacted by the Senate and House of Representatives of the United States of America in Congress assembled, That it shall be lawful for the President of the United States at any time during the continuance of this act, to order all such aliens as he shall judge dangerous to the peace and safety of the United States, or shall have reasonable grounds to suspect are concerned in any treasonable or secret machinations against the government thereof, to depart out of the territory of the United States . . . ." An Act concerning Aliens, 1Stat. 570, 570–571.

The Kentucky and Virginia Resolutions, written in denunciation of these Acts, insisted that the power to exclude unwanted aliens rested solely in the States. Jefferson's Kentucky Resolutions insisted "that alien friends are under the jurisdiction and protection of the laws of the state wherein they are [and] that no power over them has been delegated to the United States, nor prohibited to the individual states, distinct from their power over citizens." Kentucky Resolutions of 1798, reprinted in J. Powell, Languages of Power: A Sourcebook of Early American Constitutional History 131 (1991). Madison's Virginia Resolutions likewise contended that the Alien Act purported to give the President "a power nowhere delegated to the federal government." Virginia Resolutions of 1798, reprinted in Powell, supra, at 134 (emphasis omitted). Notably, moreover, the Federalist proponents of the Act defended it primarily on the ground that "[t]he removal of aliens is the usual preliminary of hostility" and could therefore be justified in exercise of the Federal Government's war powers. Massachussets Resolutions in Reply to Virginia, reprinted in Powell, supra, at 136.

In Mayor of New York v. Miln, this Court considered a New York statute that required the commander of any ship arriving in New York from abroad to disclose "the name, place of birth, and last legal settlement, age and occupation . . . of all passengers . . . with the intention of proceeding to the said city." 11 Pet., at 130–131. After discussing the sovereign authority to regulate the entrance of foreigners described by De Vattel, the Court said:

"The power . . . of New York to pass this law having undeniably existed at the formation of the constitution, the simply inquiry is, whether by that instrument it was taken from the states, and granted to congress; for if it were not, it yet remains with them." Id., at 132.

And the Court held that it remains. Id., at 139.

II

One would conclude from the foregoing that after the adoption of the Constitution there was some doubt about the power of the Federal Government to control immigration, but no doubt about the power of the States to do so. Since the founding era (though not immediately), doubt about the Federal Government's power has disappeared. Indeed, primary responsibility for immigration policy has shifted from the States to the Federal Government. Congress exercised its power "[t]o establish an uniform Rule of Naturalization," Art. I, §8, cl. 4, very early on, see An Act to establish an uniform Rule of Naturalization, 1Stat. 103. But with the fleeting exception of the Alien Act, Congress did not enact any legislation regulating immigration for the better part of a century. In 1862, Congress passed "An Act to prohibit the 'Coolie Trade' by American Citizens in American Vessels," which prohibited "procuring [Chinese nationals] . . . to be disposed of, or sold, or transferred, for any term of years or for any time what-ever, as servants or apprentices, or to be held to service or labor." 12Stat. 340. Then, in 1875, Congress amended that act to bar admission to Chinese, Japanese, and other Asian immigrants who had "entered into a contract or agreement for a term of service within the United States, for lewd and immoral purposes." An act supplementary to the acts in relation to immigration, ch. 141, 18Stat. 477. And in 1882, Congress enacted the first general immi-gration statute. See An act to regulate Immigration, 22Stat. 214. Of course, it hardly bears mention that Federal immigration law is now extensive.

I accept that as a valid exercise of federal power—not because of the Naturalization Clause (it has no necessary connection to citizenship) but because it is an inherent attribute of sovereignty no less for the United States than for the States. As this Court has said, it is an " 'accepted maxim of international law, that every sovereign nation has the power, as inherent in sovereignty, and essential to self-preservation, to forbid the entrance of foreigners within its dominions.' " Fong Yue Ting v. United States, 149 U. S. 698, 705 (1893) (quoting Ekiu v. United States, 142 U. S. 651, 659 (1892)). That is why there was no need to set forth control of immigration as one of the enumerated powers of Congress, although an acknowledgment of that power (as well as of the States' similar power, subject to federal abridgment) was contained in Art. I, §9, which provided that "[t]he Migration or Importation of such Persons as any of the States now existing shall think proper to admit, shall not be prohibited by the Congress prior to the Year one thousand eight hundred and eight . . . ."

In light of the predominance of federal immigration restrictions in modern times, it is easy to lose sight of the States' traditional role in regulating immigration—and to overlook their sovereign prerogative to do so. I accept as a given that State regulation is excluded by the Constitution when (1) it has been prohibited by a valid federal law, or (2) it conflicts with federal regulation—when, for example, it admits those whom federal regulation would exclude, or excludes those whom federal regulation would admit.

Possibility (1) need not be considered here: there is no federal law prohibiting the States' sovereign power to exclude (assuming federal authority to enact such a law). The mere existence of federal action in the immigration area—and the so-called field preemption arising from that action, upon which the Court's opinion so heavily relies, ante, at 9–11—cannot be regarded as such a prohibition. We are not talking here about a federal law prohibiting the States from regulating bubble-gum advertising, or even the construction of nuclear plants. We are talking about a federal law going to the core of state sovereignty: the power to exclude. Like elimination of the States' other inherent sovereign power, immunity from suit, elimination of the States' sovereign power to exclude requires that "Congress . . . unequivocally expres[s] its intent to abrogate," Seminole Tribe of Fla. v. Florida, 517 U. S. 44, 55 (1996) (internal quotation marks and citation omitted). Implicit "field preemption" will not do.

Nor can federal power over illegal immigration be deemed exclusive because of what the Court's opinion solicitously calls "foreign countries['] concern[s] about the status, safety, and security of their nationals in the United States," ante, at 3. The Constitution gives all those on our shores the protections of the Bill of Rights—but just as those rights are not expanded for foreign nationals because of their countries' views (some countries, for example, have recently discovered the death penalty to be barbaric), neither are the fundamental sovereign powers of the States abridged to accommodate foreign countries' views. Even in its international relations, the Federal Government must live with the inconvenient fact that it is a Union of independent States, who have their own sovereign powers. This is not the first time it has found that a nuisance and a bother in the conduct of foreign policy. Four years ago, for example, the Government importuned us to interfere with thoroughly constitutional state judicial procedures in the criminal trial of foreign nationals because the international community, and even an opinion of the International Court of Justice, disapproved them. See Medellín v. Texas, 552 U. S. 491 (2008) . We rejected that request, as we should reject the Executive's invocation of foreign-affairs considerations here. Though it may upset foreign powers—and even when the Federal Government desperately wants to avoid upsetting foreign powers—the States have the right to protect their borders against foreign nationals, just as they have the right to execute foreign nationals for murder.

What this case comes down to, then, is whether the Arizona law conflicts with federal immigration law—whether it excludes those whom federal law would admit, or admits those whom federal law would exclude. It does not purport to do so. It applies only to aliens who neither possess a privilege to be present under federal law nor have been removed pursuant to the Federal Government's inherent authority. I proceed to consider the challenged provisions in detail.

§2(B)

"For any lawful stop, detention or arrest made by a law enforcement official . . . in the enforcement of any other law or ordinance of a county, city or town or this state where reasonable suspicion exists that the person is an alien and is unlawfully present in the United States, a reasonable attempt shall be made, when practicable, to determine the immigration status of the person, except if the determination may hinder or obstruct an investigation. Any person who is arrested shall have the person's immigration status determined before the person is released. . . ." S. B. 1070, §2(B), as amended, Ariz. Rev. Stat. Ann. §11–1051(B) (West 2012).

The Government has conceded that "even before Section 2 was enacted, state and local officers had state-law authority to inquire of DHS [the Department of Homeland Security] about a suspect's unlawful status and other-wise cooperate with federal immigration officers." Brief for United States 47 (citing App. 62, 82); see also Brief for United States 48–49. That concession, in my view, obviates the need for further inquiry. The Government's conflict-pre-emption claim calls on us "to determine whether, under the circumstances of this particular case, [the State's] law stands as an obstacle to the accomplishment and execution of the full purposes and objectives of Congress." Hines v. Davidowitz, 312 U. S. 52, 67 (1941) (emphasis added). It is impossible to make such a finding without a factual record concerning the manner in which Arizona is implementing these provisions—something the Government's pre-enforcement challenge has pretermitted. "The fact that [a law] might operate unconstitutionally under some conceivable set of circumstances is insufficient to render it wholly invalid, since we have not recognized an 'overbreadth' doctrine outside the limited context of the First Amendment." United States v. Salerno, 481 U. S. 739, 745 (1987) . And on its face, §2(B) merely tells state officials that they are authorized to do something that they were, by the Government's con-cession, already authorized to do.

The Court therefore properly rejects the Government's challenge, recognizing that, "[a]t this stage, without the benefit of a definitive interpretation from the state courts, it would be inappropriate to assume §2B will be construed in a way that creates a conflict with federal law." Ante, at 23. Before reaching that conclusion, however, the Court goes to great length to assuage fears that "state officers will be required to delay the release of some detainees for no reason other than to verify their immigration status." Ante, at 22. Of course, any investigatory detention, including one under §2(B), may become an "unreasonable . . . seizur[e]," U. S. Const., Amdt. IV, if it lasts too long. See Illinois v. Caballes, 543 U. S. 405, 407 (2005) . But that has nothing to do with this case, in which the Government claims that §2(B) is pre-empted by federal immigration law, not that anyone's Fourth Amendment rights have been violated. And I know of no reason why aprotracted detention that does not violate the Fourth Amendment would contradict or conflict with any federal immigration law.

§6

"A peace officer, without a warrant, may arrest a person if the officer has probable cause to believe . . . [t]he person to be arrested has committed any public offense that makes the person removable from the United States." S. B. 1070, §6(A)(5), Ariz. Rev. Stat. Ann. §13–3883(A)(5) (West Supp. 2011).

This provision of S. B. 1070 expands the statutory list of offenses for which an Arizona police officer may make an arrest without a warrant. See §13–3883. If an officer has probable cause to believe that an individual is "removable" by reason of a public offense, then a warrant is not required to make an arrest. The Government's primary contention is that §6 is pre-empted by federal immigration law because it allows state officials to make arrests "without regard to federal priorities." Brief for United States 53. The Court's opinion focuses on limits that Congress has placed on federal officials' authority to arrest removable aliens and the possibility that state officials will make arrests "to achieve [Arizona's] own immigration policy" and "without any input from the Federal Government." Ante, at 17.

Of course on this pre-enforcement record there is no reason to assume that Arizona officials will ignore federal immigration policy (unless it be the questionable policy of not wanting to identify illegal aliens who have committed offenses that make them removable). As Arizona points out, federal law expressly provides that state officers may "cooperate with the Attorney General in the identification, apprehension, detention, or removal of aliens not lawfully present in the United States," 8 U. S. C. §1357(g)(10)(B); and "cooperation" requires neither identical efforts nor prior federal approval. It is consistent with the Arizona statute, and with the "cooperat[ive]" system that Congress has created, for state officials to arrest a removable alien, contact federal immigration authorities, and follow their lead on what to do next. And it is an assault on logic to say that identifying a removable alien and holding him for federal determination of whether he should be removed "violates the principle that the removal process is entrusted to the discretion of the Federal Government," ante, at18. The State's detention does not represent commencement of the removal process unless the Federal Government makes it so.

But that is not the most important point. The most important point is that, as we have discussed, Arizona is entitled to have "its own immigration policy"—including a more rigorous enforcement policy—so long as that does not conflict with federal law. The Court says, as though the point is utterly dispositive, that "it is not a crime for a removable alien to remain present in the United States," ante, at 15. It is not a federal crime, to be sure. But there is no reason Arizona cannot make it a state crime for a removable alien (or any illegal alien, for that matter) to remain present in Arizona.

The Court quotes 8 U. S. C. §1226(a), which provides that, "[o]n a warrant issued by the Attorney General, an alien may be arrested and detained pending a decision on whether the alien is to be removed from the United States." Section 1357(a)(2) also provides that a federal immigration official "shall have power without warrant . . . to arrest any alien in the United States, if he has reason to believe that the alien so arrested is in the United States in violation of any [federal immigration] law or regulation and is likely to escape before a warrant can be obtained for his arrest." But statutory limitations upon the actions of federal officers in enforcing the United States' power to protect its borders do not on their face apply to the actions of state officers in enforcing the State's power to protect its borders. There is no more reason to read these provisions as implying that state officials are subject to similar limitations than there is to read them as implying that only federal officials may arrest removable aliens. And in any event neither implication would constitute the sort of clear elimination of the States' sovereign power that our cases demand.

The Court raises concerns about "unnecessary harassment of some aliens . . . whom federal officials determine should not be removed." Ante, at 17. But we have no license to assume, without any support in the record, that Arizona officials would use their arrest authority under §6 to harass anyone. And it makes no difference that federal officials might "determine [that some unlawfully present aliens] should not be removed," ibid. They may well determine not to remove from the United States aliens who have no right to be here; but unless and until these aliens have been given the right to remain, Arizona is entitled to arrest them and at least bring them to federal officials' attention, which is all that §6 necessarily entails. (In my view, the State can go further than this, and punish them for their unlawful entry and presence in Arizona.)

The Government complains that state officials might not heed "federal priorities." Indeed they might not, particularly if those priorities include willful blindness or deliberate inattention to the presence of removable aliens in Arizona. The State's whole complaint—the reason this law was passed and this case has arisen—is that the citizens of Arizona believe federal priorities are too lax. The State has the sovereign power to protect its borders more rigorously if it wishes, absent any valid federal prohibition. The Executive's policy choice of lax federal enforcement does not constitute such a prohibition.

§3

"In addition to any violation of federal law, a person is guilty of willful failure to complete or carry an alien registration document if the person is in violation of 8 [U. S. C.] §1304(e) or §1306(a)." S. B. 1070, §3(A), as amended, Ariz. Rev. Stat. Ann. §13–1509(A).

It is beyond question that a State may make violation of federal law a violation of state law as well. We have held that to be so even when the interest protected is a distinctively federal interest, such as protection of the dignity of the national flag, see Halter v. Nebraska, 205 U. S. 34 (1907), or protection of the Federal Government's ability to recruit soldiers, Gilbert v. Minnesota, 254 U. S. 325 (1920) . "[T]he State is not inhibited from making the national purposes its own purposes to the extent of exerting its police power to prevent its own citizens from obstructing the accomplishment of such purposes." Id., at 331 (internal quotation marks omitted). Much more is that so when, as here, the State is protecting its own interest, the integrity of its borders. And we have said that explicitly with regard to illegal immigration: "Despite the exclusive federal control of this Nation's borders, we cannot conclude that the States are without any power to deter the influx of persons entering the United States against federal law, and whose numbers might have a discernible impact on traditional state concerns." Plyler v. Doe, 457 U. S. 202, n. 23 (1982).

The Court's opinion relies upon Hines v. Davidowitz, supra. Ante, at 9–10. But that case did not, as the Court believes, establish a "field preemption" that implicitly eliminates the States' sovereign power to exclude those whom federal law excludes. It held that the States are not permitted to establish "additional or auxiliary" registration requirements for aliens. 312 U. S., at 66–67. But §3 does not establish additional or auxiliary registration requirements. It merely makes a violation of state law the very same failure to register and failure to carry evidence of registration that are violations of federal law. Hines does not prevent the State from relying on the federal registration system as "an available aid in the enforcement of a number of statutes of the state applicable to aliens whose constitutional validity has not been questioned." Id., at 75–76 (Stone, J., dissenting). One such statute is Arizona's law forbidding illegal aliens to collect unemployment benefits, Ariz. Rev. Stat. Ann. §23–781(B) (West 2012). To enforce that and other laws that validly turn on alien status, Arizona has, in Justice Stone's words, an interest in knowing "the number and whereabouts of aliens within the state" and in having "a means of their identification," 312 U. S., at 75. And it can punish the aliens' failure to comply with the provisions of federal law that make that knowledge and identification possible.

In some areas of uniquely federal concern—e.g., fraud in a federal administrative process (Buckman Co. v. Plaintiffs' Legal Comm., 531 U. S. 341 (2001)) or perjury in violation of a federally required oath (In re Loney, 134 U. S. 372 (1890))—this Court has held that a State has no legitimate interest in enforcing a federal scheme. But the federal alien registration system is certainly not of uniquely federal interest. States, private entities, and individuals rely on the federal registration system (including the E-Verify program) on a regular basis. Arizona's legitimate interest in protecting (among other things) its unemployment-benefits system is an entirely adequate basis for making the violation of federal registration and carry requirements a violation of state law as well.

The Court points out, however, ante, at 11, that in some respects the state law exceeds the punishments prescribed by federal law: It rules out probation and pardon, which are available under federal law. The answer is that it makes no difference. Illegal immigrants who violate §3 violate Arizona law. It is one thing to say that the Supremacy Clause prevents Arizona law from excluding those whom federal law admits. It is quite something else to say that a violation of Arizona law cannot be punished more severely than a violation of federal law. Especially where (as here) the State is defending its own sovereign interests, there is no precedent for such a limitation. The sale of illegal drugs, for example, ordinarily violates state law as well as federal law, and no one thinks that the state penalties cannot exceed the federal. As I have discussed, moreover, "field preemption" cannot establish a prohibition of additional state penalties in the area of immigration.

Finally, the Government also suggests that §3 poses an obstacle to the administration of federal immigration law, see Brief for United States 31–33, but "there is no conflict in terms, and no possibility of such conflict, [if] the state statute makes federal law its own," California v. Zook, 336 U. S. 725, 735 (1949) .

It holds no fear for me, as it does for the Court, that "[w]ere §3 to come into force, the State would have the power to bring criminal charges against individuals for violating a federal law even in circumstances where federal officials in charge of the comprehensive scheme determine that prosecution would frustrate federal policies." Ante, at 11. That seems to me entirely appropriate when the State uses the federal law (as it must) as the criterion for the exercise of its own power, and the implementation of its own policies of excluding those who do not belong there. What I do fear—and what Arizona and the States that support it fear—is that "federal policies" of nonenforcement will leave the States helpless before those evil effects of illegal immigration that the Court's opinion dutifully recites in its prologue (ante, at 6) but leaves unremedied in its disposition.

§5(C)

"It is unlawful for a person who is unlawfully present in the United States and who is an unauthorized alien to knowingly apply for work, solicit work in a public place or perform work as an employee or independent contractor in this state." S. B. 1070, §5(C), as amended, Ariz. Rev. Stat. Ann. §13–2928(C).

Here, the Court rightly starts with De Canas v. Bica, 424 U. S. 351 (1976), which involved a California law providing that " '[n]o employer shall knowingly employ an alien who is not entitled to lawful residence in the United States if such employment would have an adverse effect on lawful resident workers.' " Id., at 352 (quoting California Labor Code Ann. §2805(a)). This Court concluded that the California law was not pre-empted, as Congress had neither occupied the field of "regulation of employment of illegal aliens" nor expressed "the clear and manifest purpose" of displacing such state regulation. Id., at 356–357 (internal quotation marks omitted). Thus, at the time De Canas was decided, §5(C) would have been indubitably lawful.

The only relevant change is that Congress has since enacted its own restrictions on employers who hire illegal aliens, 8 U. S. C. §1324a, in legislation that also includes some civil (but no criminal) penalties on illegal aliens who accept unlawful employment. The Court concludes from this (reasonably enough) "that Congress made a deliberate choice not to impose criminal penalties on aliens who seek, or engage in, unauthorized employment," ante, at 13. But that is not the same as a deliberate choice to prohibit the States from imposing criminal penalties. Congress's intent with regard to exclusion of state law need not be guessed at, but is found in the law's express pre-emption provision, which excludes "any State or local law impos-ing civil or criminal sanctions (other than through licensing and similar laws) upon those who employ, or recruit or refer for a fee for employment, unauthorized aliens," §1324a(h)(2) (emphasis added). Common sense, reflected in the canon *expressio unius est exclusio alterius*, suggests that the specification of pre-emption for laws punishing "those who employ" implies the lack of pre-emption for other laws, including laws punishing "those who seek or accept employment."

The Court has no credible response to this. It quotes our jurisprudence to the effect that an "express pre-emption provisio[n] does not bar the ordinary working of conflict pre-emption principles." Ante, at 14 (quoting Geier v. American Honda Motor Co., 529 U. S. 861(2000) (internal quotation marks omitted)). True enough—conflict preemption principles. It then goes on say that since "Congress decided it would be inappropriate to impose criminal penalties on aliens who seek or engage in unauthorized employment," "[i]t follows that a state law to the contrary is an obstacle to the regulatory system Congress chose." Ante, at 15. For " '[w]here a comprehensive federal scheme intentionally leaves a portion of the regulated field without controls, then the pre-emptive inference can be drawn.' " Ibid. (quoting Puerto Rico Dept. of Consumer Affairs v. ISLA Petroleum Corp., 485 U.S. 495, 503 (1988)). All that is a classic description not of conflict pre-emption but of field pre-emption, which (concededly) does not occur beyond the terms of an express pre-emption provision.

The Court concludes that §5(C) "would interfere with the careful balance struck by Congress," ante, at 15, (another field pre-emption notion, by the way) but that is easy to say and impossible to demonstrate. The Court relies primarily on the fact that "[p]roposals to make unauthorized work a criminal offense were debated and discussed during the long process of drafting [the Immigration Reform and Control Act of 1986 (IRCA)]," "[b]ut Congress rejected them." Ante, at 14. There is no more reason to believe that this rejection was expressive of a desire that there be no sanctions on employees, than expressive of a desire that such sanctions be left to the States. To tell the truth, it was most likely expressive of what inaction ordinarily expresses: nothing at all. It is a "naïve assumption that the failure of a bill to make it out of committee, or to be adopted when reported to the floor, is the same as a congressional rejection of what the bill contained." Crosby v. National Foreign Trade Council, 530 U. S. 363, 389 (2000) (Scalia, J., concurring in judgment) (internal quotation marks and alterations omitted).

* * *

The brief for the Government in this case asserted that "the Executive Branch's ability to exercise discretion and set priorities is particularly important because of the need to allocate scarce enforcement resources wisely." Brief for United States 21. Of course there is no reason why the Federal Executive's need to allocate its scarce enforcement resources should disable Arizona from devoting its resources to illegal immigration in Arizona that in its view the Federal Executive has given short shrift. Despite Congress's prescription that "the immigration laws of the United States should be enforced vigorously and uniformly," IRCA §115, 100Stat. 3384, Arizona asserts without contradiction and with supporting citations:

"[I]n the last decade federal enforcement efforts have focused primarily on areas in California and Texas, leaving Arizona's border to suffer from comparative neglect. The result has been the funneling of an increasing tide of illegal border crossings into Arizona. Indeed, over the past decade, over a third of the Nation's illegal border crossings occurred in Arizona." Brief for Petitioners 2–3 (footnote omitted).

Must Arizona's ability to protect its borders yield to the reality that Congress has provided inadequate funding for federal enforcement—or, even worse, to the Executive's unwise targeting of that funding?

But leave that aside. It has become clear that federal enforcement priorities—in the sense of priorities based on the need to allocate "scarce enforcement resources"—is not the problem here. After this case was argued and while it was under consideration, the Secretary of Homeland Security announced a program exempting from immigration enforcement some 1.4 million illegal immigrants under the age of 30. 4 If an individual unlawfully present in the United States

"• came to the United States under the age of sixteen;

"• has continuously resided in the United States for at least five years . . .,

"• is currently in school, has graduated from high school, has obtained a general education development certificate, or is an honorably discharged veteran . . .,

"• has not been convicted of a [serious crime]; and

"• is not above the age of thirty," 5

then U. S. immigration officials have been directed to "defe[r] action" against such individual "for a period of two years, subject to renewal." 6 The husbanding of scarce enforcement resources can hardly be the justification for this, since the considerable administrative cost of conducting as many as 1.4 million background checks, and ruling on the biennial requests for dispensation that the nonenforcement program envisions, will necessarily be deducted from immigration enforcement. The President said at a news conference that the new program is "the right thing to do" in light of Congress's failure to pass the Administration's proposed revision of the Immigration Act. 7 Perhaps it is, though Arizona may not think so. But to say, as the Court does, that Arizona contradicts federal law by enforcing applications of the Immigration Act that the President declines to enforce boggles the mind.

The Court opinion's looming specter of inutterable horror—"[i]f §3 of the Arizona statute were valid, every State could give itself independent authority to prosecute federal registration violations," ante, at 10—seems to me not so horrible and even less looming. But there has come to pass, and is with us today, the specter that Arizona and the States that support it predicted: A Federal Government that does not want to enforce the immigration laws as written, and leaves the States' borders unprotected against immigrants whom those laws would exclude. So the issue is a stark one. Are the sovereign States at the mercy of the Federal Executive's refusal to enforce the Nation's immigration laws?

A good way of answering that question is to ask: Would the States conceivably have entered into the Union if the Constitution itself contained the Court's holding? Today's judgment surely fails that test. At the Constitutional Convention of 1787, the delegates contended with "the jealousy of the states with regard to their sovereignty." 1 Records of the Federal Convention 19 (M. Farrand ed. 1911) (statement of Edmund Randolph). Through ratification of the fundamental charter that the Convention produced, the States ceded much of their sovereignty to the Federal Government. But much of it remained jealously guarded—as reflected in the innumerable proposals that never left Independence Hall. Now, imagine a provision—perhaps inserted right after Art. I, §8, cl. 4, the Naturalization Clause—which included among the enumerated powers of Congress "To establish Limitations upon Immigration that will be exclusive and that will be enforced only to the extent the President deems appropriate." The delegates to the Grand Convention would have rushed to the exits.

As is often the case, discussion of the dry legalities that are the proper object of our attention suppresses the very human realities that gave rise to the suit. Arizona bears the brunt of the country's illegal immigration problem. Its citizens feel themselves under siege by large numbers of illegal immigrants who invade their property, strain their social services, and even place their lives in jeopardy. Federal officials have been unable to remedy the problem, and indeed have recently shown that they are unwilling to do so. Thousands of Arizona's estimated 400,000 illegal immigrants—including not just children but men and women under 30—are now assured immunity from enforcement, and will be able to compete openly with Ari-zona citizens for employment.

Arizona has moved to protect its sovereignty—not in contradiction of federal law, but in complete compliance with it. The laws under challenge here do not extend or revise federal immigration restrictions, but merely enforce those restrictions more effectively. If securing its territory in this fashion is not within the power of Arizona, we should cease referring to it as a sovereign State. I dissent.

Notes to Justice Scalia's dissent in Arizona v. United States (June 25, 2012)

1 Many of the 17th-, 18th-, and 19th-century commentators maintained that states should exclude foreigners only for good reason. Pufendorf, for example, maintained that states are generally expected to grant "permanent settlement to strangers who have been driven from their former home," though acknowledging that, when faced with the prospect of mass immigration, "every state may decide after its own custom what privilege should be granted in such a situation." 2 Of the Law of Nature and Nations, bk. III, ch. III, §10, p. 366 (C. Oldfather & W. Oldfather eds. 1934). See generally Cleveland, Powers Inherent in Sovereignty: Indians, Aliens, Territories, and the Nineteenth Century Origins of Plenary Power over Foreign Affairs, 81 Tex. L. Rev. 1, 83–87 (2002). But the authority to exclude was universally accepted as inherent in sovereignty, whatever prudential limitations there might be on its exercise.

2 E.g., Va. Code Tit. 54, ch. 198, §39 (1849) ("If a master of a vessel or other person, knowingly, import or bring into this state, from any place out of the United States, any person convicted of crime . . . he shall be confined in jail for three months, and be fined one hundred dollars").

3 There were two Alien Acts, one of which dealt only with enemy aliens. An Act respecting Alien Enemies, 1Stat. 577.

4 Preston & Cushman, Obama to Permit Young Migrants to Remain in U. S., N. Y. Times, June 16, 2012, p. A1.

5 Memorandum from Janet Napolitano, Secretary of Homeland Security, to David V. Aguilar, Acting Commissioner, U. S. Customs and Border Protection; Alejandro Mayorkas, Director, U. S. Citizenship and Immigration Services; and John Morton, Director, U. S. Immigration and Customs Enforcement, p. 1 (June 15, 2012), online at http://www.dhs.gov (all Internet materials as visited June 22, 2012, and available in Clerk of Court's case file).

6 Id., at 2.

7 Remarks by the President on Immigration (June 15, 2012), online at http://www.whitehouse.gov.

Mandatory Health Insurance: Justice Scalia's (or Justice Kennedy's?) dissent in National Federation of Independent Business v. Sebelius (June 28, 2012)

Justice Scalia, Justice Kennedy, Justice Thomas, and Justice Alito, dissenting.

Congress has set out to remedy the problem that the best health care is beyond the reach of many Americans who cannot afford it. It can assuredly do that, by exercising the powers accorded to it under the Constitution. The question in this case, however, is whether the complex structures and provisions of the Patient Protection and Affordable Care Act (Affordable Care Act or ACA) go beyond those powers. We conclude that they do.

This case is in one respect difficult: it presents two questions of first impression. The first of those is whether failure to engage in economic activity (the purchase of health insurance) is subject to regulation under the Commerce Clause. Failure to act does result in an effect on commerce, and hence might be said to come under this Court's "affecting commerce" criterion of Commerce Clause jurisprudence. But in none of its decisions has this Court extended the Clause that far. The second question is whether the congressional power to tax and spend, U. S. Const., Art. I, §8, cl. 1, permits the conditioning of a State's continued receipt of all funds under a massive state-administered federal welfare program upon its acceptance of an expansion to that program. Several of our opinions have suggested that the power to tax and spend cannot be used to coerce state administration of a federal program, but we have never found a law enacted under the spending power to be coercive. Those questions are difficult.

The case is easy and straightforward, however, in another respect. What is absolutely clear, affirmed by the text of the 1789 Constitution, by the Tenth Amendment ratified in 1791, and by innumerable cases of ours in the 220 years since, is that there are structural limits upon federal power—upon what it can prescribe with respect to private conduct, and upon what it can impose upon the sovereign States. Whatever may be the conceptual limits upon the Commerce Clause and upon the power to tax and spend, they cannot be such as will enable the Federal Government to regulate all private conduct and to compel the States to function as administrators of federal programs.

That clear principle carries the day here. The striking case of Wickard v. Filburn, 317 U. S. 111 (1942), which held that the economic activity of growing wheat, even for one's own consumption, affected commerce sufficiently that it could be regulated, always has been regarded as the ne plus ultra of expansive Commerce Clause jurisprudence. To go beyond that, and to say the failure to grow wheat (which is not an economic activity, or any activity at all) nonetheless affects commerce and therefore can be federally regulated, is to make mere breathing in and out the basis for federal prescription and to extend federal power to virtually all human activity.

As for the constitutional power to tax and spend for the general welfare: The Court has long since expanded that beyond (what Madison thought it meant) taxing and spending for those aspects of the general welfare that were within the Federal Government's enumerated powers, see United States v. Butler, 297 U. S. 1–66 (1936).

Thus, we now have sizable federal Departments devoted to subjects not mentioned among Congress' enumerated powers, and only marginally related to commerce: the Department of Education, the Department of Health and Human Services, the Department of Housing and Urban Development. The principal practical obstacle that prevents Congress from using the tax-and-spend power to assume all the general-welfare responsibilities traditionally exercised by the States is the sheer impossibility of managing a Federal Government large enough to administer such a system. That obstacle can be overcome by granting funds to the States, allowing them to administer the program. That is fair and constitutional enough when the States freely agree to have their powers employed and their employees enlisted in the federal scheme. But it is a blatant violation of the constitutional structure when the States have no choice.

The Act before us here exceeds federal power both in mandating the purchase of health insurance and in denying nonconsenting States all Medicaid funding. These parts of the Act are central to its design and operation, and all the Act's other provisions would not have been enacted without them. In our view it must follow that the entire statute is inoperative.

I

The Individual Mandate

Article I, §8, of the Constitution gives Congress the power to "regulate Commerce . . . among the several States." The Individual Mandate in the Act commands that every "applicable individual shall for each month beginning after 2013 ensure that the individual, and any dependent of the individual who is an applicable individual, is covered under minimum essential coverage." 26 U. S. C. §5000A(a) (2006 ed., Supp. IV). If this provision "regulates" anything, it is the failure to maintain minimum essential coverage. One might argue that it regulates that failure by requiring it to be accompanied by payment of a penalty. But that failure—that abstention from commerce—is not "Commerce." To be sure, purchasing insurance is "Commerce"; but one does not regulate commerce that does not exist by compelling its existence.

In Gibbons v. Ogden, 9 Wheat. 1, 196 (1824), Chief Justice Marshall wrote that the power to regulate commerce is the power "to prescribe the rule by which commerce is to be governed." That understanding is consistent with the original meaning of "regulate" at the time of the Constitution's ratification, when "to regulate" meant "[t]o adjust by rule, method or established mode," 2 N. Webster, An American Dictionary of the English Language (1828); "[t]o adjust by rule or method," 2 S. Johnson, A Dictionary of the English Language (7th ed. 1785); "[t]o adjust, to direct according to rule," 2 J. Ash, New and Complete Dictionary of the English Language (1775); "to put in order, set to rights, govern or keep in order," T. Dyche & W. Pardon, A New General English Dictionary

(16th ed. 1777). 1 It can mean to direct the manner of something but not to direct that something come into being. There is no instance in which this Court or Congress (or anyone else, to our knowledge) has used "regulate" in that peculiar fashion. If the word bore that meaning, Congress' authority "[t]o make Rules for the Government and

Regulation of the land and naval Forces," U. S. Const., Art. I, §8, cl. 14, would have made superfluous the later provision for authority "[t]o raise and support Armies," id., §8, cl. 12, and "[t]o provide and maintain a Navy," id., §8, cl. 13.

We do not doubt that the buying and selling of health insurance contracts is commerce generally subject to federal regulation. But when Congress provides that (nearly) all citizens must buy an insurance contract, it goes beyond "adjust[ing] by rule or method," Johnson, supra, or "direct[ing] according to rule," Ash, supra; it directs the creation of commerce.

In response, the Government offers two theories as to why the Individual Mandate is nevertheless constitutional. Neither theory suffices to sustain its validity.

A

First, the Government submits that §5000A is "integral to the Affordable Care Act's insurance reforms" and "necessary to make effective the Act's core reforms." Brief for Petitioners in No. 11–398 (Minimum Coverage Provision) 24 (hereinafter Petitioners' Minimum Coverage Brief). Congress included a "finding" to similar effect in the Act itself. See 42 U. S. C. §18091(2)(H).

As discussed in more detail in Part V, infra, the Act contains numerous health insurance reforms, but most notable for present purposes are the "guaranteed issue" and "community rating" provisions, §§300gg to 300gg–4. The former provides that, with a few exceptions, "each health insurance issuer that offers health insurance coverage in the individual or group market in a State must accept every employer and individual in the State that applies for such coverage." §300gg–1(a). That is, an insurer may not deny coverage on the basis of, among other things, any pre-existing medical condition that the applicant may have, and the resulting insurance must cover that condition. See §300gg–3.

Under ordinary circumstances, of course, insurers would respond by charging high premiums to individuals with pre-existing conditions. The Act seeks to prevent this through the community-rating provision. Simply put, the community-rating provision requires insurers to calculate an individual's insurance premium based on only four factors: (i) whether the individual's plan covers just the individual or his family also, (ii) the "rating area" in which the individual lives, (iii) the individual's age, and (iv) whether the individual uses tobacco. §300gg(a)(1)(A). Aside from the rough proxies of age and tobacco use (and possibly rating area), the Act does not allow an insurer to factor the individual's health characteristics into the price of his insurance premium. This creates a new incentive for young and healthy individuals without pre-existing conditions. The insurance premiums for those in this group will not reflect their own low actuarial risks but will subsidize insurance for others in the pool. Many of them may decide that purchasing health insurance is not an economically sound decision—especially since the guaranteed-issue provision will enable them to purchase it at the same cost in later years and even if they have developed a pre-existing condition. But without the contribution of above-risk premiums from the young and healthy, the community-rating provision will not enable insurers to take on high-risk individuals without a massive increase in premiums.

The Government presents the Individual Mandate as a unique feature of a complicated regulatory scheme governing many parties with countervailing incentives that must be carefully balanced. Congress has imposed an extensive set of regulations on the health insurance industry, and compliance with those regulations will likely cost the industry a great deal. If the industry does not respond by increasing premiums, it is not likely to survive. And if the industry does increase premiums, then there is a serious risk that its products—insurance plans—will become economically undesirable for many and prohibitively ex-pensive for the rest.

This is not a dilemma unique to regulation of the health-insurance industry. Government regulation typically imposes costs on the regulated industry—especially regulation that prohibits economic behavior in which most market participants are already engaging, such as "piecing out" the market by selling the product to different classes of people at different prices (in the present context, providing much lower insurance rates to young and healthy buyers). And many industries so regulated face the reality that, without an artificial increase in demand, they cannot continue on. When Congress is regulating these industries directly, it enjoys the broad power to enact " 'all appropriate legislation' " to " 'protec[t]' " and " 'advanc[e]' " commerce, NLRB v. Jones & Laughlin Steel Corp., 301 U. S. 1–37 (1937) (quoting The Daniel Ball, 10 Wall. 557, 564 (1871)). Thus, Congress might protect the imperiled industry by prohibiting low-cost competition, or by according it preferential tax treatment, or even by granting it a direct subsidy.

Here, however, Congress has impressed into service third parties, healthy individuals who could be but are not customers of the relevant industry, to offset the undesirable consequences of the regulation. Congress' desire to force these individuals to purchase insurance is motivated by the fact that they are further removed from the market than unhealthy individuals with pre-existing conditions, because they are less likely to need extensive care in the near future. If Congress can reach out and command even those furthest removed from an interstate market to participate in the market, then the Commerce Clause becomes a font of unlimited power, or in Hamilton's words, "the hideous monster whose devouring jaws . . . spare neither sex nor age, nor high nor low, nor sacred nor profane." The Federalist No. 33, p. 202 (C. Rossiter ed. 1961).

At the outer edge of the commerce power, this Court has insisted on careful scrutiny of regulations that do not act directly on an interstate market or its participants. In New York v. United States, 505 U. S. 144 (1992), we held that Congress could not, in an effort to regulate the disposal of radioactive waste produced in several different industries, order the States to take title to that waste. Id., at 174–177. In Printz v. United States, 521 U. S.898 (1997), we held that Congress could not, in an effort to regulate the distribution of firearms in the interstate market, compel state law-enforcement officials to perform background checks. Id., at 933–935. In United States v. Lopez, 514 U. S. 549

(1995), we held that Congress could not, as a means of fostering an educated interstate labor market through the protection of schools, ban the possession of a firearm within a school zone. Id., at 559–563. And in United States v. Morrison, 529 U. S. 598 (2000), we held that Congress could not, in an effort to ensure the full participation of women in the interstate economy, subject private individuals and companies to suit for gender-motivated violent torts. Id., at 609–619. The lesson of these cases is that the Commerce Clause, even when supplemented by the Necessary and Proper Clause, is not carte blanche for doing whatever will help achieve the ends Congress seeks by the regulation of commerce. And the last two of these cases show that the scope of the Necessary and Proper Clause is exceeded not only when the congressional action directly violates the sovereignty of the States but also when it violates the background principle of enumerated (and hence limited) federal power.

The case upon which the Government principally relies to sustain the Individual Mandate under the Necessary and Proper Clause is Gonzales v. Raich, 545 U. S. 1 (2005). That case held that Congress could, in an effort to restrain the interstate market in marijuana, ban the local cultivation and possession of that drug. Id., at 15–22. Raich is no precedent for what Congress has done here. That case's prohibition of growing (cf. Wickard, 317 U. S. 111), and of possession (cf. innumerable federal statutes) did not represent the expansion of the federal power to direct into a broad new field. The mandating of economic activity does, and since it is a field so limitless that it converts the Commerce Clause into a general authority to direct the economy, that mandating is not "consist[ent] with the letter and spirit of the constitution." McCulloch v. Maryland, 4 Wheat. 316, 421 (1819).

Moreover, Raich is far different from the Individual Mandate in another respect. The Court's opinion in Raich pointed out that the growing and possession prohibitions were the only practicable way of enabling the prohibition of interstate traffic in marijuana to be effectively enforced. 545 U. S., at 22. See also Shreveport Rate Cases, 234 U. S. 342 (1914) (Necessary and Proper Clause allows regulations of intrastate transactions if necessary to the regulation of an interstate market). Intrastate marijuana could no more be distinguished from interstate marijuana than, for example, endangered-species trophies obtained before the species was federally protected can be distinguished from trophies obtained afterwards—which made it necessary and proper to prohibit the sale of all such trophies, see Andrus v. Allard, 444 U. S. 51 (1979).

With the present statute, by contrast, there are many ways other than this unprecedented Individual Mandate by which the regulatory scheme's goals of reducing insurance premiums and ensuring the profitability of insurers could be achieved. For instance, those who did not purchase insurance could be subjected to a surcharge when they do enter the health insurance system. Or they could be denied a full income tax credit given to those who do purchase the insurance.

The Government was invited, at oral argument, to suggest what federal controls over private conduct (other than those explicitly prohibited by the Bill of Rights or other constitutional controls) could not be justified as necessary and proper for the carrying out of a general regulatory scheme. See Tr. of Oral Arg. 27–30, 43–45 (Mar. 27, 2012). It was unable to name any. As we said at the outset, whereas the precise scope of the Commerce Clause and the Necessary and Proper Clause is uncertain, the proposition that the Federal Government cannot do everything is a fundamental precept. See Lopez, 514 U. S., at 564 ("[I]f we were to accept the Government's arguments, we are hard pressed to posit any activity by an individual that Congress is without power to regulate"). Section 5000A is defeated by that proposition.

B

The Government's second theory in support of the Individual Mandate is that §5000A is valid because it is actually a "regulat[ion of] activities having a substantial relation to interstate commerce, . . . i.e., . . . activities that substantially affect interstate commerce." Id., at 558–559. See also Shreveport Rate Cases, supra. This argument takes a few different forms, but the basic idea is that §5000A regulates "the way in which individuals finance their participation in the health-care market." Petitioners' Minimum Coverage Brief 33 (emphasis added). That is, the provision directs the manner in which individuals purchase health care services and related goods (directing that they be purchased through insurance) and is therefore a straightforward exercise of the commerce power.

The primary problem with this argument is that §5000A does not apply only to persons who purchase all, or most, or even any, of the health care services or goods that the mandated insurance covers. Indeed, the main objection many have to the Mandate is that they have no intention of purchasing most or even any of such goods or services and thus no need to buy insurance for those purchases. The Government responds that the health-care market involves "essentially universal participation," id., at 35. The principal difficulty with this response is that it is, in the only relevant sense, not true. It is true enough that everyone consumes "health care," if the term is taken to include the purchase of a bottle of aspirin. But the health care "market" that is the object of the Individual Mandate not only includes but principally consists of goods and services that the young people primarily affected by the Mandate do not purchase. They are quite simply not participants in that market, and cannot be made so (and thereby subjected to regulation) by the simple device of defining participants to include all those who will, later in their lifetime, probably purchase the goods or services covered by the mandated insurance. 2 Such a definition of market participants is unprecedented, and were it to be a premise for the exercise of national power, it would have no principled limits.

In a variation on this attempted exercise of federal power, the Government points out that Congress in this Act has purported to regulate "economic and financial decision[s] to forego [sic] health insurance coverage and [to] attempt to self-insure," 42 U. S. C. §18091(2)(A), since those decisions have "a substantial and deleterious effect on interstate commerce," Petitioners' Minimum Coverage Brief 34. But as the discussion above makes clear, the decision to forgo participation in an interstate market is not itself commercial activity (or indeed any activity at all) within Congress' power to regulate. It is true that, at the end of the day, it is inevitable that each American will affect commerce and become a part of it, even if not by choice. But if every person comes within the Commerce Clause power of Congress to regulate by the simple reason that he will one day engage in commerce, the idea of a limited Government power is at an end.

Wickard v. Filburn has been regarded as the most expansive assertion of the commerce power in our history. A close second is Perez v. United States, 402 U. S. 146 (1971), which upheld a statute criminalizing the eminently local activity of loan-sharking. Both of those cases, however, involved commercial activity. To go beyond that, and to say that the failure to grow wheat or the refusal to make loans affects commerce, so that growing and lending can be federally compelled, is to extend federal power to virtually everything. All of us consume food, and when we do so the Federal Government can prescribe what its quality must be and even how much we must pay. But the mere fact that we all consume food and are thus, sooner or later, participants in the "market" for food, does not empower the Government to say when and what we will buy. That is essentially what this Act seeks to do with respect to the purchase of health care. It exceeds federal power.

C

A few respectful responses to Justice Ginsburg's dissent on the issue of the Mandate are in order. That dissent duly recites the test of Commerce Clause power that our opinions have applied, but disregards the premise the test contains. It is true enough that Congress needs only a " 'rational basis' for concluding that the regulated activity substantially affects interstate commerce," ante, at 15 (emphasis added). But it must be activity affecting commerce that is regulated, and not merely the failure to engage in commerce. And one is not now purchasing the health care covered by the insurance mandate simply because one is likely to be purchasing it in the future. Our test's premise of regulated activity is not invented out of whole cloth, but rests upon the Constitution's requirement that it be commerce which is regulated. If all inactivity affecting commerce is commerce, commerce is everything. Ultimately the dissent is driven to saying that there is really no difference between action and inaction, ante, at 26, a proposition that has never recommended itself, neither to the law nor to common sense. To say, for example, that the inaction here consists of activity in "the self-insurance market," ibid., seems to us wordplay. By parity of reasoning the failure to buy a car can be called participation in the non-private-car-transportation market. Commerce becomes everything.

The dissent claims that we "fai[l] to explain why the individual mandate threatens our constitutional order." Ante, at 35. But we have done so. It threatens that order because it gives such an expansive meaning to the Commerce Clause that all private conduct (including failure to act) becomes subject to federal control, effectively destroying the Constitution's division of governmental powers. Thus the dissent, on the theories proposed for the validity of the Mandate, would alter the accepted constitutional relation between the individual and the National Government. The dissent protests that the Necessary and Proper Clause has been held to include "the power to enact criminal laws, . . . the power to imprison, . . . and the power to create a national bank," ante, at 34–35. Is not the power to compel purchase of health insurance much lesser? No, not if (unlike those other dispositions) its application rests upon a theory that everything is within federal control simply because it exists.

The dissent's exposition of the wonderful things the Federal Government has achieved through exercise of its assigned powers, such as "the provision of old-age and survivors' benefits" in the Social Security Act, ante, at 2,is quite beside the point. The issue here is whether the federal government can impose the Individual Mandate through the Commerce Clause. And the relevant history is not that Congress has achieved wide and wonderful results through the proper exercise of its assigned powers in the past, but that it has never before used the Commerce Clause to compel entry into commerce. 3 The dissent treats the Constitution as though it is an enumeration of those problems that the Federal Government can address—among which, it finds, is "the Nation's course in the economic and social welfare realm," ibid., and more specifically "the problem of the uninsured," ante, at 7.The Constitution is not that. It enumerates not federally soluble problems, but federally available powers. The Federal Government can address whatever problems it wants but can bring to their solution only those powers that the Constitution confers, among which is the power to regulate commerce. None of our cases say anything else. Article I contains no whatever-it-takes-to-solve-a-national-problem power.

The dissent dismisses the conclusion that the power to compel entry into the health-insurance market would include the power to compel entry into the new-car or broccoli markets. The latter purchasers, it says, "will be obliged to pay at the counter before receiving the vehicle or nourishment," whereas those refusing to purchase health-insurance will ultimately get treated anyway, at others' expense. Ante, at 21. "[T]he unique attributes of the health-care market . . . give rise to a significant free-riding problem that does not occur in other markets." Ante, at 28. And "a vegetable-purchase mandate" (or a car-purchase mandate) is not "likely to have a substantial effect on the health-care costs" borne by other Americans. Ante, at 29. Those differences make a very good argument by the dissent's own lights, since they show that the failure to purchase health insurance, unlike the failure to purchase cars or broccoli, creates a national, social-welfare problem that is (in the dissent's view) included among the unenumerated "problems" that the Constitution authorizes the Federal Government to solve. But those differences do not show that the failure to enter the health-insurance market, unlike the failure to buy cars and broccoli, is an activity that Congress can "regulate." (Of course one day the failure of some of the public to purchase American cars may endanger the existence of domestic automobile manufacturers; or the failure of some to eat broccoli may be found to deprive them of a newly discovered cancer-fighting chemical which only that food contains, producing health-care costs that are a burden on the rest of us—in which case, under the theory of Justice Ginsburg's dissent, moving against those inactivities will also come within the Federal Government's unenumerated problem-solving powers.)

II

The Taxing Power

As far as §5000A is concerned, we would stop there. Congress has attempted to regulate beyond the scope of its Commerce Clause authority, 4 and §5000A is therefore invalid. The Government contends, however, as expressed in the caption to Part II of its brief, that "the minimum coverage provision is independently authorized by congress's taxing power." Petitioners' Minimum Coverage Brief 52. The phrase "independently authorized" suggests the existence of a creature never hitherto seen in the United States Reports: A penalty for constitutional purposes that is also a tax for constitutional purposes. In all our cases the two are mutually exclusive. The provision challenged under the Constitution is either a penalty or else a tax. Of course in many cases what was a regulatory mandate enforced by a penalty could have been imposed as a tax upon permissible action; or what was imposed as a tax upon permissible action could have been a regulatory mandate enforced by a penalty. But we know of no case, and the Government cites none, in which the imposition was, for constitutional purposes, both. 5 The two are mutually exclusive. Thus, what the Government's caption should have read was "alternatively, the minimum coverage provision is not a mandate-with-penalty but a tax." It is important to bear this in mind in evaluating the tax argument of the Government and of those who support it: The issue is not whether Congress had the power to frame the minimum-coverage provision as a tax, but whether it did so.

In answering that question we must, if "fairly possible," Crowell v. Benson, 285 U. S. 22, 62 (1932), construe the provision to be a tax rather than a mandate-with-penalty, since that would render it constitutional rather than un-constitutional (*ut res magis valeat quam pereat*). But we cannot rewrite the statute to be what it is not. " ' "[A]l-though this Court will often strain to construe legislation so as to save it against constitutional attack, it must not and will not carry this to the point of perverting the purpose of a statute . . ." or judicially rewriting it.' " Commodity Futures Trading Comm'n v. Schor, 478 U. S. 833, 841 (1986) (quoting Aptheker v. Secretary of State, 378 U. S. 500, 515 (1964), in turn quoting Scales v. United States, 367 U. S. 203, 211 (1961)). In this case, there is simply no way, "without doing violence to the fair meaning of the words used," Grenada County Supervisors v. Brogden, 112 U. S. 261, 269 (1884), to escape what Congress enacted: a mandate that individuals maintain minimum essential coverage, enforced by a penalty.

Our cases establish a clear line between a tax and a penalty: " '[A] tax is an enforced contribution to provide for the support of government; a penalty . . . is an exaction imposed by statute as punishment for an unlawful act.' " United States v. Reorganized CF&I Fabricators of Utah, Inc., 518 U. S. 213, 224 (1996) (quoting United States v. La Franca, 282 U. S. 568, 572 (1931)). In a few cases, this Court has held that a "tax" imposed upon private conduct was so onerous as to be in effect a penalty. But we have never held—never—that a penalty imposed for violation of the law was so trivial as to be in effect a tax. We have never held that any exaction imposed for violation of the law is an exercise of Congress' taxing power—even when the statute calls it a tax, much less when (as here) the statute repeatedly calls it a penalty. When an act "adopt[s] the criteria of wrongdoing" and then imposes a monetary penalty as the "principal consequence on those who transgress its standard," it creates a regulatory penalty, not a tax. Child Labor Tax Case, 259 U. S. 20, 38 (1922).

So the question is, quite simply, whether the exaction here is imposed for violation of the law. It unquestionably is. The minimum-coverage provision is found in 26 U. S. C. §5000A, entitled "Requirement to maintain minimum essential coverage." (Emphasis added.) It commands that every "applicable individual shall . . . ensure that the individual . . . is covered under minimum essential coverage." Ibid. (emphasis added). And the immediately following provision states that, "[i]f . . . an applicable individual . . . fails to meet the requirement of subsection (a) . . . there is hereby imposed . . . a penalty." §5000A(b) (emphasis added). And several of Congress' legislative "findings" with regard to §5000A confirm that it sets forth a legal requirement and constitutes the assertion of regulatory power, not mere taxing power. See 42 U. S. C. §18091(2)(A) ("The requirement regulates activity . . ."); §18091(2)(C) ("The requirement . . . will add millions of new consumers to the health insurance market . . ."); §18091(2)(D) ("The requirement achieves near-universal coverage"); §18091(2)(H) ("The requirement is an essential part of this larger regulation of economic activity, and the absence of the requirement would undercut Federal regulation of the health insurance market"); §18091(3) ("[T]he Supreme Court of the United States ruled that insurance is interstate commerce subject to Federal regulation").

The Government and those who support its view on the tax point rely on New York v. United States, 505 U. S. 144, to justify reading "shall" to mean "may." The "shall" in that case was contained in an introductory provision—a recital that provided for no legal consequences—which said that "[e]ach State shall be responsible for providing . . . for the disposal of . . . low-level radioactive waste." 42 U. S. C. §2021c(a)(1)(A). The Court did not hold that "shall" could be construed to mean "may," but rather that this preliminary provision could not impose upon the operative provisions of the Act a mandate that they did not contain: "We . . . decline petitioners' invitation to construe §2021c(a)(1)(A), alone and in isolation, as a command to the States independent of the remainder of the Act." New York, 505 U. S., at 170. Our opinion then proceeded to "consider each [of the three operative provisions] in turn." Ibid. Here the mandate—the "shall"—is contained not in an inoperative preliminary recital, but in the dispositive operative provision itself. New York provides no support for reading it to be permissive.

Quite separately, the fact that Congress (in its own words) "imposed . . . a penalty," 26 U. S. C. §5000A(b)(1), for failure to buy insurance is alone sufficient to render that failure unlawful. It is one of the canons of interpretation that a statute that penalizes an act makes it unlawful: "[W]here the statute inflicts a penalty for doing an act, although the act itself is not expressly prohibited, yet to do the act is unlawful, because it cannot be supposed that the Legislature intended that a penalty should be inflicted for a lawful act." Powhatan Steamboat Co. v. Appomattox R. Co., 24 How. 247, 252 (1861). Or in the words of Chancellor Kent: "If a statute inflicts a penalty for doing an act, the penalty implies a prohibition, and the thing is unlawful, though there be no prohibitory words in the statute." 1 J. Kent, Commentaries on American Law 436 (1826).

We never have classified as a tax an exaction imposed for violation of the law, and so too, we never have classified as a tax an exaction described in the legislation itself as a penalty. To be sure, we have sometimes treated as a tax a statutory exaction (imposed for something other than a violation of law) which bore an agnostic label that does not entail the significant constitutional consequences of a penalty—such as "license" (License Tax Cases, 5 Wall. 462 (1867)) or "surcharge" (New York v. United States, supra.). But we have never—never—treated as a tax an exaction which faces up to the critical difference between a tax and a penalty, and explicitly denominates the exaction a "penalty." Eighteen times in §5000A itself and else-where throughout the Act, Congress called the exaction in §5000A(b) a "penalty."

That §5000A imposes not a simple tax but a mandate to which a penalty is attached is demonstrated by the fact that some are exempt from the tax who are not exempt from the mandate—a distinction that would make no sense if the mandate were not a mandate. Section 5000A(d) exempts three classes of people from the definition of "applicable individual" subject to the minimum coverage requirement: Those with religious objections or who participate in a "health care sharing ministry," §5000A(d)(2); those who are "not lawfully present" in the United States, §5000A(d)(3); and those who are incarcerated, §5000A(d)(4). Section 5000A(e) then creates a separate set of exemptions, excusing from liability for the penalty certain individuals who are subject to the minimum coverage requirement: Those who cannot afford coverage, §5000A(e)(1); who earn too little income to require filing a tax return, §5000A(e)(2); who are members of an Indian tribe, §5000A(e)(3); who experience only short gaps in coverage, §5000A(e)(4); and who, in the judgment of the Secretary of Health and Human Services, "have suffered a hardship with respect to the capability to obtain coverage," §5000A(e)(5). If §5000A were a tax, these two classes of exemption would make no sense; there being no requirement, all the exemptions would attach to the penalty (renamed tax) alone.

In the face of all these indications of a regulatory requirement accompanied by a penalty, the Solicitor General assures us that "neither the Treasury Department nor the Department of Health and Human Services interprets Section 5000A as imposing a legal obligation," Petitioners' Minimum Coverage Brief 61, and that "[i]f [those subject to the Act] pay the tax penalty, they're in compliance with the law," Tr. of Oral Arg. 50 (Mar. 26, 2012). These self-serving litigating positions are entitled to no weight. What counts is what the statute says, and that is entirely clear. It is worth noting, moreover, that these assurances contradict the Government's position in related litigation. Shortly before the

Affordable Care Act was passed, the Commonwealth of Virginia enacted Va. Code Ann. §38.2–3430.1:1 (Lexis Supp. 2011), which states, "No resident of [the] Commonwealth . . . shall be required to obtain or maintain a policy of individual insurance coverage except as required by a court or the Department of Social Services . . . ." In opposing Virginia's assertion of standing to challenge §5000A based on this statute, the Government said that "if the minimum coverage provision is unconstitutional, the [Virginia] statute is unnecessary, and if the minimum coverage provision is upheld, the state statute is void under the Supremacy Clause." Brief for Appellant in No. 11–1057 etc. (CA4), p. 29. But it would be void under the Supremacy Clause only if it was contradicted by a federal "require[ment] to obtain or maintain a policy of individual insurance coverage."

Against the mountain of evidence that the minimum coverage requirement is what the statute calls it—a requirement—and that the penalty for its violation is what the statute calls it—a penalty—the Government brings forward the flimsiest of indications to the contrary. It notes that "[t]he minimum coverage provision amends the Internal Revenue Code to provide that a non-exempted individual . . . will owe a monetary penalty, in addition to the income tax itself," and that "[t]he [Internal Revenue Service (IRS)] will assess and collect the penalty in the same manner as assessable penalties under the Internal Revenue Code." Petitioners' Minimum Coverage Brief 53. The manner of collection could perhaps suggest a tax if IRS penalty-collection were unheard-of or rare. It is not. See, e.g., 26 U. S. C. §527(j) (2006 ed.) (IRS-collectible penalty for failure to make campaign-finance disclosures); §5761(c) (IRS-collectible penalty for domestic sales of tobacco products labeled for export); §9707 (IRS-collectible penalty for failure to make required health-insurance premium payments on behalf of mining employees). In Reorganized CF&I Fabricators of Utah, Inc., 518 U. S. 213, we held that an exaction not only enforced by the Commissioner of Internal Revenue but even called a "tax" was in fact a penalty. "[I]f the concept of penalty means anything," we said, "it means punishment for an unlawful act or omission." Id., at 224. See also Lipke v. Lederer, 259 U. S. 557 (1922) (same). Moreover, while the penalty is assessed and collected by the IRS, §5000A is administered both by that agency and by the Department of Health and Human Services (and also the Secretary of Veteran Affairs), see §5000A(e)(1)(D), (e)(5), (f)(1)(A)(v), (f)(1)(E) (2006 ed., Supp. IV), which is responsible for defining its substantive scope—a feature that would be quite extraordinary for taxes.

The Government points out that "[t]he amount of the penalty will be calculated as a percentage of household income for federal income tax purposes, subject to a floor and [a] ca[p]," and that individuals who earn so little money that they "are not required to file income tax returns for the taxable year are not subject to the penalty" (though they are, as we discussed earlier, subject to the mandate). Petitioners' Minimum Coverage Brief 12, 53. But varying a penalty according to ability to pay is an utterly familiar practice. See, e.g., 33 U. S. C. §1319(d) (2006 ed., Supp. IV) ("In determining the amount of a civil penalty the court shall consider . . . the economic impact of the penalty on the violator"); see also 6 U. S. C. §488e(c); 7 U. S. C. §§7734(b)(2), 8313(b)(2); 12 U. S. C. §§1701q–

1(d)(3), 1723i(c)(3), 1735f–14(c)(3), 1735f–15(d)(3), 4585(c)(2); 15 U. S. C. §§45(m)(1)(C), 77h–1(g)(3), 78u–2(d), 80a–9(d)(4), 80b–3(i)(4), 1681s(a)(2)(B), 1717a(b)(3), 1825(b)(1), 2615(a)(2)(B), 5408(b)(2); 33 U. S. C. §2716a(a).

The last of the feeble arguments in favor of petitioners that we will address is the contention that what this statute repeatedly calls a penalty is in fact a tax because it contains no scienter requirement. The presence of such a requirement suggests a penalty—though one can imagine a tax imposed only on willful action; but the absence of such a requirement does not suggest a tax. Penalties for absolute-liability offenses are commonplace. And where a statute is silent as to scienter, we traditionally presume a mens rea requirement if the statute imposes a "severe penalty." Staples v. United States, 511 U. S. 600, 618 (1994). Since we have an entire jurisprudence addressing when it is that a scienter requirement should be inferred from a penalty, it is quite illogical to suggest that a penalty is not a penalty for want of an express scienter requirement.

And the nail in the coffin is that the mandate and penalty are located in Title I of the Act, its operative core, rather than where a tax would be found—in Title IX, containing the Act's "Revenue Provisions." In sum, "the terms of [the] act rende[r] it unavoidable," Parsons v. Bedford, 3 Pet. 433, 448 (1830), that Congress imposed a regulatory penalty, not a tax.

For all these reasons, to say that the Individual Mandate merely imposes a tax is not to interpret the statute but to rewrite it. Judicial tax-writing is particularly troubling. Taxes have never been popular, see, e.g., Stamp Act of 1765, and in part for that reason, the Constitution requires tax increases to originate in the House of Representatives. See Art. I, §7, cl. 1. That is to say, they must originate in the legislative body most accountable to the people, where legislators must weigh the need for the tax against the terrible price they might pay at their next election, which is never more than two years off. The Federalist No. 58 "defend[ed] the decision to give the origination power to the House on the ground that the Chamber that is more accountable to the people should have the primary role in raising revenue." United States v. Munoz-Flores, 495 U. S. 385, 395 (1990). We have no doubt that Congress knew precisely what it was doing when it rejected an earlier version of this legislation that imposed a tax instead of a requirement-with-penalty. See Affordable Health Care for America Act, H. R. 3962, 111th Cong., 1st Sess., §501 (2009); America's Healthy Future Act of 2009, S. 1796, 111th Cong., 1st Sess., §1301. Imposing a tax through judicial legislation inverts the constitutional scheme, and places the power to tax in the branch of government least accountable to the citizenry.

Finally, we must observe that rewriting §5000A as a tax in order to sustain its constitutionality would force us to confront a difficult constitutional question: whether this is a direct tax that must be apportioned among the States according to their population. Art. I, §9, cl. 4. Perhaps it is not (we have no need to address the point); but the meaning of the Direct Tax Clause is famously unclear, and its application here is a question of first impression that deserves more thoughtful consideration than the lick-and-a-promise accorded by the Government and its supporters. The Government's opening brief did not even address the question—perhaps because, until today, no federal court has accepted the implausible argument that §5000A is an exercise of the tax power. And once respondents raised the issue, the Government devoted a mere 21 lines of its reply brief to the issue. Petitioners' Minimum Coverage Reply Brief 25. At oral argument, the most prolonged statement about the issue was just over 50 words. Tr. of Oral Arg. 79 (Mar. 27, 2012). One would expect this Court to demand more than fly-by-night briefing and argument before deciding a difficult constitutional question of first impression.

III

The Anti-Injunction Act

There is another point related to the Individual Mandate that we must discuss—a point that logically should have been discussed first: Whether jurisdiction over the challenges to the minimum-coverage provision is precluded by the Anti-Injunction Act, which provides that "no suit for the purpose of restraining the assessment or collection of any tax shall be maintained in any court by any person," 26 U. S. C. §7421(a) (2006 ed.).

We have left the question to this point because it seemed to us that the dispositive question whether the minimum-coverage provision is a tax is more appropriately addressed in the significant constitutional context of whether it is an exercise of Congress' taxing power. Having found that it is not, we have no difficulty in deciding that these suits do not have "the purpose of restraining the assessment or collection of any tax." 6

The Government and those who support its position on this point make the remarkable argument that §5000A is not a tax for purposes of the Anti-Injunction Act, see Brief for Petitioners in No. 11–398 (Anti-Injunction Act), but is a tax for constitutional purposes, see Petitioners' Minimum Coverage Brief 52–62. The rhetorical device that tries to cloak this argument in superficial plausibility is the same device employed in arguing that for constitutional purposes the minimum-coverage provision is a tax: confusing the question of what Congress did with the question of what Congress could have done. What qualifies as a tax for purposes of the Anti-Injunction Act, unlike what qualifies as a tax for purposes of the Constitution, is entirely within the control of Congress. Compare Bailey v. George, 259 U. S. 16, 20 (1922) (Anti-Injunction Act barred suit to restrain collections under the Child Labor Tax Law), with Child Labor Tax Case, 259 U. S., at 36–41 (holding the same law unconstitutional as exceeding Congress' taxing power). Congress could have defined "tax" for purposes of that statute in such fashion as to exclude some exactions that in fact are "taxes." It might have prescribed, for example, that a particular exercise of the taxing power "shall not be regarded as a tax for purposes of the Anti-Injunction Act." But there is no such prescription here. What the Government would have us believe in these cases is that the very same textual indications that show this is not a tax under the Anti-Injunction Act show that it is a tax under the Constitution. That carries verbal wizardry too far, deep into the forbidden land of the sophists.

IV

The Medicaid Expansion

We now consider respondents' second challenge to the constitutionality of the ACA, namely, that the Act's dramatic expansion of the Medicaid program exceeds Congress' power to attach conditions to federal grants to the States.

The ACA does not legally compel the States to participate in the expanded Medicaid program, but the Act authorizes a severe sanction for any State that refuses to go along: termination of all the State's Medicaid funding. For the average State, the annual federal Medicaid subsidy is equal to more than one-fifth of the State's expenditures. 7 A State forced out of the program would not only lose this huge sum but would almost certainly find it necessary to increase its own health-care expenditures substantially, requiring either a drastic reduction in funding for other programs or a large increase in state taxes. And these new taxes would come on top of the federal taxes already paid by the State's citizens to fund the Medicaid program in other States.

The States challenging the constitutionality of the ACA's Medicaid Expansion contend that, for these practical reasons, the Act really does not give them any choice at all. As proof of this, they point to the goal and the struc-ture of the ACA. The goal of the Act is to provide near-universal medical coverage, 42 U. S. C. §18091(2)(D), and without 100% State participation in the Medicaid program, attainment of this goal would be thwarted. Even if States could elect to remain in the old Medicaid program, while declining to participate in the Expansion, there would be a gaping hole in coverage. And if a substantial number of States were entirely expelled from the program, the number of persons without coverage would be even higher.

In light of the ACA's goal of near-universal coverage, petitioners argue, if Congress had thought that anything less than 100% state participation was a realistic possibility, Congress would have provided a backup scheme. But no such scheme is to be found anywhere in the more than 900 pages of the Act. This shows, they maintain, that Congress was certain that the ACA's Medicaid offer was one that no State could refuse.

In response to this argument, the Government contends that any congressional assumption about uniform state participation was based on the simple fact that the offer of federal funds associated with the expanded coverage is such a generous gift that no State would want to turn it down.

To evaluate these arguments, we consider the extent of the Federal Government's power to spend money and to attach conditions to money granted to the States.

A

No one has ever doubted that the Constitution authorizes the Federal Government to spend money, but for many years the scope of this power was unsettled. The Constitution grants Congress the power to collect taxes "to . . . provide for the . . . general Welfare of the United States," Art. I, §8, cl. 1, and from "the foundation of the Nation sharp differences of opinion have persisted as to the true interpretation of the phrase" "the general welfare." Butler, 297 U. S., at 65. Madison, it has been said, thought that the phrase "amounted to no more than a reference to the other powers enumerated in the subsequent clauses of the same section," while Hamilton "maintained the clause confers a power separate and distinct from those later enumerated [and] is not restricted in meaning by the grant of them." Ibid.

The Court resolved this dispute in Butler. Writing for the Court, Justice Roberts opined that the Madisonian view would make Article I's grant of the spending power a "mere tautology." Ibid. To avoid that, he adopted Hamilton's approach and found that "the power of Congress to authorize expenditure of public moneys for public purposes is not limited by the direct grants of legislative power found in the Constitution." Id., at 66. Instead, he wrote, the spending power's "confines are set in the clause which confers it, and not in those of section 8 which bestow and define the legislative powers of the Congress." Ibid.; see also Steward Machine Co. v. Davis, 301 U. S. 548–587 (1937); Helvering v. Davis, 301 U. S. 619, 640 (1937).

The power to make any expenditure that furthers "the general welfare" is obviously very broad, and shortly after Butler was decided the Court gave Congress wide leeway to decide whether an expenditure qualifies. See Helvering, 301 U. S., at 640–641. "The discretion belongs to Congress," the Court wrote, "unless the choice is clearly wrong, a display of arbitrary power, not an exercise of judgment." Id., at 640. Since that time, the Court has never held that a federal expenditure was not for "the general welfare."

B

One way in which Congress may spend to promote the general welfare is by making grants to the States. Monetary grants, so-called grants-in-aid, became more frequent during the 1930's, G. Stephens & N. Wikstrom, Ameri-can Intergovernmental Relations—A Fragmented Federal Polity 83 (2007), and by 1950 they had reached $20 billion 8 or 11.6% of state and local government expenditures from their own sources. 9 By 1970 this number had grown to $123.7 billion 10 or 29.1% of state and local government expenditures from their own sources. 11 As of 2010, fed-eral outlays to state and local governments came to over $608 billion or 37.5% of state and local government expenditures. 12

When Congress makes grants to the States, it customarily attaches conditions, and this Court has long held that the Constitution generally permits Congress to do this. See Pennhurst State School and Hospital v. Halderman, 451 U. S. 1, 17 (1981); South Dakota v. Dole, 483 U. S. 203, 206 (1987); Fullilove v. Klutznick, 448 U. S. 448, 474 (1980) (opinion of Burger, C. J.); Steward Machine, supra, at 593.

C

This practice of attaching conditions to federal funds greatly increases federal power. "[O]bjectives not thought to be within Article I's enumerated legislative fields, may nevertheless be attained through the use of the spending power and the conditional grant of federal funds." Dole, supra, at 207 (internal quotation marks and citation omitted); see also College Savings Bank v. Florida Prepaid Postsecondary Ed. Expense Bd., 527 U. S. 666, 686 (1999) (by attaching conditions to federal funds, Congress may induce the States to "tak[e] certain actions that Congress could not require them to take").

This formidable power, if not checked in any way, would present a grave threat to the system of federalism created by our Constitution. If Congress' "Spending Clause power to pursue objectives outside of Article I's enumerated legislative fields," Davis v. Monroe County Bd. of Ed., 526 U. S. 629, 654 (1999) (Kennedy, J., dissenting) (internal quotation marks omitted), is "limited only by Congress' notion of the general welfare, the reality, given the vast financial resources of the Federal Government, is that the Spending Clause gives 'power to the Congress to tear down the barriers, to invade the states' jurisdiction, and to become a parliament of the whole people, subject to no restrictions save such as are self-imposed,' " Dole, supra, at 217 (O'Connor, J., dissenting) (quoting Butler, 297 U. S., at 78). "[T]he Spending Clause power, if wielded without concern for the federal balance, has the potential to obliterate distinctions between national and local spheres of interest and power by permitting the Federal Government to set policy in the most sensitive areas of traditional state concern, areas which otherwise would lie outside its reach." Davis, supra, at 654–655 (Kennedy, J.,dissenting).

Recognizing this potential for abuse, our cases have long held that the power to attach conditions to grants to the States has limits. See, e.g., Dole, supra, at 207–208; id.,at 207 (spending power is "subject to several general restrictions articulated in our cases"). For one thing, any such conditions must be unambiguous so that a State at least knows what it is getting into. See Pennhurst, supra, at 17. Conditions must also be related "to the federal interest in particular national projects or programs," Massachusetts v. United States, 435 U. S. 444, 461 (1978), and the conditional grant of federal funds may not "induce the States to engage in activities that would themselves be unconstitutional," Dole, supra, at 210; see Lawrence County v. Lead-Deadwood School Dist. No. 40–1, 469 U. S.256, 269–270 (1985). Finally, while Congress may seek to induce States to accept conditional grants, Congress may not cross the "point at which pressure turns into compulsion, and ceases to be inducement." Steward Machine, 301 U. S., at 590. Accord, College Savings Bank, supra, at 687; Metropolitan Washington Airports Authority v. Citizens for Abatement of Aircraft Noise, Inc., 501 U. S. 252, 285 (1991) (White, J., dissenting); Dole, supra, at 211.

When federal legislation gives the States a real choice whether to accept or decline a federal aid package, the federal-state relationship is in the nature of a contractual relationship. See Barnes v. Gorman, 536 U. S. 181, 186 (2002); Pennhurst, 451 U. S., at 17. And just as a contract is voidable if coerced, "[t]he legitimacy of Congress' power to legislate under the spending power . . . rests on whether the State voluntarily and knowingly accepts the terms of the 'contract.' " Ibid. (emphasis added). If a federal spending program coerces participation the States have not "exercise[d] their choice"—let alone made an "informed choice." Id., at 17, 25.

Coercing States to accept conditions risks the destruction of the "unique role of the States in our system." Davis, supra, at 685 (Kennedy, J., dissenting). "[T]he Constitution has never been understood to confer upon Congress the ability to require the States to govern according to Congress' instructions." New York, 505 U. S., at 162.

Congress may not "simply commandeer the legislative processes of the States by directly compelling them to enact and enforce a federal regulatory program." Id., at 161 (internal quotation marks and brackets omitted). Congress effectively engages in this impermissible compulsion when state participation in a federal spending program is coerced, so that the States' choice whether to enact or administer a federal regulatory program is rendered illusory.

Where all Congress has done is to "encourag[e] state regulation rather than compe[l] it, state governments remain responsive to the local electorate's preferences; state officials remain accountable to the people. [But] where the Federal Government compels States to regulate, the accountability of both state and federal officials is diminished." New York, supra, at 168.

Amici who support the Government argue that forcing state employees to implement a federal program is more respectful of federalism than using federal workers to implement that program. See, e.g., Brief for Service Employees International Union et al. as Amici Curiae in No. 11–398, pp. 25–26. They note that Congress, instead of expanding Medicaid, could have established an entirely federal program to provide coverage for the same group of people. By choosing to structure Medicaid as a cooperative federal-state program, they contend, Congress allows for more state control. Ibid.

This argument reflects a view of federalism that our cases have rejected—and with good reason. When Congress compels the States to do its bidding, it blurs the lines of political accountability. If the Federal Government makes a controversial decision while acting on its own, "it is the Federal Government that makes the decision in full view of the public, and it will be federal officials that suffer the consequences if the decision turns out to be detrimental or unpopular." New York, 505 U. S., at 168. But when the Federal Government compels the States to take unpopular actions, "it may be state officials who will bear the brunt of public disapproval, while the federal officials who devised the regulatory program may remain insulated from the electoral ramifications of their decision." Id., at 169; see Printz, supra, at 930. For this reason, federal officeholders may view this "departur[e] from the federal structure to be in their personal interests . . . as a means of shifting responsibility for the eventual decision." New York, 505 U. S., at 182–183. And even state officials may favor such a "departure from the constitutional plan," since uncertainty concerning responsibility may also permit them to escape accountability. Id., at 182. If a program is popular, state officials may claim credit; if it is unpopular, they may protest that they were merely responding to a federal directive.

Once it is recognized that spending-power legislation cannot coerce state participation, two questions remain: (1) What is the meaning of coercion in this context? (2) Is the ACA's expanded Medicaid coverage coercive? We now turn to those questions.

D

1

The answer to the first of these questions—the meaning of coercion in the present context—is straightforward. As we have explained, the legitimacy of attaching conditions to federal grants to the States depends on the voluntariness of the States' choice to accept or decline the offered package. Therefore, if States really have no choice other than to accept the package, the offer is coercive, and the conditions cannot be sustained under the spending power. And as our decision in South Dakota v. Dole makes clear, theoretical voluntariness is not enough.

In South Dakota v. Dole, we considered whether the spending power permitted Congress to condition 5% of the State's federal highway funds on the State's adoption of a minimum drinking age of 21 years. South Dakota argued that the program was impermissibly coercive, but we disagreed, reasoning that "Congress ha[d] directed only that a State desiring to establish a minimum drinking age lower than 21 lose a relatively small percentage of certain federal highway funds." 483 U. S., at 211. Because "all South Dakota would lose if she adhere[d] to her chosen course as to a suitable minimum drinking age [was] 5%of the funds otherwise obtainable under specified high-way grant programs," we found that "Congress ha[d] offered relatively mild encouragement to the States to enact higher minimum drinking ages than they would otherwise choose." Ibid. Thus, the decision whether to comply with the federal condition "remain[ed] the prerogative of the States not merely in theory but in fact," and so the program at issue did not exceed Congress' power. Id., at 211–212 (emphasis added).

The question whether a law enacted under the spending power is coercive in fact will sometimes be difficult, but where Congress has plainly "crossed the line distinguishing encouragement from coercion," New York, supra, at 175, a federal program that coopts the States' political processes must be declared unconstitutional. "[T]he federal balance is too essential a part of our constitutional structure and plays too vital a role in securing freedom for us to admit inability to intervene." Lopez, 514 U. S., at 578 (Kennedy, J., concurring).

2

The Federal Government's argument in this case at best pays lip service to the anticoercion principle. The Federal Government suggests that it is sufficient if States are "free, as a matter of law, to turn down" federal funds. Brief for Respondents in No. 11–400, p. 17 (emphasis added); see also id., at 25. According to the Federal Government, neither the amount of the offered federal funds nor the amount of the federal taxes extracted from the taxpayers of a State to pay for the program in question is relevant in determining whether there is impermissible coercion. Id., at 41–46.

This argument ignores reality. When a heavy federal tax is levied to support a federal program that offers large grants to the States, States may, as a practical matter, be unable to refuse to participate in the federal program and to substitute a state alternative. Even if a State believes that the federal program is ineffective and inefficient, withdrawal would likely force the State to impose a huge tax increase on its residents, and this new state tax would come on top of the federal taxes already paid by residents to support subsidies to participating States. 13

Acceptance of the Federal Government's interpretation of the anticoercion rule would permit Congress to dictate policy in areas traditionally governed primarily at the state or local level. Suppose, for example, that Congress enacted legislation offering each State a grant equal to the State's entire annual expenditures for primary and secondary education. Suppose also that this funding came with conditions governing such things as school curriculum, the hiring and tenure of teachers, the drawing of school districts, the length and hours of the school day, the school calendar, a dress code for students, and rules for student discipline. As a matter of law, a State could turn down that offer, but if it did so, its residents would not only be required to pay the federal taxes needed to support this expensive new program, but they would also be forced to pay an equivalent amount in state taxes. And if the State gave in to the federal law, the State and its subdivisions would surrender their traditional authority in the field of education. Asked at oral argument whether such a law would be allowed under the spending power, the Solicitor General responded that it would. Tr. of Oral Arg. 44–45 (Mar. 28, 2012).

E

Whether federal spending legislation crosses the line from enticement to coercion is often difficult to determine, and courts should not conclude that legislation is unconstitutional on this ground unless the coercive nature of an offer is unmistakably clear. In this case, however, there can be no doubt. In structuring the ACA, Congress unambiguously signaled its belief that every State would have no real choice but to go along with the Medicaid Expansion. If the anticoercion rule does not apply in this case, then there is no such rule.

1

The dimensions of the Medicaid program lend strong support to the petitioner States' argument that refusing to accede to the conditions set out in the ACA is not a realistic option. Before the ACA's enactment, Medicaid funded medical care for pregnant women, families with dependents, children, the blind, the elderly, and the disabled. See 42 U. S. C. §1396a(a)(10) (2006 ed., Supp. IV). The ACA greatly expands the program's reach, making new funds available to States that agree to extend coverage to all individuals who are under age 65 and have incomes below 133% of the federal poverty line. See §1396a(a)(10)(A)(i)(VIII). Any State that refuses to expand its Medicaid programs in this way is threatened with a severe sanction: the loss of all its federal Medicaid funds. See §1396c (2006 ed.).

Medicaid has long been the largest federal program of grants to the States. See Brief for Respondents in No. 11–400, at 37. In 2010, the Federal Government directed more than $552 billion in federal funds to the States. See Nat. Assn. of State Budget Officers, 2010 State Expenditure Report: Examining Fiscal 2009–2011 State Spending, p. 7 (2011) (NASBO Report). Of this, more than $233 billion went to pre-expansion Medicaid. See id., at 47. 14 This amount equals nearly 22% of all state expenditures combined. See id., at 7.

The States devote a larger percentage of their budgets to Medicaid than to any other item. Id., at 5. Federal funds account for anywhere from 50% to 83% of each State's total Medicaid expenditures, see §1396d(b) (2006 ed., Supp. IV); most States receive more than $1 billion in federal Medicaid funding; and a quarter receive more than$5 billion, NASBO Report 47. These federal dollars total nearly two thirds—64.6%—of all Medicaid expenditures nationwide. 15 Id., at 46.

The Court of Appeals concluded that the States failed to establish coercion in this case in part because the "states have the power to tax and raise revenue, and therefore can create and fund programs of their own if they do not like Congress's terms." 648 F. 3d 1235, 1268 (CA11 2011); see Brief for Sen. Harry Reid et al. as Amici Curiae in No. 11–400, p. 21 ("States may always choose to decrease expenditures on other programs or to raise revenues"). But the sheer size of this federal spending program in relation to state expenditures means that a State would be very hard pressed to compensate for the loss of federal funds by cutting other spending or raising additional revenue. Arizona, for example, commits 12% of its state expenditures to Medicaid, and relies on the Federal Government to provide the rest: $5.6 billion, equaling roughly one-third of Arizona's annual state expenditures of $17 billion. See NASBO Report 7, 47. Therefore, if Arizona lost federal Medicaid funding, the State would have to commit an additional 33% of all its state expenditures to fund an equivalent state program along the lines of pre-expansion Medicaid. This means that the State would have to allocate 45% of its annual expenditures for that one purpose. See ibid.

The States are far less reliant on federal funding for any other program. After Medicaid, the next biggest federal funding item is aid to support elementary and secondary education, which amounts to 12.8% of total federal outlays to the States, see id., at 7, 16, and equals only 6.6% of all state expenditures combined. See ibid. In Arizona, for example, although federal Medicaid expenditures are equal to 33% of all state expenditures, federal education funds amount to only 9.8% of all state expenditures. See ibid. And even in States with less than average federal Medicaid funding, that funding is at least twice the size of federal education funding as a percentage of state expenditures. Id., at 7, 16, 47.

A State forced out of the Medicaid program would face burdens in addition to the loss of federal Medicaid funding. For example, a nonparticipating State might be found to be ineligible for other major federal funding sources, such as Temporary Assistance for Needy Families (TANF), which is premised on the expectation that States will participate in Medicaid. See 42 U. S. C. §602(a)(3) (2006 ed.) (requiring that certain beneficiaries of TANF funds be "eligible for medical assistance under the State['s Medicaid] plan"). And withdrawal or expulsion from the Medicaid program would not relieve a State's hospitals of their obligation under federal law to provide care for patients who are unable to pay for medical services. The Emergency Medical Treatment and Active Labor Act, §1395dd, requires hospitals that receive any federal funding to provide stabilization care for indigent patients but does not offer federal funding to assist facilities in carrying out its mandate. Many of these patients are now covered by Medicaid. If providers could not look to the Medicaid program to pay for this care, they would find it exceedingly difficult to comply with federal law unless they were given substantial state support. See, e.g., Brief for Economists as Amici Curiae in No 11–400, p. 11.

For these reasons, the offer that the ACA makes to the States—go along with a dramatic expansion of Medicaid or potentially lose all federal Medicaid funding—is quite unlike anything that we have seen in a prior spending-power case. In South Dakota v. Dole, the total amount that the States would have lost if every single State had refused to comply with the 21-year-old drinking age was approximately $614.7 million—or about 0.19%of all state expenditures combined. See Nat. Assn.of State Budget Officers, 1989 (Fiscal Years 1987–1989 Data) State Expenditure Report 10, 84 (1989), http://www.nasbo.org/publications-data/state-expenditure-report/archives. South Dakota stood to lose, at most, funding that amounted to less than 1% of its annual state expenditures. See ibid. Under the ACA, by contrast, the Federal Government has threatened to withhold 42.3% of all federal outlays to the states, or approximately $233 billion. See NASBO Report 7, 10, 47. South Dakota stands to lose federal funding equaling 28.9% of its annual state expenditures. See id., at 7, 47. Withholding $614.7 million, equaling only 0.19% of all state expenditures combined, is aptly characterized as "relatively mild encouragement," but threatening to withhold $233 billion, equaling 21.86% of all state expenditures combined, is a different matter.

2

What the statistics suggest is confirmed by the goaland structure of the ACA. In crafting the ACA, Congress clearly expressed its informed view that no State could possibly refuse the offer that the ACA extends.

The stated goal of the ACA is near-universal health care coverage. To achieve this goal, the ACA mandates that every person obtain a minimum level of coverage. It attempts to reach this goal in several different ways. The guaranteed issue and community-rating provisions are designed to make qualifying insurance available and affordable for persons with medical conditions that may require expensive care. Other ACA provisions seek to make such policies more affordable for people of modest means. Finally, for low-income individuals who are simply not able to obtain insurance, Congress expanded Medicaid, transforming it from a program covering only members of a limited list of vulnerable groups into a program that provides at least the requisite minimum level of coverage for the poor. See 42 U. S. C. §§1396a(a)(10)(A)(i)(VIII) (2006 ed., Supp. IV), 1396u–7(a), (b)(5), 18022(a). This design was intended to provide at least a specified minimum level of coverage for all Americans, but the achievement of that goal obviously depends on participation by every single State. If any State—notto mention all of the 26 States that brought this suit—chose to decline the federal offer, there would be a gaping hole in the ACA's coverage.

It is true that some persons who are eligible for Medicaid coverage under the ACA may be able to secure private insurance, either through their employers or by obtaining subsidized insurance through an exchange. See 26 U. S. C. §36B(a) (2006 ed., Supp. IV); Brief for Respondents in No. 11–400, at 12. But the new federal subsidies are not available to those whose income is below the federal poverty level, and the ACA provides no means, other than Medicaid, for these individuals to obtain coverage and comply with the Mandate. The Government counters that these people will not have to pay the penalty, see, e.g., Tr. of Oral Arg. 68 (Mar. 28, 2012); Brief for Respondents in No. 11–400, at 49–50, but that argument misses the point: Without Medicaid, these individuals will not have coverage and the ACA's goal of near-universal coverage will be severely frustrated.

If Congress had thought that States might actually refuse to go along with the expansion of Medicaid, Congress would surely have devised a backup scheme so that the most vulnerable groups in our society, those previously eligible for Medicaid, would not be left out in the cold. But nowhere in the over 900-page Act is such a scheme to be found. By contrast, because Congress thought that some States might decline federal funding for the operation of a "health benefit exchange," Congress provided a backup scheme; if a State declines to participate in the operation of an exchange, the Federal Government will step in and operate an exchange in that State. See 42 U. S. C. §18041(c)(1). Likewise, knowing that States would not necessarily provide affordable health insurance for aliens lawfully present in the United States—because Medicaid does not require States to provide such coverage—Congress extended the availability of the new federal insurance subsidies to all aliens. See 26 U. S. C. §36B(c)(1)(B)(ii) (excepting from the income limit individuals who are "not eligible for the medicaid program . . . by reason of [their] alien status"). Congress did not make these subsidies available for citizens with incomes below the poverty level because Congress obviously assumed that they would be covered by Medicaid. If Congress had contemplated that some of these citizens would be left without Medicaid coverage as a result of a State's withdrawal or expulsion from the program, Congress surely would have made them eligible for the tax subsidies provided for low-income aliens.

These features of the ACA convey an unmistakable message: Congress never dreamed that any State would refuse to go along with the expansion of Medicaid. Congress well understood that refusal was not a practical option.

The Federal Government does not dispute the inference that Congress anticipated 100% state participation, but it argues that this assumption was based on the fact that ACA's offer was an "exceedingly generous" gift. Brief for Respondents in No. 11–400, at 50. As the Federal Government sees things, Congress is like the generous benefactor who offers $1 million with few strings attached to 50 randomly selected individuals. Just as this benefactor might assume that all of these 50 individuals would snap up his offer, so Congress assumed that every State would gratefully accept the federal funds (and conditions) to go with the expansion of Medicaid.

This characterization of the ACA's offer raises obvious questions. If that offer is "exceedingly generous," as the Federal Government maintains, why have more than half the States brought this lawsuit, contending that the offer is coercive? And why did Congress find it necessary to threaten that any State refusing to accept this "exceed-ingly generous" gift would risk losing all Medicaid funds? Congress could have made just the new funding provided under the ACA contingent on acceptance of the terms of the Medicaid Expansion. Congress took such an approach in some earlier amendments to Medicaid, separating new coverage requirements and funding from the rest of the program so that only new funding was conditioned on new eligibility extensions. See, e.g., Social Security Amendments of 1972, 86Stat. 1465.

Congress' decision to do otherwise here reflects its understanding that the ACA offer is not an "exceedingly generous" gift that no State in its right mind would decline. Instead, acceptance of the offer will impose very substantial costs on participating States. It is true that the Federal Government will bear most of the initial costs associated with the Medicaid Expansion, first paying 100% of the costs of covering newly eligible individuals between 2014 and 2016. 42 U. S. C. §1396d(y). But that is just part of the picture. Participating States will be forced to shoulder substantial costs as well, because after 2019 the Federal Government will cover only 90% of the costs associated with the Expansion, see ibid., with state spending projected to increase by at least $20 billion by 2020 as a consequence. Statement of Douglas W. Elmendorf, CBO's Analysis of the Major Health Care Legislation Enacted in March 2010, p. 24 (Mar. 30, 2011); see also R. Bovbjerg, B. Ormond, & V. Chen, Kaiser Commission on Medicaid and the Uninsured, State Budgets under Federal Health Reform: The Extent and Causes of Variations in Estimated Impacts 4, n. 27 (Feb. 2011) (estimating new state spending at $43.2 billion through 2019). After 2019, state spending is expected to increase at a faster rate; the CBO estimates new state spending at $60 billion through 2021. Statement of Douglas W. Elmendorf, supra, at 24. And these costs may increase in the future because of the very real possibility that the Federal Government will change funding terms and reduce the percentage of funds it will cover. This would leave the States to bear an increasingly large percentage of the bill. See Tr. of Oral Arg. 74–76 (Mar. 28, 2012). Finally, after 2015, the States will have to pick up the tab for 50% of all administrative costs associated with implementing the new program, see §§1396b(a)(2)–(5), (7) (2006 ed., Supp. IV), costs that could approach $12 billion between fiscal years 2014 and 2020, see Dept. of Health and Human Services, Center for Medicaid and Medicare Services, 2010 Actuarial Report on the Financial Outlook for Medicaid 30.

In sum, it is perfectly clear from the goal and structure of the ACA that the offer of the Medicaid Expansion was one that Congress understood no State could refuse. The Medicaid Expansion therefore exceeds Congress' spending power and cannot be implemented.

F

Seven Members of the Court agree that the Medicaid Expansion, as enacted by Congress, is unconstitutional. See Part IV–A to IV–E, supra; Part IV–A, ante, at 45–55 (opinion of Roberts, C. J., joined by Breyer and Kagan, JJ.). Because the Medicaid

Expansion is unconstitutional, the question of remedy arises. The most natural remedy would be to invalidate the Medicaid Expansion. However, the Government proposes—in two cursory sentences at the very end of its brief—preserving the Expansion. Under its proposal, States would receive the additional Medicaid funds if they expand eligibility, but States would keep their pre-existing Medicaid funds if they do not expand eligibility. We cannot accept the Government's suggestion.

The reality that States were given no real choice but to expand Medicaid was not an accident. Congress assumed States would have no choice, and the ACA depends on States' having no choice, because its Mandate requires low-income individuals to obtain insurance many of them can afford only through the Medicaid Expansion. Furthermore, a State's withdrawal might subject everyone in the State to much higher insurance premiums. That is because the Medicaid Expansion will no longer offset the cost to the insurance industry imposed by the ACA's insurance regulations and taxes, a point that is explained in more detail in the severability section below. To make the Medicaid Expansion optional despite the ACA's structure and design " 'would be to make a new law, not to enforce an old one. This is no part of our duty.' " Trade-Mark Cases, 100 U. S. 82, 99 (1879).

Worse, the Government's proposed remedy introduces a new dynamic: States must choose between expanding Medicaid or paying huge tax sums to the federal fisc for the sole benefit of expanding Medicaid in other States. If this divisive dynamic between and among States can be introduced at all, it should be by conscious congressional choice, not by Court-invented interpretation. We do not doubt that States are capable of making decisions when put in a tight spot. We do doubt the authority of this Court to put them there.

The Government cites a severability clause codified with Medicaid in Chapter 7 of the United States Code stating that if "any provision of this chapter, or the application thereof to any person or circumstance, is held invalid, the remainder of the chapter, and the application of such provision to other persons or circumstances shall not be affected thereby." 42 U. S. C. §1303 (2006 ed.). But that clause tells us only that other provisions in Chapter 7 should not be invalidated if §1396c, the authorization for the cut-off of all Medicaid funds, is unconstitutional. It does not tell us that §1396c can be judicially revised, to say what it does not say. Such a judicial power would not be called the doctrine of severability but perhaps the doctrine of amendatory invalidation—similar to the amendatory veto that permits the Governors of some States to reduce the amounts appropriated in legislation. The proof that such a power does not exist is the fact that it would not preserve other congressional dispositions, but would leave it up to the Court what the "validated" legislation will contain. The Court today opts for permitting the cut-off of only incremental Medicaid funding, but it might just as well have permitted, say, the cut-off of funds that represent no more than x percent of the State's bud-get. The Court severs nothing, but simply revises §1396c to read as the Court would desire.

We should not accept the Government's invitation to attempt to solve a constitutional problem by rewriting the Medicaid Expansion so as to allow States that reject it to retain their pre-existing Medicaid funds. Worse, the Government's remedy, now adopted by the Court, takes the ACA and this Nation in a new direction and charts a course for federalism that the Court, not the Congress, has chosen; but under the Constitution, that power and authority do not rest with this Court.

V

Severability

The Affordable Care Act seeks to achieve "near-universal" health insurance coverage. §18091(2)(D) (2006 ed., Supp. IV). The two pillars of the Act are the Individual Mandate and the expansion of coverage under Medicaid. In our view, both these central provisions of the Act—the Individual Mandate and Medicaid Expansion—are invalid. It follows, as some of the parties urge, that all other provisions of the Act must fall as well. The following section explains the severability principles that require this conclusion. This analysis also shows how closely interrelated the Act is, and this is all the more reason why it is judicial usurpation to impose an entirely new mechanism for withdrawal of Medicaid funding, see Part IV–F, supra, which is one of many examples of how rewriting the Act alters its dynamics.

A

When an unconstitutional provision is but a part of a more comprehensive statute, the question arises as to the validity of the remaining provisions. The Court's authority to declare a statute partially unconstitutional has been well established since Marbury v. Madison, 1 Cranch 137 (1803), when the Court severed an unconstitutional provision from the Judiciary Act of 1789. And while the Court has sometimes applied "at least a modest presumption in favor of . . . severability," C. Nelson, Statutory Interpretation 144 (2010), it has not always done so, see, e.g., Minnesota v. Mille Lacs Band of Chippewa Indians, 526 U. S. 172–195 (1999).

An automatic or too cursory severance of statutory provisions risks "rewrit[ing] a statute and giv[ing] it an effect altogether different from that sought by the measure viewed as a whole." Railroad Retirement Bd. v. Alton R. Co., 295 U. S. 330, 362 (1935) . The Judiciary, if it orders uncritical severance, then assumes the legislative function; for it imposes on the Nation, by the Court's decree, its own new statutory regime, consisting of policies, risks, and duties that Congress did not enact. That can be a more extreme exercise of the judicial power than striking the whole statute and allowing Congress to address the conditions that pertained when the statute was considered at the outset.

The Court has applied a two-part guide as the framework for severability analysis. The test has been deemed "well established." Alaska Airlines, Inc. v. Brock, 480 U. S. 678, 684 (1987) . First, if the Court holds a statutory provision unconstitutional, it then determines whether the now truncated statute will operate in the manner Congress intended. If not, the remaining provisions must be invalidated. See id., at 685. In Alaska Airlines, the Court clarified that this first inquiry requires more than ask-ing whether "the balance of the legislation is incapable of functioning independently." Id., at 684. Even if the remaining provisions will operate in some coherent way, that alone does not save the statute. The question is whether the provisions will work as Congress intended. The "relevant inquiry in evaluating severability is whether the statute will function in a manner consistent with the intent of Congress." Id., at 685 (emphasis in original). See also Free Enterprise Fund v. Public Company Accounting Oversight Bd., 561 U. S. ___, ___ (2010) (slip op., at 28) (the Act "remains fully operative as a law with these tenure restrictions excised") (internal quotation marks omitted); United States v. Booker, 543 U. S. 220, 227 (2005) ("[T]wo provisions . . . must be invalidated in order to allow the statute to operate in a manner consistent with congressional intent"); Mille Lacs, supra, at 194 ("[E]m-bodying as it did one coherent policy, [the entire order] is inseverable").

Second, even if the remaining provisions can operate as Congress designed them to operate, the Court must determine if Congress would have enacted them standing alone and without the unconstitutional portion. If Congress would not, those provisions, too, must be invalidated. See Alaska Airlines, supra, at 685 ("[T]he unconstitutional provision must be severed unless the statute cre-ated in its absence is legislation that Congress would not have enacted"); see also Free Enterprise Fund, supra, at ___ (slip op., at 29) ("[N]othing in the statute's text or historical context makes it 'evident' that Congress, faced with the limitations imposed by the Constitution, would have preferred no Board at all to a Board whose members are removable at will"); Ayotte v. Planned Parenthood of Northern New Eng., 546 U. S. 320, 330 (2006) ("Would the legislature have preferred what is left of its statute to no statute at all"); Denver Area Ed. Telecommunications Consortium, Inc. v. FCC, 518 U. S. 727, 767 (1996) (plurality opinion) ("Would Congress still have passed §10(a) had it known that the remaining provisions were invalid" (internal quotation marks and brackets omitted)).

The two inquiries—whether the remaining provisions will operate as Congress designed them, and whether Congress would have enacted the remaining provisions standing alone—often are interrelated. In the ordinary course, if the remaining provisions cannot operate according to the congressional design (the first inquiry), it almost necessarily follows that Congress would not have enacted them (the second inquiry). This close interaction may explain why the Court has not always been precise in distinguishing between the two. There are, however, occasions in which the severability standard's first inquiry (statutory functionality) is not a proxy for the second inquiry (whether the Legislature intended the remaining provisions to stand alone).

B

The Act was passed to enable affordable, "near-universal" health insurance coverage. 42 U. S. C. §18091(2)(D). The resulting, complex statute consists of mandates and other requirements; comprehensive regulation and penalties; some undoubted taxes; and increases in some governmental expenditures, decreases in others. Under the severability test set out above, it must be determined if those provisions function in a coherent way and as Congress would have intended, even when the major provisions establishing the Individual Mandate and Medicaid Expansion are themselves invalid.

Congress did not intend to establish the goal of near-universal coverage without regard to fiscal consequences. See, e.g., ACA §1563, 124Stat. 270 ("[T]his Act will reduce the Federal deficit between 2010 and 2019"). And it did not intend to impose the inevitable costs on any one industry or group of individuals. The whole design of the Act is to balance the costs and benefits affecting each set of regulated parties. Thus, individuals are required to obtain health insurance. See 26 U. S. C. §5000A(a). Insurance companies are required to sell them insurance regardless of patients' pre-existing conditions and to comply with a host of other regulations. And the companies must pay new taxes. See §4980I (high-cost insurance plans);42 U. S. C. §§300gg(a)(1), 300gg–4(b) (community rating); §§300gg–1, 300gg–3, 300gg–4(a) (guaranteed issue); §300gg–11 (elimination of coverage limits); §300gg–14(a) (dependent children up to age 26); ACA §§9010, 10905, 124Stat. 865, 1017 (excise tax); Health Care and Education Reconciliation Act of 2010 (HCERA) §1401, 124Stat. 1059 (excise tax). States are expected to expand Medicaid eligibility and to create regulated marketplaces called ex-changes where individuals can purchase insurance. See 42 U. S. C. §§1396a(a)(10)(A)(i)(VIII) (2006 ed., Supp. IV) (Medicaid Expansion), 18031 (exchanges). Some persons who cannot afford insurance are provided it through the Medicaid Expansion, and others are aided in their purchase of insurance through federal subsidies available on health-insurance exchanges. See 26 U. S. C. §36B (2006 ed., Supp. IV), 42 U. S. C. §18071 (2006 ed., Supp. IV) (federal subsidies). The Federal Government's increased spending is offset by new taxes and cuts in other federal expenditures, including reductions in Medicare and in federal payments to hospitals. See, e.g., §1395ww(r) (Medicare cuts); ACA Title IX, Subtitle A, 124Stat. 847 ("Rev-enue Offset Provisions"). Employers with at least 50employees must either provide employees with adequate health benefits or pay a financial exaction if an employee who qualifies for federal subsidies purchases insurance through an exchange. See 26 U. S. C. §4980H (2006 ed., Supp. IV).

In short, the Act attempts to achieve near-universal health insurance coverage by spreading its costs to individuals, insurers, governments, hospitals, and employers— while, at the same time, offsetting significant portions of those costs with new benefits to each group. For ex-ample, the Federal Government bears the burden of paying billions for the new entitlements mandated by the Medicaid Expansion and federal subsidies for insurance purchases on the exchanges; but it benefits from reductions in the reimbursements it pays to hospitals. Hospitals lose those reimbursements; but they benefit from the decrease in uncompensated care, for under the insurance regulations it is easier for individuals with pre-existing conditions to purchase coverage that increases payments to hospitals. Insurance companies bear new costs imposed by a collection of insurance regulations and taxes, including "guaranteed issue" and "community rating" requirements to give coverage regardless of the insured's pre-existing conditions; but the insurers benefit from the new, healthy purchasers who are forced by the Individual

Mandate to buy the insurers' product and from the new low-income Medicaid recipients who will enroll in insurance companies' Medicaid-funded managed care programs. In summary, the Individual Mandate and Medicaid Expansion offset insurance regulations and taxes, which offset reduced reimbursements to hospitals, which offset increases in federal spending. So, the Act's major provisions are interdependent.

The Act then refers to these interdependencies as "shared responsibility." See ACA Subtitle F, Title I, 124Stat. 242 ("Shared Responsibility"); ACA §1501, ibid. (same); ACA §1513, id., at 253 (same); ACA §4980H, ibid. (same). In at least six places, the Act describes the Individual Mandate as working "together with the other pro-visions of this Act." 42 U. S. C. §18091(2)(C) (2006 ed., Supp. IV) (working "together" to "add millions of new consumers to the health insurance market"); §18091(2)(E) (working "together" to "significantly reduce" the economic cost of the poorer health and shorter lifespan of the uninsured); §18091(2)(F) (working "together" to "lower health insurance premiums"); §18091(2)(G) (working "together" to "improve financial security for families"); §18091(2)(I) (working "together" to minimize "adverse selection and broaden the health insurance risk pool to include healthy individuals"); §18091(2)(J) (working "together" to "significantly reduce administrative costs and lower health insurance premiums"). The Act calls the Individual Mandate "an essential part" of federal regulation of health insurance and warns that "the absence of the requirement would undercut Federal regulation of the health insurance market." §18091(2)(H).

C

One preliminary point should be noted before applying severability principles to the Act. To be sure, an argument can be made that those portions of the Act that none of the parties has standing to challenge cannot be held nonseverable. The response to this argument is that our cases do not support it. See, e.g., Williams v. Standard Oil Co. of La., 278 U. S. 235–244 (1929) (holding nonseverable statutory provisions that did not burden the parties). It would be particularly destructive of sound government to apply such a rule with regard to a multifaceted piece of legislation like the ACA. It would take years, perhaps decades, for each of its provisions to be adjudicated separately—and for some of them (those simply expending federal funds) no one may have separate standing. The Federal Government, the States, and private parties ought to know at once whether the entire legislation fails.

The opinion now explains in Part V–C–1, infra, why the Act's major provisions are not severable from the Mandate and Medicaid Expansion. It proceeds from the insurance regulations and taxes (C–1–a), to the reductions in reimbursements to hospitals and other Medicare reductions (C–1–b), the exchanges and their federal subsidies (C–1–c), and the employer responsibility assessment (C–1–d).Part V–C–2, infra, explains why the Act's minor provisions also are not severable.

1

The Act's Major Provisions

Major provisions of the Affordable Care Act—i.e., the insurance regulations and taxes, the reductions in federal reimbursements to hospitals and other Medicare spending reductions, the exchanges and their federal subsidies, and the employer responsibility assessment—cannot remain once the Individual Mandate and Medicaid Expansion are invalid. That result follows from the undoubted inability of the other major provisions to operate as Congress intended without the Individual Mandate and Medicaid Expansion. Absent the invalid portions, the other major provisions could impose enormous risks of unexpected bur-dens on patients, the health-care community, and the federal budget. That consequence would be in absolute conflict with the ACA's design of "shared responsibility," and would pose a threat to the Nation that Congress did not intend.

a

Insurance Regulations and Taxes

Without the Individual Mandate and Medicaid Expansion, the Affordable Care Act's insurance regulations and insurance taxes impose risks on insurance companies and their customers that this Court cannot measure. Those risks would undermine Congress' scheme of "shared responsibility." See 26 U. S. C. §4980I (2006 ed., Supp.IV) (high-cost insurance plans); 42 U. S. C. §§300gg(a)(1) (2006 ed., Supp. IV), 300gg–4(b) (community rating); §§300gg–1, 300gg–3, 300gg–4(a) (guaranteed issue); §300gg–11 (elimination of coverage limits); §300gg–14(a) (dependent children up to age 26); ACA §§9010, 10905, 124Stat. 865, 1017 (excise tax); HCERA §1401, 124Stat. 1059 (excise tax).

The Court has been informed by distinguished economists that the Act's Individual Mandate and Medicaid Expansion would each increase revenues to the insurance industry by about $350 billion over 10 years; that this combined figure of $700 billion is necessary to offset the approximately $700 billion in new costs to the insurance industry imposed by the Act's insurance regulations and taxes; and that the new $700-billion burden would otherwise dwarf the industry's current profit margin. See Brief for Economists as Amici Curiae in No. 11–393 etc. (Severability), pp. 9–16, 10a.

If that analysis is correct, the regulations and taxes will mean higher costs for insurance companies. Higher costs may mean higher premiums for consumers, despite the Act's goal of "lower[ing] health insurance premiums." 42 U. S. C. §18091(2)(F) (2006 ed., Supp. IV). Higher costs also could threaten the survival of health-insurance companies, despite the Act's goal of "effective health insurance markets." §18091(2)(J).

The actual cost of the regulations and taxes may be more or less than predicted. What is known, however, is that severing other provisions from the Individual Mandate and Medicaid Expansion necessarily would impose significant risks and real uncertainties on insurance companies, their customers, all other major actors in the sys-tem, and the government treasury. And what also is known is this: Unnecessary risks and avoidable uncertainties are hostile to economic progress and fiscal stability and thus to the safety and welfare of the Nation and the Nation's freedom. If those risks and uncertainties are to be imposed, it must not be by the Judiciary.

b

Reductions in Reimbursements to Hospitals and Other Reductions in Medicare Expenditures

The Affordable Care Act reduces payments by the Federal Government to hospitals by more than $200 billion over 10 years. See 42 U. S. C. §1395ww(b)(3)(B)(xi)–(xii) (2006 ed., Supp. IV); §1395ww(q); §1395ww(r); §1396r–4(f)(7).

The concept is straightforward: Near-universal coverage will reduce uncompensated care, which will increase hospitals' revenues, which will offset the government's reductions in Medicare and Medicaid reimbursements to hospitals. Responsibility will be shared, as burdens and benefits balance each other. This is typical of the whole dynamic of the Act.

Invalidating the key mechanisms for expanding insurance coverage, such as community rating and the Medicaid Expansion, without invalidating the reductions in Medicare and Medicaid, distorts the ACA's design of "shared responsibility." Some hospitals may be forced to raise the cost of care in order to offset the reductions in reimbursements, which could raise the cost of insurance premiums, in contravention of the Act's goal of "lower[ing] health insurance premiums." 42 U. S. C. §18091(2)(F) (2006 ed., Supp. IV). See also §18091(2)(I) (goal of "lower[ing] health insurance premiums"); §18091(2)(J) (same). Other hospitals, particularly safety-net hospitals that serve a large number of uninsured patients, may be forced to shut down. Cf. National Assn. of Public Hospitals, 2009 Annual Survey: Safety Net Hospitals and Health Systems Fulfill Mission in Uncertain Times 5–6 (Feb. 2011). Like the effect of preserving the insurance regulations and taxes, the precise degree of risk to hospitals is unknowable. It is not the proper role of the Court, by severing part of a statute and allowing the rest to stand, to impose unknowable risks that Congress could neither measure nor predict. And Congress could not have intended that result in any event.

There is a second, independent reason why the reductions in reimbursements to hospitals and the ACA's other Medicare cuts must be invalidated. The ACA's $455 billion in Medicare and Medicaid savings offset the $434-billion cost of the Medicaid Expansion. See CBO Estimate, Table 2 (Mar. 20, 2010). The reductions allowed Congress to find that the ACA "will reduce the Federal deficit between 2010 and 2019" and "will continue to reduce budget deficits after 2019." ACA §§1563(a)(1), (2), 124Stat. 270.

That finding was critical to the ACA. The Act's "shared responsibility" concept extends to the federal budget. Congress chose to offset new federal expenditures with budget cuts and tax increases. That is why the United States has explained in the course of this litigation that "[w]hen Congress passed the ACA, it was careful to ensure that any increased spending, including on Medicaid, was offset by other revenue-raising and cost-saving provisions." Memorandum in Support of Government's Motion for Summary Judgment in No. 3–10–cv–91, p. 41.

If the Medicare and Medicaid reductions would no longer be needed to offset the costs of the Medicaid Expansion, the reductions would no longer operate in the manner Congress intended. They would lose their justification and foundation. In addition, to preserve them would be "to eliminate a significant quid pro quo of the legislative compromise" and create a statute Congress did not enact. Legal Services Corporation v. Velazquez, 531 U. S. 533, 561 (2001) (Scalia, J., dissenting). It is no secret that cutting Medicare is unpopular; and it is most improbable Congress would have done so without at least the assurance that it would render the ACA deficit-neutral. See ACA §§1563(a)(1), (2), 124Stat. 270.

c

Health Insurance Exchanges and Their Federal Subsidies

The ACA requires each State to establish a health-insurance "exchange." Each exchange is a one-stop marketplace for individuals and small businesses to compare community-rated health insurance and purchase the policy of their choice. The exchanges cannot operate in the manner Congress intended if the Individual Mandate, Medicaid Expansion, and insurance regulations cannot remain in force.

The Act's design is to allocate billions of federal dollars to subsidize individuals' purchases on the exchanges. Individuals with incomes between 100 and 400 percent of the poverty level receive tax credits to offset the cost of insurance to the individual purchaser. 26 U. S. C. §36B (2006 ed., Supp. IV); 42 U. S. C. §18071 (2006 ed., Supp. IV). By 2019, 20 million of the 24 million people who will obtain insurance through an exchange are expected to receive an average federal subsidy of $6, 460 per person. See CBO, Analysis of the Major Health Care Legislation Enacted in March 2010, pp. 18–19 (Mar. 30, 2011). Without the community-rating insurance regulation, however, the average federal subsidy could be much higher; for community rating greatly lowers the enormous premiums unhealthy individuals would otherwise pay. Federal subsidies would make up much of the difference.

The result would be an unintended boon to insurance companies, an unintended harm to the federal fisc, and a corresponding breakdown of the "shared responsibility" between the industry and the federal budget that Congress intended. Thus, the federal subsidies must be invalidated.

In the absence of federal subsidies to purchasers, insurance companies will have little incentive to sell insurance on the exchanges. Under the ACA's scheme, few, if any, individuals would want to buy individual insurance policies outside of an exchange, because federal subsidies would be unavailable outside of an exchange. Difficulty in attracting individuals outside of the exchange would in turn motivate insurers to enter exchanges, despite the exchanges' onerous regulations. See 42 U. S. C. §18031. That system of incentives collapses if the federal subsidies are invalidated. Without the federal subsidies, individuals would lose the main incentive to purchase insurance inside the exchanges, and some insurers may be unwilling to offer insurance inside of exchanges. With fewer buyers and even fewer sellers, the exchanges would not operate as Congress intended and may not operate at all.

There is a second reason why, if community rating is invalidated by the Mandate and Medicaid Expansion's invalidity, exchanges cannot be implemented in a manner consistent with the Act's design. A key purpose of an exchange is to provide a marketplace of insurance options where prices are standardized regardless of the buyer's pre-existing conditions. See ibid. An individual who shops for insurance through an exchange will evaluate different insurance products. The products will offer different benefits and prices. Congress designed the exchanges so the shopper can compare benefits and prices. But the comparison cannot be made in the way Congress designed if the prices depend on the shopper's pre-existing health conditions. The prices would vary from person to person. So without community rating—which prohibits insurers from basing the price of insurance on pre-existing conditions—the exchanges cannot operate in the manner Congress intended.

d

Employer-Responsibility Assessment

The employer responsibility assessment provides an incentive for employers with at least 50 employees to provide their employees with health insurance options that meet minimum criteria. See 26 U. S. C. §4980H (2006 ed., Supp. IV). Unlike the Individual Mandate,the employer-responsibility assessment does not require employers to provide an insurance option. Instead, it re-quires them to make a payment to the Federal Government if they do not offer insurance to employees and if insurance is bought on an exchange by an employee who qualifies for the exchange's federal subsidies. See ibid.

For two reasons, the employer-responsibility assessment must be invalidated. First, the ACA makes a direct link between the employer-responsibility assessment and the exchanges. The financial assessment against employers occurs only under certain conditions. One of them is the purchase of insurance by an employee on an exchange. With no exchanges, there are no purchases on the exchanges; and with no purchases on the exchanges, there is nothing to trigger the employer-responsibility assessment.

Second, after the invalidation of burdens on individuals (the Individual Mandate), insurers (the insurance regulations and taxes), States (the Medicaid Expansion), the Federal Government (the federal subsidies for exchanges and for the Medicaid Expansion), and hospitals (the reductions in reimbursements), the preservation of the employer-responsibility assessment would upset the ACA's design of "shared responsibility." It would leave employers as the only parties bearing any significant responsibility. That was not the congressional intent.

2

The Act's Minor Provisions

The next question is whether the invalidation of the ACA's major provisions requires the Court to invalidate the ACA's other provisions. It does.

The ACA is over 900 pages long. Its regulations include requirements ranging from a break time and secluded place at work for nursing mothers, see 29 U. S. C. §207(r)(1) (2006 ed., Supp. IV), to displays of nutritional content at chain restaurants, see 21 U. S. C. §343(q)(5)(H).The Act raises billions of dollars in taxes and fees, including exactions imposed on high-income taxpayers, see ACA §§9015, 10906; HCERA §1402, medical devices, see 26 U. S. C. §4191 (2006 ed., Supp. IV), and tanning booths, see §5000B. It spends government money on, among other things, the study of how to spend less government money. 42 U. S. C. §1315a. And it includes a number of provisions that provide benefits to the State of a particular legislator. For example, §10323, 124Stat. 954, extends Medicare coverage to individuals exposed to asbestos from a mine in Libby, Montana. Another provision, §2006, id., at 284, increases Medicaid payments only in Louisiana.

Such provisions validate the Senate Majority Leader's statement, " 'I don't know if there is a senator that doesn't have something in this bill that was important to them. . . . [And] if they don't have something in it important to them, then it doesn't speak well of them. That's what this legislation is all about: It's the art of compromise.' " Pear, In Health Bill for Everyone, Provisions for a Few, N. Y. Times, Jan. 4, 2010, p. A10 (quoting Sen. Reid). Often, a minor provision will be the price paid for support of a major provision. So, if the major provision were unconstitutional, Congress would not have passed the minor one.

Without the ACA's major provisions, many of these minor provisions will not operate in the manner Congress intended. For example, the tax increases are "Revenue Offset Provisions" designed to help offset the cost to the Federal Government of programs like the Medicaid Expansion and the exchanges' federal subsidies. See Title IX, Subtitle A—Revenue Offset Provisions, 124Stat. 847. With the Medicaid Expansion and the exchanges invalidated, the tax increases no longer operate to offset costs, and they no longer serve the purpose in the Act's scheme of "shared responsibility" that Congress intended.

Some provisions, such as requiring chain restaurants to display nutritional content, appear likely to operate as Congress intended, but they fail the second test for severability. There is no reason to believe that Congress would have enacted them independently. The Court has not previously had occasion to consider severability in the con-text of an omnibus enactment like the ACA, which includes not only many provisions that are ancillary to its central provisions but also many that are entirely unrelated— hitched on because it was a quick way to get them passed despite opposition, or because their proponents could exact their enactment as the quid pro quo for their needed support. When we are confronted with such a so-called "Christmas tree," a law to which many nongermane ornaments have been attached, we think the proper rule must be that when the tree no longer exists the ornaments are superfluous. We have no reliable basis for knowing which pieces of the Act would have passed on their own. It is certain that many of them would not have, and it is not a proper function of this Court to guess which. To sever the statute in that manner " 'would be to make a new law, not to enforce an old one. This is not part of our duty.' " Trade-Mark Cases, 100 U. S., at 99.

This Court must not impose risks unintended by Congress or produce legislation Congress may have lacked the support to enact. For those reasons, the unconstitutionality of both the Individual Mandate and the Medicaid Expansion requires the invalidation of the Affordable Care Act's other provisions.

* * *

The Court today decides to save a statute Congress did not write. It rules that what the statute declares to be a requirement with a penalty is instead an option subject to a tax. And it changes the intentionally coercive sanction of a total cut-off of Medicaid funds to a supposedly noncoercive cut-off of only the incremental funds that the Act makes available.

The Court regards its strained statutory interpretation as judicial modesty. It is not. It amounts instead to a vast judicial overreaching. It creates a debilitated, inoperable version of health-care regulation that Congress did not enact and the public does not expect. It makes enactment of sensible health-care regulation more difficult, since Congress cannot start afresh but must take as its point of departure a jumble of now senseless provisions, provisions that certain interests favored under the Court's new design will struggle to retain. And it leaves the public and the States to expend vast sums of money on requirements that may or may not survive the necessary congressional revision.

The Court's disposition, invented and atextual as it is, does not even have the merit of avoiding constitutional difficulties. It creates them. The holding that the Individual Mandate is a tax raises a difficult constitutional question (what is a direct tax?) that the Court resolves with inadequate deliberation. And the judgment on the Medicaid Expansion issue ushers in new federalism concerns and places an unaccustomed strain upon the Union. Those States that decline the Medicaid Expansion must subsidize, by the federal tax dollars taken from their citizens, vast grants to the States that accept the Medicaid Expansion. If that destabilizing political dynamic, so antagonistic to a harmonious Union, is to be introduced at all, it should be by Congress, not by the Judiciary.

The values that should have determined our course today are caution, minimalism, and the understanding that the Federal Government is one of limited powers. But the Court's ruling undermines those values at every turn. In the name of restraint, it overreaches. In the name of constitutional avoidance, it creates new constitutional questions. In the name of cooperative federalism, it undermines state sovereignty.

The Constitution, though it dates from the founding of the Republic, has powerful meaning and vital relevance to our own times. The constitutional protections that this case involves are protections of structure. Structural protections—notably, the restraints imposed by federalism and separation of powers—are less romantic and have less obvious a connection to personal freedom than the provisions of the Bill of Rights or the Civil War Amendments. Hence they tend to be undervalued or even forgotten by our citizens. It should be the responsibility of the Court to teach otherwise, to remind our people that the Framers considered structural protections of freedom the most important ones, for which reason they alone were embodied in the original Constitution and not left to later amendment. The fragmentation of power produced by the structure of our Government is central to liberty, and when we destroy it, we place liberty at peril. Today's decision should have vindicated, should have taught, this truth; instead, our judgment today has disregarded it.

For the reasons here stated, we would find the Act invalid in its entirety. We respectfully dissent.

Notes to Justice Scalia (or Justice Kennedy's?) dissent in National Federation of Independent Business v. Sebelius (June 28, 2012)

1 The most authoritative legal dictionaries of the founding era lack any definition for "regulate" or "regulation," suggesting that the term bears its ordinary meaning (rather than some specialized legal meaning) in the constitutional text. See R. Burn, A New Law Dictionary 281 (1792); G. Jacob, A New Law Dictionary (10th ed. 1782); 2 T. Cunningham, A New and Complete Law Dictionary (2d ed. 1771).

2 Justice Ginsburg is therefore right to note that Congress is "not mandating the purchase of a discrete, unwanted product." Ante, at 22 (opinion concurring in part, concurring in judgment in part, and dissenting in part). Instead, it is mandating the purchase of an unwanted suite of products—e.g., physician office visits, emergency room visits, hospital room and board, physical therapy, durable medical equipment, mental health care, and substance abuse detoxification. See Selected Medical Benefits: A Report from the Dept. of Labor to the Dept. of Health & Human Services (April 15, 2011) (reporting that over two-thirds of private industry health plans cover these goods and services), online at http://www.bls.gov/ncs/ebs/sp/selmedbensreport.pdf (all Inter-net materials as visited June 26, 2012, and available in Clerk of Court's case file).

3 In its effort to show the contrary, Justice Ginsburg's dissent comesup with nothing more than two condemnation cases, which it says demonstrate "Congress' authority under the commerce power to compel an 'inactive' landholder to submit to an unwanted sale." Ante, at 24. Wrong on both scores. As its name suggests, the condemnation power does not "compel" anyone to do anything. It acts in rem, against the property that is condemned, and is effective with or without a transfer of title from the former owner. More important, the power to condemn for public use is a separate sovereign power, explicitly acknowledged in the Fifth Amendment, which provides that "private property [shall not] be taken for public use, without just compensation." Thus, the power to condemn tends to refute rather than supportthe power to compel purchase of unwanted goods at a prescribed price: The latter is rather like the power to condemn cash for public use. If it existed, why would it not (like the condemnation power) be accompanied by a requirement of fair compensation for the portion of the exacted price that exceeds the goods' fair market value (here, the difference between what the free

market would charge for a health-insurance policy on a young, healthy person with no pre-existing conditions, and the government-exacted community-rated premium)?

4 No one seriously contends that any of Congress' other enumerated powers gives it the authority to enact §5000A as a regulation.

5 Of course it can be both for statutory purposes, since Congress can define "tax" and "penalty" in its enactments any way it wishes. That is why United States v. Sotelo, 436 U. S. 268 (1978), does not disprove our statement. That case held that a "penalty" for willful failure to pay one's taxes was included among the "taxes" made non-dischargeable under the Bankruptcy Code. 436 U. S., at 273–275. Whether the "penalty" was a "tax" within the meaning of the Bankruptcy Code had absolutely no bearing on whether it escaped the constitutional limitations on penalties.

6 The amicus appointed to defend the proposition that the Anti-Injunction Act deprives us of jurisdiction stresses that the penalty for failing to comply with the mandate "shall be assessed and collectedin the same manner as an assessable penalty under subchapter B of chapter 68," 26 U. S. C. §5000A(g)(1) (2006 ed., Supp. IV), and that such penalties "shall be assessed and collected in the same manneras taxes," §6671(a) (2006 ed.). But that point seems to us to confirmthe inapplicability of the Anti-Injunction Act. That the penalty is tobe "assessed and collected in the same manner as taxes" refutes the proposition that it is a tax for all statutory purposes, including with respect to the Anti-Injunction Act. Moreover, elsewhere in the Internal Revenue Code, Congress has provided both that a particular payment shall be "assessed and collected" in the same manner as a tax and that no suit shall be maintained to restrain the assessment or collection of the payment. See, e.g., §§7421(b)(1), §6901(a); §6305(a), (b). Thelatter directive would be superfluous if the former invoked the Anti-Injunction Act. Amicus also suggests that the penalty should be treated as a tax because it is an assessable penalty, and the Code's assessment provision authorizes the Secretary of the Treasury to assess "all taxes (in-cluding interest, additional amounts, additions to the tax, and as-sessable penalties) imposed by this title." §6201(a) (2006 ed., Supp.IV). But the fact that such items are included as "taxes" for purposes of assessment does not establish that they are included as "taxes" for purposes of other sections of the Code, such as the Anti-Injunction Act, that do not contain similar "including" language.

7 "State expenditures" is used here to mean annual expenditures from the States' own funding sources, and it excludes federal grants unless otherwise noted.

8 This number is expressed in billions of Fiscal Year 2005 dollars.

9 See Office of Management and Budget, Historical Tables, Budget of the U. S. Government, Fiscal Year 2013, Table 12.1—Summary Comparison of Total Outlays for Grants to State and Local Governments: 1940–2017 (hereinafter Table 12.1), http://www.whitehouse.gov/omb/budget/Historicals; id., Table 15.2—Total Government Expenditures: 1948–2011 (hereinafter Table 15.2).

10 This number is expressed in billions of Fiscal Year 2005 dollars.

11 See Table 12.1; Dept. of Commerce, Bureau of Census, Statistical Abstract of the United States: 2001, p. 262 (Table 419, Federal Grants-in-Aid Summary: 1970 to 2001).

12 See Statistical Abstract of the United States: 2012, p. 268 (Table 431, Federal Grants-in-Aid to State and Local Governments: 1990 to 2011).

13 Justice Ginsburg argues that "[a] State . . . has no claim on the money its residents pay in federal taxes." Ante, at 59, n. 26. This is true as a formal matter. "When the United States Government taxes United States citizens, it taxes them 'in their individual capacities' as 'the people of America'—not as residents of a particular State." Ante, at 58, n. 26 (quoting U. S. Term Limits, Inc. v. Thornton, 514 U. S. 779, 839 (1995) (Kennedy, J., concurring)). But unless Justice Ginsburg thinks that there is no limit to the amount of money that can be squeezed out of taxpayers, heavy federal taxation diminishes the practical ability of States to collect their own taxes.

14 The Federal Government has a higher number for federal spending on Medicaid. According to the Office of Management and Budget, federal grants to the States for Medicaid amounted to nearly $273 billion in Fiscal Year 2010. See Office of Management and Bud-get, Historical Tables, Budget of the U. S. Government, Fiscal Year 2013, Table 12.3—Total Outlays for Grants to State and Local Gov-ernments by Function, Agency, and Program: 1940–2013, http://www.whitehouse.gov/omb/budget/Historicals. In that Fiscal Year, total federal outlays for grants to state and local governments amounted to over $608 billion, see Table 12.1, and state and local government expenditures from their own sources amounted to $1.6 trillion, see Table 15.2. Using these numbers, 44.8% of all federal outlays to both state and local governments was allocated to Medicaid, amounting to 16.8% of all state and local expenditures from their own sources.

15 The Federal Government reports a higher percentage. Accordingto Medicaid.gov, in Fiscal Year 2010, the Federal Government made Medicaid payments in the amount of nearly $260 billion, repre-senting 67.79% of total Medicaid payments of $383 billion. See www.medicaid.gov/Medicaid-CHIP-Program-Information/By-State/By-State.html.

Searches and Seizures of DNA: Justice Scalia's dissent in Maryland v. King (June 2, 2013)

Justice Scalia, with whom Justice Ginsburg, Justice Sotomayor, and Justice Kagan join, dissenting.

The Fourth Amendment forbids searching a person for evidence of a crime when there is no basis for believing the person is guilty of the crime or is in possession of incriminating evidence. That prohibition is categorical and without exception; it lies at the very heart of the Fourth Amendment. Whenever this Court has allowed a suspicionless search, it has insisted upon a justifying motive apart from the investigation of crime.

It is obvious that no such noninvestigative motive exists in this case. The Court's assertion that DNA is being taken, not to solve crimes, but to identify those in the State's custody, taxes the credulity of the credulous. And the Court's comparison of Maryland's DNA searches to other techniques, such as fingerprinting, can seem apt only to those who know no more than today's opinionhas chosen to tell them about how those DNA searches actually work.

I

A

At the time of the Founding, Americans despised the British use of so-called "general warrants"—warrants not grounded upon a sworn oath of a specific infraction by a particular individual, and thus not limited in scope and application. The first Virginia Constitution declared that "general warrants, whereby any officer or messenger may be commanded to search suspected places without evidence of a fact committed," or to search a person "whose offence is not particularly described and supported by evidence," "are grievous and oppressive, and ought not be granted." Va. Declaration of Rights §10 (1776), in 1 B. Schwartz, The Bill of Rights: A Documentary History 234, 235 (1971). The Maryland Declaration of Rights similarly provided that general warrants were "illegal." Md. Declaration of Rights §XXIII (1776), in id., at 280, 282.

In the ratification debates, Antifederalists sarcastically predicted that the general, suspicionless warrant would be among the Constitution's "blessings." Blessings of the New Government, Independent Gazetteer, Oct. 6, 1787, in 13 Documentary History of the Ratification of the Constitution 345 (J. Kaminski & G. Saladino eds. 1981). "Brutus" of New York asked why the Federal Constitution contained no provision like Maryland's, Brutus II, N. Y. Journal, Nov. 1, 1787, in id., at 524, and Patrick Henry warned that the new Federal Constitution would expose the citizenry to searches and seizures "in the most arbitrary manner, without any evidence or reason." 3 Debates on the Federal Constitution 588 (J. Elliot 2d ed. 1854).

Madison's draft of what became the Fourth Amendment answered these charges by providing that the "rights of the people to be secured in their persons . . . from all unreasonable searches and seizures, shall not be violated by warrants issued without probable cause . . . or not particularly describing the places to be searched." 1 Annals of Cong. 434–435 (1789). As ratified, the Fourth Amendment's Warrant Clause forbids a warrant to "issue" except "upon probable cause," and requires that it be "particula[r]" (which is to say, individualized) to "the place to be searched, and the persons or things to be seized." And we have held that, even when a warrant is not constitution-ally necessary, the Fourth Amendment's general prohibition of "unreasonable" searches imports the same requirement of individualized suspicion. See Chandler v. Miller, 520 U. S. 305, 308 (1997).

Although there is a "closely guarded category of constitutionally permissible suspicionless searches," id., at 309, that has never included searches designed to serve "the normal need for law enforcement," Skinner v. Railway Labor Executives' Assn., 489 U. S. 602, 619 (1989) (internal quotation marks omitted). Even the common name for suspicionless searches—"special needs" searches—itself reflects that they must be justified, always, by concerns "other than crime detection." Chandler, supra, at 313–314. We have approved random drug tests of railroad employees, yes—but only because the Government's need to "regulat[e] the conduct of railroad employees to ensure safety" is distinct from "normal law enforcement." Skinner, supra, at 620. So too we have approved suspicionless searches in public schools—but only because there the government acts in furtherance of its "responsibilities . . . as guardian and tutor of children entrusted to its care." Vernonia School Dist. 47J v. Acton, 515 U. S. 646, 665 (1995).

So while the Court is correct to note (ante, at 8–9) that there are instances in which we have permitted searches without individualized suspicion, "[i]n none of these cases . . . did we indicate approval of a [search] whose primary purpose was to detect evidence of ordinary criminal wrongdoing." Indianapolis v. Edmond, 531 U. S. 32, 38 (2000). That limitation is crucial. It is only when a governmental purpose aside from crime-solving is at stake that we engage in the free-form "reasonableness" inquiry that the Court indulges at length today. To put it another way, both the legitimacy of the Court's method and the correctness of its outcome hinge entirely on the truth of a single proposition: that the primary purpose of these DNA searches is something other than simply discovering evidence of criminal wrongdoing. As I detail below, that proposition is wrong.

B

The Court alludes at several points (see ante, at 11, 25) to the fact that King was an arrestee, and arrestees may be validly searched incident to their arrest. But the Court does not really rest on this principle, and for good reason: The objects of a search incident to arrest must be either (1) weapons or evidence that might easily be destroyed, or (2) evidence relevant to the crime of arrest. See Arizona v. Gant, 556 U. S. 332–344 (2009); Thornton v. United States, 541 U. S. 615, 632 (2004) (Scalia, J., concurring in judgment). Neither is the object of the search at issue here.

The Court hastens to clarify that it does not mean to approve invasive surgery on arrestees or warrantless searches of their homes. Ante, at 25. That the Court feels the need to disclaim these consequences is as damning a criticism of its suspicionless-search regime as any I can muster. And the Court's attempt to distinguish those hypothetical searches from this real one is unconvincing. We are told that the "privacy-related concerns" in the search of a home "are weighty enough that the search may require a warrant, notwithstanding the diminished expectations of privacy of the arrestee." Ante, at 26. But why are the "privacy-related concerns" not also "weighty" when an intrusion into the body is at stake? (The Fourth Amendment lists "persons" first among the entities protected against unreasonable searches and seizures.) And could the police engage, without any suspicion of wrongdoing, in a "brief and . . . minimal" intrusion into the home of an arrestee—perhaps just peeking around the curtilage a bit? See ante, at 26. Obviously not.

At any rate, all this discussion is beside the point. No matter the degree of invasiveness, suspicionless searches are never allowed if their principal end is ordinary crime-solving. A search incident to arrest either serves other ends (such as officer safety, in a search for weapons) or is not suspicionless (as when there is reason to believe the arrestee possesses evidence relevant to the crime of arrest).

Sensing (correctly) that it needs more, the Court elaborates at length the ways that the search here served the special purpose of "identifying" King. 1 But that seems to me quite wrong—unless what one means by "identifying" someone is "searching for evidence that he has committed crimes unrelated to the crime of his arrest." At points the Court does appear to use "identifying" in that peculiar sense—claiming, for example, that knowing "an arrestee's past conduct is essential to an assessment of the danger he poses." Ante, at 15. If identifying someone means finding out what unsolved crimes he has committed, then identification is indistinguishable from the ordinary law-enforcement aims that have never been thought to justify a suspicionless search. Searching every lawfully stopped car, for example, might turn up information about unsolved crimes the driver had committed, but no one would say that such a search was aimed at "identifying" him, and

no court would hold such a search lawful. I will therefore assume that the Court means that the DNA search at issue here was useful to "identify" King in the normal sense of that word—in the sense that would identify the author of Introduction to the Principles of Morals and Legislation as Jeremy Bentham.

1

The portion of the Court's opinion that explains the identification rationale is strangely silent on the actual workings of the DNA search at issue here. To know those facts is to be instantly disabused of the notion that what happened had anything to do with identifying King.

King was arrested on April 10, 2009, on charges unrelated to the case before us. That same day, April 10, the police searched him and seized the DNA evidence at issue here. What happened next? Reading the Court's opinion, particularly its insistence that the search was necessary to know "who [had] been arrested," ante, at 11, one might guess that King's DNA was swiftly processed and his identity thereby confirmed—perhaps against some master database of known DNA profiles, as is done for fingerprints. After all, was not the suspicionless search here crucial to avoid "inordinate risks for facility staff" or to "existing detainee population," ante, at 14? Surely, then—surely—the State of Maryland got cracking on those grave risks immediately, by rushing to identify King with his DNA as soon as possible.

Nothing could be further from the truth. Maryland officials did not even begin the process of testing King's DNA that day. Or, actually, the next day. Or the day after that. And that was for a simple reason: Maryland law forbids them to do so. A "DNA sample collected from an individual charged with a crime . . . may not be tested or placed in the statewide DNA data base system prior to the first scheduled arraignment date." Md. Pub. Saf. Code Ann. §2–504(d)(1) (Lexis 2011) (emphasis added). And King's first appearance in court was not until three days after his arrest. (I suspect, though, that they did not wait three days to ask his name or take his fingerprints.)

This places in a rather different light the Court's solemn declaration that the search here was necessary so that King could be identified at "every stage of the criminal process." Ante, at 18. I hope that the Maryland officials who read the Court's opinion do not take it seriously. Acting on the Court's misperception of Maryland law could lead to jail time. See Md. Pub. Saf. Code Ann. §2–512(c)–(e) (punishing by up to five years' imprisonment anyone who obtains or tests DNA information except as provided by statute). Does the Court really believe that Marylanddid not know whom it was arraigning? The Court's response is to imagine that release on bail could take so long that the DNA results are returned in time, or perhaps that bail could be revoked if the DNA test turned up incriminating information. Ante, at 16–17. That is no answer at all. If the purpose of this Act is to assess "whether [King] should be released on bail," ante, at 15, why would it possibly forbid the DNA testing process to begin until King was arraigned? Why would Maryland resign itself to simply hoping that the bail decision will drag out long enough that the "identification" can succeed before the arrestee is released? The truth, known to Maryland and increasingly to the reader: this search had nothing to do with establishing King's identity.

It gets worse. King's DNA sample was not received by the Maryland State Police's Forensic Sciences Division until April 23, 2009—two weeks after his arrest. It sat in that office, ripening in a storage area, until the custodians got around to mailing it to a lab for testing on June 25, 2009—two months after it was received, and nearly three since King's arrest. After it was mailed, the data from the lab tests were not available for several more weeks, until July 13, 2009, which is when the test results were entered into Maryland's DNA database, together with information identifying the person from whom the sample was taken. Meanwhile, bail had been set, King had engaged in discovery, and he had requested a speedy trial—presumably not a trial of John Doe. It was not until August 4, 2009—four months after King's arrest—that the forwarded sample transmitted (without identifying information) from the Maryland DNA database to the Federal Bureau of Investigation's national database was matched with a sample taken from the scene of an unrelated crime years earlier.

A more specific description of exactly what happened at this point illustrates why, by definition, King couldnot have been identified by this match. The FBI'sDNA database (known as CODIS) consists of two distinct collections. FBI, CODIS and NDIS Fact Sheet, http://www.fbi.gov/about-us/lab/codis/codis-and-ndis-fact-sheet (all Internet materials as visited May 31, 2013, and available in Clerk of Court's case file). One of them, the one to which King's DNA was submitted, consists of DNA samples taken from known convicts or arrestees. I will refer to this as the "Convict and Arrestee Collection." The other collection consists of samples taken from crime scenes; I will refer to this as the "Unsolved Crimes Collection." The Convict and Arrestee Collection stores "no names or other personal identifiers of the offenders, arrestees, or detainees." Ibid. Rather, it contains only the DNA profile itself, the name of the agency that submitted it, the laboratory personnel who analyzed it, and an identification number for the specimen. Ibid. This is because the submitting state laboratories are expected already to know the identities of the convicts and arrestees from whom samples are taken. (And, of course, they do.)

Moreover, the CODIS system works by checking to see whether any of the samples in the Unsolved Crimes Collection match any of the samples in the Convict and Arrestee Collection. Ibid. That is sensible, if what one wants to do is solve those cold cases, but note what it requires: that the identity of the people whose DNA has been entered in the Convict and Arrestee Collection already be known. 2 If one wanted to identify someone in custody using his DNA, the logical thing to do would be to compare that DNA against the Convict and Arrestee Collection: to search, in other words, the collection that could be used (by checking back with the submittingstate agency) to identify people, rather than the collection of evidence from unsolved crimes, whose perpetrators are by definition unknown. But that is not what was done. And that is because this search had nothing to do with identification.

In fact, if anything was "identified" at the moment that the DNA database returned a match, it was not King—his identity was already known. (The docket for the original criminal charges lists his full name, his race, his sex, his height, his weight, his date of birth, and his address.) Rather, what the August 4 match "identified" was the previously-taken sample from the earlier crime. That sample was genuinely mysterious to Maryland; the State knew that it had probably been left by the victim's attacker, but nothing else. King was not identified by his association with the sample; rather, the sample was identified by its association with King. The Court effectively destroys its own "identification" theory when it acknowledges that the object of this search was "to see what [was] already known about [King]." King was who he was, and

volumes of his biography could not make him any more or any less King. No minimally competent speaker of English would say, upon noticing a known arrestee's similarity "to a wanted poster of a previously unidentified suspect," ante, at 13, that the arrestee had thereby been identified. It was the previously unidentified suspect who had been identified—just as, here, it was the previously unidentified rapist.

2

That taking DNA samples from arrestees has nothing to do with identifying them is confirmed not just by actual practice (which the Court ignores) but by the enabling statute itself (which the Court also ignores). The Maryland Act at issue has a section helpfully entitled "Purpose of collecting and testing DNA samples." Md. Pub. Saf. Code Ann. §2–505. (One would expect such a section to play a somewhat larger role in the

Court's analysis of the Act's purpose—which is to say, at least some role.) That provision lists five purposes for which DNA samples may be tested. By this point, it will not surprise the reader to learn that the Court's imagined purpose is not among them.

Instead, the law provides that DNA samples are collected and tested, as a matter of Maryland law, "as part of an official investigation into a crime." §2–505(a)(2). (Or, as our suspicionless-search cases would put it: for ordinary law-enforcement purposes.) That is certainly how everyone has always understood the Maryland Act until today. The Governor of Maryland, in commenting on our decision to hear this case, said that he was glad, because "[a]llowing law enforcement to collect DNA samples . . . is absolutely critical to our efforts to continue driving down crime," and "bolsters our efforts to resolve open investigations and bring them to a resolution." Marbella, Supreme Court Will Review Md. DNA Law, Baltimore Sun, Nov. 10, 2012, pp. 1, 14. The attorney general of Maryland remarked that he "look[ed] forward to the opportunity to defend this important crime-fighting tool," and praised the DNA database for helping to "bring to justice violent perpetrators." Ibid. Even this Court's order staying the decision below states that the statute "provides a valuable tool for investigating unsolved crimes and thereby helping to remove violent offenders from the general population"—with, unsurprisingly, no mention of identity. 567 U. S. ___, ___ (2012) (Roberts, C. J., in chambers) (slip op.,at 3).

More devastating still for the Court's "identification" theory, the statute does enumerate two instances in which a DNA sample may be tested for the purpose of identification: "to help identify human remains," §2–505(a)(3) (emphasis added), and "to help identify missing individuals," §2–505(a)(4) (emphasis added). No mention of identifying arrestees. Inclusio unius est exclusio alterius. And note again that Maryland forbids using DNA records "for any purposes other than those specified"—it is actually a crime to do so. §2–505(b)(2).

The Maryland regulations implementing the Act confirm what is now monotonously obvious: These DNA searches have nothing to do with identification. For example, if someone is arrested and law enforcement determines that "a convicted offender Statewide DNA Data Base sample already exists" for that arrestee, "the agency is not required to obtain a new sample." Code of Md. Regs., tit. 29, §05.01.04(B)(4) (2011). But how could the State know if an arrestee has already had his DNA sample collected, if the point of the sample is to identify who he is? Of course, if the DNA sample is instead taken in order to investigate crimes, this restriction makes perfect sense: Having previously placed an identified someone's DNA on file to check against available crime-scene evidence, there is no sense in going to the expense of taking a new sample. Maryland's regulations further require that the "individ-ual collecting a sample . . . verify the identity of the individual from whom a sample is taken by name and,if applicable, State identification (SID) number." §05.01.04(K). (But how?) And after the sample is taken, it continues to be identified by the individual's name, fingerprints, etc., see §05.01.07(B)—rather than (as the Court believes) being used to identify individuals. See

§05.01.07(B)(2) ("Records and specimen information shall be identified by . . . [the] [n]ame of the donor" (emphasis added)).

So, to review: DNA testing does not even begin until after arraignment and bail decisions are already made. The samples sit in storage for months, and take weeks to test. When they are tested, they are checked against the Unsolved Crimes Collection—rather than the Convict and Arrestee Collection, which could be used to identify them. The Act forbids the Court's purpose (identification), but prescribes as its purpose what our suspicionless-search cases forbid ("official investigation into a crime"). Against all of that, it is safe to say that if the Court's identification theory is not wrong, there is no such thing as error.

II

The Court also attempts to bolster its identification theory with a series of inapposite analogies. See ante, at 18–23.

Is not taking DNA samples the same, asks the Court, as taking a person's photograph? No—because that is not a Fourth Amendment search at all. It does not involve a physical intrusion onto the person, see Florida v. Jardines, 569 U. S. 1, ___ (2013) (slip op., at 3), and we have never held that merely taking a person's photograph invades any recognized "expectation of privacy," see Katz v. United States, 389 U. S. 347 (1967) . Thus, it is unsurprising that the cases the Court cites as authorizing photo-taking do not even mention the Fourth Amendment. See State ex rel. Bruns v. Clausmier, 154 Ind. 599, 57 N. E. 541 (1900) (libel), Shaffer v. United States, 24 App. D. C. 417 (1904) (Fifth Amendment privilege against self-incrimination).

But is not the practice of DNA searches, the Court asks, the same as taking "Bertillon" measurements—noting an arrestee's height, shoe size, and so on, on the back of a photograph? No, because that system was not, in the ordinary case, used to solve unsolved crimes. It is possible, I suppose, to imagine situations in which such measurements might be useful to generate leads. (If witnesses described a very tall burglar, all the "tall man" cards could then be pulled.) But the obvious primary purpose of such measurements, as the Court's description of them makes clear, was to verify that, for example, the person arrested today is the same person that was arrested a year ago. Which is to say, Bertillon measurements were actually used as a system of identification, and drew their primary usefulness from that task. 3

It is on the fingerprinting of arrestees, however, that the Court relies most heavily. Ante, at 20–23. The Court does not actually say whether it believes that taking a person's fingerprints is a Fourth Amendment search, and our cases provide no ready answer to that question. Even assuming so, however, law enforcement's post-arrest use of fingerprints could not be more different from its post-arrestuse of DNA. Fingerprints of arrestees are taken primarily to identify them (though that process sometimes solves crimes); the DNA of arrestees is taken to solve crimes(and nothing else). Contrast CODIS, the FBI's nationwide DNA database, with IAFIS, the FBI's IntegratedAutomated Fingerprint Identification System. See FBI, Integrated Automated Fingerprint

Identification System, http://www.fbi.gov/about-us/cjis/fingerprints_biometrics/iafis/iafis (hereinafter IAFIS).

    The Court asserts that the taking of fingerprints was "constitutional for generations prior to the introduction" of the FBI's rapid computer-matching system. Ante, at 22. This bold statement is bereft of citation to authoritybecause there is none for it. The "great expansion in fingerprinting came before the modern era of Fourth Amendment jurisprudence," and so we were never asked to decide the legitimacy of the practice. United States v. Kincade, 379 F. 3d 813, 874 (CA9 2004) (Kozinski, J., dissenting). As fingerprint databases expanded from convictedcriminals, to arrestees, to civil servants, to immigrants,to everyone with a driver's license, Americans simply "became accustomed to having our fingerprints on filein some government database." Ibid. But it is wrongto suggest that this was uncontroversial at the time, or that this Court blessed universal fingerprinting for"generations" before it was possible to use it effectively for identification.

    The Court also assures us that "the delay in processing DNA from arrestees is being reduced to a substantial degree by rapid technical advances." Ante, at 22. The idea, presumably, is that the snail's pace in this case is atypical, so that DNA is now readily usable for identification. The Court's proof, however, is nothing but a pair of press releases—each of which turns out to undercut this argument. We learn in them that reductions in backlog have enabled Ohio and Louisiana crime labs to analyze a submitted DNA sample in twenty days. 5 But that is still longer than the eighteen days that Maryland needed to analyze King's sample, once it worked its way through the State's labyrinthine bureaucracy. What this illustrates is that these times do not take into account the many other sources of delay. So if the Court means to suggest that Maryland is unusual, that may be right—it may qualify in this context as a paragon of efficiency. (Indeed, the Governor of Maryland was hailing the elimination of that State's backlog more than five years ago. See Wheeler, O'Malley Wants to Expand DNA Testing, Baltimore Sun, Jan. 11, 2008, p. 5B.) Meanwhile, the Court's holdingwill result in the dumping of a large number of arrestee samples—many from minor offenders—onto an already overburdened system: Nearly one-third of Americans will be arrested for some offense by age 23. See Brame, Turner, Paternoster, & Bushway, Cumulative Prevalence of Arrest From Ages 8 to 23 in a National Sample, 129 Pediatrics 21 (2011).

    The Court also accepts uncritically the Government's representation at oral argument that it is developing devices that will be able to test DNA in mere minutes. At most, this demonstrates that it may one day be possible to design a program that uses DNA for a purpose other than crime-solving—not that Maryland has in fact designed such a program today. And that is the main point, which the Court's discussion of the brave new world of instant DNA analysis should not obscure. The issue before us is not whether DNA can some day be used for identification; nor even whether it can today be used for identification; but whether it was used for identification here.

Today, it can fairly be said that fingerprints really are used to identify people—so well, in fact, that there would be no need for the expense of a separate, wholly redundant DNA confirmation of the same information. What DNA adds—what makes it a valuable weapon in the law-enforcement arsenal—is the ability to solve unsolved crimes, by matching old crime-scene evidence against the profiles of people whose identities are already known. That is what was going on when King's DNA was taken, and we should not disguise the fact. Solving unsolved crimes is a noble objective, but it occupies a lower place in the American pantheon of noble objectives than the protection of our people from suspicionless law-enforcement searches. The Fourth Amendment must prevail.

* * *

The Court disguises the vast (and scary) scope of its holding by promising a limitation it cannot deliver. The Court repeatedly says that DNA testing, and entry into a national DNA registry, will not befall thee and me, dear reader, but only those arrested for "serious offense[s]." Ante, at 28; see also ante, at 1, 9, 14, 17, 22, 23, 24 (repeatedly limiting the analysis to "serious offenses"). I cannot imagine what principle could possibly justify this limitation, and the Court does not attempt to suggest any. If one believes that DNA will "identify" someone arrested for assault, he must believe that it will "identify" someone arrested for a traffic offense. This Court does not base its judgments on senseless distinctions. At the end of the day, logic will out. When there comes before us the taking of DNA from an arrestee for a traffic violation, the Court will predictably (and quite rightly) say, "We can find no significant difference between this case and King." Make no mistake about it: As an entirely predictable consequence of today's decision, your DNA can be taken and entered into a national DNA database if you are ever arrested, rightly or wrongly, and for whatever reason.

The most regrettable aspect of the suspicionless search that occurred here is that it proved to be quite unnecessary. All parties concede that it would have been entirely permissible, as far as the Fourth Amendment is concerned, for Maryland to take a sample of King's DNA as a consequence of his conviction for second-degree assault. So the ironic result of the Court's error is this: The only arrestees to whom the outcome here will ever make a difference are those who have been acquitted of the crime of arrest (so that their DNA could not have been taken upon conviction). In other words, this Act manages to burden uniquely the sole group for whom the Fourth Amendment's protections ought to be most jealously guarded: people who are innocent of the State's accusations.

Today's judgment will, to be sure, have the beneficial effect of solving more crimes; then again, so would the taking of DNA samples from anyone who flies on an airplane (surely the Transportation Security Administration needs to know the "identity" of the flying public), applies for a driver's license, or attends a public school. Perhaps the construction of such a genetic panopticon is wise. But I doubt that the proud men who wrote the charter of our liberties would have been so eager to open their mouths for royal inspection.

I therefore dissent, and hope that today's incursion upon the Fourth Amendment, like an earlier one, 6 will some day be repudiated.

Notes to Justice Scalia's dissent in Maryland v. King (June 2, 2013)

1 The Court's insistence (ante, at 25) that our special-needs cases "do not have a direct bearing on the issues presented in this case" is perplexing. Why spill so much ink on the special need of identification if a special need is not required? Why not just come out and say that any suspicionless search of an arrestee is allowed if it will be useful to solve crimes? The Court does not say that because most Members of the Court do not believe it. So whatever the Court's major premise—the opinion does not really contain what you would call a rule of decision—the minor premise is "this search was used to identify King." The incorrectness of that minor premise will therefore suffice to demonstrate the error in the Court's result.

2 By the way, this procedure has nothing to do with exonerating the wrongfully convicted, as the Court soothingly promises. See ante, at 17. The FBI CODIS database includes DNA from unsolved crimes. I know of no indication (and the Court cites none) that it also includes DNA from all—or even any—crimes whose perpetrators have already been convicted.

3 Puzzlingly, the Court's discussion of photography and Bertillon measurements repeatedly cites state cases (such as Clausmier) that were decided before the Fourth Amendment was held to be applicable to the States. See Wolf v. Colorado, 338 U. S. 25 (1949); Mapp v. Ohio, 367 U. S. 643 (1961) . Why the Court believes them relevant to the meaning of that Amendment is therefore something of a mystery.

4 See, e.g., FBI, Privacy Impact Assessment: Integrated Automated Fingerprint Identification System (IAFIS)/Next Generation Identification (NGI) Repository for Individuals of Special Concern (RISC),http://www.fbi.gov/foia/privacy-impact-assessments/iafis-ngi-risc (searches of the "Unsolved Latent File" may "take considerably more time").

5 See Attorney General DeWine Announces Significant Drop inDNA Turnaround Time (Jan. 4, 2013), http://ohioattorneygeneral.gov/Media/News-Releases/January-2013/Attorney-General-DeWine-Announces-Significant-Drop; Gov. Jindal Announces Elimination of DNA Backlog(Nov. 17, 2011), http://www.gov.state.la.us/index.cfm?md=newsroom&tmp=detail&articleID=3102.

6 Compare, New York v. Belton, 453 U. S. 454 (1981) (suspicionless search of a car permitted upon arrest of the driver), with Arizona v. Gant, 556 U. S. 332 (2009) (on second thought, no).

We have no power to decide this case, and the law is legal: Justice Scalia's dissent in United States v. Windsor (June 26, 2013)

Justice Scalia, with whom Justice Thomas joins, and with whom The Chief Justice joins as to Part I, dissenting.

This case is about power in several respects. It is about the power of our people to govern themselves, and the power of this Court to pronounce the law. Today's opinion aggrandizes the latter, with the predictable consequence of diminishing the former. We have no power to decide this case. And even if we did, we have no power under the Constitution to invalidate this democratically adopted legislation. The Court's errors on both points spring forth from the same diseased root: an exalted conception of the role of this institution in America.

I

A

The Court is eager—hungry—to tell everyone its view of the legal question at the heart of this case. Standing in the way is an obstacle, a technicality of little interest to anyone but the people of We the People, who created it as a barrier against judges' intrusion into their lives. They gave judges, in Article III, only the "judicial Power," a power to decide not abstract questions but real, concrete "Cases" and "Controversies." Yet the plaintiff and the Government agree entirely on what should happen in this lawsuit. They agree that the court below got it right; and they agreed in the court below that the court below that one got it right as well. What, then, are we doing here?

The answer lies at the heart of the jurisdictional portion of today's opinion, where a single sentence lays bare the majority's vision of our role. The Court says that we have the power to decide this case because if we did not, then our "primary role in determining the constitutionality of a law" (at least one that "has inflicted real injury on a plaintiff") would "become only secondary to the President's." Ante, at 12. But wait, the reader wonders—Windsor won below, and so cured her injury, and the President was glad to see it. True, says the majority, but judicial review must march on regardless, lest we "undermine the clear dictate of the separation-of-powers principle that when an Act of Congress is alleged to conflict with the Constitution, it is emphatically the province and duty of the judicial department to say what the law is." Ibid. (internal quotation marks and brackets omitted).

That is jaw-dropping. It is an assertion of judicial supremacy over the people's Representatives in Congress and the Executive. It envisions a Supreme Court standing (or rather enthroned) at the apex of government, empowered to decide all constitutional questions, always and every-where "primary" in its role.

This image of the Court would have been unrecognizable to those who wrote and ratified our national charter. They knew well the dangers of "primary" power, and so created branches of government that would be "perfectly co-ordinate by the terms of their common commission," none of which branches could "pretend to an exclusive or superior right of settling the boundaries between their respective powers." The Federalist, No. 49, p. 314 (C. Rossiter ed. 1961) (J. Madison). The people did this to protect themselves. They did it to guard their right to self-rule against the black-robed supremacy that today's majority finds so attractive. So it was that Madison could confidently state, with no fear of contradiction, that there was nothing of "greater intrinsic value" or "stamped with the authority of more enlightened patrons of liberty" than a government of separate and coordinate powers. Id., No. 47, at 301.

For this reason we are quite forbidden to say what the law is whenever (as today's opinion asserts) " 'an Act of Congress is alleged to conflict with the Constitution.' " Ante, at 12. We can do so only when that allegation will determine the outcome of a lawsuit, and is contradicted by the other party. The "judicial Power" is not, as the major-ity believes, the power " 'to say what the law is,' " ibid., giving the Supreme Court the "primary role in determining the constitutionality of laws." The majority must have in mind one of the foreign constitutions that pronounces such primacy for its constitutional court and allows that primacy to be exercised in contexts other than a lawsuit. See, e.g., Basic Law for the Federal Republic of Germany, Art. 93. The judicial power as Americans have understood it (and their English ancestors before them) is the power to adjudicate, with conclusive effect, disputed government claims (civil or criminal) against private persons, and disputed claims by private persons against the government or other private persons. Sometimes (though not always) the parties before the court disagree not with regard to the facts of their case (or not only with regard to the facts) but with regard to the applicable law—in which event (and only in which event) it becomes the " 'province and duty of the judicial department to say what the law is.' " Ante, at 12.

In other words, declaring the compatibility of state or federal laws with the Constitution is not only not the "primary role" of this Court, it is not a separate, free-standing role at all. We perform that role incidentally—by accident, as it were—when that is necessary to resolve the dispute before us. Then, and only then, does it become " 'the province and duty of the judicial department to say what the law is.' " That is why, in 1793, we politely declined the Washington Administration's request to "say what the law is" on a particular treaty matter that was not the subject of a concrete legal controversy. 3 Correspondence and Public Papers of John Jay 486–489 (H. Johnston ed. 1893). And that is why, as our opinions have said, some questions of law will never be presented to this Court, because there will never be anyone with standing to bring a lawsuit. See Schlesinger v. Reservists Comm. to Stop the War, 418 U. S. 208, 227 (1974); United States v. Richardson, 418 U. S. 166, 179 (1974) . As Justice Brandeis put it, we cannot "pass upon the constitutionality of legislation in a friendly, non-adversary, proceeding"; absent a " 'real, earnest and vital controversy between individuals,' " we have neither any work to do nor any power to do it. Ashwander v. TVA, 297 U. S. 288, 346 (1936) (concurring opinion) (quoting Chicago & Grand Trunk R. Co. v. Wellman, 143 U. S. 339, 345 (1892)). Our authority begins and ends with the need to adjudge the rights of an injured party who stands before us seeking redress. Lujan v. Defenders of Wildlife, 504 U. S. 555, 560 (1992) .

That is completely absent here. Windsor's injury was cured by the judgment in her favor. And while, in ordinary circumstances, the United States is injured by a directive to pay a tax refund, this suit is far from ordinary. Whatever injury the United States has suffered will surely not be redressed by the action that it, as a litigant, asks us to take. The final sentence of the Solicitor General's brief on the merits reads: "For the foregoing reasons, the judgment of the court of appeals should be affirmed." Brief for United States (merits) 54 (emphasis added). That will not cure the Government's injury, but carve it into stone. One could spend many fruitless afternoons ransacking our library for any other petitioner's brief seeking an affirmance of the judgment against it. 1 What the petitioner United States asks us to do in the case before us is exactly what the respondent Windsor asks us to do: not to provide relief from the judgment below but to say that that judgment was correct. And the same was true in the Court of Appeals: Neither party sought to undo the judgment for Windsor, and so that court should have dismissed the appeal (just as we should dismiss) for lack of jurisdiction. Since both parties agreed with the judgment of the District Court for the Southern District of New York, the suit should have ended there. The further proceedings have been a contrivance, having no object in mind except to elevate a District Court judgment that has no precedential effect in other courts, to one that has precedential effect throughout the Second Circuit, and then (in this Court) precedential effect throughout the United States.

We have never before agreed to speak—to "say what the law is"—where there is no controversy before us. In the more than two centuries that this Court has existed as an institution, we have never suggested that we have the power to decide a question when every party agrees with both its nominal opponent and the court below on that question's answer. The United States reluctantly conceded that at oral argument. See Tr. of Oral Arg. 19–20.

The closest we have ever come to what the Court blesses today was our opinion in INS v. Chadha, 462 U. S. 919 (1983) . But in that case, two parties to the litigation disagreed with the position of the United States and with the court below: the House and Senate, which had intervened in the case. Because Chadha concerned the validity of a mode of congressional action—the one-house legislative veto—the House and Senate were threatened with destruction of what they claimed to be one of their institutional powers. The Executive choosing not to defend that power, 2 we permitted the House and Senate to intervene. Nothing like that is present here.

To be sure, the Court in Chadha said that statutory aggrieved-party status was "not altered by the fact that the Executive may agree with the holding that the statute in question is unconstitutional." Id., at 930–931. But in a footnote to that statement, the Court acknowledged Arti-cle III's separate requirement of a "justiciable case or controversy," and stated that this requirement was satisfied "because of the presence of the two Houses of Congress as adverse parties." Id., at 931, n. 6. Later in its opinion, the

Chadha Court remarked that the United States' announced intention to enforce the statute also sufficed to permit judicial review, even absent congressional participation. Id., at 939. That remark is true, as a description of the judicial review conducted in the Court of Appeals, where the Houses of Congress had not intervened. (The case originated in the Court of Appeals, since it sought review of agency action under 8 U. S. C. §1105a(a) (1976 ed.).) There, absent a judgment setting aside the INS order, Chadha faced deportation. This pas-sage of our opinion seems to be addressing that initial standing in the Court of Appeals, as indicated by its quotation from the lower court's opinion, 462 U. S., at 939–940. But if it was addressing standing to pursue the appeal, the remark was both the purest dictum (as congressional intervention at that point made the required adverseness "beyond doubt," id., at 939), and quite incorrect. When a private party has a judicial decree safely in hand to prevent his injury, additional judicial action requires that a party injured by the decree seek to undo it. In Chadha, the intervening House and Senate fulfilled that requirement. Here no one does.

The majority's discussion of the requirements of Article III bears no resemblance to our jurisprudence. It accuses the amicus (appointed to argue against our jurisdiction) of "elid[ing] the distinction between . . . the jurisdictional requirements of Article III and the prudential limits on its exercise." Ante, at 6. It then proceeds to call the requirement of adverseness a "prudential" aspect of standing. Of standing. That is incomprehensible. A plaintiff (or appellant) can have all the standing in the world—satisfying all three standing requirements of Lujan that the majority so carefully quotes, ante, at 7—and yet no Article III controversy may be before the court. Article III requires not just a plaintiff (or appellant) who has standing to complain but an opposing party who denies the validity of the complaint. It is not the amicus that has done the eliding of distinctions, but the majority, calling the quite separate Article III requirement of adverseness between the parties an element (which it then pronounces a "prudential" element) of standing. The question here is not whether, as the majority puts it, "the United States retains a stake sufficient to support Article III jurisdiction," ibid. the question is whether there is any controversy (which requires contradiction) between the United States and Ms. Windsor. There is not.

I find it wryly amusing that the majority seeks to dismiss the requirement of party-adverseness as nothing more than a "prudential" aspect of the sole Article III requirement of standing. (Relegating a jurisdictional requirement to "prudential" status is a wondrous device, enabling courts to ignore the requirement whenever they believe it "prudent"—which is to say, a good idea.) Half a century ago, a Court similarly bent upon announcing its view regarding the constitutionality of a federal statute achieved that goal by effecting a remarkably similar but completely opposite distortion of the principles limiting our jurisdiction. The Court's notorious opinion in Flast v. Cohen, 392 U. S. 83–101 (1968), held that standing was merely an element (which it pronounced to be a "prudential" element) of the sole Article III requirement of adverseness. We have been living with the chaos created by that power-grabbing decision ever since, see Hein v.

Freedom From Religion Foundation, Inc., 551 U. S. 587 (2007), as we will have to live with the chaos created by this one.

The authorities the majority cites fall miles short of supporting the counterintuitive notion that an Article III "controversy" can exist without disagreement between the parties. In Deposit Guaranty Nat. Bank v. Roper, 445 U. S. 326 (1980), the District Court had entered judgment in the individual plaintiff's favor based on the defendant bank's offer to pay the full amount claimed. The plaintiff, however, sought to appeal the District Court's denial of class certification under Federal Rule of Civil Procedure 23. There was a continuing dispute between the parties concerning the issue raised on appeal. The same is true of the other case cited by the majority, Camreta v. Greene, 563 U. S. ___ (2011). There the District Court found that the defendant state officers had violated the Fourth Amendment, but rendered judgment in their favor because they were entitled to official immunity, application of the Fourth Amendment to their conduct not having been clear at the time of violation. The officers sought to appeal the holding of Fourth Amendment violation, which would circumscribe their future conduct; the plaintiff continued to insist that a Fourth Amendment violation had occurred. The "prudential" discretion to which both those cases refer was the discretion to deny an appeal even when a live controversy exists—not the discretion to grant one when it does not. The majority can cite no case in which this Court entertained an appeal in which both parties urged us to affirm the judgment below. And that is because the existence of a controversy is not a "prudential" requirement that we have invented, but an essential element of an Article III case or controversy. The majority's notion that a case between friendly parties can be entertained so long as "adversarial presentation of the issues is assured by the participation of amici curiae prepared to defend with vigor" the other side of the issue, ante, at 10, effects a breathtaking revolution in our Article III jurisprudence.

It may be argued that if what we say is true some Presidential determinations that statutes are unconstitutional will not be subject to our review. That is as it should be, when both the President and the plaintiff agree that the statute is unconstitutional. Where the Executive is enforcing an unconstitutional law, suit will of course lie; but if, in that suit, the Executive admits the unconstitutionality of the law, the litigation should end in an order or a consent decree enjoining enforcement. This suit saw the light of day only because the President enforced the Act (and thus gave Windsor standing to sue) even though he believed it unconstitutional. He could have equally chosen (more appropriately, some would say) neither to enforce nor to defend the statute he believed to be unconstitu-tional, see Presidential Authority to Decline to Execute Un-constitutional Statutes, 18 Op. Off. Legal Counsel 199 (Nov. 2, 1994)—in which event Windsor would not have been injured, the District Court could not have refereed this friendly scrimmage, and the Executive's determination of unconstitutionality would have escaped this Court's desire to blurt out its view of the law. The matter would have been left, as so many matters ought to be left, to a tug of war between the President and the Congress, which has innumerable means (up to and including impeachment) of compelling the President to enforce the laws it has written. Or the President could have evaded presentation of the constitutional issue to this Court simply by declining to appeal the District Court and Court of Appeals dispositions he agreed with. Be sure of this much: If a President wants to insulate his judgment of unconstitutionality from our review, he can. What the views urged in this dissent produce is not insulation from judicial review but insulation from Executive contrivance.

The majority brandishes the famous sentence from Marbury v. Madison, 1 Cranch 137, 177 (1803) that "[i]t is emphatically the province and duty of the judicial department to say what the law is." Ante, at 12 (internal quotation marks omitted). But that sentence neither says nor implies that it is always the province and duty of the Court to say what the law is—much less that its responsibility in that regard is a "primary" one. The very next sentence of Chief Justice Marshall's opinion makes the crucial qualification that today's majority ignores: "Those who apply the rule to particular cases, must of necessity expound and interpret that rule." 1 Cranch, at 177 (emphasis added). Only when a "particular case" is before us—that is, a controversy that it is our business to resolve under Article III—do we have the province and duty to pronounce the law. For the views of our early Court more precisely addressing the question before us here, the majority ought instead to have consulted the opinion of Chief Justice Taney in Lord v. Veazie, 8 How. 251 (1850):

"The objection in the case before us is . . . that the plaintiff and defendant have the same interest, and that interest adverse and in conflict with the interest of third persons, whose rights would be seriously affected if the question of law was decided in the manner that both of the parties to this suit desire it to be.

"A judgment entered under such circumstances, and for such purposes, is a mere form. The whole proceeding was in contempt of the court, and highly reprehensible . . . . A judgment in form, thus procured, in the eye of the law is no judgment of the court. It is a nullity, and no writ of error will lie upon it. This writ is, therefore, dismissed." Id., at 255–256.

There is, in the words of Marbury, no "necessity [to] expound and interpret" the law in this case; just a desire to place this Court at the center of the Nation's life. 1 Cranch, at 177.

B

A few words in response to the theory of jurisdiction set forth in Justice Alito's dissent: Though less far reaching in its consequences than the majority's conversion of constitutionally required adverseness into a discretionary element of standing, the theory of that dissent similarly elevates the Court to the "primary" determiner of constitutional questions involving the separation of powers, and, to boot, increases the power of the most dangerous branch: the "legislative department," which by its nature "draw[s] all power into its impetuous vortex." The Federalist, No. 48, at 309 (J. Madison). Heretofore in our national his-tory, the President's failure to "take Care that the Laws be faithfully executed," U. S. Const., Art. II, §3, could only be brought before a judicial tribunal by someone whose concrete interests were harmed by that alleged failure. Justice Alito would create a system in which Congress can hale the Executive before the courts not only to vindicate its own institutional powers to act, but to correct a perceived inadequacy in the execution of its laws. 3 This would lay to rest Tocqueville's praise of our judicial system as one which "intimately bind[s] the case made for the law with the case made for one man," one in which legislation is "no longer exposed to the daily aggression of the parties," and in which "[t]he political question that [the judge] must resolve is linked to the interest" of private litigants. A. de Tocqueville, Democracy in America 97 (H. Mansfield & D. Winthrop eds. 2000). That would be replaced by a system in which Congress and the Executive can pop immediately into court, in their institutional capacity, whenever the President refuses to implement a statute he believes to be unconstitutional, and whenever he implements a law in a manner that is not to Congress's liking.

Justice Alito's notion of standing will likewise enormously shrink the area to which "judicial censure, exercised by the courts on legislation, cannot extend," ibid. For example, a bare majority of both Houses could bring into court the assertion that the Executive's implementation of welfare programs is too generous—a failure that no other litigant would have standing to complain about. Moreover, as we indicated in Raines v. Byrd, 521 U. S. 811, 828 (1997), if Congress can sue the Executive for the erroneous application of the law that "injures" its power to legislate, surely the Executive can sue Congress for its erroneous adoption of an unconstitutional law that "injures" the Executive's power to administer—or perhaps for its protracted failure to act on one of his nominations. The opportunities for dragging the courts into disputes hitherto left for political resolution are endless.

Justice Alito's dissent is correct that Raines did not formally decide this issue, but its reasoning does. The opinion spends three pages discussing famous, decades-long disputes between the President and Congress—regarding congressional power to forbid the Presidential removal of executive officers, regarding the legislative veto, regarding congressional appointment of executive officers, and regarding the pocket veto—that would surely have been promptly resolved by a Congress-vs.-the-President lawsuit if the impairment of a branch's powers alone conferred standing to commence litigation. But it does not, and never has; the "enormous power that the judiciary would acquire" from the ability to adjudicate such suits "would have made a mockery of [Hamilton's] quotation of Montesquieu to the effect that 'of the three powers above mentioned . . . the JUDICIARY is next to nothing.'" Barnes v. Kline, 759 F. 2d 21, 58 (CADC 1985) (Bork, J., dissenting) (quoting The Federalist No. 78 (A. Hamilton)).

To be sure, if Congress cannot invoke our authority in the way that Justice Alito proposes, then its only recourse is to confront the President directly. Unimaginable evil this is not. Our system is designed for confrontation. That is what "[a]mbition . . . counteract[ing] ambition," The Federalist, No. 51, at 322 (J. Madison), is all about. If majorities in both Houses of Congress care enough about the matter, they have available innumerable ways to compel executive action without a lawsuit—from refusing to confirm Presidential appointees to the elimination of funding. (Nothing says "enforce the Act" quite like ". . . or you will have money for little else.") But the condition is crucial; Congress must care enough to act against the President itself, not merely enough to instruct its lawyers to ask us to do so. Placing the Constitution's entirely anticipated political arm wrestling into permanent judicial receivership does not do the system a favor. And by the way, if the President loses the lawsuit but does not faithfully implement the Court's decree, just as he did not faithfully implement Congress's statute, what then? Only Congress can bring him to heel by . . . what do you think? Yes: a direct confrontation with the President.

II

For the reasons above, I think that this Court has, and the Court of Appeals had, no power to decide this suit. We should vacate the decision below and remand to the Court of Appeals for the Second Circuit, with instructions to dismiss the appeal. Given that the majority has volunteered its view of the merits, however, I proceed to discuss that as well.

A

There are many remarkable things about the majority's merits holding. The first is how rootless and shifting its justifications are. For example, the opinion starts with seven full pages about the traditional power of States to define domestic relations— initially fooling many readers, I am sure, into thinking that this is a federalism opinion. But we are eventually told that "it is unnecessary to decide whether this federal intrusion on state power is a violation of the Constitution," and that "[t]he State's power in defining the marital relation is of central relevance in this case quite apart from principles of federalism" be-cause "the State's decision to give this class of persons the right to marry conferred upon them a dignity and status of immense import." Ante, at 18. But no one questions the power of the States to define marriage (with the concomitant conferral of dignity and status), so what is the point of devoting seven pages to describing how long and well established that power is? Even after the opinion has formally disclaimed reliance upon principles of federalism, mentions of "the usual tradition of recognizing and accepting state definitions of marriage" continue. See, e.g., ante, at 20. What to make of this? The opinion never explains. My guess is that the majority, while reluctant to suggest that defining the meaning of "marriage" in federal statutes is unsupported by any of the Federal Government's enumerated powers, 4 nonetheless needs some rhetorical basis to support its pretense that today's prohibition of laws excluding same-sex marriage is confined to the Federal Government (leaving the second, state-law shoe to be dropped later, maybe next Term). But I am only guessing.

Equally perplexing are the opinion's references to "the Constitution's guarantee of equality." Ibid. Near the end of the opinion, we are told that although the "equal protection guarantee of the Fourteenth Amendment makes [the] Fifth Amendment [due process] right all the more specific and all the better understood and preserved"—what can that mean?—"the Fifth Amendment itself withdraws from Government the power to degrade or demean in the way this law does." Ante, at 25. The only possible interpretation of this statement is that the Equal Protection Clause, even the Equal Protection Clause as incorporated in the Due Process Clause, is not the basis for today's holding. But the portion of the majority opinion that explains why DOMA is unconstitutional (Part IV) begins by citing Bolling v. Sharpe, 347 U. S. 497 (1954), Department of Agriculture v. Moreno, 413 U. S. 528 (1973), and Romer v. Evans, 517 U. S. 620 (1996) —all of which are equal-protection cases. 5 And those three cases are the only authorities that the Court cites in Part IV about the Constitution's meaning, except for its citation of Lawrence v. Texas, 539 U. S. 558 (2003) (not an equal-protection case) to support its passing assertion that the Constitution protects the "moral and sexual choices" of same-sex couples, ante, at 23.

Moreover, if this is meant to be an equal-protection opinion, it is a confusing one. The opinion does not resolve and indeed does not even mention what had been the central question in this litigation: whether, under the Equal Protection Clause, laws restricting marriage to a man and a woman are reviewed for more than mere rationality. That is the issue that divided the parties and the court below, compare Brief for Respondent Bipartisan Legal Advisory Group of U. S. House of Representatives (merits) 24–28 (no), with Brief for Respondent Windsor (merits) 17–31 and Brief for United States (merits) 18–36 (yes); and compare 699 F. 3d 169, 180–185 (CA2 2012) (yes), with id., at 208–211 (Straub, J., dissenting in part and concurring in part) (no). In accord with my previously expressed skepticism about the Court's "tiers of scrutiny" approach, I would review this classification only for its rationality. See United States v. Virginia, 518 U. S. 515–570 (1996) (Scalia, J., dissenting). As nearly as I can tell, the Court agrees with that; its opinion does not apply strict scrutiny, and its central propositions are taken from rational-basis cases like Moreno. But the Court certainly does not apply anything that resembles that deferential framework. See Heller v. Doe, 509 U. S. 312, 320 (1993) (a classification " 'must be upheld . . . if there is any reason-ably conceivable state of facts' " that could justify it).

The majority opinion need not get into the strict-vs.-rational-basis scrutiny question, and need not justify its holding under either, because it says that DOMA is unconstitutional as "a deprivation of the liberty of the person protected by the Fifth Amendment of the Constitution," ante, at 25; that it violates "basic due process" principles, ante, at 20; and that it inflicts an "injury and indignity" of a kind that denies "an essential part of the liberty protected by the Fifth Amendment," ante, at 19. The majority never utters the dread words "substantive due process," perhaps sensing the disrepute into which that doctrine has fallen, but that is what those statements mean. Yet the opinion does not argue that same-sex marriage is "deeply rooted in this Nation's history and tradition," Washington v. Glucksberg, 521 U. S. 702–721(1997), a claim that would of course be quite absurd. So would the further suggestion (also necessary, under our substantive-due-process precedents) that a world in which DOMA exists is one bereft of " 'ordered liberty.' " Id., at 721 (quoting Palko v. Connecticut, 302 U. S. 319, 325 (1937)).

Some might conclude that this loaf could have used a while longer in the oven. But that would be wrong; it is already overcooked. The most expert care in preparation cannot redeem a bad recipe. The sum of all the Court's nonspecific hand-waving is that this law is invalid (maybe on equal-protection grounds, maybe on substantive-due-process grounds, and perhaps with some amorphous federalism component playing a role) because it is motivated by a " 'bare . . . desire to harm' " couples in same-sex marriages. Ante, at 20. It is this proposition with which I will therefore engage.

B

As I have observed before, the Constitution does not forbid the government to enforce traditional moral and sexual norms. See Lawrence v. Texas, 539 U. S. 558, 599 (2003) (Scalia, J., dissenting). I will not swell the U. S. Reports with restatements of that point. It is enough to say that the Constitution neither requires nor forbids our society to approve of same-sex marriage, much as it neither requires nor forbids us to approve of no-fault divorce, polygamy, or the consumption of alcohol.

However, even setting aside traditional moral disapproval of same-sex marriage (or indeed same-sex sex), there are many perfectly valid—indeed, downright boring—justifying rationales for this legislation. Their existence ought to be the end of this case. For they give the lie to the Court's conclusion that only those with hateful hearts could have voted "aye" on this Act. And more importantly, they serve to make the contents of the legislators' hearts quite irrelevant: "It is a familiar principle of constitutional law that this Court will not strike down an otherwise constitutional statute on the basis of an alleged illicit legislative motive." United States v. O'Brien, 391 U. S. 367, 383 (1968) . Or at least it was a familiar principle. By holding to the contrary, the majority has declared open season on any law that (in the opinion of the law's opponents and any panel of like-minded federal judges) can be characterized as mean-spirited.

The majority concludes that the only motive for this Act was the "bare . . . desire to harm a politically unpopular group." Ante, at 20. Bear in mind that the object of this condemnation is not the legislature of some once-Confederate Southern state (familiar objects of the Court's scorn, see, e.g., Edwards v. Aguillard, 482 U. S. 578 (1987)), but our respected coordinate branches, the Congress and Presidency of the United States. Laying such a charge against them should require the most extraordinary evidence, and I would have thought that every attempt would be made to indulge a more anodyne explanation for the statute. The majority does the opposite—affirmatively concealing from the reader the arguments that exist in justification. It makes only a passing mention of the "arguments put forward" by the Act's defenders, and does not even trouble to paraphrase or describe them. See ante, at 21. I imagine that this is because it is harder to maintain the illusion of the Act's supporters as unhinged members of a wild-eyed lynch mob when one first describes their views as they see them.

To choose just one of these defenders' arguments, DOMA avoids difficult choice-of-law issues that will now arise absent a uniform federal definition of marriage. See, e.g., Baude, Beyond DOMA: Choice of State Law in Federal Statutes, 64 Stan. L. Rev. 1371 (2012). Imagine a pair of women who marry in Albany and then move to Alabama, which does not "recognize as valid any marriage of parties of the same sex." Ala. Code §30–1–19(e) (2011). When the couple files their next federal tax return, may it be a joint one? Which State's law controls, for federal-law purposes: their State of celebration (which recognizes the marriage) or their State of domicile (which does not)? (Does the answer depend on whether they were just visiting in Albany?) Are these questions to be answered as a matter of federal common law, or perhaps by borrowing a State's choice-of-law rules? If so, which State's? And what about States where the status of an out-of-state same-sex marriage is an unsettled question under local law? See Godfrey v. Spano, 13 N. Y. 3d 358, 920 N. E. 2d 328 (2009). DOMA avoided all of this uncertainty by specifying which marriages would be recognized for federal purposes. That is a classic purpose for a definitional provision.

Further, DOMA preserves the intended effects of prior legislation against then-unforeseen changes in circumstance. When Congress provided (for example) that a special estate-tax exemption would exist for spouses, this exemption reached only opposite-sex spouses—those being the only sort that were recognized in any State at the time of DOMA's passage. When it became clear that changes in state law might one day alter that balance, DOMA's definitional section was enacted to ensure that state-level experimentation did not automatically alter the basic operation of federal law, unless and until Congress made the further judgment to do so on its own. That is not animus—just stabilizing prudence. Congress has hardly demonstrated itself unwilling to make such further, revising judgments upon due deliberation. See, e.g., Don't Ask, Don't Tell Repeal Act of 2010, 124Stat. 3515.

The Court mentions none of this. Instead, it accuses the Congress that enacted this law and the President who signed it of something much worse than, for example, having acted in excess of enumerated federal powers—or even having drawn distinctions that prove to be irrational. Those legal errors may be made in good faith, errors though they are. But the majority says that the supporters of this Act acted with malice—with the "purpose" (ante, at 25) "to disparage and to injure" same-sex couples. It says that the motivation for DOMA was to "demean," ibid.; to "impose inequality," ante, at 22; to "impose . . . a stigma," ante, at 21; to deny people "equal dignity," ibid.; to brand gay people as "unworthy," ante, at 23; and to "humiliat[e]" their children, ibid. (emphasis added).

I am sure these accusations are quite untrue. To be sure (as the majority points out), the legislation is called the Defense of Marriage Act. But to defend traditional marriage is not to condemn, demean, or humiliate those who would prefer other arrangements, any more than to defend the Constitution of the United States is to condemn, demean, or humiliate other constitutions. To hurl such accusations so casually demeans this institution. In the majority's judgment, any resistance to its holding is beyond the pale of reasoned disagreement. To question its high-handed invalidation of a presumptively valid statute is to act (the majority is sure) with the purpose to "disparage," "injure," "degrade," "demean," and "humiliate" our fellow human beings, our fellow citizens, who are homosexual. All that, simply for supporting an Act that did no more than codify an aspect of marriage that had been unquestioned in our society for most of its existence—indeed, had been unquestioned in virtually all societies for virtually all of human history. It is one thing for a society to elect change; it is another for a court of law to impose change by adjudging those who oppose it hostes humani generis, enemies of the human race.

* * *

The penultimate sentence of the majority's opinion is a naked declaration that "[t]his opinion and its holding are confined" to those couples "joined in same-sex marriages made lawful by the State." Ante, at 26, 25. I have heard such "bald, unreasoned disclaimer[s]" before. Lawrence, 539 U. S., at 604. When the Court declared a constitutional right to homosexual sodomy, we were assured that the case had nothing, nothing at all to do with "whether the government must give formal recognition to any relationship that homosexual persons seek to enter." Id., at 578. Now we are told that DOMA is invalid because it "demeans the couple, whose moral and sexual choices the Constitution protects," ante, at 23—with an accompanying citation of Lawrence. It takes real cheek for today's majority to assure us, as it is going out the door, that a constitutional requirement to give formal recognition to same-sex marriage is not at issue here—when what has preceded that assurance is a lecture on how superior the majority's moral judgment in favor of same-sex marriage is to the Congress's hateful moral judgment against it. I promise you this: The only thing that will "confine" the Court's holding is its sense of what it can get away with.

I do not mean to suggest disagreement with The Chief Justice's view, ante, p. 2–4 (dissenting opinion), that lower federal courts and state courts can distinguish today's case when the issue before them is state denial of marital status to same-sex couples—or even that this Court could theoretically do so. Lord, an opinion with such scatter-shot rationales as this one (federalism noises among them) can be distinguished in many ways. And deserves to be. State and lower federal courts should take the Court at its word and distinguish away.

In my opinion, however, the view that this Court will take of state prohibition of same-sex marriage is indicated beyond mistaking by today's opinion. As I have said, the real rationale of today's opinion, whatever disappearing trail of its legalistic argle-bargle one chooses to follow, is that DOMA is motivated by " 'bare . . . desire to harm' " couples in same-sex marriages. Supra, at 18. How easy it is, indeed how inevitable, to reach the same conclusion with regard to state laws denying same-sex couples marital status. Consider how easy (inevitable) it is to make the following substitutions in a passage from today's opinion ante, at 22:

"FONT DOMA's FONT This state law's principal effect is to identify a subset of FONT state-sanctioned marriages FONT constitution-ally protected sexual relationships, see Lawrence, and make them unequal. The principal purpose is to impose inequality, not for other reasons like govern-mental efficiency. Responsibilities, as well as rights, enhance the dignity and integrity of the person. And FONT DOMA FONT this state law contrives to deprive some couples FONT married under the laws of their State FONT enjoying constitutionally protected sexual relationships, but not other couples, of both rights and responsibilities."

Or try this passage, from ante, at 22–23:

"FONT [DOMA] FONT This state law tells those couples, and all the world, that their otherwise valid FONT marriages FONT relationships are unworthy of FONT federal FONT state recognition. This places same-sex couples in an unstable position of being in a second-tier FONT marriage FONT relationship. The differentiation demeans the couple, whose moral and sexual choices the Constitution protects, see Lawrence, ..."

Or this, from ante, at 23—which does not even require alteration, except as to the invented number:

"And it humiliates FONT tens of FONT thousands of children now being raised by same-sex couples. The law in question makes it even more difficult for the children to understand the integrity and closeness of their own family and its concord with other families in their community and in their daily lives."

Similarly transposable passages—deliberately transposable, I think—abound. In sum, that Court which finds it so horrific that Congress irrationally and hatefully robbed same-sex couples of the "personhood and dignity" which state legislatures conferred upon them, will of a certitude be similarly appalled by state legislatures' irrational and hateful failure to acknowledge that "personhood and dig-nity" in the first place. Ante, at 26. As far as this Court is concerned, no one should be fooled; it is just a matter of listening and waiting for the other shoe.

By formally declaring anyone opposed to same-sex marriage an enemy of human decency, the majority arms well every challenger to a state law restricting marriage to its traditional definition. Henceforth those challengers will lead with this Court's declaration that there is "no legitimate purpose" served by such a law, and will claim that the traditional definition has "the purpose and effect to disparage and to injure" the "personhood and dignity" of same-sex couples, see ante, at 25, 26. The majority's limiting assurance will be meaningless in the face of language like that, as the majority well knows. That is why the language is there. The result will be a judicial distortion of our society's debate over marriage—a debate that can seem in need of our clumsy "help" only to a member of this institution.

As to that debate: Few public controversies touch an institution so central to the lives of so many, and few inspire such attendant passion by good people on all sides. Few public controversies will ever demonstrate so vividly the beauty of what our Framers gave us, a gift the Court pawns today to buy its stolen moment in the spotlight: a system of government that permits us to rule ourselves. Since DOMA's passage, citizens on all sides of the question have seen victories and they have seen defeats. There have been plebiscites, legislation, persuasion, and loud voices—in other words, democracy. Victories in one place for some, see North Carolina Const., Amdt. 1 (providing that "[m]arriage between one man and one woman is the only domestic legal union that shall be valid or recognized in this State") (approved by a popular vote, 61% to 39%on May 8, 2012), 6 are offset by victories in other places for others, see Maryland Question 6 (establishing "that Maryland's civil marriage laws allow gay and lesbian couples to obtain a civil marriage license") (approved by a popular vote, 52% to 48%, on November 6, 2012). 7 Even in a single State, the question has come out differently on different occasions. Compare Maine Question 1 (permitting "the State of Maine to issue marriage licenses to same-sex couples") (approved by a popular vote, 53% to 47%, on November 6, 2012) 8 with Maine Question 1 (rejecting "the new law that lets same-sex couples marry") (approved by a popular vote, 53% to 47%, on November 3, 2009). 9

In the majority's telling, this story is black-and-white: Hate your neighbor or come along with us. The truth is more complicated. It is hard to admit that one's political opponents are not monsters, especially in a struggle like this one, and the challenge in the end proves more than today's Court can handle. Too bad. A reminder that dis-agreement over something so fundamental as marriage can still be politically legitimate would have been a fit task for what in earlier times was called the judicial temperament. We might have covered ourselves with honor today, by promising all sides of this debate that it was theirs to settle and that we would respect their resolution. We might have let the People decide.

But that the majority will not do. Some will rejoice in today's decision, and some will despair at it; that is the nature of a controversy that matters so much to so many. But the Court has cheated both sides, robbing the winners of an honest victory, and the losers of the peace that comes from a fair defeat. We owed both of them better. I dissent.

Notes to Justice Scalia's dissent in United States v. Windsor (June 26, 2013)

1 For an even more advanced scavenger hunt, one might search the annals of Anglo-American law for another "Motion to Dismiss" like the one the United States filed in District Court: It argued that the court should agree "with Plaintiff and the United States" and "not dismiss" the complaint. (Emphasis mine.) Then, having gotten exactly what it asked for, the United States promptly appealed.

2 There the Justice Department's refusal to defend the legislation was in accord with its longstanding (and entirely reasonable) practice of declining to defend legislation that in its view infringes upon Presidential powers. There is no justification for the Justice Department's abandoning the law in the present case. The majority opinion makes a point of scolding the President for his "failure to defend the constitutionality of an Act of Congress based on a constitutional theory not yet established in judicial decisions," ante,

at 12. But the rebuke is tongue-in-cheek, for the majority gladly gives the President what he wants. Contrary to all precedent, it decides this case (and even decides it the way the President wishes) despite his abandonment of the defense and the consequent absence of a case or controversy.

3 Justice Alito attempts to limit his argument by claiming that Congress is injured (and can therefore appeal) when its statute is held unconstitutional without Presidential defense, but is not injured when its statute is held unconstitutional despite Presidential defense. I do not understand that line. The injury to Congress is the same whether the President has defended the statute or not. And if the injury is threatened, why should Congress not be able to participate in the suit from the beginning, just as the President can? And if having a statute declared unconstitutional (and therefore inoperative) by a court is an injury, why is it not an injury when a statute is declared unconstitutional by the President and rendered inoperative by his consequent failure to enforce it? Or when the President simply declines to enforce it without opining on its constitutionality? If it is the inoperativeness that constitutes the injury—the "impairment of [the legislative] function," as Justice Alito puts it, post, at 4—it should make no difference which of the other two branches inflicts it, and whether the Constitution is the pretext. A principled and predictable system of jurisprudence cannot rest upon a shifting concept of injury, designed to support standing when we would like it. If this Court agreed with Justice Alito's distinction, its opinion in Raines v. Byrd, 521 U. S. 811 (1997), which involved an original suit by Members of Congress challenging an assertedly unconstitutional law, would have been written quite differently; and Justice Alito's distinguishing of that case on grounds quite irrelevant to his theory of standing would have been unnecessary.

4 Such a suggestion would be impossible, given the Federal Government's long history of making pronouncements regarding marriage—for example, conditioning Utah's entry into the Union upon its prohibition of polygamy. See Act of July 16, 1894, ch. 138, §3, 28Stat. 108 ("The constitution [of Utah]" must provide "perfect toleration of religious sentiment," "Provided, That polygamous or plural marriages are forever prohibited").

5 Since the Equal Protection Clause technically applies only against the States, see U. S. Const., Amdt. 14, Bolling and Moreno, dealing with federal action, relied upon "the equal protection component of the Due Process Clause of the Fifth Amendment," Moreno, 413 U. S., at 533.

6 North Carolina State Board of Elections, Official Results: Primary Election of May 8, 2012, Constitutional Amendment.

7 Maryland State Board of Elections, Official 2012 Presidential General Election Results for All State Questions, Question 06.

8 Maine Bureau of Elections, Nov. 3, 2009, Referendum Tabulation (Question 1).

9 Maine Bureau of Elections, Nov. 6, 2012, Referendum Election Tabulations (Question 1).

Justice Scalia's dissent from denial of application for stay in Brown v. Plata [and Coleman] (August 2, 2013)

    The application for stay presented to JUSTICE KENNEDY and by him referred to the Court is denied. JUSTICE ALITO would grant the application for stay.

    JUSTICE SCALIA, with whom JUSTICE THOMAS joins, dissenting.

    When this case was here two Terms ago, I dissented from the Court's affirmance of the injunction, because the District Court's order that California release 46,000 prisoners violated the clear limitations of the Prison Litigation Reform Act, 18 U. S. C. §3626(a)(1)(A)—"besides defying all sound conception of the proper role of judges." Brown v. Plata, 563 U. S. ____, ____ (2011) (slip op., at 16). The Court's opinion approving the order concluded with what I described as a "bizarre coda," id., at ____ (slip op., at 12), which said that "[t]he State may wish to move for modification" of the injunction, and that the District Court "may grant such a request provided that the State satisfies necessary and appropriate preconditions," ibid. (internal quotation marks omitted). More specifically, the opinion suggested that modification might be in order if the State makes "significant progress . . . toward remedying the underlying constitutional violations" and "demonstrate[s] that further population reductions are not necessary." Id., at ____ (slip op., at 47). These "deliberately ambiguous . . . suggestions on how to modify the injunction," were, I observed, "just deferential enough so that [the Court] can say with a straight face that it is 'affirming,' just stern enough to put the District Court on notice that it will likely get reversed if it does not follow them." Id., at ____ (slip op., at 13) (dissenting opinion). That was in my view "a compromise solution" that is "unknown in our legal system," which does not permit appellate courts to pre- scribe in advance the exercise of district-court discretion. Id., at ____, ____ (slip op., at 13, 14). I warned, moreover, that "the judges of the District Court are likely to call [the Court's] bluff, since they know full well it cannot possibly be an abuse of discretion to refuse to accept the State's proposed modifications in an injunction that has just been approved (affirmed) in its present form." Id., at ____ (slip op., at 14).

    The bluff has been called, and the Court has nary a pair to lay on the table. The State, seeking to invoke the ex ante appellate control of district-court discretion, and to compel the modification decreed by the Court's raised eyebrow, provided evidence that it has made meaningful progress and that population reductions to the level required by the injunction are unnecessary. But the latter argument was made and rejected in the last round, and the former hardly requires (demands) modification of the injunction. It was predictable two Terms ago that the State would make progress—indeed, it promised to do so. If the reality of incremental progress makes the injunction now invalid, the probability (indeed, one might say the certainty) of incremental progress made the injunction an overreach two Terms ago. Surely it is not the case that when a party subject to an injunction makes substantial progress toward compliance it is an abuse of discretion not to revise the injunction.

But as I suggested in my dissent, perhaps the Court never meant to follow through on its revision suggestions. Perhaps they were nothing more than "a ceremonial washing of the hands—making it clear for all to see, that if the terrible things sure to happen as a consequence of this outrageous order do happen, they will be none of this Court's responsibility. After all, did we not want, and indeed even suggest, something better?" Ibid. So also today, it is not our fault that California must now release upon the public nearly 10,000 inmates convicted of serious crimes—about 1,000 for every city larger than Santa Ana—three-quarters of whom are moderate (57%) or high (74%) recidivism risks. Reply in Support of Application 34.

It appears to have become a standard ploy, when this Court vastly expands the Power of the Black Robe, to hint at limitations that make it seem not so bad. See, e.g., Lawrence v. Texas, 539 U. S. 558, 604 (2003) (SCALIA, J., dissenting); United States v. Windsor, 570 U. S. ___, ___ (2013) (slip op., at 25–26) (SCALIA, J., dissenting). Comes the moment of truth, the hinted-at limitation proves a sham. As for me, I adhere to my original view of this terrible injunction. It goes beyond what the Prison Litigation Reform Act allows, and beyond the power of the courts. I would grant the stay and dissolve the injunction.

Equal Treatment and Non-discrimination: Justice Scalia's concurrence in Schuette v. BAMN (April 22, 2014)

Justice Scalia, with whom Justice Thomas joins, concurring in the judgment.

It has come to this. Called upon to explore the jurisprudential twilight zone between two errant lines of precedent, we confront a frighteningly bizarre question: Does the Equal Protection Clause of the Fourteenth Amendment forbid what its text plainly requires? Needless to say (except that this case obliges us to say it), the question answers itself. "The Constitution proscribes government discrimination on the basis of race, and state-provided education is no exception." Grutter v. Bollinger, 539 U. S. 306, 349 (2003) (Scalia, J., concurring in part and dissenting in part). It is precisely this understanding—the correct understanding—of the federal Equal Protection Clause that the people of the State of Michigan have adopted for their own fundamental law. By adopting it, they did not simultaneously offend it.

Even taking this Court's sorry line of race-based-admissions cases as a given, I find the question presented only slightly less strange: Does the Equal Protection Clause forbid a State from banning a practice that the Clause barely—and only provisionally—permits? Reacting to those race-based-admissions decisions, some States—whether deterred by the prospect of costly litigation; aware that Grutter's bell may soon toll, see 539 U. S., at 343; or simply opposed in principle to the notion of "benign" racial discrimination—have gotten out of the racial-preferences business altogether. And with our express encouragement: "Universities in California, Flor-ida, and Washington State, where racial preferences in admissions are prohibited by state law, are currently engaging in experimenting with a wide variety of alternative approaches. Universities in other States can and should draw on the most promising aspects of these race-neutral alternatives as they develop." Id., at 342 (emphasis added). Respondents seem to think this admonition was merely in jest. 1 The experiment, they maintain, is not only over; it never rightly began. Neither the people of the States nor their legislatures ever had the option of directing subordinate public-university officials to cease considering the race of applicants, since that would deny members of those minority groups the option of enacting a policy designed to further their interest, thus denying them the equal protection of the laws. Never mind that it is hotly disputed whether the practice of race-based admissions is ever in a racial minority's interest. Cf. id., at 371–373 (Thomas, J., concurring in part and dissenting in part). And never mind that, were a public university to stake its defense of a race-based-admissions policy on the ground that it was designed to benefit primarily minorities (as opposed to all students, regardless of color, by enhancing diversity), we would hold the policy unconstitutional. See id., at 322–325.

But the battleground for this case is not the constitutionality of race-based admissions—at least, not quite. Rather, it is the so-called political-process doctrine, derived from this Court's opinions in Washington v. Seattle School Dist. No. 1, 458 U. S. 457 (1982), and Hunter v. Erickson, 393 U. S. 385 (1969) . I agree with those parts of the plurality opinion that repudiate this doctrine. But I do not agree with its reinterpretation of Seattle and Hunter, which makes them stand in part for the cloudy and doctrinally anomalous proposition that whenever state action poses "the serious risk . . . of causing specific injuries on account of race," it denies equal protection. Ante, at 9. I would instead reaffirm that the "ordinary principles of our law [and] of our democratic heritage" require "plaintiffs alleging equal protection violations" stemming from fa-cially neutral acts to "prove intent and causation and not merely the existence of racial disparity." Freeman v. Pitts, 503 U. S. 467, 506 (1992) (Scalia, J., concurring) (citing Washington v. Davis, 426 U. S. 229 (1976)). I would further hold that a law directing state actors to provide equal protection is (to say the least) facially neutral, and cannot violate the Constitution. Section 26 of the Michigan Constitution (formerly Proposal 2) rightly stands.

I

A

The political-process doctrine has its roots in two of our cases. The first is Hunter. In 1964, the Akron City Council passed a fair-housing ordinance " 'assur[ing] equal opportunity to all persons to live in decent housing facilities regardless of race, color, religion, ancestry or national origin.' " 393 U. S., at 386. Soon after, the city's voters passed an amendment to the Akron City Charter stating that any ordinance enacted by the council that " 'regulates' " commercial transactions in real property " 'on the basis of race, color, religion, national origin or ancestry' "—including the already enacted 1964 ordinance—"must first be approved by a majority of the electors voting on the question" at a later referendum. Id., at 387. The question was whether the charter amendment denied equal protection. Answering yes, the Court explained that "although the law on its face treats Negro and white, Jew and gentile in an identical manner, the reality is that the law's impact falls on the minority. The majority needs no protection against discrimination." Id., at 391. By placing a "special burden on racial minorities within the governmental processes," the amendment "disadvantage[d]" a racial minority "by making it more difficult to enact legislation in its behalf." Id., at 391, 393.

The reasoning in Seattle is of a piece. Resolving to "eliminate all [racial] imbalance from the Seattle public schools," the city school board passed a mandatory busing and pupil-reassignment plan of the sort typically imposed on districts guilty of de jure segregation. 458 U. S., at 460–461. A year later, the citizens of the State of Washington passed Initiative 350, which directed (with exceptions) that " 'no school . . . shall directly or indirectly require any student to attend a school other than the school which is geographically nearest or next nearest the student's place of residence . . . and which offers the course of study pursued by such student,' " permitting only court-ordered race-based busing. Id., at 462. The lower courts held Initiative 350 unconstitutional, and we affirmed, announcing in the prelude of our analysis—as though it were beyond debate—that the Equal Protection Clause forbade laws that "subtly distor[t] governmental processes in such a way as to place special burdens on the ability of minority groups to achieve beneficial legislation." Id., at 467.

The first question in Seattle was whether the subject matter of Initiative 350 was a " 'racial' issue," triggering Hunter and its process doctrine. 458 U. S., at 471–472. It was "undoubtedly. . . true" that whites and blacks were "counted among both the supporters and the opponents of Initiative 350." Id., at 472. It was "equally clear" that both white and black children benefitted from desegre-gated schools. Ibid. Nonetheless, we concluded that desegre-gation "inures primarily to the benefit of the minority, and is designed for that purpose." Ibid. (emphasis added). In any event, it was "enough that minorities may consider busing for integration to be 'legislation that is in their interest.' " Id., at 474 (quoting Hunter, supra, at 395 (Harlan, J., concurring)).

So we proceeded to the heart of the political-process analysis. We held Initiative 350 unconstitutional, since it removed "the authority to address a racial problem—and only a racial problem—from the existing decisionmaking body, in such a way as to burden minority interests." Seattle, 458 U. S., at 474. Although school boards in Washington retained authority over other student-assignment issues and over most matters of educational policy generally, under Initiative 350, minorities favoring race-based busing would have to "surmount a considerably higher hurdle" than the mere petitioning of a local assembly: They "now must seek relief from the state legislature, or from the statewide electorate," a "different level of government." Ibid.

The relentless logic of Hunter and Seattle would point to a similar conclusion in this case. In those cases, one level of government exercised borrowed authority over an apparently "racial issue," until a higher level of government called the loan. So too here. In those cases, we deemed the revocation an equal-protection violation regardless of whether it facially classified according to race or reflected an invidious purpose to discriminate. Here, the Court of Appeals did the same.

The plurality sees it differently. Though it, too, dis-avows the political-process-doctrine basis on which Hunter and Seattle were decided, ante, at 10–14, it does not take the next step of overruling those cases. Rather, it reinterprets them beyond recognition. Hunter, the plurality suggests, was a case in which the challenged act had "target[ed] racial minorities." Ante, at 8. Maybe, but the Hunter Court neither found that to be so nor considered it relevant, bypassing the question of intent entirely, satisfied that its newly minted political-process theory sufficed to invalidate the charter amendment.

As for Seattle, what was really going on, according to the plurality, was that Initiative 350 had the consequence (if not the purpose) of preserving the harms effected by prior de jure segregation. Thus, "the political restriction in question was designed to be used, or was likely to be used, to encourage infliction of injury by reason of race." Ante, at 17. That conclusion is derived not from the opinion but from recently discovered evidence that the city of Seattle had been a cause of its schools' racial imbalance all along: "Although there had been no judicial finding of de jure segregation with respect to Seattle's school district, it appears as though school segregation in the district in the 1940's and 1950's may have been the partial result of school board policies." Ante, at 9. 2 That the district's effort to end racial imbalance had been stymied by Initiative 350 meant that the people, by passing it, somehow had become complicit in Seattle's equal-protection-denying status quo, whether they knew it or not. Hence, therewas in Seattle a government-furthered "infliction of a specific"—and, presumably, constitutional—"injury." Ante, at 14.

Once again this describes what our opinion in Seattle might have been, but assuredly not what it was. The opinion assumes throughout that Seattle's schools suffered at most from de facto segregation, see, e.g., 458 U. S., at 474, 475—that is, segregation not the "product . . . of state action but of private choices," having no "constitutional implications," Freeman, 503 U. S., at 495–496. Nor did it anywhere state that the current racial imbalance was the (judicially remediable) effect of prior de jure segregation. Absence of de jure segregation or the effects of de jure segregation was a necessary premise of the Seattle opinion. That is what made the issue of busing and pupil reassignment a matter of political choice rather than judicial mandate. 3 And precisely because it was a question for the political branches to decide, the manner—which is to say, the process—of its resolution implicated the Court's new process theory. The opinion itself says this: "[I]n the absence of a constitutional violation, the desirability and efficacy of school desegregation are matters to be resolved though the political process. For present purposes, it is enough [to hold reallocation of that political decision to a higher level unconstitutional] that minorities may consider busing for integration to be legislation that is in their interest." 458 U. S., at 474 (internal quotation marks omitted).

B

Patently atextual, unadministrable, and contrary to our traditional equal-protection jurisprudence, Hunter and Seattle should be overruled.

The problems with the political-process doctrine begin with its triggering prong, which assigns to a court the task of determining whether a law that reallocates policy-making authority concerns a "racial issue." Seattle, 458 U. S., at 473. Seattle takes a couple of dissatisfying cracks at defining this crucial term. It suggests that an issue is racial if adopting one position on the question would "at bottom inur[e] primarily to the benefit of the minority, and is designed for that purpose." Id., at 472. It is irrelevant that, as in Hunter and Seattle, 458 U. S., at 472, both the racial minority and the racial majority benefit from the policy in question, and members of both groups favor it. Judges should instead focus their guesswork on their own juridical sense of what is primarily for the benefit of minorities. Cf. ibid. (regarding as dispositive what "our cases" suggest is beneficial to minorities). On second thought, maybe judges need only ask this question: Is it possible "that minorities may consider" the policy in question to be "in their interest"? Id., at 474. If so, you can be sure that you are dealing with a "racial issue." [4]

No good can come of such random judicial musing. The plurality gives two convincing reasons why. For one thing, it involves judges in the dirty business of dividing the Nation "into racial blocs," Metro Broadcasting, Inc. v. FCC, 497 U. S. 547, 603, 610 (1990) (O'Connor, J., dissenting); ante, at 11–13. That task is as difficult as it is unappealing. (Does a half-Latino, half–American Indian have Latino interests, American-Indian interests, both, half of both? [5]) What is worse, the exercise promotes the noxious fiction that, knowing only a person's color or ethnicity, we can be sure that he has a predetermined set of policy "interests," thus "reinforc[ing] the perception that members of the same racial group—regardless of their age, education, economic status, or the community in which they live—think alike, [and] share the same political interests." [6] Shaw v. Reno, 509 U. S. 630, 647 (1993) . Whether done by a judge or a school board, such "racial stereotyping [is] at odds with equal protection mandates." Miller v. Johnson, 515 U. S. 900, 920 (1995) .

But that is not the "racial issue" prong's only defect. More fundamentally, it misreads the Equal Protection Clause to protect "particular group[s]," a construction that we have tirelessly repudiated in a "long line of casesunderstanding equal protection as a personal right." Adarand Constructors, Inc. v. Peña, 515 U. S. 200, 224, 230 (1995) . It is a "basic principle that the Fifth and Fourteenth Amendments to the Constitution protect persons, not groups." Id., at 227; Metro Broadcasting, supra, at 636 (Kennedy, J., dissenting). [7] Yet Seattle insists that only those political-process alterations that burden racial minorities deny equal protection. "The majority," after all, "needs no protection against discrimination." 458 U. S., at 468 (quoting Hunter, 393 U. S., at 391). In the years since Seattle, we have repeatedly rejected "a reading of the guarantee of equal protection under which the level of scrutiny varies according to the ability of different groups to defend their interests in the representative process." Richmond v. J. A. Croson Co., 488

U. S. 469, 495 (1989) . Meant to obliterate rather than endorse the practice of racial classifications, the Fourteenth Amendment's guarantees "obtai[n] with equal force regardless of 'the race of those burdened or benefitted.' " Miller, supra, at 904 (quoting Croson, supra, at 494 (plurality opinion)); Adarand, supra, at 223, 227. The Equal Protection Clause "cannot mean one thing when applied to one individual and something else when applied to a person of another color. If both are not accorded the same protection it is not equal." Regents of Univ. of Cal. v. Bakke, 438 U. S. 265–290 (1978) (opinion of Powell, J.).

The dissent trots out the old saw, derived from dictum in a footnote, that legislation motivated by " 'prejudice against discrete and insular minorities' " merits " 'more exacting judicial scrutiny.' " Post, at 31 (quoting United States v. Carolene Products, 304 U. S. 144–153, n. 4). I say derived from that dictum (expressed by the four-Justice majority of a seven-Justice Court) because the dictum itself merely said "[n]or need we enquire . . . whether prejudice against discrete and insular minorities may be a special condition," id., at 153, n. 4 (emphasis added). The dissent does not argue, of course, that such "prejudice" produced §26. Nor does it explain why certain racial minorities in Michigan qualify as " 'insular,' " meaning that "other groups will not form coalitions with them—and, critically, not because of lack of common interests but because of 'prejudice.' " Strauss, Is Carolene Products Obsolete? 2010 U. Ill. L. Rev. 1251, 1257. Nor does it even make the case that a group's "discreteness" and "insu-larity" are political liabilities rather than political strengths 8 —a serious question that alone demonstrates the prudence of the Carolene Products dictumizers in leaving the "enquir[y]" for another day. As for the question whether "legislation which restricts those political processes which can ordinarily be expected to bring about repeal of undesirable legislation . . . is to be subjected to more exacting judicial scrutiny," the Carolene Products Court found it "unnecessary to consider [that] now." 304 U. S., at 152, n. 4. If the dissent thinks that worth considering today, it should explain why the election of a university's governing board is a "political process which can ordinarily be expected to bring about repeal of undesirable legislation," but Michigan voters' ability to amend their Constitution is not. It seems to me quite the opposite. Amending the Constitution requires the approval of only "a majority of the electors voting on the question." Mich. Const., Art. XII, §2. By contrast, voting in a favorable board (each of which has eight members) at the three major public universities requires electing by majority vote at least 15 different candidates, several of whom would be running during different election cycles. See BAMN v. Regents of Univ. of Mich., 701 F. 3d 466, 508 (CA6 2012) (Sutton, J., dissenting). So if Michigan voters, instead of amending their Constitution, had pursued the dissent's preferred path of electing board members promising to "abolish race-sensitive admissions policies," post, at 3, it would have been harder, not easier, for racial minorities favoring affirmative action to overturn that decision. But the more important point is that we should not design our jurisprudence to conform to dictum in a footnote in a four-Justice opinion.

C

Moving from the appalling to the absurd, I turn now to the second part of the Hunter-Seattle analysis—which is apparently no more administrable than the first, compare post, at 4–6 (Breyer, J., concurring in judgment) ("This case . . . does not involve a reordering of the political process"), with post, at 25–29 (Sotomayor, J., dissenting) (yes, it does). This part of the inquiry directs a court to determine whether the challenged act "place[s] effective decisionmaking authority over [the] racial issue at a different level of government." Seattle, 458 U. S., at 474. The laws in both Hunter and Seattle were thought to fail this test. In both cases, "the effect of the challengedaction was to redraw decisionmaking authority over racial matters—and only over racial matters—in such a way as to place comparative burdens on minorities." 458 U. S., at 475, n. 17. This, we said, a State may not do.

By contrast, in another line of cases, we have emphasized the near-limitless sovereignty of each State to design its governing structure as it sees fit. Generally, "a State is afforded wide leeway when experimenting with the appropriate allocation of state legislative power" and may create "political subdivisions such as cities and counties . . . 'as convenient agencies for exercising such of the governmental powers of the state as may be entrusted to them.'" Holt Civic Club v. Tuscaloosa, 439 U. S. 60, 71 (1978) (quoting Hunter v. Pittsburgh, 207 U. S. 161, 178 (1907)). Accordingly, States have "absolute discretion" to determine the "number, nature and duration of the powers conferred upon [municipal] corporations and the territory over which they shall be exercised." Holt Civic Club, supra, at 71. So it would seem to go without saying that a State may give certain powers to cities, later assign the same powers to counties, and even reclaim them for itself.

Taken to the limits of its logic, Hunter-Seattle is the gaping exception that nearly swallows the rule of structural state sovereignty. If indeed the Fourteenth Amendment forbids States to "place effective decisionmaking authority over" racial issues at "different level[s] of government," then it must be true that the Amendment's ratification in 1868 worked a partial ossification of each State's governing structure, rendering basically irrevocable the power of any subordinate state official who, the day before the Fourteenth Amendment's passage, happened to enjoy legislatively conferred authority over a "racial issue." Under the Fourteenth Amendment, that subordinate entity (suppose it is a city council) could itself take action on the issue, action either favorable or unfavorable to minorities. It could even reverse itself later. What it could not do, however, is redelegate its power to an even lower level of state government (such as a city-council committee) without forfeiting it, since the necessary effect of wresting it back would be to put an additional obstacle in the path of minorities. Likewise, no entityor official higher up the state chain (e.g., a county board) could exercise authority over the issue. Nor, even, could the state legislature, or the people by constitutional amendment, revoke the legislative conferral of power to the subordinate, whether the city council, its subcommittee, or the county board. Seattle's logic would createaffirmative-action safe havens wherever subordinate offi-cials in public universities (1) traditionally have enjoyed "effective decisionmaking authority" over admissions policy but (2) have not yet used that authority to prohibit race-conscious admissions decisions. The mere existence of a subordinate's discretion over the matter would work a kind of reverse pre-emption. It is "a strange notion—alien to our system—that local governmental bodies can forever pre-empt the ability of a State—the sovereign power—to address a matter of compelling concern to the State." 458 U. S., at 495 (Powell, J., dissenting). But that is precisely what the political-process doctrine contemplates.

Perhaps the spirit of Seattle is especially disquieted by enactments of constitutional amendments. That appears to be the dissent's position. The problem with §26, it suggests, is that amending Michigan's Constitution is simply not a part of that State's "existing" political process. E.g., post, at 4, 41. What a peculiar notion: that a revision of a State's fundamental law, made in precisely the manner that law prescribes, by the very people who are the source of that law's authority, is not part of the "political process" which, but for those people and that law, would not exist. This will surely come as news to the people of Michigan, who, since 1914, have amended their Constitution 20 times. Brief for Gary Segura et al. as Amici Curiae 12. Even so, the dissent concludes that the amendment attacked here worked an illicit "chang[ing] [of] the basic rules of the political process in that State" in "the middle of the game." Post, at 2, 4. Why, one might ask, is not the amendment provision of the Michigan Constitution one (perhaps the most basic one) of the rules of the State's political process? And why does democratic invocation of that provision not qualify as working through the "existing political process," post, at 41? 9

II

I part ways with Hunter, Seattle, and (I think) the plurality for an additional reason: Each endorses a version of the proposition that a facially neutral law may deny equal protection solely because it has a disparate racial impact. Few equal-protection theories have been so squarely and soundly rejected. "An unwavering line of cases from this Court holds that a violation of the Equal Protection Clause requires state action motivated by discriminatory intent," Hernandez v. New York, 500 U. S. 352–373 (1991) (O'Connor, J., concurring in judgment), and that "official action will not be held unconstitutional solely because it results in a racially disproportionate impact," Arlington Heights v. Metropolitan Housing Development Corp., 429 U. S. 252–265 (1977). Indeed, we affirmed this principle the same day we decided Seattle: "[E]ven when a neutral law has a disproportionately adverse effect on a racial minority, the Fourteenth Amendment is violated only if a discriminatory purpose can be shown." Crawford v. Board of Ed. of Los Angeles, 458 U. S. 527–538 (1982).

Notwithstanding our dozens of cases confirming the exception-less nature of the Washington v. Davis rule, the plurality opinion leaves ajar an effects-test escape hatch modeled after Hunter and Seattle, suggesting that state action denies equal protection when it "ha[s] the serious risk, if not purpose, of causing specific injuries on account of race," or is either "designed to be used, or . . . likely to be used, to encourage infliction of injury by reason of race." Ante, at 9, 17 (emphasis added). Since these formulations enable a determination of an equal-protection violation where there is no discriminatory intent, they are inconsistent with the long Washington v. Davis line of cases. 10

Respondents argue that we need not bother with the discriminatory-purpose test, since §26 may be struck more straightforwardly as a racial "classification." Admitting (as they must) that §26 does not on its face "distribut[e] burdens or benefits on the basis of individual racial classifications," Parents Involved in Community Schools v. Seattle School Dist. No. 1, 551 U. S. 701, 720 (2007), respondents rely on Seattle's statement that "when the political process or the decisionmaking mechanism used to address racially conscious legislation—and only such legislation—is singled out for peculiar and disadvantageous treatment," then that "singling out" is a racial classification. 458 U. S., at 485, 486, n. 30. But this is just the political-process theory bedecked in different doctrinal dress. A law that "neither says nor implies that persons are to be treated differently on account of their race" is not a racial classification. Crawford, supra, at 537. That is particularly true of statutes mandating equal treatment. "[A] law that prohibits the State from classifying individuals by race . . . a fortiori does not classify individuals by race." Coalition for Economic Equity v. Wilson, 122 F. 3d 692, 702 (CA9 1997) (O'Scannlain, J.).

Thus, the question in this case, as in every case in which neutral state action is said to deny equal protection on account of race, is whether the action reflects a racially discriminatory purpose. Seattle stresses that "singling out the political processes affecting racial issues for uniquely disadvantageous treatment inevitably raises dangers of impermissible motivation." 458 U. S., at 486, n. 30. True enough, but that motivation must be proved. And respondents do not have a prayer of proving it here. The District Court noted that, under "conventional equal protection" doctrine, the suit was "doom[ed]." 539 F. Supp. 2d 924, 951 (ED Mich. 2008). Though the Court of Appeals did not opine on this question, I would not leave it for them on remand. In my view, any law expressly requiring state actors to afford all persons equal protection of the laws (such as Initiative 350 in Seattle, though not the charter amendment in Hunter) does not—cannot—deny "to any person . . . equal protection of the laws," U. S. Const., Amdt. 14, §1, regardless of whatever evidence of seemingly foul purposes plaintiffs may cook up in the trial court.

*   *   *

As Justice Harlan observed over a century ago, "[o]ur Constitution is color-blind, and neither knows nor tolerates classes among citizens." Plessy v. Ferguson, 163 U. S. 537, 559 (1896) (dissenting opinion). The people of Michigan wish the same for their governing charter. It would be shameful for us to stand in their way. 11

Notes to Justice Scalia's dissent in Schuette v. BAMN (April 22, 2014)

1 For simplicity's sake, I use "respondent" or "respondents" throughout the opinion to describe only those parties who are adverse to petitioner, not Eric Russell, a respondent who supports petitioner.

2 The plurality cites evidence from Justice Breyer's dissent in Parents Involved in Community Schools v. Seattle School Dist. No. 1, 551 U. S. 701 (2007), to suggest that the city had been a "partial" cause of its segregation problem. Ante, at 9. The plurality in Parents Involved criticized that dissent for relying on irrelevant evidence, for "elid[ing the] distinction between de jure and de facto segregation," and for "casually intimat[ing] that Seattle's school attendance patterns reflect[ed] illegal segregation." 551 U. S., at 736–737, and n. 15. Today's plurality sides with the dissent and repeats its errors.

3 Or so the Court assumed. See 458 U. S., at 472, n. 15 ("Appellants and the United States do not challenge the propriety of race-conscious student assignments for the purpose of achieving integration, even absent a finding of prior de jure segregation. We therefore do not specifically pass on that issue").

4 The dissent's version of this test is just as scattershot. Since, according to the dissent, the doctrine forbids "reconfigur[ing] the political process in a manner that burdens only a racial minority," post, at 5 (opinion of Sotomayor, J.) (emphasis added), it must be that that the reason the underlying issue (that is, the issue concerning which the process has been reconfigured) is "racial" is that the policy in question benefits only a racial minority (if it also benefitted persons not belonging to a racial majority, then the political-process reconfiguration would burden them as well). On second thought: The issue is "racial" if the policy benefits primarily a racial minority and " '[is] designed for that purpose,' " post, at 44. This is the standard Seattle purported to apply. But under that standard, §26 does not affect a "racial issue," because under Grutter v. Bollinger, 539 U. S. 306 (2003), race-based admissions policies may not constitutionally be "designed for [the] purpose," Seattle, supra, at 472, of benefitting primarily racial minorities, but must be designed for the purpose of achieving educational benefits for students of all races, Grutter, supra, at 322–325. So the dissent must mean that an issue is "racial" so long as the policy in question has the incidental effect (an effect not flowing from its design) of benefiting primarily racial minorities.

5 And how many members of a particular racial group must take the same position on an issue before we suppose that the position is in the entire group's interest? Not every member, the dissent suggests, post, at 44. Beyond that, who knows? Five percent? Eighty-five percent?

6 The dissent proves my point. After asserting—without citation, though I and many others of all races deny it—that it is "common-sense reality" that affirmative action benefits racial minorities, post, at 16, the dissent suggests throughout, e.g., post, at 30, that that view of "reality" is so necessarily shared by members of racial minorities that they must favor affirmative action.

7 The dissent contends, post, at 39, that this point "ignores the obvious: Discrimination against an individual occurs because of that individual's membership in a

particular group." No, I do not ignore the obvious; it is the dissent that misses the point. Of course discrimination against a group constitutes discrimination against each member of that group. But since it is persons and not groups that are protected, one cannot say, as the dissent would, that the Constitution prohibits discrimination against minority groups, but not against majority groups.

8 Cf., e.g., Ackerman, Beyond Carolene Products, 98 Harv. L. Rev. 713, 723–724 (1985) ("Other things being equal, 'discreteness and insularity' will normally be a source of enormous bargaining advantage, not disadvantage, for a group engaged in pluralist American politics. Except for special cases, the concerns that underlie Carolene should lead judges to protect groups that possess the opposite characteristic from the ones Carolene emphasizes—groups that are 'anonymous and diffuse' rather than 'discrete and insular' ").

9 The dissent thinks I do not understand its argument. Only when amending Michigan's Constitution violates Hunter-Seattle, it says, is that constitutionally prescribed activity necessarily not part of the State's existing political process. Post, at 21, n. 7. I understand the argument quite well; and see quite well that it begs the question. Why is Michigan's action here unconstitutional? Because it violates Hunter-Seattle. And why does it violate Hunter-Seattle? Because it is not part of the State's existing political process. And why is it not part of the State's existing political process? Because it violates Hunter-Seattle.

10 According to the dissent, Hunter-Seattle fills an important doctrinal gap left open by Washington v. Davis, since Hunter-Seattle's rule—unique among equal-protection principles—makes clear that "the majority" may not alter a political process with the goal of "prevent[ing] minority groups from partaking in that process on equal footing." Post, at 33. Nonsense. There is no gap. To "manipulate the ground rules," post, at 34, or to "ri[g] the contest," post, at 35, in order to harm persons because of their race is to deny equal protection under Washington v. Davis.

11 And doubly shameful to equate "the majority" behind §26 with "the majority" responsible for Jim Crow. Post, at 1–2 (Sotomayor, J., dissenting).

Separation of Powers, Treaties: Justice Scalia's dissent in Bond v. United States (June 2, 2014)

Justice Scalia, with whom Justice Thomas joins, and with whom Justice Alito joins as to Part I, concurring in the judgment.

Somewhere in Norristown, Pennsylvania, a husband's paramour suffered a minor thumb burn at the hands of a betrayed wife. The United States Congress—"every where extending the sphere of its activity, and drawing all power into its impetuous vortex" 1 — has made a federal case out of it. What are we to do?

It is the responsibility of "the legislature, not the Court, . . . to define a crime, and ordain its punishment." United States v. Wiltberger, 5 Wheat. 76, 95 (1820) (Marshall, C. J., for the Court). And it is "emphatically the province and duty of the judicial department to say what the law [including the Constitution] is." Marbury v. Madison, 1 Cranch 137, 177 (1803) (same). Today, the Court shirks its job and performs Congress's. As sweeping and unsettling as the Chemical Weapons Convention Implementation Act of 1998 may be, it is clear beyond doubt that it covers what Bond did; and we have no authority to amend it. So we are forced to decide—there is no way around it—whether the Act's application to what Bond did was constitutional.

I would hold that it was not, and for that reason would reverse the judgment of the Court of Appeals for the Third Circuit.

I. The Statutory Question

A. Unavoidable Meaning of the Text

The meaning of the Act is plain. No person may knowingly "develop, produce, otherwise acquire, transfer directly or indirectly, receive, stockpile, retain, own, possess, or use, or threaten to use, any chemical weapon." 18 U. S. C. §229(a)(1). A "chemical weapon" is "[a] toxic chemical and its precursors, except where intended for a purpose not prohibited under this chapter as long as the type and quantity is consistent with such a purpose." §229F(1)(A). A "toxic chemical" is "any chemical which through its chemical action on life processes can cause death, temporary incapacitation or permanent harm to humans or animals. The term includes all such chemicals, regardless of their origin or of their method of production, and regardless of whether they are produced in facilities, in munitions or elsewhere." §229F(8)(A). A "purpose not prohibited" is "[a]ny peaceful purpose related to an industrial, agricultural, research, medical, or pharmaceutical activity or other activity." §229F(7)(A).

Applying those provisions to this case is hardly complicated. Bond possessed and used "chemical[s] which through [their] chemical action on life processes can cause death, temporary incapacitation or permanent harm." Thus, she possessed "toxic chemicals." And, because they were not possessed or used only for a "purpose not prohibited," §229F(1)(A), they were "chemical weapons." Ergo, Bond violated the Act. End of statutory analysis, I would have thought. 2

The Court does not think the interpretive exercise so simple. But that is only because its result-driven antitextualism befogs what is evident.

B. The Court's Interpretation

The Court's account of the clear-statement rule reads like a really good lawyer's brief for the wrong side, relying on cases that are so close to being on point that someone eager to reach the favored outcome might swallow them. The relevance to this case of United States v. Bass, 404 U. S. 336 (1971), and Jones v. United States, 529 U. S. 848 (2000), is, in truth, entirely made up. In Bass, we had to decide whether a statute forbidding " 'receiv[ing], possess[ing], or transport[ing] in commerce or affecting commerce . . . any firearm' " prohibited possessing a gun that lacked any connection to interstate commerce. 404 U. S., at 337–339. Though the Court relied in part on a federalism-inspired interpretive presumption, it did so only after it had found, in Part I of the opinion, applying traditional interpretive tools, that the text in question was ambiguous, id., at 339–347. Adopting in Part II the narrower of the two possible readings, we said that "unless Congress conveys its purpose clearly, it will not be deemed to have significantly changed the federal-state balance." Id., at 349 (emphasis added). Had Congress "convey[ed] its purpose clearly" by enacting a clear and even sweeping statute, the presumption would not have applied.

Jones is also irrelevant. To determine whether an owner-occupied private residence counted as a " 'property used in interstate or foreign commerce or in any activity affecting interstate or foreign commerce' " under the federal arson statute, 529 U. S., at 850–851, our opinion examined not the federal-jurisdiction-expanding consequences of answering yes but rather the ordinary meaning of the words—and answered no, id., at 855–857. Then, in a separate part of the opinion, we observed that our reading was consistent with the principle that we should adopt a construction that avoids "grave and doubtful constitutional questions," id., at 857, and, quoting Bass, the principle that Congress must convey its purpose clearly before its laws will be " 'deemed to have significantly changed the federal-state balance,' " 529 U. S., at 858. To say that the best reading of the text conformed to those principles is not to say that those principles can render clear text ambiguous. 3

The latter is what the Court says today. Inverting Bass and Jones, it starts with the federalism-related consequences of the statute's meaning and reasons backwards, holding that, if the statute has what the Court considers a disruptive effect on the "federal-state balance" of criminal jurisdiction, ante, at 14, that effect causes the text, even if clear on its face, to be ambiguous. Just ponder what the Court says: "[The Act's] ambiguity derives from the improbably broad reach of the key statutory definition . . . the deeply serious consequences of adopting such a boundless reading; and the lack of any apparent need to do so . . . ." Ibid. (emphasis added). Imagine what future courts can do with that judge-empowering principle: Whatever has improbably broad, deeply serious, and apparently unnecessary consequences . . . is ambiguous!

The same skillful use of oh-so-close-to-relevant cases characterizes the Court's pro forma attempt to find ambiguity in the text itself, specifically, in the term "[c]hemical weapon." The ordinary meaning of weapon, the Court says, is an instrument of combat, and "no speaker in natural parlance would describe Bond's feud-driven act of spreading irritating chemicals on Haynes's door knob and mailbox as 'combat.' " Ante, at 15–16. Undoubtedly so, but undoubtedly beside the point, since the Act supplies its own definition of "chemical weapon," which unquestionably does bring Bond's action within the statutory prohibition. The Court retorts that "it is not unusual to consider the ordinary meaning of a defined term, particularly when there is dissonance between that ordinary meaning and the reach of the definition." Ante, at 16. So close to true! What is "not unusual" is using the ordinary meaning of the term being defined for the purpose of resolving an ambiguity in the definition. When, for example, "draft," a word of many meanings, is one of the words used in a definition of "breeze," we know it has nothing to do with military conscription or beer. The point is illustrated by the almost-relevant case the Court cites for its novel principle, Johnson v. United States, 559 U. S. 133 (2010). There the defined term was "violent felony," which the Act defined as an offense that " 'has as an element the use . . . of physical force against the person of another.' " Id., at 135 (quoting §924(e)(2)(B)(i)). We had to figure out what "physical force" meant, since the statute "d[id] not define" it. Id., at 138 (emphasis added). So we consulted (among other things) the general meaning of the term being defined, "violent felony." Id., at 140.

In this case, by contrast, the ordinary meaning of the term being defined is irrelevant, because the statute's own definition—however expansive—is utterly clear: any "chemical which through its chemical action on life proc-esses can cause death, temporary incapacitation or permanent harm to humans or animals," §229F(8)(A), unless the chemical is possessed or used for a "peaceful purpose," §229F(1)(A), (7)(A). The statute parses itself. There is no opinion of ours, and none written by any court or put forward by any commentator since Aristotle, which says, or even suggests, that "dissonance" between ordinary meaning and the unambiguous words of a definition is to be resolved in favor of ordinary meaning. If that were the case, there would hardly be any use in providing a definition. No, the true rule is entirely clear: "When a statute includes an explicit definition, we must follow that definition, even if it varies from that term's ordinary meaning." Stenberg v. Carhart, 530 U. S. 914, 942 (2000) (emphasis added). Once again, contemplate the judge-empowering consequences of the new interpretive rule the Court today announces: When there is "dissonance" between the statutory definition and the ordinary meaning of the defined word, the latter may prevail.

But even text clear on its face, the Court suggests, must be read against the backdrop of established interpretive presumptions. Thus, we presume "that a criminal statute derived from the common law carries with it the requirement of a culpable mental state—even if no such limitation appears in the text." Ante, at 11. And we presume that "federal statutes do not apply outside the United States." Ibid. Both of those are, indeed, established interpretive presumptions that are (1) based upon realistic assessments of congressional intent, and (2) well known to Congress—thus furthering rather than subverting genuine legislative intent. To apply these presumptions, then, is not to rewrite clear text; it is to interpret words fairly, in light of their statutory context. But there is nothing either (1) realistic or (2) well known about the presumption the Court shoves down the throat of a resisting statute today. Who in the world would have thought that a definition is inoperative if it contradicts ordinary meaning? When this statute was enacted, there was not yet a "Bond presumption" to that effect—though presumably Congress will have to take account of the Bond presumption in the future, perhaps by adding at the end of all its definitions that depart from ordinary connotation "and we really mean it."

C. The Statute as Judicially Amended

I suspect the Act will not survive today's gruesome surgery. A criminal statute must clearly define the conduct it proscribes. If it does not " 'give a person of ordi-nary intelligence fair notice' " of its scope, United Statesv. Batchelder, 442 U. S. 114, 123 (1979), it denies due process.

The new §229(a)(1) fails that test. Henceforward, a person "shall be fined . . ., imprisoned for any term of years, or both," §229A(a)(1)—or, if he kills someone, "shall be punished by death or imprisoned for life," §229A(a)(2)—whenever he "develop[s], produce[s], otherwise acquire[s], transfer[s] directly or indirectly, receive[s], stockpile[s], retain[s], own[s], possess[es], or use[s], or threaten[s] to use," §229(a)(1), any chemical "of the sort that an ordinary person would associate with instruments of chemical warfare," ante, at 15 (emphasis added). Whether that test is satisfied, the Court unhelpfully (and also illogically) explains, depends not only on the "particular chemicals that the defendant used" but also on "the circumstances in which she used them." Ibid. The "detergent under the kitchen sink" and "the stain remover in the laundry room" are apparently out, ante, at 16—but what if they are deployed to poison a neighborhood water fountain? Poisoning a goldfish tank is also apparently out, ante, at 17, but what if the fish belongs to a Congressman or Governor and the act is meant as a menacing message, a small-time equivalent of leaving a severed horse head in the bed? See ibid. (using the "concerns" driving the Convention—"acts of war, assassination, and terrorism"—as guideposts of statutory meaning). Moreover, the Court's illogical embellishment seems to apply only to the "use" of a chemical, ante, at 15, but "use" is only 1 of 11 kinds of activity that the statute prohibits. What, one wonders, makes something a "chemical weapon" when it is merely "stockpile[d]" or "possess[ed]?" To these questions and countless others, one guess is as bad as another.

No one should have to ponder the totality of the circumstances in order to determine whether his conduct is a felony. Yet that is what the Court will now require of all future handlers of harmful toxins—that is to say, all of us. Thanks to the Court's revisions, the Act, which before was merely broad, is now broad and unintelligible. "[N]o standard of conduct is specified at all." Coates v. Cincinnati, 402 U. S. 611, 614 (1971) . Before long, I suspect, courts will be required to say so.

II. The Constitutional Question

Since the Act is clear, the real question this case presents is whether the Act is constitutional as applied to petitioner. An unreasoned and citation-less sentence from our opinion in Missouri v. Holland, 252 U. S. 416 (1920), purported to furnish the answer: "If the treaty is valid"—and no one argues that the Convention is not—"there can be no dispute about the validity of the statute under Article I, §8, as a necessary and proper means to execute the powers of the Government." Id., at 432. 4 Petitioner and her amici press us to consider whether there is anything to this ipse dixit. The Constitution's text and structure show that there is not. 5

A. Text

Under Article I, §8, cl. 18, Congress has the power "[t]o make all Laws which shall be necessary and proper for carrying into Execution the foregoing Powers and all other Powers vested by this Constitution in the Government of the United States, or in any Department or Officer thereof." One such "other Powe[r]" appears in Article II, §2, cl. 2: "[The President] shall have Power, by and with the Advice and Consent of the Senate, to make Treaties, provided two thirds of the Senators present concur." Read together, the two Clauses empower Congress to pass laws "necessary and proper for carrying into Execution . . . [the] Power . . . to make Treaties."

It is obvious what the Clauses, read together, do not say. They do not authorize Congress to enact laws for carrying into execution "Treaties," even treaties that do not execute themselves, such as the Chemical Weapons Convention. 6 Surely it makes sense, the Government contends, that Congress would have the power to carry out the obligations to which the President and the Senate have committed the Nation. The power to "carry into Execution" the "Power . . . to make Treaties," it insists, has to mean the power to execute the treaties themselves.

That argument, which makes no pretense of resting on text, unsurprisingly misconstrues it. Start with the phrase "to make Treaties." A treaty is a contract with a foreign nation made, the Constitution states, by the President with the concurrence of "two thirds of the Senators present." That is true of self-executing and non-self-executing treaties alike; the Constitution does not distinguish between the two. So, because the President and the Senate can enter into a non-self-executing compact with a foreign nation but can never by themselves (without the House) give that compact domestic effect through legislation, the power of the President and the Senate "to make" a Treaty cannot possibly mean to "enter into a compact with a foreign nation and then give that compact domestic legal effect." We have said in another context that a right "to make contracts" (a treaty, of course, is a contract) does not "extend . . . to conduct . . . after the contract relation has been established . . . . Such postformation conduct does not involve the right to make a contract, but rather implicates the performance of established contract obligations." Patterson v. McLean Credit Union, 491 U. S. 164, 177 (1989) (emphasis added). Upon the President's agreement and the Senate's ratification, a treaty—no matter what kind—has been made and is not susceptible of any more making.

How might Congress have helped "carr[y]" the power to make the treaty—here, the Chemical Weapons Convention—"into Execution"? In any number of ways. It could have appropriated money for hiring treaty negotiators, empowered the Department of State to appoint those negotiators, formed a commission to study the benefits and risks of entering into the agreement, or paid for a bevy of spies to monitor the treaty-related deliberations of other potential signatories. See G. Lawson & G. Seidman, The Constitution of Empire: Territorial Expansion and American Legal History 63 (2004). The Necessary and Proper Clause interacts similarly with other Article II powers: "[W]ith respect to the executive branch, the Clause would allow Congress to institute an agency to help the President wisely employ his pardoning power . . . . Most important, the Clause allows Congress to establish officers to assist the President in exercising his 'executive Power.' " Calabresi & Prakash, The President's Power to Execute the Laws, 104 Yale L. J. 541, 591 (1994).

But a power to help the President make treaties is not a power to implement treaties already made. See generally Rosenkranz, Executing the Treaty Power, 118 Harv. L. Rev. 1867 (2005). Once a treaty has been made, Congress's power to do what is "necessary and proper" to assist the making of treaties drops out of the picture. To legislate compliance with the United States' treaty obligations, Congress must rely upon its independent (though quite robust) Article I, §8, powers.

B. Structure

"[T]he Constitutio[n] confer[s] upon Congress . . . not all governmental powers, but only discrete, enumerated ones." Printz v. United States, 521 U. S. 898, 919 (1997) . And, of course, "enumeration presupposes something not enumerated." Gibbons v. Ogden, 9 Wheat. 1, 195 (1824). But in Holland, the proponents of unlimited congressional power found a loophole: "By negotiating a treaty and obtaining the requisite consent of the Senate, the President . . . may endow Congress with a source of legislative authority independent of the powers enumerated in Article I." L. Tribe, American Constitutional Law §4–4, pp. 645–646 (3d ed. 2000). Though Holland's change to the Constitution's text appears minor (the power to carry into execution the power to make treaties becomes the power to carry into execution treaties), the change to its structure is seismic.

To see why vast expansion of congressional power is not just a remote possibility, consider two features of the modern practice of treaty making. In our Nation's early history, and extending through the time when Holland was written, treaties were typically bilateral, and addressed only a small range of topics relating to the obli-gations of each state to the other, and to citizens of the other—military neutrality, for example, or military alliance, or guarantee of most-favored-nation trade treatment. See Bradley, The Treaty Power and American Federalism, 97 Mich. L. Rev. 390, 396 (1998). But beginning in the last half of the last century, many treaties were "detailed multilateral instruments negotiated and drafted at international conferences," ibid., and they sought to regulate states' treatment of their own citizens, or even "the activities of individuals and private entities," A. Chayes & A. Chayes, The New Sovereignty: Compliance with International Regulatory Agreements 14 (1995). "[O]ften vague and open-ended," such treaties "touch on almost every aspect of domestic civil, political, and cultural life." Bradley & Goldsmith, Treaties, Human Rights, and Condi-tional Consent, 149 U. Pa. L. Rev. 399, 400 (2000).

Consider also that, at least according to some scholars, the Treaty Clause comes with no implied subject-matter limitations. See, e.g., L. Henkin, Foreign Affairs and the United States Constitution 191, 197 (2d ed. 1996); but see Bradley, supra, at 433–439. On this view, "[t]he Tenth Amendment . . . does not limit the power to make treaties or other agreements," Restatement (Third) of Foreign Relations Law of the United States §302, Comment d, p. 154 (1986), and the treaty power can be used to regulate matters of strictly domestic concern, see id., at Comment c, p. 153; but see post, at 3–16 (Thomas, J., concurring in judgment).

If that is true, then the possibilities of what the Federal Government may accomplish, with the right treaty in hand, are endless and hardly farfetched. It could begin, as some scholars have suggested, with abrogation of this Court's constitutional rulings. For example, the holding that a statute prohibiting the carrying of firearms near schools went beyond Congress's enumerated powers, United States v. Lopez, 514 U. S. 549, 551 (1995), could be reversed by negotiating a treaty with Latvia providing that neither sovereign would permit the carrying of guns near schools. Similarly, Congress could reenact the invalidated part of the Violence Against Women Act of 1994 that provided a civil remedy for victims of gender-motivated violence, just so long as there were a treaty on point—and some authors think there already is, see MacKinnon, The Supreme Court, 1999 Term, Comment, 114 Harv. L. Rev. 135, 167 (2000).

But reversing some of this Court's decisions is the least of the problem. Imagine the United States' entry into an Antipolygamy Convention, which called for—and Congress enacted—legislation providing that, when a spouse of a man with more than one wife dies intestate, the surviv-ing husband may inherit no part of the estate. Constitu-tional? The Federalist answers with a rhetorical ques-tion: "Suppose by some forced constructions of its authority (which indeed cannot easily be imagined) the Federal Legislature should attempt to vary the law of descent in any State; would it not be evident that . . . it had exceeded its jurisdiction and infringed upon that of the State?" The Federalist No. 33, at 206 (A. Hamilton). Yet given the Antipolygamy Convention, Holland would uphold it. Or imagine that, to execute a treaty, Congress enacted a statute prohibiting state inheritance taxes on real prop-erty. Constitutional? Of course not. Again, The Federalist: "Suppose . . . [Congress] should undertake to abrogate a land tax imposed by the authority of a State, would it not be equally evident that this was an invasion of that concurrent jurisdiction in respect to this species of tax which its constitution plainly supposes to exist in the State governments?" No. 33, at 206. Holland would uphold it. As these examples show, Holland places Congress only one treaty away from acquiring a general police power.

The Necessary and Proper Clause cannot bear such weight. As Chief Justice Marshall said regarding it, no "great substantive and independent power" can be "implied as incidental to other powers, or used as a means of executing them." McCulloch v. Maryland, 4 Wheat. 316, 411 (1819); see Baude, Rethinking the Federal Eminent Domain Power, 122 Yale L. J. 1738, 1749–1755 (2013).No law that flattens the principle of state sovereignty, whether or not "necessary," can be said to be "proper." As an old, well-known treatise put it, "it would not be a proper or constitutional exercise of the treaty-making power to provide that Congress should have a general legislative authority over a subject which has not been given it by the Constitution." 1 W. Willoughby, The Constitutional Law of the United States §216, p. 504 (1910).

We would not give the Government's support of the Holland principle the time of day were we confronted with "treaty-implementing" legislation that abrogated the freedom of speech or some other constitutionally protected individual right. We proved just that in Reid v. Covert, 354 U. S. 1 (1957), which held that commitments made in treaties with Great Britain and Japan would not permit civilian wives of American servicemen stationed in those countries to be tried for murder by court-martial. The plurality opinion said that "no agreement with a foreign nation can confer power on the Congress, or on any other branch of Government, which is free from the restraints of the Constitution." Id., at 16.

To be sure, the Reid plurality purported to distinguish the ipse dixit of Holland with its own unsupported ipse dixit. "[T]he people and the States," it said, "have delegated [the treaty] power to the National Government [so] the Tenth Amendment is no barrier." 354 U. S., at 18. The opinion does not say why (and there is no reason why) only the Tenth Amendment, and not the other nine, has been "delegated" away by the treaty power. The distinction between provisions protecting individual liberty, on the one hand, and "structural" provisions, on the other, cannot be the explanation, since structure in general—and especially the structure of limited federal powers—is designed to protect individual liberty. "The federal structure . . . secures the freedom of the individual. . . . By denying any one government complete jurisdiction over all the concerns of public life, federalism protects the liberty of the individual from arbitrary power." Bond v. United States, 564 U. S. ___, ___ (2011) (slip op., at 9–10).

The Government raises a functionalist objection: If the Constitution does not limit a self-executing treaty to the subject matter delineated in Article I, §8, then it makes no sense to impose that limitation upon a statute implementing a non-self-executing treaty. See Tr. of Oral Arg. 32–33. The premise of the objection (that the power to make self-executing treaties is limitless) is, to say the least, arguable. But even if it is correct, refusing to extend that proposition to non-self-executing treaties makes a great deal of sense. Suppose, for example, that the self-aggrandizing Federal Government wishes to take over the law of intestacy. If the President and the Senate find in some foreign state a ready accomplice, they have two options. First, they can enter into a treaty with "stipulations" specific enough that they "require no legislation to make them operative," Whitney v. Robertson, 124 U. S. 190, 194 (1888), which would mean in this example something like a comprehensive probate code. But for that to succeed, the President and a supermajority of the Senate would need to reach agreement on all the details—which, when once embodied in the treaty, could not be altered or superseded by ordinary legislation. The second option—far the better one—is for Congress to gain lasting and flexible control over the law of intestacy by means of a non-self-executing treaty. "[Implementing] legislation is as much subject to modification and repeal by Congress as legislation upon any other subject." Ibid. And to make such a treaty, the President and Senate would need to agree only that they desire power over the law of intestacy.

The famous scholar and jurist Henry St. George Tucker saw clearly the danger of Holland's ipse dixit five years before it was written:

"[The statement is made that] if the treaty-making power, composed of the President and Senate, in discharging its functions under the government, finds that it needs certain legislative powers which Congress does not possess to carry out its desires, it may . . . infuse into Congress such powers, although the Framers of the Constitution omitted to grant them to Congress. . . . Every reputable commentator upon the Constitution from Story down to the present day, has held that the legislative powers of Congress lie in grant and are limited by such grant. . . . [S]hould such a construction as that asserted in the above statement obtain through judicial endorsement, our system of government would soon topple and fall." Limitations on the Treaty-Making Power Under the Constitution of the United States §113, pp. 129–130 (1915).

* * *

We have here a supposedly "narrow" opinion which, in order to be "narrow," sets forth interpretive principles never before imagined that will bedevil our jurisprudence (and proliferate litigation) for years to come. The immediate product of these interpretive novelties is a statute that should be the envy of every lawmaker bent on trapping the unwary with vague and uncertain criminal prohibitions. All this to leave in place an ill-considered ipse dixit that enables the fundamental constitutional principle of limited federal powers to be set aside by the President and Senate's exercise of the treaty power. We should not have shirked our duty and distorted the law to preserve that assertion; we should have welcomed and eagerly grasped the opportunity—nay, the obligation—to consider and repudiate it.

Notes

1 The Federalist No. 48, p. 333 (J. Cooke ed. 1961) (J. Madison) (hereinafter The Federalist).

2 Petitioner offers one textual argument that the Court does not consider. She argues that the exception for "peaceful purposes" is best understood as a term of art meaning roughly any purpose that is not "warlike." Brief for Petitioner 50–57. Though that reading is more defensible than the Court's, the Act will not bear it. If "peaceful" meant "nonwarlike," the statute's exception for "any individual self-defense device, including . . . pepper spray or chemical mace," §229C—the prosaic uses of which are surely nonwarlike—would have been unnecessary.

3 Other cases in the Bass line confirm that broad text "need only be plain to anyone reading [it]" in order to be given its obvious meaning. Salinas v. United States, 522 U. S. 52, 60 (1997) (internal quotation marks omitted); see also Pennsylvania Dept. of Corrections v. Yeskey, 524 U. S. 206, 209 (1998); cf. United States v. Lopez, 514 U. S. 549, 562 (1995).

4 Nineteen years earlier, the Court embraced a similar view—also without reasoning. See Neely v. Henkel, 180 U. S. 109, 121 (1901) ("The power of Congress to

make all laws necessary and proper for carrying into execution . . . all [powers] vested in the Government of the United States . . . includes the power to enact such legislation as is appropriate to give efficacy to any stipulations which it is competent for the President by and with the advice and consent of the Senate to insert in a treaty with a foreign power"). There is also dictum arguably favorable to Holland in Prigg v. Pennsylvania, 16 Pet. 539, 619 (1842) ("[T]he power is nowhere in positive terms conferred upon Congress to make laws to carry the stipulations of treaties into effect. It has been supposed to result from the duty of the national government to fulfill all the obligations of treaties"). But see Mayor of New Orleans v. United States, 10 Pet. 662, 736 (1836) ("The government of the United States . . . is one of limited powers. It can exercise authority over no subjects, except those which have been delegated to it. Congress cannot, by legislation, enlarge the federal jurisdiction, nor can it be enlarged under the treaty-making power").

5 I agree with the Court that the Government waived its defense of the Act as an exercise of the commerce power. Ante, at 8–9.

6 Non-self-executing treaties are treaties whose commitments do not "automatically have effect as domestic law," Medellín v. Texas, 552 U. S. 491, 504 (2008), and "can only be enforced pursuant to legislation to carry them into effect," Whitney v. Robertson, 124 U. S. 190, 194 (1888) .

Recess Appointments: Justice Scalia's concurrence in National Labor Relations Board v. Noel Canning (June 26, 2014)

Justice Scalia, with whom The Chief Justice, Justice Thomas, and Justice Alito join, concurring in the judgment.

Except where the Constitution or a valid federal law provides otherwise, all "Officers of the United States" must be appointed by the President "by and with the Advice and Consent of the Senate." U. S. Const., Art. II, §2, cl. 2. That general rule is subject to an exception: "The President shall have Power to fill up all Vacancies that may happen during the Recess of the Senate, by granting Commissions which shall expire at the End of their next Session." Id., §2, cl. 3. This case requires us to decide whether the Recess Appointments Clause authorized three appointments made by President Obama to the National Labor Relations Board in January 2012 without the Senate's consent.

To prevent the President's recess-appointment power from nullifying the Senate's role in the appointment process, the Constitution cabins that power in two significant ways. First, it may be exercised only in "the Recess of the Senate," that is, the intermission between two formal legislative sessions. Second, it may be used to fill only those vacancies that "happen during the Recess," that is, offices that become vacant during that intermission. Both conditions are clear from the Constitution's text and structure, and both were well understood at the founding. The Court of Appeals correctly held that the appointments here at issue are invalid because they did not meet either condition.

Today's Court agrees that the appointments were in-valid, but for the far narrower reason that they were made during a 3-day break in the Senate's session. On its way to that result, the majority sweeps away the key textual limitations on the recess-appointment power. It holds, first, that the President can make appointments without the Senate's participation even during short breaks in the middle of the Senate's session, and second, that those appointments can fill offices that became vacant long before the break in which they were filled. The majority justifies those atextual results on an adverse-possession theory of executive authority: Presidents have long claimed the powers in question, and the Senate has not disputed those claims with sufficient vigor, so the Court should not "upset the compromises and working arrangements that the elected branches of Government themselves have reached." Ante, at 9.

The Court's decision transforms the recess-appointment power from a tool carefully designed to fill a narrow and specific need into a weapon to be wielded by future Presidents against future Senates. To reach that result, the majority casts aside the plain, original meaning of the constitutional text in deference to late-arising historical practices that are ambiguous at best. The majority's insistence on deferring to the Executive's untenably broad interpretation of the power is in clear conflict with our precedent and forebodes a diminution of this Court's role in controversies involving the separation of powers and the structure of government. I concur in the judgment only.

I. Our Responsibility

Today's majority disregards two overarching principles that ought to guide our consideration of the questions presented here.

First, the Constitution's core, government-structuring provisions are no less critical to preserving liberty than are the later adopted provisions of the Bill of Rights. Indeed, "[s]o convinced were the Framers that liberty of the person inheres in structure that at first they did not consider a Bill of Rights necessary." Clinton v. City of New York, 524 U. S. 417, 450 (1998) (Kennedy, J., concurring). Those structural provisions reflect the founding generation's deep conviction that "checks and balances were the foundation of a structure of government that would protect liberty." Bowsher v. Synar, 478 U. S. 714, 722 (1986) . It is for that reason that "the claims of individuals—not of Government departments—have been the principal source of judicial decisions concerning separation of powers and checks and balances." Bond v. United States, 564 U. S. ____, ____ (2011) (slip op., at 10); see, e.g., Free Enterprise Fund v. Public Company Accounting Oversight Bd., 561 U. S. 477 (2010); Clinton, supra; Plaut v. Spendthrift Farm, Inc., 514 U. S. 211 (1995); Bowsher, supra; INS v. Chadha, 462 U. S. 919 (1983); Northern Pipeline Constr. Co. v. Marathon Pipe Line Co., 458 U. S. 50 (1982) . Those decisions all rest on the bedrock principle that "the constitutional structure of our Government" is designed first and foremost not to look after the interests of the respective branches, but to "protec[t] individual liberty." Bond, supra, at ____ (slip op., at 11).

Second and relatedly, when questions involving the Constitution's government-structuring provisions are presented in a justiciable case, it is the solemn responsibility of the Judicial Branch " 'to say what the law is.' " Zivotofsky v. Clinton, 566 U. S. ___, ___ (2012) (slip op., at 7) (quoting Marbury v. Madison, 1 Cranch 137, 177 (1803)). This Court does not defer to the other branches' resolution of such controversies; as Justice Kennedy has previously written, our role is in no way "lessened" because it might be said that "the two political branches are adjusting their own powers between themselves." Clinton, supra, at 449 (concurring opinion). Since the separation of powers exists for the protection of individual liberty, its vitality "does not depend" on "whether 'the encroached-upon branch approves the encroachment.' " Free Enterprise Fund, supra, at 497 (quoting New York v. United States, 505 U. S. 144, 182 (1992)); see also Freytag v. Commissioner, 501 U. S. 868–880 (1991); Metropolitan Washington Airports Authority v. Citizens for Abatement of Aircraft Noise, Inc., 501 U. S. 252–277 (1991). Rather, policing the "enduring structure" of constitutional government when the political branches fail to do so is "one of the most vital functions of this Court." Public Citizen v. Department of Justice, 491 U. S. 440, 468 (1989) (Kennedy, J., concurring in judgment).

Our decision in Chadha illustrates that principle. There, we held that a statutory provision authorizing one House of Congress to cancel an executive action taken pursuant to statutory authority—a so-called "legislative veto"—exceeded the bounds of Congress's authority under the Constitution. 462 U. S., at 957–959. We did not hesitate to hold the legislative veto unconstitutional even though Congress had enacted, and the President had signed, nearly 300 similar provisions over the course of 50 years. Id., at 944–945. Just the opposite: We said the other branches' enthusiasm for the legislative veto "sharpened rather than blunted" our review. Id., at 944. Likewise, when the charge is made that a practice "enhances the President's powers beyond" what the Constitution permits, "[i]t is no answer . . . to say that Congress surrendered its authority by its own hand." Clinton, 524 U. S., at 451 (Kennedy, J., concurring). "[O]ne Congress cannot yield up its own powers, much less those of other Congresses to follow. Abdication of responsibility is not part of the constitutional design." Id., at 452 (citations omitted).

Of course, where a governmental practice has been open, widespread, and unchallenged since the early days of the Republic, the practice should guide our interpretation of an ambiguous constitutional provision. See, e.g., Alden v. Maine, 527 U. S. 706–744 (1999); Bowsher, supra, at 723–724; Myers v. United States, 272 U. S. 52–175 (1926); see also Youngstown Sheet & Tube Co. v. Sawyer, 343 U. S. 579, 610 (1952) (Frankfurter, J., concurring) (arguing that "a systematic, unbroken, executive practice, long pursued to the knowledge of the Congress and never before questioned" should inform interpretation of the "Executive Power" vested in the President); Rutan v. Republican Party of Ill., 497 U. S. 62, and n. 1 (1990) (Scalia, J., dissenting). But " '[p]ast practice does not, by itself, create power.' " Medellín v. Texas, 552 U. S. 491, 532 (2008) (quoting Dames & Moore v. Regan, 453 U. S. 654, 686 (1981)). That is a necessary corollary of the principle that the political branches cannot by agreement alter the constitutional structure. Plainly, then, a self-aggrandizing practice adopted by one branch well after the founding, often challenged, and never before blessed by this Court—in other words, the sort of practice on which the majority relies in this case—does not relieve us of our duty to interpret the Constitution in light of its text, structure, and original understanding.

Ignoring our more recent precedent in this area, which is extensive, the majority relies on The Pocket Veto Case, 279 U. S. 655, 689 (1929), for the proposition that when interpreting a constitutional provision "regulating the relationship between Congress and the President," we must defer to the settled practice of the political branches if the provision is " ' "in any respect of doubtful meaning." ' " Ante, at 7; see ante, at 8, 16, 23, 33. The language the majority quotes from that case was pure dictum. The Pocket Veto Court had to decide whether a bill passed by the House and Senate and presented to the President less than 10 days before the adjournment of the first session of a particular Congress, but neither signed nor vetoed by the President, became a law. Most of the opinion analyzed that issue like any other legal question and concluded that treating the bill as a law would have been inconsistent with the text and structure of the Constitution. Only near the end of the opinion did the Court add that its conclusion was "confirmed" by longstanding Presidential practice in which Congress appeared to have acquiesced. 279 U. S., at 688–689. We did not suggest that the case would have come out differently had the longstanding practice been otherwise. 1

II. Intra-Session Breaks

The first question presented is whether "the Recess of the Senate," during which the President's recess-appointment power is active, is (a) the period between two of the Senate's formal sessions, or (b) any break in the Senate's proceedings. I would hold that "the Recess" is the gap between sessions and that the appointments at issue here are invalid because they undisputedly were made during the Senate's session. The Court's contrary conclusion—that "the Recess" includes "breaks in the midst of a session," ante, at 9—is inconsistent with the Constitution's text and structure, and it requires judicial fabrication of vague, unadministrable limits on the recess-appointment power (thus defined) that overstep the judicial role. And although the majority relies heavily on "historical practice," no practice worthy of our deference supports the majority's conclusion on this issue.

A. Plain Meaning

A sensible interpretation of the Recess Appointments Clause should start by recognizing that the Clause uses the term "Recess" in contradistinction to the term "Session." As Alexander Hamilton wrote: "The time within which the power is to operate 'during the recess of the Senate' and the duration of the appointments 'to the end of the next session' of that body, conspire to elucidate the sense of the provision." The Federalist No. 67, p. 455 (J. Cooke ed. 1961).

In the founding era, the terms "recess" and "session" had well-understood meanings in the marking-out of legislative time. The life of each elected Congress typically consisted (as it still does) of two or more formal sessions separated by adjournments "sine die," that is, without a specified return date. See GPO, Congressional Directory, 113th Cong., pp. 524–542 (2013–2014) (hereinafter Congressional Directory) (listing sessions of Congress from 1789 through 2013); 705 F. 3d 490, 512, and nn. 1–2 (CADC 2013) (case below); ante, at 9. The period between two sessions was known as "the recess." See 26 Annals of Cong. 748 (1814) (Sen. Gore) ("The time of the Senate consists of two periods, viz: their session and their recess"). As one scholar has thoroughly demonstrated, "in government practice the phrase 'the Recess' always referred to the gap between sessions." Natelson, The Origins and Meaning of "Vacancies that May Happen During the Recess" in the Constitution's Recess Appointments Clause, 37 Harv. J. L. & Pub. Pol'y 199, 213 (2014) (hereinafter Natelson); see id., at 214–227 (providing dozens of examples). By contrast, other provisions of the Constitution use the verb "adjourn" rather than "recess" to refer to the commencement of breaks during a formal legislative session. See, e.g., Art. I, §5, cl. 1; id., §5, cl. 4. 2

To be sure, in colloquial usage both words, "recess" and "session," could take on alternative, less precise meanings. A session could include any short period when a legislature's members were "assembled for business," and a recess could refer to any brief "suspension" of legislative "business." 2 N. Webster, American Dictionary of the English Language (1828). So the Continental Congress could complain of the noise from passing carriages disrupting its "daily Session," 29 Journals of the Continental Congress 1774–1789, p. 561 (1785) (J. Fitzpatrick ed. 1933), and the House could "take a recess" from 4 o'clock to 6 o'clock, Journal of the House of Representatives, 17th Cong., 2d Sess., p. 259 (1823). But as even the majority acknowledges, the Constitution's use of "the word 'the' in 'the [R]ecess' " tends to suggest "that the phrase refers to the single break separating formal sessions." Ante, at 10.

More importantly, neither the Solicitor General nor the majority argues that the Clause uses "session" in its loose, colloquial sense. And if "the next Session" denotes a formal session, then "the Recess" must mean the break between formal sessions. As every commentator on the Clause until the 20th century seems to have understood, the "Recess" and the "Session" to which the Clause refers are mutually exclusive, alternating states. See, e.g., The Federalist No. 67, at 455 (explaining that appointments would require Senatorial consent "during the session of the Senate" and would be made by the President alone "in their recess"); 1 Op. Atty. Gen. 631 (1823) (contrasting vacancies occurring "during the recess of the Senate" with those occurring "during the session of the Senate"); 2 Op. Atty Gen. 525, 527 (1832) (discussing a vacancy that "took place while the Senate was in session, and not during the recess"). It is linguistically implausible to suppose—as the majority does—that the Clause uses one of those terms ("Recess") informally and the other ("Session") formally in a single sentence, with the result that an event can occur during both the "Recess" and the "Session."

Besides being linguistically unsound, the majority's reading yields the strange result that an appointment made during a short break near the beginning of one official session will not terminate until the end of the following official session, enabling the appointment to last for up to two years. The majority justifies that result by observing that the process of confirming a nominee "may take several months." Ante, at 17. But the average duration of the confirmation process is irrelevant. The Clause's self-evident design is to have the President's unilateral appointment last only until the Senate has "had an opportunity to act on the subject." 3 J. Story, Commentaries on the Constitution of the United States §1551, p. 410 (1833) (emphasis added).

One way to avoid the linguistic incongruity of the majority's reading would be to read both "the Recess" and "the next Session" colloquially, so that the recess-appointment power would be activated during any temporary suspension of Senate proceedings, but appointments made pursuant to that power would last only until the beginning of the next suspension (which would end the next colloquial session). See, e.g., Rappaport, The Original Meaning of the Recess Appointments Clause, 52 UCLA L. Rev. 1487, 1569 (2005) (hereinafter Rappaport, Original Meaning). That approach would be more linguistically defensible than the majority's. But it would not cure the most fundamental problem with giving "Recess" its colloquial, rather than its formal, meaning: Doing so leaves the recess-appointment power without a textually grounded principle limiting the time of its exercise.

The dictionary definitions of "recess" on which the majority relies provide no such principle. On the contrary, they make clear that in colloquial usage, a recess could include any suspension of legislative business, no matter how short. See 2 S. Johnson, A Dictionary of the English Language 1602 (4th ed. 1773). Webster even provides a stark illustration: "[T]he house of representatives had a recess of half an hour." 2 Webster, supra. The notion that the Constitution empowers the President to make unilateral appointments every time the Senate takes a half-hour lunch break is so absurd as to be self-refuting. But that, in the majority's view, is what the text authorizes.

The boundlessness of the colloquial reading of "the Recess" thus refutes the majority's assertion that the Clause's "purpose" of "ensur[ing] the continued functioning of the Federal Government" demands that it apply to intra-session breaks as well as inter-session recesses. Ante, at 11. The majority disregards another self-evident purpose of the Clause: to preserve the Senate's role in the appointment process—which the founding generation regarded as a critical protection against " 'despotism,' " Freytag, 501 U. S., at 883—by clearly delineating the times when the President can appoint officers without the Senate's consent. Today's decision seriously undercuts that purpose. In doing so, it demonstrates the folly of interpreting constitutional provisions designed to establish "a structure of government that would protect liberty," Bowsher, 478 U. S., at 722, on the narrow-minded assumption that their only purpose is to make the government run as efficiently as possible. "Convenience and efficiency," we have repeatedly recognized, "are not the primary objectives" of our constitutional framework. Free Enterprise Fund, 561 U. S., at 499 (internal quotation marks omitted).

Relatedly, the majority contends that the Clause's supposed purpose of keeping the wheels of government turning demands that we interpret the Clause to maintain its relevance in light of the "new circumstance" of the Senate's taking an increasing number of intra-session breaks that exceed three days. Ante, at 17. Even if I accepted the canard that courts can alter the Constitution's meaning to accommodate changed circumstances, I would be hard pressed to see the relevance of that notion here. The rise of intra-session adjournments has occurred in tandem with the development of modern forms of communication and transportation that mean the Senate "is always available" to consider nominations, even when its Members are temporarily dispersed for an intra-session break. Tr. of Oral Arg. 21 (Ginsburg, J.). The Recess Appointments Clause therefore is, or rather, should be, an anachronism—"essentially an historic relic, something whose original purpose has disappeared." Id., at 19 (Kagan, J.). The need it was designed to fill no longer exists, and its only remaining use is the ignoble one of enabling the President to circumvent the Senate's role in the appointment process. That does not justify "read[ing] it out of the Constitution" and, contra the majority, ante, at 40, I would not do so; but neither would I distort the Clause's original meaning, as the majority does, to ensure a prominent role for the recess-appointment power in an era when its influence is far more pernicious than beneficial.

To avoid the absurd results that follow from its collo-quial reading of "the Recess," the majority is forced to declare that some intra-session breaks—though undisputedly within the phrase's colloquial meaning—are simply "too short to trigger the Recess Appointments Clause." Ante, at 21. But it identifies no textual basis whatsoever for limiting the length of "the Recess," nor does it point to any clear standard for determining how short is too short. It is inconceivable that the Framers would have left the circumstances in which the President could exercise such a significant and potentially dangerous power so utterly indeterminate. Other structural provisions of the Constitution that turn on duration are quite specific: Neither House can adjourn "for more than three days" without the other's consent. Art. I, §5, cl. 4. The President must return a passed bill to Congress "within ten Days (Sundays excepted)," lest it become a law. Id., §7, cl. 2. Yet on the majority's view, when the first Senate considered taking a 1-month break, a 3-day weekend, or a half-hour siesta, it had no way of knowing whether the President would be constitutionally authorized to appoint officers in its absence. And any officers appointed in those circumstances would have served under a cloud, unable to determine with any degree of confidence whether their appointments were valid. 3

Fumbling for some textually grounded standard, the majority seizes on the Adjournments Clause, which bars either House from adjourning for more than three days without the other's consent. Id., §5, cl. 4. According to the majority, that clause establishes that a 3-day break is always "too short" to trigger the Recess Appointments Clause. Ante, at 19. It goes without saying that nothing in the constitutional text supports that disposition. If (as the majority concludes) "the Recess" means a recess in the colloquial sense, then it necessarily includes breaks shorter than three days. And the fact that the Constitution includes a 3-day limit in one clause but omits it from the other weighs strongly against finding such a limit to be implicit in the clause in which it does not appear. In all events, the dramatically different contexts in which the two clauses operate make importing the 3-day limit from the Adjournments Clause into the Recess Appointments Clause "both arbitrary and mistaken." Rappaport, Original Meaning 1556.

And what about breaks longer than three days? The majority says that a break of four to nine days is "presumptively too short" but that the presumption may be rebutted in an "unusual circumstance," such as a "national catastrophe . . . that renders the Senate unavailable but calls for an urgent response." Ante, at 21. The majority must hope that the in terrorem effect of its "presumptively too short" pronouncement will deter future Presidents from making any recess appointments during 4-to-9-day breaks and thus save us from the absurd spectacle of unelected judges evaluating (after an evidentiary hearing?) whether an alleged "catastrophe" was sufficiently "urgent" to trigger the recess-appointment power. The majority also says that "political opposition in the Senate would not qualify as an unusual circumstance." Ibid. So if the Senate should refuse to confirm a nominee whom the President considers highly qualified; or even if it should refuse to confirm any nominee for an office, thinking the office better left vacant for the time being; the President's power would not be triggered during a 4-to-9-day break, no matter how "urgent" the President's perceived need for the officer's assistance. (The majority protests that this "should go without saying—except that Justice Scalia compels us to say it," ibid., seemingly forgetting that the appointments at issue in this very case were justified on those grounds and that the Solicitor General has asked us to view the recess-appointment power as a "safety valve" against Senatorial "intransigence." Tr. of Oral Arg. 21.)

As for breaks of 10 or more days: We are presumably to infer that such breaks do not trigger any "presumpt[ion]" against recess appointments, but does that mean the President has an utterly free hand? Or can litigants seek invalidation of an appointment made during a 10-day break by pointing to an absence of "unusual" or "urgent" circumstances necessitating an immediate appointment, albeit without the aid of a "presumpt[ion]" in their favor? Or, to put the question as it will present itself to lawyers in the Executive Branch: Can the President make an appointment during a 10-day break simply to overcome "political opposition in the Senate" despite the absence of any "national catastrophe," even though it "go[es] without saying" that he cannot do so during a 9-day break? Who knows? The majority does not say, and neither does the Constitution.
4

Even if the many questions raised by the majority's failure to articulate a standard could be answered, alarger question would remain: If the Constitution's text empowers the President to make appointments during any break in the Senate's proceedings, by what right does the majority subject the President's exercise of that power to vague, court-crafted limitations with no textual basis? The majority claims its temporal guideposts are informed by executive practice, but a President's self-restraint cannot "bind his successors by diminishing their powers." Free Enterprise Fund, 561 U.

S., at 497; cf. Clinton v. Jones, 520 U. S. 681, 718 (1997) (Breyer, J., concurring in judgment) ("voluntary actions" by past Presidents "tel[l] us little about what the Constitution commands").

An interpretation that calls for this kind of judicial adventurism cannot be correct. Indeed, if the Clause really did use "Recess" in its colloquial sense, then there would be no "judicially discoverable and manageable standard for resolving" whether a particular break was long enough to trigger the recess-appointment power, making that a nonjusticiable political question. Zivotofsky, 566 U. S., at ___ (slip op., at 5) (internal quotation marks omitted).

B. Historical Practice

For the foregoing reasons, the Constitution's text and structure unambiguously refute the majority's freewheeling interpretation of "the Recess." It is not plausible that the Constitution uses that term in a sense that authorizes the President to make unilateral appointments during any break in Senate proceedings, subject only to hazy, atextual limits crafted by this Court centuries after ratification. The majority, however, insists that history "offers strong support" for its interpretation. Ante, at 11. The historical practice of the political branches is, of course, irrelevant when the Constitution is clear. But even if the Constitution were thought ambiguous on this point, history does not support the majority's interpretation.

1. 1789 to 1866

To begin, the majority dismisses the 78 years of history from the founding through 1866 as "not helpful" because during that time Congress took hardly any "significant" intra-session breaks, by which the majority evidently means breaks longer than three days. Ibid. (citing table in Appendix A, which does not include breaks of three or fewer days). In fact, Congress took 11 intra-session breaks of more than three days during that time, see Congressional Directory 524–527, and it appears Presidents made recess appointments during none of them.

More importantly, during those eight decades, Congress must have taken thousands of breaks that were three days or shorter. On the majority's reading, every one of those breaks would have been within the Clause's text—the majority's newly minted limitation not yet having been announced. Yet there is no record of anyone, ever, having so much as mentioned the possibility that the recess-appointment power was activated during those breaks. That would be surprising indeed if the text meant what the majority thinks it means. Cf. Printz v. United States, 521 U. S. 898–908 (1997).

2. 1867 and 1868

The first intra-session recess appointments in our his-tory almost certainly were made by President Andrew John-son in 1867 and 1868. 5 That was, of course, a period of dramatic conflict between the Executive and Congress that saw the first-ever impeachment of a sitting President. The Solicitor General counts 57 intra-session recess appointments during those two years. App. to Brief for Petitioner 1a–9a. But the precise nature and historical understanding of many of those appointments is subject to debate.

See, e.g., Brief for Constitutional Law Scholars as Amici Curiae 23–24; Rappaport, Nonoriginalism 27–33. It seems likely that at least 36 of the 57 appointments were made with the understanding that they took place during a recess between sessions. See id., at 27–31.

As for the remainder, the historical record reveals nothing about how they were justified, if at all. There is no indication that Johnson's Attorney General or anyone else considered at the time whether those appointments were made between or during formal legislative sessions or, if the latter, how they could be squared with the constitutional text. The majority drives that point home by citing a judicial opinion that upheld one of the appointments nearly two decades later with no analysis of the question presented here. See ante, at 11 (citing Gould v. United States, 19 Ct. Cl. 593 (1884)). Johnson's intra-session appointments were disavowed by the first Attorney General to address that question, see infra, at 20, and were not followed as precedent by the Executive Branch for more than 50 years, see infra, at 22. Thus, the relevance of those appointments to our constitutional inquiry is severely limited. Cf. Brief for Political Scientists and Historians as Amici Curiae 21 (Johnson's appointments "should be viewed as anomalies" that were "sui generis in the first 130 years of the Republic").

3. 1869 to 1920

More than half a century went by before any other President made an intra-session recess appointment, and there is strong reason to think that during that period neither the Executive nor the Senate believed such a power existed. For one thing, the Senate adjourned for more than 3 days 45 times during that period, and 43 of those adjournments exceeded 10 days (and thus would not even be subject to the majority's "presumption" against the availability of recess appointments). See Congres-sional Directory 527–529. Yet there is no evidence that a single appointment was made during any of those adjournments or that any President before the 20th century even considered making such appointments.

In 1901 Philander Knox, the first Attorney General known to have opined on the question, explicitly stated that the recess-appointment power was limited to the period between formal sessions. 23 Op. Atty. Gen. 599. Knox advised President Theodore Roosevelt that he could not appoint an appraiser of merchandise during an intra-session adjournment. He explained:

"[T]he Constitution and laws make it clear that in our legislative practice an adjournment during a session of Congress means a merely temporary suspension of business from day to day . . . whereas the recess means the period after the final adjournment of Congress for the session, and before the next session begins. . . . It is this period following the final adjournment for the session which is the recess during which the President has power to fill vacancies . . . . Any intermediate temporary adjournment is not such recess, although it may be a recess in the general and ordinary use of that term." Id., at 601. 6

Knox went on to observe that none of the "many elaborate opinions" of previous Attorneys General concerning the recess-appointment power had asserted that the power could be exercised "during a temporary adjournment of the Senate," rather than "during the recess of the Senate between two sessions of Congress." Id., at 602. He acknowledged the contrary example furnished by Johnson's appointments in 1867 and 1868, but noted (with perhaps too much tact) that "[t]he public circumstances producing this state of affairs were unusual and involved results which should not be viewed as precedents." Id.,at 603.

That was where things stood when, in 1903, Roosevelt made a number of controversial recess appointments. At noon on December 7, the Senate moved seamlessly from a special session into a regular one scheduled to begin at that hour. See 37 Cong. Rec. 544; 38 Cong. Rec. 1. Roosevelt claimed to have made the appointments in a "constructive" recess between the two sessions. See Special Session Is Merged Into Regular, N. Y. Times, Dec. 8, 1903, p. 1. He and his allies in the Senate justified the appointments on the theory that "at the moment the gavel falls to summon the regular session into being there is an infinitesimal fraction of a second, which is the recess between the two sessions." Extra Session Muddle, N. Y. Times, Dec. 7, 1903, p. 3. In 1905, the Senate Judiciary Committee published a report criticizing the appointments on the ground that "the Constitution means a real recess, not a constructive one." S. Rep. No. 4389, 58th Cong., 3d Sess., p. 4. The report explained that the recess is "the period of time when the Senate is not sitting in regular or extraordinary session . . . when its members owe no duty of attendance; when its Chamber is empty; when, because of its absence, it can not receive communications from the President or participate as a body in making appointments." Id., at 2 (emphasis deleted).

The majority seeks support in this episode, claiming that the Judiciary Committee embraced a "broad and functional definition of 'recess' " consistent with the one the majority adopts. Ante, at 16. On the contrary, the episode powerfully refutes the majority's theory. Roosevelt's legal justification for his appointments was extremely aggressive, but even he recognized that "the Recess ofthe Senate" could take place only between formal sessions. If the majority's view of the Clause had been considered plausible, Roosevelt could have strengthened his position considerably by making the appointments during an intra-session break of a few days, or at least a few hours. (Just 10 minutes after the new session began on December 7, the Senate took "a recess for one hour." 38 Cong. Rec. 2.) That he instead strained to declare a dubious inter-session recess of an "infinitesimal fraction of a second" is powerful evidence that the majority's view of "the Recess" was not taken seriously even as late as the beginning of the 20th century.

Yet the majority contends that "to the extent that the Senate or a Senate committee has expressed a view, that view has favored a functional definition of 'recess' [that] encompasses intra-session recesses." Ante, at 14. It rests that contention entirely on the 1905 Judiciary Committee Report. This distorts what the committee said when it denied Roosevelt's claim that there had been a recess. If someone avers that a catfish is a cat, and I respond by pointing out that a catfish lives in water and does not have four legs, I have not endorsed the proposition that every land-dwelling quadruped is a cat. Likewise, when the Judiciary Committee explained that an instantaneous transition from one session to another is not a recess because the Senate is never absent, it did not suggest that the Senate's absence is enough to create a recess. To assume otherwise, as the majority does, is to commit the fallacy of the inverse (otherwise known as denying the antecedent): the incorrect assumption that if P implies Q, then not-P implies not-Q. Contrary to that fallacious assumption, the Judiciary Committee surely believed, consistent with the Executive's clear position at the time, that "the Recess" was limited to (actual, not constructive) breaks between sessions.

4. 1921 to the Present

It is necessary to skip over the first 13 decades of our Nation's history in order to find a Presidential legal ad-viser arguably embracing the majority's interpretation of "the Recess." In 1921 President Harding's Attorney General, Harry Daugherty, advised Harding that he could make recess appointments while the Senate stood adjourned for 28 days during the session because "the term 'recess' must be given a practical construction." 33 Op. Atty. Gen. 20, 25. Daugherty acknowledged Knox's 1901 opinion to the contrary, id., at 21, but he (committing the same fallacy as today's majority) thought the 1905 Judiciary Committee report had come to the opposite conclusion, id., at 23–24. He also recognized the fundamental flaw in this interpretation: that it would be impossible to "accurately dra[w]" a line between intra-session breaks that constitute "the Recess" and those that do not. Id., at 25. But he thought the absence of a standard gave the President "discretion to determine when there is a real and genuine recess." Ibid. While a "palpable abuse of discretion might subject his appointment to review," Daugherty thought that "[e]very presumption [should] be indulged in favor of the validity of whatever action he may take." Ibid. [7]

Only after Daugherty's opinion did the flow of intra-session recess appointments start, and for several years it was little more than a trickle. The Solicitor General has identified 22 such appointments made by Presidents Harding, Coolidge, Hoover, and Franklin Roosevelt between 1921 and 1944. App. to Brief for Petitioner 9a–12a. Intra-session recess appointments experienced a brief heyday after World War II, with President Truman making about 150 such appointments to civilian positions and several thousand to military posts from 1945 through 1950. Id., at 12a–27a. (The majority's impressive-sounding claim that "Presidents have made thousands of intra-session recess appointments," ante, at 12, depends entirely on post-war military appointments that Truman made in just two years, 1947 and 1948.) President Eisenhower made only 43 intra-session recess appointments, id., at 27a–30a, after which the practice sank back into relative obscurity. Presidents Kennedy, Lyndon Johnson, and Ford made none, while Nixon made just 7. Id., at 30a–31a. The practice rose again in the last decades of the 20th century: President Carter made 17 intra-session recess appointments, Reagan 72, George H. W. Bush 37, Clinton 53, and George W. Bush 135. Id., at 31a–61a. When the Solicitor

General filed his brief, President Obama had made 26. Id., at 62a–64a. Even excluding Truman's military appointments, roughly 90 percent of all the intra-session recess appointments in our history have been made since 1945.

Legal advisers in the Executive Branch during this period typically endorsed the President's authority to make intra-session recess appointments by citing Daugherty's opinion with little or no additional analysis. See, e.g., 20 Opinions of Office of Legal Counsel (Op. OLC) 124, 161 (1996) (finding the question to have been "settled within the executive branch" by Daugherty's "often-cited opinion"). The majority's contention that "opinions of Presidential legal advisers . . . are nearly unanimous in determining that the Clause authorizes [intra-session recess] appointments," ante, at 12, is thus true but misleading: No Presidential legal adviser approved that practice before 1921, and subsequent approvals have rested more on precedent than on independent examination.

The majority is correct that during this period, the Senate "as a body" did not formally repudiate the emerging executive practice. Ante, at 14. And on one occasion, Comptroller General Lindsay Warren cited Daugherty's opinion as representing "the accepted view" on the question, 28 Comp. Gen. 30, 34 (1948), although there is no evidence he consulted any Senators or that his statement reflected their views. But the rise of intra-session recess appointments in the latter half of the 20th century drew sharp criticism from a number of Senators on both sides of the aisle. At first, their objections focused on the length of the intra-session breaks at issue. See, e.g., 130 Cong. Rec. 22774–22776 (1984) (Sen. Sarbanes) (decrying recess appointment during a 3-week intra-session adjournment as "a circumvention of the Senate confirmation power"); id., at 23235 (resolution offered by Sen. Byrd, with 39 cosponsors, urging that no recess appointments occur during intra-session breaks of fewer than 30 days).

Later, many Senators sought to end intra-session recess appointments altogether. In 1993, the Senate Legal Counsel prepared a brief to be filed on behalf of the Senate in Mackie v. Clinton, 827 F. Supp. 56 (DC 1993), vacated in part as moot, 1994 WL 163761 (CADC 1994) (percuriam), but "Republican opposition" blocked the filing. 139 Cong. Rec. 15266–15267. The brief argued that "the recess[-appointment] power is limited to Congress' annual recess between sessions," that no contrary executive practice "of any appreciable magnitude" had existed before "the past fifty years," and that the Senate had not "acquiesced in this steady expansion of presidential power." Id., at 15268, 15270. It explained that some Senators had limited their objections to shorter intra-session breaks out of a desire "to coexist with the Executive" but that "the Executive's subsequent, steady chipping away at the length of recess sufficient for making recess appointments ha[d] demonstrated the need to return to the Framers' original intent and limit the power to intersession adjournments." Id., at 15267, 15272. Senator Kennedy reiterated that position in a brief to this Court in 2004. Brief for Sen. Edward M. Kennedy as Amicus Curiae in Franklin v. United States, O. T. 2004, No. 04–5858, p. 5. Today the partisan tables are turned, and that position is urged on us by the Senate's Republican Members. See Brief for Sen. McConnell et al. as Amici Curiae 26.

* * *

What does all this amount to? In short: Intra-session recess appointments were virtually unheard of for the first 130 years of the Republic, were deemed unconstitutional by the first Attorney General to address them, were not openly defended by the Executive until 1921, were not made in significant numbers until after World War II, and have been repeatedly criticized as unconstitutional by Senators of both parties. It is astonishing for the majority to assert that this history lends "strong support," ante, at 11, to its interpretation of the Recess Appointments Clause. And the majority's contention that recent executive practice in this area merits deference because the Senate has not done more to oppose it is utterly divorced from our precedent. "The structural interests protected by the Appointments Clause are not those of any one branch of Government but of the entire Republic," Freytag, 501 U. S., at 880, and the Senate could not give away those protections even if it wanted to. See Chadha, 462 U. S., at 957–958; Clinton, 524 U. S., at 451–452 (Kennedy, J., concurring).

Moreover, the majority's insistence that the Senate gainsay an executive practice "as a body" in order to prevent the Executive from acquiring power by adverse possession, ante, at 14, will systematically favor the expansion of executive power at the expense of Congress. In any con-troversy between the political branches over a separation-of-powers question, staking out a position and defendingit over time is far easier for the Executive Branch thanfor the Legislative Branch. See generally Bradley and Morrison, Historical Gloss and the Separation of Powers, 126 Harv. L. Rev. 411, 439–447 (2012). All Presidents have a high interest in expanding the powers of their office, since the more power the President can wield, the more effectively he can implement his political agenda; whereas individual Senators may have little interest in opposing Presidential encroachment on legislative prerogatives, especially when the encroacher is a President who is the leader of their own party. (The majority would not be able to point to a lack of "formal action" by the Senate "as a body" challenging intra-session recess appointments, ante, at 15–16, had the appointing President's party in the Senate not blocked such action on multiple occasions.) And when the President wants to assert a power and establish a precedent, he faces neither the collective-action problems nor the procedural inertia inherent in the legislative process. The majority's methodology thus all but guarantees the continuing aggrandizement of the Executive Branch.

III. Pre-Recess Vacancies

The second question presented is whether vacancies that "happen during the Recess of the Senate," which the President is empowered to fill with recess appointments, are (a) vacancies that arise during the recess, or (b) all vacancies that exist during the recess, regardless of when they arose. I would hold that the recess-appointment power is limited to vacancies that arise during the recess in which they are filled, and I would hold that the appointments at issue here—which undisputedly filled pre-recess vacancies—are invalid for that reason as well as for the reason that they were made during the session. The Court's contrary conclusion is inconsistent with the Constitution's text and structure, and it further undermines the balance the Framers struck between Presidential and Senatorial power. Historical practice also fails to support the majority's conclusion on this issue.

A. Plain Meaning

As the majority concedes, "the most natural meaning of 'happens' as applied to a 'vacancy' . . . is that the vacancy 'happens' when it initially occurs." Ante, at 22. The majority adds that this meaning is most natural "to a modern ear," ibid., but it fails to show that founding-era ears heard it differently. "Happen" meant then, as it does now, "[t]o fall out; to chance; to come to pass." 1 Johnson, Dictionary of the English Language 913. Thus, a vacancy that happened during the Recess was most reasonably understood as one that arose during the recess. It was, of course, possible in certain contexts for the word "happen" to mean "happen to be" rather than "happen to occur," as in the idiom "it so happens." But that meaning is not at all natural when the subject is a vacancy, a state of affairs that comes into existence at a particular moment in time. 8

In any event, no reasonable reader would have understood the Recess Appointments Clause to use the word "happen" in the majority's "happen to be" sense, and thus to empower the President to fill all vacancies that might exist during a recess, regardless of when they arose. For one thing, the Clause's language would have been a surpassingly odd way of giving the President that power. The Clause easily could have been written to convey that meaning clearly: It could have referred to "all Vacancies that may exist during the Recess," or it could have omitted the qualifying phrase entirely and simply authorized the President to "fill up all Vacancies during the Recess." Given those readily available alternative phrasings, the reasonable reader might have wondered, why would any intelligent drafter intending the majority's reading have inserted the words "that may happen"—words that, as the majority admits, make the majority's desired reading awkward and unnatural, and that must be effectively read out of the Clause to achieve that reading?

For another thing, the majority's reading not only strains the Clause's language but distorts its constitutional role, which was meant to be subordinate. As Hamilton explained, appointment with the advice and consent of the Senate was to be "the general mode of appointing officers of the United States." The Federalist No. 67, at 455. The Senate's check on the President's appointment power was seen as vital because " 'manipulation of official appointments' had long been one of the American revolutionary generation's greatest grievances against executive power." Freytag, 501 U. S., at 883. The unilateral power conferred on the President by the Recess Appointments Clause was therefore understood to be "nothing more than a supplement" to the "general method" of advice and consent. The Federalist No. 67, at 455.

If, however, the Clause had allowed the President to fill all pre-existing vacancies during the recess by granting commissions that would last throughout the following session, it would have been impossible to regard it—as the Framers plainly did—as a mere codicil to the Constitution's principal, power-sharing scheme for filling federal offices. On the majority's reading, the President would have had no need ever to seek the Senate's advice and consent for his appointments: Whenever there was a fair prospect of the Senate's rejecting his preferred nominee, the President could have appointed that individual unilaterally during the recess, allowed the appointment to expire at the end of the next session, renewed the appointment the following day, and so on ad infinitum. (Circumvention would have been especially easy if, as the majority also concludes, the President was authorized to make such appointments during any intra-session break of more than a few days.) It is unthinkable that such an obvious means for the Executive to expand its power would have been overlooked during the ratification debates. 9

The original understanding of the Clause was consistent with what the majority concedes is the text's "most natural meaning." Ante, at 22. In 1792, Attorney General Edmund Randolph, who had been a leading member of the Constitutional Convention, provided the Executive Branch's first formal interpretation of the Clause. He advised President Washington that the Constitution did not authorize a recess appointment to fill the office of Chief Coiner of the United States Mint, which had been created by Congress on April 2, 1792, during the Senate's session. Randolph wrote: "[I]s it a vacancy which has happened during the recess of the Senate? It is now the same and no other vacancy, than that, which existed on the 2nd. of April 1792. It commenced therefore on that day or may be said to have happened on that day." Opinion on Recess Appointments (July 7, 1792), in 24 Papers of Thomas Jefferson 165–166 (J. Catanzariti ed. 1990). Randolph added that his interpretation was the most congruent with the Constitution's structure, which made the recess-appointment power "an exception to the general participation of the Senate." Ibid. (footnote omitted).

President John Adams' Attorney General, Charles Lee, was in agreement. See Letter to George Washington (July 7, 1796) (the President may "fill for a limited time an old office become vacant during [the] recess" (emphasis added)), online at http://founders.archives.gov/documents/Washington/99-01-02-00702; Letter from James McHenry to John Adams (May 7, 1799) (hereinafter 1799 McHenry Letter) (conveying Lee's advice that certain offices were " 'vacanc[ies] happening during the session, which the President cannot fill, during the recess, by the powers vested in him by the constitution' "), online at http://wardepartmentpapers.org/document.php?id=31766. 10 One of the most prominent early academic commenters on the Constitution read the Clause the same way. See 1 St. George Tucker, Blackstone's Commentaries, App. 342–343 (1803) (assuming the President could appoint during the recess only if "the office became vacant during the recess").

Early Congresses seem to have shared Randolph's and Lee's view. A statute passed by the First Congress authorized the President to appoint customs inspectors "with the advice and consent of the Senate" and provided that "if the appointment . . . shall not be made during the present session of Congress, the President . . . is hereby empowered to make such appointments during the recess of the Senate, by granting commissions which shall expire at the end of their next session." Act of Mar. 3, 1791, §4,

1Stat. 200. That authorization would have been superfluous if the Recess Appointments Clause had been understood to apply to pre-existing vacancies. We have recognized that an action taken by the First Congress "provides 'contemporaneous and weighty evidence' of the Constitution's meaning." Bowsher, 478 U. S., at 723–724. And other statutes passed in the early years of the Republic contained similar authorizations. See App. to Brief for Respondent Noel Canning 1a–17a. 11

Also illuminating is the way the Third Congress interpreted the Constitution's Senate Vacancies Clause, which uses language similar to that of the Recess Appointments Clause. Before the passage of the Seventeenth Amendment, the Constitution provided that "if Vacancies [in the Senate] happen by Resignation, or otherwise, during the Recess of the Legislature of any State, the Executive thereof may make temporary Appointments until the next Meeting of the Legislature." Art. I, §3, cl. 2. Senator George Read of Delaware resigned in December 1793; the state legislature met in January and February 1794; and the Governor appointed Kensey Johns to fill the seat in March 1794. The Senate refused to seat Johns, resolving that he was "not entitled to a seat in the Senate of the United States; a session of the Legislature of the said State having intervened, between the resignation . . . and the appointment." 4 Annals of Cong. 77–78 (1794). It is thus clear that the phrase "happen . . . during the Recess" in the Senate Vacancies Clause was understood to refer to vacancies that arose, not merely existed, during the recess in which the appointment was made. It is not apparent why the nearly identical language of the Recess Appointments Clause would have been understood differently.

The majority, however, relies heavily on a contrary account of the Clause given by Attorney General William Wirt in 1823. See 1 Op. Atty. Gen 631. Wirt notably began—as does the majority—by acknowledging that his predecessors' reading was "most accordant with the letter of the constitution." Id., at 632. But he thought the "most natural" reading had to be rejected because it would interfere with the "substantial purpose of the constitution," namely, "keep[ing] . . . offices filled." Id., at 631–632. He was chiefly concerned that giving the Clause its plain meaning would produce "embarrassing inconveniences" if a distant office were to become vacant during the Senate's session, but news of the vacancy were not to reach the President until the recess. Id., at 632, 634. The majority fully embraces Wirt's reasoning. Ante, at 22–25.

Wirt's argument is doubly flawed. To begin, the Constitution provides ample means, short of rewriting its text, for dealing with the hypothetical dilemma Wirt posed. Congress can authorize "acting" officers to perform the duties associated with a temporarily vacant office—and has done that, in one form or another, since 1792. See 5 U. S. C. §3345; Act of May 8, 1792, ch. 37, §8, 1Stat. 281; 705 F. 3d, at 511; Rappaport, Original Meaning 1514–1517. And on "extraordinary Occasions" the President can call the Senate back into session to consider a nomination. Art. II, §3. If the Framers had thought those options insufficient and preferred to authorize the President to make recess appointments to fill vacancies arising late in the session, they would have known how to do so. Massachusetts, for example, had authorized its Governor to make certain recess appointments "in case a vacancy shall happen . . . in the recess of the General Court [i.e., the state legislature], or at so late a period in any session of the same Court, that the vacancy . . . shall not be supplied in the same session thereof." 1783 Mass. Acts ch. 12, in Acts and Laws of the Commonwealth of Massachusetts 523 (1890) (emphasis added).

The majority protests that acting appointments, unlike recess appointments, are an "inadequate" solution to Wirt's hypothetical dilemma because acting officers "may have less authority than Presidential appointments." Ante, at 24–25. It cites an OLC opinion which states that "an acting officer . . . is frequently considered merely a caretaker without a mandate to take far-reaching measures." 6 Op. OLC 119, 121 (1982). But just a few lines later, the majority says that "the lack of Senate approval . . . may diminish the recess appointee's ability, as a practical matter, to get a controversial job done." Ante, at 25. The majority does not explain why an acting officer would have less authority "as a practical matter" than a recess appointee. The majority also objects that requiring the President to rely on acting officers would "lessen the President's ability to staff the Executive Branch with people of his own choosing," ante, at 24—a surprising charge, since that is the very purpose of the Constitution's advice-and-consent requirement. As for special sessions, the majority thinks it a sufficient answer to say that they are "burdensome," ibid., an observation that fails to distinguish them from many procedures required by our structural Constitution.

More fundamentally, Wirt and the majority are mistaken to say that the Constitution's " 'substantial purpose' " isto " 'keep . . . offices filled.' " Ibid. (quoting 1 Op. Atty. Gen., at 632). The Constitution is not a road map for maximally efficient government, but a system of "carefully crafted restraints" designed to "protect the people from the improvident exercise of power." Chadha, 462 U. S., at 957, 959. Wirt's and the majority's argumentum ab inconvenienti thus proves far too much. There are many circumstances other than a vacancy that can produce similar inconveniences if they arise late in the session: For example, a natural disaster might occur to which the Executive cannot respond effectively without a supplemental appropriation. But in those circumstances, the Constitution would not permit the President to appropriate funds himself. See Art. I, §9, cl. 7. Congress must either anticipate such eventualities or be prepared to be haled back into session. The troublesome need to do so is not a bug to be fixed by this Court, but a calculated feature of the constitutional framework. As we have recognized, while the Constitution's government-structuring provisions can seem "clumsy" and "inefficient," they reflect "hard choices . . . consciously made by men who had lived under a form of government that permitted arbitrary governmental acts to go unchecked." Chadha, supra, at 959.

B. Historical Practice

For the reasons just given, it is clear that the Constitution authorizes the President to fill unilaterally only those vacancies that arise during a recess, not every vacancy that happens to exist during a recess. Again, however, the majority says "[h]istorical practice" requires the broader interpretation. Ante, at 26. And again the majority is mistaken. Even if the Constitution were wrongly thought to be ambiguous on this point, a fair recounting of the relevant history does not support the majority's interpretation.

1. 1789 to 1822

The majority correctly admits that there is "no undisputed record of Presidents George Washington, John Adams, or Thomas Jefferson" using a recess appointment to fill a pre-recess vacancy. Ibid. That is not surprising in light of Randolph's early conclusion that doing so would be unconstitutional. Adams on one occasion contemplated filling pre-recess vacancies but was dissuaded by, among others, Attorney General Lee, who said the Constitution did not permit him to do so. See 1799 McHenry Letter. 12 And the Solicitor General does not allege that even a single appointment made by Adams filled a pre-recess vacancy. Jefferson, too, at one point thought the Clause "susceptible of" the majority's reading, 1802 Jefferson Letter, but his administration, like Adams', appears never to have adopted that reading.

James Madison's administration seems to have rejected the majority's reading as well. In 1814, Madison wanted to appoint Andrew Jackson to a vacant major-generalship in the Army during the Senate's recess, but he accepted, without contradiction or reservation, his Secretary of War's advice that he lacked the power to do so because the post's previous occupant had resigned before the recess. He therefore ordered that Jackson be given a "brevet of Major General," i.e., a warrant conferring the nominal rank without the salary thereof. Letter from John Armstrong to Madison (May 14, 1814); Letter from Madison to Armstrong (May 17, 1814). In conveying the brevet, Madison's Secretary of War explained to Jackson that " '[t]he vacancy produced by General Hampton's resignation, not having been filled during the late session of the Senate, cannot be supplied constitutionally, during the recess.' " Letter from Armstrong to Jackson (May 22, 1814). A week later, when Madison learned that a different major general had resigned during the recess, he thought that development would enable him to appoint Jackson "at once." Letter from Madison to Armstrong (May 24, 1814); see Letter from Armstrong to Madison (May 20, 1814) (reporting the resignation). 13

The majority discounts that evidence of an occasion when Madison and his advisers actually considered the precise constitutional question presented here. It does so apparently because Madison, in acting on the advice he was given without questioning the interpretation of the recess-appointment power that was offered as the reason for that advice, did not explicitly say "I agree." The majority prefers to focus on five appointments by Madison, unremarked by anyone at the time, that "the evidence suggests" filled pre-recess vacancies. Ante, at 27. Even if the majority is correct about those appointments, there is no indication that any thought was given to their constitutionality, either within or outside the Executive Branch. A handful of appointments that appear to contravene the written opinions of Attorneys General Randolph and Lee and the written evidence of Madison's own beliefs about what the Constitution authorized, and that lack any contemporaneous explanation, are not convincing evidence of the Constitution's original meaning. 14

If Madison or his predecessors made any appointments in reliance on the broader reading, those appointments must have escaped general notice. In 1822, the Senate Committee on Military Affairs declared that the President had "no power to make [appointments] in the recess" where "the vacancies did not happen in the recess." 38 Annals of Cong. 500. The Committee believed its construction had been "heretofore observed" and that "no instance ha[d] before occurred . . . where the President ha[d] felt himself authorized to fill such vacancies, without special authority by law." Ibid.; see also T. Sergeant, Constitutional Law 373 (2d ed. 1830) ("[I]t seemed distinctly understood to be the sense of the senate, that [it] is only in offices that become vacant during the recess, that the president is authorised to exercise the right of appointing").

2. 1823 to 1862

The Executive Branch did not openly depart from Randolph and Lee's interpretation until 1823, when Wirt issued the opinion discussed earlier. Even within that branch, Wirt's view was hotly contested: William Crawford, Monroe's Treasury Secretary, argued "with great pertinacity" that the Clause authorized the President to fill only "vacancies which happen during the recess" and not those "which happen while Congress are in session." 5 Memoirs of John Quincy Adams 486–487 (C. Adams ed. 1875). Wirt's analysis nonetheless gained ground in the Executive Branch over the next four decades; but it did so slowly and fitfully.

In 1830, Attorney General Berrien disagreed with Wirt when he wrote that "[i]f the vacancy exist during the session of the Senate, . . . the President cannot appoint during the recess." 2 Op. Atty. Gen. 333, 334. Two years later, Attorney General Taney endorsed Wirt's view al-though doing so was, as he acknowledged, unnecessary to resolve the issue before him: whether the President could, during the recess, fill a vacancy resulting from the expiration of a prior recess appointment at the end of the Senate's session. 2 Op. Atty Gen. 525, 528 (1832). Addressing the same issue in 1841, Attorney General Legaré appeared to believe the dispositive question was whether the office could be said to have "becom[e] vacant" during the recess. 3 Op. Atty. Gen. 673, 674. And in 1845, Attorney General Mason thought it "well established" that "[i]f vacancies are known to exist during the session of the Senate, and nominations are not then made, they cannot be filled by executive appointments in the recess." 4 Op. Atty. Gen. 361, 363. 15

The tide seemed to turn—as far as the Executive Branch was concerned—in the mid-19th century: Attorney General Cushing in 1855 and Attorney General Bates in 1862 both treated Wirt's position as settled without subjecting it to additional analysis. 7 Op. Atty. Gen. 186, 223; 10 Op. Atty. Gen. 356. Bates, however, entertained "serious doubts" about its validity. Ibid. And as one 19th-century court shrewdly observed in rejecting Wirt's interpretation, the frequency with which Attorneys General during this period were called upon to opine on the question likely "indicate[s] that no settled administrative usage had been . . . established." In re District Attorney of United States, 7 F. Cas. 731,

738 (No. 3,924) (DC Pa. 1868). The Solicitor General identifies only 10 recess appointments made between 1823 and 1863 that filled pre-recess vacancies—about one every four years. App. to Brief for Petitioner 68a–71a. That is hardly an impressive number, and most of the appointments were to minor offices (like Deputy Postmaster for Janesville, Wisconsin, id., at 70a) unlikely to have gotten the Senate's attention. But the Senate did notice when, in 1862, President Lincoln recess-appointed David Davis to fill a seat on this Court that had become vacant before the recess, id., at 71a—and it reacted with vigor.

3. 1863 to 1939

Two months after Lincoln's recess appointment of Davis, the Senate directed the Judiciary Committee "to inquire whether the practice . . . of appointing officers to fill vacancies which have not occurred during the recess of Congress, but which existed at the preceding session of Congress, is in accordance with the Constitution; and if not, what remedy shall be applied." Cong. Globe, 37th Cong., 3d Sess., 100 (1862). The committee responded with a report denouncing Wirt's interpretation of the Clause as "artificial," "forced and unnatural," "unfounded," and a "perversion of language." S. Rep. No. 80, 37th Cong., 3d Sess., pp. 4–6 (1863). Because the majority all but ignores this evidence of the Senate's views, it is worth quoting the report at some length:

"When must the vacancy . . . accrue or spring into existence? May it begin during the session of the Senate, or must it have its beginning during the recess? We think the language too clear to admit of reasonable doubt, and that, upon principles of just construction, this period must have its inceptive point after one session has closed and before another session has begun. . . .

. . . . .

"We . . . dissent from the construction implied by the substituted reading, 'happened to exist,' for the word 'happen' in the clause. . . . [I]f a vacancy once exists, it has in law happened; for it is in itself an instantaneous event. It implies no continuance of the act that produces it, but takes effect, and is complete and perfect at an indivisible point of time, like the beginning or end of a recess. Once in existence, it has happened, and the mere continuance of the condition of things which the occurrence produces, cannot, without confounding the most obvious distinctions, be taken or treated as the occurrence itself, as Mr. Wirt seems to have done. . . .

"Again, we see no propriety in forcing the language from its popular meaning in order to meet and fulfill one confessedly great purpose, (the keeping the office filled,) while there is plainly another purpose of equal magnitude and importance (fitting qualifications)attached to and inseparable from the former." Id.,at 3–6.

The Committee acknowledged that the broad reading "ha[d] been, from time to time, sanctioned by Attorneys General . . . and that the Executive ha[d], from time to time, practiced upon it," but it said the Executive's practice was entitled to no weight because the Constitution's text was "too plain to admit of a doubt or to need interpretation." Id., at 7.

On the same day the Committee published its scathing report, its chairman, Senator Trumbull, proposed a law barring the payment of any officer appointed during the recess to fill a pre-recess vacancy. Cong. Globe, 37th Cong., 3d Sess., 564. Senator Fessenden spoke in support of the proposal:

"It ought to be understood distinctly, that when an officer does not come within the rules of law, and is appointed in that way in defiance of the wishes of the Senate, he shall not be paid. It may not be in our power to prevent the appointment, but it is in our power to prevent the payment; and when payment is prevented, I think that will probably put an end to the habit of making such appointments." Id., at 565.

The amendment was adopted by the Senate, ibid., and after passing the House became the Pay Act, which provided that "no money shall be paid . . . out of the Treasury, as salary, to any person appointed during the recess of the Senate, to fill a vacancy . . . which . . . existed while the Senate was in session." Act of Feb. 9, 1863, §2, 12Stat. 646 (codified at Rev. Stat. §1761; subsequently codified as amended at 5 U. S. C. §56 (1925–1926 ed.)).

The Pay Act would remain in force without significant modification for nearly eight decades. The Executive Branch, however, refused to acknowledge that the Act embodied the Senate's rejection of the broad reading of "happen." Several Attorneys General continued to treat Wirt's interpretation as settled without so much as mentioning the Act. See 12 Op. Atty. Gen. 32 (1866); 12 Op. Atty. Gen. 449 (1868); 14 Op. Atty. Gen. 562 (1875); 15 Op. Atty. Gen. 207 (1877). And when, 17 years after its passage, Attorney General Devens deigned to acknowledge the Act, he preposterously described it as "conced[ing]" the President's power to make the appointments for which the Act barred payment. 16 Op. Atty. Gen. 522, 531 (1880).

The majority is not that bold. Instead, it relegates the 1863 Judiciary Committee report to a pair of anodyne sentences in which it says only that the committee "dis-agreed with" Wirt's interpretation. Ante, at 30. (With like understatement, one could say that Shakespeare's Mark Antony "disagreed with" Caesar's detractors.) Even more remarkably, the majority goes on to claim that the Senate's passage of the Pay Act on the same day the committee issued its report was not a strong enough statement to impede the constitutionalization-by-adverse-possession of the power asserted by the Executive. Why not? Because, the majority says, some Senators may have disagreed with the report, and because the Senate did not go so far as to make acceptance of a recess appointment that filled a pre-recess vacancy "a federal crime." Ante, at 30–31. That reasoning starkly illustrates the excessive burden the majority places on the Legislative Branch in contests with the Executive over the separation of powers. See supra,at 26.

Despite its minimization by subsequent Attorneys General and by today's majority, there is no reason to doubt that the Pay Act had a deterrent effect. The Solicitor General has identified just 40 recess appointments that filled pre-recess vacancies during the nearly eight decades between the Act's passage in 1863 and its amendment in 1940. App. to Brief for Petitioner 71a–79a. 16

4. 1940 to the Present

The majority finds it highly significant that in 1940, Congress created a few carefully limited exceptions to the Pay Act's prohibition on paying recess appointees who filled pre-recess vacancies. See Act of July 11, 1940, ch. 580, 54Stat. 751, now codified with nonsubstantive amendments at 5 U. S. C. §5503. Under the current version of the Act, "[p]ayment for services may not be made from the Treasury of the United States to an individual appointed during a recess of the Senate to fill a vacancy" that "existed while the Senate was in session" unless either the vacancy arose, or a different individual's nomination to fill the vacancy was rejected, "within 30 days before the end of the session"; or a nomination was pending before the Senate at the end of the session, and the individual nominated was not himself a recess appointee. §5503(a)(1)–(3). And if the President fills a pre-recess vacancy under one of the circumstances specified in the Act, the law requires that he submit a nomination for that office to the Senate "not later than 40 days after the beginning of the next session." §5503(b).

The majority says that by allowing salaries to be paid to recess appointees in these narrow circumstances, "the 1940 Senate (and later Senates) in effect supported" the majority's interpretation of the Clause. Ante, at 32. Nonsense. Even as amended, the Act strictly regulates payment to recess appointees who fill pre-recess vacancies, and it still forbids payment to many officers whose appointments are constitutional under the majority's interpretation. As amici Senators observe, the 1940 amendments "reflect at most a desire not to punish public servants caught in the crossfire" of interbranch conflict. Brief for Sen. McConnell et al. as Amici Curiae 30. Surely that inference is more reasonable than the majority's supposition that Congress, by permitting some of the appointees covered by the Act to be paid, meant to signal that it now believed all of the covered appointments were valid.

Moreover, given the majority's interpretation of the Recess Appointments Clause, it is fairly debatable whether the current version of the Pay Act is constitutional (and a fortiori, whether the pre-1940 version was constitutional). Even as amended, the Act seeks to limit and channelthe President's exercise of the recess-appointment power by prohibiting payment to officers whose appointmentsare (per the majority) within the President's sole constitutional authority if those appointments do not comply with conditions imposed by Congress, and by requiring the President to submit a nominee to the Senate in the first 40 days of the ensuing session. There is a colorable argument—which is routinely made by lawyers in the Executive Branch—that Congress " 'cannot use the appropriations power to control a Presidential power that is beyond its direct control.' " 33 Op. OLC ___, ___ (2009), online at http://www.justice.gov/olc/opiniondocs/section7054.pdf (quoting 20 Op. OLC 253, 267 (1996)). Consistent with that view, the Office of Legal Counsel has maintained that Congress could not "condition . . . the funding of an officer's salary on being allowed to appoint the officer." 13 Op. OLC 258, 261 (1989).

If that is correct, then the Pay Act's attempt to control the President's exercise of the recess-appointment power at least raises a substantial constitutional question under the majority's reading of the Recess Appointments Clause. See Rappaport, Original Meaning 1544–1546. The Executive has not challenged the Act's constitutionality in this case, and I express no opinion on whether such a challenge would succeed. I simply point out that it is impossible to regard the amended Pay Act as evidence of Senatorial acquiescence in the majority's reading when that reading has the potential to invalidate the Act.

Since the Pay Act was amended, individual Senators have continued to maintain that recess appointments may not constitutionally be used to fill pre-recess vacancies. See, e.g., 130 Cong. Rec. 22780 (statement of seven Senators that a recess appointment to the Federal Reserve Board in 1984 was unconstitutional because the vacancy "did not happen during the recess"); Brief for Sen. McConnell et al. as Amici Curiae 26 (45 Senators taking that view of the Clause). And there is no evidence that the watering-down of the Pay Act produced an immediate flood of recess appointments filling pre-recess vacancies. The Solicitor General has pointed us to only 40 such appointments between 1940 and the present. App. to Brief for Petitioner 79a–89a.

The majority, however, finds it significant that in two small "random sample[s]" of contemporary recess appointments—24 since 1981 and 21 since 2000—the bulk of the appointments appear to have filled pre-existing vacancies. Ante, at 29. Based on that evidence, the majority thinks it "a fair inference that a large proportion of the recess appointments in the history of the Nation have filled pre-existing vacancies." Ibid. The extrapolation of that sweeping conclusion from a small set of recent data does not bear even the slightest scrutiny. The majority ignores two salient facts: First, from the founding until the mid-19th century, the President's authority to make such appointments was far from settled even within the Executive Branch. Second, from 1863 until 1940, it was illegal to pay any recess appointee who filled a pre-recess vacancy, which surely discouraged Presidents from making, and nominees from accepting, such appointments. Consequently, there is no reason to assume that the majority's sampling—even if it accurately reflects practices during the last three decades—is at all typical of practices that prevailed throughout "the history of the Nation." 17

* * *

In sum: Washington's and Adams' Attorneys General read the Constitution to restrict recess appointments to vacancies arising during the recess, and there is no evidence that any of the first four Presidents consciously departed from that reading. The contrary reading was first defended by an executive official in 1823, was vehemently rejected by the Senate in 1863, was vigorously resisted by legislation in place from 1863 until 1940, and is arguably inconsistent with legislation in place from 1940 to the present. The Solicitor General has identified only about 100 appointments that have ever been made under the broader reading, and while it seems likely that a good deal more have been made in the last few decades, there is good reason to doubt that many were made before 1940 (since the appointees could not have been compensated). I can conceive of no sane constitutional theory under which this evidence of "historical practice"—which is actually evidence of a long-simmering inter-branch conflict—would require us to defer to the views of the Executive Branch.

IV. Conclusion

What the majority needs to sustain its judgment is an ambiguous text and a clear historical practice. What it has is a clear text and an at-best-ambiguous historical practice. Even if the Executive could accumulate power through adverse possession by engaging in a consistent and unchallenged practice over a long period of time, the oft-disputed practices at issue here would not meet that standard. Nor have those practices created any justifiable expectations that could be disappointed by enforcing the Constitution's original meaning. There is thus no ground for the majority's deference to the unconstitutional recess-appointment practices of the Executive Branch.

The majority replaces the Constitution's text with a new set of judge-made rules to govern recess appointments. Henceforth, the Senate can avoid triggering the President's now-vast recess-appointment power by the odd contrivance of never adjourning for more than three days without holding a pro forma session at which it is understood that no business will be conducted. Ante, at 33–34. How this new regime will work in practice remains to be seen. Perhaps it will reduce the prevalence of recess appointments. But perhaps not: Members of the President's party in Congress may be able to prevent the Senate from holding pro forma sessions with the necessary frequency, and if the House and Senate disagree, the President may be able to adjourn both "to such Time as he shall think proper." U. S. Const., Art. II, §3. In any event, the limitation upon the President's appointment power is there not for the benefit of the Senate, but for the protection of the people; it should not be dependent on Senate action for its existence.

The real tragedy of today's decision is not simply the abolition of the Constitution's limits on the recess-appointment power and the substitution of a novel framework invented by this Court. It is the damage done to our separation-of-powers jurisprudence more generally. It is not every day that we encounter a proper case or controversy requiring interpretation of the Constitution's structural provisions. Most of the time, the interpretation of those provisions is left to the political branches—which, in deciding how much respect to afford the constitutional text, often take their cues from this Court. We should therefore take every opportunity to affirm the primacy of the Constitution's enduring principles over the politics of the moment. Our failure to do so today will resonate well beyond the particular dispute at hand. Sad, but true: The Court's embrace of the adverse-possession theory of executive power (a characterization the majority resists but does not refute) will be cited in diverse contexts, including those presently unimagined, and will have the effect of aggrandizing the Presidency beyond its constitutional bounds and undermining respect for the separation of powers.

I concur in the judgment only.

Notes to Justice Scalia's concurrence in National Labor Relations Board v. Noel Canning (June 26, 2014)

  1 The other cases cited by the majority in which we have afforded significant weight to historical practice, ante, at 8, are consistent with the principles described above. Nearly all involved venerable and unchallenged practices, and constitutional provisions that were either deeply ambiguous or plainly supportive of the practice. See Dames & Moore v. Regan, 453 U. S. 654–681, and n. 8, 686 (1981) (citing Presidential practice dating from 1799 and never questioned by Congress to inform meaning of "Executive Power"); Ex parte Grossman, 267 U. S. 87–119 (1925) (citing unchallenged Presidential practice dating from 1841 as support for a construction of the pardon power based on the "common law," the "history of the clause in the Convention," and "the ordinary meaning of its words"); United States v. Midwest Oil Co., 236 U. S. 459–471, 474 (1915) (citing Presidential practice dating from "an early period in the history of the government," "uniformly and repeatedly acquiesced in" by Congress and previously upheld by this Court, to establish "a recognized administrative power of the Executive in the management of the public lands"); McPherson v. Blacker, 146 U. S. 1–35 (1892) (citing method of choosing Presidential electors prevalent among the States "from the formation of the government until now," as to the constitutionality of which " 'no question ha[d] ever arisen,' " in support of construction consistent with the constitutional text and its drafting history); McCulloch v. Maryland, 4 Wheat. 316, 401–402 (1819) (citing power "exercised by the first Congress elected under the present constitution," "recognized by many successive legislatures, and . . . acted upon by the judicial department," in support of the conclusion that the Necessary and Proper Clause allowed Congress to incorporate a bank); Stuart v. Laird, 1 Cranch 299, 309 (1803) (citing practice that "commence[d] with the organization of the judicial system" in rejecting challenge to Supreme Court Justices' riding circuit). Even Mistretta v. United States, 488 U. S. 361 (1989), which concluded that the constitutional text did not prohibit judges from undertaking extrajudicial duties and found "additional evidence" for that conclusion in a longstanding practice that it acknowledged had been "controversial," emphasized that it was relying on "contemporaneous practice by the Founders themselves" that had been "frequent and continuing" since ratification. Id., at 397–400.

  2 The majority claims that "the phrase 'the recess' was used to refer to intra-session recesses at the time of the founding," ante, at 10, but it offers strikingly little support for that assertion. It first cites a letter from George Washington that is quite obviously an example of imprecise, colloquial usage. See 3 Records of the Federal Convention of 1787, p. 76 (M. Farrand rev. 1966) ("I had put my carriage in the hands of a workman to be repaired and had not the means of mooving [sic] during the recess"). It next cites an example from the New Jersey Legislature that simply reflects that body's practice of dividing its time not only into "sessions" but also into distinct, formal "sittings" within each session, with "the recess" denoting the period between sittings. See

Brief for Respondent Noel Canning 23; see also Natelson 207. Finally, the majority cites three pages from the Solicitor General's brief without acknowledging the arguments offered in response to the Solicitor General's few supposed counterexamples. See, e.g., Brief for Respondent Noel Canning 21–24; Natelson 222, n. 120.

3 The majority insists that "the most likely reason the Framers did not place a textual floor underneath the word 'recess' is that they did not foresee the need for one" because they did not anticipate that intra-session breaks "would become lengthier and more significant than inter-session ones." Ante, at 19. The majority's logic escapes me. The Framers' supposed failure to anticipate "length[y]" intra-session breaks might explain why (as I maintain) they did not bother to authorize recess appointments during intra-session breaks at all; but it cannot explain why (as the majority holds) they would have enacted a text that authorizes appointments during all intra-session breaks—even the short ones the majority says they did anticipate—without placing a temporal limitation on that power.

4 The majority erroneously suggests that the "lack of a textual floor raises a problem that plagues" both interpretations of "the Recess." Ante, at 19. Not so. If the Clause is given its plain meaning, the President cannot make recess appointments during the session but can make recess appointments during any break between sessions, no matter how short. Contra the majority, that is not a "problem." True, the recess-appointment power applies even during very short inter-session breaks. But inter-session breaks typically occur at most a few times a year, and the recess-appointment power is of limited utility during very short inter-session breaks since, as explained below, the President can fill only those vacancies that arise during the break. See Part III, infra. Of course, as the Senate Judiciary Committee has argued, the break must be actual and not "constructive"; the Senate must adjourn for some measurable period of time between the two sessions. See infra, at 20–22. But the requirement that there actually be a recess does not involve anywhere near the level of indeterminacy entailed by the majority's requirement that the recess be long enough (or the circumstances unusual enough), as determined by a court, to trigger the recess-appointment power.

5 The majority does not contend otherwise. The Solicitor General claims that President Lincoln appointed a handful of brigadier generals during intra-session breaks in 1862 and 1863, but he does not include those appointments in his list of known intra-session recess appointments. Compare Brief for Petitioner 22 with App. to Brief for Petitioner 1a. Noel Canning convincingly argues that the generals were not given recess appointments but only unofficial "acting appointments" for which they received no commissions. Brief for Respondent Noel Canning 25; see Rappaport, Why Nonoriginalism Does Not Justify Departing from the Original Meaning of the Recess Appointments Clause (manuscript, at 27, n. 79) (hereinafter Rappaport, Nonoriginalism), online at http://papers.ssrn.com/sol3/papers.cfm?abstract_id=2374563 (all Internet materials as visited June 24, 2014, and available in the Clerk of Court's case file).

6 The majority dismisses Knox's opinion as overly formalistic because it "relied heavily upon the use of the word 'the' " in the phrase "the Recess." Ante, at 13. It did not. As the passage quoted above makes clear, Knox was relying on the common understanding of what "the Recess" meant in the context of marking out legislative time.

7 I say Daugherty "arguably" embraced the majority's view because he may have been endorsing, not the majority's position, but the intermediate view that reads both "the Recess" and "the next Session" in functional terms, so that intra-session appointments would last only until the next intra-session break. See supra, at 10; Rappaport, Nonoriginalism 34–35.

8 Despite initially admitting that the text "does not naturally favor" its interpretation, the majority halfheartedly suggests that the " 'happen to be' " reading may be admissible when the subject, like "vacancy," denotes a "continuing state." Ante, at 22–23. That suggestion distorts ordinary English usage. It is indeed natural to say that an ongoing activity or event, like a war, a parade, or a financial crisis, is "happening" for as long as it continues. But the same is not true when the subject is a settled state of affairs, like death, marriage, or vacancy, all of which "happen" when they come into being.

9 The majority insists that "character and politics" will ordinarily prevent the President from circumventing the Senate, and that the Senate has "political resources" to respond to attempts at circumvention. Ante, at 25. Neither character nor politics prevented Theodore Roosevelt from proclaiming a fictitious recess lasting an "infinitesimal fraction of a second." In any event, the Constitution does not entrust the Senate's role in the appointments process to the vagaries of character and politics. See, e.g., Freytag v. Commissioner, 501 U. S. 868–880 (1991).

10 The majority does not deny that Lee took those positions, but it claims he also "later informed [Thomas] Jefferson that, in the Adams administration, 'whenever an office became vacant, so short a time before Congress rose, as not to give an opportunity of enquiring for a proper character, they let it lie always till recess.' " Ante, at 27 (quoting Letter from Jefferson to Wilson Cary Nicholas (Jan. 26, 1802), in 36 Papers of Thomas Jefferson 433 (B. Oberg ed. 2009) (hereinafter 1802 Jefferson Letter)). Assuming Lee in fact made the statement attributed to him by Jefferson, and further assuming that Lee endorsed the constitutionality of the practice described in that statement (which Jefferson does not say), that practice could only have been regarded as a pragmatic exception to the general view of the Clause that Lee, like Randolph, espoused. And the practice must not have been extensive, since the Solicitor General has been unable to identify even a single appointment made by Adams that filled a pre-recess vacancy. See infra, at 36.

11 The majority suggests that these statutes may have reflected, not a belief that the recess-appointment power was limited to vacancies arising during the recess, but a "separate" belief that the power could not be used for "new offices" created by Congress and not previously filled. Ante, at 30. But the latter view (which the majority does not endorse) was inseparably linked with the former (which the majority rejects), as is made

clear by the very source the majority cites. See Letter from Alexander Hamilton to James McHenry (May 3, 1799), in 23 Papers of Alexander Hamilton 94 (H. Syrett ed. 1976) ("[T]he power to fill the vacancy is not the power to make an original appointment. The phrase 'Which may have happened' serves to confirm this construction. . . . [I]ndependent of the authority of a special law, the President cannot fill a vacancy which happens during a session of the Senate"); see also 2 Op. Atty. Gen., at 334 ("If the vacancy exist during the session of the Senate, as in the first creation of an office by law, it has been held that the President cannot appoint during the recess, unless he is specially authorized so to do by law"); W. Rawle, A View of the Constitution of the United States of America 163 (2d ed. 1829) (reprint 2009) ("It has been held by [the Senate], that if new offices are created by congress, the president cannot, after the adjournment of the senate, make appointments to fill them. The vacancies do not happen during the recess of the senate").

12 See also Letter from Adams to James McHenry (April 16, 1799), in 8 Works of John Adams 632 (C. Adams ed. 1853) (proposing the appointments); Letter from Adams to McHenry (May 16, 1799), in id., at 647 (agreeing to "suspend [the appointments] for the present, perhaps till the meeting of the Senate"). Before advising Adams, McHenry also consulted Alexander Hamilton, who agreed that the appointments would be unlawful. See Letter from McHenry to Hamilton (Apr. 26, 1799), in 23 Papers of Alexander Hamilton, at 69, 70 ("It would seem that, under this Constitutional power, the President cannot alone . . . fill up vacancies that may happen during a session of the senate"); Letter from Hamilton to McHenry (May 3, 1799), in id., at 94 ("It is clear, that independent of the authority of a special law, the President cannot fill a vacancy which happens during a session of the Senate").

13 All the letters cited in this paragraph are available onlinecourtesy of the Library of Congress. See James Madison Papers, http://memory.loc.gov/ammem/collections/madison_papers.

14 The same can be said of the Solicitor General's claim to have found two recess appointments by Washington and four by Jefferson that filled pre-existing vacancies. Noel Canning disputes that claim, pointing out that Washington told the Senate the offices in question had " 'fallen vacant during the recess' " and arguing that Jefferson may have removed the incumbent officers during the recess. Brief for Respondent Noel Canning 44. Suffice it to say that if either Washington or Jefferson had adopted the broader reading, against the written advice of Attorneys General Randolph and Lee, one would expect a good deal more evidence of that fact.

15 A year later Mason, like Taney and Legaré before him, concluded that when a recess appointment expired at the end of the Senate's session, the President could fill the resulting vacancy during the ensuing recess. In reaching that conclusion, Mason reiterated that the recess-appointment power "depends on the happening of vacancies when the Senate is not in session" and said the vacancy at issue was "within the meaning

of" the Clause because the happening of the vacancy and the termination of the session had "occurred eo instanti." 4 Op. Atty. Gen. 523, 526–527 (1846).

16 In the early 20th century, some Senators acceded to the majority's reading of the Clause, as the majority is eager to point out, ante, at 31. In 1904, Senator Tillman allowed that "the Senate ha[d] acquiesced" in the President's use of the recess-appointment power to fill pre-existing vacancies, 38 Cong. Rec. 1606, though he also quoted at length from the 1863 Judiciary Committee report and said he did "not see how anybody can find any argument to controvert the position [the report] takes," id., at 1608. And in 1916, Senators Robinson and Sutherland accepted the majority's reading without analysis. 53 Cong. Rec. 4298. The reader can decide whether those statements by three Senators justify the assertion that the Senate "abandoned its hostility" to the broad reading, ante, at 31.

17 The majority also notes that many of the intra-session recess appointments identified by the Solicitor General were made "within two weeks of the beginning of the recess," which, according to the majority, "strongly suggests that many of the vacancies initially arose prior to the recess." Ante, at 29. The inference is unwarranted, since there are many circumstances other than random chance that could cause a vacancy to arise early in the recess: For example, the prior officeholder may have been another recess appointee whose commission expired at the end of the Senate's session, or he may have waited until the recess to resign so that his successor could be compensated without violating the Pay Act. In any event, the overwhelming majority of the intra-session recess appointments on the Solicitor General's list occurred after 1945 and do not shed light on earlier practices.

Redistricting: Justice Scalia's dissent in Alabama Legislative Black Caucus v. Alabama (March 25, 2015)

Justice Scalia, with whom The Chief Justice, Justice Thomas, and Justice Alito join, dissenting.

Today, the Court issues a sweeping holding that will have profound implications for the constitutional ideal of one person, one vote, for the future of the Voting Rights Act of 1965, and for the primacy of the State in managing its own elections. If the Court's destination seems fantastical, just wait until you see the journey.

Two groups of plaintiffs, the Alabama Democratic Conference and the Alabama Legislative Black Caucus, brought separate challenges to the way in which Alabama drew its state legislative districts following the 2010 census. These cases were consolidated before a three-judge District Court. Even after a full trial, the District Court lamented that "[t]he filings and arguments made by the plaintiffs on these claims were mystifying at best." 989 F. Supp. 2d 1227, 1287 (MD Ala. 2013). Nevertheless, the District Court understood both groups of plaintiffs to argue, as relevant here, only that "the Acts as a whole constitute racial gerrymanders." Id., at 1287. It also understood the Democratic Conference to argue that "Senate Districts 7, 11, 22, and 26 constitute racial gerrymanders," id., at 1288, but held that the Democratic Conference lacked standing to bring "any district-specific claims of racial gerrymandering," id., at 1292 (emphasis added). It then found for Alabama on the merits.

The Court rightly concludes that our racial gerrymandering jurisprudence does not allow for statewide claims. Ante, at 5–12. However, rather than holding appellants to the misguided legal theory they presented to the District Court, it allows them to take a mulligan, remanding the case with orders that the District Court consider whether some (all?) of Alabama's 35 majority-minority districts result from impermissible racial gerrymandering. In doing this, the Court disregards the detailed findings and thoroughly reasoned conclusions of the District Court—in particular its determination, reached after watching the development of the case from complaint to trial, that no appellant proved (or even pleaded) district-specific claims with respect to the majority-minority districts. Worse still, the Court ignores the Democratic Conference's express waiver of these claims before this Court. It does this on the basis of a few stray comments, cherry-picked from district-court filings that are more Rorschach brief than Brandeis brief, in which the vague outline of what could be district-specific racial-gerrymandering claims begins to take shape only with the careful, post-hoc nudging of appellate counsel.

Racial gerrymandering strikes at the heart of our democratic process, undermining the electorate's confidence in its government as representative of a cohesive body politic in which all citizens are equal before the law. It is therefore understandable, if not excusable, that the Court balks at denying merits review simply because appellants pursued a flawed litigation strategy. But allowing appellants a second bite at the apple invites lower courts similarly to depart from the premise that ours is an adversarial system whenever they deem the stakes sufficiently high. Because I do not believe that Article III empowers this Court to act as standby counsel for sympathetic litigants, I dissent.

I. The Alabama Democratic Conference

The District Court concluded that the Democratic Conference lacked standing to bring district-specific claims. It did so on the basis of the Conference's failure to present any evidence that it had members who voted in the challenged districts, and because the individual Conference plaintiffs did not claim to vote in them. 989 F. Supp. 2d, at 1292.

A voter has standing to bring a racial-gerrymandering claim only if he votes in a gerrymandered district, or if specific evidence demonstrates that he has suffered the special harms that attend racial gerrymandering. United States v. Hays, 515 U. S. 737–745 (1995). However, the Democratic Conference only claimed to have "chapters and members in almost all counties in the state." Newton Plaintiffs' Proposed Findings of Fact and Conclusions of Law in No. 12–cv–691, Doc. 195–1, pp. 3–4 (Democratic Conference Post-Trial Brief) (emphasis added). Yet the Court concludes that this fact, combined with the Conference's self-description as a " 'statewide political caucus' " that endorses candidates for political office, "supports an inference that the organization has members in all of the State's majority-minority districts, other things being equal." Ante, at 13. The Court provides no support for this theory of jurisdiction by illogical inference, perhaps because this Court has rejected other attempts to peddle more-likely-than-not standing. See Summers v. Earth Island Institute, 555 U. S. 488, 497 (2009) (rejecting a test for organizational standing that asks "whether, accepting [an] organization's self-description of the activities of its members, there is a statistical probability that some of those members are threatened with concrete injury").

The inference to be drawn from the Conference's statements cuts in precisely the opposite direction. What is at issue here is not just counties but voting districts within counties. If the Conference has members in almost every county, then there must be counties in which it does not have members; and we have no basis for concluding (or inferring) that those counties do not contain all of the majority-minority voting districts. Morever, even in those counties in which the Conference does have members, we have no basis for concluding (or inferring) that those members vote in majority-minority districts. The Conference had plenty of opportunities, including at trial, to demonstrate that this was the case, and failed to do so. This failure lies with the Democratic Conference, and the consequences should be borne by it, not by the people of Alabama, who must now shoulder the expense of further litigation and the uncertainty that attends a resuscitated constitutional challenge to their legislative districts.

Incredibly, the Court thinks that "elementary principles of procedural fairness" require giving the Democratic Conference the opportunity to prove on appeal what it neglected to prove at trial. Ante, at 14. It observes that the Conference had no reason to believe it should provide such information because "the State did not contest its membership in every district," and the opinion cites an affidavit lodged with this Court providing a list of the Conference's members in each majority-minority district in Alabama. Ibid. I cannot imagine why the absence of a state challenge would matter. Whether or not there was such a challenge, it was the Conference's responsibility, as "[t]he party invoking federal jurisdiction," to establish standing. See Lujan v. Defenders of Wildlife, 504 U. S. 555, 561 (1992) . That responsibility was enforceable, challenge or no, by the court: "The federal courts are under an independent obligation to examine their own jurisdiction, and standing 'is perhaps the most important of [the jurisdictional] doctrines.' " FW/PBS, Inc. v. Dallas, 493 U. S. 215–231 (1990) (citations omitted). And because standing is not a "mere pleading requiremen[t] but rather an indispensable part of the plaintiff's case, each element must be supported in the same way as any other matter on which the plaintiff bears the burden of proof, i.e., with the manner and degree of evidence required at the successive stages of the litigation." Defenders of Wildlife, supra, at 561.

The Court points to Parents Involved in Community Schools v. Seattle School Dist. No. 1, 551 U. S. 701, 718 (2007), as support for its decision to sandbag Alabama with the Democratic Conference's out-of-time (indeed, out-of-court) lodging in this Court. The circumstances in that case, however, are far afield. The organization of parents in that case had established organizational standing in the lower court by showing that it had members with children who would be subject to the school district's "integration tiebreaker," which was applied at ninth grade. Brief for Respondents, O. T. 2006, No. 05–908, p. 16. By the time the case reached this Court, however, the youngest of these children had entered high school, and so would no longer be subject to the challenged policy. Ibid. Accordingly, we accepted a lodging that provided names of additional, younger children in order to show that the organization had not lost standing as a result of the long delay that often accompanies federal litigation. Here, by contrast, the Democratic Conference's lodging in the Supreme Court is its first attempt to show that it has members in the majority-minority districts. This is too little, too late.

But that is just the start. Even if the Democratic Conference had standing to bring district-specific racial-gerrymandering claims, there remains the question whether it did bring them. Its complaint alleged three counts: (1) Violation of §2 of the Voting Rights Act, (2) Racial gerrymandering in violation of the Equal Protection Clause, and (3) §1983 violations of the Voting Rights Act and the Fourteenth and Fifteenth Amendments. Complaint in No. 2:12–cv–1081, Doc. 1, pp. 17–18. The racial gerrymandering count alleged that "Alabama Acts 2012-602 and 2012-603 were drawn for the purpose and effect of minimizing the opportunity of minority voters to participate effectively in the political process," and that this "racial gerrymandering by Alabama Acts 2012-602 and 2012-603 violates the rights of Plaintiffs." Id., at 17. It made no reference to specific districts that were racially gerrymandered; indeed, the only particular jurisdictions mentioned anywhere in the complaint were Senate District 11, Senate District 22, Madison County Senate Districts, House District 73, and Jefferson and Montgomery County House Districts. None of the Senate Districts is majority-minority. Nor is House District 73. Jefferson County does, admittedly, contain 8 of the 27 majority-minority House Districts in Alabama, and Montgomery County contains another 4, making a total of 12. But they also contain 14 majority-white House Districts between them. In light of this, it is difficult to understand the Court's statement that appellants' "evidence and . . . arguments embody the claim that individual majority-minority districts were racially gerrymandered." Ante, at 8.

That observation would, of course, make sense if the Democratic Conference had developed such a claim in the course of discovery and trial. But in its post-trial Proposed Findings of Fact and Conclusions of Law, the Conference hewed to its original charge of statewide racial gerrymandering—or, rather, it did so as much as it reasonably could without actually proposing that the Court find any racial gerrymandering, statewide or otherwise. Instead, the Conference chose only to pursue claims that Alabama violated §2 of the Voting Rights Act under two theories. See Democratic Conference Post-Trial Brief 91–103 (alleging a violation of the results prong of Voting Rights Act §2) and 103–124 (alleging a violation of the purpose prong of Voting Rights Act §2).

To be sure, the Conference employed language and presented factual claims at various points in its 126-page post-trial brief that are evocative of a claim of racial gerrymandering. But in clinging to these stray comments to support its conclusion that the Conference made district-specific racial-gerrymandering claims, ante, at 9–10, the Court ignores the context in which these comments appear—the context of a clear Voting Rights Act §2 claim. Voting Rights Act claims and racial-gerrymandering claims share some of the same elements. See League of United Latin American Citizens v. Perry, 548 U. S. 399, 514 (2006) (Scalia, J., concurring in judgment in part and dissenting in part). Thus, allegations made in the course of arguing a §2 claim will often be indistinguishable from allegations that would be made in support of a racial-gerrymandering claim. The appearance of such allegations in one of the Conference's briefs might support reversal if this case came to us on appeal from the District Court's grant of a motion to dismiss. See Johnson v. City of Shelby, 574 U. S. ___, ___ (2014) (per curiam) (slip op., at 1) (noting that the Federal Rules of Civil Procedure "do not countenance dismissal of a complaint for imperfect statement of the legal theory supporting the claim as-serted"). But here the District Court held a full trial be-fore concluding that the Conference failed to make or prove any district-specific racial-gerrymandering claims with respect to the majority-minority districts. In this posture, and on this record, I cannot agree with the Court that the Conference's district-specific evidence, clearly made in the course of arguing a §2 theory, should be read to give rise to district-specific claims of racial gerrymandering with respect to Alabama's majority-minority districts.

The Court attempts to shift responsibility for the Democratic Conference's ill-fated statewide theory from the Conference to the District Court, implying that it was the "legally erroneous" analysis of the District Court, ante, at 12, rather than the arguments made by the Conference, that conjured this "legal unicorn," ante, at 7, so that the Conference did not forfeit the claims that the Court now attributes to it, ante, at 12. I suspect this will come as a great surprise to the Conference. Whatever may have been presented to the District Court, the Conference un-equivocally stated in its opening brief: "Appellants challenge Alabama's race-based statewide redistricting policy, not the design of any one particular election district." Brief for Appellants in No. 13–1138, p. 2 (emphasis added). It drove the point home in its reply brief: "[I]f theCourt were to apply a predominant-motive and narrow-tailoring analysis, that analysis should be applied to the state's policy, not to the design of each particular district one-by-one." Reply Brief in No. 11–1138, p. 7. How could anything be clearer? As the Court observes, the Conference attempted to walk back this unqualified description of its case at oral argument. Ante, at 11–12. Its assertion that what it really meant to challenge was the policy as applied to every district (not every majority-minority district, mind you) is not "clarification," ante, at 12, but an entirely new argument—indeed, the same argument it expressly disclaimed in its briefing. "We will not revive a forfeited argument simply because the petitioner gestures toward it in its reply brief." Republic of Argentina v. NML Capital, Ltd., 573 U. S.

___, ___, n. 2 (2014) (slip op., at 5, n. 2); we certainly should not do so when the issue is first presented at oral argument.

II. The Alabama Legislative Black Caucus

The Court does not bother to disentangle the independent claims brought by the Black Caucus from those of the Democratic Conference, but it strongly implies that both parties asserted racial-gerrymandering claims with respect to Alabama's 35 majority-minority districts. As we have described, the Democratic Conference brought no such claims; and the Black Caucus's filings provide even weaker support for the Court's conclusion.

The Black Caucus complaint contained three counts: (1) Violation of One Person, One Vote, see Reynolds v. Sims, 377 U. S. 533 (1964); (2) Dilution and Isolation of Black Voting Strength in violation of §2 of the Voting Rights Act; and (3) Partisan Gerrymandering. Complaint in No. 2:12–cv–691, Doc. 1, pp. 15–22. The failure to raise any racial-gerrymandering claim was not a mere oversight or the consequence of inartful pleading. Indeed, in its amended complaint the Black Caucus specifically cited this Court's leading racial-gerrymandering case for the proposition that "traditional or neutral districting principles may not be subordinated in a dominant fashion by either racial or partisan interests absent a compelling state interest for doing so." Amended Complaint in No. 2:12–cv–691, Doc. 60, p. 23 (citing Shaw v. Reno, 509 U. S. 630, 642 (1993); emphasis added). This quote appears in the first paragraph under the "Partisan Gerrymandering" heading, and claims of subordination to racial interests are notably absent from the Black Caucus complaint.

Racial gerrymandering was not completely ignored, however. In a brief introductory paragraph to the amended complaint, before addressing jurisdiction and venue, the Black Caucus alleged that "Acts 2012-602 and 2012-603 are racial gerrymanders that unnecessarily minimize population deviations and violate the whole-county provisions of the Alabama Constitution with both the purpose and effect of minimizing black voting strength and isolating from influence in the Alabama Legislature legislators chosen by African Americans." Amended Complaint, at 3. This was the first and last mention of racial gerrymandering, and like the Democratic Conference's complaint, it focused exclusively on the districting maps as a whole rather than individual districts. Moreover, even this allegation appears primarily concerned with the use of racially motivated districting as a means of violating one person, one vote (by splitting counties), and §2 of the Voting Rights Act (by minimizing and isolating black voters and legislators).

To the extent the Black Caucus cited particular districts in the body of its complaint, it did so only with respect to its enumerated one-person, one-vote, Voting Rights Act, and partisan-gerrymandering counts. See, e.g., id., at 13–14 (alleging that the "deviation restriction and disregard of the 'whole county' requirements . . . facilitated the Republican majority's efforts to gerrymander the district boundaries in Acts 2012–602 and 2012–603 for partisan purposes. By packing the majority-black House and Senate districts, the plans remove reliable Democratic voters from adjacent majority-white districts . . ."); id., at 36 ("The partisan purpose of [one] gerrymander was to remove predominately black Madison County precincts to SD 1, avoiding a potential crossover district"); id., at 44–45 (asserting that "splitting Jefferson County among 11 House and Senate districts" and "increasing the size of its local legislative delegation and the number of other counties whose residents elect members" of the delegation "dilut[es] the votes of Jefferson County residents" by diminishing their ability to control county-level legislation in the state legislature). And even these claims were made with a statewide scope in mind. Id., at 55 ("Viewed in their entirety, the plans in Acts 2012-602 and 2012-603 have the purpose and effect of minimizing the opportunities for black and white voters who support the Democratic Party to elect candidates of their choice").

Here again, discovery and trial failed to produce any clear claims with respect to the majority-minority districts. In a curious inversion of the Democratic Conference's practice of pleading racial gerrymandering and then effectively abandoning the claims, the Black Caucus, which failed to plead racial gerrymandering, did clearly advance the theory after the trial. See Alabama Legislative Black Caucus Plaintiffs' Post-Trial Proposed Findings of Fact and Conclusions of Law in No. 2:12–cv–691, Doc. 194, pp. 48–51 (Black Caucus Post-Trial Brief). The Black Caucus asserted racial-gerrymandering claims in its post-trial brief, but they all had a clear statewide scope. It charged that Alabama "started their line drawing with the majority-black districts" so as to maximize the size of their black majorities, which "impacted the drawing of majority-white districts in nearly every part of the state." Id., at 48–49. "[R]ace was the predominant factor in drafting both plans," id., at 49, which "drove nearly every districting decision," "dilut[ing] the influence of black voters in the majority-white districts," id., at 50.

The Black Caucus did present district-specific evidence in the course of developing its other legal theories. Al-though this included evidence that Alabama manipulated the racial composition of certain majority-minority districts, it also included evidence that Alabama manipulated racial distributions with respect to the districting maps as a whole, id., at 6 ("Maintaining the same high black percentages had a predominant impact on the entire plan"), and with respect to majority-white districts, id., at 10–11 ("Asked why [majority-white] SD 11 was drawn in a semi-donut-shape that splits St. Clair, Talladega, and Shelby Counties, Sen. Dial blamed that also on the need to preserve the black majorities in Jefferson County Senate districts"), and 43–44 ("Sen. Irons' quick, 'primative' [sic] analysis of the new [majority-white] SD 1 convinced her that it was designed to 'shed' the minority population of Sen. Sanford's [majority-white] SD 7 to SD 1" in order to "crack a minority influence district"). The Black Caucus was attacking the legislative districts from every angle. Nothing gives rise to an inference that it ever homed in on majority-minority districts—or, for that matter, any particular set of districts. Indeed, the fair reading of the Black Caucus's filings is that it was presenting illustrative evidence in particular districts—majority-minority, minority-influence, and majority-white—in an effort to make out a claim of statewide racial gerrymandering. The fact that the Court now concludes that this is not a valid legal theory does not justify its repackaging the claims for a second round of litigation.

III. Conclusion

Frankly, I do not know what to make of appellants' arguments. They are pleaded with such opacity that, squinting hard enough, one can find them to contain just about anything. This, the Court believes, justifies demanding that the District Court go back and squint harder, so that it may divine some new means of construingthe filings. This disposition is based, it seems, on the implicit premise that plaintiffs only plead legally correct theories. That is a silly premise. We should not reward the practice of litigation by obfuscation, especially when we are dealing with a well-established legal claim that numerous plaintiffs have successfully brought in the past. See, e.g., Amended Complaint and Motion for Preliminary and Permanent Injunction in Cromartie v. Hunt, No. 4:96–cv–104 (EDNC), Doc. 21, p. 9 ("Under the March 1997 redistricting plan, the Twelfth District and First District have boundaries which were drawn pursuant to a predominantly racial motivation," which were "the fruit of [earlier] racially gerrymandered plans"). Even the complaint in Shaw, which established a cause of action for racial gerrymandering, displayed greater lucidity than appellants', alleging that defendants "creat[ed] two amorphous districts which embody a scheme for segregation of voters by race in order to meet a racial quota" "totally unrelated to considerations of compactness, contiguous, and geographic or jurisdictional communities of interest." Complaint and Motion for Preliminary and Permanent Injunction and for Temporary Restraining Order in Shaw v. Barr, No. 5:92–cv–202 (EDNC), Doc. 1, pp. 11–12.

The Court seems to acknowledge that appellants never focused their racial-gerrymandering claims on Alabama's majority-minority districts. While remanding to consider whether the majority-minority districts were racially gerrymandered, it admits that plaintiffs "basically claim that the State, in adding so many new minority voters to majority-minority districts (and to others), went too far." Ante, at 3 (emphasis added). It further concedes that appellants "relied heavily upon statewide evidence," and that they "also sought to prove that the use of race to draw the boundaries of the majority-minority districts affected the boundaries of other districts as well." Ante, at 10.

The only reason I see for the Court's selection of the majority-minority districts as the relevant set of districts for the District Court to consider on remand is that this was the set chosen by appellants after losing on the claim they actually presented in the District Court. By playing along with appellants' choose-your-own-adventure style of litigation, willingly turning back the page every time a strategic decision leads to a dead-end, the Court discourages careful litigation and punishes defendants who are denied both notice and repose. The consequences of this unprincipled decision will reverberate far beyond the narrow circumstances presented in this case.

Accordingly, I dissent.

Bait-and-Switch: Justice Scalia's concurrence and dissent in City and County of San Francisco v. Sheehan (May 18, 2015)

    JUSTICE SCALIA, with whom JUSTICE KAGAN joins, concurring in part and dissenting in part.

    The first question presented (QP) in the petition for certiorari was "Whether Title II of the Americans with Disabilities Act [(ADA)] requires law enforcement officers to provide accommodations to an armed, violent, and mentally ill suspect in the course of bringing the suspect into custody." Pet. for Cert. i. The petition assured us (quite accurately), and devoted a section of its argument to the point, that "The Circuits Are In Conflict On This Question." Id., at 18. And petitioners faulted the Ninth Circuit for "holding that the ADA's reasonable accommodation requirement applies to officers facing violent circumstances," a conclusion that was "in direct conflict with the categorical prohibition on such claims adopted by the Fifth and Sixth Circuits." Ibid. Petitioners had expressly advocated for the Fifth and Sixth Circuits' position in the Court of Appeals. See Appellees' Answering Brief in No. 11–16401 (CA9), pp. 35–37 ("[T]he ADA does not apply to police officers' responses to violent individuals who happen to be mentally ill, where officers have not yet brought the violent situation under control").

    Imagine our surprise, then, when the petitioners' principal brief, reply brief, and oral argument had nary a word to say about that subject. Instead, petitioners bluntly announced in their principal brief that they "do not assert that the actions of individual police officers [in arresting violent and armed disabled persons] are never subject to scrutiny under Title II," and proclaimed that "[t]he only ADA issue here is what Title II requires of individual officers who are facing an armed and dangerous suspect." Brief for Petitioners 34 (emphasis added). In other words, the issue is not (as the petition had asserted) whether Title II applies to arrests of violent, mentally ill individuals, but rather how it applies under the circumstances of this case, where the plaintiff threatened officers with a weapon. We were thus deprived of the opportunity to consider, and settle, a controverted question of law that has divided the Circuits, and were invited instead to decide an ADA question that has relevance only if we assume the Ninth Circuit correctly resolved the antecedent, unargued question on which we granted certiorari. The Court is correct to dismiss the first QP as improvidently granted.

    Why, one might ask, would a petitioner take a position on a Circuit split that it had no intention of arguing, or at least was so little keen to argue that it cast the argument aside uninvited? The answer is simple. Petitioners included that issue to induce us to grant certiorari. As the Court rightly observes, there are numerous reasons why we would not have agreed to hear petitioners' first QP if their petition for certiorari presented it in the same form that it was argued on the merits. See ante, at 7–10. But it is also true that there was little chance that we would have taken this case to decide only the second, fact-bound QP—that is, whether the individual petitioners are entitled to qualified immunity on respondent's Fourth Amendment claim.

This Court's Rule 10, entitled "Considerations Governing Review on Certiorari," says that certiorari will be granted "only for compelling reasons," which include the existence of conflicting decisions on issues of law among federal courts of appeals, among state courts of last resort, or between federal courts of appeals and state courts of last resort. The Rule concludes: "A petition for a writ of certiorari is rarely granted when the asserted error con- sists of erroneous factual findings or the misapplication of a properly stated rule of law." The second QP implicates, at most, the latter. It is unlikely that we would have granted certiorari on that question alone.

But (and here is what lies beneath the present case) when we do grant certiorari on a question for which there is a "compelling reason" for our review, we often also grant certiorari on attendant questions that are not independently "certworthy," but that are sufficiently connected to the ultimate disposition of the case that the efficient administration of justice supports their consideration. In other words, by promising argument on the Circuit conflict that their first question presented, petitioners got us to grant certiorari not only on the first question but also on the second.

I would not reward such bait-and-switch tactics by proceeding to decide the independently "uncertworthy" second question. And make no mistake about it: Today's judgment is a reward. It gives the individual petitioners all that they seek, and spares San Francisco the significant expense of defending the suit, and satisfying any judgment, against the individual petitioners.* I would not encourage future litigants to seek review premised on arguments they never plan to press, secure in the knowledge that once they find a toehold on this Court's docket, we will consider whatever workaday arguments they choose to present in their merits briefs.

There is no injustice in my vote to dismiss both questions as improvidently granted. To be sure, ex post—after the Court has improvidently decided the uncertworthy question—it appears that refusal to reverse the judgment below would have left a wrong unrighted. Ex ante, how- ever—before we considered and deliberated upon the second QP but after petitioners' principal brief made clear that they would not address the Circuit conflict presented by the first QP—we had no more assurance that this question was decided incorrectly than we do for the thousands of other uncertworthy questions we refuse to hear each Term. Many of them have undoubtedly been decided wrongly, but we are not, and for well over a century have not been, a court of error correction. The fair course—the just course—is to treat this now-nakedly uncertworthy question the way we treat all others: by declining to decide it. In fact, there is in this case an even greater reason to decline: to avoid being snookered, and to deter future snookering.

Because I agree with the Court that "certiorari jurisdiction exists to clarify the law," ante, at 9 (emphasis added), I would dismiss both questions presented as improvidently granted.

*San Francisco will still be subject to liability under the ADA if the trial court determines that the facts demanded accommodation. The Court of Appeals vacated the

District Court's judgment that the ADA was inapplicable to police arrests of violent and armed disabled persons, and remanded for the accommodation determination.

Exchanges established by the state: Justice Scalia's dissent in King v. Burwell (June 25, 2015)

Justice Scalia, with whom Justice Thomas and Justice Alito join, dissenting.

The Court holds that when the Patient Protection and Affordable Care Act says "Exchange established by the State" it means "Exchange established by the State or the Federal Government." That is of course quite absurd, and the Court's 21 pages of explanation make it no less so.

I

The Patient Protection and Affordable Care Act makes major reforms to the American health-insurance market. It provides, among other things, that every State "shall . . . establish an American Health Benefit Exchange"—a marketplace where people can shop for health-insurance plans. 42 U. S. C. §18031(b)(1). And it provides that if a State does not comply with this instruction, the Secretary of Health and Human Services must "establish and operate such Exchange within the State." §18041(c)(1).

A separate part of the Act—housed in §36B of the Internal Revenue Code—grants "premium tax credits" to subsidize certain purchases of health insurance made on Exchanges. The tax credit consists of "premium assistance amounts" for "coverage months." 26 U. S. C. §36B(b)(1). An individual has a coverage month only when he is covered by an insurance plan "that was enrolled in through an Exchange established by the State under [§18031]." §36B(c)(2)(A). And the law ties the size of the premium assistance amount to the premiums for health plans which cover the individual "and which were enrolled in through an Exchange established by the State under [§18031]." §36B(b)(2)(A). The premium assistance amount further depends on the cost of certain other insurance plans "offered through the same Exchange." §36B(b)(3)(B)(i).

This case requires us to decide whether someone who buys insurance on an Exchange established by the Secretary gets tax credits. You would think the answer would be obvious—so obvious there would hardly be a need for the Supreme Court to hear a case about it. In order to receive any money under §36B, an individual must enroll in an insurance plan through an "Exchange established by the State." The Secretary of Health and Human Services is not a State. So an Exchange established by the Secretary is not an Exchange established by the State—which means people who buy health insurance through such an Exchange get no money under §36B.

Words no longer have meaning if an Exchange that is not established by a State is "established by the State." It is hard to come up with a clearer way to limit tax credits to state Exchanges than to use the words "established by the State." And it is hard to come up with a reason to include the words "by the State" other than the purpose of limiting credits to state Exchanges. "[T]he plain, obvious, and rational meaning of a statute is always to be preferred to any curious, narrow, hidden sense that nothing but the exigency of a hard case and the ingenuity and study of an acute and powerful intellect would discover." Lynch v. Alworth-Stephens Co., 267 U. S. 364, 370 (1925) (internal quotation marks omitted). Under all the usual rules of interpretation, in short, the Government should lose this case. But normal rules of interpretation seem always to yield to the overriding principle of the present Court: The Affordable Care Act must be saved.

II

The Court interprets §36B to award tax credits on both federal and state Exchanges. It accepts that the "most natural sense" of the phrase "Exchange established by the State" is an Exchange established by a State. Ante, at 11. (Understatement, thy name is an opinion on the Afford-able Care Act!) Yet the opinion continues, with no semblance of shame, that "it is also possible that the phrase refers to all Exchanges—both State and Federal." Ante, at 13. (Impossible possibility, thy name is an opinion on the Affordable Care Act!) The Court claims that "the context and structure of the Act compel [it] to depart from what would otherwise be the most natural reading of the pertinent statutory phrase." Ante, at 21.

I wholeheartedly agree with the Court that sound interpretation requires paying attention to the whole law, not homing in on isolated words or even isolated sections. Context always matters. Let us not forget, however, why context matters: It is a tool for understanding the terms of the law, not an excuse for rewriting them.

Any effort to understand rather than to rewrite a law must accept and apply the presumption that lawmakers use words in "their natural and ordinary signification." Pensacola Telegraph Co. v. Western Union Telegraph Co., 96 U. S. 1, 12 (1878) . Ordinary connotation does not always prevail, but the more unnatural the proposed interpretation of a law, the more compelling the contex-tual evidence must be to show that it is correct. Today's interpretation is not merely unnatural; it is unheard of. Who would ever have dreamt that "Exchange established by the State" means "Exchange established by the State or the Federal Government"? Little short of an express statutory definition could justify adopting this singular reading. Yet the only pertinent definition here provides that "State" means "each of the 50 States and the District of Columbia." 42 U. S. C. §18024(d). Because the Secretary is neither one of the 50 States nor the District of Columbia, that definition positively contradicts the eccentric theory that an Exchange established by the Secretary has been established by the State.

Far from offering the overwhelming evidence of meaning needed to justify the Court's interpretation, other contextual clues undermine it at every turn. To begin with, other parts of the Act sharply distinguish between the establishment of an Exchange by a State and the establishment of an Exchange by the Federal Government. The States' authority to set up Exchanges comes from one provision, §18031(b); the Secretary's authority comes from an entirely different provision, §18041(c). Funding for States to establish Exchanges comes from one part of the law, §18031(a); funding for the Secretary to establish Exchanges comes from an entirely different part of the law, §18121. States generally run state-created Ex-changes; the Secretary generally runs federally created Exchanges. §18041(b)–(c). And the Secretary's authority to set up an Exchange in a State depends upon the State's "[f]ailure to establish [an] Exchange." §18041(c) (emphasis added). Provisions such as these destroy any pretense that a federal Exchange is in some sense also established by a State.

Reading the rest of the Act also confirms that, as relevant here, there are only two ways to set up an Exchange in a State: establishment by a State and establishment by the Secretary. §§18031(b), 18041(c). So saying that an Exchange established by the Federal Government is "established by the State" goes beyond giving words bizarre meanings; it leaves the limiting phrase "by the State" with no operative effect at all. That is a stark violation of the elementary principle that requires an interpreter "to give effect, if possible, to every clause and word of a statute." Montclair v. Ramsdell, 107 U. S. 147, 152 (1883) . In weighing this argument, it is well to remember the difference between giving a term a meaning that duplicates another part of the law, and giving a term no meaning at all. Lawmakers sometimes repeat themselves—whether out of a desire to add emphasis, a sense of belt-and-suspenders caution, or a lawyerly penchant for doublets (aid and abet, cease and desist, null and void). Lawmakers do not, however, tend to use terms that "have no operation at all." Marbury v. Madison, 1 Cranch 137, 174 (1803). So while the rule against treating a term as a redundancy is far from categorical, the rule against treating it as a nullity is as close to absolute as interpretive principles get. The Court's reading does not merely give "by the State" a duplicative effect; it causes the phrase to have no effect whatever.

Making matters worse, the reader of the whole Act will come across a number of provisions beyond §36B that refer to the establishment of Exchanges by States. Adopting the Court's interpretation means nullifying the term "by the State" not just once, but again and again throughout the Act. Consider for the moment only those parts of the Act that mention an "Exchange established by the State" in connection with tax credits:

The formula for calculating the amount of the tax credit, as already explained, twice mentions "an Exchange established by the State." 26 U. S. C. §36B(b)(2)(A), (c)(2)(A)(i).

The Act directs States to screen children for eligibility for "[tax credits] under section 36B" and for "anyother assistance or subsidies available for coverage obtained through" an "Exchange established by the State." 42 U. S. C. §1396w–3(b)(1)(B)–(C).

The Act requires "an Exchange established by the State" to use a "secure electronic interface" to determine eligibility for (among other things) tax credits. §1396w–3(b)(1)(D).

The Act authorizes "an Exchange established by the State" to make arrangements under which other state agencies "determine whether a State resident is eligible for [tax credits] under section 36B." §1396w–3(b)(2).

The Act directs States to operate Web sites that allow anyone "who is eligible to receive [tax credits] under section 36B" to compare insurance plans offered through "an Exchange established by the State." §1396w–3(b)(4).

One of the Act's provisions addresses the enrollment of certain children in health plans "offered through an Exchange established by the State" and then dis-cusses the eligibility of these children for tax credits. §1397ee(d)(3)(B).

It is bad enough for a court to cross out "by the State" once. But seven times?

Congress did not, by the way, repeat "Exchange established by the State under [§18031]" by rote throughout the Act. Quite the contrary, clause after clause of the law uses a more general term such as "Exchange" or "Exchange established under [§18031]." See, e.g., 42 U. S. C. §§18031(k), 18033; 26 U. S. C. §6055. It is common sense that any speaker who says "Exchange" some of the time, but "Exchange established by the State" the rest of the time, probably means something by the contrast.

Equating establishment "by the State" with establishment by the Federal Government makes nonsense of other parts of the Act. The Act requires States to ensure (on pain of losing Medicaid funding) that any "Exchange established by the State" uses a "secure electronic interface" to determine an individual's eligibility for various benefits (including tax credits). 42 U. S. C. §1396w–3(b)(1)(D). How could a State control the type of electronic interface used by a federal Exchange? The Act allows a State to control contracting decisions made by "an Exchange established by the State." §18031(f)(3). Why would a State get to control the contracting decisions of a federal Exchange? The Act also provides "Assistance to States to establish American Health Benefit Exchanges" and directs the Secretary to renew this funding "if the State . . . is making progress . . . toward . . . establishing an Exchange." §18031(a). Does a State that refuses to set up an Exchange still receive this funding, on the premise that Exchanges established by the Federal Government are really established by States? It is presumably in order to avoid these questions that the Court concludes that federal Exchanges count as state Exchanges only "for purposes of the tax credits." Ante, at 13. (Contrivance, thy name is an opinion on the Affordable Care Act!)

It is probably piling on to add that the Congress that wrote the Affordable Care Act knew how to equate two different types of Exchanges when it wanted to do so. The Act includes a clause providing that "[a] territory that . . . establishes . . . an Exchange . . . shall be treated as a State" for certain purposes. §18043(a) (emphasis added). Tellingly, it does not include a comparable clause providing that the Secretary shall be treated as a State for purposes of §36B when she establishes an Exchange.

Faced with overwhelming confirmation that "Exchange established by the State" means what it looks like it means, the Court comes up with argument after feeble argument to support its contrary interpretation. None of its tries comes close to establishing the implausible conclusion that Congress used "by the State" to mean "by the State or not by the State."

The Court emphasizes that if a State does not set up an Exchange, the Secretary must establish "such Exchange." §18041(c). It claims that the word "such" implies that federal and state Exchanges are "the same." Ante, at 13. To see the error in this reasoning, one need only consider a parallel provision from our Constitution: "The Times, Places and Manner of holding Elections for Senators and Representatives, shall be prescribed in each State by the Legislature thereof; but the Congress may at any time by Law make or alter such Regulations." Art. I, §4, cl. 1 (emphasis added). Just as the Affordable Care Act directs States to establish Exchanges while allowing the Secretary to establish "such Exchange" as a fallback, the Elections Clause directs state legislatures to prescribe election regulations while allowing Congress to make "such Regulations" as a fallback. Would anybody refer to an election regulation made by Congress as a "regulation prescribed by the state legislature"? Would anybody say that a federal election law and a state election law are in all respects equivalent? Of course not. The word "such" does not help the Court one whit. The Court's argument also overlooks the rudimentary principle that a specific provision governs a general one. Even if it were true that the term "such Exchange" in §18041(c) implies that federal and state Exchanges are the same in general, the term "established by the State" in §36B makes plain that they differ when it comes to tax credits in particular.

The Court's next bit of interpretive jiggery-pokery involves other parts of the Act that purportedly presuppose the availability of tax credits on both federal and state Exchanges. Ante, at 13–14. It is curious that the Court is willing to subordinate the express words of the section that grants tax credits to the mere implications of other provisions with only tangential connections to tax credits. One would think that interpretation would work the other way around. In any event, each of the provisions mentioned by the Court is perfectly consistent with limiting tax credits to state Exchanges. One of them says that the minimum functions of an Exchange include (alongside several tasks that have nothing to do with tax credits) setting up an electronic calculator that shows "the actual cost of coverage after the application of any premium tax credit." 42 U. S. C. §18031(d)(4)(G). What stops a federal Exchange's electronic calculator from telling a customer that his tax credit is zero? Another provision requires an Exchange's outreach program to educate the public about health plans, to facilitate enrollment, and to "distribute fair and impartial information" about enrollment and "the availability of premium tax credits." §18031(i)(3)(B). What stops a federal Exchange's outreach program from fairly and impartially telling customers that no tax credits are available? A third provision requires an Exchange to report information about each insurance plan sold—including level of coverage, premium, name of the insured, and "amount of any advance payment" of the tax credit. 26 U. S. C. §36B(f)(3). What stops a federal Exchange's report from confirming that no tax credits have been paid out?

The Court persists that these provisions "would make little sense" if no tax credits were available on federal Exchanges. Ante, at 14. Even if that observation were true, it would show only oddity, not ambiguity. Laws often include unusual or mismatched provisions. The Affordable Care Act spans 900 pages; it would be amazing if its provisions all lined up perfectly with each other. This Court "does not revise legislation . . . just because the text as written creates an apparent anomaly." Michigan v. Bay Mills Indian Community, 572 U. S. ___, ___ (2014) (slip op., at 10). At any rate, the provisions cited by the Court are not particularly unusual. Each requires an Exchange to perform a standardized series of tasks, some aspects of which relate in some way to tax credits. It is entirely natural for slight mismatches to occur when, as here, lawmakers draft "a single statutory provision" to cover "different kinds" of situations. Robers v. United States, 572 U. S. ___, ___ (2014) (slip op., at 4). Lawmakers need not, and often do not, "write extra language specifically exempting, phrase by phrase, applications in respect to which a portion of a phrase is not needed." Ibid.

 Roaming even farther afield from §36B, the Court turns to the Act's provisions about "qualified individuals." Ante, at 10–11. Qualified individuals receive favored treatment on Exchanges, although customers who are not qualified individuals may also shop there. See Halbig v. Burwell, 758 F. 3d 390, 404–405 (CADC 2014). The Court claims that the Act must equate federal and state establishment of Exchanges when it defines a qualified individual as someone who (among other things) lives in the "State that established the Exchange," 42 U. S. C. §18032(f)(1)(A). Otherwise, the Court says, there would be no qualified individuals on federal Exchanges, contradicting (for example) the provision requiring every Exchange to takethe " 'interests of qualified individuals' " into accountwhen selecting health plans. Ante, at 11 (quoting §18031(e)(1)(b)). Pure applesauce. Imagine that a university sends around a bulletin reminding every professor to take the "interests of graduate students" into account when setting office hours, but that some professors teach only undergraduates. Would anybody reason that the bulletin implicitly presupposes that every professor has "graduate students," so that "graduate students" must really mean "graduate or undergraduate students"? Surely not. Just as one naturally reads instructions aboutgraduate students to be inapplicable to the extent a particular professor has no such students, so too would one naturally read instructions about qualified individuals to be inapplicable to the extent a particular Exchange has no such individuals. There is no need to rewrite the term "State that established the Exchange" in the definition of "qualified individual," much less a need to rewrite the separate term "Exchange established by the State" in a separate part of the Act.

 Least convincing of all, however, is the Court's attempt to uncover support for its interpretation in "the structure of Section 36B itself." Ante, at 19. The Court finds it strange that Congress limited the tax credit to state Exchanges in the formula for calculating the amount of the credit, rather than in the provision defining the range of taxpayers eligible for the credit. Had the Court bothered to look at the rest of the Tax Code, it would have seen that the structure it finds strange is in fact quite common. Consider, for example, the many provisions that initially make taxpayers of all incomes eligible for a tax credit, only to provide later that the amount of the credit is zero if the taxpayer's income exceeds a specified threshold. See, e.g., 26 U. S. C. §24 (child tax credit); §32 (earned-income tax credit); §36 (first-time-homebuyer tax credit). Or consider, for an even closer parallel, a neighboring provision that initially makes taxpayers of all States eligible for a credit, only to provide later that the amount of the credit may be zero if the taxpayer's State does not satisfy certain requirements. See §35 (health-insurance-costs tax credit). One begins to get the sense that the Court's insistence on reading things in context applies to "established by the State," but to nothing else.

For what it is worth, lawmakers usually draft tax-credit provisions the way they do—i.e., the way they drafted §36B—because the mechanics of the credit require it. Many Americans move to new States in the middle of the year. Mentioning state Exchanges in the definition of "coverage month"—rather than (as the Court proposes) in the provisions concerning taxpayers' eligibility for the credit—accounts for taxpayers who live in a State with a state Exchange for a part of the year, but a State with a federal Exchange for the rest of the year. In addition, §36B awards a credit with respect to insurance plans "which cover the taxpayer, the taxpayer's spouse, or any dependent . . . of the taxpayer and which were enrolled in through an Exchange established by the State." §36B(b)(2)(A) (emphasis added). If Congress had mentioned state Exchanges in the provisions discussing taxpayers' eligibility for the credit, a taxpayer who buys insurance from a federal Exchange would get no money, even if he has a spouse or dependent who buys insurance from a state Exchange—say a child attending college in a different State. It thus makes perfect sense for "Exchange established by the State" to appear where it does, rather than where the Court suggests. Even if that were not so, of course, its location would not make it any less clear.

The Court has not come close to presenting the compelling contextual case necessary to justify departing from the ordinary meaning of the terms of the law. Quite the contrary, context only underscores the outlandishness of the Court's interpretation. Reading the Act as a whole leaves no doubt about the matter: "Exchange established by the State" means what it looks like it means.

III

For its next defense of the indefensible, the Court turns to the Affordable Care Act's design and purposes. As relevant here, the Act makes three major reforms. The guaranteed-issue and community-rating requirements prohibit insurers from considering a customer's health when deciding whether to sell insurance and how much to charge, 42 U. S. C. §§300gg, 300gg–1; its famous individ-ual mandate requires everyone to maintain insurance coverage or to pay what the Act calls a "penalty," 26 U. S. C. §5000A(b)(1), and what we have nonetheless called a tax, see National Federation of Independent Business v. Sebelius, 567 U. S. ___, ___ (2012) (slip op., at 39); and its tax credits help make insurance more affordable. The Court reasons that Congress intended these three reforms to "work together to expand insurance coverage"; and because the first two apply in every State, so must the third. Ante, at 16.

This reasoning suffers from no shortage of flaws. To begin with, "even the most formidable argument concerning the statute's purposes could not overcome the clarity [of

] the statute's text." Kloeckner v. Solis, 568 U. S. ___, ___, n. 4 (2012) (slip op., at 14, n. 4). Statutory design and purpose matter only to the extent they help clarify an otherwise ambiguous provision. Could anyone maintain with a straight face that §36B is unclear? To mention just the highlights, the Court's interpretation clashes with a statutory definition, renders words inoperative in at least seven separate provisions of the Act, overlooks the contrast between provisions that say "Exchange" and those that say "Exchange established by the State," gives the same phrase one meaning for purposes of tax credits but an entirely different meaning for other purposes, and (let us not forget) contradicts the ordinary meaning of the words Congress used. On the other side of the ledger, the Court has come up with nothing more than a general provision that turns out to be controlled by a specific one, a handful of clauses that are consistent with either understanding of establishment by the State, and a resemblance between the tax-credit provision and the rest of the Tax Code. If that is all it takes to make something ambiguous, everything is ambiguous.

Having gone wrong in consulting statutory purpose at all, the Court goes wrong again in analyzing it. The purposes of a law must be "collected chiefly from its words," not "from extrinsic circumstances." Sturges v. Crowninshield, 4 Wheat. 122, 202 (1819) (Marshall, C. J.). Only by concentrating on the law's terms can a judge hope to uncover the scheme of the statute, rather than some other scheme that the judge thinks desirable. Like it or not, the express terms of the Affordable Care Act make only two of the three reforms mentioned by the Court applicable in States that do not establish Exchanges. It is perfectly possible for them to operate independently of tax credits. The guaranteed-issue and community-rating requirements continue to ensure that insurance companies treat all customers the same no matter their health, and the individual mandate continues to encourage people to maintain coverage, lest they be "taxed."

The Court protests that without the tax credits, the number of people covered by the individual mandate shrinks, and without a broadly applicable individual mandate the guaranteed-issue and community-rating requirements "would destabilize the individual insurance market." Ante, at 15. If true, these projections would show only that the statutory scheme contains a flaw; they would not show that the statute means the opposite of what it says. Moreover, it is a flaw that appeared as well in other parts of the Act. A different title established a long-term-care insurance program with guaranteed-issue and community-rating requirements, but without an individual mandate or subsidies. §§8001–8002, 124Stat. 828–847 (2010). This program never came into effect "only because Congress, in response to actuarial analyses predicting that the [program] would be fiscally unsustainable, repealed the provision in 2013." Halbig, 758 F. 3d, at 410. How could the Court say that Congress would never dream of combining guaranteed-issue and community-rating requirements with a narrow individual mandate, when it combined those requirements with no individual mandate in the context of long-term-care insurance?

Similarly, the Department of Health and Human Services originally interpreted the Act to impose guaranteed-issue and community-rating requirements in the Federal Territories, even though the Act plainly does not make the individual mandate applicable there. Ibid.; see 26 U. S. C. §5000A(f)(4); 42 U. S. C. §201(f). "This combination, predictably, [threw] individual insurance markets in the territories into turmoil." Halbig, supra, at 410. Responding to complaints from the Territories, the Department at first insisted that it had "no statutory authority" to address the problem and suggested that the Territories "seek legislative relief from Congress" instead. Letter from G. Cohen, Director of the Center for Consumer Information and Insurance Oversight, to S. Igisomar, Secretary of Commerce of the Commonwealth of Northern Mariana Islands (July 12, 2013). The Department changed its mind a year later, after what it described as "a careful review of [the] situation and the relevant statutory language." Letter from M. Tavenner, Administrator of the Centers for Medicare and Medicaid Services, to G. Francis, Insurance Commissioner of the Virgin Islands (July 16, 2014). How could the Court pronounce it "implausible" for Congress to have tolerated instability in insurance markets in States with federal Exchanges, ante, at 17, when even the Government maintained until recently that Congress did exactly that in American Samoa, Guam, the Northern Mariana Islands, Puerto Rico, and the Virgin Islands?

Compounding its errors, the Court forgets that it is no more appropriate to consider one of a statute's purposes in isolation than it is to consider one of its words that way. No law pursues just one purpose at all costs, and no statutory scheme encompasses just one element. Most relevant here, the Affordable Care Act displays a congressional preference for state participation in the establishment of Exchanges: Each State gets the first opportunity to set up its Exchange, 42 U. S. C. §18031(b); States that take up the opportunity receive federal funding for "activities . . . related to establishing" an Exchange, §18031(a)(3); and the Secretary may establish an Exchange in a State only as a fallback, §18041(c). But setting up and running an Exchange involve significant burdens—meeting strict deadlines, §18041(b), implementing requirements related to the offering of insurance plans, §18031(d)(4), setting up outreach programs, §18031(i), and ensuring that the Exchange is self-sustaining by 2015, §18031(d)(5)(A). A State would have much less reason to take on these burdens if its citizens could receive tax credits no matter who establishes its Exchange. (Now that the Internal Revenue Service has interpreted §36B to authorize tax credits everywhere, by the way, 34 States have failed to set up their own Exchanges. Ante, at 6.) So even if making credits available on all Exchanges advances the goal of improving healthcare markets, it frustrates the goal of encouraging state involvement in the implementation of the Act. This is what justifies going out of our way to read "established by the State" to mean "established by the State or not established by the State"?

Worst of all for the repute of today's decision, the Court's reasoning is largely self-defeating. The Court predicts that making tax credits unavailable in States that do not set up their own Exchanges would cause disastrous economic consequences there. If that is so, however, wouldn't one expect States to react by setting up their own Exchanges? And wouldn't that outcome satisfy two of the Act's goals rather than just one: enabling the Act's reforms to work and promoting state involvement in the Act's implementation? The Court protests that the very existence of a federal fallback shows that Congress expected that some States might fail to set up their own Exchanges. Ante, at 19. So it does. It does not show, however, that Congress expected the number of recalcitrant States to be particularly large. The more accurate the Court's dire economic predictions, the smaller that number is likely to be. That reality destroys the Court's pretense that applying the law as written would imperil "the viability of the entire Affordable Care Act." Ante, at 20. All in all, the Court's arguments about the law's purpose and design are no more convincing than its arguments about context.

IV

Perhaps sensing the dismal failure of its efforts to show that "established by the State" means "established by the State or the Federal Government," the Court tries to palm off the pertinent statutory phrase as "inartful drafting." Ante, at 14. This Court, however, has no free-floating power "to rescue Congress from its drafting errors." Lamie v. United States Trustee, 540 U. S. 526, 542 (2004) (internal quotation marks omitted). Only when it is patently obvious to a reasonable reader that a drafting mistake has occurred may a court correct the mistake. The occurrence of a misprint may be apparent from the face of the law, as it is where the Affordable Care Act "creates three separate Section 1563s." Ante, at 14. But the Court does not pretend that there is any such indication of a drafting error on the face of §36B. The occurrence of a misprint may also be apparent because a provision decrees an absurd result—a consequence "so monstrous, that all mankind would, without hesitation, unite in rejecting the application." Sturges, 4 Wheat., at 203. But §36B does not come remotely close to satisfying that demanding standard. It is entirely plausible that tax credits were restricted to state Exchanges deliberately—for example, in order to encourage States to establish their own Exchanges. We therefore have no authority to dismiss the terms of the law as a drafting fumble.

Let us not forget that the term "Exchange established by the State" appears twice in §36B and five more times in other parts of the Act that mention tax credits. What are the odds, do you think, that the same slip of the pen occurred in seven separate places? No provision of the Act—none at all—contradicts the limitation of tax credits to state Exchanges. And as I have already explained, uses of the term "Exchange established by the State" beyond the context of tax credits look anything but accidental. Supra, at 6. If there was a mistake here, context suggests it was a substantive mistake in designing this part of the law, not a technical mistake in transcribing it.

V

The Court's decision reflects the philosophy that judges should endure whatever interpretive distortions it takes in order to correct a supposed flaw in the statutory machinery. That philosophy ignores the American people's decision to give Congress "[a]ll legislative Powers" enumerated in the Constitution. Art. I, §1. They made Congress, not this Court, responsible for both making laws and mending them. This Court holds only the judicial power—the power to pronounce the law as Congress has enacted it. We lack the prerogative to repair laws that do not work out in practice, just as the people lack the ability to throw us out of office if they dislike the solutions we concoct. We must always remember, therefore, that "[o]ur task is to apply the text, not to improve upon it." Pavelic & LeFlore v. Marvel Entertainment Group, Div. of Cadence Industries Corp., 493 U. S. 120, 126 (1989).

Trying to make its judge-empowering approach seem respectful of congressional authority, the Court asserts that its decision merely ensures that the Affordable Care Act operates the way Congress "meant [it] to operate." Ante, at 17. First of all, what makes the Court so sure that Congress "meant" tax credits to be available everywhere? Our only evidence of what Congress meant comes from the terms of the law, and those terms show beyond all question that tax credits are available only on state Exchanges. More importantly, the Court forgets that ours is a government of laws and not of men. That means we are governed by the terms of our laws, not by the unenacted will of our lawmakers. "If Congress enacted into law something different from what it intended, then it should amend the statute to conform to its intent." Lamie, supra, at 542. In the meantime, this Court "has no roving license . . . to disregard clear language simply on the view that . . . Congress 'must have intended' something broader." Bay Mills, 572 U. S., at ____ (slip op., at 11).

Even less defensible, if possible, is the Court's claim that its interpretive approach is justified because this Act "does not reflect the type of care and deliberation that one might expect of such significant legislation." Ante, at 14–15. It is not our place to judge the quality of the care and deliberation that went into this or any other law. A law enacted by voice vote with no deliberation whatever is fully as binding upon us as one enacted after years of study, months of committee hearings, and weeks of debate. Much less is it our place to make everything come out right when Congress does not do its job properly. It is up to Congress to design its laws with care, and it is up to the people to hold them to account if they fail to carry out that responsibility.

Rather than rewriting the law under the pretense of interpreting it, the Court should have left it to Congress to decide what to do about the Act's limitation of tax credits to state Exchanges. If Congress values above everything else the Act's applicability across the country, it could make tax credits available in every Exchange. If it prizes state involvement in the Act's implementation, it could continue to limit tax credits to state Exchanges while taking other steps to mitigate the economic consequences predicted by the Court. If Congress wants to accommodate both goals, it could make tax credits available everywhere while offering new incentives for States to set up their own Exchanges. And if Congress thinks that the present design of the Act works well enough, it could do nothing. Congress could also do something else altogether, entirely abandoning the structure of the Affordable Care Act. The Court's insistence on making a choice that should be made by Congress both aggrandizes judicial power and encourages congressional lassitude.

Just ponder the significance of the Court's decision to take matters into its own hands. The Court's revision of the law authorizes the Internal Revenue Service to spend tens of billions of dollars every year in tax credits on federal Exchanges. It affects the price of insurance for millions of Americans. It diminishes the participation of the States in the implementation of the Act. It vastly expands the reach of the Act's individual mandate, whose scope depends in part on the availability of credits. What a parody today's decision makes of Hamilton's assurances to the people of New York: "The legislature not only commands the purse but prescribes the rules by which the duties and rights of every citizen are to be regulated. The judiciary, on the contrary, has no influence over . . . the purse; no direction . . . of the wealth of society, and can take no active resolution whatever. It may truly be said to have neither force nor will but merely judgment." The Federalist No. 78, p. 465 (C. Rossiter ed. 1961).

* * *

Today's opinion changes the usual rules of statutory interpretation for the sake of the Affordable Care Act. That, alas, is not a novelty. In National Federation of Independent Business v. Sebelius, 567 U. S. ___, this Court revised major components of the statute in order to save them from unconstitutionality. The Act that Congress passed provides that every individual "shall" maintain insurance or else pay a "penalty." 26 U. S. C. §5000A. This Court, however, saw that the Commerce Clause does not authorize a federal mandate to buy health insurance. So it rewrote the mandate-cum-penalty as a tax. 567 U. S., at ___–___ (principal opinion) (slip op., at 15–45). The Act that Congress passed also requires every State to accept an expansion of its Medicaid program, or else risk losing all Medicaid funding. 42 U. S. C. §1396c. This Court, however, saw that the Spending Clause does not authorize this coercive condition. So it rewrote the law to withhold only the incremental funds associated with the Medicaid expansion. 567 U. S., at ___–___ (principal opinion) (slip op., at 45–58). Having transformed two major parts of the law, the Court today has turned its attention to a third. The Act that Congress passed makes tax credits available only on an "Exchange established by the State." This Court, however, concludes that this limitation would prevent the rest of the Act from working as well as hoped. So it rewrites the law to make tax credits available everywhere. We should start calling this law SCOTUScare.

Perhaps the Patient Protection and Affordable Care Act will attain the enduring status of the Social Security Act or the Taft-Hartley Act; perhaps not. But this Court's two decisions on the Act will surely be remembered through the years. The somersaults of statutory interpretation they have performed ("penalty" means tax, "further [Medicaid] payments to the State" means only incremental Medicaid payments to the State, "established by the State" means not established by the State) will be cited by litigants endlessly, to the confusion of honest jurisprudence. And the cases will publish forever the discouraging truth that the Supreme Court of the United States favors some laws over others, and is prepared to do whatever it takes to uphold and assist its favorites.

I dissent.

Same-Sex Marriage: Justice Scalia's dissent in Obergefell v. Hodges (June 26, 2015)

Justice Scalia, with whom Justice Thomas joins, dissenting.

I join The Chief Justice's opinion in full. I write separately to call attention to this Court's threat to American democracy.

The substance of today's decree is not of immense personal importance to me. The law can recognize as marriage whatever sexual attachments and living arrangements it wishes, and can accord them favorable civil consequences, from tax treatment to rights of inheritance. Those civil consequences—and the public approval that conferring the name of marriage evidences—can perhaps have adverse social effects, but no more adverse than the effects of many other controversial laws. So it is not of special importance to me what the law says about marriage. It is of overwhelming importance, however, who it is that rules me. Today's decree says that my Ruler, and the Ruler of 320 million Americans coast-to-coast, is a majority of the nine lawyers on the Supreme Court. The opinion in these cases is the furthest extension in fact—and the furthest extension one can even imagine—of the Court's claimed power to create "liberties" that the Constitution and its Amendments neglect to mention. This practice of constitutional revision by an unelected committee of nine, always accompanied (as it is today) by extravagant praise of liberty, robs the People of the most important liberty they asserted in the Declaration of Independence and won in the Revolution of 1776: the freedom to govern themselves.

I

Until the courts put a stop to it, public debate over same-sex marriage displayed American democracy at its best. Individuals on both sides of the issue passionately, but respectfully, attempted to persuade their fellow citizens to accept their views. Americans considered the arguments and put the question to a vote. The electorates of 11 States, either directly or through their representatives, chose to expand the traditional definition of marriage. Many more decided not to.[1] Win or lose, advocates for both sides continued pressing their cases, secure in the knowledge that an electoral loss can be negated by a later electoral win. That is exactly how our system of government is supposed to work.[2]

The Constitution places some constraints on self-rule—constraints adopted by the People themselves when they ratified the Constitution and its Amendments. Forbidden are laws "impairing the Obligation of Contracts,"[3] denying "Full Faith and Credit" to the "public Acts" of other States,[4] prohibiting the free exercise of religion,[5] abridging the freedom of speech,[6] infringing the right to keep and bear arms,[7] authorizing unreasonable searches and seizures,[8] and so forth. Aside from these limitations, those powers "reserved to the States respectively, or to the people"[9] can be exercised as the States or the People desire. These cases ask us to decide whether the Fourteenth Amendment contains a limitation that requires the States to license and recognize marriages between two people of the same sex. Does it remove that issue from the political process?

Of course not. It would be surprising to find a prescription regarding marriage in the Federal Constitution since, as the author of today's opinion reminded us only two years ago (in an opinion joined by the same Justices who join him today):

"[R]egulation of domestic relations is an area that has long been regarded as a virtually exclusive province of the States."[10]

"[T]he Federal Government, through our history, has deferred to state-law policy decisions with respect to domestic relations."[11]

But we need not speculate. When the Fourteenth Amendment was ratified in 1868, every State limited marriage to one man and one woman, and no one doubted the constitutionality of doing so. That resolves these cases. When it comes to determining the meaning of a vague constitutional provision—such as "due process of law" or "equal protection of the laws"—it is unquestionable that the People who ratified that provision did not understand it to prohibit a practice that remained both universal and uncontroversial in the years after ratification.[12] We have no basis for striking down a practice that is not expressly prohibited by the Fourteenth Amendment's text, and that bears the endorsement of a long tradition of open, widespread, and unchallenged use dating back to the Amendment's ratification. Since there is no doubt whatever that the People never decided to prohibit the limitation of marriage to opposite-sex couples, the public debate over same-sex marriage must be allowed to continue.

But the Court ends this debate, in an opinion lacking even a thin veneer of law. Buried beneath the mummeries and straining-to-be-memorable passages of the opinion is a candid and startling assertion: No matter what it was the People ratified, the Fourteenth Amendment protects those rights that the Judiciary, in its "reasoned judgment," thinks the Fourteenth Amendment ought to protect.[13] That is so because "[t]he generations that wrote and ratified the Bill of Rights and the Fourteenth Amendment did not presume to know the extent of freedom in all of its dimensions . . . ."[14] One would think that sentence would continue: ". . . and therefore they provided for a means by which the People could amend the Constitution," or perhaps ". . . and therefore they left the creation of additional liberties, such as the freedom to marry someone of the same sex, to the People, through the never-ending process of legislation." But no. What logically follows, in the majority's judge-empowering estimation, is: "and so they entrusted to future generations a charter protecting the right of all persons to enjoy liberty as we learn its meaning."[15] The "we," needless to say, is the nine of us. "History and tradition guide and discipline [our] inquiry but do not set its outer boundaries."[16]

Thus, rather than focusing on the People's understanding of "liberty"—at the time of ratification or even today—the majority focuses on four "principles and traditions" that, in the majority's view, prohibit States from defining marriage as an institution consisting of one man and one woman.[17]

This is a naked judicial claim to legislative—indeed, super-legislative—power; a claim fundamentally at odds with our system of government. Except as limited by a constitutional prohibition agreed to by the People, the States are free to adopt whatever laws they like, even those that offend the esteemed Justices' "reasoned judgment." A system of government that makes the People subordinate to a committee of nine unelected lawyers does not deserve to be called a democracy.

Judges are selected precisely for their skill as lawyers; whether they reflect the policy views of a particular constituency is not (or should not be) relevant. Not surprisingly then, the Federal Judiciary is hardly a cross-section of America. Take, for example, this Court, which consists of only nine men and women, all of them successful lawyers[18] who studied at Harvard or Yale Law School. Four of the nine are natives of New York City. Eight of them grew up in east- and west-coast States. Only one hails from the vast expanse in-between. Not a single Southwesterner or even, to tell the truth, a genuine Westerner (California does not count). Not a single evangelical Christian (a group that comprises about one quarter of Americans[19]), or even a Protestant of any denomination. The strikingly unrepresentative character of the body voting on today's social upheaval would be irrelevant if they were functioning as judges, answering the legal question whether the American people had ever ratified a constitutional provision that was understood to proscribe the traditional definition of marriage. But of course the Justices in today's majority are not voting on that basis; they say they are not. And to allow the policy question of same-sex marriage to be considered and resolved by a select, patrician, highly unrepresentative panel of nine is to violate a principle even more fundamental than no taxation without representation: no social transformation without representation.

II

But what really astounds is the hubris reflected in today's judicial Putsch. The five Justices who compose today's majority are entirely comfortable concluding that every State violated the Constitution for all of the 135 years between the Fourteenth Amendment's ratification and Massachusetts' permitting of same-sex marriages in 2003.[20] They have discovered in the Fourteenth Amendment a "fundamental right" overlooked by every person alive at the time of ratification, and almost everyone else in the time since. They see what lesser legal minds—minds like Thomas Cooley, John Marshall Harlan, Oliver Wendell Holmes, Jr., Learned Hand, Louis Brandeis, William Howard Taft, Benjamin Cardozo, Hugo Black, Felix Frankfurter, Robert Jackson, and Henry Friendly—could not. They are certain that the People ratified the Fourteenth Amendment to bestow on them the power to remove questions from the democratic process when that is called for by their "reasoned judgment." These Justices know that limiting marriage to one man and one woman is contrary to reason; they know that an institution as old as government itself, and accepted by every nation in history until 15 years ago,[21] cannot possibly be supported by anything other than ignorance or bigotry. And they are willing to say that any citizen who does not agree with that, who adheres to what was, until 15 years ago, the unanimous judgment of all generations and all societies, stands against the Constitution.

The opinion is couched in a style that is as pretentious as its content is egotistic. It is one thing for separate concurring or dissenting opinions to contain extravagances, even silly extravagances, of thought and expression; it is something else for the official opinion of the Court to do so.[22] Of course the opinion's showy profundities are often profoundly incoherent. "The nature of marriage is that, through its enduring bond, two persons together can find other freedoms, such as expression, intimacy, and spirituality."[23] (Really? Who ever thought that intimacy and spirituality [whatever that means] were freedoms? And if intimacy is, one would think Freedom of Intimacy is abridged rather than expanded by marriage. Ask the nearest hippie. Expression, sure enough, is a freedom, but anyone in a long-lasting marriage will attest that that happy state constricts, rather than expands, what one can prudently say.) Rights, we are told, can "rise . . . from a better informed understanding of how constitutional imperatives define a liberty that remains urgent in our own era."[24] (Huh? How can a better informed understanding of how constitutional imperatives [whatever that means] define [whatever that means] an urgent liberty [never mind], give birth to a right?) And we are told that, "[i]n any particular case," either the Equal Protection or Due Process Clause "may be thought to capture the essence of [a] right in a more accurate and comprehensive way," than the other, "even as the two Clauses may converge in the identification and definition of the right."[25] (What say? What possible "essence" does substantive due process "capture" in an "accurate and comprehensive way"? It stands for nothing whatever, except those freedoms and entitlements that this Court really likes. And the Equal Protection Clause, as employed today, identifies nothing except a difference in treatment that this Court really dislikes. Hardly a distillation of essence. If the opinion is correct that the two clauses "converge in the identification and definition of [a] right," that is only because the majority's likes and dislikes are predictably compatible.) I could go on. The world does not expect logic and precision in poetry or inspirational pop-philosophy; it demands them in the law. The stuff contained in today's opinion has to diminish this Court's reputation for clear thinking and sober analysis.

* * *

Hubris is sometimes defined as o'erweening pride; and pride, we know, goeth before a fall. The Judiciary is the "least dangerous" of the federal branches because it has "neither Force nor Will, but merely judgment; and must ultimately depend upon the aid of the executive arm" and the States, "even for the efficacy of its judgments."[26] With each decision of ours that takes from the People a question properly left to them—with each decision that is unabashedly based not on law, but on the "reasoned judgment" of a bare majority of this Court—we move one step closer to being reminded of our impotence.

Notes

1 Brief for Respondents in No. 14–571, p. 14.

2 Accord, Schuette v. BAMN, 572 U. S. ___, ___–___ (2014) (plurality opinion) (slip op., at 15–17).

3 U. S. Const., Art. I, §10.

4 Art. IV, §1.

5 Amdt. 1.

6 Ibid.

7 Amdt. 2.

8 Amdt. 4.

9 Amdt. 10.

10 United States v. Windsor, 570 U. S. ___, ___ (2013) (slip op., at 16) (internal quotation marks and citation omitted).

11 Id., at ___ (slip op., at 17).

12 See Town of Greece v. Galloway, 572 U. S. ___, ___–___ (2014) (slip op., at 7–8).

13 Ante, at 10.

14 Ante, at 11.

15 Ibid.

16 Ante, at 10–11.

17 Ante, at 12–18.

18 The predominant attitude of tall-building lawyers with respect to the questions presented in these cases is suggested by the fact that the American Bar Association deemed it in accord with the wishes of its members to file a brief in support of the petitioners. See Brief for American Bar Association as Amicus Curiae in Nos. 14–571 and 14–574, pp. 1–5.

19 See Pew Research Center, America's Changing Religious Landscape 4 (May 12, 2015).

20 Goodridge v. Department of Public Health, 440 Mass. 309, 798 N. E. 2d 941 (2003).

21 Windsor, 570 U. S., at ___ (Alito, J., dissenting) (slip op., at 7).

22 If, even as the price to be paid for a fifth vote, I ever joined an opinion for the Court that began: "The Constitution promises liberty to all within its reach, a liberty that includes certain specific rights that allow persons, within a lawful realm, to define and express their identity," I would hide my head in a bag. The Supreme Court of the United States has descended from the disciplined legal reasoning of John Marshall and Joseph Story to the mystical aphorisms of the fortune cookie.

23 Ante, at 13.

24 Ante, at 19.
25 Ibid.
26 The Federalist No. 78, pp. 522, 523 (J. Cooke ed. 1961) (A. Hamilton).

Printed in Great Britain
by Amazon